W9-BKD-070

ANTIQUES Handbook & Price Guide

Miller's Antiques Handbook & Price Guide
By Judith Miller

First published in Great Britain in 2015 by Miller's, a division of Mitchell Beazley,
imprints of Octopus Publishing Group Ltd,
Carmelite House, 50 Victoria Embankment, London, EC4Y 0DZ
www.octopusbooks.co.uk

An Hachette UK Company
www.hachette.co.uk

Distributed in the US by Hachette Book Group
1290 Avenue of the Americas, 4th and 5th Floors, New York, NY 10020

Distributed in Canada by Canadian Manda Group
664 Annette St., Toronto, Ontario, Canada M6S 2C8

US ISBN: 9781784720896

A CIP record for this book is available from the British Library.

Set in Frutiger

Printed and bound in China

1 3 5 7 9 10 8 6 4 2

Publisher Alison Starling
Managing Editor Sybella Stephens
Editorial Co-ordinator Christina Webb
Contributor Julie Brooke
Proofreader John Wainwright
Advertising Sales Daniel Goode
Indexer Hilary Bird

Art Director Jonathan Christie
Design and Prepress Ali Scrivens, TJ Graphics

Production Controller Sarah-Jayne Johnson

Photograph of Judith Miller by Chris Terry

Page 1: One of a pair of early 19thC French Empire parcel gilt and ebonized fauteuils. $12,000-15,000 L&T
Page 2: A Gallé tin-glazed earthenware model of a cat, designed by Emile Gallé. $2,700-3,300 WW
Page 4 from left to right: A Della Robbia sgraffito vase, marked 'R.B.' with Della Robbia mark. $1,500-2,250 DRA
A pair of Finn Juhl 'Diplomat' rosewood chairs, by France and Son, Denmark. $1,500-2,250
A late 19thC French gilt-bronze cased cartel wall clock, with twin-train movement. $3,000-4,500 DN
A pre-war Marklin locomotive and tender. $750-900 POOK
Page 5 from left to right: A George III silver tankard, London 1756, by Robert Albion Cox, London. $3,000-4,000 LOCK
A fine early 19thC Italian micromosaic of the Roman Forum. $6,750-8,250 WW
An 18thC Staffordshire white saltglaze bear-baiting jug and cover. $1,200-1,800 L&T
A Gallé cameo glass small vase, in amethyst over clear frosted glass, signed. $750-1,000 DN

ANTIQUES Handbook & Price Guide

Judith Miller

MILLER'S

Contents

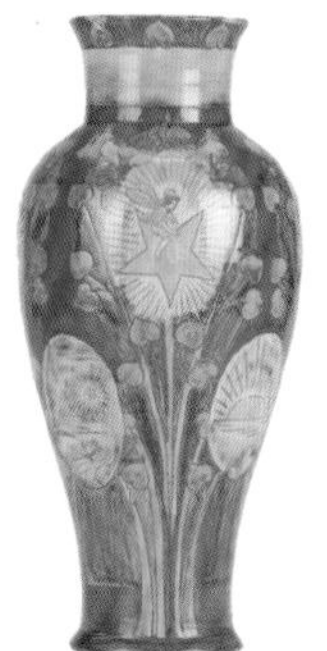

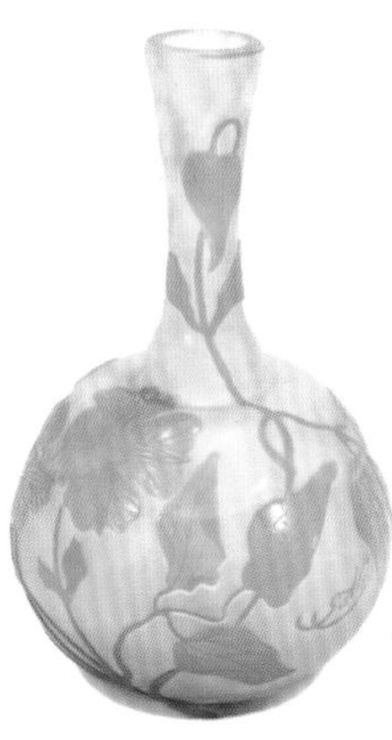

LIST OF CONSULTANTS

At Miller's we are extremely lucky to be able to call on a large number of specialists for advice. My colleagues and friends on the BBC Antiques Roadshow have a wealth of knowledge and their advice on the state of the market is invaluable. It is also important to keep in touch with dealers as they are really at the coalface dealing directly with collectors. Certain parts of the market have been extremely volatile over the past year, so up-to-date information is critical.

CERAMICS

John Axford
Woolley & Wallis
51-61 Castle Street
Salisbury SP1 3SU

Fergus Gambon
Bonhams
101 New Bond Street
London W1S 1SR

John Howard
Heritage
6 Market Place, Woodstock
OX20 1TA

John Mackie
Lyon & Turnbull
33 Broughton Place
Edinburgh EH1 3RR

Will Farmer
Fieldings
Mill Race Lane
Stourbridge DY8 1JN

Mike Moir
www.manddmoir.co.uk

DECORATIVE ARTS

Michael Jeffrey
Woolley & Wallis
51-61 Castle Street
Salisbury, SP1 3SU

FURNITURE

Lennox Cato
1 The Square, Edenbridge
Kent TN8 5BD

Lee Young
Lyon & Turnbull
33 Broughton Place
Edinburgh EH1 3RR

ORIENTAL

John Axford
Woolley & Wallis
51-61 Castle Street
Salisbury SP1 3SU

Lee Young
Lyon & Turnbull
33 Broughton Place
Edinburgh EH1 3RR

GLASS

Jeanette Hayhurst
www.antiqueglasslondon.com

SILVER

Alistair Dickenson
90 Jermyn Street
London SW1 6JD

JEWELLERY

Trevor Kyle
Lyon & Turnbull
33 Broughton Place
Edinburgh EH1 3RR

Steven Miners
Cristobal
26 Church Street
London NW8 8EP

CLOCKS & BAROMETERS

Paul Archard
Derek Roberts
25 Shipbourne Road
Tonbridge TN10 3DN

MODERN DESIGN

Mark Hill
www.markhillpublishing.com

John Mackie
Lyon & Turnbull
33 Broughton Place
Edinburgh EH1 3RR

HOW TO USE THIS BOOK

Running head Indicates the sub-category of the main heading.

Page tab This appears on every page and identifies the main category heading as identified in the Contents List on pages 4-5.

Essential Reference Gives key facts about the factory, maker or style, along with stylistic identification points, value tips and advice on fakes.

Closer Look Does exactly that. We show identifying aspects of a factory or maker, point out rare colors or shapes, and explain why a particular piece is so desirable.

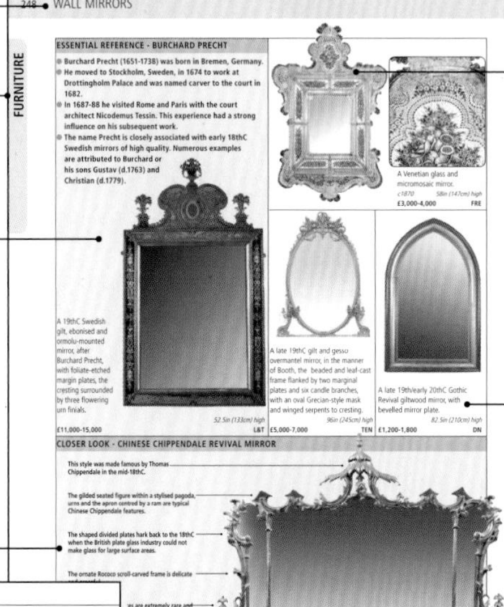

Judith Picks

When I first began collecting, I fell in love with 18thC Worcester. There was something about these pots that struck a chord. Much as I admire the superior quality of Meissen and Sèvres, there is something special about the early soft-paste porcelain produced in Worcester. I love this octagonal shape with the slightly misshapen lid, and the attempt to compete with the Chinese porcelain that was flooding the market, much as now, with the enamelled Chinese famille verte-style decoration. I believe Worcester porcelain to be undervalued and certainly some of the more common patterns are cheaper than when I bought them 20-30 years ago. Unfortunately, antiques are not always a good investment, although some of my rarer patterns have seen a substantial increase in value.

Judith Picks Items chosen specially by Judith, either because they are important or interesting, or because they're good investments.

The object The antiques are shown in full color. This is a vital aid to identification and valuation. With many objects, a slight color variation can signify a large price differential.

Caption The description of the item illustrated, including when relevant, the period, the maker or factory, medium, the year it was made, dimensions and condition. Many captions have **footnotes** which explain terminology or give identification or valuation information.

The price guide These price ranges give a ball park figure of what you should pay for a similar item. The great joy of antiques is that there is not a recommended retail price. The price ranges in this book are based on actual prices, either what a dealer will take or the full auction price.

A late 19thC gilt and gesso overmantel mirror, in the manner of Booth, the beaded and leaf-cast frame flanked by two marginal plates and six candle branches, with an oval Grecian-style mask and winged serpents to cresting.
96in (245cm) high
£5,000-7,000 TEN

Source code Every item has been specially photographed at an auction house, a dealer, an antiques market or a private collection. These are credited by code at the end of the caption, and can be checked against the Key to Illustrations on pages 632-633.

INTRODUCTION

Welcome to the 2016-2017 edition of Miller's Antiques Handbook & Price Guide. The Guide is, as always, packed with over 8,000 images of antiques and fine decorative objects that are completely new to this edition. I am often asked if we update the prices in each edition. We don't. When we publish an edition we start again – trying to reflect changes and developments in the antiques market.

It seems unbelievable to think the first Guide was published in 1979. How the antiques world has changed! When I was collecting in the early 1970s there were many more antiques shops in every High Street. There were more general auction sales where potential 'sleepers' (unidentified treasures) could be found. There was no internet and collectors scoured the country and abroad to find that hidden gem. The recession and changing tastes have hit the antiques market. Many shops have closed. And many traditional areas of the market are struggling to survive. However there are indications of an up-turn. Many dealers have joined together in antiques centers, many travel all over the country to display their antiques at fairs and many deal primarily online. Some areas are very strong – the Oriental, Russian, and Indian markets for example. And any good quality top end antique in original condition that is fresh to the market will excite collectors' interest.

I took part in a panel discussion in New York based on 'Do Antiques have a Future?' It's an interesting question. Some people quote the fact that young people seem less interested in collecting and seem keener on a minimal look. Antiques are seen as 'granny's style'. But there is always demand for antiques. When people can buy the same commodity anywhere in the world, they appear to be willing to pay more for the uniqueness of an antique. There is a shortage of good antiques – the dealers' lament is that the hardest part of the business today is finding good stuff. Consequently only a comparatively few people can own them. The difference between houses furnished with antiques and those that are not includes taste and wealth but rests finally on exclusiveness and rarity. Good contemporary furniture may be tasteful and expensive, but it is not rare: Another piece can always be produced to meet a demand. Antiques are not like that. The more globalized our world becomes, the more that people with certain tastes will desire antiques for their uniqueness. The conditions of the mass market appear to be increasing the number of those people, but there is no commensurate increase in the supply of antiques. This scarcity of good antiques will surely see prices increasing. The reduced size of the market (i.e., its exclusiveness) may well improve the investment qualities of antiques.

A 19thC French singing birds automaton, the birds with movement to the heads, beaks and tails, on a mahogany plinth base with gilt metal mounts. 23in (58cm) high $5,250–6,750 L&T

An early 18thC porcelain Chinese celadon crackle glaze and gilt-bronze mounted vase. 19.5in (49cm) high $19,500-24,000 L&T

There is still also the 'green' argument. Buying solid mahogany furniture is more ethically sound than buying disposable MDF pieces. And in many cases it is cheaper than the alternative and no one is going to convince me that MDF will prove to be a good investment. That solid, plain mahogany mid-19th century chest of drawers will still be a practical storage piece in another 200 or 300 years.

The internet has meant that antiques are more accessible than ever. We can browse large numbers of pieces of different styles and periods. Also, due to the power of the internet, smaller less well-known auction houses outside the big cities are getting record prices for rare pieces.

It really is an exciting time in the world of antiques. I am constantly asked what is the next 'big' thing? My answer is always the same. Buy something that will bring you pleasure - if it increases in value that's a bonus. But one thing is certain: however high or low antiques rank as good investments, no other investment brings with it the daily pleasure that an antique does. People buy them in order to live with them, not to sell them in the near future. It's a great time to buy. Use the Guide to increase your knowledge and enjoyment. Those hidden treasures are still out there just waiting to be discovered.

Judith Miller.

THE PORCELAIN MARKET

Although there is a certain feeling that the market is improving, there has been a continued nervousness fueled by porcelain collectors' very real concern that the ceramic market is 'soft'. Private collectors are, however, prepared to buy when items that are rare and of excellent quality are on offer. The market leaders Sèvres and Meissen have remained very much in demand, particularly for early 18thC examples. The 'golden age' of Meissen, from the early years of the factory to the end of the Seven Years War (1710-1759) is still very strong and, in this area, collectors are even prepared to accept some damage. Later 18thC pieces have tended to struggle, unless the piece has some rare features. Dresden, Vienna and Limoges pieces have to be particularly impressive to sell well. The Paris factories have also struggled and buyers are suspicious of many so-called 'Samson' pieces that do not have the quality of the true Samson copies. Good quality 'genuine' Samson continues to attract collectors.

Another area that is still struggling is British blue-and-white from both the 18th and 19th centuries. What buyers really want is pieces in exceptional condition and with a rare early pattern. Large platters are also in demand but not if they have a transfer-printed common pattern. Worcester has been in demand but only the First Period Dr. Wall pieces with rare hand-painted patterns. Later transfer-printed pieces have struggled to find pre-recession prices, with many auctioneers combining pieces in job lots. If someone is considering starting a collection of 18thC English porcelain, this is a good time to start. Many pieces fail to find the price levels that I was paying 30 years ago.

However rarity is again a key fact. A Lund's Bristol cream pail c1750 sold at Bonhams in May 2015 for $30,000. It was a rare and distinctive shape and there are just six recorded examples.

Another factory that has really bucked the trend is Lowestoft – again this is particularly true when rare shapes and patterns are on offer. Nantgarw is also still in demand due in part to rarity and superb quality. A plate in the same Bonham's sale sold for over $16,500. Unrecorded early Derby figures always excite the market. Royal Worcester ewers and vases painted by such artists as Charles Baldwin, Harry Davis and the Stintons still have their collectors and prices have remained steady.

Top Left:
A Worcester teabowl and saucer, painted with the 'Landslip' pattern.
c1755-58 *4.75in (12cm) diam*
$750-900 **WW**

Above: A Meissen pastille burner, modeled as a timber-framed and thatched farmhouse.
c1750 *6in (15cm) high*
$7,500-10,500 **WW**

INTRODUCTION - BERLIN

Wilhelm Kaspar Wegely founded the first porcelain factory in Berlin in 1752. Early Berlin porcelain wares imitated Meissen wares, with naturalistic flowers, landscapes and figures painted in the manner of French pastoral painter, Antoine Watteau.

- **Molded flowers and foliage and basketwork rims were specialities of the factory under Wegely's direction.**
- **Nine years after it opened its doors, the factory closed due to financial difficulties. It was finally reopened in 1763 as the Royal Porcelain Factory thanks to Frederick the Great, King of Prussia.**
- **Early 19thC porcelain was characterized by finely tooled gilt borders and gilt-ground sections framing paintings, highly finished to resemble works in oil.**
- **Profile portraits within oval medallions, Classical themes, silhouettes and topographical views of buildings in Berlin, such as the Royal Palace, decorated porcelain wares, especially those intended for display.**
- **From c1850 Rococo Revival elements such as curling scrollwork and flowers appeared on tablewares and vases.**
- **During the last third of the 19thC the themes became less ostentatious: maidens, nymphs and religious subjects replaced copies of Old Master works.**
- **Porcelain produced between 1752-7 was marked with a 'W' in underglaze blue. From 1832 onward, Berlin porcelain was identifiable by the 'KPM' (Königliche Porzellan-Manufaktur) mark. Between 1849 and 1870, a mark featuring a Prussian eagle holding an orb and scepter in its claws was used.**
- **Remarkably, the Berlin Royal Porcelain Factory continues to produce fine porcelain ware until this day.**

A 19thC Berlin plaque, 'Helena Fourment with her Son Francis', after Rubens, the central seated figure in 17thC dress accompanied by her nude infant son, impressed KPM and scepter marks, in a giltwood frame.

11.5in (29cm) wide

$30,000-38,000 **L&T**

A late 19thC Berlin porcelain plaque, painted with a portrait of a Spanish young woman holding a basket of fruit, impressed KPM and scepter mark.

10in (25.5cm) wide

$4,000-4,500 **MAB**

A late 19thC Berlin porcelain plaque, 'The Finding of Moses', impressed KPM and scepter marks above the letter H, and incised mark '12-9 3/4' verso, in contemporary giltwood frame.

10in (25.5cm) wide

$5,250–6,750 **FRE**

A 19thC porcelain plaque, 'Brunhilde and Grane', depicting a semi-clad young beauty leaning against a white horse in a wood, signed 'Wagner', impressed KPM and scepter marks, in a gilt frame.

10in (25cm) wide

$12,000-15,000 **L&T**

A late 19thC Berlin plaque, after Rudolf Henneberg, painted with 'Die Fagd nach dem Gluck', Neuschwanstein Castle visible on the far left, impressed marks, within a gilt frame.

This plaque is a depiction of 'The Pursuit of Fortune', with Avarice personified as a horseman in pursuit of Fortune across a bridge, closely followed by Death who rides a black horse over the prostrate body of a maiden.

8.5in (28.5cm) wide

$9,000-12,000 **WW**

A large 19thC Berlin plaque, outside decorated by Ludwig Sturm (1844-1926), inscribed verso 'Kinder Lust v. Lasch./ L. Sturm Wien/' with Vienna shield mark, impressed KPM scepter mark, mounted and framed.

15.75in (40cm) wide

$15,000-22,500 **L&T**

A late 19thC Berlin plaque, painted after Wilhelm Kray by C Met, of 'Psyche at the Sea', the winged diaphanously draped nymph with a butterfly on her finger, seated on a rocky outcrop, impressed KPM and scepter, and incised '420_314'.

12.5in (32cm) wide

$10,500-12,000 HT

A large 19thC porcelain plaque, depicting the Penitent Magdalene after Pompeo Battoni, framed, impressed KPM and scepter mark, inscribed verso.

15.75in (40cm) wide

$3,000-4,500 L&T

A late 19thC KPM porcelain plaque, 'Rebecka', painted by R. Dittrich, with the biblical figure wearing a head-dress and beaded open kaftan, signed, impressed marks, inscribed title.

12.75in (32.5cm) high

$4,500-6,000 HT

A pair of Berlin armorial cups and saucers, brightly painted with red armorial medallions suspended from pink and white ribbons within laurel garlands, the rims with floral swags and gilt diaper panels, blue scepter marks.

c1770 *5in (13cm) wide.*

$1,150-1,300 WW

A early 19thC Berlin porcelain allegorical group, of Diana wearing an off the shoulder sprigged cloak, one breast bared, above Vulcan hammering an arrow, a putto and armor around them, underglaze blue scepter, printed orb and KPM, losses.

13in (33.5cm) high

$1,000-1,400 SWO

A late 19thC Berlin porcelain cobalt ground vase, the raised gold foliage decorated with coral and turquoise enamels, underglaze scepter mark.

6.5in (16.6cm) high

$1,400-1,700 SK

A pair of late 19thC Berlin figures of a singer and her companion, modeled wearing 18thC dress on square bases, orb and scepter marks, the violinist restored, most notably the instrument, her head off and glued back.

2in (5.5cm) & 6.5in (16.5cm) high

$450-600 DN

A large Berlin urn, of campana form, the sides painted with a view of a building surrounded by trees and flowers, to the reverse a gilt inscription 'Glück auf B zum 1.10.1926 M', beneath a pair of crossed mallets, reserved against a white gilt enriched ground painted with scattered floral sprays and insects, raised on a circular socle base, red printed KPM and underglaze blue scepter marks.

c1926 *17in (44cm) high*

$1,800-4,000 L&T

A rare and early Bow chamberstick, painted with scattered flowers in the famille rose palette.

c1748-50 *5in (13cm) wide*

$450-600 **WW**

A rare Bow mug, crisply applied with sprigs of prunus, the unusual molded handle with incised details, incised mark to the base.

c1750-55 *6in (15.5cm) high*

$4,000-4,500 **WW**

A Bow plate, painted with the 'Broken Scroll' pattern, the unfurled manuscript depicting flowering peony and bamboo, painted numeral 15.

There are Dublin delftware versions of this pattern.

c1750 *9in (23.5cm) wide*

$550-700 **WW**

A rare Bow high-footed sauceboat, molded in high relief with garlands of flowers and gilded with further sprays.

c1750 *8.5in (22cm) wide*

$1,200-1,500 **WW**

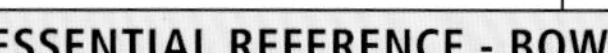

ESSENTIAL REFERENCE - BOW

The first patent for a porcelain formula was taken out c1744, but was probably not fully developed before 1748.

- **Bow porcelain was coarse, and the burnt animal bones (bone-ash), a principal ingredient at Bow, created a body that was liable to stain.**
- **Press-molded rather than slip-cast, Bow figures are heavy; early figures mainly left in the white, later examples decorated in colorful enamels.**
- **Bow copied Meissen figures; many were clumsy, but have a rustic charm.**
- **The glaze is soft and slightly blue with a tendency to pool around the base. Its decoration is underglaze; the 'quail' pattern being Bow's most popular design.**
- **Early Bow is generally unmarked, but after c1765 the 'anchor and dagger' mark was painted in red enamel.**
- **Bow closed in 1776.**

A Bow mug, painted with the Dragon pattern, with grooved strap handle, workman's number 12 to the base.

c1755-58 *6in (15cm) high*

$1,150-1,300 **WW**

A Bow mug, painted with a landscape scene of a two-storeyed house flying a pennant flag beneath pine trees, painter's numeral on footrim.

Compare with Phillips, 'The Watney Collection Part III', lot 834 for an earlier mug with the same pattern, which has been copied direct from Chinese porcelain. This is a typical Bow pattern from this period.

c1758-60 *6in (15cm) high*

$1,000-1,400 **WW**

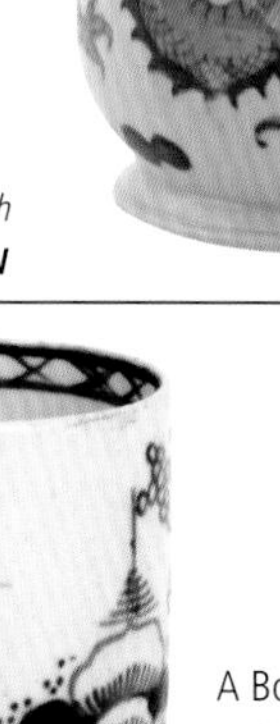

A Bow coffee can, with a heavily potted body, with a stylized chinoiserie landscape.

c1760 *2.5in (6.3cm) high*

$225-300 **SWO**

A rare Bow child's chamber pot, painted in blue with Chinese landscape vignettes of birds in flight above pagodas and trees, the grooved strap handle with a heart-shaped terminal.

Similar pots, but of a slightly smaller size, are known to have been imported to England from China in the middle of the 18thC. These objects are extremely rare in English porcelain of this period.

c1760-65 *6.75in (17.5cm) wide.*

$1,800-3,000 **WW**

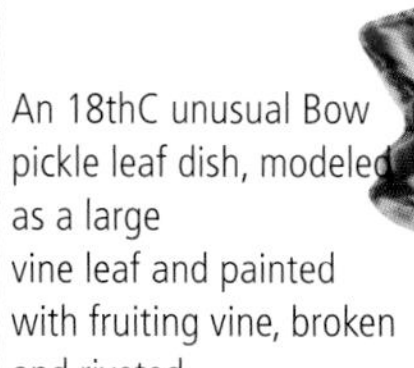

An 18thC unusual Bow pickle leaf dish, modeled as a large vine leaf and painted with fruiting vine, broken and riveted.

4in (10.5cm) wide

$400-550 **WW**

A set of four rare Bow porcelain fork handles, the steel forks 19thC, enameled with fruiting grapevine on a rich yellow ground.

c1755-60 *8.5in (21.5cm) long*

$1,200-1,400 **WW**

A Bow figure of a sailor's lass, modeled holding a handerchief.

c1758 *7in (18cm) high*

$1,500-1,800 **DN**

A Bow double leaf dish, decorated in the Kakiemon palette with the 'Two Quail' pattern, flying insects swirling above the two birds.

The shape of this dish was copied from Meissen, who in turn were emulating a Japanese shape.

c1758 *11.5in (29cm) long*

$1,000-1,200 **WW**

A set of Bow figures, possibly emblematic of the 'Senses', including a male musician and three female figures, all cut with apertures for candle-branches.

c1758 *5in (12.5) to 6in (15cm) high*

$4,500-5,250 **DN**

A Bow figure of a nun, on a simple pad base applied with flowers.

c1760 *5.5in (14cm) high*

$450-550 **DN**

A Bow group representing 'Autumn', modeled as a putto riding a goat, another putto seated below feeding it grapes.

c1760 *6.5in (16cm) high*

$3,000-4,000 **BELL**

A pair of Bow finches, each perched on a stump applied with flowers and leaves.

c1762-65 *3in (8cm) high*

$900-1,200 **WW**

A pair of Bow figures emblematic of 'Spring' and 'Autumn' from a series of the 'Four Seasons', on rocaille scroll bases.

c1765 *16.5cm (18cm) high*

$750-900 **DN**

A pair of late 18thC Bow figures, one of a female 'New Dancer', the other of a putto carrying a basket of flowers, red anchor and dagger marks.

6in (16cm) high

$750-900 **WW**

ESSENTIAL REFERENCE - CAUGHLEY

The Caughley factory was established near Broseley in Shropshire, c1750. Although initially a pottery factory, it began producing porcelain (known as Salopian ware) after it was taken over by Thomas Turner in 1772.

- **Caughley deliberately imitated Worcester pieces, both in pattern and shape.**
- **Its blue pigment is slightly brighter than Worcester's; Caughley's soapstone type-body shows orange to transmitted light, whereas Worcester's shows pale green.**
- **Painted wares are generally earlier than printed ones.**
- **In 1775, transfer-printing was introduced by Robert Hancock, formerly of Worcester.**
- **Demand for Caughley increased after the East India Company discontinued the import of Chinese porcelain tableware in 1791.**
- **Surviving miniature toy services are highly collectable, as are eye baths.**
- **The blue printed patterns are generally marked with a crescent (in imitation of Worcester's earliest mark) or with 'S' for Salopian.**
- **The Caughley Works closed in c1812.**

A Caughley mug, printed with 'La Promenade Chinoise', the reverse with 'La Pêche', with figures in pagoda landscapes, blue 'S' mark.
c1780-85 *6in (15cm) high*
$750-900 **WW**

A rare Caughley inkwell, printed with the reversed 'Bell Toy' pattern, later enameled with flowers and a pale green ground to the rim, printed 'C' mark.
c1780-85 *3.75in (9cm) diam*
$750-900 **WW**

A Caughley coffee cup, printed with the 'Travellers' pattern, with a dog running alongside figures on and beside a donkey, printed 'S' mark.

This pattern was taken from an etching by Paul Sandby who was famous for portraying realistic images of the poor of the streets of mid-18thC London.
c1780-85 *2.75in (6.5cm) high*
$1,500-1,800 **WW**

A Caughley miniature sucrier and cover, painted with the 'Island' pattern, the cover with two small sailing boats.
c1785 *2.5in (6cm) high*
$900-1,000 **WW**

A Caughley spittoon, printed with the 'Temple' pattern.
c1785 *4in (10.5cm) high*
$750-900 **WW**

A Caughley mug, decorated with the gilt monogram 'JEW', with a border of ears of corn.

This mug was exhibited at the Caughley Bicentenary Exhibition in Ironbridge in 1999.
1790 *5.5in (14cm) high*
$975-1,200 **WW**

A Caughley dish, enameled with a central rose motif, the rim with a wide 'S' scroll border within a band of gilt and turquoise husks.
c1790 *10.5in (26.5cm) wide*
$600-750 **WW**

A Caughley spoon tray, painted in underglaze blue and overpainted in gilt with flowerheads, script 'S' in blue.
c1790 *6.5in (16.5cm) wide*
$225-300 **HT**

A Caughley eyebath printed with portions of the 'Fisherman' or 'Pleasure Boat' pattern.
c1790 *2in (5.5cm) high*
$1,800-2,250 **WW**

A Caughley cabbage-leaf molded mask jug, printed with the 'Fisherman and Cormorant' pattern and 'S' mark.

c1790 *8.75in (22cm) high*

$330-450 **DN**

A pair of rare Caughley ice pails, covers and liners, printed with the 'Fisherman and Cormorant' pattern, printed 'S' marks.

c1790 *10.25in (26cm) high*

$6,000-7,500 **DN**

A pair of Caughley leaf-shaped blue and white pickle dishes, printed with the 'Fisherman and Cormorant' pattern, both un-marked.

c1790 *3.5in (9cm) long*

$300-450 **DN**

A Caughley lozenge-shaped dish, printed with the 'Fisherman and Cormorant' pattern, un-marked.

c1790 *11.5in (29.5cm) long*

$450-600 **DN**

A Caughley baking dish, printed with the 'Fisherman and Cormorant' pattern, impressed 'SALOPIAN' mark.

c1790 *9.25in (23.5cm) long*

$450-750 **DN**

A Caughley mug, printed with the 'Fisherman' or 'Pleasure Boat' pattern.

c1780-90 *4.5in (11.5cm) high*

$1,000-1,200 **WW**

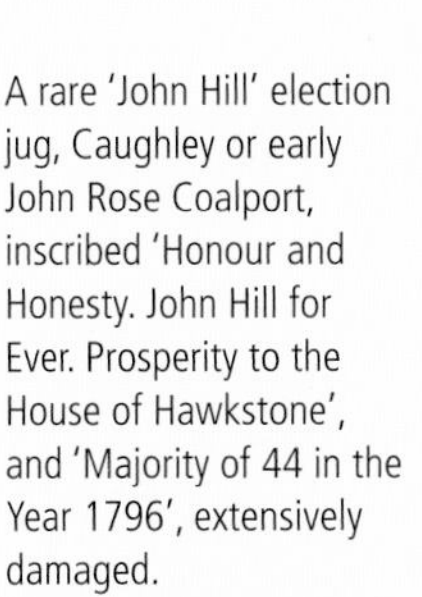

A dated Caughley cabbage leaf jug, printed with the 'Fisherman' pattern, inscribed 'Manlove Vernon Lawrence 1782', printed 'S' mark.

Manlove Vernon Lawrence of Leese Hill, Uttoxeter, was christened in Shropshire on 4th January 1782, the eldest son of Ellen Hartshorne and the Reverend Thomas Lawrence. His unusual Christian name and his middle name came from his grandmother, Ellen Vernon (née Manlove) from whom his mother inherited her vast estate.

1782 *9in (23.5cm) high*

$4,500-6,000 **WW**

ELECTION JUG

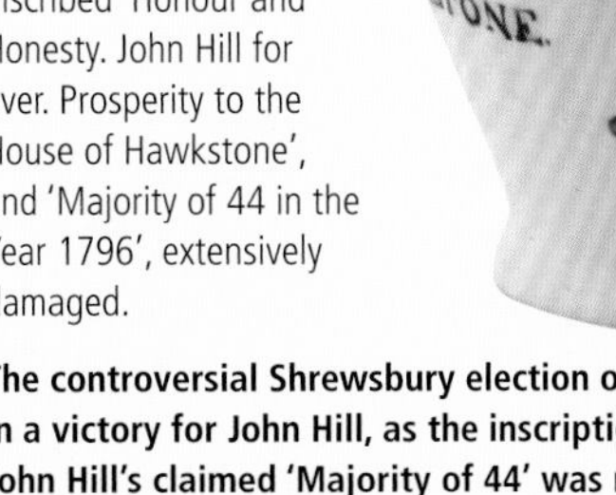

A rare 'John Hill' election jug, Caughley or early John Rose Coalport, inscribed 'Honour and Honesty. John Hill for Ever. Prosperity to the House of Hawkstone', and 'Majority of 44 in the Year 1796', extensively damaged.

The controversial Shrewsbury election of 1796 did not in fact result in a victory for John Hill, as the inscription on this jug suggests. John Hill's claimed 'Majority of 44' was reached by adding spoilt ballot papers to his valid votes, and amounted only to a majority over his younger kinsman, William Hill, rather than to the overall victor, William Pulteney. The confusion regarding attribution of the jug itself lies in the closeness of the two factories and the fact that several molds exist. It is possible that both factories produced these Election jugs, although it has sometimes been quoted as the earliest known dated Coalport porcelain.

c1796 *8.5in (22cm) high*

$600-750 **WW**

ESSENTIAL REFERENCE - BRISTOL

In its early years, The Bristol China Manufactory was run by British chemist William Cookworthy (1705-80) and Bristol merchant Richard Champion (1743-91).

- **After the discovery of Kaolin (china clay) in Cornwall, Cookworthy patented several formulas containing this mineral to produce hard-paste English porcelain.**
- **Champion purchased and improved Cookworthy's patent for hard-paste porcelain in 1774.**
- **Bristol porcelain achieved a distinct whiteness and occasionally marked its wares with a crossed-swords symbol, elements that are usually associated with Meissen porcelain.**
- **Champion manufactured good quality porcelain pieces, but never in large quantities because of persisting difficulties that occurred during the firing process of porcelain.**
- **According to the British Museum, Champion experienced financial difficulties in the 1770s because of his 14-year petition to have the porcelain patent renewed.**
- **The Bristol factory may have closed in 1781, but Champion sold his patent to a consortium of manufacturers in Staffordshire in 1782 that adapted his formula for mass production. The consortium opened a new factory under the name New Hall Co.**
- **New Hall continued into the 1830s, but its later products are not as collectable.**

A Bristol teacup and saucer, and a similar coffee cup, decorated with garlands of flowers, blue 'B' marks to the cup and saucer, blue 'X' mark to the coffee cup.

c1770-75 *5in (12.5cm)*

$300-450 **WW**

A Champion's Bristol sauceboat, molded with floral festoons and painted with garlands, a band of stiff leaves molded around the foot.

c1775 *6.5in (16.5cm) wide*

$1,500-2,000 **WW**

A pair of Bristol coffee cups and saucers, the larger finely painted with colorful sprays of flowers within gilt line and dentil rims, the smaller similarly decorated with larger floral sprays, blue 'X' marks with numbers 24 and 10.

c1775-80 *5in (12.5cm) high*

$850-975 **WW**

A Bristol fluted teabowl and saucer, painted with sprays of polychrome flowers and single scattered leaves.

c1775-80 *5in (12.5cm) high*

$750-900 **WW**

CLOSER LOOK - CHAMPION'S BRISTOL MUG

The bell-shape was a much favored style at Champion's Bristol.

The decoration of polychrome enamels with flower sprays beneath a laurel garland border is well executed.

The grooved strap handle with a puce foliate motif is typical.

The mug is marked with the Bristol blue cross mark.

A large Champion's Bristol mug.

c1775 *5in (12.5cm) high*

$1,400-1,500 **WW**

ESSENTIAL REFERENCE - CHELSEA

Founded in c1744 by Nicholas Sprimont, the Chelsea factory was the first porcelain factory in England.

- **Pieces from the Raised Anchor Period (c1749-52) are typically decorated with copies of Japanese Kakiemon wares or Meissen-style European landscapes.**
- **During the Red Anchor period (c1752-56) Chelsea was known for innovative decoration, which included painted fruit and botanical motifs.**
- **Porcelain produced during the Gold Anchor Period (c1756-69) was strongly influenced by Sèvres.**
- **The Chelsea factory was sold in 1770 to William Duesbury of Derby, who ran it until 1784. Pieces from this period are known as Chelsea-Derby.**

A pair of Chelsea 'Japanesque' teabowls and saucers, decorated with alternate panels of iron-red and green and yellow scrolling foliage, one with raised anchor mark.

c1750 *saucers 4.5in (11cm) diam*

$6,750-8,250 **DN**

A Chelsea 'Kakiemon' teabowl and saucer, painted with radiating shrubs.

c1750 *5.5in (13.5cm) diam*

$1,800-3,000 **DN**

A Chelsea 'Kakiemon' teabowl and saucer, painted with alternate panels of iron-red and gilt scrolls and flowers and objects.

c1750

$1,400-1,700 **DN**

CLOSER LOOK - CHELSEA

A Chelsea teabowl, with brown line rim.

c1750-52 *3.5in (9cm) high*

$1,800-3,000 **WW**

A Chelsea fluted teabowl or beaker, painted in the 'Kakiemon' palette, with squirrels scampering over hedges and bamboo.

c1752 *2in (5cm) high*

$1,800-2,250 **WW**

A Chelsea peony dish, the center of the flower finely detailed in purple, the overlapping leaf veined in brown with yellow detailing to the edges, red anchor mark.

c1755 *9in (23cm) wide*

$2,100-2,700 **WW**

A Chelsea silver-shaped dish, painted with small floral sprigs and sprays, brown line rim.

c1755 *8.25in (21cm) wide*

$750-900 **WW**

A Chelsea cup and saucer, painted with sprays of European flowers, the cup's handle issuing from flowering branches, red anchor marks.

c1755 *4.75in (12cm) high*

$1,000-1,400 **WW**

A pair of Chelsea plates, the osier-molded rims painted with panels of fancy birds, the wells with sprays of European flowers, red anchor marks.
c1755 *8.5in (21.5cm) diam*
$2,000-2,400 **WW**

A Chelsea 'Kakiemon' soup dish, painted with a version of the 'Two Quails' pattern, red anchor mark.
c1756 *10.25in (26cm) wide*
$3,000-4,000 **DN**

A Chelsea dish, painted with flowers within a brown-line bordered rim, red anchor mark.
c1756 *9in (23.5cm) long*
$255-300 **DN**

A Chelsea porcelain model of 'Boreas and Oreithyia', modeled after the Meissen original by F.Meyer, small red anchor mark.
c1756 *9.5in (24cm) high*
$1,500-2,250 **DN**

A pair of Chelsea 'Kakiemon' plates, painted with a large central mon within a landscape of flowering shrubs and with scalloped rim, red anchor marks.
c1756 *9.5in (24cm) diam*
$3,000-4,000 **DN**

A pair of Chelsea sunflower dishes, each molded as a flower with two leaves issuing from a stalk handle, the raised centers detailed in shades of brown, pink and yellow, red anchor marks, damages.
c1756 *9in (22.5cm) wide*
$1,650-2,000 **WW**

A Chelsea chinoiserie bouquetiere figure of a lady, modeled seated beside a pierced urn, sparsely colored and gilt.
c1760 *7.5in (19cm) high*
$1,000-1,400 **DN**

A Chelsea figure of a musician, gold anchor mark.
c1760 *10.6in (27cm) high*
$900-1,200 **DN**

A Chelsea fluted teabowl or beaker, painted with small sprays of flowers, brown line rim.

c1753 *2in (5cm) high*

$1,200-1,500 **WW**

A Chelsea silver-shaped dish, painted with sprays of flowers including pink rose.

c1756 *8.5in (21.5cm) wide*

$1,200-1,500 **WW**

A pair of Chelsea tripod stands, a bunch of grapes hung between each scrolling foot, the top of which terminates in a shell, puce anchor marks.

c1760 *3in (8.5cm) high*

$1,200-1,800 **WW**

A Chelsea bell-shaped cup and matched saucer, finely pencilled with fancy birds standing amidst leafy foliage, gold anchor marks.

c1760-64 *4.75in (12cm) high*

$1,200-1,500 **WW**

A Chelsea plate, well painted with a posy of English flowers and single scattered blooms, the molded rim with vignettes of colorful birds, gold anchor mark.

c1760 *9in (23cm) diam*

$750-900 **WW**

A Chelsea figure of a reaper, modeled standing against a tree stump holding a sheaf of corn, a flail and small barrel at his feet, gold anchor mark, some damage.

c1760-65 *12.5in (32cm) high*

$2,400-3,000 **BELL**

A pair of Chelsea figural candlesticks, depicting a musician and his companion, before blossoming bocage, gold anchor marks.

These are a true pair and are recorded with differing bocage.

c1765 *10in (26cm) high*

$1,800-3,000 **WW**

ESSENTIAL REFERENCE - DERBY

Derby porcelain was first made c1748 by Andrew Planché. In 1770 Duesbury bought the ailing Chelsea factory and ran it until 1784 in conjunction with the Derby works.

- **Chinoiserie figure groups in the white are some of the most desirable Derby figures.**
- **Influenced by Meissen, Derby figures of the 1750s and 1760s are Rococo in style, standing on scrolled bases.**
- **To prevent kiln adhesion during firing, the unglazed bases of the figures were supported on raised clay pads that left distinctive 'patch marks'.**
- **Derby's slightly creamy, glass-like glaze dribbled freely during the firing. To prevent adhesion to the kiln shelves, the glaze was wiped away from around the bases of figures and cream-jugs, giving an appearance known as 'dry-edge'.**
- **Derby developed distinctive styles of bird and flower painting. Forms were tureens, leaf shapes, baskets.**
- **During Derby's 'transitional' phase (c1755–6) the glaze, over a chalky paste, became whiter, and was lightly decorated in distinctive, rather delicate enamels, which have earned figure groups of this period the title 'Pale Family'.**
- **Derby's porcelain body meant that its teawares were prone to cracking during use, and examples are rare.**
- **Derby porcelain is usually unmarked before 1770; from c1770 a model number was often scratched into the base of a figure, greatly assisting identification.**
- **There are two marks from the Chelsea-Derby period (1770–84); the gold with Chelsea's anchor, the second is usually marked in blue enamel.**
- **c1782 to mid-19thC: the mark can be incised, or painted in purple, black, blue, or, after 1800, in red.**

A Derby gadrooned globular teapot and cover, painted with sprays of flowers in the Meissen manner, red-line rims.

c1756 *6.5in (16.5cm) high*

$1,000-1,400 **DN**

A Derby bowl, painted in the famille rose palette with pink peony and other flowers beside tall blue rockwork.

c1760 *4.25in (11cm) high*

$225-300 **WW**

A pair of Derby figures of bullfinches.

c1760-65 *4.75in (12cm) and 5.25in (13.5cm) high*

$3,400-4,000 **BELL**

A pair of dry-edge Derby sweetmeat figures, modeled seated with shells upon their knees.

The 'Dry Edge' period ran from 1750-56. This period got its name from the base that is unglazed.

c1755 *6.4in (16.5cm) high*

$2,000-2,400 **DN**

A pair of Derby figures of a bagpiper and a dancer, with patch marks.

c1760 *tallest 7in (18cm) high*

$1,200-1,500 **DN**

A Derby flower-encrusted and pierced frill pot pourri vase and cover, painted with insects and applied with two mask handles, the cover surmounted by a bird.

c1765 *12in (31cm) high*

$1,275-1,425 **DN**

A Derby figure of Winter, modeled as a putto seated before a flaming brazier and wrapped in a fur-lined cloak.

c1765 *6.75in (17cm) high*

$750-1,000 **WW**

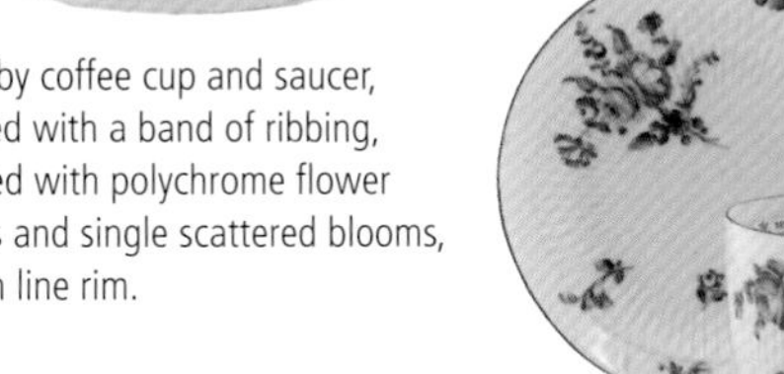

A Derby coffee cup and saucer, molded with a band of ribbing, painted with polychrome flower sprays and single scattered blooms, brown line rim.

c1765-70 *5in (12.5cm) high*

$600-900 **WW**

A pair of Derby porcelain baskets, painted with exotic birds and scattered sprigs, the basket molded exteriors with molded flowers on a pale yellow ground.

c1765 *8in (20cm) wide*

$1,800-2,100 **TEN**

A Derby butter boat, molded with wheat ears and painted with flower and leaf trails and a moth.

c1770 *4in (10cm) wide*

$400-450 **SWO**

A Derby wall pocket, molded with rococo scrolls and painted with disheveled birds.

c1770 *9.75in (24.5cm) high*

$600-750 **WW**

A Derby sweetmeat stand or centerpiece, the lobed dish divided into six sections around a central removable bowl, decorated with husk swags and a stylized scroll border.

c1770 *6.25in (16cm) high*

$900-1,200 **WW**

A Derby ewer creamer, of shell-molded form, with two entwined dolphins beneath the spout.

c1770 *3.25in (8cm) high*

$280-340 **WW**

A Derby ewer, of high-handled French form, painted with a basket of flowers including pink rose and tulip, puce mark, some restoration to the handle.

c1790-1800 *13.25in (33.5cm) high*

$400-450 **WW**

A Derby custard cup and cover, decorated with horizontal gilt and cobalt blue designs, puce crowned crossed batons mark.

c1790 *3.25in (8.5cm) high*

$1,000-1,400 **WW**

Two late 18thC Derby figures, one of a musician playing the flageolet, the other of a shepherdess holding a lamb.

5.75in (14.5cm) high

$750-1,000 **WW**

A pair of Derby bough pots, painted with topographical views of Wales and Italy, a sailing boat before a village in one, ruins atop a rugged hillside in the other, iron red marks and titles, minor damages.

c1815 *7.5in (19cm) wide*

$1,400-1,800 **WW**

A Derby 'Long Tom' vase, painted in the manner of Daniel Lucas, with cottagers in a wooded landscape with a house with smoking chimney and distant ruins.

c1820 *21in (53cm) high*

$1,150-1,425 **M&K**

A Bloor Derby vase, painted with flowers including sunflower, narcissus, nasturtium, heartsease and peony, on a white ground decorated with gilt scrolls and stylized designs, red printed mark.

c1830-40 *11.5in (29cm) high*

$850-1,125 **WW**

A Royal Crown Derby vase, painted by William Dean, with a shaped panel shipping scene, iron-red script marks.

1903 *3.5in (9cm) high*

$150-210 **DN**

A Royal Crown Derby vase and cover, painted by W Mosley, with a medallion of a church, printed mark.

1911 *7in (18cm) high*

$3,400-3,900 **M&K**

A pair of 19thC Dresden porcelain vases, the lids surmounted by a crowned heraldic crest flanked by putti, the sides painted with romantic scenes, blue crossed swords marks.

24.5in (62cm) high

$3,000-4,500 **L&T**

A pair of late 19thC Dresden urns, the bodies with reserves painted with 'deutsche blumen' and 'fetes galant', blue Augustus Rex mark.

Although having the Augustus Rex mark, therefore portending to come from the Meissen factory in the early 18thC, these vases were made in one of the many porcelain factories in Dresden at the end of the 19thC. Although not Meissen, they are of good quality.

25.25in (64cm) high

$1,800-3,000 **L&T**

A late 19thC Dresden bowl, painted with courting figures and flowers, impressed Meissen over painted Dresden.

9.5in (24cm) wide

$105-150 **DA&H**

A Dresden porcelain letter-rack, painted with flower-sprays and Watteauesque panels, script marks, cracked.

c1900 *8in (20.5cm) long*

$105-150 **DN**

A late 19thC/early 20thC Dresden porcelain charger, painted with a courting couple and sprays of flowers to center.

16in (41.5cm) long

$225-300 **ROS**

A pair of early 20thC Dresden mirrors, encrusted with flowers and leaves, the top mounted with a crowned portrait of Louis XVI flanked by putti.

36in (91cm) high

$4,500-6,000 **ROS**

An early 20thC Dresden vase and cover, the handles with snake finials, the center with flowers and foliage, marked Dresden to base.

16in (40cm) high

$450-600 **ROS**

ESSENTIAL REFERENCE - LIVERPOOL

Several porcelain factories were established in 1750s Liverpool. Many used copies of Worcester's porcelain formula, leading to confusion over attribution of their wares.

- **Richard Chaffers & Partners (c1754-65) were the most successful Liverpool porcelain maker. Chaffers bought Worcester's porcelain recipe in 1755, and produced thin teawares with blue-and-white Chinese-style patterns.**
- **Philip Christian (c1765-76) took over from Chaffers.**
- **James, John and Seth Pennington (c1769-99) were brothers with separate works around the city. Their glaze is sometimes tinted.**
- **Samuel Gilbody (c1754-61): the rarest of all Liverpool wares.**
- **William Reid (c1755-61) produced mainly blue-and-white wares with a semi-opaque body, going bankrupt in 1761.**
- **William Ball (c1755-69) took over from Reid. The decoration often resembled delftware.**

A rare William Reid blue and white teapot, painted with a Chinese pagoda landscape, the cover lacking.

Although the foot is unusual for a teapot, it is often seen on barrel-shaped mugs and jugs produced by the Reid factory at this time.

c1756-61 *7.5in (19cm) diam*

$750-1,000 **WW**

A William Reid bowl, enameled with a Chinese figure standing beside a large pot over a roaring fire.

c1756-61 *6in (15.5cm) diam*

$900-1,200 **WW**

A Chaffers Liverpool hexagonal beaker, painted with a Chinese floral pattern, a stylized spray of Oriental flowers to each facet.

c1756-60 *2.25in (6cm) high*

$1,275-1,700 **WW**

A Chaffers Liverpool tea cup, painted with the 'Jumping Boy' pattern, four character script mark.

c1758 *3.5in (8.5cm) wide*

$300-450 **WW**

A Chaffers Liverpool teapot stand, molded and painted with the Chrysanthemum pattern.

c1760 *5.5in (14cm) diam*

$600-900 **WW**

A Chaffers Liverpool teapot and cover, decorated with a bird perched on flowering Oriental branches.

This was decorated in underglaze blue and then overpainted in red and gilt to emulate the fashionable Imari palette.

c1760 *7.75in (20cm) wide*

$550-700 **WW**

A Chaffers Liverpool teabowl and saucer, printed in black with the 'Rock Garden' pattern, a couple seated and conversing beneath trees and Classical ruins.

c1760-65 *5in (12.5cm) high*

$450-550 **WW**

A James Pennington Liverpool plate, painted with bamboo and a large spray of peony issuing from jagged rockwork, star crack.

c1765-70 *8.75in (22.5cm) diam*

$300-400 **WW**

A James Pennington's Liverpool sauceboat, with gadroon molding, painted with the 'Cannonball' pattern.

c1768-73 *6.25in (16cm) wide*

$550-700 **WW**

A Christian Liverpool teacup, decorated in the Worcester manner with panels of flowers reserved on a blue scale ground.

c1770-75 *3.75in (9.5cm) diam*

$450-550 **WW**

A Christian Liverpool reeded teacup and saucer, painted in dry blue.

c1775 *5.25in (13.5cm) high*

$300-450 **WW**

A Seth Pennington Liverpool sauceboat, molded with 'Liver Bird' motifs and a smiling mask above fruiting grapevine.

c1780 *7.75in (19.5cm)*

$600-900 **WW**

A Liverpool serving dish or tureen stand, painted with flower sprays within a diaper band border.

c1780 *13.5in (34.5cm) long*

$600-900 **DN**

A pair of late 18thC Liverpool coffee cans, variously painted with flowers and scattered leaves, each with a grooved loop handle.

2.5in (6.5cm) high

$400-550 **WW**

ESSENTIAL REFERENCE - LONGTON HALL

Longton Hall, founded c1749 in rural Staffordshire, was far removed from the changing fashions of London.

- **Longton Hall porcelain had a thick, semi-opaque white glaze that has earned the name 'snowman class' for early figures.**
- **The factory made soft-paste porcelain; sometimes the body contains 'moons' – tiny air bubbles that appear as pale spots against a strong light.**
- **Meissen-style flowers are attributed to an artist known as the 'trembly rose painter'.**
- **By c1752, Longton Hall produced porcelain that could be molded quite thinly – ideal for making the forms such as fruit, vegetables, and leaves that the factory specialized in.**
- **The figures, which are not dissimilar to those of Bow and Derby, show the influence of Meissen.**
- **The variable quality of Longton Hall porcelain, coupled with heavy kiln losses, led to the factory's bankruptcy and closure in 1760.**
- **No mark was used.**

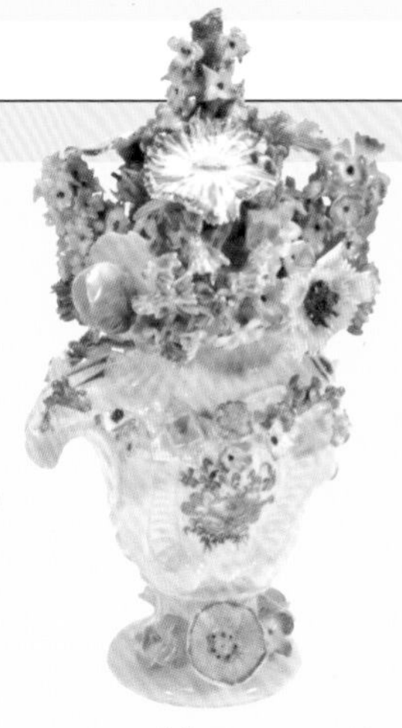

A Longton Hall flower-encrusted asymmetrical vase and cover, modeled en rocaille and painted with sprays of flowers.
c1755 *7.75in (20cm) high*
$750-1,000 **DN**

A Longton Hall figure of 'Ceres', goddess of agriculture, modeled holding a sheaf of corn, a child at her side.
c1755-58 *6.5in (16.5cm) high*
$1,650-2,100 **DN**

A Longton Hall mug, painted with three birds in a landscape with others in flight, the molded handle with puce detailing.
c1755 *3.75in (9.5cm) high*
$2,000-2,400 **WW**

A Longton Hall black-printed mug, the horse head crested armorial within rococo framing above stag hunting scenes, with a hair crack.

Although the handle shape conforms to Longton Hall, the printing can be attributed to Liverpool.
6.5in (16cm) high
$850-1,125 **CHEF**

A Longton Hall coffee cup, brightly enameled with pink peony above a red fence.
c1755-60 *2.5in (6.5cm)*
$600-900 **WW**

A Longton Hall teabowl, decorated in the 'Castle Painter' style with a turreted building beside a river, a church in the near distance.

While John Hayfield is often the name put forward as the identity of the Castle Painter, the style is actually known to have been executed by several hands.
c1756-58 *3in (7.5cm) diam*
$600-750 **WW**

A Longton Hall strawberry bowl, well painted in 'Trembly Rose' style, with a loose bouquet, with small shallow footrim chip.
c1756 *9.5in (24cm) wide*
$750-1,000 **CHOR**

A model of 'Hercules and the Nemean Lion', Longton Hall or Vauxhall, modeled wrestling on a scrolling base.
c1755 *5.75in (14.5cm) high*
$3,000-4,500 **DN**

ESSENTIAL REFERENCE - LOWESTOFT

Blue-and-white porcelain became a highly desirable commodity in 17th and 18thC Europe as a result of trade with China. However, Chinese porcelain was pricey which prompted English manufacturers to experiment with making their own hard-paste porcelain. This particular mug was made around 1760 at a factory located in the fishing port of Lowestoft in East Anglia. Although this mug isn't personalized with an inscription or date – an aspect of Lowestoft porcelain that appeals to collectors – the naively painted scene of a Chinese pagoda amongst trees is characteristic of the early Lowestoft style and has its own unique charm.

A Lowestoft mug, painted with a Chinese pagoda beneath trees with birds in flight above, a sailing vessel and pavilion to the other side, painter's numeral to the inside footrim, cracked.
c1760-65 *3.5in (9cm) high*
$850-975 **WW**

A Lowestoft 'Redgrave' pattern coffee cup, saucer and bowl, painted in underglaze blue, iron-red and gold with pheasants amongst rocks and flowers.
c1760
$280-340 **SWO**

A rare Lowestoft blue and white eyebath, painted with an Oriental flower spray to each side.
c1765 *2.25in (5.5cm) high*
$5,250-6,750 **WW**

A pair of Lowestoft sauceboats, printed with sprays of flowers within molded floral panels.
c1770 *5.5in (14cm) wide*
$600-900 **WW**

A Lowestoft guglet, of pear shape with garlic neck, painted with stylized chinoiserie foliage and insects, number 5 mark.
c1770 *9.8in (25cm) high*
$2,100-2,400 **TEN**

A Lowestoft teapot and cover, painted with bouquets of flowers and sprays.
c1770-1780, *6in (15.5cm) high*
$400-450 **SWO**

A Lowestoft coffee pot and cover, painted with a version of the 'Mansfield' pattern.
c1785 *9.5in (24cm) high*
$1,800-2,250 **DN**

A pair of Lowestoft teabowls and saucers, the fluted bodies painted in the Curtis manner with a naive spray of flowers within unusual purple ribbon garlands suspended from green and red paterae.

The pattern is similar to New Hall pattern 195, but is based on an original design from Chinese export porcelain, variations of which are also found on wares at other English factories in the period 1795-1805.
c1795 *4.75in (12cm) high*
$700-850 **WW**

A Lowestoft birth tablet, for 'Eallathe Leggett Liffen Born December 9th 1798', decorated verso with a floral sprig.
1798 *1in (3cm) diam*
$12,750-14,250 **KEY**

ESSENTIAL REFERENCE – MEISSEN

The experiments of Johann Friedrich Böttger (1682-1719) and Ehrenfried Walther von Tschirnhausen (1651-1708) led to the discovery of white hard-paste porcelain at the beginning of the 18thC. Thanks to Böttger's efforts, Augustus the Strong, Elector of Saxony, opened Europe's first hard-paste porcelain factory in Meissen in 1710.

- **Johann Joachim Kändler (1706-75) was responsible for producing some of the most striking porcelain figures during the 1730s and 1740s.**
- **From the 1750s onward, wares in the newly popular Roccoco style were decorated with pastel colors and had elaborately scrolled bases.**
- **After the war, figures were being made using molds from the 1730s, but lacked the liveliness of the originals.**
- **In 1774, new director Count Camillo Marcolini (1739-1814) introduced Neo-classicism.**
- **During the 19thC, the introduction of new styles such as Biedermeier, Roccoco and Renaissance Revival - characterized Meissen wares.**

A Meissen cup, painted with a flying insect above plants and rockwork in the Chinese manner, blue crossed swords mark.
c1730 *3in (7.5cm) high*
$400-550 **WW**

A Meissen tureen and cover, painted in 'Kakiemon' style with a bird singing on a peony branch, crossed swords mark in underglaze blue, one handle terminal missing.
c1735 *6in (15.5cm) wide*
$2,700-3,300 **MAB**

A Meissen basket, the handles issuing from maskheads emblematic of the Four Seasons, the interior painted in the Kakiemon palette, some damage.
c1735-40 *10in (25.5cm) wide*
$1,800-2,250 **WW**

A Meissen teapot and cover, painted in the Kakiemon palette, a bird in flight beneath the spout, blue crossed swords mark.
c1735 *6.25in (16cm) high*
$1,800-2,250 **WW**

A Meissen teabowl, probably decorated at Augsburg with gold chinesen, some rubbing.
c1725 *3in (7.5cm) diam*
$1,150-1,300 **TRI**

A Meissen teabowl and saucer, painted in Schwartzlot with scenes of merchants loading and unloading ships in a harbour scene, surmounted by Chinese figures, blue crossed swords mark, gilt 'J'.
c1730 *5in (12.5cm) diam*
$4,400-4,800 **WW**

CLOSER LOOK - MEISSEN PLATES

This 'Japanese Hunting' service was ordered for the collection of Augustus the Strong.

It is the only Meissen dinner service of the time with a colored ground.

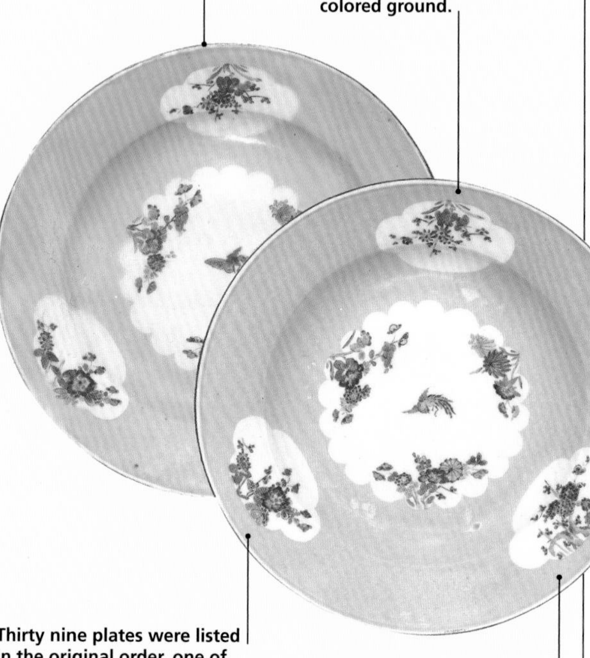

Thirty nine plates were listed in the original order, one of which is recorded as having been broken in two in 1777 at a dinner held for the King of Prussia.

The yellow is derived from the livery of the Electoral Huntsmen.

A rare pair of Meissen plates, decorated in the 'Kakiemon' manner, blue crossed swords marks, incised Johanneum numbers N=148.
c1733-34 *9.25in (23.5cm) diam*
$37,500-45,000 **WW**

A late 19thC Meissen group of 'The Drunken Silenus', typically modeled, incised 2784, blue crossed swords mark, some damage.

8.5in (21.5cm) high

$1,800-2,250 DN

A pair of late 19thC Meissen figures of 'Night and Day', personified as children, blue crossed swords marks, incised M105 and M106, minor damages.

7in (18cm) high

$1,800-3,000 WW

A late 19thC Meissen porcelain group, modeled as Scaramouche attending to a seated female, blue crossed swords and incised 279/36.

6.5in (16.5cm) high

$1,150-1,425 HT

A 19thC Meissen figure group, incised 932, with underglaze blue crossed swords mark to base, some damage.

6in (15cm) high

$1,800-2,250 BELL

A 19thC Meissen figure group, incised 932, with underglaze blue crossed swords mark to base, some damage.

6in (15cm) high

$1,800-2,250 BELL

A pair of late 19thC large Meissen kingerbusts, after a model by J J Kändler, depicting Prince Louis Charles de Bourbon and Princess Marie Zephyrine de Bourbon, blue cross swordmarks.

9in (23cm) high

$4,500-6,000 L&T

A set of eight 20thC Meissen figures of musicians from the Gallant Orchestra, after models by J J Kändler and Meyer, blue crossed swords marks, each in its original box.

6.25in (16cm) high

$4,000-5,250 WW

A Meissen chocolate pot and cover, decorated with Indianische Blumen in a variation of the Kakiemon palette, the cover sprung and with later gilt metal mounts, blue crossed swords mark.

c1735 *7.5in (19cm) high*

$3,000-4,500 WW

A Meissen chocolate pot and cover, painted with panels of merchants in harbour scenes, iron red 'J' to the inside cover and base.

c1735-40 *5.5in (14cm) high*

$13,500-19,500 WW

A Meissen cream pot and cover, outside decorated with a huntress and her dog, blue crossed swords mark and puce painter's mark.

c1740 *5.75in (14.5cm) high*

$1,800-2,400 WW

A Meissen cup and saucer, the cup painted with an equestrian figure beside a harbour, the saucer with merchants on the quayside, blue crossed swords and gilt 'S' marks.

c1740 *5.25in (13.5cm) diam*

$1,800-2,250 WW

A pair of rare Meissen Continent groups, of Africa and Europe, modeled by Eberlein and P. Reinicke after J J Kändler. Africa is personified as a negress seated on a lion, Europe is seated on a bench before a white horse, with a faint blue crossed swords mark.

Copies of Kändler's original models were frequently made (of smaller stature than these) throughout the 19thC, but the 18thC examples are seldom seen. Kändler's original figures were again slightly smaller than these groups.

c1745 *12.5in (32cm) high*

$42,000-51,000 WW

A Meissen white-glazed model of a quail, naturalistically modeled by J J Kändler, the plumage finely incised.

c1745 *5.5in (14cm) wide*

$750-1,000 WW

A Meissen figure of a Chinaman, modeled by P. Reinicke, on an ormolu mount, minor rubbing to gilding.

c1750 *5.5in (14cm) high*

$3,000-4,000 DN

A Meissen figure of a shepherdess, modeled by J J Kändler and P. Reinicke, faint blue crossed swords mark to the underside, some restoration to her fingers.

c1750 *6.5in (16.5cm) high*

$1,800-2,250 WW

J. J. KÄNDLER

A rare pair of Meissen figures of red squirrels, modeled by J J Kändler, seated on their haunches facing to the left and right, the oval mound bases applied with flowers, indistinct blue crossed swords marks, some restoration and small chips.

Kändler first modeled a pair of squirrels in 1732, his work records for August that year listing 'Zwei Eichhörnigen' (two squirrels) and in September 1733, 'Ein kleines Eichhörnigen' (a small squirrel). For the model see C.Albiker, 'Die Meissener Porrzellantiere im 18.Jahrundert (1935), no.164'. There is also an example of the squirrel holding a nut from the Collection of Sir Gawaine and Lady Baillie.

c1750 *7.75in (19.5cm) and 8.75in (22cm) high*

$82,500-97,500 BELL

A Meissen écuelle, cover and stand, painted with flowers on a blue scale ground, blue crossed swords marks, a small section of the stand restored.

c1750-60 *9.75in (24.5cm) wide*

$1,800-2,250 **WW**

A mid-18thC Meissen teapot and cover, the spout molded as a grotesque, painted with moths and other insects, the cover with a caterpillar, blue crossed swords mark.

7in (18cm) wide

$7,200-8,100 **WW**

A mid-18thC Meissen figure group of the 'Chinese Family', modeled by P. Reinicke.

6.5in (16.5cm) high

$9,000-10,500 **WW**

A pair of Meissen figures of a fisherman and companion, modeled by J J Kändler, crossed swords marks to the backs of the bases.

c1750 *6in (15.5cm) high*

$6,000-9,000 **WW**

A Meissen figure of a pastry seller, blue crossed swords mark to the reverse of the base.

c1750 *7.5in (19cm) high*

$4,950-5,400 **WW**

A mid-18thC Meissen 'Malabar' figure group.

8.75in (22cm) high

$5,100-5,700 **WW**

A mid-18thC Meissen group of Venus and Cupid, the goddess riding in a rocaille-molded shell-chariot.

7in (18cm) long

$8,250-9,750 **BELL**

J. J. KÄNDLER

Whenever possible Kändler drew his designs from nature and in 1747 he had an encounter with a rhinoceros named Clara, who had been captured as a baby in India and brought to Europe in 1741. For two weeks in April 1747, Clara's keeper, Douwe Mout von der Meer, showed her in Dresden and Kändler took every opportunity to sketch her from all angles. These drawings were to serve as the basis for all future Meissen rhinoceros figures. Kändler himself modeled Clara twice - once in a group with a seated mandarain and a rhinoceros under a palm tree, in 1750, and two years later for the figure here. He blithely disregarded the fact that the rhino was to be found neither in China nor in the Ottoman Empire.

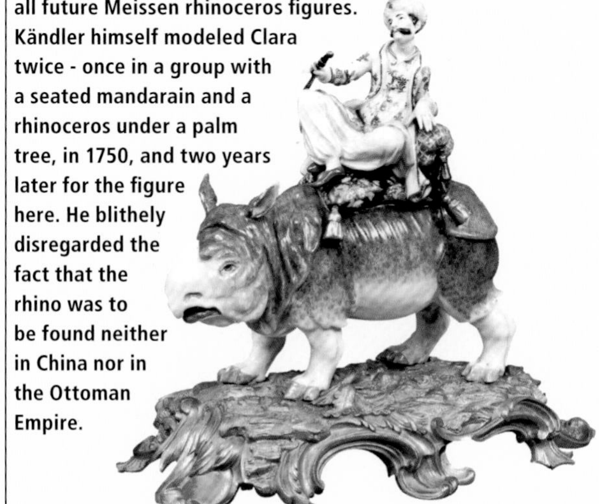

A Meissen bronze-mounted figure of a 'Turkish Sultan on a Rhinocerous', modeled by J J Kändler and P. Reinecke.

1752 *13in (33cm) high*

$90,000-105,000 **MTZ**

A Meissen figure of a coppersmith, modeled by J J Kändler, from the Artisan series, blue crossed swords marks to the rear.

c1750 *7in (18cm)*

$6,750-8,250 **WW**

A Meissen figure of a small girl, blue crossed swords mark, chips to fingers.

c1760 *4.5in (11.5cm) high*

$600-750 **DN**

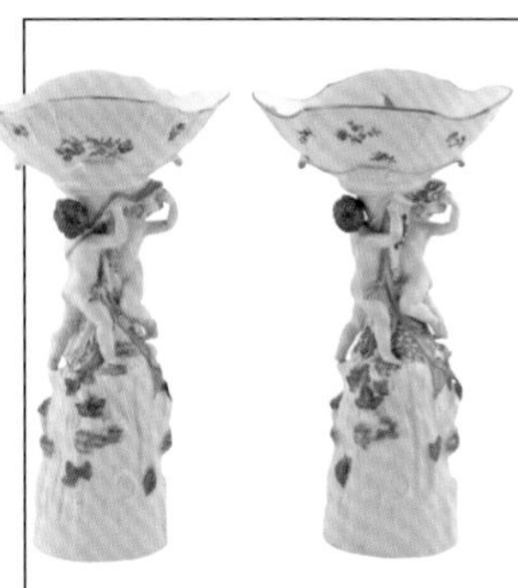

A pair of mid-18thC Meissen figural centerpieces, modeled by J J Kändler, blue crossed swords marks.

14.5in (37cm) high

$2,700-3,300 **WW**

A pair of 18thC Meissen figures of beggar musicians, blue crossed swords mark to the back of the bases.

13.25in (33.5cm) high

$1,800-3,000 **WW**

A Meissen figural group of 'The Toilette of the Little Princess', modeled by J J Kändler, blue crossed swords mark.

The group is modeled after the painting 'The Morning Toilet' by Jean-Baptiste-Siméon Chardin.

c1770 *7.25in (18.5cm) high*

$5,700-6,600 **WW**

An 18thC German porcelain scent bottle, perhaps Meissen, modeled as a small plum, with a gilt metal mount and hinged cover, a small internal stopper.

2.25in (6cm) wide

$750-1,000 **WW**

An early 19thC Meissen Marcolini period cup and saucer, painted with figures and cattle in riverside views, with a matching cup, underglaze blue cross swordmarks.

The Marcolini period of Meissen takes its name from Count Camillo Marcolini, Prime Minister of the German kingdom of Saxony, who was director of the Meissen works from 1774 until 1814. Meissen products from the Marcolini period were marked with the traditional crossed swords plus a star (sometimes looking like an asterisk) located near the short ends of the swords.

saucer 5in (13cm) diam

$750-900 **L&T**

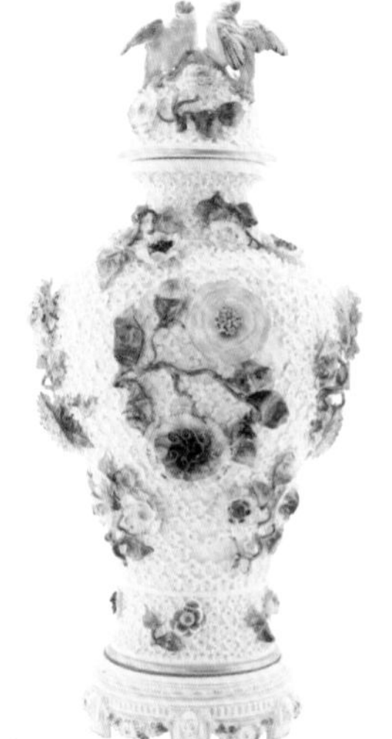

An early 19thC large Meissen Marcolini period 'schneeballen' vase, blue cross swordmark.

24in (61cm) high

$2,100-2,400 **L&T**

A mid-19thC Meissen 'Cris de Paris' figure of a lemonade seller, after the original model by P. Reinicke, blue crossed swords mark.

5.5in (14cm) high

$975-1,150 **DN**

A pair of 19thC Meissen pâte-sur-pâte porcelain vases, the reticulated covers with laurel wreath finials, the sides with serpent handles, blue crossed swords marks.

11in (28cm) high

$7,500-9,000 **L&T**

A pair of late 19thC Meissen pâte-sur-pâte vases, the sides with twin serpent handles, blue crossed swords marks, lacking covers.

9.25in (23.5cm) high

$3,600-4,400 **L&T**

A 19thC Meissen blue ground vase and cover, decorated in white and black enamel with a classical maiden, blue crossed swords mark.

8.5in (22cm) high

$1,800-3,000 **SK**

A 19thC Meissen group of the Broken Bridge, after the model by Acier, blue crossed swords mark, incised F63, a small amount of restoration.

This allegorical group shows the lady tentatively stepping onto wooden planks that Cupid strews with roses, her companion urging her forward while a further putto pushes her on to womanhood from behind.

9.75in (24.5cm) high

$2,100-2,700 WW

A pair of 19thC Meissen pot pourri vases and covers, each painted with courting couples, the pierced covers surmounted with tall floral finials, blue crossed swords marks.

16.5in (42cm) high

$5,250-6,750 WW

A 19thC Meissen figure group, depicting two winged cherubs, cornucopia and female figure, crossed swords mark with incised line through, patent number 193.

20in (50.5cm) high

$6,000-7,500 MITC

A 19thC Meissen charger, painted with a hunting party within a border marked with classical portraits en grisaille, signed 'nach Wouvermann', blue crossed swords mark.

15.5in (39cm) diam

$1,800-2,250 L&T

A pair of late 19thC Meissen figures of parrots, blue cross swordmarks.

5.75in (14.5cm) high

$850-975 L&T

A late 19thC Meissen allegorical figure group, emblematic of Autumn, blue cross swordmark.

6.5in (16.5cm) high

$975-1,150 L&T

A late 19thC Meissen figure of a cockerel, after a model by J J Kändler, blue cross swordmark.

9.75in (24.5cm) high

$1,200-1,800 L&T

A pair of Meissen figures, of a gallant with his dog and a lady with her cat, inscribed L162 and L163, impressed and painted marks, with loss.

c1890 *9in (23cm) high*

$4,000-4,500 SWO

ESSENTIAL REFERENCE - NANTGARW

Nantgarw was founded in South Wales by William Billingsley in 1813.

- **Pieces are marked 'NANTGARW' with impressed 'C.W.' (china works). Many forgeries have a red mark.**
- **Billingsley was known for his rose painting. Much decoration was done by decorators in London.**
- **By 1817 the Swansea venture was failing; Billingsley moved back to Nantgarw, erecting new kilns.**
- **Nantgarw porcelain was still difficult to control, resulting in a scarcity of teawares. Instead, plates could be fired with some success.**
- **The factory closed in 1822.**

A Nantgarw tazza, London-decorated with a butterfly and ladybird between two floral arrangements and further single scattered blooms.

This shape is unrecorded at Swansea and associated very much with the Nantgarw factory.

c1818-20 *4.25in (11cm) diam*

$900-1,200 **WW**

An unusual Nantgarw taperstick, painted probably by Thomas Pardoe with pink roses within a gilt husk border, with double C-scroll handle, some retouching to the gilding.

c1818-20 *3in (7.5cm) high*

$2,000-2,400 **WW**

A rare Nantgarw cabinet cup, painted to the exterior and interior with flower sprays, in the manner of William Billingsley, with griffon handle.

c1818-20 *3.75in (9.5cm) high*

$6,000-9,000 **WW**

A Nantgarw cabinet plate, London-decorated with flowers, the rim with three floral panels within gilt borders, impressed mark.

c1818-20 *9.25in (23.5cm) diam*

$1,500-2,100 **WW**

A Nantgarw 'chocolate'-edged plate, molded with a 'piecrust' rim and naively painted, probably by Thomas Pardoe, impressed mark.

c1820 *9.25in (23.5cm) diam*

$600-900 **WW**

A Nantgarw plate, decorated probably by William Billingsley, with roses and sprigs of other flowers and leaves, with the impressed mark 'Nantgarw CW'.

$2,500-3,000 **JON**

A Nantgarw coffee can, painted by Thomas Pardoe, with a songbird perched on a berried branch and a further bird in flight, gilt initial L.

c1818-20 *2.5in (6cm) high*

$1,200-1,800 **WW**

ESSENTIAL REFERENCE - PARIS

Following the relaxation of laws protecting the Sèvres monopoly, a large number of porcelain factories were established in Paris in the late 18thC.

- **Paris porcelain was decorative, especially late 18thC tablewares, but rarely innovative.**
- **François-Maurice Honoré founded a factory in the petite rue Saint-Gilles in 1785. By 1807 it had become the leading Paris porcelain factory. It closed in 1867.**
- **Jean-Baptiste Locré de Roissy's La Courtille factory (1771-c1840) was the most productive of the Paris factories.**

A late 18thC Paris white biscuit musical group, modeled as three musicians standing around a tree, some damage.

12.25in (31cm) high

$450-750 BELL

A Charles X Paris porcelain gold-ground vase, festooned with biscuit rose swags, the matt ground painted with classical motifs.

c1825 12.5in (32cm) high

$1,000-1,400 DN

A Paris porcelain urn, richly decorated with trophies, flowers and swags.

c1830 11.5in (29cm) high

$225-300 DN

A 19thC Paris porcelain tête-à-tête service, painted with rural and waterside scenes, comprising a teapot and cover, a hot water jug and cover, a milk jug and cover, a sucrièr and cover, two cans, two saucers and an oval tray.

$4,000-4,500 WW

Paris Porcelain Group

A late 18thC Dihl et Guerhard, Paris, biscuit porcelain figure group, possibly modeled by Charles Gabriel Sauvage, depicting a young man showing a birds nest in his hat to a young girl, the reverse modeled with a child asleep beneath a tree stump, impressed mark 'Mfre de Mgr le duc d'Angoulême à Paris'.

12.25in (31cm) high

$1,800-2,250 BELL

A pair of French porcelain Arab scent bottles and stoppers, probably Jacob Petit.

c1870 14.25in (36cm) high

$4,500-6,000 SWO

A late 19thC/early 20thC Paris porcelain bisque bust of a lady, dressed in gilt lined 18thC clothing and hat, signed A. Carrier.

18in (45cm) high

$550-700 ROS

ESSENTIAL REFERENCE – PRE-SÈVRES VINCENNES

The Vincennes factory was established in c1740. In 1745 it was granted a 20-year monopoly for the production of decorative porcelain. In 1753 Louis XV became the principal shareholder and the factory became known as the 'Manufacture Royale de Porcelaine'.

- **All pieces were of soft-paste porcelain.**
- **The factory's 'great period' began in 1751 with the appointment of Jean-Jacques Bachelier as art director.**
- **The crossed 'L's of the Royal cypher were adopted as the Vincennes (and later Sèvres) mark in 1753.**
- **The factory moved to Sèvres in 1756.**

A Sèvres bisque porcelain and gilt bronze mounted figure, 'L'amour Menacent', after Etienne-Maurice Falconet (1716-1791).

This is after an original marble statue created by Falconet for Louis XV's mistress Mme. de Pompadour in 1755, now in the Louvre. Falconet was appointed director of the sculpture atelier at Sèvres from 1757–1766 and was extremely influential in creating small figural sculptures produced in unglazed white porcelian. This model, and its companion Psyche, was extremely popular in the 18thC at Sèvres and was bought by many members of the court, including Mme. de Pompadour. The first Sèvres version was made in 1758.

c1760 *10.5in (27cm) high*

$1,800-2,250 **L&T**

A Sèvres biscuit figure of 'La Moissonneuse', raised on a mound base, some damage.

The figure was first modeled, along with its pair, 'Le Moissonneur', by Pierre Blondeau in 1752, after designs by Francois Boucher.

7.5in (18.5cm) high

$600-750 **BELL**

A Sèvres seau à liqueur, painted with colorful birds, interlaced 'LL' marks and blue painter's mark.

c1770 *12.25in (31cm) wide*

$1,800-3,000 **WW**

A Sèvres biscuit figure of 'Le Jeune Suppliant', on a rockwork base, incised arrows marks, minor chips.

The figure was first modeled by Pierre Blondeau in 1752, after Francois Boucher. The original drawing is still at Sèvres.

c1755 *8.7in (22cm) high.*

$5,250-6,750 **BELL**

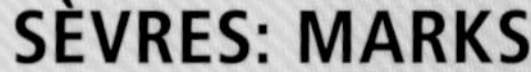

SÈVRES: MARKS

A Sèvres coffee can and saucer, painted with landscape panels, the can with auricular handle, script marks date letter 'Y'.

1776

$1,800-3,000 **DN**

An 18thC Sèvres porcelain coffee can and saucer, painted with garlands and roses, interlaced blue mark.

6in (15cm) diam

$1,500-2,000 **L&T**

An 18thC Sèvres blue ground cup and saucer or Gobelet Litron Et Soucoupe, the cup painted with cupid uniting Minover and Venus, the saucer with central script 'L'Amour Unit La Sagesse Et La Beauté', each piece bearing gold interlaced 'L's and the initials of Etinne-Henry Le Guay, the cup also with incised numbers, the saucer with under glazed capital 'C'.

6in (15cm) diam

$9,000-10,500 **CLV**

An 18thC Sèvres saucer, with a nude classical maiden in a landscape, base with interlaced 'L's with two 'G's for 1784 and with small k below for Dodin.

5.25in (13.5cm) diam

$3,000-4,000 **CLV**

A Sèvres cabinet can and stand, painted with mythical scenes of Pyramus and Thisbe, and Cadmus and Hermione, interlaced 'LL' mark, date code 'nn' and painter's mark probably for Charles-Antoine Didier Père.

c1790 *5.75in (14.5cm) diam*

$1,500-2,000 **WW**

A mid-19thC Sèvres porcelain gilt-metal mounted pot pourri, painted with figures on a terrace and architectural ruins, printed marks.

10.75in (27.5cm) high

$600-750 **L&T**

A pair of late 19thC Sèvres porcelain plates, painted with a chateau, the borders with three panels painted with musical trophies, printed marks and entitled verso.

9.75in (25cm) diam

$700-900 **L&T**

A pair of 19thC Sèvres jeweled porcelain cabinet portrait plates, one depicting Pierre Corneille, the other Embegirde Femme de Pharamond, identified and with factory marks on the reverse.

9.5in (24cm) diam

$3,000-4,000 **SK**

A pair of gilt-bronze-mounted Sèvres porcelain urns and covers, with allegorical subjects with landscapes on the reverse, nymph handles, signed under covers.

c1900 *17.25in (43.5cm) high*

$750-900 **SK**

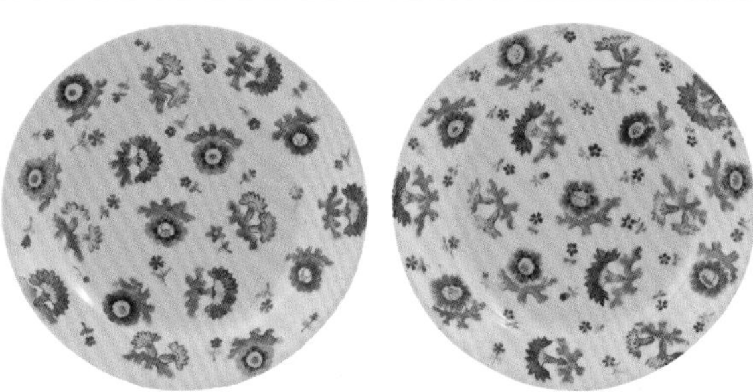

A pair of Swansea porcelain plates, from the Marino Ballroom Service, impressed marks.

The Marino Ballroom Service contained over 200 pieces, and was ordered from the Swansea factory by Mr J H Vivian of Marino, Swansea. The pattern is reminiscent of Indian flowers on contemporary chintz wall-papers and textiles.

c1815-17 *8.75in (22.5cm) diam*

$400-450 **WW**

A Swansea cabinet plate, probably painted by William Pollard.

c1815-17 *8.25in (21cm) diam*

$1,200-1,500 **WW**

A 19thC Swansea cup and saucer.

3.5in (8.8cm) high

$600-750 **ROS**

A 19thC Swansea vase, attributed to William Billingsley, of urn form with ram head handles, the spreading gilt foot on a marbled porcelain plinth.

10.25in (26.5cm) high

$1,800-3,000 **ROS**

A Swansea muffin dish, simply decorated with sprigs of pink rose and blue convolvulus, rare red Bevington mark.

The Swansea chinaworks was leased to brothers John and Timothy Bevington in the summer of 1817. Pieces made under their ownership more frequently bear an impressed mark, and it is possible that the few pieces with an overglaze mark were made during the Dillwyn period and decorated later.

c1817-20 *8.75in (22.5cm) diam*

$280-340 **WW**

A Vauxhall blue and white teabowl, painted with two Chinese figures either side of a triangular fence.

c1758-60 *2.75in (7cm) diam*

$750-900 **WW**

A Vauxhall saucer, printed and colored with butterflies in flight around flowers.

c1758-60 *4.75in (12cm) diam*

$750-900 **WW**

ESSENTIAL REFERENCE - VIENNA

The first porcelain factory in Vienna was founded in 1718 by Claudius Du Paquier with the assistance of former Meissen employees C. C. Hunger and Samuel Stölzel.

- **Vienna was the second European factory to make hard-paste porcelain after Meissen.**
- **Early wares were similar in form to those of Meissen, but have denser decoration.**
- **Du Paquier sold the factory to the state in 1744. Around this time, the Rococo style was introduced and chief modeller Johann Josef Niedermayer began producing a wide variety of figures.**
- **In 1784 Konrad Sörgel von Sorgenthal was made director. The Rococo style was abandoned during this era in favor of the Neo-classical style.**
- **The factory declined in the 1820s and closed in 1864.**

An early 19thC Vienna porcelain baluster mug.

3.25in (8.5cm) high

$40-50 **CHOR**

A Vienna porcelain dish, painted with 'The Parzen', underglazed beehive mark, impressed '4'.

c1875 *14.25in (36cm) diam*

$750-1,000 **SWO**

A pair of late 19thC Vienna porcelain vases and covers, enameled with classical figures, artist signed 'Feier', pierced covers with laurel wreath finial, beehive marks.

13in (33cm) high

$3,000-4,500 **SK**

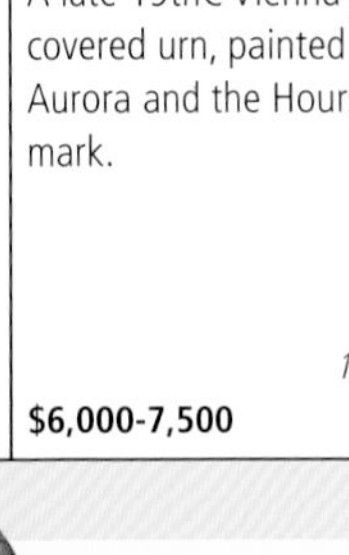

A late 19thC Vienna porcelain covered urn, painted with a scene of Aurora and the Hours, blue beehive mark.

17.5in (44cm) high

$6,000-7,500 **FRE**

CLOSER LOOK - VIENNA VASES

The vases display the fine figural painting associated with late 19thC Vienna porcelain.

W. Rosner is a well-known prolific Vienna artist - many of his pieces are in major collections.

The gilding is also of exceptional quality.

The condition is superb - any damage would considerably reduce the value.

These are titled under the base of one Romulus and Remus and Galathea, the other with Diana and Bade and Telemachus and Calypso.

A pair of 19thC Vienna porcelain covered urns, decorated with allegorical figures in polychrome enamels, artist signed 'W. Rosner', blue beehive marks.

21in (53.5cm) high

$13,500-16,500 **SK**

A late 19thC Vienna iridescent teal-ground 'jeweled' porcelain vase, painted with a semi-nude portrait of Erbluth, after Asti, blue beehive mark with red serial nos., signed 'Otto Zwierzina'.

vase17.25in (44cm) high

$15,000-19,500 **FRE**

A 19thC Vienna porcelain potpourri vase on stand.

12.5in (32cm) high

$450-750 **ROS**

A late 19thC Vienna porcelain inset gilt-metal-mounted gesso and giltwood tabletop, centered by a porcelain charger depicting Marie Antoinette and her children, surrounded by eleven plaques depicting French ladies of nobility, with impressed and factory marks, and titled in German.

20.5in (52cm) diam

$4,000-4,500 **FRE**

A 19thC Vienna cup and cover, made for the Turkish market, with blue Vienna mark to base.

7.5in (19cm) high

$1,200-1,800 **ROS**

A 19thC Vienna cup and cover, made for the Turkish market, with blue Vienna mark to base.

7.5in (19cm) high

$1,200-1,800 **ROS**

An early 20thC Vienna covered urn, painted with a Classical scene, raised on incurved fluted legs with paw feet, blue beehive mark.

17.5in (44cm) high

$4,050-4,500 **FRE**

An early 20thC Vienna-style cabinet plate, painted with the Madonna and Child and St John the Baptist, after Raphael, signed 'L. Gurkna', blue shield mark.

$450-750 **DN**

ESSENTIAL REFERENCE - WORCESTER BLUE AND WHITE

The Worcester factory begain production in 1751, later to become England's most successful porcelain factory.

- **The factory suffered heavy kiln losses, but from 1752, its use of Cornish soapstone gave Worcester porcelain increased durability, enabling its teapots to withstand hot liquids – those of most other British makers tended to crack in contact with boiling water. As a result, plenty of examples have survived.**
- **In Worcester, there were no local deposits of clay or coal; these had to be brought in by river.**
- **Shapes derived from English silverware, but adorned with Chinese-style fishing scenes, and a series of patterns derived from Oriental prototypes, many executed in an English manner.**
- **Robert Hancock invented printing on porcelain at Worcester in c1767, and it used this technique extensively to produce overglaze black enamel and underglaze-blue printed decoration.**
- **Worcester is famous for its 'scale blue' pattern, in which the underglaze blue ground was painted using a tiny fish-scale pattern.**
- **Most Worcester blue-and-white wares bear a workman's mark, usually a simple sign of unknown meaning. Marks used on printed wares (1758-85) were a crescent moon shape, where marks used on blue-ground wares (c1762-85) were an 'x' shape within a square box. The crescent mark was still used between 1774-92 in addition to a cursive 'W' printed in blue.**

A Worcester molded coffee can, painted with a chinoiserie landscape, 'Chinese' dragon scroll handle, firing crack to base of handle, minute chip to rim.

c1752-55 *2.5in (6cm) high*
$975-1,300
SWO

An early Worcester silver-shaped sauceboat, each side painted with a 'Long Eliza' figure, red workman's mark to the base.

c1753-54 *9in (23cm)*
$550-700 **WW**

A Worcester sauceboat, of small silver-shape, painted in the 'Famille Verte' palette, one side with a fisherman, the reverse with a figure in a sampan.

c1753-54 *6.75in (17cm) wide*
$1,800-2,250 **WW**

A Worcester mug, painted with the 'Zigzag Fence' pattern, scratch cross mark and workman's mark.

c1753-54 3.5in (9cm) high
$3,000-4,000 **WW**

A Worcester teabowl, painted in the 'Famille Verte' palette.

c1753-54 *3.5in (9cm) diam*
$2,000-2,400 **WW**

A Worcester shell-shaped pickle dish, painted with a shell and seaweed motif, the fluted border with flowers and insects.

c1753-54 *3.25in (8.5cm) wide*
$1,200-1,800 **WW**

A Worcester feather-molded coffee cup, painted in the 'Kakiemon' palette with the 'Banded Hedge' pattern, a Ho-Ho bird in flight.

c1754-56 *2.25in (6cm) high*
$1,800-3,000 **WW**

A Worcester sparrow beak jug, pencilled in black with the 'Boy on Buffalo' pattern, black workman's mark.
c1754 *3in (8cm) high*
$2,500-3,000 **WW**

A Worcester teapot and cover, pencilled in black with the 'Boy on a Buffalo' pattern, workman's mark to the base.
c1755-57 *7in (17.5cm) wide*
$1,650-2,000 **WW**

CLOSER LOOK - WORCESTER MUG

This rare shape is seldom found in porcelain, having originated from earlier stoneware examples.

It is boldly painted with the 'Cormorant' pattern, a lone fisherman casting his line from his boat behind the seabird perched on a large rock.

Only three other Worcester examples are known in different patterns; one in the 'High Island' pattern, and two others decorated with the 'Zig-zag fence' pattern.

It was originally thought this was a Lund's Bristol piece, where it is believed the shape originated.

A fine and very rare early Worcester mug, scratch cross mark to the base, a workman's mark beneath the handle.
c1754-55 *4.5in (11.5cm)*
$60,000-75,000 **WW**

A Worcester feather-molded teabowl and saucer, painted with sprigs of Oriental flowers.
c1755-60 *4.75in (11.7cm) high*
$300-450 **WW**

A Worcester teapot and cover, painted with the 'Weeping Willow' pattern, painted blue 'x' beneath handle, small chips to spout.
c1755-56 *3.75in (9.5cm) high*
$1,400-1,800 **BELL**

A Worcester teapot and cover, painted with the'Weeping Willow' pattern, painted blue 'x' beneath handle, small chips to spout.
c1755-56 *3.7in (9.5cm) high*
$1,400-1,800 **BELL**

A Worcester mug, decorated in the 'Kakiemon' palette with the 'Two Quail' pattern.
c1756-58 *3.25in (8cm) high*
$3,450-3,900 **WW**

A Worcester cup and saucer, painted with the 'Valentine' pattern, a pair of doves perched on a quiver of arrows beneath a breadfruit tree.

The pattern is a copy of a Chinese export porcelain pattern, drawn by Lieutenant Piercy Brett and used on a service for Commodore George Anson in 1743.
c1758-60 *4.5in (11.5cm) diam*
$2,000-2,400 **WW**

A Worcester butter boat, painted with leaf scrolls and molded with acanthus leaves, minute chip.

c1760 *3.25in (8cm) high*

$280-400 **SWO**

A rare miniature Worcester teapot and cover, painted with the 'Prunus Root' pattern, open crescent mark to the base.

Miniature Worcester wares painted with the 'Prunus Root' pattern are believed to have been produced for the Dutch market.

c1760-65 *4in (10cm) high*

$1,800-3,000 **WW**

A Worcester mug, transfer-printed in black, engraved 'George III King of Great Britain', signed 'L Sadler, Liverpool', slight wear.

The portrait was apparently engraved by Billinge after Jeremiah Mayer for a competition for the Society for the Encouragement of Arts. It was once held that the mugs were sold in the white to Liverpool for the transfer to be applied. This is obviously not feasible.

c1761 *4.5in (11.5cm) high*

$4,500-6,000 **SWO**

A Worcester small tray, printed in black with the 'Tea Party' (Version 2), signed 'RH' in the print for Robert Hancock, anchor rebus for Richard Holdship.

Robert Hancock (1730-1817) was apprenticed as an engraver to George Anderton in Birmingham and moved to Worcester in late 1756 or early 1757. He took with him a method of transfer-printing originated by John Brooks, later of the Battersea Enamel Works. This was known at Worcester as 'black printing'. The monogram 'RH' is that of Hancock and the anchor rebus of Richard Holdship, one of the partners and managers of the factory.

c1758 *5.5in (14cm) wide*

$405-480 **WW**

A rare Worcester teabowl and saucer printed in purple with 'The Windmill', a traveller and his dog standing before a gatehouse and looking at the mill.

c 1762-65 *4.7in (12cm) high*

$900-1,200 **WW**

A First Period Worcester 'Japan' pattern coffee cup, depicting Japanese figures, rubbing to gilt, small chip to underside of foot.

c1765 *2.5in (6cm) high*

$850-975 **L&T**

A rare Worcester mustard spoon, painted with a peony spray.

c1765 *4in (10cm) long*

$1,200-1,700 **WW**

A Worcester mug, painted with the 'Gardener' pattern, crescent mark.

c1765-70 *3.5in (8.5cm) high*

$1,150-1,425 **WW**

A Worcester teacup and saucer, decorated in the 'Giles' atelier, painted with naturalistic English flowers, blue crossed swords and 9 mark.

c1765 *5.25in (13.5cm) high*

$900-1,400 **WW**

A pair of Worcester dessert plates, decorated in the Kakiemon palette with the 'Sir Joshua Reynolds' pattern, script 'W' marks.
c1765-70 *8.25in (21cm) diam*
$3,000-4,000 **WW**

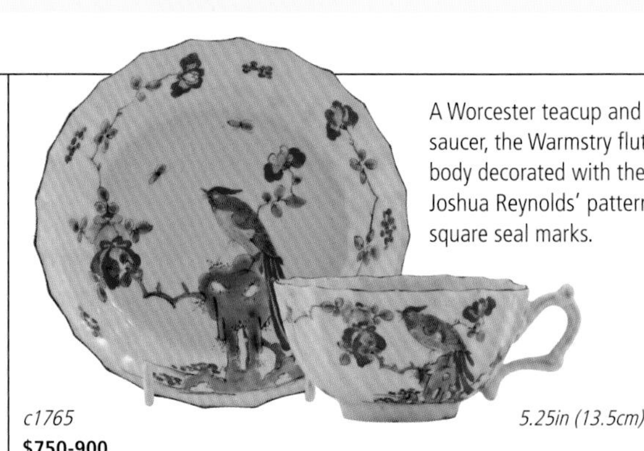

A Worcester teacup and saucer, the Warmstry fluted body decorated with the 'Sir Joshua Reynolds' pattern, square seal marks.
c1765 *5.25in (13.5cm) high*
$750-900 **WW**

A Worcester sparrowbeak jug, painted with the 'Conjurer' pattern.
c1765-70 *3.25in (8.5cm) high*
$750-1,000 **WW**

A Worcester teapot stand, painted with the 'Prunus Root' pattern, branches creeping over the rim.
c1765 *5.5in (13.5cm) wide*
$600-900 **WW**

A Worcester coffee cup, decorated in the 'Giles' atelier, pencilled in black, then filled in green with gilt highlights.

This design is a known Giles staple and is believed to have been developed from an earlier simpler and more naively painted pattern.
c1770-75 *2.5in (6.5cm) high*
$750-1,000 **WW**

A Worcester trio, the Warmstry fluted bodies enameled with the 'Dragons in Compartments' pattern, square seal marks.
c1770 *5.25in (13.5cm) wide*
$1,200-1,500 **WW**

A Worcester sparrowbeak jug, perhaps decorated in the 'Giles' atelier, boldly painted with Chinese figures.
c1770 *3.75in (9.5cm) high*
$1,000-1,400 **WW**

A Worcester dolphin ewer creamer.
c1770 *3.25in (8.5cm) high*
$750-900 **WW**

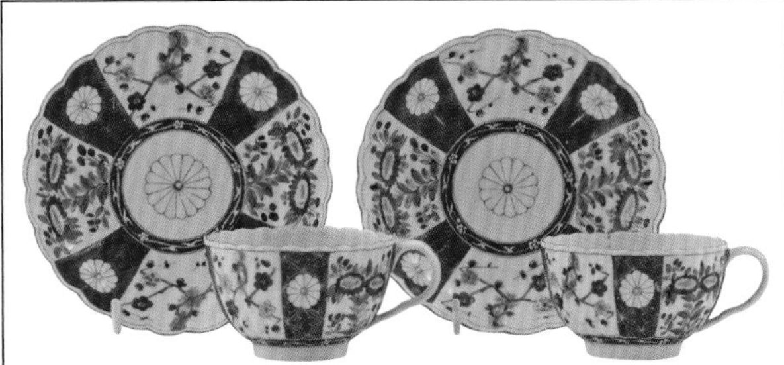

A pair of Worcester fluted teacups and saucers, decorated in the 'Scarlet Japan' pattern.

c1770 *5.5in (13.5cm) high*

$750-900 **WW**

A Worcester fluted teacup and saucer, square seal marks.

c1770 *5.5in (13.5cm) diam*

$300-450 **WW**

A Worcester teabowl and saucer, enameled with butterflies around a central caterpillar.

c1770 *4.75in (12cm) diam*

$360-420 **WW**

A Worcester 'Chelsea' ewer creamer, painted with the 'Mansfield' pattern.

The usual Chelsea Ewer creamer has a band of molded leaves around the foot. This plain version was introduced around 1772, but very few appear to have been made.

c1772 *2.75in (7cm) high*

$1,150-1,425 **WW**

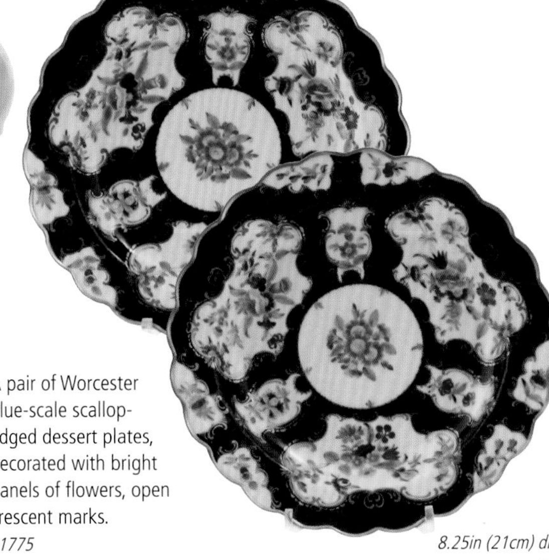

A pair of Worcester blue-scale scallop-edged dessert plates, decorated with bright panels of flowers, open crescent marks.

c1775 *8.25in (21cm) diam*

$900-1,200 **WW**

A Worcester fluted 'Hop Trellis' teacup and saucer, decorated with a version of the 'Earl Manvers' pattern.

c1775 *5.25in (13.5cm) diam*

$2,000-2,400 **WW**

A pair of Worcester scallop-edged plates, painted with Chinese figures.

c1775 *7in (17.5cm) diam*

$600-900 **WW**

A Worcester teapot stand, decorated with the 'Dragons in Compartments' pattern.

c1775-80 *5.6in (14.3cm) wide*

$600-900 **WW**

A Worcester mug, painted with flowers.

c1780-85 *3.5in (9cm) high*

$550-700 **WW**

A Flight cabbage-leaf molded mask jug, painted with swags including 'Dry Blue' flowers, framing the gilt initials 'RN'.

The flower painting on this jug is almost identical to that found on the Bostock service and also on the several mugs made for the Bishop of Lincoln, c1785.

c1785-90 *8.75in (22.5cm) high*

$1,650-2,100 **M&K**

A pair of Chamberlain's Worcester spill vases, painted with panels of feathers within oeil de perdrix borders, red script marks.

c1805-10 *3.25in (8cm) high*

$3,400-4,000 **WW**

A Barr, Flight & Barr mug, bat-printed with a portrait of Queen Caroline, flanked by a cornucopia and a dove of peace, impressed crown and 'BFB', slight wear.

Made to commemorate the Golden Jubilee of George III in 1809. The King and Queen had visited the Worcester factory in 1788, bought several services and gave permission for them to use the crown in their mark.

c1810 *3.5in (8.5cm) high*

$2,000-2,400 **SWO**

A Barr, Flight & Barr Worcester cup and saucer, decorated with a band of red and gilt flowers and leaves, impressed marks.

c1810 *5.5in (14cm) high*

$600-750 **WW**

A Flight, Barr & Barr Worcester potpourri vase, painted with pink roses, passion flower, nasturtiums and other blooms, painted and impressed marks.

c1815-20 *12in (30.5cm) high*

$3,000-4,000 **WW**

A Flight, Barr & Barr vase and cover, painted with a view of Virginia Water and also Muckross Abbey, Great Lake Killarney, the knop restored.

c1820 *18in (46cm) high*

$3,900-4,500 **TCAL**

A pair of Flight, Barr & Barr Worcester ice pails, covers and liners, incised 'FBB', damage to liners, one knop loose.

c1820s *13.75in (35cm) high*

$6,750-7,500 **TCAL**

A Flight, Barr & Barr 'Imari' pattern serving dish, printed and impressed marks.

8.6in (21cm) wide

$720-780 **L&T**

A Chamberlain's Worcester commemorative 'Warwick' vase.

The vase is inscribed 'Facsimile of the vase presented to Captain Parry by the inhabitants of Bath in commemoration of his Voyage of Discovery to the Polar Sea, made in the years 1819 & 1820'.

c1822 *6.5in (16.5cm) high*

$750-1,000 **WW**

A Chamberlain's Worcester charger, painted with iris, auricula, rose and tulip, iron red and impressed marks, a riveted crack to the footrim.

This dish is reputedly from a service presented to the Grand Duchess of Hesse by Queen Victoria.

c1840 *16.25in (41cm) diam*

$900-1,200 **WW**

A Royal Worcester ewer and stand, by Thomas Bott, decorated in Limoges-enamel style with scenes of Classical figures, gilding probably by Josiah Davis, some damage, stand signed 'T. Bott/66' and ewer 'T. Bott 1867'.

1866 and 1867 *12.25in (31cm) high*

$7,500-9,000 **WW**

An early 20thC Royal Worcester potpourri vase, inner cover and spire cover, signed Chivers, smudged blue marks obscuring date code,

c1903 *10.25in (26cm) high*

$850-975 **FLD**

A pair of Royal Worcester vases and covers, decorated with a peacock and a peahen, signed 'Sedgley', model no.1957.

c1911 *15.75in (40cm) high*

$9,000-10,500 **TCAL**

A Royal Worcester cabinet plate, painted by J Stinton, with a titled view of the Castle of Doune, with a border possibly decorated by Edward Raby, puce printed marks and date code.

1912 *9.25in (23.5cm) diam*

$900-1,200 **DN**

A Royal Worcester vase, painted by Harry Stinton with Highland Cattle, signed, puce mark, shape F126?.

1918 *5in (12.7cm) high*

$1,300-1,575 **HT**

A Capodimonte Écuelle and cover, painted by Giovanni Caselli, some restoration, cracks and losses.

c1750 *7.5in (19cm) diam*

$1,200-1,800 MAB

A pair of Chantilly vases, painted with garlands of flowers and single stems.

c1760 *8.75in (20cm) high*

$1,425-1,725 WW

A Coalport porcelain tankard, transfer-printed in black with a portrait of George III and a banner inscribed 'Glorious Jubilee to England', restored.

George III was, at this date, in the throes of porphyria and unable to reign effectively. His son, later George IV, was Regent. It is interesting to note that the molded handle has been borrowed from a contemporary Chinese example.

1809 *4in (10cm) high*

$900-1,200 SWO

A Coalport presentation plate, made for Queen Victoria to present to Tsar Nicholas of Russia, the center with the Order of St. Andrew within a border of other Russian orders, gilt retailer's mark for 'A.B. & R.P. Daniell London'.

c1845 *10in (25.5cm) wide*

$12,000-15,000 DN

A Coalport porcelain botanical dish.

c1800 *8.25in (21cm) diam*

$300-400 L&T

A Coalport centerpiece, painted by William Billingsley with tulip, nasturtium, poppy and convolvulus.

c1802 *12.5in (32cm) wide*

$700-975 WW

A pair of mid-19thC Coalport vases, with Kashmir shawl derived patterns in blue, red, green and gold between pink bands, printed 'Coalport AD1750'.

Kashmir shawls were one of the 'hits' of the 1851 Exhibition and were immediately copied in Paisley near Glasgow, Scotland. It is, however, surprising that so little porcelain was decorated to reflect the vogue, possibly because it was so labor-intensive.

4.75in (12cm) high

$600-900 SWO

A Copeland Parian figure of 'The Bride', modeled by Raphaelle Monti for the Crystal Palace Art Union, incised and impressed marks.

c1861 *14.75in (37.5cm) high*

$2,700-3,300 WW

An H & R Daniel porcelain trio.

c1827-28 *6in (15cm)*

$1,000-1,400 WW

ESSENTIAL REFERENCE - DAVENPORT

In c1793 John Davenport founded a pottery factory in Longport, Staffordshire. A porcelain factory was added in c1820.

- **Davenport was one of the most productive of all the Staffordshire factories.**
- **Wares were decorated in the style of Derby, partly because several of the Davenport painters also worked at Derby. One of the most notable was Thomas Steel (1772-1850), who was best known for painting fruit.**
- **Tea and dessert services were staple products of the factory.**
- **It developed a type of luster glaze in the early 19thC.**
- **The factory closed in 1887.**

An early 19thC Davenport porcelain vase, painted in the 'Chinese Temple' pattern.

This pattern was used for the extensive Royal Service, ordered by the Prince of Wales in 1806.

6.25in (16cm) high

$240-280 **WW**

A Fulda jug and associated cover, decorated with scenes of family life.

c1760 *5.5in (14cm) high*

$1,500-2,250 **WW**

A Herculanuem porcelain campana vase, painted with flowers spilling out onto a marble plinth, printed mark.

c1815 *5.5in (14cm) high*

$900-1,200 **WW**

A Le Nove porcelain model of a man, modeled wearing 18thC dress.

c1785 *5.7 in (14.5cm) high*

$1,150-1,425 **DN**

A Ludwigsburg figure of 'Air', modeled by Pierre François Lejeune, crowned interlaced 'CC' mark.

c1770 *7.75in (20cm) tall*

$975-1,300 **WW**

A pair of Mennecy pomade pots and covers, painted with flower sprays, the covers with fruit finials.

c1760 *3in (8cm) high*

$850-1,125 **MAB**

A Minton pâte-sur-pâte plaque by Louis Solon, decorated in white slip on a black ground with a young maiden freeing Cupid from a cage, signed and dated, impressed Mintons to the reverse.

This plaque was retailed by the Mayfair firm of Thomas Goode which was established in 1827. This is another guarantee of quality. Among its many notable customers were Queen Victoria and the Tsar of Russia.

1880 *7in (18cm) high*

$7,500-9,000 **WW**

A Mintons part dessert service, painted with rustic views, comprising two dishes and five plates, printed and impressed marks.

c1892

$975-1,300 **DN**

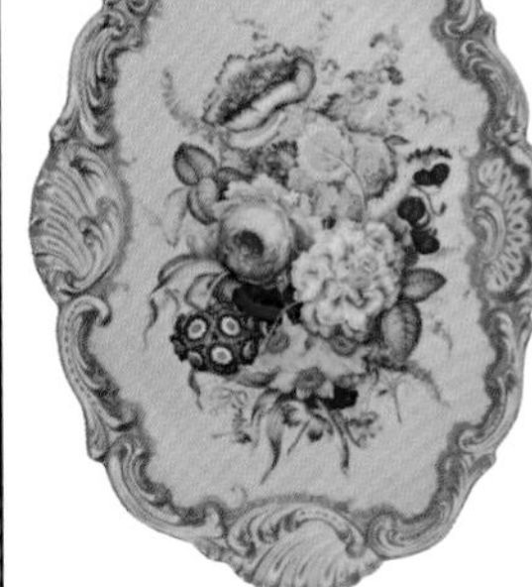

A Minton porcelain tray, painted in the manner of Thomas Steel, with flowers including rose, narcissus, honeysuckle, delphinium and chrysanthemum.

c1840 *16.5in (42cm) long*

$1,500-2,100 **WW**

A 19thC Minton figural spill vase, depicting a woodcutter leaning against the trunk, blue crossed swords mark, some chipping.
8.25in (21cm) high
$330-450 WW

A Nymphenburg eyebath, modeled as a biscuit porcelain putto, impressed shield and incised 'H' mark.
c1820 *2.75in (7cm) high*
$1,200-1,500 WW

A Plymouth pickle leaf dish.
c1770 *4in (10cm) wide*
$900-1,200 WW

ESSENTIAL REFERENCE - SAMSON

Edmé Samson's factory was established in Paris in 1845 with the aim of making exact copies of European and Oriental porcelain for collectors and museums.

- **Prior to this he had great success making replacements for broken pieces of dinner services.**
- **The factory is particularly well known for its excellent copies of Meissen and Chinese porcelain. English soft-paste porcelain copies are easier to detect due to the Continental hard-paste body.**
- **Samson wares can also be distinguished by a lack of sharp modelling and inaccurate palettes.**
- **French faience, Dutch Delft and some Strasbourg wares, as well as enamel and ormolu pieces, were also copied. Samson et Cie did not intend their replicas to be passed off as the real thing. Reportedly each piece was made with a letter 'S' contained within the copied factory's mark. However, this can be easily removed.**
- **The factory closed in 1969. Its molds were sold in 1979.**
- **Today Samson pieces are sought after in their own right, due to their decorative qualities.**

A late 19thC Samson white-glazed porcelain and gilt-metal mounted pot pourri jar and cover, some restoration and chips.
6in (15.5cm) high
$1,200-1,500 MAB

A late 19thC Samson Worcester-style plate, painted with exotic birds, square seal mark.
12.25in (31cm) diam
$150-210 WW

A Samson 'Compagnies des Indes' tea canister and cover, pseudo seal mark.
c1890 *6in (14.5cm) high*
$150-225 SWO

A late 19thC Samson porcelain figure group, in the Meissen manner, pseudo blue crossed swords mark, contained in a contemporary case.
9.5in (24cm) high
$550-825 WW

A 19thC Samson porcelain figure group of 'Virtue', after Meissen, a young maiden being crowned while a figure behind holds the French Royalist flag, another holding a plaque engraved 'La Vertu 1775', pseudo crossed swords mark.
14.5in (37cm) high
$975-1,300 WW

A pair of Spode câchepots and stands, of 'New Shape', painted in pattern '1926' with solitary figures in landscape scenes, painted factory marks and pattern numbers.

c1820 *5.5in (14cm) high*

$975-1,300 **WW**

A Spode vase, decorated in pattern '1166' with flowers, the handles issuing from satyr mask heads, iron red factory mark and pattern number.

c1815-20 *8.25in (21cm) high*

$1,200-1,500 **WW**

A late 18thC Zurich porcelain wall pocket, painted with miniature landscapes in the style of Heinrich Füssli, underglaze blue 'Z' mark, some damage.

$4,500-5,250 **HALL**

An English porcelain flower-encrusted Rococo-revival inkstand, of Coalbrokedale type, with candle stick, inkwell, cover and liner.

c1830

$150-200 **DN**

A pair of English porcelain demi-lune bough pots, possibly painted by William Billingsley, pain ted with shipping scenes, 'W' mark.

The factory that made this fine group of porcelains has long been disputed. See Geoffrey Godden, Staffordshire Porcelain (1983), Appendix VI, p556-569 for a discussion on this problem group of porcelains and several illustrations of this form.

c1800 *7.3in (18.5cm) long*

$1,800-3,000 **DN**

An English porcelain small vase, one side painted with feathers, the reverse with seashells.

c1810-15 *5in (12.5cm) high*

$1,000-1,400 **WW**

A late 19thC Sèvres-style porcelain and gilt-bronze mounted oval plaque.

9in (23cm) wide

$700-850 **L&T**

A late 19thC porcelain Sèvres-style floor vase, gilt-metal mounted with a pair of lion mask handles, painted with a Watteauesque scene.

34.75in (88cm) high

$2,700-3,300 **DN**

A 20thC large Sèvres-style hand-painted and gilt decorated bronze mounted urn.

46in (117cm) high

$7,500-9,000 **FRE**

A late 19thC German porcelain plaque, painted with the bust portrait of a woman in the Northern Renaissance manner.

9.5in (24.5cm) high

$1,500-2,250 **DN**

THE POTTERY MARKET

As with most areas, pottery collectors have been affected by the economic climate. There is some evidence that things are looking up. As always when good, rare, early pieces, and especially dated, come fresh to the market, top prices are paid. Mid-priced and low-end pieces have struggled, particularly if they were produced in large quantities, like some of the more common transfer-printed Staffordshire patterns. Some Staffordshire is doing considerably better with US collectors.

In fact to generalize the American market for pottery is generally stronger than the UK market at the moment. Business is mainly through the internet as we are still not seeing the number of American buyers travelling around the country as in the past, although there are indications that the collectors are returning. Good quality pre-1830 pottery is still in demand. Quite a few excellent big collections have come onto the market. At the other end of the scale, Victorian pottery and Staffordshire figures have to be exceptionally rare to attract any interest. As I always say it is an excellent time to start a collection.

There is still the problem of fake 'Staffordshire' coming from China. I have seen examples on both sides of the Atlantic. These are made from porcelain and not pottery and are really quite easy to spot, and they don't have the quality of period examples. If in any doubt you should buy from a reputable dealer or auction house.

Delftware again has to be early and a rare shape to achieve strong prices. Dates also help. For the more modest collector who is interested in delft and slipware it is an excellent time to buy. At many sales there is strong competition for the top-end pieces but the market is generally sluggish for the more common pieces. It is often worth waiting until the end of the sale.

Again there have been some dramatic prices paid for some early pottery, particularly the Italian maiolica istoriato ware plates, dishes and apothecary jars created in the 16thC. Interest in good and early (16thC) Hispano Moresque pottery remains strong - but little comes to the market. Mason's ironstone has to be an interesting shape with good strong colors to make money. Good quality early Wedgwood seems to be selling better in the US rooms.

American stoneware continues to have a strong collectors market, particularly for rare shapes and makers and unusual designs. Redware has seen a sluggish period where only the most unusual pieces fetch high prices. Early spatterware continues to fetch substantial prices when it comes onto the market.

Top Left: A Staffordshire creamware horse.
c1765 *8.75in (22cm) long*
$6,750-7,500 **SK**

Above: A 19thC Reading, Pennsylvania redware wall pocket, impressed 'D.P. Shenfelder, Reading, Pennsylvania'.
10.75in (27.3cm) high
$18,000-22,500 **POOK**

ESSENTIAL REFERENCE - BRITISH DELFT

British delftware is a type of earthenware with an opaque white glaze made with oxide of tin.

- **The name 'delftware' stems from the Dutch city 'Delft', one of the most important centers of earthenware production in the Netherlands, but became a generic name used for all British ware of this kind in the 18thC.**
- **The most notable centers of production in Britain were Southwark, Aldgate, and Lambeth in London, Norwich, Brislington, Bristol, Liverpool, Glasgow, Dublin and Wincanton.**
- **A record from 1567 documents the arrival of skilled laborers from the Netherlands. Jaspar Andried and Jacob Jansen, who escaped religious prosecution in their home country, established potteries in Norwich and later in Aldgate, in the east of London.**
- **'Blue-dash' chargers from the 17thC were boldly decorated in polychrome with stylized tulips, carnations, oak leaves, biblical subjects, and portraits, particularly of Charles II, William and Mary, and Queen Anne.**
- **Contemporary British subjects (figures, buildings, and landscapes) and chinoiserie themes (pagodas, pavilions, Chinese figures, birds, and flowers) adorned the earthenware.**
- **Production of British delftware diminished considerably at the end of the 18thC because of growing competition from creamware.**

A rare London delftware tile, probably Pickleherring Pothouse, decorated with a figure running with a spear, the corners with petal motifs.

The presence of oval nail holes in the corners of this tile suggests a London manufacture.

c1625 *5.25in (13.5cm) wide*

$600-900 WW

A Brislington delftware charger, decorated with a seated Chinese figure among stylized rockwork.

c1670 *13in (33cm) diam*

$600-900 WW

A late 17thC rare Bristol blue dash delftware tulip charger, with crack.

13.5in (34cm) diam

$3,000-4,000 SWO

An English delft Royal charger, depicting King William III.

c1694 *13.25in (33.5cm) diam*

$3,000-4,000 POOK

A Brislington delft posset pot, decorated in the 'Transitional' style.

c1685 *7in (18cm) wide*

$900-1,000

DN

A delft lobed dish, decorated with a seated Chinese figure, the rim with further figures in garden settings, blue mark to the reverse.

c1700 *13.5in (34.5cm) diam*

$600-900 WW

A Bristol or London delftware charger, decorated with a putto and two birds amidst flowering branches, restored.

c1705 *13.25in (33.5cm) diam*

$600-900 **WW**

An English delft posset pot and cover, painted with birds, insects and foliage, the handles and spout with scrolls.

c1710 *9in (23cm) high*

$750-1,000 **SWO**

An early 18thC London delftware plate, painted with figures beside water, a church and village scene in the distance.

9in (23cm) diam

$450-750 **WW**

A Bristol delftware bowl, decorated with four groups of two cottages with smoking chimneys, repaired, wear.

c1720 *11.5in (29cm) diam*

$1,150-1,450 **SWO**

An early 18thC Bristol delftware posset pot and cover, the loop handles and spout with blue dashes, the lid matching, lid repaired, tip of spout missing, minor chips.

7.5in (19cm) high

$4,950-6,000 **SWO**

A Bristol delft tulip charger.

c1720 *13.75in (35cm) diam*

$3,000-4,000 **POOK**

A Bristol delftware farmhouse dish, painted with a strutting cockerel.

c1720-30 *8.75in (22cm) diam*

$1,150-1,450 **WW**

A pair of Vauxhall delftware plates, painted with vases of flowers, a little chipping to the rims.

c1730-40 *6.5in (17cm) diam*

$600-750 **WW**

A London delftware panel, painted with birds in flight above a tree, a flag flying from a tower in the bottom right corner, set in an old lead mount.

These 12 tiles formed part of a larger panel, which would probably have been made for a specific building.

c1730-40 *15in (38cm) wide*

$1,800-2,250 WW

A delft slipper, painted with flowers and an imitation seam down the front, the kitten heel painted blue.

c1740 *5in (12.5cm) wide*

$600-750 WW

A delftware charger, Bristol or Wincanton, painted with a stylized flowerhead, the rim with blue-scale panels and carnation heads.

c1748 *12.75in (32.5cm) diam*

$1,700-2,100 WW

An early 18thC Bristol delft punch bowl, painted with panels of flowers.

12in (30.5cm) diam

$600-900 DN

An English delft flower-brick, possibly Bristol, painted with chinese figures, some cracks to side and base, chip to one corner and rim.

c1740 *14.5in (37cm) long*

$750-900 DN

An English delftware teapot and associated cover, London or Bristol, painted with stylized trees and rockwork, with wishbone handle and straight spout.

This is based on a Meissen porcelain shape.

c1740 *7.75in (19.5cm) wide*

$1,150-1,425 WW

An 18thC English delft posset pot, painted with reserves depicting a leaping stag.

7.5in (19cm) wide

$700-850 L&T

An English delft polychrome dish, probably Bristol, Richard Franks Factory, cracked from center.

c1760 *13.25in (33.5cm) diam*

$200-350 DN

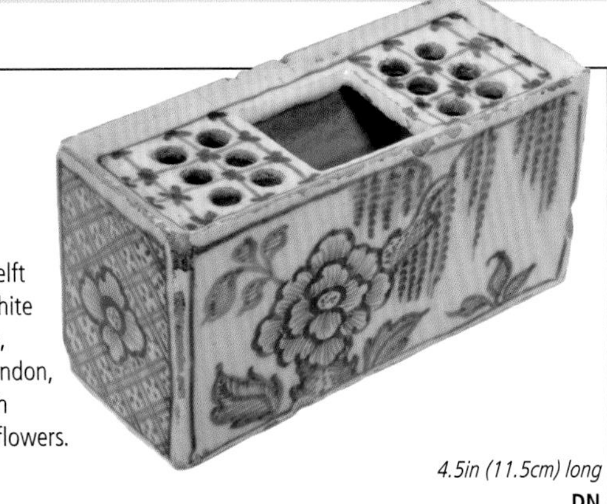

A English delft blue-and-white flower-brick, probably London, painted with chinoiserie flowers.

c1760 *4.5in (11.5cm) long*

$600-750 **DN**

A delft bowl, the exterior painted with flowering plants, and bamboo stems with a bird, the interior naively inscribed 'God bles is Magsty armes Botach By Say and Land' (sic).

c1760 *11.75in (30cm) diam*

$2,100-2,700 **H&C**

A Lambeth delft plate, painted with pine trees and rabbits.

c1760 *9in (22.5cm) diam*

$750-1,000 **L&T**

A Lambeth delft dish, attributed to Abigail Griffith, painted with a parrot beside a stylized tree stump.

c1765 *13.5in (34.5cm) diam*

$700-850 **L&T**

CLOSER LOOK - ENGLISH DELFT OINTMENT POT

Ointment pots from this period are rare as they were usually thrown away.

The inscription was a reference to Jacob Hemet, a Huguenot dental practitioner, who was made Operator for the Teeth to Queen Charlotte in 1766.

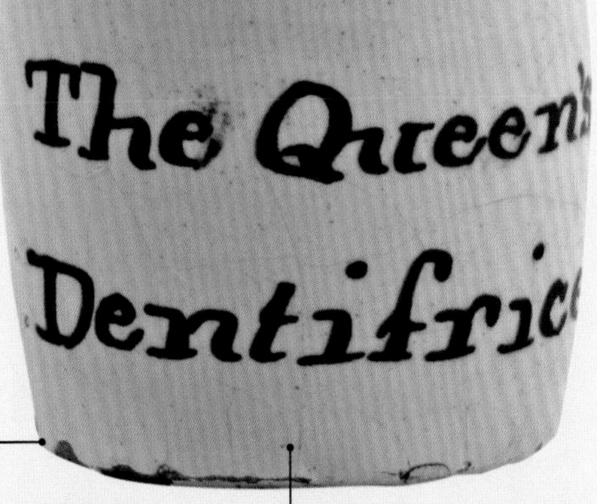

Like many other practising dentists of the time, Hemet concocted his own mouthwashes and dentifrices but was unusual in taking the trouble to patent them.

Appealing to a variety of collectors, jars provide one of the livelier niches within the delft marketplace.

A English delftware ointment pot, of small cylindrical form, painted in manganese with 'The Queen's Dentifrice'.

c1775 *2in (5cm)*

$3,400-4,000 **WW**

An 18thC delft plate, painted with two swans, red '5' to the reverse.

13.5in (34.5cm) diam

$850-975 **WW**

A late 18thC English delft clock dial, painted with Roman numeral hours and Arabic minutes.

9.5in (24cm) diam

$1,200-1,500 **WW**

A late18thC Liverpool delft pill slab, painted with the arms of the Worshipful Society of Apothecaries, the motto 'Opiferque Per Orbem Dicor' picked out in manganese.

10.5in (27cm) high

$6,750-8,250 **WW**

A Dutch Delft jar, painted with Chinese exotic birds, vegetation and peonies, with geometric flower heads on the neck partially obscured by the mount.

A smaller but similarly shaped baluster vase dated 1678 is in the Gemeentemuseum Den Haag. A faceted double-gourd jar with a similar foot, painted in the same colors, is in the V&A reserve collections (C466.1927) and attributed to Delft 1660-1680.

c1670 *18.5in (46.5cm) high*

$4,500-6,000 L&T

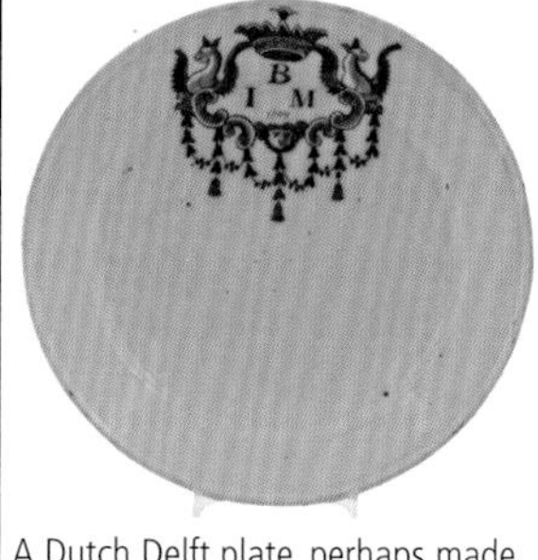

A Dutch Delft plate, perhaps made for the English market, painted with the initials 'IBM' within a cartouche of wyverns with a crown and an angel head.

1709 *10in (25.5cm) diam*

$1,000-1,400 WW

A mid-18thC Dutch Delft model of a horse.

8.5in (21.5cm) high

$400-550 SK

A pair of mid-18thC Dutch Delft chinoiseries decorated vases, each inscribed '4'.

14.5in (36.5cm) high

$1,800-3,000 SK

One of a pair of 18thC Dutch Delft vases, with birds and Chinese courtesans, inscribed 'AK', possibly attributed to Aelbrech De Kiser.

11in (27.5cm) high

$1,200-1,500 SK

A late 18thC Dutch Delft dish, painted with a head and shoulders portrait of William of Orange, base painted 720/15.

8.5in (21.5cm) diam

$1,500-1,800 HT

A pair of early 19thC Delft drug jars, one labeled 'POPUL', the other 'ALB:CAMPH'.

7.5in (19cm) high

$975-1,150 L&T

A pair of 19thC Dutch Delft parrots, bearing a monogram 'PAK', possibly Pieter Adriaen Kock.

9.75in (25cm) high

$900-1,000 HW

A late 17thC Nevers faïence cachepot, painted with Chinese figures in a Transitional-style landscape, chips and flakes to rims and handles.

Faience, also spelled faïence or fayence, is tin-glazed earthenware made in France, Germany, Spain, and Scandinavia. It is distinguished from tin-glazed earthenware made in Italy, which is called or maiolica and that made in the Netherlands and England, which is called Delft and delft.

11.75in (30cm) wide

$900-1,000 MAB

An Italian faïence albarello, painted with a church, possibly by the Levantino family of Albissola, Savona.

c1718 9in (23cm) high

$280-340 TRI

A Rouen faïence jug, painted with lambrequins and foliage, the spout with a bearded mask in a feathered headdress, cracks, handle re-stuck.

c1730 12.25in (31cm) high

$2,000-2,400 MAB

A pair of mid-18thC French faïence dry drug Jars, possibly Nevers, painted with a void scroll between flowering and leafy garlands, cracks and chips.

8.25in (21cm) high

$400-550 SWO

A pair of 19thC faïence tureens and cover, perhaps Brussels, one a red-legged partridge, the other a fancy pigeon, the pigeon with crowned monogram mark, some small chips.

10in (25cm) long

$850-975 DN

A pair of late 19thC French faïence 'fu' lions, possibly Luneville, in the 'Japonesque' manner.

24.5in (62cm) high

$2,400-3,000 L&T

One of a pair of late 19thC Nove faïence montheiths, sepia painted marks.

8.75in (22cm) wide

$400-450 pair L&T

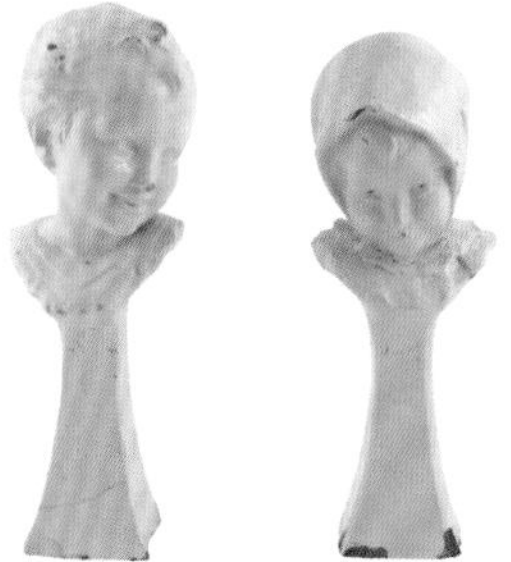

A pair of early 20thC Fabbrica Fratelli Minardi faïence busts of children, MF monogram marks, some damages.

Virginio and Venturino Minardi opened a studio in Faenza in 1899. Prior to this, both had worked at the Cantagalli factory and were influenced by what they learnt during this time.

14in (36.5cm) high

$900-1,000 WW

ESSENTIAL REFERENCE - MAIOLICA

'Maiolica' is the term for Italian tin-glazed earthenware. It is probably from the Tuscan name for the island of Majorca.

- **The earliest period of maiolica production is known as the 'Archaic' period and covers wares made until c1400. The wares tend to be basic in form: simple bowls, dishes, basins, or jugs.**
- **'Archaic' decoration was executed mainly in manganese brown on a copper-green ground, although yellow and blue were also used. Designs were mostly of stylized birds, animals, ribbonwork, hatching and geometric motifs.**
- **Most surviving early figural subjects on wares are attributed to Faenza or Florence.**
- **From the early 14thC, maiolica became appropriate for elevated patrons, with designs washed in green and outlined in manganese brown (c1425–50), and 'blue relief' wares (c1430–60), painted in thick, rich, cobalt blue, a technique known as 'impasto', with detailing in manganese brown and copper green.**
- **Wares included albarelli (drug jars for use in pharmacies and spice stores) decorated with birds, animals, human figures, coats of arms, or oak leaves.**
- **In the late 15thC Italian potters produced tiles, albarelli, and dishes painted in blue, green, a translucent turquoise, yellow, and ocher.**

A Faenza albarello, painted with a putto with a tambourine, minor rim chips.

c1540 *9.75in (25cm) high*
$2,700-3,300 **MAB**

A Castelli maiolica apothecary drug jar, probaby workshop of Orazio Pompei, painted with the portrait caricature of an old man above an inscription that reads 'GRAS.D.GALL'.

The inscription is probably for grasso di gallina (chicken fat).

c1550 *7in (18cm) high*
$18,000-22,500 **L&T**

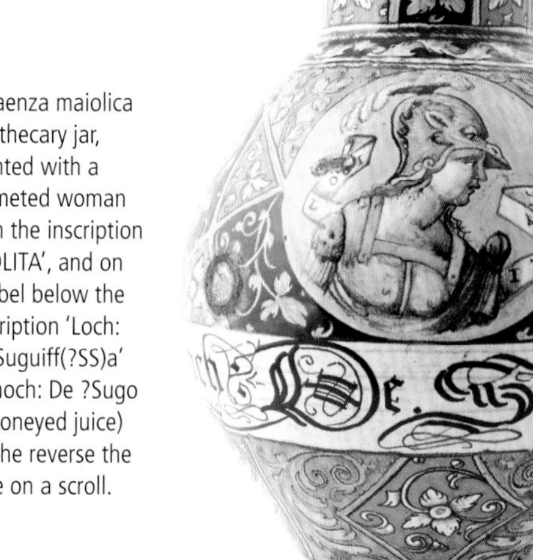

A Faenza maiolica apothecary jar, painted with a helmeted woman with the inscription 'IPOLITA', and on a label below the inscription 'Loch: De Suguiff(?SS)a' (Lohoch: De ?Sugo - ?honeyed juice) on the reverse the date on a scroll.

1548 *14.25in (36cm) high*
$34,500-39,000 **L&T**

A mid-16thC Deruta maiolica 'Galloping Horseman' dish, possibly from the Mancini workshop, painted with a Turkish horseman with a sword carrying a standard.

16.25in (41cm) diam
$13,500-18,000 **L&T**

A mid-16thC Italian maiolica apothecary bottle, Faenza or Montelupo, with a scroll label 'de consolida' for comfrey.

The decoration on this bottle was inspired by the blue painting on rarely obtained, at this period, white Chinese translucent hard paste porcelains.

8.75in (22cm) high
$975-1,150 **L&T**

A mid-16thC Castel Durante maiolica albarello or pharmacy jar, inscribed 'Gra.de.Anetra' on a scrolled banner, and the initials of the pharmacy 'GF' (Grasso de Anetra: duck or goose fat).

7.75in (19.5cm) high
$1,200-1,500 **WW**

A Faenza maiolica apothecary jar, with the inscription 'SALAMONO' on a ribbon behind, the inscription 'ELL ELESCOPH' (elettuario elescoph - The Bishop's electuary, a purgative electuary), the base with three letters '(?RZZ)'.

There is also a mark on the base incised after firing, probably a reference to the weight of the jar when empty, or its capacity, price or contents.

c1555 *7.5in (19cm) high*

$10,500-12,000 L&T

A Venice maiolica jar, probably workshop of Domenego da Venezia, painted with a Franciscan with a halo.

c1565 *13.25in (33.5cm) high*

$5,250-6,750 L&T

A Venetian maiolica jar, probably workshop of Domenego da Venezia, painted with images of an old bearded man and on the reverse a young woman.

c1565 *11.5in (29cm) high*

$7,500-9,000 L&T

A Venetian maiolica jar, probably workshop of Domenego da Venezia, on one side a woman in contemporary costume, on the other, the bust of a bearded man.

c1565 *11.5 (29cm) high*

$9,000-10,500 L&T

A 17thC Urbino maiolica 'Istoriata' footed dish, painted depicting Constantine the Great on horseback with soldiers in battle with Emperor Maxentius' cavalry.

The subject of this dish is most likely 'Constantine the Great 's Victory over the Tyrant Maxentius'. The composition for this scene may have been derived from an engraving by Giulio Bonasone after designs by Raphael, executed by Giulio Romano, for the Sala del Constantino, in the Vatican Palace.

11in (28cm) diam

$9,000-10,500 L&T

A 17thC Sicilian maiolica albarello, painted with a profile portrait.

9.75in (24.5cm) high

$1,500-2,250 WW

An Italian maiolica apothecary syrup jar with matching cover, Pesaro or Castel Durante, painted with the female figure of 'Fortune' standing on a sea monster with an inscription on a band below the handle 'O.D.CODOGNE', dated.

The inscription is probably for Olio di Codium - poppy-head oil.

1579 *10in (25.5cm) high*

$7,500-9,000 L&T

A pair of 19thC Italian maiolica drug jars, each inscribed in Latin.

17.25in (44cm) high

$1,500-1,800 L&T

CLOSER LOOK - MAIOLICA JARDINIERE

This is typical of the maiolica that was produced in Italy at the end of the 19thC. It has the painted blue crowned Ginori mark.

Although Classically inspired, its depiction of putti and grotesques is much later than other examples on the page.

Its majestic molded lion mask lug handles with hanging floral garlands make it very decorative.

Although badly chipped, which is a problem with tin-glazed earthenware, it still has the 'wow' factor.

A late 19thC Italian Ginori maiolica jardiniere.

13.5in (34cm) diam

$1,150-1,425 L&T

ESSENTIAL REFERENCE - CREAMWARE

The invention and development of creamware or cream-colored earthenware can be attributed to Thomas Astbury (1686-1743), Enoch Booth, and Josiah Wedgwood (1730-95).

- **Creamware was a success due to its versatility; it could be used in dinner services, tablewares and teawares meant for daily use as well as more ornamental vases and figures.**
- **The body provided a background that could be molded, cut in great detail and covered in a smooth lead glaze. It equally lent itself well to underglaze blue, overglaze enamelling, or printing.**
- **A mixture of Devon clay and flint produced a close-grained body and its chemical composition was similar to that of salt-glazed stoneware.**
- **Wedgwood's creamware received attention from Queen Charlotte, who commissioned a tea service in 1765, which included coffee cups, fruit baskets and stands, melon preserve pots and six-hand candlesticks. It was subsequently renamed 'Queen's ware'.**
- **Empress Catherine II of Russia (1773-4) commissioned a 926-piece Wedgwood dinner and dessert service for her Gothic summer palace 'La Grenouillière', which can be identified by a frog motif. This is an example of the acceptance of creamware amongst the higher classes of society and ensured that it remained a financial success.**

A Staffordshire creamware cauliflower teapot and cover.
c1760 *4.5in (11.5cm) high*
$2,100-2,700 SK

A Staffordshire creamware teapot and cover, hexagonal shape press-molded with scale ground and foliate cartouches to each corner, inscribed freehand 'MK' under base.
c1760 *4in (10cm) high*
$3,600-7,500 SK

A Wedgwood creamware teapot and cover, decorated with flowers, traces of gilding to knop center and handle terminals, impressed lower case mark.
c1770 *4.75in (12cm) high*
$1,150-1,300 SK

A creamware teapot and cover, painted with a man wearing a hat and carrying two bird cages.
c1770 *4.75in (12cm) high*
$550-700 HT

Judith Picks: Creamware Teapot

Out of this good selection of creamware teapots with their characteristic naive charm, this is the one that I would choose. The melon-form is unusual and the crabstock handle is desirable. This is a large size pot with an engine-turned body with strong decorative alternating green and yellow stripes. It has excellent proportions and has a quite modern appeal. Along with these desirable features, it is also one of the more expensive examples.

A Staffordshire creamware teapot and cover.
c1775 *6in (15cm) high*
$6,000-7,500 SK

A Staffordshire creamware teapot and cover, leaf-molded spout with entwined handle terminating at florets.
c1775 *5.25in (13.5cm) high*
$850-975 SK

A Staffordshire creamware teapot and cover, attributed to Swansea, with inscription 'Edith Johns July the 21st 1789'.
1789 *7in (17.5cm) high*
$1,800-3,000 SK

A Staffordshire creamware creamer and cover, attributed to William Greatbatch.

Apart from the various members of the Wood family, William Greatbatch (1735-1813) was the most talented and prolific designer and maker of potters' molds during the second half of the 18thC.

c1760 *5.75in (14.5cm) high*

$1,800-3,000 SK

A Staffordshire creamware coffee pot and cover, attributed to William Greatbatch.

c1760 *8.5in (21.5cm) high*

$1,800-2,400 SK

A Staffordshire creamware coffee cup, with molded S-scroll handle.

c1765 *3in (7.5cm) high*

$600-750 SK

A George III creamware mug, 'The Triumph of Liberty' 'The First Attack of The Bastille Taken by Storm After a Conflict of Three Hours by The Citizens of Paris July 14th 1789'.

This rare mug produced by the Staffordshire potters for the British supporters of the French Revolution. The potters were never known to miss a promotional opportunity. They famously produced wares in favor of the American struggle against the British in the War of Independence.

1789 *6.5in (16.5cm) high*

$6,750-7,500 MITC

A creamware mug, printed with a portrait inscribed 'George.III King' and with 'Britons Rejoyce; Cheer Up and Sing; And Drink His Health Long Live the KING', minor cracks.

Probably made to commemorate George III's return to sanity in 1789, although he lapsed in and out for many years.

c1789 *2.5in (6.5cm) high*

$975-1,150 SWO

An early Liverpool creamware mug, printed and colored with 'An East View of Liverpool Light House and Signals on Bidston Hill', the tower beside 56 colored flags.

Examples of this print post-1793 usually have Flag 40 listed as 'Enemies' and have at least 58 flags, while a jug dated 1790 had only 52 flags listed.

c1790-93 *5in (13cm) high*

$450-600 WW

A creamware mug, printed with a portrait of King George III, wearing full dress uniform.

This mug probably commemorates the death of George III in 1820.

c1820 *2.5in (6.5cm) high*

$1,200-1,500 SWO

A creamware Coronation mug, with a portrait of the young Queen in a wreath of national emblems.

This is an unusual print.

1837 *2.5in (6cm) high*

$900-1,000 SWO

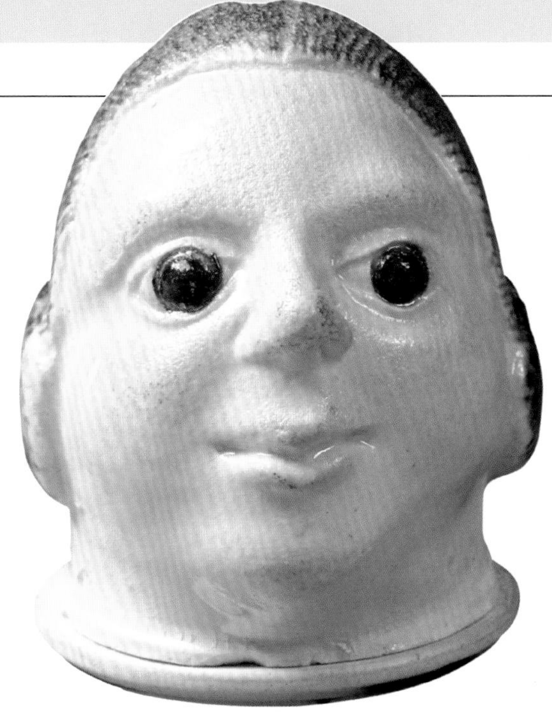

A Staffordshire creamware patch box and cover, modeled as a man's head, believed to depict George III, decorated with black hair, brown eyes, and a screw lid with mottled manganese, gray, blue, yellow, and green, each part inscribed with a number 6.

c1755 *2.5in (6.5cm) high*

$1,000-1,400 **SK**

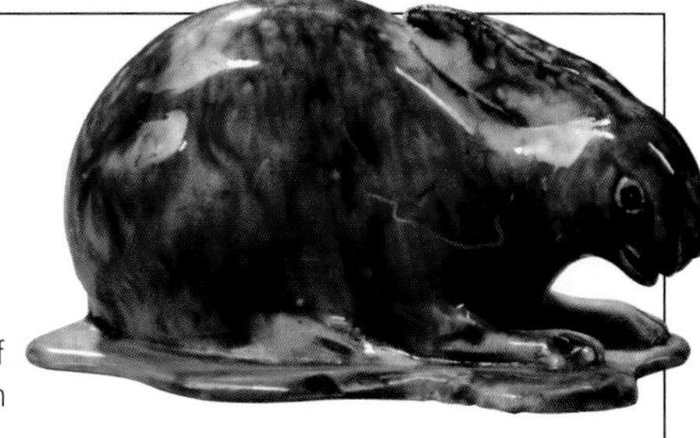

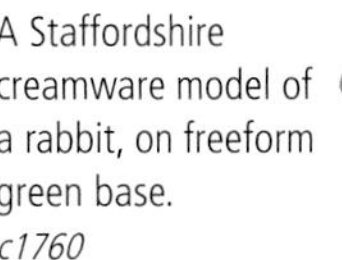

A Staffordshire creamware model of a rabbit, on freeform green base.

c1760 *3.5in (9cm) wide*

$700-850 **SK**

A Staffordshire creamware sugar bowl and cover, attributed to William Greatbatch, allover basket and fruit molded design underglaze decorated in translucent enamels.

c1760 4.5in (11.5cm) diam

$4,000-4,500 **SK**

A Staffordshire creamware leaf dish, the press-molded body naturalistically modeled with flowers and decorated with a translucent green and brown enamel.

c1765 *7.75in (19.5cm) long*

$750-900 **SK**

A Staffordshire creamware model of a cat.

c1760 *5.5in (13.5cm) high*

$450-600 **SK**

A Staffordshire creamware cauliflower sauceboat, molded and enameled body with white florets above broad green leaves.

c1770 *8in (20.5cm) long*

$8,250-9,750 **SK**

A Staffordshire creamware plate, with a basketweave border and fruit banding, translucent green, yellow, and brown glazes.

c1770 *9.5in (24cm) diam*

$975-1,150 **SK**

A Staffordshire creamware tea canister, impressed pheasant's-eye-framed cartouches of Flora in high relief to either side, translucent green, brown, and yellow glazes.

c1770 *6.75in (17cm) high*

$1,400-1,700 **SK**

A Staffordshire creamware pineapple tea canister, the molded body with yellow fruit atop stiff green leaves.

c1770 *4.5in (11.5cm) high*

$1,500-2,250 **SK**

A Staffordshire creamware tea canister, with three molded panels of Flora, the fourth an inscription 'Abraham Randell Alice Randell 1779'.

1779 *5in (12.5cm) high*

$1,400-1,800 **SK**

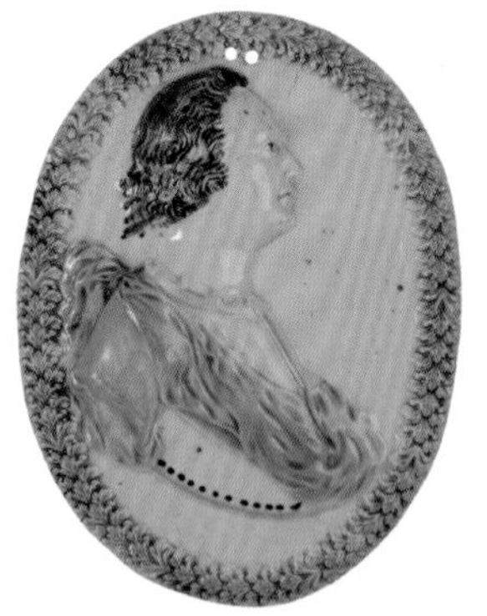

A creamware plaque, painted in the 'Ralph Wood' palette with a portrait of a gentleman, possibly the Duke of Cumberland, hairline crack.

c1790 *6in (15.5cm) high*

$900-1,200 **MOR**

An unusual creamware two-handled pot à jus and cover, decorated in blue, red and gilt with a continuous stylized foliate design.

c1790 *3.5in (9cm) high*

$700-850 **WW**

A creamware stirrup cup, crisply modeled as a dog's head with mouth slightly open to reveal a tongue and teeth, the exterior decorated in a rich brown glaze.

c1800 *5in (12.5cm)*

$450-600 **WW**

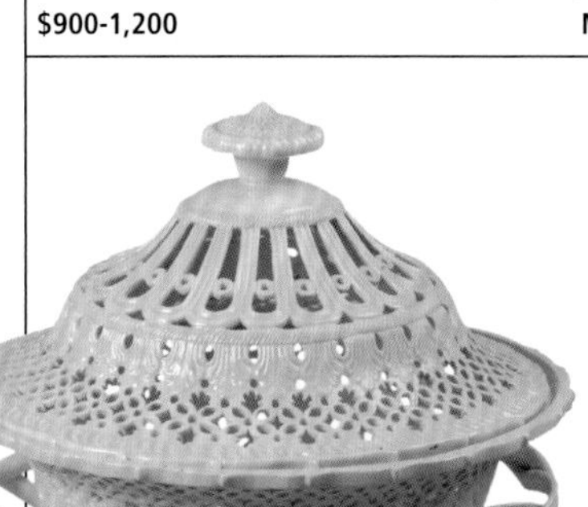

An imposing early 20thC Leeds Pottery creamware chestnut basket and cover, of two-handled circular form, overall pierced and leaf-molded, the entwined strap handles with flowerhead terminals, the domed cover with large flowerhead finial, impressed mark.

Several light brown spotted firing marks to upper surface of cover. Other minor pinhole firing marks. Numerous small modelling/firing faults around latticework of base but mostly seen on the inside. Some very light brown spotted firing marks to top and underside of foot. All over light crazing to base and cover. Base does not quite sit square on the foot.

9.5in (24cm) high x 10.5in (27cm) diam

$600-750 **MOR**

An early 20thC Leeds Pottery creamware chestnut basket and cover, of circular two-handled form, elaborately pierced allover and molded with foliage, paterae and swags, the interlacing strap handles with flowerhead terminals, the high domed cover with flowerhead finial, incised mark 'Leeds Pottery GWS' (for George W.Senior).

All over light crazing to cover and base. Cover with some light brown spotted firing marks on upper surface near finial. Two very small chips on rim. Base with two small brown firing marks to inner flange of rim. Three small firing cracks and a small hairline crack in same area. Four small areas of glaze loss on edge of foot. Other very minor firing faults to foot.

11.25in (28.5cm) high

$700-850 **MOR**

ESSENTIAL REFERENCE - PEARLWARE

Introduced by Wedgwood in c1779, Pearlware was an attempt to improve creamware.

- **Pearlware includes more white clay and flint in the body than creamware and thus has a whiter body.**
- **Suggesting an iridescent appearance, 'pearlware' is a misleading term; the addition of cobalt oxide to the glaze imparted a blueish-white cast, particularly visible where there is pooling.**
- **Pearlware is often decorated in underglaze blue by painting or transfer-printing. One of the most famous printed patterns is the chinoiserie 'Willow' pattern.**
- **Much pearlware is useful ware, such as dishes, plates, teapots and jugs.**
- **In the early 19thC, manufacturers broadened the range of patterns to include Classical designs and English landscapes.**
- **Many figure groups were also made.**

A rare pair of early 19thC Staffordshire pearlware groups, of Obadiah Sherratt-type, depicting, the 'Flight in to Egypt' and the 'Return from Egypt', minor repairs.

8in (20cm) high

$4,500-5,250 WW

A pair of Staffordshire pearlware models of a ram and ewe, decorated in splashes of blue, yellow, and brown, green glazed base.

These are particularly fine early examples with fine molding and modelling. They are also in exceptional condition.

c1780 *5in (13cm) long*

$7,500-9,000 SK

A Staffordshire pearlware figure of a lion.

c1800 *11.5in (29cm) wide*

$1,500-2,250 POOK

An 18thC English pearlware figure emblematic of 'Winter'.

8.75in (22cm) high

$300-450 L&T

A pair of early 19thC Staffordshire pearlware figures of Venus and Neptune, standing beside a dolphin on a shell-encrusted rocky mound.

9.5in (24cm) high

$2,100-2,700 L&T

An early 19thC pearlware figure of St Sebastian, his raised arm broken and restuck.

9.75in (25cm) high

$550-600 WW

An early 19thC pearlware figure of St Sebastian, his raised arm broken and restuck.

9.75in (25cm) high

$550-600 WW

A Scottish pearlware salt, probably Portobello, modeled as a horse and cart with rider, large chip to base.

c1820 *4.75in (12cm) long*

$200-350 DN

A pearlware pottery plaque, relief molded and underglaze painted with two lions, some small firing cracks.

c1820 *10in (24.8cm) wide*

$750-900 MOR

A rare Cambrian pearlware mug, transfer-printed with silhouettes of George III, Caroline, Louis XVI and Marie-Antoinette formed from the outlines of two candelabra, the French 'portraits' of France flanked by a broken crown, and all inscribed 'A New Puzzle of Portraits Striking Likenefses of the King & Queen of England and the late King & Queen of France'.

The Mysterious Urn was copied from a print drawn for the Loyalists of the guillotined Louis XVI and Queen Antoinette (1783), the disguised portraits ensuring that, if raided, their oppressors would not link the 'innocent' urn with their royal support. They ordered copies from the Chinese very soon after the atrocity. Since Britain was at war with France at the date of this mug, it is unlikely to have been supportive, although revolutionary France was much admired by the lower orders who hated the ghastly (as they saw it) Hanoverians (particularly Prinny). More likely it was simply made as an amusing trick.

c1790 *3.5in (9cm) high*

$1,500-2,000 SWO

A pearlware loving cup, printed with portraits of 'Queen Charlotte, George III, His Royal Highness Prince of Wales and the Honourable Willm. Pitt'.

c1793 *6in (15cm) high*

$6,000-6,750 SWO

A pearlware mug, printed with portraits of George III and Charlotte, inscribed 'A King Revered, a Queen Beloved', above 'Long May They Live', chips filled, crack.

c1809 *5in (12.5cm) high*

$700-850 SWO

A rare molded pearlware tankard, the portrait of George IV wearing military style uniform above a banner impressed 'King George IIII', on a pink luster ground.

This mug may well be Scottish and commemorating the visit of George to Scotland, much against his courtiers' advice. He devised his own uniform to the horror of his advisers, but to the delight of his Scottish people.

c1822 *5.25in (13.5cm) high*

$4,400-4,800 SWO

Judith Picks: Pearlware Mug

I love a good piece of history on a ceramic. 'Prinny' while having married Mrs Fitzherbert morganatically, was forced by his father to divorce her and marry his choice, the German Princess Caroline. On her arrival in London, she was nothing like the portrait miniature supplied and she bathed very infrequently. He went to the wedding drunk. Despite this, on that, his wedding night, they managed to conceive - the only time he slept with her. He then tried to divorce her, which needed an Act of Parliament. The evidence he concocted was presented to parliament in green cloth bags and largely comprised soiled bed sheets from her supposed relationship with an Italian Count. She returned to England for the coronation in 1821. The populous loathed Prinny and rooted for Caroline. At Westminster Abbey, Prinny had lodged gatekeepers, including the World Champion pugilist, Tom Cribb, preventing her entering on the grounds that she hadn't got a ticket. Distraught, Caroline turned away and died some months later, some saying she was poisoned. Despite his monstrosity, Prinny, a gambler, spendthrift and womanizer, was actually a man of great aesthetic taste. He built Carlton House (hence the desk) to his design, the Brighton Pavilion and formed its Sèvres collection. The print shows the scales of justice overseen by John Bull with speech bubbles reading 'Well done Caroline, they think to make light of you, but it won't do, I'll see fair play', the lighter Prinny, trying to be dragged down by courtiers and the law beneath bags titled 'Green' and 'Secrets', but much outweighed by Caroline, with justice on her side.

A rare pearlware mug, printed with a commemoration of the Parliamentary Bill to divorce Caroline (which failed), the mouth pink luster, some wear.

c1820 *3.5in (9cm) high*

$1,400-1,800 SWO

A 19thC pearlware Temperance teapot and cover, printed by J Aynsley of Lane End, then hand-colored, one side with a man, the reverse with a woman, standing beneath a pair of compasses with admonitions around.

9in (22.5cm) high

$280-340 WW

A Prattware plaque, molded and painted with of 'Jack on a Cruise', some restoration to lower edge.

c1800 *8.5in (25cm) high*

$1,400-1,800 **MOR**

A Prattware plaque, molded and painted with a portrait of 'Captain Cook', some areas of restoration to rim.

c1800 *5in (13.5cm) high*

$1,200-1,800 **MOR**

A Prattware pearlware plaque, molded and painted with a depiction of Venus, standing in a shell pulled by dolphins, Cupid in attendance.

c1800 *7in (17.5cm) wide*

$850-975 **MOR**

ESSENTIAL REFERENCE - PRATTWARE

Prattware is associated with the Pratt family from Lane Delph in Staffordshire, although it was also made by a number of other factories.

- **The body is similar to pearlware in weight and color, but the ware is distinguished by a strong, high-temperature palette comprising ocher, brown, green, and blue.**
- **Wares include molded teapots, jugs, and figures.**
- **It takes its name from the Staffordshire factory F. & R. Pratt, founded by William Pratt c1775.**
- **From the 1840s the firm of F. & R. Pratt & Co. was famous for multicolored printing, used extensively on pot lids.**
- **Other factories that produced similar pieces include Leeds and Bristol.**
- **In the 1840s Pratt's factory became the leading manufacturers of pot lids. These are also collectible although the market is not what it was.**

A Prattware pearlware plaque, molded with a portrait of Charles I, considerable restoration to foliate edge, hairline firing crack, overall fine crazing.

c1800 *8.5in (22cm) high*

$600-750 **MOR**

A Prattware model of a bear.

c1800 *2in (5cm) high*

$550-700 **H&C**

A pearlware harvest jug, decorated in Pratt-type colors, inscribed 'God Speed the plough'.

c1810 *7in (17.5cm) high*

$550-700 **WW**

A Yorkshire Prattware cow group, with a panting dog and a farmer wearing a top hat and holding a bowl of eggs.

c1810 *5.5in (14cm) high*

$3,400-4,000 **WW**

An unusual pair of Yorkshire Prattware cow groups, one with her tail flicked over her back, a calf between the feet, a panting dog below the other.

c1810-20 *7in (17.5cm) high*

$4,500-5,250 **WW**

A Prattware model of a lion the front paw resting upon a ball.

c1810 *2in (6cm) high*

$900-1,000 **H&C**

ESSENTIAL REFERENCE - SALT-GLAZED STONEWARE

At the highest temperature during the firing of stoneware, salt (sodium chloride) is thrown into the kiln, and, as it vaporizes, the sodium reacts with the silica in the stoneware body to form a thin, sometimes pitted glaze.

- **The iron impurities present in many stoneware clays cause most salt-glazed stonewares to be brown in color.**
- **A few wares are whitish or light buff in color.**
- **Red lead was sometimes added with the salt to make the glaze glassier.**
- **The glaze may have a slightly pitted surface, an effect known as 'orange peel'.**
- **Clays need to be rich in silica.**

A Staffordshire salt-glazed stoneware camel teapot and cover.
c1740 *5.25in (13.5cm) high*
$2,700-3,300 SK

A Staffordshire solid agate cream jug and cover, set on three lion mask and paw feet.
c1750 *6.5in (16.5cm) high*
$3,400-4,800 SK

A Staffordshire drab ground salt-glazed stoneware jug and cover, white pipe clay floral and scrollwork sprigging.
c1750 *6.25in (16cm) high*
$2,550-3,000 SK

A Staffordshire salt-glazed stoneware teapot and cover, decorated with a Chinaman to either side amongst flowers.
c1760 *7in (18cm) long*
$2,700-3,300 SK

A Staffordshire salt-glazed stoneware teapot and cover.
c1760 *7.5in (19cm) high*
$2,700-3,300 SK

A Staffordshire salt-glazed stoneware teapot and cover, on three molded peacock feet, 'Chinese Precious Ornaments' motif.
c1760 *5.5in (14cm) high*
$2,550-3,000 SK

A Staffordshire salt-glazed stoneware fruit basket and stand.
c1750 *9in (23cm) long*
$2,100-3,000 SK

A Staffordshire salt-glazed stoneware figure of a maiden, possibly a candle snuffer.
c1750 *3.5in (9cm) high*
$1,500-2,250 SK

A Staffordshire salt-glazed stoneware cup, molded with a central crest surrounded by mythical beasts and figures.
c1760 *3in (7.5cm) high*
$1,500-2,250 SK

A 17thC German stoneware flagon, possibly Frechen, decorated with a rosette medallion and shield devices.

7.5in (14.5cm) high

$600-700 **SWO**

An English stoneware silver-mounted tankard, possibly London, with embossed metal cartouche with portrait of King William III.

c1700 7in (18cm) high

$1,800-2,250 **DN**

A Staffordshire salt-glazed stoneware tea canister, possibly Bovey Tracy, metal replacement lid.

c1755 5.25in (13.5cm) high

$1,800-2,250 **SK**

A Staffordshire enameled salt-glazed stoneware sauceboat, with Chinese figures and flowers.

c1760 7in (17.5cm) long

$3,000-4,000 **SK**

A 19thC Pennsylvania stoneware jug, impressed 'Cowden & Wilcox Harrisburg'.

11in (27.5cm) high

$750-975 **POOK**

A late 19thC Victoria and Albert stoneware flask, impressed W. Cooper, Goodramgate, York.

11in (28cm) high

$700-750 **LOCK**

An early 19thC stoneware jug of Napoleon, some damages.

13.5in (34.5cm) high

$280-300 **WW**

A 19thC rare salt-glazed stoneware figure of a Highlander, holding a flask in one hand and a glass in the other.

9.5in (24cm) high

$1,200-1,800 **BELL**

An early 19thC fox's head stoneware stirrup flask, a chip to one ear.

6in (16cm) long

$450-600 **WW**

ESSENTIAL REFERENCE - TRANSFER-PRINTED 'BEAUTIES OF AMERICA' VIEWS

'Beauties of America' is a series of transfer-printed pottery decorated with American views and buildings created by John Ridgway for the American export market.

- **English pottery was exported to North America in large numbers from the third quarter of the 18thC onward, and again after the peace treaty was signed (1812-1815).**
- **Ridgway, the owner of a pottery factory in Staffordshire, toured America in 1822 to gather views of cities and to establish relationships with American merchants.**
- **According to his travel journal, Ridgway also hired artists to accompany him during parts of his American tour.**
- **Most 'Beauties of America' objects were almost entirely covered in a dark blue transfer print; dark blue wares were popular with the North American market.**
- **Patterns were applied underneath the glaze, which protected the colors from fading. This explains why most transfer-printed wares still appear relatively new today.**
- **Famous views and buildings transferred onto Ridgway's ceramicware included the Boston Athenaeum, Capitol Washington, Governor's Island in New York, as well as various hospitals, alms-houses, and insane asylums.**

A 19thC Staffordshire 'Franklin's Tomb' teapot.

5.25in (13cm) high

$400-450 POOK

A 19thC Staffordshire 'Boston State House' teapot.

5.75in (14.5cm) high

$450-550 POOK

A 19thC Staffordshire 'Washington at Tomb' coffee pot.

11in (28cm) high

$1,800-3,000 POOK

A 19thC Staffordshire 'Deaf and Dumb Asylum' pitcher, Hartford, Connecticut and 'Alms House', New York.

10.75in (27cm) high

$975-1,150 POOK

A 19thC Staffordshire 'Seal of United States' pitcher.

5.75in (14.5cm) high

$1,200-1,500 POOK

A 19thC Staffordshire 'Washington and Lafayette' pitcher.

6in (15cm) high

$600-750 POOK

CLOSER LOOK - STAFFORDSHIRE PLATE

This is a wonderful print of the Mt. Pleasant Classical Institute with deep multi-toned cobalt.

The pattern is executed to an extremely high standard with the floral surround giving it a three-dimensional effect.

This plate is extremely rare - being one of only three known.

It is impressed Clews for Ralph and James Clews who were Potters in Cobridge, near Burslem from 1813 and developed an enormous export trade to the US. They went bankrupt in c1834.

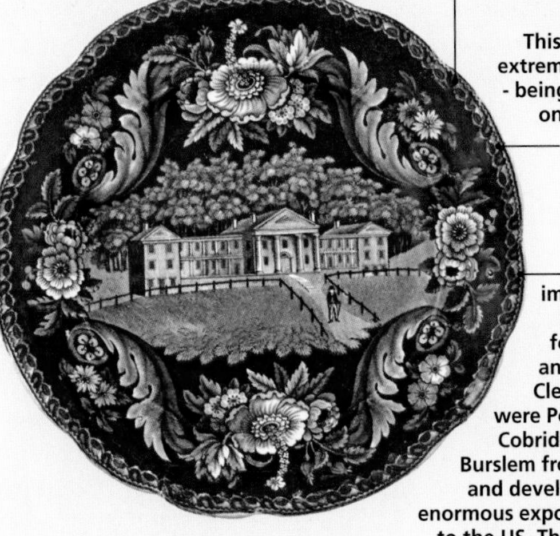

A 19thC Staffordshire plate.

10.5in (26.7cm) diam

$22,500-30,000 **POOK**

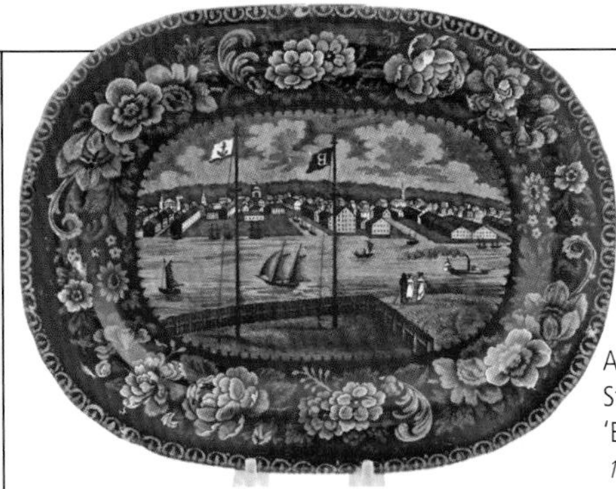

A 19thC Staffordshire 'Baltimore' platter.

11.75in (30cm) wide

$7,500-9,000 **POOK**

A 19thC Staffordshire 'Arms of Delaware' platter, with a blue printed eagle mark on the underside.

16.75in (42.5cm) wide

$6,000-6,750 **POOK**

A 19thC Staffordshire 'Capitol Washington' strainer, stamped 'Beauties of America Capitol Washington, J & W Ridgway'.

15in (38cm) wide

$3,400-4,800 **POOK**

An early 19thC Staffordshire 'General Lafayette' toddy plate, impressed Clews.

4.5in (11.4cm) diam

$4,000-4,500 **POOK**

A 19thC Staffordshire 'Customs House of Philadelphia' cup plate.

3.5in (9cm) diam

$3,400-4,000 **POOK**

A 19thC Staffordshire 'The Junction of the Sacandaga & Hudson Rivers' platter, impressed Stevenson.

14.25in (36cm) wide

$4,500-5,250 **POOK**

A 19thC Staffordshire 'Landing of Lafayette' platter, impressed Clews.

18.25in (46.4cm) wide

$3,000-3,900 **POOK**

A 19thC Staffordshire 'Highlands near Newburgh' plate, impressed Wood & Sons.

6.5in (16.5cm) diam

$3,400-4,000 **POOK**

A 19thC Staffordshire 'Baltimore Court House' waste bowl.

4.75in (12cm) diam

$1,500-2,100 **POOK**

A 19thC Staffordshire 'Boston State House' pate dish.

4.5in (11cm) wide

$1,800-3,000 **POOK**

An early 19thC Staffordshire 'Landing of Lafayette' fruit compote, impressed Clews.

10in (25.4cm) wide

$1,200-1,500 **POOK**

An early 19thC Staffordshire 'Landing of Lafayette' fruit compote, impressed Clews.

10in (25.4cm) wide

$1,200-1,500 **POOK**

A 19thC Staffordshire 'View of Governor's Island, New York' shallow soup bowl, impressed Stevenson.

10.25in (26cm) diam

$2,000-2,400 **POOK**

A 19thC Staffordshire 'Capitol Washington' serving bowl.

10in (25.4cm) diam

$600-700 **POOK**

CLOSER LOOK - STAFFORDSHIRE SOUP BOWL

This bowl has the rare 'Church and Buildings Adjoining Murray Street, New York' print.

The print is of superb quality with a good border pattern.

It has the impressed mark 'Stevenson' which is for Ralph Stevenson who had a factory in Cobridge, Staffordshire from c1810-35.

A 19thC Staffordshire soup bowl.

10in (25.4cm) diam

$6,750-7,500 **POOK**

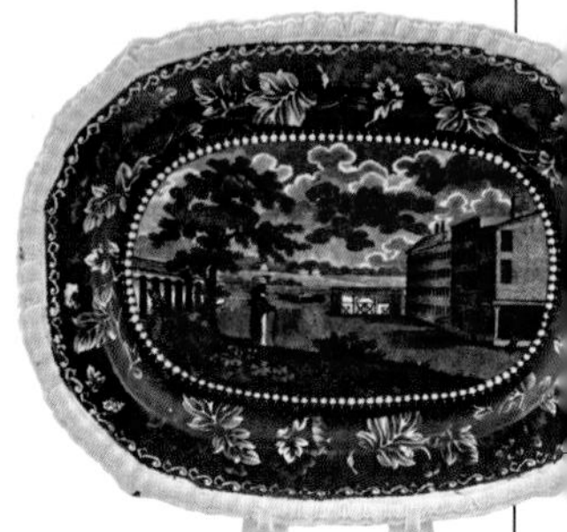

A 19thC Staffordshire 'Brooklyn Ferry' serving dish, impressed 'Stevenson'.

10in (25.5cm) diam

$5,250-6,000 **POOK**

A 19thC Staffordshire 'Woodlands near Philadelphia' vegetable bowl.

11in (28cm) wide

$600-750 **POOK**

A 19thC Staffordshire tureen, 'Alms House', Boston, with a 'Deaf and Dumb Asylum', Hartford, Connecticut cover and undertray, stamped J & W Ridgway.

tureen 17.5in (44.4cm) wide

$5,250-6,000 **POOK**

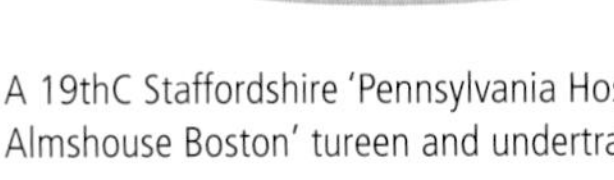

A 19thC Staffordshire 'Pennsylvania Hospital/ Almshouse Boston' tureen and undertray.

The tureen is mismarked 'Capitol Washington'. This adds to the value of this already rare tureen.

tureen 11in (27.9cm) high

$9,750-10,500 **POOK**

A 19thC Staffordshire 'Landing of Lafayette' tureen base, impressed Clews.

8.5in (21.2cm) wide

$3,400-4,800 **POOK**

A 19thC Staffordshire 'Boston State House' ladies spittoon.

4in (10cm) high

$7,500-8,250 **POOK**

A 19thC Staffordshire 'Boston State House' reticulated basket and undertray, impressed Rogers.

basket 9.75in (25cm) wide

$4,500-6,000 **POOK**

A 19thC Staffordshire 'Arms of South Carolina' leaf dish.

5.5in (14cm) long

$3,400-4,800 **POOK**

A 19thC Staffordshire 'Highlands Hudson River' reticulated tray.

10in (25.4cm) wide

$3,400-4,800 **POOK**

A 19thC Staffordshire 'Fort Gansevoort' ladle.

9.5in (24cm) long

$2,000-3,000 **POOK**

A 19thC Staffordshire 'Boston State House' egg stand, impressed Rogers.

4.75in (12cm) high

$1,800-3,000 **POOK**

A 19thC Staffordshire 'Catholic Cathedral, New York' gravy boat.

4in (10cm) high

$975-1,150 **POOK**

ESSENTIAL REFERENCE - STAFFORDSHIRE DOGS

Staffordshire figurines came in a wide variety of forms and were in high demand during the Victorian era.

- **The figures portrayed royalty, politicians, military and naval heroes, sportsmen, theatrical celebrities, religious figures, villains, and animals.**
- **Pairs of dogs were a common form of Staffordshire pottery and depicted breeds like greyhounds, pugs, poodles, dalmatians, and spaniels.**
- **Queen Victoria's pet dog Dash, a King Charles spaniel, was the likely inspiration behind the many spaniel figures that emerged during the 19thC. Spaniels made in Sunderland were often decorated with copper luster patches on their bodies or as chains around their necks.**
- **The figures were often designed for mantelpieces so not much attention was given to their backs, earning them the nickname 'flatbacks'. Placed on mantels or ledges, they would have been viewed from the front only.**
- **A pair of figures is worth more than a single piece and later examples are not as well executed as earlier ones.**
- **There are many fakes on the market.**

A extremely rare pair of Staffordshire 'Grace' and 'Majesty' spaniel dogs' with pink and green bases.
c1850 *10in (25.5cm) high*
$7,500-9,000 **PC**

A pair of mid-19thC Staffordshire pottery spaniels, each smoking a pipe, restoration to pipes.
8.75in (22cm) high
$1,800-2,250 **MAB**

A pair of 19thC Staffordshire Afghan hounds, each with a child standing between its forepaws, the dogs' coats decorated with red wheels of fire.
12in (31cm) high
$750-900 **WW**

A pair of Staffordshire pottery 'Disraeli' spaniels, some flaking.

'Disraeli' spaniels, called after the Prime Minister, have curls on their foreheads. These are also desirable as they are well painted and have baskets of flowers in their mouths.
c1860 *8in (20cm) high*
$600-750 **MAB**

A pair of mid-19thC Staffordshire spaniels, each wearing a gilt collar and smoking a pipe, raised on green bases, restoration to one pipe, minor chips.
8.75in (22cm) high
$1,800-2,250 **MAB**

A pair of mid-19thC large spaniels, each brown streaky treacle glazed and wearing a padlocked collar, molded oval plinth base, some crazing, on ewith chip.
16.7in (42.5cm) high
$2,100-2,700 **MOR**

A pair of 19thC Staffordshire figures of dalmations, on a naturalistic style ground.
8in (20cm) high
$450-600 **L&T**

ESSENTIAL REFERENCE - COW CREAMERS

Inspired by forms originally modeled in silver and pottery, pottery cow creamers are good examples of the qualities of early 19thC British pottery.

- **Staffordshire creamers were made in salt-glazed stoneware, creamware, glossy black 'Jackfield ware', pearlware and bone china.**
- **Luster glazes were used, but the most common finish was tan dappled in green, black, yellow, blue or orange.**
- **Early Welsh pieces were in splashed lusterware, and later ones had transfer-printed rural scenes.**
- **Yorkshire cows had oblong, waisted bases with chamfered corners, and colorful lusterware creamers were usually made in Sunderland.**
- **German creamers were made at the beginning of the 20thC and are significantly larger than English ones and were probably designed to hold milk rather than cream.**
- **Milk jugs modeled as cows were popular for almost 100 years from the mid-18thC. This ended when it was discovered that they might be unhygienic.**
- **Those made before 1830 tend to be rough to the touch.**
- **Because of their desirability, creamers have been widely copied.**

A late 18thC Staffordshire earthenware cow creamer with milkmaid.

7in (17.5cm) long

$850-975 **SK**

A Staffordshire earthenware bocage cow creamer, with calf by its feet.

c1800 *6.75in (17cm) long*

$1,500-2,250 **SK**

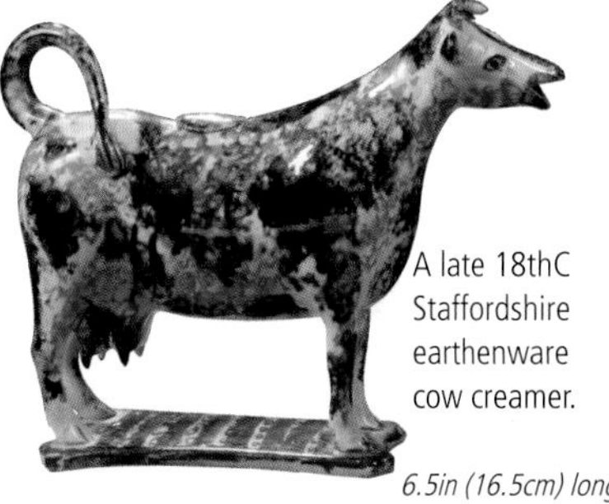

A late 18thC Staffordshire earthenware cow creamer.

6.5in (16.5cm) long

A late 18thC Staffordshire earthenware cow creamer with milkmaid.

6.25in (15.8cm) long

$450-550 **SK**

An early 19thC Staffordshire pearlware cow creamer, spongeware decorated in black, blue and yellow, canted rectangular base, tail restored, minor chips, small firing flaws.

6in (15cm) high

$975-1,150 **MOR**

A pair of mid 19thC Staffordshire earthenware rabbits, possibly WW Stubles.

9.5in (24.13cm) long

$1,800-3,000 **SK**

An early 19thC Yorkshire earthenware model of a horse, the base sponged in a green glaze.

6.25in (15.8cm) high

$4,000-4,500 **SK**

A 19thC Staffordshire pair of sheep beside a tree.

5.5in (24cm) high

$150-210 **TRI**

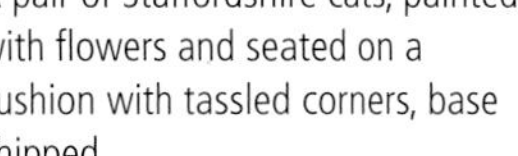

A pair of Staffordshire cats, painted with flowers and seated on a cushion with tasseled corners, base chipped.

7in (17.5cm) high

$135-180 **TRI**

A Ralph Wood group, of the 'Vicar and Moses' the Vicar asleep while the clerk preaches from a book, the pulpit applied with angel heads and swags.

c1782-90 *9.5in (24cm) high*

$750-1,200 **WW**

A late 18thC Ralph Wood figure of Cupid and a lion, some restoration.

8.3in (21cm) high

$1,800-2,250 **WW**

An early 19thC 'Night Watchman' character jug.

9in (23cm) high

$300-450 **WW**

An early 19thC Staffordshire pearlware group, 'Persuasion', in the manner of John Walton, modeled as a young couple, he holding a gold ring, some restoration.

8in (20cm) high

$3,000-4,000 **MOR**

Judith Picks:

A potter known as Obadiah Sherratt potted in the early 1800s. We do not know for certain that he was a figure potter, for the only wares bearing his name are two frog mugs. Despite this, many figures with a particulary vigorous earthiness are traditionally attributed to Sherratt. There is no denying the existence of a group of figures with common distinctive characteristics; they need to be called something, and the label 'Sherratt style' or 'Obadiah Sherratt' recognizes that credit for this work may go to an unknown potter. There are many figures which are given an Obadiah Sherratt attribution with no justification, except to increase the price! So care should be taken.

An 'Obadiah Sherratt' Staffordshire pottery bull-baiting group, the bull tossing one terrier in the air and fighting another, the handler holding a club in his hand, slight restoration or repairs.

c1820 *7in (17.5cm) long*

$4,500-6,000 **SWO**

An early 19thC Staffordshire pearlware group, modeled as a showman with dancing bears, a bocage to the rear, restored.

6in (15.5cm) high

$700-850 **MOR**

An early 19thC Staffordshire pearlware 'tithe pig' group, in the manner of John Walton, slight loses to bocage, small losses to enamels.

John Walton was a figure potter who potted in the Staffordshire Potteries from around 1806 until the late 1830s. His mark is found impressed or raised on a decorative scroll on the rear of figures, or sometimes beneath.

7.7in (19.5cm) high

$975-1,150 **MOR**

ESSENTIAL REFERENCE - TOBY JUGS

Toby jugs are ceramic pitchers and generally depict historical, fictional or popular characters wearing period attire and tri-corn hats, often in sitting positions.

- **The introduction of Toby jugs can be attributed to Ralph Wood I and II of Burslem, Enoch Wood, Thomas Hollins and William Pratt who worked in various parts of England like Staffordshire, Leeds and Portobello.**
- **The exact origin of the name 'Toby jug' is uncertain, but the most likely theory illustrates that it was named after an 18thC Yorkshire drinker called Henry Elwes, whose nickname was Toby Fillpot (or Philpot).**
- **His nickname was inspired by 'The Brown Jug', an English drinking song written in 1761.**
- **Many versions exist, including, for example, the 'Squire', the 'Thin Man' and the 'Toper'. The latter represents an ale drinker, which is the most frequently found type of Toby jug.**
- **Most jugs were modeled after male figures, but a female version portraying Martha Gunn, Brighton's most famous bathing woman, also exists.**
- **Figures appear disproportionate because their heads are modeled much larger than the bodies and their facial features are exaggerated, much like caricatures.**
- **Translucent, colored lead glazes are used to highlight the different parts of the figures and give them a slightly unfinished look. They have been popular since they were first made in the 1760s and are very sought-after by collectors.**

A creamware 'Step' or 'Twyford' Toby jug, decorated in Whieldon type glazes.

c1780 *9.5in (24cm) high*

$1,500-2,000 WW

A creamware 'Step' or 'Twyford' Toby jug and associated cover, the empty jug in his left hand decorated with a pattern of spots and stripes in brown, some damages.

c1780-90 *9.5in (24cm) high*

$6,000-6,750 WW

CLOSER LOOK - TOBY JUG

There are many unusual features to this early jug, making it rare. Even with the damage it was highly desirable to collectors.

The colors are good. It is enameled in washes of green and blue, and manganese brown.

The foamy head of his ale escapes down one side of his jug and his long clay pipe rests against his chin.

The quirkiest detail is that his mouth is slightly agape reveal a missing front tooth.

A creamware 'Step' or 'Twyford' Toby jug, some faults.

c1780 *9.5in (24cm) high*

$8,250-9,750 WW

A pearlware Toby jug, some damage to the hat.

Most Toby jugs of this period are modeled with an upright barrel, while far fewer are known with the barrel in this position.

c1780-90 *9.75in (25cm) high*

$2,700-3,300 WW

A rare 'Convict' Toby jug, of 'Thin Man' type, his coat with a design of arrows and loose stripes.

See John Bedford, 'Toby Jugs', p29 for a description of the 'Convict' class of Toby jugs.

c1790 *10in (25cm) high*

$5,700-6,300 WW

A Ralph Wood Toby jug and cover, his wrinkled face with mouth agape to reveal gaps in his teeth, some faults, the cover associated.

c1790 *9.5in (24.5cm) high*

$2,100-2,700 WW

A creamware 'Sailor' Toby jug, enameled in Pratt-type colors, seated on a sea chest with a spoiled anchor between his feet.

c1790 *11.5in (29cm) high*

$1,800-3,000 WW

An 18thC Whieldon type Toby jug, 'Ordinary' model.

9.75in (25cm) high

$4,400-4,800 **FLD**

A late 18thC Ralph Wood Toby jug.

9in (23cm) high

$4,400-4,800 **FLD**

A late 18thC Ralph Wood Toby jug, his face and hands flesh colored in manganese with a wart to his nose.

9.5in (24cm) high

$4,000-4,500 **FLD**

A Ralph Wood creamware Toby jug.

c1790 *9.5in (24cm) high*

$2,100-2,700 **WW**

A rare late 18th/early 19thC Prattware 'Sharp-Face' Toby jug, of Ralph Wood type.

9.75in (25cm) high

$1,500-2,250 **WW**

A large Yorkshire 'Crown Mark' Toby jug, his hat with an unusual scalloped rim, decorated in Prattware enamels, some restoration.

c1800-10 *10in (26cm) high*

$1,400-1,800 **WW**

A Yorkshire 'Crown Mark' Toby jug, a miniature Toby resting on one knee, the handle elaborately leaf-scrolled, some restoration.

c1800-10 *10in (26cm) high*

$4,000-4,500 **WW**

A 'Trafalgar' or 'Victory' Toby jug, seated on a sea chest bearing the legend 'Trafalgar' and an applied medallion of Nelson's flagship Victory.

This model is based on the 'Rodney's Sailor' Toby jugs made some 20 years earlier.

c1815-18 *11in (28cm) high*

$3,000-4,000 **WW**

A 'Drunken Parson' Toby jug, his bewigged head turned to the right.

c1815-20 *8in (20.5cm) high*

$600-750 **WW**

A Prattware 'Hearty Good Fellow Sailor' Toby jug, restoration to his hat.

c1820 *9.25in (23.5cm) high*

$1,800-2,250 **WW**

A small 'American Sailor' Toby jug, seated on a sea chest bearing the inscription 'Dollars' to two sides, his foaming jug of ale inscribed 'Success to the Wooden Walls', some faults.

Provenance: The Property of the late Surgeon Rear Admiral P. D. Gordon-Pugh.

c1820 *10in (26cm) high*

$600-900 **WW**

ESSENTIAL REFERENCE - WEDGWOOD JASPERWARE

Jasperware is a type of hard, fine-grained and unglazed stoneware introduced in 1774-5.

- **It is the most famous type of Wedgwood ware, typically with applied white decoration of Classical figures and motifs.**
- **Wedgwood produced the finest jasperware around 1780.**
- **John Flaxman (1755-1826), George Stubbs (1724-1806), and other artists produced designs for ornamental wares, including vases, plaques, cameos, and medallions.**
- **Jasperware first came in a variety of colors such as pale blue, sage green, olive green, lilac, lavender, and black.**
- **The most popular and most recognizable example of jasperware is the pale blue (also referred to as 'Wedgwood blue') and white color combination.**
- **The white relief ornaments that form such an attractive contrast would have been molded separately and then attached to the wares.**
- **The Portland vase is perhaps the most famous example of jasperware. The original Portland vase, dated from antiquity, was made of cameo glass.**

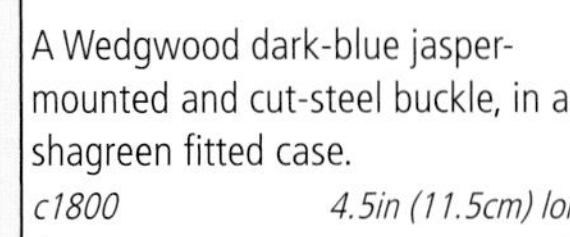

A Wedgwood dark-blue jasper-mounted and cut-steel buckle, in a shagreen fitted case.
c1800 *4.5in (11.5cm) long*
$975-1,150 SK

A mid-19thC Wedgwood light-blue jasper 'Apotheosis of Virgil' vase and cover, with snake handles terminating at Medusa masks, with Pegasus finial, impressed mark.
17.75in (45cm) high
$12,000-14,250 SK

A 19thC Wedgwood solid white jasper Portland vase, with a man wearing a Phrygian cap under the base, impressed mark.
9.75in (25cm) high
$850-975 SK

A 19thC Wedgwood dark-blue jasper dip Portland vase, a man wearing a Phrygian cap under the base, impressed mark.

The original Portland Vase was made of cameo glass and dated from about 30-20 BC. The Wedgwood copies were produced in a 'first edition' of about 50, potted during Wedgwood's lifetime. Although Wedgwood had borrowed the original vase as early as June 1786, it was not until October 1789 that he succeeded in making the first good copies.

10in (25.5cm) high
$1,800-3,000 SK

A Wedgwood solid black jasper Portland vase, a man wearing a Phrygian cap below the base, inscribed 'Executed for Charles Bellows at Etruria 1913 No. 2', impressed mark.
1913 *10in (25.5cm) high*
$9,000-10,500 SK

A Wedgwood crimson jasper Portland vase, applied classical figures in white relief, impressed mark.
c1920 *6in (15.5cm) high*
$2,700-3,300 SK

A Wedgwood crimson jasper dip jug, with applied white Classical figures below a fruiting grapevine border, with impressed mark.
c1920 *7.75in (19.5cm) high*
$300-450 SK

Wedgwood Black Basalt

A late 19thC Wedgwood black basalt bust of Nelson, impressed title and mark, inscribed 'Pubd July 22nd 1798 R. Shout Holborn'.

Josiah Wedgwood introduced a black stoneware body in 1768. He called it 'Black Basaltes'; we know it as black basalt. Made from reddish-brown clay which burned black in firing, this ceramic body was superior in its appearance to the local 'Egyptian Black' wares produced in the area prior to that date. Wedgwood's black basalt body owed its richer color to the addition of manganese.

11in (28cm) high

$1,000-1,200 **SK**

A Wedgwood and Bentley black basalt vase and cover, with applied figure of Apollo holding a lyre in high relief, impressed circular mark.

Thomas Bentley and Josiah Wedgwood were in partnership from c1769 until Bentley's death in 1780.

c1775 *9in (22.5cm) high*

$750-900 **SK**

A pair of early 20thC Wedgwood black basalt bough pots.

$1,150-1,450 **SK**

A pair of Wedgwood Art Deco black basalt 'Stag and Tree' book ends, designed by Erling B. Olsen, losses to antlers.

6.25in (16cm) high

$600-750 **WW**

A pair of Wedgwood surface agate potpourri vases and covers, with gilded trim and Pearlware drapery swags in relief, impressed Wedgwood, each cover restored.

c1785 *9in (23cm) high*

$1,200-1,800 **SK**

A Wedgwood Emile Lessore decorated Queensware double urn, artist signed and impressed mark.

c1845 *8.75in (22cm) high*

$3,000-4,000 **SK**

A pair of Wedgwood jeweled pink ground vases and covers' with gilt acorn knop and satyr mask handles, printed mark.

1878-91 *8.75in (22cm) high*

$1,150-1,450 **M&K**

A 16thC Hispano-Moresque copper luster charger.

16.25in (41cm) diam

$1,500-2,100 **L&T**

A Staffordshire redware miniature teapot and cover, with scrollwork border above trees and grazing animals.

c1760 *3in (7.5cm) high*

$1,200-1,500 **SK**

A Staffordshire redware miniature teapot and cover, with scrollwork border above trees and grazing animals.

c1760 *3in (7.5cm) high*

$1,500-2,000 **SK**

A pottery flask, marking 1837 Proclamation of Queen Victoria.

6in (15cm) high

$1,000-1,400 **H&C**

An early 19thC Sunderland transfer printed luster jug, with images comprising 'Success to Sailors', a verse, 'Success to all Lovers' and 'Success to the Shipping Trade', some damage.

9.5in (24cm) high

$600-750 **MOR**

A mid-19thC Sunderland transfer printed luster jug, with images comprising 'William Darling & his Daughter Grace Horsley Darling. The Forfarshire Steamer lost on Sept 7th:1838', a portrait of Grace Horsley Darling and a verse 'Forget not Christ the Lord of Hosts', crack restored.

7.3in (18.5cm) high

$1,800-2,250 **MOR**

A West Country pottery documentary jug, incised 'John Can Jug, September 1845', and verse 'Success to the Farmer...', and a further verse within a heart shape, 'Long may we Live Happy...', dated.

1845 *10.75in (27.5cm) high*

$3,000-4,000 **SWO**

A 19thC British red-pottery ocher-glazed jar and cover, probably Ewenny, the cover with a man and woman in 18thC dress, possibly commemorative of a marriage.

11in (28.5cm) high

$750-900 **DN**

A late 19thC large Mason's Ironstone covered ice pail, decorated in the 'Imari' palette with blossoming foliage, printed blue mark.

15.25in (38.5cm) high

$4,950-6,000 **L&T**

A pair of late 19thC English Stone China 'Amherst Japan' pattern covered urns, decorated in the 'Imari' palette, blue printed marks.

13.25in (34cm) high

$1,150-1,425 **L&T**

THE ORIENTAL MARKET

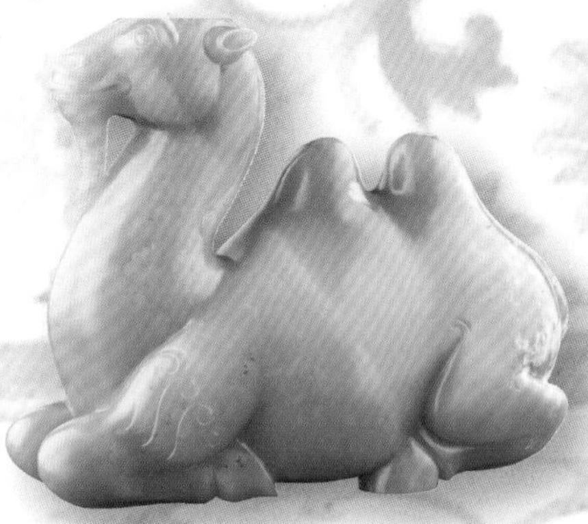

In the past few years, in a depressed economic climate, oriental works of art have bucked the trend. It seems that not a week passes without some record being broken: whether jade or ceramic. However the market is getting a lot more discerning, with top prices being reserved for rare early pieces with Imperial provenance. Also prices fluctuate – a lot may fetch a record price in Hong Kong and a similar piece fail to meet its much lower reserve in London, or the reverse.

On 20th May 2015 Woolley and Wallis sold a rare Chinese doucai small lingzhi bowl for $510,000. It had a six character Yongzheng mark and it was of the period (1723-35).

Bonhams in Hong Kong sold a rare Imperial Yongzheng famille rose bottle vase for $1,432,285. The vase is a superb example of the high technical standards and artistry gained on famille rose porcelains from the Yongzheng reign. With the innovation of the famille rose palette including opaque and semi-opaque enamels, a wider range of colors fired on porcelain that appeared softer and gentler was perfected in the Yongzheng period. There is a strong demand for rare and unusual snuff bottles, but they must be top quality.

Jade continues to excite buyers. In November 2014 Woolley and Wallis sold an Imperial dark celadon jade seal of Empress Xiaoyiren for $225,000. Although relatively late, probably made in the Forth Year of Jiaqing, corresponding to 1801, the seal was robustly carved with two five-clawed dragons, snarling to reveal their fangs, teeth and tongues.

On 14th March 2015 Freemans in Philadelphia sold a rare and important Chinese gilt bronze ritual bell for $725,000 (over £500,000). Also known as *bianzhong*, this heavily cast gilt-bronze bell was an exclusive and important part of imperial court rituals and ceremonies. As depicted in court paintings, *bianzhong* would have been suspended in two tiers of eight over tall and elaborate wooden frames.

On the market for Japanese antiques, Lee Young, head of Asian Art at Lyon & Turnbull in Edinburgh said. 'We have, over the last few years, seen a noticeable increase in the number of buyers for Japanese items, resulting in higher prices in key areas such as cloisonné and mixed metal wares... However, the regained vigour of the Japanese market is still considerably overshadowed by the incredible strength of the Chinese market. With European and American collectors now often unable to compete with newly and extremely affluent Chinese purchasers intent on buying back their heritage, it's likely they will turn their attention to the equally fine and more affordable wares of the Japanese craftsmen.'

Left A large Qianlong doucai 'lotus and bats' jar and cover, decorated with lotus scrolls and iron red bats in flight, mark and period.

The lotus is the symbol of enlightenment and bats of good fortune.

1736-95 *18in (46cm) high*

$600,000-750,000 **PW**

Top Left: A carved celadon jade of a recumbent camel.

6.75in (17cm) wide

$6,000-7,500 **L&T**

CHINESE REIGN PERIODS AND MARKS

Imperial reign marks were adopted during the Ming dynasty, and some of the most common are illustrated here. Certain emperors forbade the use of their own reign mark, lest they should suffer the disrespect of a broken vessel bearing their name being thrown away. This is where the convention of using earlier reign marks comes from – a custom that was enthusiastically adopted by potters as a way of showing their respect for their predecessors.

It is worth remembering that a great deal of Imperial porcelain is marked misleadingly, and pieces bearing the reign mark for the period in which they were made are, therefore, especially sought after.

EARLY PERIODS AND DATES

Xia Dynasty	*c2000 - 1500BC*	Three Kingdoms	*221 - 280*	The Five Dynasties	*907 - 960*
Shang Dynasty	*1500 - 1028BC*	Jin Dynasty	*265 - 420*	Song Dynasty	*960 - 1279*
Zhou Dynasty	*1028 - 221BC*	Northern & Southern Dynasties	*420 - 581*	Jin Dynasty	*1115 - 1234*
Qin Dynasty	*221 - 206BC*	Sui Dynasty	*581 - 618*	Yuan Dynasty	*1260 - 1368*
Han Dynasty	*206BC - AD220*	Tang Dynasty	*618 - 906*		

EARLY MING DYNASTY REIGNS

Hongwu	*1368 - 1398*	Zhengtong	*1436 - 1449*
Jianwen	*1399 - 1402*	Jingtai	*1450 - 1457*
Yongle	*1403 - 1424*	Tianshun	*1457 - 1464*
Hongxi	*1425 - 1425*	Chenghua	*1465 - 1487*
Xuande	*1426 - 1435*		

MING DYNASTY MARKS

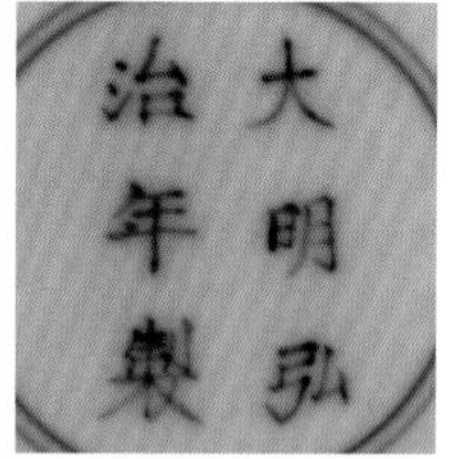

Hongzhi
1488–1505

Zhengde
1506–21

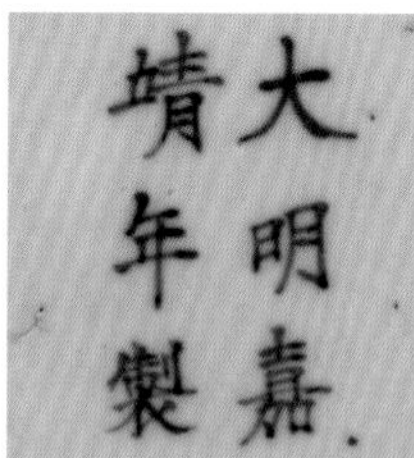

Jiajing
1522–66

Wanli
1573–1619

Chongzhen
1628–44

QING DYNASTY MARKS

Kangxi
1662–1722

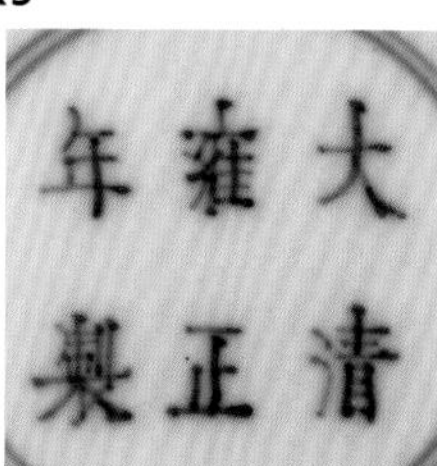

Yongzheng
1723–35

Qianlong
1736–95

Jiaqing
1796–1820

Xianfeng
1851–61

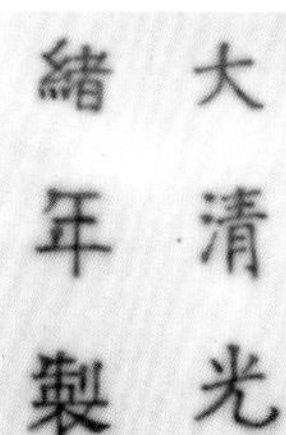

Tongzhi
1862–74

Guangxu
1875–1908

Xuantong
1909–11

Hongxian
1915–16

ESSENTIAL REFERENCE - TANG POTTERY HORSES

These horses have been tested for age and have Oxford Authentication certificates.

- **The Tang dynasty (618–907 AD) was an imperial dynasty of China preceded by the Sui dynasty and followed by the Five Dynasties and Ten Kingdoms period. It was founded by the Li family. The dynasty was briefly interrupted when Empress Wu Zetian seized the throne, proclaiming the Second Zhou dynasty (October 8, 690 – March 3, 705). The Tang dynasty, with its capital at Chang'an (present-day Xi'an), which at the time was the most populous city in the world, is generally regarded as a high point in Chinese civilization: a golden age of culture. Its territory, acquired through the military campaigns of its early rulers, rivaled that of the Han dynasty. In two censuses of the 7th and 8th centuries, the Tang records estimated the population by number of registered households at about 50 million people, although it was probably higher.**

A Tang dynasty fine pair of grey pottery horses, each superbly sculpted as the horses prancing with heads turned to one side.

19.75in (50cm) high

$30,000-45,000 L&T

A Chinese Tang dynasty pottery model of a horse, decorated with a rich chestnut glaze, on a modern wood stand.

Provenance: formerly in the collection of Walter Dick, Vice-Consul in Shanghai 1958-1962.

618-906AD *12.5in (31.5cm) high*

$4,000-4,500 WW

A set of two Chinese Tang dynasty pottery models of Zodiac figures, one modeled as a monkey, the other a dragon, each with traces of red and green pigments.

618-906AD *13in (33cm) high*

$1,200-1,500 WW

A Chinese dynasty yueyao whistle.

618-907AD *2in (5cm) high*

$3,400-4,000 WW

A large Chinese Song dynasty or later Junyao deep bowl, decorated with a sky-blue glaze deepening to lavender at the rim, the well unglazed.

See M Tregear, 'Song Ceramics', p.118, no.142, where a comparable bowl dated to the Northern Song dynasty from the Percival David Foundation is illustrated. The bowl has an Oxford Authentication Thermoluminescence Analysis Report, sample no. P112n80, which states, 'it is not possible to issue a result for this piece as the clay is too insensitive for TL measurements and cannot be dated'.

7.25in (18.3cm) diam

$12,000-15,000 WW

A small Chinese Song dynasty Junyao flared bowl, decorated with a pale blue glaze irregularly splashed with cerise and mottled celadon.

See F Xiaoqi, 'The Specimens of Ancient Chinese Kilns in the Collection of the Palace Museum, Henan Volume I', p.383, no.343, where a comparable bowl is illustrated.

960-1279AD *3.75in (9cm) diam*

$22,500-30,000 WW

A massive Chinese Yuan/early Ming dynasty Longquan celadon dish, the center crisply carved with two flowering peony stems and leaves encircled by a wide band of flowerheads and scrolling foliage.

18.25in (46cm) diam

$45,000-60,000 **WW**

A Longquan celadon censer, Ming dynasty, the sides carved with peony blooms and foliage, with Japanese kintsugi repairs, extensively damaged and restored in gold lacquer.

Kintsugi is the Japanese art of fixing broken pottery with lacquer resin dusted or mixed with powdered gold, silver, or platinum, a method similar to the maki-e technique. As a philosophy it treats breakage and repair as part of the history of an object, rather than something to disguise.

12.5in (31.5cm) diam

$900-1,200 **DN**

A large Longquan jardiniere, Yuan dynasty, carved in low-relief with lotus flowers and foliage above a vertically striped border, all beneath a rich green glaze, chips, a couple of body cracks, glaze crazing.

13in (34cm) high

$3,000-4,500 **DN**

A Chinese Kangxi celadon vase and cover, decorated in underglaze blue and red with the eight horses of Mu Wang.

1662-1722 *10.5in (26.2cm) high*

$5,250-6,750 **WW**

ESSENTIAL REFERENCE - YONGZHENG CHARGER

Sotheby's New York sold an identical charger on 23rd March 2004. Apart from this dish, no other chargers of this type appear to be recorded. The design is known in chargers of plain monochrome celadon, one example of which is in the Victoria & Albert Museum, London. The rarity of this combination of colors in the Yongzheng era and the minor firing flaws suggest that these chargers were part of an experimental group. The Yongzheng emperor was known to challenge his potters to produce increasingly advanced designs with exceptional glazes.

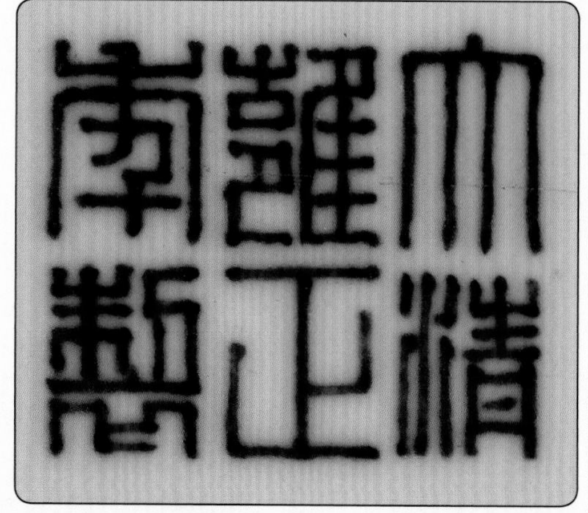

An exceptionally rare Yongzheng celadon and blue glazed dragon charger, carved with an archaic style three-clawed chilong dragon suspended in flight amongst swirls of cloud, his face with a determined expression and heavy brow, a single horn curling above his mane, his tail terminating in scrolls, with six character seal mark, Yongzheng mark.

19.75in (49.8cm) diam

$400,000-450,000 **L&T**

An 18thC Chinese celadon crackle glaze and gilt bronze porcelain mounted vase.

19.2in (49cm) high

$19,500-22,500 **L&T**

A pair of celadon ground and iron red 'Phoenix' medallion bowls, the interiors painted with a central phoenix roundel, blue underglaze seal mark Daoguang seal mark and of the period.

5.7in (14.5cm) diam

$15,000-21,000 **L&T**

A small Chinese probably Qing dynasty celadon wine ewer, the spout and handle formed as mythical beasts.

6.75in (17cm) high

$3,000-4,000 **WW**

A 19thC Chinese celadon jardinière, decorated in underglaze blue, containing fu shou characters.

Fu and Shou stand for prosperity and longevity.

11in (28cm) wide

$3,000-4,000 **WW**

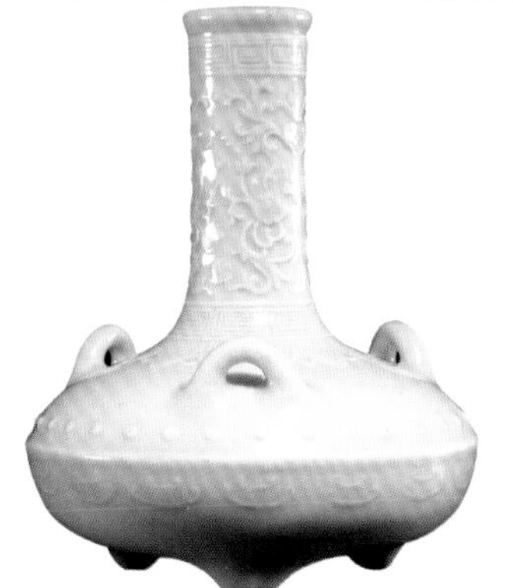

A 19thC Chinese celadon bottle vase, crisply carved with flowerheads and foliage between bands of key fret and stiff leaves, six character Qianlong seal mark.

5.75in (14.5cm) high

$9,750–11,250 **WW**

A pair of 19thC Qing dynasty celadon glazed cockerels, with incised plumage and with iron-red combs and feet.

12in (30cm) high

$3,000-4,500 **L&T**

A 19thC Chinese celadon vase, after a bronze archaic shape, the body divided into quarters, with an incised six character Qianlong seal. mark.

9.75in (24.5cm) high

$750-1,200 **WW**

A pair of 19thC Chinese celadon glazed vases, one with two peacocks below a flowering prunus, the other with auspicious objects.

23.5in (59.5cm) high

$750–1,500 **WW**

A Chinese late Ming Dynasty Blanc de Chine model of Guanyin, with two attendant children and a stem bowl before her, a bird and a meiping vase at her sides.

Blanc de Chine ('White from China') is the European term for a type of white Chinese porcelain, made at Dehua in the Fujian province. It has been produced from the Ming Dynasty (1368–1644). Large quantities were exported to Europe in the early 18th century and it was copied at Meissen and elsewhere. It was also exported to Japan in large quantities.

9in (22.7cm) high

$4,500–7,500 WW

A 17thC Blanc de Chine figure of Guanyin.

6in (15.2cm) high

$1,200-1,500 L&T

A Kangxi period Blanc de Chine figure of a man holding a towel around his waist.

9.25in (23.3cm) high

$1,500-2,250 L&T

A pair of 18thC Blanc de Chine hawks.

9.5in (24cm) high

$1,500-2,250 TEN

A rare 18thC Chinese Blanc de Chine figure of Guanyin.

5.75in (14.3cm) high

$4,000–5,250 WW

An 18thC Chinese Blanc de Chine double-walled tea bowl.

3in (7.5cm) high

$850-975 WW

A large 19thC Chinese Blanc de Chine model of Guanyin, standing on a base of waves and lotus, her long hair trailing across her shoulders, a scroll in her right hand, a wood stand.

22.25in (56.5cm) high

$7,500-9,000 WW

A 19thC Qing dynasty Blanc de chine figure of Guanyin, holding a ruyi scepter, with child and attendant, impressed mark.

12in (30cm) high

$4,000–5,250 L&T

A late 19thC large Chinese Blanc de Chine Guanyin, with flowing robes and elaborate jewelry, her hair tied up in a chignon held by a tiara, holding a scroll.

22.5in (57cm) high

$15,000–18,000 DN

A Peach Bloom glaze beehive waterpot, the sides with three incised medallions, Kangxi six character mark.

Peach Bloom glazes were used in China during the Qing dynasty (1644–1911) to decorate objects for the emperor's writing table, like water pots and ink wells, as well as decorative vases and bowls.

What is most intriguing is that the secrets of this glaze and firing technique have remained a mystery for centuries. However, at its core, Peach Bloom is a copper-based glaze that gives the impression of ripening fruit. So it may be a transparent green that blushes pink or a pinkish background with green or red speckling.

4in (10cm) high

$2,000-2,400 **L&T**

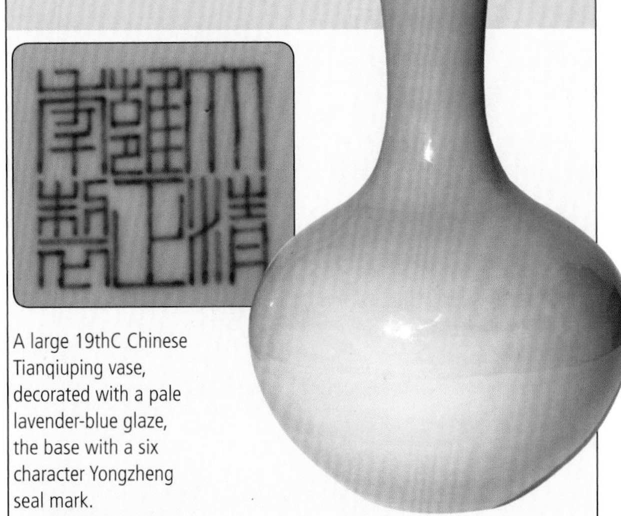

A large 19thC Chinese Tianqiuping vase, decorated with a pale lavender-blue glaze, the base with a six character Yongzheng seal mark.

'Tianqiuping' was named after its globular body as it appeared to be falling from the heavens.

20.5in (52cm) high

$22,500-30,000 **WW**

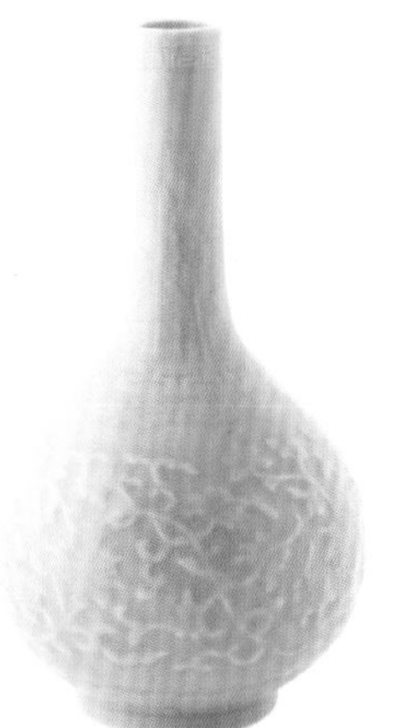

A 'clair-de-lune' glaze bottle vase, the sides with stylized lotus, Qianlong seal mark and of the period.

8.75in (22cm) high

$6,000-7,500 **L&T**

A powder blue ground 'bats and cloud' Yuhuchunping, blue seal mark, Qianlong mark and of the period.

A Yuhuchunping is a pear-shaped vase. The shape was much favored by ceramic decorators from the 14thC.

11.8in (30cm) high

$4,500-6,000 **L&T**

A large Chinese bottle vase, with a rich midnight-blue glaze stopping short of the footrim, six character Qianlong mark.

1736-95 *18in (45.3cm) high*

$9,000–12,000 **WW**

An 18thC Qing dynasty flambé jar, with rich raspberry-red glaze streaked with turquoise-blue.

9in (23cm) high

$1,500-2,250 **L&T**

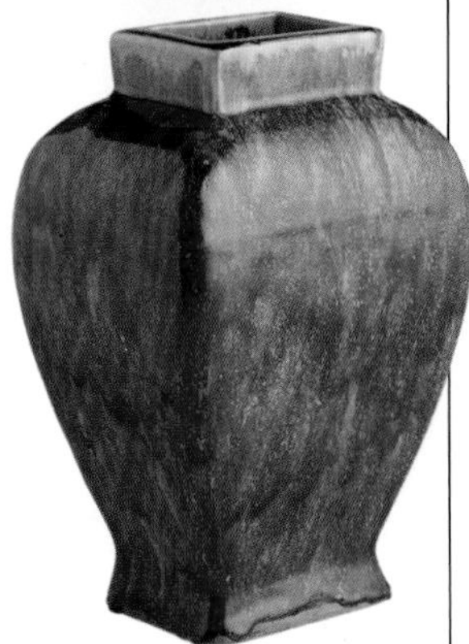

An 18thC Qing dynasty flambé vase, decorated in a rich purple glaze with turquoise-blue inclusions.

10.75in (27cm) high

$1,400-1,700 **L&T**

An 18thC blue-glazed bottle vase, the glaze settling in drops around the rim, the base with Qianlong seal mark.

16.5in (41.5cm) high

$6,000-7,500 L&T

An 18thC Qing dynasty vase, covered in a deep blue glaze.

19.5in (49cm) high

$1,000-1,400 L&T

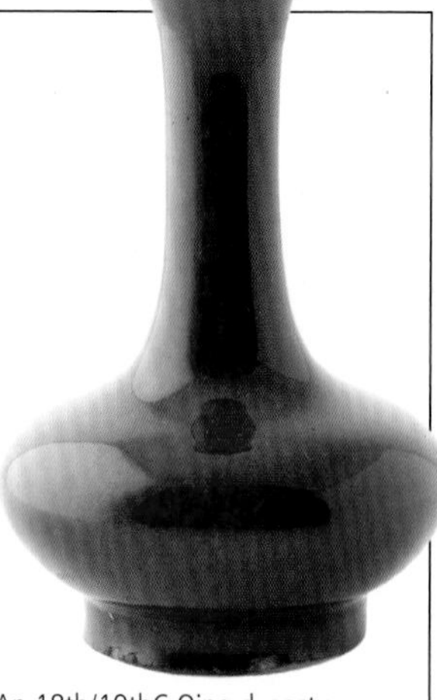

An 18th/19thC Qing dynasty miniature sang-de-boeuf bottle vase.

4.75in (12cm) high

$1,500-2,250 L&T

A Chinese ox-blood brush pot, six character seal mark, mark and period Xianfeng (1851-1861).

5in (12.7cm) high

$24,750-27,750 SWO

A Qing dynasty Langyao-type sang-de-boeuf vase, with crackled glaze of black raspberry color at the foot thinning to a pale cream color.

Sang-de-boeuf, ('oxblood') also called flambé glaze, was a glossy, rich, blood red glaze often slashed with streaks of purple or turquoise used to decorate pottery, particularly porcelain. The effect is produced by a method of firing that incorporates copper, a method first discovered by the Chinese in the Ming dynasty, probably during the reign of Wanli (1573–1620). The process was at first difficult to control, but it had been mastered by the time of Kanxi (1661–1722).

16.75in (42cm) high

$21,000-24,000 L&T

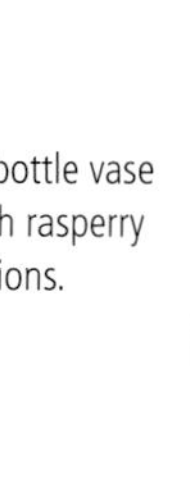

A Qing dynasty flambé bottle vase with garlic mouth, in rich rasperry glaze with purple inclusions.

17.25in (43.5cm) high

$1,800-3,000 L&T

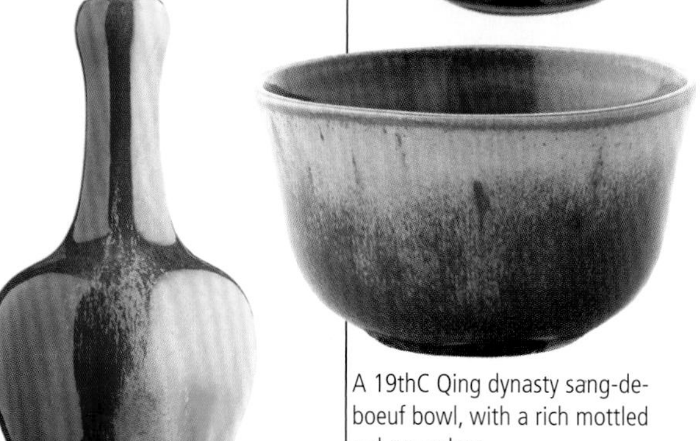

A 19thC Qing dynasty sang-de-boeuf bowl, with a rich mottled red-grey glaze.

4.5in (11cm) diam

$400-550 L&T

A 19thC Chinese sang-de-boeuf vase,

14in (36cm) high

$600-900 ROS

An early 18thC Chinese Yixing phoenix teapot and cover, the cover formed as clouds, unmarked.

6.5in (16cm) high

$1,800–4,000 **WW**

An 18thC Chinese Yixing teapot and cover, the cover and footrim formed from eight overlapping petals.

4.5in (11cm) high

$6,750-7,500 **WW**

Judith Picks

These teapots continue to fascinate me. They are made from unglazed red-brown stoneware. They have been produced in the Yixing (pronounced yeeshing) potteries in the Jiangsu province from the late Ming dynasty. Legend has it that the first one made was potted by a monk. They say that he formed the first teapot out of Yixing clay, using his bare hands. He then fired it in a friend's kiln. He left his simple, rustic pots unglazed. Was he the first to feel the magic a Yixing pot can bring to tea? It is said that with an old Yixing teapot, you can brew tea by simply pouring boiling water into the empty pot. It is also interesting to think who else has brewed tea using the pot.

A large and rare 18thC Chinese Yixing teapot and cover, decorated with molded with peony and phoenix, the cover with four stylized characters, the knop as a pierced cash symbol, the base with two seal marks which read 'Xing Xi', 'Zheng Kong Jiazhi'.

10.5in (27cm) long

$37,500–45,000 **WW**

A rare 18thC Chinese Yixing teapot and cover, the duanni body modeled as bamboo, the knop, spout and handle formed as branches and with a leaf sprig to the cover, decorated with darker brown spots (xiang fei zhu), unmarked.

6.25in (16cm) high

$105,000–120,000 **WW**

A Chinese Yixing teapot and cover, decorated with molded peony and phoenix, the knop as a Buddhist lion dog, the handle as a fish, the spout as a mask-head, unmarked.

8.5in (21.5cm) high

$7,500-9,000 **WW**

A 19thC Chinese Yixing Meng Chen teapot and cover, made for the Thai market, the finial, spout and rims with gilt, the lid marked 'Shui Ping', the base with a poem which reads 'shan shui zuo zhu ren.

5.25in (13.2cm) high

$4,500-6,000 **WW**

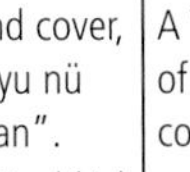

A small 19th or 20thC Chinese Yixing Meng Chen teapot and cover, the circular body inscribed "yu nü quan peng guang rong yi pian".

4.25in (10.2cm) high

$4,400-4,800 **WW**

A Yixing robin's egg glazed teapot of traditional form, with associated cover.

4in (10cm) high

$700-850 **L&T**

A rare Chinese bowl, the exterior painted in soft tones of cobalt blue with a continuous leaf scroll issuing ten large lingzhi heads, the foot with a stylized ruyi-shaped scroll and a band of lappets, with a six-character Xuande mark.

This particular form of bowl was an innovation of the 15th century, and it has been suggested they perhaps served as brush washers for scholars, for playing dice, or for cricket fights.

1426-35 *11.5in (29cm) diam*
$195,000-240,000 **WW**

A rare late 15th-early 16thC Chinese dish, painted with peony.

13.5in (34cm) diam
$45,000–52,500 **WW**

A Chinese Wanli Kraak ewer and cover, painted with floral blooms and auspicious objects, the spout mounted with silver-colored metal, the cover associated.

Kraak porcelain is a type of Chinese export porcelain produced mainly from the Wanli reign (1573–1620) until around 1640. It was among the first Chinese export ware to arrive in Europe in mass quantities, and was frequently featured in Dutch still life paintings. Kraak porcelain is believed to be named after the Portuguese ships (carracks), in which it was transported.

1573-1620 8in (20cm) high
$1,200-1,800 **WW**

A Chinese Wanli Kraak kendi, molded with leaves, the rim formed as pomegranate petals, painted with flowers, with a bird perched on rockwork to the neck.

1573-1620 *7.5in (19cm) high*
Est $8,250-9,750 **WW**

A Chinese Kraak dish, painted with a jardinière of peony and chrysanthemum, with a band of fruit and auspicious objects to the rim.

c1600 *14.5in (37cm) diam*
$2,000-2,400 **WW**

IMMORTALS BOWL

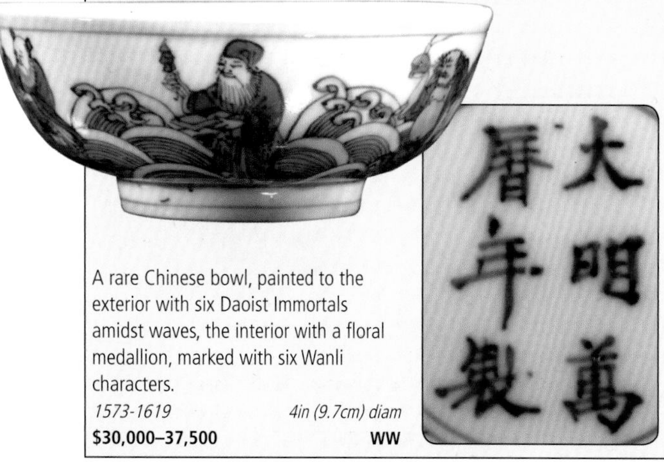

A rare Chinese bowl, painted to the exterior with six Daoist Immortals amidst waves, the interior with a floral medallion, marked with six Wanli characters.

1573-1619 *4in (9.7cm) diam*
$30,000–37,500 **WW**

CLOSER LOOK - WANLI VASE

This is a particularly well painted example and very large - showing the decoration to the best advantage. It dates from the Wanli period (1573-1619) - a high point in Chinese culture.

Each side painted with five ascending and descending five-clawed dragons - representing the emperor's sacred symbol of imperial power, representing its dignity.

The shape is based on an archaic bronze fang gu - a sacrificial vessel with great symbolic significance.

It has excellent provenance having been owned by Field Marshal Earl Kitchener of Khartoum (1850-1916), and thence by descent.

A Chinese Wanli archaistic temple vase, marked with six Wanli characters.

30in (75cm) high
$270,000-360,000 **WW**

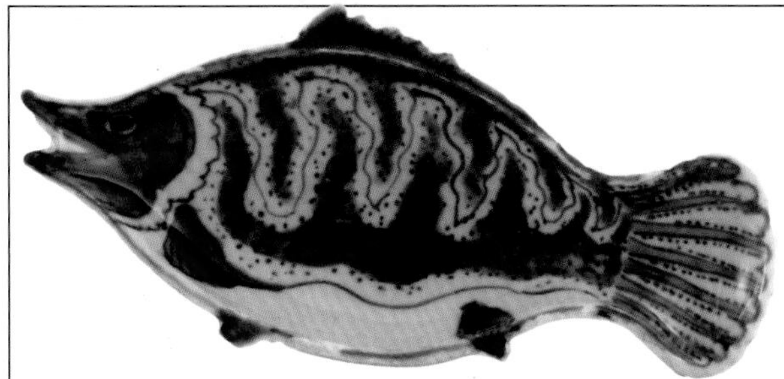

A Chinese Tianqi 'Ko-Sometsuke' sweetmeat dish, made for the Japanese market.

This is an example of an intriguing group of ko-sometsuke food dishes, known as mukozuke, which were produced in a variety of shapes, including fish, horses, oxen, leaves, peaches, aubergines, shells, fans and musical instruments, amongst others.

Ko-sometsuke ('old blue and white') porcelain was produced specifically for the Japanese market during the final decades of the Ming dynasty (1368-1644). The lack of Chinese Imperial patronage during this period prompted the potters at the Jingdezhen kilns, Jiangxi province, to seek out new markets for their porcelain. Ko-sometsuke wares were made to Japanese taste, in an astonishing variety of odd, asymmetrical and occasionally humorous forms. Ko-sometsuke porcelain was deliberately potted in a rough manner and bears numerous flaws and imperfections as a result. The mushikui or 'moth-eaten' edges, which are so prevalent among these wares, were particularly prized in Japan.

1621-1627 *8in (20cm) long*

$4,500-6,000 **WW**

ESSENTIAL REFERENCE - TRANSITIONAL

The Transitional Period was from c1620-83. In this period the Chinese Imperial court reduced its orders for porcelain and the Jingdezhen factories had to find new clients. The VOC (Dutch East India Company, 1602–1799) was an important customer for export wares. The Company now had a trading settlement on Formosa (Taiwan) from where porcelain had been ordered in China from 1634. Many dishes and plates were made in the traditional Kraak styles. Chinese shapes were very diverse, and included bowls, covered jars, bottles, teapots or wine ewers. Transitional porcelain is relatively thick, well potted, and beautifully finished with a smooth, clear glaze. The decorations in underglaze cobalt blue frequently show a continuous figurative scene in a landscape. Porcelain painters often used woodcut illustrations from Chinese books as sources for their decorations. The decorations show a spontaneous, naturalistic style. As with Kraak porcelain, the shapes and decorations of Transitional porcelain were frequently copied by Delft potters.

A Transitional blue-and-white bottle vase, painted with cockerels and butterflies.

8in (20cm) high

$18,000-22,500 **BE**

A Chinese Dehua incense burner, decorated with scrolling lotus designs separating characters.

1650-1700 *10.5in (26.5cm) diam*

$2,000-2,400 **WW**

A 17thC Chinese transitional style covered jar, decorated with peonies, narcissus, bamboo and lotus.

14.25in (36cm) high

$3,000-4,500 **L&T**

A pair of 17thC Chinese bottle vases, decorated with songbirds, peonies, prunus and chrysanthemums, unmarked.

11.5in (29cm) high

$6,000-6,750 **L&T**

A 19thC bottle vase, painted with kylin and precious objects, with six character mark of Kangxi.

18in (46cm) high

$6,000-7,500 **SWO**

A 17thC Chinese bowl, painted with large peony blooms emerging from rockwork with leaves and grasses, the rim with a metal band.

14in (35.2cm) diam

$15,000–22,500 **WW**

A pair of Chinese Kangxi jardinières and stands, painted with scholars in garden settings, and with women playing games or reading, the stands each with a metal liner.

1662-1722 *8.75in (22cm) wide*

$37,500–45,000 **WW**

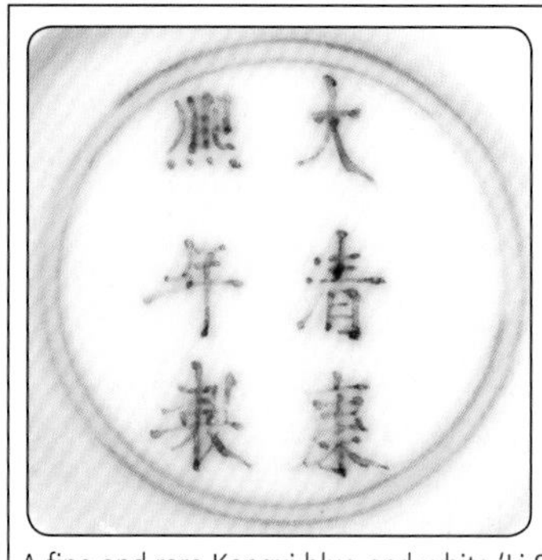

A fine and rare Kangxi blue-and-white 'Li Shizi' wine cup, painted with a scene from the poem 'Eight Immortal of the Wine Cup' by Du Fu, the central seated figure of Li Shizi drinking from a wine cup surrounded by attendants carrying ewers and further cups, in an interior with vases and a scholar's rock, the reverse side with inscription describing the scene, with original fitted zitan box, six-character Kangxi mark within double ring to the base.

The poem on the reverse reads: 'The Premier [Li Shi-zhi] spends ten thousand cash each day [on drink]; his imbibing matches the great whale's gulping down of the hundred streams; holding the wine cup, joyous sage, he calls himself 'avoider of the worthy".

The Eight Immortals of the Wine Cup were a group of scholars renowned for their love of alcoholic beverages. The extract above is from a poem dedicated to them by the acclaimed Tang poet Du Fu. Li Shizi, Duke of Qinghe (died 747), is the third Immortal to appear in the poem. He served as a chancellor during the reign of Emperor Xuanzong. Li Shizhi particularly enjoyed entertaining guests and was said to be able to drink two litres of wine without losing his lucidity.

This cup would have been part of a set of eight, each depicting one of the Immortals.

2.75in (6.7cm) diam

$45,000–52,500 **L&T**

A Chinese Kangxi 'yen yen' vase, painted with villagers and fishermen in a rocky landscape with pine and pagodas.

1662-1722 *17.75in (45cm) high*

$14,250-15,750 **WW**

A Chinese Kangxi bottle vase, painted with a chrysanthemum-head and scrolling hibiscus, between ribbon-tied pearls, with ruyi-shaped lappets to the shoulder.

1662-1722 *9.25in (23.5cm) high*

$4,400-4,800 **WW**

A Chinese Kangxi vase, painted with four young women representing the four female virtues, and with sixteen boys at play, with a wooden cover and stand.

This subject is derived from the Shang dynasty story of Jiang Ziya, the senior military counsellor who famously appointed sixteen good generals.

1662-1722 *15.25in (38.5cm) high*

$11,500–13,000 **WW**

A Chinese Kangxi vase, painted with deer and a crane amidst pine and rocky outcrops, the rim with Buddhist symbols, with a wooden cover and stand.

13.75in (35cm) high

$4,000-4,500 **WW**

A Chinese Kangxi dish, painted with a kylin in a fenced garden with plantain.

1662-1722 *6.5in (16.2cm) diam*

$1,500-2,000 **WW**

A Chinese Kangxi teapot and cover, painted with floral sprigs and ladies in fenced gardens beneath a band of ruyi-heads.

1662-1722 *6.5in (16cm) diam*

$2,250-2,700 **WW**

A Chinese Kangxi teapot and cover, painted with lotus flowers and a fishing boat in a mountainous landscape, the base with a Chenghua mark.

1662-172 *6.75in (17cm) high*

$3,000-4,000 **WW**

A Chinese bowl, painted with a maiden and attendants in a pavilion and equestrian riders, separated by columns of calligraphy, the interior painted with boys to the well, with six character Kangxi mark.

1662-1722 *8.5in (21.5cm) diam*

$4,950-5,700 **WW**

A Chinese Kangxi vase and cover, painted with prunus, chrysanthemum and peony branches above a band of auspicious objects to the shoulder.

1662-1722 *24.5in (62cm) high*

$1,500-2,250 **WW**

A Chinese Kangxi ginger jar, decorated with prunus blossom, with a later hardwood cover, with four character mark.

10.25in (26cm) high

$3,000-4,500 **L&T**

A Chinese lotus bowl, painted with a scrolling foliate design above bands of stiff leaves to the exterior, a single lotus flower to the interior, marked with six Kangxi characters.

1662-1722 *7.5in (19cm) diam*

$9,750–11,250 **WW**

A Chinese Kangxi vase, painted with vases of flowers, ladies seated in gardens, equestrian hunters and mountainous river landscapes, the base with a rabbit mark.

1662-1722 *9.25in (23cm) high*

$6,000-7,500 **WW**

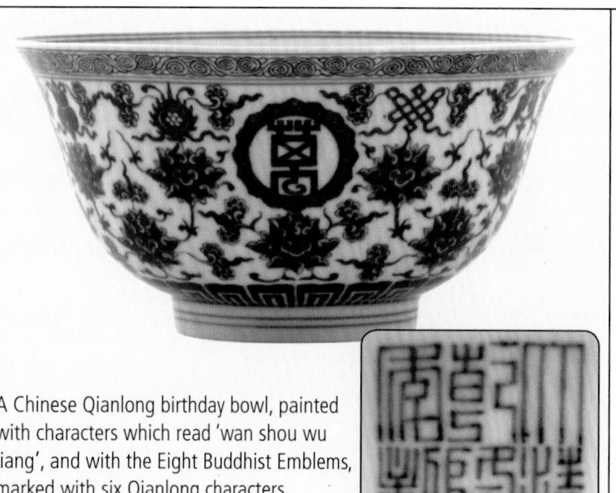

A Chinese Qianlong birthday bowl, painted with characters which read 'wan shou wu jiang', and with the Eight Buddhist Emblems, marked with six Qianlong characters.

7.25in (18.2cm) diam

$11,500–13,000 **WW**

A pair of Kangxi Chinese dishes, painted with a shepherd and a shepherdess, with six character Chenghua mark.

1662-1722 *6.5in (16.5cm) diam*

$1,800-3,000 **WW**

A rare 18thC Chinese 'Baptism of Christ' dish, painted with Christ as a young man with John the Baptist, standing beneath the holy Ghost, with cherubs with a fabulous bird, with the inscription 'Mat 3.16'.

See D Howard and J Ayers, 'China for the West' no.306, where a slightly larger dish is illustrated dated to c.1725, and where it is noted that 'it is possible that this ware was first designed for use in China and Japan, and only incidentally exported to Europe as a curiosity (and perhaps of evidence of the missionary work being done there).

17.75in (45cm) diam

$52,500–60,000 **WW**

A pair of Chinese Kangxi triple-gourd vases, painted with bands of taotie masks, restoration to rims.

Taotie is a monster mask commonly found on ancient Chinese ritual bronze vessels and implements. Typical features of the mask include large, protuberant eyes; stylized depictions of eyebrows, horns, nose crest, ears, and two peripheral legs; and a line of a curled upper lip with exposed fangs and no lower jaw. The function of the taotie motif has been variously interpreted: it may be totemic, protective, or a symbolic representation of the forces of nature.

9.5in (24cm) high

$1,500-2,250 **BELL**

A pair of Kangxi covered jars, painted with hanging grape vines, the leaves filled with unusual crossing-hatching patterns, with leaf mark.

17.75in (45cm) high

$4,500–7,500 **L&T**

A Chinese Yongzheng jarlet, painted with Ruyi and pointed leaves, marked with six Yongzheng characters.

2.75in (6.7cm) high

$4,500-5,250 **WW**

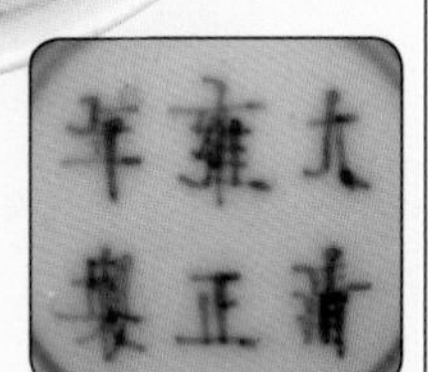

A Chinese dragon bowl, painted with a sinuous scaly dragon which continues to the exterior, marked with six Yongzheng characters.

1723-35 *4.5in (11.5cm) diam*

$3,000-4,000 **WW**

A Chinese bowl, decorated with figures being served tea in a garden, the interior with a boy flying a kite, with six character Yongzheng marks.

7.25in (18cm) diam

$6,000-6,750 **L&T**

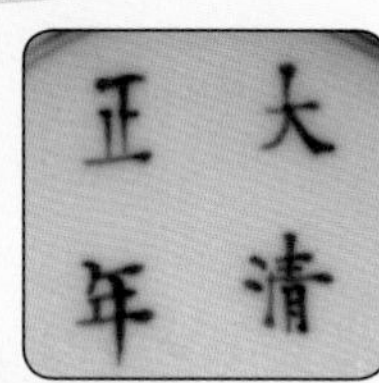

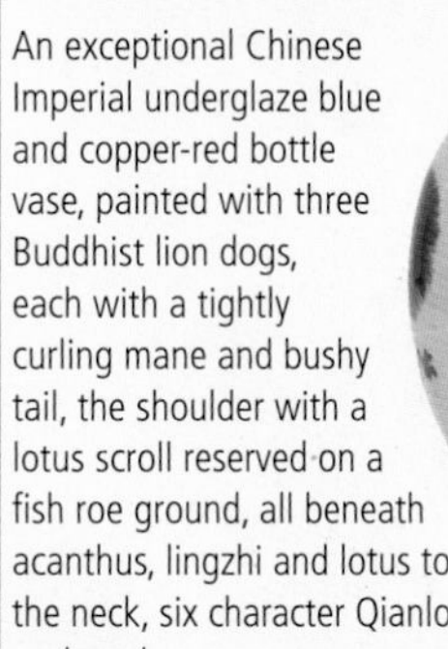

An exceptional Chinese Imperial underglaze blue and copper-red bottle vase, painted with three Buddhist lion dogs, each with a tightly curling mane and bushy tail, the shoulder with a lotus scroll reserved on a fish roe ground, all beneath acanthus, lingzhi and lotus to the neck, six character Qianlong seal mark.

See 'The Complete Collection of Treasures of the Palace Museum, Blue and White Porcelain with Underglaze Red (III)', p.235, no.215, where a circular box and cover with a seal mark of similar style is illustrated.

1736-95 *14.5in (36.3cm) high*

$525,000–675,000 **WW**

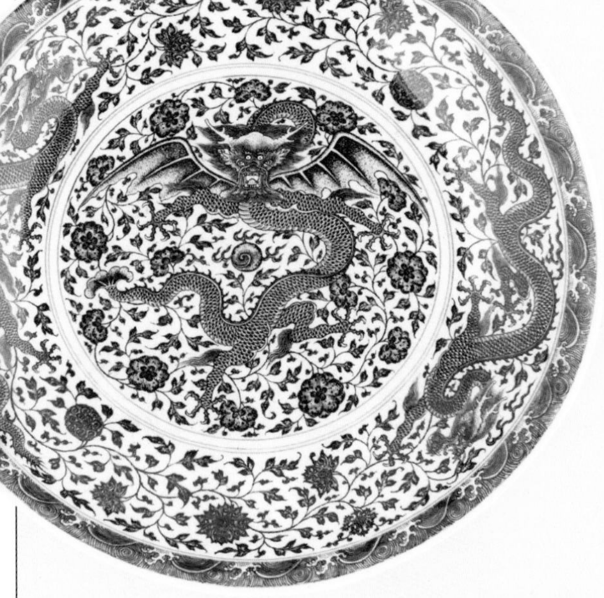

A Ming style large 'dragon' charger, the center decorated with a coiling five-toed dragon encircling a flaming pearl and enclosed by a band with two further running dragons, all against a scrolling foliate field with lotus and chrysanthemum and a wave border, Qianlong seal mark to the underside.

20in (51cm) diam

$675,000–750,000 **L&T**

A Chinese Imperial Ming style dish, painted with a lotus, marked with six Qianlong character seals.

1736-95 *8.5in (21.5cm) diam*

$13,500–15,000 **WW**

An 18thC Chinese vase, painted with lotus flowerheads and foliage between bands of stiff leaves, with an associated cover.

20.5in (51.5cm) high

$7,500-9,000 **WW**

An 18thC Qing dynasty bottle vase, with cracked ice ground, reserves of the four flowers of the seasons, chrysanthemum, peony, plum blossom and lotus.

16in (40.5cm) high

$4,500-5,250 **L&T**

A Chinese 'Five Dragons' vase, painted with five sinuous, scaly, five-clawed dragons in pursuit of a flaming pearl, with vaporous clouds and bats above a band of crashing waves at the foot and below a ruyi band at the mouth rim, Jiaqing seal mark and period.

1796-1820 *12.5in (32cm) high*

$450,000-600,000 **DN**

An early 19thC Chinese export platter, decorated with a fishing hamlet, a pagoda and houses.

19.25in (48.5cm) wide

$400-450 **L&T**

A 19thC Chinese Yenyen vase, painted with deer and birds in landscapes.

17.5in (44cm) high

$750-900 **BELL**

A late 19thC Chinese porcelain figure of Guanyin.

$12,750–14,250 **MAR**

A Ming style charger, decorated with two warriors on horseback, unmarked.

30.25in (78cm) diam

$1,800-2,250 **L&T**

A 19thC Chinese transitional style wine jar and cover, painted with coiled dragons, flaming pearl and clouds over waves, unmarked.

16.75in (42cm) high

$2,000–2,700 **L&T**

A 19thC Chinese 'dragon' bowl, decorated with a coiling dragon and pomegranate branches.

16.5in (41.5cm) diam

$3,000-4,500 **L&T**

A late 19thC large Chinese covered jar, decorated with a sage seated on a qilin with two boy attendants.

11.5in (29cm) high

$450-750 **L&T**

ESSENTIAL REFERENCE - FAMILLE VERTE

Developed from the 'wucai' (the 'five colors') palette during the reign of Kangxi, the fourth emperor of the Qing dynasty, who ruled China from 1661-1722, the 'famille verte' (or 'green family') palette is characterized by the use of yellow, blue, red, purple and, of course, green over-glaze enamels. The wares were mostly vases, jars, bowls, plates, and dishes.

- **Always exquisitely hand-painted, they often depict scenes from contemporary Chinese life and are often imbued with symbolism, for example, chrysanthemum (denoting health and longevity); peony (royalty, wealth, and honour); lotus (purity); heron (success); and butterflies (young love). Many depict traditional scenes for example elegant women depicted engaged in activities – painting, calligraphy, playing qin (a stringed musical instrument), and weiqi (a strategic board game).**

A Chinese Kangxi famille verte dish, painted with a lady playing a qin, with an attendant, while a small boy looks on from a pagoda.

1662-1722 *14.5in (37cm) diam*

$4,500-5,250 WW

A Chinese Kangxi famille verte dish, painted with flowers and foliage and with butterflies, the reverse with lingzhi mark.

The lingzhi is the sacred fungus of immortality, considered by the Daoist mystics as the food of the Immortals. It was believed that lingzhi funguses grew in the abodes of the Immortals, the Three Islands of the Blest, and that whoever ate the sacred fungus attained immortality.

1662-1722 *14in (35.2cm) diam*

$4,500-5,250 WW

A Chinese porcelain jar, painted with panels of a dragon chasing the flaming pearl, with painted 'scroll' divisions.

7.5in (19cm) high

$42,000–48,000 HAD

A Chinese Kangxi famille verte covered tureen, enameled with flowering plants and precious objects, surmounted by a blue glazed fu lion finial.

10in (25cm) high

$3,000-4,000 L&T

A pair of Kangxi famille verte vases, decorated with boys engaged in pursuits in a garden, the neck with auspicious objects.

10in (25cm) high

$4,500-5,250 L&T

A Chinese Kangxi famille verte plate, enameled with four deer in a fenced garden, with two cranes above, with panels containing lotus, chrysanthemum, peony, prunus, the reverse with a ding mark.

1662-1722 *10.75in (27.5cm) diam*

$1,800-3,000 WW

A pair of Chinese Kangxi famille verte plates, painted with a vase containing peony, chrysanthemum and prunus.

These plates were formerly in the collection of Augustus The Strong, Elector of Saxony and King of Poland. The reverse has the Johanneum marks "N:99 I".

1662-1722 *8.5in (21.5cm) diam*

$3,400-4,000 WW

A Chinese famille verte covered jar, decorated with a continuous scene of ladies on a terrace, with four character Kangxi mark.

15in (38cm) high

$1,200-1,800 **L&T**

A Chinese Kangxi famille verte 'yenyen' vase, the neck decorated with phoenix, the body with with chrysanthemums, unmarked.

16.25in (41cm) high

$1,500-2,000 **L&T**

A Kangxi famille verte covered jar, decorated with panels of dragons.

14in (35cm) high

$2,000–2,700 **L&T**

A 19thC famille verte jardinière, decorated with reserves depicting birds, flowering shrubs, and auspicious objects interspersed with chrysanthemums.

13.25in (33.5cm) high

$4,500-5,250 **L&T**

A 19thC Chinese famille verte porcelain crackle ware jar and cover, painted with finches and shrubs in mountain landscapes.

21in (53cm) high

$3,000-4,500 **HW**

A 19thC famille verte planter, painted with figures in a court scene.

16.5in (42cm) high

$4,000-4,500 **CHEF**

A late Qing dynasty famille verte jardinière, decorated with songbirds and flowering plants.

16.25in (41cm) high

$6,000–9,000 **L&T**

A Qing dynasty famille verte fish bowl, decorated with dignitaries, officials and attendants, the interior decorated with goldfish and water weeds, on a giltwood tripod stand.

31.5in (80cm) high

$1,500-2,250 **L&T**

A pair of late 19thC Chinese famille verte porcelain vases, painted with equestrian scenes and figures in interiors.

15.25in (38.5cm) high

$9,000–12,000 **TEN**

A fine and rare pair of Chinese Imperial famille rose semi-eggshell porcelain wine cups, decorated with the Eight Immortals, each painted to the well with Li Tai Bai, with six character Yonghzheng marks.

1723-35 *2.5in (6cm) diam*

$18,000-22,500 **WW**

A Chinese Qianlong famille rose and pink ground medallion bowl, decorated with reserves depicting Europeans, with Qianlong marks.

7.25in (18cm) diam

$4,000-4,500 **L&T**

A Qianlong famille rose decorated wall vase, encloses a eulogy to ru ware, the lavender glazed vessels made for the Song court.

This vase was thought to be a Guangxu (1871-1908) period reproduction but it actually belonged to the group of wares produced at the Imperial kilns and inscribed with poems written by the emperor Qianlong himself. Such vases were intended for use in the palace or in the Imperial sedan chairs.

$48,000–52,500 **SWO**

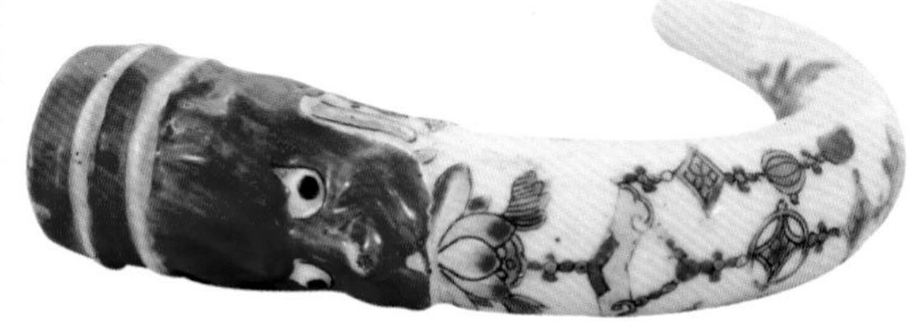

An export porcelain famille rose parasol handle, the top molded in the form of a human face.

c1770 *4.5in (11.5cm) long*

$1,800-2,250 **SWO**

A Chinese famille rose chicken bowl, painted with a boy and a cockerel, the reverse with a hen and her chicks below a poetic inscription, six character Qianlong seal mark.

3.25in (8.5cm) diam

$37,500–45,000 **WW**

Judith Picks: Eye Bath

I love the quirkiness of this eye bath and it is a rare piece. With its scrolling flower and leaf design, it is more English than French, but would have been a special order via a super- or supra-cargo, rather than through the East India Company. The most charming facet of this piece is that the Chinese, perhaps unfamiliar with the use of the object, have fired it upside-down.

A famille rose eye bath, painted with flowers, hair crack, slight wear.

c1775 *2.25in (5.5cm) high*

$1,500-2,250 **SWO**

An 18thC famille rose lotus brushwasher, of naturalistic form the lotus pad applied with budding stems, blossoms and a toad.

9in (23cm) long

$11,500–13,000 **L&T**

A Jiaqing lime-green ground famille rose tea tray, painted with an Imperial poem, inscribed and dated. The inscribed poem reads:

Fine tea is a great gift for an emperor, drinking and writing poetry by the light of the moon,
Adding new fire to the bamboo stove, the water boils like rushing waves,
Tea leaves flutter like fish and crabs eyes, gathering like shadows of banners and spears,
A cup of tea clears the mind, and keeps away the cold chills of spring.

1797 *6.5in (16cm) wide*

$4,000–5,250 **L&T**

A Chinese Jiaqing famille rose green ground basin, enameled with lotus, peony and prunus, bats, peaches and stylized ruyi heads.

1796-1820 *12.75in (32.5cm) long*

$60,000–67,500 **WW**

A Chinese Jiaqing famille rose green ground basin, decorated in enamels with bats, lotus blossoms, butterflies, gourds and ruyi scepters, unmarked.

17.5in (44cm) diam

$27,000–33,000 **L&T**

A Jiaqing lime-green ground famille rose meiping vase, enameled with bats, peaches and endless knots, with lotus blooms, the neck with geometric scrolls, red Jiaqing seal mark.

9.25in (23cm) high

$67,500–75,000 **L&T**

A Chinese famille rose green ground jar, enameled with a fruiting melon vine, butterflies, flowerheads and leafy tendrils, with six character Jiaqing mark.

1796-1820 *8.25in (20.5cm) high*

$37,500–45,000 **WW**

An early 19thC Chinese famille rose cockerel ewer and cover, the bird's tail forming the handle, its head forming the spout, the cover's finial a smaller bird.

7.5in (19cm) high

$1,800-3,000 **WW**

A Chinese famille rose ruby ground medallion bowl, enameled with figures in landscapes and engaged in agricultural activities, with six character Daoguang seal mark.

1821-50 *4.75in (12cm) diam*

$42,000–48,000 **WW**

A pair of 19thC Chinese vases and covers, made for the Islamic market, decorated with Arabic calligraphy and scrolling foliate designs in famille rose enamels, hardwood stands.

1800-1850 *16.75in (42cm) high*

$18,000-22,500 **WW**

A pair of 19thC Chinese export porcelain famille rose garden seats, enameled withwarriors in landscapes, some studs chipped.

18in (45.75cm) high

$4,000-4,500 **FRE**

A fine mid-19thC famille rose plaque, painted with an emperor and courtiers.

16.75in (42cm) high

$6,000–9,000 **L&T**

大清同治年製

A Chinese famille rose bottle vase, painted with chrysanthemum, peony and lotus blooms and butterflies in flight, with six character Tonghzi mark.

12.5in (31.5cm)

Est $4,000-4,500 **WW**

A pair of 19thC Chinese famille rose jardinières, painted with peony and magnolia.

14.5in (36.5cm) wide

$7,500-9,000 **WW**

A Chinese Guangxu famille rose bottle vase, decorated with dragons, flaming pearls and clouds, six character mark.

(1875-1908) *15.5in (39cm) high*

$6,000-6,750 **TEN**

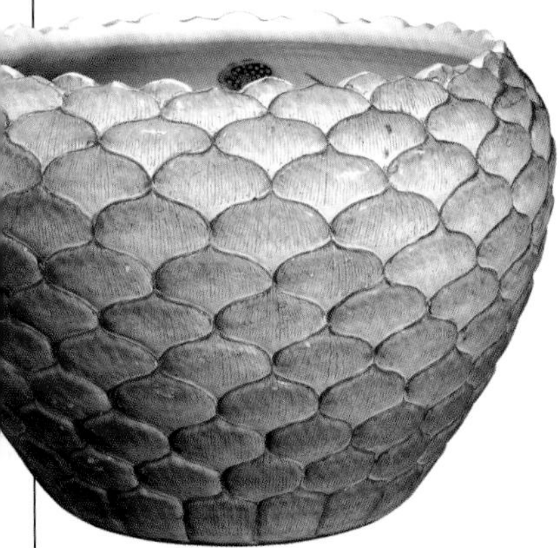

A large late 19th-early 20thC Chinese famille rose fish bowl, molded as a lotus, the interior painted with insects and an aquatic bird with an iron-red five-clawed dragon clutching at a sacred pearl, with a stand.

22.25in (56cm) high

$33,000–37,500 **WW**

An early 20thC Chinese famille rose nine peaches bottle vase, enameled with a peach tree, bamboo and lingzhi fungus, the reverse with three iron-red bats, the base with a six character Qianlong mark.

12.25in (31cm)

$12,000–13,500 **WW**

Three 20thC Chinese famille rose ladies, wearing elaborate formal floral and dragon robes with a large necklace, impressed with four character marks.

22.5in (57cm) high

$18,000-22,500 **WW**

A pair of 19thC Cantonese famille rose vases and covers, with one damaged pomegranate finial.

17.5in (44.5cm) high

$6,750-7,500 TRI

A pair of 19thC Chinese export rose mandarin vases, gilt qilong to neck, enameled with figures, birds, butterflies and foliage.

32in (81.5cm) high

$11,500–13,000 FRE

A late 19thC Chinese Canton famille rose floor vase, decorated with a battle scene and an emperor addressed by military officials in a court interior.

35.5in (90cm) high

$15,000–18,000 L&T

A mid-19thC Cantonese famille rose vase, and decorated with dignitaries on a terrace enclosed by flowers, birds and insects.

24.75in (63cm) high

$4,500–7,500 TEN

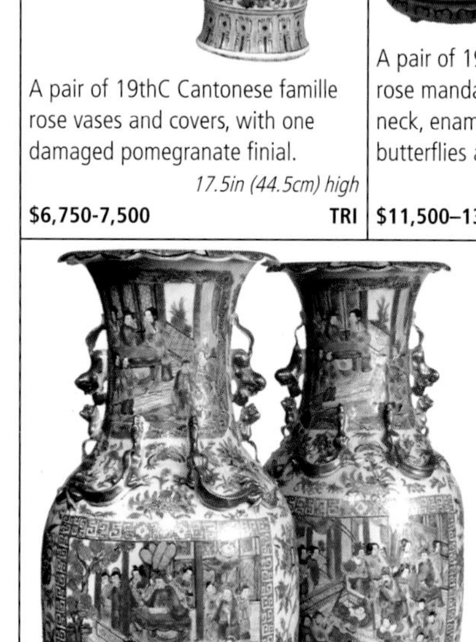

A pair of 19thC Canton vases, the four figure reserves within thunder scroll frames with Buddhist objects, flowers and butterflies.

24.25in (61.5cm) high

$6,000-7,500 CHEF

A pair of mid-19thC Cantonese porcelain famille rose vases, painted with court scenes and birds.

25.5in (64.5cm) high

$1,800-3,000 TEN

A 19thC Chinese famille jaune fish bowl and stand, the interior decorated with goldfish and aquatic plants, the exterior decorated with warriors and officials, with carved hardwood stand.

24in (61cm) high overall

$1,500-2,250 L&T

A Chinese export rose-mandarin hunt bowl, decorated with fox hunt scenes.

c1785 *6.5in (16.5cm) high*

$10,500–13,500 POOK

A mid-19thC Canton famille rose bowl, painted with figures, flowers and insects.

11.5in (29.5cm) diam

$1,150-1,300 BELL

A rare Chinese export famille rose 'Mandarin' wall sconce, painted with courtiers and pavilions.

c1775 *9.5in (24cm) high*

$7,500-9,000 L&T

A Chinese Kangxi tea canister, for the Portuguese market, painted with a debased version of the arms of Don Pedro de Lancastre Silveira Valente Castelo Branco Vasconcelos Barreto e Meneses.

See N De Castro, Chinese Porcelain and the Heraldry of the Empire, p.51 for a silver-mounted canister of this design, and where the author notes, 'It is known that two services were rejected at this period due to the coat of arms being full of errors'.

1662-1722) *6.5in (16.2cm)*
$7,500-9,000 WW

An 18thC Chinese armorial dish, made for the Portuguese market, painted with the arms of Ginori.

11.25in (28cm) diam
$6,750-7,500 WW

A Chinese famille rose armorial bowl decorated with the arms of Skinner.

c1728 *10.75in (26.9cm) diam*
$1,800-3,000 WW

A Yongzheng armorial punch bowl, with the arms of Menzies above the motto 'Will. God.I.Shall.' between painted flowers, repairs and cracks.

1723-1735 *13.75in (35cm) diam*
$1,000-1,400 SWO

A Chinese famille rose armorial saucer, decorated with the arms of Way impaling Page, with a gilt metal mount.

c1734 *4.75in (11.5cm) diam*
$850-975 WW

A pair of armorial plates, painted with the arms of Amyas of Norfolk, conferred 1576, rim with boar head crest and also with precious objects in a Kakiemon style, minor chips and wear.

c1750 *6in (16cm) diam*
$3,900-4,500 SWO

A Chinese famille rose armorial mug, with the arms for Purdon, a few small chips.

This service perhaps made for Simon Purdon, High Sheriff of Co. Limerick and grandson of Sir Nicholas Purdon, MP for Baltimore in Co. Cork.

c1765 *4.75in (12cm) high*
$850-975 WW

One of a pair of Chinese export armorial platters, with Lennox of Woodhead coat of arms and the motto 'I'll Defend'.

c1765 *11.25in (28.5cm) wide*
$4,000-4,500 the pair L&T

An early 18thC Chinese Yongzheng period Imperial doucai wine pot and cover, painted with the 'Three Friends of Winter', the base with six-character mark.

Doucai porcelain was very difficult to produce, as it required two firings, the first for the outline of the design at high temperature, the second for the overglaze colored enamels at a lower temperature.This wine pot was painted in delicate colors with the so-called Three Friends of Winter: bamboo, blossoming plum and pine trees. In Chinese iconography these are symbols of longevity and perseverance, as they flourish even in adverse conditions.

5in (13cm) high

$4,500,000+ **NAG**

An 18thC Chinese doucai porcelain vase, painted with phoenix and flowers, in later gilt bronze mounts.

12.5in (31.5cm) high excluding fittings

$6,000-6,750 **FRE**

A wucai box and cover, probably of the Wanli period, decorated with birds in a weeping willow tree, with six character Wanli mark.

9.5in (24cm) diam

$10,500-12,000 **CLV**

A Wanli wucai transitional period vase, decorated with warriors and officials within a fenced garden, underglaze blue six character Wanli mark.

12.75in (32cm) high

$3,300-3,900 **L&T**

Judith Picks

Antiques do not have a fixed retail price. Prices can vary considerably and experts do not always agree on the period or value of an object. Whilst the auction house expert, an authority and specialist academic in his field, appraised this as early 20thC and the general opinion of the English 'trade' agreed with the auction house, the purchaser and under-bidders thought otherwise. In fact they must have considered the vase to be at least 200 years earlier.The answer as always is that the value of an antique is what a willing buyer will pay for it. And that is always the excitement of this business.

An early 20thC Chinese doucai vase and associated cover, decorated with dragons amidst cloud scrolls, Tien mark, hardwood base.

4in (10cm) high

$37,500–45,000 **AS&S**

A rare Chinese wucai box and cover, painted with two parrots in a willow tree, with insects in flight and flowers in bloom beneath, six character Wanli mark in underglaze blue.

(1573-1620) *9.5in (24cm) diam*

$75,000-90,000 **WW**

A Chinese wucai incense burner, painted with two scaly dragons and a flaming pearl of wisdom, with flames and a lozenge mark.

c1640 *9.25in (23cm) diam*

$7,500-9,000 WW

A Chinese wucai vase, with scenes from 'The Plum in the Golden Vase', painted with equestrian riders and attendants, ladies in a pagoda.

c1640 *12in (30.5cm) high*

$6,000-6,750 WW

A Chinese Wucai baluster vase, painted with figures in a fenced garden.

c1650 *13in (33cm) diam*

$4,000-4,500 WW

A pair of Chinese Shunzhi or early Kangzi wucai boys, each wearing a loin cloth decorated with a peony bloom, and holding a vase containing lotus.

10.75in 27.5cm

$4,500-6,000 WW

A 17thC Chinese wucai vase, painted with general Guan Yu and his attendant Zhou Cang, with distant pagoda in a rocky landscape.

The subject of the general and his attendant is taken from the Romance of the Three Kingdoms.

7.25in (18cm)

$10,500-12,000 WW

A Chinese Imperial wucai dish, painted with two scaly five-clawed dragons and a pair of phoenix amidst peony, encircled by dragons, phoenix and flowers, six character Kangxi mark.

1662-1722 *12.75in (32cm) diam*

$10,500-12,000 WW

A Chinese Kangxi wucai dish, painted with five fishes, lotus, prunus and chrysanthemum, mounted with metal handles.

9in (22.5cm) diam

$3,000-4,000 WW

A 19thC wucai vase, decorated with fire-breathing kylins, planters with flowering shrubs and bands of peonies, lotus and chrysanthemum.

12in (30cm) high

$1,800-2,400 L&T

A 17thC Chinese wucai jar, painted with an official riding a kylin and holding a ruyi scepter, with two attendants amidst rockwork and plantain, some damage.

9.5in (24cm) high

$1,800-3,000 WW

Two Chinese models of Immortals, their robes decorated with phoenix and Buddhist lion dogs, flowers and cloud scrolls, one holding a lingzhi fungus, the other a peach branch, Jiajing.

1522-66 *11.7in (29.8cm) high*

$27,000–33,000 **WW**

A Chinese Chongzheng pottery incense burner, with a writhing dragon the handles formed as two large kylin, the body raised on three ferocious animal mask feet, with a hardwood cover.

The inscription to the neckrim reads 'Chong Zhen jin nian si yue chu ba ri Yuan Guo Si', (made for the Guoyuan Temple on the eight day of the fourth month in the ninth year of the reign of Chongzhen, 8th April 1636).

1628-44 *19in (48.2cm)*

$18,000-22,500 **WW**

A Kangxi period pair of spinach and egg glazed ducks.

5.75in (14.5cm) high

$1,500-2,250 **L&T**

A pair of 18thC Kangxi period 'foreigner' candle holders, modeled as crouching men holding a candle nozzle on their heads.

8.75in (22cm) high

$7,500–12,000 **L&T**

A pair of Chinese porcelain dragon bowls, painted with a five-clawed dragon, amidst flaming clouds in a five-color way palette, one with staple repair and the other with tiny rim chip and hairline crack, with a six character Yongzheng mark.

7.75in (19.5cm) diam

$60,000–75,000 **SHAP**

A pair of Yongzheng 'dragon' bowls, decorated in the center with a medallion of a dragon chasing the flaming pearl, the exterior with four medallions and clouds.

5.75in (14.5cm) diam

$45,000-60,000 **L&T**

Judith Picks

Just as at the Antiques Roadshow auctioneers never know what they are going to find on a routine home valuation, this vase was spotted by Andrew Marlborough, an Oriental specialist with Duke's Auctioneers in Dorchester. He saw the vase on top of an old corner cupboard in the hallway being used as a table lamp. On closer inspection, he realized it was a vase from the reign of Emperor Qianlong (1711-1799). Ceramics from this period are highly sought after at auction as they were produced during the 'golden age' of the arts in China when the country was at its wealthiest. Artefacts from the period are rare and incredibly desirable, and the Isle of Wight specimen was unmarked although the base had been drilled to accommodate an electrical wire to convert it into a lamp base. During the course of the pre-sale viewing, there was some speculation that the drill hole may have removed the Imperial reign mark. The irony is that if the vase had not been drilled and turned into a lamp base, it could easily have fetched $150,000. If the Imperial reign mark was still intact, the vase would have sold for more than $750,000.

A Qianlong underglaze blue and red bottle vase, decorated with buddhistic lions playing with balls and ribbons, with a hardwood stand, drilled for use as a lamp.

14.25in (36cm) high

$75,000–90,000 **DUK**

A mid 18thC Chinese export porcelain teapot and cover, painted with the 'Stand' pattern, unmarked.

7.5in (19cm) wide

$300-400 **HT**

A Monumental Fencai flower and landscape vase from the Imperial Qianlong period, multi-tiered baluster form vase with two chilong-inspired gilt-bronze ears on the neck, each tier with a different glaze, with a six-character turquoise Qianlong mark to the base.

This important vase was likely made for the Emperor so he could appreciate the technical achievements illustrated in the vase. It required multiple firings of the fifteen different glazes and enamels that resulted in the exquisite floral and landscape designs. This was the high point of the ceramic techniques employed by the Jingdezhen Imperial potters.

34.5in (88cm) high.

$21.3m+ **SK**

A pair of Kangxi clobbered mallet-form vases, painted with landscapes, daisies and chrysanthemum, the necks with butterflies and florets, nibbles.
c1780 *14.5in (36.5cm) high*
$9,000-10,500 **SWO**

A pair of Chinese Imperial dragon wine cups, painted with two scaly five-clawed dragons amidst clouds, each with a six character Daoguang mark and of the period.
1821-50 *2.4in (cm) diam*
$22,500-30,000 **WW**

A mid-19thC incense burner and cover, of bronze form, painted with two dragons and a pearl, the feet, handles and neck with bats amongst clouds, two minor chips.
13.25in (33.5cm) high
$7,500-9,000 **SWO**

A 19thC Chinese wig stand, with painted figures and extensive calligraphy.
10.5in (27cm) high
$2,000-2,400 **TRI**

A bottle vase, painted with five figures playing go below a pine tree, an iron-red oval seal opposite for 'Eternal Fortune and Enduring Spring' and a three character mark to one side for 'Studio of Great Culture', the four character base mark 'Yong Qing Chang Chun'.

This vase was bought in Hong Kong in 1934. The inscriptions and style are typical of the porcelains made for the Dowager Empress Cixi's 60th birthday in 1894.
16.25in (41cm) high
$6,000–9,000 **CHEF**

A 19thC Qing dynasty green crackled glaze vase of flattened form with two molded fu lions on the front and one on the back, a gilt-bronze base and metal handles in the form of kylins.
9.5in (24cm) high
$1,800–2,700 **L&T**

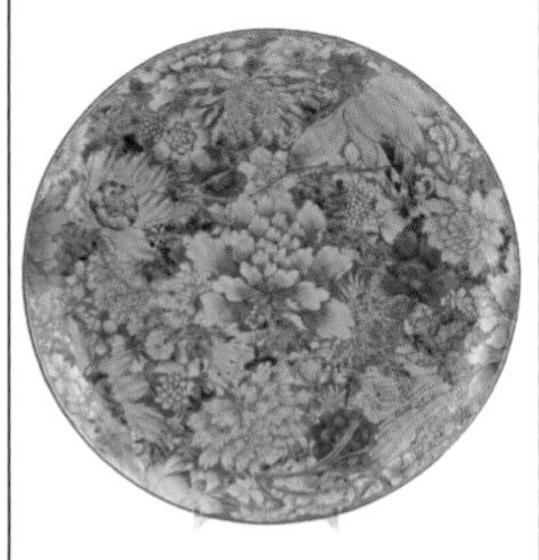

A large Chinese millefleurs dish, brightly enameled with many large flower blooms, all reserved on a gilt ground, the reverse pink, six character Guangxu mark in iron-red.
1875-1908 *13.5in (34.5cm)*
$2,000–2,700 **WW**

A pair of green and aubergine glaze yellow ground 'Dragon' bowls, the sides incised with two five-clawed dragons amidst clouds and flames, chasing flaming pearls, with fitted box, Guangxu six character mark and of the period.

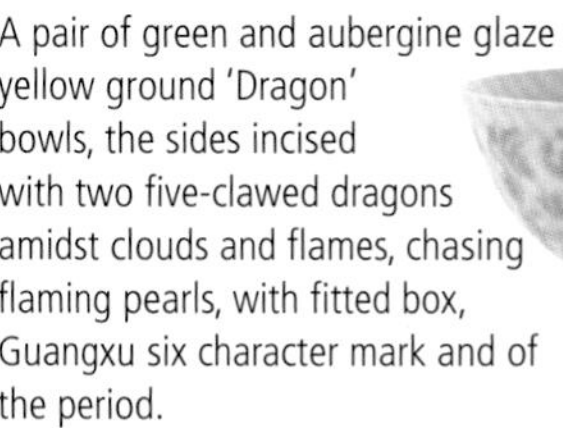

5.25in (13cm) diam
$3,000-4,500 **L&T**

A 20thC Chinese porcelain tureen, in the form of a goose.
14.5in (37cm) high
$450-600 **ROS**

A Japanese Imari charger, painted with a gnarled prunus tree issuing from rockwork, with plantain and chrysanthemum in a fenced garden.
c1700 *21.4in (54.3cm) diam*
$4,500-6,000 **WW**

A Japanese Imari bowl, decorated with peony, chrysanthemum and prunus.
c1700 *15.5in (39cm) diam*
$6,000-7,500 **WW**

A Japanese Imari dish, painted with two cranes and a minogame beneath pine and a flowering prunus tree, the border painted with Buddhist lion dogs, flowers, leaves and ribbons.
c1700 *20in (50.5cm) diam*
$5,250-6,000 **WW**

A pair of 19thC Japanese Imari porcelain vases, painted to show flowers, scrolls, and foliate forms, the laurel-cast gilt bronze bases.
c1725 *24in (70cm) high*
$18,000–24,000 **FRE**

ESSENTIAL REFERENCE - IMARI

Imari porcelain is the name for Japanese porcelain made in the town of Arita, in the former Hizen Province, northwestern Kyushu. They were exported to Europe extensively from the port of Imari, between the second half of the 17thC and the first half of the 18thC. The Japanese as well as Europeans called them Imari. Though there are many types of Imari, the term is mainly associated with a type of Imari produced and exported in large quantity in the mid-17thC. Imari is colored porcelain with cobalt blue underglaze and red and gold overglaze. The subject matter of Imari is diverse, ranging from flora and fauna to people and scenery. Some Imari design, such as 'kraak style', were adopted from China, but most designs were uniquely Japanese.

A pair of 18thC Japanese Edo period Imari vases, unmarked.
19in (48cm) high
$3,000-4,500 **L&T**

A 19thC Japanese Imari covered jar.
22.25in (56cm) high
$750-1,000 **L&T**

A pair of Japanese Imari plates, painted with a jardinière of flowers.
c1700 *14.5in (37cm) diam*
$700-850 **WW**

A pair of late 19thC Japanese Imari porcelain vases, covers and stands, painted with landscape panels on a scroll and phoenix ground, unmarked.
9.25in (23.5cm) high
$1,500-2,250 **HT**

An early 20thC Imari jar and cover.
21.75in (55cm) high
$450-750 **CHEF**

A Kinkozan Satsuma vase by Sozan, signed 'Dai Nihon Satsuma Kinkozan Sei', with a further signature on the reserve, 'Sozan Ga', and a Kinkozan paper label to base.

Few pieces are decorated with such elaborately pierced and molded upper sections, a feat of technical virtuosity for both the potter and the kiln handlers. After Yabu Meizan, Sozan is arguably the most sought-after of the Meiji Satsuma artists and this was clearly a deluxe production. It also is in its original wooden box that also carried a paper label reading 'S. Kinkozan Manufacturer of Fine Porcelains Kyoto, Japan, Established 1643'.

12in (30cm) high

$60,000–75,000 **DN**

A Japanese Meiji period Satsuma vase, decorated with figures and pavilions, signed.

4.75in (12cm) high

$850-975 **L&T**

A Meiji period Kinkozan Satsuma koro, decorated with a phoenix amongst foliage.

6.25in (15.5cm) high

$1,500-2,250 **L&T**

A Sobei Kinkozan Kyoto jar and cover, with women entertaining figures on a hillside.

c1890 *4in (10cm) high*

$1,000–1,500 **SWO**

A Sobei Kinkozan Satsuma vase, with a samurai on horseback with attendants, a wild man of the mountains, a girl kneeling at his feet, gilt Kinkozan zo on a black ingot.

c1885 *9.25in (23cm) high*

$7,500–12,000 **SWO**

A pair of Kyoto Satsuma gu, each of archaic Chinese bronze form, painted with The Seven Gods of Good Fortune, gilt Yasuda trade mark and Ryozan in gilding.

c1885 *4.75in (12cm) high*

$1,800–2,250 **SWO**

A Meizan Kyoto Satsuma vase, painted with a procession emanating from a temple, gilt Yabu Meizan.

c1890 *5.25in (13cm) high*

$4,500-6,000 **SWO**

A Meiji period Satsuma vase, decorated with chrysanthemum, wisteria, prunus and geometric panels, signed.

10.25in (26cm) high

$1,500-2,100 **L&T**

A Japanese Meiji period Satsuma vase, painted with mountainous landscapes, with stilt villages and waterfalls, bearing seal mark for Gyokuzan.

9.75in (25cm) high

$150–225 **HW**

A pair of Japanese Satsuma vases, painted and gilded with panels of figures.

16.7in (42.5cm) high

$750-900 **DA&H**

A Kinkozan Satsuma vase, Meiji period, decorated with children catching fireflies in a garden and sparrows above chrysanthemum, irises, peonies and other flowers, with impressed mark and gilt mark 'Kinkozan sei'.

4.75in (12cm) high

$3,000-4,000 **DN**

A Meiji period Satsuma Kinkozan vase, decorated with families picnicing on the banks of a stream with Fujiyama on the horizon, with impressed seal 'Kinkozan sei'.

6in (15cm) high

$4,000-4,500 **DN**

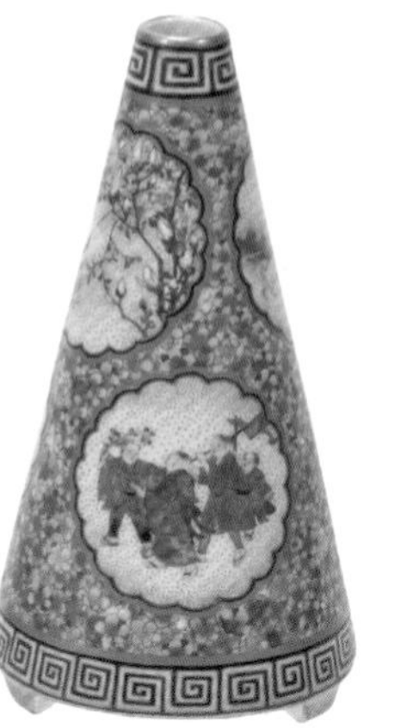

A pair of Meiji period Kozan Satsuma vases, decorated with genre scenes and floral subjects, gilt signature 'Kozan sei', slight rubbing.

4.5in (11.5cm) high

$3,000-4,500 **DN**

A Japanese Meiji period Satsuma earthenware bowl, decorated with figures before a bursting sun, Kinkozan mark to base.

12in (30.5cm) diam

$4,000-4,500 **FRE**

A small Meiji period Ryozan, Kyoto Satsuma tray, decorated with gentlemen and ladies in a garden accompanied by two boys, signed on reverse.

8in (20cm) wide

$2,700-3,300 **L&T**

A Kinkozan teapot, enameled and gilt with immortals and other figures, the edge with flying Manchurian cranes.

c1880 *5.5in (14cm) wide*

$3,400–4,500 **SWO**

A late 17thC Japanese Edo period Arita export dish, decorated with citron and peony enclosing a central monogram of the Dutch East India Company, 'VOC'.

14in (35.5cm) diam

$1,400-1,800 **L&T**

A large Arita dish, painted with a jardinière of flowers on a terrace, the border with lotus, florets, ammonite scrolls and leaves.

c1690 *21.75in (55cm) diam*

$2,550-3,000 **SWO**

A late Japanese Edo period vase, painted with landcsape views.

19.75in (50cm) high

$1,800-3,000 **L&T**

A late 19thC Japanese Arita jardinière, with diaper-pattern panels against a scrolling foliate and cloud-filled field.

12.75in (32cm) high

$1,500-2,250 **L&T**

A Yabu Meizan vase, enameled with scenes from a novel or a festival, gilt Meizan Sei, slight wear.

c1890 *4.75in (12cm)*

$3,000-4,000 **SWO**

A Japanese Meiji period Miyagawa (Makuzu) Kozan relief-molded earthenware vase, applied with three bears in a rocky, leafy cave, impressed mark.

11.5in (29cm) high

$4,500–7,500 **L&T**

A Makazu Kozan porcelain vessel, modeled as a Ho-Ho bird or phoenix, decorated with waves and auspicious emblems, seal to the base 'Miyakawa Kozan'.

7.75in (19.5cm) long

$900-1,200 **DN**

A Japanese Kutani vase, decorated with figures in landscapes, the base with a square seal mark.

c1900 *32.5in (82cm) high*

$750-1,000 **WW**

A 20thC Japanese vase, decorated with Mandarin ducks standing on a snow-covered prunus branch, the base impressed with Kinkozan Tsukuru.

16in (40.5cm) high

$1,800-3,000 **WW**

ESSENTIAL REFERENCE - IZNIK

Iznik pottery, named after the town in western Anatolia where it was made, is a decorated ceramic that was produced from the end of the 15th century until the end of the 17th century. In the last quarter of the 15th century, craftsmen began to manufacture high quality pottery with a fritware body painted with cobalt blue under a colorless transparent lead glaze. The designs combined traditional Ottoman arabesque patterns with Chinese elements. During the 16th century the decoration of the pottery became looser and more flowing. Additional colors were introduced. Initially turquoise was combined with the dark shade of cobalt blue and then the pastel shades of sage green and pale purple were added. Finally, in the middle of the century, a very characteristic bole red replaced the purple and a bright emerald green replaced the sage green.

A Turkish Ottoman Iznik pottery jug, some chips and cracks, handle restored.

c1600 *8.75in (22cm) high*

$4,000-4,500 **MAB**

A Turkish Ottoman Iznik pottery bowl, the interior with hyacinth sprigs, chips and repair.

c1600 *7.5in (19cm) diam*

$5,250-6,000 **MAB**

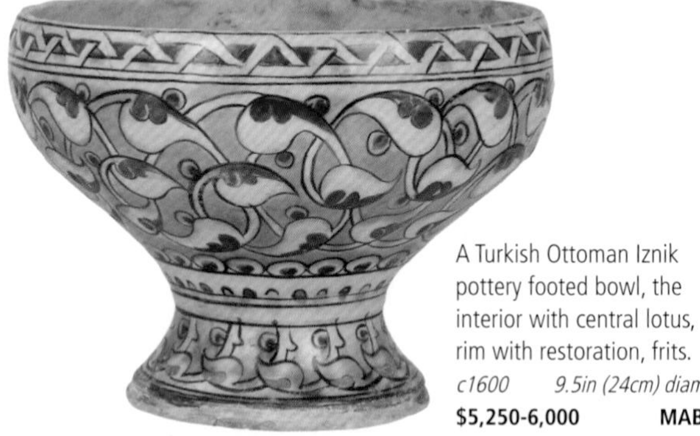

A Turkish Ottoman Iznik pottery footed bowl, the interior with central lotus, rim with restoration, frits.

c1600 *9.5in (24cm) diam*

$5,250-6,000 **MAB**

A Turkish Ottoman Iznik pottery bowl, restored, rim chips and frits.

c1600 *9.75in (24.5cm) diam*

$2,700-3,300 **MAB**

A Persian Cantagalli charger, painted with flowers and foliage, old restoration and glaze chips.

15.25in (39cm) diam

$750-1,000 **WW**

A late 19thC Persian Qajar pottery tile, framed.

Qajar art is characterized by an exuberant style and flamboyant use of color, which became more emphatic as the 19th century progressed. A particularly important feature of Qajar art is the richness of its iconography. Nostalgia for Persia's past is reflected in scenes of Sasanian rulers, traditional themes of Persian literature, and more recent battles with the Ottoman Turks and Mughals.

11.75in (30cm) wide

$750-1,000 **L&T**

A 19thC Persian Qajar pottery tile, framed.

5.5in (14cm) wide

$300-450 **L&T**

An 18thC cloisonné hat box, hardwood cover and stand, possibly Imperial, the top with central flower enclosed within bands of stylized scrolling foliage, stylized bats and clouds, all housed with stand and yellow silk lined hardwood case.

Cloisonné is an ancient technique for decorating metalwork objects, in recent centuries using vitreous enamel. The decoration is formed by first adding compartments (cloisons, in French) to the metal object by soldering or adhering copper, silver or gold wires. These remain visible in the finished piece. Cloisonné enamel objects are worked on with enamel powder made into a paste, which then is fired in a kiln. The technique was known in the Byzantine Empire. By the 14thC the technique had spread to China, where it was soon used for much larger vessels.

12in (31cm) wide

$30,000–37,500 ROS

An 18thC Qianlong gilt copper and cloisonné twin-handled incense burner and cover, of archaistic form.

11in (28cm) high

$18,000–27,000 ROW

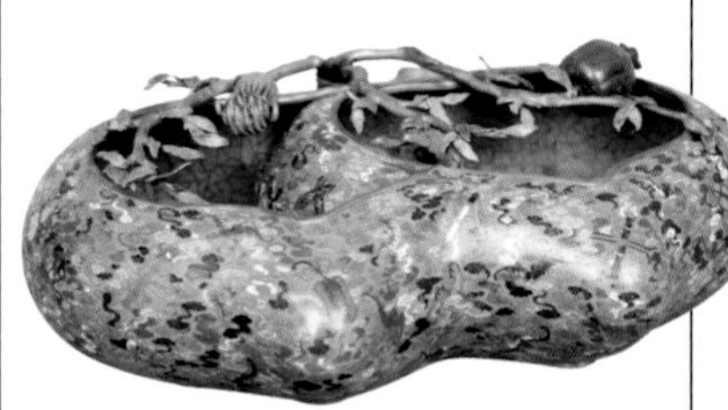

A Qianlong cloisonné, enamel and gilt washer, formed as twin peaches, decorated with bats and precious objects amongst stylized clouds, four character Qianlong mark to base, cased.

17.5in (44cm) wide

$18,000-22,500 ROW

An 18thC pair of cloisonné enamel models of quails, with separately made wings forming the aperture in the back.

6in (16cm) high

$4,000-4,500 DN

One of a pair of Qianlong period cloisonné figures of cranes.

12in (30cm) high

$15,000–22,500 pair L&T

An 18thC cloisonné bowl and cover, decorated with a dragon and tiger amongst trees.

10in (25.5cm) diam

$22,500–27,000 TEN

An 18thC dou cloisonné altar vase and cover, decorated with a foliate lotus scroll above a band of stylized stiff leaves.

5.5in (14cm)

$22,500-30,000 WW

A Qing dynasty cloisonné tripod incense burner and cover, with a panel of continuous scrolling lotus and acanthus, the legs with stylized taotie masks and C-scrolls, the finial depicting a five-clawed dragon, four character Qianlong mark.

15.25in (39cm)

$75,000–90,000 WW

A pair of Qing dynasty cloisonné enamel elephants, each supporting a vase, bejeweled and inset with cabochon-cut garnets and other stones around a foliate saddlecloth enriched with ruyi and lotus devices, hinged fringe ends.

c1800 *10.5in (26.5cm) high*

$112,500–127,500 **TEN**

A 19thC ormolu-mounted cloisonné vase, with a pair of dragon shoulder mounts, incised four character Jiaqing mark to base.

5.75in (14.5cm) high

$12,000-15,000 **ROW**

A 19thC cloisonné box and cover, formed as a vase with a central gilt animal mask handle, depicting two stylized dragons encircled by scrolling lotus and ruyi-head designs, with a four character Qianlong mark.

6.5in (16.5cm) wide

$2,000–2,700 **WW**

A massive 19thC cloisonné box and cover, the cover with a mountainous landscape and a waterfall, with pagodas and a small bridge crossing the river, with peony, chrysanthemum, lotus and prunus.

17in (43cm) diam

$3,000-4,500 **WW**

A pair of 19thC Qing dynasty cloisonné candlesticks, modeled as standing cranes.

17.75in (45cm) high

$3,000-4,000 **TEN**

A pair of 19thC cloisonné incense burners and covers, decorated with lotus, the covers pierced as cash symbols.

3.5in (9cm) high

$1,400-1,800 **WW**

A 19thC Qing dynasty cloisonné urn and stand, decorated with blossoming stems within a ruyi band, with two dragon mask scroll handles.

12.25in (31cm) high

$1,800–4,000 **L&T**

A pair of 19thC cloisonné quail incense burners.

6.5in (16.5cm) high

$3,400–4,500 **DN**

A 19thC cloisonné jar, decorated with birds perched on fruiting branches.

3.75in (9cm) diam

$600-900 **WW**

A cloisonné jardinière, decorated with birds, butterflies and flowers.

c1900 *15in (38cm) diam*

$450-750 **WW**

IMPERIAL BOX

A rare late 18thC Chinese Imperial documentary enameled silver gilt filigree box and cover, decorated with a stone chime or qing suspended from a stylized bat encircled by scrolling foliage, flowers and peaches, the sides with bats and lotus, all on a ground of tight scrolls,

The interior of the lid is inscribed 'Taken by General John Hart Dunne from the Summer Palace, Pekin, 1860, and given by him to his uncle, the Revd. Richard Hart of Catton, Norwich, with whom and his widow Jane Hart it remained until 1897'.

Provenance: The Summer Palace, Beijing, 1860. General Sir John Dunne (d.20th April 1924).

2.8in (7.2cm) wide

$82,500–97,500 **WW**

A rare Chinese Kangxi parcel-gilt silver teapot and cover, decorated with figures, pagodas, flowers, trees and birds, the handle modeled as a gnarled branch, the spout as a tapering section of bamboo, the neck with Buddhist emblems, unmarked.

The Victoria & Albert Museum, in London, have a related teapot dated to c1680.

1662-1722 *7in (18cm) high*

$60,000–75,000 **WW**

A 19thC Chinese silver cream jug, chased with figures in landscape settings, dragon scroll handle, marked with Chinese characters.

5in (13cm) high 6.3oz

$5,250-6,000 **WW**

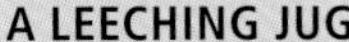

A LEECHING JUG

A 19thC Chinese silver mug, with dragon scroll handle, chased figural scenes, maker's mark of LC for Leeching.

3.75in (9.5cm) high 4.5oz

$2,000–2,700 **WW**

A Chinese export silver cigar case, by Leeching, Hong Kong, with scenes of warriors in battle, the base inscribed '1 Talbot Square, 1865 Hyde Park'.

4.75in (12cm) high

$1,150-1,425 **L&T**

A silver dragon bowl, offered by Thomas R. Callan of Ayr on November 23, marked for Luen Wo of Shanghai.

Luen Wo of Shanghai, was a prolific but high-quality maker and retailer operating from various premises in Nanking Road in Shanghai in the late 19th and early 20thC. The additional marks in Chinese characters indicate the artisan or workshop which made the piece, while a small presentation inscription dated 1897 gives an idea of its probable date.

12in (30cm) diam 62oz

$30,000–37,500 **TCAL**

A Chinese parcel-gilt silver reticulated fish, marked MK, 88 and with Chinese characters.

8.25in (21cm) wide 4oz

$450-600 **WW**

A 20thC silver model of a junk, probably Tonkinese, with twelve oarsmen and other figures, fitted with two masts and sails below pennants, both stamped 'Hop Thanh' struck with post-1893 French import marks.

24.5in (62.5cm) long 198oz

$15,000–18,000 **MAB**

A Chinese Shanghai export silver preserve jar and cover, with embossed naturalistic floral displays and birds, marked 'Zee Sung', character mark.

c1920 *3.5in (8.5cm) high 6.6oz*

$450-600 **L&T**

A pair of 18thC Canton enamel bowls, covers and stands, the yellow grounds painted with scrolling flowers, with blue dragons coiled within the foot rims. the bowls

The enamelling was compared to the enamelling on a kang table in the Palace Museum, Beijing.

4.75in (12cm) diam

$97,500–115,000 CHEF

A Qianlong Canton enamel basin, painted with figures on a walled terrace beside the ocean with peacocks flying overhead.

18.25in (46cm) wide

$4,000–5,250 L&T

A fine enameled bronze censer, of archaic form, decorated in colored enamels with bats and ruyi motifs, Qianlong seal mark.

8.7in (22cm) high (including stand)

$8,250-9,750 L&T

A Chinese late Western Zhou dynasty gui bronze wine vessel and cover.

The vessel has an inscription to the underside which is mirrored in the base's interior which reads 'wei sheng zuo bao zun gui, wei sheng qi shou kao wan, nian zi sun yong bao yong' (the ruler had this precious wine vessel made. May his sons and grandsons make eternal and precious use of it for a thousand years).

c1100-771BC 11.6in (29.5cm) wide

$45,000–52,500 WW

A pair of Ming dynasty bronze caparisoned elephant incense holders, with wood stands.

Symbolic of strength and wisdom, and when combined with a vase as in the present piece, the elephant represents the wish for peaceful times- 'vase', ping, in fact, is homophone with 'peace', pingan.

7.5in (19cm) high

$7,500-9,000 DN

A 17thC late Ming dynasty bronze tripod censer, with a later pierced hardwood cover.

12.25in (31cm) high

$2,700-3,300 L&T

A 17thC/18thC Chinese bronze gold-splash censer, the base with Xuande marks.

7.75in (19.5cm) diam

$37,500–45,000 JN

A rare 17th/18thC Chinese cast-bronze scholar's table screen, with pine sprays, cloud scrolls, a crane and a deer and other auspicious objects with lotus and a turtle below, with a hardwood stand.

This screen depicts the famous meeting of literati at the Orchid Pavilion, Lan Ting Wen Hui, in the year 353 AD.

14.25in (35.5cm) high

$18,000-22,500 WW

A large 19thC bronze Hu, cast in archaic style with taotie masks and birds, repairs.

22.5in (57cm) high

$4,500-5,250 SWO

A large 19thC Chinese bronze incense burner, the base with six character Xuande mark.

12in (30.5cm) wide

$15,000–18,000 WW

A Japanese bronze and mixed metal vase, Meiji period, decorated with pagodas and exotic birds.

10in (25cm) high

$7,500–10,500 **L&T**

A Japanese bronze koro and cover, Meiji period, decorated in relief within a coiled dragon.

11.8in (30cm) high

$3,000-4,500 **L&T**

A Japanese bronze koro and cover, Meiji period, the cover with a fish final, the sides with dragon handles.

20.5in (52cm) high

$2,700-3,300 **L&T**

A Japanese komai mixed metal censer, Meiji period, decorated with exotic birds and scrolling foliage

8in (20cm) high

$9,000–12,000 **L&T**

A Japanese bronze vase, cast in low-relief with a carp, mottled-green copper patina.

c1900 *11in (28cm) high*

$1,800-2,250 **SWO**

A Japanese Shibayama, enamel and silver mounted urn, Meiji period.

5.3in (13.5cm) high

$1,800-2,250 **L&T**

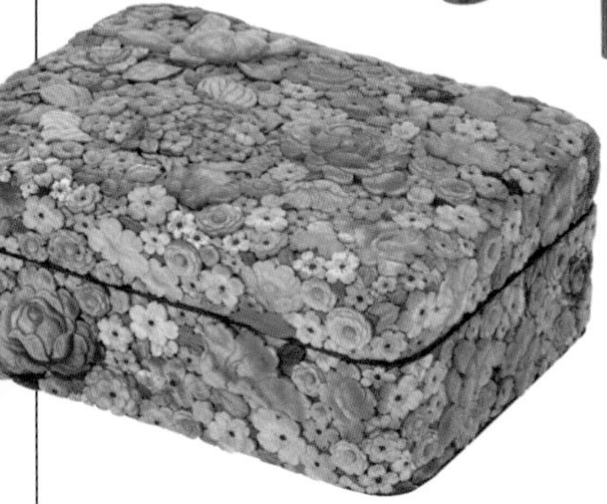

A Japanese Shibiyama lacquer box, Meiji period, decorated with mother of pearl flowers, the Makie lacquered interior with signed seal mark.

4.3in (11cm) wide

$6,000–9,000 **L&T**

A Japanese metal work inkwell, Meiji period, modeled as a cachepot, decorated with crabs, shells and star fish.

2in (5cm) high

$1,200-1,800 **L&T**

A Japanese Meiji period Shibayama lacquered tray, the ivory panel carved as basket weave and inlaid in ivory, mother of pearl, horn and lacquer.

19in (48.5cm) wide

$1,300–1,575 **HT**

ORIENTAL

A Japanese bronze and ivory figure, Meiji period, modeled as a standing warrior.

figure 7in (17cm) high

$2,700-3,300 **L&T**

A Japanese mixed metal bronze gonge, Meiji period, formed as a standing oni with a dragon coiled around his torso.

23in (58cm) high

$10,500–13,500 **L&T**

A Meiji period Miyao Eisuke, Yokohama style patinated and gilt bronze figure group, modeled as a musician and a boy with a Kitsune mask, with inscriptions to the robes reading 'Momoki' and 'Roraku'.

7in (18cm) high

$5,250-6,000 **L&T**

A Meiji period Japanese bronze and wood figure group, modeled as an old man offering food to a small boy, on a wood plank bench, the man with a seal mark signature.

25in (63cm) wide

$7,500-9,000 **L&T**

A Japanese reticulated bronze figure of a crab, Meiji period.

1868-1912 *8.75in (22cm) wide*

$3,000-4,000 **L&T**

A Japanese bronze figures of fighting cockerels, by Seiya Chu, Meiji period.

11.5in (29cm) high

$5,250-6,000 **L&T**

A late 19thC Japanese bronze fighting cock, with traces of silver and gilt patination.

27.25in (69cm) high

$12,000-15,000 **SWO**

A Meiji period bronze censer, in the form of a raven, with a removable cover on the back, unmarked.

10.25in (26cm) high

$2,700-3,300 **L&T**

A large Japanese Meiji period bronze model of a lion, signed to the base.

16in (41cm) long

$750-1,200 **ROS**

A Japanese silver box, with a bird of paradise and scroll borders, with twin character marks.

3in (7.8cm) diam 5oz

$1,000–1,500 **L&T**

A Japanese silver and enamel vase, with applied trailing floral decoration with enamel highlights, signature mark and initials VM to base.

7in (18cm) high 9.74oz

$1,500-2,250 **L&T**

A Japanese silver vase, Taisho period, engraved and chased with peonies, prunus and dogwood, with engraved signature, two character mark to base.

11in (28cm) high 26.4oz

$2,550-3,000 **L&T**

A Japanese silver vase, with a chased and engraved lake and landscape scene, with three character marks to base.

10.6in (27cm) high 35.4oz

$3,000-4,000 **L&T**

A Japanese silver coffee pot, with chased chrysanthemum decoration, character mark to base.

11in (28cm) high 24.3oz

$4,500-6,000 **L&T**

A Japanese silver doubled-walled bowl, apparently unmarked, decorated with carp and irises.

9in (23cm) high 52.3oz

$15,000–22,500 **L&T**

A fine Meiji period cloisonné koro, with phoenix and temple lions, mounted with stylized scroll metal handles and feet.

7in (18cm) high

$1,400-1,800 **L&T**

A Japanese Meiji period fine cloisonné tripod censer, decorated with carp.

6in (15cm) high

$6,000–9,000 **L&T**

A Japanese cloisonné vase, Meiji period, attributed to Namikawa Yasuyuki, decorated with flying phoenix.

3in (8cm) high

$450-750 **L&T**

A Japanese silver and enamel vase, decorated with flowers, bamboo and birds.

7.25in (18.5cm) high

$3,000-4,500 **WW**

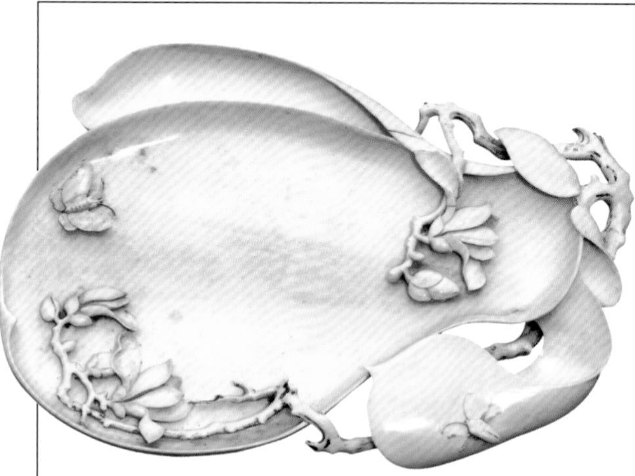

A Qianlong Imperial carved ivory brush washer, formed as a large magnolia flower bud, a small insect and a butterfly rest upon the petals, traces of cold painted pigments.

1736-95 *7.75in (19.5cm) long*

$40,500–45,000 **WW**

A late 19thC ivory seal, carved with five scaly dragons contesting flaming pearls of wisdom the base with a four character seal mark.

4in (10cm) high

$4,000–5,250 **WW**

A Canton ivory casket, carved with landscapes with figures amidst pagodas, pine and willow.

c1800 *9in (23cm) long*

$4,500-5,250 **WW**

A 19thC carved ivory puzzle ball tower, surmounted by a monkey and supported on a circular base with four elephants, in a fitted case.

26.5in (67cm) high

$1,500-2,250 **L&T**

A 19thC Canton Qing dynasty carved ivory brush pot, carved with lohans and ladies playing weiqi beneath a tree with mountains in the distance.

5.25in (13cm) high

$3,400–4,500 **L&T**

A fine 19thC Qing dynasty ivory tusk, carved with warriors, equestrian figures, and an official within a pavillion, on a later wood stand.

$7,500–10,500 **L&T**

An early 19thC ivory model of a pleasure boat, with guards and attendants, with wood stand, damage and losses.

24in (61cm) long

$4,500-6,000 **SWO**

A 19thC carved ivory figure of a maiden, on a hardwood stand.

10.5in (26.5cm) high

$1,500-2,250 **WW**

A 19thC Qing dynasty Canton ivory puzzle ball, with two deer over a pierced central column and large dragon carved ball with fourteen reticulated balls to the interior, the base carved with warriors on horseback.

18.25in (46cm) high

$4,000–5,250 **L&T**

A Meiji period carved ivory group of a figure, seated on a bundle of faggots beside a basket of fruit, signed on red tablet to base.

4.25in (11cm) high

$4,000-4,500 **TRI**

A Meiji period ivory carving of Quan Yin, highlighted with black ink, the base signed and with carved wood stand, in original box.

30in (76.5cm) high

$9,000-10,500 **TRI**

A Meiji period ivory carving of a bijin, signed 'Masanobu' to the base.

1868-1912 *8.75in (22cm) high*

$1,150-1,300 **WW**

An ivory figure of a farmer, mark to base which reads 'Sadatsune'.

c1900 *12.5in (31.5cm) high*

$700-850 **WW**

An ivory model of a fisherman, signed 'Yoshiyama'.

c1900 *7in (17.5cm) high*

$600-750 **WW**

A Meiji period carved ivory okimono, depicting a pair of wrestlers, signed.

5.75in (14.5cm) high

$1,400-1,800 **L&T**

A pair of Meiji period carved ivory okimono, each modeled as a sarumawashi (monkey trainer).

7.75in (19.5cm) and 7.5in (19cm) high

$1,800-2,250 **L&T**

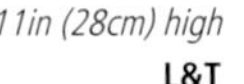

A Meiji period carved ivory okimono, of a farmer, single character signature.

11in (28cm) high

$300-450 **L&T**

A Meiji period ivory and boxwood okimono of a noh mask maker, on a naturalistic wood base.

4in (10cm) high

$975-1,150 **L&T**

A Meiji period ivory okimono of a barber, red lacquer inset signature panel to base.

7.5in (18.5cm) high

$1,500-2,250 **L&T**

A Meiji period ivory okimono of an egg seller, red lacquer inset signature panel to underside.

8.5in (21.5cm) high

$1,400-1,800 **L&T**

A Meiji period ivory okimono of a fisherman, holding his trident over his shoulder, from which hangs a large fish and a basket containing two further fish, the other hand holding a bait bucket, two character signature to base.

17in (43cm) high

$6,750-8,250 **L&T**

A Tokyo School ivory bijin, the girl, with sensitively carved features, wearing a gown and obi with relief chrysanthemums, walking in geta holding an umbrella with crawling froglet, her other hand with a double gourd, engraved mark 'Nihon'.

c1900 *11in (27.9cm)*

$4,500–6,000 **SWO**

An ivory Gama Sennin, his staff with a toad and another balancing on the scroll in his hand, engraved 'kayamin'.

Gama Sennin is a benign sage with a lot of magical knowledge about pills and drugs. He is always accompanied by a toad and he can assume the shape of a toad. He could also change his skin and become young again.

c1880 *12.25in (31cm) high*

$4,500-6,000 **SWO**

An Edo period ivory okimono of a monkey, seated with two turtles, two character signature panel.

1.5in (3.5cm) high

$16,500–22,500 **L&T**

A Meiji period Masayuki style carved walrus ivory and Shibayama inlaid elephant, engraved and inlaid in mother-of-pearl, green and red stones, with a lotus on its back supporting a glass sphere.

1868-1912 *5.5in (14cm) high*

$1,800-3,000 **TEN**

An ivory and lacquer okimono, in the form of a red-headed Shojo woman on all fours, grasping a gold-lacquered bowl, with various beasts, gilt ju, Buddhist pearl, minor damage.

Shojo are always depicted in Japanese art with long flowing red hair, and associated with inebriation; they were probably based in the idigenous tribes living in Honshu Island. In all probability, when conceived, turning the top made the monsters revolve.

c1870 *1.5in (3.6cm) wide*

$4,000–5,250 **SWO**

A Meiji period carved ivory okimono, carved as a partially husked ear of corn.

11in (28cm) long

$975-1,150 **L&T**

A 17thC Chinese Ming (or Kangxi) rhino horn libation cup, with hollow-carved opposing dragons to interior, with small rim flaw.

All these items are sold with a letter from AHVLA confirming that it can be legally traded in the UK without any further CITES certification. There has, however, been a change to the laws regarding the exporting of worked rhino horn items, in line with EC Guidance (issued March 2012). All items will require a CITES re-export certificate to be exported outwith the EU. Responsibility for obtaining this certificate lies with the owner. For more information, please visit the DEFRA website (www.defra.gov.uk).

6in (15cm) wide 8oz

$140,000–180,000 JN

A rare 17th/18thC Chinese carved rhinoceros horn libation cup, carved with taotie masks, between bands of key fret, the handle with a single crab above a rhomboid and C-scroll design.

5in (12.5cm) high

$60,000–75,000 WW

A 19thC Qing dynasty full tip carved rhinoceros horn, carved with the figure of Shou Lao, deer, scholars, attendants and monkeys with peaches, among bamboo, pine, prunus and lingzhi.

25.25in (64cm) high 1.63kg

$105,000–120,000 L&T

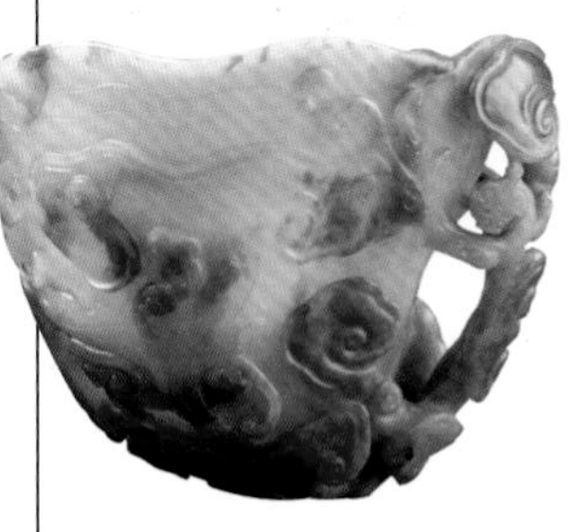

A 17thC Gong jade libation cup, of Lingxi form, carved with Lingxi and Chilong, the hardwood stand similarly carved.

3.25in. (9.5cm) high

$45,000-60,000 A&G

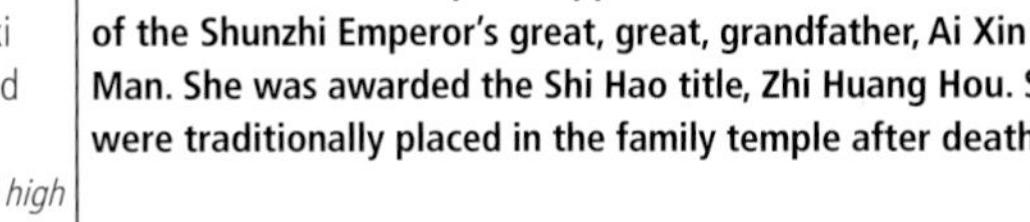

A large Imperial celadon dragon jade seal, with greyish and white striations and inclusions.

Dating from possibly the early 18thC (seals of similar color stone and design have been dated to the Kangxi period), the face is covered with the characters zhi huang hou bao in relief in both Chinese and Manchu zhuanshu scripts. It appears to be made in honour of the wife of the Shunzhi Emperor's great, great, grandfather, Ai Xin Jue Luo Fu Man. She was awarded the Shi Hao title, Zhi Huang Hou. Such seals were traditionally placed in the family temple after death.

6in (15cm) high

$400,000+ WW

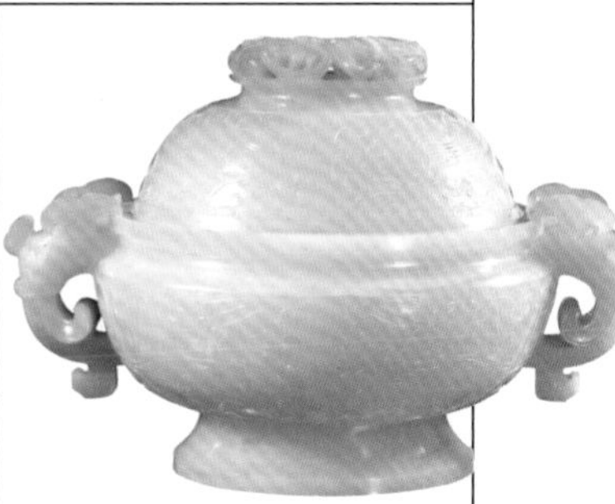

A Chinese Qianlong white jade incense burner and cover, carved in relief in archaistic style with stylized taotie, the handles as the heads of mythical beasts.

1736-95 7.25in (18.2cm) wide

$180,000–225,000 WW

Judith Picks: Jade

The large size, pale color, and fine carving on this impressive brush washer shows all the technical and artisctic skill of the jade carvings produced during the reign of the emperor Qianlong. The 'dragon amongst clouds' motif is one that can be found on related Imperial wares and are related to the famous 'black jade' wine bowl in the Round Fort in Beijing, created during the Yuan dynasty (1279-1368) and once considered one of the wonders of the Mongol court. This black jade vessel is also carved with dragons among clouds and waves. It was rescued by the Qianlong emperor from a temple where the monks used it as a vegetable container.

An impressive and large Qing dynasty carved pale celadon jade 'Dragon' brush washer, carved with a complex composition of six coiling five-clawed dragons chasing flaming pearls set amongst a cloud-filled ground, the base with a calligraphy poem inscription and Imperial Qianlong seal marks.

9.5in (24cm) long 3.5kg

$270,000–330,000 L&T

A Chinese pale celadon jade dish probably late Ming dynasty, carved with two catfish, the exterior with a crab and a dragonfly.

3.25in (8cm) wide

$8,250-9,750 WW

CLOSER LOOK - INCENSE BURNER

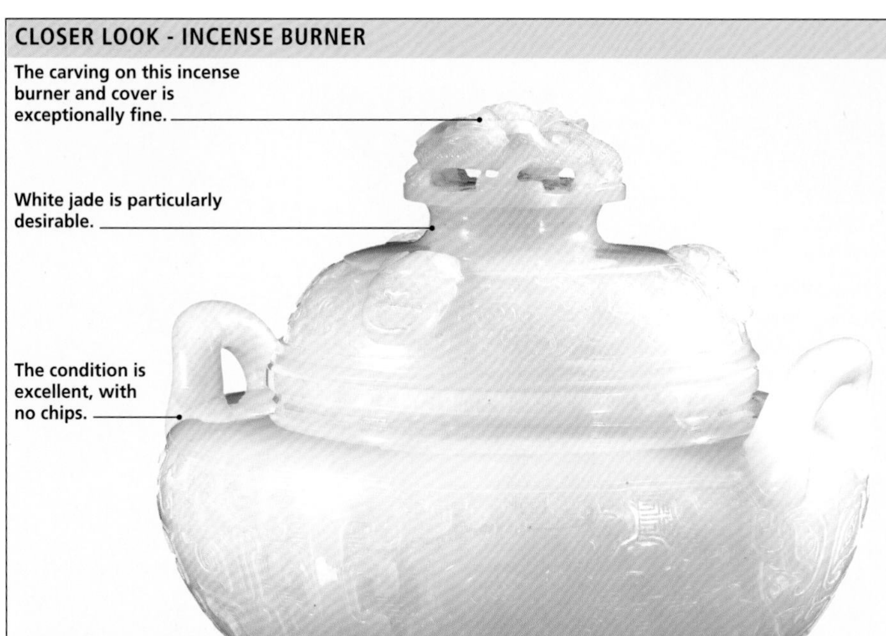

A Chinese Qianlong/Jiaqing white jade incense burner and cover, carved in shallow relief with stylized taotie masks on a wide key fret band and with loop handles to the shoulders above further stylized masks, the reticulated finial carved as a twin horned dragon, the cover with three mask and ring knops on an archaistic band.

5.75in (15cm)

$440,000-510,000 **WW**

An 18th/19thC Chinese pale celadon jade belt buckle, carved with a sinuous scrolling chilong.

5.75in (14.5cm) wide

$10,500-12,000 **WW**

An 18th/early 19thC Chinese pale celadon jade carving of a pair of Mandarin ducks, sitting on a lotus leaf, with a wood stand.

Mandarin ducks, yuanyang, depicted together with lotus, are representative of the wish for a harmonious marriage and illustrious sons.

3.75in (9.5cm) wide

$75,000–90,000 **WW**

A white jade 'champion' vase.

Twin-tube vases worked with an eagle standing atop a bear are usually referred to as 'champion vases' or 'hero vases', because the Chinese words 'eagle' and 'bear' together have similar pronounciation to 'yingxiong', the word for 'hero'.

4in (10cm) high

$52,500–60,000 **ADA**

A late 18th/early 19thC spinach green jade bamboo vase, carved with a bird on the top of the bamboo shoot, lingzhih fungus growing at its base.

4.5in (11cm) high

$4,500-5,250 **CHEF**

An 18th/19thC Chinese carved pale celadon jade carving 'Washing the Sacred Elephant', the elephant bejeweled and with saddle cloth, with two figures.

3in (7.5cm) long

$30,000–37,500 **TEN**

A 19thC Chinese celadon jade carving of a lady, with a prunus blossom in her hand, with a basket containing lingzhi fungus at her side, the base carved as swirling waves.

4.75in (12cm) wide

$4,000-4,500 **WW**

A Chinese yellow jade vase, archaic form, the sides carved with a mythical beast.

5.5in (13.5cm) high

$6,750-8,250 **L&T**

A Chinese Qianlong white jade carving of a horse, with its head turned toward a monkey which climbs upon its back and holds a flowering blossom spray, with a hardwood stand.

The horse, ma, carrying a monkey, hou, represents the wish to be conferred with high rank. Such a piece would have been given to an aspiring official.

1736-95 *4.5in (11cm) wide*

$135,000-150,000 **WW**

A Chinese Qianlong pale celadon jade carving of Shoulao, standing holding a lotus spray, with a small boy attendant who offers him a large peach, a wood stand.

1736-95 *4.25in (10.5cm) high*

$90,000-105,000 **WW**

A Chinese Qianlong period pale celadon jade bowl, carved with taotie on a keywork ground, six character mark, Fanggu mark.

The inscription of this bowl may be translated as 'exemplifying antiquity during the Qianlong reign' and this mark can be found on a number of important archaic pieces commissioned from the Palace Workshop by the Emperor Qianlong copying ancient jade and bronze forms.

6.25in (15.5cm) wide

$45,000-60,000 **TEN**

A Chinese Qianlong pale celadon jade carving of a recumbent water buffalo, with a kylin at its side, with a wood stand.

The water buffalo and kylin depicted together are representative of the Gods of peace and prosperity, and symbolize rivers and oceans.

1736-95 *4.75in (12cm) wide*

$42,000–48,000 **WW**

A Qianlong period celadon jade raft-form vase, carved with a figure holding a scroll and a lotus branch and a boy holding a peach, the small cover to the vase a later addition.

12in (30cm) long

$40,000-52,500 **L&T**

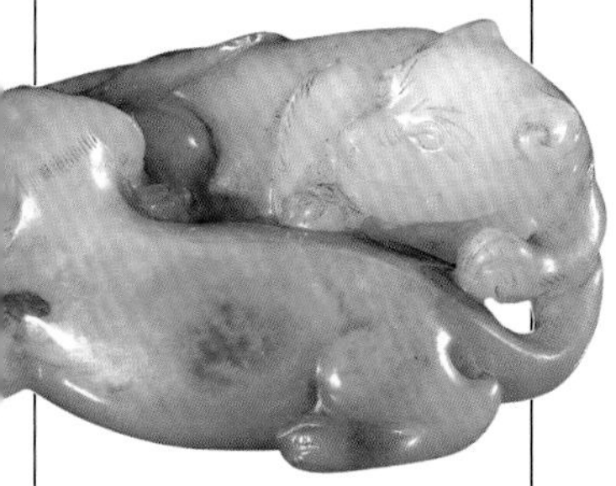

An 18thC Chinese Huan pale celadon jade carving of two recumbent cats.

2.25in (5.6cm) wide

$90,000-105,000 **WW**

An 18thC Chinese celadon jade carving, depicting an elephant's forequarters, possibly the leg for a vessel.

3in (7.5cm) high

$3,000-4,500 **WW**

A Chinese pale celadon jade carving of a luohan.

4in (10cm) high

$11,500–13,000 **WW**

A 19th/20thC Chinese russet and celadon jade carving of a gourd.

2.25in (6cm) high

$4,000-4,500 **WW**

A probably late 18thC Chinese white jade boy, clasping leafy branches in his hands, wood stand.

2.75in (6.75cm) long

$6,000-6,750 **BELL**

A Chinese Qianlong/Jiaqing Imperial pale celadon jade model of a sampan, with Ma Gu steering with an oar, with a vase of lingzhi fungi to the stern, a small deer and a crane holding a peach spray sit on the bow.

7in (17.5cm) wide

$82,500–97,500 **WW**

A Chinese Qianlong/Jiaqing celadon jade marriage bowl, the bowl carved with twin fish, and with animal mask loose ring handles to the sides, the four feet carved as lingzhi.

8.5in (21cm) wide

$30,000-45,000 **WW**

A 20thC Chinese pale celadon jade double vase and cover, carved with cloud scrolls and archaistic designs, the handles formed as dragons and mythical beasts with loose rings, bats and scrolling foliage, with two sinuous chilongs to one side, the cover surmounted by a Buddhist lion dog.

8in (20cm) wide

$18,000-22,500 **WW**

An early 20thC carved jade figure of Quan Yin.

7in (18cm) high

$450-600 **TRI**

An early 20thC carved jade figure of a recumbent buffalo, with stand.

4.25in (11cm) long

$600-750 **TRI**

A 20thC Chinese celadon jade ewer and cover, carved with two rams' heads, the spout a larger ram's head, the handle with scroll ends, contained in a fitted silk box.

7.25in (18.3cm)

$5,250-6,000 **WW**

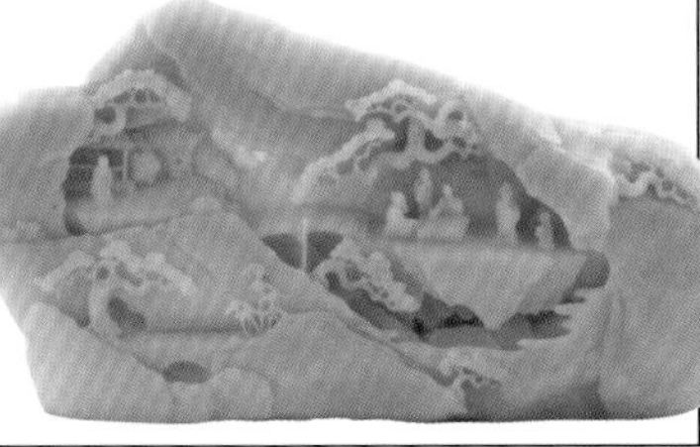

A large modern Chinese pale celadon jade boulder carving, depicting a mountain with figures, pagodas and pine trees.

18.25in (46cm) wide

$7,500-9,000 **WW**

A 19thC Chinese coral vase and cover, the vase emerging from waves, carved with two scaly dragons contesting a flaming pearl, with two further dragons, the cover's finial a phoenix.

7in (18cm) high

$16,500–21,000 **WW**

A 19thC Chinese coral carving of a boy.

3.25in (8cm) high

$3,000-4,000 **WW**

A 19thC coral 'phoenix and tree' group, the phoenix's plumage entwined around the branches.

9in (23cm) high

$5,250-6,000 **L&T**

A 19thC Chinese amber vase and cover, carved with seven boys, holding auspicious objects, an eighth boy to the cover, and with a hare, a three-legged toad and a phoenix.

4in (10.5cm) high

$15,000–18,000 **WW**

A Lapis Lazuli inkstone and cover in the shape of a cat, the cover carved in low-relief with the animal's snout and paws, the interior with grey inclusions and carved with a bat carrying a string of cash, with gilt inscription to the underside of the cover.

Lapis lazuli is a deep blue semi-precious stone that has been prized since antiquity for its intense color. Lapis takes an excellent polish and can be made into jewelry, carvings, boxes, mosaics, and ornaments. It was also ground and processed to make the pigment ultramarine, widely used during the Renaissance in frescoes and oil painting.

5.75in (14cm) long

$5,250-6,750 **L&T**

A Qing dynasty carved Lapis Lazuli boulder, carved with a mountainous landscape with pine trees, and a deer resting by a stream, two figures and a crane near a pavilion.

8in (20cm) long

$8,250-9,750 **L&T**

A large 20thC Chinese lapis lazuli model of a water buffalo, the stone with pyrite inclusions.

8.5in (21cm) long

$6,000-7,500 **WW**

An 18thC Chinese soapstone figure of Shou Lao, holding a fruiting peach branch.

10in (25.5cm)

$9,000-10,500 **WW**

An 18thC Chinese white soapstone model of Guanyin, with a small child and a parrot, a four character mark which reads 'Wang Zhu', jing xie, and with a seal mark for the artist.

This rare figure relates to a small group of carvings by Wang Zhu, an artist prevalent in the Qianlong reign, which includes an elaborate soapstone mountain in the Tianjin Museum, China.

6.5in (16cm) high

$112,500–127,500 **WW**

An 18th/19thC Qing dynasty soapstone figure of Guanyin, holding a ruyi scepter.

9in (23cm) high

$3,000-4,500 **L&T**

A pair of late 18th/early 19thC carved and stained soapstone musician figures, with painted decoration.

3.75in (9cm) high

$6,000–9,000 **L&T**

A Qing dynasty soapstone seal, carved with a dragon with a flaming pearl in high relief.

3.5in (8.5cm) high

$4,500-6,000 **L&T**

A 19thC Chinese soapstone model of the dragon luohan, holding a pearl, with a dragon emerging from a bowl, the base carved with a poem, including an inscription for the Qianlong reign.

6.5in (16cm) high

$4,500-6,000 **WW**

Judith Picks

Jeweled collars or torques were listed in the Huangchao Liqi Tushi (The Regulations for Ceremonial Paraphernalia of the Qing Dynasty) as an essential part of court dress for members of the Imperial family and noblewomen. Called a ling yue, they are made in gold or silver-gilt and set with semi-precious stones such as pearls, coral, rubies and lapis lazuli, the number of stones determining rank. They are worn and fastened with silk braids which hang down the back, ending in drop pendants which match the stones of the collar. The Huangchao Liqi Tushi, prepared for the Qianlong Emperor c1759, illustrates a ling yue, set with eleven pearls.

An extremely rare Chinese Yongzheng/Qianlong Imperial Beijing enamel and gold filigree ling yue, the crescent-shaped torque set with twelve Beijing enamel plaques, each painted with two stylized phoenix, with seven replacement cultured and simulated pearls mounted in elaborate gold filigree, tooled as scrolling flames or lingzhi.

7.5in (19cm)

$400,000-450,000 **WW**

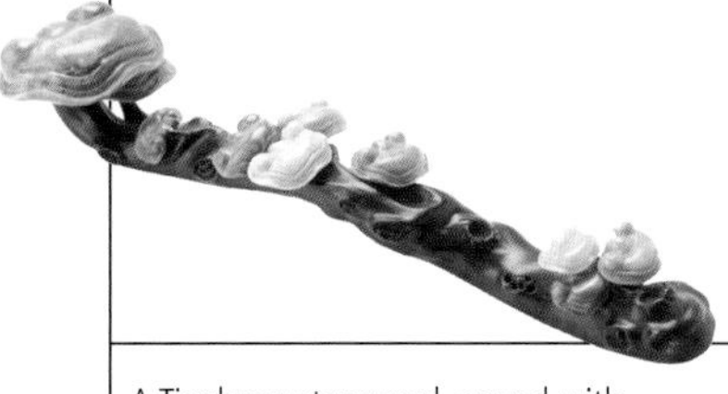

A late Qing Dynasty Chinese hardstone and wood ruyi scepre, of naturalistic form,

14.5in (37cm) long

$1,800–2,700 **L&T**

A Tianhuan stone seal, carved with mythological animals.

The seal reads 'Over 10,000 miles of rivers and mountains the goose's claws have flown; throughout a skyful of wind and moonlight the horse's hooves run free', signed with Gao Shixian's style name 'Ke'an/Ko'an at the Pavilion of the Plum King' and inscribed for the 29th year of the Guangxu period, winter.

1903 *3in (7cm) high*

$4,500-6,000 **L&T**

A Chinese Kangxi bamboo bitong, carved in relief with the Er Qiao Gong Du, of the two Qiao sisters reading together.

This scene, from the 'The Romance of the Three Kingdoms', tells the famous story of two beautiful and virtuous sisters, who both lost their husbands in battle, never remarrying and remaining faithful in memory of their husbands.

1662-1722 *5.5in (13.6cm) high*

$37,500–45,000 **WW**

SHOU LAO

A large rosewood Shou Lao, the immortal in robes inlaid with cranes, clouds and grapes in silvered metal, holding a peach and on a rockwork base, staff missing.

Shou Lou was the Chinese god of longevity. Usually recognizable by his tall, over sized forehead, representing wisdom and long beard representing long life. Attributes include peach and a staff, both symbols of longevity themselves. The God of Longevity (Shou) along with the God of Wealth (Lu) God of Prosperity (Fu) are known as the 'Three Stargods' or San xing.

1850-1875 *33.5in (85cm) high*

$7,500-9,000 **SWO**

A bamboo brush pot (Bitong), with cyclical date probably 1829, carved with literati served by a girl at a table, with rocks and pine, bamboo, maple and other trees, engraved Xishan Huiyou Tu, Jichou Nian Xia, Meilin Zhi (Picture of Meeting Friends at Xishan, Summer of Year Jichou, made by Meilin).

The three possible cyclical dates are 1769, 1829 and 1889, 1829 seeming most likely. The renowned mid-Qing bamboo carver, Wang Meilin, came from a family who ran a bamboo carving business for four generations; he was active from Qianlong to Jiaqing.

7in (17.5cm) high

$1,800-3,000 **SWO**

A late 18thC 'Hundred Boys' large zitan brush pot, carved with figures on a rocky mountainside below clouds, one side with the boys entertaining a dragon, natural split, base missing.

The Hundred Boys is a popular Chinese subject and lends itself to the imagination of the painter, sculpture or craftsman. No other Zitan brush pot of this importance seems to be recorded. The carving of numerous small figures - often Buddhist monks, or families - on a rocky mountainside is familiar from Canton carving of ivory card cases, fan guards and boxes.

9.75in (24.5cm)

$270,000–330,000 **SWO**

A pair of Japanese carved bamboo brushpots, Meiji period, carved with a toad on a tightrope with another toad, with a monkey beating a drum.

6.75in (17cm) high

$1,800–4,000 **L&T**

A Japanese Meiji period boxwood and ivory okimono, of a family group in a boat, the wood boat inset with red lacquer panels and a red lacquer signature.

19in (48cm) long, 10.25in (26cm) long

$4,500-5,250 **L&T**

A Japanese Meiji period carved wood okimono, modeled as boys climbing atop an elephant, signed to underside.

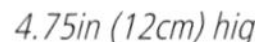

4.75in (12cm) high

$4,000–5,250 **L&T**

A Meiji/Taisho period boxwood figure group, carved as two comical men in robes.

4.75in (11.5cm) high

$1,800-3,000 **L&T**

A 17th-18thC bamboo brush pot, well carved with the drunken poet, Li Bai, seated beneath a pine tree, with a wine cup by his side, an attendant standing behind him, some cracks to the body, wear to the interior.

5.25in (13.5cm) high

$6,000–9,000 **DN**

A Chinese Qianlong Imperial red cinnabar lacquer box and cover, carved with panels of seasonal flowers, inset in jade, hardstones, ivory and turquoise with auspicious things, the inlays to the cover perhaps later additions.

1736-95 *12.5in (31.5cm) diam*

$37,500–45,000 **WW**

An 18thC Chinese red cinnabar lacquer box and cover, carved with a ferocious scaly dragon writhing amongst crashing waves.

4in (10cm) diam

$33,000–37,500 **WW**

An 18thC Chinese cinnabar lacquer tray, carved with figures crossing a bridge beneath pine tree whilst two ladies watch from a house.

13in (33cm) diam

$37,500–45,000 **L&T**

A Chinese red cinnabar lacquer ruyi scepter, decorated with figures, bats, stylized foliage and Buddhistic symbols, six character Qianlong mark.

19in (48cm) long

$12,000–18,000 **L&T**

An 18thC Chinese red cinnabar lacquer box and cover, decorated with a seated elderly gentleman playing a pipe above onlooking figures, the base decorated with deer, herons and other animals, six character Qianlong mark to base.

10.5in (27cm) diam

$45,000–52,500 **ROS**

A massive pair of 19thC Chinese red cinnabar lacquer vases, carved with five-clawed dragons contesting flaming pearls of wisdom, reserved on scrolling lotus flowerheads.

25.25in (64cm) high

$24,000–30,000 **WW**

A cinnabar lacquer horse, with a saddle carved with lotus and phoenix and mounted with jade cabochons, the bridle and harness mounted with jade, malachite and turquoise.

37in (94cm) high

$22,500-30,000 **L&T**

A pair of 19thC Chinese red cinnabar lacquer boxes and covers, carved with peony flowers and foliage on a soft metal base.

5in (12.5cm) wide

$1,800-2,250 **WW**

A Qing dynasty cinnabar lacquer box and cover, carved with chrysanthemum and scrolling foliage.

6.5in (16cm) diam

$1,800–4,000 **L&T**

ESSENTIAL REFERENCE - DOLL'S DAY

Hina-matsuri, or Doll's Day, takes place on 3rd March. This Japanese custom of displaying dolls began in the Heian period, with the belief that they had the ability to contain bad spirits. Dolls made of straw were kept in the house and then sent down river taking any bad spirits with them. By the Edo and Meiji periods, this custom had evolved into a much more elaborate tradition of collecting dolls dressed in traditional Heian costume, miniature furniture and objects related to the Imperial court. These would be displayed in strictly structured tiers illustrating the hierarchy of the court officials, attendants and entertainers all under the gaze of the Emperor and Empress who occupied the top tier. In the late 19thC collecting hina-ningyo became popular in the West with the opening of trade with Japan.

A collection of Japanese Ningyo dolls from Meiji period, comprising an Emperor and Empress, two musicians and singer, two ministers, a court lady in traditional dress with miniature lacquer screens, furniture and accessories, and with six figures of bejin and geishas.

$15,000–22,500 L&T

An 18th/19thC Japanese gold lacquer three-case inro, inlaid with aogai, together with an ivory netsuke in the shape of a man carrying a pheasant.

3in (7.5cm) high

$1,800-2,100 WW

An early 19thC Japanese gold lacquer four-case inro, decorated with a red oni on the nashiji ground, the reverse with a woman holding a fan, together with a bead ojime and ivory manju netsuke, signed Jokasai.

3in (8cm) high

$1,800-3,000 WW

A Meiji/Taisho period single-case lacquer inro, decorated with egrets in raised takamaki-e, with signature inscription.

3.5in (8.5cm) wide

$900-1,200 L&T

A lacquer five-case inro, decorated in gold lacquer and kirigane, with red lacquer koro, signed Kajikawa in gold, saku (made), minor chips.

The Kajikawa family worked as lacquerers in the late Edo period. The seal character on the koro may read 'ho' (fragrance) - appropriate on an incense burner.

c1800 *3.75in (9.5cm)*

$1,800-3,000 SWO

A 19thC Japanese lacquer box, decorated with the Buitenzorg Palace, the interior with four small boxes and one large lidded box, containing a collection of approximately 360 Chinese Mother-of-pearl gaming counters.

Bogor is a city on the Island of Java. It was named Buitenzorg by the Dutch who used it as their administrative center during the 19thC. The Buitenzorg Palace was built from August 1744 as a country retreat for the Dutch Governors. This building was substantially damaged by an earthquake in 1834. The palace was rebuilt in its present form in 1856, this time with only one storey instead of the original three, as a precaution against further earthquakes.

$1,800-3,000 ROS

ESSENTIAL REFERENCE - SNUFF

Tobacco was introduced by the Portuguese to the court at Beijing some time during the mid-to late 16thC. It was originally smoked in pipes before the establishment of the Qing dynasty. The use of snuff and snuff bottles spread through the upper class, and by the end of the 17thC it had become a part of social ritual to use snuff. This lasted through most of the 18thC. Eventually, the trend spread into the rest of the country and into every social class. It was common to offer a pinch of snuff as a way to greet friends and relatives. Snuff bottles soon became an object of beauty and a way to represent status. The highest status went to whoever had the rarest and finest snuff bottle. The peak of snuff bottle manufacture was during the 18thC. The use of snuff increased and decreased with the rise and fall of the Qing dynasty and died away soon after the establishment of the Republic of China.

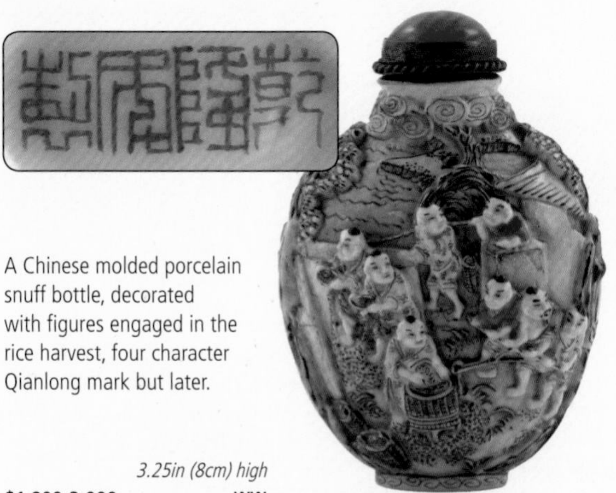

A Chinese molded porcelain snuff bottle, decorated with figures engaged in the rice harvest, four character Qianlong mark but later.

3.25in (8cm) high
$1,800-3,000 WW

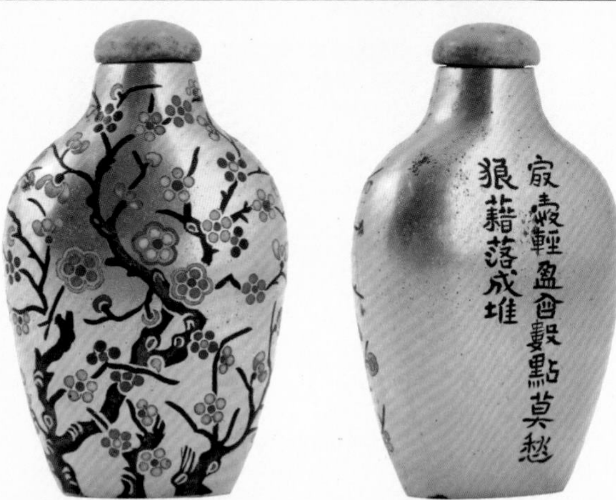

A rare Chinese Beijing Palace workshops inscribed champlevé enamel snuff bottle, decorated with prunus branches, the reverse with two lines of calligraphy from a poem written by the Qianlong emperor.

The calligraphy reads 'zui ai qing yin han shu dian mo chou lang ji luo cheng dui' (you feel the loneliness just as falling plum blossom petals).

1736-95 *2.75in (7cm) high*
$52,500–60,000 WW

A Chinese porcelain snuff bottle, painted with seven cockerels, the base with a six character Yongzheng mark.

The cockerel represents reliability, and is the epitome of fidelity and punctuality and the number seven represents togetherness and is a lucky number in relationships.

c1900 *3in (7.5cm) high*
$1,800-2,250 WW

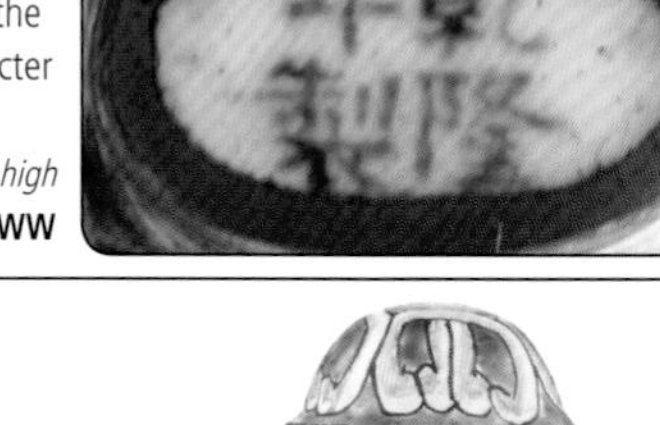

A Chinese Beijing enamel snuff bottle, painted with European ladies, a small child and a dog in landscapes, the stopper gilded, four character Qianlong mark.

1736-95 *2.75in (6.5cm) high*
$4,000-4,500 WW

A Chinese enamel-on-copper snuff bottle, painted with puppies, birds and a pine tree, blue four character seal mark to base.

2.5in (6cm) high
$1,500-2,100 L&T

A Chinese Qing dynasty moss agate snuff bottle, the green stem with red and white inclusions.

2.75in (6.5cm) high

$750-1,000 **L&T**

A 19thC Chinese agate snuff bottle, with shaded brown, russet and red inclusions, with faux handles carved in the form of mythical beasts.

3in (7.5cm) high

$1,150-1,300 **L&T**

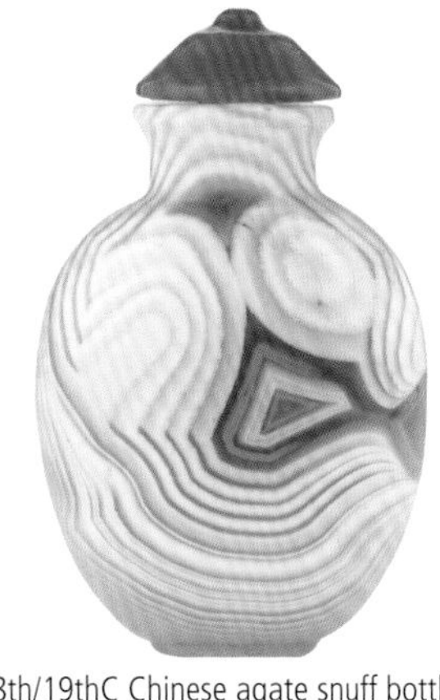

An 18th/19thC Chinese agate snuff bottle, with white, grey and brown striations.

2.5in (6cm) high

$1,200-1,500 **L&T**

A Chinese Qing dynasty shadow agate snuff bottle, with sepia carving depicting two figures under a bonsai tree.

3in (7cm) high

$900-1,200 **L&T**

A Chinese Qing dynasty cameo agate snuff bottle, carved with stylized figures and flame decoration, the honey-toned stem with darker inclusions.

2.5in (6cm) high

$1,800-2,400 **L&T**

A Chinese cameo agate snuff bottle, perhaps Suzhu, carved with a monkey amongst fruiting peach branches by a rock, with lighter agate domed stopper.

c1750-1850 *3in (7.5cm) high*

$2,700-3,300 **TEN**

A 19thC 'peanut' agate snuff bottle, carved with peanuts, peapods, peas and flowers, stem-like stopper.

3in (7cm) high

$700-850 **L&T**

A 19thC Chinese ivory snuff bottle, carved depicting Yu Boya visiting Zhong Ziqi to discuss the music of qin.

3.75in (9cm) high

$3,000-4,500 **WW**

A Chinese Qing dynasty burgaute lacquer snuff bottle, decorated with figures by a pavilion, the reverse with a bird and prunus blossom, four character mark to base.

3.5in (8.3cm) high

$4,500-5,250 **L&T**

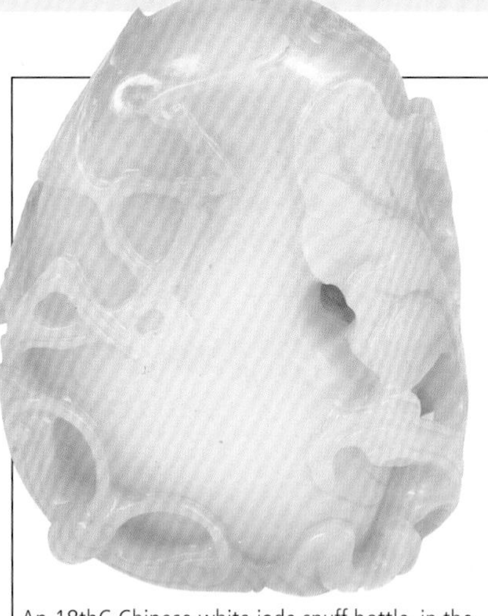

An 18thC Chinese white jade snuff bottle, in the form of a gourd, of pale celadon tone with russet inclusion, carved in relief and pierced with a butterfly and leafy tendrils.

2.25in (6cm) high

$22,500-30,000 **MAB**

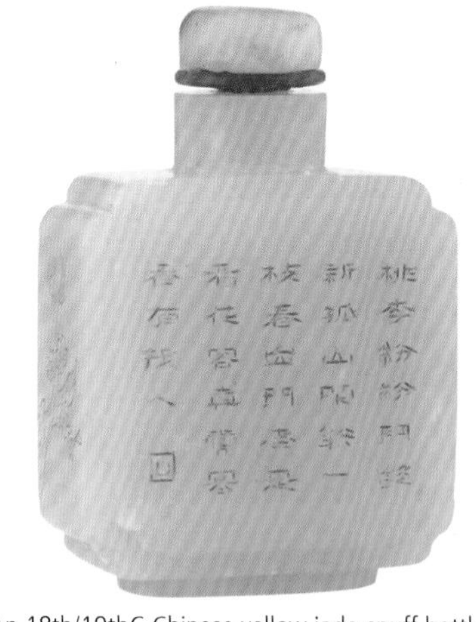

An 18th/19thC Chinese yellow jade snuff bottle, with gilt calligraphy, also gilt bamboo and prunus decoration, three character mark to base.

2.5in (6cm) high

$1,800–4,000 **L&T**

An 18th/19thC Chinese jade snuff bottle, carved in relief to one side with a deer beneath a pine tree and a lingzhi fungus, the stone a creamy-brown tone with darker striations.

3in (7.5cm) high

$2,000-2,400 **WW**

An 18th/19thC yellow jade snuff bottle, with calcite inclusions, the red stopper with silver collar.

3in (7.8cm) high

$1,800-3,000 **L&T**

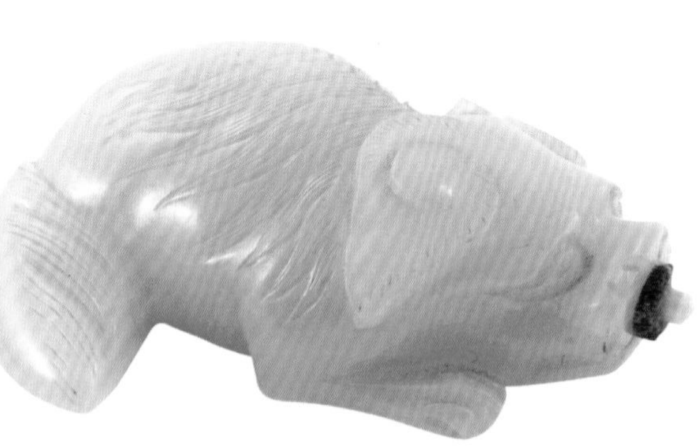

An unusual 19thC Chinese white jade snuff bottle, carved as a crouching Pekingese dog.

2.25in (5.5cm) high

$22,500-30,000 **WW**

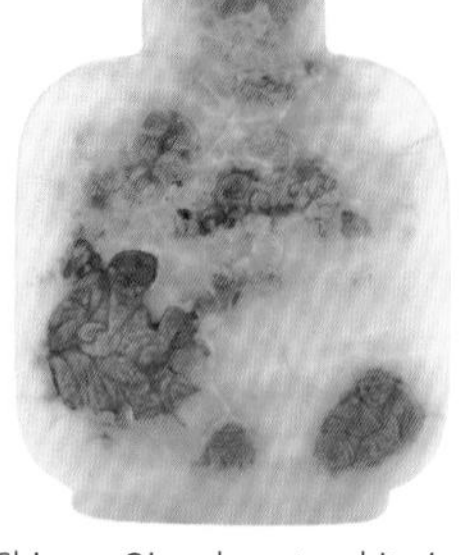

A Chinese Qing dynasty white jade snuff bottle, with russet inclusions and caned decoration of a dignitary seated with an attendant, flowering peony and bird carving to reverse.

29.75in (75cm) high

$1,500-2,250 **L&T**

A Chinese white jade snuff bottle, with incised gilded calligraphy, gilt four character mark to base.

3.25in (8cm) high

$1,800–2,700 **L&T**

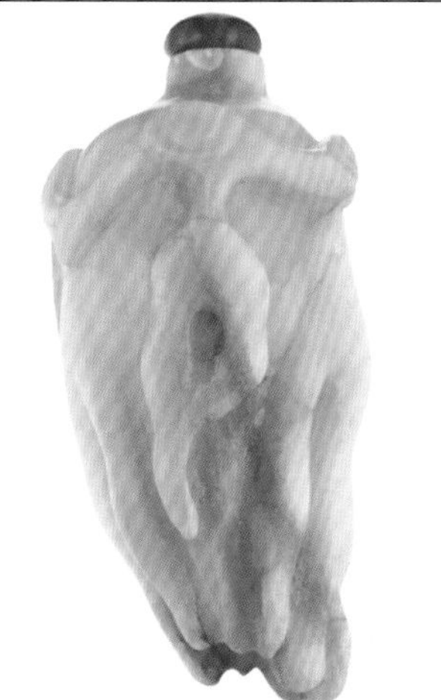

A 19thC Chinese Qing dynasty celadon jade snuff bottle, modeled as a citron.

3.25in (8cm) high

$1,500-2,250 **L&T**

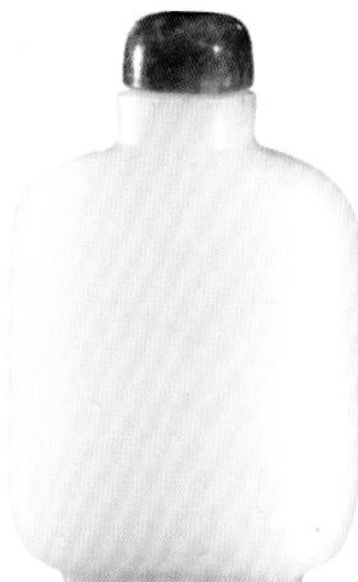

A 19th/20thC Chinese white jade snuff bottle, one side carved with Da Mo, the other with the tiger Luohan.

The monk Bodidharma, or Da Mo in Chinese, is the man credited with establishing Zen Buddhism in China, approximately one thousand five hundred years ago.

3in (7.5cm) high

$8,250-9,750 **WW**

A 19thC Chinese hair crystal snuff bottle, carved with two bats in flight amidst clouds above rockwork, a fan-shaped inclusion to one side, the jade stopper mounted in silver-colored metal.

3.25in (8cm)

$4,000-4,500 WW

A late 19thC smoky crystal carved snuff bottle, with eight facets carved with gilt characters, the neck with a ruyi collar, with mustard-yellow agate stopper.

2.75in (6.8cm) high

$900-1,200 L&T

A late 19th/early 20thC Chinese enamel-on-glass snuff bottle, painted with two birds, the reverse with peonies, with a tourmaline stopper, blue Qianlong four character seal mark to base.

3in (7cm) high

$1,150-1,300 L&T

A Chinese white overlay ruby glass snuff bottle, carved with tree shrews on flowering branches.

3.75in (9cm) high

$900-1,200 L&T

A Chinese Qianlong yellow glass water pot, carved with peony and prunus, with a fitted hardwood stand carved as a large lotus leaf, a seed pod and a snail shell forming the feet.

1736-95 *2.75in (6.8cm) high*

$15,000–22,500 WW

A pair of Qianlong Peking blue and gilt glass bowls, decorated in gilt with dragons and blossoming branches, with wood stands, four character Qianlong mark.

4.5in (11cm) diam

$900-1,200 L&T

A Peking glass vase and cover, molded with lotus petal, iris and exotic birds, seal mark to underside.

8.5in (21cm) high

$750-1,000 L&T

A Peking yellow glass vase, with allover basketweave decoration.

3.5in (8.5cm) high

$1,500-2,250 L&T

A Peking glass jar and cover, with globular diamond-cut green-to-white sides.

7.5in (19cm) wide

$1,200-1,800 L&T

ORIENTAL

ESSENTIAL REFERENCE - NETSUKE

Netsuke are decorative 'toggles' that were used to suspend small storage containers, such as pouches or boxes (inro), below the sash of a kimono. They were in everyday use throughout the Edo and Meiji periods of Japanese history but fell out of use with the kimono. Netsuke, like the inro and ojime, evolved over time from being strictly utilitarian into objects of great artistic merit and an expression of extraordinary craftsmanship. Such objects have a long history reflecting the important aspects of Japanese folklore and life. Netsuke production was most popular during the Edo period in Japan, around 1615–1868. From the middle Edo period onward, ivory was one of the most popular materials for netsuke. This fashion probably came from China. They were also often made of wood, as well as amber stone, coral, tortoiseshell and even cast-bronze.

Though most netsuke were less than five centimetres high, they were carved with extraordinary detail: the hairs of a tiger's coat would be individually incised; hidden parts, such as individual toes and fingers were all perfectly reproduced.

- **Today, the art lives on, and some modern works can command high prices.**

A Japanese boxwood netsuke of Daruma, standing on a palm frond as he sails to paradise, signed Chikudo.
1850-1900 *2.25in (5.6cm) high*
$1,150-1,450 **WW**

A late 19th/early 20thC Japanese standing boxwood netsuke carved as a Sarumawashi, his monkey rests on top of the bundle lying across his shoulder, the eyes of the figure and the monkey inlaid, unsigned.
4in (9.5cm) high
$1,500-1,800 **WW**

A mid-19thC Japanese boxwood netsuke, in the form of a female mask, signed Shumin with kao.
2.25in (5.7cm) high
$900-1,200 **WW**

An 18thC Japanese wood netsuke of a Dutchman, holding a cockerel, his eyes inlaid with horn, unsigned.
3.25in (8.5cm) high
$1,150-1,450 **WW**

A Japanese Edo period boxwood netsuke, carved as a ferocious-looking shishi protecting a brocade ball, its eyes inlaid, the base signed Tomokazu.
1615-1868 *2in (5cm) high*
$1,500-2,250 **WW**

A Japanese Meiji period fruitwood netsuke, carved as the thwarted rat catcher, the eyes inlaid, unsigned.
1868-1912 *2.5in (6.5cm)*
$3,000-4,500 **WW**

A Japanese Meiji boxwood erotic netsuke, carved as a nude beauty sitting by a basket, signed Mingyoku.
1868-1912 *2.25in (5.5cm) high*
$2,700-3,300 **WW**

A 19thC Japanese wood netsuke of an ape, clutching a peach in its paws, the eyes inlaid, unsigned.
2in (5cm) high
$1,000–1,500 **WW**

A 20thC Japanese wood netsuke, carved in the form of a mokugyo, itself formed as a dragon fish, signed 'Ikkyu to with kao'.
1.25in (3c m) high
$600-750 **WW**

UMIMATSU

Umimatsu translates as 'Tree of the Ocean' which, given the allusive nature of the Japanese language, does not accurately describe the material. Supposedly brought up from the very depths of the ocean, it is thought to be a form of coral and, indeed, there are concentric rings where branches could be. However, this would also be true were the material to be fossilized wood, another suggested material. This, like jet, is warm to the touch (as is umimatsu), whereas coral is cold.

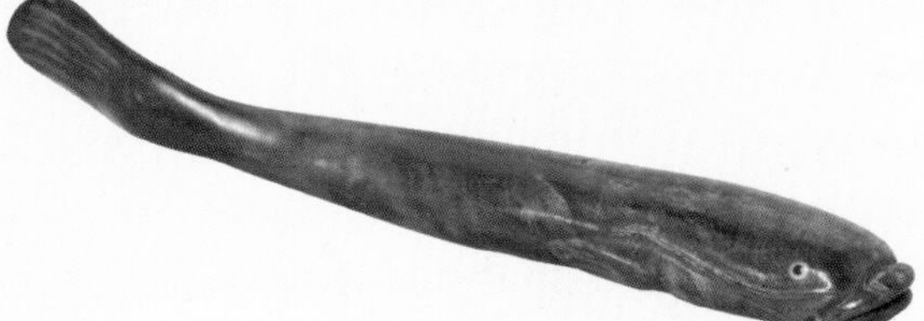

A late 18th/early 19thC Umimatsu Obi-Hasami netsuke, in the form of an earthquake fish, its eyes inlaid in abalone and black horn.
6.5in (16.5cm) long
$3,300-3,900 **SWO**

A 19thC Japanese ivory netsuke, depicting a naked man, the figure with a pained expression as he pulls his fundoshi too tight, unsigned.

2.5in (6m) high

$1,150-1,300 **WW**

An 18thC Japanese ivory netsuke, in the shape of Tekkai Sennin, holding a gourd over his shoulders, unsigned.

3.75in (9.5cm) high

$1,800-2,250 **WW**

An 18thC Japanese ivory netsuke, carved as Chokaro Sennin, holding a gourd across his shoulders with a boy on top, unsigned.

3.75in (9.5cm) high

$2,000-2,400 **WW**

An 18thC Japanese ivory netsuke of a sennin, wearing mugwort leaves, holding a hossu fly whisk and a lotus flowerhead, a smaller figure reading a makimono amongst the petals, unsigned.

3.75in (9cm) high

$1,800-2,250 **WW**

A late 18th/early 19thC ivory netsuke, depicting a Dutchman stooping to gather up two chickens.

1.75in (4cm) high

$850-975 **CHEF**

A Japanese Meiji period ivory netsuke of an oni, the demon digging for treasure, a large pot half-buried at its feet, signed Gyokuzan in a lacquer reserve.

1868-1912 *2in (5cm) high*

$1,500-2,100

WW

A Japanese Meiji period fruitwood netsuke, carved as a blind masseur holding his hypertrophied testicle, a tumour on the back of his head, his lifeless eye and teeth inlaid with shell or ivory, signed Gyokkei in an ivory cartouche at the base.

In a recent article of the International Netsuke Society Journal, J Kurstin and Y Yoshida described the subject as suffering from Elephantiasis, a disease that is characterized by the thickening of the skin.

1868-1912 *2in (4.5cm) high*

$1,500-2,100 **WW**

A Japanese Edo ivory netsuke of Shoki, the demon-queller, his arm raised as he struggles with a small oni on his shoulder, another one at his feet, unsigned.

3.5in (8.5cm) high

$1,200–1,400 **WW**

A 19thC Japanese ivory netsuke, carved as two shishi fighting, signed Tomochika.

1.75in (4.5cm) high

$2,400-3,000 **WW**

A Japanese ivory netsuke, carved as a water buffalo, two character signature.

2.5in (6cm) long

$550-700 **WW**

A Japanese ivory netsuke, carved in the form of two puppies, their eyes inlaid with dark horn, signed Hidechika.

c1870 *1.75in (4cm) wide*

$1,200-1,500 **WW**

A 19thC Japanese ivory netsuke of a rat, holding a chestnut, inlaid eyes, signed 'Masatsugu'.

1.5in (3.5cm) long

$4,500-5,250 **BELL**

A 19thC Japanese ivory netsuke, carved as a seated tiger, the eyes later inlaid with opals, unsigned.

1.75in (4cm) long

$400-450 **WW**

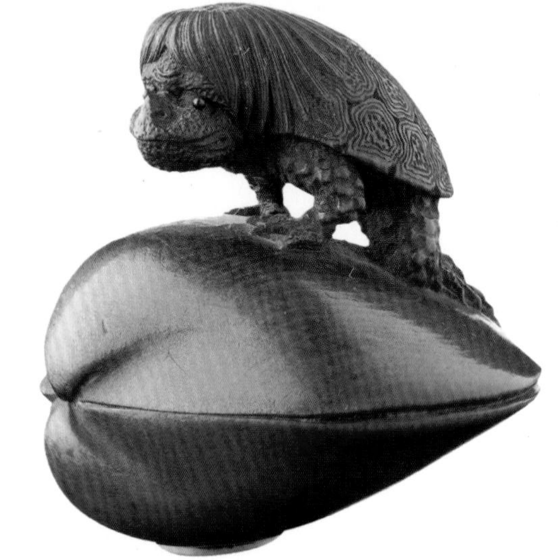

A 19thC Suketada, Takayama wood netsuke of Kappa, signed.

$6,000–9,000 **L&T**

A Rantei marine ivory netsuke, carved as a goat with inlaid eyes.

2in (5cm) wide

$1,150-1,300 **CHEF**

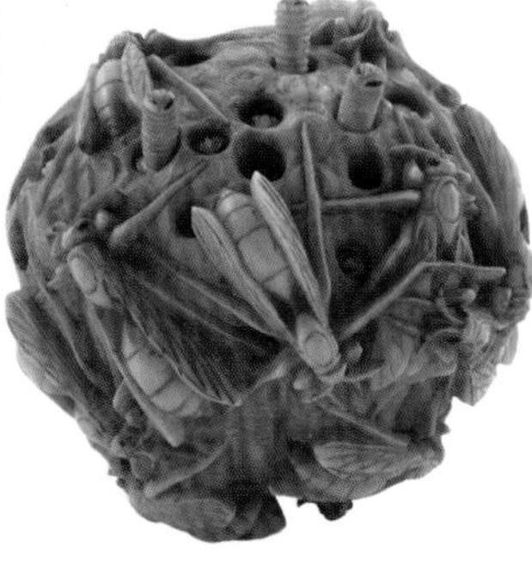

A Japanese Meiji ivory netsuke, of a broken wasps' nest, the insects crawling over the honeycomb, six of them articulated and protruding from their cells, the eyes of the adults inlaid with horn, signed Tadakazu/Chuichi.

1868-1912 *2in (5.4cm) high*

$6,000-7,500 **WW**

ESSENTIAL REFERENCE - SYMBOLS

The Twelve Symbols of Imperial Authority were rooted in ancient customs and their origination is unclear. Each symbol had a specific meaning and when appearing together represented the emperor's authority and unquestionable sovereignty. They are the Sun, Moon, Constellation, Fu symbol, Dragon, Axe-head, Flowery Creature, Sacrificial Vessels, Water Plant, Flames, Grain, and Rock. Their placement on imperial robes was strictly regulated as established by the Qianlong emperor in the 18thC. While some members of the imperial family were allowed to wear garments embroidered with combinations of the Twelve Symbols, only the Emperor wore garments displaying all of them. This strict adherence to custom relaxed toward the end of the Qing Dynasty, and it is known that the Empress Dowager Cixi, who named herself regent and essentially ruled China during the Tongzhi and Guangxu Emperor's reigns, wore robes bearing the twelve symbols.

- **It can be assumed that the present lot, which is a woman's robe, was designed for her use.**

A late Qing dynasty rare dowager Empress Cixi Imperial twelve-symbol festive summer 'dragon' robe (Long Pao), embroidered with the Twelve Symbols of Imperial Authority and nine five-clawed dragons above blue standing waves at the hem.
$112,500–127,500 L&T

A late Qing dynasty Ji Fiu Imperial silk embroidered 'dragon' robe, embroidered with ten dragons, cranes, bats, flames and clouds.
$7,500-9,000 L&T

A 19thC Chinese silk-embroidered panel, decorated with figures playing games, music, beneath a band decorated with a basket of flowers and a bat.
90.25in (229cm) long
$9,000-10,500 WW

A Chinese symbol robe in blue Kossu silk, with gauze dragons and flaming pearls with cranes in flight.
53in (135cm) long
$7,500-9,000 HT

A 19thC Qing dynasty Imperial Kesi ground formal court robe (Chi'fu), woven with a gold dragon, with dragon roundel damask silk sleeves and striped borders.
$30,000–37,500 L&T

A 19thC Chinese blue gauze court 'dragon robe', jifu, depicting nine five-clawed dragons with flaming pearls, amidst lingzhi shaped clouds, auspicious emblems and bats above foaming waves and lishui stripes, slightly worn.
54.5in (138.5cm) high
$5,250-6,000 DN

ESSENTIAL REFERENCE - A HANGING

Because of its large size, the panel would have surely been hung in a Buddhist temple in Tibet after been assembled from panels of Chinese silk garments and other articles that were sent from China as diplomatic gifts from as early as the 13thC.

- **The central, large velvet panel is very rare; it would have probably hung in the Imperial halls or temples. The squares were probably intended for a Ming dragon robe, or chaofu. The borders were probably intended for 17thC bed hangings and bed covers for the Western market. In their original shape, these covers probably enclosed a large central medallion in the field and quarter medallion in the corners. After reaching Tibet, many of these textiles were donated by the aristocrats as acts of devotion to monasteries and were thus completely transformed to create brilliant patchworks gracing the altars, sutra covers and mandalas.**
- **Whereas woven dragons were suggestive of the emperor's presence, in Tibet, they were re-interpreted as majestic signs of the Buddha's teachings.**

A rare 17thC transitional Ming/Qing dynasty large hanging, depicting two large swirling dragons surrounded by a lotus border, the outer borders are made from further dragon panels woven in the Kesi technique and parts of a late Ming period costume (Chaofu) in the Imperial color of incense, (jin huang) embroidered with dragons and mythical creatures.
144in (366cm) high
$19,500–24,000 DN

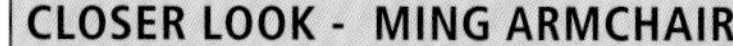

CLOSER LOOK - MING ARMCHAIR

A pair of 17thC Ming dynasty yumu armchairs, above carved and shaped spandrels, the rounded legs joined by stepped stretchers and a well-worn footrest above a plain apron.

Chairs such as these, carved in a naive style with 'architectural' taper, were made in Shanxi province during the late Ming period.

39in (99cm) high

$1,800–4,000 **L&T**

A pair of 19thC Chinese hongmu armchairs, the projecting back panel carved with two Buddhistic vases.

35in (89cm) high

$2,700-3,300 **FELL**

A Chinese mid-Qing dynasty huanghuali master's armchair, the back set with a grey and white marble panel with stylized linghzi open scroll spacers.

42.25in (107cm) high

$6,000-7,500 **L&T**

A pair of Chinese Qing dynasty jichimu horseshoe armchairs, the curved arms with scrolled handholds.

40in (101cm) high

$6,750-8,250 **L&T**

A pair of 19thC Jumu spindle-back armchairs, the top rails carved as ruyi heads with cloud scrolls and flower motifs.

31.5in (80cm) high

$1,200-1,500 **L&T**

A pair of 19thC Qing dynasty Chinese hongmu mother of pearl and marble top stools.

20.5in (52cm) high

$6,000-7,500 **L&T**

An 18th/19thC Chinese hardwood bench, carved with archaic key decoration.

41in (104cm) wide

$18,000-22,500 **JN**

An early 20thC huanghuali bench, the back with pierced scrolling panels and molded ruyi head opening, above an apron similarly pierced and carved.

54.5in (138cm) wide

$3,000-4,500 **L&T**

An 18th/19thC Chinese black lacquer table, the top decorated with flowering peony and a frieze carved with dragons.

30in (78cm) high

$1,800-2,250 **WW**

Judith Picks

We all love a bit of Imperial provenence and it certainly helps the price. This stand was estimated at $7,500–12,000 and sold for over $120,000. It is a good early date and exquisitely decorated. The top is set with a zitan panel, the border is inlaid with silver wire above a reticulated frieze decorated with stylized scrolling chilong - hornless dragons or mountain demons - the apron applied with four carved bats - a symbol of happiness and joy - and the legs with tassels suspended from eight mythical beasts, and the feet are the acanthus-capped. The book 'Classics of The Forbidden City, Imperial Furniture of The Qing Dynasties', no.344 has a closely related stand, which helps the Imperial provenance. Another lovely little touch is that the stand is accompanied by an original invoice. It was purchased from Kaneko's Art Studio, Yokohama, Japan, April 26th 1940 for $180.

A Chinese Imperial hardwood stand, Qianlong.

1736-95 *36.5in (92.5cm) high*

$120,000-135,000 **WW**

An early Qing dynasty Chinese hongmu stand, the top enclosed in a mitered frame.

31.25in (79cm) high

$3,000-4,500 **L&T**

A pair of Qing dynasty huanghuali tea tables, the cleated tops above a pierced frieze carved with fruiting vines and shou symbols.

The Chinese character shòu, representing longevity, is found on textiles, furniture, ceramics, jewelry and virtually every object conceivable. The shòu symbol may appear alone or be surrounded by flowers, bats, or other good luck symbols, but will always hold a central position.

31.25in (79cm) high

$5,250-6,750 **L&T**

A Qing dynasty hongmu and marble-top stand.

32in (81cm) high

$1,800–2,700 **L&T**

A late Qing dynasty stained softwood marble-top tea table, the top over a key and leaf carved frieze, raised on straight cabriole legs joined by a further marble tier on paw feet.

35in (89cm) high

$1,800–2,700 **L&T**

A good mid-Qing dynasty Chinese huanghuali and burr wood side table.

46in (117cm) wide

$6,000-7,500 **L&T**

A mid-Qing dynasty Chinese huanghuali high table, the top with scrolled ends fitted with drawers, above a pierced frieze carved with cloud scrolls and bi discs.

48in (122cm) wide

$11,500–13,000 **L&T**

A mid-Qing dynasty Chinese huanghuali kang table, the pierced frieze carved with dragons and clouds.

35.5in (90cm) wide

$1,500-2,100 **L&T**

A mid-Qing dynasty Chinese huanghuali kang table, the pierced frieze carved with dragons and clouds.

35.5in (90cm) wide

$1,500-2,100 **L&T**

A Ming dynasty lao-huali recessed leg altar table.

56in (142cm) wide

$12,000–13,500 **L&T**

A mid-Qing dynasty huanghuali and burrwood side table, the triple burrwood panel top with scrolled ends above an interlaced openwork frieze.

46in (117cm) wide

$6,750-8,250 **L&T**

A Qing dynasty jumu altar table, the single plank top above a pierced key pattern frieze with dragon carved corner brackets.

134.5in (341cm) long

$7,500–12,000 **L&T**

ESSENTIAL REFERENCE - CHINESE WOODS

Many of the hardwoods used in antique Chinese furniture were not native to China, but were introduced to China through trade.

- **Huali (rosewood) has a lighter hue than other rosewoods. It is one of the least valuable.**
- **Huanghuali (yellow rosewood) was popular for Ming scholar's furniture.**
- **Hongmu (mahogany) was often used for Qing dynasty furniture.**
- **Jichimu (native Chinese wood, known as 'chicken-wing wood') is an expensive, highly patterned wood, sometimes used for Ming and Qing palace furniture.**
- **Nanmu (southern elm) was popular in the Ming dynasty as it was resistant to decay.**
- **Zitan (red-purple sandal wood) is the most prized and expensive wood used in Ming and Qing furniture.**

A 19thC hongmu painting table, the cleated top raised on pedestal bases each with two short drawers.

49in (124cm) wide

$1,400-1,800 **L&T**

A 19thC Chinese Qing dynasty hongmu pedestal desk.

61in (155cm) wide

$3,000-4,000 **L&T**

An early 20thC Chinese rosewood writing desk, the frieze decorated with scrolling clouds, with drawers and compartments.

$1,800-3,000 **DN**

A 19thC Chinese Canton hardwood side-cabinet, shaped arched cresting above an asymmetric arrangement of shelves, niches and cupboards, pierced and carved throughout with scrolling leaves, prunus, bamboo and grasses.

c1880 *91.5in (232cm) high*

$18,000-22,500 **BAM**

A 19thC Qing dynasty Chinese Hongmu and mother of pearl inlay kang display shelves, the pierced and carved pediment with lotus and foliate scrolls, the shelves outlined in floral mother of pearl inlay.

48in (122cm) wide

$6,000-7,500 **L&T**

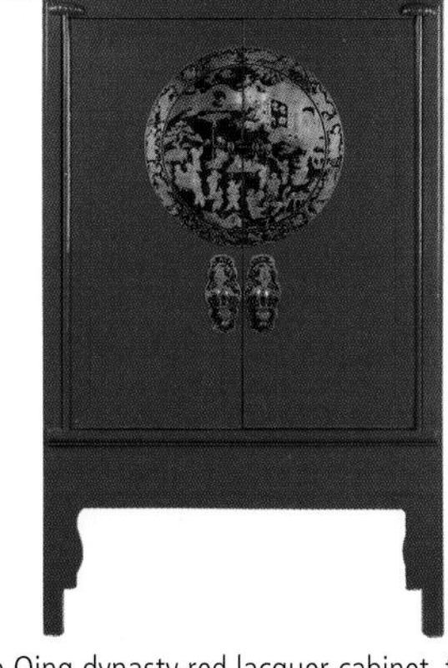

A late Qing dynasty red lacquer cabinet, the cornice with gilt foliate and linghzhi carvings, the doors centered by a black metal roundel depicting playing boys.

68.25in (173cm) high

$1,500-2,250 **L&T**

A 20thC Chinese carved, painted and giltwood side cabinet, carved doors carved with figures, within borders of trailing flowers and birds.

55.25in (140cm) high,

$600-750 **DN**

A 19thC Japanese carved hardwood and shibayama decorated cabinet-on-stand, the doors decorated with birds, vases, urns of flowers and figures in garden landscapes, heightened in ivory and gilt lacquer.

75.75in (192cm) high

$1,500-2,100 **TEN**

A Japanese Meiji period Shibayama cabinet, with sliding panel doors, open tiers, cupboard doors and drawers, inlaid and mounted with ivory, mother-of-pearl, and jade, the case carved with lions, dragons, and bamboo.

57.5in (146cm) high

$7,500-9,000 **L&T**

A late 19th/early 20thC Japanese black lacquer, specimen parquetry and mother-of-pearl inlaid cabinet-on-stand, gilt metal mounted throughout.

47.75in (121cm) high

$850-975 **DN**

A late 18thC Chinese export lacquer cabinet on stand, with two doors gilt with watery landscapes and with hammered gilt furniture opening to a theatrical galleried interior, considerable wear.

64.5in (164cm) high

$6,000-7,500 **SWO**

An 18thC Chinese lacquered cabinet-on-stand, the doors enclosing seven small drawers, two drawers below, with an English stand.

50in (127cm) high

$6,000-7,500 **CHOR**

A Qing dynasty huanghuali cabinet on stand, originally the top part of a compound cabinet, the doors opening to shelves, the later stand carved with stylized scrolls, flowerheads and fruiting vines.

56in (142cm) wide

$7,500-9,000 **L&T**

A pair of 19thC Qing dynasty Chinese black lacquer cabinets, the doors decorated in gilt with court scenes with dignitaries and attendants.

78.75in (200cm) high

$8,250-9,750 **L&T**

A Chinese late Qing dynasty hardwood cabinet, with drawers and cupboard doors carved with scaly dragons amidst clouds, the brass handles and hinges engraved with dragons, phoenix, bats and shou characters.

38.25in (97cm) wide

$7,500-9,000 **WW**

An early 20thC Chinese carved padouk wood cabinet on stand, the doors carved with figures in a boat and mountainous landscapes in the foreground.

By repute this cabinet was commissioned around 1900 in Hong Kong for the Matheson family, almost certainly of Jardine Matheson & Co.

49.25in (125cm) wide

$3,000-4,000 **TEN**

A 20thC Chinese carved, painted and giltwood side cabinet, doors with figures, within borders of trailing flowers and birds.

55.25in (140cm) high

$600-750 **DN**

A 19thC Qing Dynasty Chinese embroidered silk, hongmu and Moher-of-pearl table screen, embroidered with peacocks, cranes, parrot and songbirds with a pine tree and peonies.

32.75in (83cm) high

$6,000-7,500 **L&T**

A pair of 19thC spinach-green jade screens for a scholarly table, carved with scholars engaging in leisurely pursuits and banner carrying attendants amid a lush mountainous landscapes, with a gilded inscription commemorating the birthday of the Qianlong Emperor (AD 1736-1795), on cloisonné stands.

11in (27.5cm) high

$7,500-9,000 **DN**

A late Qing dynasty/early Republic hardwood and ivory five-panel table screen, the panels carved with warriors within mountainous landscapes, framed with a wire-inlaid surround inset with further lotus scroll openwork panels.

19in (48cm) high

$21,000-27,000 **L&T**

An 18th/19thC Chinese twelve panel lacquer screen, with peacocks, cranes and other exotic birds amongst plants and flowers within a border filled with scholar's objects.

78.75in (200cm) high

$22,500-30,000 **L&T**

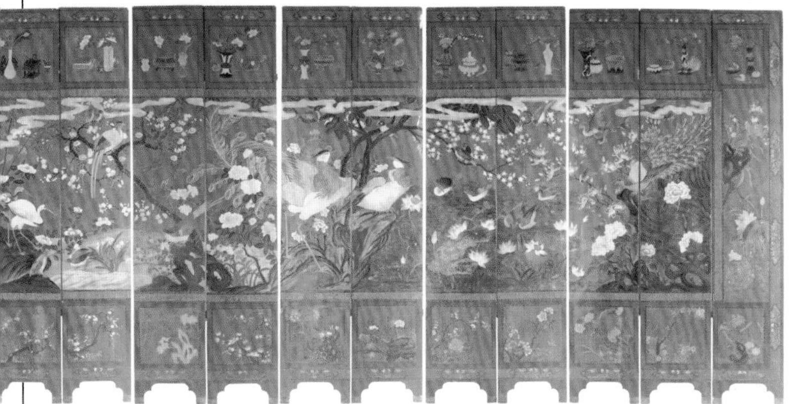

A large 19thC Chinese twelve panel double-sided red lacquer screen, carved and decorated with birds amidst peony, lotus and other flowers, the reverse with figures in an extensive mountainous pagoda landscape.

Provenance: Field Marshal Earl Kitchener of Khartoum (1850-1916).

110in (280cm) high

$7,500-9,000 **WW**

A late 19thC Chinese lacquer four fold screen, depicting ladies and boys in pavilions and gardens, the reverse with birds in trees and scholar's objects.

78.75in (200cm) high

$1,200-1,800 **L&T**

THE FURNITURE MARKET

The furniture market has continued to be very polarized. The 'brown furniture' market has continued to fall. Most auctioneers are reporting that the plain utilitarian 18thC and 19thC mahogany is proving difficult, if not impossible, to sell. Some dealers are quoting a substantial drop in prices and a general lack of interest. At the other end, quality furniture that is really top quality, fresh to the market and 'honest', continues to rise in value. It is not just age that determines the value of a piece of furniture, quality and condition and 'eye appeal' are all important factors.

The reasons for the decline in value of 'average', mid-range furniture is complex, most of it is down to fashion. Younger buyers believe that old mahogany furniture is just not 'cool' and does not fit into today's interiors. There is also a lack of really good quality examples on the market. Another problem is that vendors are reluctant to enter good antique furniture to auction while prices are depressed.

Pieces that are too bulky for modern interiors need to be of exceptional quality to attract buyers. There is no doubt that Georgian and especially Regency pieces sell better than their heavy Victorian counterparts. Also pieces like the davenport, Canterbury and bureau do not have any real function in today's interiors. 'Georgian brown' or just brown furniture has nose-dived in value whereas 20th century, especially mid-century modern, furniture has continued its renaissance. Many dealers record that American buyers are still not coming in their previous numbers and this has had a dramatic effect on export sales.

So has the low- to-mid range furniture market reached its nadir? Some of the prices achieved at auction are ridiculously low. These pieces are made of solid wood, by craftsmen and not merely fashioned out of MDF (Medium-density fibreboard- which is quite simply wood fibres, combined with wax and a resin binder). There are some indicators that prices may be beginning to climb slightly. People are being persuaded that 'antiques are green' and that recycling old furniture is more responsible than cutting down more of the Amazon jungle. Also with some prices so low, younger buyers are looking at auctions when furnishing their first flat or house. Sturdy, good-quality, highly functional pieces are excellent value for money: a solid wood mahogany Victorian chest of drawers can be found at around $150. These pieces could well provide good investment potential, as prices must surely increase with a strengthening economy.

Above: A pair of 18thC satinwood and marquetry inlaid bedside commodes, attributed to Mayhew & Ince. These were originally thought to be Edwardian reproductions, but the quality of the materials and workmanship suggests they are by Mayhew & Ince. John Mayhew and William Ince were among the first furniture-makers to embrace Robert Adam's Neo-classical style and exploit the possibilities of marquetry decoration when it regained popularity in the 1760s.

23in (57cm) wide

$195,000-225,000

Top Left: A late 18thC Italian Neo-classical commode, by Giovanni Maffezzoli, veneered in precious woods and decorated with marquetry scenes, two sans traverse drawers, with green marble top, on conical legs.

Giovanni Maffezzoli (1766-1818) was born in Cremona. A pupil of the famous cabinet maker Giuseppe Maggiolini (1738-1814), he was renowned for his characteristic intarsia work.

47in (119cm) wide

$52,500-67,500 **DOR**

A Charles I oak wainscot chair, the paneled back with downswept arms above a solid plank seat, raised on spiral turned supports, united by a peripheral stretcher.

Provenance: By repute once part of Sir Walter Scott's collection at Abbotsford.

38in (96cm) high

$6,000-7,500 L&T

A Charles I oak armchair, the triple paneled back with a fluted arched crest rail and downswept scroll arms, raised on turned legs joined by a peripheral stretcher.

40.5in (103cm) high

$4,000–5,250 L&T

A Charles II oak panel back armchair, Lancashire, the cartouche shaped back carved profusely with scrolling foliage and scroll motifs, above the solid seat flanked by downswept arms with scroll terminals above square-section and turned legs joined by peripheral stretchers.

c1660 48.5in (123cm) high

$10,500–13,500 DN

A Charles II oak panel back settle, the rectangular back with entwined link carved frieze above four lozenge and scroll carved panels above a solid seat flanked by rectangular arms and turned supports, above square section legs with peripheral stretchers.

Provenance: By repute the settle was used at the The Angel Inn, Hetton, Yorkshire until it was sold in 1983.

c1660 47.25in (120cm) high

$4,500-6,000 DN

A Charles II oak panel back armchair, the cartouche-shaped back carved profusely with lunettes, foliage and scroll motifs centered by a panel carved with a tree motif, the solid seat flanked by downswept arms with scroll terminals marked with initials 'IM' four times, above square-section and turned legs joined by peripheral stretchers.

c1660 53in (135cm) high

$5,250–8,250 DN

A Charles II carved walnut open armchair, the caned back with spiral turned uprights and acanthus carved downswept arms, above a cane seat and raised on spiral turned legs united by stretchers.

42.5in (108cm) high

$850–1,150 L&T

A pair of Charles II oak backstools, Derbyshire, each rectangular back with a pair of arched and profusely scroll carved rails, above a solid seat, turned and square section legs with bobbin turned stretchers and turned feet.

c1660 41.5in (106cm) high

$7,500–10,500 DN

A set of six Charles II walnut dining chairs, each back centered by a caned panel, surmounted by an armorial eagle, each caned seat with an additional damask covered drop in seat, on spiral turned legs and stretchers and turned feet.

c1680 46.5in (118cm) high

$8,500–11,500 DN

A Charles II walnut child's wainscot chair, the paneled back carved with lunettes, interlaced scrolls and flower-head motifs, with downswept arms above a solid seat, raised on turned legs united by peripheral stretchers.

c1680 37.75in (96cm) high

$8,500–11,500 L&T

A mid-17thC Scottish oak and fruitwood panel armchair, the scrolling arched back panel carved with strapwork above a fielded panel back and scroll arms and plank seat, raised on turned column legs joined by peripheral stretchers.

25in (64cm) wide

$3,000-4,500 **L&T**

CLOSER LOOK - CHARLES II OAK CAQUETEUSE

A caqueteuse traditionally has a flared seat and open arms. It's name comes from the French word caqueter - 'to chatter' - as these chairs were comfortable to use when having a conversation.

The French influence can be seen in the general form of the chair and in the architectural nature of the back.

This chair is similar to a group of chairs executed in the Scottish vernacular style and assembled at Trinity Hall, Aberdeen, whose significant features include a tall narrow back, a seat of almost triangular shape and the arms sweeping round to hold the sitter.

Research suggestes that the initials on the back of this chair may relate to the Gunn family of Lybster, Caithness. The Gunn family, of Norwegian descent, is an old clan who can trace their presence in the country to the early 13thC; they claim descent from the legendary Sweyn Asleifsson, the so-called 'Ultimate Viking'.

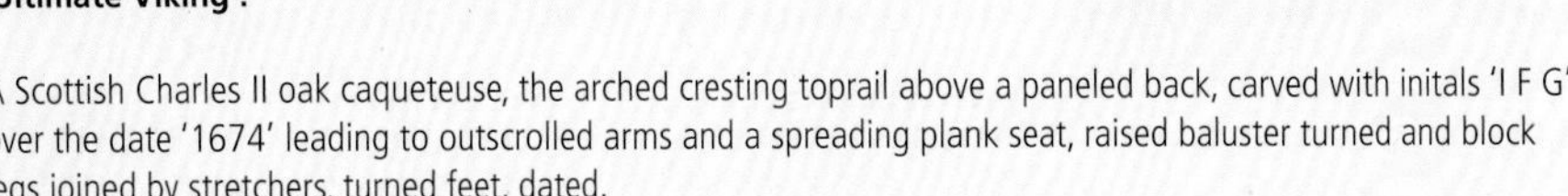

A Scottish Charles II oak caqueteuse, the arched cresting toprail above a paneled back, carved with initals 'I F G' over the date '1674' leading to outscrolled arms and a spreading plank seat, raised baluster turned and block legs joined by stretchers, turned feet, dated.

This distinctive type of chair is a fine example of the Franco-Scottish cacqueteuse chairs popular in the 17thC. The seaports on the eastern coast of Scotland supported a thriving trade and import business most notably from France to Aberdeen, which was a major center of furniture craftsmanship.

1674 *45.5in (116cm) high*

$9,000–12,000 **L&T**

A Scottish Charles II oak caqueteuse, the acanthus-carved and pierced toprail centered by a crown, above a panel back and outscrolled arms, the spreading plank seat raised on baluster turned and block legs joined by stretchers and ending on turned feet, bearing a white metal plaque inscribed: 'OLD SCOTTISH CROWN CHAIR FROM LINLITHGOW PALACE'.

The small plaque on this chair states that it came from Linlithgow Palace, once a stronghold for Scottish royalty and called home by many Stuart kings and queens. Legend has it that the towns people rushed to salvage the valuable pieces of furniture as the palace was burned down by the Duke of Cumberland in January 1746 during the Jacobite rebellion. Over time pieces of furniture bearing similar plaques stating their Linlithgow Palace provenance have come to light.

46.5in (118cm) high

$19,500-22,500 **L&T**

A Charles I oak caqueteuse, the pierced scrolling crest rail above a panel back carved with a sunburst and flower motifs, above a three plank seat and scroll arms, above a chip carved seat rail and raised on turned legs joined by peripheral stretchers.

22.5in (57cm) wide

$9,000–12,000 **L&T**

A William & Mary oak child's chair, the bobbin-turned frame with rectangular back centered by a twin lozenge-carved panel and above rectangular shaped arms and a solid seat, on conforming turned legs and peripheral stretchers.

Provenance: The Lygo Collection

c1690 *23in (58cm) high*

$2,700–3,600 **DN**

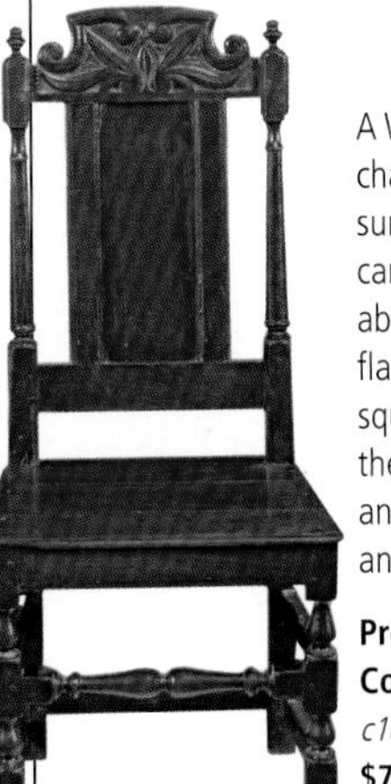

A William & Mary oak side chair, the rectangular back surmounted by a foliate carved and shaped panel above a paneled splat flanked by turned and square section uprights, the solid seat on turned and square section legs and stretchers.

Provenance: The Lygo Collection

c1690 *42.5in (108cm) high*

$750-1,200 **DN**

A late 17thC French oak back stool, the panel back centered by a rosette-carved lozenge, above a molded plank seat raised on turned and block legs joined by stretchers.

$900-1,200 **L&T**

A New London County, Connecticut, William & Mary great chair, with boldly turned finials above three slats and mushroom-capped arms, over a rush seat and sausage-turned stretchers.

c1710

$6,000-7,500 **POOK**

An 18thC primitive stick back Windsor armchair, in ash and elm, curved stay rail and bowed arm rail, curved arm supports, square fronted seat, raised on splayed legs, traces of original green paint under seat.

44in (112cm) high

$1,500-2,250 **HT**

CLOSER LOOK - TRIPLE-BACK WINDSOR SETTEE

The back consists of three overlapping chairbacks which give an elegant finish. The spindles extend from the seat to the top rail.

The patina of the wood is rich and attractive and the wear is consistent with use. Country furniture like this was made all over the States but quality varies - this example is the work of a skilled carftsman.

The detail on the knuckle arms shows that a talented wood carver made them and the tapered spindles, turned legs and stretchers supporting the settee.

A stepped back and arm rail lends additional strength to the construction.

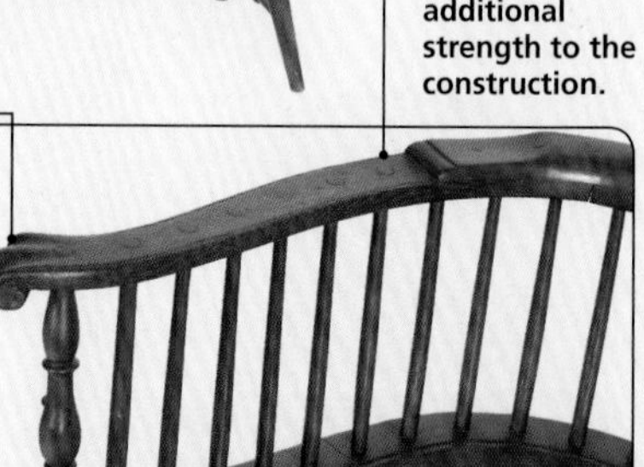

An extremely rare Philadelphia triple-chair-back Windsor settee, with knuckle arms.

c1780 *69.5in (177cm) wide*

$18,000-22,500 **POOK**

ESSENTIAL REFERENCE - WINDSOR CHAIRS

The 18thC was a golden age of British furniture production – the age of Chippendale, Adam and Hepplewhite. Outside of the large cities, a less fashionable but equally dynamic vernacular industry was also thriving.

- **One popular regional style was the Windsor chair. It was produced in centers all over England, but particularly around the town of High Wycombe in Buckinghamshire from c1700. They were also made elsewhere in the Thames Valley (including Windsor) as well as the South West, East Midlands and North East.**
- **The most important part of the Windsor chair is the saddle seat, usually carved from elm and into which the other components were directly fitted.**
- **Legs and spindles were often made from beech, which is ideally suited to turning on a lathe.**
- **Pliable yew wood was used for the stretchers, arms and top rail – these parts of the chair were often curved using a steam bending process.**
- **Many different types of Windsor chair were made and can still be found on the market.**
- **The Windsor chair was adopted by the American market.**

An early 19thC yew, ash and beech Windsor armchair in the Gothic taste, arched back, pierced splats incorporating Gothic arches and incorporating a curved arm rail, dished solid seat, cabriole legs and pad feet at the front.

37.7in (96cm) high

$1,500-2,250 **DN**

An early 19thC set of four fruitwood and elm Windsor chairs, hooped backs, pierced vase-shaped splats flanked by spindle splats, solid seats, turned tapering legs and stretchers.

$600-750 **DN**

A 19thC yew high back Windsor armchair, with a pierced splat back, an elm seat and a crinoline stretcher.

$550-700 **WW**

A 19thC yew low back Windsor armchair, with a pierced splat back, to an elm seat and a crinoline stretcher.

$550-700 **WW**

A 19thC child's Windsor chair, hoop back with spindle supports, dished seat, on turned legs and stretchers, damage and repairs.

24in (60.5cm) high

$440–480 **DN**

A 19thC yew and elm Windsor armchair, low hoop back with central shaped and pierced splat, baluster-turned end arm supports, on similar legs joined by crinoline stretcher.

$280-340 **DA&H**

A 19thC yew and elm Windsor armchair, low hoop back with pierced and shaped central splat, baluster-turned end arm supports on similar legs joined by a crinoline stretcher, stamped "F Walker, Rockley".

$400-550 **DA&H**

A 19thC child's ash and elm high back Windsor elbow chair, on turned baluster legs and stretchers.

$150–225 **FLD**

A late 19thC Yorkshire Windsor chair, high back with pierced splat, scroll end arms raised on underturnings, a shaped elm seat on ring turned legs with H cross stretchers, possibly by Young of Halifax.

$400-550 **HW**

A 19thC Orkney Islands pine armchair, with scroll arms, a drop-in seat and stretchered supports.

$750-1,200 **WW**

A 19thC painted comb-back Windsor armchair, with a pierced splat to a dished seat on stretchered supports, the back of the seat stamped '8978', with a black/red painted finish, possibly West Country.

$1,500-2,250 **WW**

An early 20thC elm Windsor armchair, the high hoop back with shaped and pierced central splat, baluster end arm supports on turned legs joined by an H-stretcher.

$150–300 **DA&H**

A Boston William & Mary maple dining chair, with a carved crest and medial stretcher.
c1720
$3,000-4,500 **POOK**

A Massachusetts William & Mary banisterback side chair, with a carved crest and Spanish feet.
c1730
$4,500-6,000 **POOK**

ESSENTIAL REFERENCE - AMERICAN QUEEN ANNE CHAIRS

In the American colonies, the Queen Anne style developed between 1720 and 1750. The style took its cue from British Queen Anne chairs which, in turn, had been inspired by the high-backed chairs developed in the Netherlands in the late 1600s.

- **Early English Queen Anne chairs had a solid vase- or baluster-shaped splat, round or balloon-shaped drop-in seat and the legs were joined by flat or turned stretchers.**
- **In the early 1700s the chair backs developed serpentine crest rails and wider, more ornate, splats.**
- **Stretchers were eventually rendered unnecessary by the addition of corner blocks in the interior edges of the frame and enabled cabinetmakers to make chairs with elegant cabriole legs, often terminating in claw-and-ball feet.**
- **American chairs are taller and slimmer than English examples with more restrained decoration, although the curve of the crest rail can be more pronounced.**
- **In America, claw-and-ball feet were used after c1740 but pad or slipper feet remained fashionable into the second half of the century.**
- **Chairs made on both sides of the Atlantic often featured carved shells on the crest rail and the knees.**
- **The chairs were often made from walnut, or walnut veneers over an oak frame.**

A Philadelphia Queen Anne walnut compass seat dining chair, the shell-carved crest with double volutes above a highly figured solid vasiform splat and supported by cabriole legs with shell and volute carved knees terminating in trifid feet.
c1750
$52,500–67,500 **POOK**

A pair of Pennsylvania Queen Anne walnut dining chairs, with a vasiform splat and flat 'H' stretcher.
c1745
$4,000-4,500 **POOK**

A mid-18thC mahogany open armchair, with leaf capped cabriole legs to Braganza front feet.
$1,200-1,800 **WW**

A Delaware Valley Queen Anne cherry armchair, with scrolled handholds and a rush seat, supported by cabriole legs terminating in trifid feet.
c1755
$2,700-3,300 **POOK**

A pair of Queen Anne walnut dining chairs, probably Massachusetts, each with a solid splat and compass slip seat supported by cabriole legs and turned cross stretchers.
c1760
$1,800-3,000 **POOK**

A set of twelve Queen Anne-style mahogany and upholstered dining chairs, the padded rounded rectangular backs over wide spreading seats raised on cabriole legs ending in pad feet, in modern foliate upholstery.
21.5in (55cm) wide
$2,700-3,300 set **L&T**

ESSENTIAL REFERENCE - IRISH CHIPPENDALE

English cabinetmaker and furniture designer Thomas Chippendale (1718–79) is among the best-known designers of all time. Thanks to his book 'The Gentleman and Cabinet-Maker's Director' the style of furniture he made found international fame and is still copied today.

- **Chippendale moved to London c1747 and within six years he had opened his own workshop in St Martin's Lane.**
- **His most celebrated pieces are in the early Rococo taste and typically decorated with trailing husks, foliage and carved shells. As he did not mark or sign the pieces made in his workshop, the term "Chippendale" usually means pieces made in the Chippendale style.**

Two Irish mahogany single chairs, one with a broken leg.

These highly desirable chairs were rescued from an outhouse. They sold for a considerable sum even though one had a broken leg, which shows the appeal of Irish Chippendale furniture.

c1750

$30,000–37,500 **ADA**

A Delaware Valley Chippendale walnut armchair, the shell and volute-carved crest above a pierced and voluted splat with a trapezoidal slip seat, resting in a shell carved frame supported by cabriole legs terminating in ball and claw feet.

c1770

$37,500–45,000 **POOK**

A pair of Philadelphia Chippendale carved mahogany dining chairs, possibly from the workshop of Thomas Tufft, each with a foliate carved crest above a Gothic splat and trapezoidal slip seat, resting in a frame with a central plume element supported by cabriole legs terminating in ball and claw feet.

c1770

$45,000-60,000 **POOK**

One of a pair of Philadelphia Chippendale walnut dining chairs.

c1770

$12,000-15,000 pair **POOK**

A set of eight George III mahogany dining chairs, comprising seven side chairs and one armchair, the backs with an arched top rail over three vertical rails carved with lotus, above a drop-in seat raised on square tapered legs joined by H-form stretcher; together with a shield back mahogany armchair.

20in (51cm) wide

$3,000-4,500 **L&T**

One of a set of six George III mahogany dining chairs, shaped toprail, pierced splat, drop-in needlework seats, square legs and stretchers.

c1780

$1,200-1,800 set **DN**

An assembled set of twenty Hepplewhite-style mahogany dining chairs, all with shield-shaped backs and serpentine stuff-over seats on square tapered legs.

21.25in (54cm) wide

$9,000–12,000 **L&T**

A set of twelve George III mahogany dining chairs, in the manner of George Seddon, comprising two armchairs and ten sidechairs, the shaped wavy spindle back over scroll carved arms and shaped upholstered seat, raised on acanthus carved cabriole legs terminating in trifid feet.

George Seddon (1727–1801) was an English cabinetmaker and in 1795 was Master of the Joiners Company of London. At one time his furniture making business was the largest and most successful in London, employing over 400 craftsmen.

c1800 *armchair 23in (58.5cm) wide*

$9,000–12,000 **FRE**

A matched set of fifteen oak dining chairs, each rectangular back with molded vertical splats, solid seats, square section legs and stretchers.

c1800

$1,200-1,800 set **DN**

A set of six Regency ebonized and parcel gilt open armchairs in the manner of John Gee, each with a lyre back decorated with ribbon tied drapes and crossed arrows with a laurel wreath, with spiral fluted arm supports to a cane seat and squab cushions, on turned supports, the seat rails stamped with workmen's marks 'R', 'SB', 'H', 'E H', 'AC' and 'E R'.

John Gee worked as chairmaker and turner working on Wardour Street, London, from 1779 until c1824. He worked with his son Thomas Aycliffe Gee and they were awarded a Royal Warrant in 1804. The company was occasionally referred to as Gee & Sons.

$5,250-6,750 WW

A set of ten Regency mahogany chairs, each with shaped top panel rail with reeded detail above a shaped lower rail, raised above upholstered drop in seats on square section tapering legs, includes two carvers.

$4,000–5,250 L&T

A matched set of six Regency dining chairs, shaped rectangular backs, patera carved pierced splats, drop-in seats and sabre legs.

c1815

$1,500-2,250 set DN

A set of six Lancaster, PA, painted plank seat chairs, stamped by maker J. Swint, retaining their original floral decoration on a yellow ground.

$1,800–2,700 POOK

A set of twelve Regency rosewood and brass inlaid dining chairs, the gadrooned and acanthus carved bar backs inlaid with scrolling foliage, above caned seats, raised on sabre legs.

c1820 *18in (46cm) wide*

$22,500-30,000 L&T

A set of six early 19thC six rosewood dining chairs, of open balloon back form with dished top rail and leaf-carved horizontal splat, drop-in seats with a blue and cream brocade covering, on lotus-carved turned tapering front legs and splayed back legs.

$900-1,200 set HT

A set of seven Regency simulated rosewood children's dining chairs, comprising an elbow chair and six single chairs, the bar backs set with a pierced brass anthemion mounted lyre splat and brass studded rondel to rail, with caned seats, turned frame and legs.

c1820 *16.5in (42cm) wide*

$1,800–2,700 DN

A set of twelve George IV mahogany dining chairs, including a pair of armchairs, one 20thC, each rectangular back with a wrythen-turned bar splat above a drop in seat and molded sabre legs.

c1825 *17.5in (44cm) wide*

$5,250-6,750 DN

A set of six George IV mahogany dining chairs, comprising four side chairs and two armchairs, the curved tablet backs over a carved swag horizontal splat, and drop-in padded seats in natural linen upholstery, raised on turned and faceted tapered legs.

c1825 *21.25in (54cm) wide*

$1,500-2,250 L&T

A set of 19thC mahogany and satinwood dining chairs, including a pair of armchairs, bar backs with central satinwood inset panels, green leatherette upholstered seats, on square legs and spade feet.

$1,800–2,700 SET DN

A set of eight 19thC mahogany dining chairs, including a pair of armchairs, stick backs, needlework drop-in seats, on square legs.

$600-900 DN

A set of six Victorian dining chairs upholstered in a cream and white tapestry, the molded and scroll carved open spoon back with arched top rail and horizontal splat, overstuffed seat, raised on slender scroll carved cabriole front legs with knurled feet.

$750-1,200 HT

One of a set of eight Victorian mahogany and leather upholstered dining chairs, molded arched back, lappet carved splats, lotus carved turned tapering legs, brass caps and ceramic castors.

c1880

$1,800–2,700 set DN

A set of six mahogany dining chairs in the George III style, shaped toprail, pierced vase splat, dished studded covered seats, on square legs and stretchers.

c1900

$600-750 DN

A set of eight early 20thC mahogany dining chairs, in the George III style, including a pair of armchairs, pieced splats, green leather upholstered seats, square legs and stretchers.

$900-1,200 DN

A set of ten mahogany dining chairs, in the George III style, eight date from 20thC, remainder early 20thC or 19thC.

$3,000-4,000 DN

One of a set of eight mid-20thC mahogany dining chairs, in the George III style, shaped backs, pierced vase splats, on square legs and stretchers, comprising six chairs and two elbow chairs.

$1,500-2,250 set DN

A set of eight 20thC mahogany and leather upholstered dining chairs in George III style, including a pair of armchairs with molded shield shaped backs, carved and pierced vase splats, serpentine fronted seats, molded square tapering legs.

$900-1,200 DN

A Charles II silvered and gesso side chair, the arched rectangular back above a stuffover seat, upholstered in gold cut velvet, on carved and gadrooned inverted baluster, front legs united by a pierced and scroll carved apron, on turned and gadrooned feet with splayed square section rear legs united by baulster turned H-stretchers.

51.5in (131cm) high

$1,800–4,000 **L&T**

A 19thC Charles II-style oak and upholstered side chair, the padded back and stuffover seat covered in studded green fabric, raised on spiral turned legs, united by stretchers.

20in (51cm) wide

$300-450 **L&T**

A William & Mary stained beech framed and upholstered side chair, the arched back and seat covered in red tartan fabric, on knopped legs joined by an X-stretcher, on scroll feet.

22in (56cm) wide

$900-1,200 **L&T**

A pair of Queen Anne walnut side chairs, with shaped top rails carved with shell and foliate cresting above a pierced vasiform splat, the drop-in seats with rounded corners raised on plain cabriole legs.

c1710 *21in (53cm) wide*

$2,700-3,300 **L&T**

An 18thC and later Queen Anne-style walnut side chair, the pierced and carved top rail centered by a helmet above a pierced spat carved with shell and foliate motifs, over a stuff over seat in blue plush fabric, raised on carved cabriole legs ending in hoof feet and joined by an H-stretcher.

21in (53cm) wide

$300–600 **L&T**

A set of six George I walnut side chairs, each with a scroll-carved and molded back with later damask upholstery, originally caned, the shaped friezes centered on a carved shell, on leaf capped cabriole legs and Braganza type feet, each with a paper label to the seat rail inscribed 'MATTHEW EDWARD GORGES 10/8/909'.

$6,000–9,000 **WW**

A mid-18thC George II mahogany and upholstered side chair, the square back and stuffed over seat covered in later needlework, raised on carved stop-fluted cabriole legs ending in scroll feet.

22.5in (57cm) wide

$975-1,300 **L&T**

A pair of George II mahogany side chairs with upholstered seats and padded backs, on acanthus carved cabriole legs and lion paw feet, upholstered in blue velvet.

38in (96.5cm) high

$19,500-22,500 **CHOR**

A pair of George III Chinese Chippendale side chairs, the rectangular padded backs with serpentine top rails over wide stuff-over seats in yellow damask upholstery and nail head detailing, raised on square tapered legs with fishscale panels and pierced corner brackets and ending in block feet with recessed leather castors.

c1760 *23in (59cm) wide*

$5,250-6,750 **L&T**

One of a pair of Chippendale-style mahogany side chairs, carved crest rail above a pierced back, upholstered seat, on blind fret carved square section legs and pierced stretchers.

c1770 and later

$700-850 pair **DN**

A pair of Louis XVI giltwood chaises, each with a ribbon tied cresting, upholstered with associated Aubusson tapestry, one stamped 'PLS DES TUILES', the other with 'three fleur de lys below a crown' and 'TH', both with copper inventory labels '1209', originally with caned seats, gilding and some decoration later.

Provenance: The Palais des Tuileries; close to the Louvre in Paris, where Louis XVI and Marie Antoinette once lived. In the 19thC it was used as the main royal palace, with some furniture from the Royal chateaux.

$3,000–4,500 **WW**

One of a pair of early 19thC rosewood bobbin-turned side chairs, with a cane seat and squab cushion.

$1,000-1,400 pair **WW**

A set of eight Regency faux rosewood painted Gothic-style side chairs, the pointed arch backs with cluster column rails above caned seats, raised on triple column legs with pierced corner brackets.

19in (48cm) high

$5,250-6,750 **L&T**

A pair of Victorian painted hall chairs, the scroll molded backs painted with wheat and a coronet, above a plank seat, raised on turned and tapered legs; one bearing old ivorine trade label for 'James Phillips & Sons, Union Street, Bristol'.

c1840 *16in (41cm) wide*

$450-750 **L&T**

One of a pair of 19thC Italian walnut and bone inlay side chairs, the serpentine top rail over a pierced splat inlaid with a cartouche, putti, masks, urns and flowering garlands, above a drop-in seat raised on square cabriole legs.

22.5in (57cm) wide

$600-900 pair **L&T**

One of a pair of 19thC George II-style walnut side chairs, with vasiform splats above needlework upholstered drop-in seats, raised on cabriole legs joined by turned stretchers and ending on pad feet.

21in (53cm) wide

$700-750 pair **L&T**

A set of five Victorian walnut side chairs, the upholstered backs with carved floral cresting above a padded seat, raised on cabriole legs.

19in (48cm) wide

$750-900 **L&T**

A mid-19thC Black Forest walnut carved owl hall chair, the circular back carved in bas-relief with two perched owls, one with inset glass eyes, enclosed by a pierced floret border above a solid seat on barley twist tapered legs.

39.5in (100.5cm) high

$400-550 **L&T**

A George II Irish walnut corner chair, crescent shaped back with twin vase splats, drop-in seat and serpentine seat rail, central leg carved with acanthus and central shell, carved claw and ball foot.

c1740 *31in (79cm) high*

$750-1,200 **DN**

A George II mahogany corner armchair, the scrolled backrail above double vasiform splats and turned supports, over a drop-in red silk upholstered seat, raised on cabriole legs ending on pad feet.

25.5in (65cm) wide

$1,800-3,000 **L&T**

A CLOSER LOOK AT A WILLIAM KENT HALL BENCH

The scrolled-over back follows a design for a bench by William Kent at Houghton Hall, Norfolk.

The design of the scrolled arm terminals is identical to the Houghton Hall bench.

The seat is constructed from a single board resting on a coved frame identical to the Houghton Hall bench.

The apron is carried to the floor at each end, forming scrolled trusses at right angles to the front legs. This is highly decorative and also adds strength.

The arched, leaf-carved apron below the seat is similar to the William Kent bench at Houghton Hall, Norfolk.

The highly enriched apron but plain moldings beneath the seat and around the back and side panels are unique to this bench.

A George II mahogany hall bench, the design attributed to William Kent, with a double-paneled back, a scrolled top and arm terminals above a double-arched acanthus leaf carved apron, foliate carved legs and scrolled feet.

Architectural-style benches such as this one were made to stand in formal entrance halls. They are associated with the English Palladian Revival of the late 1720s and 1730s, and in particular with houses where the architect/designer William Kent worked. Some are of painted deal or oak, but most surviving examples are mahogany. While all are of a broadly similar form, the benches differ in style and detail, and were probably made by more than one workshop.

c1730 *55in (140cm) wide*

$67,500–75,000 **SWO**

A Regency mahogany hall chair, with a gorget back, a dished bell seat and ring-turned supports.

$550-700 **WW**

A pair of George IV mahogany hall chairs, each with a leaf scroll carved back to a solid seat on ribbed tapering front legs.

$750-1,200 **WW**

A pair of Victorian mahogany framed hall chairs, each with circular backs centered by a cartouche, over serpentine solid seats on turned supports.

$400-550 **BELL**

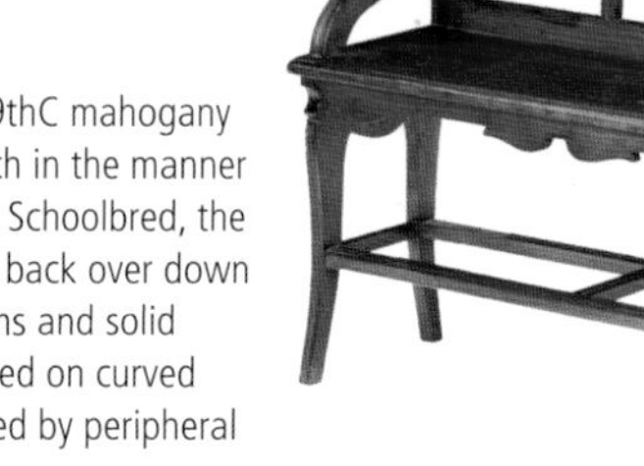

A late 19thC mahogany hall bench in the manner of James Schoolbred, the galleried back over down scroll arms and solid seat, raised on curved legs joined by peripheral stretchers.

36in (91cm) wide

$750-1,200 **L&T**

A Victorian walnut and painting hunting scene chair, the bar back formed as a harness with brass and silvered mounts, the drop-in seat painted with a hunting scene, raised on turned front legs formed as hunting horns and linked by stretchers mounted with a horseshoe.

c1900 *17in (43cm) wide*

$1,000-1,400 **L&T**

A pair of Victorian antler chairs, each with back and legs formed from entwined antlers, with oak framed seats with close nailed leather upholstered panel seats.

c1900 *36.5in (93cm) high*

$1,800–2,700 **L&T**

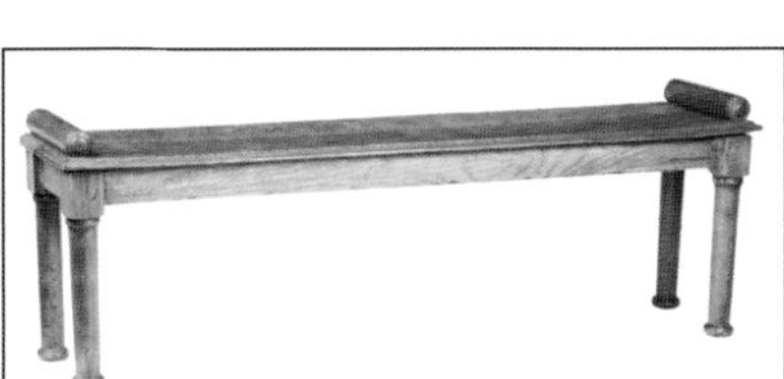

A George IV oak hall bench, the long rectangular seat with a molded edge and bar ends, raised on straight cyllindrical legs.

c1835 *60in (152cm) long*

$600-900 **L&T**

A pair of Victorian mahogany hall benches, each with a long rectangular seat with scrolled ends raised on six baluster-turned legs with toupie feet.

72in (183cm) long

$4,500–7,500 **L&T**

A Victorian oak hall bench, the frieze centered with a circular tablet painted with a sun face and a native carrying a club, on faceted tapering legs.

48in (122.5cm) wide

$750-1,200 **WW**

A Victorian oak hall bench, the solid seat flanked by scroll terminals, roundel mounted frieze, turned and octagonal tapering legs.

c1860 *51in (129cm) wide*

$1,500-2,250 **DN**

A matched pair of George III-style, mahogany upholstered window seats, the bowed seats flanked by scrolling arms, inset with stringing and circular inlay, square section tapering legs, one example with spade feet.

c1900 *39.75in (101cm) wide*

$750-1,200 **DN**

ESSENTIAL REFERENCE - BLACK FOREST FURNITURE

The term "Black Forest" is used to described highly carved furniture featuring bears and other forest creatures such as deer and birds made from the early 19thC onward.

- **Despite its name, the first pieces were made in Switzerland and not Germany's Black Forest region.**
- **They were made fashionable when wealthy Victorians brought them home as souvenirs from trips to Swiss resorts such as Interlaken, Brienz and Lucerne.**
- **After 1850 the carvings received further international recognition when they were exhibited at International exhibitions in London, Paris and Chicago.**
- **The most common animals are bears (either freestanding or as parts of furniture) but stags, dogs and birds were also popular. American buyers favored pieces carved with eagles.**
- **The carvings were made from the trunks of walnut and linden trees.**
- **Pieces signed by the maker – especially those by important makers like the Huggler family – are particularly desirable.**

A late 19thC carved Black Forest bench, modeled as two bears supportig a naturalistic plank seat, the openwork back carved with fruiting vines and centered by a further bear.

63in (160cm) wide

$1,500-2,250 **L&T**

A George II carved mahogany and upholstered window seat, one side with serpentine outline.

c1760 *38.5in (98cm) wide*

$3,000-4,000 **TEN**

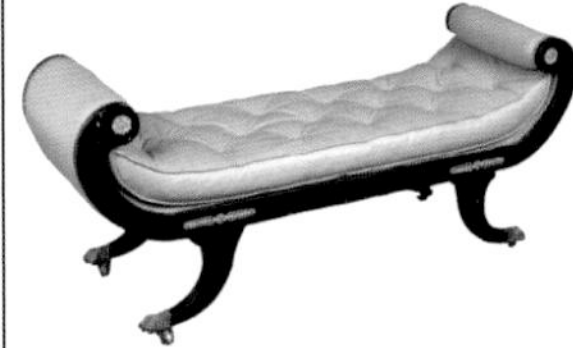

A late Regency ebonized window seat, upholstered in lilac leather, with gilt mounts and scroll ends, leather seat cushion, on sabre legs, brass paw feet and castors.

52.25in (133cm) wide

$975-1,300 **CHEF**

A late Victorian Adam-style mahogany window seat, upholstered with gingham fabric, the frame carved with paterae and ribbon tied husks.

30.25in (77cm wide)

$600-900 **WW**

A pair of George III-style mahogany and upholstered window seats, each shaped rectangular seat flanked by a pair of scrolling rests, above a fluted frieze cornered by carved patera terminals and turned tapering stop fluted legs.

c1900 *45.25in (115cm) wide*

$1,500-2,250 **DN**

An early 18thC William & Mary red japanned footstool, the square padded seat upholstered in floral needlework with a blue border, raised on turned and tapered legs joined by an X-form stretcher on flattened bun feet.

14in (36cm) wide

$1,400-1,800 **L&T**

A George II walnut fruitwood stool.

c1730

$4,500-6,000 **TARQ**

A George II walnut upholstered stool, the padded rectangular top covered in needlework upholstery, raised on cabriole legs ending in pad feet and joined by turned H-form stretchers.

21.5in (55cm) wide

$400-550 **L&T**

A Regency rosewood and upholstered stool, the padded square top in foliate and scroll needlework, raised on X-frame supports joined by turned stretchers.

c1820 *18.5in (47cm) wide*

$750-1,200 **L&T**

A pair of William IV mahogany and upholstered footstools, the scrolled ends with turned stretchers and floral needlework drop-in pads.

c1835 *13.5in (34cm) wide*

$450-750 **L&T**

An early Victorian rosewood stool, with a needlework seat on a scroll molded frame and cabriole legs.

19.5in (49.5cm) square

$600-900 **WW**

A mid-19thC walnut and upholstered ottoman, the large rectangular padded top raised on cabriole legs ending in porcelain castors.

39in (99cm) wide

$1,500-2,250 **L&T**

A pair of ebonized and parcel gilt stools, each with a stuffed-over seat on rope twist effect legs united by stretchers.

24in (61cm) square

$700-850 **WW**

A French ormolu mounted footstool.

c1900 *20in (50cm) wide*

$1,500-2,250 **POOK**

A 20thC beech-framed and needlepoint upholstered stool, in the 18thC style.

33.5in (85cm) long

$450-750 **DN**

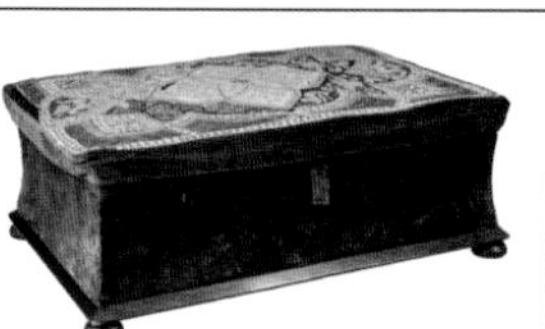

A Victorian rosewood and upholstered ottoman, the rectangular hinged top with a loose tapestry cover, opening to reveal a lined void interior, the waisted velvet upholstered sides above a molded apron raised on bun feet with countersunk castors.

c1860 *41.25in (105cm) wide*

$1,800-3,000 **L&T**

A leather-bound ottoman, the rectangular button-upholstered hinged seat opening to a lined void inerior, the tapered leather-paneled sides on molded base with castors.

c1890 *50.5in (128.5cm) wide*

$1,800-3,000 **L&T**

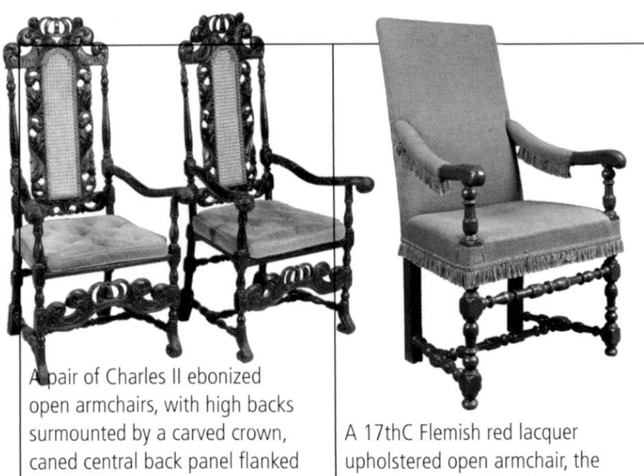

A pair of Charles II ebonized open armchairs, with high backs surmounted by a carved crown, caned central back panel flanked by columns, caned seats with loose seat cushions, outswept arms, carved stretcher centered by a crown, on turned legs and stretchers.

c1660 *27in (69cm) wide*

$450-600 **DN**

A 17thC Flemish red lacquer upholstered open armchair, the square back, padded downswept arms and stuffed seat covered in salmon-pink fabric, raised on turned legs, united by a conforming H-shaped stretcher.

25in (64cm) wide

$450-750 **L&T**

An 18thC Queen Anne walnut armchair, the solid vasiform splat and outscrolling arms above a drop-in seat covered in tapestry fabric, raised on shell carved cabriole legs ending in trefoil feet.

25in (62cm) wide

$3,000-4,500 **L&T**

A Queen Anne upholstered oak armchair, the serpentine top rail over a padded back and seat, with straight arms, raised on turned legs joined by peripheral stretchers, upholstered in green suede with brass stud detail.

21in (54cm) wide

$900-1,200 **L&T**

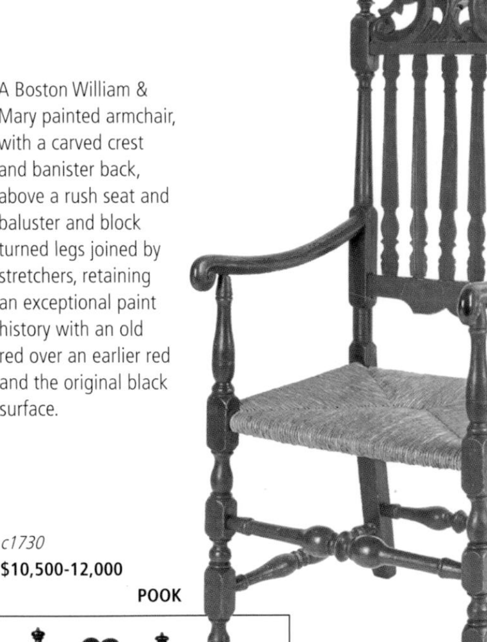

A Boston William & Mary painted armchair, with a carved crest and banister back, above a rush seat and baluster and block turned legs joined by stretchers, retaining an exceptional paint history with an old red over an earlier red and the original black surface.

c1730

$10,500-12,000 **POOK**

A Connecticut William & Mary painted heart and crown armchair, retaining an old black surface.

This chair is attributed to the workshop of Thomas Salmon, Stratford, Connecticut, Connecticut.

c1735

$6,000-7,500 **POOK**

A New London County William & Mary banister-back armchair, retaining an old black surface with gilt highlights.

c1750

$1,400-1,700 **POOK**

A New England Queen Anne painted banister-back armchair, with a carved crest and Spanish feet, retaining an old black surface with gilt highlights.

c1750

$1,800-3,000 **POOK**

A George II carved mahogany library armchair, the arched back and serpentine seat flanked by outscrolling arms with foliate and shell-carved terminals, over a lattice carved apron centered by a ruffled shell and foliate scrolls, raised on shell and foliate carved cabriole legs ending in scrolled toes, in later green and yellow floral silk upholstery.

The inspiration for this elegant armchair is undoubtedly taken from French fashion of the period as interpreted by a mid-18thC cabinetmaker. Thomas Chippendale illustrated several examples of 'French' chairs in his 'Gentleman and Cabinet Makers Director', published in 1754, and other important cabinet makers of the St. Martin's Lane Academy worked in this style. The pattern of this chair, with its incised trellis ground, enjoyed considerable popularity in the mid-18thC, making identifying the specific maker a mystery.

c1755 *26.5in (68cm) wide.*

$15,000–22,500 L&T

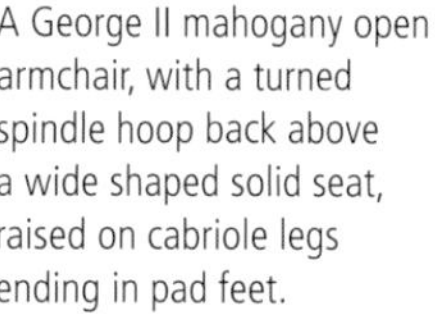

A George II mahogany open armchair, with a turned spindle hoop back above a wide shaped solid seat, raised on cabriole legs ending in pad feet.

25.5in (65cm) wide

$15,000–22,500 L&T

A good pair of George III mahogany and beech Chinese Chippendale armchairs, each with an arched and foliate scroll carved top rail over a lattice work straight back and slightly scrolling open lattice work arms, over a plank seat and blind fret carved seat rail, raised on straight square blind fret carved legs joined by an H-form stretcher.

The design for these chairs is taken almost exactly from Thomas Chippendale's 'Gentleman and Cabinet-Maker's Director', plate XXVII. It incorporates a number of Chinese influences including the blind fret carving and open trellis found throughout Chippendale's design book.

23.5in (60cm) wide

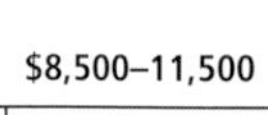

$8,500–11,500 L&T

An early George III mahogany ladderback elbow chair, the channelled back with four pierced ladders, scrolled arms on shaped scroll carved supports, overstuffed seat in gros-point covering, on molded and chamfered front legs and splayed back legs joined by H-stretchers.

$600-750 HT

A George III mahogany 'Gothic' armchair, the carved back with tracery arches flanked by cluster column stiles with acorn finials above a leather button-upholstered seat and flanked by scrolled acanthus carved arms with scrolling hand holds, raised on block and turned legs joined by a conforming H-form stretcher.

25in (63cm) wide

$3,000-4,500 L&T

One of a pair of 18thC George III mahogany open armchairs, each with a serpentine top rail with carved ears above a pierced and carved splat and scrolling arms over wide stuff-over seats, in beige velvet upholstery, raised on molded Marlborough legs.

38in (96cm) high

$750-1,200 pair L&T

A Philadelphia Chippendale mahogany armchair, with a Gothic splat and ball and claw feet, the seat insert inscribed John Folwell.

John Folwell was a well-known Philadelphia cabinet maker.

c1770

$1,800-3,000 POOK

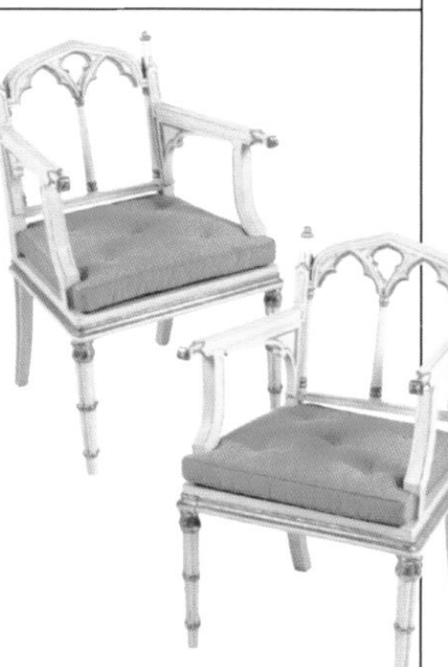

A pair of painted open armchairs in Gothic Chippendale style, with parcel gilt decoration each with a lancet arch back to a cane seat with a squab cushion on cluster column front legs.

$1,500-2,250 WW

A 19thC French Hepplewhite-style mahogany armchair, the cartouche shaped and padded back carved with anthemions above padded scroll arms and a wide stuff-over serpentine seat, raised on acanthus carved cabriole legs, in blue and gold damask upholstery.

25.5in (65cm) wide

$150–300 L&T

CLOSER LOOK - A 19THC LOUIS XV-STYLE ARMCHAIRS

This chair is based on an 18thC design. As a result its upholstery in deeper, and the fabric more exuberant, than the original would have been. The upholstered seat, back and arm rests ensured the chairs were comfortable to sit in.

The chair frames are decorated with gilding. The foliate and scroll carving on the back are more profuse than would be seen on an earlier chair.

The curved arm supports and molded seat rails show the elegant proportions and gentle curves often used by French cabinetmakers of the time. The arms terminate in scroll hand-holds.

The arms were set back from the front of the seat and the seat shaped to accommodate ladies' extravagant skirts.

A 19thC Louis XV-style giltwood fauteuil, upholstered in cream foliate fabric and raised on cabriole legs ending in scrolled toes.

31.5in (80cm)

$1,500-2,250 L&T

A set of four mid-18thC Louis XVI gilt, gesso and carved armchairs, with original Aubusson tapestry covers decorated with animals and children in pastoral settings, the frames with gadrooned crestings and carved finials above curved arm supports and overstuffed seats above molded seat rails, raised on stop-fluted supports.

20in (51cm) wide

$6,750-8,250 TEN

A George III mahogany and upholstered Gainsborough chair, the square back and padded downswept arms over a stuffover seat covered in blue fabric, raised on square legs united by an H-stretcher.

c1760 *27.5in (70cm) wide*

$1,500-2,250 L&T

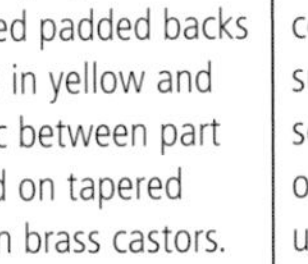

A 19thC Louis XVI-style giltwood armchairs, the arched padded backs and stuff over seats in yellow and apricot foliate fabric between part padded arms, raised on tapered fluted legs ending in brass castors.

26in (67cm) wide

$1,800-3,000 L&T

A pair of Regency rosewood tub armchairs, the curved padded backs with bobbin-turned spindles continuing to C-scroll arms and supports, over a wide padded seat above wide seat rail, raised on reeded scroll legs, in kelim upholstery.

29.5in (75cm) wide

$4,500-6,000 L&T

A pair of Regency mahogany and leather upholstered reading armchairs, the horseshoe shaped back and arms above Gothic arch splats and shaped brackets, over a shaped seat in button upholstered brown leather, raised on lotus carved and turned legs ending in brass caps and pad feet.

From a design in 'Ackermans Repository'.

c1820 *23.5in (60cm) wide*

$9,000–12,000 L&T

One of a pair of 19thC French beechwood fauteuil in the Louis XV-style, with molded frames.

$180–270 WW

A 19thC mahogany Gainsborough armchair, upholstered damask plush fabric, with blind fret carved decoration in 'Chinese Chippendale' style.

$1,400–2,000 WW

A French Empire-style mahogany tub chair, with ormolu mounts.

$400-550 **WW**

A 19thC Irish George II-style mahogany open armchair, the serpentine top rail over a pierced splat carved with acanthus and centered by a shell motif, above a needlework upholstered seat flanked by scrolling arms and hand holds, above a scroll carved seat rail raised on shell carved cabriole legs ending in hairy paw feet.

27in (69cm) wide

$1,800–2,700 **L&T**

A pair of 19thC George II-style walnut and plum pudding mahogany writing chairs, possibly Gillows, the cartouche-shaped backs with a molded edge leading to shepherd's crook arms, over a circular drop in seat, raised on cabriole legs carved with C-scrolls and ending on pad feet.

24in (61cm) wide

$7,500–10,500 **L&T**

An unusual mid-19thC French mahogany dolphin desk chair.

c1860

$3,000-4,500 **TARQ**

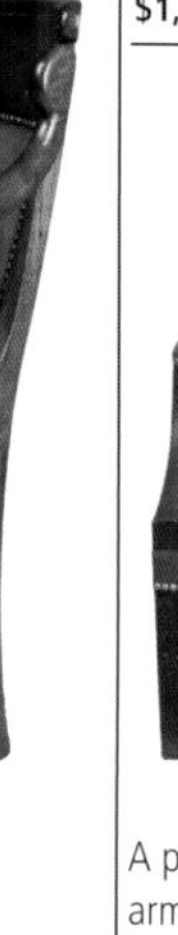

A pair of 19thC George III-style mahogany and upholstered Gainsborough armchairs, buttoned rectangular backs above rectangular arms with downswept uprights, rectangular seats on square section legs and H-shaped stretchers.

26in (67cm) wide

$4,500-6,000 **DN**

A 19thC George II-style walnut armchair, the shell-carved top rail over a vasiform splat and scroll arms, above a drop in seat with floral needlework, on cabriole legs and pad feet.

23.5in (60cm) wide

$450-600 **L&T**

A pair of Victorian carved walnut armchairs, each padded back with foliate carved cresting rail, scrolling lappet and roundel-carved arms, fluted square-section tapering legs, spade feet.

c1870 *28in (72cm) wide*

$1,800–2,700 **DN**

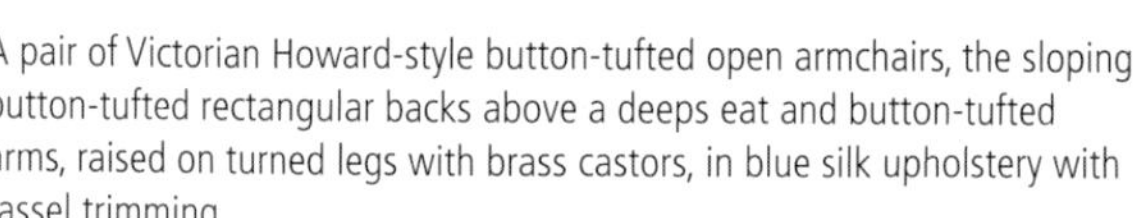

A pair of Victorian Howard-style button-tufted open armchairs, the sloping button-tufted rectangular backs above a deeps eat and button-tufted arms, raised on turned legs with brass castors, in blue silk upholstery with tassel trimming.

23in (59cm) wide

$2,700–4,000 **L&T**

A pair of Victorian oak and leather upholstered open armchairs, the button-tufted backs in a laurel and foliate-carved frame above a wide seat and padded arms raised on baluster spindles, on turned and fluted legs with brass castors, with trade label 'James Winter & Sons, 100-101 Wardour St, Soho'.

27.5in (70cm) wide

$2,100-2,700 **L&T**

A matched pair of Victorian oak easy armchairs, each upholstered with studded red leather, with fluted and leaf-carved supports on conforming front legs and brass castors.

$4,000–5,250 **WW**

One of a set of six painted fauteuils, in Louis XVI style, with oval backs, open arms, and cane seats on tapering fluted legs.

23.5in (60cm) wide

$1,800-3,000 set **DN**

A late 19thC Continental beech tub armchair, with a cane seat and a squab cushion, on stretchered turned front legs.

$120–180 **WW**

A late 19thC French mahogany fauteuil in the Empire style, with ormolu mounts.

$400-550 **WW**

A late 19thC Italian walnut Savonarola-type armchair, with carved dragon head arms on stretchered 'X'-shaped supports.

$300-450 **WW**

One of a pair of early 20thC George III-style mahogany armchairs, in the Hepplewhite style, the serpentine top rails above curved Gothic arch pierced splats carved with flowerheads, ribbons and swags above shaped stuffed over seats in yellow fabric, raised on square fluted cabriole legs ending in block feet and headed by patera.

24.5in (62cm) wide

$1,800–2,700 pair **L&T**

A pair of early 20thC George I-style mahogany elbow armchairs, with scroll-carved top rails above vase shaped splats and needlework upholstered drop-in seats raised on cabriole front legs with pad feet.

23in (59cm) wide

$1,200-1,800 **L&T**

A Louis XV walnut chaise à la reine, the padded flat back, stuff over seat and part padded arms in a foliate and C-scroll carved frame, raised on cabriole legs ending in pronounced scroll toes.

28.5in (73cm) wide

$2,100-2,700 **L&T**

A George III mahogany armchair in the manner of Chippendale, the shaped back and dished seat upholstered in green damask fabric to a brass nailed border, on blind fret carved legs.
c1770 *30in (76cm) wide*
$4,000–5,250 **CHEF**

A Regency mahogany library bergère, with scroll-shaped back, leather arm rests, cushion back and seat, on turned legs and castors.
24.25in (61cm) wide
$1,800-3,000 **CHEF**

A Regency mahogany bergère, the curved caned square back and sides above a square seat, raised on turned and reeded legs ending in ceramic castors.
c1820 *23in (59cm) wide*
$900-1,200 **L&T**

A George IV mahogany bergère armchair, in the manner of Gillows, arched rectangular back, molded downswept arms with turned and reeded supports, conforming legs at the front with brass caps and castors.
c1825 *27in (69cm) wide*
$1,150-1,300 **DN**

A William IV mahogany open armchair, arched caned back, arms and seat, leather padded arms, scroll arm terminals, on fluted tapered legs, on castors.
c1835 *25in (64cm) wide*
$750-1,200 **DN**

A chair from a suite of three carved-frame bergères, molded top rail, sweeping down turned scroll end arms with finely carved acanthus leaves, double cane work to back and sides, carved scroll and floral front rail, acanthus leaf knees and paw feet.
Three-seater settee: 75in (190cm) long
$3,000-4,500 set **TCAL**

A pair of Regency-style mahogany library armchairs, with cane backs, seats and loose cushions raised on reeded turned tapered legs ending in brass caps and castors, bearing SHOOLBRED AND CO./ LONDON labels and stamped castors.
22.5in (57cm) wide
$5,250-6,750 **L&T**

A pair of ebonized and parcel gilt bergère armchairs in Regency style, rectangular backs, molded downswept arms with scroll terminals, molded square section tapering legs.
c1900 *25.5in (65cm) wide*
$700-850 **DN**

A Queen Anne upholstered wing armchair, possibly Irish, the rectangular back with a serpentine top rail and deep serpentine wings, over patted scroll arms and a loose cushion seat, raised on ebonized shaped cabriole legs, joined by a scroll-cut stretcher and ending on pad feet, in green velvet upholstery.
c1710 *30in (77cm) wide*
$7,500–12,000 **L&T**

A George II mahogany cockfighting chair, with close-nailed scarlet hide upholstery, fitted with later hinged board, raised on simple shaped and molded cabriole supports joined by turned stretchers.
$2,000-2,400 **HW**

A Scottish George I upholstered wing armchair, the high straight back with an arched toprail and deep curved wings, above scroll arms and a loose cushion seat, raised on cabriole legs ending in pad feet and joined by turned stretchers.
33.5in (85cm) wide
$6,000–9,000 **L&T**

An 18thC Scottish George III elm upholstered wing armchair, the high back with an arched top rail, over curved wings and short scroll arms and loose cushion seat, raised on square cabriole legs, joined by block-turned stretchers.
29in (73.5cm) wide
$1,500-2,250 **L&T**

A pair of Louis XV green-painted fauteuils, with cartouche-shaped backs, upholstered backs, arms and seats, on cabriole legs.

$4,000–5,250 **SWO**

A Scottish George III wing armchair, the wide padded back with a serpentine top rail flanked by deep curved wings, over wide scrolling arms and loose cushion seat, raised on straight molded legs, joined by stretchers, in pea-green velvet upholstery.

35in (89cm) wide

$3,000-4,500 **L&T**

A George III tub armchair, upholstered in blue and white chintz and raised on painted square tapered legs terminating in leather and brass caps and castors.

37in (95cm) wide

$1,200-1,800 **L&T**

A George III mahogany and leather upholstered wing armchair, covered in studded brown leather with a loose cushion seat, raised on square tapered legs ending in brass caps,

c1790 *26in (67cm) wide*

$6,000-7,500 **L&T**

A George III mahogany-framed wing armchair, the generously proportioned back stuffover upholstered, loose-cushioned seat, on chamfered square section supports joined by an H-shaped stretcher.

28in (71cm)

$975-1,300 **MOR**

A Regency mahogany and upholstered armchair, the square wide back over a loose cushion seat and low enclosed arms, raised on tapered reeded legs ending in brass caps and castors, in yellow silk damask upholstery.

c1815 *28in (71cm) wide*

$1,800–2,700 **L&T**

A Regency stained beech and leather upholstered library armchair, the arched padded back, padded outswept arms with carved arm terminals, the padded seat, on reeded tapered legs, caps and castors.

c1815 *30in (77cm) wide*

$1,000–1,500 **DN**

CLOSER LOOK - GEORGE IV LIBRARY CHAIR

Many chairs made between c1800 and c1830 reflect the exuberant taste of the Prince of Wales during his regency and his reign as George IV. This includes elegant upholstery, often in silk and damask.

The scroll arm facings are carved with palmettes. Both were inspired by the Classical styles of Ancient Rome which were fashionable at the time following the archaeological discoveries at Herculaneum and Pompeii.

A skilled craftsmen turned the wood for the front legs and carved them with facets.

The elegant rear legs splay outward from the chair back, adding to the extravagant effect.

A George IV simulated rosewood and upholstered library chair, the legs terminating in brass cappings and castors.

c1825 *31in (79cm) wide*

$1,800–4,000 **L&T**

A George IV rosewood library armchair, upholstered green leather with brass edging on brass castors.

$1,000–1,500 **WW**

A pair of 19thC mahogany bergère armchairs, each with the same upholstered padded seats and armrests.

$1,800–4,000 **WW**

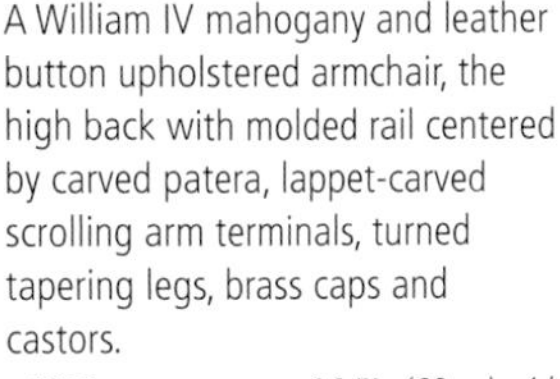

A William IV mahogany and leather button upholstered armchair, the high back with molded rail centered by carved patera, lappet-carved scrolling arm terminals, turned tapering legs, brass caps and castors.

c1835 *26.5in (68cm) wide*

$750-1,200 **DN**

An early Victorian mahogany and leather upholstered desk chair, on ceramic castors.

$700-850 WW

A 19thC George IV rosewood tub armchair, the curved enclosed back and arms ending in scrolled hand holds, over a loose cushion seat, raised on lappet carved tapered legs and foliate-carved ball feet with brass castors.

22in (56cm) wide

$1,500-2,250 L&T

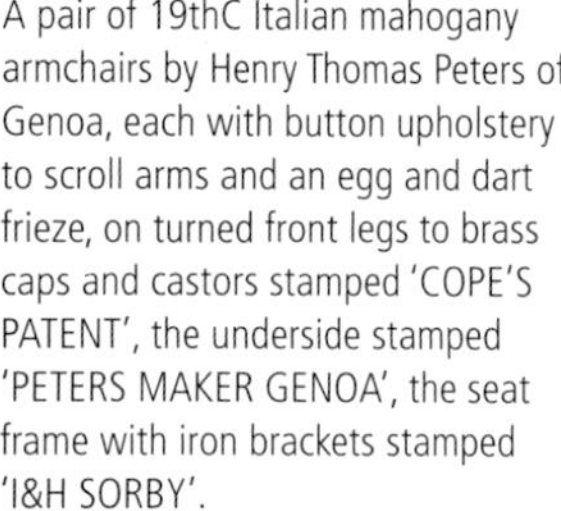

A pair of 19thC Italian mahogany armchairs by Henry Thomas Peters of Genoa, each with button upholstery to scroll arms and an egg and dart frieze, on turned front legs to brass caps and castors stamped 'COPE'S PATENT', the underside stamped 'PETERS MAKER GENOA', the seat frame with iron brackets stamped 'I&H SORBY'.

Henry Thomas Peters (d.1852) was active in Genova around 1830-1850 and was one of the leading cabinetmakers of the period. He was appointed cabinetmaker to the Court of Savoy and produced furniture for the Palazzo Reale in Genova. Peters produced furniture with the technical accuracy typical of English pieces but adapted it to a late Italian Empire style.

c1840

$6,000-7,500 WW

An early Victorian walnut framed chair, the button tufted back and stuffed-over seat in natural linen fabric, raised on cabriole legs ending in castors.

19in (49cm) wide

$600-900 L&T

A Victorian walnut library chair, upholstered back on molded scroll uprights, padded arms on end scroll supports, having serpentine seat on short-turned front legs and castors.

$300–600 DA&H

A pair of green leather upholstered tub armchairs, square backs with brass-studded border decoration, on tapering square legs, stamped 'GVS 57233'.

27.25in (69cm) wide

$4,000–5,250 CHEF

An armchair covered in Morris & Co 'Bird' woven woollen double cloth textile, probably retailed by Morris & Co, the textile designed by William Morris in 1878

42.5in (108cm) high

$1,000–1,500 WW

A Victorian walnut and leather upholstered armchair, buttoned overscolling rectangular back, pair of padded and arcaded rectangular arms, turned tapering legs, brass caps and ceramic castors at the front.

c1870 *27in (69cm) wide*

$900–1,400 DN

A 19thC George III-style wing armchair, on fluted mahogany front legs and later brass caps and castors.

$600-900 WW

A Victorian mahogany elbow chair, padded curved button-upholstered back and sides, with floral carved scrolling arm supports, on cabriole legs and ceramic castors.

c1880 *25.5in (65cm) wide*

$400–700 **DN**

A 19thC American chair attributed to J and JW Meeks of New York, carved and upholstered back on cabriole legs.

$225–400 **ECGW**

A late Victorian easy armchair, on turned walnut front legs to brass caps and castors stamped 'HOWARD & SONS, LONDON', the inside of the back left leg stamped '10370 3778'.

1880

$4,500-6,000 **WW**

A Queen Anne-style upholstered wing armchair, with upholstered back, seat and sides, on walnut cabriole legs with pad feet and a turned H-stretcher.

c1900 *31.5in (80cm) wide*

$550–850 **DN**

A George III-style upholstered tub armchair, high fluted back, scroll arms and cushion seat, on square tapered legs.

32in (82cm) wide

$600-900 **DN**

One of a pair of Edwardian upholstered club armchairs, with loose cushion seats, raised on bun feet with later castors.

31.5in (80cm) wide

$700–975 pair **L&T**

A pair of 20thC George II-style leather upholstered wing armchairs, the deep buttoned leather backs and scrolling arms over a loose cushion seat, raised on shell carved cabriole legs.

33in (84cm) wide

$6,000–9,000 **L&T**

A pair of 20thC Regency-style mahogany and upholstered armchairs, the curved padded backs and stuff over-seats upholstered in pale yellow check upholstery, within mahogany frames carved with lotus, acanthus and trailing bell flowers, raised on tapered square curved legs.

26in (67cm) wide

$1,800–4,000 **L&T**

A George II walnut and upholstered settee, the acanthus carved serpentine-shaped back, padded arms and stuffed over seat covered in green silk, raised on acanthus carved cabriole scroll legs united by a shell-carved apron.

c1740 *54in (138cm) wide*

$1,800–4,000 **L&T**

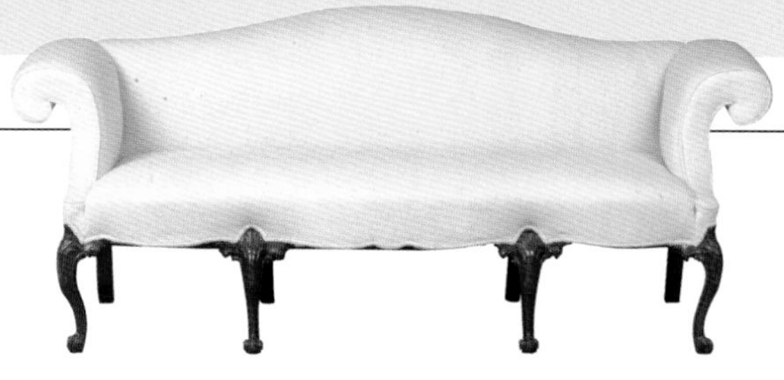

A George III upholstered sofa, the low padded back and high scroll arms above a padded seat, raised on scroll and foliate carved cabriole legs ending in scroll toes.

84.5in (215cm) wide

$5,250-6,750 **L&T**

A George III mahogany frame sofa, the slightly arched low back and downswept arms over a loose cushion seat, raised on square tapered legs.

59in (150cm) wide

$1,200-1,800 **L&T**

An 18thC continental painted and parcel gilt settee, the serpentine padded back and enclosed arms within a faux rosewood and parcel gilt frame centered by foliate carved cresting, in taupe plush fabric, raised on short cabriole legs.

76in (194cm)

$2,700-3,300 **L&T**

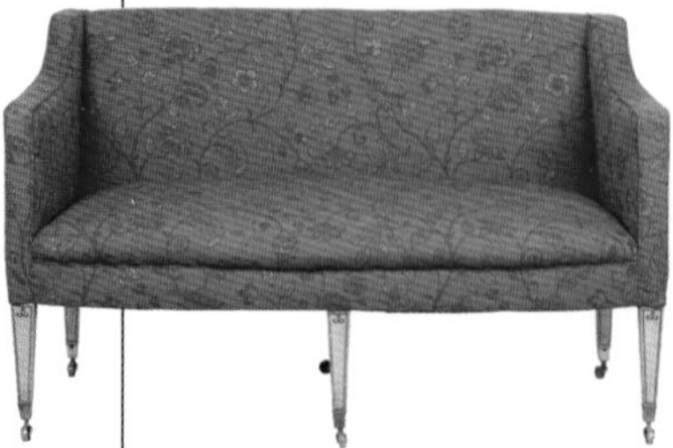

A late George III painted sofa, the straight upholstered back and squared enclosed arms raised on yellow painted square tapered legs ending in brass caps and castors, in modern coral foliate pattern upholstery.

c1800 *54in (138cm) wide*

$1,500–3,000 **L&T**

A Scottish Regency ebonized settee, with gilt metal mounts, the shaped back, scroll arms and loose cushion seat covered in cream fabric raised on bobbin-turned tapered legs terminating in brass cappings and castors, with two bolster cushions.

c1810 *76in (194cm) wide*

$1,800–4,000 **L&T**

ESSENTIAL REFERENCE - AMERICAN CLASSICAL/LATE FEDERAL STYLE

The American Classical style is among the Neo-classical styles that developed between c1760 and c1830.

- **The Neo-classical style began with rectilinear shapes taking over from curved Rococo ones. Pieces were inspired by examples from Classical antiquity and borrowed shapes and motifs from Greek and Roman architecture.**
- **In America the style was first seen in Federal pieces which were understated and inspired by designs produced by Adam, Sheraton and Hepplewhite in Britain.**
- **The Classical style – like the Regency style in Britain – is more exuberant than its predecessor. It is particularly associated with New York city and developed after c1815.**
- **Most pieces were made from mahogany and feature deeply carved Neo-classical motifs.**
- **Some examples have hints of the exoticism and flamboyancy seen on British examples.**
- **On sofas, curved and scrolled arms were popular, as were scrolled and shaped back rails.**

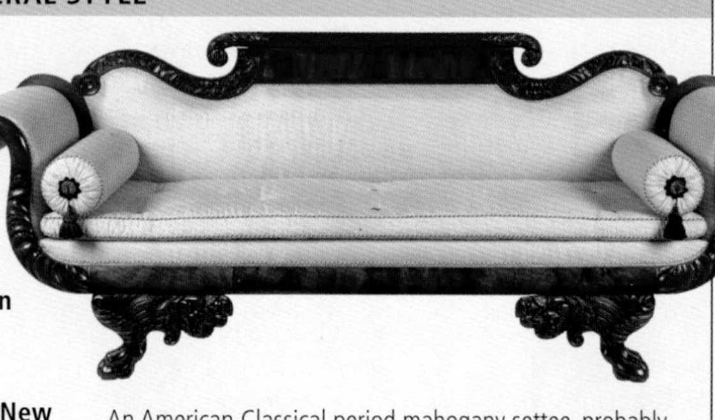

An American Classical period mahogany settee, probably New York, the serpentine back with a scroll end top rail carved with fruit and acanthus over a loose cushion seat and high scrolled arms, in yellow silk damask upholstery with two bolster cushions, the seat rail and corner brackets carved with acanthus and fruiting cornucopia, raised on carved lion paw feet.

c1825 *88in (224cm) wide*

$6,000-12,000 **L&T**

A Regency ebonized and parcel gilt three-seater sofa in the manner of John Gee, with a pierced top rail decorated with ribbon tied drapes, to fluted twist arms, with a cane seat, sides and seat, and a squab cushion and bolsters, the frame stamped 'TF'.

76.5in (195cm) wide

$4,000–5,250 **WW**

A 19thC Anglo-Indian carved hardwood settee, the slatted back and outscrolled arms above a cushioned seat, raised on carved outswept legs, carved throughout with scrolling lotus and poppies.

52.5in (134cm) wide

$1,500-2,250 **L&T**

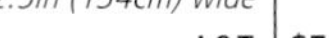

A 19thC Victorian Knole sofa, of typical form in faded green velvet with tassel edging and a brocade back panel.

63.5in (162cm) wide

$750-1,200 **L&T**

A late 19thC Louis XVI-style carved giltwood settee, arched and padded rectangular back carved with central ribbon and foliate terminal, molded downswept arms with scroll terminals, turned and fluted legs, brass caps and ceramic castors.

49in (124cm) wide

$1,000–1,500 **DN**

A Victorian walnut-framed sofa of curved outline upholstered in pale green velvet, oval padded back with pierced foliate carved crest, on scrolled supports, padded open arms on similar supports, overstuffed serpentine seat, raised on cabriole legs with scrolled feet and china castors.

60in (152cm) wide

$550–850 **HT**

A Louis XVI-style walnut and upholstered settee, the foliate-carved shaped back, padded scroll arms and stuffed-over seat covered in gold foliate-patterned fabric, raised on cabriole legs with castors.

c1880 *68in (173cm) long*

$750-1,200 **L&T**

A Victorian Chesterfield sofa, of typical form with a button-tufted back and arms upholstered in blue plush fabric, raised on bun feet.

87in (221cm) wide

$900–1,400 **L&T**

A late 19thC William & Mary-style walnut upholstered sofa, the high triple arch back over a loose cushion seat and scrolled arms, raised on carved legs with lobed buns and ending on scroll feet, joined by a shaped stretcher, in green velvet upholstery with tassel trim.

76in (193cm) wide

$3,000-4,500 **L&T**

A late Victorian Chesterfield sofa, button-upholstered on turned oak legs and unusual wooden ball castors, the back leg stamped 'GILLOW' and numbered '566 513749'.

89in (226cm) wide

$750-1,200 **WW**

A Louis XVI-style cream painted and parcel gilt sofa and pair of armchairs, arched rectangular backs, downswept arms with scrolling acanthus terminals, loose cushion seats, turned tapering fluted legs.

c1900 *the sofa 77in (195cm) wide*

$1,500-2,250 set **DN**

An early 20thC George II-style mahogany chair-back settee, with a serpentine and scroll top rail with pierced vasiform splat between splayed arm supports, above an upholstered drop-in seat raised on shell carved cabriole legs, terminating in hairy paw feet.

36in (92cm) wide

$2,100-2,700 **L&T**

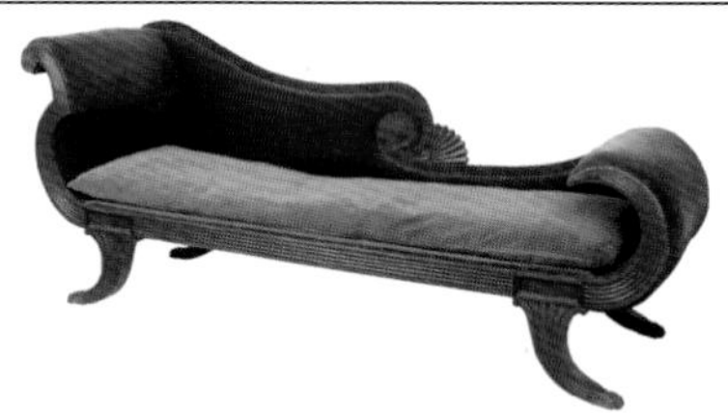

A Scottish Regency mahogany chaise longue, in the manner of William Trotter, the padded shaped back, scroll arm and loose cushion seat with reeded facings, raised on conforming reeded sabre legs terminating in brass hairy paw cappings.

c1815 *82in (208cm) wide*

$2,100-2,700 **L&T**

A Regency ebonized and parcel gilt chaise longue, shaped back and scrolling arm rest, painted with scrolling acanthus, on turned legs, caps and castors.

c1815 *75in (190cm) long*

$1,200-1,800 **DN**

A Scottish William IV mahogany chaise longue, the curved shaped padded back with bead-and-reel carving over a padded seat flanked by scroll arms faced by carved urn and scrolling foliate panels, raised on carved lyre form legs and lobed bun feet, in red faux leather upholstery.

c1830 *82.5in (210cm) long*

$2,400-3,000 **L&T**

ESSENTIAL REFERENCE - METAMORPHIC FURNITURE

Metamorphic furniture was designed to change form or function, and often incorporates space-saving features. Typical examples include chairs or tables that convert into library steps. Collapsible and extendable dining tables and buffets were also made.

- **The first pieces were made in the mid-18thC when people became fascinated by mechanical furniture, and between 1770 and 1820 a wide variety of designs emerged which gave cabinetmakers the opportunity to exploit their technical expertise and satisfy public demand for innovative designs.**
- **The style was pioneered by German-born American cabinetmaker George Hunzinger who made functional, mechanical furniture.**
- **While the furniture was innovative, the mechanisms were generally simple to use. For example, many library chairs were converted to steps by releasing a small catch on the rear stretcher of the chair, allowing the back and seat to hinge forward to reveal a set of steps.**

A Victorian oak metamorphic chair, the hinged seat allowing the frame to revolve and become a set of library steps, rectangular back shaped and pierced splat, solid seat, pierced and shaped trestle legs.

c1870 *16.5in (42cm) wide*

$975-1,300 **DN**

A Victorian rosewood chaise longue, with buttoned back and foliate carving on cabriole legs with brass castors.

c1880 *69in (175cm) wide*

$400-550 **DN**

A Victorian mahogany and upholstered chaise longue, in blue patterned fabric with tufted back and arm, raised on turned tapered legs with brass caps and ceramic castors.

70in (178cm) long

$1,000-1,800 **L&T**

A Victorian chaise longue, later upholstered and on turned walnut legs and brass caps and castors stamped 'COPE & COLLINSON PATENT', the beechwood stretcher to the underside with a paper label inscribed 'EASY CHAIR & SOFA FACTORY, HOWARD & SONS UPHOLSTERERS, 27 BERNERS STREET, LONDON, PATENT DINING TABLES', inscribed in pencil '153265277'.

60.5in (154cm) wide

$1,000-1,800 **WW**

A 19thC mahogany reclining chair, button-upholstered armrests, cushion back and seat, on turned legs and brass castors.

36in (63cm) wide

$600-900 **CHEF**

A mahogany framed leather gaming chair, leather back and seat, the arms with hinged compartments opening to divisions including two decanters and a glass, with an adjustable leather inset footrest, on castors, bearing a label for Glenisters Patent and listing the Patent and design numbers.

c1900 *31.5 in (80cm) wide*

$1,800–2,700 **DN**

A 17thC oak refectory table, with a removable cleated end three board top, above a carved frieze having a chevron parquetry border and turned legs, front stretcher with wear and old worm, feet tipped, basically reconstructed using earlier elements.

82.25in (208.5cm) long

$1,500-2,250 WW

A 17thC oak refectory table, the plank top with cleated ends on acorn and turned knop legs united by floor-level stretchers.

78.5in (199cm) long

$1,800–2,700 CHEF

A Charles II refectory table, the three board cleated top over a plain frieze, raised on turned baluster legs ending on octagonal block feet and joined by an H-form stretcher.

83.5in (212cm) long

$3,000-4,000 L&T

A 17th or 18thC Italian walnut refectory table, the large planked rectangular top over two boldly carved scroll supports with caryatids to the center, united by similarly carved stretcher.

93in (244cm) long

$11,500–13,000 FRE

An early 19thC French chestnut refectory table, the twin plank top above three frieze drawers, shaped apron, on cabriole shaped square section legs.

83in (211cm) long

$1,800-3,000 DN

A 19thC Flemish oak draw-leaf table, with earlier elements the created rectangular top above a molded frieze, raised on bulbous baulster turned legs, united by a peripheral stretcher.

100in (255cm) long when extended

$1,800–2,700 L&T

A 19thC French provincial walnut dining table, the cleated plank top over deep frieze with four fielded drawers on each long side having brass pear-drop handles, raised on ring-and-baluster-turned and block legs with bun feet joined by square stretchers.

83.5in (212cm) long

$1,500-2,250 HT

An early 18thC oak gateleg table, the elm drop-leaf top above an end frieze drawer, on block and turned supports and scroll feet.

51in (130cm) long extended

$750-1,200 WW

A Boston William & Mary maple gateleg dining table, with a single drawer, retaining an old red stained surface.

c1720 *46.5in (118cm) long*

$15,000-21,000 POOK

A New England William & Mary maple and pine gateleg tavern table, probably Massachusetts, with a single demi-lune dropleaf and a drawer supported by baluster-turned legs joined by a box stretcher, retaining an old red surface.

c1740 *40.5in (103cm) long closed*

$10,500-12,000 POOK

A mid-18thC Georgian mahogany drop-leaf table, the oval top with drop sides raised on straight legs ending on pad feet.

39in (99cm) long

$1,200-1,800 L&T

A Victorian dwarf burr walnut and ash Sutherland table, the oval top with drop sides and a molded edge raised on bobbin-turned legs joined by a bobbin-turned stretcher, on scroll trestle feet, the gate legs with porcelain castors.

25in (64cm) wide

$900-1,200 L&T

A pair of 19thC small faux rosewood painted and gilt drop-leaf tables, the oval tops with drop sides raised on bell and baluster-turned slender legs joined by peripheral stretchers.

20in (74cm) long

$750-1,200 L&T

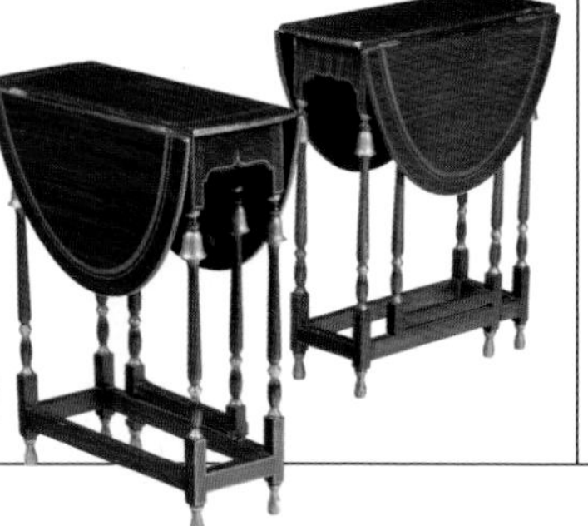

A Victorian bird's eye maple Sutherlund table, turned double gate section, turned trestle supports and stretcher, on knopped downswept feet.

c1860 *41in (105cm) wide*

$850-975 DN

A George III mahogany three-pillar dining table, with a drop-leaf center section fitted with two frieze drawers and two 'D' ends with a tilt-top action, each supported on a vase-shaped turned pedestal and downswept tripod legs.

110in (280cm) long

$9,000-10,500 **SWO**

A Regency mahogany extending dining table, the rectangular top with rounded corners and a reeded edge over a deep frieze with bead molding, raised on squared baluster end supports joined by a turned cross-stretcher raised on reeded sabre legs ending in brass paw caps and castors, with two leaf inserts.

c1815 *95in (242cm) long extended*

$9,000–12,000 **L&T**

An early 19thC mahogany pedestal dining table, the rounded rectangular top with one leaf insert, raised on baluster-turned columns ending on sabre legs with brass caps and castors.

75.5in (192cm) long

$3,000-4,500 **L&T**

A Regency twin-pedestal dining table, the rounded rectangular top on twin pedestal supports, each end with a drop leaf over a frieze drawer to one side and a dummy drawer opposing, raised on turned column supports ending on four outswept legs ending in brass caps and castors, with one leaf extension.

Provenance: Previously Somerville College, Oxford. Reportedly the boardroom table at Somerville. Founded in 1879, Somerville College, Oxford was among the first colleges in the country to be created to allow women to benefit from higher education. It was named after Mary Somerville, an important scientist of the nineteenth century and also an author, mathematician, astronomer, landscape artist and suffragette. Illustrious alumnae include Dorothy Hodgkin, the only British woman to win a Nobel Prize in science, Indira Gandhi and Margaret Thatcher. Male undergraduates first gained admission in 1994.

c1815 *87in (221cm) long*

$1,800–4,000 **L&T**

A George IV mahogany D-end extending dining table, the rounded rectangular top above a plain frieze raised on turned, tapered, reeded legs terminating in brass cappings and castors, with five leaf extensions.

c1825 *55in (139cm) long*

$5,250-6,750 **L&T**

An early Victorian mahogany metamorphic twin-pedestal dining table, the rounded rectangular top with four end sections to form two breakfast tables, raised on baluster turned column supports ending in downswept scroll legs with brass castors.

c1840 *53.5in (136cm) wide*

$9,000-15,000 **L&T**

A Victorian A. D. Narramore Ltd mahogany extending dining table, the pull-out action with five separate leaves, the banded rounded oblong top with ebony stringing and hinged end flaps, molded edged frieze, raised on three square section supports each with twin reeded downswept legs having brass toes and castors, together with maker's original drawings in watercolor.

107in (271cm) long

$1,800-3,000 **HT**

A 20thC Regency-style mahogany and gilt-mounted twin-pedestal dining table, with an additional leaf, oval top with metal mounted edge, each turned and reeded stem, on stepped and fluted downswept legs, brass caps and castors.

110in (280cm) long

$750-1,200 **DN**

A George III mahogany three-pillar dining table, the gun barrel column on tripod supports, fitted with two extra leaves.

140in (356cm) long

$10,500-12,000 **CHOR**

CLOSER LOOK - REGENCY EXTENDING DINING TABLE

A Regency mahogany extending dining table, the rectangular top with rounded corners with two leaf inserts.

c1815 *95in (242cm) long extended*

$9,000–12,000 **L&T**

A George III mahogany dining table, comprising of two D-end sections, central Pembroke twin gate leg table section with two hinged leaves, rectangular top with molded edge, rounded corners, plain frieze on turned tapering legs.

c1790 *174in (442cm) long*

$1,800–2,700 **DN**

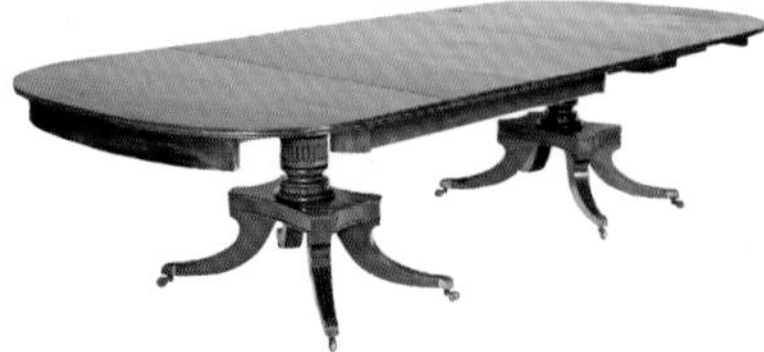

A Regency mahogany extending dining table of rounded oblong form with three separate leaves and pull-out action, reeded edged top, plain frieze, raised on twin pedestal supports each with reeded banding, concave platform base, and four downswept legs with brass toes and castors.

112in (284cm) long

$5,250-6,750 **HT**

A Regency mahogany extending dining table, in the manner of Gillows, the rounded rectangular top with a reeded edge, raised on turned and reeded tapered legs ending in brass caps and castors, with four leaf extensions.

c1820 *131.5in (334cm) long*

$12,000-15,000 **L&T**

A William IV mahogany extending dining table, with two additional leaf insertions, the rectangular top with molded edge, molded frieze, lappet-carved tapering legs, brass caps and castors.

c1835 *93.5in (238cm) long extended*

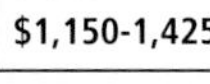

$1,150-1,425 **DN**

A Victorian mahogany extending dining table, with four additional leaf insertions in a leaf rack, rectangular top with molded edge, conforming frieze, turned and reeded legs, brass caps and castors.

c1870 *132in (335cm) long*

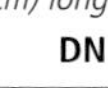

$1,800–4,000 **DN**

A Victorian mahogany extending dining table of D-end form with wind-out action and four leaves, molded edged top over a curved plain frieze, raised on lobed and fluted baluster turned tapering legs with brass toes and china castors, paper label for Roadhouse & Sons Ltd, Leeds, and ivorine label for W Richardson & Sons, Leeds.

172.5in (438cm) long

$10,500–13,500 **HT**

A mahogany extending dining table, the circular top with molded edge extending with three additional leaf insertions, molded frieze, turned and reeded tapering legs.

c1890 *94in (239cm) long extended*

$1,800–4,000 **DN**

A Georgian-style mahogany triple pillar dining table, of large proportions, the reeded edge with seven extra leaves, each pillar raised on four-ring turned stands, on downswept legs, with brass paw caps and castors.

91in (232cm) long closed

$12,000–18,000 **SWO**

A mahogany circular dining table with ebony crossbanding and brass stringing, after a Regency design by George Bullock, raised on a graduated square platform base with carved claw feet and acanthus carved scrolls.

80in (203cm) diam

$5,250-6,750 **TEN**

A circular mahogany concentric extending dining table, of recent manufacture, with five curved extensions.

84in (213cm) diam extended

$1,500-2,250 **DN**

A George III mahogany breakfast table, the rectangular drop-leaf top with a molded edge, over a single frieze drawer to one end raised on square tapered legs joined by a shaped X-form stretcher and ending in tassel feet with brass castors.
c1760 *43.5in (111cm) long open*
$1,500-2,250 L&T

A George III mahogany supper table, the oval top with drop-down sides above a single frieze drawer over a pair of in-curved wire mesh lined doors and side panels, raised on square tapered legs ending on brass caps and castors.
38in (97cm) wide
$450-750 L&T

A Regency rosewood and calamander crossbanded breakfast table, the rounded rectangular tilt top with line inlaid edge raised on four turned column supports over a rectangular undertier, raised on scrolling sabre legs ending in brass hairy paw feet and castors.
c1815 *84.5in (123cm) wide*
$1,500–3,000 L&T

A Regency mahogany breakfast table, the rectangular top with molded edge, turned stem on triple-hipped downswept legs, brass caps and castors.
c1815 *48.5in (123cm) long*
$600-900 DN

A mahogany breakfast table, the molded edge crossbanded tilt-top on a ring turned stem and hipped downswept legs and brass caps and castors, early 19thC top.
62in (158cm) long
$750-1,200 WW

ESSENTIAL REFERENCE - WILLIAM TROTTER

In the early 19thC, William Trotter (1772–1833) became the most important and successful cabinetmaker in Scotland. His work often used rosewood and is known for its restrained and understated decoration, including reeding, paterae and molding. It is rarely marked. Much of his furniture was commissioned for fashionable new homes in Edinburgh's burgeoning New Town.

- **Trotter was a descendent of John Knox, a founding father of the Protestant Reformation in Scotland, and of the Church of Scotland. His father was a merchant and he became a member of The Merchant Company in 1797 and was elected master in 1819. As well as running a successful business he was Lord Provost of Edinburgh from 1825–27.**
- **The writer Thomas Dibdin described his workshop in Princes Street, Edinburgh: 'The locality of this great warehouse is rather singular. It is on the ground floor, lighted by a skylight. Of great length, and vistas filled with Mahogany and Rosewood objects of temptation. Of all styles, including the modern form'.**

A Regency burrwood and ebony inlaid breakfast table, in the manner of William Trotter, the circular top with a double band of ebony inlay above a frieze with bead-molded edge, raised on a waisted square support with a foliate carved collar, on a quatreform base raised on lobed bun feet.
c1815 *50.5in (129cm) diam*
$5,250-6,750 L&T

A Regency rosewood and brass inlaid breakfast table, the circular top above a gilt-molded frieze inlaid with brass flowerheads and lotus, on a tapered ring-turned column raised on downswept brass inlaid legs ending in hairy paw caps and castors.
c1815 *48in (122cm) diam*
$1,500-2,250 L&T

A Regency mahogany, rosewood, crossbanded and ebony breakfast table, the round crossbanded and inlaid top over a turned baluster support and quatreform platform with gadroon molding, raised on downswept scrolling legs ending in reeded brass caps and castors.
c1815 *49in (125cm) diam*
$1,500-2,250 L&T

A William IV rosewood breakfast table, the circular tilt-top on a turned and acanthus carved stem, the triform base with scroll feet and sunken brass castors.
50in (127cm) diam
$2,550-3,000 WW

A William IV rosewood breakfast table, the circular tilt-top with egg and dart moldings on a triform base with scroll feet and brass castors.
48in (122cm) diam
$1,500-2,250 WW

A mid-Victorian burr walnut breakfast table, the circular top with a molded edge above a lobed baluster column on paneled tripod legs terminating in scrolled feet.
c1860 *51in (130cm) diam*
$600-900 L&T

A George II and later walnut center table, the molded edge top above a shaped frieze centered either side a carved shell, on shell-capped legs terminating in fluted square-section feet, possibly Irish.

37in (94cm) wide

$1,800-2,700 **WW**

A Regency rosewood brass-inlaid center table, the circular tilt top inlaid in brass with a wide band of stylized foliate scrolls, over a frieze with a beaded edge, raised on a triform acanthus carved column support, ending in a triform base with brass bun feet.

c1815 *50in (127cm) diam*

$9,000–12,000 **L&T**

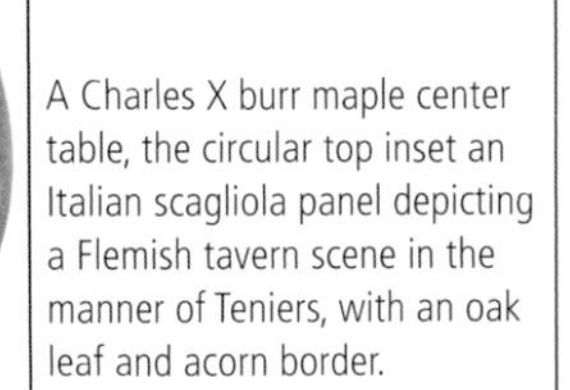

A Charles X burr maple center table, the circular top inset an Italian scagliola panel depicting a Flemish tavern scene in the manner of Teniers, with an oak leaf and acorn border.

38.75in (98.5cm) diam

$4,000–5,250 **WW**

A George IV rosewood and brass marquetry center table, with a tilt-top.

49in (124.5cm) diam

$7,500-13,500 **WW**

A George IV rosewood breakfast table, the circular top with a plain frieze on a turned tapered column carved with gadroon molding and acanthus scrolls, on a triform platform base raised on lobed bun feet.

c1825 *52in (132cm) diam*

$1,800–2,700 **L&T**

A William IV rosewood center table, the circular tilt-top with an applied scrolling leaf edge above a well carved lappet stem and a leaf and petal base with conforming scroll feet to castors.

58.75in (147cm) diam

$1,800–4,000 **WW**

An Anglo-Indian padouk center table, the large circular top with a foliate-carved edge, on a baluster turned and foliate carved column and four reeded and acanthus-carved scroll supports, on a quatreform base raised on ball feet.

c1840 *64.5in (164cm) diam*

$4,500–7,500 **L&T**

CLOSER LOOK - RENT TABLE

This table is an example of the 19thC practice of creating commemorative furniture from materials taken from buildings, ships or wood in particular locations. It is made from timber and stone from different locations in Yorkshire and was made for Sheffield steel manufacturer Benjamin Sayle (1770-1846).

The molded edge features an applied brass band with the remains of an inscription which may have related to the story behind the table.

The turned stem, quatreform base and sunken wood castors are typical features of William I tables of this style.

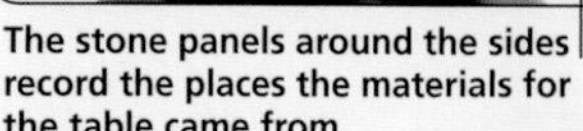

The stone panels around the sides record the places the materials for the table came from.

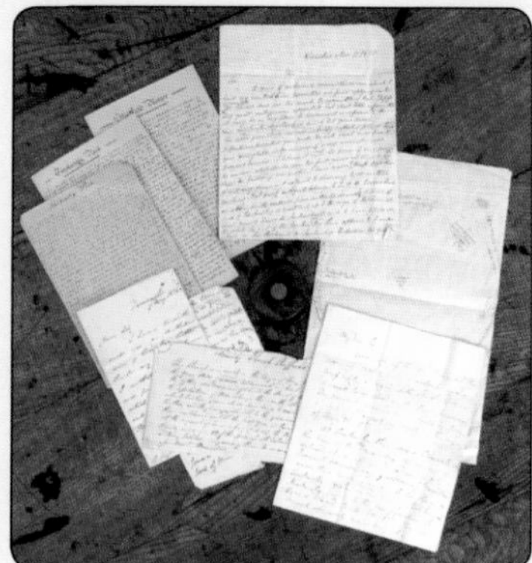

A William IV oak and brass mounted rent table by Benjamin Sayle Esq., constructed from timber and stone donated by among others the Duke of Norfolk and Earl Fitzwilliam from Roche Abbey, Tankersley Hall, York Minster and Pontefract Castle, the revolving top has a central brass plaque within a circular section of oak, inscribed 'PONTEFRACT CASTLE 1074', above four frieze drawers and four false fronts, with applied stone panel with inscriptions, together with letters and documents relating to the table and the donation of the oak and stone.

48in (123cm) diam

$12,750-15,750 **WW**

An unusual 19thC Louis Phillipe Moorish-style parquetry and marquetry inlaid octagonal center table, the octagonal top inlaid to the center to show a quiver of arrows and a horn, surrounded by parquetry inlay in various fruitwoods, above conforming galleried sides united by stepped undertier surmounted by an urn, raised on ebonized bun feet.

38.75in (98cm) diam

$5,250-6,750 **FRE**

A 19thC gonccalo alves center table, the circular top with a plain edge, on a lappet-carved stem, concave sided platform, on leaf-carved scroll feet.

48in (122cm) diam

$975-1,300 **DN**

A Victorian burr walnut and walnut circular center table, the circular top with molded edge, turned and gadrooned stem, on three molded downswept legs, scroll carved feet and concealed castors.

c1880 *47in (120cm) diam*

$1,200-1,500 **DN**

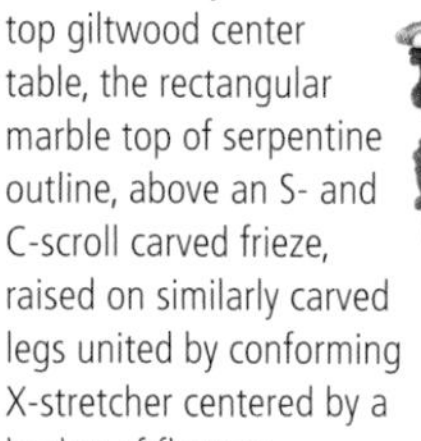

A Louis XV-style marble top giltwood center table, the rectangular marble top of serpentine outline, above an S- and C-scroll carved frieze, raised on similarly carved legs united by conforming X-stretcher centered by a basket of flowers.

c1900 *66in 167cm) diam*

$12,000–18,000 **FRE**

A pair of 20thC French Louis XV-style kingwood center tables, each with a shaped verde antico marble top and with ormolu mounts, on cabriole legs united by an X-stretcher with a flaming finial.

24.5in (62cm) wide.

$1,800–2,700 **WW**

A George III mahogany drum library table, the circular top with a green leather insert, above four real and four dummy frieze drawers with boxwood stringing, on a baluster column and reeded sabre legs ending in carved paw feet with brass castors.

50in (127cm) diam

$3,000-4,500 L&T

A Regency mahogany library table, the molded rectangular top with gilt tooled leather inset, a pair of frieze drawers with ivory handles, molded rectangular trestle supports, plinth bases , brass caps and castors.

c1815 *42in (107cm) wide*

$750-1,200 DN

INTRODUCTION TO LIBRARY TABLES

In the early 19thC a number of new types of furniture were developed with specific uses. These include library tables.

- **They usually have fixed ends to make the tops sturdy enough to hold piles of books; others can be extended to support large maps or other documents. The surfaces were generally covered with leather to make them comfortable for use when writing. The legs are positioned to allow plenty of room for a reader's or writer's legs to sit under the table top. It may be fitted with drawers.**
- **Early writing tables were made in the then fashionable Neo classical, Regency style and may feature decorative inlays and stringing and gilt brass mounts.**
- **Library tables can be rectangular or circular.**

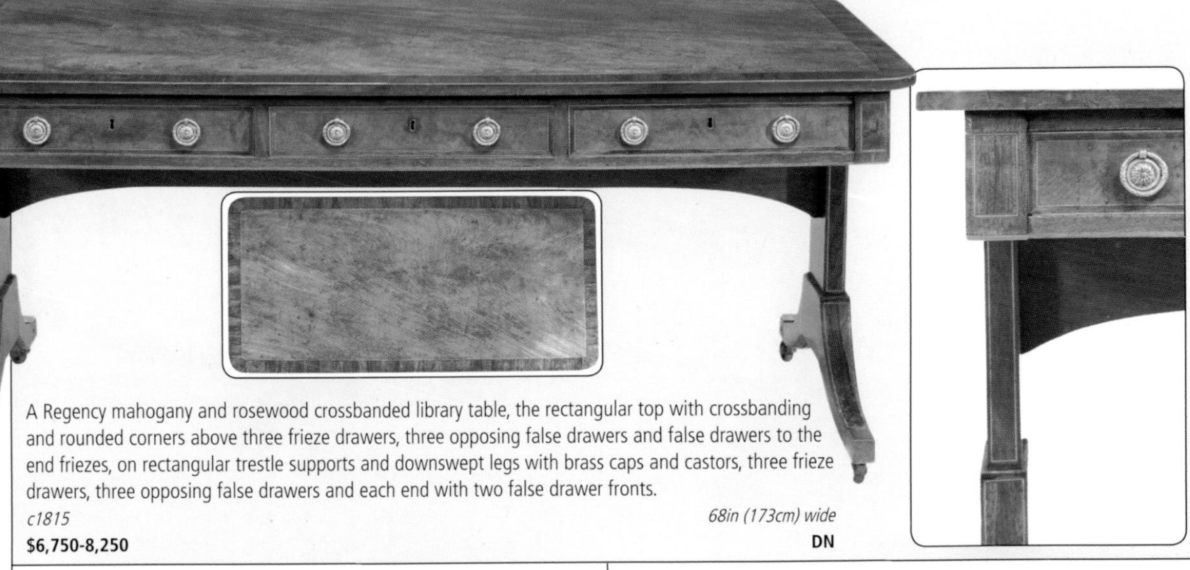

A Regency mahogany and rosewood crossbanded library table, the rectangular top with crossbanding and rounded corners above three frieze drawers, three opposing false drawers and false drawers to the end friezes, on rectangular trestle supports and downswept legs with brass caps and castors, three frieze drawers, three opposing false drawers and each end with two false drawer fronts.

c1815 *68in (173cm) wide*

$6,750-8,250 DN

A Regency mahogany library table, the rounded rectangular top with a green leather writing surface over two short frieze drawers, with two dummy drawers opposing and blue leather lined lateral slides, raised on square end supports and trestle bases with scrolled brackets.

c1815 *48in (122cm) wide*

$3,000-4,500 L&T

A Regency mahogany library table, formerly from Windsor Castle, the rounded rectangular top with a green tooled leather insert, above two short frieze drawers with brass star escutcheons, with two dummy drawers opposing, raised on squared lotus carved side supports on reeded sabre legs ending in brass caps and castors; stamped on the underside 'Windsor Castle / Room 6411' under a crowned VR, with a paper inventory label with item no. 20.

c1815 *47in (119cm) wide*

$5,250-6,750 L&T

A George IV mahogany drum-top library table, with crossbanding and stringing, the top with green leather inset above an arrangement of four frieze drawers and four false drawers, on a turned stem and four hipped downswept legs, brass caps and castors.

c1825 *43.5 in (110cm) diam*

$4,500-6,000 **DN**

A William IV rosewood library table, the rectangular top with curved corners on lappet-carved supports and scroll feet to brass castors.

50in (127cm) wide

$1,800-3,000 **WW**

A William IV rosewood library table, the rectangular top with rounded corners and gilt tooled leather inset, a pair of frieze drawers and an opposing pair of false drawers, molded rectangular trestle uprights, plinth bases, scroll carved feet and concealed castors.

c1835 *45in (114cm) wide*

$900-1,200 **DN**

A William IV rosewood library table, with rectangular top, pair of freize drawers, each end with two barley twist supports united by a turned and square-section stretcher.

c1835 *55in (140cm) wide*

$1,200-1,800 **DN**

An early Victorian rosewood library table, with a pair of frieze drawers fitted with turned knob handles, on solid trestle ends united by a turned beech stretcher, on disc feet with sunken brass castors.

53.5in (136cm) wide

$300-450 **WW**

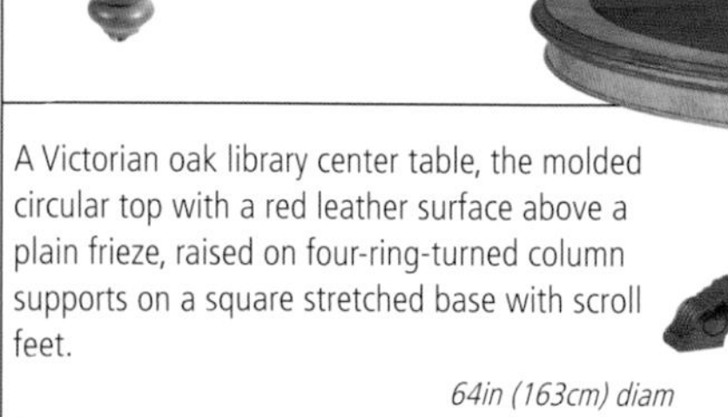

A Victorian oak library center table, the molded circular top with a red leather surface above a plain frieze, raised on four-ring-turned column supports on a square stretched base with scroll feet.

64in (163cm) diam

$700-850 **L&T**

An early 20thC Regency-style mahogany library table, the rectangular top over a line-inlaid frieze fitted with an arrangement of real and dummy drawers, raised on reeded tapered legs.

53.5in (136cm) wide

$1,500-2,250 **L&T**

CLOSER LOOK - IRISH PIER TABLE

The extravagant frieze features a tongue and dart border above a pounced lattice panel and ribbon tied rods. These motifs are typical of the period.

The gilding all over the table is of a high quality.

The lion mask in the center of the table creates a strong focal point enhanced by the swags of oak leaves, shells and foliate scrolls.

The bold leaf-capped broken square cabriole legs terminate in bold claw-and-ball feet.

A George II Irish giltwood and gesso pier table, with a later breccia marble top.
c1740 *25in (63cm) wide*
$115,000-150,000 **ADA**

A Louis XV marble-top console table, the yellow and orange veined marble top with rounded fore-corners, over shaped frieze centered by a scallop shell, raised on cabriole legs.
56in (142cm) wide
$3,000-4,500 **FRE**

An Adam-style giltwood and gesso console table, the veined and mottled marble top above an egg and dart and fluted frieze, flanked and divided by foliate roundel motifs, raised on square tapered legs decorated with enclosed guilloche panels and with doric capitals, terminated in ball feet.
c1830 *59in (150cm) wide*
$12,000–18,000 **L&T**

A William IV mahogany and marble mounted console table, variegated grey marble top, molded frieze, scrolling molded tapering legs at the front, above a shaped plinth, turned bun feet.
36in (92cm) wide
$600-750 **DN**

ESSENTIAL REFERENCE - MATTIAS LOCK

Matthias Lock (d.1765) was an accomplished carver and designer who worked in London in the 18thC.

- **He was apprenticed to his father, also named Matthias, who was a joiner, and Richard Goldsaddle, the carver, in 1724. By the 1740s he was working for himself.**
- **Between 1740 and his death he published numerous books of designs for furniture, including mirrors and girandoles.**
- **He was described by a pupil, and fellow designer and carver, Thomas Johnson, as 'the famous Matthias Lock, the most excellent carver, and reputed to be the best ornament draughts-man in Europe'.**
- **He probably also supplied some of the furniture designs for the first edition of Thomas Chippendale's 'The Gentleman and Cabinet-Maker's Director', published in 1754.**
- **Lock's 1746 publication 'Six designs for Tables' include patterns for marble tables in this French 'Picturesque' manner, with flowered festooned Roman acanthus and scalloped cartouches.**

A George II carved giltwood console table, in the manner of Matthias Lock, the marble top with molded edge and rounded outset corners the foliate and scroll carved frieze cornered by female mask terminals and on foliate carved cabriole legs and hoof feet.
c1750
$6,000-7,500 **DN**

One of a pair of Russian Empire-style mahogany and brass mounted console tables, the three-quarter galleried top above a paneled frieze flanked and divided by roundel motifs, raised on square tapered legs ending in spade feet.

86in (219cm) wide

$15,000–22,500 pair **L&T**

An Italian giltwood console table, the later marble top over a deep carved edge, pierced aprons with floral husks and centered with flowerhead and lattice shields, the C- and S-scroll legs united with a shaped stretcher, with an urn finial.

56in (143cm) wide

$4,000–5,250 **SWO**

A 19thC Continental ebonized and parcel gilt slate top console table, the rectangular black slate top raised on ram's head monopodia on a faux marble painted plinth base with a mirror back.

50.5in (129cm) wide

$1,800–2,700 **L&T**

A 19thC French mahogany console table, the later crossbanded and molded edge rosewood top above a frieze drawer, with front turned columns with brass mounts.

45in (115cm) wide

$600-900 **WW**

A 19thC Continental painted and parcel gilt marble-top console table, the thick Breche marble breakfront top with a molded edge over a frieze carved with rosettes and patera and centered by an oval portrait medallion above a pierced and carved foliate apron, raised on scrolling volute legs carved with acanthus and joined by a stretcher rail.

53in (135cm) wide

$4,500–7,500 **L&T**

A 19thC French carved and painted pine console table, in the form of a spread eagle supporting a Serpentine white marble top.

48in (123cm) wide

$3,000-6,000 **SWO**

A 19thC mahogany console table, with a Breche marble top, with a paneled frieze and carved scroll supports to a serpentine plinth base.

47in (119cm) wide

$1,800–4,000 **WW**

A 19thC Bombay blackwood console table, profusely carved, on cross stretchers and with carved legs.

c1860 *63in (160cm) wide*

$3,000-4,500 **CHEF**

A George III mahogany serving table, the crossbanded and boxwood strung top above two frieze drawers and raised on square tapered legs terminating in spade feet.

70in (177cm) wide

$1,800–2,700 L&T

A George III mahogany breakfront serving table, of shallow breakfront outline, raised on square tapered legs with spade feet and headed by patera.

95in (242cm) wide

$1,500-2,250 L&T

A George III mahogany, satinwood and inlay serpentine serving table, the serpentine top over a conforming crossbanded frieze with ebony and boxwood stringing, raised on square tapered legs with line inlay.

c1780 *84in (213cm) wide*

$3,000-4,500 L&T

A large Scottish George IV mahogany serving table, the stepped arch back panel carved with foliate scrolls, over an inverted breakfront top with a gadrooned carved edge, raised on reeded and lotus carved legs capped by flower carved blocks, on foliate carved bun feet.

c1825 *111in (282cm) long*

$9,750–11,250 L&T

A George IV mahogany serpentine serving table, the molded serpentine top over a deep frieze and raised on chamfered straight legs ending on block feet.

c1825 *72in (183cm) wide*

$10,500-15,000 L&T

A 19thC George III-style mahogany and brass mounted serving table, stamped Gillows & Co, the breakfront rectangular top with a brass gallery with urn finials, above a conforming frieze with a central drawer carved with an urn and ribbon tied laurel swags flanked by fluted panels, raised on scrolling volute legs carved with acanthus and ending on scroll toes on block feet, the drawer stamped "Gillows & Co" and the number L41766.

95.5in (243cm) wide

$6,000–9,000 L&T

An early 17thC oak Salisbury credence table, with a canted folding top, the guilloche and chevron banded frieze with stamped decoration, having a later central drawer, above three arches and ring-turned legs to a conforming base with an undertier, the back with a single gate.

38.5in (97cm) wide

$5,250-6,750 **WW**

CLOSER LOOK - SIDE TABLE

The alabaster-veneered top reflects the Italian baroque influence in William Kent and William Kent-style furniture.

Carved acanthus and Vitruvian scrolls on the frieze are motifs from Classical antiquity.

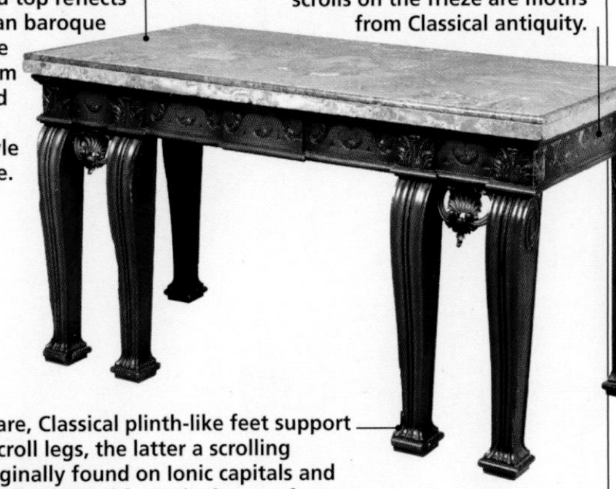

The square, Classical plinth-like feet support volute scroll legs, the latter a scrolling form originally found on Ionic capitals and purportedly derived from the horns of a ram.

A George II mahogany and alabaster side table in the manner of William Kent, the rectangular alabaster veneered top with a molded verde antico edge above a wide frieze with carved acanthus and Vitruvian scrolls, the apron with pierced and carved shells, raised on six reeded volute scroll legs ending in spreading square feet.

59.5 in (151cm) wide

$150,000-225,000 **L&T**

A William & Mary side table, with rectangular quarter-veneered top, frieze drawer, spiral turned legs with an X-shaped stretcher and turned feet.

c1690 *34in (86cm) wide*

$1,500-2,250 **DN**

A George II mahogany silver table, the rounded rectangular dish top above a plain frieze raised on lappet carved turned tapered legs ending in pad feet.

c1750 *30in (76cm) wide*

$1,200-1,800 **L&T**

One of a pair of George II fruitwood side tables, the white marble tops painted and grained in veined green to simulate variegated green marble, the frieze with Greek key blind fretwork on square chamfered legs.

54in (137cm) wide

$15,000–18,000 pair **CHOR**

An 18thC Irish George III mahogany marble top side table, the later rectangular white veined marble top over a plain frieze centered by a carved shell motif, raised on scroll carved cabriole legs ending on claw and ball feet.

37.5in (95cm) wide

$7,500–12,000 **L&T**

A George III oak side table, with rectangular top, two frieze drawers, on square legs united by a stretcher.

c1780 36in (91cm) wide

$1,500-2,250 **DN**

A 19thC Regency mahogany inverted bowfront side table, the shaped rectangular top with rounded outset forecorners, over three frieze drawers, raised on fluted and turned tapered legs ending in turned feet.

41.5in (106cm) wide

$1,800–4,000 **L&T**

FURNITURE

A Regency mahogany side table, with rectangular top, molded frieze, twin turned trestle supports, downswept sabre legs, brass lion-paw caps and castors.
c1815 *33in (84cm) wide*
$750-1,200 **DN**

A Regency mahogany side table, with rectangular top, an arrangement of three drawers, turned tapering legs, brass caps and castors.
c1815 *37in (95cm) wide*
$750-1,200 **DN**

A Victorian painted and parcel gilt side table, rectangular top, two frieze drawers, with painted frieze, on fluted turned tapered legs, stamped HOLLAND & SONS.
28in (72cm) high
$2,700-3,300 **DN**

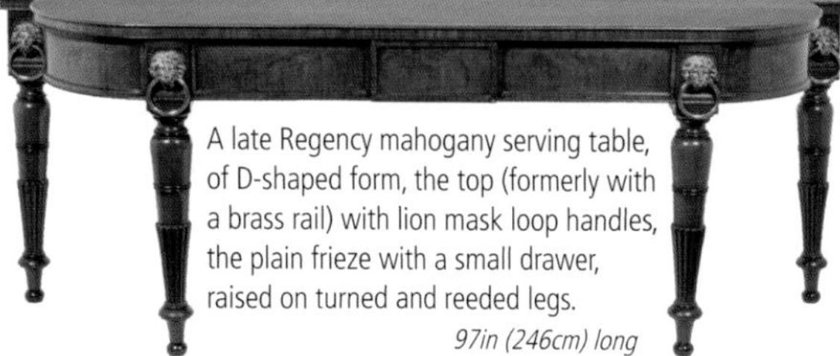

A late Regency mahogany serving table, of D-shaped form, the top (formerly with a brass rail) with lion mask loop handles, the plain frieze with a small drawer, raised on turned and reeded legs.
97in (246cm) long
$4,000–5,250 **TEN**

An 18thC-style carved giltwood and marble side table, the serpentine marble top over a foliate and scroll-carved frieze, on slender cabriole legs with pointed pad feet.
c1900 *38.5in (98cm) wide*
$3,000-4,500 **DN**

A 20thC George II-style giltwood and marble top side table, the rectangular green marble top with a molded edge over a vitruvian scroll frieze, raised on shell carved cabriole legs ending in hairy paw feet.
54in (137cm) wide
$900-1,200 **L&T**

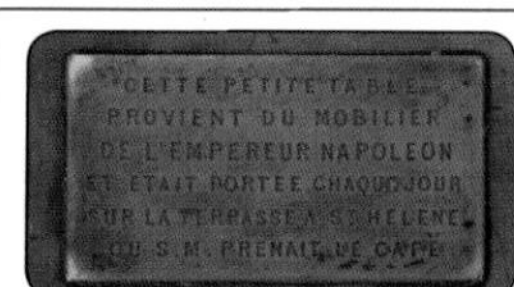

An early 19thC Regency mahogany side table of Napoleonic interest, the rectangular top with crossbanding and line inlay and a molded edge, raised on turned and tapered slender column legs joined by trestle supports and a flat stretcher rail, previously from a set of quartetto tables; the top mounted with a silver plaque engraved 'CETTE PETITE TABLE PROVIENT DU MOBILIER DE L'EMPEREUR NAPOLEON ET ETAIT PORTEE CHACQUE JOUR SUR LA TERRASSE A St HELENE OU S.M. PRENAIT LE CAFE'.

When Napoleon was exiled to the British controlled island of St. Helena in the south Atlantic in 1815, he was housed in Longwood House, a modest single story residence built specifically for this purpose. Simply furnished, it was a far cry from the lavish surroundings he had enjoyed as Emperor. The present lot, by repute used by Napoleon to take his coffee on the terrace of Longwood House, is similar to a side table visible in several paintings made of Napoleon on his deathbed, and a possibly matching table from the original quartet can be seen today in the sitting room at Longwood.
13in (34cm) wide
$4,000–5,250 **L&T**

CLOSER LOOK - LOUIS XV-STYLE SIDE TABLE

Gervais-Maximilien-Eugène Durand established the Maison Durand firm in 1870, with workshops at 12, rue de la Crisaie and then at 23., rue Beautrellis. The firm specialized in very high quality furniture in the 18thC style, and it was awarded a silver medal at the Exposition Universelle in 1889.

The top of the table is decorated with luxury materials: it is crossbanded and quarter veneered with satinwood and features an ebony line inlay.

The edge of the table top is decorated by a band of gilt bronze.

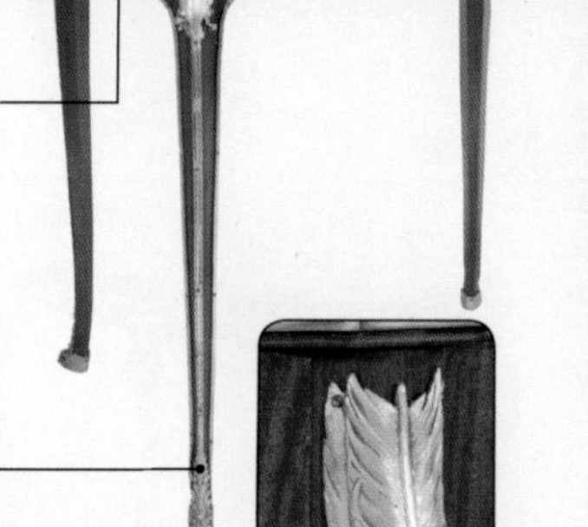

The exceptional detail continues to the feet which are fitted with acanthus-cast sabots.

The top of each leg is embellished with a high-quality case-bronze arrow.

A late 19thC French Louis XV-style gilt bronze mounted tulipwood side table, by Gervais-Maximilien-Eugène Durand, Stamped twice 'G. Durand", to underside.

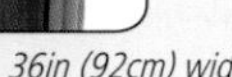

36in (92cm) wide
$4,500-6,000 **FRE**

ESSENTIAL REFERENCE - SPECIMEN TOP TABLES

Items decorated with elaborate Italian marble inlays were highly prized as souvenirs of the Grand Tour – the trip undertaken by young gentlemen to complete their education in the arts. The concept of the Grand Tour developed in the late 16thC and early 17thC but was most popular during the 18th, when visitors to Italy went to admire ancient Roman sculpture and architecture, and Renaissance and Baroque painting.

- **Specimen marble table tops were brought home by these early tourists, or imported by furniture makers, to be turned into decorative tables. They took advantage of the colorful marbles quarried in Italy.**
- **The decoration usually consists of geometric patterns, although more elaborate examples may show views or feature fashionable motifs such as swags and bows.**
- **The inlay technique began in ancient Rome and was revived during the Renaissance and again in the 18thC when visitors admired the Roman artefacts at Herculaneum and Pompeii. They would also have seen Roman antiquities in Rome.**
- **Specimen marble tops were usually used for console and occasional tables – the finest examples feature gilded bases.**
- **Some examples were made in Russia using malachite and the UK using colored stones from Derbyshire.**
- **Marble inlays were also used to decorate jewelry and wall plaques.**

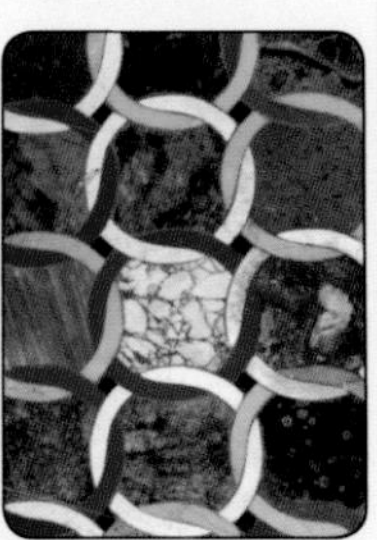

A pair of 19thC and later specimen marble-top tables, each with rectangular white marble tops, inlaid with pattern of interlocking circles, including assorted specimen hardstones and marbles, in the manner of Giuseppe Canart, each set within a molded gilt brass frame in the early 19thC manner, columnar supports united by glass undertier.

23.6in (60cm) wide

$19,500-22,500 **BELL**

A part-19thC gilt-metal, patinated bronze and polished hardstone occasional table, with multiple geometric veneers to the circular top, the base in the manner of George Smith.

20.5in (52cm) diam

$6,000-7,500 **TEN**

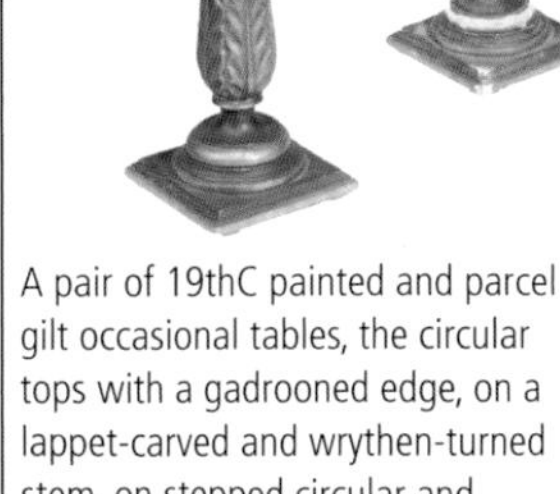

A pair of 19thC painted and parcel gilt occasional tables, the circular tops with a gadrooned edge, on a lappet-carved and wrythen-turned stem, on stepped circular and platform base, turned feet.

17in (43cm) diam

$750-1,200 **DN**

A Victorian mahogany and leather inset occasional table, the circular top with molded edge and tooled leather inset, turned and scroll carved stem, three downswept legs carved with scrolls and acanthus.

c1870 *30in (76cm) diam*

$1,200-1,800 **DN**

A Victorian walnut and marquetry circular occasional table, the top with radiating veneers and central stylized flowerhead motif, arcaded frieze, turned and flowerhead-carved stem, cabriole legs and scroll feet.

c1870 *3in (58cm) diam*

$600-900 **DN**

An early 20thC large Qajar tile-mounted low table, by Whytock & Reid, the large circular ceramic panel top depicting figures against a blue ground, in a low relief carved mahogany frame raised on stylized cabriole legs.

25.5in (65cm) diam

$3,000-4,500 **L&T**

A Chippendale-style mahogany two-tier occassional table, each shaped tier with molded edge and acanthus-carved frieze, pierced square section supports and tapering legs with shaped and pierced feet.

c1910 *20in (51cm) square*

$975-1,300 **DN**

An early 19thC Empire rosewood, gilt metal and marble top guéridon, the circular dished veined black marble top with a molded edge, above a facetted baluster support and triform base with scrolling brackets and raised on carved paw feet, with gilt metal mounts throughout.

38.5in (98cm) diam

$3,000-4,500 **L&T**

A Louis Philippe mahogany guéridon, the molded edge grey marble top on a triform base with gilt metal mounts and paw feet.

38in (96.5cm) diam

$3,000-4,500 **WW**

A Louis XV-style ormolu-mounted two-tier guéridon, each tier with floral marquetry inlaid into kingwood and well-cast ormolu mounts to edge, upper tier raised on ormolu supports topped by a winged espagnolette, lower tier with two scrolled handles, on four cabriole legs joined by an X-form stretcher surmounted by flower spray to center.

c1900 *30.5in (76cm) wide*

$33,000-42,000 **SK**

A pair of early 20thC satinwood and floral marquetry guéridons, of two tier circular form with gilt metal mounts, the banded top with pierced gallery and floral wreath, similar undershelf, on shaped square section supports with cabriole legs and splayed feet.

30in (76cm) high

$4,500-6,000 **HT**

A Louis XVI-style mahogany and gilt-bronze mounted guéridon, the oval top with a pierced brass gallery, over a single frieze drawer, raised on hipped cabriole legs united by an oval undertier, with gilt metal mounts throughout and ending on foliate sabots.

19in (49cm) wide

$600-1,200 **L&T**

INTRODUCTION TO PEMBROKE TABLES

Pembroke tables are small, occasional tables with four legs and usually set on castors to allow them to be moved around the room with ease.

- **They are usually elegant pieces of furniture, with one or two frieze drawers and two drop leaves supported by wooden brackets on hinges, known as 'elbows'.**
- **The Pembroke table was produced in England from the mid-18thC and is thought to have been named after the then Countess of Pembroke, who the furniture maker Thomas Sheraton called, "that Lady who first gave orders for one of them, who probably gave the first idea of such a table to the workmen."**
- **The tops were often elaborately inlaid with satinwood, ebony and boxwood decoration.**
- **In the 19thC, brass inlay became popular, and in the late 19th and early 20thC they were often painted in revival styles.**
- **Pembroke tables were practical as they could be used for dining, games or as worktables as required.**
- **American Pembroke tables tend to be more valuable than British ones because fewer were made.**

A George III mahogany and kingwood crossbanded oval Pembroke table, the top incorporating a pair of hinged leaves, frieze drawer and opposing false drawer, over square tapering and satinwood strung legs ending with brass caps and castors.

30cm (76cm) deep closed

$1,000–1,500 **DN**

A George III mahogany oval Pembroke table, the top with kingwood crossbanding, frieze drawer and false opposing drawer with crossbanding and boxwood inlay, on square tapered legs with shell paterae, on castors.

c1810 *30in (76cm) wide closed*

$3,000-4,500 **DN**

A Regency rosewood and brass inlaid sofa table, of rounded rectangular form with two drop leaves above two frieze drawers centered by a rectangular tablet, raised on four spindle-turned supports and quartrepartite base with four scrolling sabre legs, brass toes and castors.

35in (89cm) wide

$1,200-1,800 **TEN**

A Regency rosewood sofa table, the sliding top opening to a backgammon board, frieze drawers, two false opposing drawers, rectangular uprights, downswept legs, caps and castors.

c1815 *61in (155cm) wide*

$13,500-16,500 **DN**

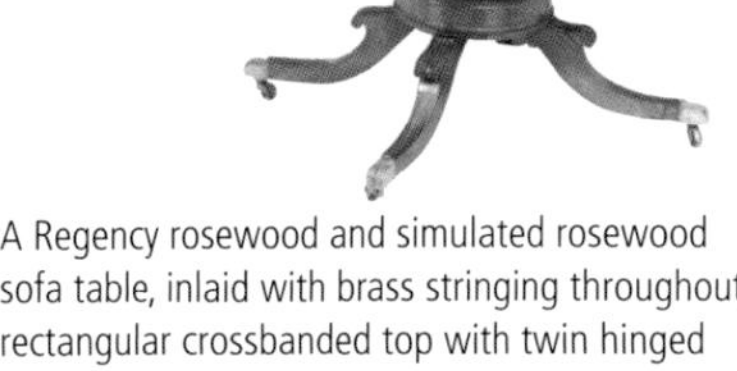

A Regency rosewood and simulated rosewood sofa table, inlaid with brass stringing throughout, rectangular crossbanded top with twin hinged ends, a pair of frieze drawers, turned acanthus carved stem, circular base, on four hipped downswept legs, brass caps and castors.

c1815 *60in (150cm) wide*

$850-1,300 **DN**

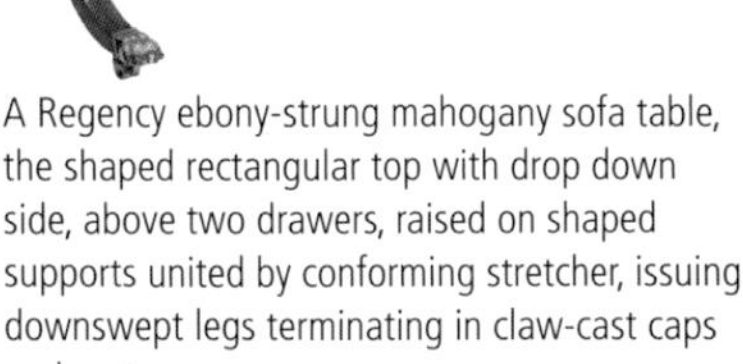

A Regency ebony-strung mahogany sofa table, the shaped rectangular top with drop down side, above two drawers, raised on shaped supports united by conforming stretcher, issuing downswept legs terminating in claw-cast caps and castors.

48in (122cm) wide

$3,000-4,500 **FRE**

A George IV mahogany sofa table, the rectangular top incorporating a pair of hinged leaves, pair of frieze drawers, pair of opposing false drawers, shaped trestle supports, acanthus carved hipped downswept legs, brass caps and castors.

c1825 *36in (92cm) wide*

$1,800–2,700 **DN**

A Regency mahogany, ebony and brass inlay sofa table, the rectangular top with canted drop down ends inlaid with ebony banding and brass star inlay, over one real and one dummy frieze drawer and the same opposing, with brass lion mask loop handles, raised on trestle supports joined by a turned stretcher rail and reeded scroll legs ending on brass caps and castors.

64.5in (164cm) wide opened

$1,200-1,800 **L&T**

A Regency yew, tulipwood and boxwood strung writing table, the square top with burr yew central panel within tulipwood crossbanding, frieze drawer opening to divisions and stationery fittings, on turned tapered leg and brass castors.

c1815 *21in (53.5cm) wide*

$1,800–2,700 **DN**

A Regency rosewood writing table in the manner of Gillows, the rectangular top cross-banded in satinwood and rosewood with inlaid stringing and a later gilt tooled green leather writing surface.

$2,550-3,300 **WW**

A William IV goncalo alves writing/work table, almost certainly by Gillows, with ratchet writing surface above twin drop leaves and an arrangement of drawers with sliding work box below, raised on turned and reeded supports with brass toes and castors.

c1830 *30.5in (78cm) wide*

$5,250-6,750 **TEN**

A Victorian mahogany writing table, the rectangular top with leather inset, three frieze drawers, on turned tapered legs, caps and castors.

c1860 *55in (140cm) long*

$1,200-1,800 **DN**

A late 19thC Louis XVs-tyle walnut bureau plat, with gilt-metal mounts and inlaid stringing, the serpentine-edge top inset with a green leather writing surface, above a pair of frieze drawers with oval panels on cabriole legs with bearded male masks.

47in (120cm wide)

$300-450 **WW**

A fruitwood, olive wood and marquetry writing table, possibly Maltese, with an arrangement of drawers and a central cupboard with 'BO' monogram, writing surface with marquetry star motif, two frieze drawers, downswept legs and hoof feet.

c1900 *42.5in (108cm) wide*

$1,800–4,000 **DN**

An Edwardian mahogany and satinwood crossbanded kidney-shaped writing table, with Waring & Gillow label , green tooled leather inset, with a central long drawer flanked by two short drawers, on tapering legs asnd brass caps and castors.

c1900 *47in (119cm) wide*

$1,500-2,250 **DN**

ESSENTIAL REFERENCE - CARD AND GAMES TABLES

Although the first tables designed for the fashionable pastime of playing cards were made in the late 17thC, the form did not become popular until the 18thC. They fell out of fashion in the 19thC following a ban on gambling during the Regency period.

- **Early card and games tables were usually veneered with walnut and had tapering legs; tables with a folding top sometimes had legs which were designed to swing out and support it.**
- **After c1720 the swing leg support was joined by a concertina-action flap support.**
- **During the 18thC, the fabric traditionally placed over the top of the table became an integral part of the design.**
- **Some tables were made with multiple leaves for different games, and in the mid- to late 18thC tables were made for different games and designs became more elaborate as cabinetmakers took the opportunity to use them to show off their skills. In France square tables were made for the game 'quadrille', circular for 'brelan', and triangular for 'tri'.**
- **By the late 18thC designs no longer included dishes for candles or counters, and marquetry decoration became less common.**

A George I walnut and burr walnut folding games table, the rectangular crossbanded and featherbanded top with rounded outset corners, opening to a baize inset interior incorporating counter well and circular corner terminals, the shaped frieze centered by a drawer and on cabriole legs with pad feet.

c1720 *34in (87cm) wide*

$10,500-16,500 DN

A George II mahogany tea/game table, two shaped rectangular foldover tops, the lower baise-lined and with counter wells and candle recesses to the angles, above a further inlaid games/reading surface, hinged and with ratchet support enclosing a well, gate-leg support to the rear, on hipped cabriole legs, pad feet.

34in (86cm) wide

$2,000–2,250 MOR

A George II walnut concertina action card table by Benjamin Crook, the hinged fold-over top inlaid feather stringing revealing a baize lined surface with candle stands and counter wells above a frieze drawer, on shell and husk capped cabriole legs and pad feet, the remains of the cabinet makers paper label, and with an ivorine label inscribed 'COWDRAY 103 1919'.

33in (83.5cm)

$15,000–22,500 WW

A George III mahogany demi-lune card table, the fold-over top crossbanded in satinwood and rosewood on twin gate supports.

36.5in (93cm) wide

$600-1,200 WW

A New York Chippendale mahogany card table, the serpentine top with blocked corners above a conforming apron with a gadrooned edge supported by cabriole legs, terminating in ball and claw feet.

c1770 *34in (86cm) wide*

$27,000–33,000 POOK

A George III mahogany serpentine triple folding combined tea and card table, on canted and fluted legs.

c1770 *36in (91cm) wide*

$1,200-1,800 DN

A Louis XVI mahogany and brass mounted semi-elliptical games table, folding top above a paneled frieze, turned tapering fluted legs.

c1770 *43in (110cm) wide*

$750-1,200 DN

A rare mid-18thC Anglo-Chinese Huanghuali demilune triple foldover tea and games table, the demi-lune top opening to a plain top and again to a playing surface, the baize now lacking, carved with foliate scrolls and gaming wells, above a deep frieze carved with foliate scrolls, raised on straight cabriole legs ending in pad feet carved with dragon masks and ruyi.

Provenance: In 1965 this table was used to sign the documents leading to the independence of Botswana (then Bechuanaland).

33in (84cm) wide

$3,000-4,500 **L&T**

A George III mahogany serpentine card table, the foldover top with ribbon and flower carved edge, having a shaped frieze supported by foliate brackets, raised on canted molded square legs.

28.5in (73cm) wide

$1,200-1,800 **L&T**

One of a pair of George III satinwood and mahogany foldover demilune games tables, the crossbanded tops opening on a double gateleg to a green baize playing surface, raised on square tapered line inlaid legs ending in spade feet.

c1790 *36in (92cm) wide*

$4,000–5,250 pair **L&T**

A George III mahogany folding card table, D-shaped crossbanded top, tablet molded frieze with satinwood crossbanding, turned tapering reeded legs.

c1800 *26in (92cm) wide*

$1,000-1,700 **DN**

A Regency rosewood and brass inlay foldover games table, the foldover D-shape top with foliate brass inlay and opening to a blue baize lined playing surface, raised on a square column support and quatreform base on reeded bun feet, inlaid all over with scrolling foliate brass inlay.

c1815 *35.5in (90cm) wide*

$4,500-6,000 **L&T**

A Regency rosewood foldover games table, the crossbanded demi-lune top opening to a red baize lined playing surface, raised on a waisted octagonal support with gilt metal leaf mounts and downswept legs ending in foliate cast brass caps and castors.

c1815 *37in (96cm) wide*

$1,400-2,100 **L&T**

A 19thC Regency mahogany games table, attributed to Gillows, the rounded rectangular top with a sliding center section reversing to a games board, the interior with an inlaid backgammon board, above a pair of short frieze drawers with two dummy drawers opposing, raised on tapered reeded legs ending in brass caps and castors.

36in (92.5cm) wide

$3,000-4,500 **L&T**

One of a pair of Scottish Regency rosewood foldover card tables, in the manner of William Trotter, Edinburgh, D-shaped twist and foldover top, gadrooned frieze raised on four scrolling supports with applied gilt metal rosette terminals on a quatre form base with square section tapering legs, terminating in brass paw caps and castors.

37.5in (96cm) wide

$18,000-22,500 pair **TCAL**

A Regency mahogany foldover card table, the reeded edge over a paneled frieze, spiral twist columns on outswept legs, with brass paw feet and castors.

36in (91cm) wide

$600-900 **SWO**

A William IV rosewood games table, the reversible sliding top inlaid a satinwood and ebony chequer board, revealing a leather backgammon board flanked by a pair of hinged counter compartments above a frieze drawer, on scroll feet and brass castors, originally with a bag.

33.5in (85cm) wide

$550-975 **WW**

A Victorian rosewood and marquetry games table, the foldover rectangular top opening to a backgammon and chess board above a long frieze drawer with floral marquetry, raised on scrolling lyre supports joined by a turned stretcher rail, on foliate carved scroll legs with castors.

24in (61cm) wide

$900–1,400 **L&T**

A Philadelphia Empire mahogany games table, attributed to Anthony Quervelle.

39.5in (100cm) wide

$1,800–2,700 **POOK**

An early Victorian rosewood card table, the swivel fold over top on a turned and lappet carved stem on disc feet and sunken brass castors.

36in (92cm) wide

$300-750 **WW**

An early Victorian walnut Serpentine card table, the fold-over and swivel top on four scroll supports and brass castors.

36in (91.5cm) wide

$1,500-2,250 **WW**

A 19thC Louis XV-style kingwood, amaranth, acajou and marquetry gilt- bronze mounted games table, the foldover serpentine top with a gilt-bronze mounted edge and opening to a baize playing surface, over a serpentine frieze with foliate marquetry, raised on square cabriole legs ending in sabots.

35in (89cm) wide

$3,000-4,500 **L&T**

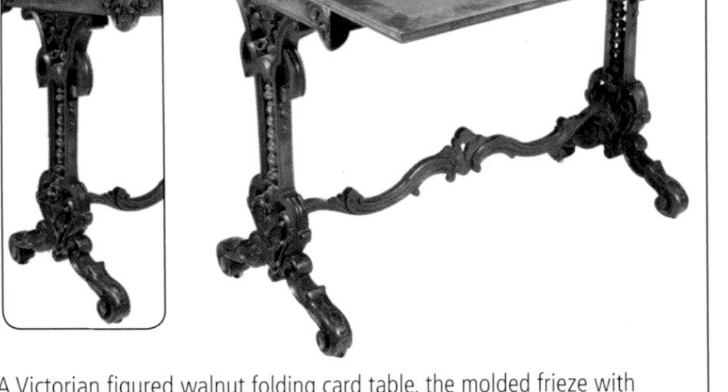

A Victorian figured walnut folding card table, the molded frieze with acanthus carved terminals, profusely carved and pierced trestle supports, hipped downswept legs with scroll feet.

c1870 *39in (99cm) wide*

$1,200-1,800 **DN**

A Victorian walnut and marquetry games table, serpentine gilt metal mounted top with central marquetry inset games board, on carved stem, three downswept legs.

c1880 *26in (66cm) wide*

$750-1,200 **DN**

A Victorian walnut, ebony and painted games table, the molded rectangular top with an inlaid games board over a single frieze drawer, the frieze mounted with painted watercolor panels of flowers, the sides with large reniform panels depicting the Coliseum and classical ruins, on foliate carved baluster end supports and acanthus carved scroll feet, on castors.

24in (61cm) wide

$1,800–4,000 **L&T**

A late Victorian walnut envelope card table by Gregory & Co., the swivel molded edge top revealing a baize-lined surface above a frieze drawer, stamped twice 'GREGORY & CO, 212 & 214 REGENT ST LONDON', and '2926', with pierced fret spandrels on turned legs united by an X-stretcher and on brass castors.

23.5in (60cm) square

$450-1,400 **WW**

An Edwardian rosewood and marquetry envelope games table, the pivoting square top with urn and foliate inlay, the leaves opening to reveal a baize playing surface, raised on square tapered legs joined by a galleried undertier, on brass castors.

22in (56cm) wide

$600-1,400 **L&T**

An Irish George III mahogany tea table, the rectangular dished top over a pierced scroll cut apron raised on cabriole legs carved with scales and acanthus and ending on faceted pad feet.

30.5in (78cm) wide

$3,000-4,500 **L&T**

CLOSER LOOK - AMERICAN QUEEN ANNE TABLE

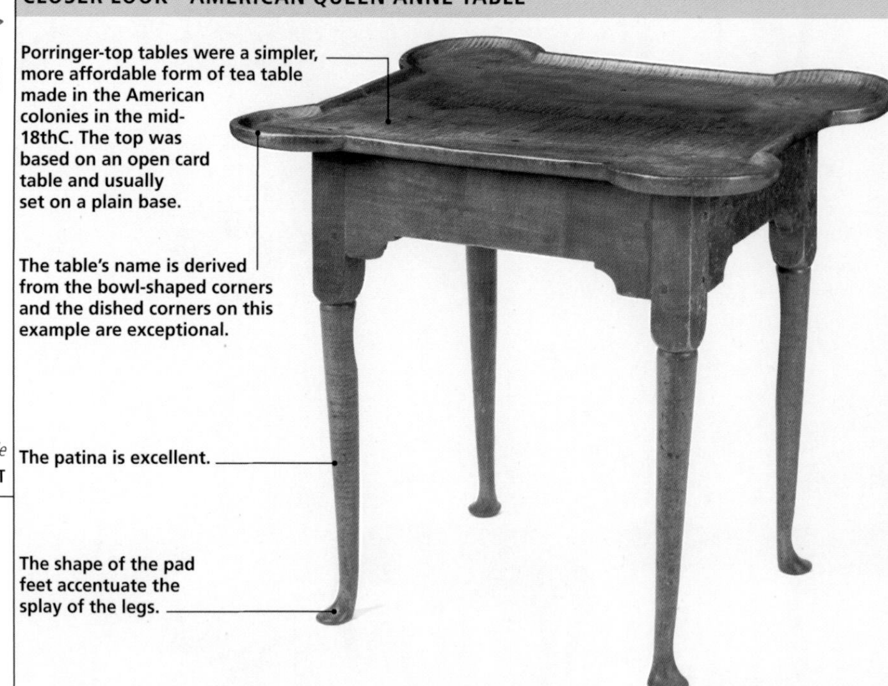

An American Queen Anne tiger maple porringer-top table, probably Rhode Island, the shaped top overhanging a straight frame with cutout apron, supported by turned legs terminating in pad feet.

c1765 *26in (66cm) wide*

$12,000-14,250 **POOK**

An 18thC mahogany candlestand, the dished circular top on baluster turned stem, raised on tripod base and pad feet, adapted.

21in (53cm) high

$1,000–1,500 **HT**

A George III mahogany and satinwood demi-lune tea table, the circular foldover top opening on double gatelegs, above a line inlaid frieze centered by a short drawer, raised on square tapered legs ending on brass caps and castors.

39in (99cm) wide

$1,500-2,250 **L&T**

A George III Chippendale mahogany tea table, with pie-crust tilt-top, with birdcage-action platform title, on three carved ball-and-claw feet, the underside stamped 'Ismay, 15 Hill St, B. Sq.'.

c1770-90 *28in (71cm) high*

$4,000–5,250 **D&H**

A George III mahogany folding tea table, of serpentine outline, hinged top with pierced corner brackets, on square legs.

c1770 *37in (95cm) wide*

$750-1,200 **DN**

A George III mahogany tilt top table, with piecrust edge, on vase column with spiral fluting and tripod feet.

c1770 *29in (73cm) diam*

$450-1,200 **DN**

A George III mahogany tripod table, with circular top, turned stem, three downswept cabriole legs and pad feet.

c1770 *33in (84cm) diam*

$750-1,200 **DN**

A Pennsylvania Queen Anne walnut candlestand, with a dish top, birdcage support, and suppressed ball standard.
c1770 *20in (50cm) wide*
$3,000-4,500 **POOK**

A George III mahogany circular tripod table, on turned vase column with bird cage mechanism, three downswept legs.
c1780 *28in (72cm) diam*
$1,000-1,700 **DN**

A mid-Georgian yew wood circular pedestal tripod table, with a ring turned tapering baluster column, supported on carved cabriole legs with pad feet.
28in (71cm) high
$1,800–2,700 **TRI**

A George III mahogany folding tea table, the rectangular top, plain frieze with a drawer, on square tapered legs, block feet.
c1790 *37in (94cm) wide*
$600-1,200 **DN**

A Regency penwork tilt-top pedestal table, the top decorated in the Greek revival manner after Thomas Hope with a standing subject wearing laurel crown, on a twist-carved column with applied brass mounts and on a triform base with brass paw feet.

The base with a crack and loss of gilding to the paw feet and a small scratch to the top

c1810 *14.75in (37cm) wide*
$2,700–4,000 **CHEF**

A Regency mahogany folding tea table, the folding top above a lattice decorated frieze, turned tapering legs, brass caps and castors.
c1815 *36in (92cm) wide*
$600-1,200 **DN**

A Regency rosewood tea table, in the manner of William Trotter, the scroll base with applied paterae and leaf cast brass sabot and castors.
42in (106cm) wide
$3,000-4,500 **WW**

A George III mahogany oval work table, the reeded sides set tapering legs with spade feet, the lift top revealing a well to each side and a fabric lined central well.

18.5in (47.5cm) wide

$550–850 **DN**

A George III mahogany oval work table, the reeded sides set tapering legs with spade feet, the lift top revealing a well to each side and a fabric lined central well.

18.5in (47.5cm) wide

$550–850 **DN**

A Regency rosewood work table, the hinged top with brass stringing and canted corners, opening to fabric lined interior and divided compartments, pleated workbag, on an ebonized and gilt metal mounted base with lyre mounts, hipped downswept legs and brass paw casp and castors.

c1815 *17.5in (44.5cm) wide*

$750-1,200 **DN**

A George IV rosewood sewing table, with nulled decoration, the hinged top on a brass ratchet to a divided interior with pin cushions, above a frieze drawer with ink compartments above a pull-out bag, on stretchered trestle ends on scroll feet and brass castors.

22in (55.5cm) wide

$1,000-1,700 **WW**

A William IV rosewood work table, twin sliding panels opening to a fitted interior incorporating lidded and paper lined divisions, one false drawer and two further long drawers, three opposing false drawers.

c1835 *21.6in (55cm) wide*

$750-1,200 **DN**

A Victorian walnut work table of circular form with stringing and foliate sprays, hinged burr walnut top revealing fitted interior over a faceted tapering well with turned pendant, raised on four turned supports with leaf carved collars, similar circular base with four scrolled feet and china castors.

18.5in (47cm) wide

$1,200-1,800 **HT**

A Victorian walnut, mahogany and inlay work/games table, the foldover top with Tunbridge Ware banding opening to a top fitted for games, above a single frieze drawer and sliding compartment, raised on turned and carved trestle supports, joined by a stretcher and raised on porcelain castors.

28in (72cm) high

$900-1,500 **L&T**

A George I walnut and elm crossbanded dressing table, the rectangular top with a molded edge over a long drawer and arched kneehole flanked by short drawers, raised on cabriole legs ending in pad feet.
c1720 *29.5in (75cm) wide*
$1,000–1,500 **L&T**

An 18thC oak lowboy, with re-entrant corners, three small drawers, on cabriole legs and shell carved feet.
34.5in (88cm)
$750-1,200 **CHEF**

ESSENTIAL REFERENCE - LOW BOYS

The lowboy developed in the 18thC as a variation on a chest-on-stand with long legs. It was a low table designed for use as a writing or dressing table.

- **They were designed to be used by ladies and typically have between one and three fitted drawers as well as space for a freestanding mirror. Long legs allowed space for the drawers and for someone to sit comfortably at it. The drawers typically do not have locks, suggesting they were not used to house valuable objects.**
- **Very early 18thC lowboys are rare and desirable.**
- **Typical 18thC features include restrained cabriole legs terminating in pad feet.**
- **The design was inspired by French dressing tables called 'poudreuse' and 'coiffeuse'. These were designed for applying powder to the face and dressing hair. The coiffeuse later developed to include a writing surface and inkwell and might be used by gentlemen as well.**

An 18th century walnut lowboy, quarter veneered with inlaid border decoration, fitted three small drawers, on cabriole legs and pad feet.
31.5in (78cm) wide
$1,800–2,700 **CHEF**

A George II pollarded oak and oak lowboy, with a rectangular molded edge top above an arrangement of four drawers with brass plate handles, above a shaped apron on cabriole legs.
36in (91cm) wide
$7,500–10,500 **WW**

A Pennsylvania Queen Anne walnut dressing table, the rectangular notched corner top overhanging a frame with three drawers and a scalloped skirt supported by cabriole legs terminating in Spanish feet.
c1760 *33.5in (85.5cm) wide*
$4,500-6,000 **POOK**

A Regency mahogany dressing table by Gillows, the three-quarter galleried top above a concave drawer flanked by two short drawers to each side, on reeded legs with brass caps and castors.
45in (114cm) wide
$5,250-6,750 **CHOR**

A George IV mahogany dressing table in the manner of Gillows, the three-quarter galleried top above one long and four short drawers, on reeded legs with brass castors.
45in (115cm) wide
$5,250-6,750 **CHOR**

A New England Classical painted two-part dresser, retaining its original vibrant red and black grained surface with gilt highlights.
c1830 *36.25in (92.5cm) wide*
$4,500-6,000 **POOK**

A late 19thC French Louis XVI-style kingwood, tulipwood and gilt metal mounted dressing table, the cartouche-shaped hinged lid opening to a mirror-mounted underside and divided tray section, square section cabriole legs and sabots.
24in (60cm) wide
$900–1,400 **DN**

A George IV mahogany architect's table, attributed to Gillows of Lancaster, the rectangular twin-ratchet height and angle adjustable top with molded edge above a frieze drawer opening to a baize inset sliding surface, on fluted square section legs and molded feet with concealed casters.

c1825 *30.5in (78cm) wide*

$4,500-6,000 **DN**

A George II walnut architect's table, the rectangular hinged top with retracting book support above a fitted drawer, on square chamfered legs.

24in (60cm) wide

$6,750-8,250 **CHOR**

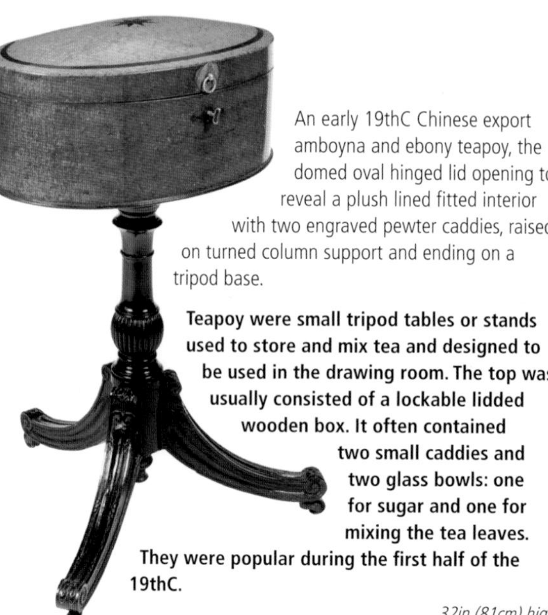

An early 19thC Chinese export amboyna and ebony teapoy, the domed oval hinged lid opening to reveal a plush lined fitted interior with two engraved pewter caddies, raised on turned column support and ending on a tripod base.

Teapoy were small tripod tables or stands used to store and mix tea and designed to be used in the drawing room. The top was usually consisted of a lockable lidded wooden box. It often contained two small caddies and two glass bowls: one for sugar and one for mixing the tea leaves. They were popular during the first half of the 19thC.

32in (81cm) high

$3,000-4,500 **L&T**

A French kingwood bijouterie table, the kidney shaped hinged lid with a beveled glass panel opening to a baize lined interior with glazed sides, raised on square cabriole legs, with gilt metal mounts.

c1870 *28in (71cm) wide*

$3,000-4,500 **L&T**

An Edwardian mahogany bijouterie table, the rectangular hinged glazed top and sides enclosing a blue plush lined interior, raised on square tapered legs joined by arched stretchers and ending on spade feet.

26in (66cm) wide

$450–900 **L&T**

CLOSER LOOK - GEORGE III HIGH DRESSER

The size of the dresser and the patina on the wood add to its attractiveness.

The quality and detail of the carving of the ogee-molded cornice and honeysuckle-pierced scrolling frieze are the work of a highly skilled craftsman.

The detail on the dresser includes fielded cabinet doors which sit between fluted uprights.

The five-drawer base is fitted with brass swing handles.

The heart-pierced and scrolling cut apron echoes the decoration on the frieze.

A George III Shropshire oak high dresser, three open shelves flanked by an open shelf, on three front cabriole legs terminating in pointed toes.

140in (355cm) wide

$18,000–27,000 **HALL**

A Welsh yewwood cupboard, with an open top.

c1750 78in (1.9m) wide

$3,000-4,500 **POOK**

A George II oak dresser, the molded cornice over a wavy frieze and three open shelves; the lower part with six short drawers above three further drawers, raised on chamfered legs joined by an undertier.

57in (145cm) wide

$1,800-3,000 **L&T**

A mid-18thC oak dresser, the raised plate rack with a pair of cupboard doors marquetry inlaid swags, husks and urns with a triad of initials 'EEG' and the date '1793' probably as a wedding gift, each enclosing a drawer, the base with a pair of fielded panel doors flanking three dummy drawers, with replaced metalwork.

73in (185cm) wide

$4,000–5,250 **WW**

A mid-18thC oak dresser, with a raised plate rack with reeded uprights, the base with three frieze drawers fitted replaced handles above three raised ogee panel doors.

74.5in (189cm) wide

$1,800–4,000 **WW**

A George III oak dresser, the molded cornice with a wavy frieze over two shelves flanked by shelved alcoves and over five short drawers, the lower part with three deep drawers raised on later baluster legs.

78.5in (200cm) wide

$4,000–5,250 **L&T**

A George III oak and inlay dresser, the molded cornice above a scroll-cut frieze over three long shelves and closed back flanked by cupboard doors and short shelves; the lower part with a molded edge above a pair of cupboard doors flanked by two pairs of short drawers above a scroll-cut apron, raised on cabriole legs ending in pointed pad feet.

71.5in (182cm) wide

$3,000-4,500 **L&T**

A George III oak dresser, with raised plate rack with shaped fret-carved cornice, open shelves and spice drawers, the base fitted a central cupboard flanked by drawers, with later handles, on bracket feet.

c1770 *63.5in (161cm) wide*

$1,800–4,000 **CHEF**

A George III oak dresser, with a plate rack incorporating a pair of cupboards, the base with three long drawers and cabriole legs with pad feet to front.

c1780 *74in (188cm) wide*

$750–1,500 **DN**

A George III stained pine dresser, the shelved superstructure above three frieze drawers and two paneled cupboard doors, centered by three further dummy drawers, raised on bracket feet.

c1800 *56in (143cm) wide*

$1,800–4,000 **L&T**

A late Georgian oak and mahogany banded dresser, the boarded delft rack with molded cornice and scrolled frieze over three shelves, flanked by two inlaid cupboard doors and three small drawers below, the base with six drawers having later turned wood handles, shaped apron, raised on square tapering legs.

76in (193cm) wide

$1,800–2,700 **HT**

A late George III oak dresser, the open shelves with later brass hooks, above three frieze drawers with later brass handles above carved fan brackets, on turned supports to a pot board base, shelves with later strengthening bars, later brass handles, back feet tipped.

83.5in (213cm) wide

$1,800–4,000 **WW**

An early 19thC oak high dresser, the molded cornice above an arrangement of open shelves flanked by a pair of cupboards, the base with an arrangement of five drawers, turned tapering legs at the front above the solid undertier.

71.5in (182cm) wide

$1,800–2,700 **DN**

A late 18thC oak dresser, having associated rack with lambrequin frieze over two shelves, the protruding base with a central bank of four drawers flanked to either side by fielded panel cupboard doors, paneled sides on stile supports.

50in (127cm) wide

$450-750 **DA&H**

A 17thC and later oak cupboard, molded top, pair of carved paneled doors, on stile feet.

60in (152cm) wide

$1,200-1,800 **DN**

A George III oak dresser base, the rectangular top above an arrangement of three drawers and thre cupboards, on stile feet.

c1770 *66.5in (169cm wide)*

$1,500-2,250 **DN**

A George III oak dresser base, the rectangular top above an inverted breakfront fitted with nine drawers around a fielded panel door, raised on a plinth base.

c1780 *80in (204cm) wide*

$4,500-6,000 **L&T**

An 18thC oak dresser base, the fitted three drawers over a shaped apron and three turned fore supports with a pot-board base, the drawers fitted with brass handles and escutcheons.

72in (183cm) wide

$3,000-4,500 **HW**

An early 19thC pine low dresser, having molded edged top over three frieze drawers with brass loop handles, on turned tapering front legs.

63.5in (162cm) wide

$1,200-1,800 **DA&H**

A Charles II paneled oak cupboard, the pair of miter-paneled cupboard doors above a drawer, with a further cupboard door and stile feet.

c1660 *66in (168cm) wide*

$1,000-1,800 DN

A 17thC three-tiered oak court cupboard, with open-hooded shelf above a middle tier with carved central cupboard bearing a date and inverted finials, the base with drawers and cupboards, on stile legs.

22.5in (57cm) wide

$3,000-4,500 CHEF

A 17thC and later oak court cupboard, extensively carved with strapwork, flowers, an arch and leaves, the frieze centered a panel with initials 'RP BP' and the date '1692' above a pair of paneled doors with cupboards below.

84in (214cm) wide

$1,800–4,000 WW

A part-17thC oak court cupboard, in two sections, the frieze carved with scrolling foliage and dated '1693', above a pair of carved cupboards, with paneled cupboards below.

54.5in (138cm)

$1,500-2,250 WW

An Albany, New York, gumwood kas, with its original removable bun feet and old surface.

c1740 *54in (137cm) wide*

$9,000-10,500 POOK

A Pennsylvania Chippendale walnut schrank, the ogee cornice over tombstone panel doors, flanked by sunken panel pilasters, above a base with two drawers and ogee bracket feet.

c1770 *60in (152.5cm) wide*

$6,750-8,250 POOK

A Pennsylvania stained pine and poplar pewter cupboard, the open top with original scalloped sides and lollipop terminals, above three drawers and two raised panel doors supported by bracket feet, retaining an old red surface.

c1770 *60in (152cm) wide*

$12,750-13,500 **POOK**

A Lancaster County, Pennsylvania painted hard pine schrank, the architectural molded cornice over raised panel doors with fluted quarter columns, resting on a molded base with faux drawers and an overall scrubbed sponge decorated surface.

c1780 *876in (193.5cm) wide*

$112,500–127,500 **POOK**

A late 18thC French provincial oak buffet a deux corps, with molded and carved decoration, the plate rack with a detachable cornice and with three shelves above two frieze drawers fitted iron handles and cupboard doors enclosing a shelf.

62in (158cm) wide

$750–1,500 **WW**

A late 18thC Pennsylvania walnut two-part corner cupboard, with a dentil molded cornice and raised panel cupboard doors.

43in (110cm) wide

$1,000-1,400 **POOK**

A Pennsylvania painted pine two-part corner cupboard, retaining an old blue surface with salmon moldings.

c1800 *47.5in (120cm) wide*

$4,500-6,000 **POOK**

An early 19thC Pennsylvania or Maryland painted pine two-part corner cupboard, the upper section with shell and pinwheel carved moldings, retaining an old ocher grain decorated surface.

44.5in (113cm) wide

$3,000-4,500 **POOK**

ESSENTIAL REFERENCE - HENRY LAPP

Henry Lapp (1862–1904) is probably one of the best-known 19thC American cabinetmakers. He was born deaf and it is believed that he painted pictures as a means of communication because his speech was hard to follow.

- **He lived and worked in Leacock Township, Lancaster County, Pennsylvania, and today his furniture is considered to be the epitome of Amish furniture design.**
- **Lapp was among the first to make furniture in a plain, undecorated style rather than the painted, Germanic-style. This may reflect the Amish belief in the value of hard work, making things to last and avoiding devices that could distract one from serving the community.**
- **He recorded customer's orders in a book of watercolor paintings which is now in the Philadelphia Museum of Art.**

A late 19thC Lancaster, Pennsylvania walnut Dutch cupboard, attributed to Henry Lapp.

48in (122cm) wide

$6,000-7,500 POOK

CLOSER LOOK - WALNUT HANGING CUPBOARD

A Chester County, Pennsylvania walnut hanging cupboard.

c1780 *18in (45cm) wide.*

$18,000–27,000 POOK

A Lancaster County, Pennsylvania walnut Dutch cupboard, signed by cabinetmaker Henry Lapp, with restoration.

1902 *48in (122cm) wide*

$750–1,500 POOK

A Pennsylvania walnut hanging cupboard, probably Lancaster County, the molded cornice over a raised panel door with original rattail hinges, above a single drawer and an open shelf with spurred sides.

c1750 *26in (66cm) wide*

$7,500-9,750 POOK

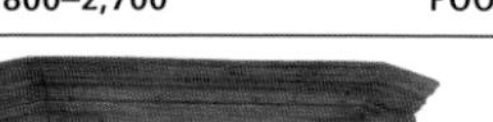

A Pennsylvania walnut hanging cupboard, probably Lancaster, with a single tombstone panel door and a relief-scalloped panel.

c1770 *24.5in (62cm) wide*

$1,800–2,700 POOK

An early 19thC Pennsylvania walnut hanging corner cupboard, with a raised panel door and fishtail base.

22.75in (58cm) wide

$1,800–2,700 POOK

An 18thC Dutch mahogany linen press, with carved and applied moldings and gilt brass and later brass mounts, with a central shelf of three short drawers, flanked by stop-fluted pilasters, the base with three long drawers, the central having a curved front.

97.5in (247.5cm) high

$3,000–6,000 **WW**

A mid-18thC mahogany secretaire linen press, the dentil cornice above a pair of fielded panel doors enclosing four slides above a secretaire drawer fitted with pigeon holes and drawers, above two short and two long drawers with brass handles on ogee bracket feet.

52in (132cm) wide

$1,800–2,700 **WW**

A late 18thC New Jersey or New York gumwood linen press.

78in (109m) high

$1,800-3,000 **POOK**

A late 18thC/early 19thC Dutch mahogany clothes press, with molded cornice, a pair of doors, three long graduated drawers flanked by acanthus carved terminals, square tapering fluted feet.

61in (155cm) wide

$750–1,500 **DN**

An early 19thC mahogany linen press, with a pair of plum pudding doors with outline moldings, enclosing five blue paper lined slides, above two short and two long drawers, on bracket feet, the back with a hand written label inscribed 'Mrs Higginson Wardrobe No 19'.

81.75in (207.5cm) high

$3,000-4,000 **WW**

ESSENTIAL REFERENCE - EGYPTIAN REVIVAL TASTE

In the 1790s, Napoleon's military campaigns in Egypt and the publications of Baron Vivant Denon contributed to the vogue for Egyptian ornaments. By the late 18thC and 19thC, this Egyptian fashion reached its apogee as it became entwined with Regency, Empire and Federal styles.

- **Motifs such as sphinxes and obelisks were employed in the applied arts from the 16thC.**
- **Egyptian Revival style refers to forms and motifs inspired by ancient Egyptian art and architecture.**
- **Hieroglyphs, winged griffins, palmettes and lotus leaves are among typical motifs.**
- **Throughout the 19thC, the fashion for Egyptian style continued as a strand of Historicism.**
- **In 1922, the discovery of Tutankhamen's tomb led to a revival in the popularity of Egyptian style, most notably in the Art Deco style.**

A Regency mahogany breakfront press, in the Egyptian Revival taste, with winged pediment cornice sections, fitted central section with slides above drawers, flanked by hanging compartments, on turned legs.

The overall color and condition is considered to be good. There is a split in the left hand door and a very small piece of molding missing from the border outline of the door of the right hand wing.

c1820 *89.5in (227cm) high 98in (249cm) wide*

$4,500-6,000 **CHEF**

One of a matched pair of William IV mahogany clothes presses, each with a molded cornice, pair of arch-molded doors flanked by pilasters with acanthus-carved terminals, opening to an arrangement of shelves, each base with three long drawers, turned feet.

c1835 *60in (153cm) wide*

$1,800–2,700 pair **DN**

An early Victorian mahogany single wardrobe, the cavetto-molded cornice over single mirrored door with cut corners and flanked on either side by an arched bead panel, the interior with hinged shoe box to base, on molded plinth.

84.5in 214cm) high

$1,000–1,500 **HT**

A 19thC mahogany linen press, the molded cornice over two paneled brass trimmed doors enclosing four slides, and later hanging rail, two long drawers below with turned wood handles, molded base and bun feet.

79in 200cm) high

$1,500-2,250 **HT**

ESSENTIAL REFERENCE - HADLEY CHESTS

Considered one of the most celebrated groups of early American furniture, Hadley chests have three panels in the front, a well, and one, two, or, rarely, three drawers. Ornamented over the entire front with flat carving usually involving a tulip motif, the chest sometimes includes the initials of the owner.

- **In the early 18thC, richly carved and brightly painted Hadley chests would have been striking additions to any home.**
- **Thanks to the writings of Henry Wood Erving in 1883, Hadley chests have been acclaimed, examined and reinterpreted.**
- **A Hadley chest was typically made for a young woman before marriage.**
- **Today, Hadley represents the largest group of American joined furniture. Some 250 Hadley chests survive.**

A Massachusetts Pilgrim Century carved oak chest, probably Hadley area, the lift lid over a fully carved case with two drawers supported by stile feet.

c1700 *46in (117cm) wide*

$10,500-12,000 **POOK**

A Massachusetts Pilgrim Century carved oak chest, probably Hadley area, the carved façade with three floral panels, the center one initialed EB, all over a single drawer supported by stile feet.

c1690 *42.5in (108cm) wide*

$12,750–14,250 **POOK**

A Massachusetts Pilgrim Century carved oak chest, probably Hadley area, the lift lid over a case profusely carved with floral decoration, initialled MS, above a single drawer and stile feet, retaining an old red stained surface.

c1700 *41in (104cm) wide*

$5,250-6,750 **POOK**

An early 17thC and later oak coffer, of planked construction, on trestle-end supports with carved rosette, plain hinged lid, the solid front carved on the upper half with stop fluting.

50in (128cm) wide

$1,000-1,700 **DN**

An mid-17thC oak two-panel coffer, probably Yorkshire, the lid panels carved with foliate scrolls within a guilloché carved frame, the front panels inlaid with geometric motifs within dog-tooth carved frames and below an S-carved frieze, the side panels carved with lunettes within dog-tooth carved frames.

32.5in (83cm) wide

$1,800–4,000 **SWO**

A Charles II paneled oak chest, hinged lid above a twin paneled front carved with lozenge and flowerheads.

c1660 *45in (115cm) wide*

$750–1,500 **DN**

A late 17thC Charles II oak coffer, the multi paneled lid inscribed 'John Hutchinson, 1637' opening to reveal a void interior, the later carved front with figural doric pilasters, raised on stile feet.

52in (132cm) wide

$1,500-2,250 **L&T**

An 18thC Dutch oak and steel-bound silver chest, the slightly domed top enclosing a void interior with shelf and lidded compartment, the steel strap work sides with brass stud decoration.

42in (107cm) wide

$1,800–2,700 **L&T**

CLOSER LOOK - BOULLE WORK CHEST ON STAND

The lid and sides are inlaid with brass and red tortoiseshell and inset in polychrome ivory and mother of pearl, with foliate scrolls and mythological beasts.

The stand is decorative as well as practical: the four scrolled supports are joined by a waved X-stretcher.

The drawers are also decorated with Boulle work – a sign of a high quality piece.

The frieze is fitted with a fall flap enclosing a red velvet lined interior with a lift out tray and four fitted drawers.

A 19thC Boulle work chest on stand, with hinged domed lid, the stand on four scrolled supports joined by a waved X-stretcher, with brass caps and castors.

Boulle work is an intricate style of marquetry developed by André-Charles Boulle (1642-1732). Born in Paris, Boulle trained as a cabinet-maker, an architect, a bronze worker, and engraver and obtained the privilege of lodging and working in the Louvre for Louis XIV. Boulle marquetry was usually of brass inlaid into a dark background of tortoiseshell or ebony, or vice versa. The style was imitated by 19thC French furniture-makers.

39in (100cm) wide

$150,000-180,000 **TCAL**

ESSENTIAL REFERENCE - BLACK UNICORN ARTIST

Black unicorn decorated chests are among the most sought after dower chests. Recorded on birth and baptismal fraktur documents, these are considered mythological art forms.

- **The Alsatian twin flat heart designed dower chests originated from father and son wood crastsmen Jacob and John Bieber.**
- **Bieber folk art twin heart motifs epitomize the Americana Pennsylvania Dutch folk techniques involving compass and geometric shapes.**
- **Most early Ducth families gave their daughters, and occasionally a son, dower chests to store personal belongings.**

A late 18thC Berks County, Pennsylvania painted pine dower chest, the decoration attributed to the Black Unicorn Artist, the façade with three arched floral decorated panels, the center panel with a figure on horseback, all on a blue ground further embellished with potted flowers and rampant lions.

49in (124cm) wide

$12,000-15,000 **POOK**

A Lehigh County, Pennsylvania painted poplar dower chest, retaining its original ocher sponge decorated surface with green tombstone panels and diamond borders.

c1800 *27.5in (69.8cm) high*

$7,500-9,000 **POOK**

A Berks County, Pennsylvania painted pine dower chest, retaining a vibrant decorated surface with tulips and pinwheel flowers on a blue ground.

c1800 *48in (121.9cm) wide*

$21,000-27,000 **POOK**

A Delaware painted hard pine diminutive blanket chest, retaining its original urn and fruit decoration on a Prussian blue background.

c1810 *36in (91.4cm) wide*

$12,000–18,000 **POOK**

An early 19thC Virginia diminutive painted pine dower chest, retaining its original red, yellow and green geometric decoration with pinwheel and heart.

31in (78.7cm) wide

$10,500-16,500 **POOK**

A Center County, Pennsylvania painted pine dower chest, the front with a large panel of a spread-winged eagle and tulips surrounded by an ocher-sponge ground with pinwheels.

1814 50in (127cm) wide

$6,000-7,500 POOK

A Pennsylvania painted pine blanket chest, retaining its original salmon swirl decorated surface.

c1815 *46.25in (117.4cm) wide*

$1,000-1,700 POOK

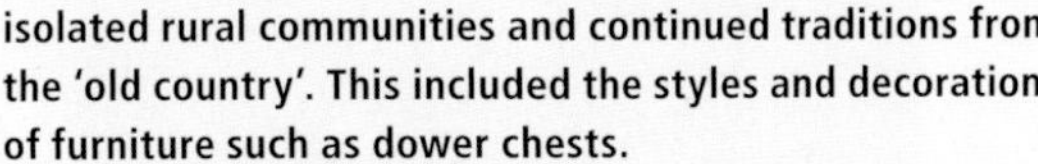

ESSENTIAL REFERENCE - PENNSYLVANIA DUTCH DOWER CHESTS

Dower – or hope – chests were given to young girls preparing for marriage and used to store household items such as embroidery and linens they were preparing for their married lives.

- **Painted chests were common in central Europe and Scandinavia, and the fashion reached its height at the end of the 18thC. Decoration included scenes from folk tales and local or imaginary views.**
- **In 18thC America, many European migrants lived in isolated rural communities and continued traditions from the 'old country'. This included the styles and decoration of furniture such as dower chests.**
- **The American chests were usually made by local craftsmen and decorated by itinerant artists to suit the person who commissioned them. Today, simpler and more naïve New World decoration is more desirable than traditional European landscapes and religious themes.**
- **Motifs may include hearts, tulips, flowers, birds and American eagles and turkeys.**
  - **A central panel may be painted with the bride's name and the date of her wedding.**
  - **Collectors pay a premium for pieces with vibrant decoration and which have not been restored; values are not affected by worn or flaking paint.**

A Center County, Pennsylvania painted pine dower chest, with flared French feet, retaining its original red and blue hex and star decoration on an ivory background, with a yellow background behind the drawers.

c1815 49in (102cm) wide

$45,000-60,000 POOK

An early to mid-19thC painted poplar blanket chest, probably Ohio, the front and sides with unusual stylized trees, flowers, and hearts, above an elaborately scalloped apron supported by bracket feet.

47.5in (120cm) wide

$4,000–5,250 POOK

FURNITURE

A Charles II paneled oak chest-of-drawers, with molded edge above three geometric long drawers, on turned feet.

c1660 *49.5in (126cm) wide*

$1,200-1,800 **DN**

A Charles II oak chest-of-drawers, in two sections, with four long drawers.

42.5in (108cm) wide

$550–850 **DN**

A Massachusetts oak and walnut joined chest-of-drawers, with two short and three long drawers and applied half columns supported by turned bun feet.

c1690 *37.5in (95cm) wide*

$19,500-22,500 **POOK**

A William & Mary oyster veneered chest of four long drawers decorated with geometric boxwood lines, on bun feet.

33in (84cm) wide

$4,500-6,000 **CHOR**

CLOSER LOOK - GEORGE I BACHELOR'S CHEST

The cabinetmaker has relied on the decorative features of the wood to decorate the surface of the chest. This is typical of English furniture of the time.

The hinged fold-over top doubled the surface of the chest.

The edges of the drawers are decorated with cross- and feather-banding.

The chest sits on bracket feet.

A George I walnut bachelor's chest, four long, graduated drawers, the bottom drawer with a paper label inscribed 'These drawers are given to Dorothy Emily Briggs on her second birthday September the 19th 1894 by her Grandma Emily Briggs'.

30in (76cm) wide

$21,000-27,000 **WW**

A Queen Anne walnut chest-of-drawers, the later rectangular branded top over a pair of short drawers and three long graduated drawers, raised on later bracket feet, some restoration.

38.5in (98cm) wide

$1,800–2,700 **L&T**

A George II walnut chest-of-drawers, rectangular top quarter-veneered, line-inlaid and crossbanded, with two short and three long drawers and on bracket feet.

c1740 *38in (97cm) wide*

$1,800-3,000 **DN**

A George II black lacquered chest-of-drawers, the rectangular top above three short and three graduated long drawers, raised on bracket feet, the front decorated with Chinoiserie scenes, the top and sides to show floral sprays.

This was probably originally the top half of a chest-on-chest.

39.5in (100cm) wide

$9,000–12,000 **FRE**

A part-early 18thC burr elm bachelor's chest, the cross-and-feather banded fold-over top with re-entrant back corners, revealing a walnut veneered surface, above two short and three long graduated drawers fitted replaced brass handles, together with a previous set of brass handles, on bracket feet.

30in (77cm) wide

$10,500–13,500 **WW**

An 18thC walnut chest-of-drawers, the rectangular top with crossbanding and molded edge, two short and three long drawers on bracket feet.

39in (100cm) wide

$1,200-1,800 **DN**

A George III mahogany chest-of-drawers, the molded rectangular top above a drawer fitted with a baize inset brushing slide supported by lopers, over three further long graduated drawers, raised on shaped bracket feet.

c1760 *40in (102cm) wide*

$5,250-6,750 **L&T**

A George III serpentine chest of drawers, the shaped molded top above four long graduated drawers flanked by canted corners, raised on shaped bracket feet.

c1760 *40in (102cm) wide*

$9,000–12,000 **L&T**

A mid-18thC George III mahogany serpentine chest of drawers, the serpentine molded top over four graduated long drawers, raised on ogee bracket feet.

36in (91cm) wide

$1,500-2,250 **L&T**

A George III mahogany bow front chest-of-drawers, the bowfront top over four graduated long drawers, the top drawer fitted with a sliding green leather writing surface opening to reveal a fitted interior with a ratchet mirror, raised on scroll bracket feet.

39.5in (101cm) wide

$2,700-3,300 **L&T**

A George III mahogany serpentine dressing chest with four long graduating drawers and lopers to support the once-fitted top drawer, within blind fret corners and on ogee bracket feet.

39.5in (100cm) wide

$10,500–13,500 **CHOR**

A George III serpentine mahogany chest of drawers the four long drawers on bracket feet.

42in (107cm)

$3,000–6,000 **SWO**

A George III mahogany bachelor's chest, the rectangular fold-over top opening to a brown leather insert surface, over a long frieze drawer and three further graduated long drawers, raised on bracket feet.

30in (76cm) wide

$1,800–4,000 **L&T**

An 18thC George III mahogany chest-of-drawers, the serpentine quarter veneered featherbanded and rosewood crossbanded top over four graduating long drawers, raised on shaped bracket feet.

42in (106cm) wide

$1,800-3,000 **FRE**

A George III mahogany chest-of-drawers, the serpentine top over a brushing slide with a brown leather insert and three long graduated drawers, raised on splay feet.

39in (100cm) wide

$1,500-2,250 **L&T**

A George III mahogany chest of drawers, rectangular crossbanded top, two short and three long drawers flanked by reeded columns, on ogee bracket feet.

c1780 *37in (94cm) wide*

$1,800–4,000 **DN**

A George III oak chest-of-drawers, with molded rectangular top, two short and three long graduated drawers, on shaped bracket feet.

c1780 *39in (100cm) wide*

$750-1,200 **DN**

A George III mahogany and inlay serpentine chest-of-drawers, the serpentine top with line inlay over four graduated crossbanded drawers flanked by inlaid angles, above a shaped apron and raised on bracket feet.

c1790 *48in (123cm) wide*

$1,800-3,000 **L&T**

A George III mahogany secretaire chest-of-drawers, the rectangular top with molded edge, the fall front drawer opening to small drawers, pigeon holes and a central cupboard, three further long drawers, outswept bracket feet.

c1790 *45in (115cm) wide*

$750-1,200 **DN**

A George III mahogany gentlemens dressing table, hinged lid, opening to a fitted interior, incorporating divisions and centered by a ratchet adjustable mirror, above a slide with a baize inset writing surface and an arrangement of drawers beneath, square section legs, brass caps and castors.

c1790 *29in (74cm) wide*

$900–1,400 **DN**

A George III mahogany chest of drawers, with rectangular molded top, two short and three long bracket feet.

c1790 *33in (85cm) wide*

$850-1,300 **DN**

A George III mahogany bowfront chest-of-drawers, the bowfront top with boxwood line inlay and stringing, over a pair of short drawers and three long graduated drawers, raised on short splay feet.

c1800 *45in (114cm) wide*

$900-1,500 **L&T**

A George III mahogany bowfront dressing chest, the top drawer with brushing slide, lidded compartments, ratchet mirror and pull-out drawer to the side, three further drawers below, raised on bracket feet.

c1800 *40.5in (103cm)*

$1,500-2,250 **TEN**

A 19thC oak chest, the molded edged top with three small drawers below, the central one concealing secret drawers behind (vacant), two short and three long drawers with foliate brass drop handles and flanked by mahogany quarter columns, molded base and bracket feet.

48in (123cm) wide

$750-1,200 **HT**

An 18thC north Italian walnut marquetry commode, the molded rectangular top above three long drawers inlaid with scrolling foliate motifs, raised on shaped bracket feet.

56in (143cm) wide

$3,000-4,500 **L&T**

An 18thC Northern European kingwood, amaranth, sycamore and marquetry gilt bronze mounted serpentine bombe commode, the quarter-veneered serpentine top with a molded edge centered by an oval cartouche with flowering urn and bird marquetry, above three serpentine and bombe drawers inlaid with floral sprays and drapery swags mounted with robust pierced foliate gilt bronze handles; the side panels with floral sprays, the angles mounted with gilt bronze satry masks and foliate scrolls, raised on short splay feet with gilt bronze foliate case sabots, the top drawers stamped 'S.S.' on the interior.

59in (150cm) wide

$37,500-52,500 **L&T**

A Louis XV kingwood and tulipwood commode, stamped 'F. FRANC JME', mottled grey and pink marble top, with acanthus and scroll cast mounts, square section tapering legs and sabots.

c1760 *50in (127cm) wide*

£3,000-4,000 **DN**

An 18thC Continental parcel gilt mahogany and rosewood commode, the serpentine top over conforming case enclosing two long drawers, above carved and pierced apron, raised on Rococo carved cabriole legs.

40in (101cm) wide

$4,500-6,000 **FR E**

An 18thC Northern European kingwood, amaranth, sycamore and marquetry gilt bronze mounted serpentine bombe commode, the quarter-veneered top with a molded edge centered by an oval cartouche with flowering urn and bird marquetry, raised on short splay feet with gilt bronze foliate cast sabots, the top drawer stamped 'S.S.' on the interior.

59in (150cm) wide

$22,500-37,500 **L&T**

An 18thC French oak commode, the serpentine front with two short and three long drawers, with all-over carved foliate and scrolled decoration within paneled sides.

47in (120cm) wide

$3,000-4,500 **SWO**

CLOSER LOOK - GEORGE III COMMODE

The floral marquetry top is typical of Langlois' commodes.

The twin doors to the serpentine front are seen on other pieces by Langlois.

Langlois shared his premises with his son-in-law, the bronze-caster and gilder Dominique Jean, who made the high quality mounts for his furniture.

A George III kingwood, rosewood and floral marquetry serpentine commode, in the manner of Pierre Langlois, the serpentine crossbanded and floral and ribbon tied marquetry top, with conforming floral marquetry doors, enclosing a later interior of two shelves, with foliate gilt metal mounts, the shaped and banded side with floral, foliate and C-scrolled marquetry sides, raised on out-swept feet terminating sabots.

The shaped sides are decorated in the same way as the front and top.

Pierre Langlois (active 1759-1767) was a French ébéniste who worked in London's Tottenham Court Road, from the 1750s. It is likely that he trained with one of the best Paris marquetry workshops, possibly that of Jean-Fran‡ois Oeben (1721-1763). Unlike many of his French contemporaries, Langlois paid a lot of attention to the interiors of his furniture, which might include lining drawers with mahogany.

36in (91cm) wide

$27,000–33,000 **ROS**

An 18thC Swedish mahogany, marquetry and parquetry marble top commode, the breakfront green marble top with outset square corners over a conforming long frieze drawer and gilt metal laurel banding and two further long drawers, with a central marquetry panel of a basket of fruit flanked by further panels with urns, raised on square tapered legs ending in gilt metal mounts.

45in (115cm) wide

$4,500-6,000 **L&T**

A French kingwood, tulipwood and gilt metal mounted serpentine commode, with later marble top above a pair of parquery decorated drawers, shaped frieze, tapered cabriole legs and sabots.

c1770 *47.6in (121cm) wide*

$6,000-7,500 **DN**

A Northern Italian olive wood, walnut and fruitwood parquetry serpentine commode, the molded serpentine top with an oval parquetry cartouche, over three long drawers centered by a further cartouche, the sides with chevron panels, above a serpentine apron and raised on short cabriole legs.

c1780 *51.5in (131cm) wide*

$3,000-4,500 **L&T**

A late 18thC George III mahogany and inlaid bowfront commode, the bow front top with outset rounded corners above a pair of short drawers and pair of tambour doors flanked by three quarter fluted columns, raised on round tapered legs.

43.5in (111cm) wide

$450-750 **L&T**

A French mahogany commode, with white marble top, fitted two long and three short drawers.

c1800 *50.5in (128cm) wide*

$3,000-4,500 **CHOR**

An early 19thC Italian Neo-classical walnut and fruitwood inlay commode, the rectangular top with banded inlay and barberpole molded edge over three long drawers with enamel and brass pulls depicting portraits of ladies, raised on square tapered legs, the top drawer stamped '5550'.

49in (125cm) wide

$4,500-6,000 L&T

ESSENTIAL REFERENCE - NICOLAS LANNUIER

French-born maître-ebeniste Charles-Honore Lannuier (1779-1819) was a leading figure in the development of a distinctive and highly refined style of furniture in the American Late Federal period. From his brother Nicolas, a Parisian cabinetmaker, he learned the 'art and mystery' of cabinetmaking before going to America in 1803.

- **He established his own workshop and wareroom at 60 Broad Street and by 1804 was listed in the New York City Directory.**
- **He provided seating furniture for the Common Council Chamber of New York's new City Hall.**
- **He applied a handsomely engraved bilingual label to his finished pieces, transmitting directly to America the Greco-Roman revival style that was popular in Republican and early empire France.**
- **While his career was cut short by his untimely death at the age of 40, documented examples of Lannuier's furniture can be found in the permanent collections of museums such as The Metropolitan Museum of Art.**

A 19thC Louis XVI-style kingwood, tulipwood and parquetry marble top commode, the rectangular black and white veined marble top of slight breakfront outline with outset square corners over three long drawers with parquetry veneers, raised on square tapered legs ending in sabots.

47in (120cm) wide

$1,500-2,250 L&T

A 19thC Louis XVI-style mahogany, black lacquer and gilt bronze mounted marble top 'commode à l'anglaise', stamped Perreau, after the model by Nicolas Lannuier, of bowfront outline, the white marble inset top within a gilt bronze border, above a gilt bronze vitruvian scroll frieze, above two black lacquered chinoiserie paneled doors, flanked by two marble galleried shelves on either side, raised on short tapering legs terminating in brass caps.

69in (175cm)

$45,000-60,000 FRE

A burr elm, kingwood and tulipwood commode, of serpentine outline, the top with marquetry inset star motif, above three drawers flanked by a pair of cupboards, on cabriole legs.

44in (112cm) wide

$2,250-3,000 DN

A pair of late 19thC Swedish kingwood and crossbanded bombe commodes, the quarter veneered serpentine and crossbanded tops over two short and two long drawers and a serpentine apron, raised on square splayed slender legs terminating in sabots.

43in (109cm) wide

$6,000–9,000 L&T

A 20thC kingwood and parquetry decorated commode, in the Louis XV/XVI transitional style, with a marble top, above an arrangement of three drawers, on downswept legs and gilt metal sabots.

41in (104cm) wide

$750-1,200 DN

A James II walnut chest-on-stand, feather-banded decoration, brass drop handles and escutcheon, on a later stand with baluster turned legs and stretchers, on bun feet.

37.5in (96cm) wide

$4,000–5,250 **CHEF**

An early 18thC walnut chest-on-stand, mirrored veneers and plain banded border decoration and brass ring handles, the stand on later cabriole legs.

40.5in (103cm) wide

$750–1,500 **CHEF**

A southern Massachusetts Queen Anne walnut high chest-of-drawers, with a bonnet top and demi-lune carved drawers.

c1765 37.5in (95cm) wide

$12,750–14,250 **POOK**

An 18thC walnut veneered chest-on-stand, with three short and four long drawers, the 19thC stand on turned and joint supports.

41.5in (106cm) wide

$750–1,500 **CHEF**

A Massachusetts Queen Anne walnut bonnet top high chest, with fan-and-line inlaid drawers.

c1765 38in (96cm) wide

$12,750–14,250 **POOK**

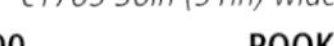

A New England Queen Anne tiger maple high chest, attributed to John Kimball, Concord or Derryfield, New Hampshire, retaining an early Spanish brown surface.

c1765 36in (91in) wide

$37,500–45,000 **POOK**

An early 20thC Queen Anne-style oak and walnut chest on stand, the molded rectangular top over three long graduated drawers; the lower part with three short frieze drawers above a scrolled apron, raised on baluster turned legs and a conforming undertier, raised on ball feet.

35.5in (91cm) wide

$1,200-1,800 **L&T**

A mid-20thC Chippendale-style walnut high chest, a well-executed bench-made copy of a fully developed Philadelphia masterpiece.

99.5in (253cm) high 43in (109.5cm) wide

$16,500–21,000 **POOK**

A part-17thC William & Mary walnut cabinet-on-chest, the later cupboard doors enclosing an arrangement of eleven drawers around a cupboard door, the chest of two short over two long drawers, raised on later bun feet.

42.5in (108cm) wide

$3,000-4,500 **TEN**

An early 18thC walnut, prince's wood and oyster veneered cabinet-on-chest, with a cushion frieze drawer, above a pair of radiating veneered doors enclosing an arrangement of eleven drawers around a cupboard with four secret drawers, the base in two sections and fitted with three drawers, the top and base associated.

45.5in (115cm) wide

$4,500-6,000 **WW**

An 18thC George II red walnut chest-on-chest, the molded cornice over a plain frieze; the upper part with two short drawers over three long graduated drawers; the lower part with three further long graduated drawers, raised on shaped bracket feet

40in (102cm) wide

$1,800–4,000 **L&T**

A George II walnut chest-on-chest, with oak sides and replaced brass handles, the base inlaid a parquetry sunburst.

75in (190cm) high

$4,500-6,000 **WW**

A George II mahogany chest on chest, of three short and three long graduated drawers flanked by fluted canted angles, fitted with brass bat's wing handles.

72in (182.5cm) high

$1,500-2,250 **WW**

An 18thC walnut and oak chest-on-chest, with a brushing slide.

41.5in (106cm) wide

$1,800–4,000 **SWO**

A George III mahogany chest-on-chest, the molded cornice with canted corners above a plain frieze and two short drawers over three long drawers flanked by fluted angles, the lower part with three further long drawers, raised on ogee bracket scroll feet.

c1760 *40.5in (103cm) wide*

$2,700-3,300 **L&T**

A George III and later carved mahogany chest-on-chest, elaborate fret-carved swan neck pediment, molded cornice, greek key and blind fret decorated frieze and repeated decoration to the carcase, gilt brass handles, on conforming carved square bracket feet.

44.5in (114cm) wide

$1,800–2,700 **CHEF**

A George III pine tall chest.

c1770 *35.5in (91cm) wide*

$1,200-1,800 **POOK**

A Connecticut Chippendale cherry bonnet top chest-on-chest, probably Colchester, with a pinwheel carved tympanum and drawer.

c1775 *41.5in (105cm) wide*

$9,750–11,250 **POOK**

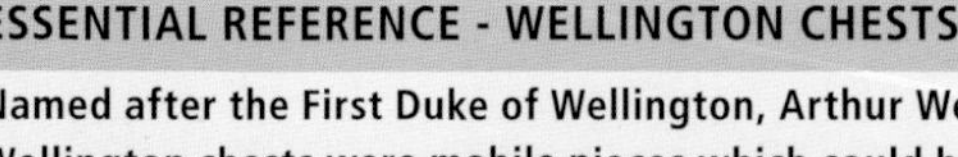

ESSENTIAL REFERENCE - WELLINGTON CHESTS

Named after the First Duke of Wellington, Arthur Wellesley, Wellington chests were mobile pieces which could be easily transported during military campaigns.

- **Popular in England and France from 1820, a Wellington chest consisted of a narrow chest-of-drawers, with up to 12 drawers and a single locking mechanism. A hinged flap ran down one side of the chest, locking over the drawers.**
- **In the Victorian period, they were made of mahogany, walnut and rosewood. Some had a fitted secretaire occupying two drawer heights.**
- **Wellington chests were also made in Continental Europe, usually in decorative timbers with gilt metal mounts without a side-locking flap.**

A George III mahogany chest-on-chest, molded cornice, two short and six long drawers, shaped bracket feet.

c1780 *45in (115cm) wide*

$900-1,500 **DN**

A William IV rosewood Wellington chest, fitted with eight drawers and with two column locking side plates, applied leaf carved capital moldings, on a plinth base.

24in (61cm) wide

$4,000–5,250 **CHEF**

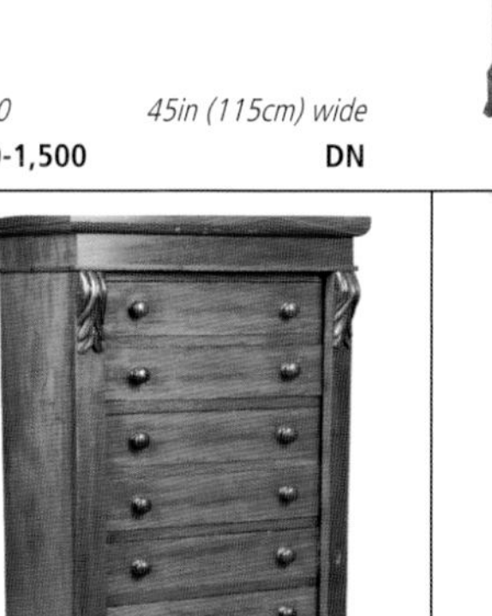

An early Victorian mahogany Wellington chest, fitted with ten drawers, with side locking plates and acanthus leaf carved capital moldings, on a plinth base.

23.5in (60cm)

$300-750 **CHEF**

A Victorian burr walnut secretaire Wellington chest with seven graduated drawers and turned bun handles.

22.5in (57cm)

$3,000-4,500 **SWO**

An early 18thC Anglo-Dutch walnut and marquetry escritoire, with a cushion frieze drawer, the hinged fall inlaid with stained bone and fruitwood urns of flowers and mythical beasts issuing tulips, enclosing an arrangement of drawers and pigeon holes around a central cupboard, above two short and two long drawers fitted later brass handles.

42.5in (108cm) wide

$3,000-4,500 WW

A George III mahogany and kingwood fall front secretaire, the rectangular top with molded outset square corners over a long frieze drawer, above a fall front opening to an arrangement of pigeon holes and drawers with a green baize writing surface; the lower part with a cupboard door opening to shelves, all outlined in chequer stringing, raised on square tapered legs ending in brass caps and castors.

30in (76cm) wide

$1,800-3,000 L&T

A George III mahogany two-part secretary, the lower section with a butler's desk.

36in (91cm) wide

$1,000–1,500 POOK

A Pennsylvania Chippendale walnut two-part secretary, the secret document drawer inscribed Mr. Bines and his Lad Made this desk in the Month of May 1785.

39.5in (100cm) wide

$3,000-4,500 POOK

A New York Federal mahogany secretary, the broken arch bonnet above two cupboard doors, resting on a base with a single drawer and two cupboard doors flanked by carved columns.

Provenance: Stanley Weiss.

c1820 *50in (127cm) wide*

$1,500-2,250 POOK

A Boston, Massachusetts Chippendale mahogany secretary, the upper section with a broken arch pediment centering a carved bust of Shakespeare, over two scalloped panel doors enclosing a fitted interior flanked by fluted pilasters with carved capitals, resting on a base with a fall front enclosing an interior with fan carved drawers and a block front case with four drawers supported by ball and claw feet.

41.5in (105cm) wide

$25,500-33,000 POOK

A Napoleon III gilt-metal and Sevres-style porcelain mounted, burl walnut, ebonized and inlaid secretaire cabinet, in two sections, the upper section with pediment top over central recess with mirrored back, flanked by two shelves each above a cupboard door centered by an oval Sevres-style porcelain plaque painted to show 18thC couples and above a short drawer, flanking two larger central glazed cupboard doors, the lower section with pull-out leather writing surface flanked by two drawers above three open shelves and two cupboard doors below flanked by shelves, raised on turned feet.

56in (142cm) wide

$10,500–13,500 FRE

A George II burl elm secretaire bookcase, in two parts, the upper section with molded breakfront cornice over twin mirrored cupboard doors etched to show a crown, the lower section with fallfront desk opening to reveal a series of pigeonholes and drawers, above four graduated long drawers flanked by fluted canted corners, raised on shaped bracket feet.

44in (111cm) wide

$3,000-4,500 **FRE**

A George III mahogany breakfront secretaire bookcase, the molded cornice above four astragal glazed doors, the interior fitted with adjustable shelves, the base with a reeded edge above a central configuration of secretaire drawer with leather sciver, enclosing pigeon holes and drawers, above two panel cupboard doors enclosing drawers, flanked by columns of five graduated drawers, furnished throughout with brass bail handles, on a plinth.

87.5in (223cm) wide

$4,500-6,000 **MOR**

A George III green lacquered secretaire bookcase, in two sections, the broken pediment top over twin arched doors (lacking panes), opening to a series of shelves, the lower section with drop down writing surface opening to a red lacquered interior with drawers and pigeon holes, above two short and two long drawers, raised on bracket feet, the whole green lacquered all over to show Chinoiserie scenes.

90in (228cm) high

$9,000–12,000 **FRE**

A late 18thC French provincial two-part fruit wood bookcase.

45in (114.5cm) wide

$1,800–2,700 **POOK**

A Maryland Hepplewhite mahogany and maple veneer two-part secretary bookcase, with butler's desk.

c1800 *37.5in (95cm) wide*

$1,500-2,250 **POOK**

A George III mahogany secretaire bookcase, the top with a pair of astragal glazed doors, opening to three shelves, the base with sliding secretaire drawer opening to a fitted interior inlaid with boxwood, above three long drawers, on bracket feet, the top of base section bearing a label inscribed 'Francis Heathed Esq. Harvledown near Canterbury'.

c1810 *43in (109cm) wide*

$600-900 **DN**

A late 19thC French mahogany and brass mounted bibliotheque, with urn finials to a broken pediment above a pair of glazed doors enclosing adjustable shelves, on toupie feet.

49in (125cm) wide

$3,000-4,500 **WW**

An early 19thC mahogany bow-fronted secretaire bookcase, the back with Gothic arched glazing bars and carved moldings, to an alcove and fitted base, baize-lined desk and cupboards below, on a plinth.

53in (134cm) wide 22.25in (56cm) deep

Est $450-750 DNS **CHEF**

CLOSER LOOK - QUEEN ANNE BUREAU BOOKCASE

The broken arch molded pediment is centered by a molded plinth above a shaped mirror insert.

The slant front opens to an interior fitted for writing with a brown leather writing surface and drawers and pigeon holes centered by an architectural niche.

The arched molded doors are decorated externally with beveled mirror plates, open to an arrangement of small drawers and pigeon holes.

The bookcase is raised on bracket feet.

A Queen Anne burr walnut and inlay bureau bookcase, with two candle slides, a pair of short drawers and two long graduated drawers.

41in (104cm) wide

$30,000–37,500 **L&T**

An early 18thC walnut bureau bookcase, with molded cornice above glass paneled doors upon a bureau with fitted interior, above two short and two long drawers on bracket feet.

c1715 *39in (99cm) wide*

$16,500-19,500 **CHOR**

An 18thC Venetian bureau bookcase, the arched upper section with painted chinoiserie decoration, molded frame to the glass paneled door, the now glass paneled fall concealing a central cupboard and four drawers painted with chinoiserie scenes above four long graduating drawers painted with figures in landscapes, the sides also with chinoiserie scenes.

35in (89cm) wide

$4,000–5,250 **CHOR**

A George II mahogany bureau bookcase, molded cornice above a pair of arched paneled cupboard doors, fall opening to a fitted interior, two short and three long graduated drawers, on bracket feet.

c1750 *45.5in (116cm) wide*

$1,200-1,800 **DN**

A George III mahogany bookcase cabinet, with a broken swan-neck pediment above a pair of oval panel doors banded in rosewood, enclosing nine short shelves above a pair of curved front drawers, above a pair of conforming doors enclosing two shelves, on ogee bracket feet.

49in (125cm) wide

$2,700-3,300 **WW**

A Philadelphia mahogany bureau bookcase, the carved swan-neck pediment terminating in flower heads over pierced trellis panels and centered by a carved urn finial, above a blind fret carved frieze and pair of astragal glazed doors opening to shelves, over two candle slides; the lower part with a slant front opening to an arrangement of pigeon holes and drawers, above four graduated long drawers, raised on ogee bracket feet.

c1770 *41in (105cm) wide*

$12,000-15,000 **L&T**

A George III mahogany bureau bookcase, the molded cornice over a frieze inlaid with alternating ebony stars and fleur-de-lys, two glass doors below with Gothic astragals enclosing adjustable shelving, the base with cylinder bureau fitted with satinwood veneer drawers and pigeon holes, over a baize-lined hinged adjustable reading/writing slide, three long drawers below with pierced brass drop handles, waved apron and splayed bracket feet.

c1800 *46.5in (118cm) wide*

$1,000-1,700 **HT**

A George III mahogany 'Chinese chippendale' bureau bookcase, the dentil-molded broken pediment centered by a raised plinth over a molded cornice with blind fret carving, over a pair of astragal glazed doors with blind fret carving opening to shelves, the sides with brass loop handles; the lower part with a slant front opening to an interior fitted for writing with an arrangement of drawers and pigeon holes, over four graduated doors flanked by fluted quarter columns, the sides with further handles, raised on short bracket feet.

42.5in (108cm) wide

$1,800–4,000 **L&T**

A 19thC Gothic Revival pitch pine bureau bookcase, the heavy carved sawtooth cornice with carved star motifs over a pair of glazed doors above a fall front with riased panels opening to a void interior; the lower part with two panel cupbaord doors raised on a plinth base.

45.5in (116cm) wide

$1,500–3,000 **L&T**

An 18thC George III mahogany bureau bookcase, the broken arch pediment centered by an urn finial above a fluted frieze, over a pair of astragal glazed doors opening to shelves; the lower part with a slant front opening to an interior fitted with pigeon holes, drawers and two secret compartments, above four graduated long drawers, and raised on shaped bracket feet.

42.5in (108cm) wide

$4,500–7,500 **L&T**

An early 18thC Queen Anne burr walnut and inlay bureau bookcase, the broken arch molded pediment centered by a molded plinth above a mirror insert, over a pair of arched molded doors with mirror plates opening to an arrangement of drawers and pigeon holes, with two candle slides below; the lower part with a slant front opening to an interior fitted with a leather writing surface and drawers and pigeon holes centered by an architectural niche, above a pair of short drawers and two long graduated drawers, and raised on bracket feet.

41in (104cm) wide

$15,000-30,000 **L&T**

A Queen Anne walnut and burr walnut bureau bookcase, cross- and feather-banded, with giltwood finials above a double domed top with later beveled glass doors, enclosing adjustable shelves, with pull-out candle slides; the hinged fall with a rest enclosing a stepped interior of pigeon holes and drawers, the central section pulls out to reveal four secret drawers above a well, above two short and two long drawers, on later bracket feet.

42in (107cm) wide

$10,500-15,500 **WW**

A George III mahogany bureau bookcase 18thC the broken arch pediment centered by an urn finial above a fluted frieze, over a pair of astragal glazed doors opening to shelves; the lower part with a slant front opening to an interior fitted with pigeon holes, drawers and two secret compartments, above four graduated long drawes, raised on shaped bracket feet

42.5in (108cm) wide

$6,000–9,000 DNS **L&T**

ESSENTIAL REFERENCE - VILE AND COBB

William Vile (c1700–1767), and John Cobb (c1715–1778) were an important cabinetmaking partnership based in St. Martin's Lane, London.

- **From 1750–1760 Vile was one of the most eminent craftsmen of his generation, with much of his work considered to be superior to that produced by Chippendale in the Rococo period. At this time the two men produced furniture for George III.**
- **Vile specialized in carving and Cobb in upholstery.**
- **After Vile's retirement in 1764, Cobb produced Neoclassical pieces decorated with floral marquetry with the help of his foreman Samuel Reynolds. His inlays used tropical woods, especially satinwood.**
- **In 1772 it was suggested that Cobb was involved in the smuggling of furniture into Britain from France.**

A mid-18thC George III mahogany breakfront bookcase, the acanthus carved swan neck pediment with fretwork panels over a dentil molded cornice and pair of astragal glazed doors opening to shelves, flanked by narrow side cabinets with matching astragal glazed doors, the lower part with a gadrooned carved edge over a pair of molded anel doors flanked by further molded panel doors, raised on conforming plinth feet.

69.5in (177cm) wide

$45,000-60,000 **L&T**

A George II mahogany breakfront bookcase, in the manner of Vile and Cobb, of shallow breakfront outline, the broken arch pediment above a pair of doors with arched glazed panels and foliate carved corner moldings opening to shelves, flanked by further set back glazed doors; the lower part with a central cupboard door with oval moldings marked at the sides with acanthus carving, flanked by cupboard doors carved with ribbon tied fruit and foliate trails, raised on shaped bracket feet.

Provenance: Collection of B. Coppinger Prichard; Property from a Highland Estate.

c1755 *65in (166cm) wide*

$105,000–120,000 **L&T**

A George III mahogany breakfront library bookcase, the breakfront cornice with key molding over a blind fret carved frieze, above astragal glazed doors opening to shelves; the conforming lower part with a matching fret carved frieze over panel cupboard doors opening to shelves and raised on a plinth base.

96.5in (246cm) wide

$19,500-27,000 **L&T**

A Gillow and Co. burr oak breakfront library bookcase fitted with adjustable shelves, the top with folding rest with pull-out supports on a plinth base, stamped Gillow & Co. 2806.

76.25in (194cm) wide

$2,700-3,300 **CHOR**

A 19thC mahogany breakfront library bookcase, the base with a pair of cupboard doors enclosing three adjustable slides, with replaced brass handles.

85in (216cm) wide

$5,250-6,750 **WW**

A Victorian mahogany breakfront bookcase, the molded cornice on plain pilasters with leaf and flower carved capitals and scrolled bases over three arched glazed doors enclosing adjustable shelving, similar protruding base with three paneled doors, on plinth.

80in (203cm) wide

$2,700-3,300 **HT**

A mid-19thC French mahogany and brass mounted breakfront open bookcase by Grohe, Paris, the arched cornice to a frieze applied with a gilt brass laurel wreath and burning torches, above three sections of adjustable shelves, stamped 'GROHE A PARIS' in several places, later adapted from a bibliotheque with later shelves and back.

80in (203cm) wide

$2,700-3,300 **WW**

A George III mahogany bookcase cabinet, the reeded and cavetto molded cornice over a pair of glazed doors with arched mullions opening to shelves and lined with chinoiserie printed fabric; the lower part with a pair of cupboard doors opening to eight short drawers, raised on bracket feet.

39in (100cm) wide

$3,000-4,500 **L&T**

A George III mahogany bookcase, the broken arch pediment with trellis panels above a dentil molded frieze, over a pair of astragal glazed doors open to a pale blue silk lined and shelved interior; the lower part similarly arranged, raised on bracket feet.

45.5in (116cm) wide

$4,500-6,000 **L&T**

A George III mahogany bookcase cabinet, the molded cornice over a Greek key carved frieze, above a pair of astragal glazed doors opening to three adjustable shelves; the lower part with four graduated long drawers, raised on bracket feet.

39in (100cm) wide

$4,500-6,000 **L&T**

A 19thC Irish mahogany library bookcase, by R. Strahan & Co., Dublin, the stepped molded cornice over four sections with open shelves divided by recessed panel columns headed by acanthus carved scrolling capitals; the lower part centered by two further sections of open shelves flanked by raised panel and molded doors, on a plinths base, the lock plates stamped 'R. Straha & Co. Dublin'.

The furniture firm of Robert Strahan & Co. was founded in Dublin in 1776 and by 1845 it had two workshops as well as its main commercial premises. It continued to trade until 1969. Known for its high quality work, the firm exhibited at the Dublin Great Industrial Exhibition in 1853 and the London International Exhibition in 1862. It supplied furniture to many of the most well-known Irish country houses including Doneraile Court, Lisnavagh, and Monte Alverno, many of which had their contents sold off in the 20thC.

204in (519cm) wide

$37,500-52,500 **L&T**

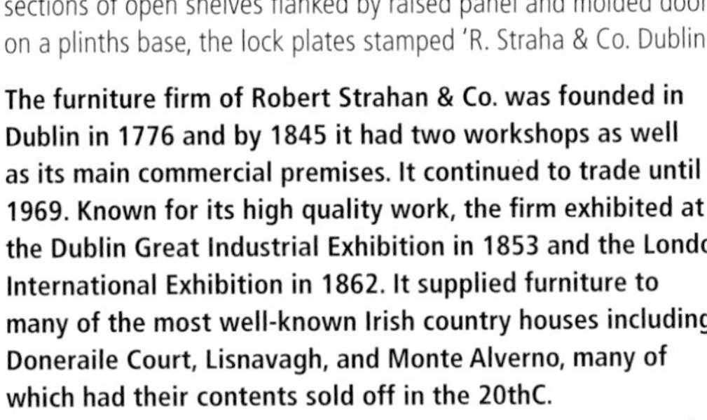

A George II-style mahogany bookcase cabinet, in two parts, the projecting cornice with dentil and dart molding above a pair of astragal glazed doors opening to shelves and flanked by blind fret carved canted angles; the lower part with two further astragal glazed doors opening to shelves and flanked by similarly carved blind fret angles, raised on ogee bracket feet; the base bearing a brass plaque inscribed 'USED BY/ DOUGLAS HAIG / 1911-1928.

Field Marshal Douglas Haig, 1st Earl Haig of Bemersyde, (1861–1928) was a British senior officer during World War I. He commanded the British Expeditionary Force (BEF) from 1915 to the end of the war. Haig was born in Charlotte Square, Edinburgh, where his father was in the whisky trade. By the time of his death, he was extremely popular, and his funeral became a day of national mourning. Haig and his military tactics have, however, been subject to criticism in more recent years, due to the high level of casualties during his command. These gained him the nickname of 'Butcher of the Somme' and make him one of the most controversial figures in British war history.

c1900 *48in (122cm) wide*

$5,250-6,750 **L&T**

A Victorian matched pair of mahogany bookcases by Maple & Co., each with molded cornice above a pair of glass paneled doors opening to adjustable shelves, each lower section with a pair of paneled cupboard doors, plinth bases, two of the doors bearing a circular enamel plaque titled 'MANUFACTURED BY MAPLE & CO. .....'.

c1880 *48in (122cm) wide and 41.5in (106cm) wide*

$15,000–18,000 **DN**

A pair of Edwardian satinwood and inlaid library bookcases, each with a molded cornice over a pair of scale pattern astragal glazed doors opening to a green plush lined shelved interior; the lower part with a pair of cupboard doors opening to a sliding tray to one side and four graduated drawers to the other, raised on shaped bracket feet.

68in (173cm) wide

$30,000-45,000 **L&T**

A Regency mahogany and ebony inlaid waterfall open bookcase, three-quarter gallery with central anthemion marquetry, two open shelves, square section tapering feet.

c1815 *43in (110cm) wide*

$750-1,200 **DN**

A Victorian carved walnut open bookcase, the square top with canted outset corners above open shelved sides, flanked and divided by applied relief carved fruit and foliate decoration, surmounted by mask motifs and Doric capitals, raised on a gadrooned platform base.

c1880 *26in (66cm) wide*

$4,000-6,750 **L&T**

A late 19thC burr walnut and brass inlaid dwarf bookcase, with gilt metal mounts, the shaped rectangular top above open adjustable shelves, flanked and divided by stop fluted corinthian style pilasters, raised on a platform base with squat bun feet.

72in (183cm) wide

$15,000–22,500 **L&T**

ESSENTIAL REFERENCE - CAMPAIGN FURNITURE

Campaign – or 'knockdown' - furniture was designed to be taken on military campaigns by officers and could be erected and taken down in a few minutes.

In his 1803 'Cabinet Directory' the designer Thomas Sheraton said his campaign furniture 'should not retard rapid movement, either after or from the enemy'.

- **The first pieces date from the Napoleonic Wars (1800-15) and include Wellington chests, chairs, beds, desks and even dining room tables to sit 20 guests.**
- **Early pieces were made for the wealthiest aristocratic officers and was as luxurious and well made as the furniture they had at home. They featured fine upholstery, leather linings and many desks had hidden compartments.**
- **By the mid-19thC merchant officials and military officers were also buying it, as well as seafarers and families emigrating to start a new life abroad.**
- **Pieces are generally lightweight and can be taken apart, and some elements folded, for ease of transport.**
- **Typical features are joints that could be joined and unjoined with screws rather than traditional joints; corners and other edges protected by brass mounts; brass handles sunk into the wood; and the cylinder Bramah lock.**
- **Pieces made for use in the tropics were designed for hot, humid climates with canvas seats and canework.**

A 19thC folding teak campaign bookcase, opening to reveal a pair of astragal glazed doors, each enclosing a pair of shelves and single drawer.

16in (41cm) wide closed

$2,400-3,150 **BELL**

A Victorian walnut and gilt metal mounted library cabinet, stamped HOLLAND & SON, pierced brass gallery, central open bookshelf flanked by a pair of paneled cupboard doors, rectangular top above a pair of small drawers, turned tapering and fluted legs, brass caps and castors.

c1870 *36in (92cm) wide*

$1,000-1,700 DN

A 19thC Dutch walnut display cabinet, the arch-molded cornice centered by a carved shell motif above a pair of astragal glazed doors opening to velvet lined shelves; the lower part of bombe form with three long drawers flanked by angles and raised on carved paw feet.

68in (173cm) wide

$1,800–2,700 L&T

A late 19thC French kingwood, marquetry and gilt metal mounted standing corner cabinet, the glass paneled door decorated with a marquetry flowering urn, square section legs and sabots.

33.5in (85cm) wide

$1,150-1,425 DN

A walnut floral marquetry and ebonized cabinet-on-stand, the molded cornice over two doors with roundels depicting knights and enclosing shelving, similar roundels to the sides, the interior of the doors inscribed "Geschenk aano Franks Hall 1640", frieze drawer, the base with arched frieze on S-scroll supports on bun feet, joined by wavy stretcher.

c1900 *39in (100cm) wide*

$2,100-2,850 HT

An Edwardian mahogany display cabinet, by Maple & Co Ltd, with cross banding and satinwood stringing of serpentine form with swan neck pediment over plain frieze and single glazed door flanked to either side by shaped glazed panels enclosing shelves, the protruding base with two frieze drawers raised on square tapering legs joined by a shaped undershelf and spade feet.

48in (122cm) wide

$1,800–2,700 DA&H

An Edwardian mahogany parlor cabinet of oblong two stage form with stringing and foliate marquetry, the upper section with central convex mirror having pierced scroll surmount and turned finials over galleried shelf and drop down writing slope revealing drawers and pigeon holes, the whole flanked by glazed cabinets, serpentine front base with two frieze drawers, raised on slender turned tapering legs with fluting and stiff leaf collars, on turned feet joined by raised scrolled cross stretchers supporting a small shelf.

54in (137cm)

$2,100-2,850 HT

A mid-20thC Louis XV-style kingwood and tulipwood veneered and gilt metal mounted serpentine fronted vitrine, the molded frieze with central scroll and foliate cast mount, glass paneled door and shaped sides, incorporating gilt metal framed reserves of floral marquetry, square section tapering legs and sabots.

41in (105cm) wide

$1,200-1,800 DN

A mid-20thC Louis XV-style tulipwood, marquetry and gilt metal mounted serpentine side cabinet, the shaped top with ogee molded edge, above a hinged door, opening to an adjustable glass shelf, three small drawers below, tapering cabriole legs and sabots.

25in (64cm) wide

$600-900 DN

A George III papier mache polychrome painted and gilded bowfront corner cabinet, probably by Henry Clay, the top and doors with Angelica Kaufmann-style decoration, raised on turned and fluted gilded legs.

31.5in (80cm) wide

$4,500–7,500 TEN

George I style walnut cabinet on stand early 20thC the cushion molded cornice above a pair of quarter-veneered cupboard doors opening to a mirrored and shelved interior; the lower part with central drawer flanked by two deep drawers and arched apron, raised on foliate carved cabriole legs ending on claw and ball feet

37in (94cm) wide

$1,800–2,700 DNS L&T

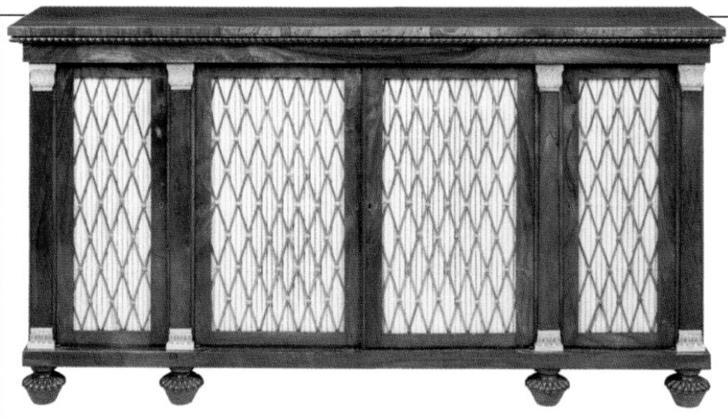

A Regency rosewood and gilt bronze mounted credenza, the rectangular top over a beaded frieze and a pair of brass grille insert doors lined with faded blue pleated silk and flanked by two further grille insert doors, all flanked and divided by square pilasters with lotus cast gilt metal capitals and bases, raised on lobed bun feet.

c1815 *63in (160cm) wide*

$8,250-9,750 **L&T**

A Regency rosewood and marble top side cabinet, the shaped demi-lune white marble top over a pair of cupboard doors with brass grille inserts backed with faded red silk and opening to shelves, flanked by three mirror-backed white marble quarter round open shelves raised on turned feet, the whole outlined with gilt metal mounts.

c1820 *60.5in (154cm)*

$6,000–9,000 **L&T**

A mid-19thC figured walnut, tulipwood and floral marquetry credenza, of serpentine shaped form, with central glazed door flanked by open wings and raised on a platform base.

50.5in (129cm)

$3,000-4,000 **TEN**

A mid-19thC figured walnut credenza, having glazed convex side windows, the shelved interior enclosed by two hinged doors, ormolu mounted and with split column pilasters, supported on a shaped plinth.

67in (170cm) wide

$1,800-3,000 **TRI**

A 19thC Victorian burr walnut, inlay and gilt metal mounted credenza, the shaped demi-lune top over a central cupboard door with line inlay outlined in gilt metal and flanked by fluted and turned columns with gilt metal urn-form capitals, with bowed glazed doors to the sides opening to red plush lined shelves, on a plinth base.

59in (150cm) wide

$2,700-3,300 **L&T**

A Victorian ebonized pier cabinet, with ornate gilt bronze mounts and a single door inset with hardstones with an urn of fruiting foliage, on a black marble ground.

37.5in (96cm) wide

$7,500–10,500 **SWO**

A Victorian burr walnut credenza with crossbanded shaped top above a central glass paneled door flanked by convex glass panels within turned pilasters.

45in (115cm) wide

$1,800-3,000 **CHOR**

A 19thC walnut pier display cabinet of oblong form with floral marquetry and gilt metal mounts, molded edged top and waisted frieze over single door with serpentine opening enclosing velvet lined interior with shelving, raised on canted base with shaped apron and bracket feet.

34in (86cm) wide

$900-1,500 **HT**

A Victorian walnut, crossbanded and ormolu mounted side cabinet with scroll capitals to the canted side pieces, enclosed by glazed door with shaped panel, on a plinth base.

33in (84cm) wide

$1,500-2,250 **DN**

A late 19thC Kingwood and gilt metal mounted breakfront side cabinet, the shaped quarter veneered and brass bound rectangular top with a three-quarter pierced gallery over a central glazed door flanked by two further glazed doors opening to shelves and glazed panels to the sides, the canted angles mounted with gilt metal caryatids, raised on gilt metal hairy paw feet.

61.5in (157cm) wide

$5,250-6,750 **L&T**

A Regency mahogany and gilt metal mounted chiffonier, the rectangular mahogany superstructure with a three-quarter brass gallery raised on cast brass supports, over a single drawer and pair of grille insert doors lined with pleated yellow silk, flanked by squared columns headed by female gilt metal busts, raised on turned feet.

39.5in (101cm) wide

$2,700-3,300 **L&T**

A George IV rosewood breakfront chiffonier, having a central frieze drawer above adjustable shelves and a pair of rectangular panel hinged doors, on carved leaf and molded pilasters and paw feet, the plinth base with applied rondels.

60in (153cm) wide

$1,800-3,000 **WW**

A Regency amboyna, mahogany, rosewood and ebony chiffonier, the stepped superstructure surmounted by a book recess with gilt bronze foliate brackets above a pair of blue silk lined doors flanked by further doors, opening to small drawers and pigeon holes, over a fold-over green leather lined writing surface; the lower part with a long frieze drawer over a pair of blue silk lined doors flanked by tapered square columns, on molded tapered square feet.

c1815 *28.5in (73cm) wide*

$4,000-6,750 **L&T**

A William IV ebonized and polychrome decorated chiffonier, richly painted with exotic birds and flowers, the superstructure with C-scroll supports above two cupboard doors, raised on a plinth base.

33.5in (86cm)

$1,500-2,250 **TEN**

A rare specimen wood chiffonier, the raised super-structure with a scalloped gallery, above a cube parquetry panel with turned and carved supports, the base with a frieze drawer and a pair of panel doors enclosing adjustable shelves flanked by turned and carved columns with part ribbed feet, with applied printed labels 'FROM Ralph v Cabinet and Upholstery MANUFACTORY, KINGSTON, JAMAICA' with the original drawing, signed and dated 1837, together with a chart of the specimen panel to the raised back, signed and dated.

1837 *19.5in (49.5cm) wide*

$9,750–11,250 **WW**

A mid-19thC rosewood chiffonier, the arched mirrored back with pierced fret surmount, the base with bead and reed edged top over two doors each with pierced front panels featuring scrolling foliage and with yellow silk backing, and flanked by flower carved pilasters, on plinth.

49.5in (125cm)

$700–975 **HT**

A George III mahogany and inlaid serving table, the rounded rectangular top with a reeded edge and raised brass gallery, above three frieze drawers, raised on square tapered legs ending in spade feet.

c1790 *61in (155cm) wide*

$1,400–2,000 **L&T**

A George III mahogany semi-elliptical sideboard, with rear brass gallery, central frieze drawer flanked by a lead lined cellaret drawer and a cupboard door, the opposing side with two drawers and a cupboard door.

-c1800 *90in (229cm) wide*

$1,200-1,800 **DN**

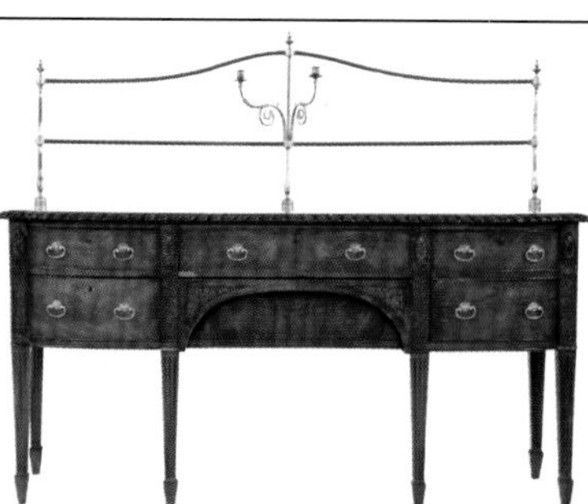

A George III mahogany sideboard with bow front, the brass rail back with a pair of scroll candle brackets, over a gadrooned edge over five drawers, with gilt brass handles, on fluted square tapering legs and spade feet, with carved and blind fret moldings.

72in (184cm)

$5,250-6,750 **SWO**

ESSENTIAL REFERENCE - HEPPLEWHITE

George Hepplewhite (c1727–86) was an English furniture-maker, known for his pattern-book 'The Cabinet-maker and Upholsterer's Guide', which was influential both in Europe and North America.

- **Published posthumously in 1788, the book featured Hepplewhite's designs for slender elegant furniture which came to epitomize Neoclassical furniture.**
- **Hepplewhite's designs simplified those introduced by Robert Adam (see page 248), making them suitable for and attractive to a wider market.**
- **American Hepplewhite-style furniture is called Federal, after the new US government, and often features its symbol the American eagle.**
- **Cabinetmakers – in particular those working in the provinces – often used his guide as a trade catalog. As a result provincial furniture in the Hepplewhite style was probably made long after it ceased to be popular in London.**
- **Typically, his work displayed inlaid and painted rather than carved decoration; motifs such as sunbursts, husks, scrolls and paterae.**
- **Hepplewhite forms include bow-and serpentine-fronted chests-of-drawers and chairs with shield-shaped backs or square backs, incorporating Prince of Wales feathers.**
- **No actual pieces of furniture can be attributed to George Hepplewhite.**

A Maryland Hepplewhite mahogany sideboard, the serpentine top over a frame with floral and rosette inlays supported by square tapering legs with bellflower chain inlays.

c1800 *72in (184cm) wide*

$12,000-15,000 **POOK**

A George III mahogany sideboard, the bowfront over a case with a bottle drawer, a central door, and a door enclosing a fitted interior with overall fan and herringbone inlays.

66.5in (170cm) wide

$3,000-4,500 **POOK**

A George III mahogany and inlaid serpentine sideboard, the raised back fitted with two cupboard doors, below are four further drawers around the shaped apron, raised on square tapered legs ending in spade feet.

c1800 *72.5in (184cm) wide*

$4,500-6,000 **L&T**

A Pennsylvania or Maryland Federal mahogany serpentine front sideboard.

c1800 *72in (183cm) wide*

$1,800–2,700 **POOK**

A William IV rosewood side cabinet, with a raised superstructure with scroll-carved crest, above a shelf on scrolling lappet gilt metal supports, breakfront base with central section incorporating open shelves flanked by leaf carved and gadrooned columns, flanked by grille fronted cupboards, plinth base.

c1835 *72in (183cm) wide*

$1,800-3,000 **DN**

New York Hepplewhite mahogany sideboard, ca. 1800, with overall line inlay.

c1800 *73in (185cm) wide*

$2,100-2,700 **POOK**

A Massachusetts Federal mahogany sideboard, with spiral and reeded legs.

c1815 *80in (200cm) wide*

$1,200-1,800 **POOK**

A Regency mahogany and ebony pedestal sideboard, the arched back above a bow front center section with two frieze drawers with brass lion's mask handles, flanked by pedestal ends each with two drawers over a cupboard door, raised on carved paw feet.

104in (265cm) wide

$1,500–3,000 **L&T**

A Regency mahogany breakfront sideboard, the breakfront top over a central drawer and arched kneehole, flanked by a deep drawer to one side and a cupboard door opposing, with brass lion's mask loop handles, raised on turned tapered legs.

60.5in (154cm) wide

$1,800–2,700 **L&T**

A George IV mahogany serving table, bowfront top, above an arrangement of four drawers, one with baize lined divisions, floral cast gilt metal handles, the frieze with foliate carved roundels, on turned legs.

c1825 *48in (123cm) wide*

$900–1,400 **DN**

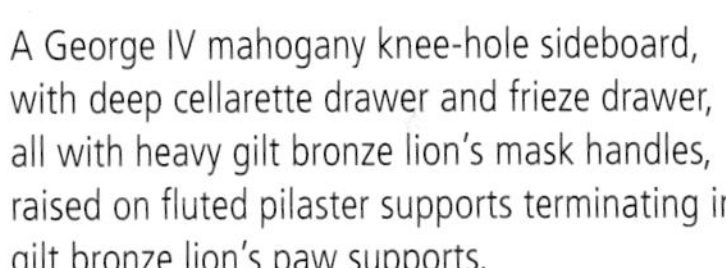

A George IV mahogany knee-hole sideboard, with deep cellarette drawer and frieze drawer, all with heavy gilt bronze lion's mask handles, raised on fluted pilaster supports terminating in gilt bronze lion's paw supports.

82in (208cm) wide

$1,200-1,800 **HW**

A Regency mahogany breakfront sideboard, the slab top above two central cock-beaded frieze drawers flanked by deep cock-beaded drawers, furnished with hollow brass ring handles and backplates, turned, tapering circular supports, brass caps and castors.

80in (203cm) wide

$975-1,450 **MOR**

A mid-19thC Scottish mahogany serving table, with two frieze ash lined drawers on lappet carved legs to carved front paw feet.

82.5in (209cm)

$4,500-6,000 **WW**

A late 17thC/early 18thC Continental walnut and ebonized table cabinet, probably Flemish or Dutch, the central cupboard door decorated with a carved architectural arch and flanked by figures, opening to three drawers concealing three secret drawer, flanked by two further small cupboard doors and an arrangement of four small drawers, plinth base.

22in (56cm) wide

$1,800–2,700 **DN**

An early 18thC faux tortoiseshell table cabinet, of plain oblong form, the hinged cover opening to reveal fitted compartments over a pair of doors enclosing two drawers and raised upon four silvered ball feet.

7in (18cm) wide

$225–400 **HT**

A George III mahogany night commode, gallery top above a drawer, pair of cupboard doors and a further drawer beneath.

c1790 *19.5in (50cm) wide*

$900–1,400 **DN**

A 19thC 17thC-style Antwerp ebonized table cabinet, of oblong form, the pagoda top with slide action dome surmounted by a cast gilt metal cymbal player seated on a camel, over a pair of doors, hinged and opening to reveal three drawers, on a projecting base raised upon four French bracket feet, inset with 25 Vienna enamel plaques painted in colors with Classical scenes and with four similar cylindrical pillars at each corner painted with wrythen swags of flowers and with gilt metal scroll appliques.

9.5in (24cm) wide

$4,500-6,000 **HT**

A Pennsylvania walnut spice cabinet, with an elaborately carved crest and with parquetry inlays.

c1860 *18.5in (53cm) wide*

$1,800–4,000 **POOK**

A 19thC continental walnut Gothic cabinet, with carved and pierced decoration, with an open front and sides with four galleried shelves.

38in (96cm) wide

$4,000–5,250 **WW**

A pair of 19thC and later mahogany bedside cupboards, with gallery above a door and opening to drawers, on plinth base.

16.5in (42cm) wide

$1,500-2,250 **DN**

A pair of French Louis XVI-style mahogany and stained sycamore banded bedside cupboards, each rectangular top with shallow gallery, a frieze drawer and a sliding tambour cupboard door, square section tapering legs and gilt metal sabots.

c1900 *17in (44cm) wide*

$1,200-1,800 **DN**

A pair of burr walnut inverted breakfront bedside chests, each of four drawers to plinth base.

c1900 *16.5in (42cm) wide*

$1,800–2,700 **ECGW**

A pair of French mid-20thC Louis XVI-style tulipwood, marquetry and gilt metal mounted circular bedside cupboards, each top with pierced three-quarter gallery, three short drawers, square section cabriole legs and sabots.

14in (36cm) diam

$1,800–2,700 **DN**

A George I walnut kneehole desk, the rectangular quarter-veneered top over a long drawer fitted with a brushing slide above a kneehole recess with a cupboard door and apron drawer, flanked by banks of three short drawers, raised on bracket feet.

c1720 *32in (82cm) wide*

$4,000–5,250 **L&T**

A George II walnut kneehole desk, with rectangular top, arrangement of seven drawers around the kneehole with recessed cupboard, set on bracket feet.

c1740 *,34in (87cm) wide*

$1,500-2,250 **DN**

CLOSER LOOK - CHIPPENDALE DESK

The fall front encloses a fitted interior with fan-carved drawers. Carved intaglio fans are typical of the Dunlap family's work.

The maple used for the drawer fronts has an attractive grain and patina which adds to its desirability.

The elegant voluted cabriole legs and ball-and-claw feet indicate that this piece of furniture was made by a master craftsman.

The Dunlap family are renowned for the egg-, dart-, and sawtooth-carving seen on the base molding of this desk.

An important New Hampshire Chippendale maple slant-lid desk, signed by cabinetmaker Samuel Dunlap, retaining an old grained surface and drawers with line borders.

Lieutenant Samuel Dunlap (1752–1830) was a member of family of American furniture-makers who lived in New Hampshire. His older brother Major John Dunlap (1746–92) is known for his inlaid cherry wood furniture. The family's furniture is characterized by the expressive use of flowered ogee moldings, basket-weave cornices, open pediments, scrolls and intaglio fans.

c1740 *38in (96cm) wide*

$97,500–115,000 **POOK**

A New England Queen Anne stained cherry child's desk on frame, retaining an old red surface.
c1765 *29in (73cm) wide*
$6,000–9,000 **DN**

A George III satinwood small cylinder desk, with kingwood banding and stringing, the tambour fall revealing pigeon holes and drawers, the a pull-out slide with a replaced green leather above a frieze drawer fitted later oval brass plate ring handles.
27.5in (77cm) wide
$2,700-3,300 **WW**

A George III mahogany bureau, the fall opening to an arrangement of small drawers, pigeon holes, central cupboard doors, two short, three long graduated drawers, set on bracket feet.
c1780 *41in (105cm) wide*
$450-750 **DN**

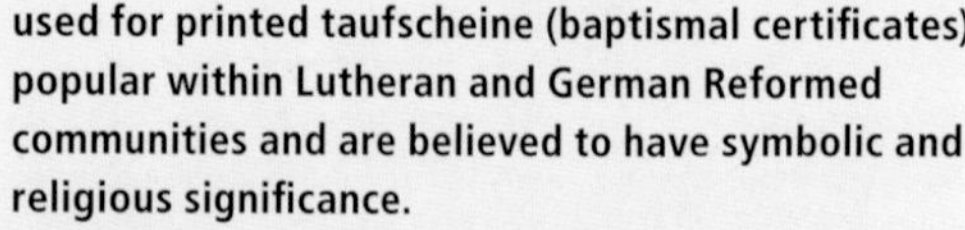

A George III mahogany writing desk, rectangular top and tambour slide, opening to small drawers, pigeon holes and sliding section with ratchet adjustable writing surface, on square tapered supports, pair of frieze drawers, square section tapering legs.
c1800 *35.5 in (91cm) wide*
$1,200-1,800 **DN**

ESSENTIAL REFERENCE - MAHANTONGO VALLEY FURNITURE

Craftsmen working in Pennsylvania's Mahantongo (or Schwaben Creek) Valley created some of the most distinctive and elaborately decorated furniture in the early 19thC.

- **Their work is considered to be among the masterpieces of Pennsylvania German decorative art and the majority of known pieces are held in museum collections, including Philadelphia Museum of Art and the Winterthur Museum.**
- **The unique form of painted decoration used on Mahantongo Valley pieces is attributed to the isolation of the rural communities there.**
- **The furniture made there included cupboards, slant-top desks, blanket chests and chests-of-drawers. Small, turned wooden items such as spice cups and sugar bowls were also made. It was made from tulip poplar and pine.**
- **The decoration typically features angels, praying children, urns, stars, rosettes, birds, horses, deer, geometric and floral designs. Many of these were inspired by designs used for printed taufscheine (baptismal certificates) popular within Lutheran and German Reformed communities and are believed to have symbolic and religious significance.**
- **Several examples bear dates and signatures of their makers or state who the piece was made for.**

A Mahantongo Valley, Pennsylvania painted poplar slant-front desk, the fall front decorated with a central potted tulip, flanked by standing figures and star devices within a potato-stamp border, over a case with four drawers with birds, stags, and floral decoration, supported by turned feet.
c1830 *37in (94cm) wide*
$67,500-90,000 **POOK**

A Regency mahogany and ebony-strung desk, the molded edge top over frieze drawer with hinged adjustable leather lined reading/writing stand and kneehole below, flanked by a pair of drawers, later brass ring handles, the carved front corners with fluted columns extending down to reeded turned tapering legs, brass toes and castors, stamped 'From W Williamson & Sons Guildford'.

48.5in (123cm) wide

$1,200-1,800 **HT**

An early 19thC French mahogany, gilt metal mounted and parcel gilt desk, with three frieze drawers to one side and leather inset slide to each end, on square tapered legs and block feet.

60.5in (154cm) wide

$1,200-1,800 **DN**

A William IV mahogany library desk, the rectangular top with gilt tooled leather inset, two frieze drawers and false opposing drawers, rectangular supports, flanked by scroll brackets, on a plinth base with bun feet.

c1835 *56in (142cm) wide*

$600-1,200 **DN**

A Victorian mahogany partners desk, stamped HOLLAND & SONS, rectangular top with tooled leather inset, above an arrangement of seven drawers on each side, one drawer with makers stamp, reeded turned tapering legs, brass caps and castors.

73in (186cm) wide

$1,500-2,250 **DN**

A 19thC mahogany pedestal partner's desk, fitted nine drawers and cupboards and frieze drawers verso, on plinth bases.

60in (152cm) wide

$1,800–2,700 **CHEF**

A Victorian mahogany partners' pedestal desk, with molded rectangular top, gilt tooled leather inset, above a pair of molded paneled doors, each decorated with acanthus carved corbels, one opening to an arrangement of four drawers, the other to a shelves interior, the opposing side with the same arrangement of cupboards and interiors, tapered square section feet.

c1880 *76.5in (195cm) wide*

$1,200-1,800 **DN**

A mahogany pedestal desk, the brown leather inset leather top raised on twin pedestals with four graduated drawers on plinth bases.

This desk belonged to the poet Robert Browning (1812-1889). Browning was born in Camberwell, London. The son of a bank clerk, he had Scottish and German descent from his mother's side, whose family had settled in Dundee. Encouraged in his youth by a creative family, his mother being a talented musician and his father possessing an extensive library comprising 6,000 volumes, Browning became the embodiment of the Victorian sage, widely regarded for his knowledge and his explorations of philosophical questions of great resonance in Victorian life. He married fellow poet Elizabeth Barrett in 1846, and while his early poetic career passed in relative obscurity, he has come to be regarded as one of the principal poets of the Victorian period. It can be assumed the present lot was used by Browing for everyday personal use and general correspondence, while his main literary work was completed on another desk which was sold by Sotheby's in 1913.

According to the present owners, descendants of Elizabeth Barrett Browning's nephew General Sir Edward Altham, this desk was kept in Robert Browing's study in his Kensington home, 29 De Vere Gardens. It was given to Edward Altham by his cousin Pen, son of Robert and Elizabeth Barrett Browning.

c1860 *48in (122cm) wide*

$6,000-7,500 **L&T**

A Victorian mahogany pedestal desk, with rectangular leather inset top, paterae-carved edge, arrangement of nine drawers around the kneehole, plinth bases and concealed castors.

66.5in (169cm) wide

$1,500-2,250 **DN**

A Victorian mahogany and ebony partners desk, the rectangular top with a faux leather insert over three frieze drawers with Vitruvian scrolls and laurel swags, the same opposing, raised on twin pedestals with molded panel doors opening to drawers and flanked by half columns with trailing husks, on plinth bases.

c1880 *69in (175cm) wide*

$2,700-3,300 **L&T**

A Victorian burr walnut pedestal desk, the rectangular leather molded top with nine drawers around the kneehole.

c1880 *48in (123cm) wide*

$3,000-4,500 **DN**

An early 19thC mahogany Carlton House Desk, the superstructure fitted with an arrangement of drawers and cupboards above a sliding writing surface, three deep drawers below, raised on square tapering legs with brass toes and castors, joined by a shaped undertier.

51in (130cm)

$1,800–2,700 **TEN**

A Victorian mahogany Carlton House desk, inlaid ebonized stringing, the top with a brass gallery and two hinged brass letter slots, above six drawers and curved cupboards with a ratcheted writing slope and three frieze drawers.

56in (142cm)

$4,500-6,000 **WW**

A late 19thC George III-style mahogany Carlton House desk, of typical form, the curved superstructure fitted with drawers, pigeon holes and sloping compartments fitted for writing, with two post slots, above a sliding writing surface over three short frieze drawers, raised on square tapered and fluted legs headed by patera and ending in spade feet.

50in (127cm) wide

$4,000–5,250 **L&T**

ESSENTIAL REFERENCE - CARLTON HOUSE DESKS

Named after the residence of the then Prince of Wales, the Carlton House desk was first referred to in a cost book of Gillows in 1796. A type of writing table or desk, it has a pierced brass gallery and drawers surrounding a leather or polished wood writing surface.

- **The desk was normally of mahogany or satinwood with a stepped or tiered superstructure of drawers an pigeonholes running along the back and curving around the side of the top.**
- **Introduced in the 1780s, the Carlton House table continued to be produced into the 20th century, though its craftsmanship and use of expensive materials made it relatively rare.**
- **An entry from the Prince of Wales' accounts in the Royal Archives reveals an insight into a table of this type supplied by John Kerr, one of the Prince's favored cabinet-makers.**
- **In 1814, Rudolph Ackermann included a French fashioned writing table in his Repository of Arts, naming it a 'Carlton House table'.**

A late 19thC satinwood, ebony and boxwood strung Carlton House desk, the superstructure with graduated drawers and cupboard doors, the sliding green leather writing surface above three frieze drawers, on square tapering legs with brass toes and castors.

51.5in (131cm) wide

$5,250-6,750 **TEN**

A late 19thC George III-style mahogany kneehole desk, the rectangular top with inset tooled leather, eleven short drawers, on bracket feet.

56in (142cm) wide

$1,200-1,800 **DN**

An Edwardian mahogany Carlton House desk, the curved superstructure fitted with an arrangement of drawers, pigeon holes and compartments and two mail slots, above three short drawers raised on square tapered and fluted legs with applied carved sunflower blocks and ending on spade feet.

51.5in (131cm) wide

$4,000–5,250 **L&T**

A mahogany 'Bradford desk' by Christopher Pratt & Sons, the frieze drawer operating a tambour top section enclosing hinged leather lined writing surface and stationery compartment, three drawers below flanked by a paneled cupboard door, fielded panel sides and back, molded base and bracket feet, on castors, maker's label and small silver presentation plaque, dated.

1905 *30in (76cm) wide*

$750-1,200 **HT**

An Edwardian mahogany and marquetry writing desk in the manner of Edwards and Roberts, with satinwood banding and inlaid stringing, a pair of stationery compartments with curved lids inlaid oval panels with putti, enclosing divisions for stationery and pens and inkwells to a gilt tooled leather lined surface with three frieze drawers, one stamped '9298' with four further drawers, all inlaid scrolling foliage with griffins and fitted with brass drop handles.

47in (120cm) wide

$4,000–5,250 **WW**

A George III satinwood and mahogany cylinder bureau, with three-quarter brass gallery to the top above tambour cupboard and cylinder bureau with writing slide, above two drawers and on square tapering legs with spade feet.

c1790 *39in (99cm) wide*

$1,200-1,800 **CHOR**

A 19thC Louis XVI-style kingwood and rosewood crossbanded bonheur du jour, the rectangular superstructure with a pierced brass gallery and fitted with drawers and cupboard doors, over a foldover brown baize lined writing surface above a long frieze drawer, raised on square tapered legs.

28.5in (73cm) wide

$1,500-2,250 **L&T**

ESSENTIAL REFERENCE - MAISON MILLET

A highly regarded furniture firm specialising in fine bronzes for furniture, founded in the mid-19thC by Blaise Millet. Maison Millet won a gold medal in the 1889 Paris Exposition Universelle, a Grand Prix in 1900 and three further diplomes d'honneur and four medailles d'or for their furniture.

- **The firm specialized in Louis XV and XVI styles, though they were also acclaimed for their own modern style.**
- **During the 1890s, the firm became an important part of the Paris luxury furniture industry.**
- **In 1902, the firm was authorized by the Palais de Versailles to replicate Marie-Antoinette's celebratred Grand Cabinet a bijoux.**
- **Under the direction of Blaise's son Theodore the firm was expanded, and after 1900 opened a branch office in Nice. Maison Millet was an active client of Francois Linke.**
- **The firm ceased trading in 1918.**

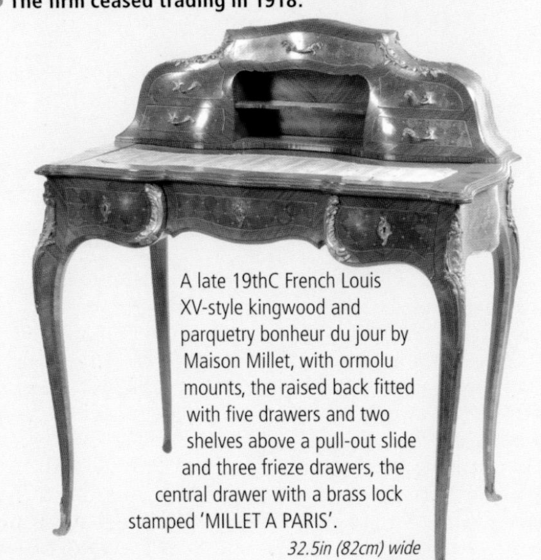

A late 19thC French Louis XV-style kingwood and parquetry bonheur du jour by Maison Millet, with ormolu mounts, the raised back fitted with five drawers and two shelves above a pull-out slide and three frieze drawers, the central drawer with a brass lock stamped 'MILLET A PARIS'.

32.5in (82cm) wide

$4,000–5,250 **WW**

A late 19thC French ebonized, porcelain-inset and gilt metal-mounted bonheur du jour, the rectangular top, above a pair of porcelain plaques painted with cherubs, two doors each inset with a porcelain plaque painted with a courting couple, opening to shelves, above two small drawers, a leather inset hinged writing surface, the top with porcelain inset panel depicting children and a goat, above a drawer, on fluted tapered legs and shaped stretcher.

35in (89cm) wide

$4,500-6,000 **DN**

A late 19thC Louis XVI-style kingwood and amaranth parquetry bonheur du jour, the superstructure fitted with drawers above a sliding writing work surface over an arched apron flanked by short drawers, raised on square tapered legs.

34.5in (88cm) wide

$750-1,200 **L&T**

A satinwood bonheur du jour, three-quarter gallery above an open shelf flanked by a pir of cupboards, the folding top opening to a tooled leather inset, the frieze drawer on square section taperings legs joined by a shaped undertier.

c1900 *0in (77cm) wide*

$750-1,200 **DN**

An Edwardian Sheraton Revival satinwood and marquetry cylinder bureau, richly decorated with flower garlands, flower bells and acanthus scrolls, the broken-neck pediment above two arched glazed doors enclosing two fixed shelves, the fall enclosing pigeon holes, small drawers and a pull-out leather writing surface, above a long frieze drawer, raised on square tapering legs with brass toes and castors.

25cm (64cm) wide

$2,000–2,700 **TEN**

An early 20thC satinwood and marquetry lady's writing desk, stamped Edwards & Roberts, the two-tier superstructure above a fall front richly inlaid with exotic birds and foliage around an urn, the interior with leather writing surface, two long drawers and four pigeon holes with a drawer below, the table richly decorated with trailing flowers above a bow front frieze drawer, raised on elegant square tapering legs.

36in (92cm) wide

$3,000-4,500 **TEN**

ESSENTIAL REFERENCE - NICOLAS SAGEOT

Nicolas Sageot (1666-1731, maître, 1706) specialized in opulent commodes, armoires and desks in Boulle marquetry from his workshop in Faubourg Saint-Antoine in Paris. In 1698, he was first recorded as working as an ouvrier libre, becoming a member of the cabinetmaker's guild eight years later.

- **In 1720, he retired from business and sold his stock to the Marchand Mercier Grossier joaillier Privilegie suivant la Cour Leonard Prieur for 16,000 livres.**
- **In 1723, he suffered a mental breakdown and two years later was committed to a psychiatric hospital where he died.**
- **Many ébénistes subcontracted the production of brass and tortoiseshell inlaid panels. These were normally cut out in series from the same design by specialized marqueteurs, Toussaint Devoye.**
- **Sageot, one of the first ébénistes to stamp his pieces, was admired by ébénistes working in metal marquetry in the Fauborg Saint-Antoine. While his maquetry was often repetitive, based upon cartoons, it was always elegant.**

A fine Louis XIV boulle marquetry and ebony bureau mazarin, attributed to Nicolas Sageot, the rectangular top with canted corners above a curved central drawers and kneehole recess with fall front compartment, flanked by two banks of three drawers, raised square tapered legs joined by a shaped stretcher rails and terminating on turned feet, the whole in premiere and contre parti red boulle marquetry with oriental figures, monkey and exotic birds.

c1700 *45.5in (116cm) wide*

$60,000-90,000 **L&T**

A George I walnut and crossbanded bureau, the slant front opening to an interior fitted with pigeon holes and drawers, over three long serpentine drawers and raised on shaped bracked feet.

48in (122cm) wide

$1,500-2,250 **L&T**

A George III Chinese export padouk bureau, the slant front opening to an arrangement of stepped tiers of shelves, pigeon holes and columns, over a long drawer, two short drawers, and two further long drawers, raised on bracket feet.

39in (99cm) wide

$900-1,500 **L&T**

A George III mahogany and inlaid bureau, the slant front opening to an arrangement of drawers and pigeon holes centered by a door with urn inlay, above four graduated long drawers, raised on scroll carved bracket feet.

42in (107cm) wide

$1,200-1,800 **L&T**

A 19thC Dutch walnut and marquetry bombe bureau, the slant front inlaid with birds and a flower-filled basket highlighted with mother of pearl, opening to an arrangement of pigeon holes, small drawers, and a recessed well with sliding cover, over a long dummy drawer and three further long drawers, with floral marquetry throughout, raised on carved claw feet.

43.5in (111cm) wide

$6,000-7,500 **L&T**

A Victorian walnut and marquetry Davenport, the upper section with a pair of doors enclosing pigeon holes and two drawers, above a frieze drawer fitted with a leather line ratcheted slope, a pen tray and a compartment for an inkwell, above a cupboard with four shelves, on ceramic castors.

23.5in (60cm) wide

$1,500-2,250 **WW**

A Victorian burr walnut, mahogany and birch davenport, the sloped top with an insert leather writing surface and hinged superstructure with a three quarter gallery opening to a fitted interior, with carved bracket supports; over a bank of four short drawers and four opposing dummy drawers on a trestle base with porcelain castors.

21in (54cm) wide

$1,200-1,800 **L&T**

A Regency mahogany canterbury/whatnot, the hinged top rising on a brass tipped easel, above twin tiers divided by turned spindles to accommodate music folios, two drawers below, terminating in original castors.

c1810 *42in (106.7cm) high*

$4,500-6,000 **RGA**

An early 19thC mahogany canterbury, the slatted superstructure with baluster turned corner posts and central loop handle, the base with drawer having turned brass handles, on baluster-turned legs with brass toes and castors.

19in 48cm) wide

$600-1,200 **HT**

A Regency mahogany canterbury, with three divisions above an apron drawer, raised on turned tapered legs ending in brass caps and castors.

c1810

$3,000-4,500 **L&T**

An early 19thC mahogany canterbury, with a pierced handgrip, above four dipped divisions and a frieze drawer, fitted replaced handles, on brass castors.

19.5in (49cm) wide

$1,000-1,700 **WW**

A late Regency rosewood canterbury, with four dipped divisions, one with a carrying handle, two that pull-out, above a frieze drawer, on turned legs and brass castors.

20in (51cm) wide

$1,500-2,250 **WW**

A William IV rosewood Canterbury after a design by J. C. Loudon, with three X-shape divisions decorated with laurel wreaths, above a frieze drawer on brass castors.

21in (53cm) wide

$1,200-1,800 **WW**

A William IV rosewood canterbury, the X-frame upper section forming three divisions, above a frieze drawer, turned tapering legs, brass caps and castors.

c1835 *20in (53cm) wide*

$600-1,200 **DN**

A Victorian painted simulated rosewood canterbury.

17in (44cm) wide

$300-750 **SWO**

A Victorian carved and figured walnut three-divisioned canterbury, pierced scroll divisions over a base drawer on turned legs and ceramic castors.

19in (49cm)

$450–900 **FLD**

A Queen Anne walnut veneer looking glass, with a scrolled crest.

c 1750 *14.5in (37cm) wide*

$1,400-1,800 POOK

A George II style carved and giltwood wall mirror, in the manner of William Kent, the frame centered with a cherub mask surrounded with scrolled floral, leaf and husk borders, with a carved diaper ground, replaced glass plate.

27in (69cm) wide

$4,500–7,500 SWO

One of a pair of Regency giltwood and gesso mirrors, the inverted breakfront cornice over a wide frieze applied with palm fronds and anthemion, above a rectangular mirror plate flanked by reeded column with acanthus capitals.

16.5in (42cm) wide

$4,000-5,250 pair L&T

A Regency giltwood overmantle mirror, the arched mirror plate in an egg-and-dart molded frame hung with floral garlands beneath foliate scroll cresting centered by a shell motif.

57in (146cm) wide

$6,000–9,000 L&T

ESSENTIAL REFERENCE - BURCHARD PRECHT

Burchard Precht (1651–1738) was a sculptor and cabinetmaker. He was born in Bremen, Germany and educated in Hamburg, but moved to Sweden in 1674 to work at Drottningholm Palace. He was named carver to the court in 1682 and is renowned for his early 18thC mirrors.

- **In 1687-88 Precht traveled to Rome and Paris with the court architect Nicodemus Tessin. The architecture and other items he saw there strongly influenced his work.**
- **Prechet's son, Gustav (1698–1763) also produced mirror frames and it is often difficult to distinguish their work. His other son, Christian (d.1779), was an important silversmith.**

A 19thC Swedish Neoclassical gilt bronze mounted mirror, in the manner of Burchard Precht, the C-scroll framed cresting with gilt metal flowering urn finials above a shield shaped beveled mirror plate, set within a mouded giltwood slip and conforming margin plates, all outlined in gilt metal.

40.5in (103cm) wide

$4,500–7,500 L&T

A pair of 19thC mahogany wall mirrors, probably Irish, acanthus and scroll carved frame, with marginal and arched upper section.

50.7in (129cm) high

$5,250-6,750 DN

A George IV gilt framed wall mirror, with split column side pilasters, concave frieze with roundel ends and conforming molded cornice.

c1825 *29in (74cm) wide*

$300-750 DN

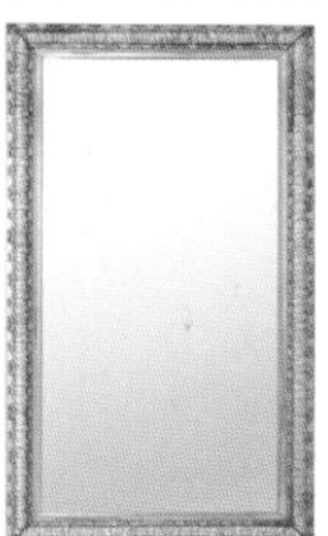

A mid-19thC giltwood and composition framed wall mirror, of large proportions, rectangular form, beveled mirror plate within lappet and leaf and berry borders.

52in (132cm) wide

$2,700-3,300 DN

A 19thC Florentine giltwood mirror.

$7,500–12,000 TARQ

A late 19thC giltwood wall mirror, the shaped rectangular plate within a profusely carved frame, surmounted by a stylized flowerhead.

29in (74cm) wide

$1,000-1,800 DN

Large 19thC giltwood and gesso overmantle mirror, the arched mirror plate within a reeded giltwood and gesso frame with bead and leaf tip moldings.

72in (183cm) wide

$1,500-2,250 L&T

A pair of giltwood overdoor mirrors, the shaped demi-lune plate with C-scroll and floral frame.

26.5in (68cm) wide

$750-1,200 **SWO**

A Regency giltwood and gesso overmantel mirror, the ball-molded breakfront cornice above a frieze with a relief-molded Neoclassical frieze depicting Mars, over three mirror plates within ebonized slips, flanked by corinthian pilasters.

58.5in (149cm) wide

$1,800–4,000 **L&T**

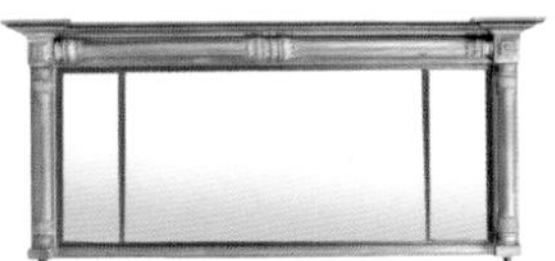

A George IV giltwood triple plate landscape overmantel mirror, half-round gilt column supports, ebonized slip frame.

c1825 *61in (155cm) wide*

$450–900 **DN**

A Victorian giltwood and composition overmantle mirror, with an elaborate scrolling crest with floral swags above guilloche molding, shaped mirror plate within molded borders and lappet headed columns, scrolling acanthus detail to outer edge.

c1880 *63in (160cm) wide*

$1,500-2,250 **DN**

CLOSER LOOK - CHINESE CHIPPENDALE MIRROR

This style of decoration is known as chinoiserie, a European style, inspired by the exotic motifs, forms and palettes used in Chinese and Japanese decorative arts. Thomas Chippendale's 'The Gentleman and Cabinet-Maker's Director' (1754) inspired a vogue for chinoiserie designs in furniture. The fashion continued throughout the Regency period, particularly at the Royal Pavilion in Brighton.

The frame is decorated with fruiting vines and fretwork with pagodas at the top, these are typical features of the Chinese Chippendale style.

The detailed carving of the seated Chinese figures on the rockwork base are evidence that this is a high quality piece.

The good condition of the glass and the frame add to its desirability.

A 19thC Chinese Chippendale-style giltwood mirror, the blued mirror plates within an elaborate carved giltwood and gesso frame.

62in (158cm) wide

$15,000–22,500 **L&T**

A George IV giltwood and composition overmantle mirror, marginal mirror plate within beveled edge, surmounted by an urn with swags and anthemion finials, reeded leaf decorated frame headed by lappet terminals.

c1825 *48in (122cm) wide*

$900-1,500 **DN**

A George II giltwood and gesso overmantel mirror, the triple beveled mirror plates in a bead-and-reel molded slip and openwork scroll frame with applied flower heads.

61.5in (157cm) wide

$1,800–4,000 **L&T**

A late 19thC giltwood and composition wall mirror, the rectangular plate within a molded and a repeated cabochon-decorated frame, scrolling acanthus and trellis decorated surmount and conforming pendant frieze.

34.5in (88cm) wide

$600-1,200 **DN**

A 19thC Baroque-style ebonized mirror, the rectangular beveled mirror plate within a wide frame applied with corner rosettes, bosses, foliate garlands, and surmounted by putti.

24.5in (62cm) wide

$450–900 **L&T**

A Regency-style giltwood overmantel mirror, with three rectangular plates, to a baton-and-bead molding, the frieze decorated with classical figures painted en grisailles.

c1900 *62.5in (159cm) wide*

$3,000-4,500 **WW**

A 20thC 18thC-style Continental painted wood-framed mirror, with a repeating lappet carved border.

47in (120cm) diameter

$900-1,500 **DN**

ESSENTIAL REFERENCE - ROBERT ADAM

Robert Adam (1728–92) was a Scottish architect, interior decorator and designer, who worked in the Neoclassical style.

- **In 1754 Adam went on a fashionable Grand Tour to gain an appreciation of architecture. While staying in Rome, he became an accomplished draughtsman, absorbing the principles and motifs of the Neoclassical style and Roman antiquity as well as meeting future aristocratic clients.**
- **He set up a practice in London in 1758 and by the early 1760s was considered to be the leading British architect of the day. He extended his talents to interior design, architectural fitting and all types of furniture, metalwork and textiles. His designs were executed by Ince & Mayhew and influenced Thomas Chippendale and George Hepplewhite.**
- **Robert and his brother James Adam published 'Works in Architecture in Britain' in 1773–79. In 1822, a third, posthumous volume was published, increasing his influence in France and the US.**
- **His designs feature light, delicate Neoclassical forms and motifs. Furniture is often painted or gilded, and used ornament rather than form for effect.**
- **Classical motifs such as palmettes and festoons, rams' heads and husks, were used to decorate commodes and girandoles, wall mirrors and pier tables.**
- **The style peaked in popularity in Britain in the 1760s and 1770s.**

A Regency giltwood and ebonized convex girondole mirror, the large circular convex mirror plate within an ebonized molded slip and giltwood frame issuing two pairs of curved candle arms and surmounted by acanthus scrolls and carved eagle cresting.

35.5in (91cm) wide

$15,000–22,500 L&T

An early 19thC giltwood and gesso convex wall mirror, with an eagle standing on rockwork and with a pineapple pendant, some later elements.

44in (111.5cm) high

$1,500-2,250 WW

A Regency carved giltwood and gesso circular mirror, the circular mirror plate within an ebonized and reeded slip and ball surmounted frame headed by an acanthus-carved pediment with eagle surmount.

44.5in (114cm) wide

$7,500–12,000 TEN

A pair of George III giltwood girandole mirrors, in the manner of Robert Adam, the oval mirror plates within further margin plates and gadrooned frames surmounted by flowering urns and ribbon-tied trailing husks, over a patera-drop finial issuing two outscrolling candle arms.

c1780 42.5in (108cm) high

$18,000–27,000 L&T

A Regency giltwood and composition convex wall mirror, leaf decorated and sphere mounted molded frame, surmounted by an eagle.

c1815 44in (113cm) high

$1,500-2,250 DN

A 19thC Louis XVI-style giltwood mirror, the beveled oval mirror within a molded frame and beveled margin plates, surmounted by a flowering urn finial and scrolling floral garlands.

39in (100cm) wide

$4,000–5,250 L&T

A 19thC French Louis Louis XVI-style giltwood mirror, the cartouche shaped mirror plate in a giltwood frame with foliate scrolls, shells and floral garlands.

33in (85cm) wide

$3,000-4,500 L&T

A 19thC Italian carved and giltwood framed double girandole, the two circular mirrors united by a pierced cartouche, each surround by four metal candle branches.

51in (130cm) wide

$450–900 DN

A 19thC Continental giltwood and composition oval wall mirror, profusely carved and pierced with scroll work.

22.5in (57cm) wide

$750-1,200 DN

A late 19thC 18thC-style Venetian clear and colored glass wall mirror, the scrolling top above a stylized mask, shaped plate with an egg-and-dart molded border with applied stylized flowers.

20in (52cm) wide

$1,200-1,800 DN

An early 18thC black japanned dressing table mirror, gilt decorated with chinoiserie, the later arched beveled plate to a lockable back, the base with seven drawers around a central cupboard, on later bracket feet.

16in (41cm) wide

$750-1,200 WW

An 18th century walnut dressing table mirror, with fret-carved cresting and tiered drawers.

17in (43cm) wide

$600-1,200 CHEF

A George III mahogany dressing table mirror, inlaid barber's pole stringing, the replaced beveled oval plate to a serpentine base fitted with three drawers, with turned bone handles.

17in (43cm) wide

$600-1,200 WW

An Edwardian satinwood dressing table mirror, oval swing plate to a serpentine base, fitted four drawers and with ivory handles, on small bracket feet.

34.5in (88cm) wide

$300-450 CHEF

A William IV Gothic Revival mahogany toilet mirror, the rectangular mirror plate between foliate carved column clusters above a breakfront base with three short drawers, raised on carved paw feet.

c1835 22in (56cm) wide

$450-750 L&T

A George II mahogany and parcel gilt toilet mirror, the molded rectangular adjustable mirror between reeded upright supports, the ogee-molded base fitted with one drawer, on later bracket feet.

16in (41cm) wide

$550–850 L&T

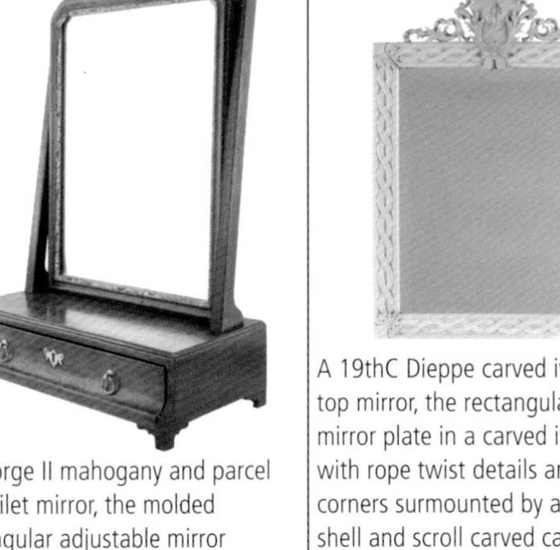

A 19thC Dieppe carved ivory table-top mirror, the rectangular beveled mirror plate in a carved ivory frame with rope twist details and foliate corners surmounted by a foliate, shell and scroll carved cartouche bearing the monogram "JC", with a hinged support with engraved metal mounts.

14in (36cm) wide

$1,500–3,000 L&T

A George III mahogany and boxwood-strung cheval mirror, the beveled plate and rectangular frame above square section supports, downswept square section legs, brass caps and castors.

c1810 25in (64cm) wide

$900–1,400 DN

A French Empire mahogany and ormolu-mounted cheval mirror, the arched mirror plate in a conforming frame with gilt bronze laurel garland mounts, flanked by tapered columns surmounted by gilt urn finials and raised on arched trestle supports on brass castors.

35in (90cm) wide

$1,500-2,250 L&T

A Regency mahogany-framed cheval glass, with urn finials and ring-turned stretcher.

27in (69cm) wide

$550–850 CHEF

A Regency mahogany, parcel gilt and brass inlay cheval mirror, the molded pediment bearing a gilt metal mount depicting a chariot drawn by horses over a rectangular swing mirror flanked by tapered square uprights with term capitals and ending in feet, on a trestle base raised on lion paw feet.

c1815 41.5in (106cm) wide

$9,000–12,000 L&T

FURNITURE

A George IV mahogany whatnot, the rectangular top over two conforming tiers with gilt metal mounts, raised and divided by spiral turned columns above a cupboard door, raised on bun feet.

c1820

$4,500–7,500 **L&T**

A Regency mahogany whatnot, attributed to Gillows, the ratcheted rectangular top over a hinged shelf and opposing sliding leaf extensions, raised on slender turned legs joined by two undertiers with a three-quarter gallery and curved front, ending on brass caps and castors.

21in (53cm) wide

$450-750 **L&T**

ESSENTIAL REFERENCE - CHARLES HEATHCOTE TATHAM

Charles Heathcote Tatham (1772-1842) was an English architect and designer.

- **He visited Rome from 1794–96 where he studied antique remains and ornament, material which was later in his book 'Etchings of Ancient Ornamental Architecture drawn from the Originals in Rome and other Parts of Italy...' (1799–1800). It was an immediate success and was followed by 'Etchings Representing Fragments of Grecian and Roman Ornaments' (1806). Both of these were used as sourcebooks for Neo-Classical design, notably by the renowned designers Charles Percier and Pierre François Léonard Fontaine as well as Thomas Hope. The style of linear engravings used in his books was copied by Thomas Hope in 'Household Furniture and Interior Decoration' (1807).**
- **During his stay in Italy he also bought a large number of antique fragments for his employer and mentor, Henry Holland (1745-1806) who was architect to the Prince of Wales. These are now in the Soane Museum, London.**

A pair of Regency rosewood and specimen marble étagères, the three-quarter brass gallery over a white marble rectangular top tier above a grey veined marble open shelf, over a faux marble painted recess and a cupboard door with a brass grille insert backed with faded red silk, raised on square legs joined by further veined grey marble undertier and ending on tapered feet, the whole outlined in gilt metal beading.

These were possibly supplied to Quidenham Hall, Norfolk, in 1820 when the interiors were redone under the supervision of the architect and designer Charles Heathcote Tatham (1742-1842) on direction of the 4th Earl of Albemarle.

c1820 *15in (38cm) wide*

$18,000–27,000 **L&T**

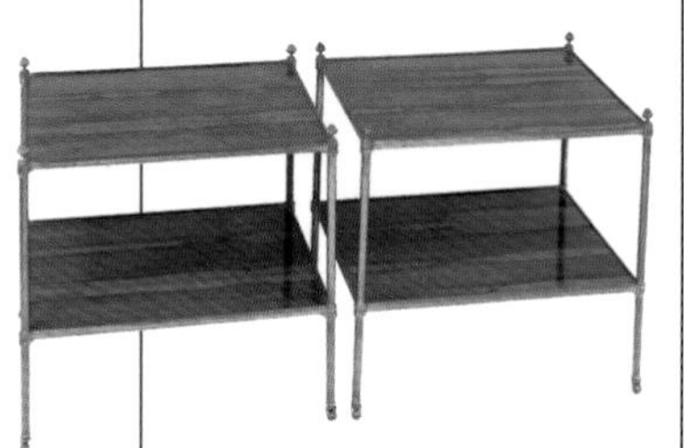

A pair of rosewood and brass rectangular two-tier étagères with pineapple finials.

21in (54cm) wide

$4,000–5,250 **CHOR**

A William IV mahogany seven-tier corner whatnot, of tapering form, each serpentine fronted tier with twin lappet carved S- scroll supports, turned feet and concealed castors.

c1835 *34in (87cm) wide*

$750-1,200 **DN**

A 19thC painted pine four-tier plant stand, retaining an old green surface.

60in (152cm) wide

$900-1,200 **POOK**

A Victorian burr walnut whatnot of rounded oblong three-tier form with pierced scroll fret galleried surmount, spiral twist shelf supports, base drawer with turned wood handles, on molded bracket feet and castors.

26in (66cm) wide

$450-750 **HT**

A late 19thC rosewood three-tier whatnot or étagère, with turned spiral and inverted baluster supports over a base drawer on turned legs and brass castors.

19in (48cm) wide

$750-1,200 **FLD**

A George III mahogany dumbwaiter, with three graduated dished circular tiers on a central baluster turned support and endingon cabriole legs with raised pad feet.

39in (100cm) high

$750-1,200 **L&T**

An Irish George II mahogany wine cooler, the oval top with brass bands and lion mask handles, and a tin liner; the stand with turned legs joined by a turned X-form stretcher and ending on ball feet ending on leather castors.

c1740 *22.5in (58cm) wide*

$4,500–7,500 **L&T**

A George III carved mahogany wine cooler on stand, the brass-bound coopered basin with associated tole liner, the cabriole and scrolled feet with concealed leather castors.

Thomas Chippendale in 'The Gentleman and Cabinet-Maker's Director' of 1762, 3rd edition, illustrates in plate CLI designs for Cisterns or Wine Coolers with similarities which include a gadrooned lip, scalloped handles and scrolled "French style" cabriole legs.

c1770 *32in (59cm)*

$10,500–13,500 **TEN**

Judith Picks: George III Wine Cooler

This wine cooler is proof that condition is not always important if the piece is exceptional. Dating from the reign of George III it features bold carving in the Neoclassical style. Its theme is the bacchanale – a typical one for wine antiques. However, it appears that it was not always used to cool alcohol: the four boxwood inlaid cartouches read Orangeade, Lemonade, Soda and Ice Water. The condition was described as 'country house', a kind way to say that it shows years of use. The cover had been split in two and some pieces of the inlay decoration were damaged. Despite this is sold for ten times more than the lower end of the auctioneer's estimate.

A George III mahogany wine cooler.

In addition to bodly carved Neoclassical decoration on the theme of the bacchanale are four boxwood inlaid cartouches, reading Orangeade, Lemonade, Soda and Ice Water. Despite its 'country house' condition, (the cover was split in two and some pieces of inlay were missing) it generated enough interest to sell at ten times its lower estimate.

$22,500-30,000 **LAW**

A George III satinwood cellarette, the hinged rectangular top opening to a later fitted interior with a lift-out tray and baize lined compartments, raised on slender square tapered legs ending in brass castors.

17in (44cm) wide

$4,000–5,250 **L&T**

A late 18thC George III mahogany cellarette on stand.

16in (41cm) wide

$750-900 **POOK**

A George III mahogany cellaret, the hinged top opening to a divided interior, with brass carrying handles, on square tapered legs on castors.

c1800 *19in (48cm) wide*

$600-900 **DN**

A Regency mahogany sarcophagus-shaped wine cooler, the hinged cover with acanthus carved knob handle, the shaped base raised on bun feet.

27.5in (70cm) high

$600-1,200 **CHOR**

A Regency mahogany wine cooler, of sarcophagus form, the hinged lid opening to a partially lead lined interior, a pair of brass ring side carrying handles, turned and gadrooned feet.

c1815 *25.5in (65cm) wide*

$1,200-1,800 **DN**

A George IV mahogany sarcophagus wine cooler, with nulled moldings and brass ring handles, the turned stem on leaf carved and molded legs and brass castors.

50.5in (52cm) wide

$1,500-2,250 **WW**

A Regency mahogany reading stand, circa 1815, rectangular top with rounded corners and reeded edge with a book rest and incorporating a drawer opening to divisions, on an adjustable turned stem and three reeded downswept legs, caps and castors.

c1815 *20.5in (53cm) wide*

$1,500-2,250 **DN**

A Victorian rosewood reading stand the hinged top above three tiers, each supported on turned spindles and feet.

18in (46cm) wide

$150–225 **FLD**

A folding mahogany stationery stand, the main section incorporating four open shelves, the folding stand incorporating square section and turned elements, on ring turned tapering legs.

c1900 *16in (41cm) wide*

$225–400 **DN**

A Delaware Valley Queen Anne walnut candlestand, with a dish top tilting on a suppressed ball standard supported by cabriole legs terminating in pad feet, retaining an old dry surface.

c1760 *21in (53cm) wide*

$4,000–5,250 **POOK**

An 18thC Anglo-Indian rosewood, ebony and bone inlay box on stand, the rectangular hinged lid and box inlaid throughout with ebony scrolling foliage and bone flowerheads, with an engraved brass escutcheon and iron loop handles to the sides, raised on an ebonized stand with spiral carved supports joined by a wavy X-form stretcher and ending on flattened bun feet.

$4,500–7,500 **L&T**

A mahogany candle stand, shaped gallery, sliding candle stand, on square legs and X-stretcher.

c1800 and later *16in (41cm) wide*

$600-900 **DN**

A Victorian rosewood travelling washstand the hinged top enclosing a mirror, fold-out drawers and a marble inset, over a frieze drawer, on twist turned supports.

22in (56cm) wide

$750–1,500 **SWO**

A late 19thC French amboyna and ebonized jardinière stand, with gilt metal mounts.

21in (54cm) wide

$550–850 **WW**

A 19thC mahogany whip and boot stand, with a brass carrying handle.

41.5in (106cm) wide

$600-1,200 **WW**

A mahogany hall stand, with an arrangement of brass hooks, above a turned rail and further rail with apertures for sticks, platform feet, scroll carved teminals.

c1900 *71.5in (182cm) wide*

$1,800–2,700 **DN**

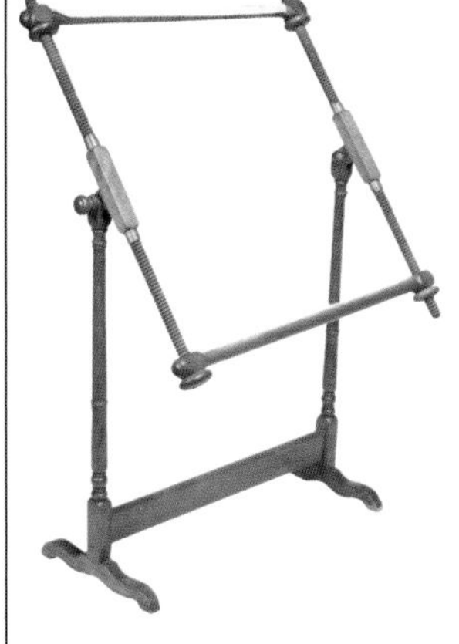

A late 19th/early 20thC mahogany needlework stand.

33in (83cm) wide

$225–400 **DN**

A Victorian gentleman's shaving stand, with a circular mirror and a shelf with a drawer, on a tripod stand.

63.5in (162cm) high

$450-600 **DN**

A mahogany wash/basin stand, fitted with two drawers, with a blue and white pottery bowl and jug.

21in (54cm) wide

$75-400 **WW**

An Edwardian mahogany display stand in Chinese Chippendale style, in two sections with leaf carved and blindfret decoration, the base with a pierced frieze on stretchered supports.

73in (185cm) wide

$8,250-9,750 **WW**

A William IV rosewood portfolio stand, the plain end standards with carved supports and carved claw feet.

31in (79cm) wide

$3,000-4,500 **CHOR**

A Victorian painted cast iron six-division stickstand.

29in (74cm) wide

$180-330 **WW**

A late 19thC Victorian mahogany snooker cue stand, upper section with central globular terminal, flanked by an arrangement of metal clasps, cirular molded base with circular apertures, turned bun feet.

49in (125cm) high

$900-1,500 **DN**

An 18thC leather three-fold screen, with arched top and scroll shaped feet.

94.5in (240cm) wide

$1,500–3,000

CHEF

A pair of Regency rosewood and brass fire screens, the rectangular framed screens with cream upholstered panels above a brass gallery and folding shelf, raised on turned columns and ending on acanthus carved trestle supports with scrolled toes and joined by a padded stretcher.

c1820 *44.5in (113cm) high*

$750-1,200 **L&T**

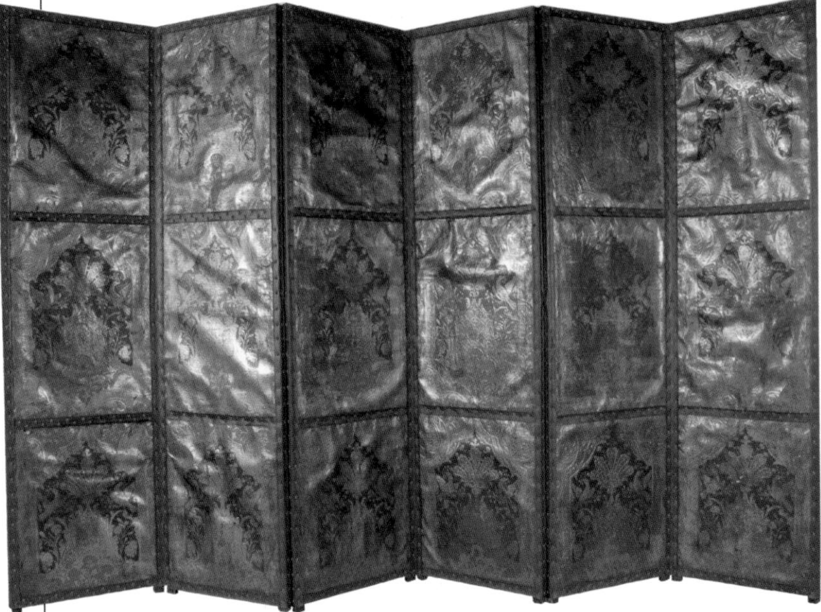

A 19thC embossed, gilt and painted leather six fold screen.

88in (233cm) high

$4,000–5,250 **WW**

A 19thC oil-on-panel dressing screen, depicting Lafayette on horseback with an American harbour in the background.

54.5in (138cm) wide

$1,800-3,000 **POOK**

A 19thC Louis XV-style giltwood and glazed three-fold screen, each fold with a glazed upper panel and silk-upholstered lower panel within a Rococo scroll giltwood frame.

63.5in (162cm) wide

$450–900 **L&T**

A large Chinese screen, the hardwood frame carved with dragons flanking a central shou character, the silk screen embroidered with birds, butterflies and bamboo, the reverse with an inscription which reads 'bei ning ruan wen nan, xin zhi'.

c1900 *53in (134cm) high*

$4,000-4,500 **WW**

A George II mahogany wine carrying tray, with pierced handle, holds six bottles, complete with stand raised on slender turned supports with castors.

18in (46cm) wide

$1,800–4,000 **HW**

A George III oval mahogany tray with two scroll handles and double brass binding.

20 in (51cm) long

$600-900 **SWO**

A George III mahogany tray, with later mahogany stand, the rectangular tray with gallery sides, pierced with handles at the two long sides.

18.5in (47cm) wide

$600-750 **DN**

A Regency mahogany dining room pedestal, in the manner of Thomas Hope, now with a grey veined marble top over a single paneled door, the sides with conforming panels, over a reeded border and carved scrolled feet, the interior tin-lined and with two slatted shelves.

13in (33cm) high excluding marble

$4,500-6,000 **SWO**

An early 19thC tôle peinte tray, painted with 'A View of High Street, Birmingham' after T. Hollins, the aquatint by J. C. Stadler, published 1st July 1812, with a gilt border and pierced handgrips.

30.5in (77cm) wide.

$1,200-1,800 **WW**

A pair of Regency green-painted and parcel-gilt torchère stands, the triform molded tops on scroll supports and tapered triform columns carved with flower swags and raised on scrolling legs.

c1815 *53in (135cm) high*

$2,700–4,000 **L&T**

A pair of 18thC-style carved wood and parcel gilt Blackamoors, each holding a cornucopia and wearing a plumed headdress, on a stepped base with vacant cartouches.

60in (152cm) high

$4,000–5,250 **WW**

A rosewood and gilt brass music stand, pair of rectangular pierced trellis rests, each ratchet adjustable, turned and lappet carved stem, on triple molded downswept legs, leaf carved feet.

c1835 *16.5in (42cm) wide*

$750-1,200 **DN**

A pair of 19thC-style mahogany music stands, each with height adjustable rest, turned stem, on three turned legs.

16in (41cm) wide

$750-1,200 **DN**

A George III mahogany jardinière with brass liner.

$1,800–2,700 **TCAL**

A late 18thC Dutch mahogany and brass mounted tea stove, of cylindrical form, with a pair of side carrying handles, deorated with blind fretworh depicting foliage and incorporating a small drawer, shaped apron, on cabriole legs, carved claw and ball feet.

12in (31cm) diam

$1,500-2,250 **DN**

One of a pair of early 19thC tôle peinte jardinieres, black and gilt painted, each with a scalloped edge one decorated with exotic birds the other with ribbon-tied swags of flowers.

1.5in (29cm) wide

$300-450 **WW**

A 19thC Empire style tôle peinte, parcel gilt and bronze mounted metal jardiniere, of octagonal section, the canted angles each with a projecting maiden bust herm descending to feet below, with twin lion's mask and ring handles, the interior with lift out liner.

10in (25cm) high

$1,800–4,000 **DN**

A 17thC and later oak three-tier buffet, each shelf with an incised dot-and-dash border over a guilloché carved frieze, supported on carved baluster front supports.

35in (89cm) wide

$12,000-15,000 **SWO**

A mahogany wall corner shelf unit, of graduated quadrant form, arched crest with finials, three mirror backed shelves with gilt beaded edging, shaped base.

c1900 *15in (38cm) wide*

$600-1,200 **HT**

A 17thC Italian walnut prie dieu, molded rectangular top above an arrangement of five drawers, three carved with masks, above a pair of figured cupboards flanked by caryatids, opening to shelves, plinth base and block feet.

41.5in (105cm) wide

$1,800–4,000 **DN**

A 17thC Italian walnut prie dieu, molded rectangular top above a drawer, flanked by male masks, paneled cupboard door below with similar central mask, flanked by female term figures, lower section with hinged lid.

31.5in (80cm) wide

$750-1,200 **DN**

A set of Victorian mahogany library or bed steps, formed of three bowfronted steps inset with gilt tooled green leather, two of the steps with hinged tops, turned tapering legs.

c1860 *18.5in (47cm) wide*

$750-1,200 **DN**

A Victorian oak set of library steps.

c1880 *24.5in (63cm) wide*

$750-1,200 **DN**

An 18thC ash spice box with fret hanging support and three drawers.

18.5in (47cm) high

$600-1,200 **CHOR**

CLOSER LOOK - 18THC NEW ENGLAND SPOON RACK

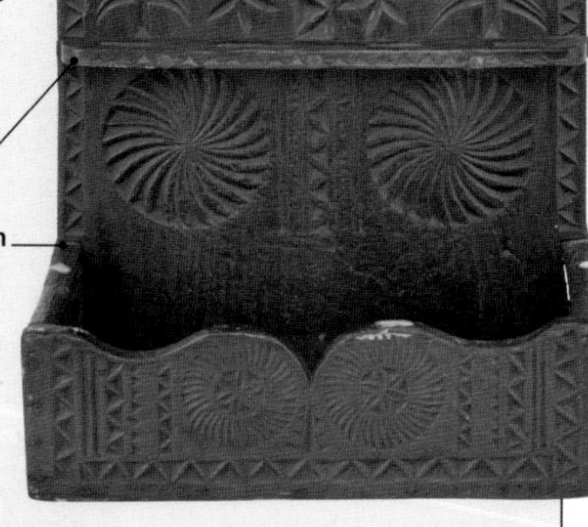

Most boxes made in this style come from Pennsylvania, New York or the mid-Atlantic states. But this is believed to be a rare, 'Friesian' New England example.

The stylized carved pine trees suggest it is from New England as the decoration is similar to that on chests known to come from that region.

The box is relatively intact despite its age and the fact that it was made for daily use in the home. The three original spoon rests are lost, and the two remaining rests have been restored

It appears to have been originally painted with a thin red wash, with a second, green coat applied in the 19thC.

A 19thC American carved white pine hanging spoon rack, with a lollipop finial and an overall pinwheel and sawtooth decoration, retaining an old blue over red surface.

13in (33cm) wide

$12,000-15,000 **POOK**

An 18thC Portuguese colonial rosewood bed, with relief-carved arched headboard and twist carved column posts.

82.5in (210cm) wide

$1,500–3,000 **CHEF**

A 19thC Caribbean carved mahogany tall post bed, probably St. Croix, the headboard with a carved basket of fruit flanked by serpents.

65in (165cm) wide

$6,000–9,000 **POOK**

A Regency birds-eye maple miniature bookcase, with brass stringing, the two glazed doors opening to reveal shelves, above two short and two long drawers, raised on bun feet.

13.5in (34cm) wide

$6,000–9,000 **CHEF**

ESSENTIAL REFERENCE - PAPIER MÂCHÉ

The first papier-mâché dates from the 17thC when a compound of plaster, bark, nettles and straw was used to create molded architectural ornaments such as cornices and rosettes for internal decoration.

- **By the late 17thC, a simpler mixture of damp pulped paper was being used to make a variety of household objects. When dry, the paper surface could be varnished and hand-painted.**
- **It was strong and versatile and was used to make heads and limbs for dolls, parts of coaches and decorative items for the home.**
- **One of the most prominent papier-mâché manufacturers in the United Kingdom was Henry Clay. In 1772 he patented a strong papier-mâché material that could be dovetailed and sawed just like wood. Jennens and Bettridge took over Clay's business c1815 and continued experimenting with papier-mâché and pearl inlay decoration. By the 1850s they were known as the foremost papier-mâché producers.**
- **In the 19thC papier-mâché was used to make everything from visiting card cases and tea caddies to ornate tables, chairs and fire screens. To strengthen the structure, layers of papier-mâché were built up on a wooden or metal skeleton.**
- **Pieces were typically finished with black lacquer and then painted to emulate Oriental lacquer work. They could also be embellished with gilt and mother-of-pearl.**

A rare Henry Clay papier mâché two compartment oval tea caddy, painted throughout with a marine scene.

6.5in (16.5cm) wide

$12,000-18,750 RGA

A George III papier-mâché oval tea caddy in the manner of Henry Clay, with a later gilt brass handle and painted with figures and cows in an arcadian idyll with Roman arches and buildings.

5in (12cm) wide

$1,800–2,700

A George III fruitwood pear-form tea caddy, with oval metal escutcheon.

6.75in (17cm) high

$3,000-4,000 L&T

A George III mahogany and marquetry tea caddy, with boxwood stringing and kingwood banding, the interior vacant.

7.5in (19.5cm) wide

$225-300 WW

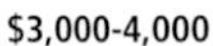

A George III satinwood tea chest, kingwood banded and boxwood stringing, with a silver plated navette shape handle and a bone escutcheon, the interior with a pair of lidded caddies with stained sycamore and red dot inlay flanking an engraved blue glass sugar bowl.

12in (30.5cm) wide

$750-900 WW

A George III harewood tea caddy, inlaid swags of bell flowers, with a zinc-lined lidded interior.

5.75in (14.5cm) wide

$550-600 WW

A George III satinwood oval caddy box, inlaid shell paterae to lid, and vases to base.

6in (15cm) wide

$300-450 HW

A George III quillwork tea caddy, with finely rolled polychrome and gilt paper under glass panels, depicting flowers, the front panel centered with faded watercolor painting of a girl.

Quilling involves rolling, curling or twisting strips of paper and then sticking them to a surface to create a decorative design. Its origins are unknown but in the 18thC and 19thC it was a popular pastime for wealthy ladies who used it to decorate tea caddies, workboxes, screens and cabinets among other items. Some cabinetmakers made boxes with recessed sides suitable for quilled decoration.

c1790 *8.5in (22cm) wide*

$900–1,400 CHEF

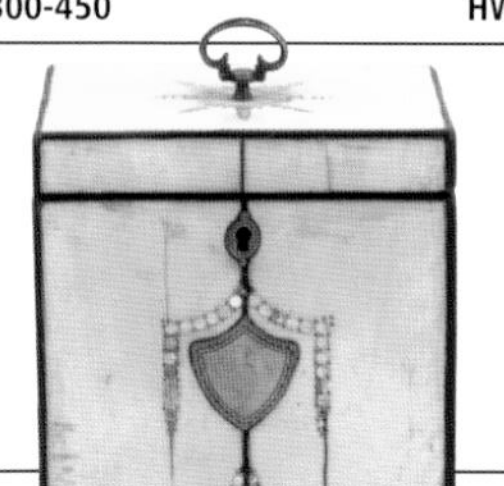

A George III mother-of-pearl inlaid ivory tea caddy with loop handle.

4in (10cm) wide

$600-1,000 BELL

A George III harewood and marquetry tea caddy, of canted form with panels of flowers, the interior with a single lid with a brass handle.

6in (15cm) wide

$700–975 WW

A George III burr yew tea caddy, inlaid stringing with oval panels, the interior with twin lidded compartments, with brass handles.

7in (18cm) wide

$300-450 WW

A George III burr yew wood tea caddy, of rounded sarcophagus shape with strung decoration and bronze lions mask ring handles, the interior with two lidded compartments.

6.5in (17cm) high

$450-600 SWO

A George III harewood and painted tea caddy, with canted corners and inlaid boxwood edges.

4.5in (11cm) high

$600-750 SWO

Judith Picks

In any collecting area, collectors are looking for the rarities - something made for a special commission or for a person of note. We don't know the history of this tea caddy but there is no doubt it is rare and desirable. The fact that it depicts a mansion house in itself is unusual, but it is the detailed execution that stands out. The breakfront panel is arranged as a two story building, with steps leading to an arched doorway flanked by three windows and a further seven windows above. The central window is flanked by columns. The hinged lid with a brass bow handle has boxwood and rosewood stringing. It encloses a cut glass mixing bowl and two lift-out tin canisters each with a domed mahogany cover. But the real excitement is a secret compartment with two silver spoons!

A rare George III mahogany tea caddy in the form of a mansion house, in restored condition.

11in (28cm) wide

$6,000–9,000 DW

A George III ivory tea caddy, with tortoiseshell stringing.

4.5in (11.5cm) high

$750-1,200 SWO

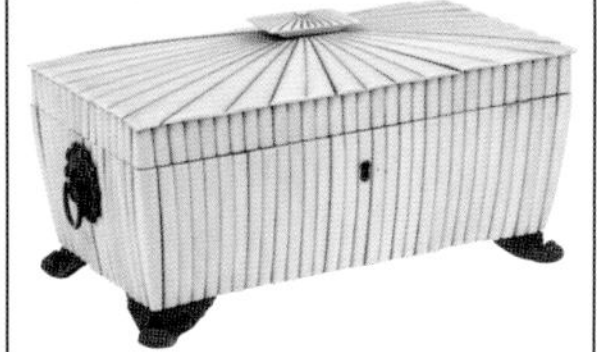

A Georgian sarcophagus-shaped caddy, finished inside and out in ivory.

$3,000-4,000 HT

A late 18thC London tortoiseshell tea caddy with silver caddy spoon, the corners with ivory line inlay, the lid of the single compartment of later date, the spoon with bright cut handle.

c1795 *3.5in (9cm) wide*

$1,200-1,800 CHEF

A very unusual and rare Continental fruit tea caddy in the form of a melon within a woven basket, the fruit of the basket inscribed 'Andenken V Baden' meaning, 'Souvenir from Baden'.

c1800 *6in (15.5cm)*

$12,000-15,000 RGA

A George III elliptical single compartment satinwood tea caddy, painted with Neoclassical decoration.

5in (12cm) high

$450–900 SWO

A Regency tortoiseshell and ivory tea caddy, inlaid with Mother-of-pearl, the lid enclosing a lidded compartment, on bun feet.

4.5in (11cm) wide

$3,000-4,500 L&T

A rare Regency green tortoiseshell tea caddy with ivory edging, with silver initial plate and silver key escutcheon, with two inner lids in green tortoiseshell.

7.5in (20cm) wide

$12,000–13,500 RGA

A rare Regency tea caddy in the form of a country house with dormer windows, with two compartments.

6.5in (16.5cm) high

$6,000-10,875 RGA

A Regency tortoiseshell veneered tea caddy, the bombe-shaped body with a canted hinged lid, opening to reveal a fitted interior with two covered compartments complete with ivory finials, all raised on four ivory bun feet.

5.5in (14cm) high 6.5in (16.5cm) wide

$900–1,400 L&T

An early 19thC fruitwood and bone inlaid tea caddy, the interior with three divisions.

12.75in (32.5cm) wide

$450-600 WW

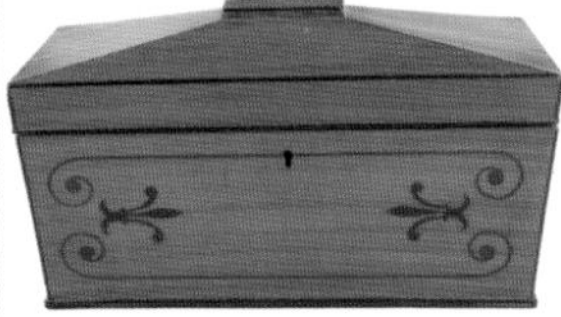

A Regency satinwood and ebony inlaid sarcophagus shape tea chest, the interior with twin lidded compartments, lacking its sugar bowl and feet, with key.

10.75in (27.5cm) wide

$345-420 WW

A Regency penwork tea caddy, painted with figures in various pursuits within penwork foliate borders, with a lidded interior.

4in (10.5cm) wide

$850-900 WW

An early 19thC French lacquer and steel-mounted tea caddy, decorated with chinoiserie scenes, the lidded interior with twin divisions.

6.25in (16cm) wide

$700-850 WW

A Regency penwork tea caddy, Chinoiserie-decorated with figures in oriental landscapes, the interior with twin-lidded compartments.

7.5in (19cm) wide

$750-1,200 **WW**

A Regency tortoiseshell tea caddy, of rectangular form, the slightly domed cover set with a brass plaque, opening to reveal two lidded compartments with ivory knops, on ivory bun feet.

7.5in (19cm) wide

$2,000–2,700 **TEN**

A Regency burr elm sarcophagus-shape tea caddy, with ebonized stringing, the interior with pull-out twin hinged lidded canisters flanking a glass sugar bowl.

12.5in (32cm) wide

$550-975 **WW**

An early 19thC satinwood and ebonized single tea caddy, the lift-off lid with a turned finial and painted with bands of leaves and flowers.

4in (10cm) diameter

$450-750 **WW**

An early 19thC tortoiseshell tea caddy, of slightly bulbous oblong form, the front inlaid with floral mother of pearl and white metal wire, the hinged lid with flattened pagoda top opening to reveal two lidded compartments with four stained ivory bun feet.

7in (18cm) wide

$750-1,200 **DA&H**

A George IV wax seal tea caddy, the bowfront body inlaid with barber's pole stringing and decorated with various red wax seals, with a brass handle with a single lidded interior with an ebonized handle.

47in (18cm)

$750-1,200 **WW**

A George IV rosewood tea caddy, opening to two covered tea canisters and a mixing bowl recess.

12.25in (31cm) wide

$225–400 **L&T**

A 19thC Napoleon III boulle tea caddy, the interior with two lidded compartments.

9.25in (23cm) wide

$900-1,000 **L&T**

An extremely rare tea caddy in the form of a teapot, the fruitwood carcass painted and decorated with trailing vines and gilt highlights, possibly Continental.

6.25in (16cm) high

$22,500–27,000 **RGA**

A 19thC Continental tortoiseshell and white metal-mounted tea caddy, with engraved corner mounts, the interior later plush-lined and with ivory edging, the lid inset a rectangular plaque engraved a coat of arms.

6in (15cm) wide

$900–1,400 **WW**

A 19thC tortoiseshell tea caddy, the interior with twin compartments on bun feet.

7in (18cm) wide

$1,200-1,800 **ECGW**

A small Victorian tortoiseshell and silver mounted caddy, of sarcophagus form, the hinged lid enclosing a lidded compartment, with twin loop handles and scroll feet; together with a Scottish silver caddy spoon.

5in (13cm) wide

$1,800-3,000 **L&T**

A 19thC tortoiseshell and Mother-of-pearl tea caddy, with shaped front, the hinged top opening to reveal two lidded compartments within, raised on bun feet.

8in (20cm) wide

$750-1,200 **CHEF**

A Napoleon III rosewood and and ivory inlaid tea caddy, with brass stringing the lid inscribed 'THE', to a vacant interior.

12in (30cm) wide

$120–180 **WW**

A Victorian brass tobacco caddy, the insides inscribed 'press tobacco shanty'.

7.25in (18cm) wide

$300-450 **L&T**

A Victorian sample wood cube parquetry, burr walnut and rosewood veneered tea caddy, of sarcophagus form, on four bun feet, the hinged cover opening to twin subsidiary caddies flanking a circular aperture.

14in (36cm) wide

$300–600 **DN**

A rare late 19thC French fruitwood coal bucket tea caddy, with an iron swing handle and oval lock escutcheon.

5.5in (14cm) wide

$4,000–5,250 **WW**

A George IV silver dressing table set in case, by George Reily, London, the plain brass-bound rosewood case fitted with twelve engine turned silver topped glass boxes and bottles, some foliate pierced and engraved, with assorted Mother-of-pearl manicure items and a jewelry drawer to the base. dated.

1826 *13.5in (34cm) long*

$1,500-2,250 TEN

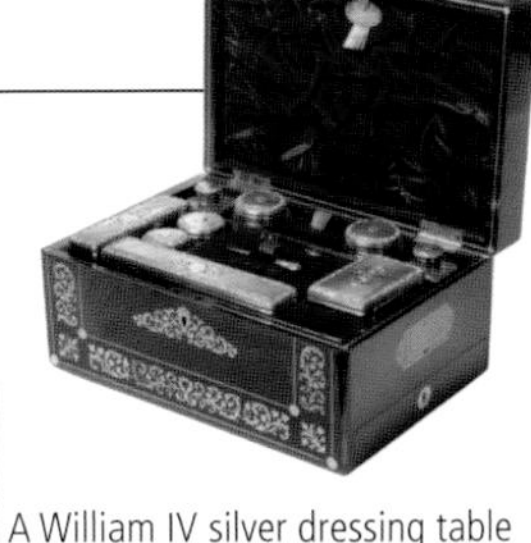

A William IV silver dressing table set in case, by Archibald Douglas, London, the rosewood case with mother-of-pearl inset foliate borders and reserves, with a velvet fitted interior accommodating nine silver top boxes and bottles, with a jewelry case drawer and fall-down correspondence flap, each cover initialled 'A', dated.

1830-1 *13in (33cm) long*

$900–1,400 TEN

A fine Victorian coromandel and brass-bound dressing cage, by Asprey, London, the hinged rectangular top opening to a fitted interior with a fall front and twin spring-release hinged side compartments, lined in blue plush and Moroccan leather, containing sterling silver-mounted cut glass boxes and scent bottles, cut-steel scissors, mother-of-pearl handled implements and an ivory hand mirror, with silvered trade label 'C&G Asprey 166 New Bond St W', the mounts with Charles and George Asprey hallmarks, dated.

1879 *12/5in (31cm) wide*

$6,000–9,000 L&T

CLOSER LOOK - LADY'S DRESSING CASE

This outstanding piece is probably unique due to the way it opens. Lifting the top of the case not only reveals the interior, but at the same time lowers the front of the case containing a vast selection of items and lifts the center section of the carousel so that it sits above the other bottles. It is possible that this piece was a commission undertaken by the maker, but was so difficult to execute that they didn't repeat it.

The interior of the lid has a central section enclosing a lift out velvet lined pad with a selection of ivory tools with glove stretcher, shoe horn, large hand-held mirror and two smaller hand mirrors, a leather stationery wallet with silk lined interior and a silver gilt clasp, two picture holders, access to a recessed compartment, two removable boxes with sliding lids, a clock and a barometer.

The box contains sixteen hobnail cut bottles all with silver gilt tops, each decorated with the owners initials D.S. in coral and seed pearls. Two rising candle holders on swing out arms, all over a long drawer which contains a large ivory hairbrush, together with a compartment for the jewelry storage. Removing this drawer reveals a secret compartment.

The drop down front contains an extensive selection of 28 differing tools, including scissors, nail tools and a napkin holder.

A George Betjemann & Sons' lady's dressing case in a large coromandel-veneered case with brass corners and brass inlaid decoration.

George Betjemann (1798-1886) began his career as an apprentice cabinetmaker and set up his own business, with his two sons, in 1855, in Clerkenwell, London. In 1859, he moved to Pentonville Road, London where he continued his business, now called George Betjemann & Sons. The company continued to expand and when George died in 1886 his family continued to run it until 1939.

c1877 *17.75in (45cm) wide*

$67,500-97,500 RGA

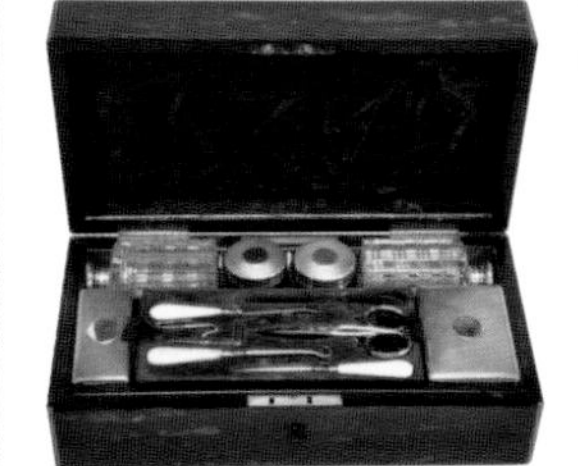

A Victorian coromandel toilet box by Chapman, Son & Co., London (Oliver & Middleton Chapman), with silver-mounted fittings, with brass edges and vacant name plate, the cover interior with a concealed mirror and stationery pocket, the base fitted with two cut-glass bottles, two circular and two rectangular jars and a tray with five mother-of-pearl and/or steel manicure items and a replacement scissors.

1871 *28cm (11in) wide*

$1,200-1,800 DN

A Victorian coromandel travelling toilet case with silver gilt-mounted fittings by Frederick Purnell, London 1884, with brass edges, the cover interior with a concealed mirror and stationery pocket, the base fitted with four square section bottles, three circular and three rectangular jars, each engraved with a monogram 'EMB', a tray with six Mother of pearl and/or steel manicure items (four missing), and a drawer beneath, with a leather outer protective case.

14in (35cm) wide

$1,800–2,700 DN

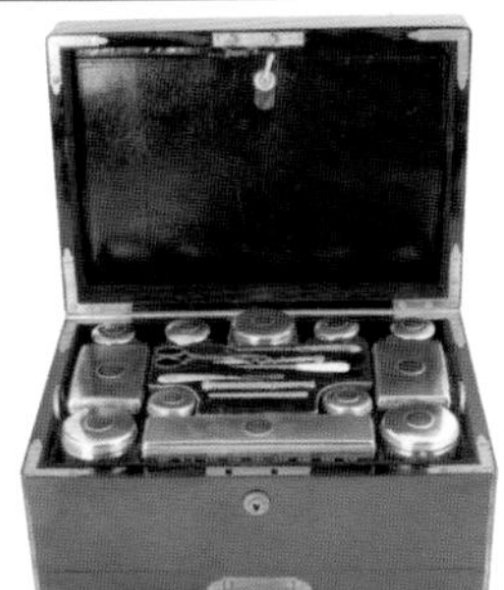

A Victorian ebony and brass-mounted travelling toilet box by F. West, the hinged lid inset a monogram 'ECC', to a plush and leather lined interior, the lid inset a pouch and previously a hand mirror, to twelve cut glass and engine-turned silver gilt topped bottles, jars and boxes, all with a monogram, by J. B, London 1870, fitted with various utensils and implements including a corkscrew, stamped 'F. WEST MANUFACTURER TO HER MAJESTY & THE ROYAL FAMILY, 1 ST. JAMES'S Street', with a Bramah lock, with side carrying handles and with a base drawer for jewelry.

14in (35cm) wide

$1,800–2,700 WW

An early 20thC black crocodile skin dressing case, the purple silk-lined interior fitted extensively with ivory brushes, boxes and jars, all monogrammed, including silver-mounted jars and a travelling clock.

20.5in (52cm) wide

$1,000-1,700 SWO

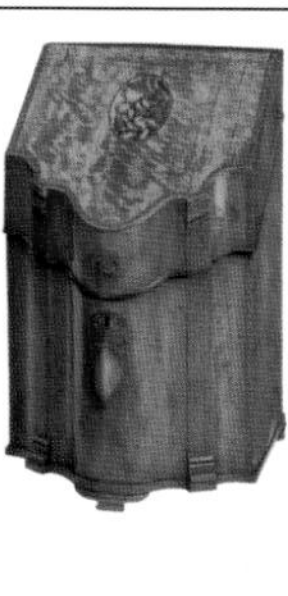

A pair of George III satinwood, tulipwood crossbanded and marquetry inlaid knife boxes, the hinged sloping lids centered by a conch shell, opening to a fitted interior, the underside of the lids inlaid to show a conch shell within a featherbanded border, the fronts inlaid to simulate pilasters, original silver escutcheon and pull, raised on shaped bracket feet.

c1770 *15.25in (39cm) high*

$6,000–9,000 **FRE**

A George III mahogany and crossbanded knifebox, with hinged sloping top and double breakfronted serpentine front, with oval white metal escutcheon, the interior with slotted panel, together with a George III mahogany and marquetry oval tray.

c1770 *9.5in (24cm) wide*

$400-550 **DN**

One of a pair of George III mahogany knife boxes, each with hinged, sloping cover and double break-fronted, with boxwood stringing overall and star patarae inside the covers, on ogee bracket feet, the interiors with slotted panels.

c1790 *15in (38.5cm) high*

$1,500-2,250 pair **DN**

A George III mahogany knife box, of serpentine form, the sloping hinged lid opening to reveal a fitted interior with various cutlery apertures and inlaid star and stringing.

12in (30cm) high

$300-450 **DA&H**

INTRODUCTION TO KNIFE BOXES

Knife boxes are decorative cases used to store cutlery. The interiors contain slotted fittings designed to hold sets of cutlery – the knives and forms handle up, and spoons bowl up.

- **The first knife boxes were made during the reign of George II and were usually supplied as a pair.**
- **At this time, they were generally of serpentine or bow form with a slanted lid and silver or brass mounts. In early examples the wooden (often mahogany) box might be covered with shagreen or silk-velvet. Mahogany or veneered knife boxes became popular in the 1760s. Vase-form knife boxes were introduced in the 1780s.**
- **During the reign of George III decoration became more lavish and might include cross- or feather-banding.**
- **Knife boxes (and cutlery urns which had been introduced in the 1780s) ceased to be used from the early 19thC as more and more sideboards contained fitted cutlery drawers.**

A George III mahogany knife box, Serpentine outline with chequered line border inlay, fitted interior and with side handles and brass lock plate and clasps.

9.25in (23cm) wide

$300-450 **CHEF**

A pair of George III Adams-design pedestal knife boxes, with turned finials, domed covers and barber pole stringing throughout, the interior with five graduated rings, raised on a molded circular base and square platform bases.

27in (69cm) high

$10,500-15,000 **TEN**

A set of twelve George III silver and ivory dessert knives and forks in a cutlery case, the silver by Moses Brent, London, the green-stained handles with blackened crests, the earlier shagreen case with brass mounts, the sloping lid revealing the original velvet-lined fitted interior, on brass dome feet.

1792 *9.75in (25cm) high*

$2,700-3,300 **DN**

ESSENTIAL REFERENCE - TUNBRIDGEWARE

Tunbridgeware is the collective name given to small wooden domestic objects decorated with intricate mosaic patterns made up of thin geometric slivers of colored woods.

- **It was first used in the late 17thC, but most pieces seen today date from the 1830s to the end of the 19thC.**
- **Its name comes from the spa town of Tunbridge Wells in Kent, England, which became a popular resort in the 19thC. Pieces were made in and around the town, often as souvenirs.**
- **Most designs feature flora and fauna, or people, buildings and landscapes surrounded by geometric borders.**
- **It was typically used to decorate stamp- and workboxes, rulers, picture frames and games boards, and also, rarely, work tables.**
- **Tunbridgeware was associated with polite, usually female, leisure activities such as sewing and writing. As a result it was often used and displayed in parlors and drawing rooms.**

A Regency Tunbridgeware sewing basket with a swing handle, the top printed with a view of Brighton Pavilion, within a painted floral border, the interior lined in pink paper and with a green paper label 'A Brighton Trifle', interior grubby and with missing division.

5in (12cm) high

$300-450 SWO

An early 19thC Tunbridgeware and rosewood sewing box, of sarcophagus shape, the hinged lid inlaid with parquetry specimen woods to a paper lined interior with a lift-out tray with divisions, a lift-out pin cushion, a white wood measure and thimble and with a silk covered pin case on cast gilt feet.

8.5in (22cm) wide

$280-340 WW

A Tunbridgeware and rosewood workbox, the convex lid with a mosaic panel depicting Shakespeare's birthplace, Stratford-upon-Avon, the inside with a panel of deer before a tree, good condition, inside divisions missing.

7in (22cm) wide

$1,200-1,800 SWO

A Tunbridgeware rosewood and walnut sewing box, the lid with a printed panel of a mother and child within tulipwood crossbanding, a pair of brass lion's mask ring handles, the green-papered interior over a drawer fitted with painted whitewood boxes, a tape measure and further accessories, on brass lions paw feet, with an applied oval-green paper label for 'Friend, Tunbridgeware Manufacturer'.

c1830 *11in (27cm) wide*

$1,200-1,800 SWO

A Tunbridgeware mosaic book stand, the spindle gallery with two scroll ends, the base with a central foliate panel within a floral border, the top surface with grained decoration, surface condition deteriorated, marks, scratches.

c1840 *15in (38cm) wide*

$750-1,200 SWO

A mosaic Tunbridgeware games box, of octagonal shape, decorated with a central flower panel within a foliate border, containing contemporary playing cards and carved Mother-of-pearl counters of different shapes, including fish, the base with a paper label for "Edmund Nye", top with split through center.

c1840

$3,000-4,500 SWO

An early Victorian Tunbridgeware and ebony tea caddy by Thomas Barton, the hinged lid with a parquetry specimen wood panel to a pair of inlaid lidded compartments, the base with a band of flowers, the underside with a paper trade label inscribed 'T. BARTON Late NYE, Manufacturer, MOUNT EPHRAIM, AND PARADE, TUNBRIDGE WELLS'.

7.5in (19cm) wide

$400-550 WW

A Tunbridgeware tea caddy, the lid with inlaid sunbursts, over all-round cube parquetry and a twin compartment interior.

c1850 *7in (18cm) wide*

$900–1,400 **SWO**

A Victorian Tunbridgeware and rosewood side table, the rectangular top with a geometric band to a central panel with a mosaic of Muckross Abbey, Killarney, Ireland, to a mahogany line inlaid base fitted with a frieze drawer.

20in (51cm) wide

$550-700 **WW**

A Victorian Tunbridgeware and walnut sewing box, inlaid parquetry and feather stringing, the hinged lid with a mosaic view of Tonbridge Castle, Kent, the front and sides with panels of flowers to a fitted interior with three lidded compartments and further divisions with a central pin cushion to the lift-out tray.

13in (33cm) wide

$400-550 **WW**

A Victorian Tunbridge ware and bird's eye maple table cabinet, with geometric bands, the top and hinged door inlaid mosaic floral sprays, fitted with three drawers with ebonized and bone handles, on disc feet.

8in (21cm) wide

$280-340 **WW**

A Victorian Tunbridgeware and rosewood box, the hinged lid with a mosaic panel of a stag within bands of flowers, to a Mother of pearl escutcheon and a paper lined vacant interior.

9in (23cm) wide

$300-450 **WW**

A Tunbridgeware box, the top with a panel depicting 'Penhurst Place'.

c1875 *9in (23cm) wide*

$300-450 **SWO**

A 17thC boarded walnut desk box, the hinged rectangular lid with iron strapwork above the fall front enclosing four geometrically molded drawers and a secret compartment, the front with an engraved escutcheon.

15in (38cm) wide

$1,800–4,000 **ROW**

A George III mahogany map box of upright rectangular form, having a sloped hinged lid and dovetailed sides.

23in (59cm) wide

$600-900 **SWO**

A 19thC Vizagapatam ivory work box, of sarcophagus form, the lobed hinged cover with a flowerhead finial and foliate engraved bands, opening to reveal a compartmented fitted interior, raised on lobed bun feet.

9in (23cm) wide

$1,500-2,250 **L&T**

A 19thC Indian Vizagapatam tortoiseshell counter box, with engraved and pierced ivory mounts and paw feet, the domed cover enclosing fourteen ivory gaming counters.

3.9in (10cm) wide

$600-900 **SWO**

A 19thC Indian Vizagapatam rosewood and ivory inlaid box, the cover and sides profusely decorated with flowers and foliage, with secret drawer on bun feet.

16in (40cm) wide

$9,000–12,000 **ECGW**

ESSENTIAL REFERENCE - VIZAGAPATUM

Vizagapatum is the term given to ivory-veneered boxes and pieces of furniture made in or near the town of the same name on the southeastern coast of India.

- **Vizagapatum fell under British control in 1668 and by the 18thC the whole of India's eastern seaboard was part of the British Empire.**
- **By the mid-18thC local merchants had started to commission fine, inlaid pieces which combined British and Indian tastes. As a rule, the forms were Western and the decoration inspired by Western and Indian tradition.**
- **Work boxes, tea caddies, writing boxes and small desks and tables were among the items made. They were veneered with ivory which was engraved and highlighted with lacquer.**
- **Pieces of Vizagapatum were exported to Europe from the early 19thC and examples were displayed at the Great Exhibition in London in 1851.**
- **The workshops went into decline in the late 19thC and early 20thC as demand for Vizagapatum faded.**

An Anglo-Indian Vizagapatam ivory and quillwork box, sarcophagus form with tented top lifting to reveal velvet pincushion and mirror, over two larger levels of fitted compartments, with "Vizagapatam 2nd Dec. 1831" inscribed in ink to one lid, over single drawer, on four-reeded ball feet.

1831 *9in (22cm) wide*

$7,500–10,500 **SK**

An early 19thC brass bound burr yew travelling writing slope with fitted interior.

12.5in (31cm) wide

$1,000–1,500 **BELL**

A 19thC ormolu-mounted tortoiseshell table-top stationery cabinet, of bombe form, the folding hinged top above a writing fall enclosing a sectional interior over a frieze drawer, standing on ormolu mounted scrolling feet.

25in (64cm) wide

$5,250-6,750 **ROW**

A William IV or early Victorian rosewood and Mother-of-pearl marquetry writing slope, of rectangular form, the top and sloping front with a border of birds and animals amongst foliage, with a recessed brass swing handle at each end, the fully fitted and satinwood lined interior with lidded apertures for pens and inkwells, above a hinged and velvet lined writing surface.

c1835 *15.5in (40cm) wide*

$450-750 **DN**

A William IV tooled leather writing box by Bramah & Prestage, with a sunken brass handle inscribed 'W. H. RICHARDS', the flame mahogany veneered interior with a writing surface and a twin lidded compartment the underside with pen loops and a letter pouch a further hinged lidded compartment with a lift-out tray and an inkwell compartment, with a green printed maker's label inscribed 'BRAMAH & PRESTAGE, 124 Piccadilly, MANUFACTURERS, By Appointment, To their Royal Highnesses THE DUCHESS of KENT and THE PRINCESS VICTORIA', the brass lock stamped 'I. BRAMAH 124 PICCADILLY'.

Bramah & Prestage set up a partnership and took out a lease on premises at 124 Piccadilly in 1836 and they parted company in 1841. W.H.Richards (1816-1885), was a mining engineer at Cuiaba and Morro Velhos gold mines in Brazil during the 1840s.

14in (35cm) wide

$750-1,200 **WW**

A late George III mahogany apothecary's cabinet, with ebonized and boxwood edging, with drawers and bottle partitions.

14in (35cm) wide

$750-1,200 WW

An early 19thC mahogany domestic medicine chest, the hinged cover with brass handle securing two fitted opening sections, each with glass medicine bottles and further small drawers with ivory handles and a set of small brass and steel scales.

6.5in (16cm) wide

$1,800-3,000 CHEF

A 19thC apothecary travelling box with recessed brass mounts and fitted interior with bottles.

$750-1,200 ECGW

A 19thC French kingwood and amboyna liquor set, with brass mounts, the hinged lid and sides to a serpentine front revealing a lift-out amaranth and ormolu-mounted decanter stand with four decanters and thirteen glasses, one damaged, all with etched and gilt decoration.

13in (34cm) wide

$900–1,400 WW

ESSENTIAL REFERENCE - ANTON SEUFFERT

Anton Seuffert (1815–87) worked as a cabinetmaker in Auckland, New Zealand. He is renowned for decorating his work with intricate marquetry inlays using New Zealand woods.

- **Anton Seuffert was born in Bohemia in 1815. He worked for Carl Leistler & Sons of Vienna, a firm which made furniture in historical revivial styles for many of the European royal houses. As foreman, he was sent to England to assemble furniture for Queen Victoria and in 1851 he set up the company's displays at the Great Exhibition.**
- **He emigrated to New Zealand in 1859 where he continued to work as a cabinetmaker.**
- **Within a few years he had begun to make writing cabinets. They remain the best examples of his work.**
- **Seuffert's designs used elements of European furniture. He was particularly influenced by the cabinet of curiosities.**
- **After Seuffert's death the company was run by his son William. The company closed in 1943.**

A 19thC marquetry and parquetry jewelry casket, by Anton Seuffert, New Zealand, of inverted bombe form with an all-over basket-weave design, the hinged lid with a scrolling foliage design, above an ivory thumbpiece and escutcheon, with a plush lined interior, on turned feet, the underside with printed pre-1869 label 'A. SEUFFERT, CABINET MAKER To His Royal Highness THE DUKE OF EDINBURGH, Elliott St, AUCKLAND, NEW ZEALAND.'

8.5in (22cm) wide

$9,000–12,000 WW

A mid-19thC Anglo-Indian ivory inlaid macassar ebony jewel stand, incorporating a miniature press.

9in (23cm) wide

$900–1,400 TEN

A tortoiseshell and brass marquetry veneered liqueur case in the style of Boulle, of rectangular form with serpentine front, with a foliate cast handle to each end and four foliate cast feet below, the hinged top and front opening to a fitted interior with four cut-glass and parcel-gilt decanters and nine drinking glasses arranged in a lift-out gilt-metal stand.

c1880 *14.5in (37cm) wide*

$1,200-1,800 DN

A Victorian coromandel decanter box of square form with brass trim, hinged lid with inset vacant brass plaque, opening to reveal a velvet lined interior, four square cut glass decanters with faceted spherical stoppers, brass campaign drop side handles.

9.5in (25cm) wide

$900–1,400 HT

A late 19thC French kingwood and gilt bronze mounted jewelry box, the lid mounted with an oval porcelain plaque of a cherub and a dove, opening to reveal a light blue satin mounted interior, raised on a shaped apron, with a decorative escutcheon.

11.5in (29cm) wide

$450-750 SWO

A 19thC necessaire in burr walnut, upright-piano musical box, the lid with gilt metal candle sconces, lifting to reveal a purple velvet tray fitted with two blue glass scent bottles with enameled gilt metal lids, gilt handled scissors, thimble, pin case and bodkin.

11.25in (28.5cm) wide

$1,200-1,800 **CHEF**

A Regency rosewood and penwork sewing box, the lid with a classical engraving, to bands of scrolling foliage and parquetry, the divided interior with a paper label inscribed 'BETTISON'S MARGATE LIBRARY', with a lift-out tray, with later lion's mask handles, originally on feet.

12in (30cm) wide

$400-550 **WW**

An early 19thC French satinwood sewing box, with a cut steel handle, barber's pole stringing and a mother of pearl plaque and escutcheon, the fitted interior with a mirror to the lid and with a plush lined tray fitted with associated steel scissors, a thimble, a button hook, a mother of pearl case and reel holders, on ivory feet.

7.5in (19cm) wide

$400-550 **WW**

A 19th century mahogany candle box, with a sliding paneled cover.

6in (15cm) wide

$150–225 **WW**

A 19thC oak salt box, with a base drawer.

10in (26cm) wide

$120–180 **WW**

A 19thC French fruitwood piano étui, in Palais Royale style, with gilt brass mounts, with a twin hinged top, one revealing a mirror and keyboard, the interior fitted with mother of pearl handled utensils flanking an engraving of putti, with further gilt metal sewing tools, with mother of pearl reels, a glass scent bottle, with a pair of metal thread embroidered lidded compartments, the lift-out keyboard with buttons activating the brass musical movement, on ebonized legs.

12in (29cm) wide

$1,200-1,800 **WW**

A 16thC French iron missal box, the oak core covered with wrought iron tracery and four suspension rings, the lock hasp cast with Gothic buttresses.

11in (28cm) wide

$9,000–12,000 **SWO**

An early 19thC wallpaper-covered hat box with a fox hunt scene.

16.75in (42cm) wide

$550-700 **POOK**

A 19thC Alphonse Giroux, Paris, French ebonized and gilt metal table casket, of canted rectangular outline, the hinged lid inset with a rectangular panel painted with a stag hunting scene, two smaller panels set to front, lined interior, figural and foliate cast mounts, on scroll cast feet, engraved 'Alph. Giroux Paris'.

14.25in (36cm) wide

$3,000-4,500 **CHEF**

A Pennsylvania or Virginia painted pine bentwood box, retaining its original red and white spotted pinwheel and floral decoration on a black ground.

c1830 *13.25in (33.5cm) wide*

$37,500–45,000 **POOK**

A Victorian rosewood and brass mounted portable card dispenser, the center with an ebony veneered press flanked by four boxes, the tops with oval panels of the card kings.

12in (31cm) wide

$450-750 **WW**

ESSENTIAL REFERENCE - COMPASS ARTIST

A number of the craftsmen working in the Pennsylvania German community in the early 19thC made and decorated small boxes known as Schmuckkastchen. The boxes were traditionally given as gifts within European Germanic communities and so it is likely that this tradition continued in German areas in the New World. The boxes were used to hold trinkets such as ribbons and keepsakes. Few of the makers signed their work, and so they are known by the style of decoration they used rather than by their names.

- **The Compass artist used a pair of compasses to draw his designs and then decorated them with paint.**
- **The boxes he decorated are usually made from pine, cedar or poplar with metal latches and fine dovetail joints. They take several forms, including dome- and slide-tops. Some of the boxes were lined with Lancaster County newspapers dating from 1812–38.**
- **Any name or initials marked on the box refer to the owner rather than the maker.**
- **The surface of each box is covered with an umber, red, blue or green ground. This is then decorated with stylized flowers, vines and pinwheels drawn with a pair of compasses.**

A Lancaster, Pennsylvania painted 'Compass Artist' box, decorated with pinwheel flowers on an umber ground.

c1800 *5.25in (13.5cm) wide*

$8,250-9,750 **POOK**

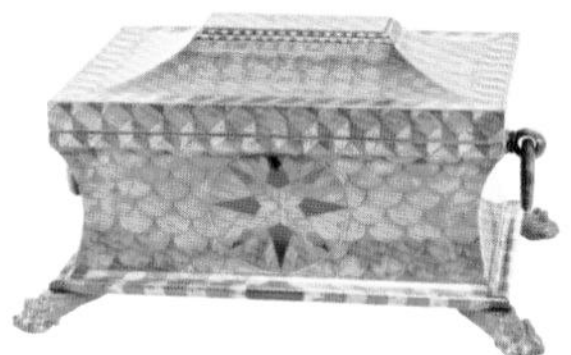

A Victorian parquetry box the lid with a raised panel inscribed 'This box composed of 2255 pieces Jan 1865(?)', with two ring handles and paw feet.

1865 *15in (39cm) wide*

$750-1,200 **SWO**

A 20thC hardwood rectangular humidor by Dunhill, Paris, with original cardboard case.

9.75in (25cm) wide

$225–400 **BELL**

SNUFF BOXES

Snuff – a finely ground, scented tobacco – arrived in Britian in the early 18thC when large quantities were seized from captured Spanish ships. Taking snuff was common on mainland Europe and quickly became popular among the British nobility. As taking snuff became fashionable, a host of conventions developed, including specially made boxes.

- **Early examples were made for aristocrats from precious metals, but as snuff became more affordable the practice became more widespread and boxes were made from wood and papier mâché.**
- **Some of the finest boxes were destined to be diplomatic gifts. They might be decorated entirely in gold, with engine turning or engraving to sparkle in the light. Further decoration was created by adding metal such as silver or iron to the gold, or adding inlays of Mother-of-pearl, tortoiseshell, porcelain, micromosaics, ivory, or Japanese lacquer. Precious stones such as diamonds were sometimes used.**
- **Enamel boxes were decorated with pictures painted on inset panels. Portraits were popular, as were hunting or mythological scenes.**
- **Tortoiseshell was veneered on to a white or colored wooden surface. To maximize the effect of the shell, decoration was kept simple.**
- **Other materials include silver decorated with pieces of shell or quartz; porcelain; papier-mâché; and wood carved into novelty shapes such as shoes.**

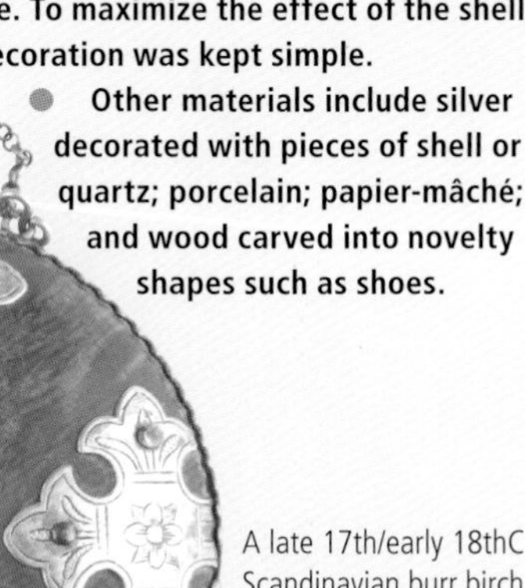

A late 17th/early 18thC Scandinavian burr birch or maple brass- and silver-mounted snuff flask, with engraved mounts, the top with a stopper on a chain, the base with a screw-off tamper.

3.5in (8cm) wide

$900–1,400 WW

A Scandinavian burr maple snuff flask, with engraved brass mounts and central bosses, one side inscribed '1675', the top with a threaded funnel, the base stopper missing.

c1675 3in (7cm) diam

$300-450 WW

A late 17th/early 18thC Scandinavian burr birch or maple brass-mounted snuff flask, the central rondel to each side with an inscription, the base with an engraved seal/tamper, stopper missing.

3.5in (8cm) wide

$550–850 WW

A French walnut snuff box, of circular form, the lift-off lid carved with a river landscape scene with numerous buildings, figures, animals and birds, etc, opening to reveal a tortoiseshell lined interior.

3in (8cm) diameter

$300-450 DA&H

An early 19thC French pressed burr maple circular snuff box, titled 'Frederick the 11nd, King of Purfsia,' Frederick the Great on horseback, marked 'DE NAYES' and indistinct text, the interior tortoiseshell lined.

3in (7cm) diameter

$450-750 WW

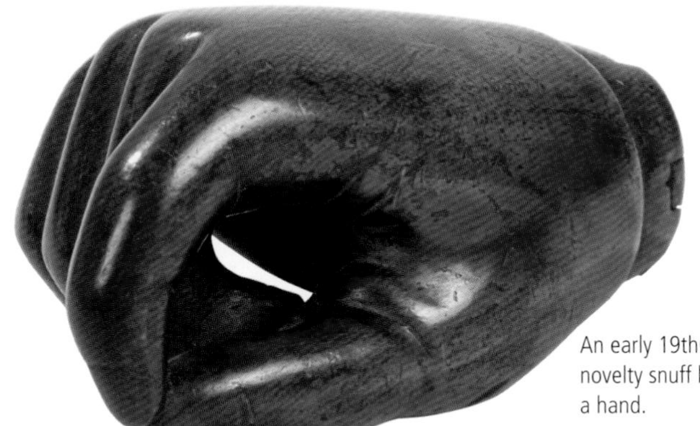

An early 19thC carved fruitwood novelty snuff box, in the form of a hand.

4in (10cm) high

$750-1,200 LOCK

A 19thC carved treen snuff box, modeled as a hand, the fingers taking a 'pinch of snuff', with a hinged lid.

4.5in (11cm) long

$300-450 L&T

A 19thC novelty snuff shoe, with a pull-off top, the sole with a sliding cover revealing a well endowed man.

4in (10cm) long

$400-550 **WW**

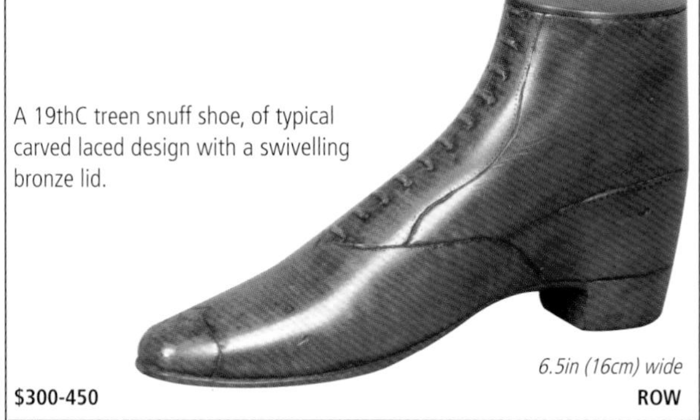

A 19thC treen snuff shoe, of typical carved laced design with a swivelling bronze lid.

6.5in (16cm) wide

$300-450 **ROW**

A French post-Revolution carved cockerel snuff box, carved with date ANIV- 1795, the base sliding out to reveal snuff box.

3in (8cm) high

$180–270 **LOCK**

A pearwood coffin-shaped snuff box, with sliding lid.

3in (7.5cm) long

$450–900 **LOCK**

A 19thC silver-mounted treen fox mask snuff box, unmarked, plain mounts, the hinged cover carved with oak leaves, with an oval cartouche with a monogram, gilded interior.

2.5in (7cm) long

$1,500-2,250 **WW**

A 19thC mahogany horse head snuff box, with brass tack harness decoration, the base with a sliding cover.

2.5in (7cm) wide

$225–400 **WW**

A 19thC treen snuff box, in the form of a peacock, with painted decoration, a hinged wing and sliding cover.

6in (15cm) wide

$400-550 **WW**

A possibly French Folk Art carved birth snuff mull, in the form of a recumbent lion with open mouth and extended tongue, the head and rump opening to reveal storage apertures.

30cm (12in) long

$1,500–3,000 **HW**

A possibly late medieval unusual treen turned fruitwood goblet, carved with George and the Dragon.
5.5in (13cm) high
$600-900 **LOCK**

A possibly 16th/17thC Welsh treen sycamore goblet or chalice, the turned bowl above a turned column and platform base.
8.75in (22cm) high
$600-900 **LOCK**

A 17thC Georgian sycamore wassail bowl and cover, the finial to the cover with turned ivory tip and unscrewing to keep a nutmeg in, the interior of the lid with nutmeg grater and the bowl standing on a circular spreading base.
8in (20cm) high
$4,500–7,500 **MLL**

A 17thC treen walnut wassail cup or loving cup, the high sides with ring turning above a turned stem and platform foot.
8.5in (22cm) high
$1,500-2,250 **LOCK**

CLOSER LOOK - NORWEGIAN TANKARD

These tankards were used at celebrations such as wedding feasts to drink a toast. Many of them have a series of pegs inside which measure out equal amounts. Each drinker was expected to drink as far as the next peg and then pass the tankard to the next person. They were treasured possessions which would have been passed from generation to generation.

The lion and ball finial was added later. The lion is the emblem of the Norwegian royal family and so was often used as a national symbol on these tankards.

The body of the tankard is carved with three oval panels, the central one with a male and female figure each holding a cornucopia and entwined by a caduceus (a winged staff with two snakes wrapped around it and an ancient astrological symbol of commerce associated with the Greek god Hermes).

The patina of the wood and the condition of the tankard add to its desirability.

A late 17thC Norwegian burr birch tankard, the hinged lid carved with a sleeping figure within a crowned serpent edge and a fruit and leaf outer border, with an S-scroll handle carved with two male mask terminals, the outer border inscribed 'ONSILIV...INNOCTE', to leaf and flower carvings with a snail, lion, a squirrel and a lamb, with two further panels each with a laurel border and depicting Apollo and Mercury, raised on later lion and ball feet, the base with a flower head with the initials 'R S' and the date.
1672 *7in (17cm) wide*
$18,000-22,500 **SWO**

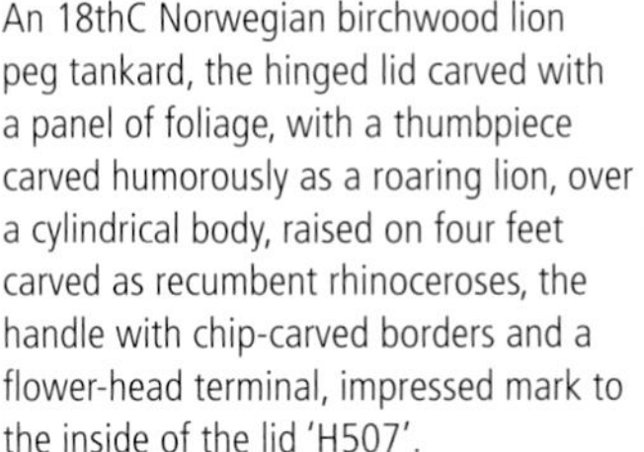

An 18thC Norwegian birchwood lion peg tankard, the hinged lid carved with a panel of foliage, with a thumbpiece carved humorously as a roaring lion, over a cylindrical body, raised on four feet carved as recumbent rhinoceroses, the handle with chip-carved borders and a flower-head terminal, impressed mark to the inside of the lid 'H507'.
10.5in (26cm) high
$600-900 **SWO**

An 18thC treen staved tankard, with bone rounded to the top above a carved tapering lid, chip carved hinged handle and bound drum base.
6.5in (16cm) high
$300-450 **LOCK**

An 18thC Norwegian birchwood lion peg tankard, the hinged lid with a flower-head boss, turned rings and a lion thumbpiece, the cylindrical body supported on three foliate carved feet, the handle with incised and carved decoration.
10.5in (26cm) high
$450-750 **SWO**

An 18thC treen Scottish staved beaker, bound with brass bands and copper nails.
4.5in (12cm) high
$225–400 **LOCK**

A late 18th/early 19thC coconut cup, with white metal mounted rim, knopped stem and coconut domed foot.
6.5in (17cm) high
$450-750 **DA&H**

A Continental hardwood lidded goblet, the lift-off lid and cylindrical body carved with scrolling leaves between beaded and stiff leaf borders with matching beaded knopped stem and drum base.
10.5in (27cm) high
$225–400 **DA&H**

A boxwood scissor-action nutcracker, in the form of a figure, the chip and scratch carved decoration includes the initials 'EW' but no date.

Most of these date from the last quarter of the 17thC or the first quarter of the 18thC.

$4,500–7,500 **GHOU**

A 19thC three-handled silver-mounted wooden quaich, probably Scottish, circular body formed with light and dark colored wooden staves, the three handles with plain mounts, on a circular foot, unmarked.

4.5in (11cm) long

$900–1,400 **WW**

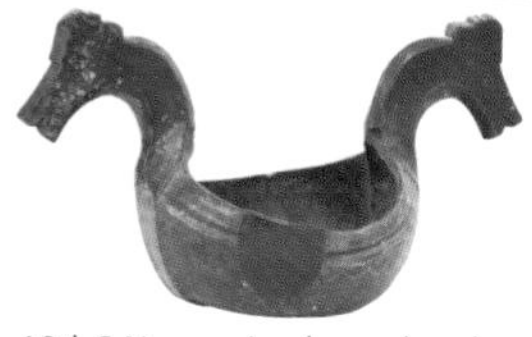

A 19thC Norwegian horse-head kasa, of traditional form, with painted decoration.

6.5in (17cm) high

$750-1,200 **SWO**

A 19th/early 20thC softwood nutcracker, carved in the form of a seated whiskered man.

10in (26cm) high

$300-450 **SWO**

A pair of 19thC Scandinavian turned softwood beer bowls, both with painted decoration and an inscription to the outer rim, each with a handwritten paper label applied to the base, 'Let this cup be passed round, and when emptied filled again' and 'Welcome friends to my house, now we'll drink merrily'.

9in (23cm) diameter

$550–850 **SWO**

A 19thC pair of turned walnut goblets.

6.5in (16cm) high

$120–180 **TRI**

An early 20thC carved novelty nutcracker, modeled as the cricketer W G Grace.

6in (16cm) long

$700–975 **SWO**

A late 18th/early 19thC carved coquilla nut nutmeg grater, the acorn finial with an ivory and steel grater with a compartment for nutmegs, the screw-off base also with a nutmeg compartment.

6.5in (16cm) high

$900-1,200 **WW**

An early 19thC carved coquilla nut nutmeg grater, of acorn form, the screw-off lid revealing an ivory and steel grater.

3in (7cm) high

$300-450 **WW**

A George III mahogany cheese coaster, with turned finials on swivel base.

15.5in (40cm) wide

$450–900 **BELL**

A George III mahogany cheese coaster, of dished form on leather roller castors.

12.5in (31cm) wide

$150–300 **WW**

A Victorian rosewood and bird's-eye maple desk tidy, with turned spindle handles, the base with a paper label inscribed in pen 'Given to Moia Daoni, by H.R.H. The Princess Royal Christmas 1946'.

8in (20cm) wide

$600-900 **WW**

A 19thC Goncalo Alvez double sided book stand, with fret-cut end supports.

15.75in (40cm) wide

$450–900 **BELL**

A 19thC rosewood book rack, in the manner of Gillows, the twin turned carrying handles above the square section gallery with turned and scrolling uprights, above a frieze drawer with a bead molded base.

16.5in (41cm) wide

$450-750 **ROW**

A 17thC treen chip-carved candle box, carved with stars inside circles, slide top bordered by carved symbols of animals, human figures and fish.

5in (13cm) wide

$180–270 LOCK

A 19thC Scandinavian treen box, with a slide lid and geometric carved sides.

3.5in (9cm) high

$120–180 LOCK

AN INTRODUCTION TO MAUCHLINWARE

Mauchlineware was a popular 19thC souvenir of visits to Scotland. Pieces were made from yellow sycamore wood and decorated with a small scenes of a view or house, usually applied as a transfer, though some early pieces were hand-painted. The whole piece was then covered in several coats of varnish. As the varnish protected the decoration, scratched or dented pieces will drop in value considerably.

- **It gets its name from the town of Mauchline in Ayrshire, Scotland. It was produced primarily by W. & A. Smith from the 1850s.**
- **Early pieces featured Scottish views or houses such as Robert Burns's Cottage, but once the style proved popular other tourist destinations began to be used. As a result some scenes are more collectible than others.**
- **Mauchlineware was primarily used to make boxes, but also napkin rings, quaiches, card holders, rulers, photograph frames and other small items.**
- **Early snuffboxes are of particular interest to collectors as they are among the first examples of Scottish inventor, John Sandy's 'hidden hinge', which was designed to prevent snuff from leaking into the owner's pocket.**

A 19thC Sudan campaign Mauchlinware pyramid sewing box, with pictures of General Gordon, Lord Wolseley and General Stewart, the hinge top with Clark sewing advertising labels and three cotton reel rods.

$750-1,200 LOCK

A 19thC unmarked white metal mounted coco de mer, formed as a box with a hinged lid, the base with pierced and scrolling dolphin form feet.

15in (39cm) high

$1,200-1,800 ROW

An early 19thC possibly Welsh or Scandinavian treen ladle, with a carved beast handle to a turned column stem containing nine balls, the bowl decorated with leaves and flowers and with the date '1810'.

14.5in (37cm) long

$150–300 WW

A set of 19thC boxwood cutlery, with a treen fork, ladle, spoon and two cawl spoons.

$150–225 LOCK

A late George III Irish mahogany and brass-bound plate bucket, with a swing handle.

14in (34cm) wide

$600-900 WW

A 17thC treen sycamore mortar, ring-turned top and base, with a later pestle.

7.5in (18cm) high

$300-450 LOCK

An unusual George III period treen oak candle holder or stick, the collapsible stick in the form of two male figures, with a plug in the candle top.

8in (20cm) high

$450-750 LOCK

An early 19thC HMS Victory interest treen, with a carved top, with a plaque inset stating 'Miss M E Eccles. Please accept this little token from grandest vessel that ever sailed H.M.S. Victory, poor Nelson was shot & died on the ship'.

This is possibly a descendant of Nelson's stepson; his granddaughter was called Eccles and wrote a book on Nelson.

3in (7cm) high

$600-900 LOCK

A late Victorian country house oak post box, of pillar box form, the hexagonal top above a hinged brass letter slot, the cylindrical trunk with hinged door, Morocco leather-lined to the interior, and on a circular section base bearing registration plaque.

17in (44cm) high

$5,250–8,250 MOR

A 16thC carved polychrome figure of John the Baptist, kneeling in prayer.

35in (89cm) high

$4,500-6,000 SWO

A 17thC carved walnut figure, modeled standing in flowing robes, mounted on a later plinth base.

29in (74cm) high

$1,500-2,250 ROW

A late 17thC Dutch carved and stained walnut armorial panel in Baroque style, the pierced surround with cresting featuring a central shield with helm flanked by putto bearers, with further putti beneath to each side, all amongst densely scrolling foliage; the central rectangular reserve later mounted with an early 16thC carved and polychrome painted model of St George.

19.5in (50cm) wide

$1,500–3,000 DN

An 18thC carved wooden model of a lady, possibly the Virgin Mary, with traces of polychrome and gilt decoration, mounted on a plinth base.

13.5in (35cm) high

$150–225 ROW

An 18thC walnut carving, modeled as a faun above scrollwork.

12.5in (31cm) high

$300-450 ROW

A pair of 19thC carved wooden cherub groups, each formed kneeling in prayer with gilt and polychrome decoration.

15.5in (39cm) wide

$225–400 ROW

An early 19thC carved and painted tobacconist shop figure, modeled as a Highlander in a black feathered cap, red jacket and tartan kilt, taking snuff from a horn mull on a stepped base.

31.5in (80cm) high

$6,000–9,000 SWO

A 19thC Continental carved fruitwood figure of St Francis, the standing figure carved with his right hand raised and holding a book in his left, some signs of original painted surface.

38.5in (98cm) high

$3,000-4,500 L&T

A late 19thC Continental carved and part polychrome painted softwood articulated figure, the head, hands and feet painted in skin tones, with inset glass eyes, with later metal stand and another late 19thC Continental carved and painted softwood articulated figure.

43.5in (111cm) high

$1,500-1,800 DN

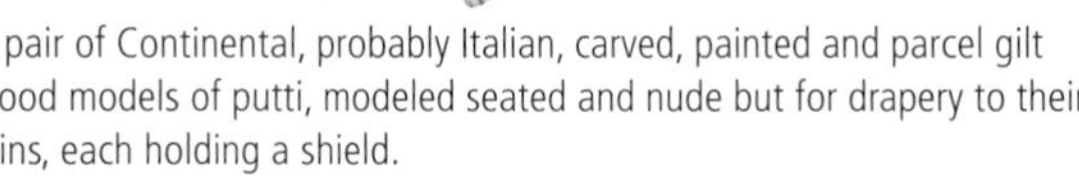

A pair of Continental, probably Italian, carved, painted and parcel gilt wood models of putti, modeled seated and nude but for drapery to their loins, each holding a shield.

c1900 *17in (43cm) high*

$1,500–3,000 DN

A 19thC Black Forest carved hall stand, formed as a bear climbing a tree, the top carved with a bear cub.

82in (208cm) high

$4,000-4,500 ROW

A late 19thC Swiss Black Forest Huggler Frères carved walnut group of two oxen, the base with an old crack running the length of the carving and with a later base holding it together, the underside with an indistinct ink signature, the naturalistic base stamped 'Huggler Frères'.

12.75in (32cm) wide

$1,500-2,250 WW

A late 19thC Black Forest bear, carved four-square looking to the left, open mouth and painted red and orange details.

19.5in (49cm) long

$4,000–5,250 SWO

A late 19thC Swiss Black Forest life-size carved linden wood model of a seated dog, with glass eyes, the base marked 'INTERLAKEN 1897'.

32in (81cm) high

$2,700-3,300 WW

A late 19thC Black Forest carving of a dog and her puppies.

26in (67cm) long

$9,000–12,000 WOT

A late 19thC Swiss carved linden wood stick stand, probably Brienz, realistically modeled as a brown bear standing on its hind legs with arms outstretched holding a molded branch, drip tray within a molded and carved base.

50in (127cm) high

$9,000–12,000 TEN

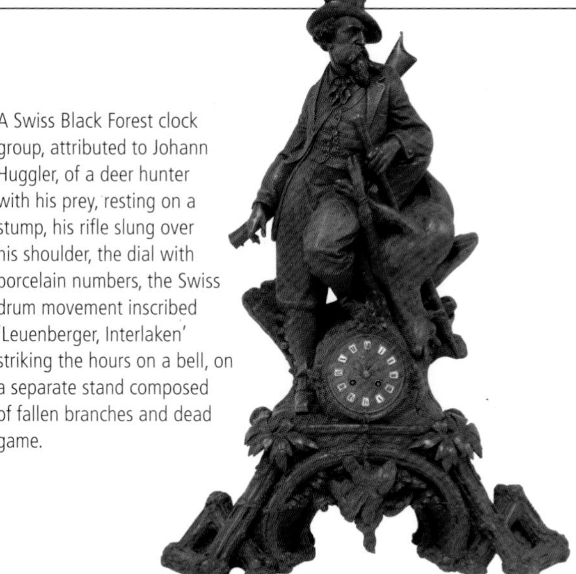

A Swiss Black Forest clock group, attributed to Johann Huggler, of a deer hunter with his prey, resting on a stump, his rifle slung over his shoulder, the dial with porcelain numbers, the Swiss drum movement inscribed 'Leuenberger, Interlaken' striking the hours on a bell, on a separate stand composed of fallen branches and dead game.

33in (84cm) high

$7,500–12,000 SWO

An early 20thC black forest carved bear stand, polychrome painted, the figure standing with one paw raised holding a carved dish, on a circular plinth base.

43in (110cm) high

$1,800–2,700 L&T

An early 20thC Swiss Black Forest carved wood and polychrome decorated model of a seated bear, with glass eyes.

16.5in (41cm) high

$1,000–1,500 WW

THE CLOCKS & BAROMETERS MARKET

The trends we wrote about in the Clocks market in the last Antiques Handbook and Price Guide have continued. Good-quality clocks in original condition by important makers are still highly desirable. London makers tend to be the most sought after, but many skilled provincial makers are beginning to fetch comparable prices.

Historically, the market was for good clocks in unrestored condition. There is a new group of buyers entering the market who are interested in the aesthetics of the clock and will accept sensitive restoration, especially with early clocks. There are also some buyers who go for a good-looking, good quality case.

The longcase clock market has again displayed two distinct trends. The most desirable 17th and early 18thC examples by well-known makers have continued to do well. Mid-to late 18thC and particularly 19thC large mahogany clocks have proved difficult to sell.

Skeleton clocks have proved popular, particularly if the clock has unusual features. Architectural clocks are also in demand, as are good quality carriage clocks, particularly by the top makers, Jacot, Drocourt, Le Roy, Dent and Garnier. Bracket clocks have to be early, be in original condition and by a recognized maker.

Barometers have been slow sellers unless by a top name like Daniel Quare or John Patrick. In 2014 Lyon & Turnbull sold a fine Scottish Regency barometer by A. Adie, Edinburgh for $15,000. Unusual features help and in general good quality 18thC examples are selling better than 19thC. Dealers report that they are finding some younger buyers, so the market may well improve.

In the 1970s a watch collector tended to be interested in 18th and 19thC pocket watches. Gold pocket watches still have their collectors but gold-plated examples are proving difficult to sell.

Fine wristwatches by the great makers such as Rolex and Patek Philippe, and to a lesser extent, Breguet and Cartier continue to have a strong following. Vintage or modern mechanical wristwatches (not the battery driven watches) have a universal appeal, and one that is growing. The market demand for well-preserved Rolex sports models the Submariners, Explorers and Daytonas has grown and they have proved to be an excellent investment. At Bonhams sale on June 10th 2015 a military Submariner, or 'MilSub', reference 5513 made in 1972 and issued in 1975, sold for just under $105,000. These watches were ordered directly from the Ministry of Defence with specific enhancements. Only around 1,700 were made. The knowledge that these watches have seen 'action' adds to their appeal.

Above: A mid-18thC japanned tavern clock, by Daniel Ray, Manningtree, with an associated four-pillar anchor escapement.

dial 24 inch (61cm) diam

$6,000-9,000 **SWO**

Top Left: A James II/William and Mary Joseph Windmills lantern clock with alarm, with restoration/rebuilding.

c1685-90 *15in (38cm) high*

$4,000-4,500 **DN**

A Charles II silver-mounted, ebony-veneered architectural longcase clock, by Johannes Fromanteel, London, the month-going movement with four latched and ringed pillars joining rectangular plates, bolt-and-shutter maintaining power, anchor escapement.

c1670 *76in (193cm) high*

$67,500-75,000 **L&T**

A William and Mary miniature longcase clock, the movement by Joseph Knibb, London, the case hood later, the door with boxwood and ebony star parquetry inlay, the movement on ball and spike feet with four ring-turned pillars, replaced knife edge verge escapement and countwheel strike on later bell.

c1685 *69in (175cm) high*

$19,500-24,000 **L&T**

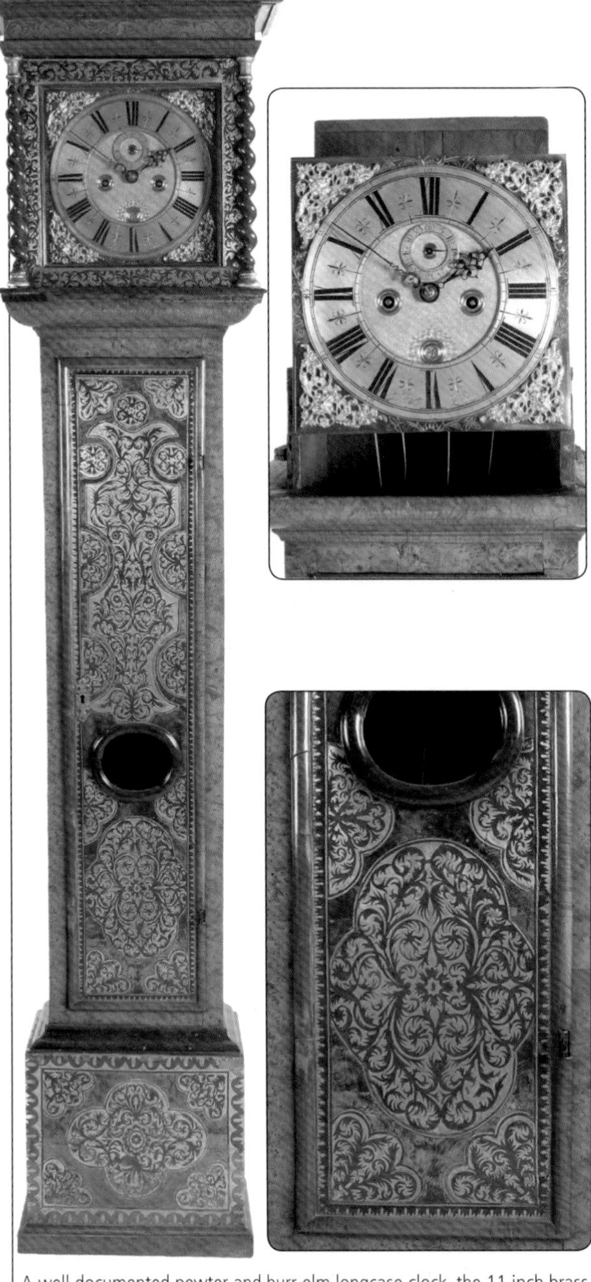

A well documented pewter and burr elm longcase clock, the 11 inch brass dial signed 'Jacob Wallis', London, eight-day movement with four turned and latched pillars, inside count wheel strike, the burr elm case with flat hood flanked by barley twist columns, decorated with seaweed marquetry of pewter, glass lenticle.

c1695-1700 *80in (203cm) high*

$37,500-45,000 **WW**

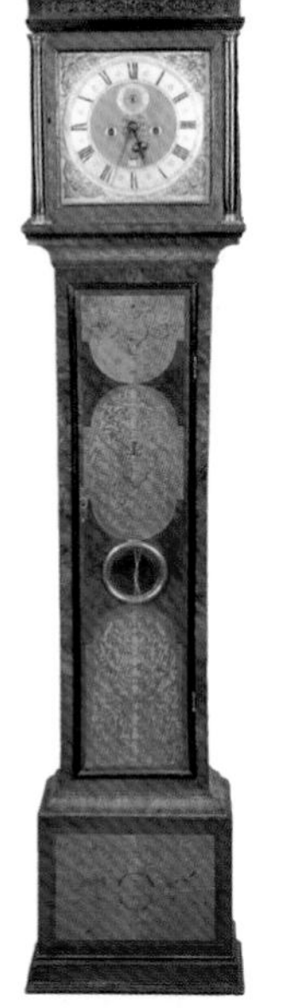

An eight-day walnut longcase clock, by Thos. Pare of London, the movement has six ringed pillars and latchplates and inside countwheel striking, the trunk door has three panels in marquetry depicting birds and foliage.

c1700 *86.5in (219.7cm) tall*

$8,250-9,750 **TRI**

A Queen Anne walnut eight-day longcase clock, by Anthony Herbert, London, the five finned pillar (center latched) rack and bell striking movement.

c1705 *88in (224cm) high*

$3,000-4,000 **DN**

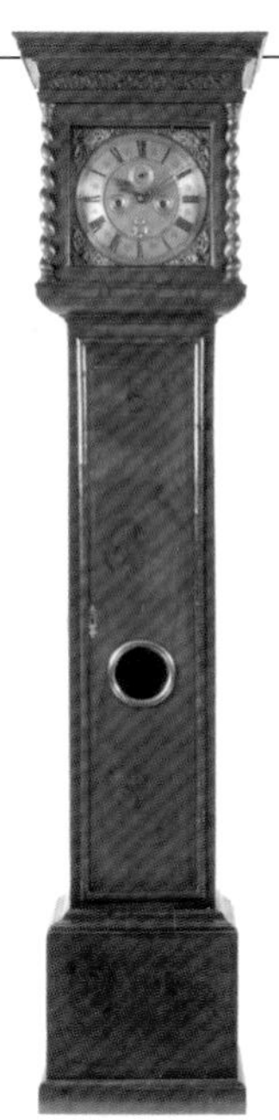

An eight-day walnut longcase clock, the brass dial signed 'Jos. Cooper, Whitchurch', the five ringed pillar movement with inside locking plate striking and anchor escapement, the flat hood with blind fret and flanked by barley twist columns, with crossbanded sides.

c1710 *83.5in (212cm) high*

$7,500-9,000 WW

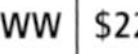

An early 18thC month-duration burr walnut longcase clock, the brass dial signed 'Chr. Gould, Londini Fecit', the six ringed pillar movement with locking plate striking and anchor escapement, the flat hood with caddy top and frets, the sides and plinth with herringbone inlays and crossbanded panels.

Christopher Gould was made a freeman of the Clockmakers Company 1682. Died 1718. He was maker of great repute, especially of longcase clocks.

88in (223cm) high

$22,500-30,000 WW

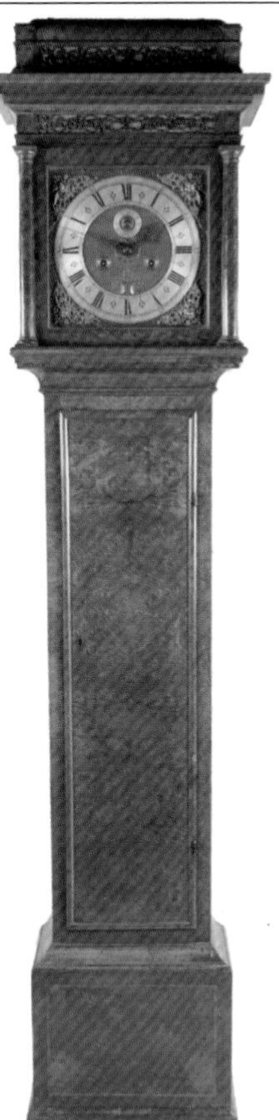

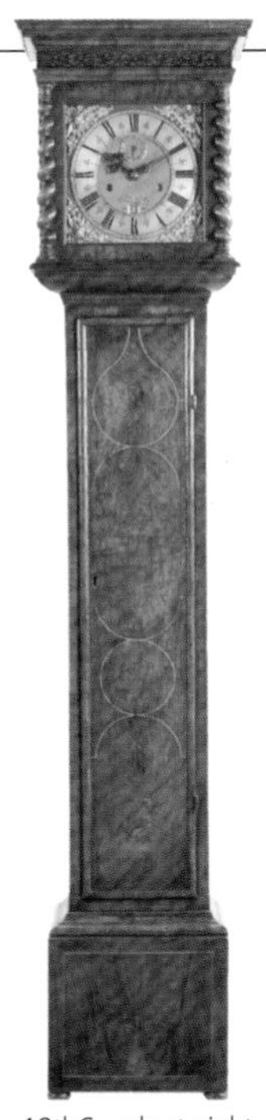

An early 18thC walnut eight-day longcase clock, the brass dial signed 'John Martin, Londini Fecit', the movement with five latched ringed pillars, bolt and shutter maintaining power, locking plate striking.

76in (193cm) high

$37,500-45,000 WW

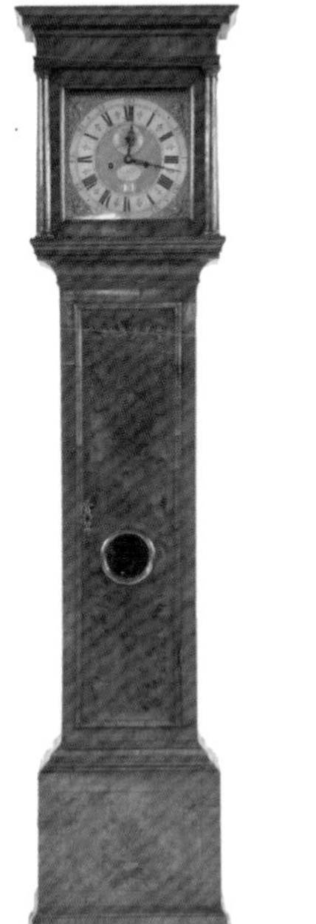

An early 18thC walnut longcase clock, the brass dial signed 'John Winkles, London', with an eight-day movement striking the hours.

84.8in (215.5cm) high

$6,000-7,500 SWO

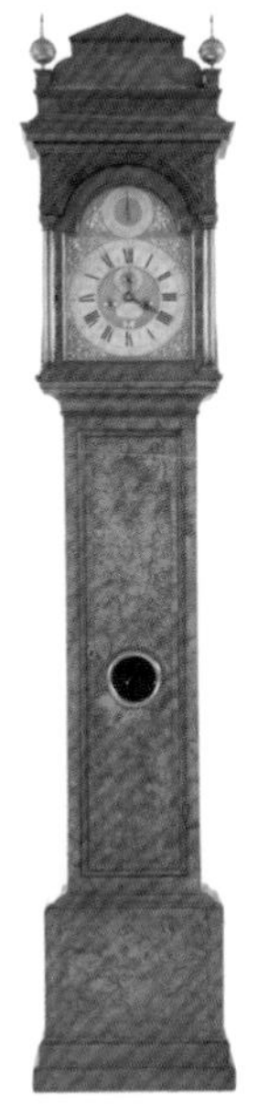

An early 18thC pollarded elm longcase clock, the silvered dial, inscribed 'John Latham, London', with eight-day movement striking the hours, in a restored case with blind fretwork.

100.4in (255cm) high

$10,500-12,000 SWO

An early 18thC marquetry longcase clock, by John Clowes, London, the movement with five finely finned pillars, the 11in dial with ringed winding holes, seconds and date mechanisms and outside count wheel.

82in (208cm) high

$19,500-24,000 SWO

A George II black Japanned longcase clock, by Richard Kenfield, Winchester, the trunk with an arched door over a plinth base, decorated all over with gilt Chinoiserie on a black ground, the eight day movement striking on a bell.

90in (228cm) high

$3,750-4,500 L&T

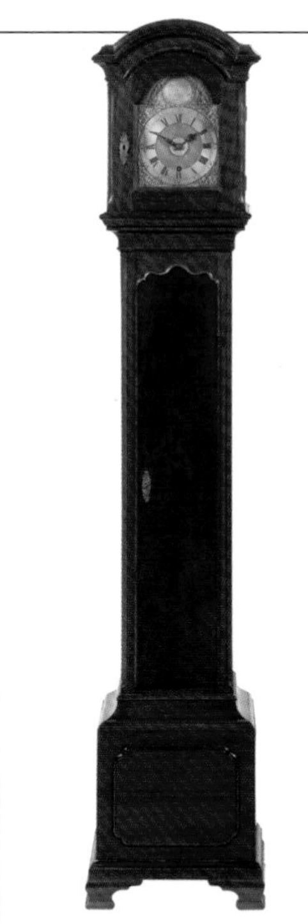

A mid-18thC George III 'Grand Daughter' mahogany longcase clock, by Thomas Page, Norwich, with a bell striking movement.

63in (160cm) high

$7,500-10,500 **L&T**

A mid-18thC George III mahogany longcase clock, by Joshua Harrocks, Lancaster, subsidiary seconds and date aperture, two winding holes and painted moon phase dial, pierced brass spandrels.

91in (231cm) high

$3,000-4,000 **L&T**

A late George II green and gilt chinoiserie longcase clock, by John Dewe (fl.1733-1764), London, the silvered dial with Roman and Arabic chapter ring, date aperture, signed with date to dial.

c1760 *90in (228cm) high*

$3,750-4,500 **ROS**

A George III longcase clock, by Joseph Herring, London, the steel chapter ring with Roman numerals, the case and hood black lacquered and gilt painted in the Chinoiserie taste.

90.25in (229cm) high

$3,000-4,500 **FRE**

An 18thC George III mahogany longcase clock, by John Greenwood, Rochester, with.subsidiary strike/ silent, seconds and calendar dials, eight-day movement.

100.8in (256cm) wide

$3,000-4,500 **L&T**

A George III mahogany longcase clock, by Higgs and Evans, made for the Spanish market, the dial signed 'Higgs, Diego Evans', Londres, with subsidary second dial, date aperture and silent/strike, the eight day three train movement striking on nine bells.

c1760 *260cm high*

$10,500-13,500 **L&T**

An 18thC longcase clock, the brass dial inscribed 'Thomas Wheeler, London', with eight-day five-pillar movement, in a later red chinoiserie lacquer case,

90in (229cm) high

$3,000-4,000 **SWO**

A George III mahogany eight-day longcase clock with moonphase, the four pillar rack and bell striking movement.

82.7in (210cm) high

$750-900 **DN**

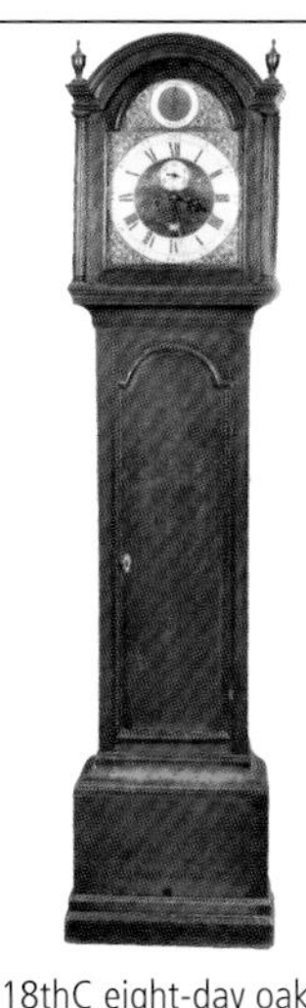

A late 18thC eight-day oak longcase clock, by John Grace, Tring and having a strike/silent lever in the arch.

John Grace is not listed as a maker in Tring and this clock bears resemblances to ones made by John Clement of Tring at this time. A John Grace was born in Tring in 1766 and it is possible that this may have been made for him by Clements in 1780/90s.

81in (205.7cm) tall

$2,100-2,700 **TRI**

A George III scarlet lacquered tall case clock, by Geo. Lumley, Bury, signed, lacquered all over to show Chinoiserie scenes.

82in (208cm) high

$3,750-4,500 **FRE**

An 18thC George III japanned longcase clock, by Richard Finch, with subsidiary seconds dial, silent/strike and date aperture, the eight-day movement striking on a bell.

78in (198cm) high

$4,000-5,250 **L&T**

A late 18thC mahogany longcase clock, the dial signed 'Sutton Liverpool', the arched brass dial with moonphase and inscribed 'Tempus Edax Rerum', with eight-day striking movement.

91in (231cm) high

$1,800-2,250 **SWO**

An 18thC oak longcase clock, the brass dial inscribed for 'Francis Swindon, Brentwood', with eight-day movement striking the hours on a bell.

86.2in (219cm) high

$750-900 **SWO**

A mahogany longcase clock, signed 'John Yonge, Liverpool', the eight day repeater movement with anchor escapement striking on a bell, the case with scrolled pediment and turned wood finials over 'verre eglomise' panels.

92in (233.7cm) high

$3,000-4,000 **HT**

An oak longcase clock, signed 'Thomas Lawson, Keighley', the thirty-hour movement with anchor escapement, outside count wheel and striking on a bell, silvered chapter ring with Arabic and Roman numerals, painted moonphase in the arch.

91.25in 231.8cm) high

$1,500-2,250 **HT**

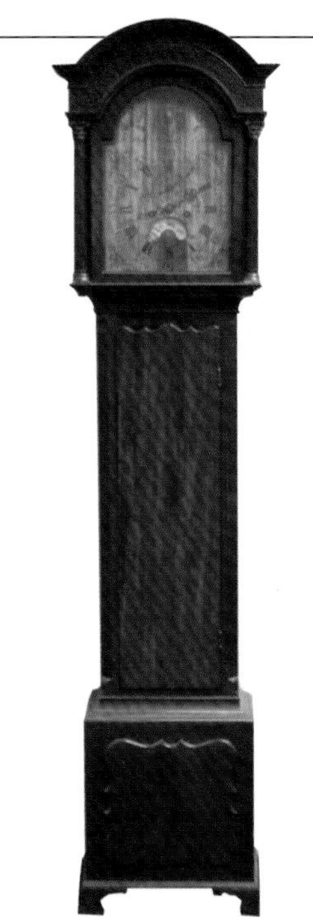

A late 18thC eight-day longcase clock, by Jas. Hine of Exeter, the four pillar movement chiming on a single bell.

86.5in (220cm) high

$750-1,200 HW

An 18thC longcase clock, with eight-day movement, the brass dial inscribed 'James Hewith, Sunderland', in oak case with cut down pagoda top, on replaced bracket feet.

89in (226cm) high

$900-1,000 DA&H

A George III mahogany longcase clock, by Wilson, London, with subsidiary seconds dial and date aperture, painted arched panel depicting a pastoral scene, eight-day movement striking on a bell.

96in (244cm) high

$3,000-4,500 L&T

A George III longcase clock, with eight-day movement with silvered dial inscribed 'William Rust, Hull', in inlaid mahogany Scottish style case with satinwood stringing.

82in (208cm) high

$2,250-3,000 DA&H

A George III oak longcase clock, the thirty-hour movement converted to eight-day, with brass dial inscribed 'Smith, Alfreton' with unused date aperture.

83in (211cm) high

$600-750 DA&H

A Scottish mahogany longcase clock, the eight-day striking half hours, the painted dial inscribed 'K Murdoch, Ayr', with subsidiary seconds and calendar dials.

80in (202cm) high

$1,000-1,400 SWO

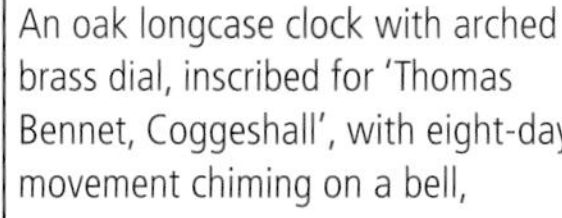

An oak longcase clock with arched brass dial, inscribed for 'Thomas Bennet, Coggeshall', with eight-day movement chiming on a bell, *c1823*

89.3in (227cm) high

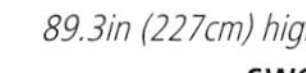

$900-1,200 SWO

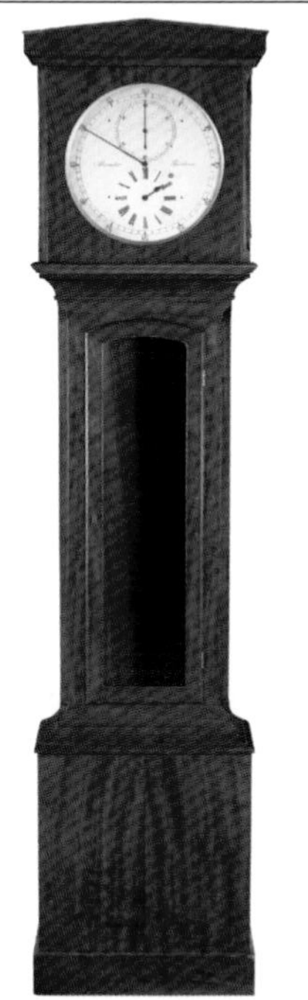

A late Regency mahogany longcase regulator clock, by Alexander Gardner, the arched pediment over a silvered dial with minutes and subsidiary seconds and hour dials.

77in (196cm) high

$4,000-5,250 **L&T**

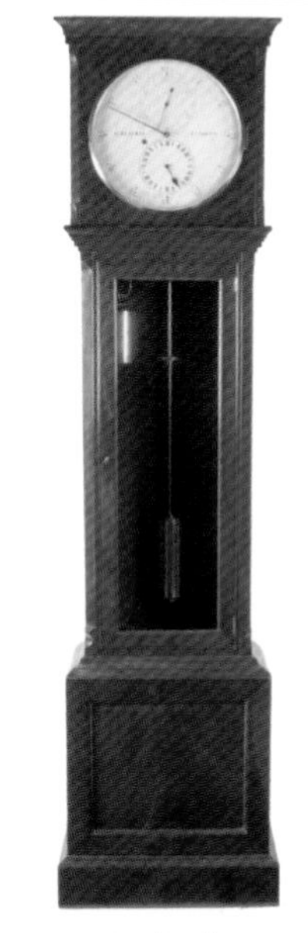

A flame-veneered mahogany longcase regulator, the painted dial singed G. Blackie, London, the four pillar rectangular plated movement with dead beat escapement and maintaining power, the pendulum with cylindrical brass bob supported from the back board.

75in (190cm) high

$6,000-7,500 **WW**

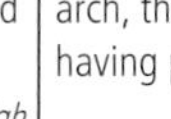

An early 19thC longcase clock, with eight-day movement, the painted dial inscribed 'J Wreghit Pattrington', with three dimensional moving Adam and Eve figures to the arch, the oak and mahogany case having pagoda top with brass orbs.

95in (241cm) high

$2,100-2,700 **DA&H**

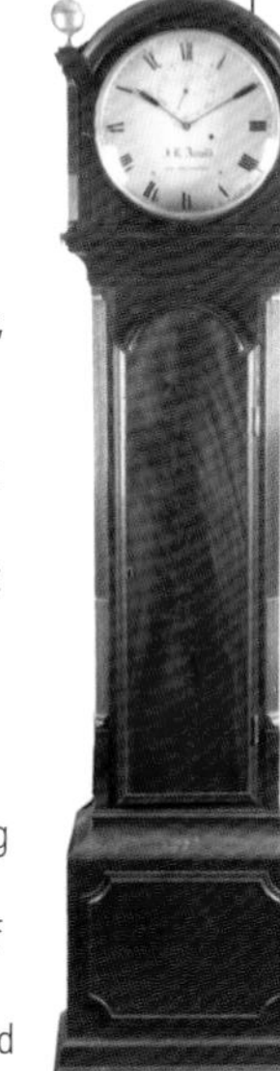

A well documented longcase domestic mahogany regulator, by John Roger Arnold, dial signed, unusual arrow flight hands, substantial five pillar movement in shouldered plates, dead beat escapement with jeweled pallets and Harrison maintaining power, set-on-beat adjustment at top of crutch, mercury jar pendulum suspended from the back lock.

Arnold was in partnership with Dent 1830-1840 so with this signature the clock must have been for personal or family use. Vandrey Mercer suggests that it could have been made to celebrate Arnold's silver wedding.

1834 86in (218cm) high

$7,500-9,000 **WW**

A Victorian mahogany longcase clock, the eight-day movement with rolling moon phase, with painted dial inscribed 'J Briscall Birmingham', case with swan neck pediment, on replaced bracket feet.

92in (234cm) high

$1,150-1,300 **DA&H**

A late 19thC oak longcase clock, with eight-day movement, with brass dial, inscribed 'Jonathan White, Kirton', with pagoda top and fluted columns, line incised trunk door and paneled base on replaced bracket feet.

96in (244cm) high

$750-900 **DA&H**

An Edwardian mahogany longcase clock, the eight-day musical movement playing 'Westminster' and 'Whittington', chimes striking on eight tubular gongs, with brass dial with copper chapter ring, traces of silvering.

101 in (257cm) high

$3,750-4,500 **DA&H**

A Gordon Russell cased longcase clock, in rosewood and bog oak, design no774, the brass dial signed 'Russell Workshops, Broadway, Worcestershire', with cottage regulator movement, label 'Cabinet Maker A Harmison'.

1928 85in (216cm) high

$7,500-9,000 **CHOR**

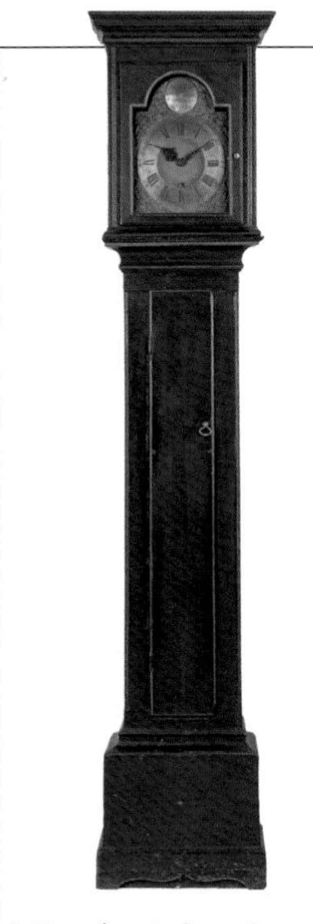

A Massachusetts Queen Anne painted pine tall case clock, with a thirty-hour works with a brass face, inscribed 'Made by David Blasdel in Amesbury MDCCLVI'.

1756 *87.5in (222cm) high*

$15,000-21,000 **POOK**

A Chester County, Pennsylvania Chippendale walnut tall case clock, the broken arch bonnet with an eight-day works with a brass face, inscribed 'B. Chandlee, N:ham', over a case with fluted quarter columns on ogee bracket feet.

c1770 *95in (241.5cm) high*

$9,000-10,500 **POOK**

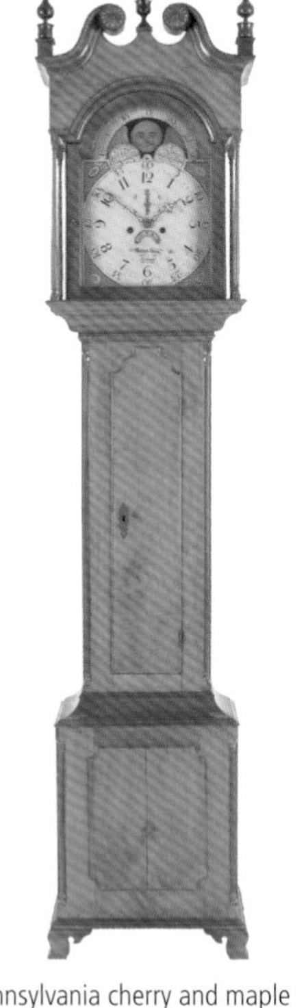

A Pennsylvania cherry and maple tall case clock, with painted dial, inscribed 'Griffith Owen Philad.', with an eight-day movement.

c1785 *100in (250cm) high*

$7,500-9,000 **POOK**

A Massachusetts Federal mahogany tall case clock, with a Roxbury case and an eight-day works, the painted dial inscribed 'Aaron Willard Boston'.

c1790 *104.5in (265.4cm) high*

$37,500-45,000 **POOK**

A Reading, Pennsylvania Chippendale walnut tall case clock, with an eight-day movement with a painted dial and moon phase.

c1790 *98in (249cm) high*

$8,250-9,750 **POOK**

A Pennsylvania Chippendale walnut tall case clock, with a thirty-hour works, signed 'John Murphy Northampton'.

c1793 *95.5in (242.5cm) high*

$3,750-4,500 **POOK**

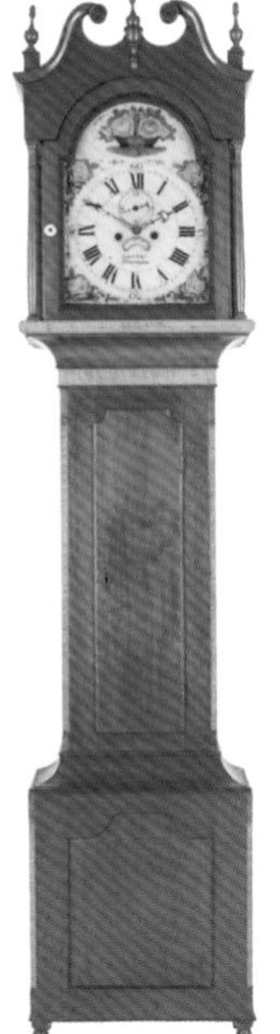

An early 19thC Pennsylvania Federal cherry and tiger maple tall case clock, with eight-day movement, the painted face inscribed 'Geo. Eby Manheim'.

94in (238.7cm) high

$5,250-6,750 **POOK**

An early 19thC Pennsylvania walnut tall case clock, with an eight-day works, signed 'Henry Hahn, Reading'.

100in (254cm) high

$4,500-5,250 **POOK**

A William & Mary ebony basket top bracket clock, by Samuel Watson, London, the movement with a silent pull cord quarter repeat and two-bell strike on the hours and quarters, verge escapement.

Samuel Watson listed working in Coventry and London and registered with the Clockmaker's Company 1687-1710.

1687 *12in (30cm) high*

$13,500-16,500 L&T

A William and Mary ebonized and repousse brass-mounted bracket clock, by George Etherington, London, the 8-day quarter repeat bell striking movement, signed 'George Etherington, London', the case with a dolphin and eagle mask handle above a pierced cushion top with ho ho birds, masks and scrolls.

c1690 *9.5in (24cm) wide*

$27,000-33,000 L&T

A Queen Anne ebonized bracket clock, by Peter Wise, London, the eight-day silent pull quarter movement striking on two bells, verge escapement.

Peter Wise listed Clockmakers Company 1693, Master 1725-41.

c1710 *14in (36cm) high*

$4,500-6,000 L&T

An early 18thC George I bracket clock, with a Japanned case, with musical works, signed Asselin London.

19.75in (50cm) high

$11,500-12,750 POOK

A Louis XV ormolu and kingwood repeating bracket clock, by Jean Baptiste Baillon, the single-train movement with recoil escapement and exterior rack and bell striking, the movement signed 'J B Baillon Paris No. 141637', with pendulum and two keys, with bracket.

the clock 19in (48cm) high

$9,000-10,500 ROS

A George III mahogany striking bracket clock, signed Rich Wilson London, twin-fusee movement with verge escapement and rack striking on a bell, with an early George III mahogany wall bracket.

c1760 *21in (53cm) high*

$11,500-12,750 TEN

A mid-18thC Louis XVI boulle marquetry clock and bracket, by Waltrin le Jeune, the case with a gilt metal relief dial depicting a profile of Louis XVI, the movement striking on a bell and engraved 'Waltrin Le Jeune * Aepinal', on a conforming bracket.

34.75in (88cm) high

$4,000-5,250 L&T

A late 18thC mahogany-cased bracket clock, the dial marked 'Thomas Best, London', the triple-fusee movement with variable chime, Air, Gigue, Minuet, March, Hornpipe, Gavotte, sounding on a rack of eight bells and a single bell for striking the hours.

Thomas Best is recorded as working from 1761.

17.5in (44cm) high

$9,000-10,500 **HW**

CLOSER LOOK - STRIKING MUSICAL BRACKET CLOCK

This is a magnificent ball-top case flanked by caryatids, drop handles and elaborate urn finials.

Decorated with gilt chinoiserie designs against a dark blue lacquer ground.

The brass dial with silvered chapter ring, concentric calendar hand, between twin subsidiaries for chime/not chime and a Jigg/ Country Dance.

With foliate-engraved backplate, the pinned barrel quarter chiming and on each hour playing music with nine hammers on eight bells.

A dark blue lacquered quarter striking musical bracket clock, signed 'Benj. Barber, London', the three-train movement with six pillars, knife edge verge escapement.

Benjamin Barber, Red Lion Square, London 1785-1794. Liveryman of the Goldsmiths Company.

c1775 *26in (66cm) high*

$33,000-45,000 **WW**

A mid-to late 18thC ebonized bracket clock, by Timothy Vernier of London, with eight-day twin-fusee movement.

15.5in (39cm) high

$8,250-9,750 **HW**

An 18thC walnut grande sonnerie bracket clock, by Boschmann, London, with three train-fusee movement, chiming on seven bells, the silvered dial with date aperture, moon phase, date and calendar dials, repeat/no repeat, strike/no strike.

17in (43cm) high

$15,000-18,000 **SWO**

A George III mahogany and brass mounted bracket clock, by 'Henry Maze, London' the three-train movement striking the quarters on eight bells, with a repeater and calendar aperture.

20.5in (51.5cm) high

$7,500-9,000 **SWO**

A striking bracket clock, the dial with strike/silent lever and 'Father Time', the five-pillar movement with anchor escapement and trip repeat, in an associated case, the backplate signed 'T.Ore, Birmingham'.

Thomas Ore, Wolverhampton, moved to Birmingham in 1788. One of his clocks is in Birmingham Cathedral.

15.5in (40cm) high

$1,800-2,250 **WW**

A Regency mahogany bracket clock, the dial inscribed 'Thos Worsfold Hampton Wick', the eight-day movement striking on a bell.

11in (28cm) wide

$2,250-3,000 **L&T**

A Regency brass inlaid mahogany bracket clock, the three-fusee musical movement chiming the quarters on eight bells, the dial signed 'J Vassalli, Scarbro.'.

25in (64cm) high

$6,000-7,500 **SWO**

An early 19thC English double-fusee bracket clock, dial signed 'Thwaites & Reed, Clerkenwell, London', the double-fusee movement has anchor escapement and strikes on a bell and has a pull repeat.

16.5in (42cm) high

$3,000-4,000 **TRI**

A Regency rosewood and brass inlay bracket clock, the eight-day movement striking on a bell.

c1820 *13.5in (34cm) high*

$3,300-4,400 **L&T**

An early 19thC Regency mahogany, ebonized and brass-mounted bracket clock, by Peter Keir, Falkirk, the eight-day movement striking on a bell with a foliate engraved brass backplate, signed.

18in (46cm) high

$1,400-1,875 **L&T**

A large late 19thC gilt and patinated bronze mantel clock, with an eight-day bell-striking movement, surmounted by a seated figure of a young woman reading a book.

14.25in (36cm) wide

$2,250-3,000 **L&T**

A late 19thC Louis XV-style gilt-bronze and tortoiseshell boulle marquetry bracket clock, signed 'Lesage a Paris', Back of movement stamped 'L.G. 2357', some brass and tortoiseshell missing.

16in (41cm) wide

$3,750-4,500 **FRE**

A late 18thC French figural ormolu and marble mantle clock, depicting Erigone seated on a lion's pelt, being presented a crown by the draped figure of Zephyr, case inscribed 'Zephir precede Bachus au coeur d'Erigone et de plaisir ses sens ... elle dit ah Zephir me Couronne', the eight-day movement striking a bell.

20.5in (52cm) high

$7,500-9,000 **L&T**

A late 18thC George III mahogany and brass mantel chronometer, by George Margetts, no97, the eight-day movement with a single winding hole to the back, the reverse bearing an ivory label inscribed 'Margetts/97/Eight Days', movement with spring detent platform and chain fusee movement.

George Margetts London (Cheapside) Freeman of Clockmakers Company 1779, Liveryman of the Clockmakers Company 1799 - 1808. A famous maker of the late 18thC in the circle of English horologists experimenting with precision timekeeping, such as: Mudge, Emery, Arnold, Earnshaw, Kendal, Brockbank, Barraud, Pennington and Haley. Examples of his work can be found in the British Museum, Guildhall Museum and the Dennison Collection.

13in (33cm) high

$21,000-27,000 **L&T**

A Regency rosewood and brass inalid mantel clock, by G Anthony, London, with a single-train fusee movement.

c1815 *6.75in (17cm) wide*

$1,500-2,100 **L&T**

A Regency gilt and patinated metal mantel clock, the sunburst dial surmounted by a griffin finial and supported by twin recumbent horses.

17in (43cm) wide

$6,000-7,500 **L&T**

A Regency ebonized balloon eight-day strike mantel clock, dial marked 'Leroux', with some alterations.

21.25in (54cm) high

$2,250-3,000 **FLD**

A Viennese enamel timepiece, signed 'Leopold Bauman, in Wien', with central camel above a dome shaped base with mythological panels, gilt fusee verge movement signed.

c1820 7in (18cm) high

$3,000-4,500 **TEN**

An unusual walnut striking mantel clock, dial signed 'Arnold, 84 Strand, London, no.457', the two-train fusee movement with anchor escapement and pull trip repeat, striking on a bell, steel rod pendulum with brass bob engraved Fast/Slow for the rating nut above.

c1838 *12in (31cm) high*

$12,750-14,250 **WW**

A Viennese grande sonnerie mantel clock, with alarm, the four-train movement signed 'Franz Schiesl, in Wien', all racks and snailwork visible on the backplate, fuse for the going train, going barrels for the others, the bells in the base behind fretwork.

8.5in (22cm) high

$15,000-21,000 **WW**

A rosewood inlaid ormolu striking mantel clock, twin-barrel movement with outside countwheel striking on a bell.

c1840 *20.25in (53cm) high*

$2,250-3,000 **TEN**

A French Paris Jean-Baptiste Delettrez Sevres-style porcelain inset ormolu mantel clock, the circular eight-day bell striking movement with Brocot-type pendulum regulation and stamped with oval 'J.B.D' trademark above serial number '31209, 21-9' to backplate, with gilt-painted wood stand applied with brass presentation plaque dated 1869.

c1865 *21.25in (54cm) high*

$4,500-6,000 **DN**

A 19thC French cold painted spelter mantel clock, modeled as a Turkish lady on an elephant.

19in (48cm) wide

$4,000-5,250 L&T

A 19thC French ebonized automaton mantel clock, by Tharin of Paris, the brass twin-drum movement with outside countwheel, depicting a musical automaton figural scene of monks at a table within a monastery interior, continental brass musical movement playing a single air.

20.5in (52cm) wide

$4,500-6,000 L&T

A late 19thC French gilt metal and porcelain mounted mantel clock, with an eight-day bell-striking movement, the case inset with porcelain panels painted with cherubs.

14in (35.5cm) high

$750-900 L&T

A rosewood-inlaid Portico striking mantel clock, twin-barrel movement with outside countwheel striking on a bell, backplate stamped 'Baschet Baullier Paris' and numbered '4274'.

c1880 18in (46cm) high

$1,400-1,800 TEN

An ormolu and porcelain mounted striking mantel clock, porcelain panels depicting figures in costume and garden scenes, twin-barrel movement striking on a bell, backplate stamped 'Hy Marc Paris' and numbered '53246'.

c1880 15.75in (40cm) high

$2,100-2,700 TEN

An ormolu and porcelain mounted striking mantel clock, surmounted by a winged cherub, twin-barrel movement striking on a bell, backplate stamped 'JBD' and numbered '33811'.

c1880 14in (36cm) high

$1,800-2,250 TEN

A late 19thC French ormolu and white marble mantel clock, the twin barrel drum movement striking on a bell and inscribed 'Var Dewint Her a Paris 162', dial signed 'J.B. Marchand Rue Richelieu 57 Paris'.

11.75in (30cm) high

$975-1,150 HT

A gilt-metal and porcelain striking mantel clock, twin-barrel movement striking on a bell.

c1890 20in (51cm) high

$1,500-2,100 TEN

A late 19thC French gilt-brass four-glass mantel timepiece, of one year duration, retailed by Mason & Son, Canterbury, the four-pillar movement fitted with large diameter spring barrel and greatwheel to backplate driving via cocked pinion the four-wheel train set between the plates regulated by visible Brocot escapement mounted within the dial and Ellicott-type compensated pendulum.

14in (35.5cm) high

$4,500-6,000 DN

A 19thC French gilt-bronze mantel clock, with a Queen holding a scroll inscribed 'Tigne Blancoe par la Rein', on a Gothic base.

25.5in (65cm) high

$3,000-4,000 SWO

A 19thC French Sèvres-style porcelain and gilt-bronze lyre clock, the case mounted with a central mask and sunburst finial, the movement signed 'Le Roy et Fils A Paris'.

25.75in (65cm) high

$9,750-11,250 **ROS**

A white marble striking lyre mantel clock, applied ormolu mounts, surmounted by a sunburst mask, twin-barrel movement with outside countwheel striking on a bell.

c1890 *17.75in (45cm) high*

$2,250-3,000 **TEN**

A French Jasperware-mounted champlevé enamel mantel clock.

16in (41cm) high

$750-900 **WW**

A French Empire-style gilt-metal mantel clock, the twin-barrel movement with outside count wheel striking on a bell, case with an allegorical classical maiden with cornucopia and wreath.

c1900 *10.5in (27cm) wide*

$1,500-2,100 **HT**

A Louis XVI-style faux tortoiseshell and gilt-bronze mantel clock, with an eight-day twin fusee movement striking on a gong, signed 'Ross, Exeter'.

c1900 18.5in (47cm) high

$1,500-2,250 **L&T**

A late 19thC 'Black Forest' mantel clock, with two birds amongst foliage, upon a naturalistic shaped base.

20in (51cm) high

$1,000-1,500 **SWO**

A late 19thC oak and elm mantel clock, the case modeled in a Gothic architectural form, the silvered chapter ring marked 'Clerke 1 Royal Exchange London', the movement with Westminster chime, pendulum and key.

32.5in (82.5cm) high

$3,000-4,000 **ROS**

A Victorian triple-fusee eight-day presentation mantle clock, with a carved oak Gothic Revival case of architectural form cased by John Hardman & Co, the dial with the Latin inscription 'Qui Habitat in Adiutorio Altissimi', dated.

1901 *23in (58cm) high*

$2,100-2,700 **HW**

An Edwardian mantel clock, by W Comyns London, the case with arched pediment, with white enamel dial with blue Arabic numerals.

1905 *8.5in (21cm) high*

$2,250-3,000 **L&T**

An early 20thC French four-glass mantel clock, the cylinder movement, stamped 'R. & Co., Paris' and numbered '5455', striking on a coiled gong and with mercury-filled pendulum, the champlevé-enameled circular dial with Arabic numerals, small dial crack.

10.75in (27cm) high

$1,800-2,250 **MOR**

An ebonized striking table clock, signed 'William Dale', London, twin-fusee movement with verge escapement and striking on a bell.

c1770 *20.5in (52cm) high*

$6,000-7,500 **TEN**

A Massachusetts Federal mahogany shelf clock, with a lunette-inlaid bonnet, a painted dial with urn and swag decoration, and French feet.

c1800 *42.5in (108cm) high*

$5,250-6,750 **POOK**

A Regency ormolu and white marble table clock, by Thomas Moss, London, with an eight-day chain-fusee movement.

c1815 *7.7in (19.5cm) high*

$1,500-2,250 **L&T**

A Regency ebonized striking table clock, signed 'Geo Beveridge', twin-fusee movement with anchor escapement and striking on a bell.

17.7in (45cm) high

$3,000-4,000 **TEN**

A Regency mahogany table clock, by Berquez, Cavendish Square, twin-fusee movement with anchor escapement and striking on a bell.

15.8in (40cm) high

$1,150-1,300 **TEN**

A mahogany striking table clock, signed 'Wm J Ainsby, Northampton', twin-fusee movement with platform lever escapement and striking on a gong.

c1870 *21.2in (54cm) high*

$1,800-2,250 **TEN**

A Victorian ebonized chiming table clock, signed 'J C Jennens, London', triple-fusee movement with anchor escapement and quarter chiming eight hammers striking a nest of eight bells and striking a further bell for the hours.

c1870 *15.8in (40cm) high*

$3,300-4,400 **TEN**

A 19thC Continental lacquered brass tabernacle table clock, with associated movement, the architectural case with spire finials and surmounted by figure of Thor.

15in (38cm) high

$2,700-3,300 **L&T**

A 19thC French stained snakeskin and gilt-bronze mounted table clock, with an eight-day movement striking on a bell.

4.7in (12cm) wide

$1,500-2,250 **L&T**

A 19thC Chinese striking table clock, twin-fusee movement with verge escapement and rack striking on a bell, on a stand with scroll feet.

19in (48.5cm) high

$2,250-3,000 **TEN**

A mahogany chiming table clock, arch with three dials for chime/silent, fast/slow and Cambridge/Westminster, triple-fusee movement with anchor escapement, quarter chiming with eight hammers striking eight bells and four hammers striking four gongs and a further hammer striking for the hours.

c1890 *28in (71cm) high*

$4,800-6,000 **TEN**

An ebonized chiming table clock, triple-barrel movement with anchor escapement, quarter chiming with four hammers striking four gongs and another hammer striking a gong for the hours, backplate stamped 'W&H Sch'.

c1890 *19.3in (49cm) high*

$1,500-2,100 **TEN**

An oak chiming table clock, three dials for chime/silent, fast/slow, Whittington/Westminster selections, triple-fusee movement with anchor escapement, quarter chiming with eight hammers striking a nest of eight bells or four hammers striking four gongs and a hammer striking a gong for the hours.

c1890 *24.8in (63cm) high*

$8,250-9,750 **TEN**

A miniature tortoiseshell table clock, by Asprey, London, the case with brass handle and ball feet, with a French movement.

c1910 *3.7in (9.5cm) high*

$1,200-1,800 **L&T**

A 20thC French champlevé enamel and onyz cased four-glass table clock, the twin barrel movement stamped 'Al 141848', twin mercury tube pendulum.

10.75in (27.3cm) high

$700-850 **HT**

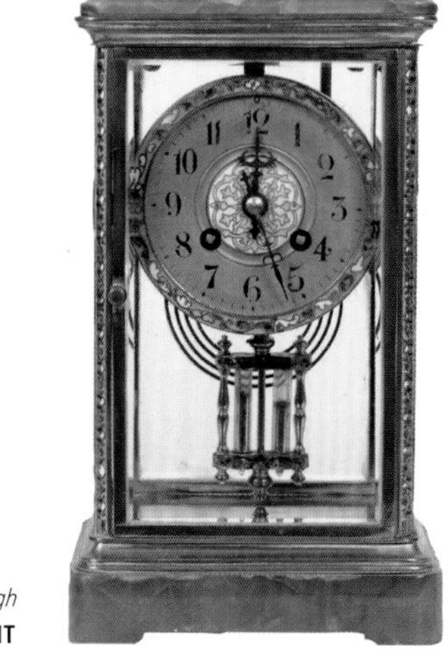

A modern orrery brass table clock, by the Devon Clock Company, the globe inscribed with motto of the year and signs of the zodiac over a two-train drum movement, with glass dome.

17.25in (44cm) high

$1,000-1,200 **HT**

ESSENTIAL REFERENCE - LANTERN CLOCKS

Thomas Knifton is recorded as born in Nottingham 1614 and apprenticed to William Sellwood in 1632 gaining his freedom of the Clockmakers' Company in 1640. He worked at the Cross Keys, Lothbury in St. Margarets Parish and at one time at the Draper's Arms. He died in January 1667 in the parish of St. Botolph's, Bishopsgate. He was a prolific maker of lantern clocks and was probably succeeded by John Ebsworth who invariably signed his early clocks with the same 'crossed keys' device. This clock was made to impress with the frame being of particularly large proportions. The incorporation of a pierced gallery above the movement top plate is perhaps first seen on a clock originally made with a balance wheel (probably dating to the 1640s) by David Bouquet. Relatively few lantern clocks with true enclosed galleries appear to have been made, however during the 1640s a pattern of fret was developed in order to give a similar visual impression; this type of fret was often used by Knifton. Technical developments, which included invention of the pendulum in 1658, resulted in a gradual overhaul of lantern clock design during the early 1660s. This clock would have been amongst one of the first made with verge escapement regulated by short bob pendulum.

A rare Charles II brass lantern clock, the posted countwheel bell striking movement with remote hour hammer pivoted between lugs above verge escapement set within the gallery and short bob pendulum now swinging within the frame of the case at the rear, the dial signed 'Thomas Knifton' at the (crossed keys) in Lothbury, London, with large 'Lothbury' type frame.

c1665 *19.75in (50cm) high*

$19,500-27,000 DN

A mid-17thC brass 'second period' lantern clock, the posted countwheel bell striking movement now with anchor escapement to the reversed going train, the dial with unusual tight concentric ring engraved center and long-tailed iron hand, with tied-asterisk half-hour markers and deep inner quarter-hour track with the first of each quarter division hatched, unsigned.

15in (38cm) high

$6,000-7,500 DN

A 17thC brass lantern clock, inscribed 'William Bowyer', single hand and concentric alarm disc, posted movement with verge escapement, top mounted bell.

15in (38cm) high

$30,000-38,000 L&T

A late 17thC Italian Lorenzo Riviera brass chamber clock, the two-train weight-driven posted countwheel bell striking movement configured with verge escapement mounted above the top plate and short bob pendulum swinging to the rear, the countwheel cut for Italian six hour striking with each count cut twice in order for the previous hour to be automatically repeated when activated by a second lifting pin positioned soon after the first, one finial, hand, escapement and elements of movement lacking, no pendulum or weights.

This appears to be a fairly typical example of an Italian 'lantern' clock dating to the end of the 17thC.

12in (30cm) high

$7,500-9,000 DN

A William III lantern clock, the posted countwheel bell striking movement with verge escapement and pendulum swinging within the frame of the clock between the trains, the dial signed 'Jos: Foster in Exchange Alley', the standard 'third period' 'Lothbury' type frame.

Joseph Foster is recorded in Baillie, G.H. Watchmakers & Clockmakers of the World as apprenticed in 1684, gaining his freedom of the Clockmakers' Company in 1691 and working from Exchange Alley, London until 1707.

c1695 *15.5in (39cm) high*

$8,250-9,750 DN

An early 18thC lantern clock, by William Jackson of Loughborough, the 30-hour movement has a verge escapement and the movement is countwheel striking on the bell, verge shaft and crown wheel renewed.

c1730 *15.5in (39.4cm) high*

$6,000-7,500 TRI

A late 19thC brass lantern clock, the chapter ring detailed 'AYSELIN LONDON', with a two-train fusee movement.

15.25in (39cm) high

$750-900 BELL

An English humpback carriage timepiece, dial signed 'DENT/82 STRAND/LONDON', nickel case with an ivory handle, the eight-day fusee movement with English lever platform escapement, stamped 'no473'.
c1835 *5.5in (14cm) high*
$27,000-36,000 **L&T**

A French chased gilt-brass carriage clock, the eight-day two-train bell striking movement with substantial transverse gilt platform lever escapement, 'N. 3294. LE ROY & FILS H'GERS DU ROI A PARIS', with conforming serial number '3294'.

The firm of Le Roy & Fils can be traced back to 1785 when the business was founded by Basille Charles Le Roy at 60 Galerie de Pierre, Palais Royal, Paris.

c1845 *6in (15cm) high excluding handle*
$850-975 **DN**

A giant patinated bronze repeating carriage clock, subsidiary seconds dial and inscribed 'JAMES MCCABE/ ROYAL EXCHANGE/LONDON/2888', the 8-day twin-chain double-fusee movement striking on a gong.

James McCabe was apprenticed to Reid and Auld, Edinburgh and became Free of the Clockmakers' Company in 1822.

c1850 *9.8in (25cm) high (handle up)*
$18,000-22,500 **L&T**

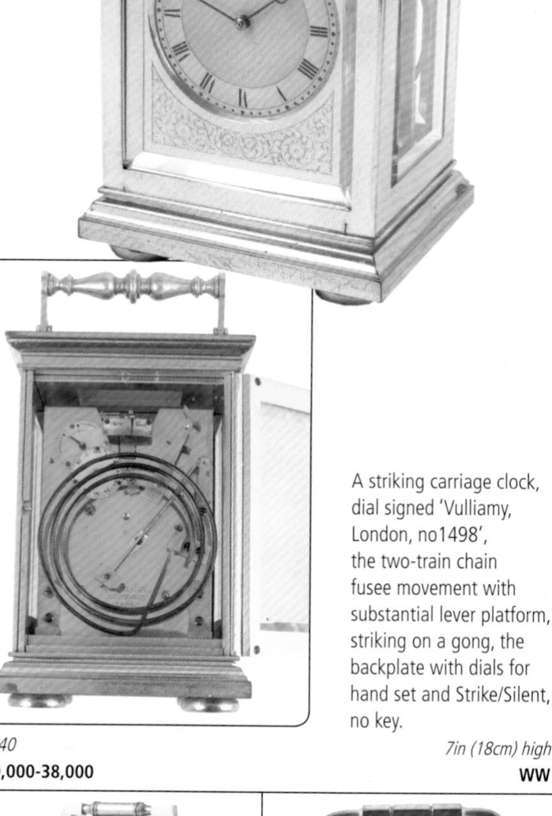

A striking carriage clock, dial signed 'Vulliamy, London, no1498', the two-train chain fusee movement with substantial lever platform, striking on a gong, the backplate with dials for hand set and Strike/Silent, no key.
c1840 *7in (18cm) high*
$30,000-38,000 **WW**

A mid-19thC English gilt brass repeating carriage clock, signed 'JAMES McCABE/ROYAL EXCHANGE/LONDON/3506', the eight-day double fusee movement with an English lever platform escapement, repeating and striking on a gong.
6.7in (17cm) high
$19,500-27,000 **L&T**

A mid-19thC French gilt brass 'pendule de voyage', by Berthoud, the reeded handle with swan neck supports, signed 'BERTHOUD', eight- day movement with spring detent platform, with remontoir, hour striking on a gong.
10.4in (26.5cm) high excluding handle
$16,500-21,000 **L&T**

A giant carriage clock, the porcelain dial decorated with birds and gilt foliage, chapter ring signed 'Vokes, Bath', the repeating movement numbered '591', with massive lever platform, in a case of pagoda form flanked by bamboo columns.
c1880 *9in (23cm) high*
$9,750-11,250 **WW**

A late 19thC French grand sonnierie brass carriage clock, a repeating gong striking movement, with a leather travelling case.
4.3in (11cm) high
$2,250-3,000 **L&T**

A late 19thC French brass repeating carriage clock, with a Hong Kong retailer's name, the double-fusee movement striking on a gong.

5.7in (14.5cm) high

$1,000-1,200 **L&T**

A late 19thC French brass carriage timepiece, with calendar, unsigned, the eight-day movement with platform cylinder escapement, with twin subsidiary day of the week and date of the month dials, case stamped 'H.A. BREVETTE S.G.D.G.', hairlines to dial.

11.5cm (4.5ins) high excluding handle

$600-750 **DN**

A gilt-brass porcelain mounted striking carriage clock, with blue porcelain side panels depicting figures in costume, twin-barrel movement with platform lever escapement and striking on a gong.

c1890 *6.7in (17cm) high (handle up)*

$4,400-5,100 **TEN**

A silver striking and repeating carriage clock, stamped for 'Drocourt', twin-barrel movement with platform lever escapement and striking on a gong, backplate stamped 'DC' and numbered '32232', with travelling case.

1895 *4.7in (12cm) high (handle up)*

$3,750-4,500 **TEN**

A striking carriage clock, bell striking movement numbered '4507', cylinder escapement, in an obis case, ticking but requires overhaul, white enamel dial restored, case with signs of wear.

5.25in (13cm) high

$280-340 **WW**

A French brass petite sonnerie striking carriage clock, with decorated porcelain panels, push-button repeat and alarm, retailed by Anglo Swiss Watch Company, Calcutta, the eight-day two-train movement ting-tang striking the quarters on two gongs and sounding the hour on the larger of the two, with silvered platform lever escapement.

c1900 *6.75in (17cm) high excluding handle*

$4,000-5,250 **DN**

A 'Pendule D'Officier' striking clock, retailed by Hunt & Roskell Ltd, 25 Old Bond St W, twin barrel movement with striking on a gong, platform lever escapement.

c1910 *8.7in (22cm) high (handle up)*

$1,500-2,100 **TEN**

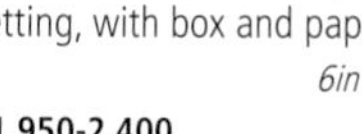

A reproduction calendar carriage clock with moonphase, the striking and repeating movement with lever platform, signed 'L'Epee', with subsidiaries for date, day and alarm setting, with box and paperwork.

6in (15cm) high

$1,950-2,400 **WW**

A late 19thC George III style mahogany carriage clock case, in the Chippendale manner, of pagoda form carved throughout with foliage, rococo scrolls and acanthus, the stand raised on molded cabriole legs terminating in claw and ball feet.

20in (50cm) high

$1,400-1,800 **L&T**

A mid-19thC Victorian lacquered brass 'Litchfield Cathedral' hour-striking skeleton clock, with trip repeat, attributed to John Smith and Sons, London, for retail by Rhodes, Bradford, the twin-chain fusee gong striking movement with anchor escapement and five-spoke wheel crossings, mounted on original inlaid rosewood stand cut with rebate for the original glass dome cover.

This clock can be attributed to John Smith and Sons of St. John's Square, Clerkenwell, and can be compared to the design published in their 1865 catalog. The firm of John Smith and Sons was established in 1780 and became one of the largest manufacturers of both domestic and public clocks throughout the 19thC.

16.25in (41cm) high

$3,750-4,500 **DN**

A mid-19thC Victorian small brass fusee skeleton timepiece, the single chain fusee movement with six-spoke wheel crossings and anchor escapement set between stepped 'Gothic' pierced plates, unsigned.

10.75in (27cm) high overall

$450-600 **DN**

A late 19thC Victorian brass skeleton clock, the single-chain fusee movement with an anchor escapement and striking on a bell, with a glass dome and stand.

clock 17.7in (45cm) high

$900-1,000 **L&T**

A late 19thC English brass Gothic cathedral clock.

18.5in (47cm) high

$1,200-1,500 **L&T**

A mid-20thC brass skeleton 'Congreve' clock, made by Varleys of Norwich, chiming on a bell, with spirit levels to front and left side, adjustment screws front and back.

clock 19.7in (50cm) high

$2,250-3,000 **SWO**

A 20thC decorative brass skeleton timepiece, the single-fusee movement with anchor escapement, with a stepped ogee-molded Carrara marble base with glass dome cover, unsigned, no key.

17.5in (44cm) high

$900-1,000 **DN**

A French marble and gilt metal crystal pendulum mystery clock, by Guilmet, the pendulum supported by a gilt lady clasping the hand of a cherub, figures have been over-painted.

23in (58cm) high

$6,750-8,250 **WW**

A miniature desk clock, the engine turned blue enamel domed case enriched with gilt, in a leather case.

c1900 *2.8in (7cm) high*

$1,500-2,250 **L&T**

A late 19thC miniature French birdcage automaton desk clock, the cage with an hours sphere and a pivoting songbird.

6in (15cm) high

$550-700 **L&T**

A gilt-bronze and porcelain striking mantel clock with garniture, signed 'Balthazard, A Paris', twin-barrel movement with outside countwheel striking, silk suspension, backplate stamped 'Villard A Paris' and 'no1619'.

c1850 *28.7in (73cm) wide*

$10,500-12,000 **TEN**

A 19thC French gilt bronze and 'jeweled' Sevres style porcelain clock garniture, by Japy Freres, the movement with Japy freres medaille d'honneur cachet, with inset porcelain plaques depicting 18thC figures.

clock 11.5in (29cm) wide

$5,250-6,000 **FRE**

A 19thC French onyx gilt brass and champlevé clock garniture, the twin-train movement striking on a gong and with a mercury pendulum.

clock *13.8in (35cm) high*

$2,100-2,700 **L&T**

An ormolu and porcelain striking mantel clock with garniture, twin-barrel movement striking on a bell, backplate stamped 'Japy Freres' and 'no6898'.

c1880 *clock 16.5in (42cm) high*

$2,400-3,000 **TEN**

An ormolu and champlevé enamel striking mantel clock with candlestick garniture, with twin-barrel movement striking on a bell, backplate stamped 'AF' and numbered '1097'.

16.5in (42cm) high

$5,250-6,750 **TEN**

A late 19thC French gilt and pocelain garniture de cheminée, comprising the clock and two four-branch candelabra. The clock's movement is rack striking on a bell.

clock 21in (53cm) high

$2,100-2,700 **TRI**

A late 19thC Louis XV-style gilt-bronze and pink ground procelain clock garniture, the eight-day movement striking on a bell.

clock 13in (33cm) high

$2,250-3,000 **L&T**

A late 19thC French Sévres-style porcelain inset gilt metal mantel clock garniture, retailed by Steel and Sons Limited, Belfast, with eight-day bell striking movement.

16.75in (42.5cm) high

$1,300-1,450 **DN**

A late 19thC French three-piece clock set, the bronze spherical clock with brass eight-day movement.

clock 8in (20cm) high

$700-850 **DA&H**

A Maple and Co. champlevé enamel and ormolu clock garniture of Louis XV style, an eight-day striking movement, with bell back plate inscribed 'Maple and Co Paris'.

clock 10.75in (27.5 cm) high

$3,000-4,000 **HW**

A late 19thC Vienna style porcelain mantel timepiece, with a matched pair of pedestal vases painted by Rosner, signed.

clock 13in (33cm) high

$1,950-2,400 **HT**

A four-glass gilt champlevé enamel striking mantel clock with garniture, twin-barrel movement striking on a gong.

c1890 *16.5in (42cm) high*

$5,250-6,000 **TEN**

A late 19thC French gilt-brass and champlevé enamel mounted green onyx four-glass mantel clock garniture, the movement by S. Marti and Cie, Paris, the eight-day circular gong striking movement stamped with 'S. Marti et Cie, Médaille d'argent 1889' roundel.

clock 13.5in (34cm) high

$2,700-3,300 **DN**

A French silvered and porcelain mounted striking mantel clock with garniture, twin-barrel movement striking on a gong, backplate stamped 'R&C for C.A Richard et Cie' and 'no2014'.

c1890 *22.4in (57cm)high 16.5in (42cm) high*

$9,000-10,500 **TEN**

A late 19thC French Noir Belge marble and bronze figural mantel clock garniture, the eight-day bell striking movement.

clock 19in (48cm) high 48cm (19ins) high

$450-600 **DN**

An onyx and champlevé enamel four-glass striking mantel clock with garniture, twin-barrel movement striking on a gong, backplate no5362.

13in (33.5cm) high

$1,500-2,100 **TEN**

A early 20thC French porcelain and gilt metal three-piece clock garniture, in the Louis XVI style, case stamped 'BRUNFAUT', the eight-day movement stamped 'P.R.7267' and striking on a bell.

clock 20in (50cm) high

$3,000-4,000 **L&T**

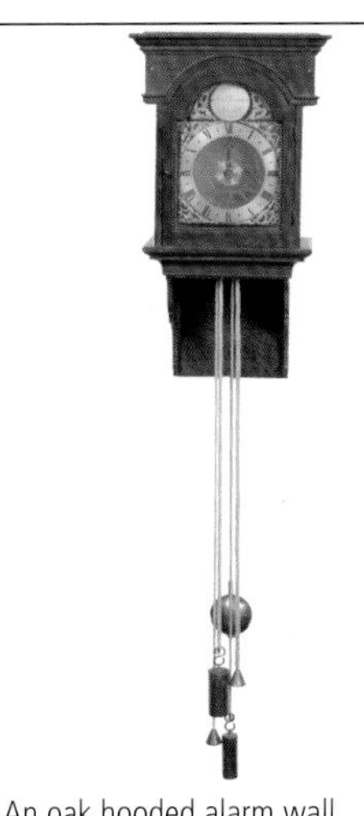

An oak hooded alarm wall timepiece, signed 'Richd Comber, Lewes', four-posted movement with anchor escapement, alarm striking on a top mounted bell.

c1780 *21in (53cm) high*

$4,500-6,000 **TEN**

A late 18thC George III black japanned tavern clock, the current six-pillar two-train rack-and-bell striking movement with four-wheel trains and anchor escapement, the case with signature 'Mann & Wall', door decorated in raised polychrome and gilt with oriental figures in an ornamental garden, the case signed for Mann and Wall, Coventry.

The partnership between Mann and Wall is recorded as working in Coventry from 1787. Evidence in the dial (unused single winding hole) suggests that the current lot was originally made as a timepiece only. The current hour-striking movement is a subsequent (possibly early) 'upgrade' which has been with the case for a long time, and was made in the late 18th/early 19th century for use in a tavern clock.

56.5in (143cm) high

$7,500-9,000 **DN**

A George III red japanned tavern timepiece, signed 'Rich. Lawrence, Bath', movement with anchor escapement in tapered plates, the door decorated with Chinese figures by a lake with pagoda in the background.

59in (150cm) high

$18,000-22,500 **WW**

A late 18th/early 19thC George III mahogany wall clock, inscribed 'Thos. Applewhite, London' with saltbox backboard.

16.5in (42cm) diam

$3,000-4,500 **L&T**

A brass inlaid drop dial wall clock, signed 'Barraud, Cornhill, London' , later single-train fusee movement.

21.5in (55cm) high

$4,500-5,250 **WW**

A Scottish Regency mahogany and brass inlaid wall clock, by Alexander Hood, Dumfermline, with a single-train fusee movement.

c1820 *17.3in (44cm) wide*

$900-1,200 **L&T**

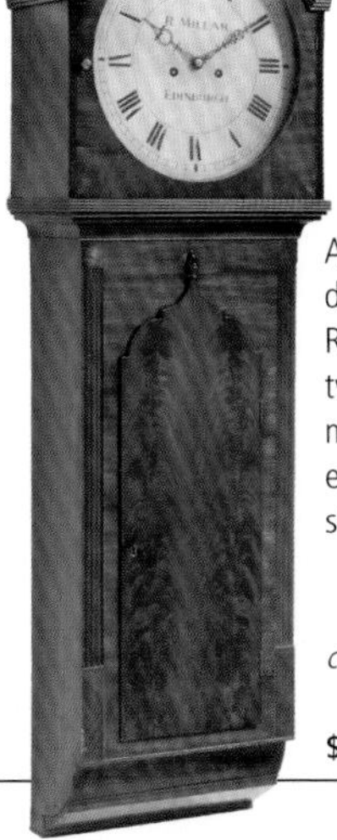

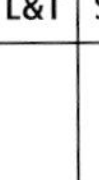

A mahogany drop dial wall clock, by R Millar, Edinburgh, twin weight-driven movement with anchor escapement and striking on a bell.

c1820 *57.5in (146cm) high*

$1,500-2,100 **TEN**

A rosewood drop dial striking wall clock, twin-fusee movement with anchor escapement and striking on a bell.

c1830 *28.4in (72cm) high*

$700-850 **TEN**

An oak striking wall clock, twin-fusee movement with anchor escapement and striking on a bell, backplate stamped 'JW Benson'.

c1850 *40.6in (103cm) high*

$975-1,150 **TEN**

A mahogany wall timepiece, by Henry Raw, Baxter Gate, Whitby, single fusee movement with anchor escapement and maintaining power, backplate no9820.

c1860 *22.4in (57cm) high*

$2,700-3,300 **TEN**

A 19thC brass wall clock, the dial inscribed 'E. Dent & Co. 61 Strand & 34, Royal Exchange, London', the single chain fusee movement with an anchor escapement.

10.6in (27cm) diam

$3,000-4,500 **L&T**

A 19thC rosewood eight-day fusee wall clock, dial marked 'William Hay, Wolverhampton', some damage.

25in (64cm) high

$1,800-2,250 **FLD**

A mahogany striking wall clock, by Whittington, Manchester, twin fusee movement with anchor escapement and striking on a bell.

c1870 *15.4in (39cm) high*

$850-975 **TEN**

ESSENTIAL REFERENCE - JOHANN BEHA

Johann Baptist Beha was born in Oberbrand in 1815 and was trained as a clockmaker by his father, Vinzenz, before setting-up on his own in Eisenbach in 1845. He specialized in cuckoo clocks and through his continuous development became the leading maker of fine and complex examples. His main export markets were to Russia, where he had a distribution warehouse in St. Petersburg, and the British Isles. He died in 1898 leaving the business to be continued by his sons Lorenz and Engelbert. The design of this clock appears in a surviving drawing by Lorenz Beha dated 1874 and was produced in very small numbers. The monk automaton is activated alongside the 'Angelus' striking which is intended to mark the time of prayer for the Catholic daily liturgy.

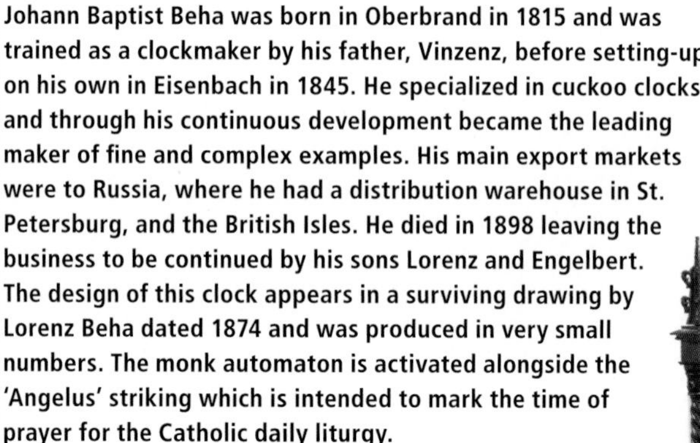

A Black Forest carved walnut weight-driven 'Angelus' cuckoo wall clock, attributed to Johann Baptist Beha, Eisenbach, the wooden-framed triple train weight-driven movement with anchor escapement and wood-rod pendulum carved with Gothic tracery to bob, the striking train with external countwheel and linkages to two bellows and a cuckoo automaton which appears from behind a pair of doors within the gable of the case to announce the hour with a two-note call followed by the hour repeated on a gong, the third train with further countwheel and linkages to a monk who appears within an arched recess beneath the dial to apparently ring a bell set within the tower at six am., twelve noon and six pm, some losses to the case.

c1875 *32.5in (82cm) high*

$9,000-10,500 **DN**

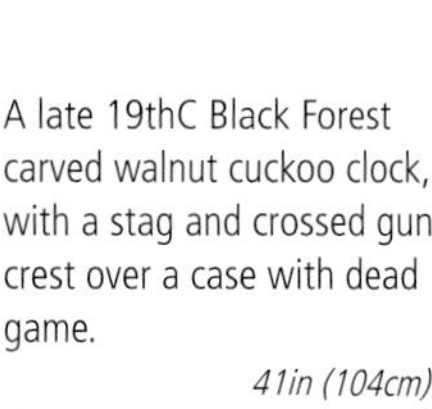

A late 19thC Black Forest carved walnut cuckoo clock, with a stag and crossed gun crest over a case with dead game.

41in (104cm) high

$1,500-2,100 **POOK**

A mahogany eight-inch drop-dial wall timepiece, by Heathcote, Derby, single fusee movement with anchor escapement.

c1890 *15.8in (40cm) high*

$1,300-1,450 **TEN**

ESSENTIAL REFERENCE - BREGUET

Breguet was founded in 1775 by Abraham-Louis Breguet, a Swiss watchmaker born to Hugenot parents in Neuchâtel. He studied watchmaking for 10 years under Ferdinand Berthoud and Jean-Antoine Lépine before setting up his own watchmaking business in Paris at 51 Quai de l'Horloge on the Île de la Cité in Paris. The dowry that came with his marriage to the daughter of a prosperous French bourgeois provided the backing which allowed him to open his own workshop. Breguet's connections made during his apprenticeship as a watchmaker and as a student of mathematics helped him to establish his business. Following his introduction to the court, Queen Marie Antoinette grew fascinated by Breguet's unique self-winding watch, Louis XVI bought several of his watches and legend has it that Marie Antoinette commissioned the watch that was to contain every watch function known at that time – Breguet's masterpiece, the 'Marie Antoinette'.

An early 20thC 18k gold cased 'Repitition' Carillon chronograph, no18813, the full hunter case opening to reveal a keyless carillon striking movement.

2.75in (6cm) diam

$2,100-2,700 **HW**

A gold and enamel verge watch, the movement signed 'Breguet a Paris no12272', in a consular case, the back with an enamel scene of lovers in a classical landscape, chip to right side

c1790 *2.1in (54mm) diam*

$7,500-9,000 **WW**

A late 18thC gold fusee verge repeating pocket watch, movement signed 'Dufalga, Geneva'.

2in (5.1cm) diam

$2,000-2,400 **ECGW**

A Victorian silver pocket watch fusee chronometer, by John Forrest, maker to the Admiralty, key not working.

2.5in (6.4cm) diam

$225-300 **ECGW**

A French gilt metal and enamel verge watch, signed 'Grissey a Paris, no129', both hands broken.

2.2in (55mm) diam

$1,950-2,400 **WW**

A silver military wristwatch, black 24 hour dial signed 'G.C.T.' (Greenwich Civil Time), keyless lever movement signed 'Hamilton Watch Co, U.S.A. 4992B', 22 jewels, back inscribed 'AN5740 Mfrs part no. 4992B, Serial no1985-43, Contract no86366'.

c1940 *2in (52mm) diam*

$1,800-2,250 **WW**

A fine 18ct gold hunting cased keyless lever split seconds chronograph, dial signed 'Hardy Bros, London & Sydney', twin subsidiaries for running seconds and 60 minute recording, the movement with micrometer adjustment, London.

1888 *2in (5.5cm) diam*

$14,250-16,500 **WW**

A heavy 18ct gold quarter repeating duplex watch, full plain movement signed 'C. Harris, Cornhill, London, no2969', flat steel three armed balance, diamond endstone, in a guilloche case London.

1820 *2.2in (56mm) diam*

$3,750-4,500 **WW**

A rare documentary English gold and enamel duplex pocket watch, made for the Chinese market, by William Ilbery, the movement profusely engraved with scrolling foliage and flowerheads, the duplex escapement with a five-armed steel balance and diamond endstone, signed 'Ilbery, London, no5825', the reverse finely decorated with eight peacock feathers, all on a dark blue basse taille enamel ground.

The interior is inscribed 'From the Summer Palace, Pekin, Chinese War 1860, Captn. T.A.J. Harrison, R.A.'.
William Ilbery (1780-1839), specialized in watches for the Chinese market, and appears to have introduced the style now known as 'la montre Chinoise', in which the decoration of the movement, as well as the highly decorated case-work, became a principal feature.

c1820 *2.3in (5.8cm) diam*

$150,000-225,000 **WW**

An 18K gold cased five minute repeater pocket watch, in full hunting cases and keyless wind, patent action for setting the hands, patented January 15th 1867, signed' Jules Jurgensen' and 'no12242', in the original fitted mahogany case.

$4,800-6,000 **L&T**

A Victorian 18ct gold half-hunter pocket watch, with lever escapement, by Lambert, Coventry Street, London, back engraved with church, Birmingham.

1885 *2in (5cm) diam*

$1,450-1,700 **ECGW**

An 18ct gold open faced keyless pocket watch, signed 'Limit', lever movement, stamped 'ALD' and 'no99341', with 18ct gold watch chain, each link stamped '18, 37g'.

1945 2in (50m) wide

$2,250-3,000 **TEN**

An 18thC enameled ball pendant ladies watch, the case with the figure of Cephisa clipping Cupid's wings, movement signed 'Mayer La Ville ??' and 'a Vienne NO 138'.

1.2in (31mm) diam

$1,950-2,400 **ECGW**

An early 20thC 'Goliath' chrome pocket watch, by M M Co Patent Light System, light apperture to XII.

2.8in (70mm) diam

$165-210 **LOCK**

A Swiss gold cased pocket watch, by Patek Capek & Co., 'no737' plain lever movement, glass lacking. Dial

1.23in (36mm) diam

$6,750-8,250 **L&T**

An 18ct gold open faced center seconds keyless pocket watch, signed ' Josh Penlington, Liverpool, No.15826', fusee lever movement, maker's initials 'HW' and numbered '15826'.

1884 *2in (51mm) wide*

$1,500-2,250 **TEN**

A quarter repeating duplex watch, attributed to Sigismund Rentzsch, the gold dial with fine foliate engraving, in a machine-turned case.

c1835 *1.6in (40mm) diam*

$3,000-4,000 WW

An 18ct gold full hunter keyless pocket watch, signed 'Russells, 18 Church St, Liverpool', lever movement no10379, stamped with maker's mark 'TR', with original box.

1884 *2in (50mm) wide*

$2,250-3,000 TEN

A 9ct gold full hunter keyless pocket watch, lever movement stamped 'S&Co, Peerless' and 'noH6 709607 55231', maker's mark 'FT' and no'2457', with two-color watch chain, T-bar and clasp stamped 18c.

1923 *2in (50mm) wide*

$1,500-2,100 TEN

A 18ct gold full hunter 'Karrusel' center seconds pocket watch, signed 'S Smith & Son, 9 Strand, London, 191-372', 'Maker's to the Admiralty', Class A Certificate Kew Observatory, karrusel lever movement no191.372/25589, diamond endstone and bimetallic balance, with 15ct gold watch chain.

1908 *2.1in (55mm) wide*

$6,750-7,500 TEN

An 18ct gold half hunter keyless pocket watch, with full armorial of Baron Llangattock, signed 'D & J Wellby, Garrick Street, London, 1898', lever movement no04754, free sprung blued overcoil hairspring, bimetallic balance, stamped 'JA'.

John Allan Rolls, 1st Baron Llangattock (1837-1912), and father of Charles Stewart Rolls, the pioneer motorist, aviator and founding partner of Rolls Royce.

1.9in (48mm) wide

$4,500-5,250 TEN

A late 19thC 18ct full hunter, crown wind pocket watch, engraved 'Presented to Inspector Bugby by the principle inhabitants in the district of the H Division of the Metropolitan Police in recognition of the gentlemanly manner in which he has performed his duties of his office during the 17 years of his service as inspector. 16th March 1886', case stamped '18k'.

$1,300-1,450 FLD

An 18ct gold full hunter pocket watch, fusee lever movement, no17597, front cover with blue enamel monogram.

1869 *1.9in (47mm) wide*

$1,650-2,100 TEN

A green enamel, 18ct gold and diamond set pendant fob watch, plain lever movement, unsigned.

0.8in (20mm) diam

$1,350-1,650 L&T

A Cartier gold and steel 'Panthere Vendome' wristwatch, serial no183964/18597, silvered dial with date at 3 o'clock and center seconds, flexible bracelet, with box.

1.3in (32mm) diam

$2,250-3,000 **WW**

A Corum Admiral's Cup GMT gentleman's stainless steel wristwatch, luminous hands, red luminous 24-hour indicator hand, a Corum logo center seconds hand and date aperture, 21 jewel Corum automatic movement, cal. ETA 2899-2, on a black crocodile strap with double fold-over clasp, ref01.0055 2238827, no0279/2000.

$1,800-2,250 **DN**

A Hamilton Automatic estoril gold-plated gentleman's wristwatch, attached to link bracelet with folding clasp.

1.4in (35mm) wide

$225-300 **LOCK**

A gentlemen's German Hanhart WW2 'Heer Kriegsmarine and Luftwaffe' pilot's watch, case marked 'Boden Edelstahl Wassergeschutzt Stossfest'.

40mm) diam

$3,000-4,000 **SWO**

A Jaeger-LeCoultre Master Control 1000 Hours a gentleman's 18-carat gold wristwatch, 36 jewel Jaeger-LeCoultre 1000 hour automatic movement adjusted to six positions, no. 2920741, ref. 984/2/447, on a brown strap with a Jaeger-LeCoultre 18-carat gold fold-over clasp, in box.

c2000 *the case 1.75in (4.3cm) wide*

$7,500-9,000 **DN**

A Jaeger-LeCoultre Master Compressor gentleman's stainless-steel chronograph wristwatch, 41 jewel Jaeger-LeCoultre 1000 hour automatic chronograph movement, cal. 751, no. 3489765, on an alligator strap with a double fold-over clasp, in box.

2in (4.9cm) wide

$10,500-12,000 **DN**

A Franck Muller Long Island lady's 18-carat gold and diamond wristwatch, 5-jewel Swiss Ronda quartz movement, cal. 772, on a black strap with an 18-carat gold and diamond-set buckle, in a Franck Muller pouch, ref. 950 QZD, no. 578.

c2000 *the case 2in (4.5cm) wide*

$9,000-10,500 **DN**

A gentleman's Longines wristwatch, the automatic movement in a plain tonneau case, on an integral polished stainless steel bracelet, cased with warranty card and instruction booklets.

$750-900 **HT**

An Omega James Bond Limited Edition steel seamaster wristwatch, Ref. 22268000, watch no. 81733698, co-axial escapement on flexible bracelet, no. 05095 of an edition of 10,007, with box and all original packaging.

c2006 *1.8in (45mm) diam*

$2,250-3,000 **WW**

A Vacheron & Constantin gentleman's 18-carat white-gold wristwatch, 17 jewel Vacheron & Constantin slim movement adjusted to heat-cold isochronisms and five positions, cal. 1003, no581269, on a black Vacheron & Constantin strap with an 18-carat white-gold buckle, ref. 6506, no409873.

c1960 *case 1.5in (3.8cm) wide*

$5,250-6,000 **DN**

A Rolex early 1930s Oyster wrist watch, movement 'Rolex Extra Prima' 15 jewels, timed six positions for all climates, case excluding winder.

1.2in (30mm) wide

$2,100-2,700 **L&T**

A Rolex gentleman's stainless-steel wristwatch, 17 jewel Rolex chronograph valjoux movement, monometallic balance and overcoil balance spring, on a black strap with Rolex buckle, in a Rolex case, ref.2508.

c1940 *case 2in (4.5cm) wide*

$15,000-21,000 **DN**

A Rolex gentleman's 18ct white gold dress watch, Cellini, dial, inscribed, with baton numerals, Rolex crown at 12, rounded rectangular bezel, integral flexible bracelet, the movement 1600 calibre, 19 rubies.

c1970

$1,500-2,250 **L&T**

A Rolex 18ct gold diamond set oyster perpetual day-date wristwatch, ref18048, serial no6446076, the dial with two baguettes and eight round diamonds, the bezel set with forty four diamonds, on president bracelet with concealed clasp, with tag and box.

c1980 *1.5in (39mm) diam*

$11,500-12,750 **WW**

A lady's 18 carat gold Rolex bracelet watch, Oyster Perpetual Datejust model, diamond markers, President bracelet with crown clasp, Reference 69178, case no. X982505, complete with original box, paperwork and seal.

c1990s

$6,000-7,500 **MAB**

A Rolex Cellini gentleman's 18-carat white gold wristwatch, 8 jewel Rolex quartz movement, cal.6620, on an 18-carat white-gold Úimler' bracelet with fold-over clasp. ref. 6622, noX606976.

c1991 *case 1.75in (4.3cm) wide*

$3,750-4,500 **DN**

A Rolex gentleman's 18-carat gold Oyster perpetual day date wrist watch, all gold case, diamond set numerals, President bracelet, fold over clasp, serial no. X623846 Model no. 18238, with leather case, gilt buckle with Rolex motif.

c1991-93 *1.1in (28mm) diam*

$10,500-12,000 **L&T**

A Rolex Oyster perpetual day-date gentleman's 18-carat gold wristwatch, 31 jewel Rolex automatic movement adjusted to five positions and temperature, cal. 3136, no. 32771669, on a block-link bracelet with fold-over clasp.

c2008 *case 2in (5cm) wide*

$19,500-24,000 **DN**

An unusual 18ct gold padlock-form bracelet watch by Rolex, the dial signed Rolex, Precision, ref 88520n an 18ct gold curb link bracelet signed 'Rolex S.A.' One link with a small padlock key attached, with box.

$6,000-7,500 **WW**

A Rolex Precision 9 carat gold gentleman`s wristwatch, the case numbered '15037', attached to 9 carat gold bracelet with folding clasp,

1.3in (33mm) wide

$1,500-2,100 **LOCK**

A mid-18thC George II mahogany stick barometer, by Joseph Hurt, London, with a silvered veneer thermometer.

Joseph Jurt, fl.1729-48 is recorded at Archimedes and Three Golden Spectacles, Ludgate Street, London.

39.4in (100cm) high

$3,000-4,000 L&T

A George III mahogany and crossbanded stick barometer, by Thomas Blunt, London, the silvered vernier signed 'Blunt, Royal Exchange, London', with a mercury thermometer, the case with broken-pediment above a hand-set hygrometer.

c1780 42.5in (108cm) high

$4,500-6,000 L&T

A late 18thC Scottish mahogany stick barometer, with a silvered brass plate with thermometer/ barometer gauges, inscribed 'P. MASINO, EDIN'.

39in (99cm) high

$1,400-1,500 L&T

A mahogany stick barometer, the silvered register plate signed 'Made by Geo. Adams in Fleet Street, London, Instrumt Maker to His Majesty'.

38.5in (98cm) high

$4,500-6,000 WW

A George III mahogany stick barometer with ivory plaque, inscribed 'Blunt, No 22 Cornhill, London', with swan neck cornice and hygrometer dial.

38in (97cm) high

$4,000-4,500 SWO

ESSENTIAL REFERENCE - EDWARD NAIRNE

Edward Nairne was born in 1726 and apprenticed to the celebrated instrument maker Matthew Loft in 1741. Latterly he worked from 20 Cornhill and published numerous booklets on navigational, pneumatic and astronomical instruments. In 1776 Nairne devised a marine barometer with a restriction in the bore of the mercury tube which served to dampen the oscillation of the mercury. He was elected to the Royal Society in the same year. In 1774 he formed a loose partnership with his former apprentice Thomas Blunt, perhaps for mutual convenience as Blunt's premises were next door to Nairne's at 22 Cornhill. Edward Nairne is believed to have retired to Chelsea in 1801 and died in 1806.

A late 18thC George III London Edward Nairne mahogany mercury stick barometer, the caddy molded arch-top case inset with circular glazed hygrometer with independent adjustment, via a brass turn-screw set beneath, operating a pair of visible geared wheels fitted to the rear, over vernier scale calibrated in barometric inches.

41in (104cm) high

$7,500-9,000 DN

An 18thC George III mahogany stick barometer, with thermometer and barometer scales, engraved 'Somalvico Lione & Co. 125 Holbn, London', the chequer-banded case ending in a ball cistern.

39.3in (100cm) high

$1,500-2,250 L&T

A George III mahogany stick barometer, the silvered vernier signed 'E. Marzorati, FECIT', with a broken arched pediment and a brass urn finial.

c1800 39.8in (101cm) high

$600-900 L&T

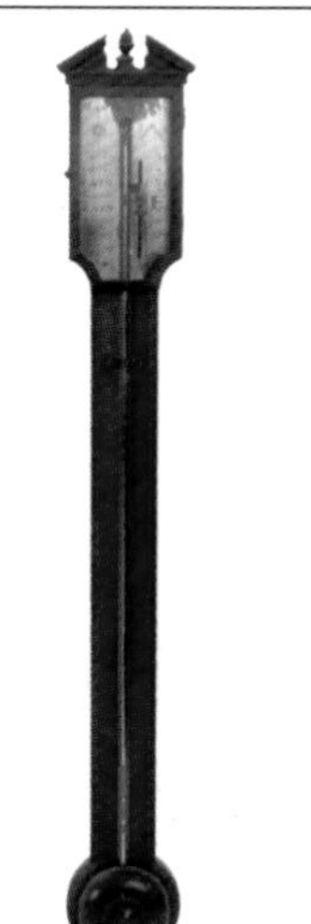

A George III mahogany stick barometer, with chequer stringing, the silvered register engraved with Masonic symbols, and inscribed 'Manticha Fecit'.

38in (97cm) high

$1,350-1,650 SWO

A George III mahogany stick barometer, the silvered dial inscribed 'Geo. Adams, Fleet St., London', with a brass urn finial and broken arm pediment, ivory knob and ebony stringing.

40.7in (103.5cm) high

$3,750-4,500 SWO

A Georgian mahogany wheel barometer with inlaid shells, and chequer stringing, the dial signed 'J M Rokelli, Holborn London'.

36in (92cm) high

$2,250-3,000 SWO

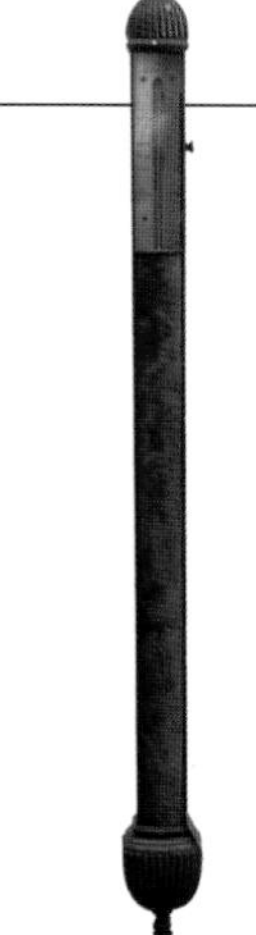

An early 19thC Scottish mahogany stick barometer, by Alexander Adie, Edinburgh, the reeded dome pediment over a bow front case and cistern cover, the silvered dial with a single gauge and sliding vernier, inscribed 'Adie, Edinburgh'.

40.6in (103cm) high

$11,500-12,750 L&T

A Mahogany Stick Barometer, signed J Poncione, Colombo & Co, No.180 High Holborn, London, circa 1820, broken arched pediment, visible mercury tube, turned cistern, single silvered vernier dial signed, thermometer tube.

38.2in (97cm) high

$375-450 TEN

A mahogany wheel barometer, signed 'Gardners, Glasgow', with hygrometer, thermometer box, rectangular framed spirit level.

c1820 *39in (99cm) high*

$1,200-1,400 TEN

ESSENTIAL REFERENCE - ADIE & SON

Born in 1774 Alexander Adie was the nephew of the renowned Scottish instrument maker, John Millar. Adie became his uncle's apprentice in 1789 and his business partner, under the name of Miller and Adie, in 1804. The business continued to flourish after Miller's death in 1815. Adie was predominately interested in meteorological instruments and notably invented the Sympiesometer, or marine barometer, in 1818. Appointed as optician to both William IV and Queen Victoria, his success was formerly recognized when he was elected a Fellow of the Royal Society of Edinburgh in 1819. He brought one of his sons, John, into partnership in 1835, while two of his other sons set up businesses in London and Liverpool.

A Scottish Regency mahogany barometer, by Adie & Son, with silvered vernier, the bow fronted case with reeded domed pagoda top and urn finial, corresponding bulbous base with lotus leaf pendant.

41.7in (106cm) high

$12,750-14,250 DN

ESSENTIAL REFERENCE - EDWARD TROUGHTON

This barometer was probably made by Edward Troughton who is recorded in 'Clifton, Gloria Directory of British Scientific Instrument Makers 1550-1851' as first working in partnership with his brother, John from several addresses in London (including Queen's Square, Bartholemew and 136 Fleet Street) from 1788 until John's death in 1804. Edward continued alone from their Fleet Street address until 1826 when he formed a partnership with William Simms which lasted until after Troughton's death in 1831. Edward Troughton was apparently quite a character, choosing to live a semi-reclusive life and was characterized by his snuff-stained wig and ear trumpet! However his skill both in the manufacture and design of fine instruments led him to be awarded lucrative contracts from The East India Company, The Board of Ordinance, the Royal Observatory and The Board of Longitude.

A George III mahogany bowfronted mercury stick barometer, with vernier scale calibrated in barometric inches and with the usual weather observations beneath signature 'Troughton, London' the flame figured trunk of bowed profile and with ebony strung edges with convex throat molding and vernier adjustment screw, glass lacking.

c1820 *39.5in (100cm) high*

$5,250-6,750 DN

A 19thC mahogany ship's stick barometer, signed 'Dollond, London', concealed mercury tube, hinged door with side latch, single vernier scale signed, thermometer tube, cylindrical cistern cover, gimbal wall bracket missing.

36.2in (92cm) high

$1,800-2,250 TEN

A Victorian oak angle barometer, the painted paper register inscribed 'Davis, Leeds', with two brass scales, with an ivory inlaid turned well.

45in (114.5cm) high

$4,800-6,000 SWO

A Victorian carved oak barometer, by Connell, 83 Cheapside, London, with double angled ivory register plates and a detachable Reaumur and Fahrenheit scale thermometer.

39.4in (100cm)

$450-750 SWO

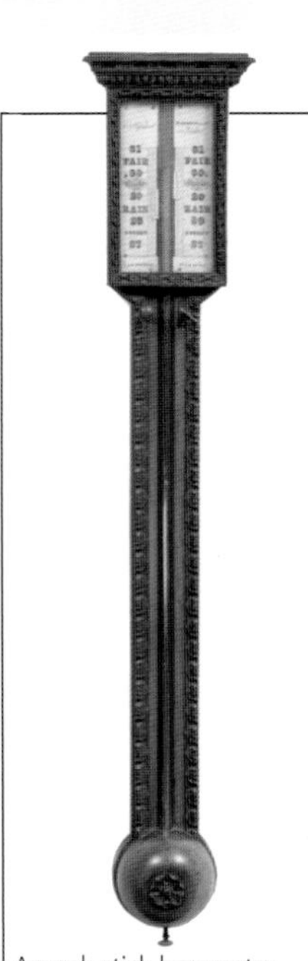

An oak stick barometer, signed 'C Shepherd, 53 Leadenhall St. London', visible mercury tube with carved acanthus leaf borders, twin ivory vernier dial signed.

c1850 *37.4in (95cm) high*

$450-600 **TEN**

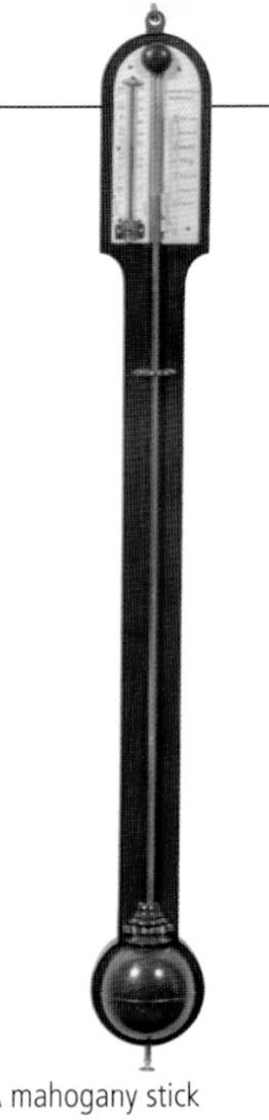

A mahogany stick barometer, signed 'J Lazars Optician, Edinburgh', exposed mercury tube with single ivory vernier dial signed, thermometer tube.

c1850 *37.4in (95cm) high*

$850-975 **TEN**

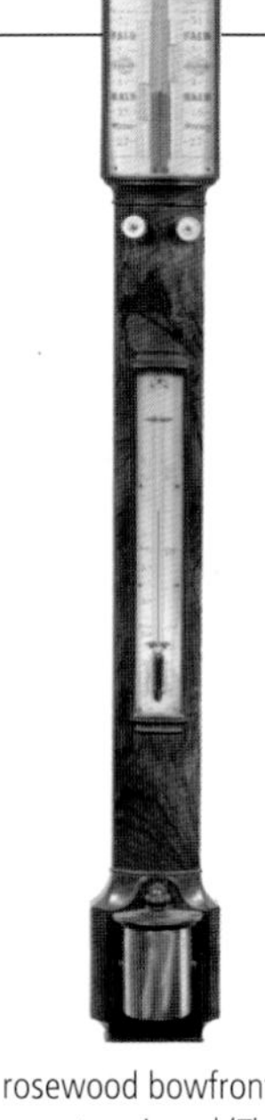

A rosewood bowfront stick barometer, signed 'Thos Underhill, 4 Old Mill Gate, Manchester', concealed mercury tube, twin ivory scale vernier signed, thermometer box.

c1850 *38in (97cm) high*

$1,150-1,300 **TEN**

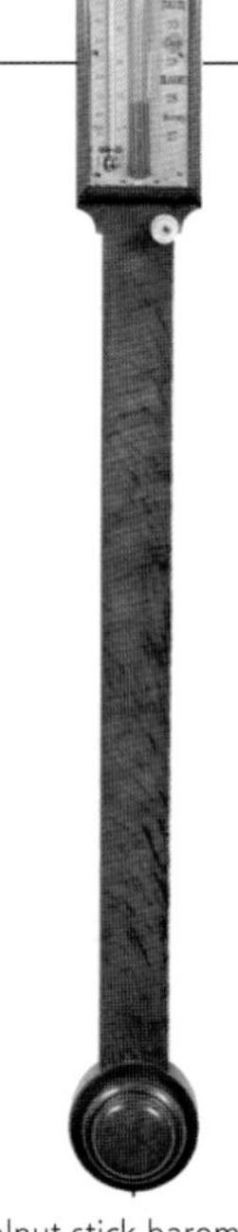

A walnut stick barometer, signed 'J Casartelli, Optician, Manchester', concealed mercury tube, single ivory vernier dial signed, thermometer tube.

c1870 *35.4in (90cm) high*

$850-975 **TEN**

A Victorian carved oak stick barometer, with an inscribed glass double register for '10 A.M Yesterday' and '10 A.M Today', with a double rack and pinion scale, over a thermometer,

40.4in (102.5cm) high

$750-900 **SWO**

A mahogany wheel barometer, dial signed 'L. Caminuel, Winchester', trunk set with hygrometer, thermometer and convex mirror.

38in (97cm) high

$180-225 **WW**

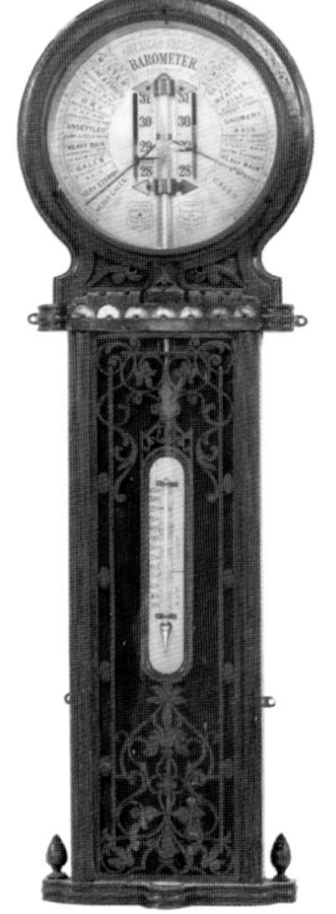

An American oak barometer, the dial inscribed 'Joseph Davis & Co., 6 Kennington Park Road, London', with vernier displays for winter and summer, the trunk with week disc registers.

c1880 *38.4in (97.5)cm high*

$750-900 **SWO**

A late 19thC Louis XV-style kingwood and ormolu barometer, the case applied with gilt metal Rococo scrolling decoration of arrows and musical instruments, the thermometer with silvered backplate above a white paper weather dial.

46in (117cm) high

$2,250-3,000 **ROS**

A late 19th/early 20thC French Louis XVI-style gilt bronze and porcelain mounted clock barometer, signed 'Thiery A Paris', the case with swags and oak leaves, wreaths and cherub heads, the body inset with Wedgwood style Jasper ware plaques of Classical taste, with thermometer, with clock.

36in (91cm) high

$6,750-8,250 **ROS**

A silver-cased pocket barometer, thermometer and compass, the case in the form of a double sovereign holder, maker's mark indistinct, London.

1912 *2.75in (7cm) wide*

$850-900 **HT**

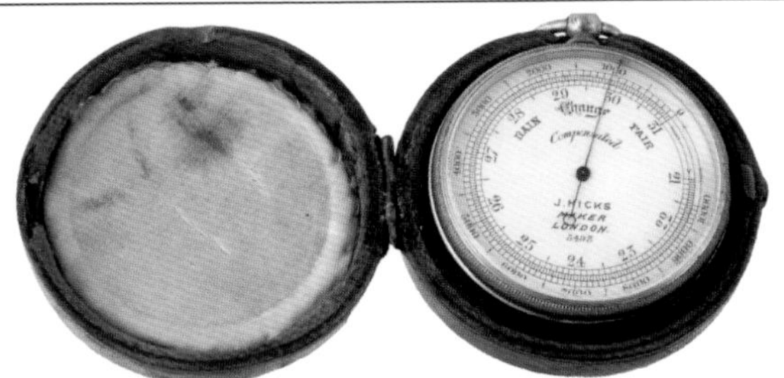

A late 19thC gilt-brass aneroid pocket barometer, with altimeter scale, signed 'J. Hicks, Maker, London, 5493' calibrated for barometric inches divided into twentieths and annotated with weather observations, within fixed outer scale calibrated in feet from 0 to 10000 and divided for 100 foot intervals, with original leather cover.

James Joseph Hicks is recorded as working from Hatton Garden, London from 1861 until after 1900. He was a committed Catholic who presented various meteorological instruments to the Vatican receiving the title of Knight Commander of St. Gregory for his services.

2in (5cm) diam

$375-450 **DN**

ESSENTIAL REFERENCE - CHARLES ASPREY

The firm of Charles Asprey and Sons was originally founded as a silk printing business in Mitcham, Surrey by William Asprey in 1781. Charles Asprey relocated the business to London in 1841 to form a partnership with Francis Kennedy, a stationer based at 46 Bond Street. This partnership lasted until 1843 after which the business was continued by Charles Asprey alone until he took in his son, also called Charles, and relocated to 166 Bond Street in 1847. In 1872 the business name was changed to 'Asprey and Son' followed by 'Asprey and Sons' in 1879 when his other son, George Edward, joined the firm. The name changed again to 'C. and G.E. Asprey' in 1888 before finally becoming 'Asprey and Company' in 1900.

A Victorian silver-cased aneroid pocket barometer, with altimeter scale, signed 'C. & G.E. Asprey, 166. New Bond St., London' beneath Improved Scale, Compensated and stamped registration number '149175', with concentric scale calibrated for barometric inches divided into tenths and annotated with the usual weather observations within rotating outer scale calibrated in feet from 0 to 12000 and divided for 50-foot intervals, marks for London.

1892 *2in (5cm) diam*

$700-850 **DN**

A combination carriage timepiece barometer, movement with lever platform with the stamp of Duverdery & Bloquel, the barometer surmounted by an inset compass.

6.5in (16cm) high

$1,000-1,200 **WW**

A mahogany barograph, by Short & Mason, the recording drum flanked by a silvered dial 'Stormograph', with eight aneroid movement.

14.5in (37cm) wide

$1,200-1,400 **WW**

A mahogany cased barograph, by R & J Beck LTD, 68 Cornhill London, with eight-section vacuum and clockwork mechanism.

14.75in (37.5cm) wide

$850-975 **BELL**

A late 19thC London wall-mounted mahogany barograph, aneroid chamber mounted with armature operating the inked pointer for recording the change in barometric pressure on a horizontally pivoted clockwork driven paper-scale lined rotating drum, engraved 'J. Hicks, London, No. 71'.

This barograph is a rare design which may have been developed for maritime use. Recording by dots would both help to lessen the chance of interruption through jolts onboard a vessel, as well as allow clear indication of sustained fall in pressure which normally precedes a storm.

10in (25.5cm) high

$1,150-1,300 **DN**

An early 20thC London lacquered and patinated brass transit theodolite, engraved 'Stanley London, 30143, Patent', with original hardwood box fitted with accessories. the box

The firm of W.F. Stanley and Co. was founded by William F. Stanley as specialising in drawing instruments in 1854. The firm expanded to become one of the largest suppliers of surveying instruments working from several addresses in London and continued in business (latterly as a subsidiary of Russell Instruments) until being wound-up 1999.

18.5in (47cm) wide

$750-900 **DN**

A Johann Gabriel Doppelmayr (1671–1750) terrestrial miniature Globe, 'Globus/Terrestris Novus/ opera /Ioh. Gab. Doppelmaieri M. P. P./ Ioh. Georg: Puschnero/ Chalcogr. Norib./A: 1736', with twelve engraved paper gores on papermache/plaster sphere, full brass meridian and hour ring, original wood stand, damages.

3.9in (10cm) diameter

$9,000-10,500 **DOR**

A pair of 15in Regency terrestrial and celetial library globes, by J.&W. Cary, London, the terrestrial globe with cartouche 'Drawn from the most recent GEOGRAPHICAL WORKS, shewing the whole of the New Discoveries with the TRACKS of the PRINCIPAL NAVIGATORS and every improvement in Geography to the Present Time. LONDON. London. Published by G. & J. Cary, St James's, St. January 4 1824', the celestial globe with cartouche 'CARY'S NEW CELESTIAL GLOBE, ON WHICH are carefully laid down the whole of the STARS AND NEBULÆ contained in the Catalogues of Wollaston, Herschel, Bode, Piazzi, Zach &c. calculated to the Year 1820', with meridian circle, supported on four quadrant supports.

1820-24 *39in (99cm) high*

$30,000-45,000 **L&T**

A Regency 18in terrestrial library globe, by John and William Cary, with twenty engraved gores, the cartouche reading 'Cary's new terrestrial globe : exhibiting the tracks and discoveries made by Captain Cook : also those of Captain Vancouver on the North West Coast of America and M. de la Pe´rouse on the coast of Tartary : together with every other improvement collected from various navigators and travellers to the present time... W. Cary, sold by S. & J. Duncan, Glasgow, 1817', with brass meridien ring, on stand.

1817 *44in (111.8cm)*

$13,500-18,000 **FRE**

A Smith & Son London terrestrial globe, 'Smiths/ Terrestrial Globe/containing the whole of/the Latest Discoveries/in/Australia Africa and/the Arctic Regions/also the directions of/ the Ocean Currents/ London/Smith & Son 63 Charing Cross', 12 colored paper gores on papier mâché plaster sphere, full brass meridian, wood stand with horizon showing zodiac, months and days, small damages.

c1870 *12in (30cm) diam*

$4,500-6,000 **DOR**

An early 20thC 14-inch terrestrial table globe, with label 'Philip's, 14-inch, Terrestrial Globe…, London, Geographical Institute, George Philip & Son Ltd. 32 Fleet Street' and annotated with principal towns, cities, rivers, mountain ranges and trans-continental railway routes to land masses, the oceans with principal steamship routes annotated in nautical miles, on inverted baluster-turned supports.

22in (56cm) high

$2,100-2,700 **DN**

A pair of English 12in terrestrial and celestial table globes, Bardin, each with twelve gores, the terrestrial globe with a cartouche inscribed 'BARDIN'S TERRESTRIAL GLOBE [...] MANUFACTURED & PUBLISHED BY S.C. TISLEY, COUCH SQUARE, LONDON'; the celestial globe inscribed 'BARDIN'S BRITISH CELESTIAL GLOBE, containing the exact positions of 4000 fixed stars, nebulae &c, on turned ebonized legs joined by an 'X' stretcher, dated. 1861

$7,500-9,000 **L&T**

An early 19thC Cary's terrestrial globe on a turned mahogany stand.

17.75in (45cm)

$1,500-2,250 **BELL**

Judith Picks: Pocket Globe

I love the descriptive terms used - 'the oceans including the Ethiopic Ocean, the Western or Atlantic Ocean, The Eastern Ocean, and Great South Sea with tracks for Anson and Cook, the South Pole unmarked and described as 'Frozen Ocean', Australia described as 'New Holland' and conjoined as one with Tasmania, national boundaries in dotted outline, cities and rivers, China, showing the Great Wall, sited next to 'Independent Tartary', Africa with details such as 'Negroland', and 'Country of the Hottentots', Canada with no northern coastline, and other details. Our globes today seem tame by comparison.

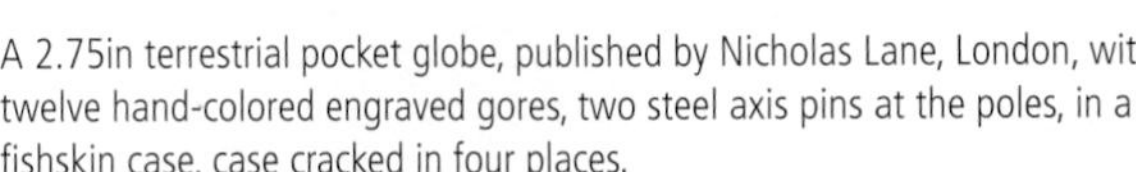

A 2.75in terrestrial pocket globe, published by Nicholas Lane, London, with twelve hand-colored engraved gores, two steel axis pins at the poles, in a fishskin case, case cracked in four places.

1807 *3in. (7.5cm.) diam*

$5,250-6,000 **CM**

A late 19thC 'THE GEOGRAPHIA' terrestrial 8in table globe, on a chrome-plated pivot and softwood base,

13in (33cm) high

$450-550 **HT**

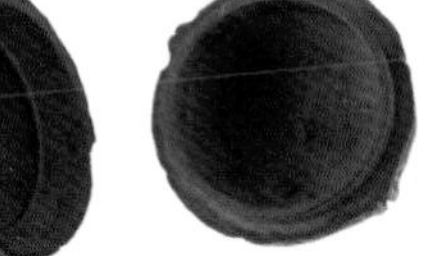

A rare early 19thC German Nuremburg Carl Bauer 1-inch miniature terrestrial globe, the sphere applied with twelve printed gores, in original carved wood case modeled as a walnut, some wear.

2.25in (5.5cm) high

$1,150-1,300 **DN**

A George V miniature 'Coronation Globe', marked ' PHILIPS' GRAPHIC GLOBE, GEORGE PHILIP & SONS LTD, THE LONDON GEOGRAPHIC INSTITUTE', on a brass tripod base, in original box.

1911 *8.8in (22.3cm) high*

$600-700 **WW**

A 7inch globe, with cream paper gores, signed 'Kelvin & Hughes Ltd, Star Globe, Epoch 1975', the meridian ring moveable within the azimuth circle and four vertical quadrants, in a mahogany box, the lid with Twilight Setting, instructions and spare cursors.

box 10.5in (27cm) square

$750-900 **WW**

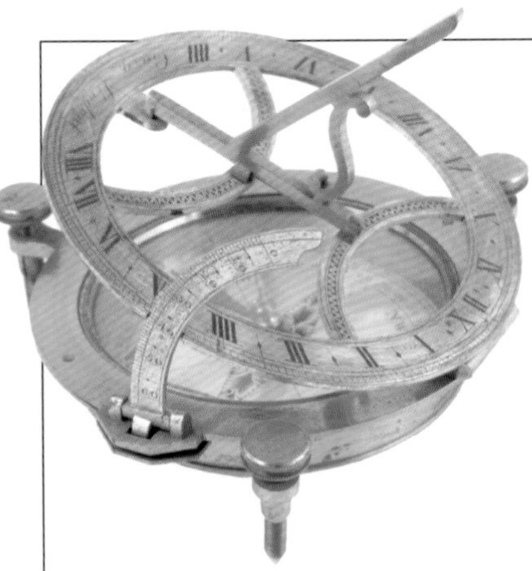

A universal equinoctial dial, signed 'Cary, London', folding gnomon and latitude scale, the base inset with compass and two levels, three levelling screws, with case.

5in (13cm) diam

$2,400-3,000 **WW**

A universal equinotcal dial, Augsburg, signed 'Ioh. G. Vogler' beneath a list of cities and latitudes, hinged hour ring and gnomon and adjustable latitude arc, inset silvered compass, in leather case.

3in (7.5cm) wide

$1,150-1,300 **WW**

An 18thC brass pocket sundial, signed 'I Coggs Fecit'.

A John Coggs is recorded as working from 'Globe & Sun against St. Dunstan's Church in Fleet Street' 1718-33. He is known to have sold universal equinoctial ring dials and advertised a full range of instruments. The name of the business was changed to 'Coggs & Wyeth' when John and William Wyeth joined the business in 1733 later becoming 'Wright & Wyeth' in 1740.

1725-50 *3.25in (8cm) diam*

$1,300-1,450 **DN**

An early 19thC Regency London William and Samuel Jones fine lacquered brass 'universal' pattern compound microscope, the original fully fitted mahogany box with a comprehensive and almost complete selection of original accessories.

The partnership between the brothers William and Samuel Jones is recorded as operating from several addresses in Holborn, London 1792-1859 (including 30 Holborn 1800-1860). This microscope is very similar to 'Jones Most Improved Compound Microscope and Apparatus' which was based upon a design originally conceived by George Adams and published in the 1798 edition of his Essays on the Microscope.

$6,750-8,250 **DN**

A brass binocular compound microscope, signed 'Smith & Son, 6 Coleman St, London', with a box containing.

c1840

$2,250-3,000 **WW**

A late 19thC London J. Swift and Son lacquered and patinated brass monocular microscope, with rack and pinion coarse and fine top-screw focus adjustment and twin-lens nosepiece, with original mahogany box fitted with various accessories.

The firm of J. Swift and Son was founded in 1853 by John Powell Swift. His son, Mansell James, joined the company in 1884. J. Swift and Son supplied microscopes for Captain Scott's 1901-4 expedition to the Antarctic on the R.R.S. Discovery. The business continued under the management of subsequent generations before being merged with E.R. Watts and Son in 1946 and was bought-out by John H. Bassett in 1968.

12in (30cm) high

$850-975 **DN**

A lacquered brass and black enameled monocular microscope, with rack-and-pinion course and micrometer focusing, a triple nosepiece, a circular stage with micrometer adjustment, a substage condenser and mirror, the tube signed 'E Leitz, Wetzlar No. 137506'.

12.25in (31cm) high

$750-900 **SWO**

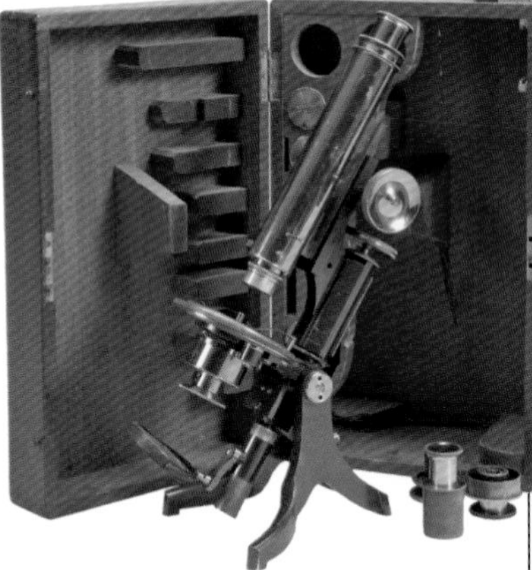

A lacquered and patinated brass polarizing monocular microscope, with rack and pinion coarse and fine top-screw focus adjustment and twin prism slides, engraved 'J. Swift & Son, 81 Tottenham Court Rd, London', with original mahogany box fitted with some accessories.

c1900 *13.5ins (34.5cm) high*

$450-600 **DN**

A universal equinoctial ring dial, by Richard Abbott, in lacquered brass, the outer meridian ring engraved with latitude scale, the reverse with nautical quadrant ring engraved 0-90° with pinhole, central bridge with sliding pinhole gnomon to calendar scale, the reverse with sun declination scale inscribed 0-20-0, the inner ring with Roman numeral hour scale engraved III-XII-IX.

c1670 *3.5in (9cm) diam*

$6,750-8,250 **CM**

A universal compass sundial, by Troughton & Simms, London, with two spirit levels and needle with clamp, with folding gnomon and latitude arm, with original sharkskin case, with maker's instruction sheet.

6in (15cm) diam

$4,500-5,250 **CM**

A marine sighting compass, by Langford, Bristol, detachable sights and glazed top with cross-hairs, gimbal-mounted, within original wooden box .

c1850 *12in (30.5cm) wide*

$900-1,200 **CM**

A marine chronometer, dial signed 'Eiffe, London, 48 Lombard St, City and South Creset. Bedford Sq.', no549, 'Little Glory', movement with spring detent escapement, blued steel helical spring, free-sprung, most unusual double-Z balance.

Eiffe was known to give fantastic names to some of his chronometers, 'Little Glory' being fairly innocuous. Gould records that the Admiralty were by no means sympathetic to this innovation.

c1835 *box 5.5in (14cm) square*

$18,000-22,500

A two-day marine chronometer, with Barraud's auxiliary compensation weight, dial signed 'Barraud, 41 Cornhill, London, Maker to the Royal Navy', no2840, subsidiary seconds at 12 o'clock, with Earnshaw spring detent escapement, blued steel helical spring, free-sprung, the bi-metallic balance carrying his 'Patent Correcting Weights'.

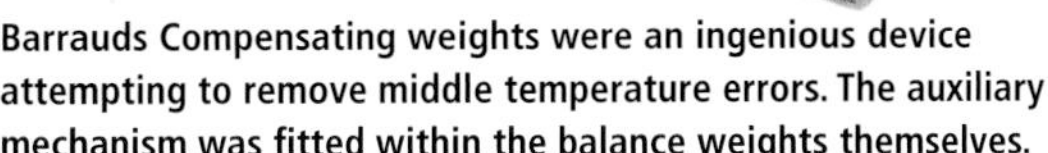

Barrauds Compensating weights were an ingenious device attempting to remove middle temperature errors. The auxiliary mechanism was fitted within the balance weights themselves.

c1845, *box 7in (18cm) square*

$16,500-22,500 **WW**

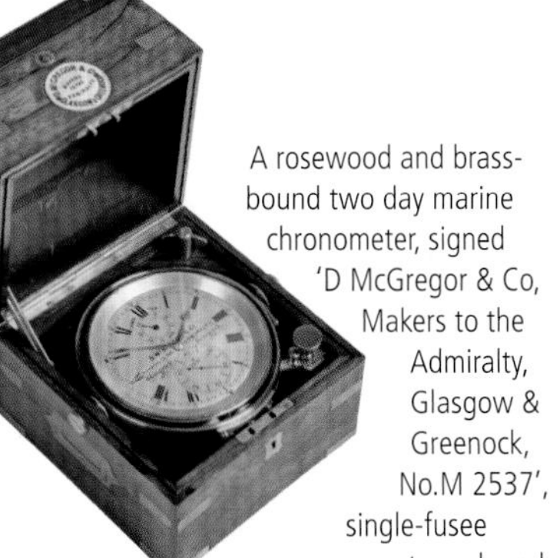

A rosewood and brass-bound two day marine chronometer, signed 'D McGregor & Co, Makers to the Admiralty, Glasgow & Greenock, No.M 2537', single-fusee movement numbered '2560', 'Earnshaws', spring detent escapement, 'Harrison's' maintaining power.

Duncan McGregor & Co are recorded at 36 Brymner St, Greenock 1859-1885 and 30 Clyde Place, Glasgow 1860-1865.

c1862. *7in (19cm) wide*

$2,250-3,000 **TEN**

A 19thC ebony two-day marine chronometer, signed 'Barraud, 41 Cornhill, London, no1749', single-fusee movement with 'Harrisons' maintaining power and 'Earnshaws' type spring detent escapement, free sprung helical hairspring, compensation balance with weights and timing screws, movement not working.

7.5in (19cm) high

$6,750-8,250 **TEN**

A two-day marine chronometer, signed 'Dobbie, McInnes Ltd, So. Shields, London, Glasgow, Liverpool, no10009, Contractors to the Admiralty', spring detent escapement elinvar helical spring, free-sprung, top lid missing. with key.

c1940 *5in (12.5cm) diam*

$1,800-2,250 **WW**

ESSENTIAL REFERENCE - MARINERS' ASTROLABE

Most mariners' astrolabes are the products of either Spain or Portugal (a tiny proportion have been attributed to British, Dutch or French makers) where the industry became highly evolved with, according to Stimson, seven distinct patterns emerging between 1500 and 1700, which is believed to be their approximate period of use at sea - this example is Type I(a), a cast wheel with base ballast. Early in the sixteenth century, the Spanish authorities required all navigational instruments to be examined by the Pilot Major of the Casa e Contratación for accuracy, with successful instruments being stamped with an approval mark. The regulation was much ignored, to the extent that it was re-issued in 1545. However, it is presumed that in the period when Portugal was a province of Spain (1580-1640) these regulations also applied, and the armillary sphere (a symbol adopted from King Henry the Navigator, 1394-1460, by Manuel I, 1469-1521, and still used on the Portuguese flag) was used as the approval mark. Francisco de Goes flourished between 1587-1632 and worked from Lisbon, signing his instruments variously as 'Gois'; 'Goes' and 'Goys'. His son Agostinho de Raposo succeeded him, and also his grandson João de Raposo, who took the family business into the third quarter of the seventeenth century.

A rare Portuguese mariner's astrolabe by Francisco de Goes, cast from bronze, signed 'GOIS 1595' and impressed with Manueline armillary sphere approval mark, divided over the top half 90°-0-90°, the alidade with countersunk pierced pinnules in the sighting vanes, secured with decorative threaded axis pin and wing nut.

1595 *7.5in (18.8cm) diam 7lb 14oz (3.57kg)*

$127,500-142,500 **CM**

A late 19thC Maghribi planispheric astrolabe, the mater with throne, hinged joint and ring containing seven double-sided latitude plates with alignment lugs at north, the reverse with upper right quadrant scale divided between 0°-90° with graduated alidade sights secured by tapering pin and horse.

6.25in (16cm) diam

$7,500-9,000 **CM**

A marine brass sextant, unsigned.

10.25in (26cm) long

$100-115 **LOCK**

A rare 16.5in brass geodetic theodolite or portable Altazimuth repeating circle, by Troughton & Simms, London, silvered meridian scale divided 0-360° with micrometer microscopes, tapering pillars with central bracing pivot supporting a pair of braced six-spoke circles, the right inset with silvered scale divided in four quadrants of 0-90°, with micrometer microscopes and a 2in telescope.

1829 *31.5in (80cm) high*

$34,500-45,000 **CM**

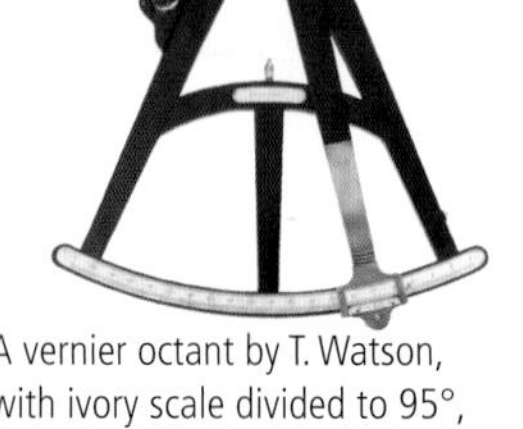

A vernier octant by T. Watson, with ivory scale divided to 95°, centralized Vernier, pinhole sights, interchangeable shades, pencil.

1767 *19.25in (49cm) high*

$3,300-4,400 **CM**

An early 19thC lacquered-brass telescope, believed to have been used by Thomas Graves R.N. on surveying missions to South American and the Mediterranean between 1827-1853, signed 'Thos. Jones Charring Crofs', with eyepiece with rack-and-pinion focus, interchangeable tubes with astronomical shade accessories, dew cuff, tripod stand, original case.

45.5in (115.5cm) long

$3,300-4,400 **CM**

A single draw telescope, signed 'Dollond, London, Achromatic Night', engraved with crest and motto, leather bound tube with gilt-brass clamp and column, on later tripod base.
The crest is for the Pelley family of naval officers. This telescope was passed down from Captain Richard Pelley (1814-1890) to Admiral Sir Henry Pelley KCVO, CB (1867-1942).

26.5in *(67cm) long (closed)*

$1,150-1,300 **WW**

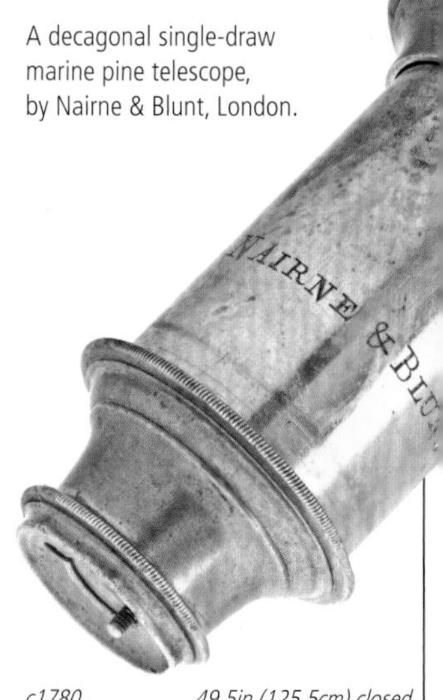

A decagonal single-draw marine pine telescope, by Nairne & Blunt, London.

c1780 *49.5in (125.5cm) closed*

$1,150-1,425 **CM**

A Bulkhead clock, believed to be from the S.S. Discovery, National Antarctic Expedition 1901-4, single winding arbor to chain fusee movement, stamped 'H.M.S. DISCOVERY / R.F. SCOTT. 6 AUG. 1901', with metal plate engraved 'H.M.S. DISCOVERY CAPTAIN SCOTT TERRA NOVA EXPEDITION 1910'.

c1900 *10.5in (27cm) diam*

$4,500-6,000 CM

A rare single-cylinder 'baby' diver's pump, by Siebe Gorman & Co. Ltd, within brass-bound mahogany box, inset pressure dial with hinged lid, water draw-off and air inlet, wooden handled crankshafts and cast iron flywheel.

37.5in (95cm) high

$12,000-15,000 CM

The brass bell, from H.M. Submarine R10, black-filled lettering as per title, molded rim and clapper.

1917 *9in (23cm) high*

$1,350-1,650 CM

An early 19thC mahogany model for a double capstan, constructed as in working practice with board pole slots and ratchet action.

8.25in (21cm) wide

$24,000-27,000 CM

An early 19thC sailor's tarred leather foul weather hat, lining stencilled 'W & Z', with original woven hat band.

14in (36cm) diam

$1,800-2,400 CM

A late 18th/early 19thC Continental carved oak ship's figurehead, depicting a young officer.

32.7in (83cm) high

$9,750-11,250 L&T

An early 19thC, possibly French, laminated limewood figurehead, of Minerve, the helmet and breast plate with relief carving, flowing hair and robes.

64in (163cm) high

$13,500-16,500 CM

ESSENTIAL REFERENCE - SLAVERY AND ANTI-SLAVERY

HMS Sharpshooter was one of the first iron steamers to be used by the Royal Navy. It was built by Ditchburn and Mare in 1846 and entered service after sea trials in 1848. In Captain Bailey's account she was, 'a brand new and experimental steam gun vessel of 489 tons and 202 horse-power, carrying eight guns, namely six 32-pounder medium guns on the broadsides, one 8-inch 68-pounder pivot gun forward, and one 10-inch 84-pounder pivot aft. She was the first iron ship to which the screw propeller had ever been applied'. After serving in the Channel Squadron and the Mediterranean, HMS Sharpshooter headed to the coast of Brazil on anti-slavery duties.

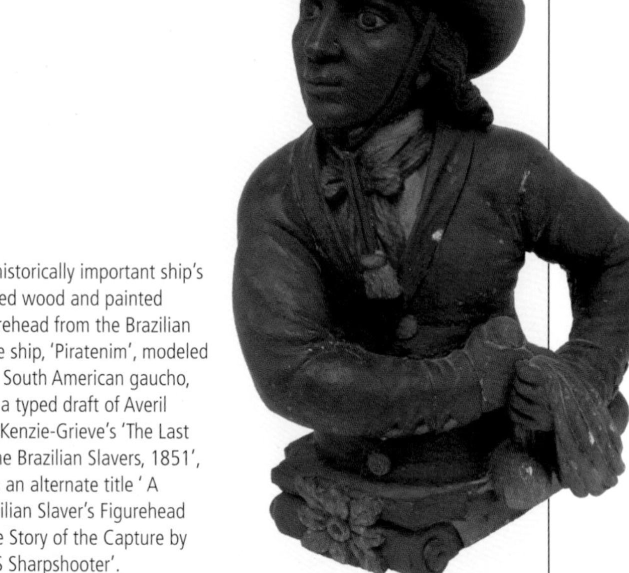

An historically important ship's carved wood and painted figurehead from the Brazilian slave ship, 'Piratenim', modeled as a South American gaucho, and a typed draft of Averil MacKenzie-Grieve's 'The Last of the Brazilian Slavers, 1851', with an alternate title ' A Brazilian Slaver's Figurehead - The Story of the Capture by HMS Sharpshooter'.

25in (63cm) high

$90,000-105,000 SWO

An early/mid-19thC New England patriotic scrimshaw whale's tooth, the obverse with a ship and an eagle holding an American flag under a row of thirteen stars, the reverse with a portrait of Grace Darling.

6.25in (16cm) high

$97,500-112,5000 **POOK**

A mid 19thC American sailorwork whalebone tusk, incised with two architectural structures and a twin-funnelled paddle steamer flying the American flag.

15.5in (39.5cm) wide

$600-750 **CM**

A 19thC Scrimshaw whale's tooth, with a figure of Lady Liberty with eagle and flag.

7in high

$9,000-12,000 **POOK**

A 19thC sailorwork scrimshaw-decorated pan bone plaque, depicting a typical whaling scene with six-man whalers from two British ships harpooning sperm whales.

13in (33cm) wide

$4,800-6,000 **CM**

A large 19thC scrimshaw marine tooth, possibly whale, carved with a ship near a fort, a cottage amongst trees and two warships at sea.

7.25in (18cm) long

$2,250-3,000 **FLD**

A 19thC scrimshaw marine tooth, possibly whale, carved with H.M.S Collingwood below a pair of pineapples, the reverse decorated with a standing native.

6.5in (16cm) high

$2,250-4,000 **FLD**

A set of three probably late 19th/early 20thC scrimshaw-decorated whales' teeth, commemorating the Battle of Flamborough Head, the two teeth engraved with the commanders and their vessels and a tooth bearing inscription as per title and note of Captain Sir Richard Pearson's defeat by John Paul Jones, contained in a wooden box.

10in (25.5cm) diam

$700-850 **CM**

A 19thC sailorwork pan bone plaque, depicting a whale ship and boats whaling, inscribed 'Frolic. London'.

8in (20cm) wide

$1,150-1,300 **CM**

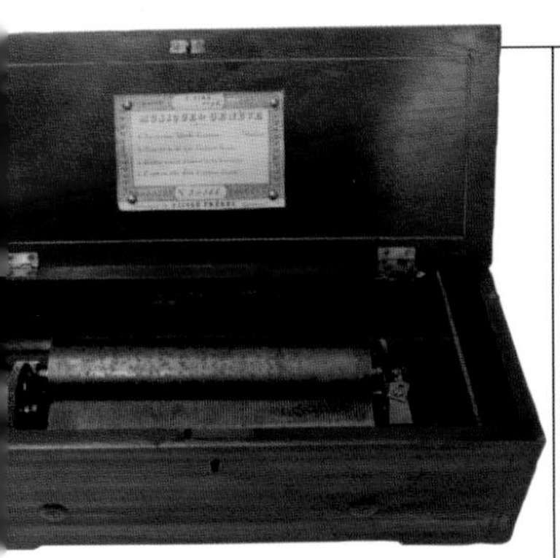

mid 19thC Nicole Frères musical box, with a eel comb and brass cylinder movement playing ur airs (overwound), with winding key.

15in (38cm) wide

1,000-1,200 HT

A Swiss eight-air musical box, the 6in (15.5cm) pinned cylinder also playing on three bells flanked by a pair of dancing dolls, numbered 28515.

19in (48cm) wide

$3,000-4,500 WW

A 12-air musical box, with six bells and castagnettes, by Nicole Freres, Geneva, serial no. 50049, single spring motor, triple section comb with zither on reeded gilt bedplate.

30.5in (77cm) wide.

$6,000-6,750 WW

10 air musical box, with drum and six bells by icole Frères, Geneve, serial no. 51170, double pring motor, triple section comb on reeded gilt edplate.

28in (70cm) wide.

4,000-5,250 WW

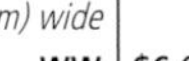

A 19thC Swiss walnut cased music box, playing eight airs, the cylinder movement with seven bells and a drum.

23in (57.5cm) wide

$4,500-7,500 ROW

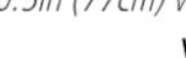

A 19thC rosewood cased music box, the cylinder movement striking on three bells and a drum and inscribed N.L. Van Gruisen, 17 Bold Street, Liverpool.

20.5in (52cm) wide

$1,200-1,800 ROW

Victorian coin-perated polyphon, omb no.10664, the rank-handled coin perated movement o.13259, turning 19 .75in (2cm) vertical iscs, in walnut case, he reel-molded ornice inscribed Polyphon', with xtra discs.

27.5in (70cm) wide

3,000-4,000 HT

A late 19th/early 20thC 'Stella' upright disc musical box, playing 25.5in (65cm) discs, with a disc bin containing 35 discs, the movement inscribed 'Chevob and Co, Geneva'.

34.25in (87cm) wide

$7,500-9,000 SWO

A Queen Anne silver taper stick, by Matthew Cooper, London.
c1707 *4in (10.5cm) high 3.5oz*
$3,000-4,000 **WW**

A Queen Anne silver taper stick, by John Barnard I, London, engraved with an armorial.
c1713 *4.25in (11cm) high 2.5oz*
$3,000-4,000 **WW**

A pair of George I Irish cast silver candlesticks, maker's mark '.. W', Dublin, each engraved under the bases with scratch-weights 10=8 and 10=10.

The maker's marks are indistinct but may be for Joseph Walker.
c1723 *6.25in (16cm) high 20.75oz*
$5,250-6,000 **DN**

Two of a set of four George II cast silver candlesticks, by James Gould, London.
1741 *9in (22.5cm) high 81oz*
$7,500-10,500 set **WW**

A pair of George II silver candlesticks, by John Cafe, London.
1746 *8.25in (20.5cm) high 34.1oz*
$4,500-5,250 **CHEF**

One of a pair of George II cast silver candlesticks, by George Boothby, London.
1748 *8.25in (21cm) high 40oz*
$4,400-5,100 pair **CHOR**

One of a set of four George II silver candlesticks, by John Cafe, London, with contemporary armorials.

The arms are probably those of Rodney, perhaps for George Brydges Rodney (1718-1792), a Commander in the Navy under Admiral Hawke in 1747. He was created a baronet in 1764 and was raised to the peerage as Baron Rodney of Rodney Stoke in 1782. He is best known for his commands in the American War of Independence, particularly his victory over the French at the Battle of the Saintes in 1782. It is often claimed that he was the commander to have pioneered the tactic of 'breaking the line'.
1752/54 *8.25in (21cm) high 71oz*
$8,250-9,000 set **MAB**

ESSENTIAL REFERENCE - GEORGE III SILVER

James Ker is without doubt one of Edinburgh, and indeed Scotland's most important goldsmiths. Working in the heart of Edinburgh's 'Golden Age' he, and within partnership with his son-in-law William Dempster as Ker & Dempster, made some of the most important mid-18thC Scottish plate. The sheer amount of silver linked to his marks would suggest a large workshop and much of the silver bearing his mark could not be the work of his hand. However the constant quality in design and manufacture is undeniable.

A pair of George III candlesticks, by Ker & Dempster, Edinburgh.
1763 *14.25in (36.5cm) high 36oz*
$9,750-11,250 **L&T**

A George II taperstick, London.
1752 *5in (13cm) high 5oz*
$1,500-2,250 **L&T**

One of a pair of Règence-style George III silver candlesticks, by Ebenezer Coker, London, the bases engraved with an early 19thC coat-of-arms and crest.

1764 *9in (23cm) high 54oz*

$6,750-8,250 pair **MAB**

A matched pair of George III silver candlesticks, one Ebenezer Coker, London, the other William Cafe, London.

1761/1765 *9in (23cm) high 33.25oz*

$1,500-2,250 **CHOR**

A pair of George III cast tapersticks, by Lothian & Robertson, Edinburgh.

As with Edinburgh-made cast candlesticks, cast tapersticks are rarely encountered. Even more so when found in pairs. This pair is obviously very closely inspired by London-made examples and perhaps cast from an original London pair in Edinburgh.

1769 *6in (15.5cm) high 6.7oz*

$5,250-6,750 **L&T**

A pair of George III silver candle sticks, J Parsons & Co, Sheffield, the simple tapered columns with acanthus border below sconce.

1784 *10.75in (27cm) high*

$3,000-4,000 **L&T**

A pair of Victorian Walker Knowles & Co, Sheffield silver candlesticks, in the mid-18thC style, crested.

1844 *9.25in (23cm) high loaded*

$1,500-2,250 **CHEF**

A set of six Rococo-style Victorian Scottish silver candlesticks, by John Crichton III, Edinburgh, with six-point foliate sconces, crested, sconces with engraved initials.

The single crest of a hand bearing arrows is that of Brodie of Lethen, Co. Elgin. The initials 'TDB' on each sconce suggest that the candlesticks belonged to Thomas Dawson Brodie. Sir Thomas Dawson Brodie (1832-1896), first and last Baronet, was Deputy Keeper of the Privy Seal of Scotland. John Critchon III was born in 1860, the son of a goldsmith. He was first apprenticed to his uncle, George Crichton I, in 1875 and then continued his apprenticeship with George Crichton II in 1879. The design for the maker's marks on these candlesticks was registered in 1875 and John Critchon III was made a freeman in 1885.

1897 *8.5in (22cm) high 102oz*

$12,000-13,500 **SWO**

A set of four Victorian silver candlesticks, by Charles Stuart Harris, London, in the late 17thC style, engraved with the badge of the Rifle Brigade.

This large business of manufacturing silversmiths, C.S. Harris & Sons Ltd, is said to have been commenced by John Mark Harris, a spoon maker, in 1817; he moved c1831 to 27 Nelson Street, City Road. It would appear that the firm was continued by John Robert Harris, who moved c1842 to 29 Kirby Street, Hatton Garden where he is listed from 1843 until 1852 as a silver spoon and fork manufacturer. The business then passed c1852 to Charles Stuart Harris, who is listed from 1854 at 29 Kirby Street as an elctro spoon and fork maker, electro plater and gilder and agent for plated wares (1856), electro spoon and fork maker, electro plater and gilder and manufacturer of plated wares and silversmith (1858), and silversmith (1871).

c1876 *8.5 in (21.5cm) high 70oz*

$9,750-11,250 **WW**

A pair of late 19thC Dutch silver candlesticks, with earlier pseudo marks, and tax marks.

8.25in (21cm) high 15oz

$1,000-1,200

WW

A matched set of four Victorian silver and electroplated candlesticks, two by Martin, Hall and Company, London, two unmarked.

c1890 *11in (28.5cm) high*

$550-700 **WW**

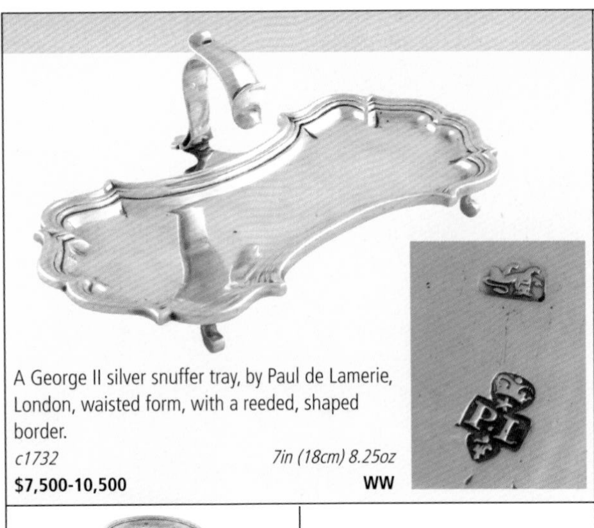

A George II silver snuffer tray, by Paul de Lamerie, London, waisted form, with a reeded, shaped border.

c1732 *7in (18cm) 8.25oz*

$7,500-10,500 **WW**

A George II snuffer tray, by William Chawner, London, the engraved crest within foliate cartouche, with S-scroll handle and raised on four claw feet.

1759 *7in (18.5cm) wide 7oz*

$450-750 **L&T**

A George III silver snuffer tray, by Peter and Jonathan Bateman, London.

c1790 *10in (25.5cm) long 4oz*

$900-1,000 **WW**

A George III chamberstick, London.

1791 *6in (15cm) diam 9oz*

$600-900 **L&T**

A pair of Irish George III wick trimmers, by James Scott, Dublin.

1793 *7in (18cm) long 3.5oz*

$750-900 **L&T**

A George III silver eccentric candle snuffer, maker's mark 'W..', London, the scissor action with a steel-edged blade, engraved with a later crest.

The crest of an upright wing charged with two 6-pointed molets gules is not identified.

1799 *6.75in (17cm) long 4.5oz*

$240-300 **DN**

Judith Picks: George III chamberstick

What a difference a name makes. This is a reasonably plain and elegant chamberstick but it was made by arguably the greatest late18th/19thC silversmith Paul Storr. Paul Storr (1771-1844) was an English goldsmith and silversmith working in the Neo-classical style during the late eighteenth and early nineteenth centuries. He perfected the works styles and designs of the Regency period. His works range from simple tableware to magnificent sculptural pieces made for royalty. Storr was apprenticed to Andrew Fogelberg, who was of Swedish origin, when he was 14. On completion of his apprenticeship he started his own shop in 1796. In 1807, he began an association with Rundell and Bridge (later Rundell, Bridge and Rundell), a firm of royal goldsmiths, for whom he carried out many commissions ranging from simple tableware to highly ornate and intricate work. In many cases he produced work following the firm's designs. Though he held no official title, Storr enjoyed patronage from many important and powerful figures of the period, including King George III. His first major work was a gold font commissioned by the Duke of Portland in 1797 and in 1799 he created the 'Battle of the Nile Cup' for Lord Nelson.Some of his own designs were inspired by ancient Roman silver, while others were in a Rococo style. He left the firm in 1819 and by 1822 had entered a partnership with John Mortimer, which was to last until 1838. Storr retired from silversmithing at the age of 68, moving to Tooting in 1839. He died just five years later. Paul Storr's legacy is a remarkable body of work with far-reaching influences. Storr imparted a level of craftsmanship and superior quality that has seldom been seen since. Every piece of Storr silver was given the same superior level of quality, including this chamberstick, receiving the benefit of being created from the finest high-gauge silver.

A George III silver chamberstick, by Paul Storr, London, plain circular form, with an angular handle, gadrooned border, detachable drip pan and conical snuffer, crested.

c1809 *6in (15cm) diam 13.5oz*

$3,000-4,500 **WW**

An early Victorian silver chamber candlestick, by Henry Wilkinson & Co., Sheffield, with scroll and shell borders, a central inverted bell capital, detachable conical extinguisher with a bud finial, engraved with a crest.

c1839 *6in (15cm) diam 10oz*

$975-1,150 **DN**

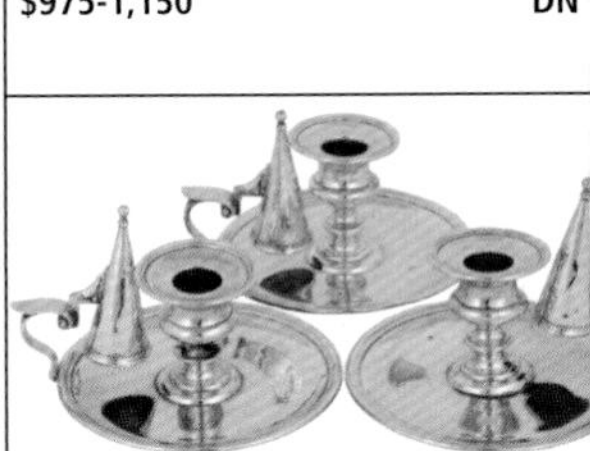

A set of three Victorian silver chamber sticks, Edward & John Barnard, London.

1852 *32oz*

$1,500-2,250 **L&T**

A Charles II silver beaker, maker's mark of a goose in a dotted circle, London, prick-dot initialed 'EAT 1680', (the AT conjoined).

c1679 *4in (10cm) high 4.5oz*

$13,500-16,500 **WW**

A Charles II provincial silver tumbler cup, by Thomas Mangy, York, later initialed 'JB'.

c1684 *3in (7.5cm) diam 2.5oz*

$6,750-8,250 **WW**

A George I silver mug, by Paul de Lamerie, London, later engraved with a coat-of-arms and crest, the scroll handle engraved with the initials Cover IM.

1719 *4in (10cm) high 9oz*

$5,250-6,750 **MAB**

A pair of George I silver mugs, by Anthony Nelme, London, Britannia Standard, engraved with armorials.

1721 *4in (10cm) high 19oz*

$5,250-6,750 **TEN**

A George I silver mug, by Simon Pantin I, London.

c1725 *3.5in (9cm) high 8.5oz*

$1,500-2,250 **WW**

A Scottish provincial mug, by Robert Luke, marked RL, S, RL, Town mark, for Glasgow.

This strong price is further evidence of the strengh of the Scottish provincial market. This mug is also of a good early date.

c1730 *3.75in (9.5cm) high 5.5oz*

$3,400-4,500 **L&T**

A George II silver tankard, by Fuller White, London.

1747 *8in (20cm) high 24oz*

$2,700-3,300 **TEN**

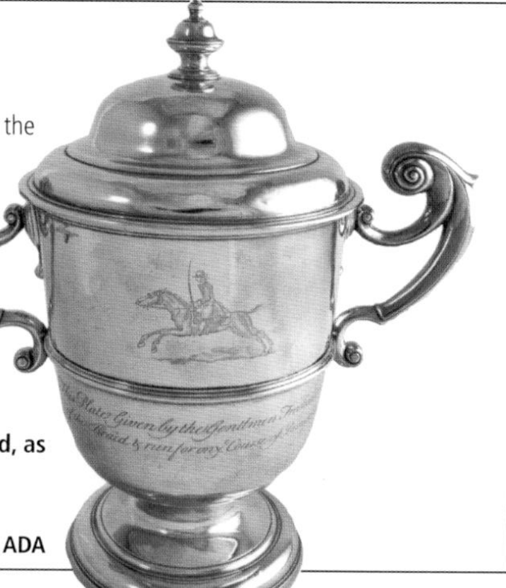

A silver cup inscribed with an engraved jockey and a racehorse, 'This Plate Given By the Gentlemen Freeholders of The Braid and Run for On Ye Course of Broughshane'.

Made in Dublin c1750, the Broughshane Cup was inscribed Dublin 1751, the year the course was founded. It precedes by five years the example by Robert Calderwood in the National Museum. The cup will stay in Ireland, as one of the earliest extant Irish racing cups.

1751

$30,000-45,000 **ADA**

A George II silver tankard, by William Shaw and William Priest, London, with traces of an armorial.

c1759 *7.5in (19cm) high 24.5oz*

$2,700-3,300 **WW**

An early George III English provincial silver tankard, by John Langlands I, Newcastle.
c1769 *7in (18cm) high 24oz*
$2,250-3,000 **DN**

A George III silver tankard, by I.K, London.
1771 *4.75in (12cm) high 10oz*
$600-750 **L&T**

A matched pair of George III Irish silver beakers, by J Jackson, Dublin.
1784/1787 *3.25in (8.5cm) high 8.5oz*
$1,800-2,250 **L&T**

A George III silver cup, maker's mark probably that of Peter and Ann Bateman, over-struck by another, London, engraved and later dated.
1797 *6in (15.5cm) 11.5oz*
$375-450 **WW**

A pair of George III silver beakers, by John Robertson II & John Walton, Newcastle.
c1815 *3.5in (9cm) high 10.75oz*
$2,250-3,000 **WW**

A late George III silver goblet, maker's mark '… A', London.
1816 *5.5in (14cm) high 8.25oz*
$750-900 **DN**

A Victorian silver mug, by James Charles Edington, London, the body chased with floral sprays, a boy and animals.
1855 *4.5in (11cm) high 7oz*
$450-600 **L&T**

A Victorian silver goblet, by Robert Hennell III, London.
c1862 *7in (18cm) high 12 oz*
$1,150-1,300 **DN**

A late Victorian collapsable silver tot cup, by G Unite, Birmingham, formed of six tapered collars.
1893 *2in (5cm) high 1oz*
$280-340 **L&T**

ESSENTIAL REFERENCE - GEORGE I BULLET TEAPOT

This is the earliest recorded Scottish teapot, matched in date with one other by Colin McKenzie. Both dating from 1714-15 it is interesting to note they are made by master and apprentice, showing not only the control that McKenzie had within the Edinburgh market but also the skills of a newly trained silversmith. Colin McKenzie was without doubt one of the most important makers in Edinburgh in the early 1700s and the legacy he left through his apprentices would follow for decades to come. Colin Campbell was made a Freeman of the Incorporation of Goldsmiths of the City of Edinburgh only two years previously in 1712, and appears to have had a successful early career. Valuable commissions such as this would rarely have gone to a relatively inexperienced and newly established goldsmith; however, the accomplished manufacture of this piece shows the skill Campbell had. Interestingly he is not just copying a style laid down by his master, or another maker, but expanding the design to what would become the standard and popular bullet teapot. The other recorded early teapots made in Edinburgh are all of apple form with tapered body and without a foot. This example with a foot stopped the immediate need for a simple teapot stand, which are also recorded at this early period. This example must be considered the forerunner of the bullet teapot and the model from which others were designed and made. This bullet style synonymous with Scottish silver can therefore now be traced further back than originally considered.

An early George I bullet teapot, by Colin Campbell, Edinburgh, Assay Master Edward Penman.
1714 *5.75in (14.5cm) high 17.2oz*
$21,000-27,000 L&T

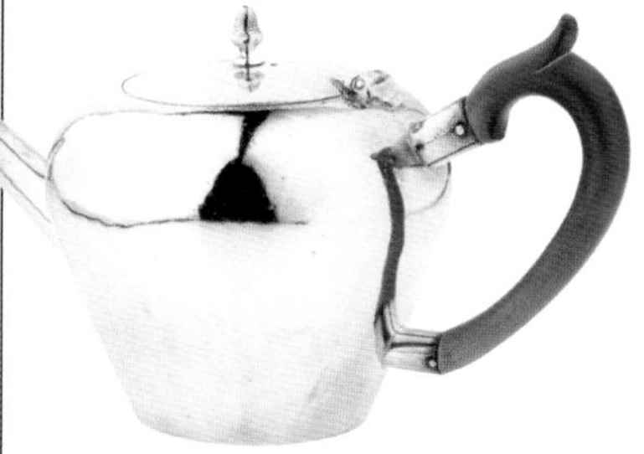

A George I Scottish tapered bullet teapot, by Henry Bethune, Edinburgh.
1719 *5in (13cm) high 13.7oz*
$9,000-10,500 L&T

A rare early English provincial George I octagonal teapot, by John Carnaby, Newcastle.
1721 *6.25in (16cm) high 11.5oz*
$6,750-8,250 L&T

A George II Scottish silver teapot, maker's mark 'RL', probably for Robert Luke, Glasgow, scroll ivory handle.
c1743 *8.5in (22cm) high 17oz*
$4,500-5,250 WW

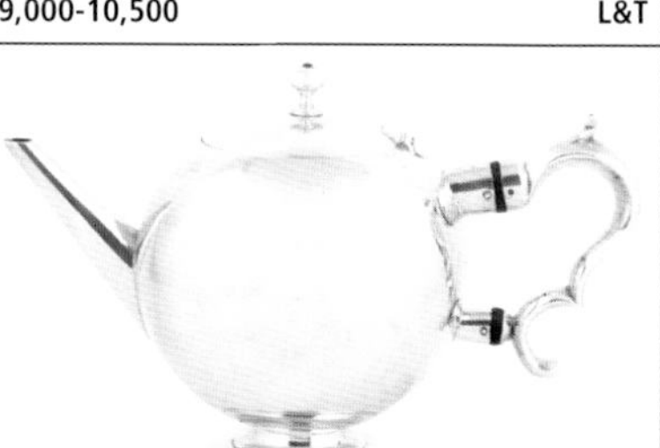

A George II bullet teapot, by James Ker, Edinburgh, Assay Master Archibald Ure.
1746 *6.75in (17cm) high 20oz*
$6,000-7,500 L&T

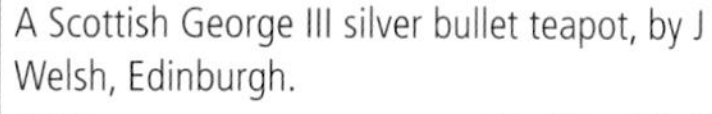

A Scottish George III silver bullet teapot, by J Welsh, Edinburgh.
1766 *6in (15cm) high 24oz*
$2,250-3,000 L&T

A George III inverted pear-shaped teapot, by William Dempster, Edinburgh.
1770 *6.5in (16.5cm) high 16.25oz*
$1,500-2,250 L&T

A George III silver teapot and stand, by Langlands & Robertson, Newcastle, profusely bright-cut engraved around two oval cartouches, the stand matching.
1788/1790 *6in (16cm) high 25oz*
$1,800-2,250 TEN

An 18thC Russian silver-gilt teapot, marks partially worn, maker's mark 'A.T', also with a later French import mark.
8in (20.5cm) wide 11oz
$1,400-1,800 WW

A George III silver teapot and stand, by Peter and Ann Bateman, London.

c1793 *11in (28cm) wide 20.5oz*

$1,800-2,250 **WW**

A George III pedestal teapot, by R & D Hennell, London, with wriggle and prick engraved borders and cartouches.

1800 *11.5in (29cm) high 25.75oz*

$975-1,150 **L&T**

A George III provincial silver teapot, by Cattle and Barber, York.

c1808 *9in (22.5cm) high 28.5oz*

$1,300-1,450 **WW**

A late Federal period coin silver teapot, by Thomas Fletcher & Sidney Gardiner, Philadelphia, Pennsylvania.

1815–30 *10.5in (26.5cm) high 58oz*

$3,000-4,500 **SK**

A George III silver teapot, by Emes and Barnard, London, of fluted melon form.

1828 *11in (28cm) wide 24oz*

$1,150-1,300 **L&T**

A George IV silver teapot, by Jonathan Hayne, London.

1820 *10.75in (27cm) wide 25oz*

$900-1,000 **MAB**

A William IV Irish teapot, by PL, Dublin, of lobed melon form.

1834 *7in (17.5cm) high 27oz*

$850-975 **L&T**

A William IV silver teapot, by Paul Storr, London.

c1836 *9in (22.5cm) wide 13oz*

$2,000-2,700 **WW**

A 19th century Dutch silver teapot, marked with pseudo earlier Amsterdam marks.

1845 *7in (17.5cm) high 10oz*

$1,150-1,300 **WW**

A Victorian silver teapot, by Charles Favell for TJ&N Creswick, Sheffield, in contemporary Japanese style, with a presentation inscription.

The inscription reads: 'Presented to the Honble. Charlotte Jane Kenyon, by her Friends and Neighbours, Hanmer, January 13th. 1876 The Hon. Charlotte Jane Kenyon (1843-1893), eldest child of Lloyd Kenyon, 3rd Baron Kenyon and his wife, Georgina (de Grey), was married on 13 January 1876 to the Rev. George Montagu Osborn (1843-1910), Rector of Campton, Bedfordshire, third son of Sir George Robert Osborn, 6th Bt, by his wife, Lady Charlotte Elizabeth Kerr.'

1873 *6.5in (16.5cm) high 15oz*

$1,500-2,250 **MAB**

A Queen Anne silver coffee pot, by William Lukin, Britannia marks for London, the hinged cover to the spout missing.

1705 *9.5in (24cm) high 27oz*

$3,750-4,500 **CHOR**

A rare George II Channel Islands silver coffee pot, by Jean Gavey, Jersey, engraved with an armorial for the Lamprière family, of Rose Manor, Jersey.

c1735 *13.75in (35cm) high 35.75oz*

$30,000-38,000 **WW**

A George II Scottish silver coffee pot, by Charles Dickson, Assay Master Hugh Gordon, Edinburgh, later embossed decoration on a matted background.

The arms are those of Mackintosh, for Aenas Mackintosh, the 23rd laird, who was created a Baronet of the UK on 30 December 1812, but died without issue after eight years when the title became extinct.

1749 *9.5in (24cm) high 25oz*

$2,700-3,300 **WW**

A George III coffee pot, by William Grundy, London.

1759 *11in (28.5cm) high 30.8oz*

$1,800-2,700 **L&T**

A George III silver coffee pot, by Charles Wright, London.

1772 *(27.5cm) high 27.6oz*

$1,400-1,800 **CHEF**

A George II silver coffee pot, marked for Anthony Danvers and struck with the Jamaican sterling standard mark of an alligator's head, possibly made by Abraham Le François, who moved to Jamaica from England in 1749, around the same time as Danvers.

c1775 *11.5in (29cm)*

$18,000-22,500 **MAB**

A George III silver coffee pot, by John Langlands I & John Robertson I, Newcastle, crested, no date letter.

8.5in (21.5cm) high 23oz

$3,000-4,000 **WW**

A George III silver coffee pot, by Charles Wright, London, later foliate chased throughout.
1778 *11in (28cm) high 29oz*
$1,400-1,800 **TEN**

A George III silver coffee pot, by Hester Bateman, London.
c1781 *12in (30.5cm) high 28.75oz*
$3,300-4,400 **WW**

A Danish silver coffee pot, marks indistinct.
c1787-1823 *8in (20cm) high 17.5oz*
$550-700 **L&T**

A George III pedestal coffee pot, by Fogelberg, London.
1802 *11.4in (29cm) high 29oz*
$1,000-1,400 **L&T**

A Victorian silver coffee pot, by R&S Garrard, London, engraved with a crest, garter motto and badge of the Order of the Bath.

The crest, motto and badge of the Order of the Bath are those of Lieutenant General James Caulfeild, CB, who was born on 30 January 1782.

Caulfeild began his army career in 1798 as a cadet in the Bengal Army of the East India Company. He rose steadily in the ranks until being appointed in 1829 Lieutenant Colonel. He was also active as a political officer in British India, publishing in 1831 'Observations on our Indian Administration, Civil and Military', the same year as he was appointed a Companion of the Most Hon. Order of the Bath (CB). Caulfeild left India for London in 1841, when he was promoted to Major General and in 1851 to Lieutenant General. Meanwhile he sat as a Director of the East India Company between 1848 and 1851; in July the following year he was successfully returned as MP for Abingdon but died at his Irish seat, Copsewood, Pallaskenry, County Limerick, on 4 November.

The design for this coffe pot was inspired by an engraving of c1760 after the furniture designer and maker, John Linnell (1723-1796).
1841 *9.5in (24cm) high 34oz*
$2,250-3,000 **MAB**

A Scottish George IV silver coffee pot, by J McKay, Edinburgh.
1821 *11in (28cm) high 28oz*
$1,300-1,450 **L&T**

A mid-19thC Swiss silver coffee pot, by Rehfuss & Cie, Bern, with a lion finial to the flat cover, the spout with a lion's head, an anthemion and dolphin band.
1840–50 *10.5in (26.5cm) high 26.5oz*
$1,000-1,400 **DN**

A Victorian silver coffee pot, by Joseph Angell I & Joseph Angell II, London.
1848 *11.25in (28.5cm) 28oz*
$900-1,000 **CHEF**

A scarce George III tea urn, by William Dempster, Edinburgh, with wrythen knop and pineapple finial.

This tea urn would have represented the larger commissions from a mid-18thC Edinburgh goldsmith. Weighing 84oz it is far heavier than the fashionable ovoid coffee urn which it would have sat beside. At this time, coming toward the end of ovoid coffee urns as a popular piece of Scottish plate, this urn is the beginning of the new trend for hot water urns/samovars as part of the highly fashionable tea equipage, and would have represented a very high status piece of plate for any family. An obvious extravagance as part of a tea set, these urns would have been commissioned in very small numbers relative to the number of tea services produced. This example appears to be one of the earliest examples of such an urn in Scottish silver.

1762 *20in (51cm) high 84oz*

$7,500-9,000 **L&T**

A George III silver tea urn and cover, by Louisa & Samuel Courtauld, London, lacking spigot.

1777 *20.5in (52cm) high 94oz*

$3,750-4,500 **MAB**

A George III silver tea urn, by Emes & Barnard, London, with the crest and motto of the Edinburgh Friendly Insurance Society.

The Friendly Insurance Society, the first of the kind formed in Scotland, was instituted in Edinburgh in the year 1720, and insured proprietors of houses in Edinburgh, Canongate, and Leith against losses by fire. In the year 1727 it obtained a Seal of Cause from the Town Council of Edinburgh, erecting it into a body-corporate, and carried on business on the original plan until 1767, when the benefits of the Society were extended over the whole of Scotland. This Society is now united with the 'Sun'.

1811 *13in (33cm) high 112oz*

$4,400-5,100 **MAB**

A George III four-piece tea service, by Ker & Dempster Edinburgh.

Although made in reasonably large numbers, the survival rate of complete mid-18thC Scottish tea services is relatively low. While some surviving teapots and other individual pieces of tea equipage would have originally been part of one of these sets, most would have been produced as single items for adding to ceramic tea sets to increase their sense of grandeur and status.

1765/1766 *Teapot 6.75in (17.5cm) high 41.5oz*

$10,500-12,000 **L&T**

A George IV silver teaset,by Edward Barnard & Sons, London, chased throughout with foliate panels against a matted ground.

1829 *6in (15cm) high, 51oz*

$2,400-3,000 **TEN**

A William IV silver tea and coffee set, by John & Joseph Angell, London.

1832 *Coffee pot 11in (28cm) high 94oz*

$4,500-5,250 **MAB**

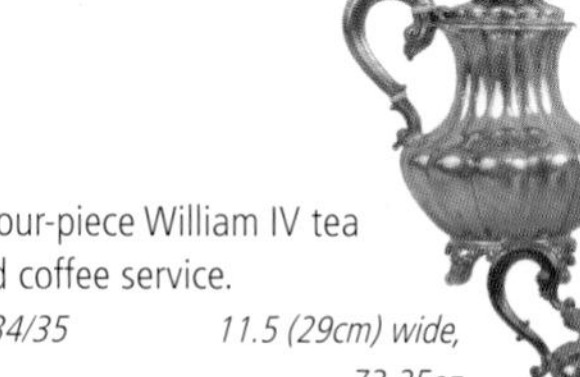

A four-piece William IV tea and coffee service.

1834/35 *11.5 (29cm) wide, 73.25oz*

$2,250-3,000 **DA&H**

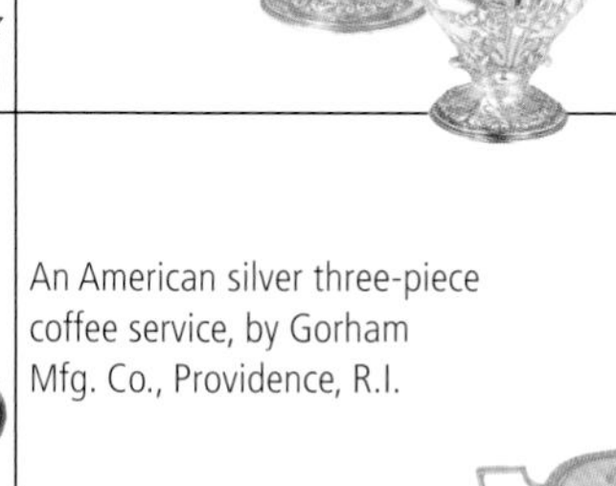

An American silver three-piece coffee service, by Gorham Mfg. Co., Providence, R.I.

1950 *9in (23cm) high 40.5 oz*

$750-900 **DN**

A George III silver tea caddy, by William & Aaron Lestourgeon, London.
c1768 *5in (12.5cm) high 19.25oz*
$7,500-9,000 **ROS**

A George III silver tea caddy, by Duncan Urquhart & Naphtali Hart, London, lacking key.
c1802 *6.75 in (17cm) high, 14.3oz*
$3,400-4,000 **WW**

A late Victorian novelty tea caddy, by E T Bryant, London import marks.
1896 *4.75in (12in) high 7oz*
$1,200-1,400 **HT**

A Continental silver tea caddy, Chester import marks.
1902 *4in (10cm) high 8.75oz*
$375-450 **L&T**

An early 19thC silver filigree caddy spoon, probably Birmingham made.
c1800 *3.25in (8.5cm) long 0.25oz*
$975-1,150 **WW**

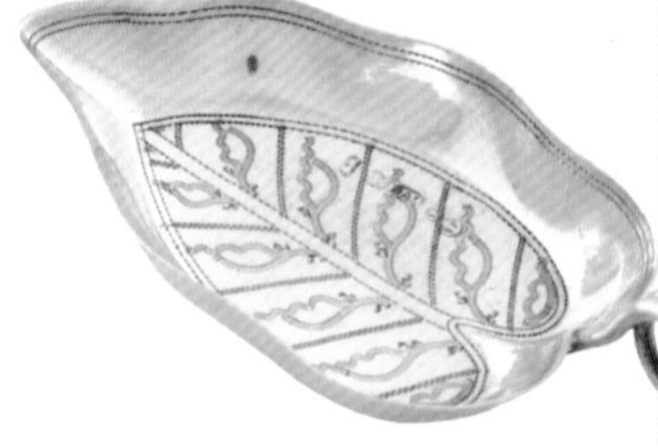
A George III silver deep leaf caddy spoon, by Joseph Willmore, Birmingham.
c1809 *3.25in (8.5cm) long*
$450-550 **WW**

A George III silver scoop form caddy spoon, by Lea & Clark, Birmingham, possible repair to front of bowl.
1816
$120-180 **ECGW**

A George III silver shell form and fiddle pattern caddy spoon, by Thomas Wheatley, Newcastle.
1817
$135-180 **ECGW**

A George IV silver caddy spoon, by L & Co., Birmingham.
1826
$240-300 **ECGW**

A Scottish provincial 'Balmoral' caddy spoon, by William J Fraser, Ballater.
3.5in (8.5cm) long 0.75oz
$550-600 **L&T**

A New Zealand silver-mounted green hardstone caddy spoon, by Joseph Swindell and Son, Christchurch.
c1900 *5.5in (14cm) long*
$115-140 **WW**

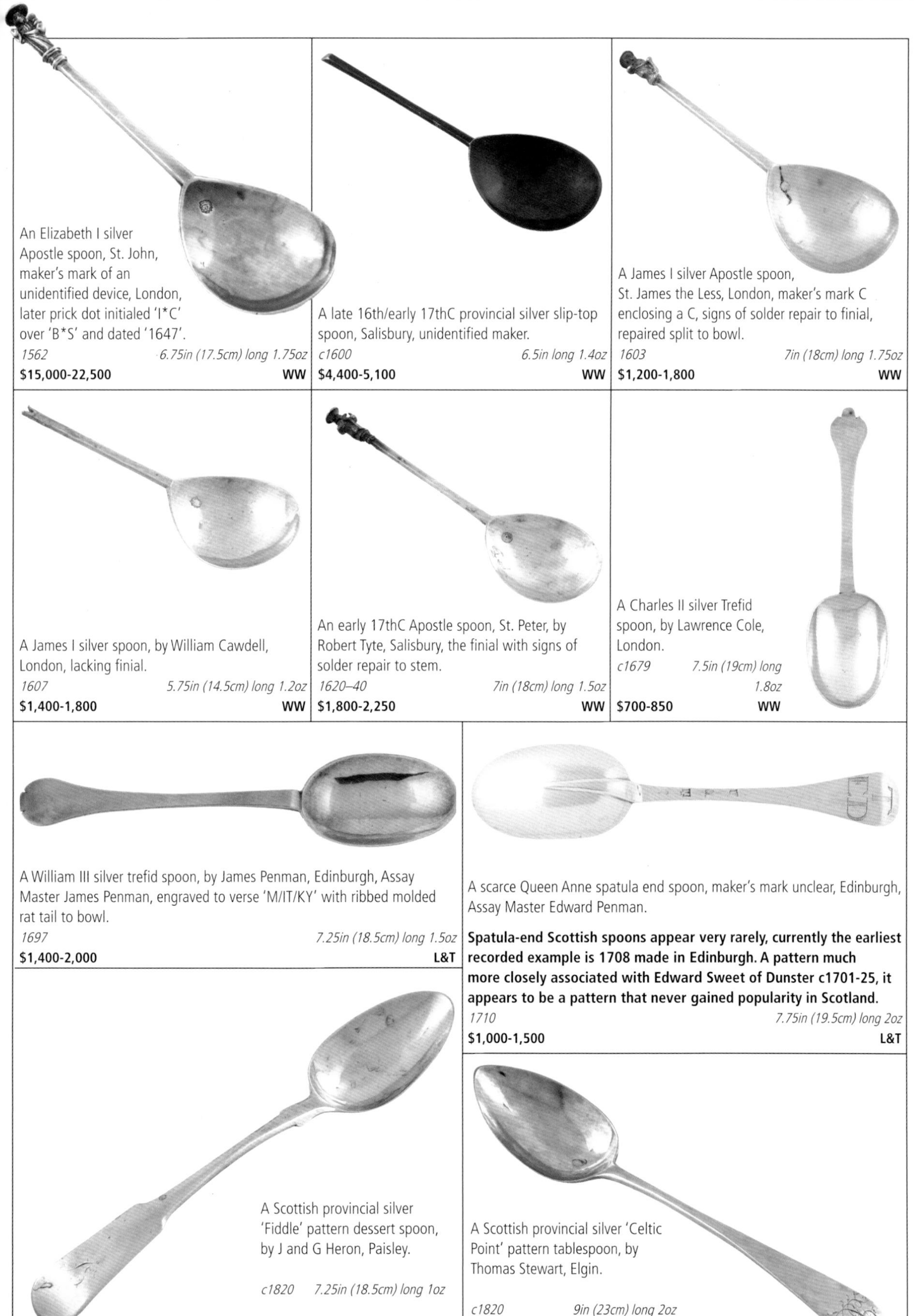

An Elizabeth I silver Apostle spoon, St. John, maker's mark of an unidentified device, London, later prick dot initialed 'I*C' over 'B*S' and dated '1647'.
1562 *6.75in (17.5cm) long 1.75oz*
$15,000-22,500 **WW**

A late 16th/early 17thC provincial silver slip-top spoon, Salisbury, unidentified maker.
c1600 *6.5in long 1.4oz*
$4,400-5,100 **WW**

A James I silver Apostle spoon, St. James the Less, London, maker's mark C enclosing a C, signs of solder repair to finial, repaired split to bowl.
1603 *7in (18cm) long 1.75oz*
$1,200-1,800 **WW**

A James I silver spoon, by William Cawdell, London, lacking finial.
1607 *5.75in (14.5cm) long 1.2oz*
$1,400-1,800 **WW**

An early 17thC Apostle spoon, St. Peter, by Robert Tyte, Salisbury, the finial with signs of solder repair to stem.
1620–40 *7in (18cm) long 1.5oz*
$1,800-2,250 **WW**

A Charles II silver Trefid spoon, by Lawrence Cole, London.
c1679 *7.5in (19cm) long 1.8oz*
$700-850 **WW**

A William III silver trefid spoon, by James Penman, Edinburgh, Assay Master James Penman, engraved to verse 'M/IT/KY' with ribbed molded rat tail to bowl.
1697 *7.25in (18.5cm) long 1.5oz*
$1,400-2,000 **L&T**

A scarce Queen Anne spatula end spoon, maker's mark unclear, Edinburgh, Assay Master Edward Penman.

Spatula-end Scottish spoons appear very rarely, currently the earliest recorded example is 1708 made in Edinburgh. A pattern much more closely associated with Edward Sweet of Dunster c1701-25, it appears to be a pattern that never gained popularity in Scotland.
1710 *7.75in (19.5cm) long 2oz*
$1,000-1,500 **L&T**

A Scottish provincial silver 'Fiddle' pattern dessert spoon, by J and G Heron, Paisley.
c1820 *7.25in (18.5cm) long 1oz*
$550-700 **WW**

A Scottish provincial silver 'Celtic Point' pattern tablespoon, by Thomas Stewart, Elgin.
c1820 *9in (23cm) long 2oz*
$550-700 **WW**

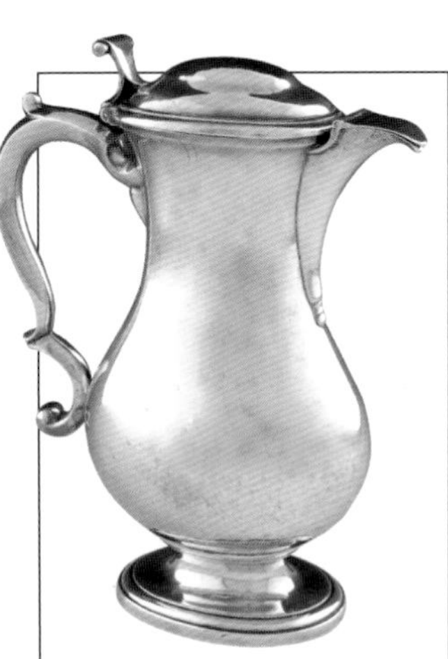

A George II silver hot-water pot, by Paul Crespin, London.

1752 *7.5in (19cm) high 15oz*

$4,500-6,000 **WW**

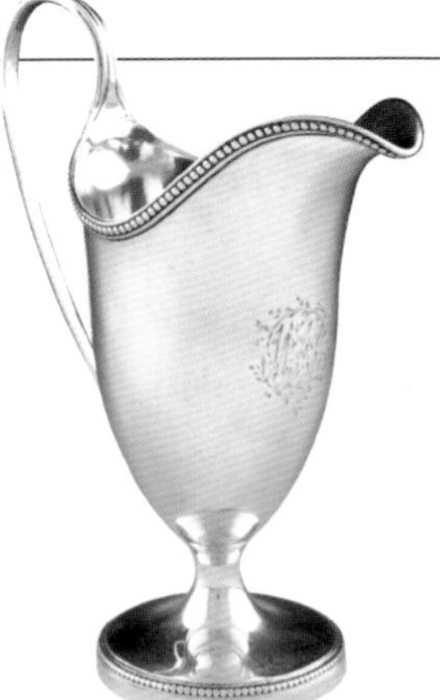

A George III silver cream jug, probably by John Scofield, London, plain helmet form.

c1780 *5.75in (14.5cm) high 3.8oz*

$340-450 **WW**

A late 18thC George III Irish silver cream jug, by William Townsend, Dublin, crests to the two roundels.

5.5in (14cm) high 5.5 oz

$330-420 **DN**

A George III silver cream jug, by Cattle and Barber, York.

c1812 *5in (12.5cm) long 4.5oz*

$600-750 **WW**

A coin silver pitcher, by Edward Lownes, of Philadelphia, inscribed 'Presented to Mr. John S. Barbour by Mr. Bayler & Daughters'.

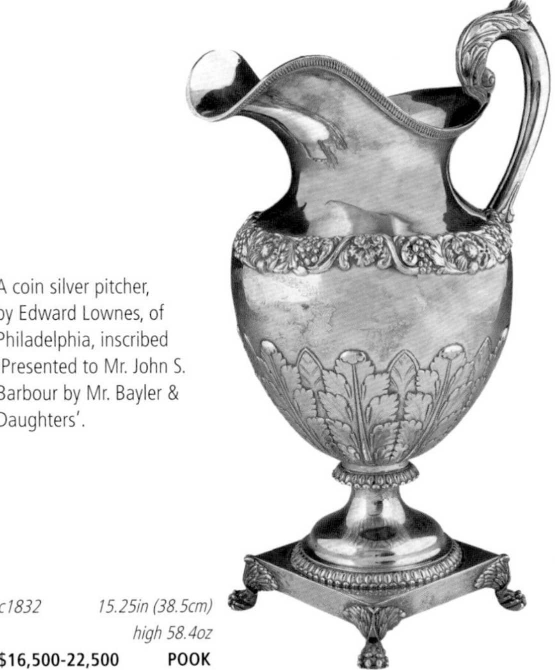

c1832 *15.25in (38.5cm) high 58.4oz*

$16,500-22,500 **POOK**

A William IV silver claret jug, Edward Barnard & Sons, London.

1836 *13.75in (35cm) high 44oz*

$4,050-4,800 **MAB**

A Victorian travelling communion set, by Fox Brothers, London, comprising small wine goblet, a paten and a jug in the form of a flagon with a cruciform finial, the goblet and paten fitting within the flagon for transport.

A paten, or diskos, is a small plate, usually made of silver or gold, used to hold Eucharistic bread which is to be consecrated. It is generally used during the service itself, while the reserved sacrament are stored in the tabernacle in a ciborium.

1851 *5.5in (14cm) high 9.6oz*

$900-1,000 **DN**

A Victorian silver ewer, by the Barnards, London, embossed with foliate scroll decoration and applied vine leaf and grape border.

c1856 *13.75in (35cm) high 42.5oz*

$3,300-4,400 **WW**

A Victorian silver Cellini pattern wine jug, by George Ivory, London, richly allover chased and embossed below a flaring covered spout with caryatid handle, silver-mounted cork stopper.

1858 *11.75in (29.5cm) high 34.3oz*

$3,000-4,500 **CHEF**

A George I silver circular sauce boat, by William Darker, London, with twin tongue-capped S-scroll handles and twin lips.

c1726 *4in (10cm) diam 5.75oz*

$700-850 **DN**

A George II sauce boat, by William Dempster, Edinburgh, Assay Master Hugh Gordon.

1757 *8.25in (21cm) wide 8.25oz*

$1,150-1,300 **L&T**

CLOSER LOOK - IRISH SAUCEBOATS

18thC Irish silver by a prominent maker is highly desirable.

The bodies have finely flat chased Rococo scrolls and fruiting vine.

The scroll formed cartouches have armorial and motto within.

The flying S-scroll handle has a fine quality griffin terminal.

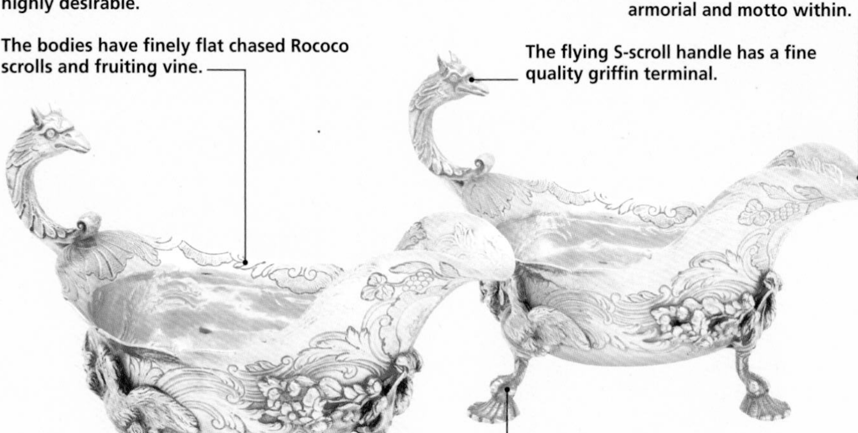

The applied case feet have displayed eagles and floral garlands with claw and ball terminals on shell caps.

A pair of George II Irish sauceboats, by Samuel Wood, Dublin.

c1755 *8.75in (22cm) long 36.25oz total*

$9,750-11,250 **L&T**

A pair of George III silver sauce boats, possibly by William Skeen, London.

c1762 *6.75in (17cm) long 12.5oz*

$1,400-1,800 **WW**

A pair of George II-style Victorian silver sauceboats, by Lambert, London.

1878 *8.25in (21cm) wide 30oz*

$1,500-2,250 **L&T**

A George III silver soup tureen and cover, by Daniel Smith & Robert Sharp, London.

1783 *18in (46cm) wide 90oz*

$6,750-8,250 **MAB**

A George III vegetable dish and cover, by McHattie & Fenwick, Edinburgh, with a cast heraldic finial.

1802 *11in (28cm) wide 29oz*

$2,250-3,000 **L&T**

A late 19thC silver covered tureen, by Ball Black & Co. New York, with stag handles and finial, marked 950.

7.75in (19.5cm) high 22.35 oz

$2,250-3,000 **POOK**

METALWARE

Judith Picks: George III silver salver

One of the fascinating reasons to collect antiques is the history the object can unlock. It is often to do with the families that commissioned or bought the item and no more so than with armorials. This quite simple salver has the arms of Sir Jacob Downing, 4th baronet of East Hatley, Cambridgeshire. He was son of Charles Downing, Comptroller of the Household, and Sarah Garrard and was heir to his cousin, Sir George Downing KCB MP, 3rd baronet.

Sir George died without issue in 1749 having bequeathed (1717) his property to his nephew, Jacob, with the proviso that if Jacob's line failed the estate should found Downing College, Cambridge. Although Sir Jacob married a Miss Price he died without issue in 1764 and after much litigation Downing College was founded in 1800.

A George II silver salver, maker's mark lacking, London, the center with rococo classical display with armorial.
1733 *17.5in (44cm) diam 89oz*
$4,500-5,250 **L&T**

A George II salver, by James Tait, Edinburgh, Assay Master Archibald Ure.
1734 *7.5in (19cm) diam 10.6oz*
$1,800-2,250 **L&T**

A George II salver, by 'FS'?, London, with scalloped edges on three hoof feet.
1735 *5.75in (14.5cm) diam 5oz*
$550-700 **L&T**

A George II silver salver, over-stamped with maker's mark of Edward Aldridge and John Stamper, London, with an armorial, on three claw-and-ball feet.
1748 *16in (40.5cm) diam 64oz*
$2,250-3,000 **WW**

A George II silver salver, by William Peaston, London, engraved beneath 'K' over 'I.A'.
1749 *11.5in (29cm) diam 22.25oz*
$750-900 **DN**

A pair of George II silver meat plates, by Edward Wakelin, London, engraved with armorials, scratch weights and numbers beneath.
1757 *19.75in (50cm) long 125.5oz*
$4,500-6,000 **DN**

A George III silver salver, by John Carter, London, the underside scratch initialed '66"0' and '53"4'.
c1770 *16in (41cm) and 15in (38.5cm) diam 118oz*
$7,500-9,000 **WW**

A George III silver dinner plate, by John Parker I & Edward Wakelin, London, engraved with a crest.
1773 *10.5in (27.5cm) diam 23.3oz*
$900-1,400 **WW**

A pair of George III salvers, by William Robertson, Edinburgh, with engraved armorial, raised on three stepped bracket feet.

1794 *8.5in (21.5cm) diam 30oz*

$1,800-2,250 **L&T**

A George III silver tray, by Thomas Hannam & John Crouch II, London.

c1804 *25.5in (65cm) wide 105oz*

$5,250-6,000 **WW**

A George III silver meat plate, by Paul Storr, London, the border with a shell and foliate rim, engraved with a crest.

1808 *21.5in (54.5cm) long 94.35 oz*

$5,250-6,750 **DN**

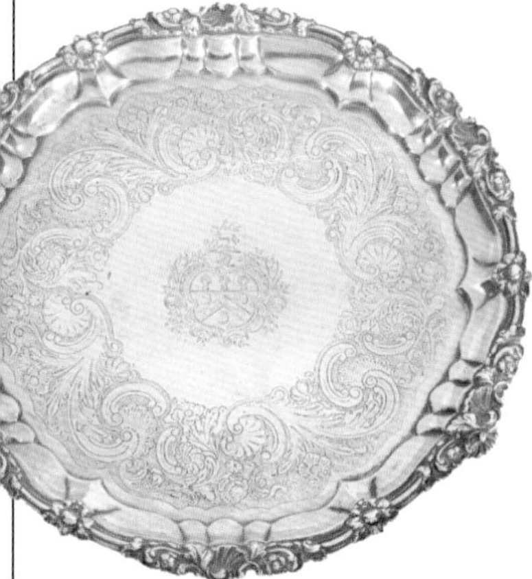

A George IV silver salver by Rebecca Emes & Edward Barnard I, London.

1825 *10.25in (26cm) diam 21.5oz*

$750-900 **DN**

A Victorian silver gilt dressing table tray, by J S Hunt, London, additionally inscribed 'Hunt & Roskell Late Storr Mortimer & Hunt', with monogrammed initials and Viscount's coronet above.

1865 *8.25in (21cm) wide 14.5oz*

$3,750-4,500 **L&T**

A Victorian silver plate, Hunt & Roskell, London, with engraved monogram and crown above.

1865 *10in (25cm) diam 20oz*

$750-1,050 **L&T**

A set of twelve Victorian silver plates, by James Garrard, London.

1888 *9.8in (25cm) diam 250.5oz*

$9,000-10,500 **WW**

A set of thirty Edwardian silver-gilt dessert plates, by Catchpole and Williams, London, guillochè borders, engraved with a crest.

c1905 *9.5in (24cm) 520oz.*

$15,000-21,000 **WW**

A silver salver, by WS over CS, Sheffield, on four gnarl feet.

1913 *20.5in (52cm) diam 100oz*

$3,450-4,400 **WW**

A William & Mary silver caster, maker's mark 'DA' crowned, London, with armorial within a wreath of plumes.
1691 *5.25in (13.5cm) high 5oz*
$3,000-4,000 **CHOR**

An early 18thC Britannia sugar caster, makers mark indistinct, engraved crest to body.
c1700 *9in (23cm) high 15.7oz*
$3,000-4,500 **L&T**

A Queen Anne silver sugar caster, by Charles Adam, London.
1708 *8in (20cm) 8.5oz*
$2,700-3,300 **WW**

A George III Irish silver sugar caster, by W Williamson (probably), Dublin.
1758/1765 *6.25in (15.5cm) high 6oz*
$550-700 **L&T**

A late 18thC Irish provincial silver pepper pot, by George Hodder, Cork.
c1760 *4.75in (12cm) high 3.5oz*
$2,250-3,000 **WW**

A late 18thC Irish provincial silver pepper pot, by George Hodder, Cork.
c1760 *4.75in (12cm) high 3.5oz*
$1,950-2,400 **WW**

A George III caster, Edinburgh (maker's mark lacking).
1761 *7.75in (20cm) high 10.6oz*
$1,500-2,250 **L&T**

A George III silver pepper pot, by John Delmester, London.
c1762 *4.75in (12cm) high 2oz*
$255-330 **WW**

A pair of Victorian silver casters, by James Jay Ltd of London, Chester.
1900 *8.75in (22.5cm) high 16oz*
$450-600 **MAB**

An Edwardian Britannia standard silver miniature Warwick cruet frame, by Maurice Freeman, London.
1907 *4in (10cm) long 40z*
$600-750 **WW**

A pair of Dutch silver casters, with flame finials.
c1920 *9.25in (23.5cm) high 34oz*
$1,500-2,100 **WW**

A Victorian silver novelty owl pepper caster, by Charles Thomas Fox & George Fox, London, with inset two-color glass eyes.

c1851 *3in (7.7cm) high 1.85oz*

$700-850 **DN**

A Victorian 'Game cock' silver cruet, by J Barclay Hennell, London, comprising a pair of pepperettes and mustard pot.

1881 *3in (7.5cm) high 7.2oz*

$1,500-2,250 **L&T**

A Continental novelty parakeet silver pepper pot, importer's mark of Samuel Landeck, Chester.

1903 *8.25in (21cm) long 6oz*

$750-850 **WW**

A pair of 'Fighting Cock' silver pepperettes, by G Gilliam London.

1904 *2.5in (6.5cm) high 10.5oz*

$900-1,000 **L&T**

A novelty silver chauffeur pepper pot, by Saunders and Shepherd, Chester.

c1906 *3.5in (8.8cm) high*

$1,150-1,300 **WW**

An Edwardian novelty silver rocking horse pepper pot, by Saunders and Shepherd, Chester.

1907 *2in (5cm) long 0.5oz*

$600-700 **WW**

A pair of silver and enamel novelty mannequin pepper pots, by Louis Willmott, London.

c1907 *4in (10cm) high*

$1,800-2,100 **WW**

A silver novelty terrier pepper pot, by William Hornby, London.

c1908 *3in (8cm) long 3.6oz*

$850-900 **WW**

A novelty silver teddy bear pepper pot, by H.V Pithey and Co, Birmingham.

c1909 *1.5in (3.7cm) high 0.2oz*

$375-450 **WW**

A pair of Zimbabwean silver hippopotomus salt and pepper pots, by Patrick Mavros.

1.5in (3.5cm) high

$900-1,000 **WW**

A Charles II silver bleeding bowl, maker's mark of CK, London, the handle part marked and scratch initialed 'W' over 'R*M'.
c1673 *8.5in (21.5cm) long 8.3oz*
$6,000-6,750 **WW**

A late Victorian punch bowl, retailed by Mappin & Webb, London.
1895 *10in (26cm) diam 31oz*
$850-1,150 **L&T**

A late Victorian silver pedestal punch bowl, by Charles Stuart Harris, London.
c1897 *15.75in (40cm) diam 86.65 oz*
$6,000-7,500 **DN**

A late Victorian punch bowl, by Walker & Hall, Sheffield, with twin lion mask drop ring handles.
1898 *10in (25.5cm) diam 41oz*
$1,500-2,100 **L&T**

An American silver fruit bowl, marked Regency, STERLING.
12in (31cm) diam 24.5oz
$700-850 **L&T**

A pair of late Victorian rose bowls, by Walker & Hall, Sheffield, with embossed acanthus lower section.
1901 *5.5in (14cm) diam 20oz*
$600-900 **L&T**

An Edwardian silver punch bowl, cover and ladle, by Goldsmiths & Silversmiths Company, London.
1904 *8.6in (22cm) diam 77.5oz*
$5,250-6,750 **L&T**

A Continental silver basket, with pierced lattice decoration to sides and handles, import marks.
1905 *20in (53cm) wide 69oz*
$3,000-4,000 **L&T**

A pair of German silver figural comports, by Neresheimer of Hanau, with import marks for Chester, importer's mark of Berthold Muller.
c1910 *9.8in (25cm) high 31oz*
$2,250-3,000 **WW**

A 20thC American silver bowl, by International Silver Co., Meriden, Connecticut.
10 in (25.5cm) diam 25.05 oz
$450-600 **DN**

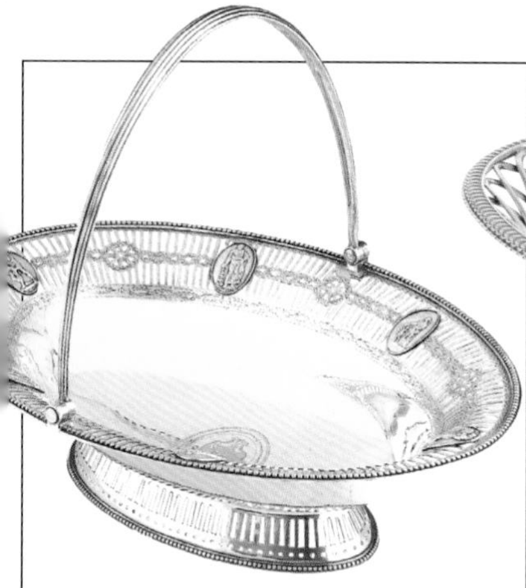

A George III silver cake basket, by Burrage Davenport.
1781-82 *14.5in (37cm) wide 29.75oz*
$4,500-6,000 **POOK**

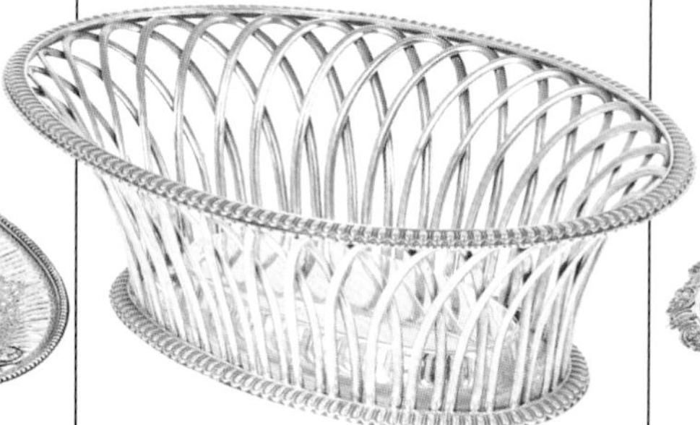

A George III silver basket, by Burwash & Sibley, London.
1809 *10.5in (26.5cm) wide 31oz*
$2,250-3,000 **MAB**

A George IV silver basket, by John Hayen, London, engraved with a coat-of-arms, crest and motto, swing handle damaged.
1821 *11.75in (30cm) diam 31oz*
$850-975 **MAB**

A Victorian silver swing-handled sugar basket, by the Barnards, London.
c1874 *5in (13cm) long 4.5oz*
$400-550 **WW**

A Victorian silver egg stand, by George Fox, London.
c1867 *5.5in (14cm) high 11oz*
$1,000-1,200 **DN**

A George II Irish silver lemon strainer, Dublin, no maker's mark.
1731 *7.25in (18.5cm) long 3.6oz*
$2,250-3,000 **WW**

An early George III silver orange or lemon strainer, maker's mark 'E …'?, London.
c1761 *. 8in (20cm) long 3.5oz*
$600-750 **DN**

A George IV Irish 'Fiddle' pattern silver fish slice, by T Farnett, Dublin.
1824 *12in (30cm) long 5.5oz*
$700-850 **L&T**

A pair of Edwardian asparagus tongs, by Goldsmiths & Silversmiths Company, London.
1904 *23cm long 4.6oz*
$225-300 **L&T**

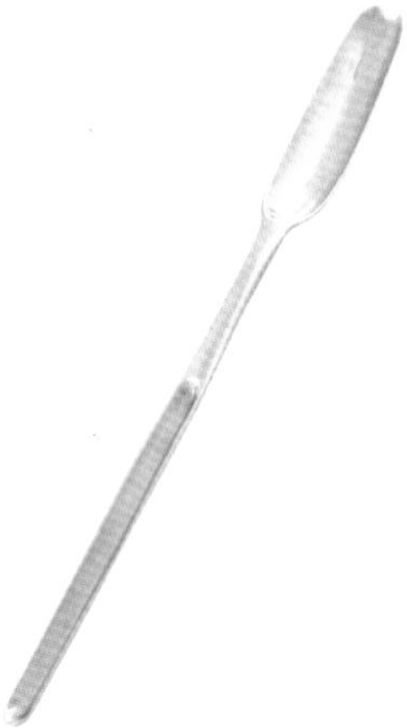

A George I silver marrow scoop, possibly by George Manjoy, London.
1721 *8.5in (21.5cm) long 1.2oz.*
$300-400 **WW**

A George III silver toast rack, by Solomon Hougham, London.
c.1816 *9.4in (23.8cm) long 9.5oz*
$360-450 **WW**

A George IV toastrack, by Emes & Barnard, London.
1820/21 *6.5in (16.5cm) long 11ozs*
$850-975 **HT**

A George IV silver toast rack, by Benjamin Smith, London.
c1827 *6in (15.8cm) long 13oz*
$975-1,150 **WW**

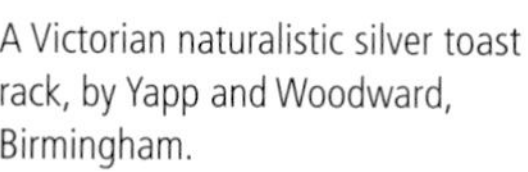

A Victorian naturalistic silver toast rack, by Yapp and Woodward, Birmingham.
1844 *7.4 in (19cm) long 4oz*
$600-700 **WW**

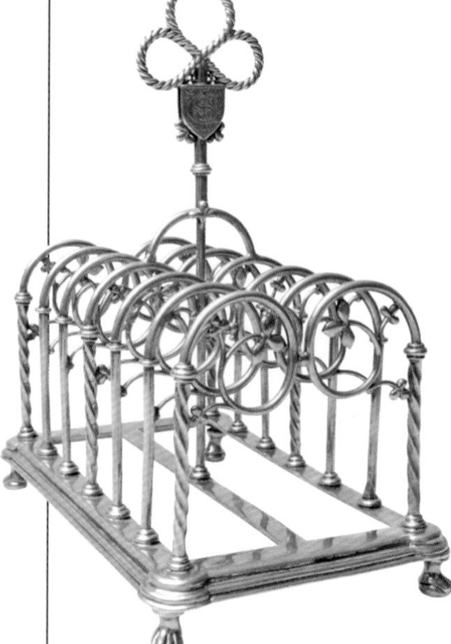

A Victorian six-section silver toast rack, in the Gothic-Revival style, by John Hardman & Co, Birmingham.
1856. *7in (18cm) long 17oz*
$12,750-14,250 **HW**

A pair of George III silver navette pedestal salt cellars, by William Plummer, London, with blue glass liners.
c1782 *5in (12.5cm) long 6.75oz*
$375-450 **DN**

A pair of George IV silver late 17thC style salt cellars, by R. & S. Garrard & Co. (Robert Garrard II), London.
1826 *3.75in (9.5cm) diam 11oz*
$450-600 **DN**

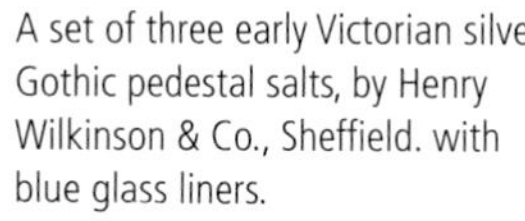

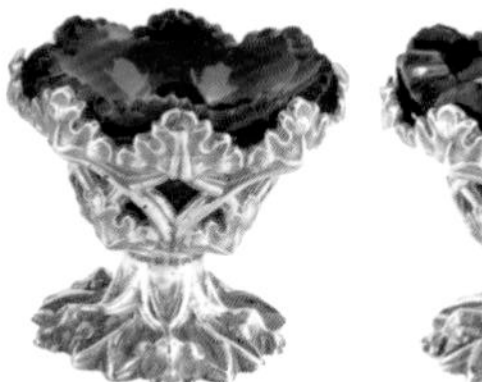

A set of three early Victorian silver Gothic pedestal salts, by Henry Wilkinson & Co., Sheffield. with blue glass liners.
1838 *2.5in (6.5cm) 8.75oz*
$450-600 **DN**

A pair of Victorian silver salts, by Joseph & Albert Savory, London.
1845 *3.25in (8.5cm) diam 6.75 oz*
$340-450 **DN**

An early Victorian silver mustard pot, by Charles Reily and George Storer, London.
1837 4in (10cm) long 4.55 oz
$550-600 **DN**

A George II silver wine label, maker's mark unidentified.
c1750 *2in (5cm) long*
$300-400 **WW**

A George III silver wine label, by Susannah Barker, London.
c1785 *2in (5cm) long*
$450-600 **WW**

A George III cast silver-gilt wine label, by Benjamin Smith, London.
c1807 *2in (5.2cm) wide*
$1,500-2,000 **WW**

A George III silver-gilt wine label, by Benjamin Smith, London.
c1807 *3in (7.8cm) long*
$1,200-1,400 **WW**

A George III silver wine label, by Solomon Hougham or Simon Harris, London, titled 'SHERRY'.
1814 *2½in (6.5cm) long 0.8oz*
$300-400 **WW**

A Scottish provincial silver wine label, by Peter Lambert of Montrose, with Edinburgh marks.
c1821 *1.4in (3.6cm) long*
$300-450 **WW**

A George IV silver wine label, by The Barnards, London.
c1827 *2.5in (6cm) long 0.8oz*
$225-300 **WW**

A George IV cast silver wine label, by Robert Garrard, London.
1828 *2.25in (5.5cm) long 1.1oz*
$600-700 **WW**

Four 19thC Wedgwood ceramic bin labels.

Wine, bin labels are the lowly but elder relations of decanter labels and served a different purpose. Their origins go back to the mid 17th century when the binning or storage of wines first became important. They then served a utilitarian purpose identifying unmarked bottles in wine cellars. They were either directly nailed to a shelf on which were stored the bottles or barrels or directly to the barrel itself. Bin labels are in the main made from pottery including delftware and creamware, or broadly speaking, earthenware. They are therefore highly susceptible to damage and destruction and therefore there are far fewer bin labels than decanter labels still in existence. Earthenware requires a glaze to make it impervious to liquids.
5½in (14cm) long
$600-750 **WW**

A William IV silver wine label, by Rawlings and Summers, London, incised 'SWEET WINE'.
1834 *2.25in (6.5cm) long 0.7oz*
$450-600 **WW**

A silver decanter label 'PORT', by Rawlings & Summers, London.
1850
$100-115 **ECGW**

METALWARE

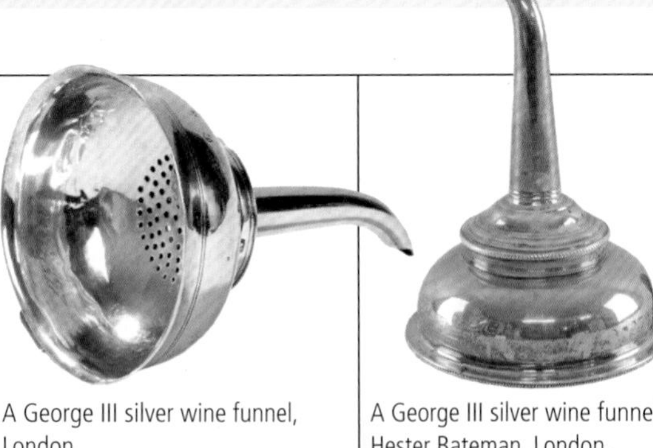

A George III silver wine funnel, London.
1774 *4.3in (11cm) high*
$300-400 **LOCK**

A George III silver wine funnel, by Hester Bateman, London.
1788 *2oz*
$550-600 **ECGW**

A George III wine funnel, by Robert Gray & Sons of Glasgow (probably), Edinburgh.
c1800 *5.5in (14cm) high 4.2oz*
$1,400-1,500 **L&T**

A George III silver wine funnel, by Thomas Wheatley, Newcastle.
1819 3.5oz
$850-900 **ECGW**

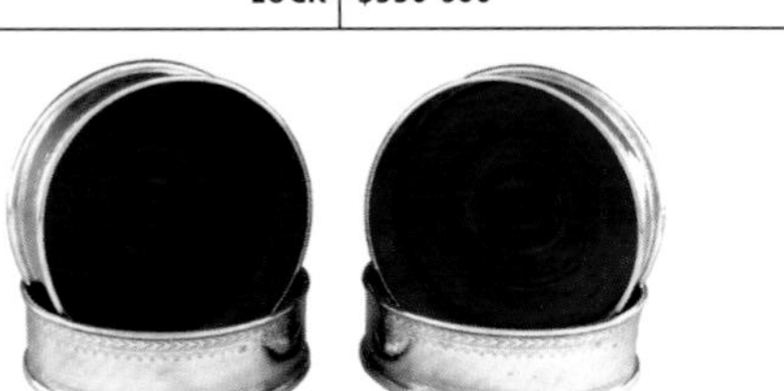

A set of four George III Irish silver wine coasters, by Christopher Haines, Dublin.
1794 *5in (12.5cm) diam*
$6,000-6,750 set **WW**

A pair of George III wine coasters, by Francis Howden, Edinburgh.
1808 *5.5in (14cm) diam*
$3,300-4,400 **L&T**

Judith Picks: wine bottle holder

Enjoying a glass of wine as I do, I think it is a great shame that some of the accoutrements of enjoying a glass have somehow gone out of fashion. Wine funnels have been known from the early 18thC. Wine coasters, or decanter stands as they are sometimes known, have been an integral part of the elegant dining table in England since the same period, when they were also known as bottle slides. A coaster serves various functions, originally more functional than aesthetic; it prevents spillage from a bottle or decanter on a tablecloth or directly on to a polished table top; it stops one decanter touching another and thus prevents chipping of cut-glass decanters; and it allows the bottle or decanter to be slid across the table, 'coasting', from one diner to another. But I am particularly struck by this fine bottle holder - an absolute must for an elegant 19thC dinner party.

A William IV silver wine bottle holder, by Robert Garrard I.
c1830 *4.5in (11cm) high 6.7 oz*
$1,150-1,300 **DN**

A George I silver brandy pan, maker's mark worn, London.
c1726 *9in (23.5cm) long 7.2oz*
$1,150-1,300 **WW**

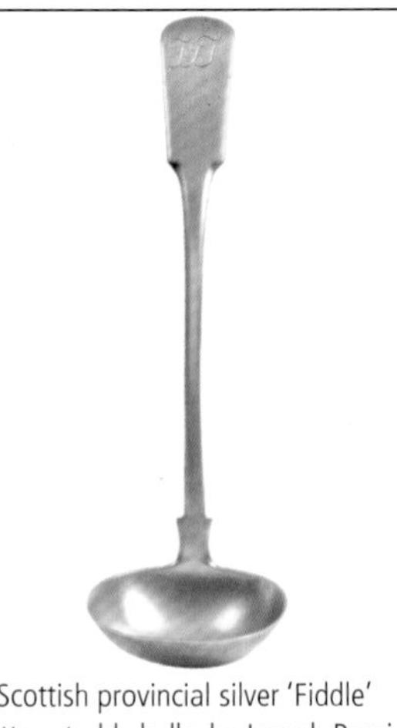

A Scottish provincial silver 'Fiddle' pattern toddy ladle, by Joseph Pozzi, Elgin.
c1840 *7in (17cm) long 0.99oz*
$900-1,400 **TEN**

A pair of Sheffield-plated wine coolers, unmarked, with twin lion mask and ring handles.

8in (20cm) high

$1,800-2,250 **L&T**

A Victorian electro-plated, cut and frosted glass spirit decanter wagon, with Registration mark for 18th September.

1863 *10.5 in (27cm) high*

$1,150-1,300 **DN**

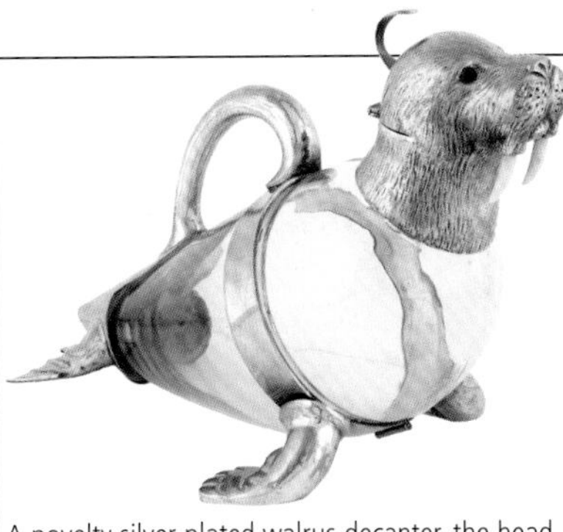

A novelty silver-plated walrus decanter, the head naturalistically formed with glass eyes and ivory tusks.

14in (35cm) long

$3,750-4,500 **L&T**

ESSENTIAL REFERENCE - SHEFFIELD PLATE

Plating was introduced by Thomas Bolsover, a cutler in Sheffield, in 1742. It was not made in any quantities until the 1770s. A silver sheet was placed onto a copper ingot, and all the air removed by hammering. Another layer of copper was applied to protect the silver and the 'sandwich' was then placed in a hot fire until the silver melted and fused to the ingot (silver melts before copper). If the ingots were then put through a rolling mill the metal could stretch to an almost infinite length without the silver leaving the copper. Sheffield plate virtually disappeared in the 1840s with the introduction of electroplate. Although an electroplate goblet is recorded as early as 1814, it was not really until Elkington & Co took out a patent in 1840 that the process became widespread. Electroplating involved putting a metal object in solution in a tank with a positive wire attached to a silver anode. A current was then passed from the positive to the negative. This resulted in a fine sheet of silver being applied to the object, which was whiter and harsher in appearance than Sheffield plate. Initially, the base metal was copper, but later nickel was used, hence the lettering EPNS (electroplated nickel silver), which is stamped on many electroplated wares.

A George III old Sheffield plated coffee pot, unmarked.

c1780 *11.6in (29.5cm) high*

$300-400 **WW**

A George III old Sheffield plated tea urn, with a stained green ivory tap, unmarked.

c1790 *14.8in (36.5cm) high*

$225-300 **WW**

An old Sheffield-plate argyle, unmarked.

6.7in (17cm) high

$600-700 **L&T**

A 19thC electroplated brass coffee pot, marked with a fleur-de-lys, and maker's mark 'I.B', re-plated.

8.4in (21.3cm) high

$975-1,150 **WW**

A pair of Old Sheffield plated three-light candelabra, unmarked.

c1830 *20.6in (52.3cm) high*

$450-550 **WW**

A pair of 19thC silver-plated twin-light wall sconces, in the 17thC style.

14in (36cm) high

$1,500-2,100 **L&T**

A George III old Sheffield plated soup tureen and cover, engraved with two armorials.
c1800 *15in (38.5cm) wide*
$550-600 **WW**

A pair of silver-plated entrèe dishes and covers, by Elkington & Co
10.6in (27cm) wide
$130-165 **L&T**

An electroplate jardinière, unmarked, probably French.
c1900 *14.5in (37cm) long*
$550-700 **MAB**

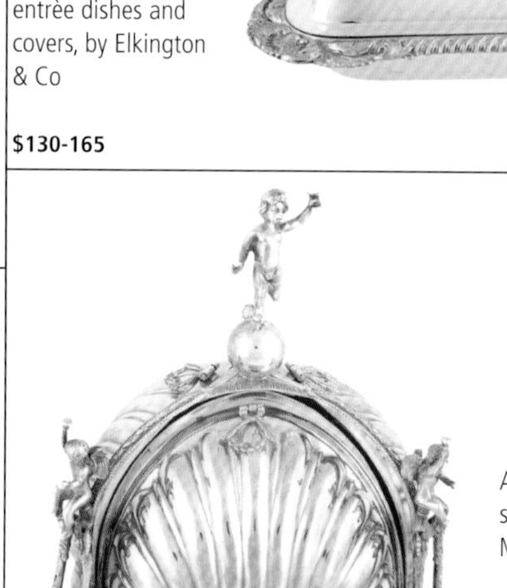

A silver plated three section biscuit box, by Mappin & Webb.
10.6in (27cm) high
$700-850 **L&T**

A Victorian electroplated epergne, by Elkington and Co, modeled as palm trees, with Robinson Crusoe.
c1858 *17.75in (45cm) high*
$700-850 **WW**

One of a pair of late George III Old Sheffield plate trays, engraved with an armorial and a motto 'Ne Cede Malis'.
c1815 *27in (66.5cm) wide*
$975-1,150 pair **DN**

An early 19thC Sheffield-plated tray.
32.3in (82cm) long
$375-450 **WW**

A large Victorian silver-plated salver, by Elkington & Co, engraved with armorial, also to reverse 'To Mary Rice Henn from her Mother 1844'.
1844 *22.8in (58cm) wide*
$550-600 **L&T**

A Victorian electroplated tray, by James Dixon and Sons.
22.6in (57.5cm) long
$180-225 **WW**

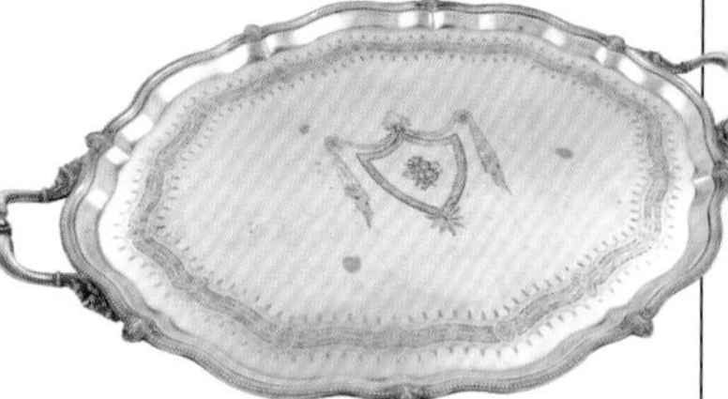

A Victorian electroplated tray, with a central shield cartouche.
28in (71cm) long
$225-300 **WW**

An 18thC pewter double-volute lidded pint measure, maker's mark worn, but probably 'TS'.

c1760-1800 *6in (15cm) high*

$300-450 WW

An 18thC Swiss pewter lidded flagon or stegkanne, with a touchmark to the handle with initials 'L R' possibly for Ludwig Roder.

12.75in (32cm) high

$900-1,000 WW

A pewter flagon, by Johann Phillip Alberti, Philadelphia, Pennsylvania, 1754-1780, with lid with heart shaped spout, the body with double C-scroll handle and the inscription 'Georg-Kirchen 1763'.

For a nearly identical example, see 'Herr Pewter in Pennsylvania German Churches', plate 166 and 167. A flagon, also inscribed "Georg-Kirchen 1763" and purchased from the Costar family of Homsburg, PA was sold at the Wichmann sale, Sotheby's June 1983, lot 154.

1763 *15in (38cm) high*

$52,500-60,000 POOK

An 18thC pewter charger, by Robert Salder, London & Newcastle.

c1750 *18.25in (46.3cm) diam*

$225-300 WW

A Pennsylvania copper kettle, impressed 'D. Bentley Phila 1840'.

1840 18in (45.5cm) high

$4,000-5,250 POOK

ESSENTIAL REFERENCE - QUEEN ANNE WEIGHT

The act of Union in 1707 demanded many changes within Scotland and this is seen not only in currency and minting of coins, but also weights and measures; attempting to bring Scotland into line with the English systems and standards. There had been many previous attempts to standardize weights and measures within Scotland and England before but without any great success until the push for it from 1707. In fact, it did not take hold completely until the 1824 act and the issue of Imperial weights in 1826 which formally and almost finally brought Scottish weights and measures into line with England.

- **This weight would originally have formed part of stacking set (not dissimilar to those commonplace on shop keepers counters). In 1707 it is recorded that 21 sets were commissioned. However only parts of 14 sets are still known to survive, mainly still residing within council and museum collections. These sets would have represented a town's official weights which all other merchant's weights would have had to be tested against to be sure of honest dealings.**

A rare Queen Anne 'Union' 8lb weight, engraved with crown above 'PRIMO MAII, AR, ANo Doni 1707, A REGNI VI, VIII AUER'.

5.5in (14cm) diam

$5,250-6,750 L&T

A Willoughby Shade Berks County, Pennsylvania wrigglework coffee pot, the base inscribed Sarah Gargas and the handle stamped W.Shade.

c1840 *11in (27.9cm) high*

$3,000-4,500 POOK

A set of three late 19thC toleware tea cannisters and covers.

25.75in (40cm) high

$340-450 CHEF

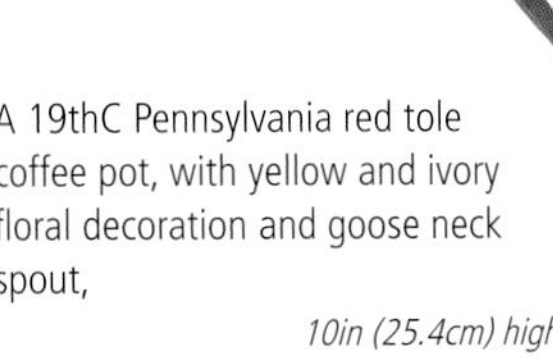

A 19thC Pennsylvania red tole coffee pot, with yellow and ivory floral decoration and goose neck spout,

10in (25.4cm) high

$24,000-30,000 POOK

METALWARE

A wine glass, with a bell-shaped bowl over a stem with beaded knop, on domed foot.

c1730 *6.5in (16.5cm) high*

$850-975 **SWO**

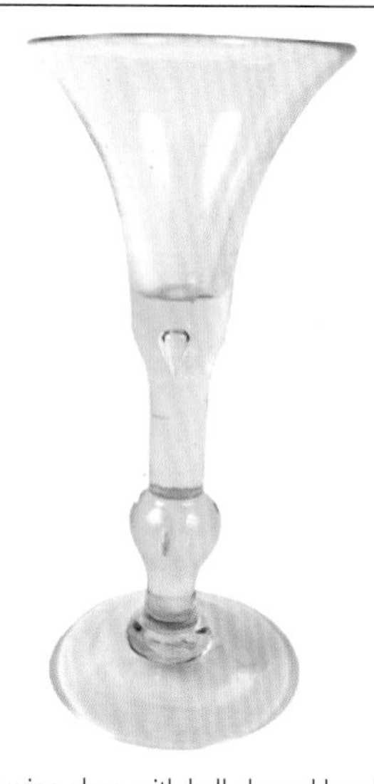

A wine glass, with bell-shaped bowl with baluster-knopped teared stem.

c1740 *6in (15.8cm) high*

$225-400 **SWO**

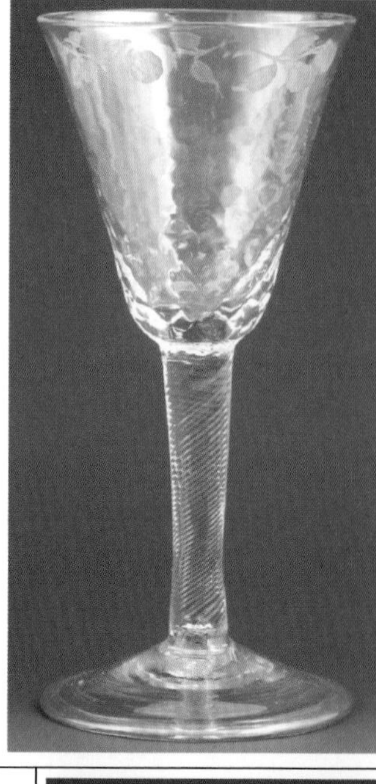

A cider glass, the bowl with hammered effect, the rim engraved with fruit, raised on an incised twist stem above a folded foot.

c1740 *7in (17.5cm) high*

$4,000-4,500 **WW**

A Newcastle goblet, the bell shaped bowl engraved, on a multi-knopped stem, small chip to foot.

c1740 *7in (18.5cm) high*

$750-1,000 **TEN**

A kit-kat type glass, the funnel bowl with diamond point engraved 'A BUMPER TO YE KING', on a balustroid stem and domed foot.

c1740 *7in (18cm) high*

$900-1,000 **TEN**

A cordial glass, with triple-knop stem on slightly domed folded foot.

c1750 *5in (13cm) high*

$280-340 **SWO**

A mid 18thC Newcastle light baluster wine glass, the funnel bowl raised on a multiple knopped stem, one knop with two rows of tears, the lower with a single teardrop.

6.5in (16cm) high

$1,200-1,400 **WW**

A mid-18thC Newcastle light baluster glass, the bowl engraved with the arms of Delft supported by two lions, raised on a multiple knopped stem with central teardrop above a folded foot.

8in (20.5cm) high

$3,000-4,000 **WW**

A George III wine glass, the funnel bowl etched in capitals 'HODGE PODGE' and the date '5 MAY 1752' within laurel wreaths, on a facet-cut stem.

This Glasgow, Scotland club was founded in the 18th century and is still in existence. Records commmence on 5th May 1752 and Dr John Moore was a famous founder member. In its original form the club had a literary nature. They started out meeting monthly at seven but this was soon changed to five – 'the dinner hour among the better classes' – according to John Strang in his 1856 'Glasgow and its clubs' where a full thirty-two pages are devoted to the history of this club. He continues 'with whist and conversation the evening passed till nine-o'clock arrived'.

c1760 *6.75in (17cm) high*

$1,800-2,250 **L&T**

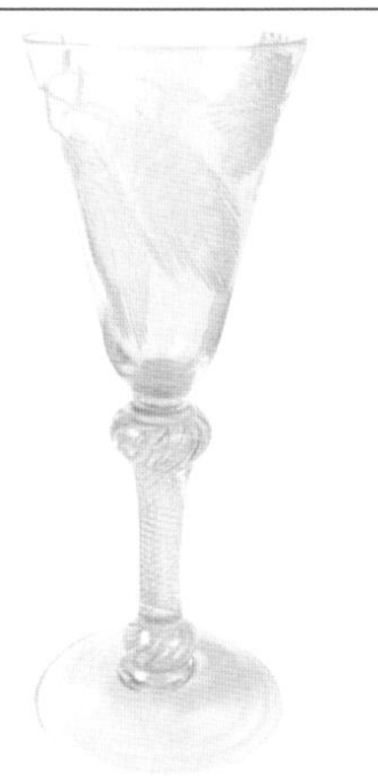

An airtwist ale glass, the funnel-shaped bowl engraved with hops and barley, on a double-knop stem.

c1750 *7in (18cm) high*

$450-550 **SWO**

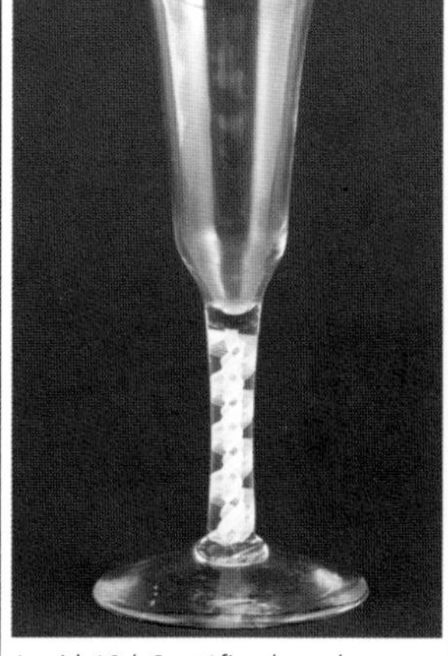

A mid-18thC ratâfia glass, the narrow funnel bowl rising from a double series opaque twist stem.

7in (18cm) high

$600-900 **WW**

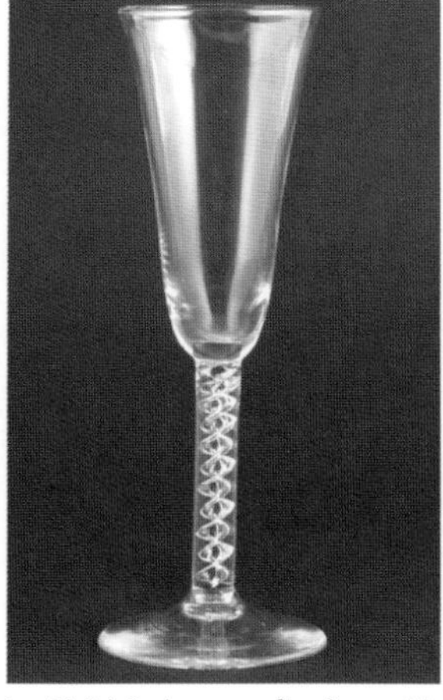

A mid-8thC ale or ratafia glass, with tall flared bowl raised on a spiraling airtwist stem.

8in (20cm) high

$340-450 **WW**

A mid-18thC wine glass, raised on a knopped opaque airtwist stem.

5.75in (14.5cm) high

$225-300 **WW**

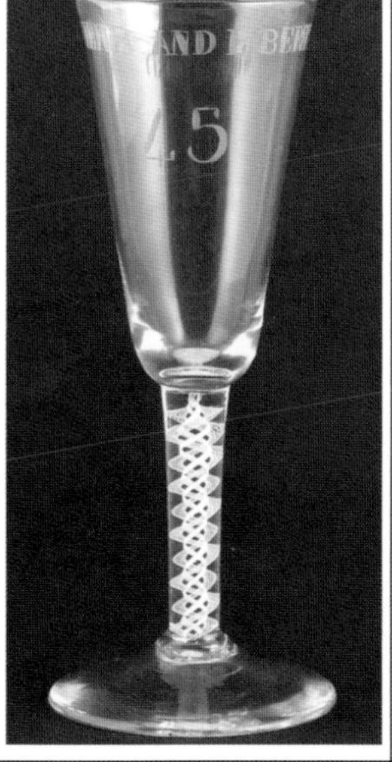

An 18thC political ale glass, engraved 'Wilkes and Liberty' above the number 45, raised on a double series opaque twist stem.

In issue 45 of his publication, 'The North Briton', John Wilkes' attack on George III's 1763 speech endorsing the Paris Peace Treaty earned him a warrant for his arrest for libel. With strong public support, Wilkes was cleared by the Lord Chief Justice.

7in (18cm) high

$4,500-5,250 **WW**

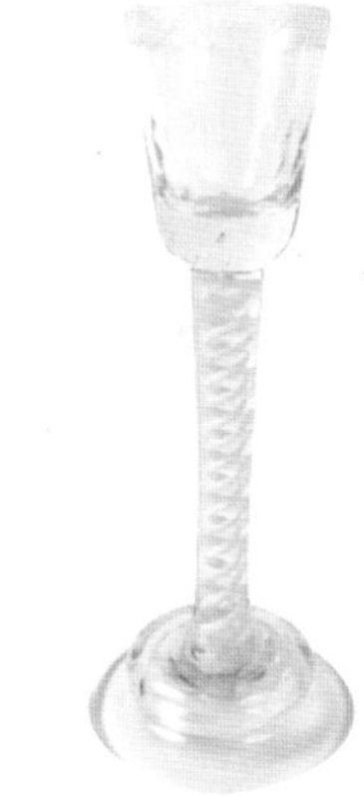

A composite stem ratafia glass, the elongated funnel bowl, the upper section with double opaque twist, the lower section with knopped air twist.

c1760 *7in (18.5cm) high*

$1,150-1,300 **SWO**

An opaque twist cordial glass, with round funnel-shaped bowl, the stem with inner solid and outer gauze corkscrews, on domed foot.

c1760 *6in (15.5cm) high*

$900-1,000 **SWO**

A wine glass, the narrow funnel bowl with an unusual flattened knop, raised on a slender opaque twist stem.

c1760 *6.5in (16.5cm) high*

$1,150-1,450 **WW**

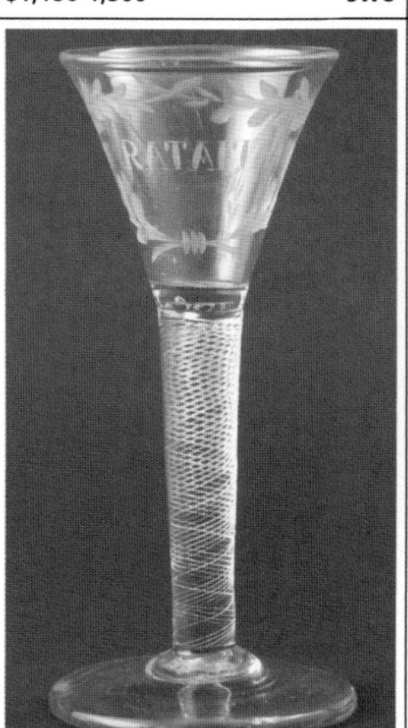

A ratafia glass, with small flared bowl raised on a diminished airtwist stem, the bowl engraved 'Ratafia' within a leaf garland.

c1760 *5.5in (14cm) high*

$1,800-3,000 **WW**

A wine glass, the bell-shaped bowl raised on a double knopped airtwist stem above a conical foot.

c1765 *7in (18cm)*

$450-750 **WW**

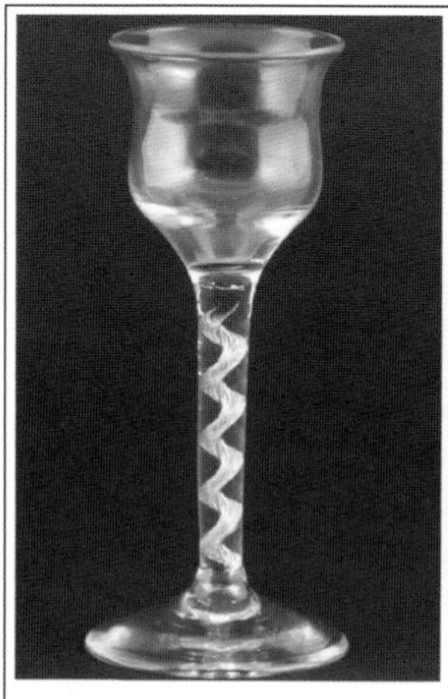

A wine glass, with bell-shaped bowl raised on an airtwist stem.

c1760 *6in (15cm) high*

$300-400 **WW**

A wine glass, the funnel bowl with honeycomb molding, raised on an airtwist stem.

c1760 *6.5in (16.5cm) high*

$600-750 **WW**

An ale glass, the tall narrow bowl engraved with hops and barley, raised on a double series opaque airtwist stem.

c1765 *7.5in (18.5cm) high*

$400-450 **WW**

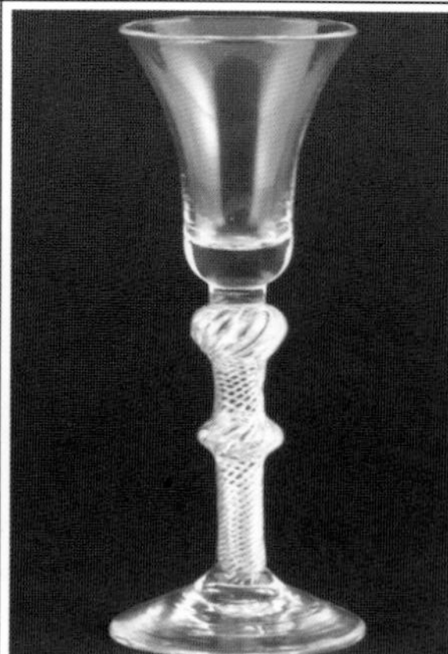

A wine glass, the bell-shaped bowl raised on a double-knopped airtwist stem.

c1760 *6.75in (17cm) high*

$400-450 **WW**

A wine glass, the funnel bowl with dimple molding, raised on an airtwist stem.

c1760 *6.5in (16.5cm) high*

$700-850 **WW**

An ale glass, the bowl engraved with hops and barley, raised on a double-knopped airtwist stem.

c1760 *7.75in (19.5cm) high*

$750-900 **WW**

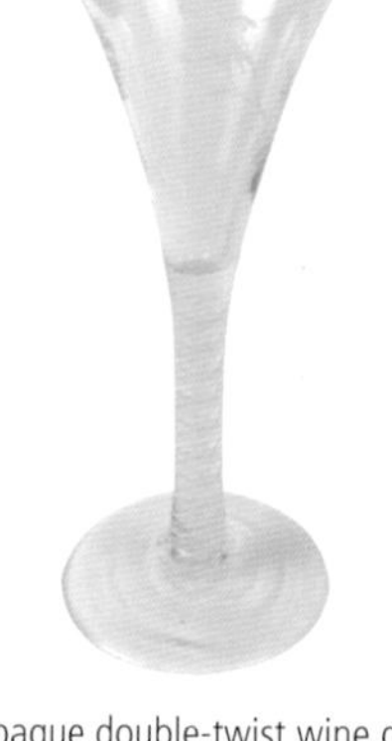

An opaque double-twist wine glass, the trumpet-shaped bowl engraved with fruiting vines and a bird.

c1765 *7in (17.5cm) high*

$600-750 **SWO**

A color-twist wine glass, with bell-shaped bowl raised on a double series opaque twist stem, one twist edged in green and red.

c1765 *6.5in (16.5cm)*

$2,400-3,000 **WW**

A Beilby firing glass, the bucket-shaped bowl enameled in white with grapevine, on a squat double series opaque twist stem.

c1765 *3.5in (9cm) high*

$5,250-6,750 **WW**

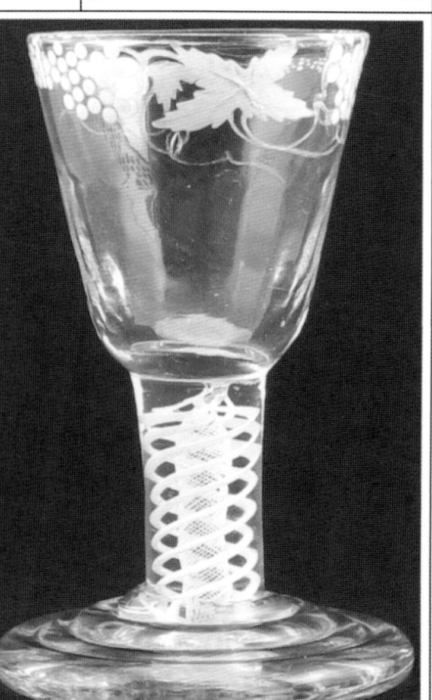

A goblet, the funnel bowl engraved with the arms of Friesland, on a composite stem with knops over an opaque twist section.

c1770 *6.5in (16.5cm) high*

$1,500-2,100 **TEN**

A late 18th/early 19thC air-twist stem glass, the bowl engraved with flowers and scrolling foliage

6in (15cm) high

$225-400 **L&T**

A baluster sweetmeat glass, with a shoulder knop above an inverted baluster lower section, on a folded conical foot.

c1700 *3in (7.5cm) high*

$550-600 **DN**

A lead glass English roemer, with a hollow stem applied with flat raspberry prunts above a trailed foot.

This was probably made for export.

c1720 *6in (15.5cm) high*

$900-1,200 **WW**

A mid-18thC Bristol green wine glass, with facet-cut base, probably gilded in the atelier of James Giles.

4.25in (10.4cm) high

$150-225 **HT**

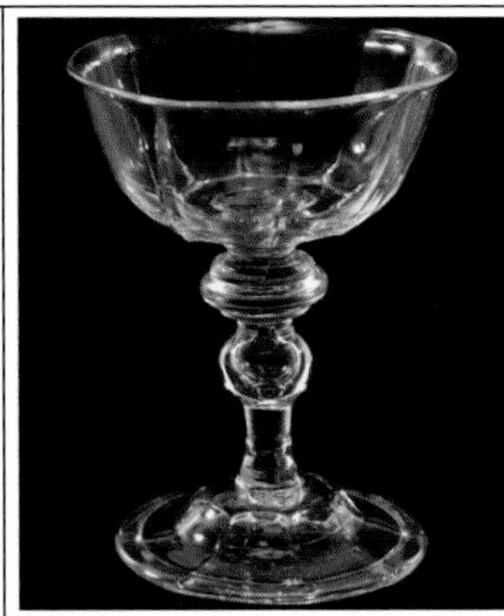

A baluster sweetmeat glass, with an annular knop and inverted baluster lower section.

c1750 *5.25in (13.5cm) high*

$600-750 **DN**

ESSENTIAL REFERENCE – 'NO EXCISE' GLASS

Plain stem wine glasses were made throughout the eighteenth century and featured any number of bowl types including the trumpet, the rounded funnel, the ogee, the pan top, the saucer top, the bell, the ovoid, the cup, the bucket and others. Feet were folded and conical, or domed, or conical without a fold, or were thickened to make a firing foot. As with the balusters the center of the foot had to be raised off the table to avoid the rough pontil mark scratching the furniture on which the glass stood. The majority of the stems were made of solid glass save for air tears, but especially towards the end of the eighteenth century, following the Glass Excise Act of 1745, hollow stem glasses were introduced. The glass tax was widely ridiculed at the time as it stated that glass was to be taxed on weight. To counter this, the glass houses produced lighter glasses by removing the folded foot and introducing 'hollow stems'.

A rare mid 18thC 'No Excise' firing glass, engraved to the bowl and raised above a short double series opaque twist stem and a thick foot.

4in (10cm) high

$3,400-4,400 **WW**

An emerald green wine glass, with a rib-molded bowl raised on a plain stem above a molded conical foot.

c1755-60 *5.5in (13.5cm) high*

$550-600 **WW**

A commemorative firing glass, the bowl engraved 'Duncan For Ever' and raised on a short plain stem above a stepped foot.

This glass commemorates Lord Viscount Duncan, whose victory against the Dutch at Camperdown in October 1797 was the most significant battle between the Dutch and the English during the French Revolutionary Wars.

c1800 *3.75in (9cm) high*

$3,000-4,000 **WW**

An early 19thC commemorative glass rummer, one side engraved with a profile portrait of Admiral Lord Nelson within a banner proclaiming 'Who Defeated the French Fleet Oct 21st 1805, Off Cape Trafalgar', the reverse with HMS Victory with sails furled and flag flying.

Provenance: Admiral George Stewart, 8th Earl of Galloway (1768-1834), former Admiral of the Blue, then to his 2nd son, Vice Admiral Hon. Keith Stewart CB (1814-1879) and thence by descent.

7.75in (19.5cm) high

$1,800-3,000 **WW**

A Russian glass, from the Country (Prigorodnyi) Service, made at the Imperial Glassworks in St Petersburg, designed by Ivan Alekseevich.

Cf. Karen Kettering, 'Russian Glass at Hillwood', which discusses the champagne flutes from the service, now housed at Hillwood Museum. The service was the first in lead glass to be made at the Glassworks and the intricate pattern was designed to sparkle in candlelight.

c1823 *5 .5in (14cm) high*

$1,000-1,400 **WW**

A ceremonial glass, for the British Bowmen society, engraved with the text 'Drink and become a member of this society, Norton Priory, 1856'.

c1856 *11in (28cm) high*

$850-900 **LOCK**

An early English sealed wine bottle, applied with a circular seal containing a shield of three fleur-de-lys.
c1660-70 *8.25in (21cm) high*
$12,000-15,000 **WW**

An 18thC green glass heavy bodied mallet form port or wine bottle.
9in (23cm) high
$225-300 **HW**

A pair of sealed wine bottles, each applied with seal titled 'T Chard 1773'.
1773 *10in (25cm) high*
$1,800-3,000 **WW**

A pair of 19thC Continental silver-mounted decanters.
10.75in (27cm) high
$975-1,300 **L&T**

A pair of Victorian silver mounted glass decanters, by Charles Reily & George Storer, stamped 'Registered London August 184..'.
c1847-48 *11.4 in (28.5cm) high*
$4,000-4,500 **DN**

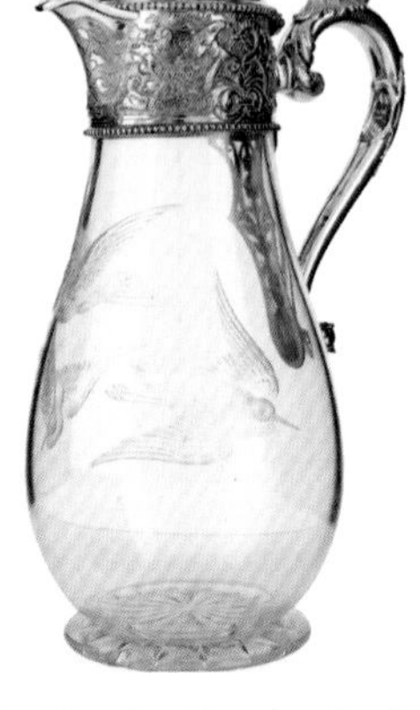

A late Victorian silver-plated and engraved glass claret jug.
11in (28cm) high
$550-600 **L&T**

A Victorian silver mounted cut glass claret jug, by Richards & Brown, London.
1867 *12in (30.5cm) high*
$1,800-2,250 **DN**

A pair of fluted green glass mallet-shaped decanters and stoppers.
c1880 *13.5in (34.5cm) high*
$450-550 **DN**

A late Victorian silver-mounted and cut glass claret jug, Sheffield.
1899
$600-700 **ECGW**

An Edwardian silver-mounted cut glass claret jug, probably by William Devenport, Birmingham.
c1906 *9.5in (24.5cm) high*
$900-1,000 **DN**

An 18thC Bohemian milch glass mug, painted with two buildings.

6.5in (16.5cm) high

$280-340 **CHEF**

A pair of Bohemian Lithyalin hexagonal vases

c1830-40 *3.5in (9cm) high*

$1,200-1,500 **WW**

A pair of Bohemian Lithyalin scent bottles with metal stoppers, probably by Friedrich Egermann,

c1830-40 *7in (18cm) high*

$9,000-11,000 **WW**

A Moser Karlsbad glass vase, with a band of acid-etched Classical warrior figures.

7.75in (19.5cm) high

$600-750 **WW**

A Moser Karlsbad glass vase, with a band of acid-etched Classical warrior figures.

4in (10cm) high

$600-850 **WW**

Two 19thC Bohemian amber flash cut glass vases.

8.75in (22cm) and 8in (20cm) high

$225-300 **L&T**

A pair of 19thC Bohemian ruby glass vases, engraved with stags in woodland landscapes.

13in (33cm) high

$4,000-4,500 **L&T**

A late 19thC 'Zwischengoldglas' Beaker, the base with a four-leaf clover, enameled and gold foiled.

Zwischengoldglas is a technique where thin layers of gold foil are trapped in a double-walled glass vessel. The design reveals itself once the glass is empty, implying that when the drinker has finished, the message can be found from the giver – 'Be Mine' as well as the four-leaf clover, being a universal symbol for luck.

3.75in (9.5cm) high

$450-750 **SWO**

A pair of Bohemian white overlay cranberry vases, cut with Eastern style panels.

11in (27.5cm) high

$1,500-2,100 **DA&H**

An 18thC George III glass candlestick, chip to top.

8.25in (21cm) high

$1,400-1,800 **L&T**

A 19thC English glass epergne.

30.5in (77cm) high

$550-700 **L&T**

A George III sweetmeat tazza, with hollow Silesian stem.

10.25in (26cm) diam

$300-450 **CHEF**

A pair of early 19thC Irish Regency cut glass covered urns, with banded hobnail and diamond cutting.

11.8in (30cm) high

$1,800-2,250 **L&T**

A Vienna enameled glass beaker (ranftbecher), by Anton Kothgasser.

c1825 *4.5in (11cm) high*

$12,750-14,250 **TEN**

A glass vase, by Steigerwald of Munich, after an Alhambra original, the whole finely gilt with scrolls and calligraphy.

c1862 *12.75in (32.3cm) high*

$4,000-4,500 **SWO**

A pair of glass whisky and old brandy dispensers and covers, labeled 'Rd. No. 179154', Henry Turner Manufacturer, Praed Street, Paddington', chips to covers,

21.2 in (54cm) high

$1,800-2,250 **SWO**

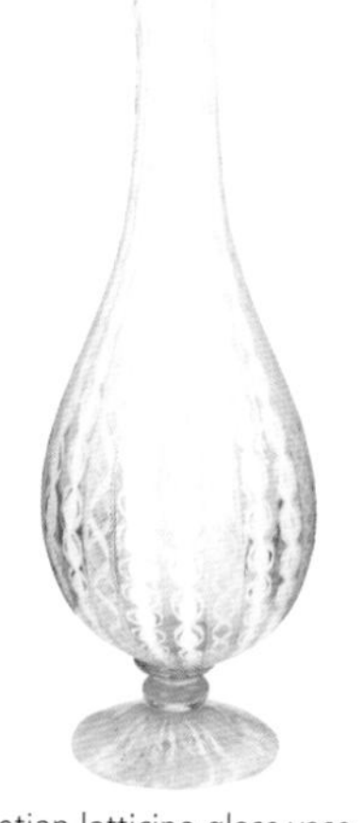

A 19thC Venetian latticino glass vase.

12in (30cm) high

$900-1,200 **L&T**

A pair of 19thC Beykoz (Ottoman Turkey) clear glass ewers and stoppers.

18.5in (47cm) high

$4,000-4,500 **WW**

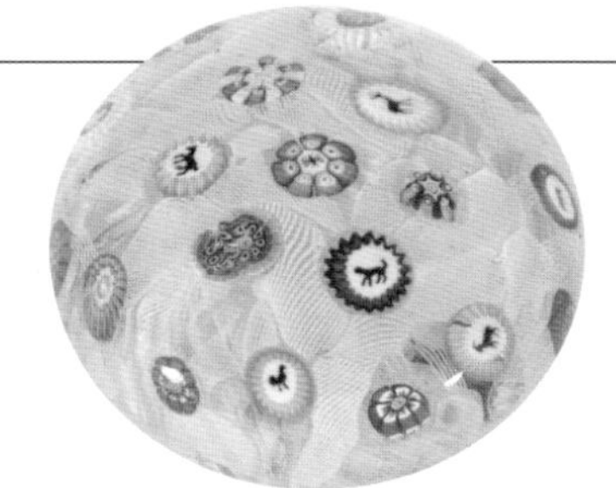

A Baccarat dated scattered millefiori silhouette paperweight, including animal canes of a horse, dog, stag and goat.

1848 *2.9 in (7.5cm) diam*

$1,150-1,450 DN

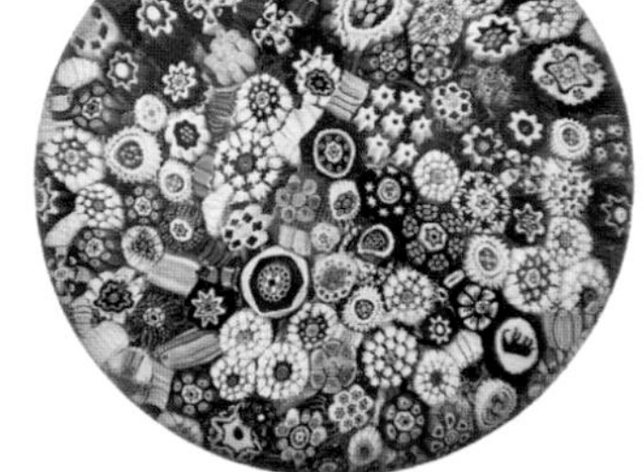

A Baccarat close pack millefiori paperweight, monogrammed JS.

1859 *2.75in (7cm) diam*

$1,000-1,200 POOK

A Clichy trefoil garland paperweight.

2.75in (6.87cm) diam

$850-900 POOK

A Clichy millefiori paperweight, with 11 red, pink and green canes separated by blue and white barber's pole segments.

2.5in (6.5cm) diam

$2,700-3,300 FELL

A mid 19thC Clichy barber's pole paperweight, a green and pink 'Clichy rose' cane to the center, a small chip to the foot.

2in (5cm) high

$2,000-2,400 WW

A mid 19thC Clichy barber's pole paperweight, set with three rows of canes including a green and pink 'Clichy rose', a small surface dint.

2in (5cm) high

$900-1,000 WW

A St. Louis scrambled paperweight.

3in (7.5cm) diam

$400-450 POOK

A St. Louis upright bouquet paperweight.

2.75in (6.87cm) diam

$750-900 POOK

PARABELLE GLASS

A Parabelle close pack millefiori paperweight, with a paper label.

Parabelle Glass began production in 1981 in Oregon, USA. Gary Scrutton melted his own glass, designed his own molds and created his own colors. His best weights are regarded highly by collectors who compare them to the best classical French weights. Production continued to 1998.

2.75in (6.8cm) diam

$450-600 POOK

A Parabelle spaced millefiori paperweight, with a paper label.

2.75in (6.8cm) diam

$550-600 POOK

An 18thC iron rushnip and candleholder, on a painted wood base.

10.6in (27cm) high

$400-450 **WW**

A late 18thC Scottish wrought iron rushnip, with a leaf shape base and scroll feet.

9.5in (24cm) high

$200-280 **WW**

An early 19thC pewter rushlight, base engraved 'W. B. 1824'.

10.8in (27.4cm) high

$150-225 **WW**

A pair of late 16th/early 17thC Italian Baroque brass and copper candlesticks.

5.75in (14.4cm) high

$900-1,200 **WW**

A pair of late 17th/early 18thC North European bell metal candlesticks.

10.5in (26.5cm) high

$225-300 **WW**

A pair of 17th/18thC Dutch brass 'Heemskerk' candlesticks.

7.25in (18cm) high

$300-450 **WW**

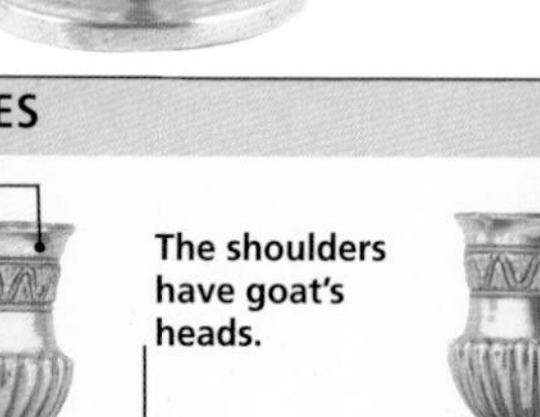

A pair of late 17th/early 18thC brass candlesticks.

5.5in (13.8cm) high

$450-600 **WW**

A pair of late 17th/early 18thC brass candlesticks.

5.5in (13.8cm) high

$750-900 **WW**

A pair of Régence bell metal candlesticks.

c1720 *10in (25cm) high*

$275-525 **WW**

CLOSER LOOK - CASSOLETTES

Ormolu mounted Blue John cassolettes are rare.

The shoulders have goat's heads.

These are of the highest quality and probably made by top craftsman Mattew Boulton.

The reversible gadrooned nozzles and tapering bodies are hung with laurel swags.

The waisted spiral fluted socle bases and square stepped plinths terminate in ball feet.

A pair of George III cassoltettes.

c1770 *8in (20cm) high*

$60,000-75,000 **L&T**

ESSENTIAL REFERENCE - PAKTONG CANDLESTICKS

Paktong is a unique, non-tarnishing metal which first appeared in China in the 12thC and was brought to London in the early 18thC by the East India Company. Although it was not considered as valuable as silver, the malleable metal was favored by certain English craftsmen for its non-tarnishing surface. There are a number of paktong tea sets dating from the mid-18thC, but the metal was more commonly used for fire grates and candlesticks, as paktong is particularly easy to maintain and polish. The Chinese import was much sought after, but supply was limited throughout the 18thC. Despite efforts to replicate paktong, the exact constitution of the alloy, a mixture of nickel, tin, and copper, was never successfully imitated in Europe. While paktong was usually shipped to Europe and then cast by silversmiths upon arrival, Chinese imitations of Western items were also exported in the late 1700s, offering slightly eccentric and outdated interpretations of Western-style teapots to English customers. However, paktong also appeared in the very fashionable interiors by Robert Adam, whose paktong fire-grates were commissioned by the Earls of Coventry and Duke of Northumberland during the second half of the 18thC.

A pair of George III paktong candlesticks.
10.5in (26.6cm) high
$600-900 **WW**

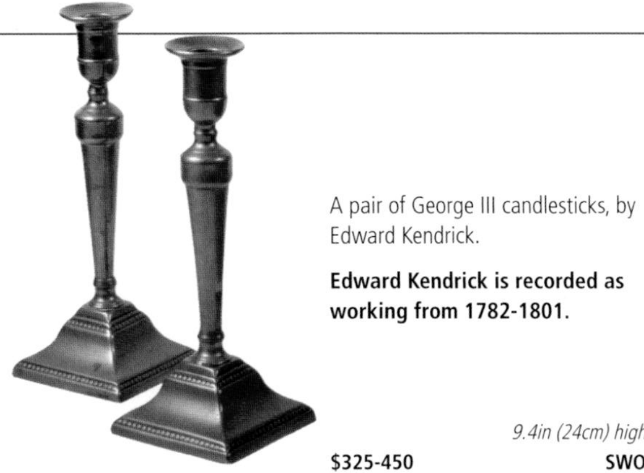

A pair of George III candlesticks, by Edward Kendrick.

Edward Kendrick is recorded as working from 1782-1801.

9.4in (24cm) high
$325-450 **SWO**

A pair of Regency gilt and patinated bronze candelabra.
c1815 *15in (38cm) high*
$6,750-8,250 **TEN**

A pair of Empire ormolu candelabra, by Pierre-Philippe Thomire, each with removable leaf sheathed candle branches, with acanthus leaf and anthemion cast stems, on paw feet, stamped 'THOMIRE À PARIS'.
c1815 *20in (50cm) high*
$18,000-22,500 **TEN**

A large early 19thC Empire gilt and patinated bronze figural candelabrum.
38.6in (98cm) high
$2,000-3,000 **L&T**

A pair of early 19thC Charles X gilt bronze candlesticks.
12.6in (32cm) high
$1,500-3,000 **L&T**

A pair of early 19thC brass and bronze candlesticks.
8.75in (21.9cm) high
$300-400 **WW**

A near pair of early 19thC brass and bronze candlesticks, the underside of one inscribed indistinctly 'Soutter'.
5.25in (13.3cm) high
$300-450 **WW**

A pair of early 19thC Empire patinated and gilt bronze twin light figural candelabra.
15.4in (39cm) high
$3,000-4,500 **DN**

One of a pair of 19thC French bronze griffin candlesticks.

5.75in (14.6cm) high

$150-225 **WW**

A pair of Victorian Gothic Revival gilt-brass altar candlesticks, by Hardman's Medieval Art Manufactory, probably after a design by A. W. N. Pugin.

Reputedly the first pair of candlesticks made by Hardman to a design by A. W. N. Pugin, probably in 1839. The foot, stem, and knop are similar to those found on a silver-gilt chalice designed by Pugin for St Mary's College, Oscott, in 1838, traditionally his first chalice design.

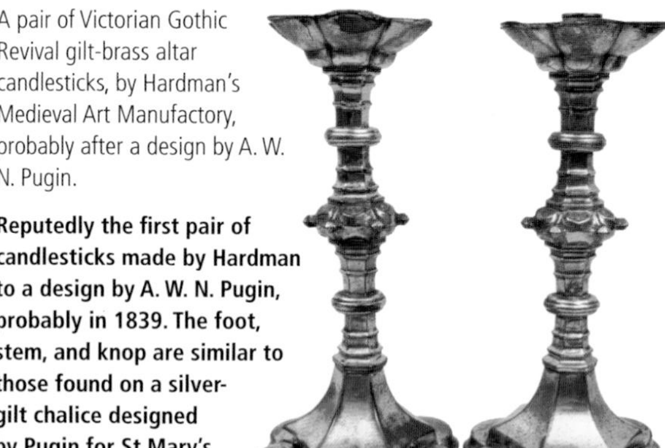

15.4in (39cm) high.

$4,000-4,500 **HW**

A pair of 19thC French bronze and gilt bronze candlesticks.

11.25in (28.3cm) high

$340-425 **WW**

A pair of 19thC French gilt bronze and marble vase lamps.

35.8in (91cm) high

$6,7500-8,250 **SWO**

A pair of Victorian Cornish serpentine candlesticks.

16in (40.3cm) high

$1,400-1,800 **WW**

A pair of 19thC ormolu-mounted rouge marble cassolettes, with reversible nozzles, the legs topped by rams' heads and ending in hooves.

7.25in (18cm) high

$550-700 **CHEF**

A set of four 19thC French ormolu pricket altar candlesticks, in early 18thC style.

23in (58.5cm) high

$575-725 **WW**

A pair of late 19thC gilt bronze mounted Sèvres style porcelain candelabra.

23.6in (60cm) high

$4,800-6,000 **TEN**

A pair of Central European bronze figural candlesticks, in 15thC style.

9in (23cm) high 5.5in (14cm) wide

$200-300 **WW**

A pair of late 19thC French bronze 'Gothic' candelabra.

27in (69cm) high

$1,800-4,000 **L&T**

A pair of 19thC Victorian brass telescopic standard lamps, previously oil lamps.

55in (140cm) high

$600-750 **L&T**

A pair of late 19thC French gilt-bronze five-light candelabra.

22.6in (57.5cm) high

$1,400-1,800 **DN**

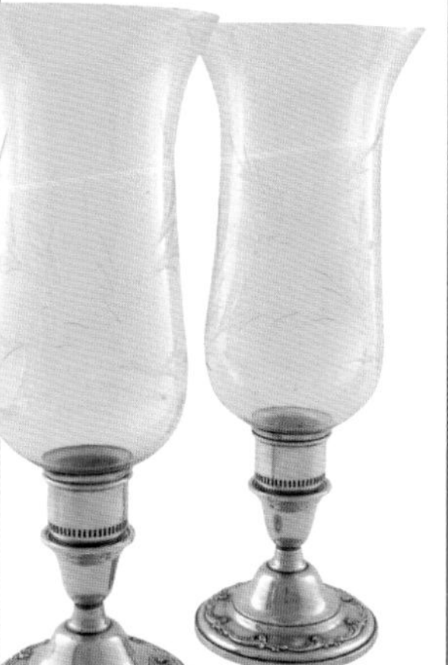

A pair of American silver storm lanterns, marked 'International Sterling'.

14.25in (36cm) high

$425-525 **WW**

A 20thC nine-light floor candelabra, in the form of a blackamoor.

82.7in (210cm) high

$900-1,200 **ROS**

A pair of Venetian style carved wood Blackamoor candelabra, fitted for electricity.

77in (195cm) high

$2,400-3,000 **WW**

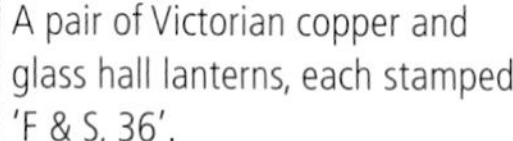

A pair of Victorian copper and glass hall lanterns, each stamped 'F & S, 36'.

16.25in (41cm) high

$900-1,000 **WW**

An early 20thC Edwardian brass and cut glass hall light, in the manner of F & C Osler.

31in (79cm) high

$1,700-2,250 **L&T**

An early 20thC French painted wrought iron and glazed ceiling lantern.

27.25in (69cm) high

$1,000-1,200 **DN**

A 20thC patinated bronze and beveled glass hall lantern.

51in (130cm) high

$1,500-2,100 **DN**

A pair of Victorian brass wall-mounted gas lights.

$550-700 **SWO**

One of a pair of late 19thC gilt and plaster three-branch wall lights.

17.7in (45cm) high

$200-280 pair **SWO**

Two of a set of four late 19thC French twin-light wall appliques, in Louis XVI style.

16.25in (41cm) high

$1,500-2,100 set **WW**

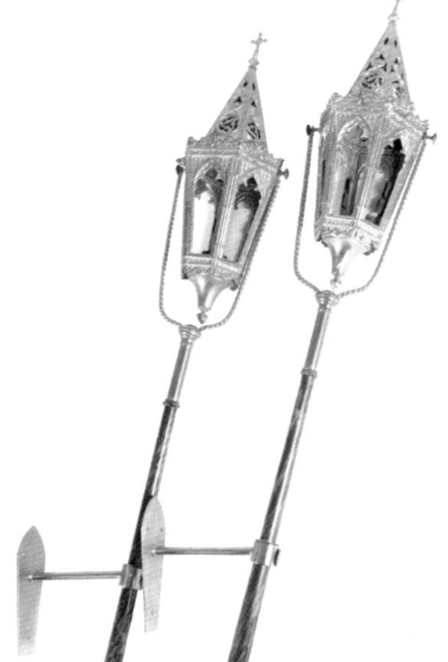

A pair of late Victorian gilt metal Gothic pole lanterns, on beech and simulated poles.

62in (157.5cm) high

$1,800-2,250 **WW**

A pair of 19thC three-light wall appliqués, gilt-bronze, unmarked.

$1,200-1,800 **KAU**

A pair of gilt-bronze twin branch wall lights, with rose flower branches.

c1900 *22.6in (57.5cm) high*

$225-300 **SWO**

A pair of early 20thC French giltwood and composition three light wall appliques, in 18thC style.

29in (74cm) high

$750-1,000 **DN**

A pair of 20thC gilt metal twin light wall appliques in the Louis XVI style.

21in (53.5cm) high

$600-750 **DN**

A set of four Regency-style wall lights.

18.5in (47cm) high

$750-1,000 **SWO**

A 19thC Louis XV style fifteen-light gilt-bronze chandelier, the stem modeled as three cherubs clutching bullrushes, fitted for electricity.

34.6in (88cm) wide

$4,500-6,000 **L&T**

A 19thC French Empire gilt and patinated bronze twelve-light chandelier.

33in (84cm) diam

$6,000-9,000 **L&T**

An early 20thC blue jasperware and gilt bronze six-light chandelier, electrified.

25.6in (65cm) high

$1,800-4,000 **L&T**

An early 20thC Continental gilt metal and glass hung six-light chandelier.

32.75in (83cm) wide

$600-900 **DN**

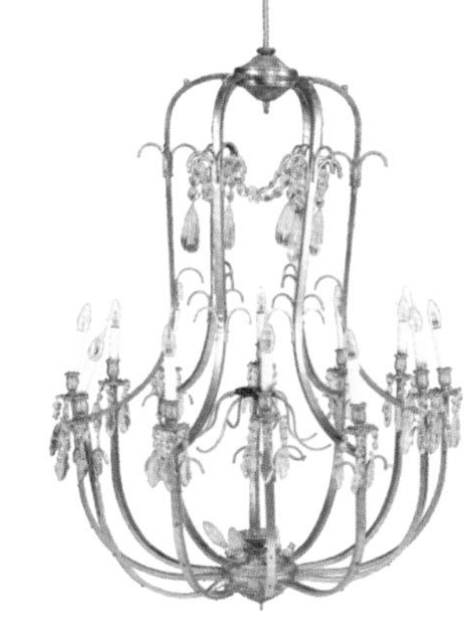

A 20thC gilt metal and cut glass mounted twelve-branch chandelier, wired for electricity.

41.5in (105cm) diam

$3,000-4,500 **DN**

An early 20thC gilt bronze six-light chandelier in the French Régence style.

23in (58cm) wide

$1,200-1,500 **DN**

One of a pair of late 20thC pair of ten-light brass and glass electroliers, in the Pompeiian revival taste.

39.5in (100cm) diam

$1,500-2,250 pair **DN**

An Edwardian gilt-bronze and cut glass eight-light wall appliqué.

15in (37.8cm) high

$300-450 **WW**

A Doulton Lambeth oil lamp, the stoneware body and domed base incised with foliage, probably by Mark Marshall.
c1884 *22.5in (57cm) high*
$1,500-2,100 **SWO**

A Victorian oil lamp, the column molded with Art Nouveau-style flowers on a cast brass and pottery base.
26in (66cm) high
$900-1,000 **SWO**

A Victorian oil lamp, with a brass Corinthian column.
26.5in (67.5cm) high
$600-750 **SWO**

A Victorian oil lamp, the column with a gilt metal Corinthian capital on a similar square base.
30in (78cm) high
$1,500-2,100 **SWO**

A Victorian oil lamp.
30in (76cm) high
$1,000-1,400 **SWO**

A Doulton Lambeth stoneware table lamp, impressed mark, incised decorator's mark 'EDL', probably Edith D Lupton.
c1882 *23in (59cm) high*
$700-850 **SWO**

An Elkington & Co. oil lamp, with a silver-plated Corinthian column, stamped '19226 Elkington & Co.'.
33in (84cm) high
$975-1,150 **SWO**

A Victorian oil lamp, with a molded green glass reservoir and a pressed metal base.
25.5in (65cm) high
$700-850 **SWO**

A Walker & Hall oil lamp, with a silver-plated Corinthian column, stamped 'W & HS'.
31.25in (79.5cm) high
$1,400-1,800 **SWO**

ESSENTIAL REFERENCE – DECADE RING

Decade rings (so called as the shank has ten nuggets) were used in the same way as a Rosary. A Hail Mary was said for each knob, then Our Father (Paternoster) for the ring head. In 1571 rosaries were forbidden in England and Wales, but decade rings were not mentioned by the Act, and they continued to be made until at least the 18thC. Until the mid-15thC the ring head usually had a saint engraved in the middle, but after Reformation the letter S was used, possibly to represent 'servant' of Christ. A bronze example can be found in the V&A Museum, London, item 775-1871.

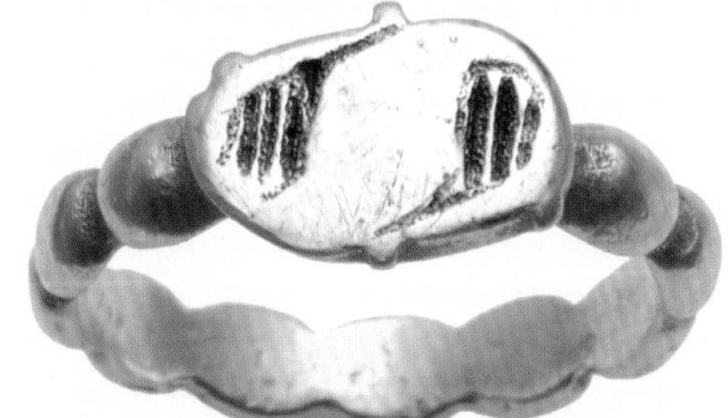

A possibly 17thC Decade ring, the shank comprises ten nuggets, to an oval head, with the letter S depicted,

finger size L

$975-1,150 **TEN**

A late 16th/early 17thC gold and turquoise ring, on a scalloped mount decorated with traces of enamel.

size N

$1,800-3,000 **MAB**

A pair of early 17thC probably Flemish earrings, enameled in green, puce, and white with black highlighting, set with emeralds and rubies, with a S J Philips retail box.

$37,500-45,000 **DUK**

A late 17thC gold memorial ring, with the initials J and S in gold wirework and beneath a skull and bones, on fabric or hair ground.

Size L 1/2.

$3,000-4,000 **WW**

A pair of purple paste set earrings.

c1740 *1.5in (4cm) long*

$3,000-4,500 **L&T**

A 16carat diamond flowerhead clip pin, the central five-pointed petals set with pear and cushion cut diamonds on an old cut diamond pavé set ground, centered with a cushion cut diamond in a pinched collet setting, with a later clip attachment, in S.J. Phillips case.

c1780

$21,000-27,000 **DN**

An 18th/19thC gold and diamond set pin, with a large baroque pearl suspension.

1in (3cm) wide

$750-900 **L&T**

An 18th/19thC diamond set ring, with a navette cut diamond, flanked to either side by a pear-shaped diamond.

Ring size: Q, principle diamond 0.5in (1.5cm) 0.1in (0.5cm)

$2,000-2,400 **L&T**

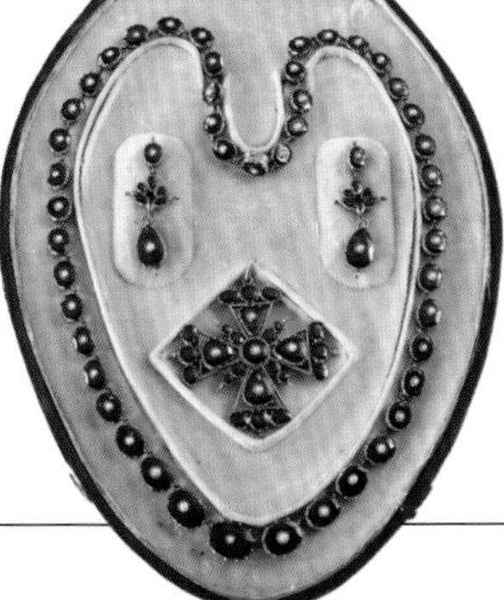

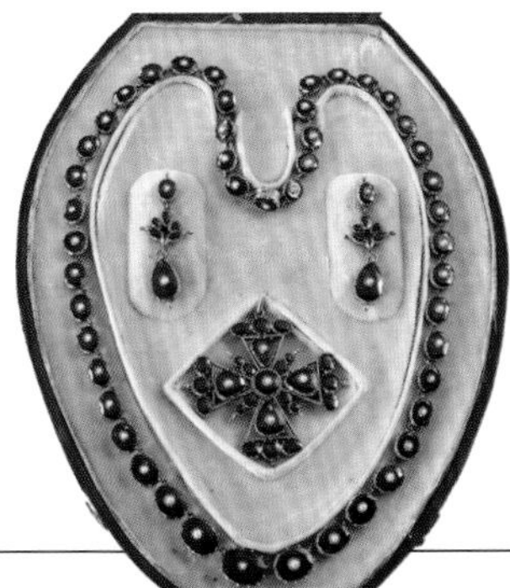

A Georgian gold, foil back garnet and seed pearl parure, consisting of a necklace, Maltese cross pendant and pendant earrings, in original case.

$6,000-7,500 **ROS**

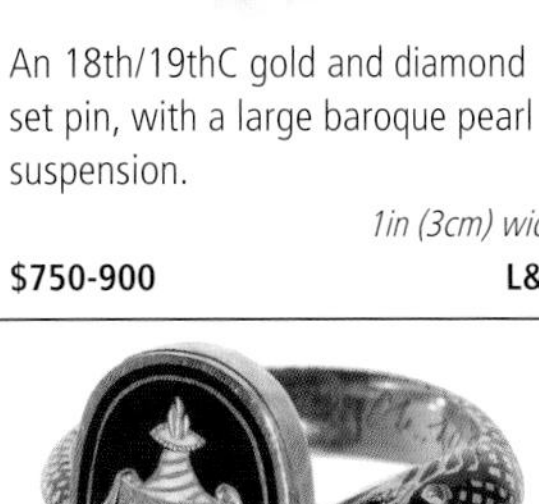

A George III gold and enamel mourning ring, reverse inscribed 'Jona[tha]n Pytts Esq', decorated with enamel scales, inside shank engraved: Nat 2nd April 1731, Ob,, 10 Decr,, 1807.

The shank of this ring has an ouroboros (symbol of eternity of a snake eating its tail).

c1808 *size K½*

$2,100-2,700 **MAB**

A hardstone cameo, carved with a portrait of a young man with vine leaf crown and sash with lion mask motif.

2in (5cm) high

$2,000-2,400 **L&T**

An early 19thC carved hardstone cameo, the male head possibly Neptune.

1.4in (4cm) high

$4,000-4,500 **L&T**

A 19thC carved hardstone cameo pin, depicting the head of a woman with her eyes closed and hair tied up, mounted in gold with pearl border.

1.75in (4.5cm) high

$1,400-1,800 **WW**

Judith Picks

Benedetto Pistrucci was a gem engraver and medalist. The work he is most famous for appears every year on Britain's gold coinage. He was responsible for the St George design on the sovereign and half sovereign. Pistrucci took over the position of Chief Medalist at the Royal Mint in London after the death of Thomas Wyon in 1817. There were difficulties in fully accepting the position owing to his Italian birth, however compromise was reached. This however didn't help the progress of his masterpiece celebrating Waterloo taking an eventual 33 years to come to fruition! An added bonus is that the subject matter is a member of the Royal Family.

An early 19thC shell cameo pin, the cameo inscribed to reverse 'DUKE OF YORK, BY PHI PISTRUCCI, 1827'.

1.5in (4cm) high

$1,800-3,000 **L&T**

An early 19thC diamond and garnet set pin, set with rose cut diamonds and graduated garnet carbuncles, in a case stamped 'Leighton... BURLINGTON ARCADE...'.

2.75in (7cm) high

$4,500-7,500 **L&T**

An early 19thC diamond set pendant, set with graduated old mine and rose cute diamonds, with similarly set bale.

2in (5cm) long

$6,000-7,500 **L&T**

A 19thC continental emerald and diamond set butterfly pin.

2.5in (6cm) wide

$450-750 **L&T**

A pair of early 19thC diamond ear pendants, 4.5cts.

2in (5cm) long

$9,750-12,750 **L&T**

A pair of early 19thC diamond and sapphire drop earrings.

$3,400-4,400 **WW**

A William IV 18ct gold memorial ring, with glazed locket to reverse, containing woven hair, flanked to either side by collet set pairs of single cut diamonds.

Ring size: L/M

$900-1,200 **L&T**

A Victorian garnet and diamond set pin, set with graduated old mine and rose cut diamonds.

1.75in (4.5cm) wide

$1,800-2,100 **L&T**

A pair of Victorian pins, the filligree balls with allover wire work detail.

$450-600 **L&T**

A 19thC micromosaic pin, of girandole design, depicting a winged beetle, with tassel drops.

1.75in (4.5cm) wide

$1,000-1,400 **L&T**

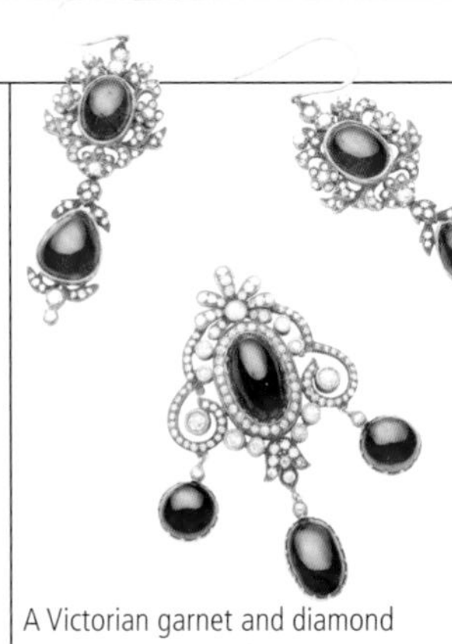

A Victorian garnet and diamond set demi-parure, collet set with graduated oval, pear or round cut garnet cabochons, and single and old European cut diamonds.

Pin: 2in (5.5cm) long

$7,500-10,500 **L&T**

A Victorian pin, with central claw set cirtrine with amethysts interspersed by collet set rose cut diamonds.

1in (2.5cm) diam

$1,500-2,250 **L&T**

A Victorian ruby and diamond set pin, with central ruby, within borders set with graduated old mine and rose cut diamonds, ruby weight 2.18cts.

1.75in (4cm) diam

$6,750-9,000 **L&T**

An early 19thC diamond set scroll pin.

1.75in (4.5cm) wide

$6,750-8,250 **WW**

A Victorian emerald and diamond pin pendant, set in gold.

Accompanied by report number 07843 from the Gem and Pearl Laboratory, London dated 31st May 2013 stating that the emerald has moderate clarity enhancement and is of Colombian origin.

0.5in (1cm) x 0.1in (0.5cm)

$30,000-38,000 **WW**

A 19thC bee pin, the body formed with a cabochon quartz catseye, with lines of diamonds and black enamel, with further diamonds on wings and antennae, with cabochon ruby eyes, case by The Goldsmiths and Silversmiths Company.

1.5in (3.5cm) long

$3,750-4,500 **WW**

A late 19thC insect pin, pavé set with graduated cushion shaped and rose cut diamonds, a line of graduated rubies and two sapphires, with a larger diamond to the head, in silver and gold, with case.

1.75in (4.5cm) long

$4,800-6,000 **WW**

A late Victorian old mine cut diamond set star pin.

1.5in (4cm) diam

$1,500-2,250 **L&T**

A Victorian diamond set star pin, set in silver and gold, cased by The Goldsmiths and Silversmiths Company.

1in (3cm) wide

$2,250-3,000 **WW**

A Victorian diamond star pin, inset with old cut and rose cut diamonds, in white claw settings, on a gold mount, total estimated diamond weight 2.60 carat in a case by J.W. Benson Ltd.

$1,300-1,450 **TEN**

A late Victorian diamond set star pin, set with old cut diamonds, in white claw settings.

1.5in (4cm) wide 1.75 carat

$750-900 **TEN**

A late Victorian diamond set crescent form pin, with old European cut diamonds flanked by borders set with rose cut diamonds.

1.5in (3.5cm) diam

$1,150-1,450 **L&T**

A 19thC diamond and ruby set bird form pin, set with old mine and rose cut diamonds and circular and pea cut rubies, the heart shaped drop with glazed locked aperture to reverse.

1.75in (4.5cm) long

$1,800-2,700 **L&T**

A late Victorian diamond foliate pin, set with old circular cut diamonds in silver and gold.

3in (7.5cm) long

$1,300-1,500 **WW**

A diamond horseshoe pin, two rows of graduated old cut diamonds, in white claw and collet settings.

c1880 *1.25in (3cm) wide 6carat*

$4,400-4,800 **TEN**

A late Victorian bow pin, inset with rose cut diamonds, in white claw and collet settings.

1.75in (3cm) wide 1.5carat

$850-1,150 **TEN**

A late 19thC pearl and diamond pin, the reverse with glazed hair panel.

$600-900 **HW**

A Scottish multi-gem set pin.

1.5in (3.5cm) diam

$300-400 **L&T**

A Victorian gold and opal set pin, collet set with a central opal in a border of smaller circular opals.

1in (2.5cm) diam

$700-975 **L&T**

A late Victorian diamond and opal pendant pin, set in unmarked white and yellow metal.

$1,500-2,100 **ECGW**

A late Victorian split pearl, coral and diamond bar pin.

2.75in (7cm) long

$550-700 **TEN**

An amethyst and diamond pin, the cut amethyst within a spaced border of old cut diamonds.

c1880 *3.2cm high*

$700-850 **TEN**

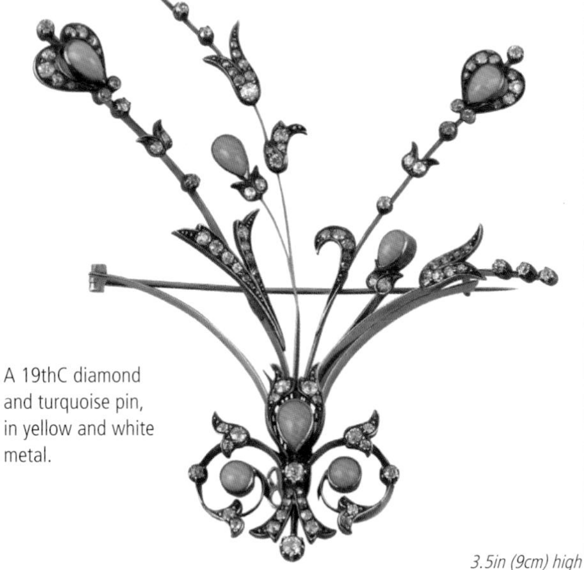

A 19thC diamond and turquoise pin, in yellow and white metal.

3.5in (9cm) high

$1,500-2,100 **DA&H**

A 19thC emerald and diamond cluster ring.

Ring size O1/2

$600-750 **L&T**

A 19thC emerald and diamond set cluster ring.

Ring size: L/M

$1,800-3,000 **L&T**

A Victorian 19ct gold mounted ruby and diamond set snake ring.

RIng size: N/O

$1,200-1,800 **L&T**

A Victorian diamond cluster ring, a cruciform of old cut diamonds centrally.

Ring size O 1.35 carat

$1,500-2,100 **TEN**

A Victorian locket, the satin finished body with three turquoise cabochons, with rose cut diamonds between.

$550-600 **L&T**

A Victorian yellow metal locket, set with lapis lazuli cabochons, in original fitted case, unmarked.

1.5in (4.5cm) long

$4,500-5,250 **L&T**

A Victorian serpent necklace, the snake head with ruby eyes and split pearl ridges to a blue enamel ground, a pearl and enamel drop suspended from the mouth.

16.25in (41.5cm) long

$1,800-3,000 **CHOR**

A late Victorian lapis lazuli, pearl and diamond pendant, with a locket back.

1.75in (4.5cm) wide

$900-1,200 **TEN**

A late Victorian stone set cross, with a cameo centrally, within a border of seed pearls, the cross inset with amethysts and rubies.

6in (15cm) high

$4,500-6,000 **TEN**

A late Victorian gold and half-pearl necklace, with case, stamped Frazer & Haws From Garrards, 31 Regent St, Piccadilly.

c1890 *15.75in (40cm) long*

$2,500-3,000 **DN**

A late Victorian bracelet, with gems including citrines, amethysts, peridot, and garnet.

7.25in 18.5cm) long

$2,100-2,700 **L&T**

A Victorian Scottish citrine set bangle of hinged design.

2.5in (6cm) diam

$1,400-1,800 **L&T**

A Victorian gold snake bracelet, set with two cabochon ruby eyes to an articulated chain body, the tail forming the clasp.

$1,500-2,100 **HT**

A pair of Victorian diamond floral cluster earrings.

1in (2.5cm) long

$6,000-7,500 **L&T**

A pair of 19thC gold amphora design earrings, with cannetille and enamel decoration.

1.5in (3.5cm) high

$4,500-6,000 **WW**

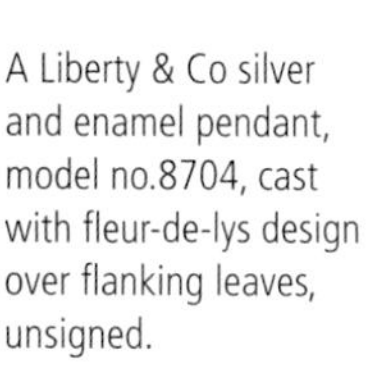

A Liberty & Co silver and enamel pendant, model no.8704, cast with fleur-de-lys design over flanking leaves, unsigned.

The original line drawing for this design is held in the Liberty Jewelry Sketches at the Westminster Library.

1.5in (3.5cm) high

$900-1,000 WW

An Arts and Crafts citrine pendant, in the style of Sybil Dunlop, cased by Pearsal.

c1920 *2in (8cm) high*

$2,100-2,700 WW

An Arts and Crafts silver and enamel pendant, by G Vale & Co, suspending a small pearl.

1in (2.5cm) wide

$300-400 WW

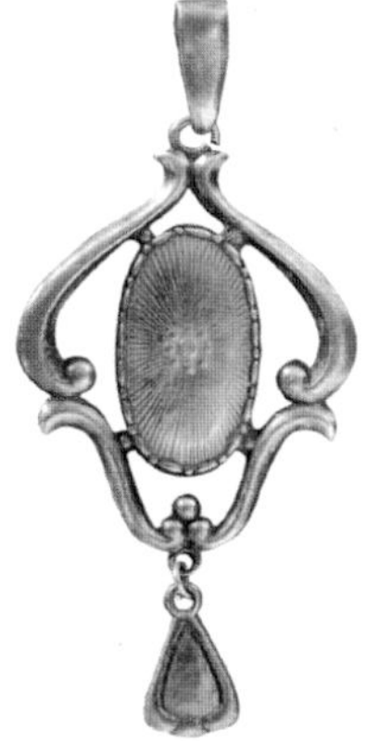

An early 20thC Charles Horner hallmarked silver open work pendant, with pale blue enamels.

1912 *2in (5cm) long*

$280-340 FLD

An Arts and Crafts enamel and amethyst pin.

3in (7.5cmm) wide

$1,150-1,450 L&T

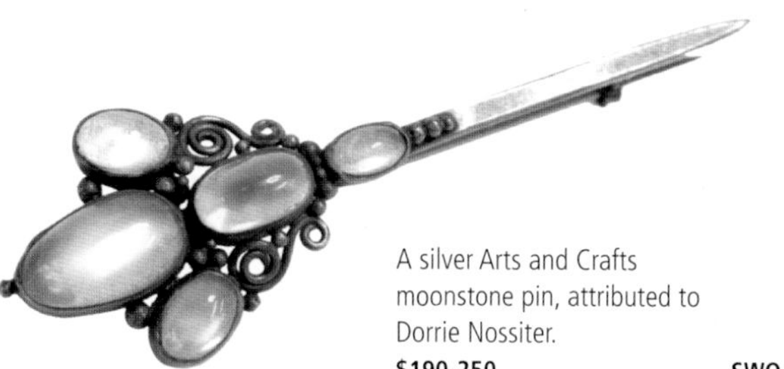

A silver Arts and Crafts moonstone pin, attributed to Dorrie Nossiter.

$190-250 SWO

A silver Arts and Crafts amethyst crescent pin, attributed to Bernard Instone.

1.75in (4.5cm) diam

$150-225 SWO

An Art Nouveau silver pendant, designed by Archibald Knox for Liberty & Co, marked WHH for William Hair Hasler.

2in (5cm) long pendant

$1,200-1,500 WW

An Art Nouveau gem set plique-à-jour enamel pendant, set with an amethyst and five rubies in silver.

$750-900 WW

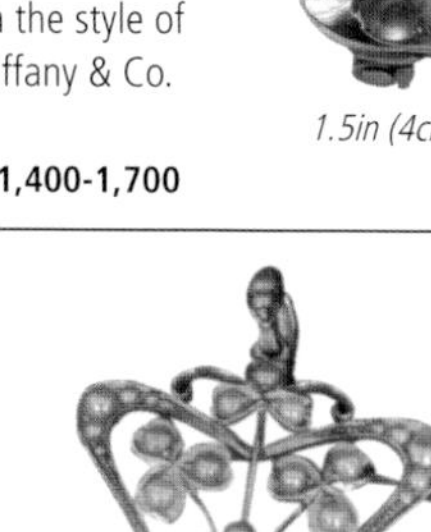

An Art Nouveau black opal pin, in the style of Tiffany & Co.

1.5in (4cm) wide

$1,400-1,700 TEN

An Art Nouveau hallmarked openwork amethyst and seed pearl pendant pin.

$376-450 FLD

ESSENTIAL REFERENCE – SUFFRAGETTE PIN

The women campaigning for suffrage in Britain pre-WWI were masters in their use of jewelry as a tool for potent political expression. The Women's Social and Political Union (WSPU) was founded in 1903 by Emmeline Pankhurst and took a more militant view on the campaign for women's suffrage than other groups from the period. By 1906, the WSPU had become well-known for their extreme line – often resorting to arson, vandalism and hunger strikes to promote their cause – all covered extensively by the national press. In 1908 the government passed The Public Meeting Act, 'to prevent disturbance of Public Meetings' that effectively made the disruptive 'Deeds not Words' of the WSPU illegal. Support for the WSPU had swelled over the years, something that did not cease even after the threat of arrest and imprisonment. In the same year as The Public Meeting Act was passed, the group devised an innovative way for supporters to show their allegiance by developing 'corporate' colors – purple (for dignity), white (for purity), and green (for hope). It did not take long for the colors to take hold and in June of 1908 30,000 women displayed their colors in a demonstration in London's Hyde Park – thought to have been watched by up to half a million spectators. This demonstration marked the beginning of a remarkable and persistent campaign for women's suffrage that continued until the outbreak of war in 1914, at which point the members of the WSPU vowed to concentrate on the war effort. In 1918 women over 30 were granted the vote, with the voting age dropping to 21 years old in 1928.

A gold and enameled amethyst pendant, the outer frame of scrolling green and white enamel scrolls with small diamond highlights.
1.5in (4cm) long
$5,250-6,000 L&T

An Edwardian pin/pendant, with a square cut amethyst within an outer rose cut diamond set foliate border.
1in (3cm) wide
$1,150-1,450 L&T

An Edwardian pin, set with old European, old mine and rose cut diamonds.
2in (5cm) wide
$1,800-3,000 L&T

An early 20thC giardenetto pin, set with rose cut diamonds, rubies (probably synthetic), an emerald, amethyst, ruby and seed pearls, suspending a pearl drop.
3.75in (9.5cm) long
$600-750 L&T

An early 20thC sapphire and diamond set crescent form pin.
2.5in (6.5cm) long
$550-700 L&T

An Edwardian pin, with trapezoid cut peridots, around the central seed pearl, within borders set with old European cut diamonds.
1.5in (3.5cm) diam
$1,800-3,000 L&T

A Belle Époque diamond set pin.

The Belle Époque – French for 'Beautiful Era' – was a period in European history that is conventionally dated as starting in 1871 and ending when World War I began in 1914. Occurring during the era of the French Third Republic (beginning 1870), it was a period characterized by optimism, peace at home and in Europe, new technology and scientific discoveries. The peace and prosperity in Paris allowed the arts to flourish, and many masterpieces of literature, music, theater, and visual art gained recognition. The Belle Époque was named, in retrospect, when it began to be considered a 'golden age' in contrast to the horrors of World War I.
1.5in (3.5cm) wide principal diamond 0.89cts
$4,000-4,500 L&T

An Edwardian openwork diamond pin set in unmarked white metal.
1.7 carat
$1,500-2,100 ECGW

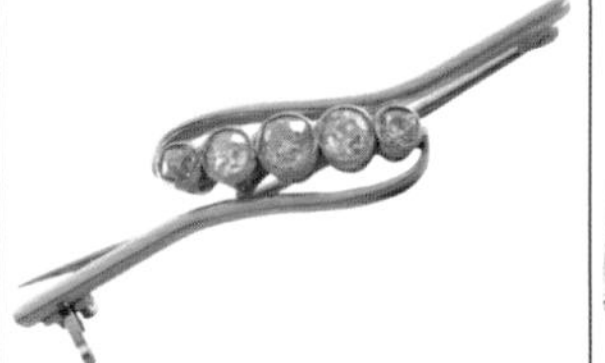

An Edwardian pin, set with diamonds in millgrain setting platinum and 15ct gold.
$200-250 ECGW

An Edwardian pin, with an old brilliant and rose-cut diamond open cluster.
c1910 *4cm wide* ***1.30 carats***
$1,200-1,500 DN

An Edwardian diamond pin, with an old cushion cut diamond.
c1915 2in (5.3cm) wide 3.50 carats
$3,000-4,000 DN

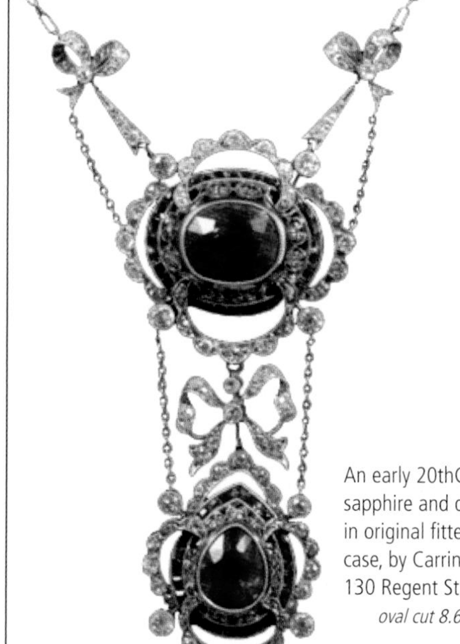

An early 20thC Belle Époque sapphire and diamond necklace, in original fitted tooled leather case, by Carrington & amp; Co., 130 Regent Street, W.

oval cut 8.66 carats, pear cut 3.50 carats

$67,500-75,000 REEM

An early 20thC diamond set necklace, with old European cut diamonds.

9in (23cm) long 0.36carats

$1,400-1,800 L&T

An Edwardian gold and pearl set necklace.

15in (38cm) long

$2,700-3,300 L&T

An early 20thC Elizabeth Bonte carved horn 'bee' necklace, signed.

Elizabeth Bonte was a French designer and maker who specialized in decorative horn jewelry, especially pendants. Her workshops were merged with her rival, George Pierre, and they worked together, mainly in the Art Nouveau style, until the mid 30s.

2.5in (6cm) diam

$750-850 L&T

An Edwardian diamond set necklace, in a fitted case.

1.75in (4.5cm) long

$1,150-1,450 L&T

An early 20thC necklace, with amethysts interspersed by emeralds and pearls flanking the central large pear cut amethyst drop.

19in (48cm) long

$1,800-3,000 L&T

A Edwardian gold bracelet, with a cultured bouton pearl, and a pair of old cut diamonds, opals, sapphires, and rubies.

8in (20cm) long

$1,500-2,100 L&T

An Edwardian sapphire and diamond set bangle.

2.5in (6cm) diam

$1,150-1,450 L&T

An early 20thC emerald and diamond set ring, 18ct white gold and platinum. ring size: N.

0.5in (1.5cm) long

$1,500-2,250 L&T

An Edwardian emerald and diamond 18ct gold crossover ring.

$300-400 ECGW

A pair of Edwardian emerald and diamond set earrings, set with a moonstone cabochon.

0.75in (2cm) long

$1,500-2,250 L&T

An Art Deco carved emerald, diamond, jadeite, pearl, and lapis lazuli pin, the plate beneath the jadeite indistinctly numbered 1694 with French assay poincon.

c1925 *10.3cm long*

$45,000-52,500 **DN**

An Art Deco diamond, sapphire and pearl pin.

42mm long

$750-900 **L&T**

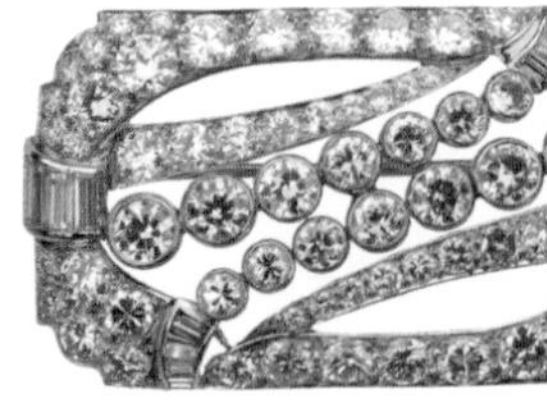

An Art Deco diamond plaque pin, in Garrard box.

4.5cm wide

$6,000-6,750 **WW**

A Russian Art Deco sapphire and pearl pin, indistinctly marked St Petersburg.

1in (3cm) wide

$750-900 **L&T**

An Art Deco sapphire and diamond pin, by Polak-Aine, the center with a single old brilliant cut diamond in run over mount, signed Polak-Aine Paris 8583.

$7,500-9,000 **HW**

An Art Deco diamond and obsidian pin, with one terminal modeled as an Indian deity, the other as an elephant.

$6,000-6,750 **CHOR**

A black opal and aquamarine pin.

c1930 *3.5cm wide*

$1,800-2,250 **TEN**

An Art Deco diamond double clip pin, in white claw settings.

6cm wide 4.00 carat

$1,800-3,000 **TEN**

An Art Deco modernist design 9 carat gold bracelet.

$600-750 **ECGW**

An Art Deco platinum bracelet, set with 60 sapphires and 72 diamonds, the clasp is engraved 'Plat' and 'U3327', one sapphire missing.

sapphires 5 carats, diamonds 3 carats

$8,250-9,750 **ECGW**

An Art Deco Bakelite and white metal bracelet.

$300-400 **SWO**

A 1940s ruby and brilliant-cut diamond set ring.

Ring size: N/O

$975-750 **L&T**

An Art Deco emerald and diamond set ring.

Ring Size: N, 3.62carats

$30,000-45,000 **L&T**

An Art Deco style sapphire and diamond set cluster ring, set with a trap-cut diamond and French cut sapphires, shank stamped 'Pt950'.

Ring Size: M/N, main diamond .50 carats

$3,000-4,500 **L&T**

An Art Deco sapphire and brilliant-cut diamond set ring, shank numbered 2562.

sapphire weight 2.13 carats

$3,000-4,000 **L&T**

An Art Deco ring, set with a large blue zircon, diamond shoulders metal unmarked.

$300-450 **ECGW**

An Art Deco emerald and diamond cluster ring.

Ring size: L diamond weight 2.00 carat

$5,250-6,000 **TEN**

An Art Deco diamond cluster ring, a central brilliant cut diamond with a border of baguette cut and smaller round brilliant cut diamonds.

Ring size P 1.00 carat

$1,800-2,250 **TEN**

An Art Deco diamond ring, the collet set square diamond, within a surround of baguette cut diamonds, stamped PLAT.

c1930 *Ring size O 1/2 1.5 carats*

$8,250-9,750 **DN**

A pair of Art Deco aquamarine and diamond set earrings.

50mm long

$4,000-5,250 **L&T**

A mid-20thC bird pin, with pear-cut ruby set eye, above the red guilloche enameled body, with sapphire set feet on branch with single cut diamonds, stamped 750.

5cm high

$900-1,000 **L&T**

A 1950s leaf clip pin, pavé-set with topaz baguettes and decorated with a spine of brilliant-cut diamonds, French gold mark.

3in (8cm) long

$1,800-2,250 **MAB**

A 1950s Cartier novelty duck pin, in 18ct gold, agate, emerald and coral.

2in (5cm) long

$30,000-35,000 **BE**

A Ben-Amun 24ct gold plate on pewter necklace, with faux pearl and resin stones part of the 'Medieval' collection.

c1985

$425-525 SCA

A Ben-Amun gold plated and faux cornelian necklace.

c1984

$450-550 SCA

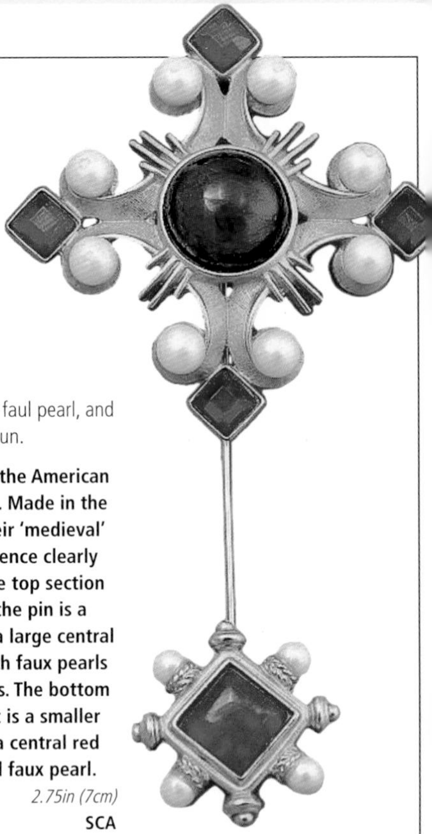

A 1980s gold-plated, faul pearl, and paste pin, by Ben-Amun.

This pin is made by the American designer Ben-Amun. Made in the 1980s as part of their 'medieval' collection, this influence clearly shines through – the top section that is attached to the pin is a stylized cross with a large central green cabochon with faux pearls and red paste finials. The bottom detachable element is a smaller stylized cross with a central red paste cabochon and faux pearl.

2.75in (7cm)

$400-450 SCA

A bronze tone metal necklace, by Hanna Bernhard, with a bronze tone drop in the shape of a woman's head with a head dress, with faux turquoise and faux onyx crystal and a black resin 'body'.

$750-900 SCA

A bronze tone metal cuff, by Hanna Bernhard, with applied head wearing a turban, claw set with a red glass cabochon stone and a white crystal flanked by claw set banded glass pear shaped cabochon stones.

$550-600 SCA

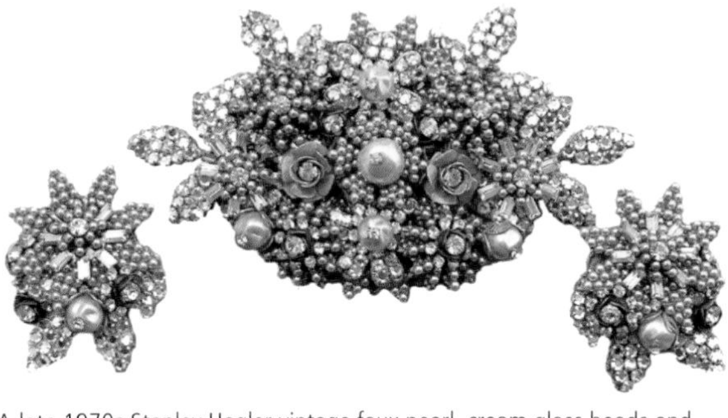

A late 1970s Stanley Hagler vintage faux pearl, cream glass beads and paste pin and clip earrings.

4.5in (11cm) wide

$600-700 SCA

A Stanley Hagler vintage coral colored glass bead and paste pin & clip earrings.

$600-750 SCA

A Stanley Hagler vintage green bead and paste necklace and matching clip earrings.

The necklace is marked 'Stanley Hagler N.Y.C.' in an oval cartouche and is therefore made after 1973 and probably in the late 1970s/early 1980s.

17.25in (43.7cm) long

$975-1,000 SCA

A Stanley Hagler vintage purple, pink and gold bead and paste pin and clip earrings.

$600-750 SCA

A 1950s vintage clear and citrus yellow glass bead & paste necklace by Miriam Haskell

18ins (46cm) long

$750-900 **SCA**

A vintage glass bead, faux pearl and paste necklace, by Miriam Haskell, signed.

This vintage glass bead, faux pearl and paste necklace is typical Haskell. Made in the 1950s-60s the faux baroque pearls are typical of Haskell's jewelry although the molded opaque lemon glass beads are more unusual.

18in (46cm) long

$850-900 **SCA**

ESSENTIAL REFERENCE – JOSEFF OF HOLLYWOOD

A pair of Joseff of Hollywood cat clip earrings, in 'Russian gold' with green crystal eyes, the reverse of each earring is signed 'Joseff' in script.

$225-280 **SCA**

A 1960s bee/insect pin, in 'Russian gold', the body of the insect has been ridged and textured, signed 'Joseff' in script on a round plaque.

3in (7.7cm) wide

$225-280 **SCA**

Eugéne Joseff moved from Chicago to California in the late 1920s to escape the Great Depression, and to try to exploit his great passion – jewelry design – in one of the few booming industries of the period: Hollywood. He soon met with incredible success, both as a designer and a supplier of jewelry to the major film studios. This success – which endured from the early 1930s, beyond his tragic death in an aircraft crash in 1948, through to the 1960s – was based on three fundamental factors. Firstly, his ability to accurately research and then simplify specific historical styles. Secondly, his development of a coppery-gold colored matte finish (known as 'Russian gold'), which minimized the traditional cameraman's problem of over-reflectivity when filming gold jewelry under powerful studio lights. And thirdly, his and his wife, Joan Castle's, considerable commercial acumen. The list of films for which Joseff designs were commissioned would overrun this article by many pages! The most mouthwatering and notable examples including: A Star is Born (1936); The Wizard of Oz and Gone With The Wind (both 1939); Casablanca (1942); Anchors Aweigh (1945); Easter Parade (1949); Singing in the Rain (1952); To Catch a Thief (1955); Ben Hur (1959); Breakfast at Tiffany's (1961); Cleopatra (1963); and My Fair Lady (1964). The list of famous Hollywood stars who actually wore the jewelry is equally impressive, and includes Greta Garbo, Vivian Leigh, Bette Davis, Marlene Dietrich and Grace Kelly, as well as Tyrone Power, Douglas Fairbanks Jnr, Clark Gable, Errol Flynn and Tony Curtis – to name but a few.

A 1960s Joseff 'Russian gold' cat pin, with marquise shaped green crystal eyes.

3in (7.7cm) wide

$400-450 **SCA**

A pair of Joseff 'Russian gold' winged putto-clip earrings.

$400-450 **SCA**

An Oscar de la Renta gilt metal daisy necklace.

$400-450 **SCA**

A Larry Vbra bronze tone metal, faux turquoise, acrylic and glass stones collar style necklace and matching clip earrings.

$1,150-1,300 **SCA**

A gold vinaigrette, unmarked, engraved with scroll decoration on an engine-turned background.

c1800 *1.25in (3cm) wide 0.72oz*

$1,450-1,800 **WW**

An early 19thC gold mounted aventurine vinaigrette, unmarked.

1.25in (3cm) wide

$975-1,150 **WW**

CLOSER LOOK - NELSON MEMORIAL VINAIGRETTE

Due to the Nelson association this vinaigrette appeals to collectors of vinaigrettes and Nelson memorabilia.

The cover has a portrait of Nelson and 'England expects every man will do his duty'.

The grille has a depiction of the Victory and 'Traf.R Oct.R 21 1805'

A George III silver Nelson memorial vinaigrette by Matthew Linwood, Birmingham.

1805 1.75in (4cm) wide

$5,250-6,000 **ECGW**

A George III silver purse vinaigrette, by Lawrence and Co, Birmingham, with two later chains and a bar pin attachment.

1817 *1in (2.5cm) long 0.2oz*

$480-600 **WW**

A gold vinaigrette, with micro mosaic of a dog to the lid with engraved foliate decoration.

0.75in (2cm) wide 0.11oz

$550-600 **L&T**

A 19thC citrine vinaigrette, the citrine claw set in a hinged lid, the sides of engine turned and beaded decoration, with a fitted case.

$2,700-3,600 **L&T**

A William IV silver-gilt and micro mosaic vinaigrette, by Robert Gray and Son, Glasgow, the cover set with a panel of Pliny's doves, around a bird bath, the hinged grille with pierced and engraved foliate decoration.

1834 *2.25in (5.5cm) long 3.2oz*

$12,000-15,000 **WW**

A silver 'castle-top' vinaigrette, of Kenilworth, by Nathaniel Mills, Birmingham.

1837 *1.75in (4cm) long 0.9oz.*

$1,800-2,250 **WW**

An early Victorian Scottish silver gilt and rock crystal combination vinaigrette and snuff box, maker's mark 'AGW' (possibly A. G. Whighton), Edinburgh.

1838 *1.5in (4cm) long*

$1,000-1,400 **DN**

An early Victorian silver castle top vinaigrette, by Gervase Wheeler, Birmingham, of Abbotsford House.

1839 *1.5in (4cm) wide*

$750-900 **LOCK**

A silver vinaigrette, by Nathaniel Mills, Birmingham, the interior with a gilded pierced grille.

1841 *1.5in (4cm) long 0.5oz*

$480-600 **WW**

A Victorian three-color gold vinaigrette, unmarked.

1in (2.5cm) 0.3oz

$550-600 **WW**

A Victorian silver vinaigrette, by Owen & Boon, Birmingham.

1856

$270-330 **ECGW**

A Victorian silver vinaigrette, with engine turned decoration by Gervaise Wheeler, Birmingham.

1866

$450-550 **ECGW**

A 19thC Austro-Hungarian silver-gilt and enamel vinaigrette, maker's mark of L.P, the interior with a pull-out pierced grille.

1in (2.5cm) high

$570-630 **WW**

A rare American silver scent bottle/ vinaigrette, by Tiffany and Co, Edward C. Moore period, modeled as a two-handled classical vase.

c1870-75 *4in (10cm) wide 2.5oz*

$4,500-5,500 **WW**

A 19thC Continental gold vinaigrette, the cover painted with a Mediterranean lakeland scene with snow capped mountain.

1.3in (3.25cm) wide.

$2,000-2,400 **MOR**

A novelty 'thistle' silver vinaigrette, by E.H. Stockwell, London.

c1876 *4in (10cm) long 2.3oz*

$3,300-3,900 **WW**

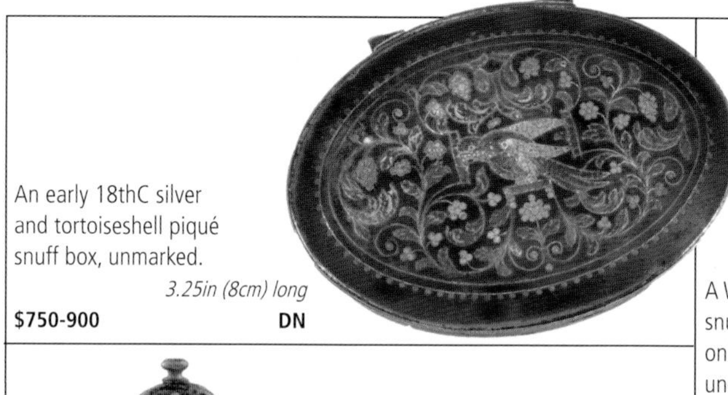

An early 18thC silver and tortoiseshell piqué snuff box, unmarked.

3.25in (8cm) long

$750-900 **DN**

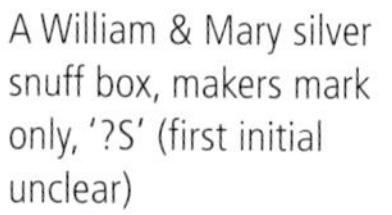

A William & Mary silver snuff box, makers mark only, '?S' (first initial unclear)

2.5in (6.5cm) wide 1.4oz

$1,500-1,800 **L&T**

A gilt metal mounted Mother-of-pearl snuff box/flask, unmarked, the top with a screw-off cover, the base with a push button to open the snuff box.

c1740-60 *3.25in (8.5cm) long*

$1,800-2,250 **WW**

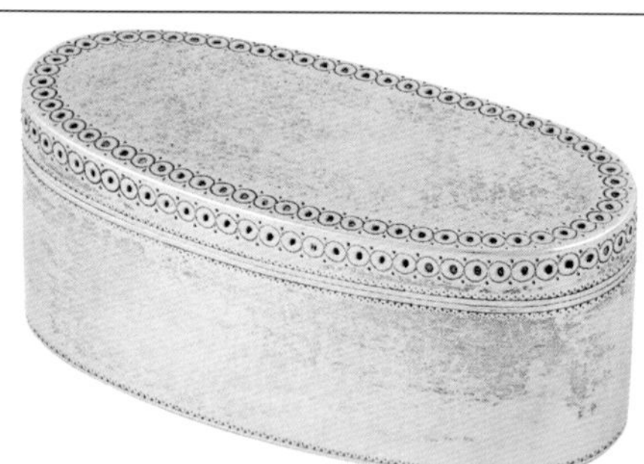

A George III silver snuff box, by Patrick Robertson, Edinburgh, the gilt interior with latin presentation inscription.

1755 *3.5in (8.5cm) wide 3.4oz*

$975-1,150 **L&T**

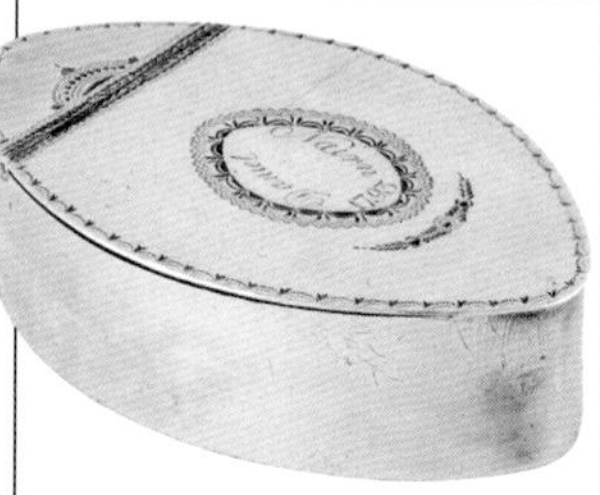

A George III silver snuff box, by IM, London, inscribed 'Daniel Nairn 1793'.

1789 *3.5in (8.5cm) long 2.6oz*

$450-550 **L&T**

An 18thC silver and carved Mother-of-pearl snuff box, the nacre-set lid decorated with a man playing the pipes.

2.75in (7cm) wide

$400-450 **SWO**

An 18thC French vari-colored gold snuff box, in the original fitted shagreen and velvet lined case.

Provenance is really important as is condition and age. The inside of the cover with a later inscription, 'Believed to be the snuff box of John Keble from whose house it came. Presented to Geoffrey and Madeline Teed by Canon Edward Keble 2nd June 1978'.

3in (7cm) long 2.7oz

$9,000-10,500 **WW**

A George III silver double snuff box, by Phipps and Robinson, London the cover later engraved with a scene of The Mansion House.

1791 *3.25in (8.5cm) wide 3.5oz*

$6,750-8,250 **WW**

A late 18thC Mother-of-pearl and silver gilt snuff box, the inner cover engraved with a scene of a shipwreck, the cover with the arms quartered of Meers, Farington, De la Fontaine, Bussy & Nevil, unmarked.

$2,700-3,300 **CHEF**

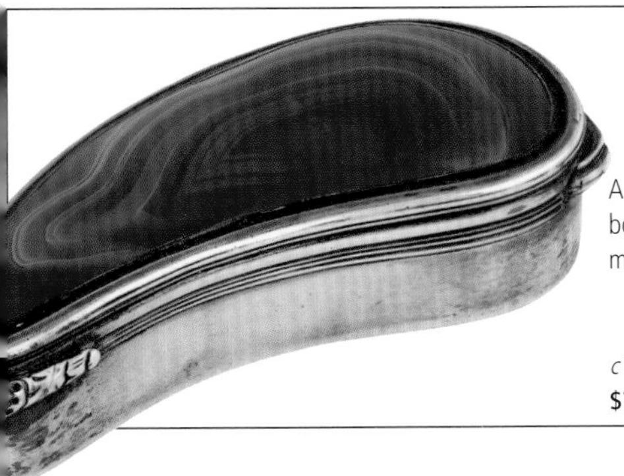

A George III agate mounted silver snuff box, by Robert Haxton, Edinburgh, makers mark only struck twice.

c1800 *3.5in (9cm) long*

$700-850 **L&T**

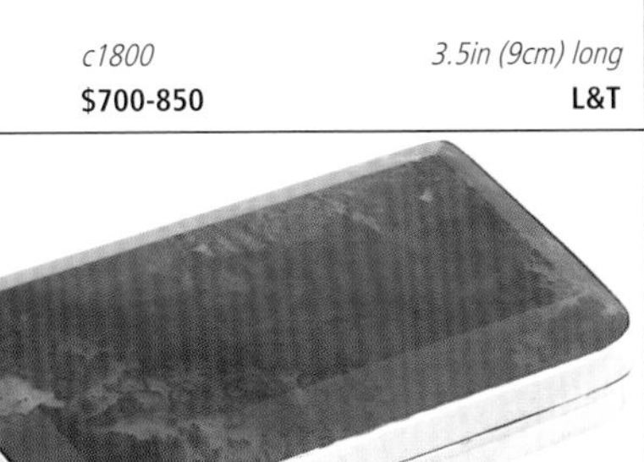

A Scottish provincial hardstone mounted snuff box, by David Gray, Dumfries, the cover and base of polished agate.

David Gray was a prolific silversmith. His known working dates were from 1778 to 1841.

3in (7.5cm) wide

$4,500-5,500 **L&T**

A George III silver-mounted Conus Textile shell snuff box, unmarked.

Conus Textile, common name the Textile Cone or the cloth of gold cone is a venomous species of sea snail, a marine gastropod mollusc in the family Conidae, the cone snails.

c1800 *3.75in (9.5cm) long*

$900-1,000 **WW**

An early 19thC Continental silver mounted tortoise snuff box, possibly Dutch.

4.25in (10.5cm) long

$2,250-3,000 **WW**

An early 19thC silver-gilt pedlar snuff box, with cancelled marks, marked with London Assay Office number 8905, with the pedlar in relief.

4in (10cm) long 6oz

$850-975 **WW**

A silver-gilt, malachite and micro mosaic table snuff box, with a scene of figures before a river and waterfall with a Neo-Classical building.

4in (10cm) wide

$18,000-22,500 **ROS**

An early 19thC gold-mounted lapis lazuli patch or snuff box, unmarked.

1.5in (3.75cm) wide

$1,500-2,100 **MOR**

An early 19thC Mauchline ware sycamore and penwork snuff box, the lid decorated with a scene taken from Robert Burns' poem the Whistle, inscribed 'The Whistle- vide Burns' and 'Then uprose our bard like a prophet in drink'.

3in (8cm) wide

$850-975 **WW**

An early 19thC French pressed burr maple circular snuff box, titled 'Frederick the IInd, King of Purfsia,' marked 'DE NAYES' and indistinct text, the interior tortoiseshell lined.

3in (7.5cm) diam

$550-600 **WW**

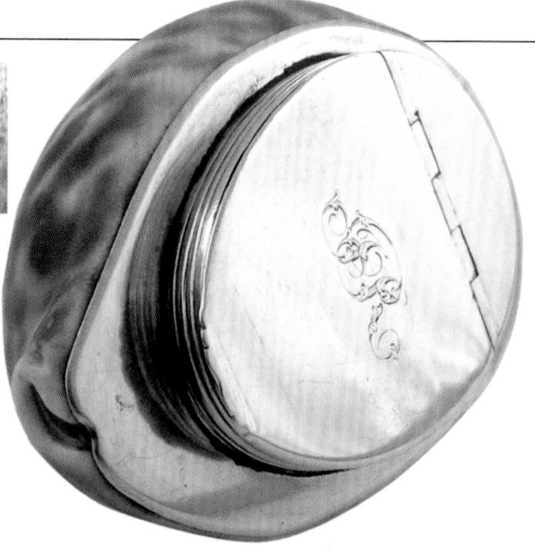

A Scottish provincial silver cowrie shell snuff box, by Robert Keay, Perth, engraved with a monogram.

c1820 *3.25in (8.5cm) wide*

$900-1,000 **WW**

A William IV Scottish silver mounted agate snuff box, by William Cross & John Carruthers, Edinburgh.

1830 *3in (7.5cm) long*

$550-600 **DN**

A William IV silver castle top snuff box, by Joseph Wilmore, Birmingham, the cover with a scene of Abbotsford House.

1834 *3.5in (9cm) wide 6.5oz*

$700-750 **L&T**

A Victorian silver table snuffbox, possibly by George Edwards, London, with the inscription.

1858 *4in (10cm) wide 7.9oz*

$2,250-3,000 **CHEF**

A large 19thC French silver and niello work hunting snuff box, the cover with a huntsman on horseback.

4.25in (11cm) long 6.5oz

$1,400-1,800 **WW**

A Victorian silver snuff box, by Reily and Storer, London, cast with a hunting scene.

1863 *3in (8cm) wide 4.7oz*

$1,400-1,800 **WW**

A French tortoiseshell piqué snuff box, the cover inset with an inlaid, painted and applied scene of Cupid, a basket of flowers, a portrait cameo and 'Souvenir' on a banner, under glass.

c1870 *3in (8cm) diam*

$600-750 **DN**

A Continental silver and gilt niello decorated snuff box, depicting the 'Duomo di Milano'.

3in (8cm) wide

$210-280 **L&T**

A late 17th/early 18thC inlaid tortoiseshell snuff box, inlaid with flower head and fruiting vine motifs, mirrored monogram and inscription 'No Recompense but Love'

2.75in (6.5cm) wide

$1,200-1,500 **L&T**

A late 18thC French gold-mounted tortoiseshell portrait snuff box, maker's mark partially worn, 'O?' over 'J.T, Paris'.

The enameled portrait of a gentleman, is believed to be Jean Baptiste de Machault d' Arnouville, (1701-1794), minister to Louis XV.

1777 *2.75in (7cm) long*

$3,300-3,900 **WW**

An 18thC George III gold and silver piqué tortoiseshell snuff box.

3.75in (9.5cm) wide

$400-450 **L&T**

A George III tortoiseshell scent bottle holder, with silver inlay, with a glass scent bottle.

2.5in (6cm) high

$700-750 **SWO**

A late 18thC two color gold-mounted blonde tortoiseshell snuff box.

2.5in (6cm) diam

$4,500-5,500 **WW**

A French tortoiseshell portrait box.

c1810 *3.5in (8.5cm) diam*

$700-850 **WW**

A French tortoiseshell souvenir cheroot case, inlaid with a view of the Eiffel Tower and a Montgolfière.

c1889 *5.75in (14.5cm) long*

$300-400 **MAB**

A silver-mounted tortoiseshell card case, by A J How, London, set with a pietra dura panel, within gold and silver floral pique borders.

1918 *4in (10cm) long*

$750-900 **WW**

A tortoiseshell toilet box, with silver banding to foot and middle, handwritten note inside 'from Queen Mary, Xmas 1923'.

3in (8cm) wide

$450-550 **L&T**

ESSENTIAL REFERENCE - VESTA BOX

The inscription probably relates to a campaign during the China War of 1860, when the Allied forces marched to Chang-Kia-Wan (mis-spelled in the inscription) encountering Chinese forces on 18th September. A battle ensued and as the party spurred their horses, encountering fire from all directions, it was reported that two men were wounded and one horse was killed. It is likely that the Charger in the inscription was this horse.

A Victorian silver-mounted hoof table vesta box, by William Summers, London, the cover inscribed 'WILFUL, 1st Charger Shot in Action on the 18th September 1860 AT CHOW-KIA-WHAU NEAR PEKIN', on a silver horse shoe.
1863 *4.75in (12cm) long*
$975-1,150 **WW**

A Victorian silver and enamel vesta case, maker's mark mis-struck, 'T?', Birmingham, applied with an enamel fox's head.
1883 *1.75in (4.5cm) long 0.6oz*
$700-850 **WW**

A Victorian silver and enamel vesta case, by L. Emmanuel, Birmingham, with a lady in a landscape.
1887 *1.75in (4cm) long 0.7oz*
$850-975 **WW**

A Victorian silver and enamel vesta case, decorated with fox hounds, by Sampson Mordan & Co., London.
1887
$2,000-2,700 **FELL**

A Victorian silver novelty vesta case, in the form of a hip flask, by M. Bros., Birmingham.
1888
$400-450 **ECGW**

A Victorian silver and enamel vesta case, maker's mark of R.B.S, Birmingham, with two racehorses, the reverse inscribed 'GARRNS SPORTS GIB'.
1897 *2in (5cm) long 1.1oz*
$550-600 **WW**

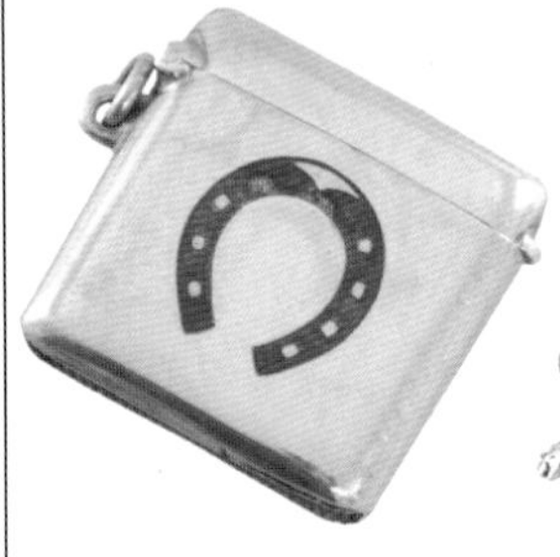

A Victorian silver novelty vesta case, with enameled horseshoe decoration, by 'HM' Birmingham.
1898
$115-130 **ECGW**

A Victorian silver-mounted tortoiseshell table vesta striker.
$900-1,000 **WW**

A Victorian silver novelty vesta case, inset with a compass, Birmingham.
1900
$150-225 **ECGW**

A silver vesta case, by Alexander Ritchie, with chased design of galleon and stylised leaves, stamped maker's marks 'AR/IONA', hallmarked Chester.
1910 *1.75in (4.5cm) high 24.5g*
$2,000-2,700 **L&T**

A silver-gilt mounted novelty table vesta box, modeled as a tortoise, by Levi and Salaman, Birmingham, the hinged tortoiseshell back opens to reveal a striker, crack to cover.
1911 *3in (7.5cm) long*
$600-750 **WW**

A French enamel and silver-mounted snuff box, probably by Antoine Leschaudel.
c1747 *3in (7cm) wide*
$1,500-1,800 **WW**

An enamel snuff box, south Staffordshire or Birmingham, painted with figures amidst classical ruins.
c1760 *2.75in (7cm) long*
$600-750 **DN**

A South Staffordshire enamel spaniel bonbonnière, minor cracks to inside of cover.
c1770 *2in (5cm) wide*
$1,500-2,100 **SWO**

An English enamel table snuff box, with a view of 'Harwood House', the cover interior with 'A trifle from Harrogate'.
c1790 *3.5in (9cm) long*
$900-1,000
DN

A Bilston enamel snuff box, painted with George Washington.
c1800 *2in (5cm) wide*
$850-975 **MOR**

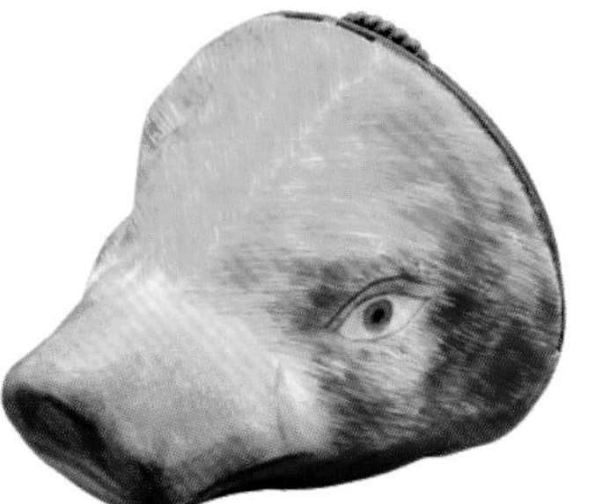

An early 19thC French enamel and hand painted boar's head snuff box.
2.75in (7cm) diam
$550-700 **SWO**

A Victorian silver and enamel scent bottle, by George Heath, London, enameled with Windsor castle.
1888 *3in (7.5cm) long*
$1,300-1,450 **WW**

A 19thC Continental gold and enamel snuff box, with Greek mythological scene, cased.
3.5in (9cm) wide 4.3oz
$7,500-9,000 **ROS**

A late 19thC French Limoges enamel pill box.
1.5in (3.5cm) diam
$450-550 **DN**

A gilt-brass and enamel 'Palais Royal' First Empire French monocular, unsigned, six draws with 1.25in objective lens, contained in gilt-brass body with six detailed enamels of putti.

$1,800-2,250 **CM**

A gilt metal and enamel opera glasses, with Mother-of-pearl eye pieces, painted with lovers in Arcadian landscapes.

c1900 *4in (10cm) wide*

$400-450 **DN**

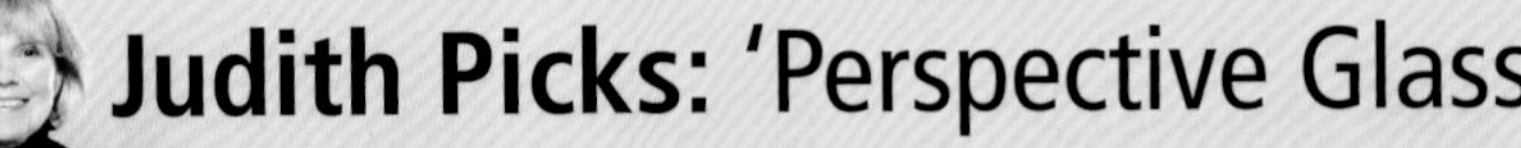

Judith Picks: 'Perspective Glass'

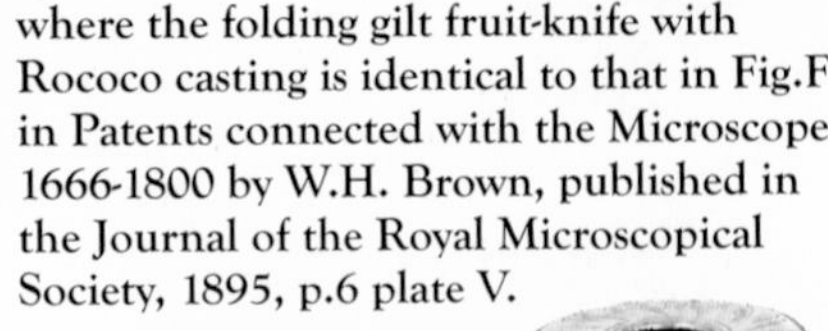

Thomas Ribright (w.1735-1772) patented this form of 'perspective glass' on 7th February, 1749 (No. 640) and fitted them with many different accessories to suit a variety of clients, and even one which doubled up as a microscope - this, where the folding gilt fruit-knife with Rococo casting is identical to that in Fig.F in Patents connected with the Microscope 1666-1800 by W.H. Brown, published in the Journal of the Royal Microscopical Society, 1895, p.6 plate V.

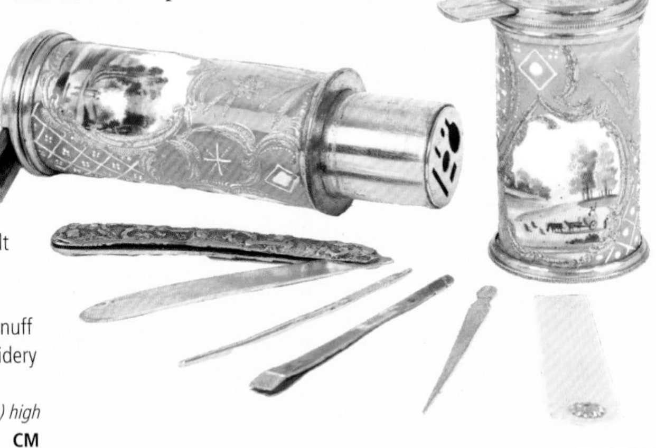

A rare Bilston enamel spyglass compendium étui, attributed to Thomas Ribright, lens and eyepieces with dust slides, fitted internally with compartments for silver-gilt accessories comprising folding fruit knife with Rococo handle, tweezers, ivory aide-memoire, snuff spoon and pin tool, and embroidery needle.

c1765 *4.75in (12cm) high*

$3,300-3,900 **CM**

An enamel watch case, London, the lid probably c1880 set with a compass.

c1760 *2in (5cm) diam*

$3,000-4,000 **MAB**

A South Staffordshire enamel chamberstick

c1770 *7in (17.5cm) wide*

$750-900 **WW**

A battersea enamel plaque, printed in purple with allegorical figures, some hairline cracks.

c1751 *4.5in (11.5cm) high*

$1,500-2,250 **MOR**

A Battersea enamel plaque, printed in iron red and sepia with an heraldic crest and motto 'For our Country', within a gilt metal paste set frame, four of the pastes are replaced and are claw set rather than collet set.

c1753-55 *4.75in (12cm high)*

$3,000-4,000 **MOR**

A Staffordshire enamel plaque, painted with a couple seated beneath a tree in a river landscape.

c1770 *3.5in (8.5cm) wide*

$1,500-2,100 **MOR**

An English enamel plaque, possibly Battersea, printed with a portrait of Horace Walpole.

c1770 *3.5in (8.5cm) high*

$2,100-2,800 **MOR**

Judith Picks: 'castle top'

This is an unusual subject for a castle top card case and is made more desirable by its association with Lord Byron. It also harks back to a time when people (mainly gentlemen) carried calling cards. During the 1800s and early 1900s the practice of 'calling' upon or visiting one's relatives, friends, and acquaintances was a middle and upper class social ritual governed by countless rules. Central to visiting etiquette was the use of the calling card. When calling upon a friend, a gentleman gave his card to the servant answering the door. If the person the gentleman was calling upon was home, the servant would take the card to them and they would come meet the gentleman. If the person being called upon was not home, the servant would leave the card for when they returned. Generally upon a gentleman's initial visit to a home, he would simply leave a card and then depart. If the new acquaintance wished to formally visit with him, he or she would send a card in return. If no card was sent, or the return card was sent in an envelope, this signaled that the new acquaintance did not wish for a personal visit to occur. How much better than emails!

A William IV silver 'castle top' card case, by Taylor & Perry, Birmingham, with a medallion titled 'George Gordon Byron, Lord Byron', the reverse with his ancestral home Newstead Abbey, the cover inscribed 'B. R. Thomas'.

1835 *3.75in (9.5cm) long*

$1,400-1,800 **DN**

A Scottish silver card case, by James Naysmith and Co, Edinburgh.

1841 *4in (9.5cm) long 2.5oz*

$700-850 **WW**

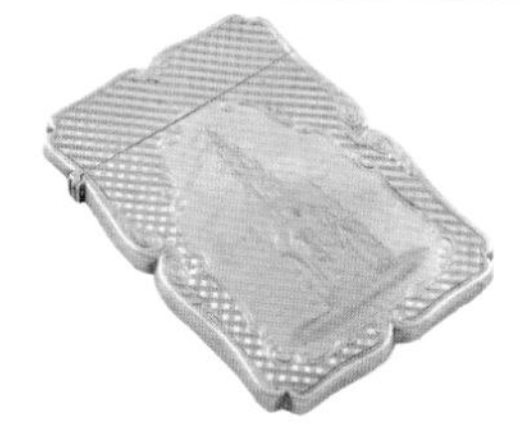

A silver visiting card case, by Nathaniel Mills, Birmingham, engraved with the Scott memorial and tartan decoration.

1843 *3.75in (9.5cm) long 2.2oz*

$1,400-1,700 **WW**

A silver card case, by Frederick Marson, Birmingham.

1854 *4in (10cm) long 2oz*

$400-450 **WW**

A silver 'castle top' card case, by Frederick Marsden, Birmingham, embossed with the Scott Monument.

1868 *4in (10cm) long 2oz*

$900-1,000 **WW**

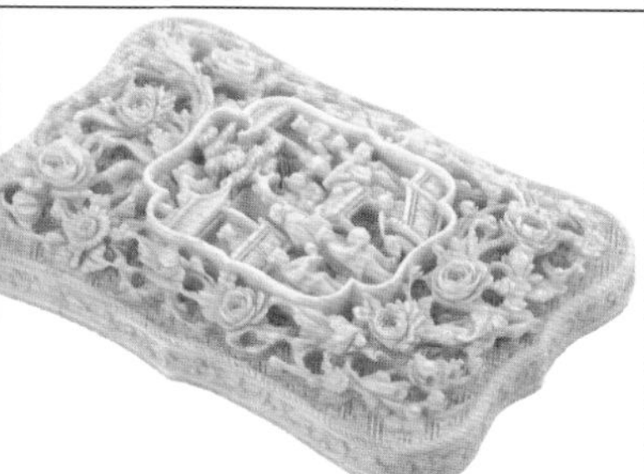

A 19thC Chinese Canton ivory card case, carved with figures, pagodas and animals, with a box.

4.5in (11.5cm) long

$2,700-3,300 **WW**

A 19thC Chinese Canton ivory card case, carved with figures in a pagoda beneath pine.

4.75in (12cm) long

$2,400-3,000 **WW**

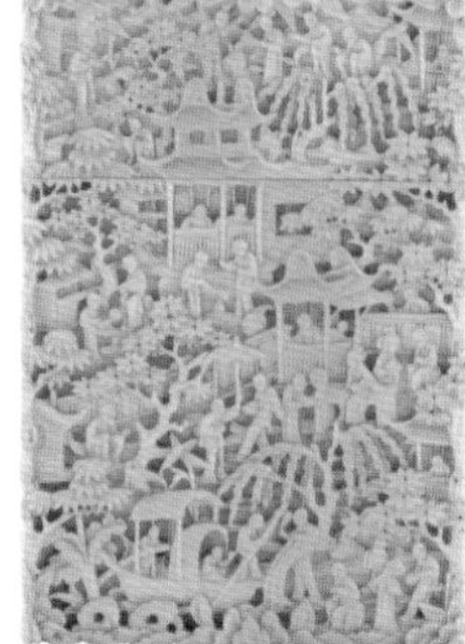

A 19thC Chinese Canton ivory card case, carved with figures in pagodas and fenced gardens.

4.5in (11.5cm) long

$2,250-3,000 **WW**

ESSENTIAL REFERENCE - NUTMEG

Nutmeg is a spice that has long been prized for its medicinal properties. The history of nutmeg goes back to the 1stC as evidenced in writings by Pliny, the Roman writer. Prized in medieval times for its uses in cuisine, nutmeg was brought to Europe in the middle ages by the Arabs through the Venetians. The spice was very popular and very expensive. It was even rumoured to ward off the plague.

- **Nutmeg is native to the Banda islands of Indonesia. When the Portuguese rounded the Cape of Good Hope in Africa in the late 1400s, they took control of the spice trade because they could transport nutmeg far more cheaply in the hold of a ship than it could be transported by caravan. Soon the Dutch became the predominant traders of this precious spice. At the time, the only source of nutmeg was on Run Island. Because the British also wanted in on the lucrative trade there were many struggles between the British and the Dutch over control of the Island.**
- **During the Napoleonic wars, the English finally gained control of Run Island and proceeded to plant nutmeg trees in Grenada and Zanzibar. This ensured that the British would not lose complete control of the Nutmeg trade should they ever decide to give up the island. The expansion of nutmeg production also had the effect of making nutmeg accessible to more people at lower prices.**

A silver 'acorn' nutmeg grater, probably by Samuel Meriton, London.
c1760 *1.75in (4.5cm) long 0.7oz*
$600-750 **WW**

An 18thC silver nutmeg grater, by Samuel Meriton, London, of egg form, with a later grater.
c1775 *1.25in (3cm) long*
$300-450 **WW**

A George III silver nutmeg grater, by Samuel Meriton II, London.
1791 *2in (5cm) long*
$900-1,000 **CHEF**

A Scottish silver nutmeg grater, by Marshall & Sons, Edinburgh, no date letter, with slide-out steel grater, engraved with a crest.

The maker's mark was entered in 1817 to 1827 and from 1835 to 1890, with George IV duty mark hence date of c1825. The crest of HOUSTON, originally of Blackadder House, Chimside, Berwickshire, and representatives of the ancient family of HOUSTON of Cotrich.
c1825 *2.5in (6cm) high*
$1,500-2,100 **DN**

A silver nutmeg grater, by Thomas & James Phipps II, London.
1816 *1.75in (4.5cm) long*
$400-450 **DN**

A silver 'melon' nutmeg grater, by Hilliard and Thomason, Birmingham.
1854 *1.5in (3.5cm) long 0.6oz*
$1,200-1,400 **WW**

A novelty silver nutmeg grater, by Hilliard and Thomason, Birmingham, modeled as a strawberry.
1859 *1.5in (3.5cm) long 0.6oz*
$7,500-8,250 **WW**

SHELL NUTMEG GRATER

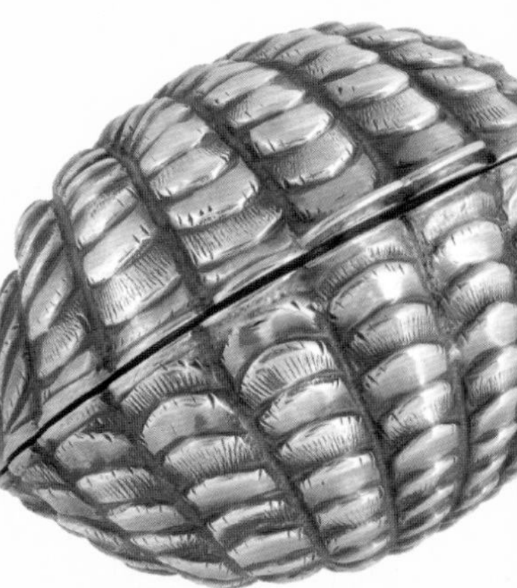

A silver novelty 'shell' nutmeg grater, by Hilliard & Thomason, Birmingham.
c1875 *2in (4.5cm) long*
$1,000-1,200 **DN**

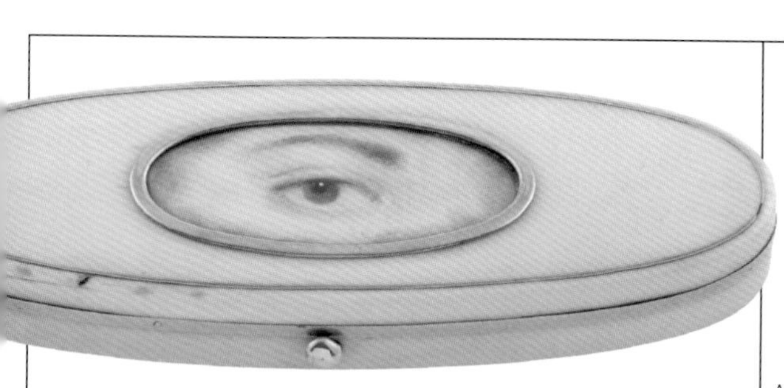

A 19thC ivory mentomori/lover's eye tooth pick box, with gold mounts and inlay.

3in (8cm) wide

$3,000-4,000 **L&T**

A late 18thC French ivory and two color gold mounted ivory carnet de bal, with inscription 'Souvenier d' Amitie'.

c1780 *3.5in (8.5cm) high*

$300-400 **L&T**

A 19thC German carved ivory tankard, with two huntsmen and dogs attacking a wolf.

7in (18cm) high

$3,000-4,000 **L&T**

A late 19thC in 17thC style German silver mounted ivory Historismus tankard, pseudo Augsburg marks, probably Hanau, the body carved with a battle.

10.25 (26cm) high

$12,750-14,250 **DN**

A late 19th/early 20thC carved ivory and multi-gem set elephant, with cabochon cat's eye chrysoberyls, faceted sapphires, rubies and emeralds.

5in (13cm) high

$9,750-10,500 **HALL**

A 19thC ivory doll's house whatnot, each tier mounted with bottles, cups and candlesticks.

3.5in (9cm) high

$450-550 **SWO**

An early 19thC Napoleonic Prisoner of War bone automaton group.

8.25in (21cm) high

$9,000-10,500 **WW**

A late 19thC French Dieppe carved ivory handle, of a lady.

5.5in (14cm) long

$550-600 **WW**

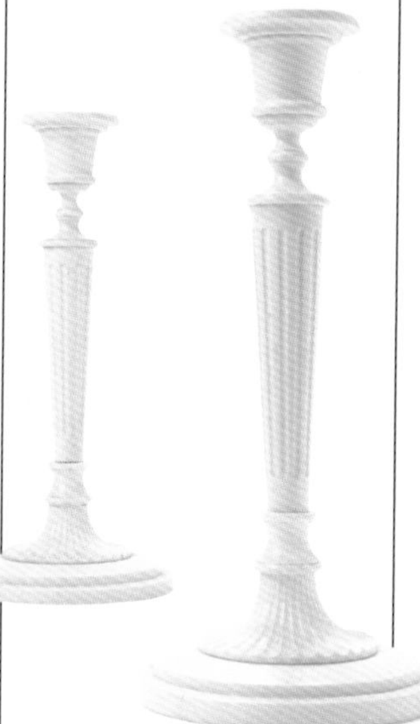

A pair of 19thC ivory candle sticks.

9.5in (24cm) high

$2,000-2,400 **L&T**

A mid-19thC ivory desk seal.

4.25in (11cm) long

$270-330 **HT**

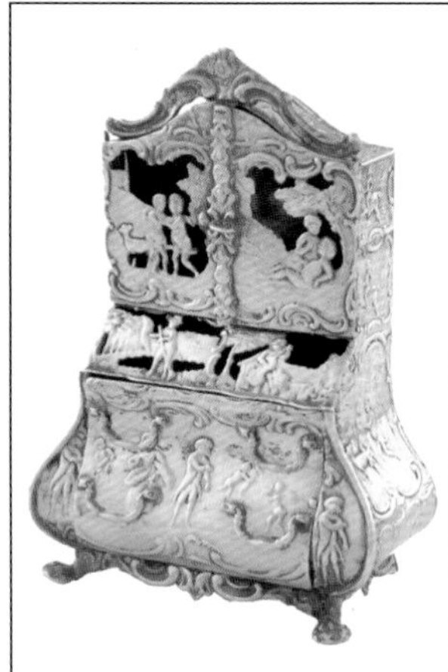

A Dutch silver miniature bureau bookcase.

4.25in (11cm) high 5oz

$270-330 **WW**

A Dutch silver miniature house box, importer's mark of Boaz Landeck, Chester.

1906 *2.75in (7cm) high 2.2oz*

$350-300 **WW**

A late 19thC Continental silver miniature bureau, importer's mark of Elly Miller, London.

1898 *3.75in (8.5cm) high 2.5oz*

$210-280 **WW**

A Continental set of six filigree chairs and a table.

table 2.5in (6.5cm) long

$450-600 **WW**

A Dutch miniature silver fire place.

3.5in (9cm) high 2.9oz

$200-350 **WW**

A miniature silver long case clock, importer's mark of Barnet Joseph, London.

1887 *5in (13cm) high 2.8oz*

$150-225 **WW**

A silver novelty 'sun dial' calendar, by James Deakin and Sons, Birmingham.

1907 *2.5in (6cm) high*

$300-400 **WW**

A novelty silver 'grenade' table lighter, Birmingham, dented.

1907

$135-180 **ECGW**

A model of a snake, by D & J Welby, London.

1910 *8.75in (22cm) high 29oz*

$4,500-5,500 **L&T**

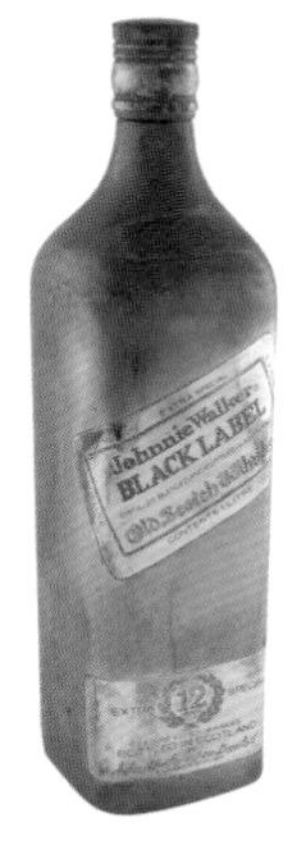

A novelty silver 'Johnnie Walker' whisky decanter.

11.5in (29.5cm) high 0.33oz

$1,400-1,800 **WW**

A silver-mounted novelty tortoise table bell, by Grey and Co, Chester.

c1910 *6in (14.5cm) long*

$1,500-1,800 **WW**

A novelty 'Boer war field gun' cigar cutter, by Alexander Clark Manufacturing Co, London.

1903 *14in (35.5cm) long*

$4,500-5,500 **HT**

A silver novelty 'George III knife box' tea caddy, by Samuel Walton Smith, Birmingham.
c1899 *3.5in (8.5cm) high 4.6oz*
$600-700 **DN**

A set of three silver and composition hunting menu card holders, by Grey & Co., Chester.
c1930 *1.5in (4cm) high*
$450-550 **DN**

A parcel-gilt silver 'watering can' scent flask, by Henry Dee, London.
1872 *1.75in (4.5cm) high 0.9oz*
$1,450-1,800 **WW**

A silver scent bottle, possibly by L. Emmanuel, Birmingham.
1890 *3.75in (10cm) long*
$210-280 **WW**

A novelty 'pillar box' propelling pencil, unmarked, probably by S. Mordan.
c1870 *1.75in (5cm) long*
$1,000-1,200 **WW**

A silver travelling apple corer, by Peter Archambo, London.
c1750 *6in (15cm) long 0.8oz*
$850-900 **WW**

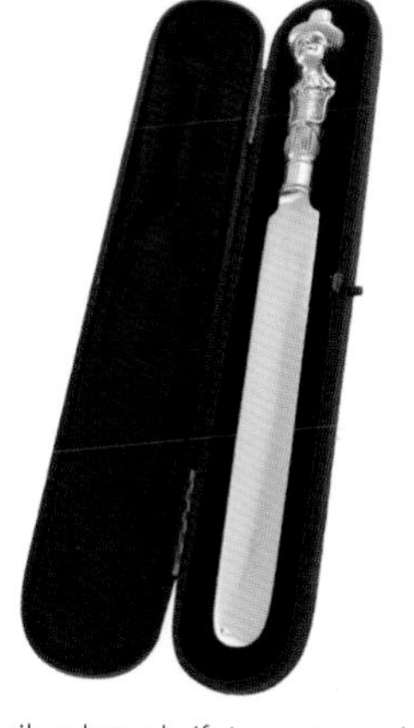

A silver letter knife/page turner, by Theobalds and Atkinson, London.
1838 *11.5in (29.5cm) long*
$600-750 **WW**

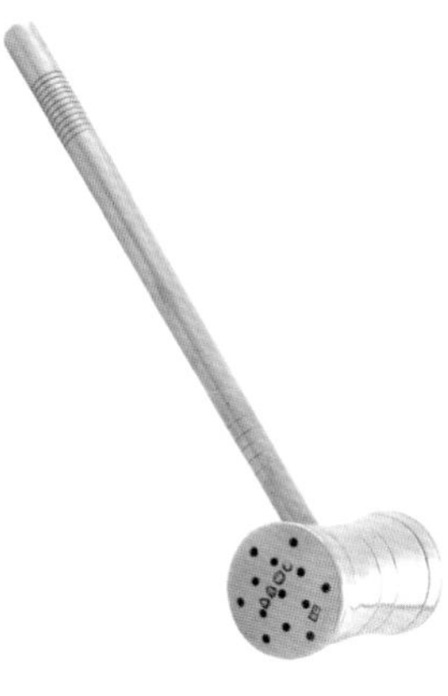

A silver novelty 'gavel' sander, by Stuart Clifford, London.
1837 *4.75in (12cm) long 0.8oz*
$450-550 **WW**

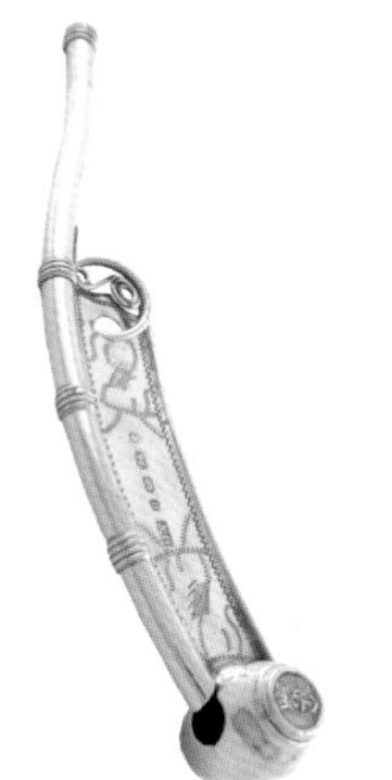

A silver bosun's call, by H. Aston, Birmingham.
1865 *5in (13cm) long 0.4oz*
$550-600 **WW**

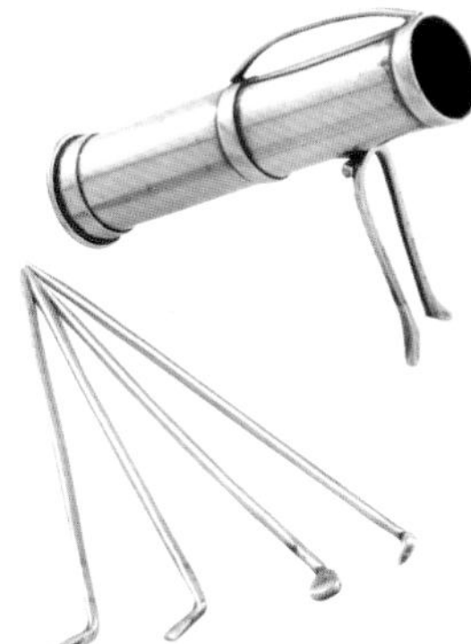

A novelty silver 'golf bag' cocktail stick holder, by Cohen and Charles, Chester, with four 'golf club' cocktail sticks.
1929 *2.25in (6cm) long 0.5oz*
$340-390 **WW**

A novelty silver 'ink pen nib' inkwell, by Saunders and Shepherd, Birmingham, with clear glass liner.
1894 *5.25in (13.5cm) high 2.4oz*
$450-550 **WW**

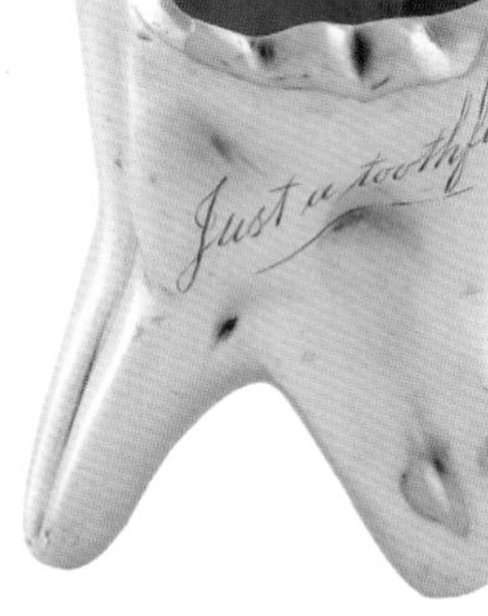

A novelty silver table 'molar tooth' shot holder, by Henry Dee, London, inscribed 'Just a Toothful'.
c1879 *2in (5.5cm) high 1.6oz*
$750-850 **WW**

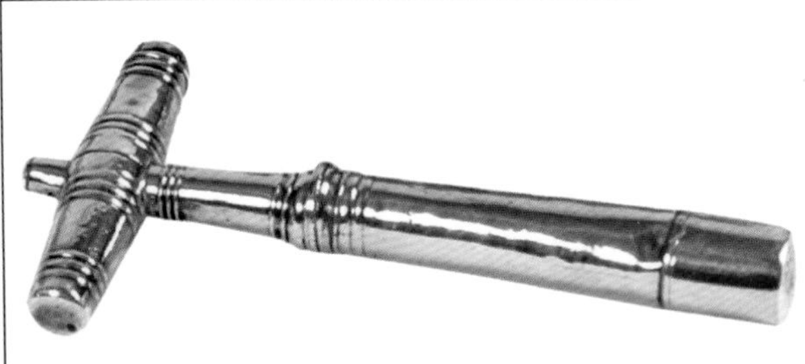

A silver travelling corkscrew, no maker's mark, London.
1832 *3.25in (8.25cm) long*
$450-550 **HT**

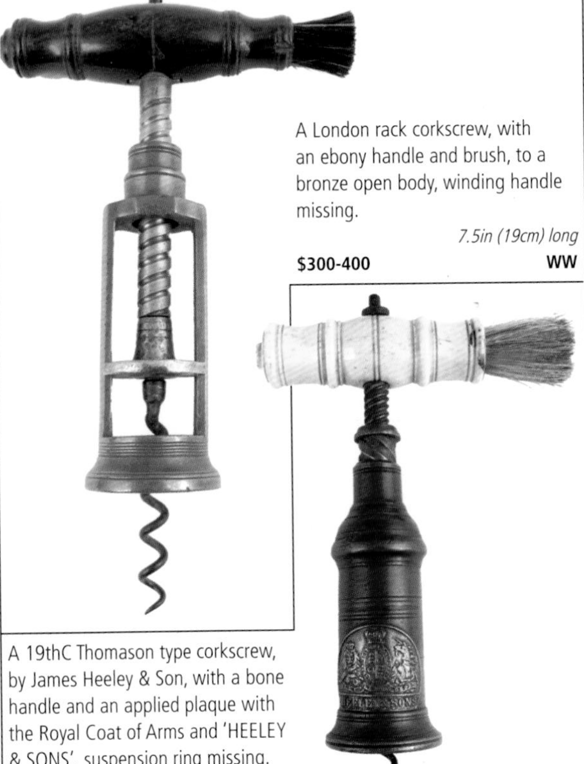

A London rack corkscrew, with an ebony handle and brush, to a bronze open body, winding handle missing.
7.5in (19cm) long
$300-400 **WW**

A 19thC Thomason type corkscrew, by James Heeley & Son, with a bone handle and an applied plaque with the Royal Coat of Arms and 'HEELEY & SONS', suspension ring missing.
7.25in (18cm) long
$450-550 **WW**

ESSENTIAL REFERENCE - CORKSCREWS

The corkscrew design may have derived from the gun worm which was a device used by musketmen to remove unspent charges from a musket's barrel in a similar fashion, from at least the early 1630s. The corkscrew is possibly an English invention, due to the tradition of beer and cider, and 'Treatise on Cider' by John Worlidge in 1676 describes 'binning of tightly corked cider bottles on their sides', although the earliest reference to a corkscrew is, 'steel worm used for the drawing of Corks out of Bottles' from 1681. In 1795, the first corkscrew patent was granted to the Reverend Samuell Henshall, in England. The clergyman affixed a simple disk, now known as the Henshall Button, between the worm and the shank. The disk prevents the worm from going too deep into the cork, forces the cork to turn with the turning of the crosspiece, and thus breaks the adhesion between the cork and the neck of the bottle. The disk is designed and manufactured slightly concave on the underside, which compresses the top of the cork and helps keep it from breaking apart.

- **A person who collects corkscrews is a helixophile.**

A 19thC Dutch silver pocket corkscrew, marked only with a 19thC tax mark.
3.5in (9cm) long
$1,500-2,100 **WW**

A Thomason type double action corkscrew, with a turned bone handle and brush, the brass barrel applied a crown.
6.5in (16.5cm) long
$200-350 **WW**

A green stained ivory corkscrew, Sheffield, with silver plated screw.
1919 *5.5in (14cm) long*
$450-600 **L&T**

A French direct pull corkscrew, with a cast vine handle.
3in (7.5cm) long
$200-350 **WW**

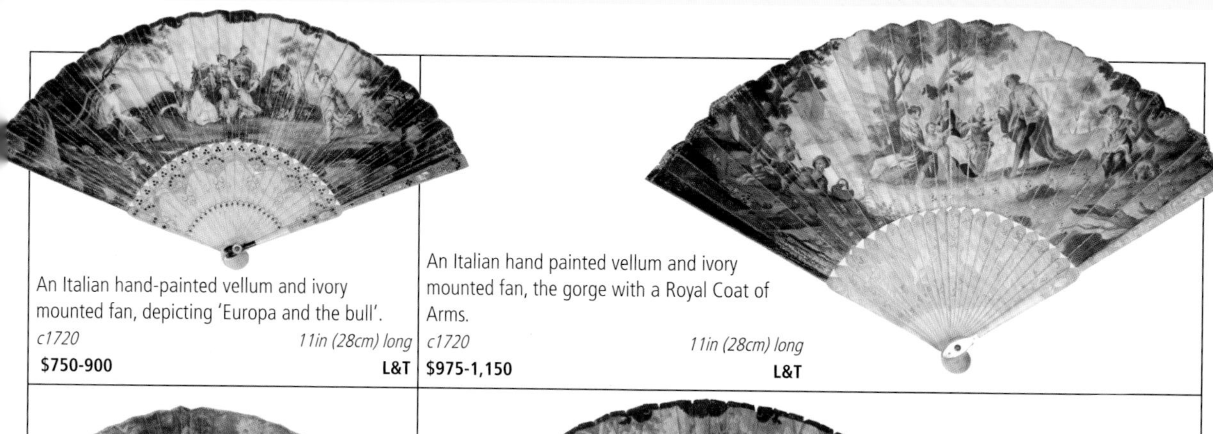

An Italian hand-painted vellum and ivory mounted fan, depicting 'Europa and the bull'.
c1720 *11in (28cm) long*
$750-900 **L&T**

An Italian hand painted vellum and ivory mounted fan, the gorge with a Royal Coat of Arms.
c1720 *11in (28cm) long*
$975-1,150 **L&T**

An English hand-painted vellum and ivory mounted fan, depicting Diana and nymphs hunting, with later guards.
c1740 *10.5in (26.5cm) long*
$600-750 **L&T**

An Italian hand-painted vellum and ivory mounted fan, depicting 'Susanna and the Elders'.
c1720 *11in (28cm) long*
$850-975 **L&T**

A Scottish hand colored and ivory mounted fan, depicting 'The Battle of Stirling Castle'.
c1746 *11in (28cm) long*
$300-400 **L&T**

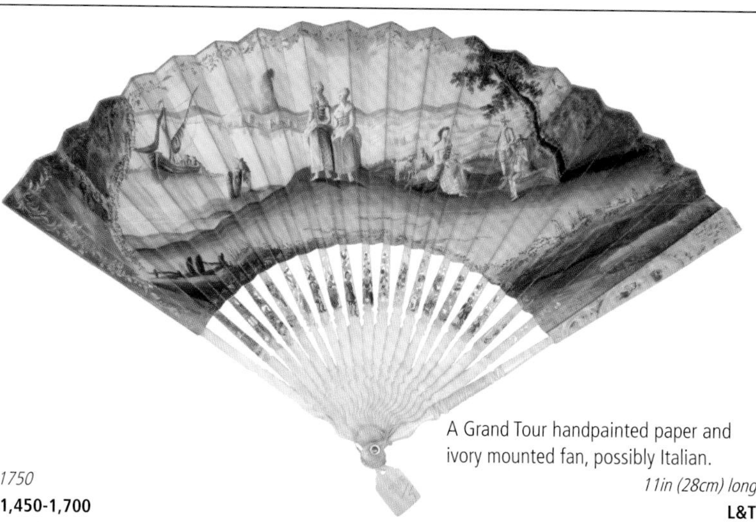

A Grand Tour handpainted paper and ivory mounted fan, possibly Italian.
c1750 *11in (28cm) long*
$1,450-1,700 **L&T**

A hand-painted paper and mother of pearl mounted fan, possibly English, depicting a religious scene, with carved gilded mother of pearl sticks.
c1750 *10.5in (26.5cm) long*
$400-450 **L&T**

A French hand painted paper and ivory mounted fan, depicting 'Achilles and the daughters of Lycomedes'.
c1780 *10in (25.5cm) long*
$975-1,150 **L&T**

A late 18thC Chinese Canton ivory brisé fan, painted with cartouches depicting mountainous pagoda landscapes.
16.75in (42cm) long
$3,000-4,500 **WW**

A Chinese Canton ivory brisé fan, carved with figures amidst pagodas and trees, a cartouche with the monogram 'H R H'.

c1800 *12.75in (32cm) long*

$3,000-4,000 **WW**

A Chinese Canton ivory brisé fan, with figures and animals amidst pagodas and trees, dragons chasing flaming pearls, phoenix and other birds, and a cartouche with the armorial for the Smith family, baronets of Sydling St Nicholas, Dorset.

c1800 *14in (35cm) long*

$3,000-4,000 **WW**

A 19thC Chinese carved ivory fan, painted with figures and attendants with fans in pagodas, the figures' faces applied in ivory, a fitted silk box.

22in (55.2cm) long

$4,000-4,500 **WW**

A 19thC Victorian signature fan, the paper folds bearing the signatures of Edward VII, Queen Alexandra, Prince Albert Victor, Prince George, Princess Louise, Princess Victoria, Princess Maud, and King Christian IX of Denmark.

13in (33cm) long

$600-750 **L&T**

A 19thC Victorian painted gauze, lace and mother of pearl fan, signed 'Standar'.

12.75in (32cm) long

$400-450 **L&T**

A 19thC Chinese Canton fan, the splines in black lacquer and gilt chinoiserie, painted with figures, flowers and birds.

22in (56cm) wide

$450-550 **TRI**

A 19thC Chinese lacquer fan, with ivory faces, a fitted box.

20.75in (52.5cm) long

$750-900 **WW**

A French hand-painted paper and ivory mounted fan, signed 'E.DUBOIS'.

c1890 *12in (30.5cm) long*

$300-400 **L&T**

A 19thC European mother of pearl fan, in original box made for Shreve Crump & Low, Boston.

20.5in (52cm) wide

$300-400 **TRI**

A Palais Royal piano form musical sewing box, the exterior veneered in stained burr maple with a mother-of-pearl and ebony keyboard, with; a pair of gilt agate boxes, a gold pique ivory needle box, a gold pencil, a pair of steel bladed scissors, a single blade folding knife, a 'fan' notelet, with miniature pencil, a gold thimble, and a gilt metal vinaigrette, the musical box with multiple 17 section comb playing two airs.

6in (15.5cm) high

$7,500-9,000 **RGA**

A late 18thC Vizagapatam Anglo-Indian ivory and lac engraved workbox, in the form of a house, the interior with pin cushions twin lidded compartments, a spool, thimble and other sewing utensils.

8.25in (20.5cm) wide

$13,500-15,000 **WW**

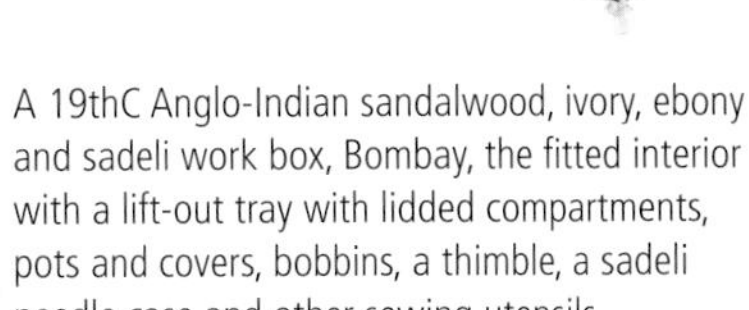

A 19thC Anglo-Indian sandalwood, ivory, ebony and sadeli work box, Bombay, the fitted interior with a lift-out tray with lidded compartments, pots and covers, bobbins, a thimble, a sadeli needle case and other sewing utensils.

Added value to this box is that it also has a silk embroidered cover and is contained with in a pine travelling box, the lid inscribed 'Mrs Sheppee's Work Box'.

12.75in (32.5cm) wide

$3,000-4,000 **WW**

A Victorian papier-mâché sarcophagus shape sewing box.

9.25in (23.5cm) wide

$300-450 **WW**

A late 19thC Pennsylvania painted pine table top sewing stand, with pinwheel and philphlot decoration.

18in (46cm) high

$2,250-3,000 **POOK**

An early 19thC Tunbridgeware sewing box, with painted scene of country house with figures in the garden.

7.5in (18.5cm) wide

$850-975 **LOCK**

A 19thC Tunbridge ware novelty tape measure.

1.75in (4cm) high

$165-225 **LOCK**

A late Victorian treen sewing clamp, with painted decoration and label 'A Brighton Present'.

2.5in (6cm) wide

$130-145 **LOCK**

A Mauchline ware thimble case, decorated with 'Bournemouth From Terrace Mount', with a Charles Horner silver thimble.

$75-90 **LOCK**

A Mauchline ware needlecase, printed with a scene of 'St. MARY'S ABBEI, YORK'.

9in (22.5cm) long

$60-75 **WW**

A novelty silver polar bear pin cushion, by Adie and Lovekin, Birmingham.
1909 *1.25in (3.5cm) long*
$1,800-2,250 **WW**

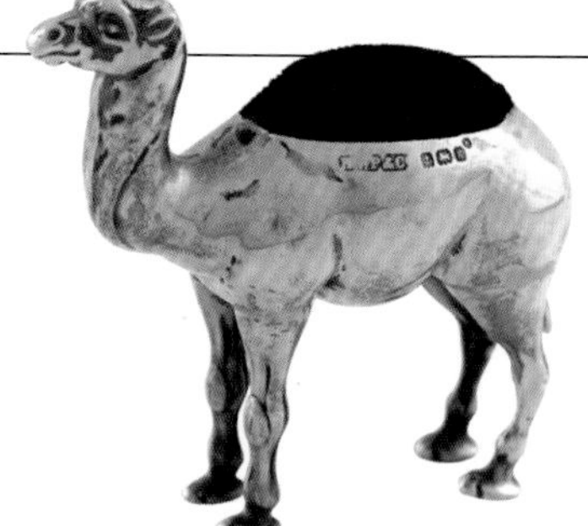

A novelty silver camel pin cushion, maker's mark worn, Birmingham.
1906 *2.5in (6.5cm) high*
$600-750 **WW**

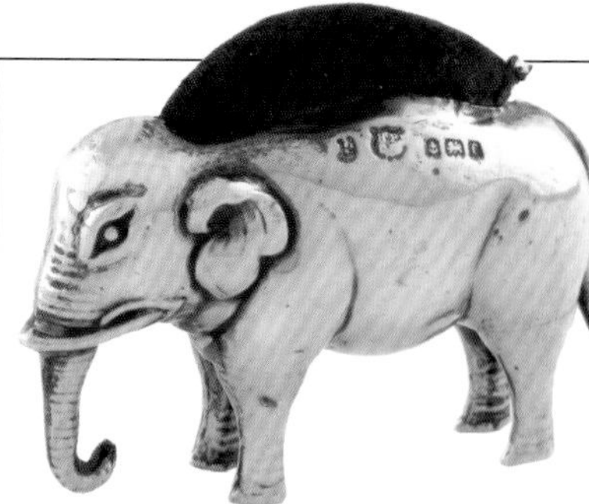

A novelty silver elephant pin cushion, by Boots Pure Drug Company Limited, Birmingham.
c1905 *2.5in (6cm) long*
$300-400 **WW**

A novelty silver swan pin cushion, by Adie and Lovekin Ltd., Birmingham.
c1907 *2.75in (7cm) long*
$550-700 **WW**

A silver novelty chick pin cushion, by Sampson Mordan & Co., Chester.
1907
$270-330 **ECGW**

A novelty George V Admiral's Cap pin cushion, by S. Blanckensee & Sons Ltd of Birmingham, Chester.
1910 *2.75in (7cm) long*
$550-700 **MAB**

A 19thC French silver gilt étui, by Alph Geroux, with needle case, bodkin, thimble, scissors.
4.5in (11.5cm) high
$600-750 **L&T**

An early 19thC tortoiseshell needle case and cover, inlaid with silver.
4in (10.5cm) long
$550-700 **SWO**

A rare novelty silver flat fish sewing case and hand mirror, by Louis Dee, London, fitted with scissors, a needle case, a thimble, a bodkin, a crochet hook and a spike.
c1884 *7.5in (19cm) long*
$6,750-7,500 **WW**

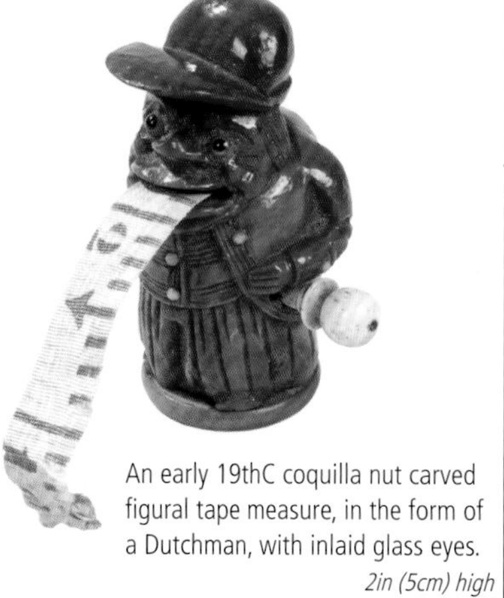

An early 19thC coquilla nut carved figural tape measure, in the form of a Dutchman, with inlaid glass eyes.
2in (5cm) high
$750-900 **LOCK**

A gilt metal mounted Mother-of-pearl scissor case.
c1750 *4in (10cm) long*
$900-1,000 **WW**

A Victorian two-colored gold thimble, in a fitted case.
1in (2.5cm) high 5.8g
$400-450 **WW**

A thornwood walking stick, carved with a bird, dated to the reverse, beak damaged and splits.

c1777 *35in (89.5cm) long*

$600-750 SWO

A late 18thC malacca walking stick, with an ivory and piqué work handle, and silver collar, lacking ferrule.

34in (86cm) long

$1,800-2,250 SWO

A late 19thC walking stick, with duck's-head handle, the shaft carved with animals, heads and birds.

37in (94cm) long

$1,400-1,700 SWO

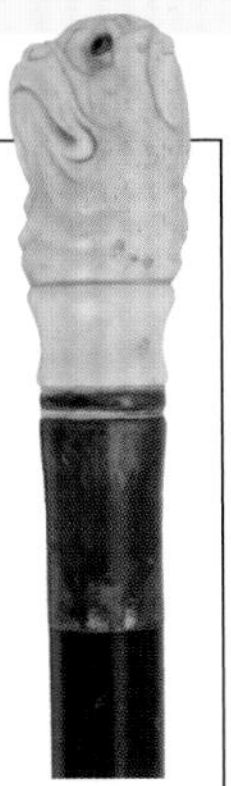

A late 19thC carved ivory and brass mounted stained hardwood walking stick, the grip modeled as a pug dog's head, with inset horn eyes.

36in (91.5cm) high

$850-975 DN

A late 19thC carved ivory and brass mounted stained hardwood walking stick, the grip modeled as a parrot, with inset horn eyes.

36in (91cm) high

$1,150-1,300 DN

An early 19thC marine ivory and tortoiseshell walking stick.

34in (87cm) long

$4,000-4,500 SWO

An unusual mid 19thC walking stick telescope, the horn handle incorporating a compass.

34in (87cm) long

$2,000-2,400 SWO

A mid 19thC Indian ivory walking stick, the terminal carved with a deer in a tiger's jaws.

36in (91cm) long

$2,000-2,400 SWO

A mid 19thC narwhal tusk walking stick, lacking pommel terminal, with CITES certificate.

35.5in (90cm) long

$8,500-9,000 SWO

A narwhal sailors' cane, with silver mounting and walrus ivory top that unscrews to a container for snuff, the collar is inscribed: 'Brought home in the Fox by Geo. Edwards' and 'Sent out by Lady Franklin 1859'.

35.5in (90cm) long

$18,000-22,500 SPL

A 19thC Scottish briar serpent walking cane, carved with a dog's head to a white metal collar inscribed 'DAVID BUR'.

30in (76.5cm) long

$1,450-1,800 WW

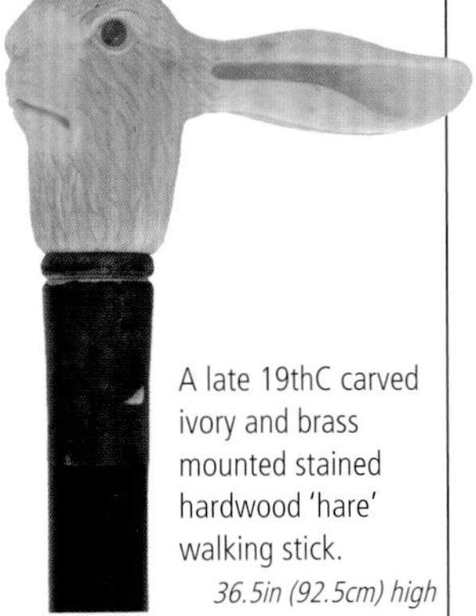

A late 19thC carved ivory and brass mounted stained hardwood 'hare' walking stick.

36.5in (92.5cm) high

$3,300-3,900 DN

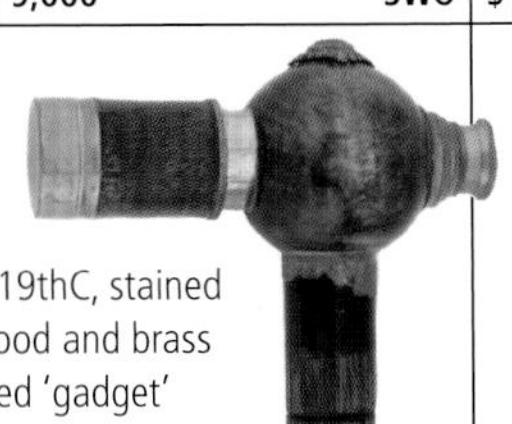

A late 19thC, stained hardwood and brass mounted 'gadget' walking stick, later adapted, the spherical grip holding a telescope, with eyepiece and five sections.

40in (100.5cm) high

$450-750 DN

A late 19thC carved fruitwood walking cane, carved with the symbols of the union of England, Scotland and Ireland.

35.75in (90.5cm) long

$975-1,150 WW

A Schtockschnitzler Simmons carved and painted cane, with a bird grip, with vibrant red and black surface.

Schtockschnitzler Simmons from Berks County, Pennsylvania was active from 1885-1910.

38.5in (98cm) long

$3,300-4,400 POOK

An early 20thC Antarctic interest walking stick, with a carved handle depicting the bust of Charles Royds wearing a balaclava inscribed 'Semper Paratus'.

Vice-Admiral Sir Charles William Rawson Royds (1876-1931) was First Lieutenant of the RRS Discovery on Robert Falcon Scott's National Antarctic Expedition from 1901 to 1904. Cape Royds in Antarctica is named after him. 'Semper Paratus' (Always Ready) is the Royds crest.

34in (86.5cm) long

$1,400-1,800 SWO

ESSENTIAL REFERENCE - GUJARAT

Gujarat, situated on the Northwest coast of India, was a prosperous and wealthy region that rose to prominence under the influence of the Mughal Empire. Its ports were busy centers of export, and during the 17thC the Portuguese, Dutch, French and English all established bases in the region to capitalise on the lucrative trade in luxury goods. Mother-of-pearl wares from Gujarat were being exported to Europe in the early part of the 16thC through the 17thC and were frequently given European made mounts. Based on a European metalware shapes, examples of these highly desirable wares like this example can be found in the inventories of royal collections of that period: one is recorded being given to Henry VIII by Oliver Cromwell in 1534 as a New Year's gift.

A 17thC Mughal, Gujarat, Mother-of-pearl ewer.

8.75in (22cm) high

$105,000-120,000 L&T

A mid 18thC Scottish pendant fob seal, yellow metal and bloodstone, engraved 'AWA WHIGS AWA'.

1in (2.5cm) long

$400-550 L&T

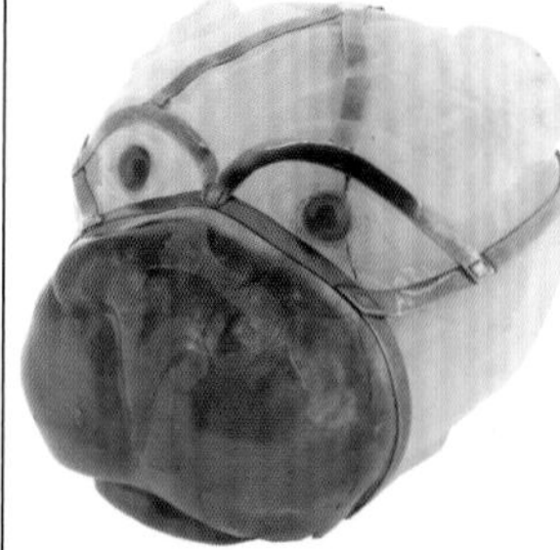

A mid 18thC carved amethyst quartz dog's head bonbonnière, probably German, with early 19thC French control mark, some damage.

2.75in (7cm) high

$1,500-1,800 WW

A Blue John goblet, monogrammed GW beneath.

7in (18cm) high

$1,500-2,100 CHOR

A pair of early 19thC Indian enamel wares, decorated with Europeans and floral panels.

3in (7.5cm) high

$600-750 L&T

An early 19thC Italian silver mounted red hardstone micromosaic inlaid bodkin case, mark for Rome, with four vignettes: the Column of Marcus Aurelius or Trajan, the Pyramid of Cestius, a ruined tower, a pair of doves, a dog, flowers and an insect, in the original fitted box.

3in (7.5cm) long

$4,500-5,500 DN

A late 18thC George III Blue John urn.

12in (30cm) high

$4,500-6,000 L&T

A late 19thC enamel-mounted music box, probably Austria.

8.5in (21cm) wide

$3,300-4,400 SK

A 19thC French singing bird automaton music box, the box in mauve guilloché enamel, opening to reveal a gilt pierced panel from which emerges a small songbird with iridescent feathers, the interior with silk lining stamped 'A. Lancel/38 Rue des Italiens/Paris', French silver import marks.

Established in 1876 by Angele Lancel in the Opera Garnier, the epynomous shop specialized in luxury decorative objects and accessories for women.

4in (10cm) long

$30,000-38,000 L&T

A 19thC mahogany-cased sea shell 'Sailor's Valentine'.

14.75in (37cm) wide

$3,300-4,400 CHEF

A Russian silver-gilt and cloisonné enamel goblet, maker's mark 'GS', Kokoshnik mark for Moscow.

1908-26 *4in (10cm) high 2.65oz (84 zolotniks)*

$1,150-1,450 **DN**

A Russian silver and enamel beaker, by the 6th Artel, Moscow, Kokoshnik mark.

The 6th Artel was one of the most famous in Russia and court supplier of high quality enameled silver.

1908-26 *2.75in (6cm) high 2oz (88 zolotniks)*

$2,250-3,000 **DN**

A Russian silver-gilt and enamel tankard, maker's mark 'IGT', assay master Yakov Lyapinov, St Petersburg, Kokoshnik mark.

1899-1908 *4in (11cm) high 12oz (84 zolotniks)*

$9,000-10,500 **DN**

A Russian silver-gilt and cloisonné enamel cup, possibly by Ivan Saltikov, Moscow, assay master Vasily Petrov.

1884 *2in (5cm) high 1.5oz (88 zolotniks)*

$1,450-1,800 **DN**

A late 19thC Russian silver-gilt and enamel beaker, maker's mark illegible, Moscow?.

2in (5cm) high 2oz

$1,450-1,800 **DN**

ESSENTIAL REFERENCE - ZOLOTNIK

A zolotnik was a small Russian unit of weight, equal to 0.1505 avoirdupois ounces. Used from the 10thC to the 20thC, its name is derived from the Russian word zoloto, meaning gold. As a unit, the zolotnik was the standard for silver manufacture, 96 zolotniks correspond to pure silver. The most frequently found proportions for silver are 84 and 88 zolotniks.

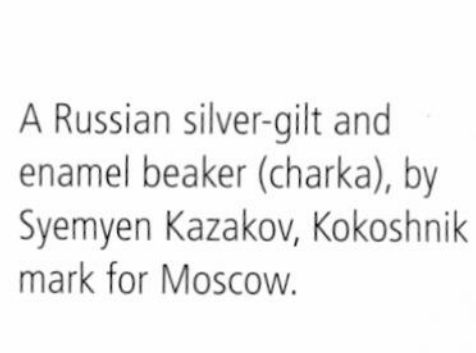

A Russian silver-gilt and enamel beaker (charka), by Syemyen Kazakov, Kokoshnik mark for Moscow.

1908-26 *2in (5.5cm) high 1.75oz (84 zolotniks)*

$1,800-2,400 **DN**

A Russian silver-gilt and cloisonné enamel cup and saucer, by Igor Samoshin, Kokoshnik mark for Moscow.

1908-26 *the cup 3in (8cm) high 6.15oz (84 zolotniks)*

$2,700-3,300 **DN**

A Russian silver and cloisonné enamel lobed cup, maker's mark illegible, Kokoshnik mark.

1899-1908 *2in (6cm) high 2.5oz (84 zolotniks)*

$1,150-1,450 **DN**

A Russian silver-gilt and cloisonné enamel cup and saucer, by Ivan Grishik, Moscow, assay master Lev Oleks.

1896 *the cup 2.5in (6.5cm) high 6.5oz (84 zolotniks)*

$4,000-4,500 **DN**

ESSENTIAL REFERENCE - KOKOSHNIK

In 1896 Tsar Nicholas II (1868-1918) issued an adict to reform the old system of silver marks and the Kokoshnik mark became the new assayer's mark. As thousands of new diestamps had to be created, the kokoshnik was not widely used until early 1899. Until 1908 the mark consisted of a left facing woman's head in profile wearing the peasant headdress known as a kokoshnik. From 1908 her profile is facing right.

A Russian silver and cloisonné enamel tea glass holder, by Pyetr Baskakov, Kokoshnik mark, Moscow.
1908-26 *4in (10cm) high 6.25oz (84 zolotniks)*
$3,300-4,400 **DN**

A Russian silver and cloisonné enamel casket, maker's mark 'VR', assay master Yakov Lyapinov, St. Petersburg, Kokoshnik mark, lacking the key.
1899-1908 *5in (12.5cm) wide 17.5oz (84 zolotniks)*
$7,500-9,000 **DN**

A Russian silver-gilt cloisonné and shaded enamel salt chair, maker's mark 'P OVCHINNIKOV, Moscow', beneath the Imperial Warrant and 84 silver standard.
1897-1908 *4in (10.5 cm) high*
$2,250-3,000 **JACK**

A Russian silver and champlevé enamel tea caddy, bearing indistinct marks, the caddy of square form, with scrolling floral design.
4.5in (11cm) high
$6,000-7,500 **L&T**

A Russian silver-gilt and shaded enamel cigarette case, Moscow, in the Pan Slavic style typical of the Ruckert workshop, dated.
1914 *3.75in (9.5cm) long*
$12,000-15,000 **JACK**

A Russian silver-gilt and shaded enamel Kovsh, by Vasiliy Agafonov, Moscow, with Art Nouveau enameled flowers, engraved with a Russian idiom in cyrillic 'When you pour the wine, remember me'.
1899-1908 *4.75in (12cm) long*
$4,000-4,500 **JACK**

A Russian silver and enamel kovsh, by Feyodor Ruckert, St Petersburg.
1899-1908 *2.75in (7cm) long 10oz*
$3,000-4,500 **TEN**

A Russian silver and enamel bowl, Solvyhegodsk region.
2in (5cm) high
$75,000-82,500 **LOCK**

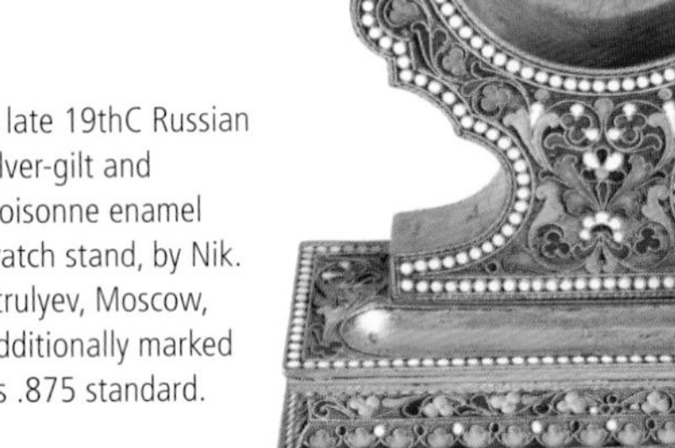

A late 19thC Russian silver-gilt and cloisonne enamel watch stand, by Nik. Strulyev, Moscow, additionally marked as .875 standard.
3.75in (9cm) high 6oz (84 zolotniks)
$2,100-2,800 **DN**

ESSENTIAL REFERENCE - FABERGÉ

This exceptionally rare early 20thC Fabergé carved hardstone figure of an Imperial bodyguard is placed on the same level of rarity as that of Fabergé's Imperial Easter eggs.

- **Well known to collectors, but its whereabous unknown, the figure was rediscovered in an attic in upstate New York. It is a carving of Nikolai Nikolaievich Pustynnikov, the personal Cossack bodyguard to the Empress Alexandra Feodorovna. Held in high esteem by the Empress and Dowager Empress, the bodyguards accompanied them each time they would leave their residences, explaining why they were memorialised in such fashion. The figure is dressed in a long nephrite and jasper coat fixed with gold and enameled orders and medals. Pustynnikov was one of just two models commissioned by Nicholas II himself and, due to the object's basis on a historical figure, the object's rarity and desirability is heightened. Even rarer still, the total number of Fabergé hardstone figure carvings is deemed to be no more than 50.**

An early 20thC Fabergé carved hardstone Imperial bodyguard figure of Pustynnikv, the heels and soles of the boots are inscribed in Cyrillic capitals Fabergé.

1912 *7in (18cm) high*

over $6,000,000 STA

A Fabergé enameled silver and hardstone cigarette box, with V-shaped iron-red and blue enamel panels of birds, with its original silk-lined sycamore box.

5in (12cm) wide

$67,500-82,500 MELL

An Imperial Russian yacht 'Tsarevna' Fabergé gold, enamel and diamond set 'life-belt' badge, by Oskar Pihl, St. Petersburg, 72 gold standard (18kt).

c1895 *1.25in (3.5cm) wide*

$20,000-27,000 JACK

A Fabergé gold and gem encrusted cameo pin, by Erik Kollin, St. Petersburg, 56 (14K) gold standard, and scratched inventory number 53477.

c1890 *1.5in (4 cm) diam*

$6,750-8,250 JACK

A Fabergé gold-mounted kovsh, by Erik Kollin, St. Petersburg, set with ruby cabochons and mounted on an agate bowl, and 56 gold standard (14K).

c1895 *4in (10.5cm) long*

$7,500-9,000 JACK

A Fabergé varicolor gold photograph frame, workmaster Henrik Wigström, St. Petersburg, 72 standard, scratched inventory number 3967.

1903-1917 *2in (5cm) high*

$12,000-13,500 SOTH

A Fabergé gilded silver evening bag, St. Petersburg, struck Fabergé in Cyrillic, 88 standard, scratched inventory number 19426.

1908-1917 *4in (11cm) wide*

$5,500-7,000 SOTH

A Fabergé silver and sandstone 'frog'match holder, workmaster Julius Rappoport, St Petersburg, with Fabergé in Cyrillic, 91 standard.

1899-1908 *4.75in (12cm) wide*

$82,500-97,500 SOTH

A Fabergé silver 'rhinoceros' table lighter, workmaster Julius Rappoport, St Petersburg, with Fabergé in Cyrillic beneath the Imperial Warrant, 88 standard, scratched inventory number 9330.

c1890 *6.25in (16cm) long*

$120,000-135,000 SOTH

A Faberge jeweled bowenite, silver-gilt and enamel gum-pot, workmaster's mark for Henrik Wigstrom, St. Petersburg.

1903-17 *2.75in (7cm) high*

$40,000-45,000 L&T

A Russian icon of the 'Tenderness Mother of God', the riza hallmarked Moscow, probably by Ivan Fedorov.

In this unidentified Mother of God type, the title 'Tenderness' (Russian - Umilinie) can be used. The Tenderness title is a generic term used to describe icons that depict Mother and child in a 'tender' cheek-to-check embrace.

c1810 *12in (30.5cm) high*

$20,000-24,000 JACK

A Russian icon of Saint Nicholas, with life scenes.

The large size of this icon would suggest that it was a church icon, probably in a small chapel dedicated to Nicholas or perhaps an altar devoted to the saint.

c1825 *52in (132cm) high*

$40,000-45,000 JACK

A Russian gilt metal filigree and enamel icon, 'The Kazan Mother of God'.

10.5in (27cm) high

$11,500-13,000 L&T

A Russian icon of Saint Sebastian Sokhotsky, by Vasily Peshekhonov, holds a scroll inscribed in Old Church Slavonic with the first two lines of Psalm 39, 'I waited patiently for the Lord; and he listened to me, and heard my prayer, and from the pit of suffering he raised me up out of the mire…'.

1855 *17.5in (44.5cm) high*

$135,000-165,000 JACK

A Russian presentation icon of Saints Kosmas and Damian, by Ivan Malyshev.

The two saints were twin brothers who lived in Asia and were martyred in the 3rdC. The title inscribed above their head includes the distinctive term 'bezsrebrennik', meaning literally 'without silver,' because they accepted no money in payment for their services. They each hold a medicine box, and are invoked for aid in studies.

1882 *14in (36cm) high*

$75,000-90,000 JACK

A Russian icon of Saints Samon, Guriy and Aviv, Mstera, possibly by Alexander Tsepkov, overlaid with a gilded silver repoussé and chased riza hallmarked Moscow, Cyrillic maker's mark IG, and 84 silver standard.

c1886 *12in (31cm) high*

$135,000-165,000 JACK

A large 19thC Russian icon of Christ pantocrator.

17.5in (44cm) high

$2,000-2,400 L&T

A 19thC Russian icon of Saint Nicholas, with Christ and the Mother of God seated on clouds.

17.5in (44.5cm) high

$4,000-4,500 L&T

A 19thC Russian silver gilt and enamel cased icon, 'The Smolensk Mother of God'.

11.25in (28.5cm) high

$6,750-8,250 L&T

A Russian icon of the archangel Michael, the borders rendered with faux cloisonné enameling.

c1890 *50.5in (128.5cm) high*

$40,000-45,000 **JACK**

A Russian icon of the unburnt Thornbush Mother of God, Mstera.

All of these scenes are considered Old Testament prefigurations of the Mother of God and Her role in the Incarnation. The sides and verso are encased in a painted coating of smoothly finished gesso, a time consuming technique usually only found on the highest quality icons produced in the most exclusive icon workshops in Moscow.

c1890 *14in (36cm) high*

$15,000-21,000 **JACK**

A Russian icon of The Three Youths in the Fiery Furnace, a rarely depicted Old Testament theme (Daniel 3,6), executed in the 15thC revivalist style.

c1890 *12.25in (31cm) high*

$19,500-30,000 **JACK**

A Russian icon of Saint Michael Metropolitan of Kiev, follows closely the same form as often found on icons from the Moscow workshop of Mstera trained iconographer Mikhail Ivanovich Dikarev.

It seems likely that this icon was produced to commemorate the 900th anniversary of the death of St. Michael, who died in Kiev in the year 992.

c1892 *35.5in (90cm) high*

$15,000-22,500 **JACK**

A Russian icon of the Mother of God of the Passion Mstera.

c1900 *12in (31cm) high*

$19,500-30,000 **JACK**

A Russian icon of Saint Nicholas, he wears a bishop's stole about his neck, with his right hand he delivers a blessing, with his left hand he holds an open book of Gospels revealing a variant of Luke 6:17, hallmarked Moscow, with Cyrillic maker's mark 'S.Zh.'

c1900 *12.25in (31cm) high*

$55,000-70,000 **JACK**

A Russian icon of the warrior Saint Dmitry, Moscow, possibly the workshop of Vasiliy Pavlovich Guryanov.

c1900 *12.25in (31cm) high*

$55,000-70,000 **JACK**

An Imperial Russian presentation icon, of Saint Savva of Storozhevsk, Dikarev Workshop, the silk lined wooden case with retailer's mark of Fabergé.

The verso with engraved dedicatory plaque which reads, 'To Her Imperial Highness, Grand Duchess Maria Pavlovna, from the Police force of the District of Zvenigorod. April 10, 1908'. The connection to Zvenigorod, of course, is Saint Savva, the highly stylized and condensed inscription identifies him as 'Holy Venerable Savva of Storozhevsk, Wonderworker of Zvenigorod'.

c1908 *10.5in (27cm) high*

$135,000-165,000 **JACK**

A Russian icon of Saints Peter and Paul.

c1915 *28in (57cm) high*

$9,000-10,500 **JACK**

A Russian Gardner Factory 'Ladies' Shoe Vendor' Inkstand, with lid, the interior with parcel-gilt inkwell and sand caster, apparently unmarked.

c1825 *8in (20cm) high*

$22,500-30,000 **SOTH**

A Russian Popov Manufactory, Gorbunovo, fishwife, after a 1750 design 'London Street Traders' by J. J. Kändler for Meissen, blue monogram factory mark.

c1845 *4.75in (12cm) high*

$4,500-6,000 **SOTH**

A Russian Gardner Factory figure of a 'Sbiten Vendor', Verbilki, stamped iron red and impressed factory marks, impressed model number 146.

The sbiten vendor, or sbitenshchik, was a common figure on Russian streets for centuries. He sold a hot spiced honey drink long popular in Russia until it was replaced by imported tea and coffee.

1870-1890 *7.5in (19cm) high*

$21,000-27,000 **SOTH**

A late 19thC Russian Gardner Factory biscuit porcelain figure group, printed red mark, impressed 34.

8.5in (21.5cm)

$2,400-3,000 **WW**

A late 19thC Russian Gardner Factory biscuit porcelain figure of Sobakevich, from Nikolai Gogol's Dead Souls, impressed and red printed marks, broken off the base and restuck.

Gogol's novel of 1842 was written to expose the flaws in the Russian middle class financial system, and to seek reform of the old-fashioned serfdom.

8in (20.5cm) high

$2,250-3,000 **WW**

A late 19thC Russian Gardner Factory biscuit porcelain figure of a Jewish man, red printed mark, impressed 147.

This figure is one of a pair of Jewish men from different classes, this being the more prosperous.

8.75in (22cm) high

$9,000-9,750 **WW**

A set of four 19thC Russian Imperial glass works champagne flutes.

6.75in (17cm) high

$2,250-3,000 **L&T**

One of a set of nine 19thC Russian Imperial glass works white wine goblets, engraved with an Imperial cypher 'EM'.

5.75in (14.5cm) high

$3,300-4,400 set **L&T**

A set of five 19thC Russian Imperial glass works decanters, with associated stoppers.

11in (28cm) high

$5,250-6,000 **L&T**

A late 19thC Russian cast iron group of a man on horseback, indistinctly dated, possibly 40172'.
15in (38cm) high
$1,400-1,700 **DN**

A Nikolai Ivanovich Lieberich bronze bear and cub inkwell, signed in Cyrillic 'Lieberich 1860'.
1828-1883 *19in (48cm) long*
$42,000-48,000 **SOTH**

A Nikolai Ivanovich Lieberich bronze pointer, signed in Cyrillic 'sculp. N. Lieberich' and Latin 'Fabr C.F. Woerffel' with 1886 foundry mark.
1828-1883 *13.5in (34.5cm) long*
$16,500-21,000 **SOTH**

An Ivan Fedorovich Kovshenkov bronze figure, Filipp Pakhomov Matveev, signed in Cyrillic 'Ivan Kovshenkov'.
1824-1898 *16in (41cm) high*
$60,000-67,500 **SOTH**

A Vasily Yakovlevich Grachev bronze, 'Circassian at a Gallop', signed in Cyrillic 'sculp. Grachev' and in Latin 'Fabr. C.F. Woerffel St Petersbourg'.
1831-1905 *17.25in (44cm) long*
$10,500-15,000 **SOTH**

A Russian silver and niello cheroot case, by Ivan Futikin, Moscow, with decoration of a rider, sledge and horse. *3.5*in (8.5cm) long 2oz
$850-975 **TEN**

A Russian carved hardstone striated agate anteater, St. Petersburg, with diamond-set eyes.
c1900 *2in (5cm) high*
$6,000-7,500 **SOTH**

A Imperial Russian army regimental silk 'color' banner, of the Life Guards' Regiments, from the reign of Pavel I, with the Imperial double-headed eagle, emblazoned in Cyrillic 'God is with Us' and surmounted by the Imperial Crown.

Surviving specimens from this period in any condition are exceedingly rare.
c1800 *56.5in (144cm) high*
$45,000-60,000 **JACK**

A unique Russian orthodox bullion and silk embroidered sticharion, from the coronation of Tsar Nicholas II and Empress Alexandra Feodorovna, by A & V Sapozhnikov, Moscow.
1896 *47in (120cm) long*
$22,500-30,000 **JACK**

A 19thC Scottish stripped pine and composition fire surround.

69in (175cm) wide

$4,500-5,500 **L&T**

A 19thC French carved limestone fire surround.

53in (135cm) wide

$3,000-4,000 **L&T**

A 19thC Regency stripped pine and gesso fire surround.

67in (170cm) wide

$3,000-4,000 **L&T**

An American Federal carved pine mantel.

c1810 *58.5in (140cm) high*

$5,250-6,000 **POOK**

A George III cast iron firegrate, in Adam style, the fire box later.

32.5in (82.5cm) long

$3,300-3,900 **WW**

A George III cast iron 'Carron' hob grate.

38in (96.5cm) long

$750-900 **WW**

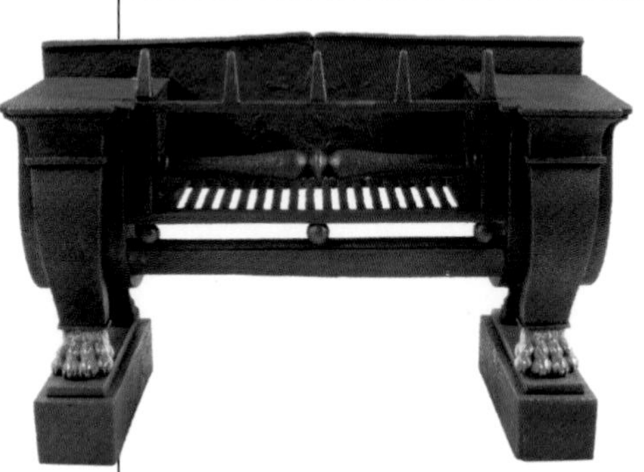

A Regency cast iron and brass mounted firegrate.

32.5in (82cm) wide

$1,450-1,700 **WW**

A George III cast iron hob grate.

33in (83.5cm) long

$1,500-1,800 **WW**

A Regency cast iron and brass-mounted fireplace insert, replaced backplates.

39.5in (100cm) high

$1,400-1,700 **SWO**

A pair of Victorian brass door stops.
16.25in (41cm) high
$600-750 WW

A pair of Victorian brass door stops, one stamped '4054'.
17in (43cm) high
$340-390 WW

A Victorian bronze pineapple door stop.
13.75in (35cm) high
$300-400 WW

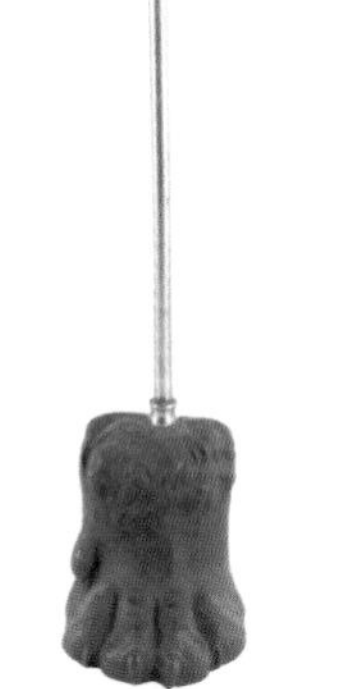

A Victorian brass and cast iron paw door stop.
19.25in (48cm) high
$200-350 WW

A 19thC gilt bronze dolphin door stop.
12in (30cm) high
$120-180 WW

A pair of 19thC iron fire dogs, with brass ball finials.
18.25in (46cm) high
$135-165 WW

A pair of 19thC brass Talbot fire dogs, one marked 'D.H'.
12.75in (32cm) high
$600-750 WW

A pair of American Federal brass and iron knife blade andirons, with a set of iron fire tools.
c1780
$550-600 POOK

A pair of 19thC Louis XV style gilt bronze chenets, by Henri Vian, cast with two Eastern gentlemen, with stamped initials HV and 443.
15in (38cm) high
$2,100-3,000 L&T

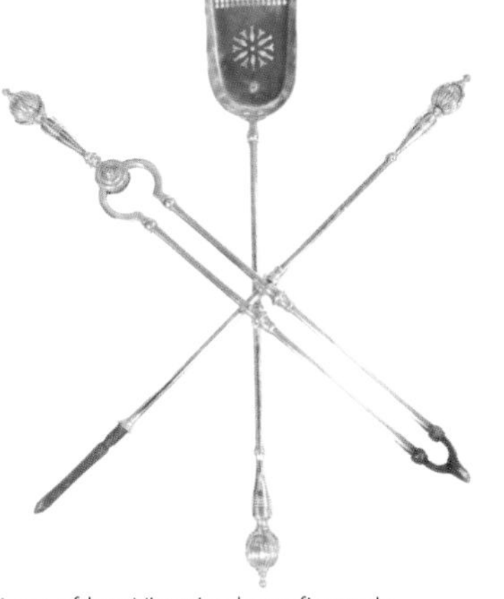

A set of late Victorian brass fire tools.
$180-225 WW

A late 19th/early 20thC brass adjustable fender, with a pair of andirons cast.

22in (56cm) high

$700-850 **SWO**

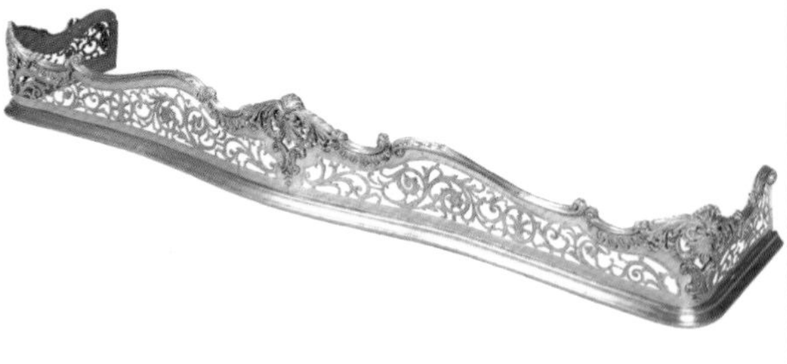

A 19thC Victorian brass fender.

56in (142cm) long

$1,700-2,100 **L&T**

An early 19thC polished steel bowfront fender.

50in (127cm) long

$340-450 **WW**

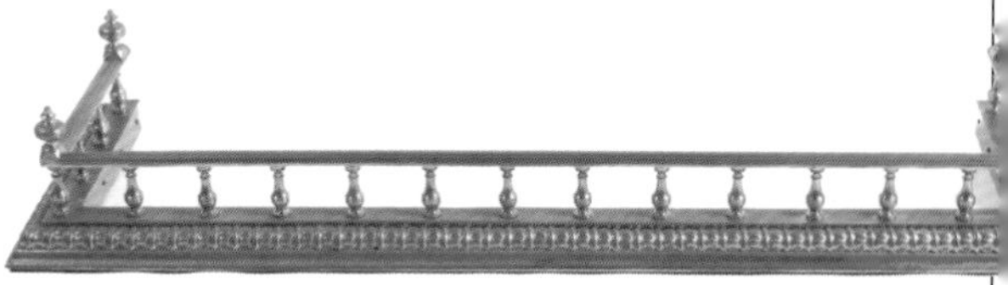

A Victorian brass fender.

57in (144.5cm) long

$300-400 **WW**

A late 19thC gilt brass fender.

55.5in (141cm) long

$300-400 **WW**

An early 19thC polished steel serpentine fender.

50.75in (129cm) long

$340-450 **WW**

An early 19thC polished steel bowfront fender.

43.75in (111cm) long

$180-225 **WW**

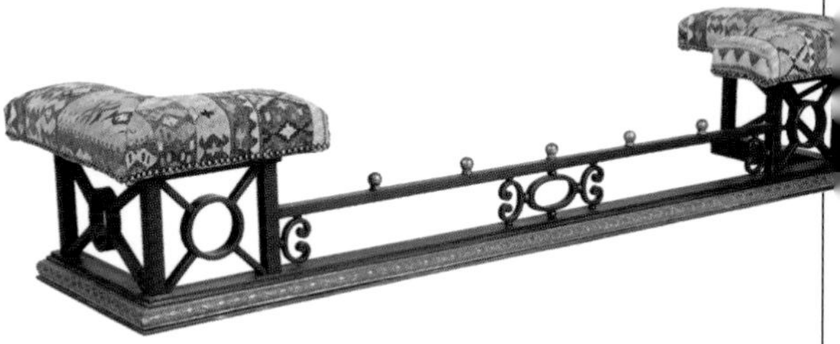

A wrought iron and brass club fender.

67in (170cm) long

$1,000-1,400 **L&T**

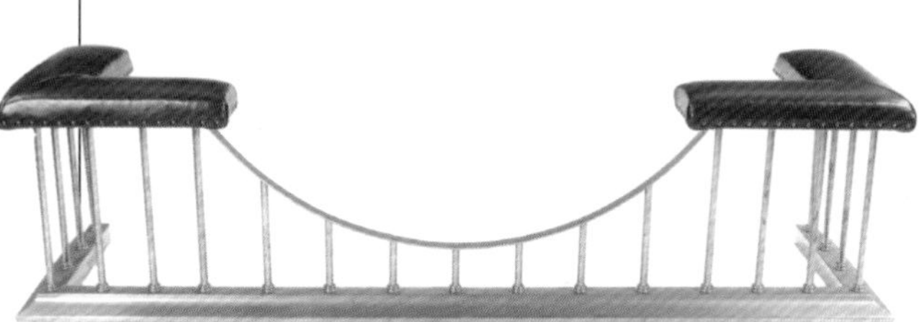

A brass club fender.

74.5in (189cm) long

$2,000-2,400 **WW**

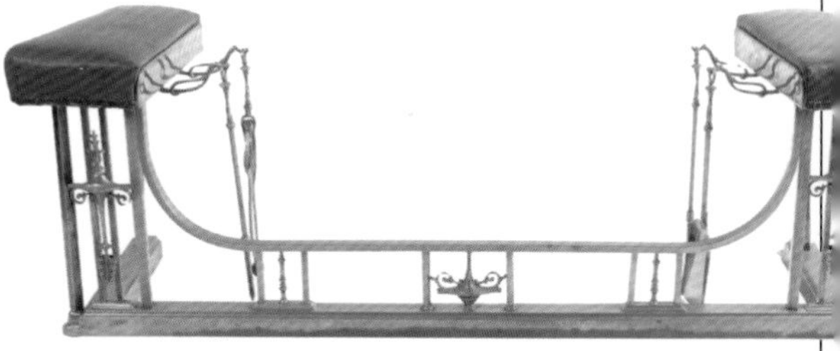

An Edwardian brass club fender, with four fire tools.

59.5in (151cm) wide

$1,150-1,300 **WW**

A cast iron fire back, and with a crowned shield with three fleur-de-lys.

1669 *23in (58cm) wide*

$340-450 **WW**

A late Victorian brass and wirework nursery fender, losses to the wire.

27in (69cm) high

$270-330 **WW**

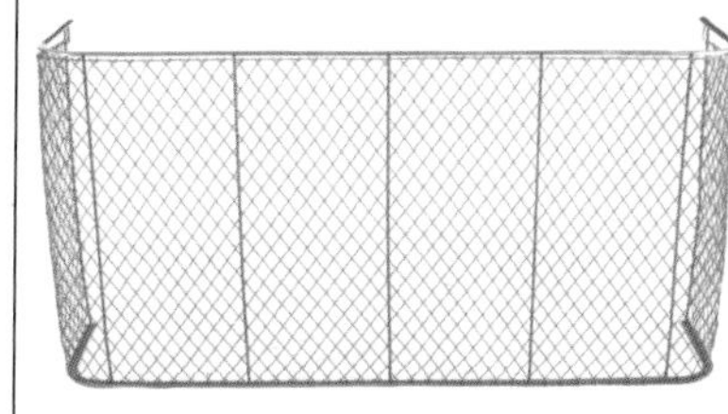

A Victorian brass and wirework fender.

26.75in (68cm) high

$440-480 **WW**

A 19thC gilt brass firescreen, with a pleated silk panel.

21in (53.5cm) long

$550-600 **WW**

A 19thC French gilt brass firescreen.

32.5in (82.5cm) high

$400-450 **WW**

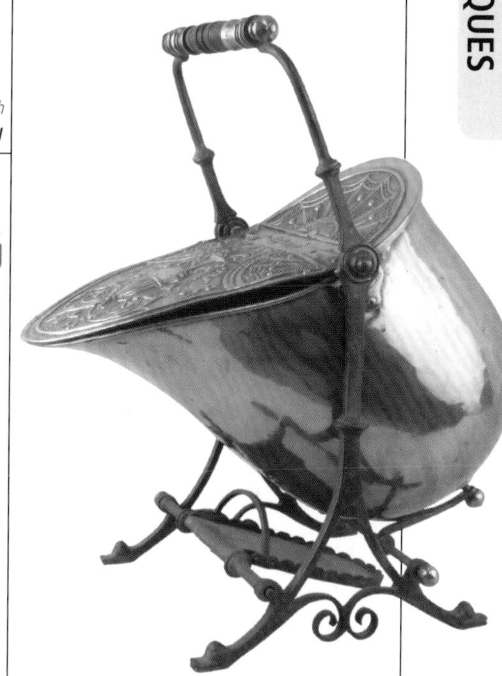

A Victorian seamed copper helmet shaped coal scuttle.

20.75in (52.5cm) high

$225-300 **DA&H**

A late 19thC copper log bin.

22in (56cm) high

$850-900 **WW**

A late 19thC Dutch coal bucket, repoussé decorated with a coat of arms.

21in (53.5cm) high

$150-225 **WW**

A Victorian brass log bin, repoussé decorated with a coat of arms for Lord Carisfort.

15.5in (39cm) high

$400-450 **WW**

A Regency iron strapwork garden seat.

35.5in (90cm) high

$850-975 **CHEF**

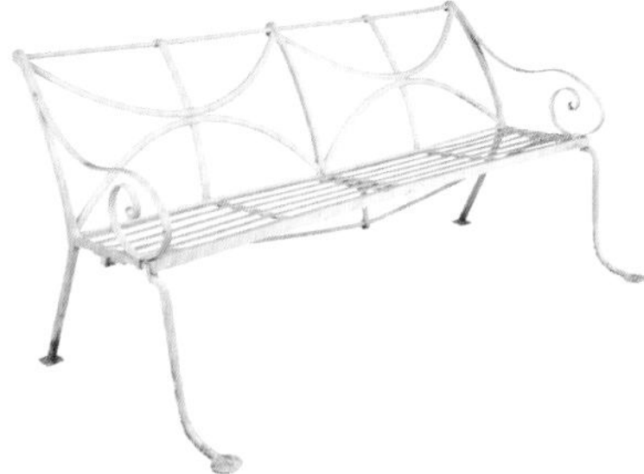

A 19thC Victorian white painted wrought iron garden bench.

71.75in (182cm) wide

$1,400-1,700 **L&T**

A 19thC Victorian 'Fern' cast iron garden bench

76in (193cm) wide

$1,300-1,450 **L&T**

A Coalbrookdale 'Nasturtium' pattern cast iron seat, fully marked with CBdale and diamond registration stamp and pattern number.

This design, number 1958629 was registered and patented at the Public Records Office by Coalbrookdale on the 1st of March 1866 and is seat number 44 in their 1875 catalog of castings.

c1870 *72in (183cm) wide*

$6,000-6,750 **SPL**

A Coalbrookdale 'Medieval' pattern cast iron seat, fully stamped Coalbrookdale and with diamond registration and pattern stamps.

c1870 *43in (109cm) long*

$8,500-9,000 **SPL**

A rare Coalbrookdale 'Osmundia Fern' pattern cast iron seat, fully stamped with Coalbrookdale registration number and pattern number.

Together with 'Osmundia Regalis', the 'Osmundia Fern' pattern is one of the rarest and most intricate of all the Coalbrookdale designs.

c1870 *56in (147cm) long*

$9,750-10,500 **SPL**

One of a pair of rare Coalbrookdale 'Horse Chestnut' pattern cast iron seats, fully stamped Coalbrookdale Co and registration stamp 217568 and with diamond registration stamps.

The design of this seat, number 217568, was registered and patented by the Coalbrookdale Iron Foundry at The Public Record Office on 23rd March 1868, and is number 46 in their 1875 Castings Catalogue, Section III, page 256.

75in (190cm) long

$42,000-48,000 pair **SPL**

A late 19thC small Victorian 'Gothic' pattern cast iron garden bench.

39.5in (100cm) wide

$1,400-1,800 **L&T**

A late 19thC Coalbrookdale 'Medallion' pattern cast iron seat, stamped with diamond registration stamp and number.

This design, number 149934 was registered and patented at the Public Records Office by Coalbrookdale on 13th March 1862 and is seat No 35 in their 1875 'Coalbrookdale Castings Catalogue' Section III page 259.

66in (168cm) long

$6,000-6,750 **SPL**

ESSENTIAL REFERENCE - CISTERN

Possibly one of those mentioned in the Chatsworth Inventory, October 1764 in the Breakfast Room.

- **The cistern that remains at the top of the Great Staircase, supplied by Burket and Finch in 1694, is very similar to this planter. That cistern has a gilded tap fitted, so that glasses might be safely rinsed and was supplied at the cost of 13s6d in 1694. The 1st Duke was particulary ambitious with his use of water. The cascade built in the garden, ten water closets and a bagnine or bathing room fitted in colorful marbles are testament to this.**

A late 17thC carved limestone planter, originally inset into a wall.
14in (35.5cm) high
$4,500-5,500 SPL

A pair of 19thC Scottish terracotta garden urns.
32.5in (82cm) high
$2,700-3,300 L&T

A 19thC French carved limestone planter.
20in (50cm) high
$4,000-4,500 SPL

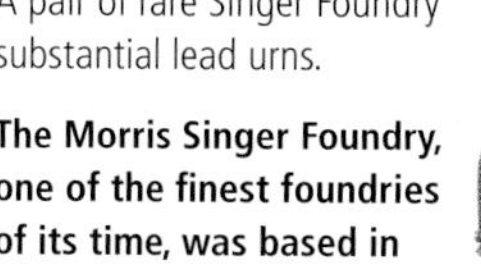

A pair of rare Singer Foundry substantial lead urns.

The Morris Singer Foundry, one of the finest foundries of its time, was based in Basingstoke and Frome. the fine chiselling and finishing in these examples is evidence of their high quality.

c1910 28in (72cm) high
$40,000-45,000 SPL

An 18thC carved marble urn.
19in (48cm) high
$7,500-8,250 WW

A terracotta colored plaster garden urn.
18.75in (48cm) high
$300-400 WW

A pair of early 20thC Continental variegated gray marble urns.
15.75in (40cm) high
$600-700 DN

A Coadestone Townley vase, stamped Coade's Lambeth.
1840 36in (92cm) high
$27,000-33,000 SPL

A possibly late 16th/17thC carved Istrian stone throne, with indistinct Greek inscription.
56in (143cm) high
$18,000-22,500 SPL

A lead statue, by the Bromsgrove Guild 'Dryad and Boar', depicting a hunter attacking a wild boar, stamped to the reverse 'Bromsgrove Guild Worcestershire'.

The Bromsgrove Guild (1898-1966) was founded by Walter Gilbert and based on the principles of the Arts and Crafts movement. The Guild worked in a variety of mediums, bronze, lead, glass, wood and textiles - employing highly skilled craftsmen and made famous for making the main gates at Buckingham Palace. The original 'Dryad and Boar' was made in bronze by Swiss sculptor Louis Weingartner of the Guild.

57in (144cm) high

$67,500-75,000 FLD

An 18thC Northern European, carved sandstone lion, almost life sized, with a slightly smaller lion.

The two lions have been at the Jacobean/ Georgian Wicken Manor near Buckingham for nearly three centuries. They were possibly commissioned for a 'menagerie' in the estate's parkland.

63in (160cm) long and 59in (150cm) long

$15,000-22,500 pair HW

A pair of 18thC carved Bath stone armorial hounds.

These would have originally been commissioned as family armorial crestings to stand on gate piers at the entrance to the family estate.

42in (106cm) high

$25,500-30,000 SPL

A cast iron garden figure of a pointer.

c1900 *30in (76.5cm) high*

$4,500-6,000 POOK

ESSENTIAL REFERENCE - ELEANOR COADE

Eleanor Coade (d.1821) opened her Lambeth Manufactory for ceramic artificial stone in 1769, and appointed the sculptor John Bacon as its manager two years later. She was employed by all the leading late 18thC architects and received commissions for a number of commemorative pieces, such as those for George III's Jubilee and for Admiral Lord Nelson. From about 1777 she began her engraved designs, which were published in 1784 in a catalog of over 700 items entitled 'A Descriptive Catalogue of Coade's Artificial Stone Manufactory'. Then in 1799, the year she entered into partnership with her cousin John Sealy, she issued a handbook of her Pedlar's Lane exhibition Gallery. The firm became Coade and Sealy from this date and following Sealy's death in 1813, it reverted to Coade and in 1821 with the death of the younger Eleanor Coade, control of the firm passed to William Croggan, who died in 1835, following bankruptcy.

- **Similar roundels may be seen at Belmont House, Faversham Kent, designed by Samuel Wyatt, elder brother of James Wyatt in 1792.**

One of a pair of late 18thC Coadestone roundels depicting Spring and Summer, one stamped Coade and indistinct stamp '**92', restorations.

32in (81cm) diam

$12,000-15,000 pair SPL

A late 18thC Georgian wrought iron grille.

45in (114cm) high

$2,250-3,000 SPL

A late 19th/early 20thC gray marble architectural archway.

87in (221cm) high

$975-1,150 DN

A rare Hope foundry lead wall sundial, with bronze gnomon.

The Hope leadworks were established in the early 20thC by Henry Hope in Jamestown, New York with showrooms in Park Avenue, New York, Montreal and Toronto.

c1930 *25in (63cm) high*

$6,000-7,500 SPL

An early 20thC painted wrought iron and hardwood child's see saw, wood replaced.

141in (358cm) long

$30,000-38,000 SPL

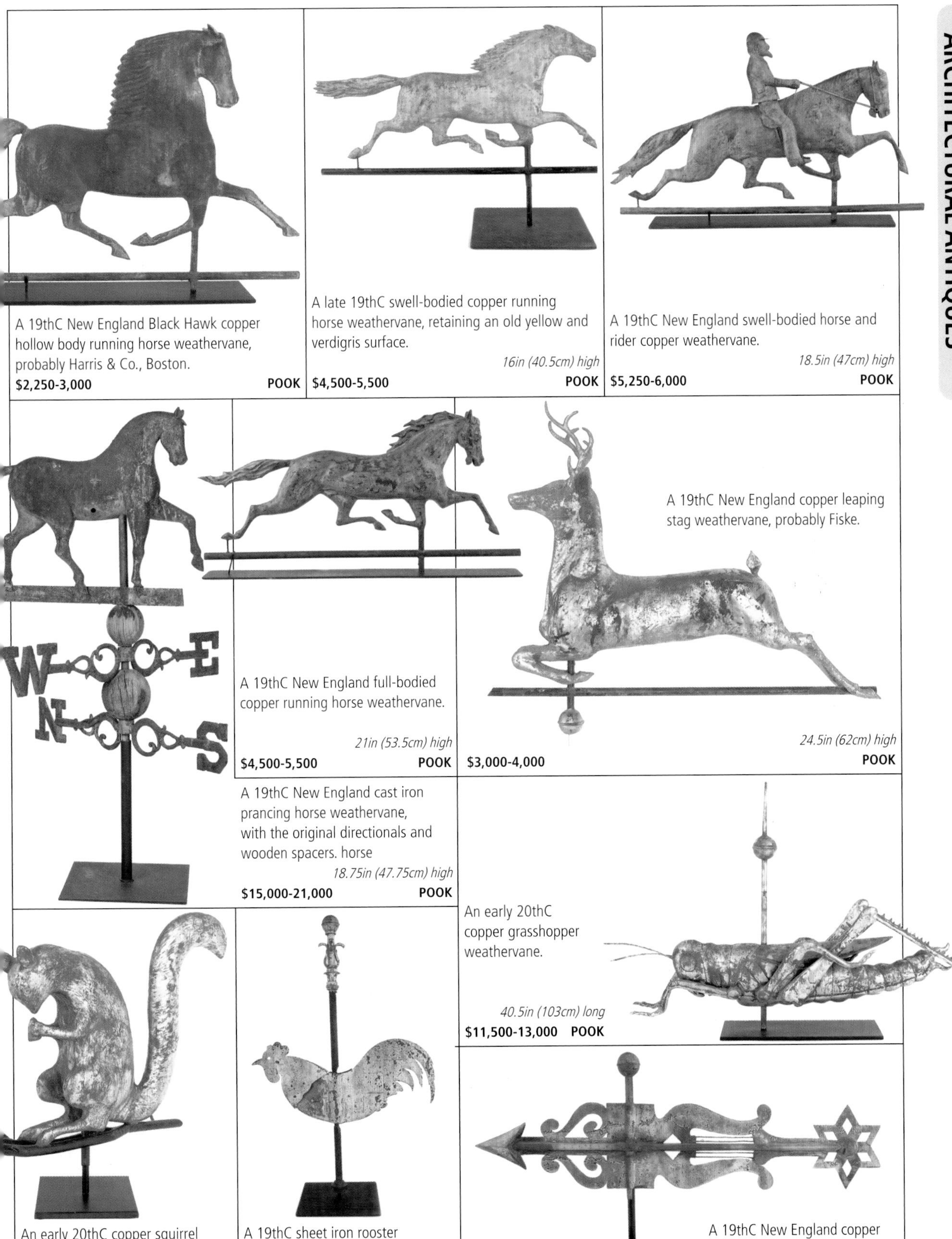

A 19thC New England Black Hawk copper hollow body running horse weathervane, probably Harris & Co., Boston.
$2,250-3,000 **POOK**

A late 19thC swell-bodied copper running horse weathervane, retaining an old yellow and verdigris surface.
16in (40.5cm) high
$4,500-5,500 **POOK**

A 19thC New England swell-bodied horse and rider copper weathervane.
18.5in (47cm) high
$5,250-6,000 **POOK**

A 19thC New England full-bodied copper running horse weathervane.
21in (53.5cm) high
$4,500-5,500 **POOK**

A 19thC New England copper leaping stag weathervane, probably Fiske.
24.5in (62cm) high
$3,000-4,000 **POOK**

A 19thC New England cast iron prancing horse weathervane, with the original directionals and wooden spacers. horse
18.75in (47.75cm) high
$15,000-21,000 **POOK**

An early 20thC copper grasshopper weathervane.
40.5in (103cm) long
$11,500-13,000 **POOK**

An early 20thC copper squirrel weathervane.
17in (43cm) high
$15,000-18,000 **POOK**

A 19thC sheet iron rooster weathervane.
41in (100cm) high
$2,250-3,000 **POOK**

A 19thC New England copper bannerette weathervane.
47.75in (121cm) long
$3,000-4,000 **POOK**

An Afshar rug.
65.75in (167cm) long
$600-700 **DN**

A 20thC Bakhtiari carpet, Northwest Persia.
197.75in (502cm) long
$3,000-4,000 **L&T**

A Bakhtiari gabbeh, with a chequerboard design, the original finishes all around.

The purely abstract design is an example of the art of surface decoration using simple but highly effective means. The three zig-zag borders are a characteristic feature of Bakhtiari gabbehs.

$10,500-12,000 **RBOS**

A large late 19thC/early 20thC Fereghan carpet, West Persia.
237in (603cm) long
$1,450-1,800 **L&T**

A Bakhtiari carpet, West Persia.
201in (512cm) long
$4,400-5,100 **TEN**

A late 19thC Kurdish Garus carpet, Northwest Persia.

When we talk about Garrus Bijars or Kurdish Bijars we are actully using different words for the same thing. Garrusi is a dialect of Kordi (Kurdish). The other name for Garrus is Bijari so a Kurd from Bijar is a Garrus Kurd. In the rug trade they use Garrus to describe simpler less sophisticated rugs from the weavers in the Bijar area. This is a distinction between commercial contract work, and also from the Bijar type rugs woven by the Afshar in the Bijar area.

207in (526cm) long
$1,800-2,250 **WW**

A Heriz carpet, of overall repeated flowerhead design.
143.75in (365cm) long
$1,000-1,200
DN

ESSENTIAL REFERENCE - HERIZ

The weavers of Heriz are rightly famous for their excellent large wool piled carpets made with outstanding dyes. During the last quarter of the 19thC small numbers of fine silk rugs (usually as here in prayer format) were produced in the region on a cottage industry basis. Typical of Heriz silk rugs this example is made on a silk foundation with excellent quality silk used in the pile. The knot count is high. By 1900 silk rug weaving ceased in the region.

A silk Heriz prayer rug, Persian Azerbaijan.
72.5in (184cm) long
$4,800-6,000 **TEN**

A large late 20thC Isfahan carpet, Central Persia.

236in (600cm) long

$7,500-9,000 L&T

A late 20thC Isfahan carpet, Central Persia.

211in (536cm) long

$4,800-5,700 L&T

An Isfahan carpet.

163in (414cm) long

$1,300-1,450 DN

A Jozan rug.

Jozan is a village situated between Malayer and Sultanabad.

$10,500-12,000 RBOS

A large 19thC carpet, in the Kelleh format, the white-ground field and the equally white ground of the border appear to merge into one another, various restored areas and signs of wear in the pile.

In his detailed description, William Robinson, traces the design to Tabriz models, but goes on to state that no directly comparable examples are known. In particular, the color scheme of this impressive Karabagh is a unique feature. It was woven in one of the workshops of the Khanate of Karabagh, which belonged to the Persian Empire at the time.

$34,500-39,000 RBOS

A Kashan carpet, losses to fringing.

168in (427cm) long

$1,500-2,250 DN

A Kashan silk carpet, West Persia, slight damage in places.

c1930 *145in (367cm) long*

$4,500-5,500 WW

An early 20thC Kashan souf silk and metal thread prayer rug, West Persia.

81.5in (207cm) long

$16,500-21,000 WW

One of a pair of late 19th/early 20thC Kashan silk prayer rugs, Central Persia.

Collected by William Semple, an engineer with The Anglo-Persian Oil Company, in Iran c1910.

80in (204cm) long

$17,250-21,000 pair L&T

One of a pair of early 20thC Kashan part silk rugs, Central Persia.
55in (140cm) wide
$8,500-9,750 pair **L&T**

A 20thC Kashan carpet.
140in (360cm) long
$1,800-2,400 **HW**

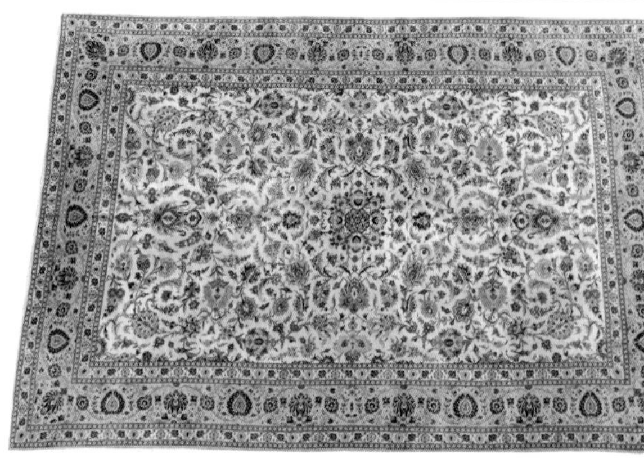

A Kashan Carpet, Central Persia.
153in (389cm) long
$1,800-2,400 **TEN**

A Kashan carpet, Central Persia.

Signed by the designer Saniia Kashan in four places.
153.5in (390cm) long
$3,900-4,500 **TEN**

A Kashkuli carpet, with several small animals scattered across the ground.

The excellent condition of this carpet is explained by the fact that in Persia, rugs of this kind used to be an investment and were not destined for use.
$27,000-33,000 **RBOS**

A Kerman carpet, Southwest Persia.
c1930 *208in (528cm) long*
$850-975 **WW**

A 19thC/early 20thC Mahal carpet, West Persia.
207in (526cm) long
$900-1,200 **L&T**

A large Nain carpet, Central Persia, modern, signature to one end.
264in (670cm) long
$8,500-9,000 **L&T**

A Qashqa'i kilim, with an abstract tile design in light patinated colors.
$5,250-6,000 **RBOS**

ESSENTIAL REFERENCE - SERAPIS

Woven in the rugged mountains of Northwest Persia, Serapis display a distinct Heriz regional style, with finer knotting and more large-scale spaciously placed designs than other rugs from this area.

- **Although it was the grandest of the antique Heriz styles, the Serapi format is seldom seen after 1910, because of the remoteness of the mountains in Northwest Persia. Carpets had to be taken by their weavers to Serab, 30 miles distant, to be marketed. 'Serapi' is not a place or tribal name; rather it is a market term derived from 'Serab-i', meaning 'of Serab'.**
- **Serapis combine design elements borrowed from many traditions. The bold geometric designs are probably connected to the tribal Caucasian traditions across the Aras River to the north. The elegant court carpets of Tabriz to the west certainly would have influenced the weavers' understanding of balance and the central medallion format.**
- **Serapi carpets were woven on the level of a family or small workshop with multiple weavers working several years to complete each rug. The weaving was done almost exclusively by women. Highly skilled artisans, they continually reinterpreted the design as they wove, creating highly spontaneous and inventive artistry. In general, the Serapis made in small workshops are more finely woven and formal, and pieces woven on a family level are more rustic and symbolic in design.**
- **The women of this area were master dyers able to deeply dye the superb, silky, local wool with a great range of soft-shaded or 'abrashed color. The wide palette of hues came from many carefully brewed plants and minerals, colors for which the recipes are now lost.**

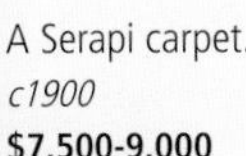

A Serapi carpet.
c1900 *141in (358cm) long*
$7,500-9,000 POOK

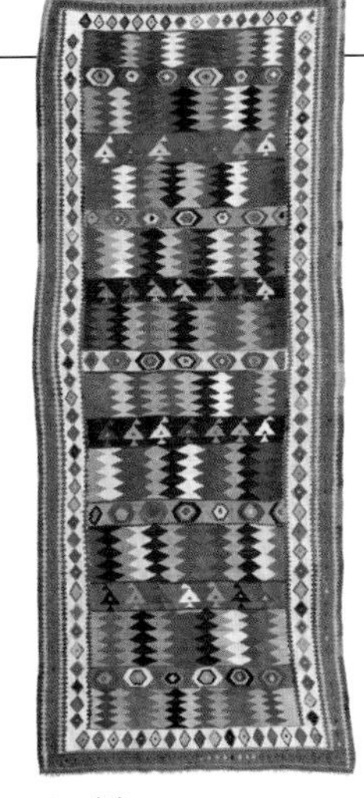

A Persian kilim.

This large kilim was woven by a Shahsavan tribal group in the Bijar region.

$6,750-8,250 RBOS

A rare Persian cover (shadda), two panels are woven separately and joined at the center, bands decorated with small plants bearing star-shaped blossoms meet at the central axis, forming flat triangular gables.

This cover is finely woven in the sumakh technique by the Moghan Shahsavan, and is a masterpiece of nomad textile art.

$60,000-67,500 RBOS

A Sultanabad carpet, Persian Azerbaijan.
136in (346cm) long
$1,800-2,400 TEN

A Tabriz pictorial carpet, Southeast Persia, woven with many animals, including giraffes, deer, rabbits, figures riding horses, and lions, signed at one end.
c1900 *250in (633cm) long*
$25,500-33,000 SWO

A fine Haji Jalili Tabriz carpet, Persian Azerbaijan.

The name Haji Jalili is occasionally heard in connection with some of the finest Tabriz carpets of the late 19thC. These carpets were made in the village of Marand 40 miles north west of Tabriz. Haji Jilili owned workshops that produced small quantitles of outstanding carpets.
175in (445cm) long
$6,000-7,500 TEN

A Tabriz carpet, Persian Azerbaijan.
221in (562cm) long
$9,000-10,500 TEN

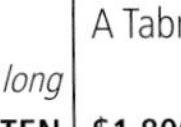

A Tabriz carpet, Persian Azerbaijan.
128in (325cm) long
$1,800-2,400 TEN

An antique Chelaberd carpet.

In the past, the carpets in this distinctive group were described as 'Eagle' kazaks by the trade, although most of them were woven in the Karabagh region. The main motif derives from the design repertoire of older Caucasian workshop pieces.

$15,000-21,000 **RBOS**

A late 19th/early 20thC 'Kasim Usag' rug, South Caucasus.

86.75in (220cm) long

$1,400-1,800 **L&T**

A late 19thC/early 20thC Kazak 'Lori Pambak' rug, Southwest Caucasus.

90in (228cm) long

$2,000-2,700 **L&T**

A late 19thC 'Sewan' Kazak rug, South Caucasus.

56.75in (144cm) wide

$2,700-3,300 **L&T**

A Kazak carpet, with unusual tree design.

c1900 *97in (246.5cm) long*

$1,800-2,250 **POOK**

A 'Karachov' Kazak carpet, the red triangles surround the central octagon are plain spaces, unlike most Karachovs, where they contain small-pattern mosaics.

The characteristic knotting structure of antique Kazaks suggest its date.

c1850

$33,000-39,000 **RBOS**

A late 19thC Kuba runner, East Caucasus.

40in (102cm) wide

$1,400-1,800 **L&T**

A late 19thC Shirvan long rug, East Caucasus.

45.75in (116cm) wide

$2,250-3,000 **L&T**

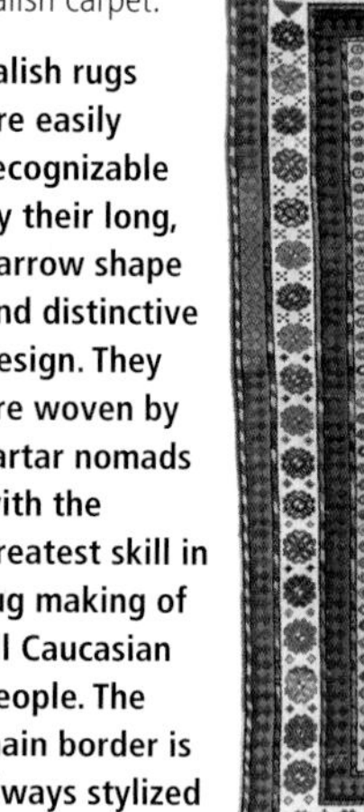

A narrow field Talish carpet.

Talish rugs are easily recognizable by their long, narrow shape and distinctive design. They are woven by Tartar nomads with the greatest skill in rug making of all Caucasian people. The main border is always stylized in a very distinguished manner. The Talish rugs with the plain solid field are the most favored by collectors.

$12,750-14,250 **RBOS**

A 20thC Hereke silk and metal threat prayer rug, West Anatolia.

62in (157cm) long

$2,000-2,400 **L&T**

A Khotan, repiled upper and lower finishes.

$22,500-30,000 **RBOS**

A mid 19thC nine-gül Salor chuval, low pile.

Nine-gül Salor chuvals are one of the pieces woven with an asymmetric knot open to the right around the mid 19thC, and thus do not belong to the so-called S-group (asymmetric knot open to the left). Although the design does not differ significantly from the S-group in the details of the drawing or the layout, the lack of silk at the center of the primary güls is striking. The warps are barely depressed, giving the weaving a softer and more flexible handle than S-group examples.

$6,000-7,500 **RBOS**

An early Salor main carpet.

Salor is the western trade name for the Salyr. The Salyr are one of the original tribes of the Ohguz confederation. S-Group refers to a structurally distinct group of Turkmen weaving which are often attributed to the Salyr.

$22,500-30,000 **RBOS**

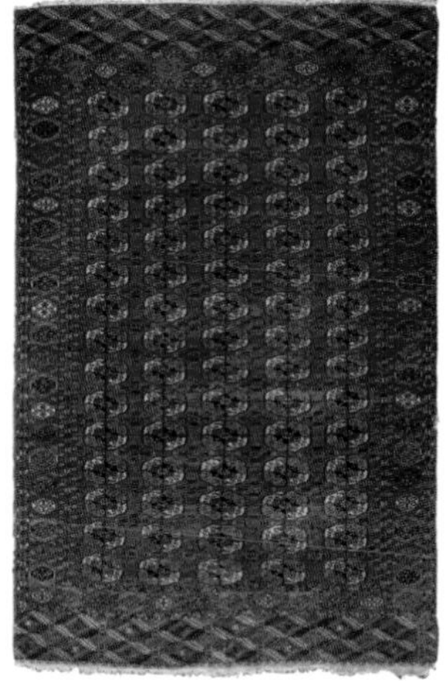

A late 19thC Tekke main carpet, Turkmenistan.

79.5in (202cm) wide

$1,800-2,250 **L&T**

A late 19thC Tekke carpet, Turkmenistan, repairs in places.

111in (290cm) long

$1,800-2,250 **WW**

A late 19thC Ushak carpet, West Anatolia.

214in (544cm) long

$4,400-4,800 **L&T**

An early 20thC Ushak carpet, West Anatolia.

169in (430cm) long

$1,500-2,250 **L&T**

A late 19thC Yomut carpet, Turkmenistan.

118in (300cm) long

$1,500-2,250 **L&T**

ESSENTIAL REFERENCE - SUZANI RUGS

Suzani is a type of embroidered and decorative tribal textile made in Tajikistan, Uzbekistan, Kazakhstan and other Central Asian countries. Suzan means needle. The art of making such textiles in Iran is called Suzandozi (needlework).

- **Suzanis usually have a cotton (sometimes silk) fabric base, which is embroidered in silk or cotton thread. Chain, satin, and buttonhole stitches are the primary stitches used. There is also extensive use of couching, in which decorative thread laid on the fabric as a raised line is stitched in place with a second thread. Suzanis are often made in two or more pieces, that are then stitched together. Popular design motifs include sun and moon disks, flowers (especially tulips, carnations, and irises), leaves and vines, fruits (especially pomegranates), and occasional fish and birds.**
- **The oldest surviving suzanis are from the late 18th and early 19thC, but it seems likely that they were in use long before that.**

A Bokhara Suzani rug.
$8,500-9,000 RBOS

A Suzani carpet, made in Pskent, a city in the north east of Uzkebistan that once belonged to the Emirate of Kokand.
$5,550-6,000 RBOS

A comparatively small-format Samarkand Suzani carpet, this piece from Samarkand appears to be very old, the cotton ground has faded to yellow with age.
$6,000-6,750 RBOS

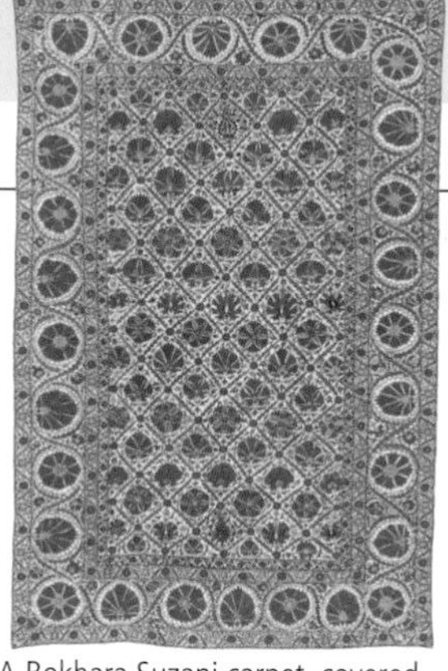

A Bokhara Suzani carpet, covered in a dense diamond lattice design, the sides have been backed with ikat fabric.
$15,000-18,000 RBOS

A Karshi Suzani, showing an eight-pointed, central floral star and two large blossoming trees.
$14,250-17,250 RBOS

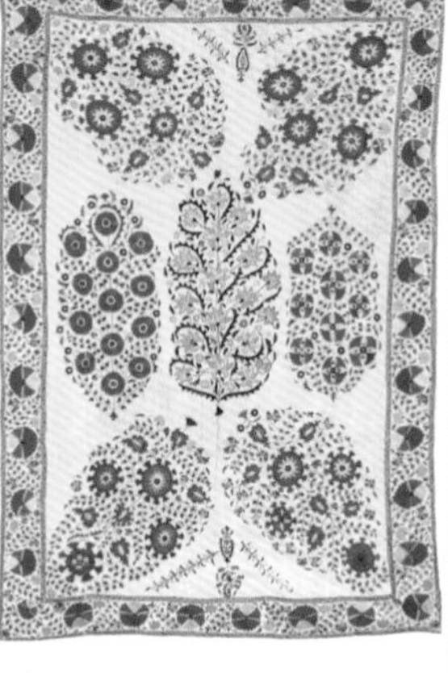

A classic Nurata Suzani, embroidered in light glossy colors.
$13,500-14,250 RBOS

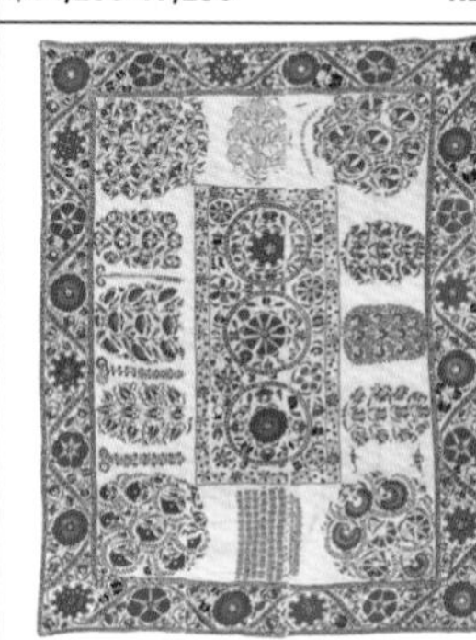

A large Nurata Suzani, woven by Bausback, represents a rather rare type in which a closed rectangle occupies the center of the field, with horizontal and diagonal flowering trees arranged around it.
$19,500-22,500 RBOS

An 18th/19thC Karakecili rug, with a cartouche border influenced by 17thC Transylvanian rugs, the sides have been cut and reselvedged.

Created when the Karakecili tribe inhabited the mountainous hinterland of the Bergama region during the 18thC and 19thC. This typical of their distinctive rugs.
$4,500-5,500 RBOS

A Saltillo serape, of soft and supple wool, backed with red fabric.

The very vibrant colors include a high proportion of cochineal. These serapes were woven for the Spanish upper class in northern Mexico, a true mounted 'caballero' wore his serape over his shoulder like a wide sash, enabling him to use it as a blanket providing warmth at night or to carry it, rolled up, behind his saddle.
$17,250-20,250 RBOS

A large early 20thC Donegal carpet, Northwest Ireland, of Ushak design.

307in (780cm) long

$9,000-13,500 L&T

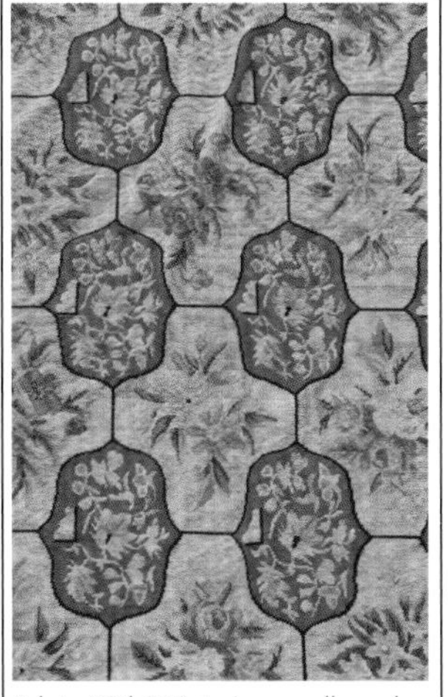

A late 19thC Victorian needlework carpet.

137.5in (349cm) long

$900-1,200 DN

A 20thC Aubusson woven carpet.

118in (300cm) long

$600-750 DN

A late 19th/early 20thC Amritsar hunting carpet, North India.

248in (630cm) long

$6,000-6,750 L&T

An Indian carpet, probably Amritsar, North India.

c1950 210in (534cm) long

$5,500-7,000 WW

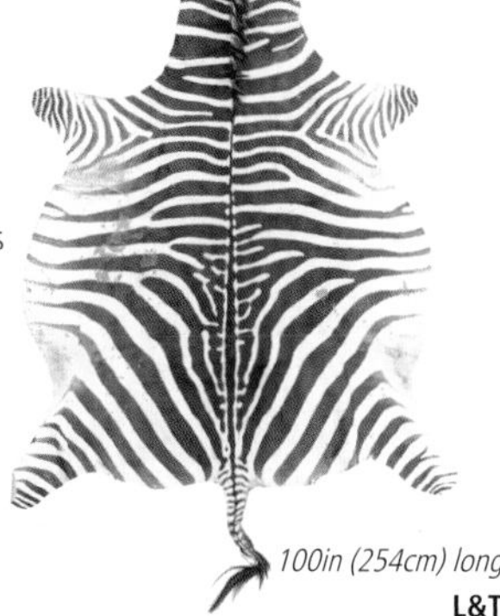

A Grant's zebra skin rug, (Equus Quagga Boehmi).

100in (254cm) long

$300-450 L&T

An early 20thC American hooked rug, of a coaching scene with fox coachman.

This is an unusual and desirable rug.

64in (160cm) wide

$900-1,000 POOK

An early 20thC American hooked rug, of a ram.

40in (101cm) wide

$300-400 POOK

CLOSER LOOK - HOOKED RUG

The rug is in remarkably good condition.

The dog is realistically portrayed with charming naivety.

The flora and fauna have a three-dimentional quality.

An early 20thC American hooked rug, of a dog.

37in (94cm) wide

$550-600 POOK

A late 19thC star variant patchwork quilt.

76in (193cm) long

$440-480 **POOK**

An early 20thC Pennsylvania patchwork quilt.

76in (193cm) long

$480-600 **POOK**

An early 19thC New England green Linsey Woolsey quilt.

104in (264cm) long

$1,500-2,250 **POOK**

A Baltimore appliqué quilt top, signed Sarah Cobb, with blocks with grapevines.

c1850 *99in (251.5cm) square*

$3,000-4,000 **POOK**

An early/mid 20thC Lancaster, Pennsylvania Amish 'Trip around the World' quilt.

75in (190.5cm) long

$975-1,150 **POOK**

A 19thC 'Star of Bethlehem' quilt, possibly done by Mary Justus of Philadelphia.

102in (259cm) square

$1,500-2,250 **POOK**

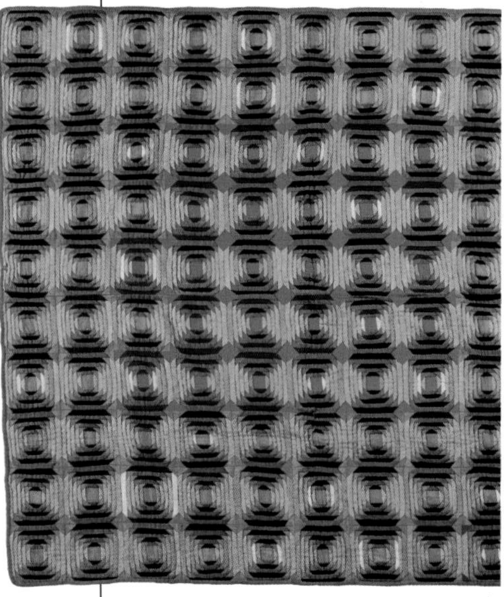

A late 19thC log cabin quilt.

67in (170cm) long

$400-450 **POOK**

A late 19thC pieced star pattern quilt.

83in (211cm) long

$600-700 **POOK**

A Victorian crib crazy quilt.

57in (145cm) long

$400-480 **POOK**

A late 16thC Flemish historical tapestry, of Alexander the Great and the capture of Tyre, possibly Tournai, woven in wool and silk, Alexander stands with the captured King of Tyre in a cart, before him are laid the shields and arms of the defeated Tyreans.

204in (519cm) long

$42,000-51,000 **L&T**

A late 16thC Dutch pastoral garden tapestry, probably Delft, after Karl Van der Madel, probably workshop of François Spiering, the border lacking.

99in (252cm) long

$14,250-15,750 **L&T**

A 17th/18thC verdure tapestry, Flanders.

112in (285cm) long

$3,000-4,000 **SK**

A late 16th/early 17thC Flemish Biblical tapestry, of Cain and Abel and fall of man, possibly Oudenaarde, woven with scenes depicting the Creation of Adam, the union of Adam and Eve, placement in the Garden of Eden, the Tempation at the Tree of Knowledge of Good and Evil, and the Fall and Expulsion from the Garden, the field with a Cross of St. George cartouche.

248in (630cm) long

$127,500-142,500 **L&T**

An 18thC Brussells verdue tapestry, depicting ducks in a lake with architecture behind.

62in (157.5cm) wide

$3,000-4,000 **FRE**

A 17thC Brussells verdure tapestry, depicting the Rape of Europa.

159.5in (405cm) long

$3,000-4,500 **FRE**

A 19thC French Aubusson tapestry, the cream ground centered by trophies, within reserves bordered by branches decorated with floral sprigs.

79.5in (202cm) wide

$2,250-3,000 **DN**

A 17thC Stuart Mirror with royal portraits, protected by a UV filtered frame.

This important and well documented raised work mirror is probably unique in that it is embroidered with a series of six royal portraits and is in outstanding condition. It represents a superb example of English embroidery from the second half of the 17thC. Its fresh colors and outstanding state of preservation along with exceptionally fine workmanship make it a rare survival from the Stuart period.

c1660-1683 *29 (74cm) high*

$127,500-135,000 **WIT**

A stumpwork framed Carolean looking glass, with stump work frame.

The beveled plate is flanked by a figure of Charles II and Queen Catherine of Braganza beneath bell top canopys, the lower panel with a lion and leopard within wreaths.

c1600 *38.5in (98cm) high*

$15,000-18,000 **LAW**

A stumpwork raised work embroidery, of Solomon and the Queen of Sheba.

When an embroidery has complex and extensive raised work in good condition and color, conserved to museum standards, expect to pay in excess of $30,000 for comparable examples.

c1660 *25in (63cm) long*

$30,000-38,000 **WIT**

A 17thC silkwork picture, of Esther before King Ahasuerus, the king beneath a canopy, the Queen with two attendants, within a garden with other figures, plants, birds, a lion and leopard, a figure hanging from a gallows to the upper left.

16.75in (42cm) wide

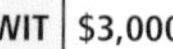

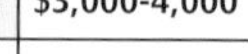

$3,000-4,000 **CHEF**

A pair of 18thC crewelwork hangings, with Tree of Life decoration depicting plants, flowers, fruit, and running deer on grassy hills, some restoration.

71.5in (181.5cm) high

$3,300-3,900 **ECGW**

A Spanish banner, with panel embroidered with flowers and butterflies, coronet and monogram in gilt metal, green silk with gold brocaded border, some damage.

c1830 *59in (150cm) high*

$550-700 **ECGW**

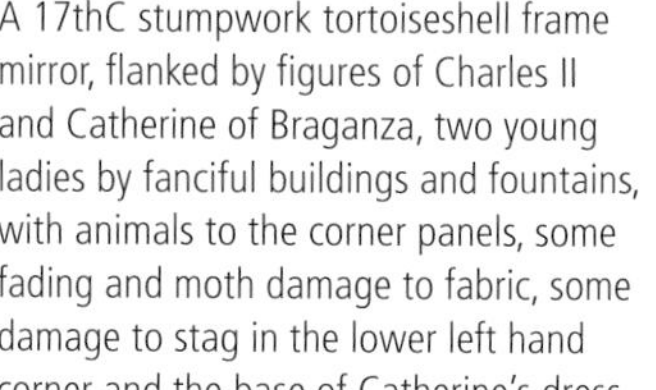

A 17thC stumpwork tortoiseshell frame mirror, flanked by figures of Charles II and Catherine of Braganza, two young ladies by fanciful buildings and fountains, with animals to the corner panels, some fading and moth damage to fabric, some damage to stag in the lower left hand corner and the base of Catherine's dress.

It is possible that the frame is a faux tortoiseshell, and probably the assemblage was put together later, including the glass; the stumpwork is all original.

c1900-1920 *25.75in (65cm) high*

$9,000-10,500 **CHEF**

A crewelwork wall hanging/bed cover, with design of trees, flowers, a squirrel and butterfly, with paneled border of plums, pears and strawberries.

c1900 *71in (180cm) wide*

$2,100-2,700 **ECGW**

A 17thC needlework cushion cover, worked in gros and petit point, satin stitch, coiled and purled needlework in wool and metallic threads on linen, with young women discovering Moses in the bullrushes, a lion in the foreground.

21.75in (55cm) wide

$1,800-2,400 **L&T**

A map of England and Wales by Mary Rogers, embroidered with colored silks outlining the county borders, dated.

1792 *19in (49cm) long*

$450-600 **DN**

An early 19thC woolwork picture of a young woman, playing a flute and seated at the base of a tree with a dog.

13in (32cm) high

$225-300 **DN**

A George III silkwork picture of Elijah.

c1800 *18in (46cm) high*

$180-240 **DN**

A mid 19thC early Victorian woolwork picture of a parrot, in a maple frame.

23.75in (60cm) wide

$550-600 **DN**

A late 18thC George III silkwork picture, of a floral arrangement, in a giltwood frame and glazed.

25in (63cm) high

$550-600 **DN**

A mid 17thC English embroidered picture of Christ, with the woman of Samaria, with two disciples and the houses of the city embellished with coiled thread and mica, worked in tent stitch with silks and metal thread.

c1660 *15.75in (40cm) wide*

$1,300-1,450 **DN**

A 19thC wool work picture of a spaniel, with flowers, some fading, in rosewood frame.

12in (30.5cm) wide

$300-400 **CHEF**

A Victorian woolwork picture, of a merchantman, flying an ensign, with inscription 'Hannah Evans Esher Wenfaw'.

c1868 *27.5in (70cm) high*

$450-600 **SWO**

ESSENTIAL REFERENCE: SAILORS' WOOLWORKS

Sailors' woolworks were produced from c1840 until they fell out of fashion around World War I. Many men passed the long hours on board by sewing scenes of their ships and landscapes. As woolworks are often unsigned, the names of the artists are largely unknown.

- **They are often dated, with the ship's name incorporated into the picture.**
- **The naiveté is what makes woolworks most charming - many are quite simple and straightforward. While it is regarded as unusual for men to have had this particular hobby for making woolwork pictures, it is actually not so strange as until the 1880s, seamen had no standard uniform and had to provide and maintain their own. Another task they faced was repair of the sails. Sailors mainly used wool thread, but cotton and silk were used when available.**

A 19thC sailor's woolwork picture, of a ship flying the red ensign and other flags, with three attendant boats including a paddle steamer.

21.25in (54cm) wide

$1,500-2,100 **WW**

A Victorian woollen threadwork picture, of a sailing ship and a fishing smack, in a rosewood frame.

20in (49.5cm) wide

$550-600 **DA&H**

A 19thC sailor's woolwork picture, of a ship flying the white ensign, in a glazed maple frame.

20.5in (52cm) wide

$600-900 **WW**

A mid 19thC sailor's woolwork picture, with busy depiction of sail/steam squadron under way, in original maple frame.

with frame 26.25in (66.5cm) wide

$1,500-2,100 **CM**

A long sampler, of whitework embroidery, drawn threadwork and needle lace, of geometric design, with the initials 'MH' which conceal the letters forming 'This is Mary Hardcastle W'.

c1640 *27in (69.5cm) high*

$4,500-5,500 **DN**

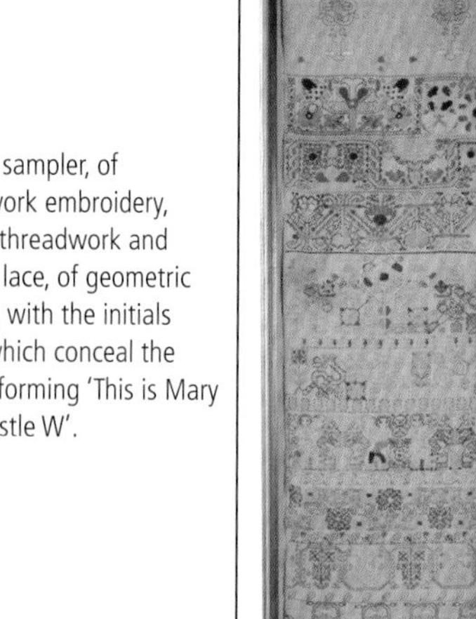

A long sampler, designed with rows of the alphabet, roses, acorns, upright and inverted plants, boxers and honeysuckle, with stem, satin, buttonhole and herringbone stitches on a linen ground.

1669 *29in (74cm) high*

$6,000-6,750 **DN**

A Queen Anne needlework sampler, with moralistic text above the alphabet, inscribed 'MARY LOWE AGED TEN YEARS JULY THE 23 DAY 1707', later framed and glazed.

1707 *39in (100cm) high*

$2,250-3,000 **DN**

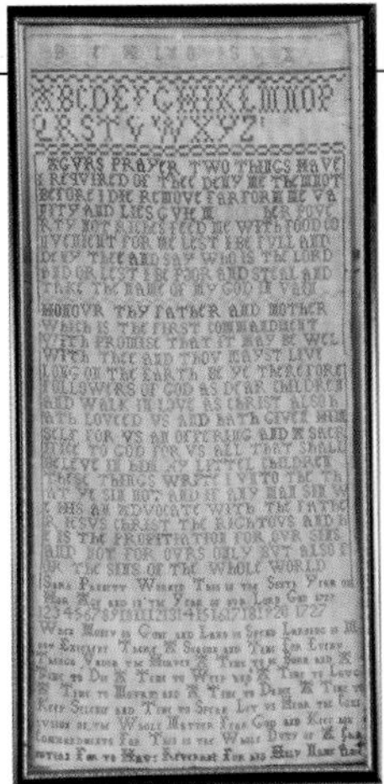

A needlework sampler, by Sarah Pannett, designed with prayers, a commandment, and verse with moral sentiment.

1727 *19in (48cm) high*

$900-1,000 DN

A Scottish needlework sampler, designed with a row of flowers, a house, crowns, initials, birds, animals and trees, on a wool ground.

c1750 *11.8in (30cm) high*

$1,800-2,250 DN

A needlework sampler, with a figure of William Shakespeare and a quote from The Tempest Act IV Scene 1, with a church, clock, flowers, houses, trees and flowering plants, by Fanney Martin.

1773 *21in (54cm) high*

$7,500-9,000 DN

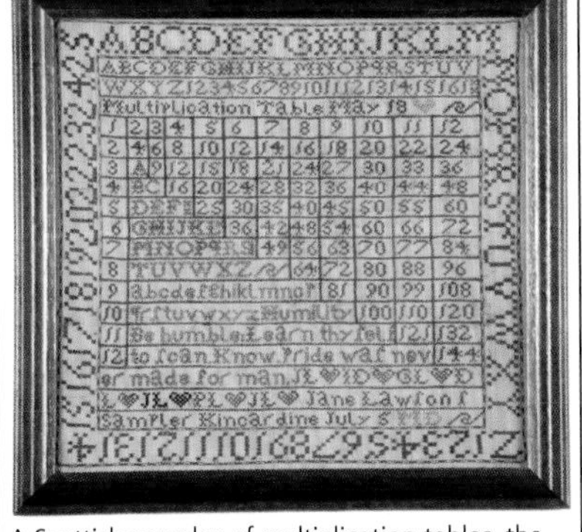

A needlework sampler, by Jane Watkins, aged 10 years, with a many windowed house, to the left Justice and to the right Adam and Eve, with rows of trees, flowers, animals, birds, crowns and figures in cross, some damage.

c1780 *17in (44cm) high*

$600-750 DN

A Scottish sampler, of multiplication tables, the left portion including a prayer, the border with the alphabet and numerals, by Jane Lawfon, Kinkardine.

c1800 *11in (28.5cm) square*

$3,600-4,400 DN

A needlework sampler, by Margaret Davie, with angels, exotic birds, butterflies and insects, figures, animals, trees and flowers.

17.25in (44cm) high

$6,000-6,750 SWO

An early 19thC needlework sampler, inscribed 'Isable Forrester Drumeldry, year 1808' with a house, a couple, alphabet and various sets of initials.

This was possibly a marriage piece. Drumeldry is in Fife, Scotland.

17in (43cm) high

$850-900 SWO

A needlework sampler, by Frances Burgum.

1811 *16.5in (42cm) high*

$1,300-1,450 CHOR

A George III petit point sampler, with figures, soldiers, animals and country house, with inscription 'Mary Alexandra and Mary Mary'.

The three soldiers appear to include a Rifleman and an Argyll and Sutherland Highlander.

1811 *17in (43cm) high*

$2,700-3,600 HW

A needlework sampler, initialed and dated 'BT', with a house, birds and animals.

1812 *11in (28cm) high*

$1,300-1,450 **CHOR**

A Dutch needlework sampler, by B.C.B. Anno, with a sailing ship, a house, a windmill, flowers, birds, angels, figures.

1821 *18in (45cm) high*

$1,000-1,200 **DN**

A Scottish schoolgirl sampler, worked by Jean Gerard, aged 12 years, with a house, flowers, birds and animals, the Lord's Prayer, six pairs of family initials and a written message from the artist.

1822 *12.5in (31.5cm) wide*

$2,700-3,300 **L&T**

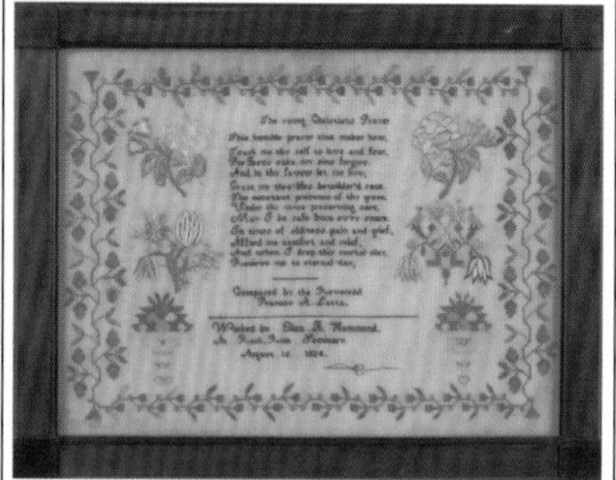

A Harford County, Maryland needlework, of 'The Young Christians Prayer', by Eliza B. Hammond at Rock Run Female Seminary.

1824 *21in (53.3cm) wide*

$4,000-4,500 **POOK**

A needlework sampler, by Elizabeth Morgan, with a house, a windmill, a church and animals.

1828 *14in (35.5cm) high*

$1,500-2,250 **DN**

A Chester County, Pennsylvania silk on linen sampler, wrought by Anna Mary Russel, Honeybrook Township Harmony School.

1832 *17in (43cm) wide*

$6,000-7,500 **POOK**

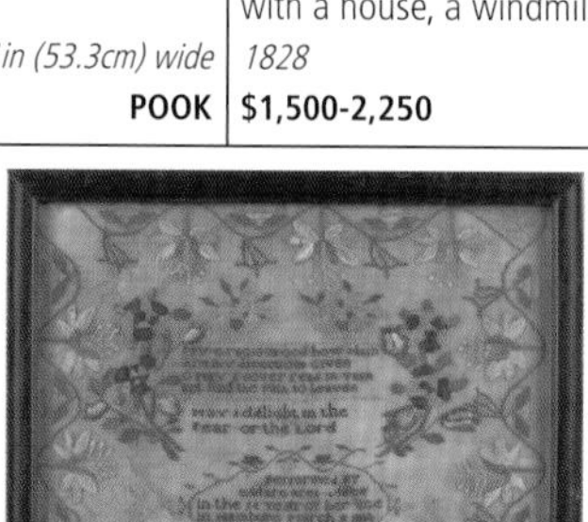

A Pennsylvania silk on linen sampler, wrought by Margaret Nice, 14 years old, Hamburg.

c1832 *17in (43cm) high*

$700-850 **POOK**

A needlework sampler, by Elizabeth Jotcham.

1832 *19in (48cm) high*

$850-975 **CHOR**

A Pennsylvania silk embroidered show towel, inscribed 'Catherine Fass Stowe'.

1848 *60in (152cm) long*

$975-1,150 **POOK**

A mid 19thC Pennsylvania embroidered show towel, by Rebeca Martin.

55in (140cm) long

$1,200-1,400 **POOK**

A Balenciaga couture blue lace dress, with boned bodice, with a blue lace overlay draped over the shoulders and a full skirt, missing petticoat.

41in (104.5cm) long

$1,200-1,800 **LHA**

A Bisang couture velvet and fur cape, labelled Bisang Couture, monogrammed 'D.P.M.' on interior lining.

size 8 35in (89cm) long

$2,000-3,000 **LHA**

A Bill Blass floral chiffon print gown, ruffle trim halter neckline with an asymmetric ruffle, tiered hem, labeled.

bust 15in

$700-850 **LHA**

A Romeo Gigli for Callaghan ivory slubbed silk gown, strapless, with tulle layers to the skirt and petticoat, labelled 'Callaghan'.

c1990 *size 42*

$2,250-3,000 **LHA**

A 1960s Chanel couture chiffon day dress, with an all-over Lurex jacquard, accordion pleated skirt, and goldtone lion's head buttons, labelled 'Chanel'/tape label '45385'.

$1,800-2,250 **LHA**

A Chanel cream wool coat, center front wood buttons, with piped seamed detailing, labeled.

size 38

$1,500-2,250 **LHA**

A Chanel bouclé skirt suit, with a double breasted jacket with a slit Nehru collar, goldtone buttons, with a fitted skirt, labeled 'Chanel Boutique'.

Size 42

$450-600 **LHA**

A Chanel couture tweed coat, with goldtone buttons in a woven motif, with a half belt to the back waist, Chanel/Tape label '52592', fabric piling.

Bust 16.5in

$850-975 **LHA**

A Chanel sequin and taffeta skirt ensemble, labeled Chanel Boutique.

Autumn/Winter 1994 *Size 42.*

$900-1,200 **LHA**

A Comme des Garcons black leather baseball glove saddle stitch jacket, labelled.

spring/summer 2005 *sizeM*

$1,500-2,100 **LHA**

A Jean Dessés couture blue ombre silk chiffon halter gown, sweetheart neckline with a ruched and interior boned bodice and a full skirt, labelled 'Jean Dessés'/tape label '1549', needs repair, tears close to the hemline.

c1955 *37in (94cm) long*

$2,700-3,300 **LHA**

A Christian Dior couture brown wool skirt suit, labeled, 'Christian Dior Paris'/stamped: '78752'.

Autumn/Winter1955 *jacket bust 17in waist*

$2,700-3,300 **LHA**

A Marc Bohan for Christian Dior black velvet dress, comprised of a sleeveless V-neck dress with a silk bodice, and a velvet bottom, together with a velvet vest, general wear.

c1960 *size16*

$400-550 **LHA**

A Madame Grés couture satin gown, with an interior corset, labelled 'GRES/1, Rue de la Paix Paris', unlined, minor runs in the satin, hem is moderately soiled.

c1958 *49in (124.5cm) long*

$1,400-1,800

LHA

A Claude Montana leather pant ensemble, comprised of a pair of high-waisted leather jodhpurs, with a white cotton button-down shirt, labeled, faint scratches to leather.

shirt size 40, pant size 38

$750-900 **LHA**

An Yves Saint Laurent khaki cotton safari tunic, labelled, small red stain to the left sleeve and purple pen mark to the label. spring/summer

1968 *30in (76.5cm) long*

$3,000-4,000 **LHA**

A 1980s Chanel quilted navy leather purse, with burgundy leather lining, gilt and leather chain strap and interlocking CC swivel clasp, with original felt bag and authenticity card No.2254407.

9in (23cm) wide

$2,400-3,000 **SWO**

A Chanel black quilted round leather bag, zipper closure, with large goldtone and leather tassle, and an interior zipped pocket.

7.5in (19cm) long

$850-975 **LHA**

A Chanel peach caviar leather wallet on a chain, with an interwoven leather and silvertone chain strap, interlocking 'C' logo.

7in (18cm) long

$1,300-1,450 **LHA**

A Chanel quilted leather bag, interwoven leather and goldtone chain shoulder strap, with a foldover flap, interlocking 'C' turnlock closure, with authenticity card, dust bag and box.

7in (18cm) long

$2,700-3,300 **LHA**

A Chanel quilted patent leather flap bag, two interwoven leather and goldtone chain straps, a goldtone interlocking 'C' turn lock closure.

12in (30.5cm) long

$2,100-2,800 **LHA**

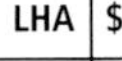

A Chanel faux tortoiseshell box bag, goldtone snake chain strap, with a push down clasp closure, and a goldtone interlocking 'C' to the top, with box, and dustbag.

5in (13cm) long

$4,000-4,500 **LHA**

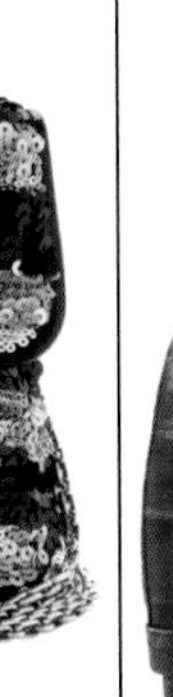

A cruise Chanel silver and black sequin bead medium flap runway bag, silvertone chain strap, with a 'Mademoiselle' turnlock closure, with dust bag.

2012 *10.5in (27cm) long*

$2,700-3,300 **LHA**

A Hermès 'Sac Mallette' golden brown crocodile purse, with key, both locks engraved.

c1950 *14.25in (36cm) high*

$1,800-2,250 **SWO**

A Hermès tan leather 'Bolide' bag, with padlock.

13in (33cm) wide

$2,100-3,000 **CHEF**

A Hermès suede 'Lydie' bag, goldtone 'H' logo, blindstamp circle 'F.' stamped 'Hermès', with dustbag.

1976 *10in (25.5cm) long*

$1,300-1,450 **LHA**

A Hermès ebene leather and toile 'Kelly' bag, gold hardware, lock and key sheath, blindstamp square 'G.' stamped 'Hermès', with dustbag.

2003 *14in (35.5cm) long*

$4,000-5,250 **LHA**

A Hermès bleu box calf leather 'Kelly' bag, gold hardware, lock and key sheath, blindstamp circle 'W.' stamped 'Hermès', with dustbag.

1993 *13in (33cm) long*

$4,000-5,250 **LHA**

A Hermès vert ostrich leather Birkin bag, gold hardware, covered lock and key sheath, with dustbag.

2001 *14in (35.5cm) long*

$16,500-21,000 **LHA**

A Hermès rouge casaque taurillon clemence leather 'Birkin' bag, palladium hardware, lock and key sheath, with dustbag.

2013 *14in (35.5cm) long*

$16,500-21,000 **LHA**

A rare Hermès custom order tricolor ostrich rigide 'Kelly' bag, cognac, vert and brown, with gold hardware, covered lock and key sheath, blindstamp circle 'X'. stamped 'Hermès', with dustbag.

1994 *13in (33cm) long*

$20,000-24,000 **LHA**

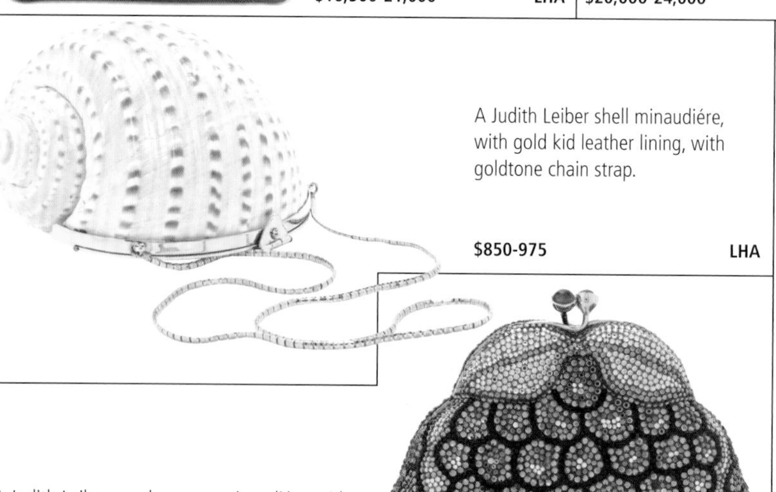

A Judith Leiber shell minaudiére, with gold kid leather lining, with goldtone chain strap.

$850-975 **LHA**

A Judith Leiber purple grapes minaudiére, with goldtone with a semiprecious stone encrusted coin purse clasp closure.

5in (13cm) high

$600-750 **LHA**

A Louis Vuitton monogram vinyl 'Cabas Ambre' tote bag, with two faux tortoise shell chain link and leather straps, comes with dustbag.

13.5in (34.5cm) high

$1,000-1,500 **LHA**

A Hermès tan leather suitcase, the rigid body with brass latches and locks, the interior with red silk lining and leather lashing straps.

21.25in (54cm) high

$3,000-4,000 **CHEF**

LOUIS VUITTON CASE

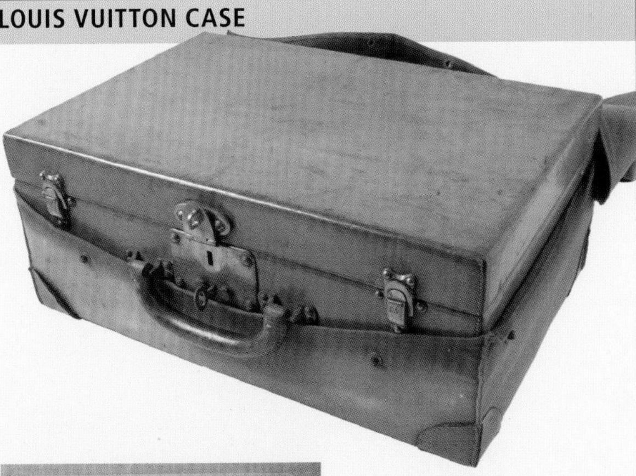

An early 20thC Louis Vuitton leather bound travelling case, with brass clasps and locks, the interior with a lift-out tray and with a paper label 'LOUIS VUITTON 767739, PARIS 70 CHAMPS ELYSEES, 149 NEW BOND ST. LONDON W., NICE 4,JARDIN ALBERT 1er, LILLE 34, RUE FAIDHERBE'.

18in (45.4cm) wide

$2,700-3,300 **WW**

A pair of Louis Vuitton suitcases, with monogrammed covers, torn leather straps and handles.

$550-700 **SWO**

An early 20thC Louis Vuitton rigid leather suitcase, serial number to label internally '918300'.

20.5in (52cm) high

$1,300-1,450 **CHEF**

A Louis Vuitton canvas hardsided suitcase, with key, monogrammed 'MRW' by Louis Vuitton, stamped 'Louis Vuitton/SN 917947'.

15in (38cm) long

$975-1,150 **LHA**

A Louis Vuitton monogram canvas trunk, leather trim, brass hardware, stamped 'Louis Vuitton'.

40in (102cm) long

$6,750-8,250 **LHA**

A Louis Vuitton flat top travelling trunk, with 'LV' monogrammed canvas, wood bracings and brass mounts, numbered '132325', lacking tray, worn.

40in (102cm) wide

$2,000-2,700 **SWO**

Carwitham, John, 'The Compleat Florist Botany', for J. Duke, published by J. & J. Robinson, emblematic frontispiece engraved by John Carwitham and 100 botanical plates, contemporary calf, rebacked, worn, 8vo.

Each plate in this beautifully colored work depicts a single variety, and includes images of tulips, roses, lilies, irises and more.

1747

$2,250-3,000 DN

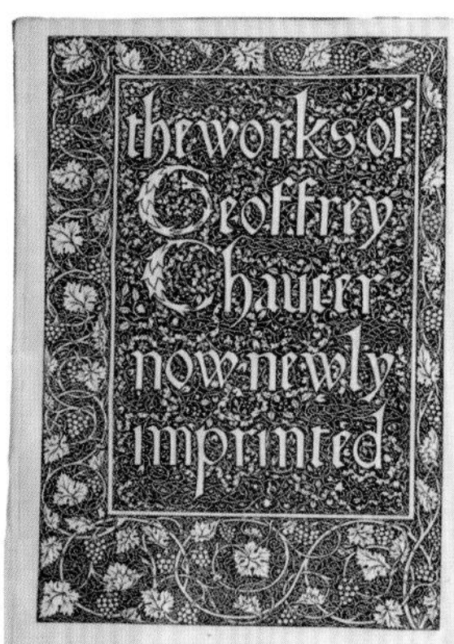

Chaucer, Geoffrey, 'The Works...now newly imprinted', edited by F.S.Ellis, folio, published by Kelmscott Press, one of 425 copies on paper, borders and initials by C.E.Keates, W.H.Hooper and W.Spielmeyer after William Morris, 87 woodcut illustrations by W.H.Hooper after Sir Edward Burne-Jones.

The most important work from the Kelmscott Press, and arguably the greatest of all private press books. Morris began discussing the project in 1891 and finally issued the book to subscribers in June 1896, a few weeks before his death.

1896

$36,000-45,000 DN

Curtis, John, 'British Entomology; Being Illustrations and Descriptions of the Genera of Insects Found in Great Britain and Ireland: Containing Colored Figures From Nature of the Most Rare and Beautiful Species and in Many Instances of the Plants Upon Which they are Found', vol1, first edition, printed for the author.

1824

$2,700-3,300 DW

Darwin, Charles, 'The Origin of Species, by means of Natural Selection', second edition, second issue, original green blind-stamped cloth.

1860

$3,000-4,000 DN

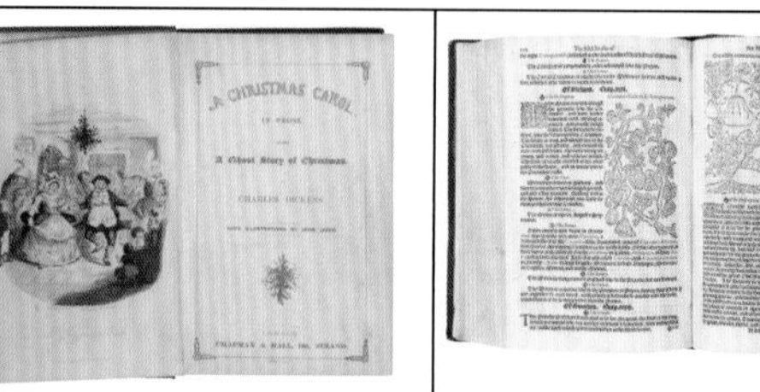

Dickens, Charles, 'A Christmas carol' first edition, first issue, 4 hand-colored etched plates by John Leech, published by Chapman and Hall, London.

1843

$4,000-4,500 L&T

Dodoens, Rembert, 'A Nievve Herball, or Historie of Plantes', first English edition, translated by Henry Lyte.

1578

$8,500-9,750 DN

Donovan, Edward, 'The Natural History of British Fishes, Including Scientific and General Descriptions of the most Interesting Species and an Extensive Selection of Accurately Finished Colored Plates', 5 volumes published by F & C Rivington.

1802-08

$2,550-3,000 DW

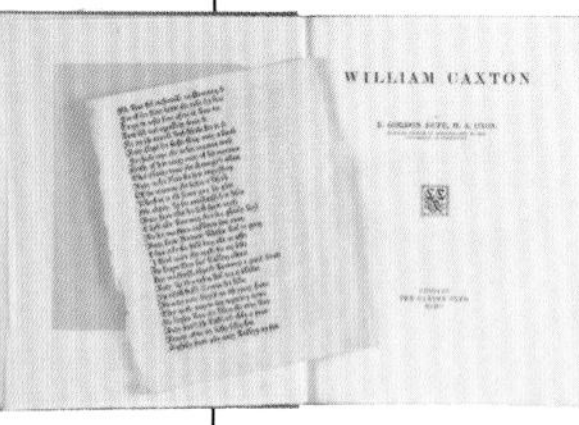

Duff, E. Gordon, 'William Caxton', published by the Caxton Club, Chicago, 26 plates, original single leaf, from Chaucer's 'Canterbury Tales', printed by William Caxton (Westminster 1476 or 1477) contained in wrapper in rear pocket, untrimmed, original cloth.

This is one of 148 copies, of a total edition of 252, with an original printed leaf from William Caxton's edition of Chaucer's 'Canterbury Tales'. The present leaf is from The Squire's Tale and numbered 199/200 in pencil at head of each side.

1905

$4,500-6,000 DW

Greene, W.T., 'Parrots in Captivity', three volumes, first edition, 81 wood-engraved plates printed in colors and finished by hand, large 8vo.

1884-87

$2,250-3,000 DN

'The English Bible', five volumes, one of 500 copies, initials in red by Edward Johnston, folio, published by the Doves Bindery.

In his book 'Four Centuries of Fine Printing' Stanley Morison states that the Doves Press Bible 'represents the finest achievement of modern English printing.'

1903-05

$9,000-10,500 DN

Judith Picks

I love the serendipity of the life of an auctioneer! Bill Forrest, valuer at the Macclesfield firm of Adam Partridge, was first shown a box of Jewish prayer books when preparing the Manchester estate of a Rothschild family descendant for sale earlier this year. The 20-leaf vellum manuscript, punctuated by numerous colored vignettes that set forth the order of the Passover Seder, was found buried toward the bottom but apparently no worse for its recent neglect. It retained its original boards of red-dyed parchment with remants of silver tooling, a type of binding typically found on manuscripts of Aaron Wolf Herligen, and was in fresh condition, save the minor staining on folios whose text relates to the ritual consumption of food. A particularly rewarding find.

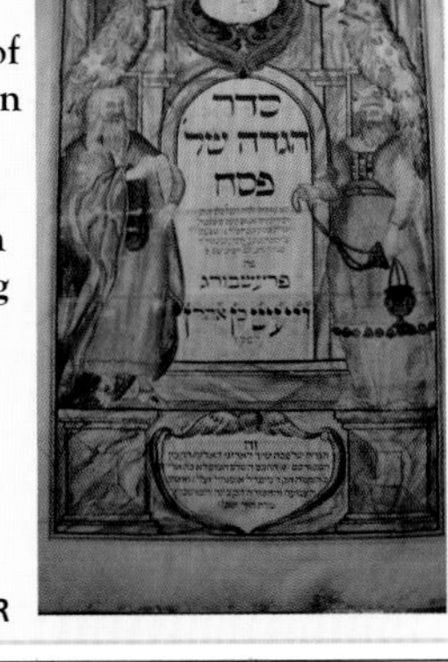

Herlingen, Aaron Wolf, a newly discovered copy of the Passover Haggadah, written and illuminated by the celebrated 18thC scribe.

$375,000-450,000 **APAR**

Keats, John, 'Poems', one of 200 copies, published by the Doves Bindery, small 4to.

1915

$5,250-6,000 **DN**

Milton, John, 'Paradise Lost [and] Paradise Regain'd', together two volumes, each one of 300 copies on paper, published by Doves Press, small 4to.

1902-05

$3,300-4,400 **DN**

Potter, Beatrix, Weatherly, Frederic, 'A Happy Pair', rare first Beatrix Potter illustrated book, published by Hildesheimer & Faulkner, London.

Unrestored copy of the first book illustrated by Potter. Thought to survive in a very limited number of copies. This copy is lacking a title-page, though it is almost certain that some of these were issued without one: the drawings appeared both as a series of separate chromolithographed prints as well as in book form. In the spring of 1890 Potter produced a series of paintings using as her subject her pet rabbit Benjamin Bouncer: 'My first act was to give Bounce ... a cupful of hemp seeds, the consequence being that when I wanted to draw him the next morning he was partially intoxicated and wholly unmanageable' (Lear, 73). Frederic Weatherly provided the verses for this publication and pre-dates Peter Rabbit (the first book of her own) by over a decade.

1890

$15,000-18,000 **SWA**

Roberts, David, 'The Holy Land, Syria, Idumea, Arabia, Egypt & Nubia', 6 volumes in three, 248 tinted lithographed plates, two uncolored maps.

1855-56

$2,250-3,000 **DW**

Spenser, Edmund, 'The Shepheardes Calender: Conteyning Twelve Aeglogues, Proportionable to the Twelve Monethes', published by Kelmscott Press.

1896

$2,550-3,000 **DW**

Tiffany, Louis C., tooled gilt leather book, 'The Artwork of Louis C. Tiffany', an unsigned copy of the volume personally commissioned by Louis C. Tiffany in a limited run of four hundred and ninety-two copies.

This book is profusely illustrated with Tiffany's favorite creations in the various disciplines of his artwork.

$4,500-5,500 **MIC**

'Dayly Observations and Meditations', a manuscript commonplace book, handwritten text in brown ink, generally in good legible condition.

A 17thC commonplace book, containing copies and extracts from literature, sermons and poetry.

c1660-70

$6,000-7,500 **DW**

ESSENTIAL REFERENCE - GULLIVER'S TRAVELS

Whistler's magnum opus of illustration. Apparently inspired by Richard Bentley's Designs for Six Poems by Mr T.Gray of 1753 he drew the illustrations within elaborate rococo frames, each one different, many reflecting his love of Baroque architecture. He spent months on the detailed pen and ink drawings; according to his brother Laurence he sat up all night drawing one wheatsheaf. Dennis Cohen, the owner of the press, bought the original illustrations from Whistler for a modest sum and sold them on at a profit, later on the artist bought them back again for considerably more.

Swift, Jonathan, 'Gulliver's Travels', three volumes, from an edition limited to 205, 12 engraved plates, 5 maps, 4 head- and 4 tail-pieces by Rex Whistler, the 12 plates hand-colored under the artist's supervision, with the additional suite of engravings all signed in ink by the artist, published by Cresset Press, folio.

1930

$33,000-45,000 **DN**

Bradbury, Ray, 'FAHRENHEIT 451', first British edition, published by Rupert Hart-Davis, London. 8vo.

1954

$450-600 L&T

Burgess, Anthony, 'A CLOCKWORK ORANGE', first edition, published by William Heinemann, London, dustwrapper in 1st state with 16s/NEt at lower right hand corner of the front flap, not price-clipped but spine faded with some chips at ends of spine and around edges, 8vo.

1962

$850-975 L&T

Burgess, Anthony, 'A CLOCKWORK ORANGE', first American edition, published by W. W. Norton, New York, spine tips lightly bumped, one corner clipped retaining price, Christopher Clark Geest bookplate to front pastedown, contents pristine, 8vo.

1963

$550-700 SWA

Burroughs, William, 'THE NAKED LUNCH', first edition, first issue, published by The Olympia Press, Paris, pictorial dust jacket after a design by Brion Gysin, spine panel slightly sunned. 8vo.

This copy is signed twice by Burroughs on the title-page including a short presentation inscription to Nelson Lyon dated 1989. A near fine copy of Burroughs' enduring and provocative Beat anti-classic. One of 5000 copies.

1959

$2,100-2,800 SWA

Burton, Virginia Lee, 'KATY AND THE BIG SNOW', first edition, published by Houghton Mifflin, Boston, in scarce dust jacket, color illustrations by Burton, price-clipped, four yellowed tape repairs on recto across spine panel to front and rear panels, square 4to.

1943

$1,150-1,200 SWA

Caspary, Vera, 'Laura', first edition, published by Houghton Mifflin, Boston, unclipped with $2.50 price, 8vo.

This book was cooly received by the critics - who later wrote nostalgic rhapsodies about it ... 'A haunting and memorable novel and a masterpiece…'. It was the basis for the classic Otto Preminger film noir.

1943

$6,000-6,750 SWA

Disney Studios, Walt, 'The Adventures of MICKEY MOUSE', Book I, first edition, published by David McKay, Philadelphia, color illustrations throughout, thin 8vo.

This dust jacket is exceptionally rare. This is considered the first Mickey Mouse book appearance, and also marks Donald Duck's first appearance in print. So it's the book debut for the most famous cartoon character ever created.

1931

$6,000-6,750 SWA

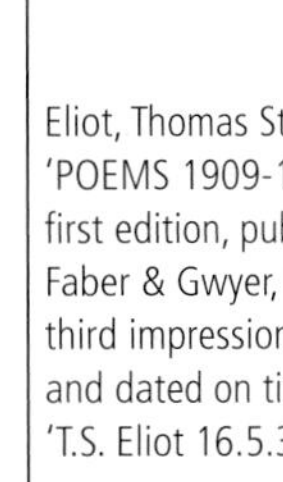

Eliot, Thomas Stearns, 'Prufrock and other observations', first edition, published by The Egoist Ltd., London, 8v0.

A very good copy of one of the first, great Modernist works. 500 copies were published by The Egoist where Eliot was working as Assistant Editor.

1917

$6,000-6,750 L&T

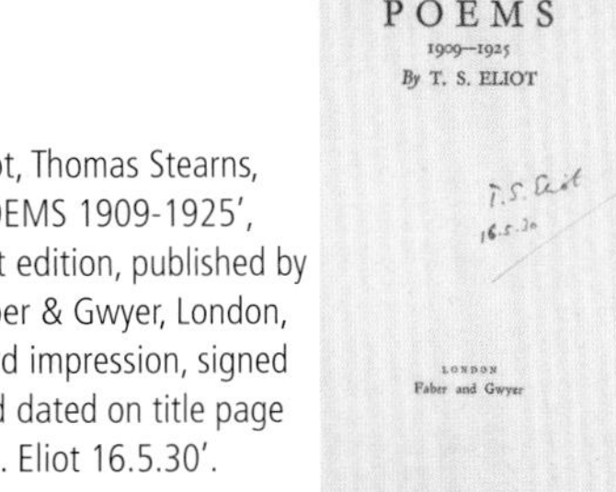
POEMS
1909—1925
By T. S. ELIOT

LONDON
Faber and Gwyer

Eliot, Thomas Stearns, 'POEMS 1909-1925', first edition, published by Faber & Gwyer, London, third impression, signed and dated on title page 'T.S. Eliot 16.5.30'.

This is an early printing of T.S. Eliot's first collection of poems, signed by him on the titlepage. This collection, first published in 1925, includes some of Eliot's finest work: 'The Love Song of J. Alfred Prufrock', 'The Hollow Men', and 'The Wasteland'.

1928

$1,500-2,250 L&T

Eliot, Thomas Stearns, 'THE WASTE LAND', first edition, published by Boni and Liveright, London, number 234 of 1000 copies, one of the first 500 copies printed with the limitation number printed in type 5mm high and bound in flexible black cloth.

This is the first edition of one of the most important poems of the 20thC. 'Eliot's Waste Land is I think the justification of the modern experiment since 1900' (Ezra Pound).

1922

$3,000-4,000 L&T

Faulks, Sebastian, 'BIRDSONG', first edition, published by Hutchinson, London, signed by the author on title, 8vo, original green boards, dustwrapper.

1993

$600-750 L&T

Fitzgerald, F. Scott, 'The GREAT GATSBY', first edition, second printing with textual corrections, published by Scribner's, New York, several old cellotape repairs on verso edges, internally pristine, 8vo.

1925

$12,750-14,250 SWA

Flack, Marjorie, and Wiese, Kurt, 'THE STORY ABOUT PING', first edition, published by Viking, New York, color lithograph illustrations by Wiese, unclipped, crisp jacket, 8vo.

1933

$900-1,000 SWA

Fleming, Ian, 'CASINO ROYALE', first edition, in dust jacket.

1953

$25,500-30,000 SAS

Gilbreth, Frank B. Jr. and Carey, Ernestine Gilbreth, 'Cheaper by The Dozen', cartoon illustrations by Donald McKay, first edition, published by Thoms Y. Crowell, New York, unclipped, contents pristine, 8vo.

This book was the basis for the classic 1950 film with Clifton Webb and Myrna Loy.

1948

$900-1,000 SWA

Grahame, Kenneth, 'THE WIND IN THE WILLOWS' first edition, published by Methuen and Co., London, frontispiece by W. Graham Robertson, 8vo.

1908

$3,000-4,000 L&T

Heaney, Seamus, 'Death of a Naturalist', first edition, published by Faber and Faber Ltd, London, signed by the author on the titlepage, 8vo.

1996

$1,000-1,500 L&T

Hemingway, Ernest, 'THE OLD MAN AND THE SEA', advance galley proofs, New York, comprising 17 galley sheets, printed on rectos only, stapled.

The book is stamped on first sheet of text 'Advance galley proofs for your personal reading only, Life publication date, Sept. 1.' Prior to magazine publication, Life distributed 5000 sets of advance galley proofs of the story for promotional purposes.

1952

$1,000-1,500 SWA

Joyce, James, 'ULYSSES', published by Shakespeare & Company, Paris.

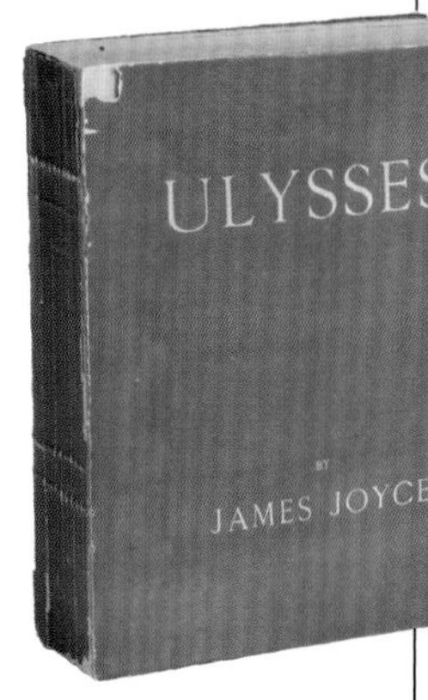

The first printing of Ulysses consisted of 1000 copies comprising: the first 100 were printed on Dutch handmade paper, numbered and signed by Joyce; copies 101-250 were printed on Vergé d'Arches paper, not signed; and the final 750, as here, were numbered 251-1000 and printed on a lesser grade of handmade paper and were not signed. The most significant and celebrated English language novel of the 20thC, its publishing trials and tribulations are legend. Stymied by obscenity charges that prevented its serial publication in The Egoist, Joyce's masterpiece was published instead by Sylvia Beach in the winter of 1922.

1922

$18,000-22,500 SWA

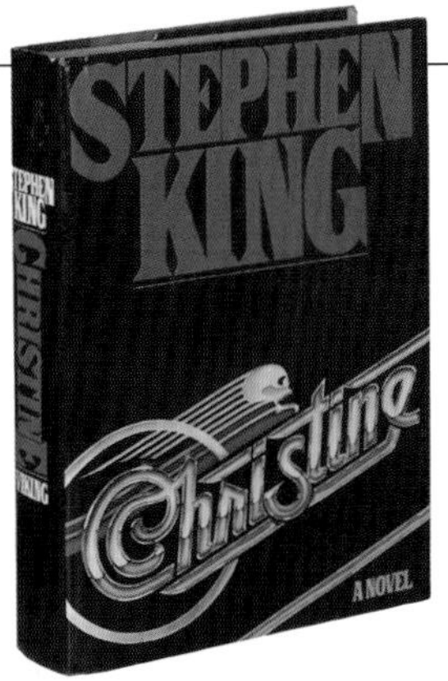

King, Stephen, 'Christine', first trade edition, published by Viking, New York, unclipped with no chips or tears, signed and inscribed by King in the year of publication on front free endpaper, 8vo.

1983

$400-450 SWA

Melville, Herman, 'MOBY DICK OR THE WHALE', three volumes, one of 1000 copies, pictorial title, plates and illustrations by Rockwell Kent, Chicago, Lakeside Press.

1930

$2,250-3,000 DN

Miller, Arthur, 'DEATH OF A SALESMAN', first edition, published by Viking, New York with loose slip of paper signed by Arthur Miller, 8vo.

1949

$850-975 L&T

Orwell, George, 'nineteen eighty-four', first edition, original cloth, with original publisher's wraparound band, 8vo.

A stunning copy of Orwell's dystopian classic, especially scarce in such condition and with the original wraparound band.

1949

$12,000-13,500 DN

Pratchett, Terry, 'THE Color OF MAGIC', first edition, first impression, Gerrards Cross, Colin Smythe.

The extremely scarce first Discworld novel, especially so in the first state dust-jacket.

1983

$4,500-5,500 DN

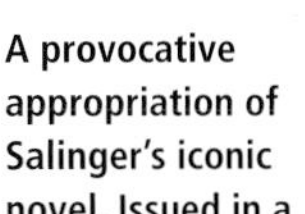

Prince, Richard, 'the CATCHER in the RYE', first edition, artist's book, published by Amerian Place, New York, dust jacket with $62.00 printed price, 8vo.

A provocative appropriation of Salinger's iconic novel. Issued in a limited edition of 500 copies. Shortly after publication, Prince peddled copies on a sidewalk along Central Park; it was also available at the Printed Matter BookFair the same year, but since then it has become rather furtive.

$850-975 SWA

Sendak, Maurice, 'WHERE THE WILD THINGS ARE', first edition, published by Harper & Row, New York, first issue dust jacket, front flap clipped twice, oblong 8vo.

1963

$3,000-4,500 SWA

Steinbeck, John, 'THE GRAPES of WRATH', first edition, published by Viking, New York, first state dust jacket, with the original $2.75 price present, internally pristine, 8vo.

This is a spectacular copy in unfaded and unrestored jacket of this American 20th Century highspot and Pulitzer Prize winner..

1939

$5,500-7,000 SWA

Steinbeck, John, 'OF MICE AND MEN', first edition, first issue, published by Covici-Freide, New York, several tape ghosts on front and rear flyleaves, small booklabel, 8vo.

1937

$600-750 SWA

Stoppard, Tom, 'ROSENCRANTZ and GUILDENSTERN are DEAD' first edition, published by Faber and Faber.

1967

$975-1,150 L&T

Seuss, Dr. (Theodor Geisel), 'THE CAT IN THE HAT', first edition, first printing, published by Random House, New York, 4to.

1957

$3,000-4,000 SWA

Tolkien, J.R.R., 'THE LORD OF THE RINGS', three volumes, first editions, volume one and three first impressions, volume two second impression, 8vo.

1954-55

$4,000-4,500 DN

Waugh, Evelyn, 'VILE BODIES', first edition, published by Chapman and Hall, London, 8vo.

This is Waugh's second novel. it's the first edition in the rare dust jacket with the price '7/6' on the spine panel and with Second Choice by Jeffery E. Jeffery as the last book on Chapman and Hall's list of Centenary Year Novels printed on the rear panel. This jacket is entirely unrestored.

1930

$20,000-24,000 SWA

Wells, H.G., 'The Time Machine', first edition in wrappers, issued simultaneously with the first cloth edition, published by William Heinemann, London, 12mo.

1895

$2,700-3,300 SWA

Wodehouse, P.G., 'THE CODE OF THE WOOSTERS', first English edition in unrestored dust jacket, published by Herbert Jenkins, London, 8vo.

This is one of the more uncommon Wodehouse titles of the period - increasingly scarce in collectable condition with jacket.

1938

$3,000-4,000 SWA

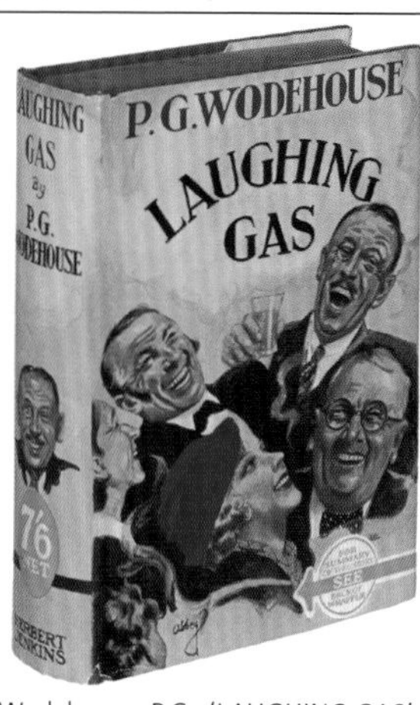

Wodehouse, P.G., 'LAUGHING GAS', first edition, published by Herbert Jenkins, London, internally pristine, 8vo.

1936

$2,700-3,300 SWA

Wodehouse, P.G., 'THE LUCK OF THE BODKINS', first edition, first issue unclipped, published by Herbert Jenkins, London, 8vo.

1935

$3,300-4,400 SWA

Woolf, Virginia, 'MONDAY OR TUESDAY', first edition, with 4 woodcuts by Vanessa Bell, published by Hogarth Press, London, one of 1,000 copies, 8vo.

1921

$1,000-1,500 SWA

Yeats, W.B., 'MOSADA', published by Cuala Press, Dublin, original parchment wrappers, uncut and unopened, original glassine wrappers, no 49 of 50 copies, 8vo.

This was privately printed and not available for sale. First included in the Dublin University Review, this dramatic poem, here reprinted, was Yeats's first publication. The orginal issue in 1886 is one of the most celebrated rarities of moden English literature.

1943

$1,800-2,250 L&T

Allard, Carel, 'Italia et Insulae circumjacentes' map of Italy, showing the mainland with the islands Corsica, Sardinia and Sicily as well as parts of Albania, with hand-coloring.

c1685 *21in (53cm) wide*

$975-1,150 **DN**

Blaeu, Johan and Willem, 'Tabula Russiae ... M.DC.XIIII' map, Amsterdam, showing Russia, with inset plan of Moscow upper left, vignette view of Arkhangelsk center right, with some hand-coloring, Dutch text verso.

c1645-50 *21.5in (54.5cm) wide*

$1,650-2,250 **DN**

Blaeu, Johan and Willem, 'Americae Nova Tabula' map, from the 'Appendix Theatri ...' of Blaeu's classic 'carte a figures' of the Americas, Amsterdam, showing portraits of native figures, with vignettes of major cities, copperplate, colored.

With an inset map of Greenland, Iceland and the mythical Frisland. California is still shown as a peninsula, only one Great Lake is seen. When first published, c1618 the map summarised the most up-to-date cartography and influenced numerous other map publications until mid-century.

1617-31 *21.5in (54.5cm) wide*

$10,500-11,250 **JPOT**

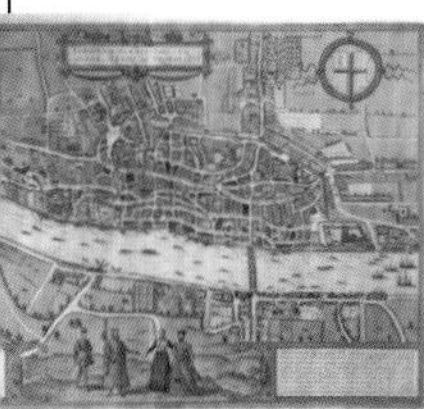

Braun, Georg and Hogenberg, Frans, 'Londinum Feracissimi Angliae Metropolis' map, Cologne, copperplate, colored.

The first printed plan of London reflected London's importance among European cities of the 16thC. London is shown from the Tower to Westminster, with the City already heavily built-up. On the south bank bull- and bear-baiting rings are prominent.

1572-1574 *19in (48.5cm) wide*

$10,500-11,250 **JPOT**

Buck, Samuel and Nathaniel, 'Untitled [Panorama Of The Thames From Westminster Bridge To London Bridge on Five Sheets]' map, London, copperplate, uncolored.

The brothers Samuel and Nathaniel Buck travelled through England from 1724 to 1738, drawing and then engraving prospects of the cities and various antiquities.

1749 *156.25in (297cm) wide*

$12,000-12,750 **JPOT**

Coronelli, V. M., 'Canada Orientale Nell'America Settentrionale' map, Venice, copperplate, colored.

1696 *23.5in (60cm) wide*

$1,500-2,250 **JPOT**

ESSENTIAL REFERENCE - WORLD MAP

A fine example of a large world map of great scientific significance. Edmond Halley, scientist and cartographer, understood the need for navigators to establish the basis of magnetic deviation to use the compass to its best effect. 'It was a sensational event when a map was published in 1701 that depicted the lines that connected points with the same declinations with each other. ... He based his map on observation data, some of which he had generated himself during scientific expeditions that had been arranged specifically for this purpose. ... This map attained great prominence and is considered both a milestone in the history of cartography and in the studies of the history of terrestrial magnetism.' Halley is probably best known now for the comet named after him, but his world map, first published in London in 1702 by Mount and Page with subsequent Dutch editions, marked a dramatic advance in the determination of longitude with all its navigational benefits. The map shows lines of equal magnetic variation, termed isolines, or isogonic lines, which proved to be an invaluable method for recording scientific data. Printed on three sheets joined, the world is shown with overlapping detail at each side, thus allowing Australia and the Orient to appear twice, and has a large inset of the North Pole.

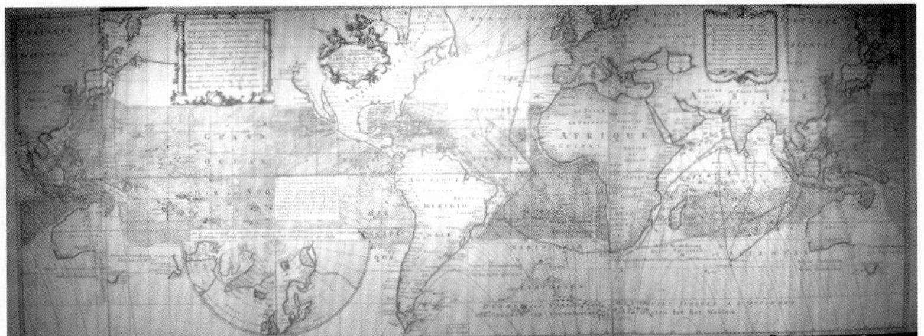

Halley, Edmond and Ottens, R and J, 'Nova & Accuratissima Totius Terrarum Orbis Tabula Nautica' map, Amsterdam, copperplate, original color.

c1730 *56.25in (143cm) wide*

$18,000-22,500 **JPOT**

Harris, John, 'A View Of The World In Divers Projections' map, London, copperplate, original color.

John Harris is relatively unknown although he produced maps for a number of publishers at a time when English cartographers, reflecting the Nation's increasing overseas activities, were creating many important and often separately published maps related particularly to the New World. Many are now very rare.

1697-c1710 *22.75in (58cm) wide*

$13,500-15,000 **JPOT**

Vanden Hoeye, Rombout, 'Londinum Celeberrimum Angliae Emporium' map, of London with the imprint of Rombout Vanden Hoeye', Amsterdam, copperplate, uncolored.

This is a scarce example of a classic pre-fire London panorama. Rombout (1622-1671) was the son of Francois (c1590-1636) and both were printers, publishers, engravers and map sellers of Amsterdam.

c1638 *20in (51cm) wide*

$6,000-7,500 **JPOT**

De Leth, A. and H., 'Carte Nouvelle De La Mer Du Sud' map, Amsterdam, showing the Pacific and discoveries there with the Americas positioned centrally on the map, with a large island California, and also the Atlantic and west coast of Africa, copperplate, original color.

1740 *37in 94cm) wide*

$21,000-22,500 **JPOT**

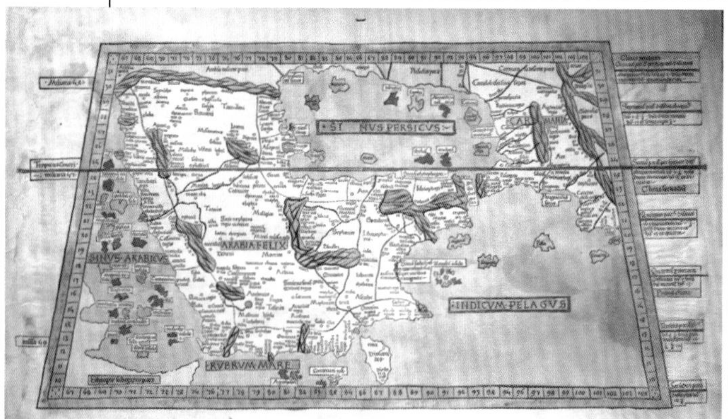

Ptolemy, Claudius and Leonhardt, Holle, 'Untitled' but verso 'Sexta Asie Tabula' map, Ulm, woodblock, original color.

One of the earliest maps ever printed. The atlas was the first published outside Italy, the first in woodblock.

1482 *21.75in (55.5cm) wide*

$33,000-37,500 **JPOT**

Homann, Johann Baptist, 'Planiglobii Terrestris cum utroq Hemisphærio Cælest' double hemisphere world map, Nuremberg, smaller celestial hemispheres above and below.

c1720 *22in (56cm) wide*

$1,500-3,000 **DN**

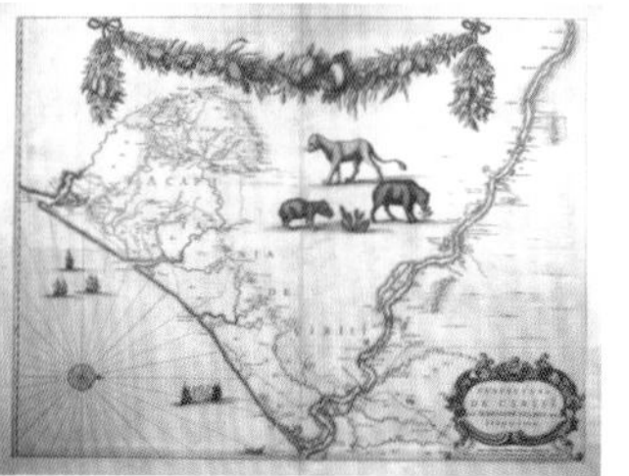

Marcgraf, G., Barlaeus, C. and Blaeu, J., 'Praefectura De Ciriii Vel Seregippe Del Rey Cum Ipatuana' map, Amsterdam, depicting part of the Brazilian south east coast and interior from below the Sao Paulo region, copperplate, original color.

1647 *21in (53.5cm) wide*

$1,000-1,200 **JPOT**

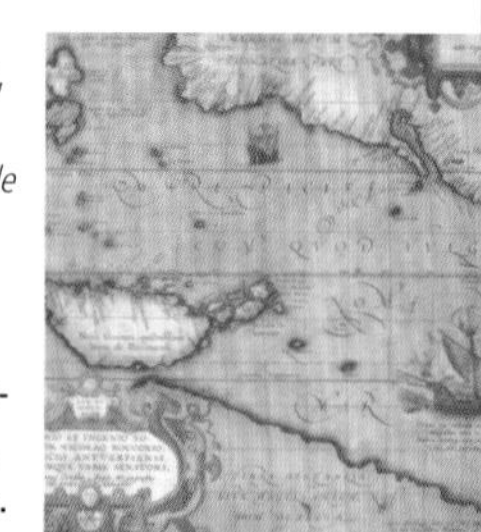

Ortelius, A., 'Maris Pacifici (Quod Vulgo Mar Del Zur)' map, of the Pacific Ocean, Antwerp, copperplate, original color.

1590 *19.5in (49.5cm) wide*

One of the most famous atlas maps ever produced, the first to focus on the Pacific Ocean, important for its inclusion of the Americas, Japan, South East Asia and Antarctica. Shown in the Pacific is Magellan's ship, the Victoria, as it circumnavigates the globe.

$1,000-1,200

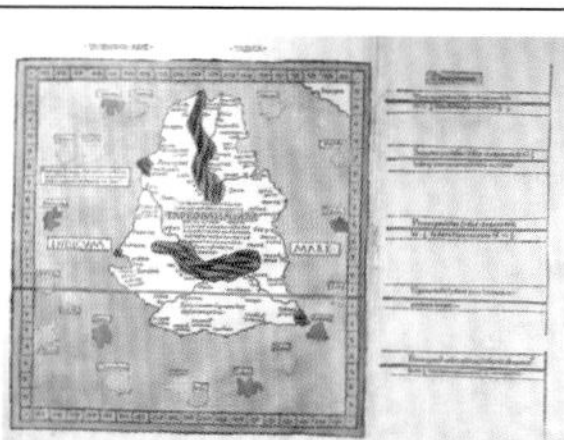

Ptolemy, Claudius and Leonhardt, Holle, 'Duodecima Asie Tabula' map, of Ceylon, Ulm, woodblock, original color.

This map shows the island of Taprobana, a name sometimes applied to Sumatra but here identifying Ceylon, now Sri Lanka.

1482-86 *15.75in (40cm) wide*

$9,750-10,800 **JPOT**

Seller, John, 'A Chart of the Westermost Part of the Mediterranean Sea' map, from the Straits of Gibraltar to the Adriatic, probably from the Atlas Maritimus.

c1675 *20.5in (52cm) wide*

$2,700-3,300 **DN**

Seutter, M., 'Le Pays De Perou Et Chili' map, Ausburg, excluding the eastern part of Brazil and, as such, effectively illustrating Spanish, from Portuguese, South America as defined in the centuries earlier Treaty of Tordesillas, copperplate, original color.

Typically, for a German publication of the period, the whole is set off by title cartouche with South American figures, a llama, foliage, ships and settlements appear against a volcanic coastline with sailing ships off-shore.

c1740 *22.75in (58cm) wide*

$1,800-2,400 JPOT

Speed, John, 'Britain As It Was Devided in the Tyme of the Englishe Saxons Especially During Their Heptarchy' map.

c1627 *20in (51cm) wide*

$3,000-4,500 DN

Speed, John, 'The Invasions of England and Ireland with al their Civill Wars Since the Conquest' map.

1676 *20.5in (52cm) wide*

$2,250-3,000 DN

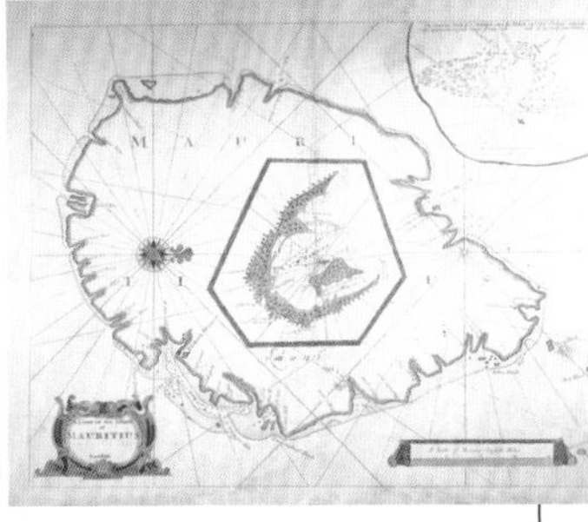

Thornton, John, (attributed) 'A Chart Of The Island Of Mauritius' map, for publication in the Third Book of the 'English Pilot ... Oriental Navigation', copperplate, colored.

A rare chart of Mauritius, this was the first detailed map or chart of the island which was, at this time, about to be abandoned by the Dutch, who had settled there almost one hundred years earlier to be succeeded by the French for the early part of the 18thC. The island coastline is shown in great detail.

1703 *21in (53.5cm) wide*

$3,000-4,000 JPOT

ESSENTIAL REFERENCE - JOHN SPEED

From the first world atlas produced in England, this sought-after map is, in its first edition of 1627, the earliest world map generally available to show the famous misconception of California as an island. This example is the rare third state with the imprint of Roger Rea the Elder. The plate is remarkable for the mass of decoration and information including allegorical figures representing the four elements - Water, Earth, Fire and 'Aire' - as well as diagrams of the 'Heavens and Elements', eclipses, celestial hemispheres and portraits of the circumnavigators Drake, Cavendish, Magellan and Van Noort. John Speed's map is a compendium of information; it shows a prominent 'Southerne Unknowne Land' described as home to "The Atlantic and many other curiosities.

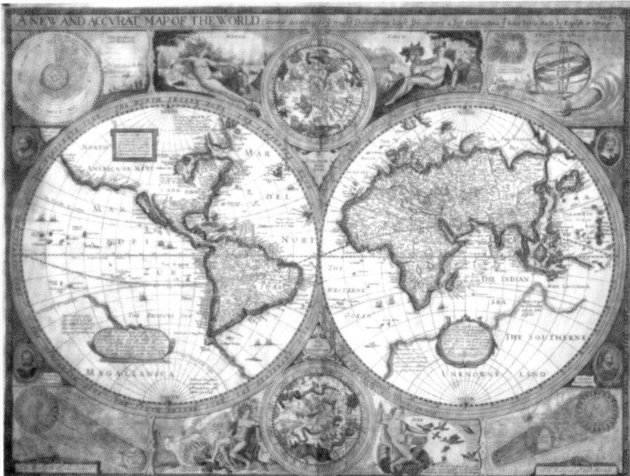

Speed, John, 'A New And Accurat Map Of The World', London.

1627-62 *20in (51cm) wide*

$14,250-15,750 JPOT

Westmorland, Hodgson (Thomas), 'Plan of the County of Westmorland' map.

Describing minutely the boundaries of wards, parishes and townships, large wall map with inset vignette views of Appleby Castle and Lowther Castle in lower corners.

1828 *63.5in (162cm) wide*

$2,250-3,000 DN

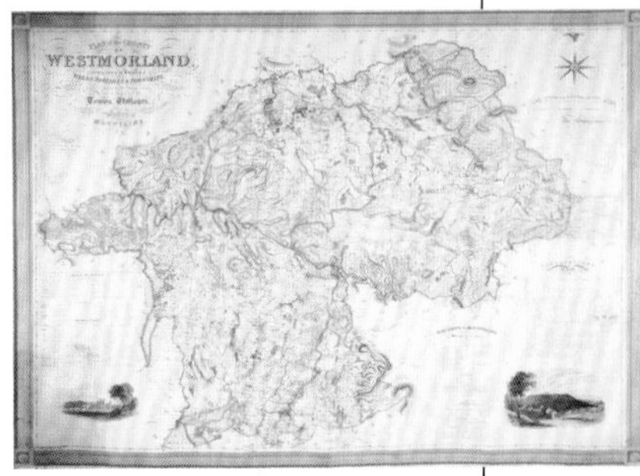

De Wit, F. and Renard, L., 'Occidentalior Tractus Indiarum Orientalium' map, Amsterdam, copperplate, colored.

A good example of a later issue of Frederic De Wit's chart, the chart extends along the East African coast from the Cape northward to include all Arabia, the Gulf and the western part of the Indian Ocean as far as India and the Maldives. De Wit's 'Atlas Maritimus' enjoyed popular acclaim, being a finely produced synopsis of current hydrographic knowledge, presented on well engraved general charts covering the whole world. De Wit's charts maintained the artistic elements of 'the Golden Age of Cartography' in the face of the more utilitarian, albeit more up-to-date, charts of the Van Keulen family and others.

1685-1715 *21.25in (54cm) wide*

$1,800-2,250 JPOT

ESSENTIAL REFERENCE - CHURCHILL LETTER

At this time, Churchill was First Lord of the Admiralty and Kitchener was the Secretary of State for War. Theirs was a frosty relationship, though Kitchener was eventually persuaded to support Winston Churchill's disastrous Gallipoli Campaign in 1915-16. Churchill lost his post at the Admiralty on 27 May 1915 over the Campaign, while Kitchener died in 1916, his ship HMS Hampshire striking a mine off the Orkney Islands. The British Authorities ordered over 150,000 Japanese guns shortly after World War One began in August 1914, a mixed batch of 30th and 38th Year type rifles. Most of these rifles were used by training battalions but T. E. Lawrence suggests that at least a few reached the Middle East and were likely 'part of a 20,000-gun consignment of Arisaka rifles issued to the Royal Navy from June 15 1915 to free Lee-Enfields for land service. Japanese rifles also served the Royal Flying Corps. and its 1918-vintage successor, the Royal Air Force. The Arisakas were soon recalled, the Navy guns being replaced by Canadian Ross-rifles in April-June 1917. About 128,000 assorted Japanese guns were subsequently sent from Britain to Russia, and the patterns were declared obsolete in British service in 1921'.

Churchill, Sir Winston Leonard Spencer (1874-1965), typed letter signed, 'Winston S. Churchill', Admiralty, Whitehall, to Lord Kitchener. Excluding ships in the Mediterranean and on foreign stations, there are at present afloat in the Grand Fleet and other Squadrons in Home Waters, and in the posession of the Royal Marines at their Headquarters, 20,000 rifles, of which 8,000 Seamen's rifles are long-charger loading, and 12,000 Marines' rifles are short-charger loading. All the Marines' rifles are in good condition. A proportion of the Seamen's rifles are rather worn. It will not be possible for us to have onboard ships of the main fleets in Home Waters two patterns of rifles requiring different kinds of ammunition. It is therefore necessary for you to replace in these ships not only the 12,000 Marines' rifles, but the 8,000 Seamen's rifles, with the Japanese weapon; and these will be handed over to you within four weeks of the delivery to us of the 20,000 Japanese rifles. With regard to ships abroad, a further statement will be made as soon as possible; and we are quite prepared as soon as it can be arranged, to replace all Admiralty rifles now afloat by Japanese weapons, if you desire it'.

8th April, 1915

$2,250-3,000 DW

Whistler, Rex, three original drawings for 'A Book of Pensées' by Ronald Hall [unpublished], comprising: 'The Man of Destiny', pen and ink, signed and dated lower right, mounted on board; 'Illustration to Death's Precipice', pen and ink with watercolor, signed lower right; 'A Man of Pedigree', pen and ink with watercolor, mounted on board, all titled in ink in lower margin, lightly browned with a few small spots or stains.

1926 *8.25in (21cm) high*

$6,000-7,500 DN

Robinson, William Heath, 'Hobart', original watercolor from Rudyard Kipling's 'A Song of the English', signed lower left, framed and glazed.

1909 *image 1.5in (4cm) high*

$5,500-7,000 DN

Whistler, Rex, 'De la Mare', the 5 original copper plates for 'Desert Islands and Robinson Crusoe', with modern pulls from the 2 tail-pieces and a copy of the first edition of the book, 8vo.

1930 *pictorial title 0.75in (2cm) long, 2 head and 2 tail pieces 0.5in (1cm) long*

$5,500-7,000 DN

Whistler, Rex, 'Design for curtain for 'Operatic Pills' original drawing, scene in C. B. Cochran's revue 'Wake Up and Dream', original drawing in pencil, pen, ink and watercolor, 2 sheets joined in center, lightly soiled with a few small stains, slight creasing to edge of one sheet at center join, framed and glazed.

The impresario Charles B.Cochran commissioned Whistler to design scenery and costumes for several of his popular London revues, starting with this curtain for 'Wake Up and Dream'. It shows a vast choir at the Albert Hall, described by Laurence Whistler as 'hideous females in short white dresses, with red or blue sashes and angels' wings, banked in front of the great organ, and bellowing'.

1929 *2.5in (6.5cm) long*

$11,500-13,000 DN

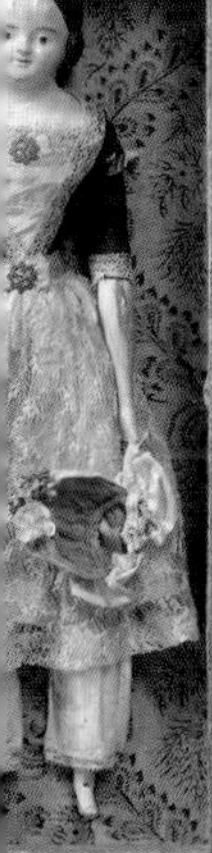

An early 19thC American papier-mâché shoulder-head doll, with painted blue eyes and red lips, carved and painted wood arms and legs, in a sealed shadow box lined with blue floral-printed wallpaper, with imperfections.

box 15.75in (40cm) high

$2,250-3,000 **SK**

A large mid-19thC papier-mâché shoulder-head doll, painted blue eyes, smiling mouth, black center-part hair with curls behind exposed ears, cloth body, white kidskin arms.

$225-300 **SK**

ESSENTIAL REFERENCE - COMPOSITION DOLLS

Papier-mâché, carton moulé, carton pâte or holz-masse are all terms describing a type of composition material made from paper sheets or paper pulp mixed with paste, oil, resin or other material to form a strong material that was pressed together. Earliest papier-mâché dolls were individually handmade, by the mid 1800s pressure mold processes made it possible for dolls to be mass produced. Ludwig Greiner dolls were made from 1840-1900.

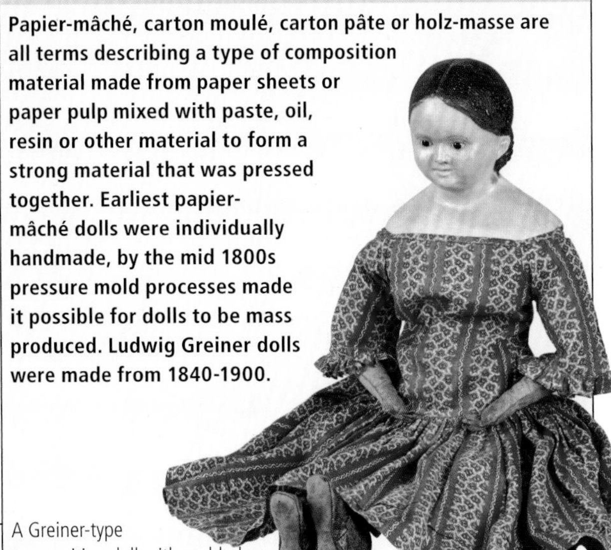

A Greiner-type composition doll with molded hair and glass eyes.

32in (81.3cm) high

$1,000-1,200 **POOK**

A 19thC Greiner-type composition doll, with molded hair and a stuffed body, stamped Holz Masse.

18in (46cm) high

$180-270 **POOK**

A late 19thC Greiner-type composition boy doll, with its original outfit, including a beaver top hat and molded hair.

23in (58.5cm) high

$975-1,150 **POOK**

A large German china head-and-shoulder doll with molded hair.

31in (79cm) high

$400-550 **POOK**

A painted papier-mâché milliner's head on a walnut stand.

c1840 *36.75in (93.5cm) high*

$1,500-2,100 **POOK**

A 19thC papier-mâché milliner's head.

15in (39cm) high

$1,150-1,300 **POOK**

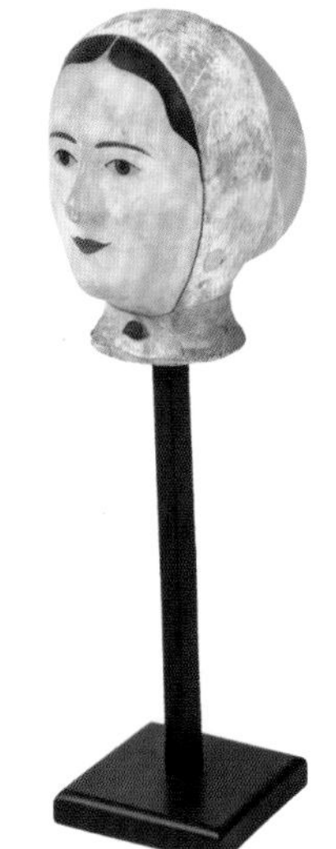

A 19thC French carved and painted wood milliner's head.

9.5in (24cm) high

$1,500-2,100 **POOK**

A 1920s Dean's Rag Book 'Miss Betty Oxo' cloth doll, having molded face with painted features, side-glancing eyes, label to foot missing.

This doll was offered in exchange for 480 Oxo cube wrappers, and comes complete with the 'Little Miss Oxo Doll Competition' card.

17.5in (44cm) high

$600-750 **AST**

A Tete Jumeau bisque-head doll, with composition body, later clothes, back of head printed in red 'Depose Tete Jumeau Bte SGDG 6'.

15in (38cm) high

$1,150-1,300 **SWO**

An early 20thC Jumeau 'Bebe' doll, with fixed brown eyes, painted features and pierced ears, blonde wig, with working voice box operated by two drawstrings, with printed mark 'Depose'.

17in (43.5cm) high

$3,000-4,000 **AST**

An early 20thC Kämmer & Reinhardt/ Simon & Halbig bisque-head girl doll, with sleeping eyes, open mouth with teeth, blonde wig, jointed composition body, head impressed 'Simon & Halbig K R Germany' with star to center, missing the tips of two fingers.

14in (35.5cm) high

$300-400 **AST**

An early 20thC Kämmer & Reinhardt/Simon & Halbig bisque-head girl doll, with painted features, blonde wig, fully jointed composition body, head impressed with 'K * R' logo.

19in (48.5cm) high

$1,500-2,250 **AST**

An early 20thC Kämmer & Reinhardt/Simon & Halbig bisque-head doll, with sleeping eyes, open mouth with teeth, fully jointed composition body, impressed 'Simon & Halbig K * R', slight damage to fingers and toes.

28in (71.5cm) high

$750-900 **AST**

A Kämmer & Reinhardt Halbig bisque-head doll, with sleep eyes and an open mouth, inscribed '80'.

30.5in (77.5cm) high

$255-330 **POOK**

A German Käthe Kruse cloth doll, with fixed head with neck seam, three pate seams to rear of head, body and limbs comprised of several pieces of cloth, and shoes, faint markings to sole of feet (one reads 'Made in Germany').

16.5in (42cm) high

$1,800-2,250 **AST**

A Lambert bisque-headed musical automaton doll, the bisque arms moving with a fan in her right hand and a posy of flowers in her left, her head moving to the left and right, up and down to the flowers, standing on a box containing the movement, the head stamped in red 'Depose Tete Jumeau, Bte S.G.D.G. 4'.

21in (53.5cm) high

$5,250-6,000 **WW**

An early 20thC Schützmeister & Quendt bisque-head baby doll, with sleeping blue eyes with open mouth with teeth, light brown wig and composition body, with working voicebox, head impressed '201' followed by S&Q logo then 'Germany'.

16in (41cm) high

$350-300 **AST**

An early 20thC S.F.B.J. bisque-head girl doll, with sleeping blue eyes, open mouth with teeth and tongue, blonde wig, composition body, impressed 'SFBJ 230 PARIS'.

21in (53.5cm) high

$450-550 **AST**

An early 20thC French SFBJ (Société Française de Fabrication de Bébé & Jouets) girl doll, with sleeping blue eyes, with open mouth with teeth, with fully jointed composition body, impressed 'SFBJ Co Paris 6/0'.

12in (30.5cm) high

$450-600 **AST**

An early 20thC Simon & Halbig bisque-head doll, with sleeping brown eyes, open mouth with teeth, and pierced ears, fully jointed composition body, impressed '1078 Germany Simon & Halbig S & H 14'.

30in (76.5cm) high

$750-900 **AST**

A Simon and Halbig 1279 bisque-head character doll.

1899

$1,800-2,400 **HALL**

A Simon and Halbig bisque-head doll, with open-close and side-to-side eyes, open mouth and jointed composition body, stamped '126 50'.

21in (53cm) high

$280-360 **FLD**

A late 19th/early 20thC bisque shoulder-head doll, with leather body, fixed blue eyes and painted features.

13in (33cm) high

$2,250-3,000 **AST**

A late 19th/early 20thC bisque-head doll, with bisque shoulders and forearms and a soft-filled body, painted features and pierced ears, unmarked.

11in (28cm) high

$1,200-1,800 **AST**

Judith Picks: Dolls' house

Wouldn't I have loved a house like this when I was a child! This dolls' house was made in 1850 by Mr & Mrs Newton of Liverpool for their daughter Emma when she was 6 years old. Mr Newton, a lawyer, was a keen amateur carpenter and it was he who designed and made most of the furniture and the house itself. Mrs Newton meanwhile made all the furnishings and bedclothes. The dolls, china, utensils and some of the more elaborate furniture were 'mass' produced in Switzerland and Germany and were added to the dolls' house during family holidays abroad. Everything is to scale.

A mid-19thC dolls' house, carpeted and fully furnished with period furniture, with two dolls, one in a pushchair, and a small dog.
c1850 *48in (122cm) high*
$67,500-82,500 **CHOR**

An Edwardian dolls' house, the two doors painted as a mock-Tudor house, the interior with six rooms, the gable with a plaque inscribed 'MJ 1904'.
39.5in (100cm) high
$1,000-1,400 **SWO**

A Bliss paper litho dolls' house.
12.75in (32.5cm) high
$550-700 **POOK**

A Bliss paper-covered wood dolls' house, with furniture and accessories.
13.25in (34cm) high
$975-1,150 **POOK**

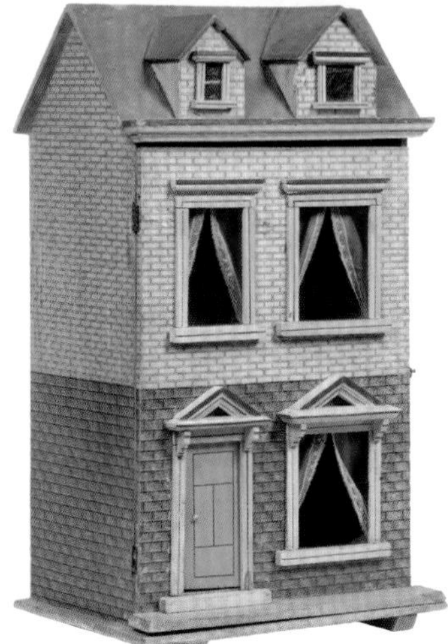

An early 20thC Moritz Gottschalk blue roof two-storey dolls' house, with brick-papered exterior enclosing two rooms, unfurnished.
21.75in (55cm) high
$600-900 **TEN**

ESSENTIAL REFERENCE - STEIFF BEAR

This is a rare and historically important bear. It's where it all began, well almost, as this is, to our knowledge, the oldest Steiff teddy bear design in existence. It incorporates the second type of limb ('rod jointing') that Steiff experimented with at the turn of the last century, and bears like this were only produced for a few years. Few survive today.

An original blond mohair Steiff five-ways rod-jointed bear with elephant button, with black shoebutton eyes, a shaved muzzle, a black hand-formed gutta percha nose.

15in (38cm) overall

$15,000-22,500 **JDJ**

A Steiff golden mohair bear, with replacement pads, missing ear button.

c1906 *24in (61cm) high*

$8,500-9,750 **BELL**

An early five-ways jointed white mohair Steiff bear with button, with pronounced back hump, long arms with curved felt paws and wrists, long narrow feet, with four claws on each paw, with working growler, with black shoebutton eyes, a trimmed muzzle a with small long trailing "F" button.

28in (71cm) high

$15,000-21,000 **JDJ**

A five-ways jointed white mohair Steiff teddy bear, with long arms, a pronounced back-hump, long narrow feet, light felt paw pads with four brown claws on each paw, with a non-working side squeaker, very light mohair thinning.

c1907 *15in (38cm) high*

$3,000-4,000 **JDJ**

A five-ways jointed Steiff bear with button, long arms, long narrow feet, and a pronounced back hump, with black shoebutton eyes, has small trailing 'F' button with working growler.

Provenance is particularly important when it comes to bears, particularly Steiffs. This bear comes with a photo of his original owners and a letter explaining his history.

c1910 *24in (61cm) high*

$22,500-30,000 **JDJ**

A rare, historically important black Steiff 'Titanic' mourning bear, with button, five-ways jointed with tan felt paw pads, solidly stuffed with excelsior, with non-working growler, professional restoration on the right paw pad.

Only 655 of these red backed eye bears were produced in response to the sinking of the Titanic in 1912 and only 78 were made in this size and mohair configuration. The red indicates crying and sadness at the tragedy.

12.5in (31cm) overall

$40,000-45,000 **JDJ**

An early Steiff clown-style rattle bear with button, five-ways jointed, with black button eyes.

The bear has a working rattle, which was made by inserting a tube filled with beads into his belly.
This item does not appear in the standard Steiff reference books.

c1912 *5in (13cm) high*

$9,000-10,500 **JDJ**

A five-ways jointed Steiff teddy bear, with oversized brown and black glass pupil eyes, hand-embroidered nose and mouth, and a slightly shorter mohair muzzle, retains long trailing 'F' Steiff button.

This amazing teddy bear design was produced because Richard Steiff, in a letter from America, insisted that Steiff bears, which had not changed significantly in design since their introduction at the turn of the last century, become more soft, colorful and warm, reflecting the culture of the time.

1925-30 *20in (50cm) high*

$13,500-18,000 JDJ

A Steiff brown-tipped teddy clown bear, five-ways jointed, with brown and black colored eyes, with original fabric clown ruff and hat, with his named, metal-rimmed chest tag, larger long trailing 'F' Steiff button and crisp and fully red, legible ear tag with working squeaker.

1926-30 *12in (28cm) high*

$30,000-38,000 JDJ

A brown-tipped blue-eyed five-jointed Steiff bear, with button and full ear tag, with wire-rimmed and posable ears, oversized eyes, traditional and distinctive center seam and facial construction, with long trailing 'F' button and legible red ear tag.

Steiff originally named 'Buschy', the name was later changed to 'Petsy', the baby bear. Overall 10,668 pieces were made through 1930.

16in (40cm) high

$20,000-24,000 JDJ

An early Steiff mid-size six-way jointed mohair cat, with button, fully posable, with green and black slit pupil eyes, and a few monofilament whiskers, with crisp fully legible white Steiff ear tag.

7.5in (19cm) high

$2,700-3,300 JDJ

A Steiff 'Fluffy' cat sitting on a pincushion, unjointed, with green and black glass pupil eyes, the bell is original but the bow is not, retains all of the original Steiff IDs.

1928-30 *7in (18cm) with pincushion*

$7,500-9,000 JDJ

A Steiff velvet cat pincushion, unjointed, with black shoebutton eyes, and monofilament whiskers, with trailing 'F' button.

This cat pincushion was made in this size only from 1902-18.

3.25in (8cm) wide

$6,000-7,500 JDJ

A Steiff 'Rabbiette' velvet doll, with mohair rabbit head, unjointed limbs, with black and brown pupil eyes, with all original IDs.

These 'play and care dolls' included 'Bulliette', the bulldog, and 'Fluffiette', the cat.

1927-32 *8in (20.5cm) high*

$1,800-2,250 JDJ

An early Steiff unjointed German Shepherd pull toy, on four regular green wooden wheels, no IDs, a finial is missing from one wheel.

1923-28 *11in (28cm) high*

$750-900 JDJ

A 1920s French CIJ Alfa Romeo P2 red large-scale pressed-steel racing car, stamped 'Made in France', some flaking to paint.

This is believed to be one of the first 1000 to be produced.

c1926 *21in (53cm) long*

$9,750-10,500 AST

A Buddy L pressed-steel bus.

28.5in (72.5cm) long

$1,800-2,250 POOK

A Hoge pressed-steel 'Popeye the Sailor' wind-up row boat.

17in (43cm) long

$4,000-4,500 POOK

A Buddy L pressed-steel 'Wrigley's Spearmint Chewing Gum International' delivery truck.

25in (63.5cm) long

$700-850 POOK

A cast-iron 'Boy on Trapeze' mechanical bank, manufactured by J. Barton and Smith Company.

8.75in (22.5cm) high

$750-900 POOK

A cast-iron 'Organ Grinder and Dancing Bear' mechanical bank, manufactured by Keyser & Rex.

5.25in (13.5cm) high

$1,800-2,250 POOK

A cast-iron 'Trick Pony' mechanical bank, manufactured by Shepard Hardware Co.

$850-975 POOK

A cast-iron 'Leap Frog' mechanical bank, manufactured by Shepard Hardware Co.

$850-975 POOK

A cast-iron 'Lion and Two Monkeys' mechanical bank, manufactured by Kyser & Rex.

$1,000-1,200 POOK

A cast-iron 'Indian Shooting Bear' mechanical bank, manufactured by J. & E. Stevens Co.

$750-900 POOK

A promotional tinplate model Citroen fixed-head coupé, replacement rear wheels.

12.75in (32cm) long

$550-600 **DN**

A German Distler Electromatic '7500 Porsche speedster' convertible, tinplate battery-operated model.

10in (25cm) long

$550-600 **AST**

A Burnett chauffeur-driven limousine.

$3,000-4,000 **RW**

A Burnett 'All Weather Bus' boxed tinplate toy.

$5,250-6,000 **RW**

A German tinplate 'Triumph' motorcycle with sidecar, rider and passenger, good to fair condition.

4.5in (11cm) long

$1,150-1,300 **AST**

A German tinplate 'Indian' motorcycle with sidecar and rider, good to fair condition.

4.5in (11.5cm) long

$850-975 **AST**

A tinplate 'Ibense' motorcycle with gun and soldier, in fair condition.

4in (10cm) long

$850-975 **AST**

A KiCo tin motorcycle, with a simulated 2-cylinder engine lithographed on the side panels, in good plus condition.

The lithography on this bike is much more finely detailed than on Distler or other tin motorcycles.

8in (20cm) long

$6,000-7,500 **JDJ**

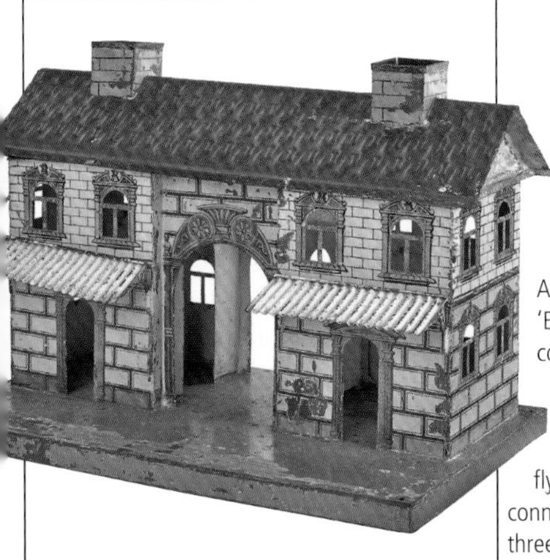

A pre-war Märklin painted tin train station.

9.75in (25cm) high

$400-550 **POOK**

A Märklin live steam 'Engine House', boiler room containing horizontal spirit fired boiler, and machine room with twin-fixed horizontal cylinder, single flywheel motor with governor connected to a line shaft with three wheels of differing sizes which could be connected through slots in the rear wall to external accessories, all original and unrestored.

20in (50cm)

$82,500-97,500 **VEC**

A rare Märklin tin freight station.

9.5in (24cm) high

$4,500-6,000 **POOK**

A German Lehmann No.640 'Zick-Zack' tinplate rocking vehicle, with two large wheels to either side, clockwork motor with fixed key to base, in original box, flaps to lid are missing.

1910-45

$1,800-2,250 **AST**

An Althof Bergmann tin clockwork carousel, with six painted gondolas and horses with riders.

20in (51cm) diam

$4,000-4,500 **POOK**

A Goodwin Walker carriage, with clockwork, the walking doll simulates a person walking, this is the patented linen head version, in the carriage is a parian style all bisque girl, not original to this toy.

patent date of 1867 *12in (30.5cm) long*

$750-900 **JDJ**

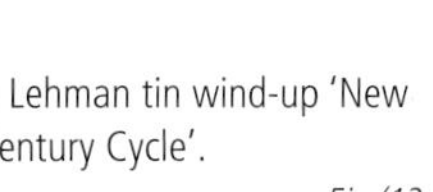

A Lehman tin wind-up 'New Century Cycle'.

5in (13cm) high

$450-550 **POOK**

A French Martin 'Le Joueur D'Orgue' tinplate clockwork organ grinder, in fair box, lacks the key and there is a rust mark to one trouser leg.

c1911 *9in (22.5cm) high*

$1,800-2,250 **AST**

A German Lehmann 790 'Nina the Cat' tinplate clockwork cat, with swaying head and tail, and mouse attached by rod, good condition.

produced 1927-41 *8.5in (21cm) long*

$750-900 **AST**

A Dinky 'Aston Martin DB3 Sports', (110), in near mint condition, good condition box.
$300-400 DN

A Dinky Supertoys 'Guy Flat Truck', (512), in blue box with applied label, showing some wear.
$120-180 W&W

A Dinky Supertoys 'Guy Van Slumberland', (514), blue boxed with applied label, with minor wear.
$180-225 W&W

A Dinky Supertoys 'Foden Flat Truck' with tailboard, (503), first type DG, in early style utility box with applied paper label, some age wear.
$225-300 W&W

A Dinky 'Guy Van Spratt's', (917), boxed, with some wear, the vehicle is in very good condition with minor chipping.
$450-550 W&W

A Dinky 'Mighty Antar with Transformer', (909), with plastic transformer load replacing the Centurion tank of the more familiar military version, boxed.
$300-400 W&W

A Tri-ang 'Spot-On Triumph TR3', (108), boxed, with paperwork, one outer end flap damaged, vehicle in mint condition.
$300-400 W&W

A Corgi Toys 'Citroen Safari Olympic Winter Sports', (475) '1964 Olympic Sports' decal to bonnet, with skier, four and four sticks, boxed with paperwork, in mint condition.
$225-300 WW

A Corgi Toys Special issue 1966 'R.A.C. International Rally B.M.C. Mini Cooper S', (333), box one end flap detached but present, vehicle very minor wear.
$200-280 W&W

A late 19thC carved and painted mechanical toy, 'The Dancers', with a hand crank which moves four pairs of couples, who rotate as a group and individually.

13in (33cm) high

$6,000-7,500 **POOK**

A German painted Noah's ark, with approximately sixty animals and figures.

c1900

22.5in (57cm) long

$1,000-1,500 **POOK**

A carved and painted pine mechanical acrobat toy, attributed to John Scholl (American 1827-1916), with eight figures operated by a hand crank pulley.

16.25in (41.5cm) high

$9,750-11,500 **POOK**

A Roullet & Decamps walking dog, with clockwork mechanism and original key, glass eyes, one wheel is jammed but otherwise in good condition.

9in (23cm) long

$900-1,200 **TEN**

An early 20thC composition Santa Claus candy container.

19.5in (49.5cm) high

$4,500-6,000 **POOK**

A composition mechanical Santa Claus, with feather tree and lantern.

25in (63.5cm) high

$4,500-6,000 **POOK**

An early 20thC carved wooden rocking horse, painted dapple gray, on a swing trestle base.

52in (132cm) wide

$400-450 **FLD**

A mid-20thC carved and painted dapple gray rocking horse, with some damage.

47.25in (120cm) high

$600-750 **DW**

A Staunton pattern boxwood and ebony chess set, in a mahogany box with sliding cover, white king stamped 'JAQUES LONDON', no label.

4in (10cm) high

$975-1,150 **WW**

A late 19thC Chinese lacquer games box, with chequer and backgammon boards, decorated with dragons, together with an associated part chess set and four bone dice.

16.75in (42cm) wide

$120-180 **WW**

A 19thC ivory Staunton pattern chess set, with a Chinese lacquer folding games board.

the king 3.5in (8.5cm) high

$750-1,000 **WW**

A late 19thC/early 20thC Staunton pattern ivory chess set in the manner of Jaques, in mahogany box.

the king 4.5in (11.5cm) high

$4,000-5,250 **WW**

A 19thC carved ivory chess set fitted in later mahogany case, attributed to George Merrifield.

13in (33cm) wide

$900-1,200 **CHEF**

An early 20thC oak-cased games compendium, the lid with chrome-plated bezique marker with red and white bone draughtsmen, counters and games markers, the compartments behind with Staunton bone chess set, dominoes and six lead racehorses.

13.5in (34cm) high

$550-700 **CHEF**

A 19thC Bermudan cedarwood chess box by J. H. Jackson, in the form of a book, the part leather-gilt tooled spine inscribed 'Bermuda Cedar Three Shades, J. H. Jackson cabinet maker Bermuda, 1854', with a drawer with divisions.

J. H. Jackson was a cabinet maker in Bermuda during the middle of the 19thC. His furniture can be found in various houses on the island, for example he made all the dining room furniture and the cedar panelling for Camden House.

16.25in (41.5cm) wide

$2,250-3,000 **WW**

A late 19thC Chinese carved ivory part chess set.

16.25in (41.5cm) wide

$2,250-3,000 **WW**

A Samuel M. Stewart Philadelphia full deck of playing cards, including the ace of spades, which is the maker's identifying card, with the original case.

c1835

$6,000-7,500 **POOK**

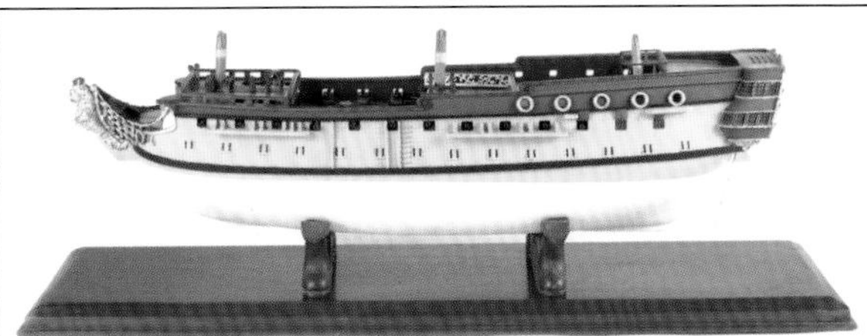

An early 18thC planked-and-framed model of a sixty-gun man-of-war, with a carved crowned lion figurehead, the bronze cannon on carriages, has been restored.

c1730 *27in (68.5cm) long*

$1,400-1,800 **WW**

A 1:64 scale model, for an 18thC sixth rate of the Royal Navy, with planked and pinned hull, finely carved unicorn and warrior figurehead, semi-planked decks revealing 'tween decks and great cabin.

33in (84cm) long the case 37.75in (96cm) long

$2,250-3,000 **CM**

ESSENTIAL REFERENCE - 'FIFTH RATE'

The name ship of a new class of 18-pounder 'fifth rate' designed by Sir William Rule in 1799, 'Lively' was the prototype of what soon came to be regarded as the most successful frigate design; a further fifteen were ordered for the fleet between 1803 and 1812. She was measured at 1,075 tons and was 154 feet long with a 39 foot beam. She mounted 38 guns. Launched in 1804, she was commissioned under Captain Graham Hamond. First in action off Cadiz on 5th October 1804, she - in company with three other frigates, 'Indefatigable', 'Medusa' and 'Amphion', captured a Spanish 'treasure fleet' of four frigates (although one was sunk) whose cargo netted almost one million pounds sterling when it was sold back at home. 'Lively' was wrecked in 1810 when she ran ashore near St. Paul's Bay, Malta, due to the incompetence of her Master, Michael Richard.

A 1:48 scale Admiralty Board frame model, probably for the 'Lively' class 38-gun frigate, c1800 constructed in steamed boxwood with pinned stringing, with a contemporary case.

45.5in (115.5cm) wide

$60,000-67,500 **CM**

A builder's model of the 'Mauretania', 1:64 scale for the famed 'North Atlantic Greyhound', built for Cunard by Swan Hunter & Wigham Richardson, Tyne and Wear, carved from laminated wood,with gilt and painted fittings and superstructure and finished in Cunard service livery, within modern two-part case.

1906 *157.5in (400cm) long*

$255,000-300,000 **CM**

A builder's-style model of the ill-fated submarine 'H.M.S. M1', modeled by D. Simpson.

M1's most distinctive feature was the massive single 12 in. gun mounted forward of her conning tower. This was to prove to be her Achilles heel as it had to be loaded when the vessel was surfaced and fired when partially submerged. On 12th November 1925 the keel of the Swedish vessel S.S. Vidar passed over her, knocking the gun turret off . She sank quickly taking with her the entire crew of 69.

1917 *64in (162.5cm) long*

$3,000-4,000 **CM**

A 1920 builder's dockyard model of the Ellerman Lines 'S.S. City of Adelaide', built by Gray of Sunderland.

71.25in (181cm) long

$13,500-16,500 **CM**

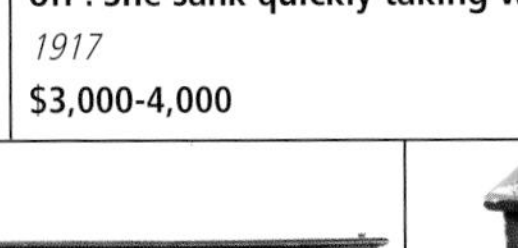

A 1921 builder's model for the 'S.S. Pencarrow', built by Irvine Shipbuilding, West Hartlepool for R.B. Chellew.

84in (213.5cm) long

$9,000-12,000 **CM**

A cut-away model of the Continental-built iron cruiser 'Scuta'.

28in (71cm) long

$210-280 **DN**

A 19thC prisoner-of-war bone ship model, in a glazed gilt metal case.

7in (18cm) high

$1,500-2,250 **L&T**

An early 19thC French Napoleonic prisoner-of-war-style bone model, for a 74-gun ship, the 6in (15.5cm) hull planked and pinned with ebony main and secondary wales, female form figurehead, oxidised-brass guns with red port lids, bound masts with yards and s'tuns'l booms, standing and running rigging, mounted on bone supports.

12.5in (32cm) long

$4,000-4,500 **CM**

An early 19thC French Napoleonic prisoner-of-war bone model, for a 74-gun ship, the 6.5in (16.5cm) planked and pinned hull with baleen main and secondary wale, brass guns with red painted port lids, warrior form figurehead, extensive deck details, mounted on bone stands.

14.5in (37cm) long

$11,500-14,500 **CM**

A French prisoner-of-war-style bone and baleen model, of the 74-gun ship 'Bellerophon', the planked and pinned hull with brass cannon, ornately carved figurehead, stern and quarter lights, mounted on a planked bone and baleen base.

27in (68.5cm) long

$22,500-27,000 **CM**

An early 19thC French Napoleonic prisoner-of-war bone model, of the 74-gun frigate 'Le Brave', with 7in (18cm) planked and pinned hull, protruding brass guns with red port lids, polychrome and gilt warrior figurehead, within later display base with glazed dome.

14in (35.5cm) long

$7,500-9,000 **CM**

An early 19thC French Napoleonic prisoner-of-war bone model, of the 4th-rate 50-gun ship 'Jupiter', the 15in (38cm) planked and pinned hull with baleen main and secondary wales, bulwark capping and central deck strake, retractable brass guns with red-painted muzzles, finely carved bone figurehead, extensive deck fittings, mounted on wooden brackets.

This Jupiter was built and launched by John Randall at Rotherhithe in 1778. In October 1799 she was in action with the 36-gun La Preneuse in the Indian Ocean and served as Admiral Sir Roger Curtis's flagship in the East Indies for several years. She was under the command of Capt. Harry Baker en route for the East Indies when, attempting to anchor near the harbour at Vigo Bay, Spain, she hit a reef. After two days, during which the stores were saved, she was abandoned as a wreck on the 10th December, 1808.

model 28in (71cm) long

$37,500-45,000 **CM**

A Napoleonic prisoner-of-war bone hull of a warship, figure head and stern cabin windows, with 63 guns, on later mahogany plinth, 2 guns missing, once with three masts.

24.25in (61.5cm) wide

$15,000-18,000 **CHEF**

An early 19thC French prisoner-of-war bone and baleen model, of a 90 gun ship of the line, fully rigged with pinned and planked hull and brass cannon, on a straw-work marquetry base within a glazed and brass case.

9.25in (23.3cm) wide

$3,000-4,000 **WW**

An American Flyer wide gauge 1927 'President's Edition' train set, to include a no.4687 Engine, an Annapolis observation car, a West Point passenger car, and a United States mail car, with the original boxes, five sections of track, and a 1927 catalog.

$3,300-4,500 **POOK**

A Bassett-Lowke 'O' gauge Stanier class 4P 2-cylinder 2-6-4T locomotive, an 8-volt DC 3-rail electric example, RN 2603, in LMS lined black livery, with vacuum pipes, drop link couplings, tank vents, hand-rails, sprung buffers.

$1,500-2,100 **W&W**

A live steam Bassett-Lowke L.M.S. Mogul 2-6-0 tender locomotive, 2945, spirit-fired, unboxed.

$400-450 **DN**

A Bing for Bassett-Lowke L.M.S. Precursor 4-4-0 tender locomotive 'George the Fifth', 5320, clockwork motor, unboxed.

$400-450 **DN**

CLOSER LOOK - BASSETT LOWKE TRAIN

A wonderful example in fabulous, all original pristine condition.

The finish is vibrant and shows virtually no sign of wear.

The box is in excellent condition and even has the original tissue paper and the corrugated cardboard wrap (very desirable to collectors).

It is in very fine overall mechanical condition.

An O Gauge Bassett Lowke 'Flying Scotsman'.

20.5in (52cm) long

$1,500-2,250 **JDJ**

A Carette for Bassett-Lowke L.N.W.R. twelve-wheeled Dining Saloon, No.13210, unboxed.

$280-340 **DN**

A live steam Bing L.N.W.R. 2-2-0 tender locomotive, 0/35, spirit-fired, unboxed.

$450-550 **DN**

A 1902 Bing L.N.W.R. 2-4-0 tender locomotive 'King Edward VII', clockwork motor, with a Bing L.N.W.R. first class coach, both unboxed.

$975-1,150 DN

A Hornby LMS Princess Royal class 4-6-2 tender locomotive, 3-rail 20 volt electric, 'Princess Elizabeth', RN 6201, with vacuum pipes, safety valves, LMS hooter, in original wooden presentation case, worn but sound.

$2,250-3,000 W&W

A Lionel standard gauge four-piece train set, to include a no.408E Engine, a parlor car, an observation car, and a dining car.

$1,500-2,100 POOK

A Marklin G.W.R. 4-6-2 tender locomotive 'The Great Bear', 111, with clockwork motor and restored lined green livery, unboxed.

Literature: Levy, Allen. A Century of Model Trains , New Cavendish, London c.1978, pp.64-65, which pictures the clockwork model alongside live steam and electrically powered versions.

$1,800-2,250 DN

A Marklin 4-4-0 tender locomotive, 1040, with lined black livery and clockwork motor, unboxed.

$300-450 DN

A Marklin Gauge 1 High Voltage 0-4-0 locomotive, silver steam dome and streamlined front, with two lamps, with Marklin monogram and '110-220 Volts Lampenvorschaltung', one lamp missing, cab roof a little misshaped.

$1,150-1,300 TEN

A large-scale live steam locomotive and tender, in a 4-2-2 configuration boiler emblazoned '147' on front, highly detailed cowcatcher, rails, various steam gauges, with some missing pieces.

33in (84cm)

$1,500-2,250 JDJ

An outstanding large electric ride-on train, in wood, steel, iron and brass consists of 4-4-0 locomotive, with some missing parts.

This has crossover appeal to Folk Art collectors.

33in (84cm) long

$1,800-2,400 JDJ

A George Cohen No.2 'Stan's XI' jersey, from the 'Stanley Matthews Farewell Match' played at Stoke City's Victoria Ground v an 'International XI' 28th April 1965, with the match program, and a Stanley Matthews-signed dinner menu for the centenary of the Sports Argus in 1997.

$2,250-3,000 **GBA**

A late 19thC leather football, with eight panels, leather lacing.

$2,400-3,000 **GBA**

An FA Cup semi-final program, 1929 Aston Villa v Portsmouth, played at Highbury 23rd March.

1929

$850-975 **MM**

An Argentina v England program, played at the River Plate Stadium in Buenos Aires 17th May 1953, also covering the Argentinian F.A. XI v The Football Association XI 14th May.

The England game was suspended after 23 minutes and then abandoned due to heavy rain waterlogging the pitch.

1953

$900-1,200 **GBA**

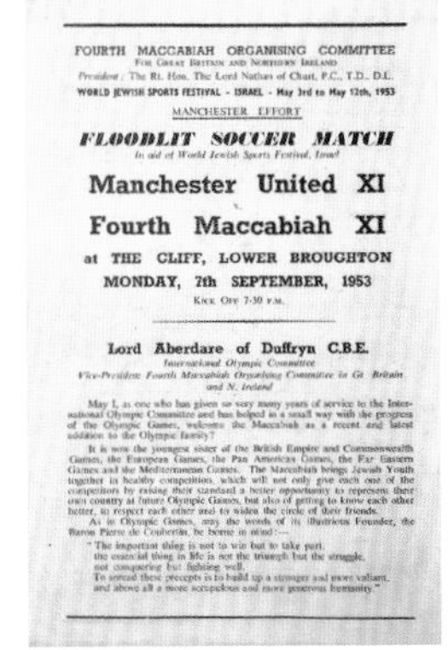

A Manchester United v Fourth Maccabiah XI football program, dated Monday 7 September 1953. played at The Cliff Lower Broughton Salford, kick-off 7.30pm.

The match was to raise funds for the Jewish Sports Festival Israel.

1953

$2,700-3,300 **MM**

A Brazilian national flag, signed by the 1970 World Cup winning squad, signatures in red felt tip pen, now quite faded, including Pele, Carlos Alberto, Piaza, Clodoaldo, Tostao, Jairzinho, Dario and Zagallo, framed.

41in (104cm) wide

$1,800-2,250 **GBA**

An official FIGC Report for the 1934 World Cup in Italy, Coppa Del Mondo, Cronistoria Del II Campionato Mondiale Di Calcio, published by the Federazione Italiana Giuoco Del Calcio, 232 pages, numerous illustrations, original pictorial wrappers.

$5,250-6,000 **GBA**

Judith Picks: 1953 FA Cup Medal

Although not a great football fan even I am impressed with this! In Coronation Year of 1953 and after 21 years as a professional footballer, Stanley Matthews finally won the F.A. Cup medal that had eluded him for so long. After a dramatic match in which Blackpool defeated Bolton Wanderers 4-3, Stanley Matthews was presented with this, the most fabled medal in the long and romantic history of the Football Association Challenge Cup by Her Majesty The Queen. Twice in three years (1948 and 1951) Matthews was on the losing side in classic final encounters, and with 55 minutes of the 1953 final elapsed, Bolton were 3-1 ahead. Then the 100,000 crowd packed into Wembley, with countless more at home witnessed the 'Wizard of Dribble' turn the game around with a vintage right- wing display. First, an outswinging center to the far post deceived the Bolton keeper, Hanson, whose fumbled catch dropped in the path of Stan Mortensen to score. With a minute of the game left, yet another Matthews' center found Mudie, who was fouled close to the penalty box. From a rehearsed free kick routine, Mortensen rescued the game for Blackpool crashing home the equaliser. In injury time Matthews embarked on another run, and with a trademark jink to the outside and a cut to the inside he fooled Banks, rolled the ball past Barrass, and crossed for Perry to score a last- gasp winner. The world's most famous footballer playing on the game's most famous stage had his medal.

Top: A signed photograph of Sir Stanley Matthews, Matthews being held aloft by his Blackpool team mates and holding his elusive FA Cup Winner's medal in 1953.

19in (49cm) wide

$300-400 GBA

Bottom: A Stanley Matthews's 1953 F.A. Cup Final winner's medal, in 9ct. gold, the reverse inscribed THE FOOTBALL ASSOCIATION, CHALLENGE CUP, WINNERS, in original case.

$375,000-450,000 GBA

A 9ct. gold Football Association England v Wales 1919 Victory International medal, inscribed 'THE FOOTBALL ASSOCIATION, ENGLAND v WALES, 1919, VICTORY INTERNATIONAL'.

$2,250-3,000 GBA

A 9ct. gold 1921-22 Football League Division Two Championship medal awarded to Sam Hardy of Nottingham Forest, inscribed 'THE FOOTBALL LEAGUE, CHAMPIONS, DIVISION 2, WINNERS, 1921-22', 'NOTTm. FOREST F.C., S. HARDY'

$1,800-2,250 GBA

A 1960 FA Cup Winner 9ct Gold Medal, embossed R Mason Wolves, in the original Fattorini case.

$4,500-6,000 MM

A silver medal, awarded by the Uruguayan Football Association to the 1930 World Cup winning footballer Ernesto Mascheroni.

1930

$4,000-4,500 GBA

A winner's prize medal from the first modern Olympic Games, at Athens in 1896, designed by Jules Chaplain, signed, struck in silver for first place, the inscription translated from the Greek reads 'INTERNATIONAL OLYMPIC GAMES, ATHENS, 1896'.

1896

$300,000-375,000 GBA

A St Louis Olympic Games athlete's participation medal, by Dieges & Clust, New York, the obverse with a naked athlete, the reverse with shields of St Louis, France & USA.

The version of this medal has a loop at the top and was worn as a badge with the medal hanging from a ribbon. The medal has no traces of a loop being removed, therefore presented to a participating athlete.

$21,000-27,000 GBA

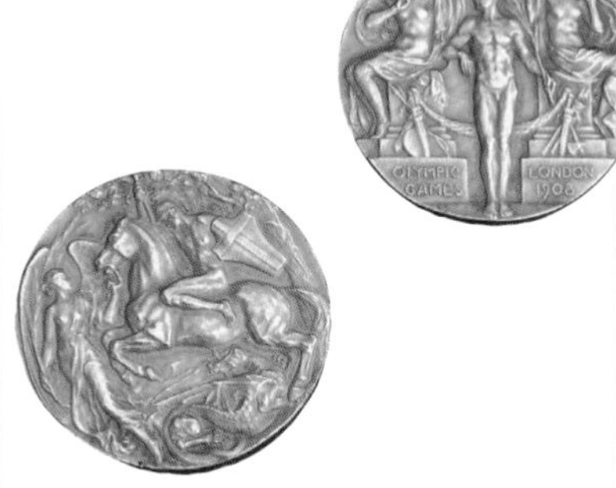

A London Olympic Games 15ct gold rowing prizewinner's medal, by Vaughton & Sons, engraved 'WINNER EIGHT-OARED RACE', in original case from Vaughton.

1908 *1.5in (3.5cm) diam 1ox*

The winning eight at the 1908 Olympics was a crew from Leander Rowing Club.

$13,500-16,500 FELL

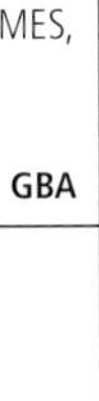

A London Olympic Games gold winner's medal, presented to Patrick Brennan, captain of the Canadian lacrosse team, designed by Bertram MacKennal.

This was lacrosse's second and final appearance at an Olympic Games following its introduction at St Louis in 1904. After South Africa's withdrawl, just Great Britain and Canada competed in the gold medal match.

1908

$21,000-27,000 GBA

An Olympic Games judge's badge, by Vaughton of Birmingham, in silvered bronze with the head of Athena, encirled by a blue enamel band inscribed 'OLYMPIC GAMES, LONDON 1908, COMMITTEE', pin fitting.

1908 *2.25in (6cm) diam*

$3,300-4,000 GBA

An Antwerp Olympic Games silver prize medal, awarded to British tennis player Winifred Geraldine Beamish, designed by Josue Dupon, inscribed 'RUNNERS-UP, LADIES' DOUBLES, MRS. A.E. BEAMISH (AND MISS E.D. HOLMAN)'.

1920

$8,500-9,000 GBA

A Paris Olympic Games gold-plated silver first place winner's medal, designed by Andre Rivaud, struck by the Paris Mint in an edition of 304.

Owned by the Norwegian fencer Raoul Heide who competed in the individual epee events at the 1924 Paris & 1928 Amsterdam Olympic Games. A collector, he did not win this medal.

1924

$30,000-38,000 GBA

A Garmisch-Partenkirchen Winter Olympic Game gold-plated silver first place winner's medal, designed by Richard Klein, struck by Deschler, Muenchen, Victory with a laurel leaf, riding in a triga, bobsled, ski, ice hockey stick and skate below, in case with Olympic Rings on the lid.

The largest Olympic winner's medal awarded ever, and one of only 36 awarded at the Games.

1936

$52,500-60,000 GBA

An extremely rare Squaw Valley 1960 Winter Olympic Games gold winner's prize medal, awarded to Helga Haase, representing the Unified Germany team in the women's 500m speed skating.

The first Olympic gold medal awarded to a woman for speed skating. One of only 50 awarded.

$90,000-97,500 GBA

ESSENTIAL REFERENCE - OLYMPIC BOBSLEIGH

Bobsledding was still a fairly young sport in 1924, having been invented in the late 19thC. The International Federation for Bobsleigh and Tobogganing (FIBT) was founded on 23 November 1923 just months before the inaugural Winter Olympic Games. The Olympics were the first major international championship in the sport, as World Championships were only established in 1930. The track at Chamonix ran for a length of 1,370 meters, starting at an altitude of 1210m and finishing at 1054m above sea level. The quality of the course was considered to be quite low and it moreover proved to be dangerous, three of the nine teams crashing. The only event was the men's 4-man bob although curiously rules at the time allowed a 5th rider. Switzerland I took gold from Great Britain II with Belgium I collecting bronze. France II finished fourth. France I, interestingly, crashed out on run 2, but evidently were allowed to complete the 3rd & 4th runs even though their subsequent times would have no count in final placings.

A Bobsleigh, used by the French team at the first Winter Olympic Games at Chamonix in 1924, a depiction of a dolphin and inscribed 'DAUPHIN', steering wheel front foot and rear hand brakes still operational, canvas seat with areas of damage, central side struts are missing, runners still in tact.

10.5in (27cm) long.

$7,500-9,000 **GBA**

A rare Cortina 1956 Winter Olympic Games bearer's torch, in superb condition complete with burner containing an unlit wick, based on Ralph Lavers's aluminum alloy pierced bowl with legend design first used at the London 1948 Summer Games, with a printed photograph of a torch being held aloft at the Opening Ceremony.

It is unrecorded how many torches were used during the 1956 Winter Games but they rarely appear and must have been quite limited in numbers.

$21,000-27,000 **GBA**

A St Louis 1904 Olympic Games bronze prize medal, won by Robert Stangland of the USA in the Running Broad Jump [Long Jump], by Dieges & Clust, New York, in original maroon leather case, inscribed gilt 'MEDAL FOR OLYMPIC GAMES UNIVERSAL EXPOSITION, ST. LOUIS U.S.A., F.J.V. SKIFF, DIR. OF EXHIBITS, JAS. E. SULLIVAN, CHIEF'.

Robert Stangland (1881-1953) was born in Kendall, New York. He won the bronze in the long jump with a mark of 6.88 metres. He also won bronze in the Triple Jump.

$30,000-38,000 **GBA**

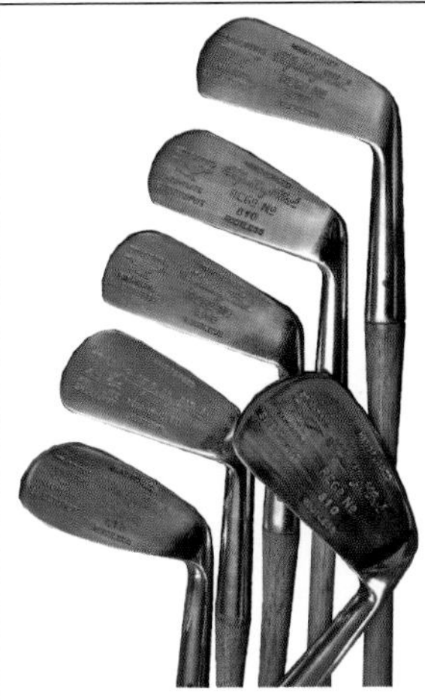

A matching set of 6 Spalding Kro-Flite 'Sweetspot' polished rustless irons, regd no 810, numbers 2 3 4 5 6 and 7 fitted with the original full length leather grips.

$600-750 MM

A Dunlop 'Caddie' papier-mâché golf ball advertising figure, inscribed to 2 panels 'We Play Dunlop', with the original ply-board base retaining 6/6 original clubs.

16in (40.6cm) high

$1,150-1,300 MM

A Bromford Man papier-mâché advertising golfing figure, inscribed 'He Played a Bromford', some knocks and damage.

c1925 *20.5in (52cm) high*

$900-1,000 MM

A Giant Dunlop 65 Golf Ball shop counter display, the base reads 'You'll do better with Dunlop', some paint wear.

19in 48cm) high

$1,000-1,200 MM

A rare Silver King square mesh dimple golf ball shop counter display, the papier mache golf ball standing its own removable tee stand, which reads 'Silver King – The Consistent Golf Ball'.

11.5in (29cm) high

$3,000-4,000 MM

A silver trophy holder, with a silver pedestal golf ball holder with sliding lever to reveal the Penfold golf ball, engraved 'The Ball used last 6 holes-Roehampton Tournament 1935 by Archie Compston and Presented to Miss Priscilla Kidston', hallmarked Birmingham.

1935 *4.25in (10.8cm) high*

$600-700 MM

A Copeland Late Spode golfing teapot, with golfers in white relief in the round, printed and impressed with the maker's mark and 'Rd. no345322'.

c1910

$700-850 MM

A rare Bobby Jones, Open Golf Champion, signature, signed in ink 'Robert T Jones Jnr' on large album page.

$1,400-1,700 MM

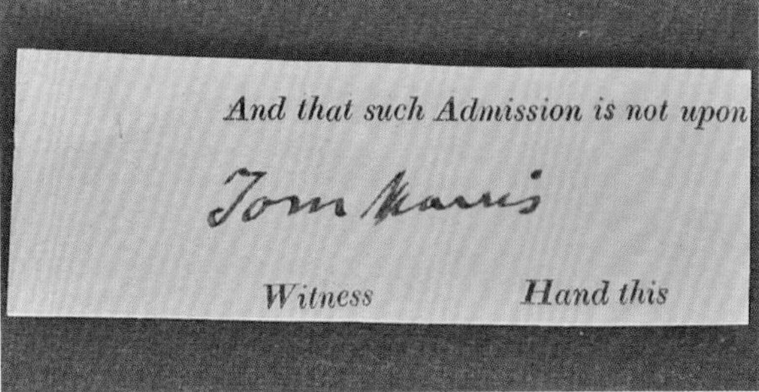

A rare Tom Morris St Andrews signature, the founding father of golf signed in ink on clipped legal document.

$1,300-1,450 MM

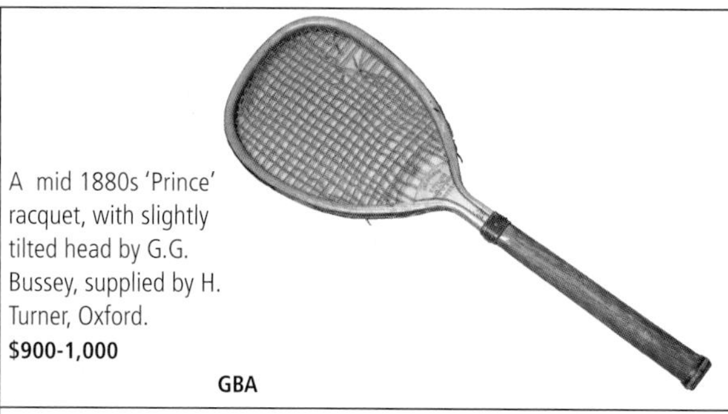

A mid 1880s 'Prince' racquet, with slightly tilted head by G.G. Bussey, supplied by H. Turner, Oxford.

$900-1,000 GBA

A bulbous tapered wooden handle tennis racket, stamped 'The Club' to the convex wedge.

$600-750 MM

The squash racquet, used by Jahangir Khan when winning the 1983 British Open Championship.

This was the second of Jahangir Khan's sequence of ten consecutive victories in the British Open Championship between 1982 and 1991.

$750-900 GBA

A Steffi Graf tennis racquet, used at a French Open, a Wilson ProStaff 7.1 Flat Beam racquet, broken stringing.

With a publicity card signed by Steffi Graf and with a hand written note that translates from the German as 'congratulations to the racquet that helped me at the French Open'.

$1,500-2,100 GBA

A Fred Perry Tennis Tournament 9ct Gold Medal, Bournemouth Lawn Tennis Hard Court Championships of Gt Britain Men's doubles winners gold medal, won by Fred Perry and J S Oliff.

$1,200-1,400 MM

A silver tennis trophy, 'The North London Hard Court Lawn Tennis Club Gentleman's Open Singles Championship' 'Spring Meeting Silver Trophy' engraved with the winners names from 1923-39, hallmarked Sheffield, with makers 'F&F' mark.

1922 *overall 7in (17.8cm) high 17oz*

$750-900 MM

A cast-iron Victorian 'Automatic Tennis Ball Cleaner', manufactured by 'H. J. Gray & Sons Ltd. Cambridge.'

It has a drum inside with brushes providing an abrasive surface to clean lawn tennis balls. The balls are inserted via an aperture at the top, the side handle is turned and the balls are pulled through the mechanism. They are ejected from the apparatus through a small sliding trap door beneath. The idea was patented by John Osmond of Clifton Kent on 30th November 1887.

13.8in (35cm) high

$750-900 MM

A Michael Schumacher 2006 British Grand Prix worn Ferrari racesuit.

This suit was worn at the British GP where reigning World Champion Michael Schumacher managed to beat his eventual Ferrari successor, Kimi Raikkonen, to 2nd place, albeit 13 seconds behind the Renault of Fernando Alonso.

$19,500-24,000 GBA

A Fernando Alonso 2006 San Marino Grand Prix worn Renault racesuit.

$9,000-12,000 GBA

A rare silver cricket trophy, inscribed 'Presented to – ALFRED SHAW – Burton Joyce Notts – for his unprecedented bowling 1875'.

Undoubtedly the trophy was awarded when he achieved his most outstanding bowling figures playing for Notts against v MCC when he returned bowling figures 41.2 overs 36 maidens and taking seven wickets for only 7 runs.

9.5in (24cm) high 19 oz

$9,750-10,500 MM

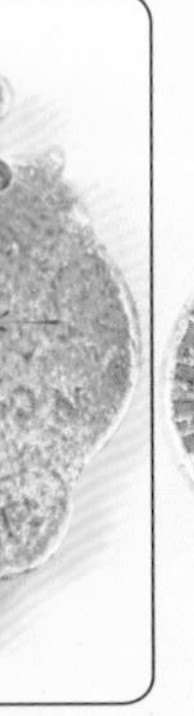

An Australia signed cricket bat, including D Bradman, W Brown, W Ponsford, S McCabe, W Woodfull, L Darling, A Chipperfield, C Grimmett, W O'Reilly, T Wall, A Kippax, B Barnett and L Fleetwood-Smith plus CB Fry and A Mailey altogether 15 signatures, the bat is stamped 'The Boundary Driver' 'Treble Spring' and by the maker Fred Milner, Harrogate.

1934

$750-900 MM

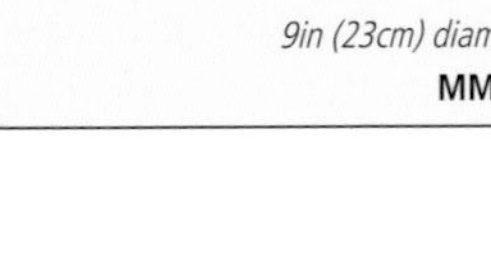

A W. G. Grace Coalport commemorative bone china plate, the front with W. G. Grace portrait, on the reverse inscribed 'In Commemoration of Dr W G Grace's Century of Centuries 1866-1895' also 'X1662', 3 small hairline cracks.

c1895 *9in (23cm) diam*

$600-750 MM

A 1905 Warrington Rugby Club 15ct gold and enamel Challenge Cup medal, inscribed 'LANCASHIRE CHESHIRE YORKSHIRE', the reverse inscribed 'Winners 1904-5 Warrington F.C. J.W. Harmer'.

This medal was awarded for Warrington rugby club's first Challenge Cup triumph in 1905. Warrington were part of the Northern Union 1895-1922 and in 1905 they made their third Challenge cup final appearance, this time winning it, a 6-0 victory over Hull Kingston Rovers before a 19,638 crowd at Headingley.

1.25in (3cm) high

$1,500-2,100 APAR

A pair of fight worn Henry Cooper Lonsdale boxing gloves, signed by Cooper and Ali, also have a faint Muhammad Ali '79 signature.

$750-900 MM

A case of five perch, inscribed 'Caught by F. Britton at Fordingbridge, Feb 3rd 1922', labeled 'Preserved by J Cooper & Sons, 28 Radnor Street, St. Lukes, London EC…'.

30in (76cm) wide

$3,300-4,400 SWO

A mirror carp stuffed and mounted, in a bow-front case.

32in (81.5cm) wide

$850-975 SWO

A mid-20thC char, set in a naturalistic setting in a bow-fronted case, caught on Lake Windermere.

25in (64cm) wide

$300-400 SWO

A carp, by J Cooper of London, gilt text reads 'Carp caught by Captain F.B. Grant at Staines, 1898'.

28in (71.5cm) wide (weight 7lb 2oz)

$1,300-1,450 SWO

An Angi maternity figure, seated on a twin support stool, holding her left breast and with an infant on her lap.

18in (46cm) high

$4,400-5,100 **WW**

A pre-1920 Kwaku Bempah (father of Osei Bonsu) Ashanti maternity figure, with the child on her back, on a later wood stand.

18in (46cm) high

$4,000-4,500 **WW**

A Bambara doll, with remains of fabric, studs removed, mounted on a wood block.

15.25in (39cm) high

$1,800-2,250 **WW**

A Baule 'Goli' mask, with a red face with black border and horns.

14in (35.5cm) high

$1,200-1,500 **WW**

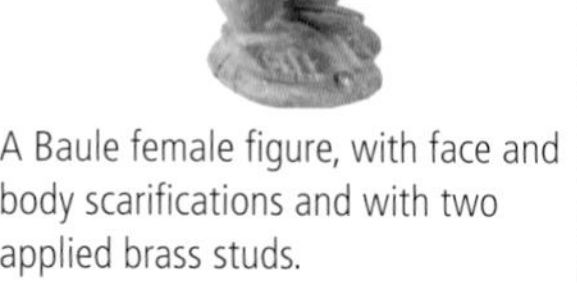

A Baule female figure, with face and body scarifications and with two applied brass studs.

17in (43cm) high

$1,500-2,100 **WW**

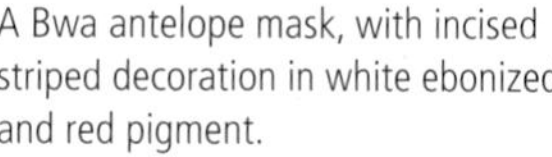

A Bwa antelope mask, with incised striped decoration in white ebonized and red pigment.

19.75in (50cm) high

$400-550 **WW**

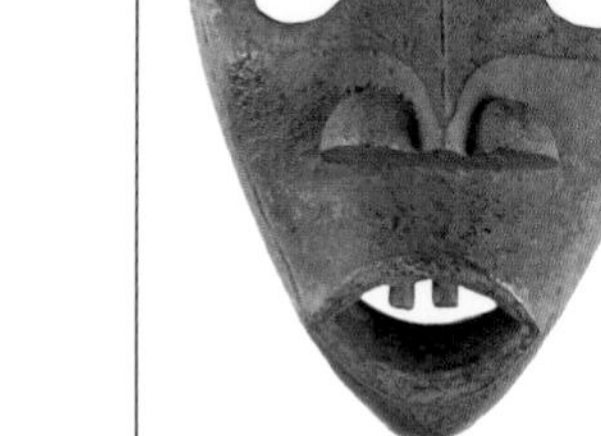

A Dan mask, with crusty patination.

12.5in (31.5cm) high

$700-850 **WW**

A Fang Mabea figure.

26.5in (67cm)

$5,250,000+ **SOTH**

A Guro heddle pulley.

7.75in (20cm) high

$1,300-1,450 **WW**

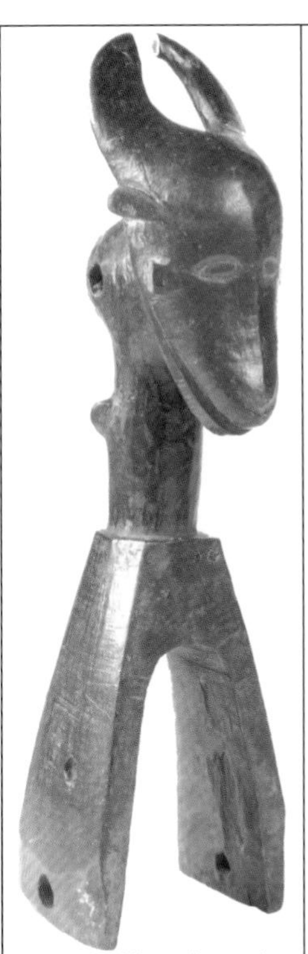

A Guro heddle pulley, with three raised notches to back of neck.

8.75in (22.5cm) high

$600-750 **WW**

An Ibo patinated and painted wood female figure.

56.75in (144cm) high

$6,000-7,500 **L&T**

A possibly Mambile Northern Nigeria male figure, the eyes with nails to an open mouth with tongue, on a later stand, the head has termite damage and the front section of one foot is missing.

16.5in (42cm) high

$2,100-2,700 **WW**

A Mumuye or Chanba male figure, dark patination with losses to his right leg, on a later square stand.

19in (48cm) high

$1,800-2,250 **WW**

A Mumuye figure, notched rectangular ears and scarification to face, long neck, angled torso and arms, on a later stand.

33.5in (85cm) high

$3,000-4,000 **WW**

A Wazaremo ebony maternity figure, with an infant on her back and wearing a loin cloth, on a later stand, the feet are damaged.

13in (33cm) high

$1,700-2,100 **WW**

A Yoruba Ibeji female twin figure, by Abegunde of Ede or his son, with five-point coiffure with blue pigment, scarifications to the face, bead necklace.

10.5in (26.5cm) high

$2,250-3,000 **WW**

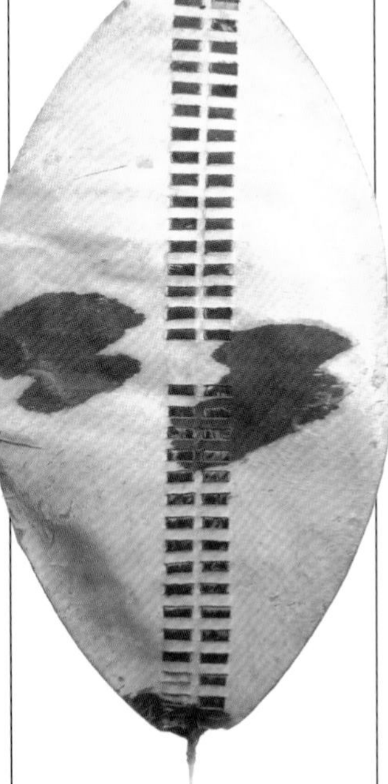

A Zulu hide shield, the reverse inscribed 'S. Reel and D.Huxley'.

58in (147.5cm) high

$1,800-2,250 **WW**

A Zulu/Tsonga carved wood staff.

37.25in (94.5cm) high

$2,250-3,000 **L&T**

A figure holding a child, in stone, by Mathew Aquigaaq (1940-2010), Baker Lake, signed in syllabics.

13in (33cm)

$4,500-6,000 WAD

A hawk, in stone, by Kenojuak Ashevak (1927-2013), E7-1035, Cape Dorset.

c1970 14.5in (37cm)

$4,000-4,500 WAD

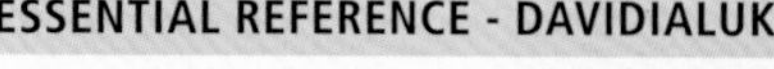

ESSENTIAL REFERENCE - DAVIDIALUK

"Born in 1910, Davidialuk – hunter, raconteur and artist – has lived intimately with the land all his life. By image and word, the memories of everyday events experienced by the hunter of yesterday are the stuff of his creativity. Nothing is too small or unworthy of notice. Pre-eminently, his themes dwell on survival: of man in conflict with man; man in conflict with animal; man in conflict with nature; woman's despair at the loss of her mate; and awe of the supernatural. Little of the tranquil is considered – nature and man seldom rest. Hand-in-hand with personal myth-making, he recalls the common legends of the people: the northern lights that decapitate him who whistles at them: the eagle and his human wife; the giant kayakman who strides the land, dwarfing the people; the spirit Katyutayuuq in the shape of a human head with breasted cheeks and vagina-clefted chin who propels herself on cloven feet; and not least the ubiquitous sea-woman simply described by Davidialuk as 'half-fish'. As the animals share with man the same problems of survival, Davidialuk presents them also in conflict or stress." From 'Davidialuk of Povungnituk: Myth Maker'.

Stone figures on a sleeping platform, by Davidialuk Alasua Amittu (1910-1976), E9-824, Povungnituk.

19in (48.5cm)

$37,500-45,000 WAD

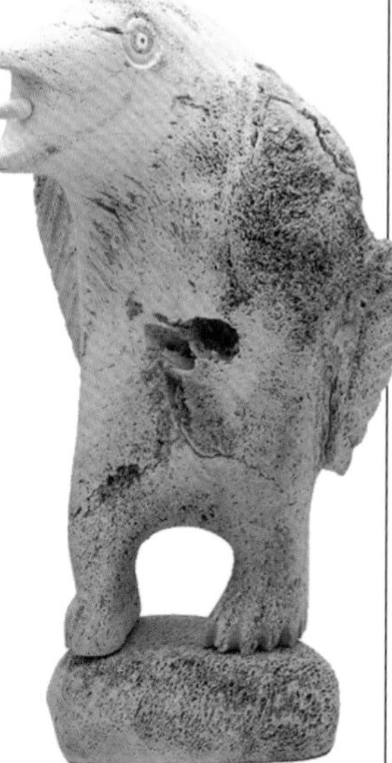

A bird guarding a nest of eggs, in bone, by Karoo Ashevak (1940-1974), E4-196, Spence Bay, signed in syllabics.

17.75in (45cm) high

$30,000-38,000 WAD

A lolling frog and shaman mask, in wood and skin, by Dempsey Bob (1948-), signed in Roman.

1981 13.5in (35cm)

$12,000-13,500 WAD

A polar bear, in stone, by Henry Evaluardjuk (1923-2007), E5-846, Iqaluit, signed in Roman with syllabics.

13in (33cm)

$4,000-4,500 WAD

A woman with braided hair, in stone, by Elizabeth Nutaraluk Aulatjut (1914-1998), E1-445, Arviat, signed in syllabics.

c1968 9.75in (25cm)

$7,500-9,000 WAD

A polar bear attacking a woman, in stone, by Davidialuk Alasua Amittu (1910-1976), E9-824, Povungnituk, signed in Roman, inscribed with disc number.

c1965 8.5in (22cm)

$6,000-7,500 WAD

A dancing walrus, in stone, by Henry Evaluardjuk (1923-2007), E5-846, Iqaluit, signed in Roman with syllabics.

c1975 14.75in (37.5cm)

$10,500-13,500 WAD

A musk osk and calf, in stone and antler, by Nuveeya Ipellie (1920-2010), E7-509, Iqaluit, signed in Roman.

14.75in (37.5cm)

$3,000-4,000 WAD

A polar bear with cub and seal, in stone, by Osuitok Ipeelee (1923-2005), E7-1154, Cape Dorset, signed in syllabics.

22.75in (58cm)

$14,250-18,000 WAD

A woman in Amautik, in stone, by John Kavik (1897-1993), E2-290, Rankin Inlet.

10in (25.5cm)

$4,500-5,250 WAD

A contemplative man, in stone, by John Kavik (1897-1993), E2-290, Rankin Inlet.

c1975 20in (51cm)

$15,000-21,000 WAD

A Qalupalik holding a head, in stone, antler and fur, by David Ruben Piqtoukun (1950-), W3-1119, Toronto, signed in Roman.

1994 14in (35.5cm)

$3,300-4,400 WAD

ESSENTIAL REFERENCE - JOE TALIRUNILI

This work is a depiction of a significant event that took place during the artist's childhood. While traveling to new hunting grounds, several families were stranded on an ice floe that split from the mainland. They built an umiak out of scarce supplies and in haste as the ice floe was melting. Some people perished during this tumultuous migration. When the group finally spotted land, it appeared to be drifting away from them therefore one man with a rifle shot at the land to prevent it from moving any further. Some of Talirunili's versions of the Migration have included a list of the names of the survivors. Although similar due to the subject matter, each boat is unique, the number of people aboard as well as their positioning varies and the occupants have been depicted as owls and hares in other versions of the Migration.

'The Migration', in stone, wood, hide and thread, by Joe Talirunili (1893-1976), E9-818, Povungnituk.

c1975 11.5in (29.5cm)

$112,500-127,500 WAD

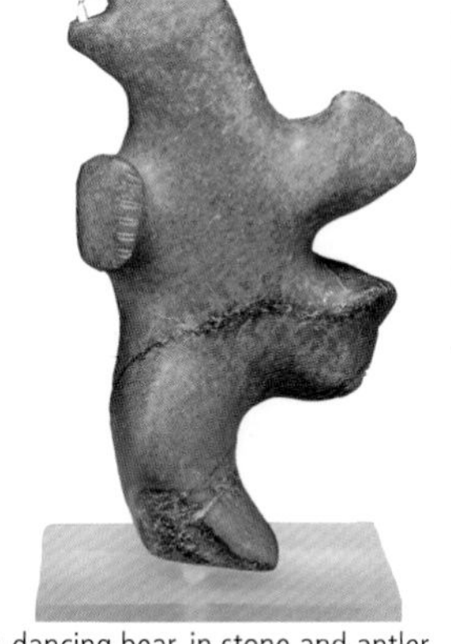

A dancing bear, in stone and antler, by Pauta Saila (1916-2009), E7-990, Cape Dorset.

c1970 12.5in (32cm) high

$9,000-12,000 WAD

A dancing polar bear, in stone, by Pauta Saila (1916-2009), E7-990, Cape Dorset, signed in syllabics.

1976 13in (33cm)

$12,750-14,250 WAD

A standing figure, in stone, by John Tiktak (1916-1981), E1-266, Rankin Inlet, signed in syllabics.

c1970 5in (13cm)

$4,000-4,500 WAD

A woman with ulu and child in amaut, in stone and antler, by Judas Ullulaq (1937-1999), E4-342, Gjoa Haven, signed in syllabics.

25in (63.5cm)

$6,000-7,500 WAD

Bright plumage, by Kenojuak Ashevak (1927-2013), E7-1035, Cape Dorset, stonecut, edition 24/50.

1963 *36in (92cm) wide*

$2,700-3,300 WAD

Multi-feathered bird, by Kenojuak Ashevak (1927-2013), E7-1035, Cape Dorset, stonecut, edition 33/50.

'The swift flight of this bird and the animated beating of its wings are revealed in an image almost entirely composed of feather forms.' Arts of the Eskimo: Prints, Patrick Furneaux and Leo Rosshandler, Ernst Roch.

1960 *21.75in (55.5cm) long*

$4,500-6,000 WAD

Birds, by Qatjuayuk Atchealak (1911-), E7-1180, Cape Dorset, stonecut, edition 13/50.

1960 *18.75in (47.75cm) wide*

$2,700-3,300 WAD

Musk Ox, by Osuitok Ipeelee (1923-2005), E7-1154, Cape Dorset, stonecut, edition 7/30.

1958 *9in (23cm) wide*

$5,250-6,750 WAD

Snow house builders, by Niviaxie (1909-1959), E7-1077, Cape Dorset, stonecut, edition 26/35.

1959 *12in (30.5cm) wide*

$5,250-6,000 WAD

Woman, by A Jessie Oonark (1906-1985), E2-384, Baker Lake, stonecut, edition 36/50.

1970 *31in (79cm)*

$7,500-9,000 WAD

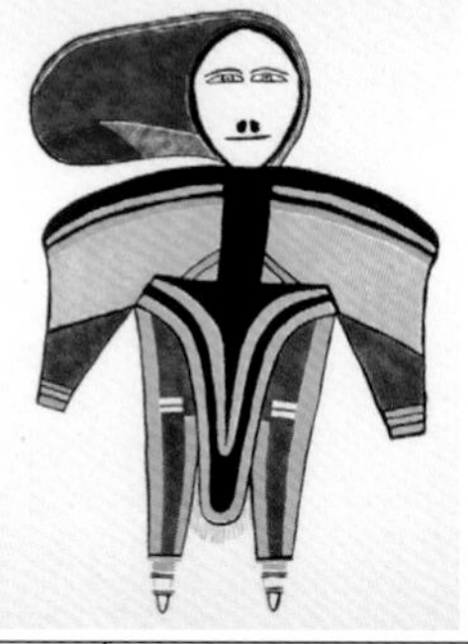

Untitled, by A Jessie Oonark (1906-1985), E2-384, Baker Lake, colored pencil drawing, signed in syllabics.

30in (76.5cm) wide

$22,500-30,000 WAD

A hunter and dog with animals, by Parr (1893-1969), E7-1022, Cape Dorset, graphite drawing, signed in syllabic.

c1960 *25.75in (65.5cm)*

$8,250-9,750 WAD

Caribou, by Josephie Pootoogook (1887-1958), E7-1166, Cape Dorset, stonecut, edition 6/30.

1958 *8in (20.5cm) wide*

$6,000-7,500 WAD

Woman and snow bird, by Pitaloosie Saila (1942-), E7-1006, Cape Dorset, stonecut and stencil, edition 16/50.

1973 *24in (61cm) wide*

$9,000-10,500 WAD

A late 19thC Athabascan beaded hide Chief's coat, smoked hide with fringe at the seams, partially beaded with glass and metallic seed beads.

35in (89cm) long

$1,400-1,800 **SK**

A Haida wood grease bowl, with inset bone cabouchon and beads, carved masks and eyes, the interior with two frogs.

14in (35.5cm) long

$850-975 **WW**

A North West Coast mask, with tufts of hair.

14in (35.5cm) high

$1,000-1,200 **WW**

A Plateau Parfleche case, painted with geometric designs and with buffalo (?) hide fringe and strap.

c1875-1900 *cylinder 15.75in (40cm) long*

$3,000-4,000 **SK**

A late 19thC Pomo coiled gift basket, decorated with beads, shell discs, and feather tufts.

11in (28cm) diam

$10,500-12,000 **SK**

CLOSER LOOK - WASCO-WISHRAMS OUTFIT

This is a rare early example with good provenance.

They are beaded with both loom and single-lane techniques with thread and sinew.

The shirt has traces of red pigment at the neck.

The bibs probably representing the mythical Tsalagle, 'the one who watches', a prominent rock art feature along the Columbia River near the Wishram area.

A rare Wasco-Wishram beaded hide man's shirt and trousers, with some restoration to red trade cloth.

1850-1875 *trousers 37in (94cm) long*

$90,000-105,000 **SK**

A Great Lakes 'Brass Vine' tomahawk, the brass head with steel bit and engraved with vines and star, moon, and sunrise, the ash shaft with sawtooth design probably dates to a later period.

c1800 *14.75in (37.5cm) long*

$6,000-7,500 **SK**

A Woodlands carved burl bowl and two mush paddles, bowl with head-like projections at each end.

17.5in (44.5cm) long

$11,500-12,750 **SK**

A Northern Plains beaded and quilled hide belt set, possibly Hidatsa, geometric beadwork with quilled rawhide slats and tin cone and horsehair danglers.

c1875-1900 *51in (129.5cm) long*

$21,000-24,000 **SK**

A Southern Cheyenne beaded and fringed hide woman's dress, the yoke stained yellow and with red pigment details, with multicolored geometric beaded detail, with minor tear.

c1850-1875 *56in (142.5cm) long*

$45,000-52,500 **SK**

A Southern Cheyenne beaded hide pipe bag, the long tabs and quill-wrapped fringe with tin cone and red trade cloth danglers.

Provenance: Thought to have been collected by Major General William August Kobbe (1840-1931), Kobbe had a long distinguished career in the military, including serving on the frontier in New Mexico and Kansas during Indian hostilities.

c1870 *20in (51cm) long*

$19,500-24,000 **SK**

ESSENTIAL REFERENCE - OUTFIT

By family repute, this highly important Native American outfit had come to Ireland through the family of Reymond Hervey de Montmorency (1835-1902), a major general in the British Army who married Rachel Mary Lumley Godolphin Michel, daughter of Field Marshal Sir John Michel, at Montreal, Canada, in 1866. Mountain-sheep hide garments of this type, intended for best-dress events, denoted a man of stature and could be worn only with the approval of his community. While all Plains Indians made war shirts, this example shares many characteristics - the porcupine quilwork, the painted colors and the motifs - of those made by the Lakota Sioux or Cheyenne communities in North Dakota and Montana. Laws surrounding the sale of eagle feathers dictate that the headdress or war bonnet could not be sold in the US, but the war shirt and leggings have great commercial value.

A late 19thC Native American outfit, comprising an eagle-feathered headdress, hide poncho, war shirt, matching leggings and purse.

$375,000-450,000 **FOM**

A Lakota beaded hide cradle, geometric designs on a white background.

1875-1900 *22in (56cm) long*

$9,750-11,500 **SK**

A Lakota trade cloth blanket, with beaded hide blanket strip, centers with twisted hide fringe with metal thimbles and green silk ribbon.

1875-1900 *60.5in (154cm) wide*

$4,500-5,250 **SK**

A Lakota buffalo hide bag, quilled with an 'Elk Dreamer' design, with geometric beadwork, with dentalium shell and horsehair danglers.

c1875-1900 *21in (53.5cm)*

$10,500-12,000 **SK**

An 1870s Lakota commercial leather 'Dispatch' bag, beaded with geometric designs done in multicolored glass and faceted brass seed beads, old period tag reads 'Sioux Indian Ammunition Pouch, found on the field of the Custer Massacre', with much leather and bead loss.

9in (23cm) high

$6,750-7,500 **SK**

Lakota buffalo hide double saddlebags, attributed to the Hunkpapa tribe, beaded with geometric designs and stylized buildings.

c1870 *72in (183cm) long*

$23,250-27,750 **SK**

Lakota buffalo hide double saddlebags, attributed to the Hunkpapa tribe, beaded with classic Lakota multicolored geometric designs, with a row of small German silver buttons along both panel tops.

c1870 *74in (188cm) long*

$37,500-45,000 **SK**

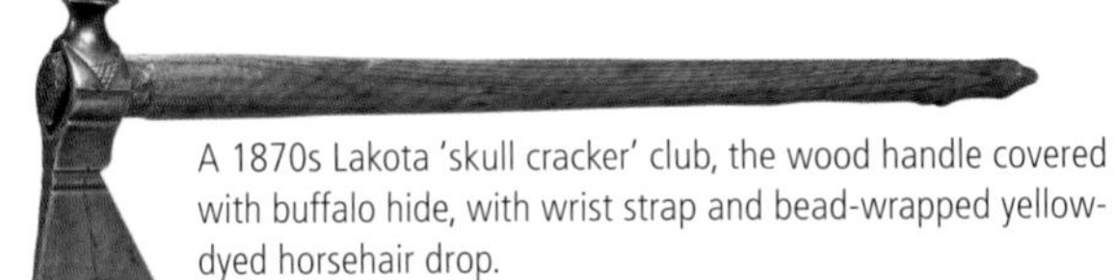

A 1870s Lakota 'skull cracker' club, the wood handle covered with buffalo hide, with wrist strap and bead-wrapped yellow-dyed horsehair drop.

27in (69cm) long

$975-1,150 **SK**

ESSENTIAL REFERENCE - PICTOGRAPHIC COAT

The Lakota people (pronounced and also known as Teton, Thíthunwan (prairie dwellers),and Teton Sioux ('snake, or enemy') are an indigenous people of the Great Plains of North America. They are part of a confederation of seven related Sioux tribes, the Ochéthi Šakówin or seven council fires, and speak Lakota, one of the three major dialects of the Sioux language. The Lakota are the westernmost of the three Siouan language groups, occupying lands in both North and South Dakota.

A Lakota hide pictographic coat, beaded with equestrian figures, both riding and leading their horses, several warriors wearing war bonnets, breastplates, and carrying society staffs.

c1890 *41in (104cm) long*

$112,500-127,500 **SK**

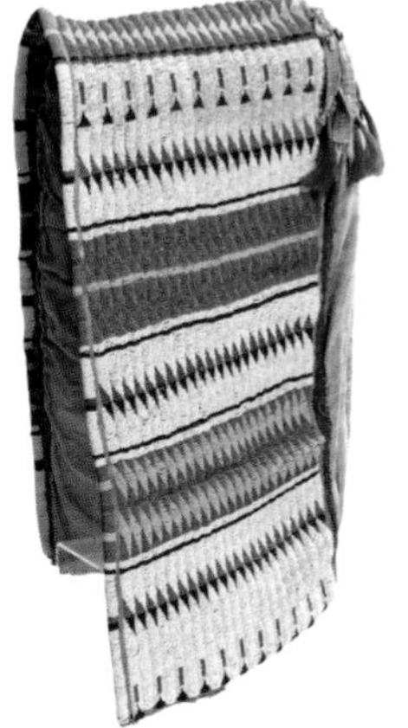

A Lakota hide cradle, with unusual geometric banded design, some cut beads, with tin cone and red horsehair danglers.

1875-1900 *21in (53.5cm) long*

$7,500-9,000 **SK**

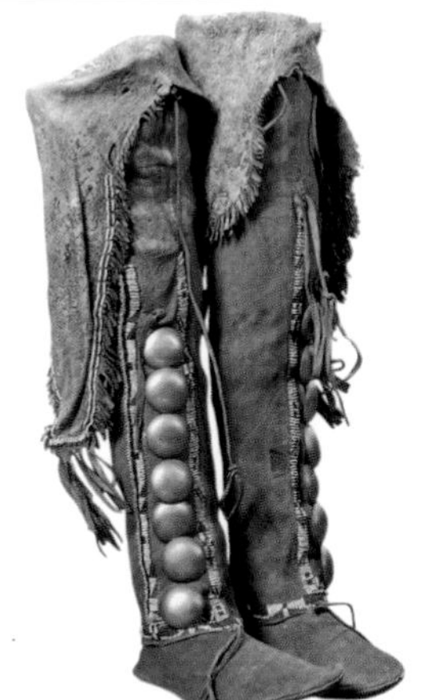

A pair of 1870s Kiowa woman's legging moccasins, large German silver conchas, and beaded detail.

22.5in (57cm) high

$52,500-60,000 **SK**

A Kiowa beaded cloth and hide model cradle, with a pair of miniature moccasins hanging off the side.

1875-1900 *24in (61cm) long*

$33,000-42,000 **SK**

A Kiowa beaded hide young girl's dress, with a row of mesal beans on fringe.

c1875-1900 *23in (58.5cm) wide*

$67,500-75,000 **SK**

An 1870s Crow beaded and fringed buffalo hide rifle scabbard, with classic Crow geometric designs.

43.5in (110.5cm) long

$25,500-30,000 **SK**

A framed photograph by Joseph K. Dixon, 'Here Custer Fell (Four Crow Scouts at Custer Battlefield)', silver print, taken during the Wanamaker Expedition 1908-13.

print c1915 *39in (99cm) long*

$10,500-13,500 **SK**

A late 19thC Crow-beaded cloth and hide horse collar, with classic Crow designs using glass and metallic seed beads.

36in (91.5cm) long

$15,000-18,000 **SK**

A mid-19thC Plains beaded buffalo hide 'possible bag', remnant tin cone danglers down the sides, includes custom stand, with bead loss.

14.5in (37cm)

$60,000-67,500 SK

A Blackfoot beaded hide warrior's bag

c1875-1900 *42in (107cm) long*

$10,500-13,500 SK

A Plains Cree buffalo hide beaded bowcase and quiver, with fringe, includes seven arrows, and a sinew-backed ash bow.

1850-1875 *35in (89cm) long*

$60,000-67,500 SK

An Arapaho beaded hide pipe bag, the tabs edged in red and white 'pony' beads, and twisted fringe.

1850-1875 *25in (63.5cm) long*

$12,750-15,000 SK

A 19thC Plains pipe tomahawk, with an iron blade, the handle with pewter lattice decoration.

19.5in (49.5cm) long

$9,750-11,500 POOK

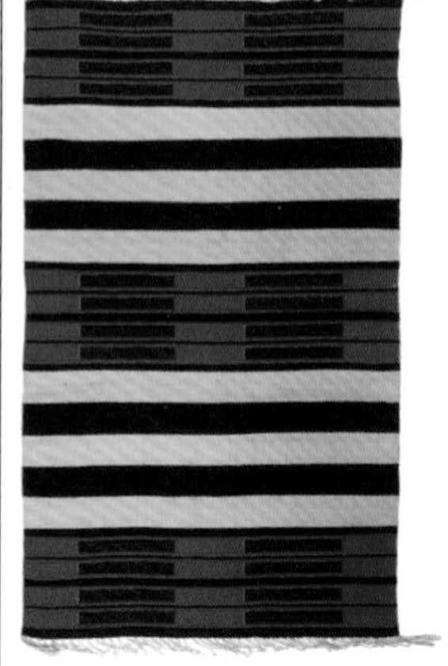

A Navajo chief's blanket, probably second phase.

79in (197.5cm) long

$600-750 POOK

ESSENTIAL REFERENCE - NAVAJO WEAVING

When the Spanish arrived, the Navajo began herding sheep and goats as a main source of trade and food, with meat becoming an essential component of the Navajo diet. Sheep also became a form of currency and status symbol among the Navajo based on the overall quantity of herds a family maintained. In addition, the practice of spinning and weaving wool into blankets and clothing became common and eventually developed into a form of highly valued artistic expression. The Spanish first used the term Apachu de Nabajo in the 1620s to refer to the people in the Chama Valley region east of the San Juan River and northwest of present-day Santa Fe, New Mexico.

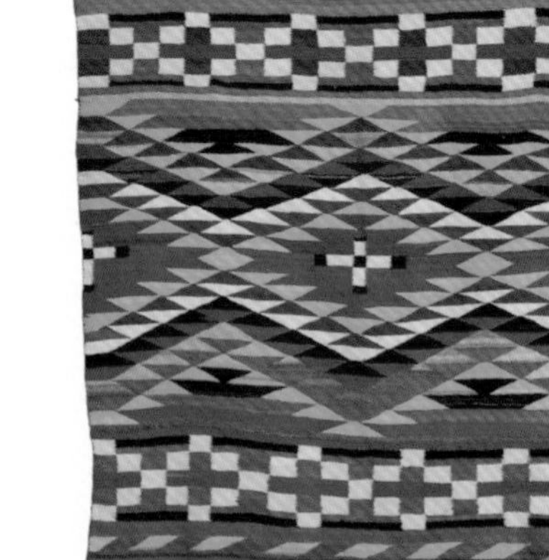

A Navajo Transitional weaving.

1875-1900 *83in (211cm) long*

$3,000-4,000 SK

A Navajo late Classic child's blanket, some old repairs.

48in (122cm) long

$1,800-2,250 SK

A Navajo late Classic wearing blanket, with some wool loss and repairs.

76in (193cm) long

$3,300-4,500 SK

A Zuni pottery Jar, with two split circles framing four heartline deer between two large rosettes.

c1900

11.5in (29.5cm) diam

$4,000-5,250 SK

An early 20thC Apache pictorial basketry bowl, the central band with human figures and multiple quadrupeds.

14.25in (36cm) diam

$3,300-3,900 SK

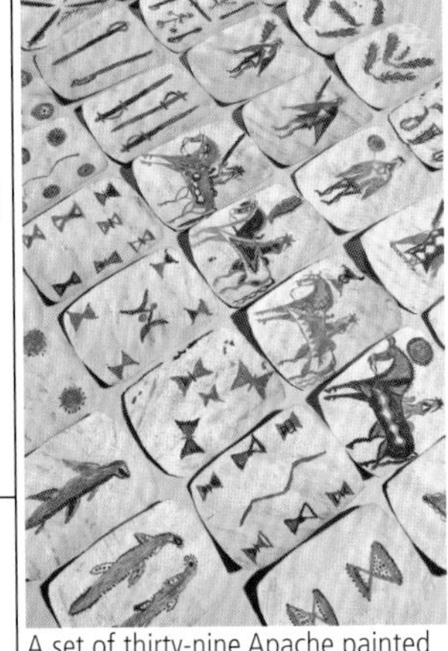

A set of thirty-nine Apache painted rawhide playing cards, possibly Chiricahua.

c1850-1900 *3.25in (8.5cm)*

$18,000-22,500 SK

A Hopi polychrome carved wood Kachina, a Hemis Maiden by Jimmy Koots.

10.75in (27.5cm) high

$1,300-1,450 SK

ESSENTIAL REFERENCE - HOPI KATSINA FIGURES

Hopi katsina figures, also known as kachina dolls are figures carved, typically from cottonwood root, by Hopi people to instruct young girls and new brides about katsinas or katsinam, the immortal beings that bring rain, control other aspects of the natural world and society, and act as messengers between humans and the spirit world. Except for major ceremonial figures, most katsina figures originated in the late 19th century. Kachinas represent the spirit of the gods who personify nature: clouds, sky, storms, trees, etc. They also represent the spirits of good people who die and become clouds, bringing much-needed rain. Shalako is a ceremony occurring during the first week of December. The participants have been practicing all year to perform their duties, seven new houses have been built to welcome the Shalakos (the Giant Couriers of the Rainmakers) and the Longhorns (Rain Gods of the North), and an enormous amount of food is prepared for both residents and visitors. Shalako brings the old year to a close and welcomes the new year, and asks for rain, the propagation of plants and animals, and the health and well being of its participants.

A Hopi carved wood Kachina doll, representing Shalako Kachina.

15.5in (39.5cm) high

$12,750-14,250 SK

A pair of Creek beaded hide child's moccasins.

c1825-1850 *6.25in (16cm) long*

$14,250-16,500 SK

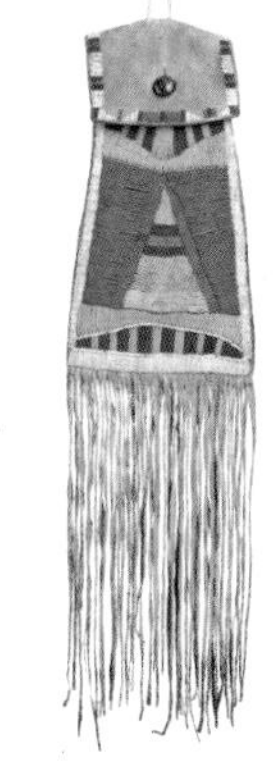

An 1870s Ute beaded hide pipe bag, the flap secured with brass military button.

25in (63.5cm) long

$10,500-12,000 SK

A late classic Saltillo serape, with some restoration.

78in (198cm)

$4,500-5,250 SK

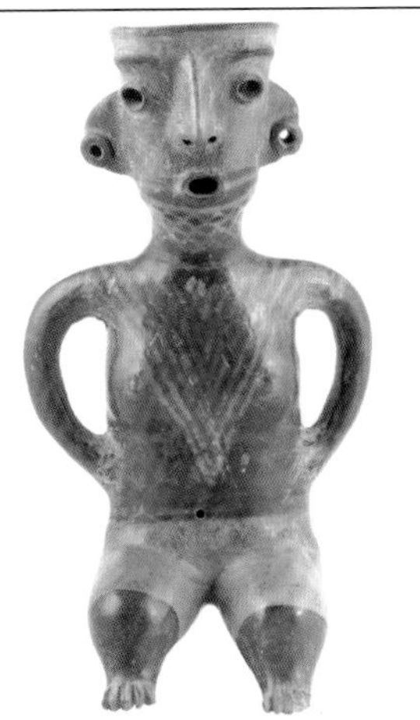

A Zacatecas pottery female figure, with disc earring.

13.75in (35cm) high

$1,150-1,300 WW

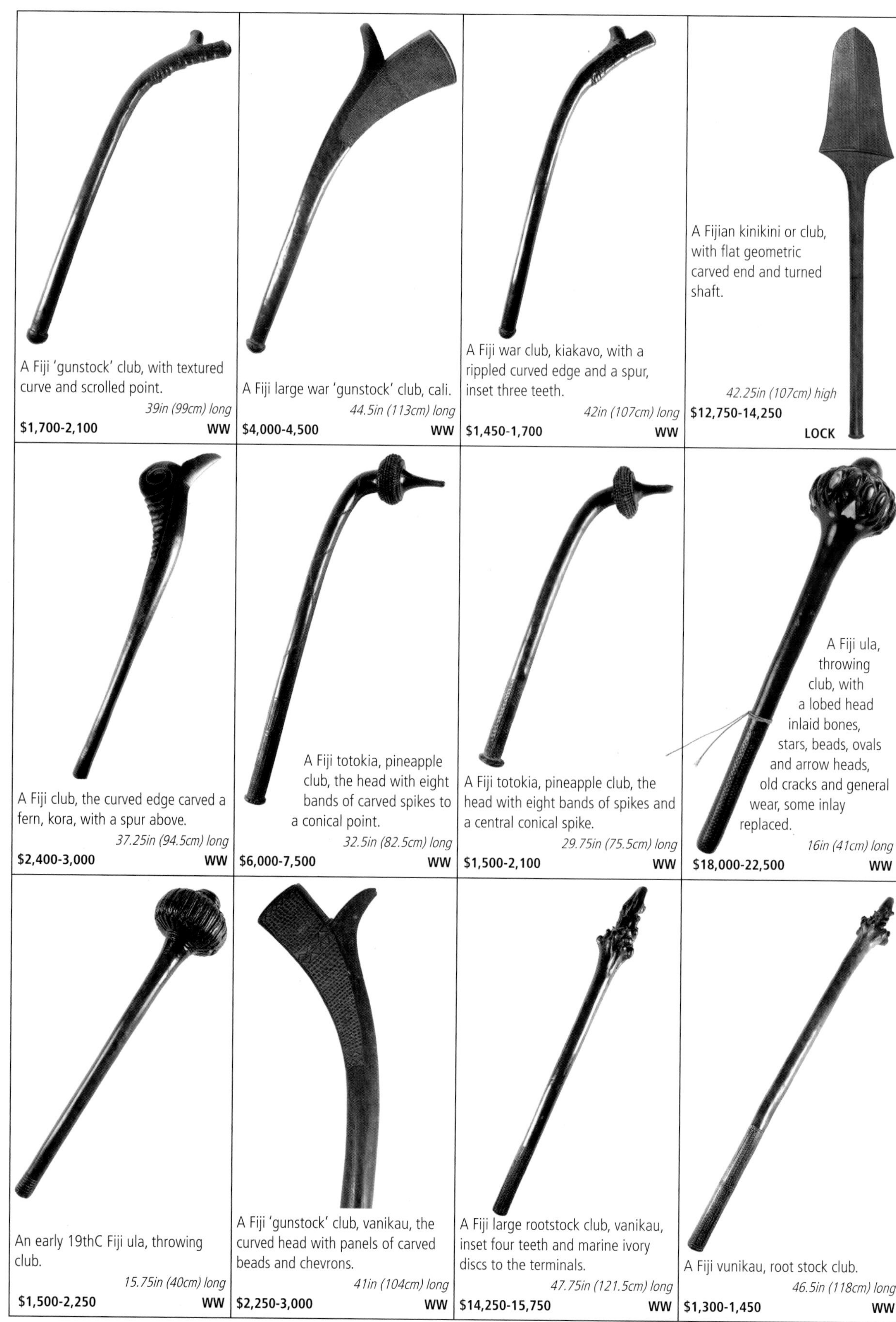

A Fiji 'gunstock' club, with textured curve and scrolled point.
39in (99cm) long
$1,700-2,100 **WW**

A Fiji large war 'gunstock' club, cali.
44.5in (113cm) long
$4,000-4,500 **WW**

A Fiji war club, kiakavo, with a rippled curved edge and a spur, inset three teeth.
42in (107cm) long
$1,450-1,700 **WW**

A Fijian kinikini or club, with flat geometric carved end and turned shaft.
42.25in (107cm) high
$12,750-14,250 **LOCK**

A Fiji club, the curved edge carved a fern, kora, with a spur above.
37.25in (94.5cm) long
$2,400-3,000 **WW**

A Fiji totokia, pineapple club, the head with eight bands of carved spikes to a conical point.
32.5in (82.5cm) long
$6,000-7,500 **WW**

A Fiji totokia, pineapple club, the head with eight bands of spikes and a central conical spike.
29.75in (75.5cm) long
$1,500-2,100 **WW**

A Fiji ula, throwing club, with a lobed head inlaid bones, stars, beads, ovals and arrow heads, old cracks and general wear, some inlay replaced.
16in (41cm) long
$18,000-22,500 **WW**

An early 19thC Fiji ula, throwing club.
15.75in (40cm) long
$1,500-2,250 **WW**

A Fiji 'gunstock' club, vanikau, the curved head with panels of carved beads and chevrons.
41in (104cm) long
$2,250-3,000 **WW**

A Fiji large rootstock club, vanikau, inset four teeth and marine ivory discs to the terminals.
47.75in (121.5cm) long
$14,250-15,750 **WW**

A Fiji vunikau, root stock club.
46.5in (118cm) long
$1,300-1,450 **WW**

A Papua New Guinea gope board, with a pierced nose and a handle.
40.5in (103cm) high
$16,500-21,000 **WW**

A Sepik River female spirit carving, Yamok, with inset shell eyes, with metal stand.
18in (46cm) high
$600-750 **WW**

A Sepik River mask, with a serrated protruding mouth, with applied animal hide and hair.
12in (30.5cm) high
$450-600 **WW**

A Sepik River carved wood maternity figure, standing holding a child, the reverse with mother breast feeding her child.
34.5in (87.5cm) high
$6,000-7,500 **WW**

A Sepik Mei mask, with cowrie shell eyes, with a beaked bead terminal and a pointed tongue under.
25.5in (65cm) high
$3,450-3,900 **WW**

A 19thC Solomon Islands axe, the handle inlaid with mother-of-pearl and shell discs, with a European trade iron blade, stamped '2'.
39in (99cm) long
$1,700-2,000 **WW**

A Tongan paddle club, with zig-zag and geometric decoration.
39.25in (100cm) long
$1,700-2,100 **WW**

A Tongan paddle club.
39.5in (100.5cm) long
$3,000-4,000 **WW**

A Tongan club, with carved figures, fish and birds.
35in (89cm) long
$15,000-18,000 **WW**

An Easter Island male figure, with inset bone and ebonized eyes.
16.25in (41.5cm) high
$3,000-4,000 **WW**

An Oceanic paddle club, with a leaf shape blade having an 'axe' protrusion to one side, the pointed terminal handle with fibre binding.
46in (117cm) long
$3,300-4,400 **WW**

A Maori carved softwood figure.

23.75in (60cm) high

$1,000-1,200 **SWO**

A Maori jade carved tiki, with the remains of red pigment to eyes.

The hei-tiki is an ornamental pendant of the Māori which is worn around the neck. Hei-tiki are usually made of pounamu which is greenstone, and are considered a taonga (treasure). They are commonly referred to as tiki, a term that actually refers to large human figures carved in wood, and, also, the small wooden carvings used to mark sacred places.

1.75in (4.5cm) high

$750-900 **WW**

A Maori tewhatewha, battleaxe, the shaft with carved decoration.

The axe has an accompanying letter from the premier of New Zealand, Richard Seddon, dated 18th Febr. 1901. The Hon William Swanson (1819 - 1903) was a noted Aukland politician and prominent Member of the Legislative Council. His wife, Ani Rangitunoa, a Maori chieftainess, descended from a chiefly line of the Ngati Kahunguna tribe.

40.75in (103.5cm) long

$3,000-4,000 **WW**

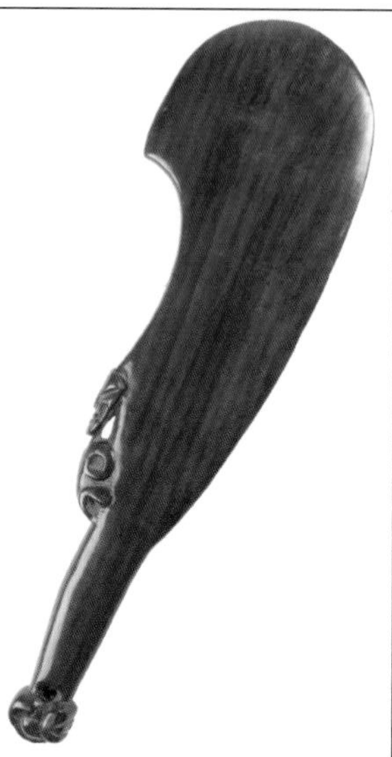

A Maori wahaika, hand club, with a carved tiki, with suspension aperture and carved tiki head terminal.

15.5in (39.5cm) long

$1,800-2,250 **WW**

A Maori carved wood wahaika, hand club, with a tiki to the curve of the blade and handle terminal.

15in (38cm) long

$2,250-3,000 **WW**

A Maori taiaha, quarter staff, with a carved tongue terminal.

54.75in (139cm) long

$900-1,000 **WW**

A Maori tewhatewha, battleaxe, carved a stylised mask toward the terminal inset with abalone eyes, one missing abalone eye.

53in (134.5cm) long

$1,700-1,800 **WW**

A Maori carved wood staff, with masks, notches and lines.

36.75in (93.4cm) long

$750-900 **WW**

A Polynesian carved handwood paddle.

38.25in (97cm) long

$6,000-7,500 **L&T**

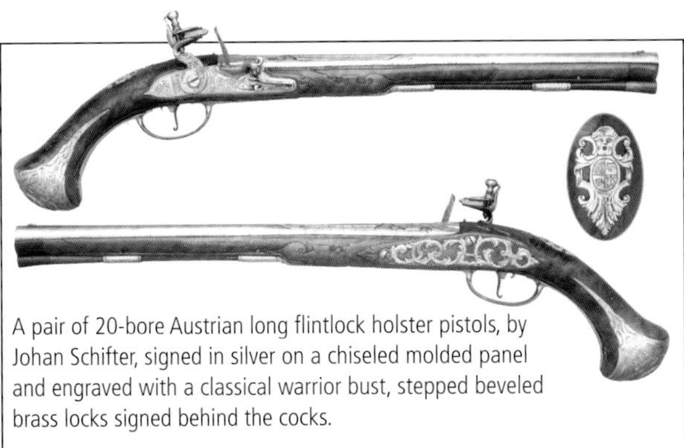

A pair of 20-bore Austrian long flintlock holster pistols, by Johan Schifter, signed in silver on a chiseled molded panel and engraved with a classical warrior bust, stepped beveled brass locks signed behind the cocks.

Johan Schifter is recorded in Wiener Neustadt c1694-1730. Two guns by this maker are preserved in the Hofjagd-und Rüstkammer, Vienna and another in the Musée de l'Armée, Paris.

c1720 *barrels 14.5in (37cm) long*

$18,000-22,500 **TDM**

A mid-18thC pair of Spanish flintlock holster pistols, by I H Deop, with brass mounts, and silver overlay.

barrels 9.5in (24cm) long

$4,000-4,500 **WW**

A pair of flintlock Queen Anne-style brass action and barreled holster pistols, by Robert Wilson, London, with silver mounts, maker JA. barrel

c1750 *7in (18cm) long*

$8,500-9,000 **WW**

A pair of flintlock boxlock cannon barrel pistols, by Hadley, London, stock silver wire inlaid, losses, silver butt cap mask, Birmingham hallmarked, trigger guard safety.

c1780 *barrels 5in (13cm) long*

$4,000-4,500 **WW**

A side by side tap action flintlock boxlock pistol, by Archer, London, the action with top safety and silver butt cap, silver maker Charles Freeth, Birmingham.

1788 *barrels 4.5in (12cm) long*

$2,400-3,000 **WW**

An 18thC Queen Anne- style flintlock overcoat pistol, by Stanton of London.

barrel 2in (5.5cm) long

$600-750 **TEN**

A pair of 19thC percussion cap pocket pistols, by J Lang Haymarket London, screw off proof marked octagonal barrels with dolphin-shaped hammers.

$6,000-6,750 **FLD**

A 19thC percussion cap overcoat pistol, by Mk. Pattison of Dublin, with a sprung bayonet retained by a sliding clip, with barrel and nipple conversion, the chequered walnut flattened bag but set with silver escutcheons.

barrel 3in (8cm) long

$1,500-2,250 **TEN**

An 18thC flintlock three-barrel tap action pocket pistol, by John Richards, London, brass box lock engraved with martial trophies.

barrels 1.2in (3cm) long

$2,250-3,000 **TEN**

A pair of cased flintlock pistols, by Boutet Paris, the tangs engraved with thunderbolts and floral motifs, locks signed 'MANUF.RE A VERSAILLES', provided with anti-friction and sealing systems, batterie with thunderbolts, in case with tools.

c1800

$97,500-105,000 **CZER**

A 15-bore flintlock pistol of livery type, by H. Nock, the steel parts pitted, cock incomplete, brass mounts of livery type and steel stirrup ramrod.

c1800 *8.75in (22.5cm) barrel long*

$900-1,200 **TDM**

A pair of French double barreled double percussion holster pistols, by Manufacture Royale, St Etienne, the stocks with silver mounts with original bone ram-rods, converted from flintlock.

barrels 8.75in (22cm) long

$3,000-4,000 **WW**

A 28-bore percussion cap travelling pistol, by Riviere, London, converted from flintlock.

barrel 4in (10.5cm) long

$750-900 **TEN**

A rare four-barreled tap action flintlock pistol, by Wheeler, London, the steel action with cut-off.

barrels 2.75in (7cm) long c1810

$4,000-4,500 **WW**

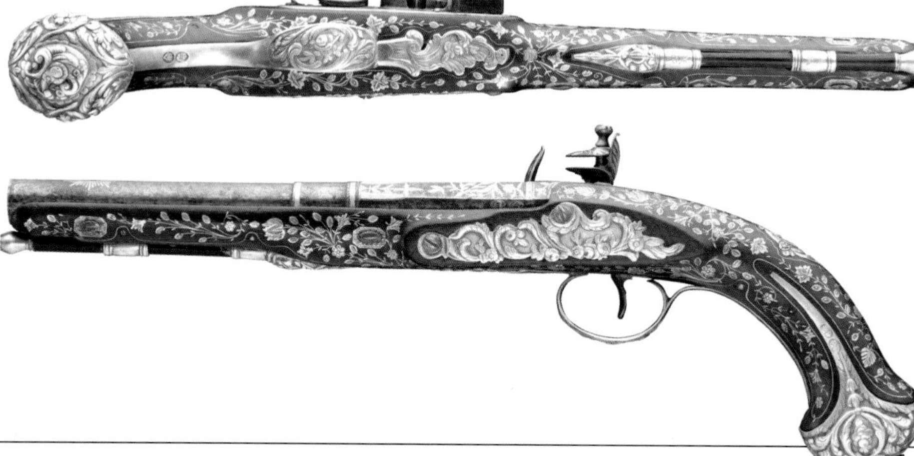

A pair of 20-bore silver-mounted flintock holster pistols, for presentation to a potentate, in the English taste, engraved and inlaid in gold, fitted with rainproof pans, rollers and 'French' cocks.

c1830 *barrels 9in (23cm) long*

$30,000-38,000 **TDM**

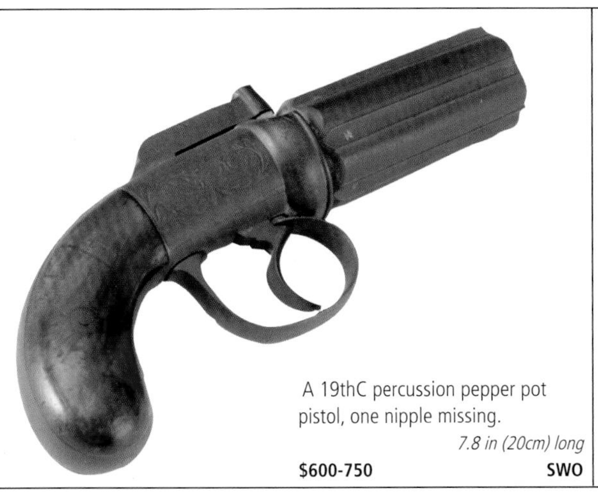

A 19thC percussion pepper pot pistol, one nipple missing.

7.8 in (20cm) long

$600-750 SWO

A Persian contract broom handle Mauser Model semi-automatic pistol, marked 'Waffenfabrik Mauser Oberndorf A Neckar', 50-1000 meter rear sight, serial #154826.

c1896

$1,000-1,200 POOK

A late 17thC Dutch snap-matchlock target gun, with two-stage barrel, fitted with fore-sight, medial sight and back-sight with folding peep aperture, spurred trigger-guard, rear stirrup, set trigger, and no provision for a ramrod, the barrel shortened at the muzzle.

barrel 48.25in (123.4cm) long

$1,400-1,800 TDM

A f25-bore Bavarian wheel-lock sporting rifle, by Abraham Dellemayr in Münche, with octagonal swamped sighted barrel rifled with eight grooves, signed, dated and engraved, dated.

Abraham Dellermayer is recorded in Münich c1669-1701.

1695 *barrel 35.5in (90cm) long*

$21,000-27,000 TDM

An early 18thC British flintlock musket, the later lock plate stamped 'TOWER' and with crowned 'GR' cypher.

barrel 54in (137cm) long

$2,700-3,300 TEN

An 18thC flintlock blunderbuss, by Jno. Mann, with London proof marks, signed steel lock plate.

Condition Report: Action works, holds at full and half cock. Old repairs to stock along each side of the barrel and around the breech.

barrel 14.6in (37cm) long

$1,800-2,250 TEN

An 18thC Tower flintlock blunderbuss, steel lock plate stamped 'TOWER' and crowned 'GR', sideplate missing.

barrel 13.8in (35cm) long

$2,100-2,700 TEN

A George III Tower flintlock 'India Pattern' 'Brown Bess' musket, lock plate stamped 'TOWER', the tang engraved 'V/G/5', with steel sling swivels, leather sling and correct socket bayonet.

barrel 39in (99.5cm) long

$3,300-4,400 TEN

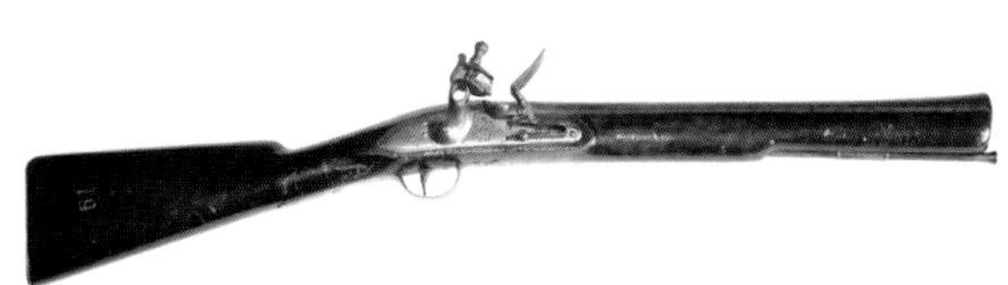

An 18thC Tower flintlock blunderbuss.

barrel 17in (43cm) long

$1,800-2,400 **TEN**

A cased J. Purdey side-by-side under lever double-barrel Express rifle, 500 cal., marked J.P. Purdey & Sons, with an English walnut stock with silver escutcheon with Earl of Shannon, ser. no14596.

barrels 28in (71cm) long

$9,000-10,500 **POOK**

A Stephen Grant & Sons side-by-side, side lock, side lever double-barrel shotgun, 12-gauge, in a fitted leather case, ser. #6957.

barrels 28in (71cm) long

$5,250-6,000 **POOK**

A John Rigby & Co. side-by-side under lever double-hammer rifle, cal. 360, inscribed 'Jno Rigby & Co., Dublin & London, serial no15093'.

barrels 26in (66cm) long

$6,000-7,500 **POOK**

An Alex Henry side-by-side under lever double-hammer Express rifle, .577/.500 cal., black powder proof barrels without ejectors, inscribed 'Alex Henry, Edinburgh & London Patent No. 3206, serial #4147'.

barrels 28in (71cm) damascus long

$6,000-7,500 **POOK**

A John Rigby & Co. side-by-side under lever double-hammer Express rifle, .577/.500 cal., inscribed 'Jno. Rigby & Co., 72 St. James St., London & Dublin, serial #16219'.

barrels 26in (66cm) long

$6,000-7,500 **POOK**

A Henry Atkin side-by-side, side lock hammerless double-barrel shotgun, with ejectors, 12 gauge, nitro proofed barrels, marked 'Henry Atkin LTD 7 Bury Street St. James London England, serial #1038'.

barrels 27in (68.5cm) long

$4,500-5,250 **POOK**

A Stephen Grant & Sons side-by-side, side lock, top lever double-barrel shotgun, 12-gauge, serial #7550.

barrels 30in (76.2cm) long

$4,500-5,250 **POOK**

A mid-19thC exceptional double-barreled shotgun, Paris, the breech signed 'GASTINNE RENETTE ARQ. DE S. M. L'EMPEREUR', 'EXP.ON' and '1855', gilded decorations picturing vine shoots and bunches of grapes ebony half stock carved with hunting scenes and the imperial coat of arms of Napoleon III, with case.

This outstanding shotgun was manufactured for the Emperor Napoleon III and presented at the Exposition Universelle held in Paris from May 15 to November 15, 1855. Paris exposition was one of the major events in France, countries from all over the world participated with their best products. The gunsmith Gastinne-Renette took part in the exhibition, exposing three objects created for the Emperor, among them is this outstanding shotgun.

$300,000-375,000 **CZER**

ESSENTIAL REFERENCE - WESTLEY RICHARDS & CO

Although the Westley Richards breech loading monkey tail carbine/rifle was popular in South Africa with many farmers and settlers, some, especially among the Boers, continued to prefer a muzzle loader. Carbines such as this were exported to meet this demand. Some were used against the British in the early days of the Anglo Boer War.

A late Westley Richards and Co. 52 bore percussion carbine, stamped 'WHITWORTH PATENT' and numbered 'C1197', with Birmingham proof marks and '.450', the lock plate stamped 'WESTLEY RICHARDS & CO'.

1876 *barrel 23.6in (60cm) long*

$975-1,150 **TEN**

ESSENTIAL REFERENCE - MEDIEVAL SWORD

This sword conforms to Oakeshott type XI. The Oakeshott typology was created by historian and illustrator Ewart Oakeshott as a way to define and catalog the medieval sword based on physical form. It categorizes the swords of the European Middle Ages (roughly 11th to 15th centuries) into 13 main types labeled X to XXII. The type XI has a tapering point and was in use c1100-1175. Sub-type XIa has a broader, shorter blade.

A 12thC medieval sword, in excavated condition, with tapering flat blade, straight cross-guard, and wheel pommel.

blade 35.25in (90cm) long

$7,500-9,000 TDM

A reproduction late 14thC/early 15thC sword, possibly English, the long crossguard with upcurled quillons, the tang lacking its grip, relic condition.

blade 29in (74.5cm) long

$1,800-2,400 TEN

A late 17thC basket hilted broadsword, with wooden grip and fullered blade.

44in (113cm) long

$1,500-2,250 SWO

A 17thC basket hilt sword, with engraved guard, blade with various stamp marks.

38in (97cm) long

$3,000-4,000 SWO

A 17thC basket hilt sword, with wire wound grip and engraved guard.

36.2in (92cm) long

$3,000-4,000 SWO

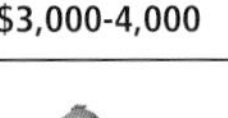

A Scottish basket hilt sword, pierced with hearts in a traditional manner, pommel, grip missing, remains of a leather lining, a German double edged blade.

c1700 blade 30in (76cm) long

$1,500-2,250 L&T

An English stirrup hilted riding sword, with double edged fullered earlier blade, signed 'Andrea Farara', steel hilt with lion's head pommel, hilt.

c1720 blade 29.5in (75cm) long

$1,800-2,250 WW

ESSENTIAL REFERENCE - SABER

Grand Duke Michael Pavlovich of Russia (St. Petersburg, 8 February 1798 – Warsaw, 8 September 1849) was younger brother of Alexander I and Nicholas I, and grandson of Frederick II and Catherine the Great. In 1824 he married Princess Charlotte of Württemberg, they had six children. He commanded the Imperial Russian Guard during the Polish revolution of 1831. It seems that Alexander I commissioned this saber to commemorate Napoleon's defeat (it was definitely manufactured before 1825, otherwise it would show Nicholas I initials). The date is concurrent with the 1831 campaign against Polish revolutionaries when Grand Duke Michael Pavlovich commanded the Imperial Guard. This weapon was very likely given on the occasion of this feat.

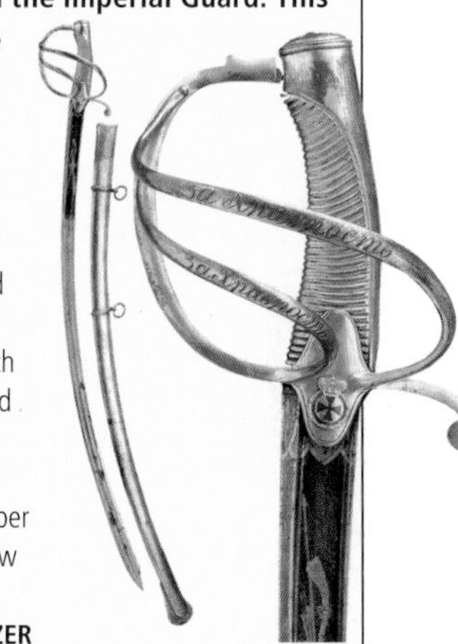

A Russian honor saber, from the property of Grand Duke Michail Pavlovich Romanov, single-and false-edged blade, both edges thickened, engraved monogram 'A I' (standing for Tzar Alexander I) surmounted by the effigy of the imperial eagle, with cartouches featuring name and date of each battle carried by the Russian Imperial Guard against Napoleon, at the back of the blade the name of 'Zlatoust' arms factory, with dedication closing with date 9th of December 1833 (December 22nd according to the new calendar), day of delivery of the sword.

$375,000-525,000 CZER

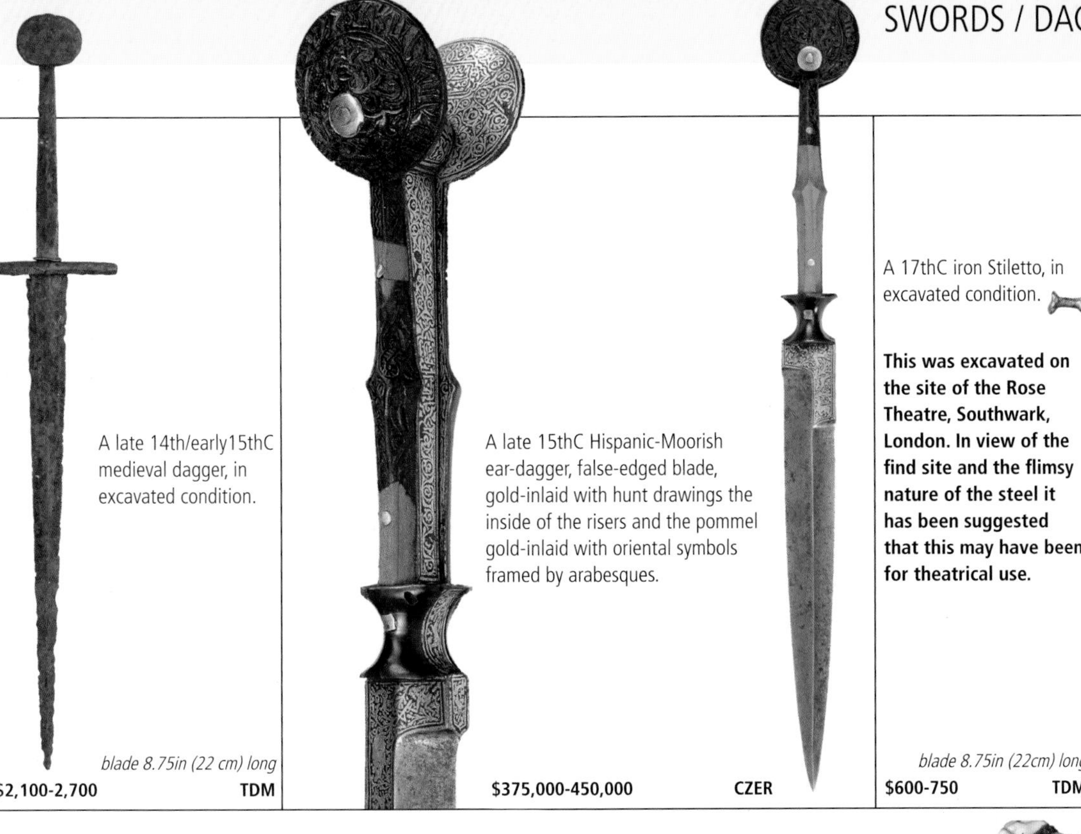

A late 14th/early15thC medieval dagger, in excavated condition.

blade 8.75in (22 cm) long

$2,100-2,700 **TDM**

A late 15thC Hispanic-Moorish ear-dagger, false-edged blade, gold-inlaid with hunt drawings the inside of the risers and the pommel gold-inlaid with oriental symbols framed by arabesques.

$375,000-450,000 **CZER**

A 17thC iron Stiletto, in excavated condition.

This was excavated on the site of the Rose Theatre, Southwark, London. In view of the find site and the flimsy nature of the steel it has been suggested that this may have been for theatrical use.

blade 8.75in (22cm) long

$600-750 **TDM**

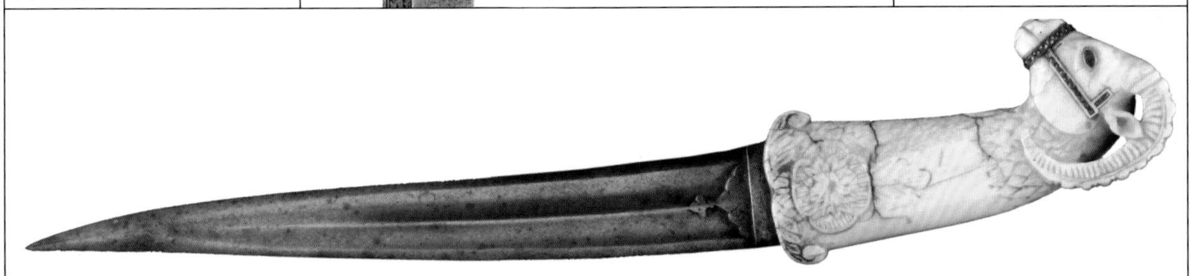

An 18thC Mughal dagger with a marine-ivory handle carved as a ram's head, two red cabochons missing to the head, blade slightly pitted.

$22,500-30,000 **CHOR**

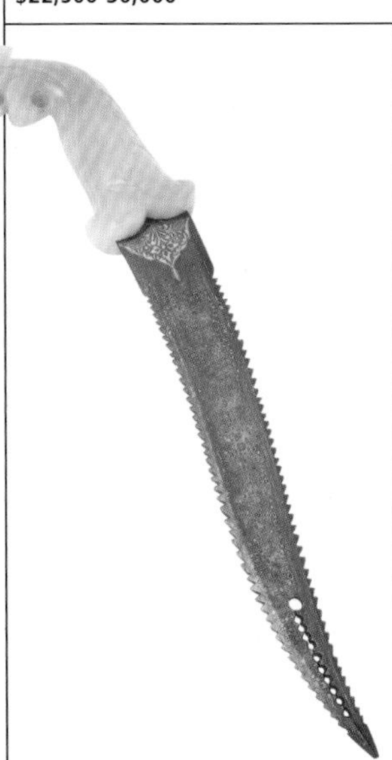

A Mughal jade-hilted dagger (khanjar), the watered steel blade with gold inlaid forte.

17in (43cm) long

$1,400-1,800 **L&T**

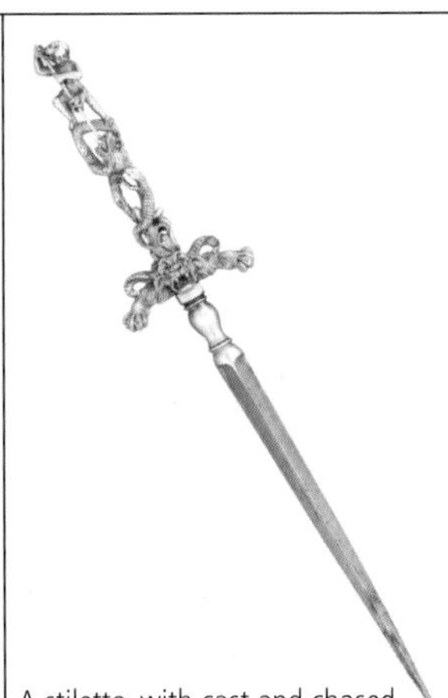

A stiletto, with cast and chased gilt-bronze hilt, cast and chased with rococo revival designs, with the fore-quarters of a gaping lion, the grip with a warrior spearing a serpent, the latter set upon by a salamander, with much early polish and gilding.

c1830 *6.2in (15.5cm) long*

$1,800-2,250 **TDM**

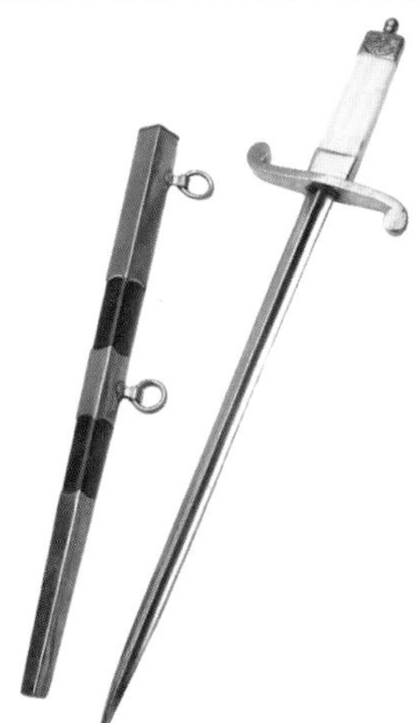

An early 20thC Russian Nicholas II naval officer's dirk, model 1914, fullered blade of diamond section to brass hilt with 'S' quillon, ivory grip and pommel bearing crowned Imperial cypher, in leather scabbard.

blade 11.5in (29cm) long

$1,150-1,300 **WAD**

A rare 18thC Austrian combined flintlock pistol and sword, by F Sturm, Salzburg, the 4in (10cm) steel cannon barrel octagonal at the breech and signed 'F.STURM IN SALZBURG', set to the right side of the 21in (54cm) single edge fullered steel blade, engraved with a running wolf.

26.5in (67.5cm) long

$1,800-2,700 **TEN**

An English or Flemish close helmet, with one-piece skull rising to a low boldly roped medial comb pierced at its apex with two large holes, the visor with stepped centrally divided vision fitted at its right side with a lifting-peg, replaced, that also serves as a pull to release the spring-catch securing it to the upper bevor, pitted and worn overall.

c1550 *11in (28cm) high*

$13,500-18,000 **TDM**

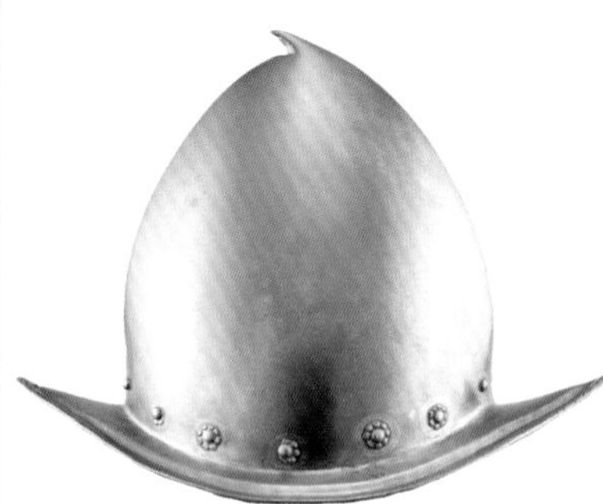

An Italian morion in the 'Spanish' fashion, formed in one piece with an almond-shaped skull rising to a short backward-directed stalk, and an integral brim turned down at each side, the base of the crown encircled by fourteen brass-capped lining-rivets, now partly rusetted.

c1580 *11.25in (28.5 cm) high*

$4,500-5,250 **TDM**

A rare English close helmet, Greenwich, with pointed one-piece skull rising to a baluster finial and formed with eight facets, its brow with a deep visor shaped to the chin, the visor secured to the skull at the right of the neck by a spring-catch, restored.

The helmet, made in the Royal Armour Workshops at Greenwich under the mastership of Jacob Halder (1576-1607/8), is one of only three recorded examples of its type. The other two, possessing the same distinctive form of hinged face-defense and peak, are respectively preserved in the Royal Armouries Museum, Leeds, and the Metropolitan Museum of Art, New York.

c1590 *9.5in (24cm) high*

$52,500-60,000 **TDM**

A European burgonet, the crown with scalloped edge, large frontal rim with pierced applied decoration, two ear flaps hinged and pierced.

c1590 *10in (25.4cm) high*

$1,800-2,700 **L&T**

A German close helmet, the scull with raised comb, with etched foliate panels, panels of decoration with female figure in armor.

c1590 *12in 30.5cm) high*

$7,500-9,000 **L&T**

An early 17thC Italian morion, etched with four panels with classical female figures, broad rope molded rim retaining some brass headed rivets, some damage.

10in (25.4cm) high

$975-1,150 **L&T**

A South German 'Gothic' breastplate and backplate, the two pieces closely matched, the first formed of a main plate with angular outward turns at its neck and arm-openings, the lowest cut with a shallow arch over the crotch, and the second formed of three downward overlapping plates, both elements extensively patched, pitted and worn, all mounted on a stand.

A very similar breastplate is in the City Museum, Vienna. The distinctive form of turned edges seen on the breastplate is also found on a cuirass in the Hofjagd- und Rüstkammer, Vienna, made for the young Philip the Handsome by Jörg (?) Treytz of Innsbruck c1490.

c1490 *23.5in (60cm)*

$30,000-38,000 **TDM**

A German backplate, the entire plate etched with two figures of knights in armor, rope molded edges.

c1590 *17in (43cm) high*

$3,000-4,500 **L&T**

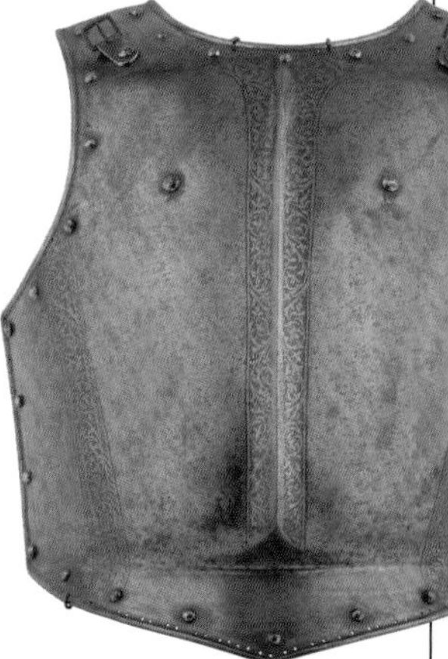

An Italian breast plate, of peascod form, with raised central rib, two neck buckles and raised rivet heads throughout.

c1600 *14in (35.6cm) high*

$1,800-2,700 **L&T**

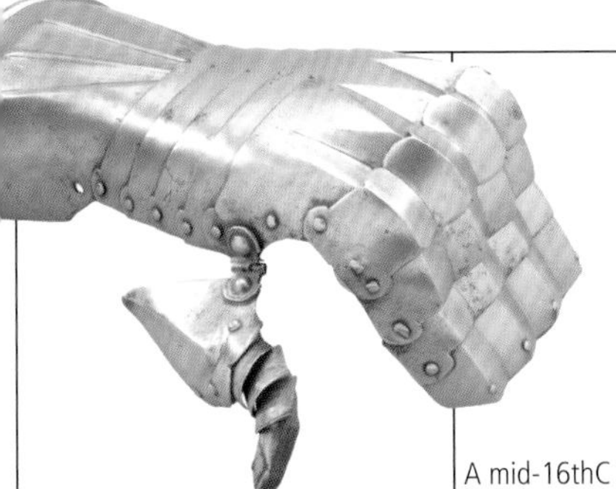

A South German half-mitten gauntlet for the left hand, formed of a short flaring gutter-shaped cuff, five metacarpal plates, a knuckle-plate and three finger-plates and an associated thumb-defense of five scales attached by a hinge to the inner end of the last metacarpal-plate.

The gauntlet can be seen as transitional in character between the so-called 'Gothic' and 'Maximilian' fashions.

c1500 *9.75in (24.5cm) high*

$4,500-5,250 TDM

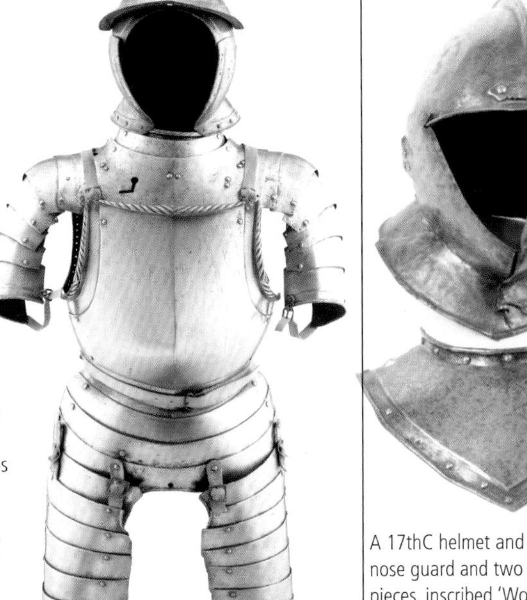

A mid-16thC composite South German infantry half-armor, comprising burgonet with one-piece skull rising to a tall roped comb, 'almain' collar of three lames front and rear with integral spaudlers of six lames each, breastplate formed of a main plate with medial ridge projecting forward over the belly, a pair of pendent tassets of seven and eight lames respectively, one-piece backplate.

$33,000-42,000 TDM

A 17thC helmet and neckpiece, with nose guard and two hinged cheek pieces, inscribed 'Worn by a retainer of the Earl of Pembroke from Wilton House'.

12.2in (31cm) high

$3,450-4,500 SWO

A Japanese full suit of armor, comprising lacquered metal kabuto with three tier shikoro, black lacquered four tier Mempo, hari-date with chased brass wreath form crest or mon of the Rattan Clan, black lacquered eight-tier cuirass, with full shoulder, arm and leg defenses formed of gilt lacquered plates and mail on fabric, some losses and areas of rust.

early Edo period and later *66in 9168cm) high*

$4,000-5,250 HT

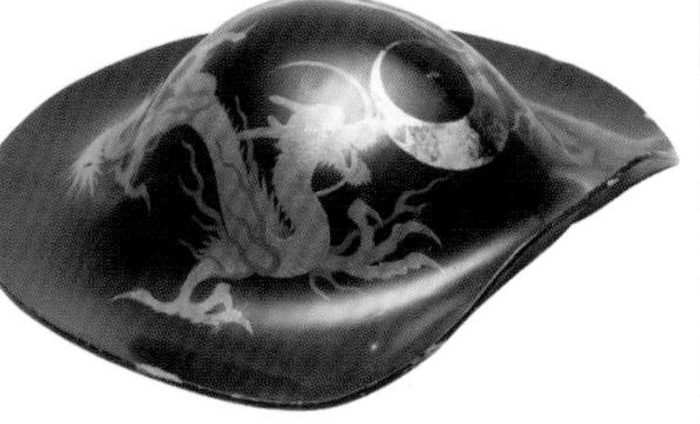

A Japanese lacquered helmet (jingasa), lacquered black and decorated in gilt polychrome with a pair of dragons divided by a gilt crescent mon,small chips.

late Edo or Meiji period *13.75in (35cm) diam*

$600-750 TDM

A rare 17th/18thC Chinese helmet, probably for a member of the imperial household, with tall skull formed of four iron plates each decorated on the outside in damascened gold with four Lentsa characters above a running five clawed dragon, the top of the skull with a large pierced iron central boss retained by four bud-shaped rivets all thickly encrusted with gold, retaining much gold throughout, the skull plates with small areas of pitting.

The five-clawed dragon was adopted as a motif on the robes of Government Officials and members of the Imperial family from the 14th Century. It is one of the twelve ornaments, all twelve being present only on the robes of the Emperor.

9in (23cm) high

$60,000-75,000 TDM

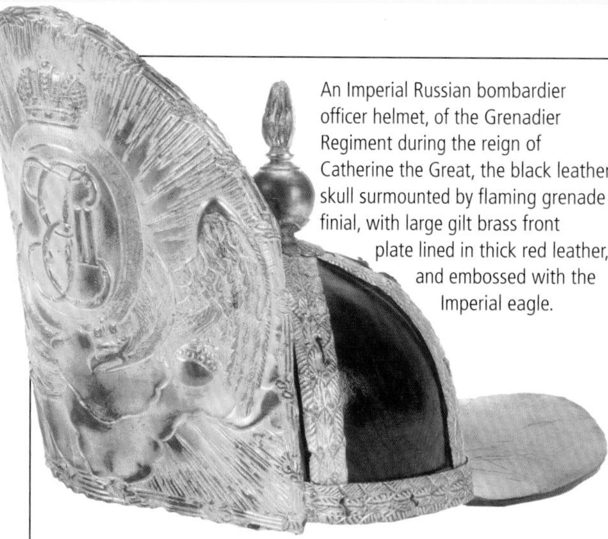

An Imperial Russian bombardier officer helmet, of the Grenadier Regiment during the reign of Catherine the Great, the black leather skull surmounted by flaming grenade finial, with large gilt brass front plate lined in thick red leather, and embossed with the Imperial eagle.

c1760 *17in (43 cm) long*

$22,500-30,000 **JACK**

A Victorian officer's helmet of the Household Cavalry, with silver-plated skull and gilt mounts, fine QVC plate flanked by oak and laurel sprays, mounted with a Garter Star, red plume of the Royal Horse Guards.

$4,500-6,000 **TDM**

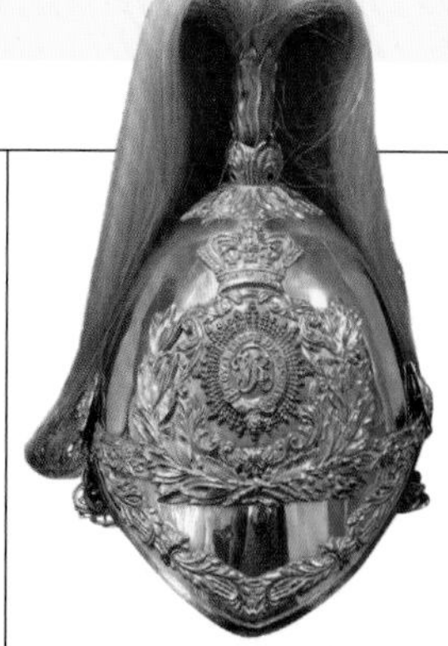

A Victorian Royal Irish Dragoon Guards officer's gilt helmet, probably worn by Lieutenant-Colonel George Ramsay Alured Denne (d.1915).

Denne entered the 4th Dragoon Guards as ensign in 1860, lieutenant in 1864, captain in 1870, major in 1881 and lieutenant colonel in 1882. He served in the Eygptian War in 1882 and was present at Tel-et-Mahuta and Mahsama, at the action of Kassasin, and was in command of the 4thDG at the Battle of Tel-el-Kebir and the capture of Cairo.

$3,000-4,500 **LOCK**

An officer's Victorian mess dress, of the 5th Dragoon Guards, with post-1901 rank-badges, companion green velvet waistcoat, and a frosted gilt waistbelt-plate of Dragoon Guards pattern, mounted with Victorian Royal Cypher and Motto all in white metal.

c1890-1902

$975-1,150 **TDM**

Two pages' miniature uniforms, of the Argyll and Sutherland Highlanders, two double-breasted short jackets with yellow collars, cuffs and shoulder-straps, two pairs of 'Government' tartan trews, waistbelts and shoulder-belts, two swords, two white shirts.

$300-450 **TDM**

An Indian Army officer's full dress tunic, of the 38th Dogra Regiment.

c1903-22

$120-180 **TDM**

An Indian Army officer's full dress tunic, of the 5th Mahratta Light Infantry, gold lace and braid ornamentation of post-1902 Infantry regulation style, twisted gold shoulder-cords bearing Major's crowns.

post 1922

$150-225 **SWO**

An Indian Army officer's mess dress, of the 3rd/6th Rajputana Rifles, by J. Dege, Conduit Street, London.

c1931

$300-450 **TDM**

Judith Picks

In a story which attracted extensive media coverage, this life-sized artefact was discovered in front of a gas fire during the house clearance of a local cottage. The owners, who had inherited the piece after the recent death of a relative, were unaware of its value and had been about to throw it in a skip. Auctioneer David Lay took the work to the British Museum where it was authenticated and dated to the 26th dynasty (c700-500BC), while further research linked the artefact to Douglas Liddell, the managing director of Spink & Sons from 1976-87. He was a close relation of the vendors and owned it on retiring to Cornwall. Mr Liddell died in 2003.

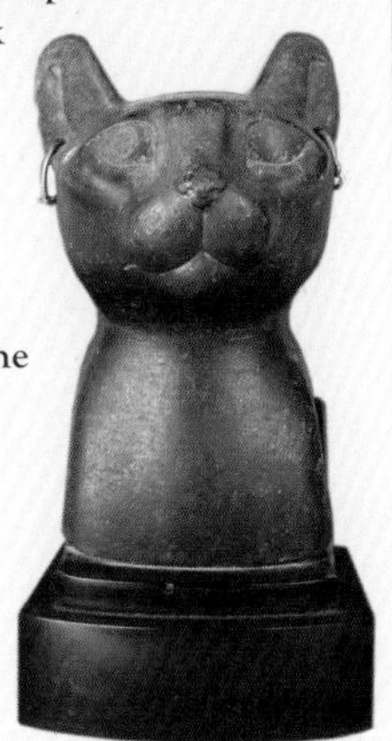

A finely modeled ancient Egyptian 26th dynasty bronze cat head, with original large gold hoop earrings.
700-500BC *7in (18cm) high*
$90,000-105,000 **LA**

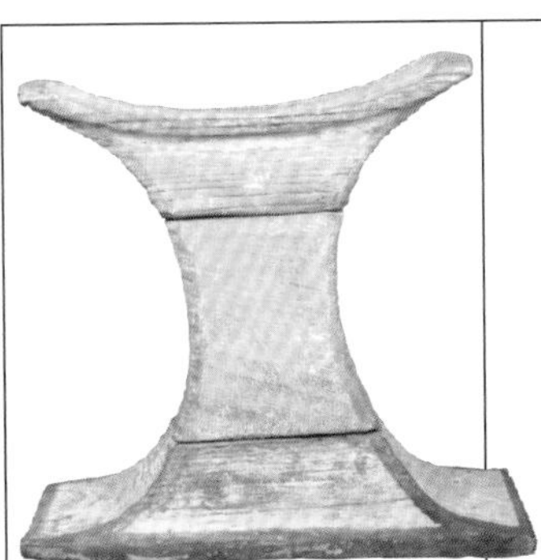

An Egyptian Middle Kingdom wood headrest, in three parts, with remains of pigment.
6.25in (15.5cm) high
$1,200-1,500 **WW**

An Egyptian carved wood 'Ba' bird, with a human face and headdress, the back with incised feather decoration.
9.25in (23.5cm) high
$4,000-4,500 **WW**

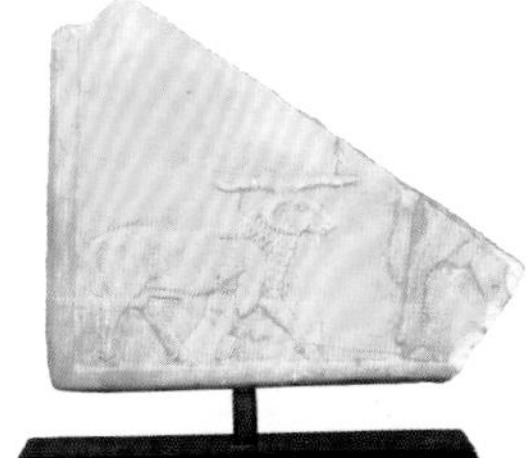

An Egyptian Ptolemaic Period limestone relief fragment, depicting a ram with curled horns.
304-330BC *3.75in (9.5cm) high*
$1,500-2,100 **WW**

An Egyptian 26th Dynasty ushabti, 'Psamtik Nefer Seshem faience Shabti (shawabti)', that translates to 'Illuminating of Osiris, the God's Father, Servant of Min, Lord of Sekret, Psamtik Nefer Seshem'.
660BCE *4.5in (11cm) high*
$2,400-2,850 **ARTM**

A Ptolemaic Egyptian limestone erotic figure, the Pataikos-like male with detailed wrap-around penis that he uses to rest on, original red pigment still evident, head invisibly reattached.
304-50BCE *4.5in (11.5cm) high*
$5,250-6,000 **ARTM**

An Egyptian cast bronze 'Apis' bull, standing on an integral plynth and wearing a uraeus and crown.

Apis was a deity worshiped primarily in Memphis and served as an intermediary between humans and Ptah, and later Osiris.

662-330BCE *2in (5cm) long*
$450-550 **ARTM**

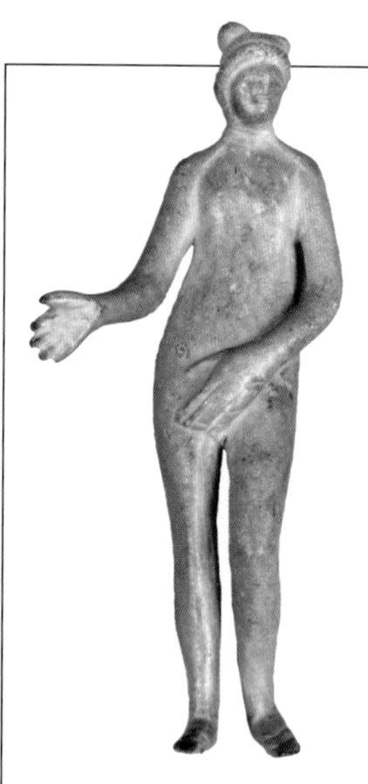

A Roman bronze figure of Aphrodite, standing nude covering her modesty with her left hand.
2nd-3rdC AD *5.5in (13.5cm) high*
$2,250-3,000 **WW**

A Roman bronze balsamarium, in the form of a male head, the hinged lid now missing.
2ndC AD *with handle 6in (15cm) high*
$1,800-2,250 **WW**

A Romano-Egyptian limestone head, carved with male head in relief, showing distinct Egyptian coiffure, with remains of original black and pink pigment.
1stC BCE *10.5in (27cm) high*
$6,750-7,500 **ARTM**

A Chimu/Inca double vessel, relief decorated stingrays and birds, with head and spout terminals linked with an arched handle.
8.75in (21.5cm) high
$1,500-2,250 **WW**

ESSENTIAL REFERENCE - MEZCALA CULTURE

The Mezcala culture (sometimes referred to as the Balsas culture) is the name given to a Mesoamerican culture that was based in the Guerrero state of southwestern Mexico, in the upper Balsas River region. The culture is poorly understood but is believed to have developed during the Middle and Late Pre-classic periods of Mesoamerican chronology, between 700 and 200BC. The culture continued into the Classic period (250-650AD) when it coexisted with the great metropolis of Teotihuacan. Archaeologists have studied the culture through limited controlled excavations, the examination of looted artifacts, and the study of Mezcala sculptures found as dedicatory offerings at the Aztec complex of Tenochtitlan.

A Mezcala stone figure.
5.25in (13cm) high
$900-1,200 **WW**

A Bactrian marble column idol, with a flared top having a central groove, the underside with a conforming groove.

2nd millennium BC *11in (28cm) high*
$4,000-4,500 **WW**

An unusual pre-Columbian Colima shaman, hollow-molded with vent hole between legs, he wears an exaggerated shaman's horn, repair to one leg and staff.
200BCE *17.75in (45cm) high*
$3,000-4,000 **ARTM**

An Etruscan bronze statue, 'Herakles & Lion Skin', with the skin of the Nemean lion draped over his arm, torch held in his right hand, crack, indentation on left hip.
4thC BCE *5.5in (14.5cm) high*
$6,750-7,500 **ARTM**

A Greek terracotta male head, with beard, painted inventory number E.65708.

2ndC BC *4.5in (11cm) high*

$1,000-1,200 **WW**

A Greek Corinthian aryballos, with a large swan confronting a lion, with palmettes, wear to pigment, repaired from 3 or 4 large sections.

These were used to hold precious oils in the bath and gymnasium.

7th-6thC BCE *4.75in (12cm) high*

$3,300-3,900 **ARTM**

A rare Greek attic right foot votive, the toenails and knuckles delineated, the pinky toe curling slightly in, on an integral plinth conforming to the shape of the foot.

Note the remaining pigment on the foot, very rare for such examples. Our initial assumption was that this is Etruscan, 300BCE. However, Dr. Florent Heintz at Sothebys is convinced this is Greek Attic, 4thC BCE.

4thC BCE

$1,000-1,400 **ARTM**

A Greek Canosan terracotta female statuette, slipped in white with pink and red accents, her face still holds much of the original white paint and red lips, while her hair takes an orange/red color, neck repaired.

3rd-2ndC CE *8.75in (22.5cm) high*

$2,700-3,300 **ARTM**

A Roman redware pottery oil lamp, central discus adorned with a dog running right, wearing collar around its neck, encircled by a band of intricately detailed and varied geometric decoration.

Lamps such as this were filled with olive oil in ancient times and lit by means of a thick wick, which protruded from the nozzle end. The flickering light of the oil lamp was the primary means of illuminating the darknes.

4th-5thC CE *2.25in (6cm) high*

$700-850 **ARTM**

A Roman marble foot fragment, 'The Greek Foot', likely from a full sized sculpture, incredibly veristic representation of the arch, muscles, and toes, including the small and purposefully malformed toe.

This foot is the idealized form of the foot in Greek Sculpture (also called the Royal Toe or the Morton's Triad) and thus followed through into Roman sculpture.

1st-2ndC CE *5.5in (14cm) long*

$4,000-4,500 **ARTM**

An iridescent Roman Empire glass jar, of pale green glass, with single wheel cut line and series of small, pulled nubbins.

200-350CE *3.75in (9.5cm) high*

$450-550 **ARTM**

A late 17th/early 18thC Italian violin, attributed to Giovanni Floreno Guidante, the one piece back of faint medium curl, unlabeled.

14in (35.40cm) high

$12,000-13,500 **GHOU**

An 18thC German violin, labeled 'Joannes Keffer, Geigen und Lautenmacher In Ischl', the one piece back of plainish wood.

1702 *14.25in (36.20cm) high*

$3,000-4,500 **GHOU**

A French violin, by and labeled 'Ch.J.B. Collin-Mezin, Luthier a Paris, Rue du Faub Poissonniere, no. 10', the two piece back of faint broad curl, with Edward Withers case.

1888 *14.2in (35.90cm) high*

$10,500-12,000 **GHOU**

A Markneukirchen violin, labeled 'Francesco Ruggieri, Gebaut 1914 Nach', the one piece back of broad wild curl, with two nickel mounted bows.

14in (35.60cm) high

$3,600-4,400 **GHOU**

An English violin, by and labeled 'John Wilkinson, London', the two piece back of wild flame.

14in (35.40cm) high

$8,250-9,750 **GHOU**

A German violoncello, of the Klotz School, labeled 'Baptiste Vuillaume a Paris...', the two piece back of faint medium curl, some damage.

c1780 *29in (74cm) high*

$6,750-8,250 **GHOU**

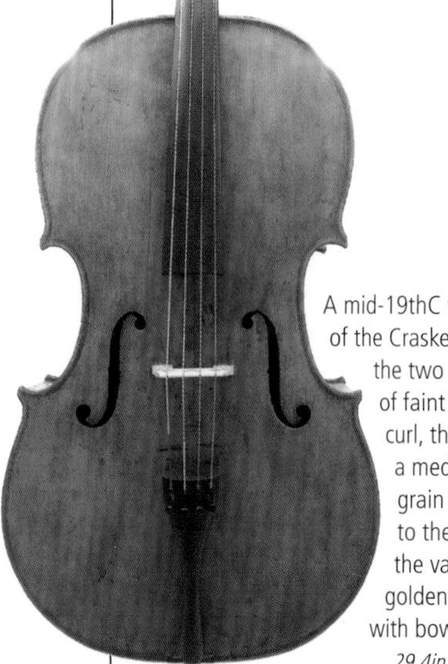

A mid-19thC violoncello, of the Craske school, the two piece back of faint medium curl, the table of a medium width grain widening to the flanks and the varnish of a golden-brown color, with bow.

29.4in (74.60cm) high

$120,000-135,000 **GHOU**

A 19thC French violoncello, branded 'Flanbau Aine a Paris', the two piece back of faint medium curl.

28.5in (72.40cm) high

$5,250-6,750 **GHOU**

An Italian violoncello, by Eugen Tenucci and labeled 'Copie Andreas Guarnerius, Hug & Co.-Zurich, Geigenbau- Atelier, Gebaut anno 19..', the jointed back of medium curl.

The purchase receipt for this instrument is from F.G. Rost, London dated September 25th 1946 for $105.

28.75in (73cm) high

$15,000-18,000 **GHOU**

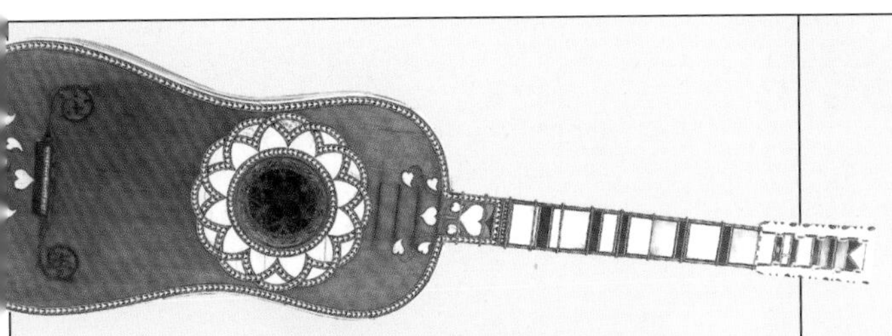

An early 17thC five-course baroque guitar, by Matteo Sellas, Venice, the back of numerous fluted ebony ribs intersected by bone stringing, the ribs with a central band of similar construction flanked by plain ebony bands.

This guitar was formerly the property of Sebastian Isepp (1884-1954), renowned picture conservator and chief restorer at the Kunsthistorischesmuseum, Vienna. He formed a collection of some thirty-five stringed instruments. Some passed to his son the renowned piano accompanist Martin Isepp (1930-2011).

string length 27in (68.5cm)

$82,500-90,000 **GHOU**

A late 18thC Italian small bodied guitar, labeled 'Gio: Battista Fabricatore, Napoli Anno 1790 in S M...', ebony banded burr walnut, spruce table.

$3,000-4,000 **GHOU**

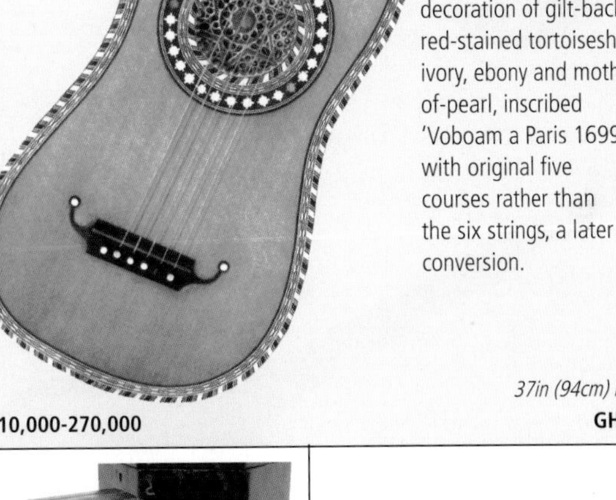

A guitar, by the celebrated French Luthier Jean-Baptiste Voboam (1658-after 1731), with intricate decoration of gilt-backed red-stained tortoiseshell, ivory, ebony and mother-of-pearl, inscribed 'Voboam a Paris 1699', with original five courses rather than the six strings, a later conversion.

37in (94cm) long

$210,000-270,000 **GHOU**

An early 20th century ukulele, by and stamped 'C. F. Martin & Co., Nazareth. PA', the headstock above a 12 fret rosewood fingerboard.

$1,000-1,200 **GHOU**

A Clifford Essex 'Paragon' five string resonator banjo, with case.

the skin 11in (28cm) diam

$1,800-2,250 **GHOU**

A Lachenal three row Anglo concertina, with thirty-three bone buttons on rosewood ends, six-fold bellows, in box.

$2,000-2,400 **GHOU**

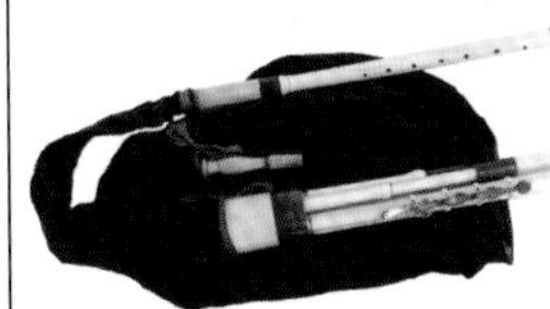

A set of ivory British silver-mounted pastoral pipes, the chanter in two joints, the leather bag with velvet cover and silk ties.

c1760 *length of chanter 20in (51cm)*

$22,500-27,000 **GHOU**

A burr maple and gilt composition harp, by Sebastian and Pierre Erard, forty six strings and eight pedals.

c1830 *70in (178cm) high*

$2,550-3,000 **L&T**

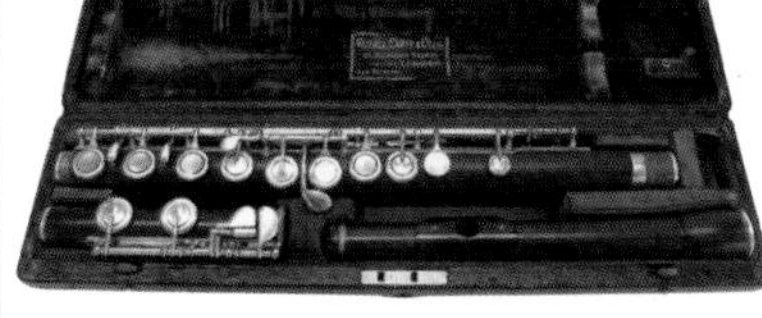

An early 20thC English flute, by and stamped 'Rudall Carte & Co. Ltd, 23 Berners Street, Oxford Street, London, no. 6729', in case.

26.8in (68cm) long

$1,800-2,250 **GHOU**

An Old Heckel maple bassoon, stamped 'Heckel, Biebrich, Sole Agent for U.S.A. Carl Fischer, New York, no. 5985'.

c1930 *53in (134.50cm) long*

$6,750-7,500 **GHOU**

A Fender Stratocaster electric guitar, made in USA, ser. no5422, tuners replaced with after-market Kluson style tuners, professional re-fret, professional re-finish, neck pickup has been rewound, neck re-lacquered, pots read 304-604, non-original case.

c1960

$7,500-9,000 **GHOU**

A Fender Telecaster electric guitar, made in USA, ser. noL76935, original condition with minimal wear, electrics in working order, a removed capacitor to enable the tone pot on the neck pickup, original case.

c1966

$10,500-12,000 **GHOU**

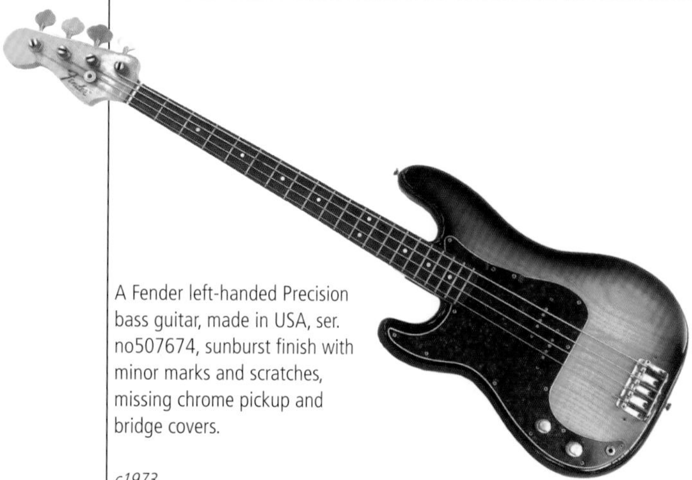

A Fender left-handed Precision bass guitar, made in USA, ser. no507674, sunburst finish with minor marks and scratches, missing chrome pickup and bridge covers.

c1973

$1,700-2,100 **GHOU**

A Gibson Les Paul Junior electric guitar, made in USA, ser. no72647, some wear to the fretboard, in working order, original case.

c1962

$4,500-6,000 **GHOU**

A Gibson 'Melody Maker' electric guitar, made in USA, ser. no. 43668, non-original bridge, repair to headstock, in working order, non-original hard case.

c1962

$1,400-1,500 **GHOU**

A Gibson ES-335 TD electric guitar, made in USA, ser. no96468, old fitted Bigsby tremolo, one replaced tuner, some crude repairs, in working order, hard case.

c1962

$6,000-6,750 **GHOU**

A Gibson Flying V Centennial 100th Anniversary series electric guitar, limited edition, only 100 made, made in USA, ser. no1970 9, with hard case.

c1994

$4,500-5,250 GHOU

A Gibson Les Paul Standard electric guitar, made in USA, ser. no02651596, in working order, hard case.

c2001

$2,100-2,700 GHOU

An Ibanez Universe seven string electric guitar, made in Japan, ser. no913465, missing truss rod cover, in working order, Ibanez hard case.

c1900

$2,700-3,300 GHOU

A Levinson Blade Texas Deluxe electric guitar, ser. no131461, 22 fret rosewood fingerboard with dot position markers, hard case

$850-975 GHOU

A Mosrite Mk. III electric guitar, made in USA, ser. noNC1438, signed by Semie Moseley, three pickups, electrics in working order, Mosrite hard case.

1988

$3,000-4,000 GHOU

A Rickenbacker model 4001 bass guitar, made in USA, ser. noTD1637, repaired buckle rash to the back, replaced like-for-like bridge saddles (originals in case) one volume knob missing cap, electrics require attention, modern hard case.

c1980

$1,800-2,250 GHOU

A 1977-78 American Telecaster, signed by Francis Rossi and Rick Parfitt, members of Status Quo, ser. noS723172, in fitted case.

The importance of provenence with rock & pop: the vendor is a friend of members of Status Quo. The guitar was signed on 8th November 1993 in Southampton at the book signing of 'Just for the Record'.

$1,500-2,250 SWO

DECORATIVE ARTS MARKET

As with many areas of collecting, Decorative Arts pieces have seen a rise in sales and prices of high-end items, and stagnation of mid-to-low-end goods.

Many Doulton wares are quite simply unfashionable. Demand for the Royal Doulton figures has fallen dramatically and only the prototypes, limited production and rare colorways are fetching good money. The opposite is true of the Doulton pieces with experimental glazes – especially anything lusterd or flambéd.

Moorcroft and Martin Brothers have continued to be strong in the market place. A James Macintyre flambé 'Carp' vase sold at Woolley & Wallis for a world record of nearly $40,500. A rare Martin Brothers stoneware bird jar and cover, dated 1884 sold at the same saleroom for over $90,000. Clarice Cliff will command high prices if the pattern and shape are rare. Lyon and Turnbull sold a 'May Avenue' conical sugar sifter for over $9,750.

Wedgwood Fairyland luster ceramics have still been on a roll, particularly in the US, Canada and Australia. Rare patterns, unusual colorways and the experimental or trial pieces are highly contested.

The Ohio school, meanwhile, including Rookwood and Roseville, has had a quiet year, with few exciting pieces coming onto the market. However Van Briggle, from Colorado, has been much in demand if it is an unusual colorway or shape, such as the 'Lorelei' vase, 1902, which David Rago sold for $274,000 (£190,000). Unusual ceramics continue to excite the Arts & Crafts market. David Rago sold a rare Arthur Baggs, Marblehead scenic tile c1908 for $100,000 (£70,000). Frederick H. Rhead at University City continues to break records. A four-part tile panel excised and enameled with a peacock c1910 sold at the same sale for $250,000 (£180,000).

20thC silver has continued to sell well, especially pieces by Charles Robert Ashbee and Omar Ramsden, as are rare and unusual Liberty pieces, particularly those by Archibald Knox.

In Art Nouveau glass, it is the big names that continue to sell: Lalique, Gallé, Tiffany, Loetz and Daum. David Rago sold a rare Lalique 'Bouchon Cassis' perfume bottle for $25,000 (£18,000).

Bronze and ivory figures by Demêtre Chiparus and Ferdinand Preiss have performed extremely well.

The sale of early 20thC furniture has been unspectacular – although when something fresh and with very good provenance appears so do the collectors. Charles Rennie Mackintosh continues to have a strong following. In their Decorative Arts sale in March 2015 Lyon and Turnbull sold an ebonized oak 'ladder back' chair designed for Miss Cranston's Willow Tearooms in 1903 for $60,000.

The work of George Nakashima continues to excite collectors. In April 2015 Freemans in Philadelphia sold 'Works from Nakashima Studios'. Highlights included a special 1981 Minguren 1 coffee table for $55,000 (almost £40,000) and a special cherry room divider for $40,000 (almost £30,000).

ght: A W.A.S. Benson Arts and Crafts silvered metal
ling light, attributed to James Powell & Co.
16in (40.5cm) wide
5,000-52,500 **MLL**

p Left: A possibly unique electroplated coffee pot,
signed by Christopher Dresser, made by James Dixon
Sons in Sheffield with facsimile signature 'CHR.
ESSER'.
881 *8.5in (22cm) high*
35,000-180,000 **L&T**

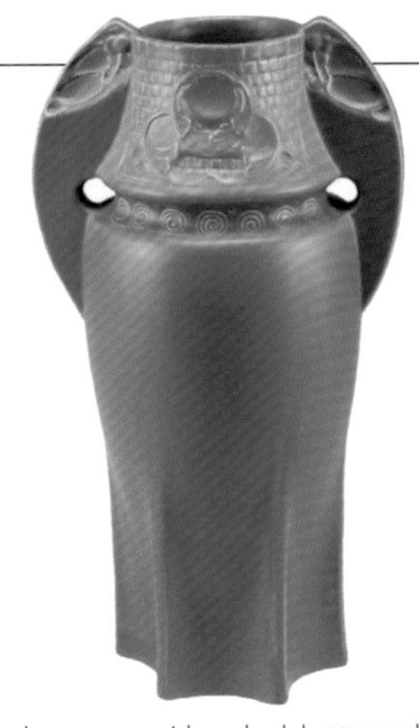

An Amphora vase, with arched, buttressed handles and scalloped base, bruise to base, Amphora mark/Austria.

17in (43cm) high

$850-975 **DRA**

An Art Nouveau Amphora Pottery vase, model no. 8357, with four loop handles, with stylised chrysanthemums, impressed marks.

5.5in (14cm) high

$600-750 **WW**

An Amphora Pottery vase, model no. 3604, with Art Nouveau maiden, minor glaze chips, hairline to body.

21in (53cm) high

$750-900 **WW**

An Amphora Art Nouveau vase, painted with a long-haired maiden, red R St K stamp, among others.

9.75in (25cm) high

$5,250-6,000 **DRA**

An Imperial Amphora figural vase, with a dragon wrapped around the rim, stamp 'IMPERIAL AMPHORA 4105 52, AUSTRIA', restoration to several areas.

17in (43cm) high

$10,500-12,000 **DRA**

An early 20thC Austrian jeweled Amphora vase, Amphora crown and oval mark.

16in (40.5cm) high

$2,000-2,400 **DRA**

A Riessner, Stellmacher & Kessel rare Amphora vase, with cockatoos, 'IMPERIAL AMPHORA' mark, '11956/46/GG'.

c1900 *12in (30.5cm) high*

$900-1,000 **DRA**

A Riessner, Stellmacher & Kessel Amphora calla lily pitcher, stamped crown 'AMPHORA AUSTRIA 531 G'.

c1900 *9in (23cm) high*

$750-900 **DRA**

A large Boch Frères Keramis Persian jardinière, painted BFK mark small hairlines to top rim.

10.25in (26cm) high

$1,150-1,300 **WW**

A Boch Frères pottery vase, impressed marks, restored.

10.25in (26cm) high

$1,150-1,300 **WW**

A Boch Frères Keramis vase, designed by Charles Catteau, pattern D.1099, with painted marks.

12.25in (31cm) high

$550-600 **WW**

A Boch Frères Keramis vase, designed by Charles Catteau, pattern D.1111, printed and painted marks, facsimile signature.

10in (25cm) high

$700-750 **WW**

A Boch Frères Keramis vase, designed by Charles Catteau, pattern D2531, with cranes wading in a river, painted marks, restoration to foot rim.

13.5in (34cm) high

$600-750 **WW**

A Boch Frères Gres Keramis vase, designed by Charles Catteau, pattern D.2300, painted with doves flying, impressed, printed and painted marks.

8.75in (22cm) high

$975-1,150 **WW**

A Boch Frères Keramis vase, 'Perseus and the Gorgons', designed by Charles Catteau, enameled with warriors fighting the Gorgons, printed and painted marks.

14in (36cm) high

$3,000-4,000 **WW**

A 1920s Charles Catteau Boch Frères Keramis glazed stoneware vase, ink stamp 'Gres Keramis D882 Ch. Catteau', stamped '886'.

10in (25.5cm) high

$975-1,150 **DRA**

A 1920s Charles Catteau Boch Frères Gres Keramis vase, marked 'Gres-Keramis 698'.

11in (28cm) high

$1,800-2,250 **DRA**

A Carlton Ware vase, 'Dragon and Traveller' pattern, printed marks.

7.5in (19cm) high

$750-900 **FLD**

A 1930s Carlton Ware 'Jazz' pattern vase, decorated with geometric patterns and shapes, printed marks, restored.

8.75in (22cm) high

$900-1,000 **FLD**

A Carlton Ware 'Fantasia' pattern champagne bucket.

8.5in (21cm) high

$495-600 **FLD**

A Carlton Ware 'Fantasia' pattern ginger jar and cover, printed script mark.

11in (28cm) high

$700-850 **FLD**

A 1920s Wiltshaw and Robinson Carlton Ware 'Tutankhamun' pattern ginger jar and cover, decorated with Egyptian scenes and motifs, printed marks, gilt hieroglyphics marks.

13.5in (34cm) high

$2,000-2,700 **FLD**

A 1930s Carlton Ware 'Egyptian Fan' pattern temple jar and cover, printed marks.

7in (18cm) high

$750-850 **FLD**

An Art Deco Carlton Ware 'Egyptian Fan' pattern plaque, printed factory marks and painted 'O/3283 3697'.

12.75in (32cm) diam

$2,250-3,000 **TEN**

A 1930s Carlton Ware 'Red Devil (Mephistopheles)' pattern trinket or cigarette box and cover, restored.

6.5in (16cm) wide

$600-700 **FLD**

A 1930s Carlton Ware 'Chinaland' pattern footed bowl, printed marks, diameter

10in (25cm) diam

$750-900 **FLD**

CLOSER LOOK - CLARICE CLIFF

Collectors look for bold, geometric patterns.

The enamel paint was applied relatively thickly, leaving behind visible brush strokes, although by this period they were slightly less dominent.

Lotus jugs are popular because they show the pattern clearly – you get a lot of pattern for your money.

This piece is in perfect condition, with no scratches or rubbing on the enamels.

This piece is made more desirable because it epitomises the designs and style of Clarice Cliff.

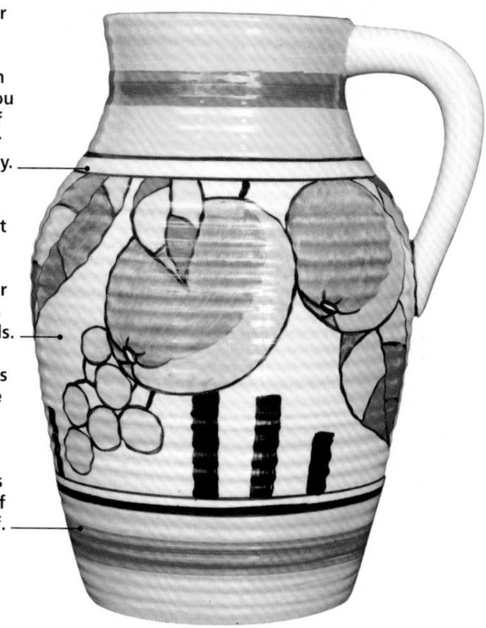

A Clarice Cliff 'Apples' pattern Lotus jug, 'FANTASQUE' and 'Bizarre' mark.
c1931 *11.5in (29cm) high*
$6,750-7,500 **FLD**

A Clarice Cliff 'Applique Lugano' pattern vase, shape 358, hand-painted 'Applique' and printed 'Bizarre' mark, some damage.
c1930 *8in (20.5cm) high*
$3,000-4,000 **FLD**

A Clarice Cliff 'Blue Autumn' pattern Lotus jug, printed 'Bizarre' marks.

This pattern is sometimes known as 'Balloon Trees'.
c1930 *11.75in (29.5cm) high*
$1,450-1,700 **L&T**

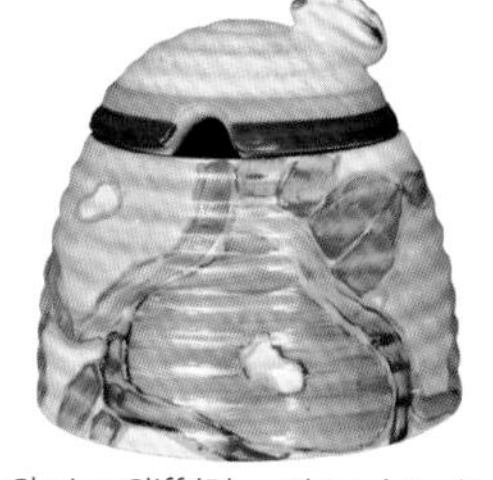

A Clarice Cliff 'Blue Chintz' Beehive honey pot, printed 'FANTASQUE' and 'Bizarre' mark.
c1932 *4in (10cm) high*
$300-400 **FLD**

A Clarice Cliff 'Branch & Squares Yellow' pattern bowl, shape 394, 'Bizarre' mark, small restoration to rim.
9in (23cm) wide
$850-975 **FLD**

A Clarice Cliff 'Bridgewater' pattern 'Lotus' jug, 'Bizarre' mark.
c1934 *11.5in (29cm) high*
$3,000-4,000 **FLD**

A Clarice Cliff 'Butterfly' pattern vase, shape 369, 'Fantasque' mark.
c1930 *8in (20cm) high*
$6,750-7,500 **FLD**

A Clarice Cliff 'Chevaux' pattern side plate, facsimile signature and factory printed marks.

This was designed by John Armstrong for the 1934 'Art in Industry' Exhibition.
8in (20cm) diam
$200-350 **SWO**

A Clarice Cliff 'Comets' pattern Lotus jug, printed 'Bizarre' mark.

This is the only known single-handled 'Lotus' jug in this pattern.

11.5in (29cm) high

$3,000-4,000 SWO

A Clarice Cliff 'Coral Firs' pattern 'As You Like It' planter, shape 657, printed marks.

4.75in (12cm) wide

$200-350 SWO

A Clarice Cliff 'Coral Firs' Mei Ping vase, printed 'Bizarre' marks.

9in (23cm) high

$2,250-3,000 WW

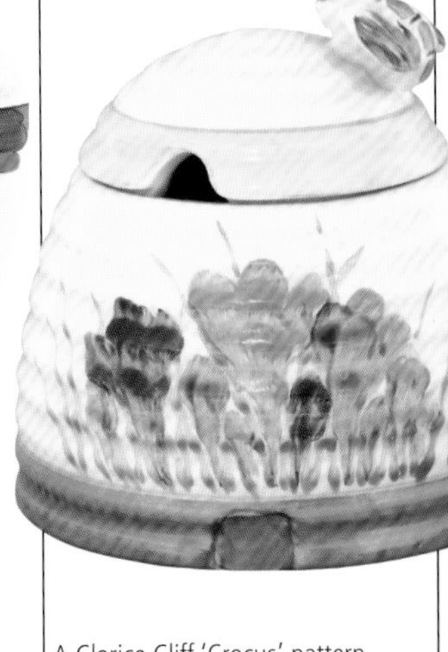

A Clarice Cliff 'Crocus' pattern honey pot and cover, printed 'Newport Pottery' mark.

3.75in (9.5cm) high

$165-225 SWO

A Clarice Cliff 'Delecia' pattern jug.

c1930 *6in (15cm) high*

$450-550 CHOR

A Clarice Cliff 'Double V' pattern miniature vase, shape 177, Newport Pottery marks.

2.75in (6.5cm) high

$1,150-1,300 FLD

A Clarice Cliff 'Double V' pattern vase, shape 269, 'Bizarre' mark.

1929 *6in (15cm) high*

$750-900 FLD

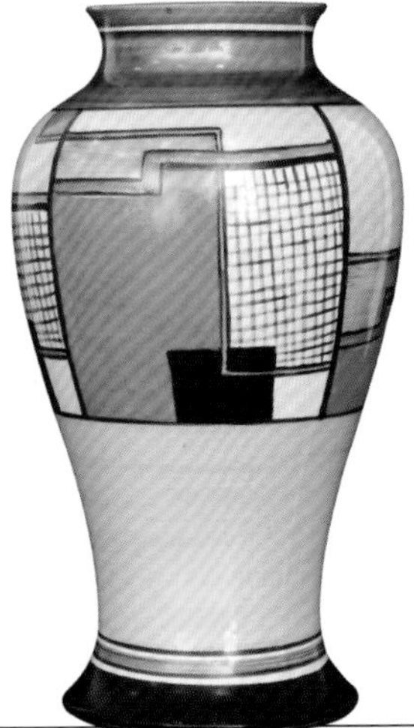

A Clarice Cliff 'Football' pattern Mei Ping vase, shape 14, 'Bizarre' mark.

c1930 *14in (36cm) high*

$7,500-9,000 FLD

A Clarice Cliff 'Forest Glen' pattern ribbed charger, with a streaked 'Delecia' effect sky, 'Bizarre' mark.

c1936 *18in (46cm) diam*

$3,000-4,000 FLD

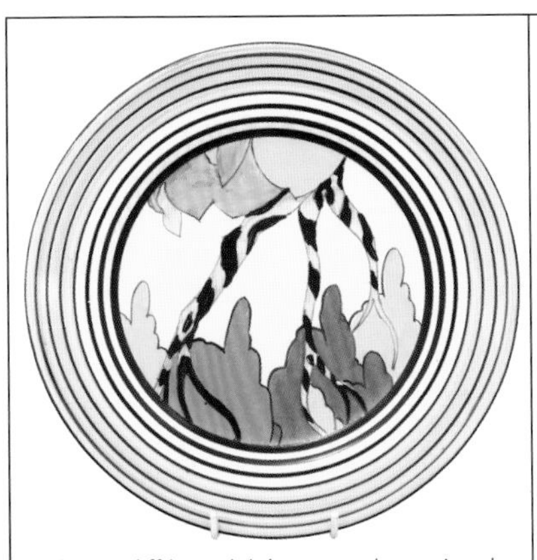

A Clarice Cliff 'Honolulu' pattern plate, printed 'Bizarre' marks, impressed date code.
1933 *10in (25cm) diam*
$550-700 **SWO**

A Clarice Cliff 'House & Bridge' pattern vase, shape 360, printed 'FANTASQUE' and Bizarre mark.
1932 *8in (20cm) high*
$2,250-3,000 **FLD**

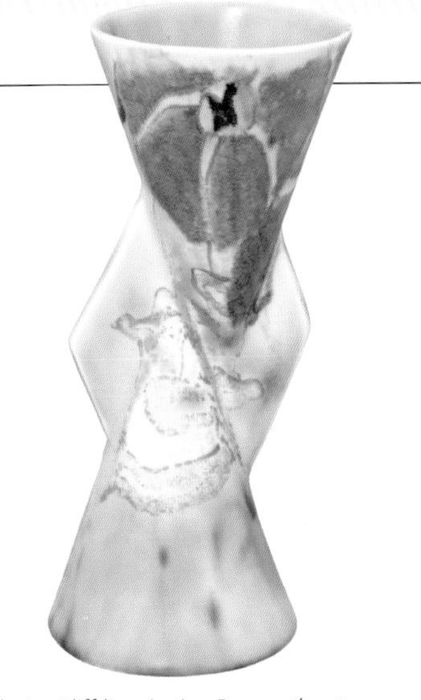

A Clarice Cliff 'Inspiration Bouquet' pattern yo-yo vase, shape 379, printed and painted marks.
9in (23cm) high
$4,000-4,500 **SWO**

A Clarice Cliff 'L'oiseau' bookend, incised signature, printed and inscribed in black.
1930s *7in (18cm) high*
$900-1,000 **HT**

A Clarice Cliff 'Latona Tree' pattern ribbed wall charger, large Clarice Cliff script signature.
c1930 *18in (46cm) diam*
$4,800-6,000 **FLD**

A Clarice Cliff 'Lightning' pattern vase, shape 265, printed and molded marks.
6in (15.5cm) high
$3,000-4,000 **SWO**

A Clarice Cliff 'Melon' pattern vase, printed 'Fantasque' mark.

This pattern is sometimes referred to as 'Picasso Fruit'.

c1930 *8.5in (21.5cm) high*
$700-750 **L&T**

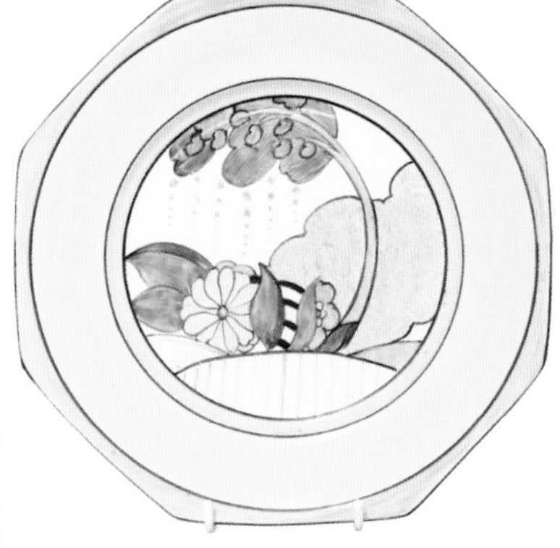

A Clarice Cliff 'Moonlight' pattern plate, printed 'Bizarre' marks.
c1933 *8.75in (22cm) wide*
$300-400 **SWO**

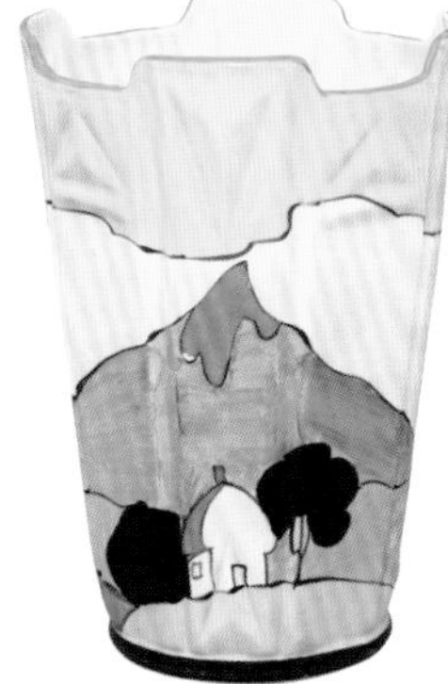

A Clarice Cliff 'Mountain' pattern vase, shape 451.
c1930 *8in (20cm) high*
$1,300-1,450 **SWO**

A Clarice Cliff 'Pastel Autumn' pattern vase, shape 515, printed 'Bizarre' marks.
c1930 *4.75in (12cm) high*
$1,150-1,300 **L&T**

A Clarice Cliff 'Poplar' pattern wall charger, printed 'Bizarre' mark, professionally restored.
13.5in (34cm) diam
$1,150-1,300 **WW**

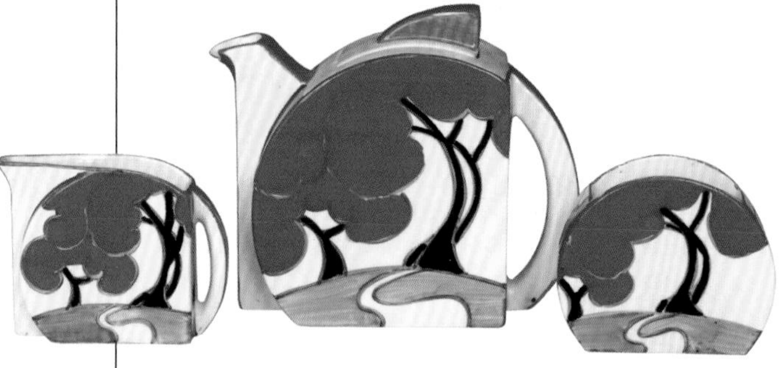

A Clarice Cliff 'Red Autumn' pattern Stamford shape teapot, milk and sugar, printed 'FANTASQUE' and 'Bizarre' mark with gold Lawleys backstamp, some damage.
c1930
$1,500-2,250 **FLD**

A Clarice Cliff 'Rudyard' pattern vase, shape 362, printed 'Bizarre' mark, restored.
8in (20cm) high
$600-700 **WW**

A Clarice Cliff 'Secrets' pattern Double D vase, shape 464, 'Bizarre' mark, some damage.
c1930 *8in (21cm) high*
$900-1,000 **FLD**

A pair of Clarice Cliff 'Solitude' pattern candlesticks, shape 310, printed 'Bizarre' marks.
c1930 *3in (8cm) high*
$600-700 **SWO**

A Clarice Cliff 'Summerhouse' pattern Lotus jug, black printed Newport Pottery and 'Bizarre' 'Fantasque' marks, small firing imperfection to the neck.
11.5in (29cm) high
$2,400-3,000 **CHEF**

A Clarice Cliff 'Sunburst' pattern vase, shape 358, 'Bizarre' back stamp.
c1930 *8in (20cm high*
$3,000-4,000 **FLD**

CLOSER LOOK - CLARICE CLIFF BOOKENDS

Clarice Cliff's iconic 'Sunray' design dating to late 1929 through to 1930.

The design represents a New York skyline and was Clarice's first landscape design, a crossover between abstract and landscape.

These are a well painted pair and the only ones known in this design.

These were illustrated in Will Farmer's 'Clarice Cliff', Shire Library, 2011, p7.

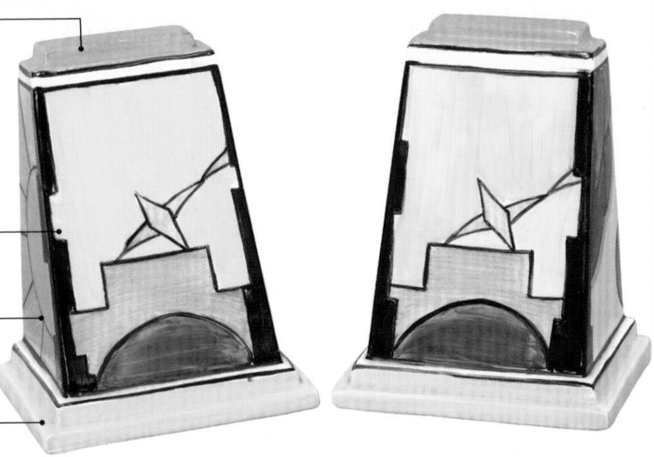

A pair of Clarice Cliff 'Sunray' pattern bookends, shape 405, printed 'Bizarre' marks.

5.75in (14.5cm) high

$4,500-5,250 **SWO**

A Clarice Cliff 'Sunrise' pattern Isis vase, printed factory marks.

9.75in (24.5cm) high

$1,150-1,300 **WW**

A Clarice Cliff 'Tennis' pattern side plate, printed 'Fantasque' marks.

c1930 *7in (18cm) diam*

$600-750 **SWO**

A Clarice Cliff 'Three Image Orange Trees' pattern vase, shape no.362, printed 'Fantasque' marks.

8in (20cm) high

$1,450-1,725 **SWO**

A Clarice Cliff 'Triangle Flower' pattern vase, shape 342, printed factory marks.

c1930 *7.5in (19cm) high*

$2,000-2,400 **WW**

A Clarice Cliff 'Umbrellas' pattern vase, printed factory marks, professional restoration to top rim.

1929 *8.75in (22cm) high*

$975-1,000 **WW**

A Clarice Cliff 'Umbrellas & Rain' pattern Lotus jug, 'Fantasque' mark.

c1929 *12in (30cm) high*

$1,300-1,450 **FLD**

A Clarice Cliff 'Windbells' pattern sardine box and cover, shape 447, 'Bizarre' mark.

c1933 *5in (13cm) wide*

$900-1,000 **FLD**

Judith Picks: William de Morgan

In 1907 William de Morgan left the London pottery he'd co-founded nineteen years earlier at Sands End, in Fulham. His parting observation was, 'all my life I have been trying to make beautiful things, and now that I can make them nobody wants them'. De Morgan's words are understandable; the enterprise had been failing commercially for some time. As far as the future was concerned, however, de Morgan got it completely wrong: aside from the fact that, prior to his death in 1917, he went on to become a highly acclaimed novelist, his distinctive ceramics are much admired nowadays, and command commensurately high prices.

A William De Morgan three tile panel, late Fulham period, with a blue Viking longship, stamped DM 98.
c1898 *24in (61cm) wide*
$10,500-12,000 **BELL**

A William De Morgan Sand's End Pottery tile, painted with a dragon-like creature in a Persian palette, framed impressed marks, minor restoration.
6in (15.5cm) square
$2,250-3,000 **WW**

A William De Morgan Chelsea Period tile, painted with a griffin being attacked by a cat-like creature, impressed marks.
6in (15.5cm) square
$3,300-4,400 **WW**

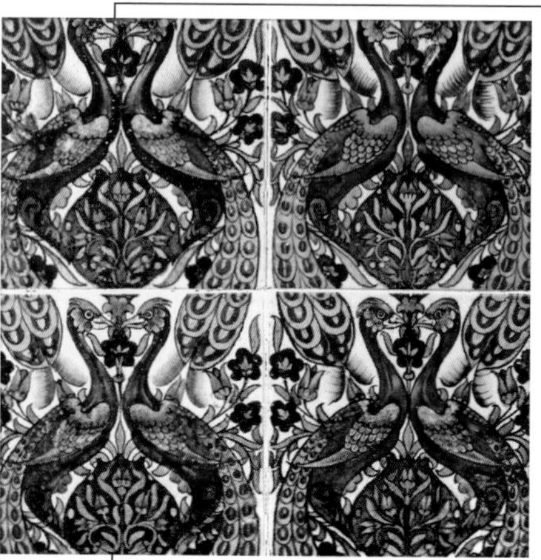

A William De Morgan group of four tiles, painted with pairs of peacocks divided by blue tulip heads. each tile
8.75in (22cm) square
$9,750-11,500 **CHEF**

A pair of William De Morgan Sand's End Pottery 'chameleon' tiles
6in (15.5cm) square
$11,250-14,250 **WW**

A William De Morgan pottery vase, painted with peacock birds, unsigned, small chip tot top rim.
8.75in (22cm) high
$3,000-4,000 **WW**

A William De Morgan ruby luster vase with dragons, unmarked.
1870s *10in (25.5cm) high*
$6,750-8,250 **DRA**

A William De Morgan pottery charger, painted with a gazelle.
14in (36cm) diam
$2,250-3,000 **WW**

CLOSER LOOK - DOULTON STONEWARE VASE

Although much Doulton stoneware is out of fashion this is by one of the great artists Hannah Barlow.

Although restored the pride of lions subject matter is unusual.

It is of extremely good quality with good tonality.

A Doulton stoneware vase, impressed mark, incised monogram, restored neck.

19in (48cm) high

$1,700-2,250 **WW**

A Doulton Lambeth vase, by Hannah Barlow, incised with ponies, impressed and incised marks and numbered 342, chip to the base and restored, dated.

1876 *13.25in (33.5cm) high*

$300-400 **SWO**

A Doulton Lambeth stoneware vase, by Frank H Butler, incised with Art Nouveau motifs, impressed and incised marks.

12.75in (32cm) high

$330-420 **SWO**

A Doulton Lambeth stoneware vase, by Edith Lupton, impressed marks, artist's monogram, chip to base rim, dated.

1880 *11in (28.5cm) high*

$300-400 **SWO**

A Doulton Lambeth vase, by Florence E. Barlow, decorated with seagulls, dated.

1887 *6.5in (16cm) high*

$300-400 **SWO**

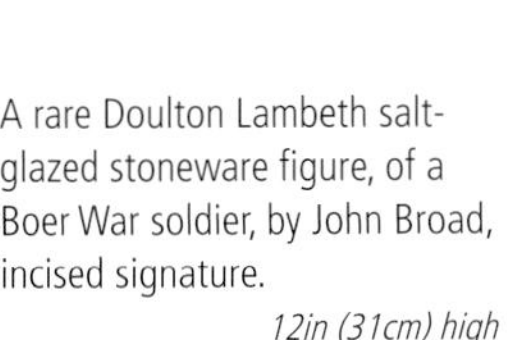

A rare Doulton Lambeth salt-glazed stoneware figure, of a Boer War soldier, by John Broad, incised signature.

12in (31cm) high

$1,800-2,250 **WW**

A Doulton Lambeth stoneware 'Galleon' finial, designed by Gilbert Bayes, minor chip.

This is a rare survivor. They were made for the washing line posts at St Pancras Housing Association Estates, London.

20in (51cm) high

$12,000-13,500 **WW**

A pair of Royal Doulton vases, by Hannah Barlow, incised with ponies and sheep, impressed marks and inscribed monograms, one rim damaged.
8.75in (22cm) high
$450-550 **SWO**

A Royal Doulton stoneware vase, by Elisa Simmance, painted with Art Nouveau cornflowers, impressed and incised marks.
14in (36cm) high
$600-750 **WW**

A Royal Doulton stoneware jardinière and stand.
41.25in (105cm) high
$300-400 **SWO**

A pair of Royal Doulton stoneware jardinières, with Art Nouveau decoration, incised 'B.W.' artist mark, shape 1884, impressed marks.
c1920 *7.75in (19.5cm) high*
$300-400 **SWO**

A Royal Doulton stoneware jardinière, impressed marks.
7.5in (19cm) high
$180-240 **SWO**

A Royal Doulton stoneware 'Foliage' bowl.
9in (22.5cm) diam
$180-240 **SWO**

Judith Picks: Inkwell

This inkwell is in the form of a Suffragette, 'The Virago', the figure standing with folded arms, an extremely unpleasand facial expression, with her apron impressed 'Votes for Women'. I think we can work out pretty clearly with the less-than-flattering portrayal of the subject what modeller Leslie Harradine's attitude was to women's suffrage! This model was one of two figures (the other similar with the head of an infant known as 'Baby') registered by Royal Doulton c1909 when the WSPU were taking their most radical and militant action.

A Royal Doulton inkwell, by L Harradine, impressed marks, with chips, damage to hinge.
3.5in (8.5cm) high
$700-750 **BW**

A Royal Doulton Titanian vase, after Cecil Aldin, printed signature.
8in (21cm) high
$450-550 **SWO**

A Royal Doulton flambé vase, by Harry Nixon, printed mark artists HN monogram.
6.5in (16.5cm) high
$2,250-3,000 WW

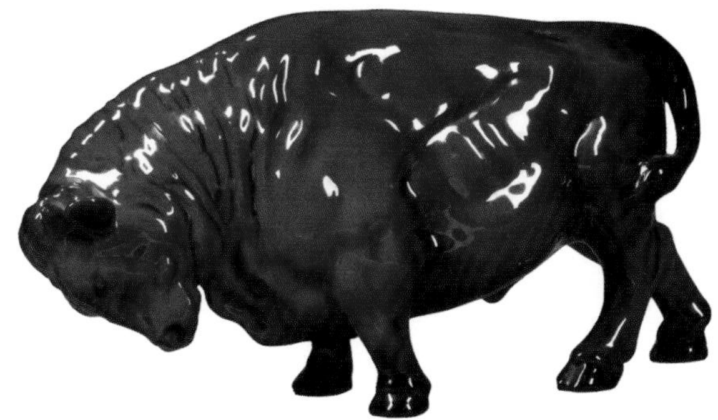

An early 20thC Royal Doulton flambé bull, signed Noke, printed mark.
10.75in (27.5cm) long
$600-750 SK

A Royal Doulton 'Bluebeard' figurine, HN75, designed by Charles Noke, missing plume on turban.

This figure was originally thought to have been modeled by E W Light, but is now thought to have been modeled by Noke. This figure is one of a number of Doulton figures from this period inspired by the costumes and sets of the Ballets Russe, in particular the 1910 production of 'One Thousand and One Arabian Nights'.
In theory this figure was produced for almost 20 years but, like many of these early figures, the surviving numbers are small.

c1917
$4,000-4,500 PFR

A Royal Doulton 'Sung Ware' flambé vase, signed monograms for Frederick Moore, printed factory mark.
c1925 *7in (18cm) high*
$1,500-2,100 SK

A Royal Doulton comical 'Seated Fox in Huntsman dark red jacket', HN100,
6.25in (16cm) high
$1,450-1,800 PSA

A Royal Doulton figure 'Dolly', HN355, after the model by Ernest William Light, printed and painted marks.

The model for this rare figure was originally ascribed to Charles Noke, until another example was discovered, signed E.W. Light. The obscured original title on the present example appears to read 'Dollie', suggesting this is a very early production, before the spelling 'Dolly' was finally fixed upon. Ernest William Light was a freelance modeller in the potteries, producing a number of the early figures for Doulton, starting in 1914, as well as working for Wedgwood.

c1919 *7.5in (18.5cm) high*
$1,500-2,250 MAB

A rare Royal Doulton figurine Dolly, HN469, designed by Harry Tittensor.
c1920
$9,000-10,500 MAR

A rare Royal Doulton figurine 'One of the Forty', HN501, designed by Charles Noke.

Inspiration was the traditional Oriental tale 'Ali Baba and the Forty Thieves', first performed as the operetta 'Chu Chin Chow' at His Majesty's Theatre in 1916.

8.5in (20cm) high
$3,000-4,500 MAR

A Royal Doulton figurine' Jack Point', HN610 from the character series depicting Sir Henry Lytton in character, designed by Charles J Noke, issued 1924 to 1949, painted and printed marks.

6.75in (17cm) high

$570-700 FLD

A Royal Doulton figurine 'Elsie Maynard', HN639, from the character series designed by Charles J Noke, issued 1924 to 1949, painted and printed marks.

c1935 *7.5in (19cm) high*

$450-550 FLD

A Royal Doulton Prestige figure, 'Jack Point', HN2080 designed by Charles Noke.

Charles J. Noke, the original Art Director at Doulton, was fascinated by jesters and legend has it that the first piece he modeled for Doulton was that of a jester. Nokes first HN jester, 'Jack Point', HN85, was modeled after the central character in Gilbert and Sullivans opera 'The Yeoman of the Guard', first performed in 1888. In the opera, 'Jack Point' is a strolling jester with a broken heart. The story ends tragically with Jack Point collapsing, apparently dead, after he is abandoned by his beloved, Elsie Maynard.

1952-2009 *16in (40.5cm) high*

$1,300-1,450 PSA

A Royal Doulton 'Sunshine Girl', HN1344, modeled by Leslie Harradine.

1929 *5in (13cm) high*

$5,250-6,000 CR

A Royal Doulton Prestige figure, 'King Charles', HN2084,

16in (41cm) high

$700-750 PSA

A Royal Doulton 'Figure Ships Figure Pocahintus', HN2930, designed by S. Keenan, limited edition of 950, with wooden stand and presentation box.

1982 *8in (20cm) high*

$400-450 PSA

A Royal Doulton Figure Henry VIII, 'Bird of Prey', HN3350, limited edition No1397, with certificate.

$700-750 PSA

A Royal Doulton Prestige figure, 'Field Marshall Montgomery', HN3405, in a limited edition with certificate.

12in (31cm) high

$400-450 PSA

A Fulper jar with pedestal, with cucumber green crystalline glaze, with raised racetrack mark.

1916-22 *11.25in (29cm) high*

$4,500-5,250 DRA

A Fulper vase, Chinese blue crystalline glaze, vertical incised mark.

1916-22 *8in (20.5cm) high*

$2,250-3,000 DRA

A Fulper vase, with gunmetal and famille rose flambé glazes, vertical raised mark.

1916-22 *8in (20.5cm) high*

$1,000-1,200 DRA

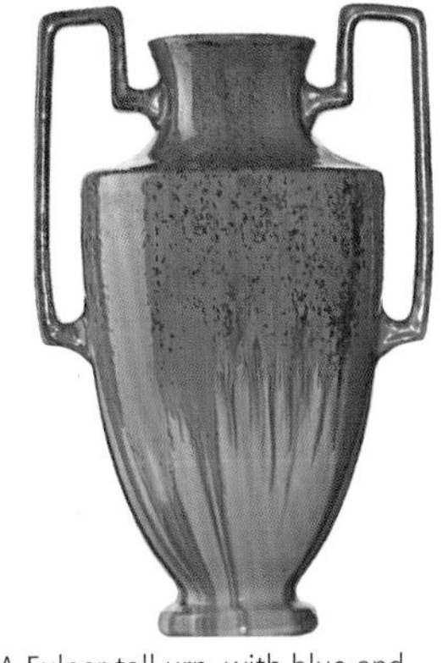

A Fulper tall urn, with blue and ivory flambé glazes, with raised racetrack mark.

1916-22 *14.5in (37cm) high*

$3,300-4,500 DRA

A rare Fulper 'Cattail' vase, with verte antique glaze, vertical incised mark.

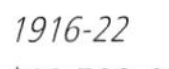

1916-22 *12.5in (32cm) high*

$10,500-12,000 DRA

A Fulper bottle-shaped vase, in famille rose glaze, on stand, vertical raised mark to both pieces.

1916-22 *18.5in (47cm) high*

$3,900-4,500 DRA

A rare Fulper 'Vasekraft' lamp, with 'Flemington green flambé' glaze, with leaded glass, two sockets, with rectangular ink stamp, patent pending, no. 22, shade numbered 22/33/28.

c1908 *22in (56cm) high*

$14,250-17,250 DRA

A rare Fulper Vasekraft lamp, 'Leopard Skin' crystalline glaze, leaded glass, two sockets, vertical rectangular stamp.

18in (46cm) high

$21,000-27,000 DRA

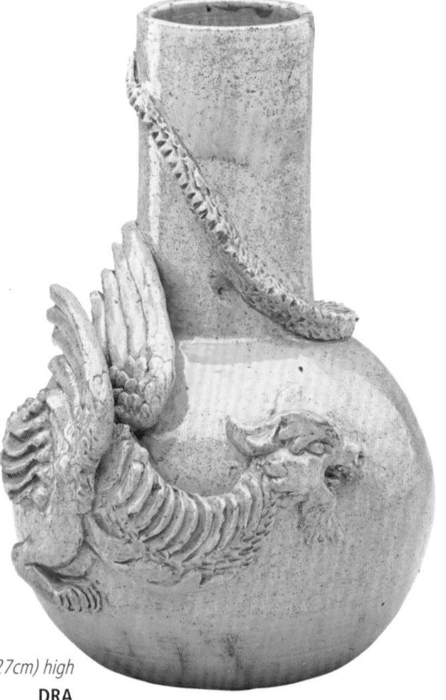

A George Ohr glazed earthenware vase, with sculpted dragon, stamped 'NEW ORLEANS ART POTTERY COMPANY 249 BARONNE STREET', 4in (10cm) hairline from rim.

c1890 *10.5in (27cm) high*

$27,000-33,000 **DRA**

A George Ohr vase, with in-body twist and ruffled rim, with pink and purple volcanic glazes, stamped 'G.E. OHR, Biloxi, Miss'.

1897-1900 *5.5in (14cm) high*

$75,000-90,000 **DRA**

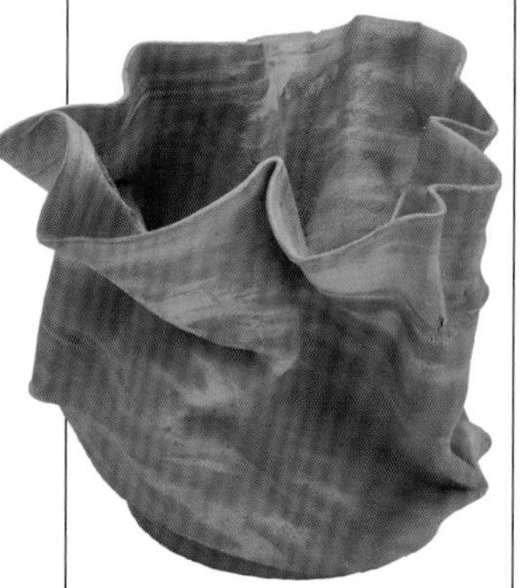

A George Ohr bisque-fired vessel, of manipulated scroddled clay, with script signature.

1898-1910 *5in (13cm) high*

$22,500-30,000 **DRA**

A George Ohr vase, with curled handles, with jade, amber, and gunmetal mottled glazes with melt fissures, stamped 'G.E. OHR, Biloxi, Miss.'.

1895-96 *7.25in (18.5cm) high*

$30,000-38,000 **DRA**

A George Ohr vessel, with ocher and red sponged-on glaze, stamped 'G.E. OHR Biloxi, Miss.'.

1897-1900 *9.25in (23.5cm) high*

$49,500-54,000 **DRA**

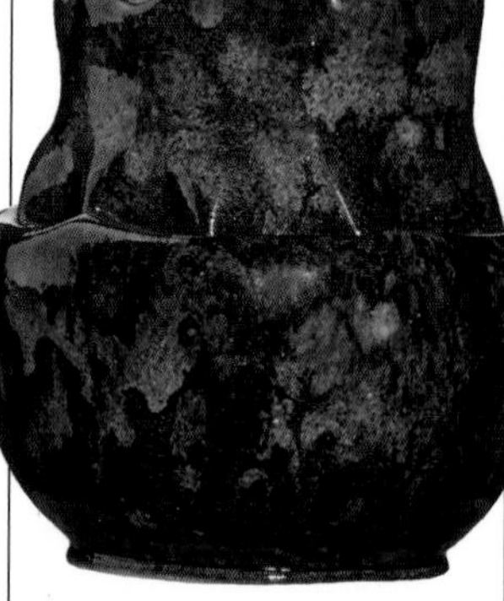

A George Ohr vase, with mottled blue and white sponged-on glaze, stamped 'G.E. OHR, Biloxi, Miss.'.

1897-1918 *5in (13cm) high*

$25,500-30,000 **DRA**

A George Ohr pitcher with ribbon handle, gunmetal, raspberry, and gray sponged-on glaze, stamped 'G.E. OHR, Biloxi, Miss.'

8in (20.5cm) high

$28,500-34,500 **DRA**

A George Ohr crumpled vessel, with pink volcanic glaze with speckled green interior, stamped 'GEO. E. OHR BILOXI, MISS'.

1895-6 *4in (10cm) wide*

$5,700-6,300 **DRA**

A George Ohr dimpled pitcher, with ocher and gunmetal glazes, stamped 'BILOXI, MISS. GEO. E. OHR'.

1895-6 *3.5in (9cm) high*

$3,000-4,000 **DRA**

A late 19thC Goldscheider earthenware bust, of a Nubian female slave, cold painted in colors and gilt, impressed marks,

22in (56cm) high

$2,250-3,000 **HT**

A 20thC Art Nouveau Goldscheider Pottery wall plaque, cast from a model by Montenave, model no. 0799, with two Symbolist maidens, facsimile signature in the cast, minor damages.

35in (90cm) wide

$3,300-4,400 **WW**

An Goldscheider figure by Lorenzl, signed on the top of the base, makers mark underneath.

c1930 *17.5in (44cm) high*

$4,500-6,000 **PC**

A Goldscheider Pottery figure of two tennis players, cast from a model by Stephan Dakon, model no. 7778, impressed marks, facsimile signature, losses.

12.75in (32cm) high

$2,000-2,700 **WW**

A Goldscheider Pottery model of a lady, designed by Josef Lorenzl/Stephan Dakon, model no.5532, dressed as a pierrot, impressed and printed marks, restored finger.

12.75in (32cm) high

$1,500-2,250 **WW**

A Goldscheider Pottery figure of a dancer, designed by Josef Lorenzl, model no. 5715, impressed and printed marks, cast signature to back.

15.5in (39cm) high

$2,400-3,000 **WW**

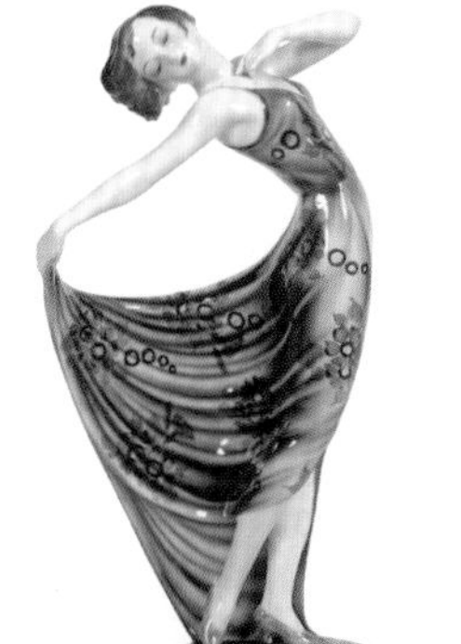

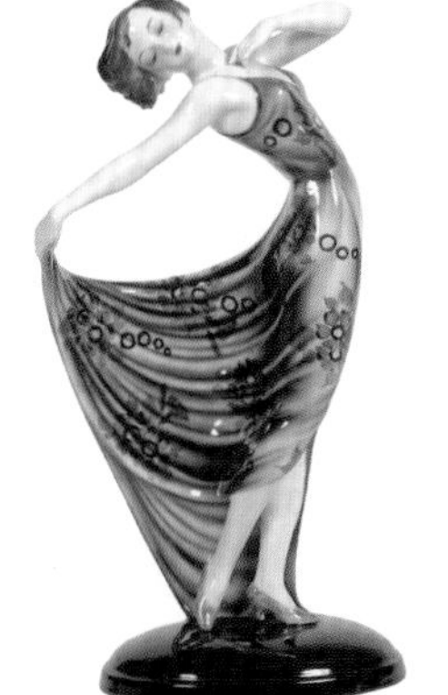

A 1930s Goldscheider figure, after Lorenzl, of a young female dancer wearing a blue floral dress, printed marks.

16in (41cm) high

$1,500-2,100 **HT**

A Goldscheider earthenware figure, by Dakon, with impressed marks, no. 7423.

9.5in (24.5cm) high

$2,250-3,000 **L&T**

A Goldscheider pottery wall mask, model no.7813, designed by Kurt Goebel, with impressed and incised mark.

c1938 *13in (33cm) high*

$600-900 **L&T**

A Goldscheider pottery wall mask, model no.7784, with impressed and printed marks.

c1935-8 *11in (28cm) high*

$400-550 **WW**

A 1930s Goldscheider mask, holding a tragedy mask, stamped 'Goldscheider Wien Made in Austria, 6288 3'.

14in (35.5cm) high

$1,200-1,500 **DRA**

A Goldscheider wall mask, model no.7784, impressed and printed marks.

10.25in (26cm) high

$420-510 **WW**

A Goldscheider wall mask.

c1925-8 *11.5in (29cm) high*

$1,400-1,700 **PC**

A 1930s Goldscheider bust, with wood stand, 'Goldscheider Wien' brass tag on base.

13.5in (24cm) high

$975-1,150 **DRA**

A 1930s Goldscheider bust, stamped 'Goldscheider Wien Made In Austria 66 7653'.

15in (38cm) high

$1,700-2,100 **DRA**

A 1950s Goldscheider bust, stamped 'Goldscheider Wien Made In Austria, 7604 66'.

12in (30cm) high

$1,200-1,500 **DRA**

A Goldscheider head, model no.585, impressed and printed marks original paper label, chips

10in (25cm) high

$400-450 **WW**

A Grueby seven-handled vase, with circular Grueby pottery stamp '5'.

c1900 *10.75in (27.5cm) high*

$37,500-45,000 **DRA**

A Grueby vase, with light green irises, with circular 'Faience' stamp 'EWR 161'.

c1900 *13in (33cm) high*

$30,000-38,000 **DRA**

A Grueby vase, with leaves and buds, with circular 'Faience' stamp.

c1900 *23in (58.5cm) high*

$22,500-30,000 **DRA**

A Grueby vase, with dark green matte glaze, with circular 'Pottery' stamp '257'artist's cipher.

c1905 *8.5in (22cm) high*

$3,000-4,000 **DRA**

A Grueby vase, by Ruth Erickson, with curdled blue glaze and carved irises, circular 'Pottery' stamp, incised 'RE'.

c1905 *14.75in (37.5cm) high*

$34,500-45,000 **DRA**

A Grueby fine two-color vase, with leaves and white buds, circular 'Pottery' stamp, incised 'HJ 8-11' (or 17).

c1905 *6.5in (16.5cm) high*

$9,750-11,500 **DRA**

A Grueby ribbed vase, circular 'Pottery' stamp.

c1905 *10.75in (27.5cm) high*

$4,500-6,000 **DRA**

A Grueby vase, with indigo blue glaze, circular 'Pottery' stamp, incised 'CH'.

c1905 *9in (23cm) high*

$2,250-3,000 **DRA**

A Grueby vase, with leaves and white buds, circular 'Pottery' stamp, incised 'FE 6/9'.

8in (20.3cm) wide

$6,000-7,500 **DRA**

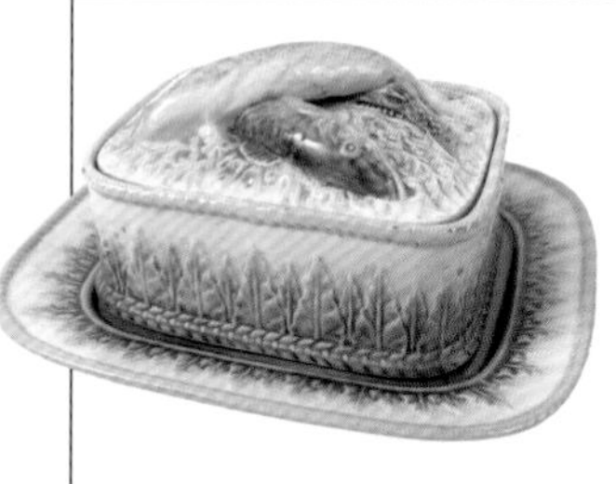

A George Jones majolica sardine dish, cover and stand, the lid with relief molded pike, perch and trout on a seaweed bed.

c1875 *8.5in (21.5cm) wide*

$450-600 **SWO**

A late 19thC George Jones majolica jardinière, applied with sparrows and damselflies.

12in (30cm) high

$1,200-1,500 **WW**

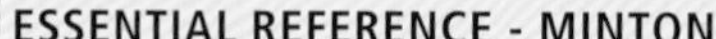

ESSENTIAL REFERENCE - MINTON

Minton majolica was created by Joseph Leon Francois Arnoux who was appointed Art Director at Minton in 1848. His primary task was to introduce and promote new products. At the time there was great interest in classical design and bright color. Arnoux decided to reintroduce the work of Bernard Palissy, whose naturalistic, bright colored 'maiolica' wares had been popular in the 16thC. However, Arnoux used a thicker body to make pieces more sturdy. This body was given a coating of opaque white glaze which provided a surface for over-painting in brightly colored opaque glazes. Later, transparent glazes were used over relief molding. Some pieces produced were uniquely Victorian, and were influenced by naturalism, Japonism, Darwin's origin of species, and the revival of Renaissance and Gothic taste introduced by Augustus Pugin. The result often being unusual and whimsical shapes. Minton's introduced their new pottery at the 1851 exhibition to great success, with Queen Victoria being one of majolica's new admirers.

A Minton majolica pie dish and cover, the cover with a hound and hunting trophy, the sides with a hare and a pheasant, impressed marks, dated cypher.

1864 *12.25in (31cm) wide*

$1,400-1,800 **L&T**

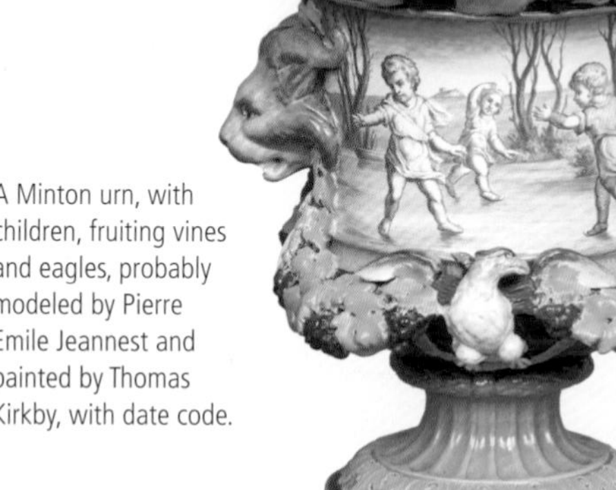

A Minton urn, with children, fruiting vines and eagles, probably modeled by Pierre Emile Jeannest and painted by Thomas Kirkby, with date code.

1856 *12in (31cm) high*

$900-1,000 **ROW**

A Minton & Co. majolica 'monkey' garden seat, impressed cipher and uppercase 'MINTON' marks, mold number 589, date cypher.

1867 *17.75in (45cm) high*

$15,000-21,000 **L&T**

A Minton majolica jardinière, painted with exotic birds, flowers and foliage, with twin dolphin mask loop handles, impressed mark, date cypher.

1876 *13in (33cm) diam*

$1,800-2,250 **L&T**

A Minton majolica centerpiece, modeled as two cats pulling on ribbons either side of a basket, impressed marks.

5.5in (14cm) high

$1,400-1,700 **GORL**

A Wedgwood majolica jardinière on pedestal base, decorated with floral urns, impressed marks.

1893 *jardiniere 41.25in (104.5cm) high*

$1,500-2,100 **SK**

A Minton majolica jardinière, with lion mask handles and paw feet, impressed number, some damage.

11in (28cm) high,

$195-270 **BELL**

A late 19thC Worcester majolica nautilus shell centerpiece, modeled on the back of a swan between lilypad dishes, impressed mark.

8.75in (22cm) high

$900-1,000 **WW**

An early 20thC Clement Massier majolica floor vase, stamped 'CLEMENT MASSIER GOLFE JUAN (A.M.)', some restoration to handles.

23.25in (59cm) high

$1,000-1,500 **DRA**

A 19thC majolica garden seat, with cranes amidst aquatic plants, the reverse with swallows.

19in (48cm) high

$1,800-2,250 **WW**

A rare 19thC majolica stick stand, modeled as a pug dog.

21in (53cm) high

$3,300-4,400 **WW**

A Victorian majolica jardinière, with the stand, badly damaged.

7in (18.5cm) high

$75-120 **DA&H**

A Continental Art Nouveau majolica jardinière on pedestal, marked 'Vulcan'.

1900 *50in (127cm) high*

$1,800-2,250 **DRA**

A Martin Brothers glazed stoneware bird tobacco jar, incised 'R.W. Martin + Bros. London + Southall 9.1886'.
1886 *12.5in (32cm) high*
$45,000-60,000 **DRA**

Judith Picks: Wally Bird

Who could not fall in love with a Wally Bird with his puffed out chest and outstretched wings, and head with forward looking staring eyes and broad beak. The Robert and Edwin Martin had apprentiships at the Doulton Lambeth factories and prior to that at the Palace of Westminster. Each of the Martin brothers had distinct roles within the studio; Robert Wallace was principally responsible for the modelling; the birds, face jugs and grotesques were largely his work. Charles ran the shop and gallery at High Holborn, London, whilst Edwin was the principle decorator and Walter the thrower. They were the early pioneers of the studio pottery movement, using salt glaze stoneware to produce their unique and hand crafted designs. It is said that their grotesque 'Wally Birds' were modeled on leading public figures of the day. I'd love to know who this bird represented!

A large Martin Brothers stoneware bird sculpture, by Robert Wallace Martin, incised 'R W Martin & Bros, London & Southall 11', small chip to neck.
1891 *16.5in (42cm) high*
$75,000-90,000 **WW**

A Martin Brothers bird salt-glazed stoneware tobacco jar, incised 'Martin Bros London & Southall 7-1892'.
1892 *11in (28cm) high*
$97,500-112,500 **DRA**

A Martin Brothers stoneware bird vase and cover, by Robert Wallace Martin, incised 'Martin Bros London & Southall', small chip to collar, dated.
1898 *14.75in (37cm) high*
$57,000-66,000 **WW**

An early 20thC Martin Brothers stoneware humidor, their heads removable as covers.
6in (15cm) high
$60,000-75,000 **SK**

A Martin Brothers glazed stoneware dog tobacco jar, head incised 'Martin Bros.10-1895'.
1895 *12.5in (32cm) high*
$21,000-27,000 **DRA**

A rare Martin Brothers stoneware spoon warmer, by Robert Wallace Martin, incised 'Martin London & Southall, 5.9', dated.
1882 *6.75in (17cm) high*
$67,500-75,000 **WW**

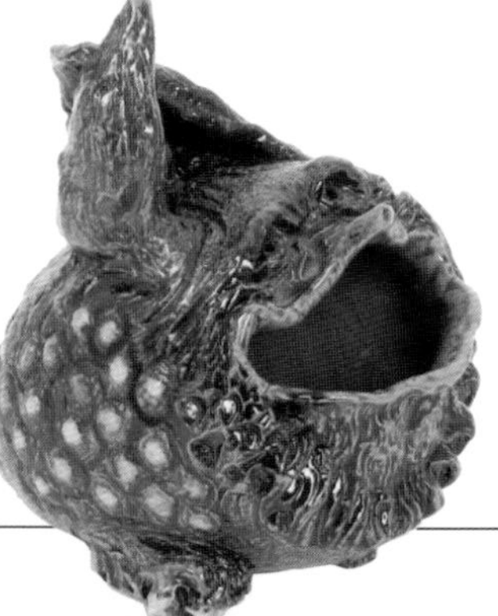

A Martin Brothers glazed stoneware armadillo flower vessel, incised 'R.W. Martin + Bros. London + Southall 1-1890'.
1890 *8.5in (21.75cm) long*
$45,000-52,500 **DRA**

A Martin Brothers stoneware aquatic vase, by Robert Wallace Martin, with grotesque fish, the handles modeled as grotesque eels, incised 'R W Martin & Bros London & Southall 5-1884', kiln kiss to body.

1884 *12.25in (31cm) high*

$8,250-9,750 **WW**

A Martin Brothers stoneware jug, by Robert Wallace Martin, with a Bacchanalian mask, incised 'R W Martin London & Southall'.

1891 *8.75in (22cm) high*

$19,500-22,500 **WW**

A Martin Brothers stoneware ewer, with grotesque fish, jelly-fish, and octopus, with white metal Japonism stopper. incised '8 1892, Martin Bros, London & Southall', neck re-stuck.

1892 *8.75in (22cm) high*

$2,400-3,000 **WW**

A Martin Brothers stoneware vase, with red squirrels, incised '4-1894, Martin Bros London & Southall'.

1894 *8in (20cm) high*

$8,250-9,750 **WW**

A Martin Brothers stoneware bird jug, by Edwin and Walter Martin, incised '2-1896 Martin Bros London & Southall'.

1896 *8in (20cm) high*

$6,000-7,500 **WW**

A Martin Brothers stoneware 'dragon' jug, incised '3 1898 Martin Bros London & Southall'.

1898 *9in (23cm) high*

$6,000-7,500 **WW**

A Martin Brothers stoneware aquatic flask, by Walter and Edwin Martin, incised with fish and eels, incised 'Martin Bros London & Southall 4-1900', body cracks.

1900 *8in (20cm) high*

$4,500-5,250 **WW**

A Martin Brothers stoneware 'Eskimo' jug, incised 'R W Martin & Bros. London & Southall. 7.7.1903.', crack to body, rim chip).

1903 *13in (33cm) high*

$4,500-6,000 **DN**

A rare Martin Brothers stoneware 'Eskimo' jug, by Robert Wallace Martin, incised 'R W Martin & Bros London & Southall', hairline to top rim.

1903 *14in (35.5cm) high*

$9,750-11,500 **WW**

A Minton flask and cover, decorated with fish and sea shells, signed William Mussill.

12in (30cm) high

$750-900 PSA

A pair of Minton Secessionist vases, probably designed by Leon Solon, printed and impressed marks, small chips to footrims.

13in (33cm)

$700-850 CHEF

CLOSER LOOK - MINTON PÂTE-SUR-PÂTE

Pâte-sur-pâte is a relief design is created on an unfired, unglazed body by applying successive layers of white slip (liquid clay) with a brush.

This vase is signed by Frederick Alfred Rhead one of the greatest porcelain designers.

It is a rare and stunningly beautiful example.

It is very unusual with text 'And when the angel with his darker draught draws up to thee-take that and do not shrink' taken from verse 48 of 'The Rubaiyat of Omar Khayyam'.

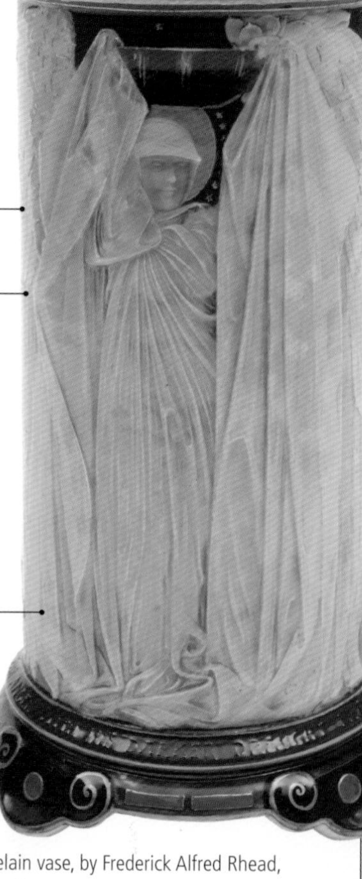

A Minton pâte-sur-pâte porcelain vase, by Frederick Alfred Rhead, decorated with an angel, signed.

12in (30.5cm) high

$30,000-38,000 BE

A Minton pilgrim flask, attributed to Dr Christopher Dresser, with gilt lug handles, decorated with cranes, scrolling clouds and leaping carp, impressed '1348'.

c1870 8in (20cm) high

$550-700 SWO

A Minton garden seat, possibly by Christopher Dresser, molded with cranes, shape number 1219, chip to rim, dated.

1877 19in (48cm) high

$150-225 SWO

A Minton's encaustic bread plate, designed by A. W. N. Pugin, inscribed 'Waste Not Want Not', impressed '430' to reverse.

13in (33.5cm) diam

$2,000-2,700 WW

A pair of late 19thC Mintons porcelain pâte-sur-pâte plates, by Albion Birks, carved with a putto, puce marks, retailers marks for Thomas Goode.

9.5in (24.5cm) diam

$2,700-3,300 DN

A Minton Hollins & Co. tile, painted with an owl, marked.

8.5in (21cm) square

$850-975 WW

A Moorcroft Macintyre 'Revived Cornflower' vase, signed in green 'W Moorcroft' with printed Macintyre mark, restored to neck and base.

c1910 10.5in (26.5cm) high

$1,200-1,500 SWO

An early 20thC James Macintyre & Co. 'Dianthus' vase, by William Moorcroft, printed marks with green flash initials.

9.5in (24cm) high

$1,500-2,100 FLD

A James Macintyre & Co. 'Eighteenth Century' vase, designed by William Moorcroft, printed mark, painted green signature.

7in (17.5cm) high

$750-900 WW

An early 20thC James Macintyre & Co 'Florian' ware 'Hazeldene on White' vase, by William Moorcroft, decorated with tubelined trees, green full signature with printed marks and retailer mark 'Made for Townsend & Co, Newcastle on Tyne'.

10in (26cm) high

$13,500-18,000 FLD

A James Macintyre 'Florian' ware 'Honesty' jardinière, designed by William Moorcroft, printed factory mark, painted green signature

7.5in (18.5cm) high

$1,500-2,100 WW

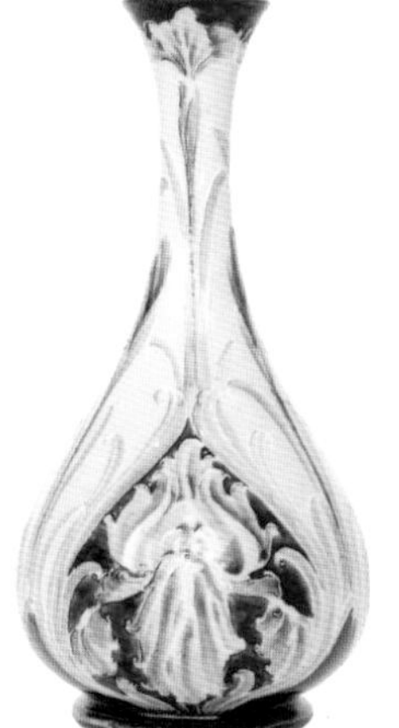

An early 20thC James Macintyre & Co. 'Iris' bottle vase, by William Moorcroft, printed marks with green flash initials.

8.5in (21cm) high

$750-900 FLD

A James Macintyre & Co. 'Pansy' vase, by William Moorcroft, impressed Burslem mark, painted green signature and date.

1914 9.5in (33.5cm) high

$4,500-5,250 WW

An early 20thC James Macintyre & Co 'Peacock Feather' vase, by William Moorcroft, decorated with tubelined feathers and foliate scrolls, printed marks with green flash initials.

5in (13cm) high

$550-600 FLD

An early 20thC James Macintyre & Co. 'Poppy on White' 'Florian' ware vase, by William Moorcroft, printed marks and green flash signature.

12.25in (31cm) high

$1,500-2,100 FLD

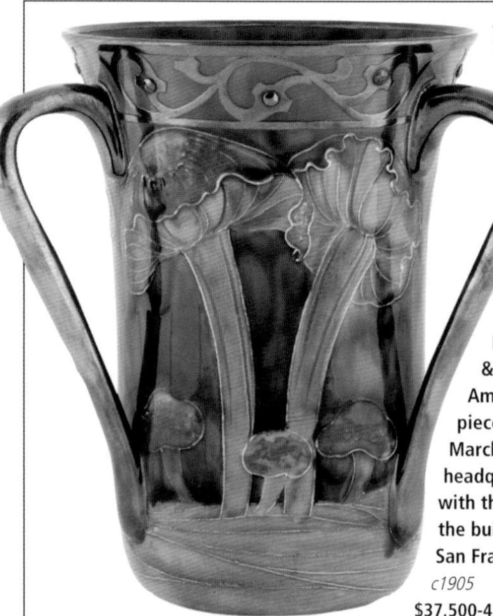

A Moorcroft silver-overlaid 'Claremont' loving cup, for Shreve, San Francisco, the silvered border executed in the Arts and Crafts taste, surmounting the squeeze bag mushroom decorated body, base numbered 'R'N' 420081', and signed 'W. Moorcroft / Shreve & Co. / San Francisco'.

This image was taken before the silver was polished. This loving cup combines the talents of William Moorcroft and the San Francisco jewellers Shreve & Co. Awarded a gold medal at the St Louis International Exhibition, Moorcroft pottery was sold by Shreve & Co. from 1904, with Tiffany and other famous American stores following shortly afterward. Many pieces were silver-mounted, specifically for export. In March 1906 Shreve & Co. opened their new 11-storey headquarters at Post Street and Grant Avenue. Built with the latest engineering technologies of the time, the building was one of only a few to survive the Great San Francisco earthquake the following month.

c1905 *7.5in (19cm) high*

$37,500-45,000 **CLAR**

A monumental William Moorcroft flambé 'Eventide Landscape' vase, tubelined with ten tall trees, impressed 'MADE IN ENGLAND', blue painted signature and dated.

16in (40.5cm)

$15,000-18,000 **TEN**

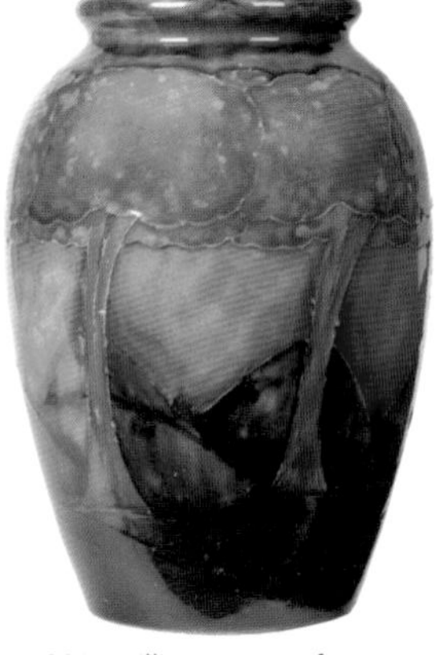

A 1920s William Moorcroft 'Eventide Landscape' vase, tubelined with six tall trees, impressed 'MOORCROFT MADE IN ENGLAND', blue painted signature.

9.5in (24cm) high

$4,000-4,500 **TEN**

A tall Moorcroft Pottery 'Moonlit Blue' candlestick, designed by William Moorcroft, impressed marks, painted green signature.

c1925 *10in (26cm) high*

$975-1,150 **WW**

A Moorcroft 'Moonlit Blue' inkwell and cover, designed by William Moorcroft, impressed marks, painted signature.

3in (8cm) high

$2,400-3,000 **WW**

A Moorcroft 'Pomegranates' wall charger, printed mark 'MADE FOR LIBERTY & CO.', signed in green 'W. MOORCROFT'.

c1910 *11.75in (29.5cm) diam*

$5,250-6,000 **L&T**

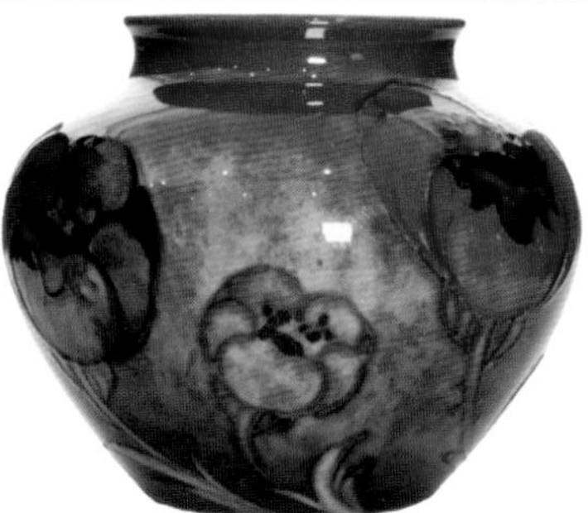

A Moorcroft 'Flambé Poppy' vase, decorated with tubelined flowers and foliage, impressed marks with flash initials.

3.5in (8.5cm)

$1,150-1,300 **FLD**

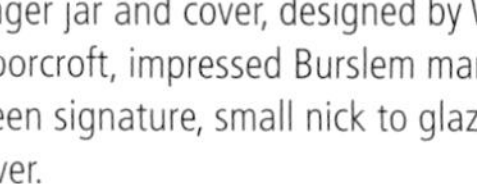

A 1920s Moorcroft Pottery 'Spanish' pattern ginger jar and cover, designed by William Moorcroft, impressed Burslem mark, painted green signature, small nick to glaze on rim of cover.

6in (15cm) high

$6,000-7,500 **WW**

A William Moorcroft flambé bear, designed by Francis Arthur Edwards, blue painted monogram 'WM'.

c1925 *6.75in (17cm) long*

$4,500-6,000 **TEN**

An early Newcomb College tyg, by Irene Borden Keep, with pomegranates, marked 'NC/JM/U/I.B.K./C50/1' in triangle.

1901 *6.5in (16.5cm) high*

$15,000-22,500 DRA

An early Newcomb College vase, by Marie de Hoa LeBlanc, with cotton blossoms, marked 'NC/MHLeB/S30'.

1902 *11in (28cm) high*

$27,000-37,500 DRA

An early Newcomb college vase, by Harriet C. Joor, carved with dogwood, marked 'NC/HJ/Y30/JM'.

1903 *8in (20.5cm) high*

$10,500-12,000 DRA

An early and unusual Newcomb College vessel, incised with fish, marked 'NC/AL52/C/JM' and unrecognized artist's cipher.

1905 *6in (15cm) high*

$25,500-30,000 DRA

A rare Newcomb College oil lamp, by Mary Sheerer, inscribed, 'Live and Love Till Life and Love Are One,' base signed 'NC JM Q BQ13 M.S.', with paper label.

1907

$97,500-112,500 DRA

An early Newcomb College vase, by Leona Nicholson, with freesia, marked 'NC/LN/JM/W/CW-4'.

1909 *8.25in (21cm) high*

$45,000-52,500 DRA

An early Newcomb College vase, by Leona Nicholson, with raised decoration of bats, marked 'NC/M/Q/LN/G91X', professional restoration to rim and base.

1913 *13.25in (34cm) high*

$52,500-60,000 DRA

A Transitional Newcomb College vase, by Henrietta Bailey, with irises, marked 'NC/JX26/268/HB/JM'.

1918 *11.25in (29cm) high*

$15,000-22,500 DRA

A Newcomb College scenic vase, by Sadie Irvine, marked 'NC/MO35/JM/AFS/211'.

1922 *11.25in (29cm) high*

$12,000-15,000 DRA

A Pilkington's 'Lancastrian' vase, by Richard Joyce, painted with birds perched on carnation stems between cypress trees, impressed marks, painted artist cipher, dated.

1906 *4.5in (11cm) high*

$1,800-2,250 **WW**

A Pilkington's 'Royal Lancastrian' vase, by Richard Joyce, painted with birds perched amongst prunus boughs, impressed marks, painted monogram.

6.75in (17cm) high

$2,250-3,000 **WW**

A Pilkington's 'Royal Lancastrian' luster vase, by Gordon Forsyth, impressed marks and inscribed marks, restored.

1906 *4in (10.5cm) high*

$550-600 **SWO**

An early 20thC Pilkington's 'Royal Lancastrian' vase, by Jessie Jones, artist cypher and impressed marks.

3.5in (9cm) high

$900-1,000 **SWO**

A Pilkington's 'Lancastrian' bottle vase, by Charles Cundall, impressed mark, painted cipher and dated.

1907 *7in (17.5cm) high*

$1,150-1,300 **WW**

A Pilkington's 'Lancastrian' vase, impressed marks, dated.

1909 *4.75in (12cm) high*

$750-900 **WW**

A Pilkington's 'Lancastrian Pottery' 'Sea Maiden' vase, designed by Walter Crane, painted by William S Mycock, painted with a classical female figure in a sailing boat, between bands of laurel and Greek Key, painted artist cypher 'WC Des' cypher and impressed marks, paper label.

10.75in (27cm) high

$9,000-10,500
WW

A large Pilkington's 'Lancastrian' vase, by William S Mycock, impressed mark and painted monogram, dated.

1913 *10.25in (26cm) high*

$6,000-6,750 **WW**

A Pilkington's 'Royal Lancastrian' vase, by Richard Joyce, impressed and painted marks, dated.

1917 *8.5in (21cm) high*

$1,400-1,800 **WW**

A Carter's Poole Pottery luster vase, designed by Owen Carter, incised marks, chips, dated.

1906 *12.75in (32cm) high*

$400-450 **WW**

A Carter Stabler & Adams Poole Pottery red earthenware vase, shape no. 958, designed by Harold Stabler, painted by Mary Brown, impressed mark 'no. 11', painter's mark and '/ CA', some crazing.

1921-34 *7.5in (18.5cm) high*

$600-700 **MOR**

A Carter Stabler Adams Poole pottery 'Leipzig Girl' charger, designed by Olive Bourne, incised 'C.S.A. POOLE, ENGLAND, 910'.

This charger takes its name from the International Exhibition of Industrial Art at Leipzig in 1927, at which Carter Stabler and Adams exhibited.

1927 *17.75in (45cm) diam*

$900-1,200 **SWO**

A Carter Stabler & Adams Poole Pottery vase, pattern HE, impressed and painted marks.

8.75in (22cm) high

$255-300 **WW**

A Carter Stabler & Adams Poole Pottery vase, by Truda Rivers, pattern ZW, impressed and painted marks.

14in (36cm) high

$900-1,000 **WW**

A 1930s Poole Pottery vase, designed by Truda Carter, shape 429, painted by Ruth Pavely in the YI pattern, impressed and hand-painted marks.

10.25in (26cm) high

$600-700 **FLD**

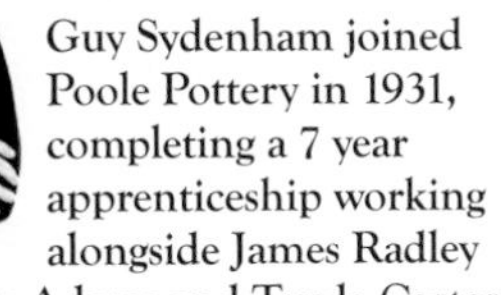

Judith Picks: Poole

Guy Sydenham joined Poole Pottery in 1931, completing a 7 year apprenticeship working alongside James Radley Young, John Adams and Truda Carter. He said himself, 'My brief after the War was to revive the old traditional majolica and Delft floral ware. I had to train a new team of throwers and when this was up and running I managed to persuade the directors to let me have a studio separate from the factory and we began...to move into more creative and individual pieces of studio pottery. The 1950's and 1960's...was a very creative and fulfilling decade; then, unfortunately, commercial pressures to standardise and economise caused a dilution of standards and quality, when freshness and spontaneity became dulled by repetition - the result was inevitable. I left'.

'People have to be led away from wanting what is traditional' [Guy Sydenham]

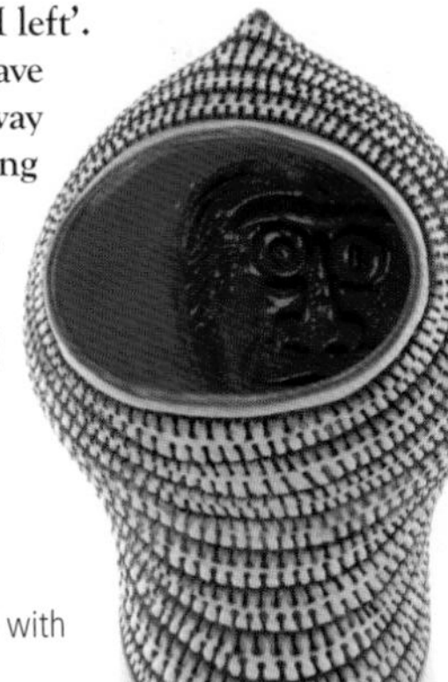

A Poole Pottery 'Atlantis' stoneware helmet table lamp, by Guy Sydenham, with carved chain-mail decoration, the interior carved with a bearded knight, impressed mark, incised monograms.

12in (30cm) high

$975-1,150 **WW**

A 1930s Poole Pottery vase, shape 660, decorated in the 'BL' pattern, painted by Ruth Pavely, impressed and painted marks.

12.25in (31cm)

$850-975 **FLD**

A Poole Pottery two-tile Egyptian panel, decorated by Nicola Massarella, mounted on a board.

10in (25cm) wide each panel

$400-450 **SWO**

An early Rookwood 'Dull Finish' vase, by Maria Longworth Nichols, with frogs, octopi, and crab in a tug-of-war, 'tamped ROOKWOOD 1882/R65' artist's cipher.

1882 *9.75in (25cm) high*

$13,500-18,000 **DRA**

A Rookwood 'Faience' umbrella stand, with carp, flame mark 'VI/1066AY/12/X'.

1906 *26in (66cm) high*

$4,000-4,500 **DRA**

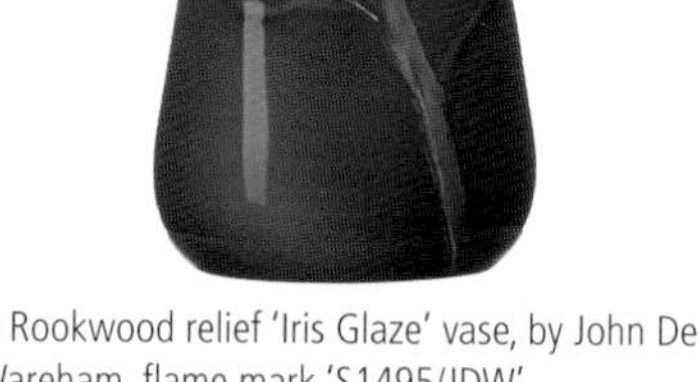

A Rookwood relief 'Iris Glaze' vase, by John Dee Wareham, flame mark 'S1495/JDW'.

1899 *11.5in (29.5cm) high*

$15,000-22,500 **DRA**

A Rookwood special-order 'Iris Glaze' vase, by Edward T. Hurley, flame mark 'III/S1611A' and artist signature.

1903 *19in (48.5cm) high*

$19,500-27,000 **DRA**

A Rookwood 'Iris Glaze' vase, by Kataro Shirayamadani, flame mark 'X/951A/W' and artist's cipher.

1910 *15in (38cm) high*

$19,500-27,000 **DRA**

A Rookwood 'Black Iris' vase, decorated by Carl Schmidt, flame mark 'X/614B/W/CS'.

David Rago, of the Rago Arts and Auction Center stated that this was the finest Iris Glaze vase he had ever seen. A similar example is in the collection of the Newark Museum.

1910 *14in (36cm) high*

$52,500-60,000 **DRA**

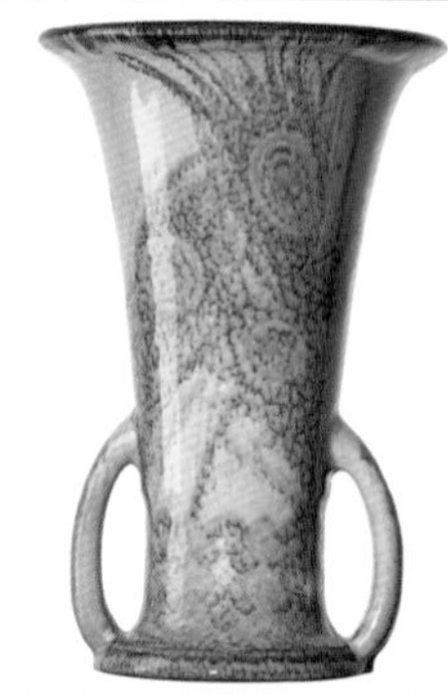

A Rookwood 'Jewel Porcelain' flaring vase, by Sara Sax, flame mark 'XXIX/6115/SX'.

1929 *10.25in (26cm) high*

$2,250-3,000 **DRA**

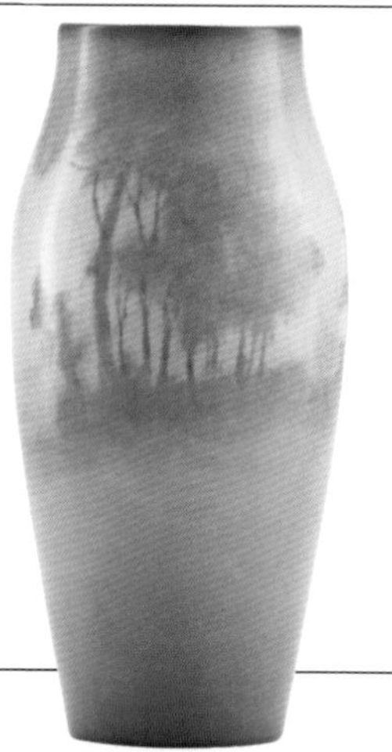

A Rookwood 'Scenic Vellum' vase, by Lenore Asbury, flame mark 'XIX/30F/V/L.A'.

1909 *7in (18cm) high*

$1,800-2,700 **DRA**

A Rookwood 'Scenic Vellum' vase, by Fred Rothenbusch, flame mark 'XIII/2040D/V' artist's cipher.

1913 *9.25in (23.5cm) high*

$2,250-3,000 **DRA**

A Rookwood 'Sea Green' vase, by Virginia B. Demarest, with bronzed overlay of seahorses, flame mark 'T1234/VBD/g'.

Shortly before the turn of the century, Rookwood Pottery began experimenting with electrodeposit, at first incorporating it into the design and then increasing its importance by enveloping the painted decoration with leaves and flowers that continue the floral scheme. In some cases, the metal became the dominant element. One of the important Rookwood artisans involved in this process was the Japanese metal worker R. Ito.

1900 *5in (12.75cm) high*

$9,750-11,500 **DRA**

A Rookwood 'Standard Glaze' puzzle mug, by Harriet Wilcox, with silver overlay, flame mark '711/W/H.E.W.', silver stamped 'GORHAM MFG. CO. R1696', crazed with one very minor spider line to bottom of base, does not go through, two minor, short splits to silver.

1894 *5in (12.7cm) high*

$1,150-1,300 **DRA**

A Rookwood early 'Barbotine' plaque, attributed to Mary Keenan, in original frame, stamped 'ROOKWOOD' dated, overall crazing.

1883 *11in (28cm) wide*

$18,000-22,500 **DRA**

A Rookwood 'Scenic Vellum' plaque, by Sara Sax, in original frame, flame mark 'XII/V', artist signature to front, crazed.

1912 *10.5in (27cm) high*

$9,000-10,500 **DRA**

A Rookwood 'Scenic Vellum' plaque, by Ed Diers, in original frame, flame mark 'XIV/V', artist initials to front, crazed.

1914 *10.75in (27.5cm) high*

$6,000-7,500 **DRA**

A Rookwood marine 'Scenic Vellum' plaque, by Carl Schmidt, in original frame, flame mark 'XVIII', artist signature to front.

1918 *15in (38cm) wide*

$6,000-7,500 **DRA**

A Rookwood large 'Scenic Vellum' plaque, by Ed Diers, depicting Yosemite's 'El Capitan', in original frame, flame mark 'XXVII', artist initials to front.

1927 *16.5in (42cm) high*

$30,000-45,000 **DRA**

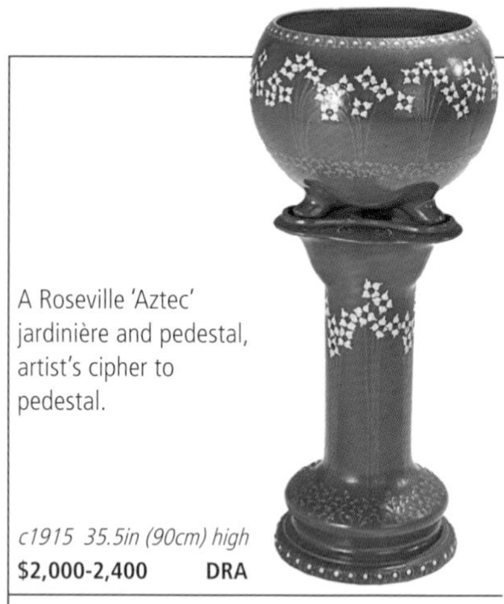

A Roseville 'Aztec' jardinière and pedestal, artist's cipher to pedestal.

c1915 35.5in (90cm) high

$2,000-2,400 DRA

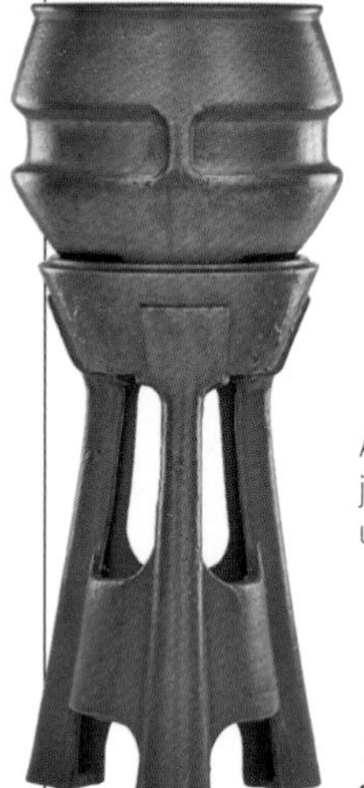

A Roseville 'Egypto' jardinière and pedestal, unmarked.

1915 30.5in (75.5cm) high

$5,250-6,000 DRA

A Roseville Rozane 'Olympic' vase, 'Persia and Ionia Yoked to the Chariot of Xerxes,' marked 'ROZANE OLYMPIC POTTERY' and title.

1910 14in (35.5cm) high

$3,300-4,400 DRA

A Roseville 'Carnelian II' vase, unmarked.

1926 14in (35.5cm) high

$3,000-4,000 DRA

A Roseville 'Carnelian II' vase, unmarked.

1926 16.5in (42cm) high

$3,000-4,000 DRA

A Roseville 'Futura' graduated spherical vase, with paper label.

1924 8.25in (21cm) high

$450-600 DRA

A Roseville 'Imperial II' vase, in golden ocher over frothy blue glaze.

11.25 (29cm) high

$750-900 DRA

A Roseville brown 'Pinecone' pitcher, die-impressed mark.

1935 10in (25.5cm) high

$300-400 DRA

A Roseville 'Sunflower' vase, unmarked.

9.5in (24cm) high

$750-900 DRA

A Rozenburg earthenware bottle vase, painted with stylised poppy heads, painted 'Rozenburg, Stork, Den Haag' and incised 'W142 L', foot chips restored.

The Rozenburg Factory at Den Haag is best known for its finely enameled egg shell porcelain, but the factory also produced fine Arts and Crafts style faience which deserves better recognition.

c1900 *15.75in (40cm) high*

$600-700 **SWO**

A Rozenburg earthenware vase, painted with stylised thistles, incised 'W47D', painted mark including anchor and '48', slight restoration to base.

c1900 *11.5in (29.5cm) high*

$450-600 **SWO**

A Rozenburg earthenware vase, painted with two fighting sparrows, restored, incised 'W1370', painted mark including anchor and '131'.

c1900 *13in (33.5cm) high*

$400-450 **SWO**

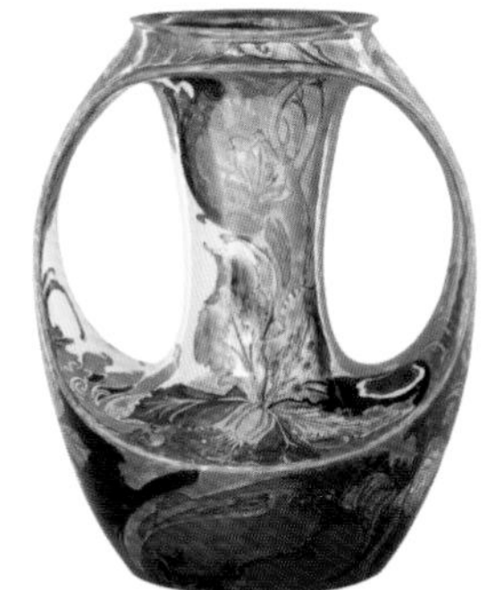

A Rozenburg earthenware vase, painted with poppies, printed mark and painted spider, crossed '2' and '653'.

c1900 *10.5in (26.5cm) high*

$330-420 **SWO**

A Rozenburg earthenware vase, painted with dragons, incised 'W176V', painted mark including '528'.

c1900 *12.75in (32.5cm) high*

$450-550 **SWO**

A Rozenburg earthenware bottle vase, incised 'W481V', painted mark including '118'.

c1900 *10.5in (27cm) high*

$400-450 **SWO**

A Rozenburg baluster vase, Rozenburg Den Haag stamp '495' with incised numbers.

c1900 *10in (25.5cm) high*

$700-850 **DRA**

A Rozenburg glazed ceramic charger, signed 'Rozenburg 6Y74 Den Haag/F.J.'.

c1900 *15.75in (40cm) diam*

$1,800-2,250 **DRA**

A Ruskin high-fired vase, impressed oval 'Ruskin Pottery, West Smethwick', dated.

1906 *7.5in (19cm) high*

$900-1,000 **SWO**

A rare Ruskin Pottery high-fired stoneware lamp base, pale silver-gray graduating to flambé with mint green and lavender spots, impressed Ruskin England mark, applied Ruskin Paper labels.

9.5in (24cm) high

$2,000-2,700 **WW**

A Ruskin Pottery chalice, with a high fired red and lavender glaze over a dove gray ground, impressed marks, dated.

1924 *8.5in (21cm) high*

$900-1,200 **FLD**

A Ruskin Pottery high fired lamp base, formed as a ginger jar and cover, in a sang-de-beouf glaze with copper green spotting, impressed marks.

15in (38cm) high

$2,700-3,600 **FLD**

A Ruskin Pottery high-fired stoneware vase, the purple glazed covered in a speckled and veined mint and white glaze, repaired chip to foot.

7in (17.5cm) high

$600-750 **WW**

A Ruskin Pottery vase, with a streaked 'Strawberry Crush' type glaze over a dove gray ground, impressed marks, restored, dated.

1925 *12in (30cm) high*

$195-270 **FLD**

A Ruskin Pottery high-fired stoneware vase, flambé covered in a lavender glaze with mint green spots, impressed marks, hairline to neck, dated.

1926 *8.75in (22cm) high*

$450-600 **WW**

A Ruskin high-fired vase, with a mottled purple, green and blue glaze, impressed marks and dated.

1926 *10.75in (27cm) high*

$3,000-4,000 **CHEF**

A Ruskin high fired vase, with a sang-de-boeuf glaze, impressed 'Ruskin, England', dated.

1933 *5.75in (14.5cm) high*

$600-750 **SWO**

A Saturday Evening Girls bowl, by Frances Rocchi, incised 'Early to bed & early to rise makes a child healthy, wealthy & wise', signed with bowl shop mark, 'SEG/FR', dated.

1909 *12.25in (31cm) diam*

$105,000-120,000 **DRA**

A Saturday Evening Girls bowl, by Ida Goldstein, signed 'IG/S.E.G.', dated.

1911 *10.25in (26cm) diam*

$4,000-4,500 **DRA**

A Saturday Evening Girls bowl, by Fannie Levine, signed 'S.E.G. FL', dated.

1914 *11.5in (29.5cm) diam*

$9,750-11,500 **DRA**

A Saturday Evening Girls bowl, by Fannie Levine, marked 'S.E.G.', dated.

1921 *11.5in (29.5cm) diam*

$6,000-7,500 **DRA**

A Saturday Evening Girls trivet, signed 'JMD/SEG/5', dated.

1920 *5.5in (14cm) diam*

$1,200-1,500 **DRA**

A Saturday Evening Girls pitcher, by Frances Rocci, incised 'This is the cock that crew in the morn', signed 'SEG/FR' and dated.

1909 *9.75in (25cm) high*

$13,500-16,500 **DRA**

A Saturday Evening Girls pitcher, by Fannie Levine, with Viking ships, signed with bowl shop mark, 'SEG/ FL 180-5-09'.

1909 *9in (23cm) high*

$6,000-6,750 **DRA**

A Saturday Evening Girls mug, by Frances Rocchi, with a French inscription, signed 'S.E.G./FR/6.13'.

1913 *4in (10.5cm) high*

$1,200-1,500 **DRA**

A Saturday Evening Girls wall pocket, by Albina Mangini, signed 'AM/12-16/S.E.G.', dated.

1916 *6in (15.5cm) high*

$3,000-4,000 **DRA**

A rare Teco massive vase, with iris blossoms, stamped 'Teco' twice.

c1905 *22.5in (57cm) high*

$217,500-232,500 **DRA**

A Teco jardinière, with lotus blossoms, stamped 'TECO', some professionally repaired chips.

c1905 *9in (23cm) high*

$22,500-30,000 **DRA**

A Teco jardinière, with irises, stamped 'TECO', one chip to rim.

c1910 *9.75in (25cm) high*

$12,000-15,000 **DRA**

A Teco Tiffany Studios oil lamp, with 'Pomegranate' shade, with original oil font, base stamped 'TECO', shade with tag stamped 'TIFFANY STUDIOS NEW YORK'.

c1910 *23.5in (60cm) high*

$6,750-8,250 **DRA**

A Teco buttressed vase, stamped 'TECO'.

c1910 *6.5in (16.5cm) high*

$1,450-1,800 **DRA**

A Teco buttressed vase, by Fernand Moreau, with charcoaling, stamped 'TECO', incised '420'.

c1910 *13.75in (35cm) high*

$3,000-4,000 **DRA**

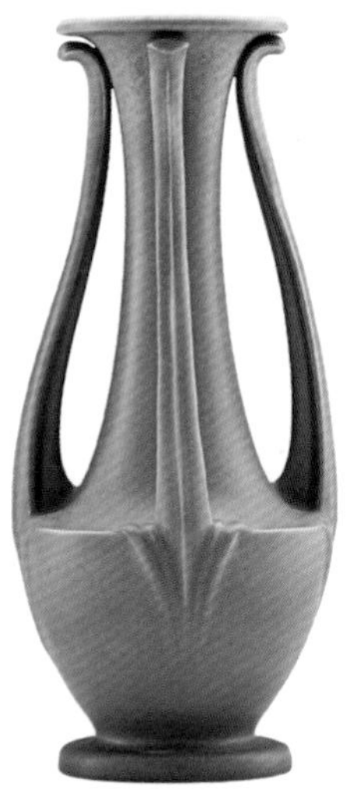

A Teco four-handled vase, stamped 'TECO'.

c1910 *11.5in (29cm) high*

$2,250-3,000 **DRA**

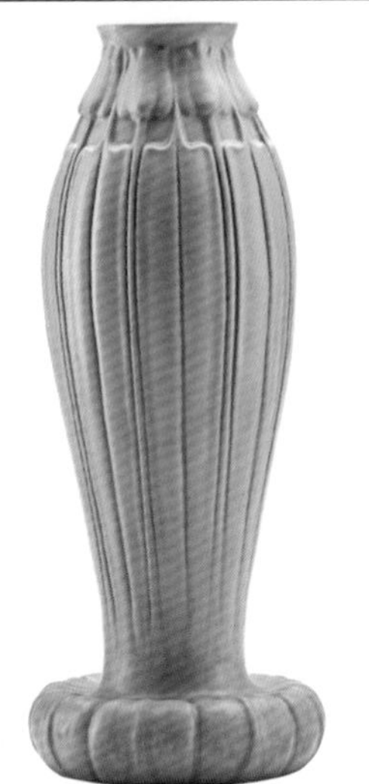

A Teco tall vase, with embossed tulips, stamped 'TECO'.

c1910 *13.5in 34.5cm) high*

$25,500-30,000 **DRA**

A Wedgwood 'Fairyland Lustre' bowl, the exterior with the 'Fairy with Large Hat' pattern, the interior of with 'Woodland Bridge' pattern, with Portland vase mark 'WEDGWOOD MADE IN ENGLAND Z-5360'.

6.5in (16.5cm) diam

$6,000-7,500 **JDJ**

A Wedgwood 'Fairyland Lustre' bowl, decorated with the 'Fairy Gondola' pattern, with printed mark to the base.

13in (33cm) diam

$6,000-7,500 **DUK**

A Wedgwood 'Fairyland Lustre' 'Fairy Gondola' lily tray, pattern number Z4968, gilt Portland vase mark.

13in (33cm) diam

$4,000-4,500 **TEN**

A Wedgwood 'Fairyland Lustre' bowl, 'Firbolgs & Thumbelina', pattern no.5200, printed Portland vase mark.

9in (22.5cm) diam

$4,500-6,000 **SWO**

A Wedgwood 'Fairyland Lustre' 'Leapfrogging Elves' fruit bowl, pattern Z5360, the interior with 'Woodland Bridge Variation I' and mermaid center, signed MJ and printed mark.

11.25in (28.5cm) diam

$19,500-27,000 **SK**

A Wedgwood 'Fairyland Lustre' footed punch bowl, the exterior with the 'Poplar Trees', the interior with 'Woodland Bridge', gilt printed mark, no. Z4968.

9.5in (24cm) diam

$4,000-4,500 **DN**

A Wedgwood 'Fairyland Lustre' chalice bowl, the exterior with 'Twyford Garlands' pattern, the interior with 'Fairy Gondola', with Portland vase mark 'WEDGWOOD MADE IN ENGLAND Z-5360'.

$10,500-12,000 **JDJ**

A Wedgwood black 'Fairyland Lustre' 'Butterfly Woman' and 'Floating Fairies' trumpet vase, printed gilt factory mark, impressed shape 'No.2810', painted 'Z4968 and H'.

9.5in (24cm) high

$3,000-4,500 **TEN**

One of a pair of Wedgwood 'Fairyland Lustre' 'Candlemas' malfrey pots, printed gilt factory mark, incised shape 'No.2311'.

8.5in (21cm) high

$9,000-10,500 **TEN**

A Wedgwood 'Fairyland Lustre' 'Ghostly Wood' malfrey pot and cover, Portland vase mark and painted 'Z4968', incised '2312'.

13in (33cm) high

$52,500-60,000 **SWO**

A Wedgwood 'Fairyland Lustre' 'Goblins' Florentine vase, printed gilt factory mark, incised '3281'.

7in (18cm) high

$4,500-6,000 **TEN**

A pair of Wedgwood 'Fairyland Lustre' vases, with the 'Rainbow' pattern.

8in (20.5cm) high

$6,000-6,750 **WHP**

A 1920s Wedgwood 'Fairyland Lustre' 'Torches' vase, pattern number Z5360, gilt Portland vase mark, painted 'Z5360' and 'B', incised shape number '3177'.

11in (28cm)

$6,000-6,750 **TEN**

A Wedgwood 'Fairyland Lustre' 'Tree Serpent/Imps on a Bridge' vase, shape no.3150, in pattern no.Z5360, with gilt factory mark.

c1925 *12in (30cm) high*

$9,000-10,500 **TEN**

A Wedgwood 'Fairyland Lustre' 'Picnic By A River' plaque, printed gilt factory mark, painted 'Z5156', with residual paper label.

10.75in (27cm) wide

$5,250-6,750 **TEN**

A rare Wedgwood 'Fairyland Lustre' Lincoln plate, 'Si Wang Mu' and 'Thumbelina', the rim with flaming pearls, printed factory mark.

10.75in (27cm) diam

$9,000-10,500 **WW**

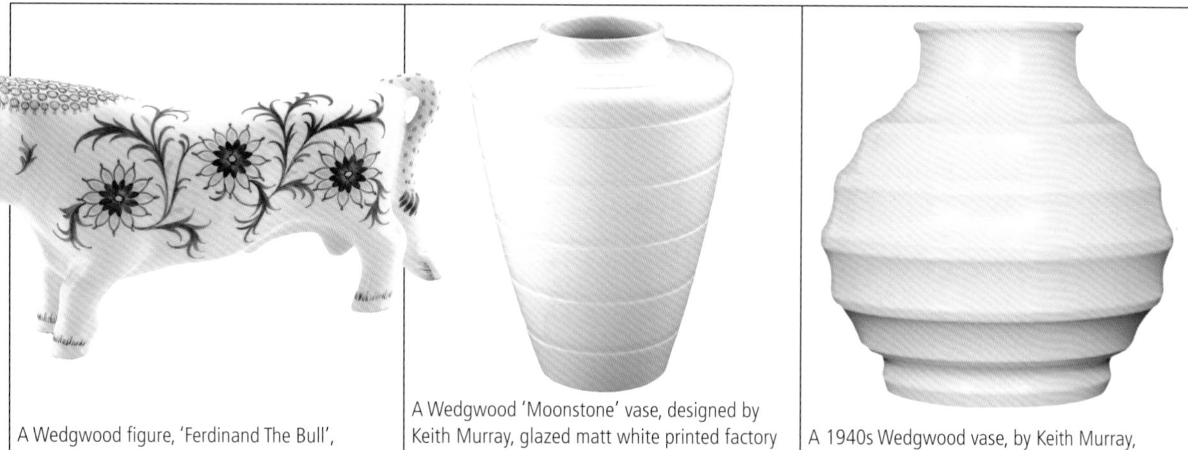

A Wedgwood figure, 'Ferdinand The Bull', designed by Arnold Machin.

1942 *12.75in (32cm) wide*

$400-450 **WW**

A Wedgwood 'Moonstone' vase, designed by Keith Murray, glazed matt white printed factory mark, facsimile signature.

11.5in (29cm) high

$550-600 **WW**

A 1940s Wedgwood vase, by Keith Murray, impressed Etruria and Barlaston mark.

6.75in (17cm) high

$300-400 **FLD**

A Wedgwood bowl, painted by Alfred Powell, the interior painted with rooks nesting in a tree, the exterior with buildings in a landscape, impressed marks, painted artist monogram.

14in (35.5cm) diam

$8,250-9,750 **WW**

A Wedgwood commemorative mug, designed by Eric Ravilious,'King George VI Queen Elizabeth 1937', impressed and printed factory marks, museum restoration.

4in (10cm) high

$450-550 **WW**

ESSENTIAL REFERENCE - ERIC RAVILIOUS

Eric William Ravilious was born in London in 1903 and grew up in Eastbourne. He studied at the Eastbourne School of Art and the Royal College of Art and later taught in both. He was introduced to Tom Wedgwood in 1935 and designed for the pottery from 1936-40. The pattern shown here is Persephone who was the Greek name for Proserpine, the daughter of Jupiter and Ceres. Designed in 1936, it was not initially a commercial success, but when it was re-introduced in 1952 it rapidly became one of Wedgwood's most popular patterns. Unfortunately Ravilious was not alive to witness this success. He was appointed official war artist in 1940, and died in 1942 while on a Royal Air Force air sea rescue mission off Iceland.

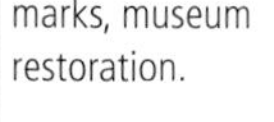

A Wedgwood model of seal on rock, by J Skeaping, in a black gloss finish.

7.5in (19cm) high

$550-700 **PSA**

A Wedgwood 'Persephone' pattern dinner service, designed by Eric Ravilious, comprising: 12 dinner plates, 12 dessert plates, 10 side plates, 12 dessert bowls, and an oval serving dish, printed and impressed marks.

$900-1,000 **SWO**

A Wedgwood bowl, by Norman Wilson, 'NW' monogram, glaze chip to top rim.

11in (27.5cm) diam

$85-115 **WW**

A rare Wemyss Ware large pig, decorated with thistles, shamrocks and cabbage roses, impressed mark 'WEMYSS WARE/ R.H.&S'.

c1900 *17.75in (45cm) long*

$9,000-10,500 **L&T**

A small Wemyss Ware pig, impressed mark 'WEMYSS WARE/R.H.&S'.

c1900 *6.75in (17cm) long*

$400-450 **L&T**

A large Wemyss Ware 'Cabbage Roses' pig, decorated by Joe Nekola, painted mark 'WEMYSS/ MADE IN ENGLAND'.

post 1930 *18in (46cm) long*

$2,400-3,000 **L&T**

A rare Wemyss Ware 'Apples' sleeping pig, decorated by James Sharp, painted and impressed mark 'WEMYSS'.

c1900 *6.5in (16.5cm) long*

$19,500-27,000 **L&T**

A Wemyss Ware 'Cabbage Roses' cat, with glass eyes, impressed 'Wemyss Ware R.H.T.S'.

13in (33cm) high

$8,500-9,000 **SWO**

A Wemyss Ware 'Apples' heart shaped tray, impressed mark 'WEMYSS WARE/ R.H.&S'.

c1900 *11.75in (30cm) long*

$750-900 **L&T**

A Wemyss Wear 'Buttercups' comb tray, impressed mark 'WEMYSS'.

c1900 *10in (25.5cm) wide*

$600-750 **L&T**

A Wemyss Ware 'Chickens' egg basket, stamped 'WEMYSS' and 'T Goode & Co. South Audley St., London, W.',

15.75in (40cm) long

$1,200-1,400 **SWO**

A Wemyss Ware 'Daffodils' Kenmore vase, decorated by James Sharp, incised mark 'WEMYSS', printed retailer's mark.

c1900 *14.5in (37cm) high*

$3,000-4,000 **L&T**

A Wemyss Ware 'Irises' Elgin vase, decorated by James Sharp, painted mark 'WEMYSS', impressed mark 'WEMYSS WARE/R.H.&S'.

c1900 *17.75in (45cm) high*

$1,000-1,200 **L&T**

A Wemyss Ware 'Iris' mug, decorated by James Sharp, painted and impressed marks 'WEMYSS', restored rim.

c1900 *5.75in (14.5cm) high*

$550-700 **L&T**

An early 20thC Wemyss Ware medium 'Lemons' preserve jar and cover, marked 'WEMYSS WARE', painted mark 'WEMYSS'.

4.5in (11.5cm) high

$750-900 **L&T**

A Wemyss Ware 'Purple Plums' muffin dish and cover, impressed mark 'WEMYSS WARE/ R.H.&S.'

9in (23cm) diam

$850-975 **L&T**

A rare Wemyss Ware 'Hybrid Poppies' Kenmore vase, impressed mark 'WEMYSS WARE/ R.H.&S.', printed retailer's mark, restoration.

c1900 *14.75in (37cm) high*

$3,000-4,000 **L&T**

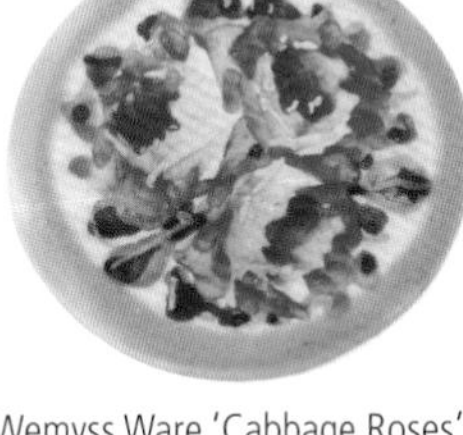

A Wemyss Ware 'Cabbage Roses' button, impressed mark 'WEMYSS'.

c1900 *1.5in (3.5cm) diam*

$1,450-1,800 **L&T**

A Wemyss Ware 'Shamrock Leaf' button, impressed mark 'WEMYSS'.

c1900 *1.5in (3.5cm) diam*

$1,300-1,450 **L&T**

A Wemyss Ware 'Tulips' basket, impressed mark 'WEMYSS', printed retailer's mark.

c1900 *8in (20.5cm) wide*

$750-900 **L&T**

A Wemyss Ware 'Violets' pin tray, with inscription 'I looked for something sweet to send you and the violets asked if they would do.', impressed mark 'WEMYSS'.

c1900 *5.75in (14.5cm) across*

$850-975 **L&T**

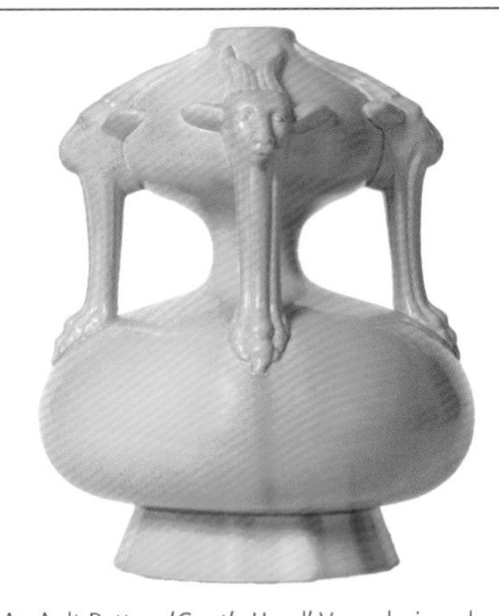

An Ault Pottery 'Goat's Head' Vase, designed by Christopher Dresser, facsimile signature 'Chr Dresser', impressed shape number.
c1890 *10.5in (26.5cm) high*
$13,500-18,000 TEN

A Baron Ware Barnstaple grotesque pocket watch-holder, by Blanche Vulliamy, incised Baron marks.
5.5in (13.5cm) high
$600-750 WW

A John Bennett covered jar, signed 'JBENNETT 412E24 N.Y.'
1879 *14in 35.5cm) high*
$37,500-45,000 DRA

A John Bennett vase, signed 'J BENNETT 412E24 N.Y'.
1880 *15in (38cm) high*
$10,500-12,000 DRA

A C.H. Brannam Barum vase, by James Dewdney, applied with dragon handles, restored wing and glaze loss, dated.
1897 *9in (23cm) high*
$600-700 WW

A Burmantoft's faïence 'Anglo Persian' floor vase, by Leonard King, model D.607, impressed marks, painted monogram, small hairline to top rim,
21in (53cm) high
$4,000-4,500 WW

A Byrdcliffe 'White Pines' vase, marked '173 A', incised 'MII'.
c1915 *6.5in (16.5cm) high*
$5,250-6,000 DRA

A Cantagalli pottery 'Fleur de Lys' spill vase, painted cockerel mark, minor glaze chips.
9in (22.5cm) high
$300-400 WW

A Clewell copper-clad vase, etched 'Clewell 272-2-6'.
11.75in (30cm) high
$3,000-4,000 DRA

A Susie Cooper Productions 'Horse and Jockey' bowl, printed factory mark.
12in (31cm) diam
$300-400 **WW**

A Susie Cooper 'Moon and Mountains' pattern jug, galleon backstamp for A E Gray & Co and pattern no 7960.
4.75in (12cm) high
$150-225 **CHOR**

A Cowan glazed ceramic 'Jazz' plate, by Viktor Schreckengost, stamped 'COWAN'.
c1930 *11.25in (28.6cm) diam*
$18,000-22,500 **DRA**

ESSENTIAL REFERENCE - DELLA ROBBIA POTTERY

The Della Robbia Pottery was a ceramic factory founded in 1894 in Birkenhead, England.

- **The business was started by Harold Steward Rathbone and Conrad Gustave d'Huc Dressler. Rathbone, had been a pupil of Ford Madox Brown, who was one of the founders of the Arts and Crafts movement. Dressler was a sculptor and potter. The pottery was established as a true Arts & Crafts pottery on the lines advocated by William Morris, using local labor and raw materials such as local red clay from Moreton, Wirral. The pottery had lustrous lead glazes and often used patterns of interweaving plants, typical of Art Nouveau, with heraldic and Islamic motifs.**
- **The wares were inspired by the work of the Florentine sculptor Luca della Robbia and his family.**
- **The Della Robbia mark is usually handwritten on the base of pieces with a ship device, and often the initials of the designer and decorator, and sometimes the date.**
- **The costs of making the Della Robbia products was greater than the prices that could be charged. The pottery closed in 1906.**

A Della Robbia pottery vase, incised in low relief with flowers and foliage, incised Della Robbia marks and 'PB' artist mark, professional restoration, dated.
1900 *17.75in (45cm) high*
$1,300-1,450 **WW**

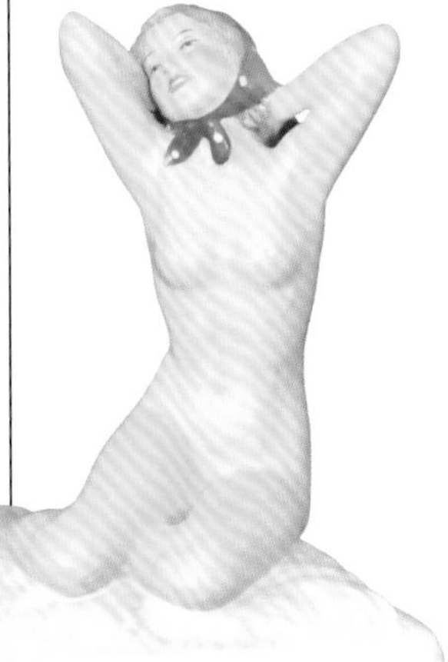

A 1930s Royal Dux figurine, of a seated nude, printed circular mark.
8.5in (21cm) high
$400-450 **FLD**

A Della Robbia pottery charger, by John Fogo, applied paper label over Della Robbia mark, incised 'JF' and painted 'PJ', probably for Aphra Pierce, hairlines.
c1900 *13.5in (34cm) diam*
$480-600 **WW**

A Foley faience charger, designed by Frederick Rhead, printed with Pre-Raphaelite musicians, printed factory mark, hairline cracks.
14.5in (37cm) diam
$600-750 **WW**

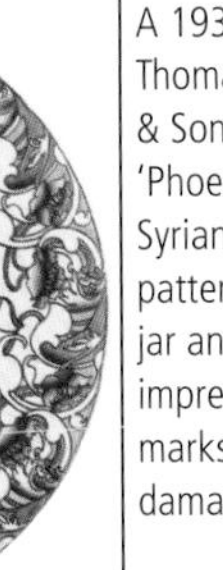

A 1930s Art Deco Thomas Forrester & Sons 'Phoenix Syrian' pattern ovoid jar and cover, impressed marks, some damage.
12.75in (32cm) high
$165-225 **FLD**

A pair of Fulham Pottery candlesticks, by John Piper, painted with Kidwelly Castle, inscribed 'John Piper Kidwelly 1x/82 Fulham Pottery', one with a chip, dated.
1982 *12in (30.5cm) high*
$1,500-2,100 **SWO**

A Gallé tin-glazed earthenware cat, by Émile Gallé, applied glass eyes, painted 'E Galle Nancy' to the foot.

12.75in (32cm) high

$3,000-4,000 **WW**

A Richard Ginori earthenware vase, designed by Gio Ponti, painted with Italian propellor planes flying amongst clouds, painted 'Ginori 36' mark to base.

7in (17.5cm) high

$1,300-1,450 **WW**

A 'Rhodian Matapan' pattern Gouda pottery lantern, with 'Lazarus Gate PZH' factory mark, pattern name, 'Holland', numbered '04/2'.

c1915 *10.5in (27cm) high*

$900-1,000 **SK**

A Gouda pottery luster vase, by J.W. van Schaik, painted temple, unique 'plazuid Gouda, Holland and JvS'.

c1910 *11in (46cm) high*

$975-1,150

SWO

A Shoji Hamada glazed stoneware jar, with ash glaze and wax-resist designs, signed, Japan, with original box.

c1960 *9in (23cm) high*

$6,750-7,500 **DRA**

A 1930s Lenci earthenware figure of a young girl, workshop of Helen (Elena) Konig-Scavini and Entico Scavini, Turin, marked 'Lenci Torino 12 (XII) Made in Italy Tk'.

16.5in (42cm) high

$12,000-13,500 **FELL**

A Lenci figural dish, by Elena Konig Scavini, modeled as a naked girl riding on the back of a fish, molded maker's mark to body 'ICNEL'.

c1930 *17.5in (44.5cm) high*

$8,500-9,000 **L&T**

An early 20thC Limoges pâte-sur-pâte vase, signed Joe Descomps, signed in gilt 'L'Art decoratif Limoges' and incised 'Joe Descomps'.

7.5in (19cm) high

$1,500-2,250 **L&T**

A Links Pottery, Kirkcaldy tankard.

c1890 *5.75in (14.5cm) high*

$1,500-2,100 **L&T**

A Linthorpe Pottery vase, shape No.168, designed by Christopher Dresser, impressed 'LINTHORPE 168', signature 'Chr Dresser', 'HT' (Henry Tooth) monogram, incised 'CFR' monogram.

19in (48cm) high

$900-975 **TEN**

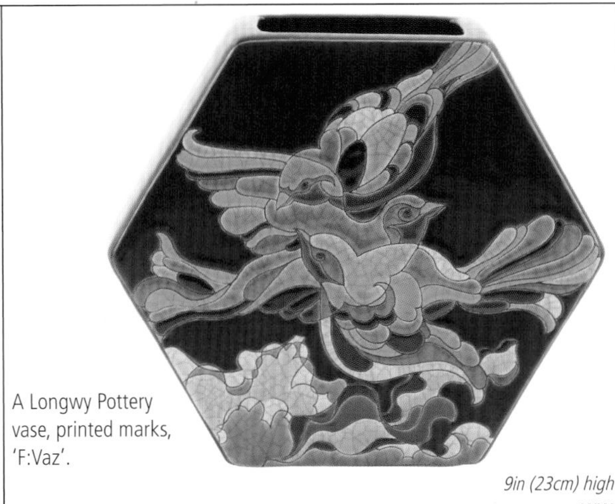

A Longwy Pottery vase, printed marks, 'F:Vaz'.

9in (23cm) high

$975-1,150 **WW**

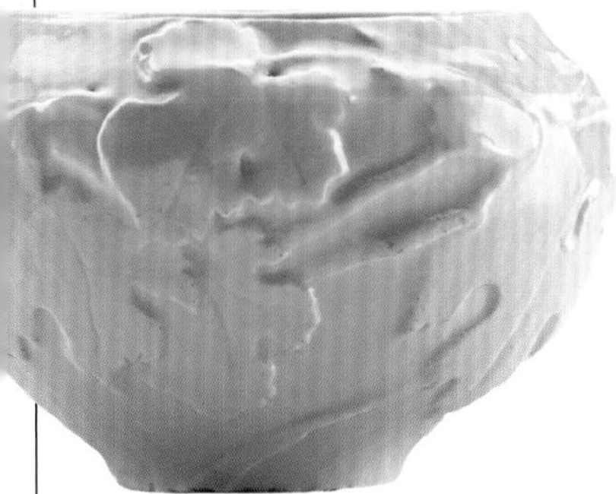

A rare Losanti bowl, carved with maple leaves, by Mary Louise Mclaughlin, marked 'Losanti/185' with artist's cipher.

c1900 *6.5in (16.5cm) diam*

$22,500-30,000 **DRA**

A rare 1920s Marblehead vase, stamped ship mark, incised 'HT'.

6in (15.5cm) high

$45,000-52,500 **DRA**

A Clément Massier Golfe Juan luster vase, impressed and painted marks, minor nicks to rim.

7in (18cm) high

$850-975 **WW**

A rare Maw & Co ship ewer, designed by Walter Crane, model no. 9420, painted factory marks to base.

12.5in (32cm) high

$9,750-11,500 **WW**

A Bernard Moore solifleur vase, printed mark.

9.5in (24cm) high

$6,000-7,500 **WW**

A North Dakota School Of Mines vase, by Julia Mattson, indigo stamp, 'JM/391'.

c1935 *3.5in (9cm) high*

$3,000-4,000 **DRA**

A Pewabic vase, matte café au lait glaze, maple leaf mark.

c1905 *14in (35.5cm) high*

$3,000-4,000 **DRA**

A Poillon Pottery glazed stoneware footed center bowl, by Clara Poillon, Woodbridge, NJ, signed 'CLP M', dated.

Works by this potter are rare. Pieces of this scale and medium, almost unheard of.

1905 *13in (33cm) diam*

$4,000-4,500 DRA

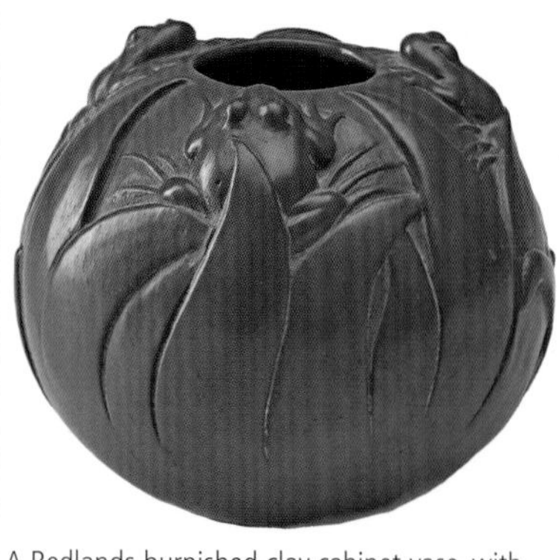

A Redlands burnished clay cabinet vase, with frogs, Redlands pottery stamp.

c1905 *3in (7.5cm) high*

$16,500-21,000 DRA

A University City important vessel, enamel-decorated with mushrooms, by Frederick Hurten Rhead and Agnes Rhead, incised 'UC/FHR/AR/AML' (for American Women's League).

1910 *6.5in (16.5cm) high*

$150,000-210,000 DRA

A Frederick H. Rhead tile panel, unmarked, Santa Barbara, CA.

Descended from Mrs. Hugh Weldon of Mission Canyon whose father, Christoph Tornoe, was one of the directors of Rhead Pottery as well as Rhead's neighbour and landlord.

1914-17 *with frame 37.75in (96cm) wide*

$120,000-135,000 DRA

A University City bowl, by Frederick H. Rhead and Agnes Rhead, incised 'UC/AWL/FHR/1911/AR/1003'.

1911 *7.75in (20cm) diam*

$60,000-67,500 DRA

An Adelaide Robineau porcelain vase, with crystalline glaze, carved 'AR/210, Syracuse, NY'.

c1905 *4.25in (11cm) diam*

$21,000-27,000 DRA

An Art Deco Rosenthal figure, of a Spanish lady, by Claire Weiss, printed and impressed marks, small chips.

9.5in (24cm) high

$280-340 ECGW

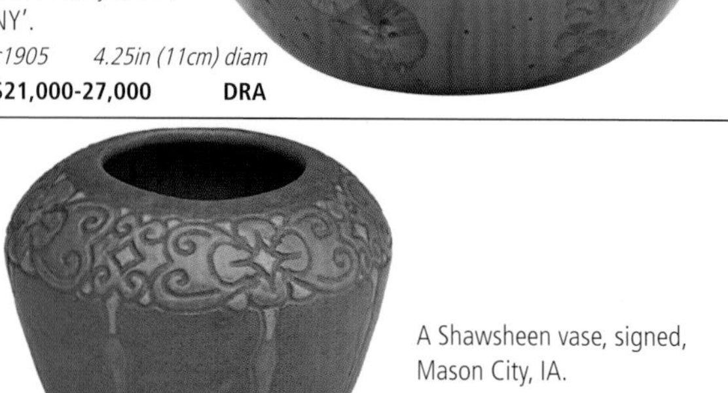

A Shawsheen vase, signed, Mason City, IA.

c1910 *5in (13cm) diam*

$4,000-4,500 DRA

A Shelley 'Sunray' 'Vogue' trio, by Eric Slater, pattern no.11742, printed and painted marks.

1930

$330-420 SWO

ESSENTIAL REFERENCE - TIFFANY

Pottery wares at Tiffany Furnaces were frequently made from living models, such as wild flowers and vegetables, which were sprayed with shellac until rigid and then electroplated with copper. These, in turn, were made into the plaster of Paris molds in which the clay was pressed into its final form. Other themes included specimens of tooled leather, American Indian pottery and forms of marine life, such as octopi, algae and coral growths. To the public, pottery was the least readily identifiable of Tiffany's mediums, and for that reason, in part, the least financially successful. Jimmy Stewart, a glassblower at Corona, later stated that a good deal of it was put out of sight whenever Mr. Tiffany was expected to visit the factory as the staff did not want him to know how little demand there was for it. The firm's pottery was offered for sale from 1905 until around 1917.

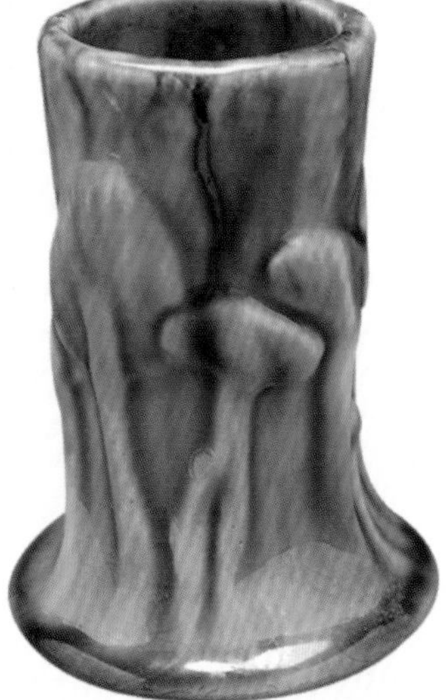

A Tiffany Studios toadstool cabinet vase, incised underglaze 'LCT' monogram.

c1910 *2.75in (7cm) high*

$7,500-9,000 MIC

A 20thC Troika Pottery mask, by Avril Bennet, painted marks.

10in (25.5cm) high

$1,000-1,200 WW

A Utrecht Pottery vase, painted with stylised flowers and leaves in the Art Nouveau manner, printed black mark and monogram for J.W.Mijnlief, two chips to base.

c1890 *16.75in (42.5cm) high*

$600-750 MOR

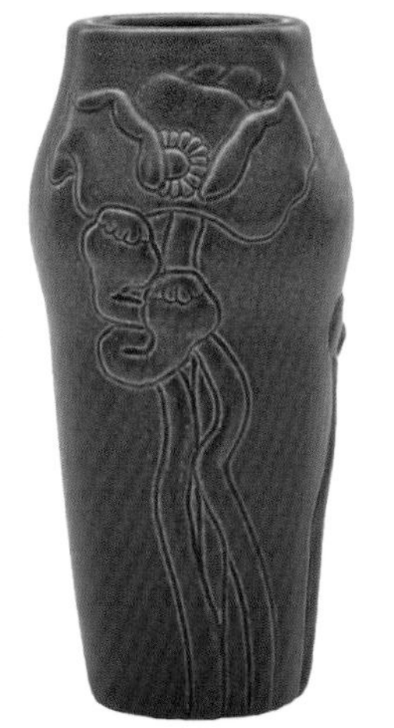

A Van Briggle vase, with poppy, blue and green glaze, 'AA VAN BRIGGLE/2D/1902/III'.

1902 *7.75in (20cm) high*

$16,500-22,500 DRA

A Van Briggle vase, with celadon and green glaze, signed 'AA VAN BRIGGLE/200/1903/III'.

1903 *5.75in (15cm) high*

$2,000-2,400 DRA

A Weller cameo vase, with birds and ferns, stamped 'Weller 2P'.

13.5in (34.5cm) high

$1,500-2,100 DRA

A J Wellard & Co Bordeaux enameled vase, model D.46, impressed marks, overpainted top rim.

13in (32cm) high

$300-450 WW

A Wheatley vase, with ocher glaze, marked 'WP', artist's cipher/621.

c1905 *19.5in (49.5cm) high*

$2,250-3,000 DRA

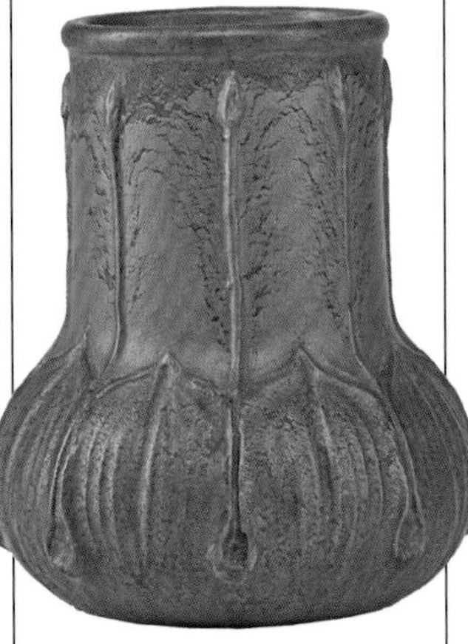

A 1900s Wheatley vase, with curdled green glaze, possible mark, covered by glaze.

9in (23cm) high

$4,000-4,500 DRA

An A.J.Wilkinson 'Lotus' jug, by John Butler, in the 'Tahiti Foam' pattern, signed, pattern name to base, printed A.J.Wilkinson mark.

c1928-29 *12in (30cm) high*

$450-550 **FLD**

A pair of Wilton Ware luster vases, pattern 116/5403.

13.5in (34cm) high

$400-450 **SWO**

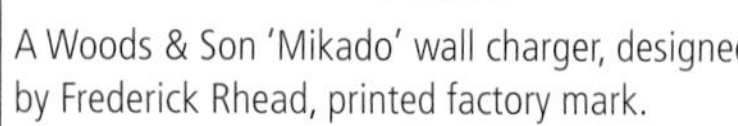

A Woods & Son 'Mikado' wall charger, designed by Frederick Rhead, printed factory mark.

16in (41cm) diam

$600-750 **WW**

A Royal Worcester figure, entitled 'The Bather Surprised', puce printed marks with date code.

1921 *15.5in (39cm) high*

$850-975 **FLD**

A Royal Worcester 'Japanese Girl' candle snuffer, printed mark and date code.

1926 *3in (7cm) high*

$280-340 **SWO**

A Royal Worcester group, of 'The Minstrel with Lester Piggott', modeled by B Winskill, printed marks, wood stand, dated.

This was the sculptor's copy.

1976 *15in (38cm) long*

$1,800-2,250 **SWO**

A Zoslnay figural vessel, with eosin glaze, raised five churches medallion, 8748.

c1900 *12.5in (32cm) long*

$7,500-9,000 **DRA**

A Zsolnay charger, with maiden, eosin glaze, five churches medallion, stamped 'ZSOLNAY PECS 47014'.

c1898 *15in (38cm) diam*

$19,500-24,000 **DRA**

A Zsolnay owl figurine, with eosin glaze, stamped 'Zsolnay', five churches medallion, illegible numbers.

c1900 *12.5in (32cm) high*

$4,500-5,250 **DRA**

A 19thC Gothic Revival carved oak center table, the underside marked 'HENRY OUSEY(?) MAKERS 18*8'.

51.5in (131cm) wide

$3,300-4,500 **L&T**

A late 19thC Aesthetic mahogany and lacquer display cabinet, with gilt metal mounts.

26in (66cm) wide

$3,000-4,000 **L&T**

An Aesthetic ebonized corner cupboard, in the Japonesque style.

65in (165cm) high

$450-600 **SWO**

An Art Nouveau walnut table, by Louis Marjorelle, inlaid decoration in the form of wisteria, the stretcher with bronze mounts cast in floral form, signed.

36in (91.5cm) high

$7,500-9,000 **ECGW**

A Gallé marquetry tray with carved dragon handles, inlaid in various woods with a ruined castle, signed 'Gallé'.

c1890 *19.5in (49.5cm) wide*

$1,300-1,450 **BELL**

A rare 20thC Carlo Bugatti copper and vellum hall chair, unsigned.

35in (90cm) high

$13,500-16,500 **WW**

A pair of Charles Rennie Mackintosh ebonized chairs, designed for Miss Cranston's Willow Tearooms.

c1905 *41in (104cm) high*

$19,500-24,000 **CHOR**

A smoking room table, attributed to Charles Rennie Mackintosh, pierced with squares.

Francis Smith is thought to have quoted for two tables of this design for the Smoking Room of the Willow Tearooms in September 1903. The form and construction is similar to a larger single table commissioned for the Billiards Room at the same time and which is now in the collection of Glasgow School of Art. Although none of these tables appear in contemporary photographs, their more robust construction gives them an affinity with the other furniture made for the Billiards Room at the same time.

c1905 *28.25in (71.5cm) high*

$6,000-7,500 **L&T**

An Arts and Crafts Spanish mahogany piano, designed by Charles Robert Ashbee for the Guild of Handicrafts, manufactured by John Broadwood and Co., model no. 8, piano no. 96376.

45in (114cm) high

$19,500-27,000 **SWO**

A Cotswold School oak occasional table, unsigned.

8.5in (21cm) diam

$6,000-6,750 **WW**

An Arts and Crafts Cotswold School oak refectory table.

$8,250-9,750 **WW**

A Heal's walnut pedestal desk.

29.75in (75.5cm) high

$4,500-6,000 **SWO**

An Arts & Crafts light oak wardrobe, retail attributed to Liberty & Co.

85in (216cm) high

$850-975 **ECGW**

ESSENTIAL REFERENCE - STANLEY DAVIES

After university Stanley Davies joined the family mill business, but decided to further his talent for woodworking with an apprenticeship under the acclaimed Cotswold School designer Romney Green.

- **In 1923, Davies started his own Arts & Crafts furniture company in Cumbria, building a house and workshop near Windermere, which he called 'Gatesbield', meaning a shelter for small animals. Most of his furniture was made here, and the manufacturing process adhered strictly to Arts & Crafts principals. Characteristic features of his tables include rounded angles and exposed tenons, as in the current example which he made for his own use in the kitchen at Gatesbield.**

A 1920s ash kitchen table, by Stanley Webb Davies (1894–1978).

53.5in (135.5cm) wide

$2,000-2,400 **L&T**

A walnut veneered display cabinet on chest, by Sir Robert Lorimer (1864-1929).

c1920 *96.75in (246cm) high*

$4,500-6,000 **L&T**

An Arts & Crafts oak side chair, by William Daniel McLennan (1872-1940).

c1910

$750-900 **L&T**

A Morris & Co ebonized wood settle, rush seat and turned bobbin back.

54in (137cm) wide

$2,700-3,300 WW

A 'Flowerpot' embroidered firescreen, by William Morris (1834–1896) for Morris & Company, stamped maker's marks.

c1890 *48.75in (123.5cm) high*

$1,500-2,250 L&T

An oak center table, by Philip Webb for Morris & Co.

Philip Webb (1831-1915) was chief furniture designer for Morris, Marshall, Faulkner and Co, and later Morris & Co. His furniture designs demonstrate a solidity and architectural presence with features drawn from his knowledge of early furniture from around the world. An example of this design can be seen in the long drawing room at Kelmscott House where Morris lived from 1878.

c1870s *71in (180cm) wide*

$15,000-21,000 CHEF

An exceptional English Arts & Crafts elm cabinet, designed by F. A. Rawlence, with wrought-iron, unsigned.

This chest has an excellent provenance. It was made for Wiltshire House, home of the Marquis of Pembroke and Montgomeryshire.

c1900 *50.75in (129cm) wide*

$52,500-60,000 DRA

A Gordon Russell mahogany and Bombay rosewood sideboard, designed by David Booth, labeled 'GORDON RUSSELL LIMITED BROADWAY WORCS.'

48in (122cm) wide

$3,000-4,000 TEN

A Gordon Russell English oak dining table, in the Cotswolds School manor, handwritten Broadway workshop label, cabinet maker C. Beadle, dated, model x133.

1929 *72in (183cm) wide*

$6,000-7,500 ECGW

An oak occasional table, attributed to Mackay Hugh Baillie Scott.

c1890s *27in (68.5cm) high*

$4,500-5,250 SWO

An Arthur W Simpson 'The Handicraft's' oak chest on stand, with heart-shaped lock escutcheon in the manner of C.F.A. Voysey.

42in (107cm) wide

$2,700-3,300 WW

A pair of oak side chairs, by Ernest Archibald Taylor (1874-1951), for Wylie & Lochhead, Glasgow.

c1910

$1,300-1,450 L&T

An Arts & Crafts oak and inlaid side cabinet, by Ernest Archibald Taylor (1874-1951) for Wylie & Lochhead, Glasgow, bears maker's label.

c1910 *72in (183cm) wide*

$1,200-1,500 L&T

A sideboard, by Ernest Archibald Taylor, for Wylie & Lochhead, Glasgow, the superstructure with roses and foliage flanked by sliding doors, above three drawers and four panelled doors below, each centered with stained and leaded glass panels depicting stylised roses.

This sideboard is similar in form to a sideboard designed by Taylor for William Douglas Weir (later Lord Weir) in Glasgow c1901, following the success of his room for Wylie & Lochhead at the Glasgow International Exhibition the same year.

c1900 *72in (183cm) wide*

$12,000-13,500 L&T

A rare Charles Voysey cabinet table secretaire.

c1900 *20in (50cm) high*

$127,500-142,500 L&T

ESSENTIAL REFERENCE - GEORGE WALTON

George Walton was born in Glasgow on 3 June 1867, the youngest of twelve children. The painter, Edward Arthur Walton, born in 1860, was his elder brother and the flower painter, Constance Walton, his sister. His father died in 1873 leaving the family in reduced circumstances and Walton had to leave school aged thirteen to become a clerk with the British Linen Bank, but while working there he also studied at Glasgow School of Art. In 1888 Miss Catherine Cranston commissioned Walton to re-design the interiors of the tea rooms at 114 Argyle Street, Glasgow. Walton gave up banking and opened showrooms entitled George Walton & Co, Ecclesiastical and House Decorators, at 152 Wellington Street. The Walton firm quickly expanded into woodwork, furniture making and stained glass. In 1896 Walton received a further commission from Miss Cranston to decorate the Buchanan Street premises. His collaborator was C. R. Mackintosh. In 1897 Walton moved to London and, as well as retaining his Glasgow showroom, opened a branch in York.

A rare mahogany gate-leg tea table, designed by George Henry Walton (1867-1933), bears maker's label.

c1905 *27.5in (70cm) high*

$6,000-7,500 L&T

A satin birch side cabinet, designed by George Walton (1867-1933).

c1898 *44.75in (114cm) wide*

$1,800-2,250 L&T

A Gustav Stickley early Morris chair (no. 2342), early red decal.

c1900 *39.5in (100.3cm) high*

$6,000-7,500 **DRA**

A Gustav Stickley drop-arm spindle Morris chair, red decal.

c1905 *40in (101.6cm) high*

$5,250-6,000 **DRA**

A Gustav Stickley spindle armchair, unmarked.

c1905 *49in (124.5cm) high*

$3,000-4,000 **DRA**

A Gustav Stickley bow-arm Morris chair, red decal.

c1905 *37in (94cm) high*

$8,500-9,000 **DRA**

A Gustav Stickley early smoker's stand, red decal.

c1900 *26.75in (68cm) high*

$8,250-9,750 **DRA**

A Gustav Stickley early quartersawn oak bride's chest, with wrought iron, unmarked.

c1902 *41in (104cm) wide*

$19,500-24,000 **DRA**

A rare early Gustav Stickley Yeddo plant stand, with Grueby ten-inch tile (no.11), unmarked.

c1900 *24in (60.9cm) high*

$19,500-24,000 **DRA**

A Gustav Stickley double-door china cabinet, (no.815), Eastwood paper label, black decal.

c1905 *63.75in (162cm) high*

$8,250-9,750 **DRA**

An extremely rare L. & J.G. Stickley rare paneled Prairie settle, 'The Work of...' decal.

c1912 *84.5in (215cm) wide*

$21,000-27,000 **DRA**

An L. &. J. G. Stickley crib settle (no.222), 'The Work of...' decal.

1912-17 *84.5in (215cm) wide*

$4,500-5,250 **DRA**

An L. &. J. G. Stickley quartersawn oak, spring seat, ladder back open-arm chair, later upholstered back, decal label.

27in (68.6cm) high

$550-600 **DRA**

An L. & J.G. Stickley Onondaga Shops chest of drawers with mirror, unmarked.

c1900 *76in (193cm) high*

$6,000-7,500 **DRA**

An L. & J. G. Stickley Onondaga Shops rare and early two-door bookcase, with mitered mullions and cathedral arches.

c1900 *75in (190.5cm) high*

$27,000-33,000 **DRA**

An L. & J.G. Stickley triple door bookcase, branded 'The Work of...'

c1915 *72.5in (184cm) wide*

$27,000-33,000 **DRA**

An L. &. J. G. Stickley nine-drawer chest, Handcraft decal.

1907-11 *53in (134.5cm) high*

$4,500-6,000 **DRA**

An L. &. J. G. Stickley sideboard, 'The Work Of...' decal.

c1912 *72in (183cm) wide*

$5,250-6,750 **DRA**

A rare L. & J. G. Stickley massive trestle table, branded mark.

c1910 *96in (243.8cm) long*

$25,500-33,000 **DRA**

A Stickley Brothers flaring even-arm settle, with drop-in foam seat, unmarked.

c1910 *83.5in (212cm) wide*

$6,000-7,500 **DRA**

A spindled hall table, attributed to L. & J. G. Stickley Onondaga Shops, unmarked.

c1904 *36in (91.4cm) high*

$1,000-1,400

DRA

A set of six Stickley Brothers tall-back chairs, with heart cut-outs, unmarked.

c1905

$4,000-4,500 **DRA**

A Stickley Brothers bookcase, with metal label.

c1910 *58.5in (148.6cm) wide*

$3,000-4,000 **DRA**

A Stickley Brothers pipe rack, with inlay of Old King Cole, unmarked.

c1904 *25.5in (64.7cm) wide*

$2,250-3,000 **DRA**

A Stickley Brothers sideboard, branded and decal label.

c1910 *50in (127cm) wide*

$2,250-3,000 **DRA**

A rare Byrdcliffe Community magazine stand, stained and carved with hollyhocks, carved 'Byrdcliffe 1904'.
1904 *36in (91.5cm) high*
$12,750-14,250 DRA

A Limbert massive rocker, (no.846), branded signature.
c1905 *38in (96.5cm) high*
$4,000-4,500 DRA

A Limbert double-oval table, unsigned.
c1905 *48in (122cm) wide*
$6,750-8,250 DRA

A Limbert sideboard, branded.
c1910 *53in (134.6cm) wide*
$3,000-4,000 DRA

A Limbert china cabinet, branded.
c1910 *58.25in (148cm) high*
$2,250-3,000 DRA

A Limbert bookcase, unmarked.
c1915 *57in (145cm) high*
$2,100-2,700 DRA

A Charles Rohlfs armchair, carved 'R'.
c1900 *24.5in (62cm) high*
$4,000-5,250 DRA

An important Charles Rohlfs (1853-1936) drop-front desk on pivoting base, unmarked.

Several clues lead us to believe that this desk is a prototype, or certainly a very early version of this form: the plain construction of the drawers, the use of a secondary wood on the drawer interiors, the butt hinges to the underside of the drop front as opposed to side-mounted knife hinges, and the lack of a signature. The wooden keys are also different from those on subsequent versions of this desk.
c1900 *56.25in (143cm) high*
$300,000-375,000 DRA

A Charles Rohlfs hall chair, carved 'R'.
c1905 *50in (127cm) high*
$8,250-9,750 DRA

A Rose Valley Community armchair, carved with monkeys and dragons, designed by William Price for the John O. Gilmore residence, 'Yorklynne', branded 'rose' and 'V' encircled with buckled belt, inscribed 'Rose Valley Shops'.

c1900 *46in (117cm) high*

$27,000-33,000 **DRA**

A Rose Valley carved oak folding chair, with owl, carved signature 'anno domini 1905 P & Mc L' and 'V' inside rose with original paint.

1905 *33in (84cm) high*

$6,000-6,750 **DRA**

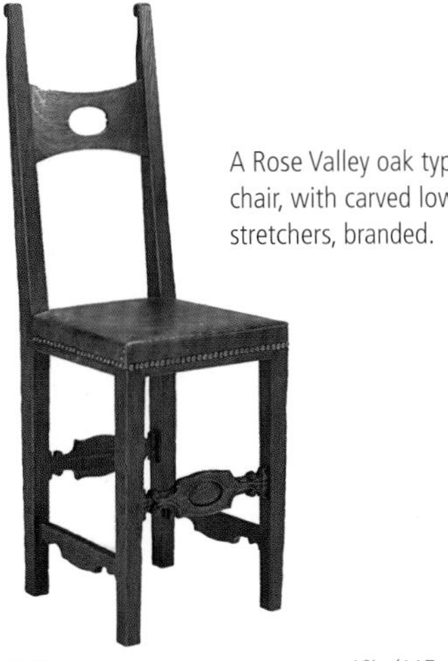

A Rose Valley oak typist's chair, with carved lower stretchers, branded.

c1905 *46in (117cm) high*

$2,100-2,700 **DRA**

An important Rose Valley Community large trestle table, designed by William Price for the John O. Gilmore residence, 'Yorklynne', unsigned.

c1900 *84in (213cm) long*

$240,000-300,000 **DRA**

A Roycroft mahogany corner chair, unmarked.

c1905 *33.5in (85cm) high*

$3,000-4,000 **DRA**

A Roycroft pedestal magazine stand, orb and cross mark, has been cut down by 1in, exterior refinished.

c1905 *63in (160cm) high*

$6,750-7,500 **DRA**

A Shop of the Crafters magazine stand, with painted panel, paper label.

c1910 *48in (122cm) high*

$1,500-2,100 **DRA**

A Shop of the Crafters Inlaid armchair, paper lable.

c1910 *46in (117cm) high*

$1,200-1,500 **DRA**

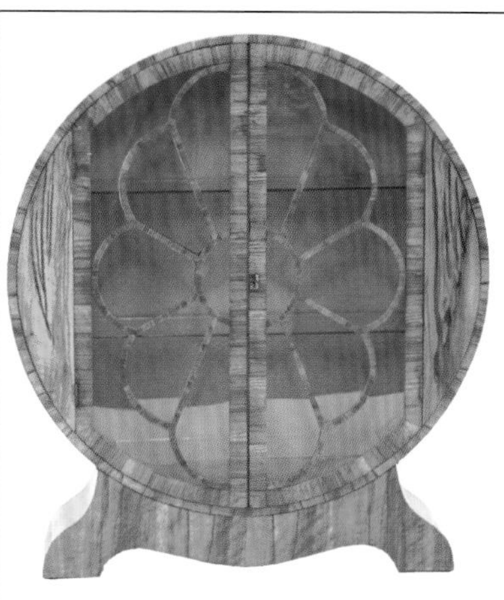

An Art Deco walnut display cabinet.

120.5cm (47.5cm) high

$1,000-1,500 **SWO**

An Art Deco walnut cocktail cabinet, the raised center opening to reveal a mirrored and fitted interior, with chrome and ivorine handles.

48.5in (123cm) high

$600-900 **SWO**

An Art Deco walnut double dome top display cabinet.

50in (127.5cm) high

$900-1,200 **SWO**

An Art Deco bird's-eye maple cocktail cabinet, the top opening to reveal glass shelves and a mirrored back, fitted cupboard below.

66in (168cm) high

$4,400-5,100 **SWO**

A pair of birch and mohair relax chairs, by Jean Royere (1902-81), unmarked.

1940s *41in (104cm) high*

$15,000-18,000 **DRA**

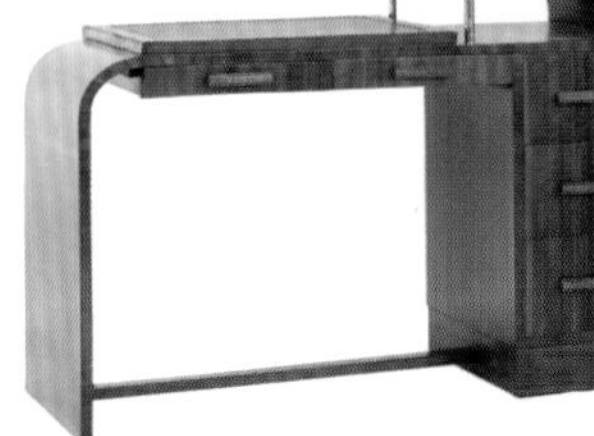

An Art Deco walnut desk, with a leather top and an arched chrome supported shelf.

38in (97cm) high

$1,800-2,250 **SWO**

A pair of Art Deco rocking chairs, with stained oak arms and stand, with 'handbrake' to the side.

$975-1,300 **SWO**

An Art Deco walnut console table, each end with a single drawer.

47.75in (121cm) wide

$900-1,200 **SWO**

An Art Deco bird's-eye maple and walnut crossbanded dining table, attributed to Hille, and six dining chairs.

table 71.75in (182cm) long

$6,000-7,500 **SWO**

ESSENTIAL REFERENCE - D'ARGENTAL

D'Argental is a mark used in France by the Compagnie des Cristalleries de St. Louis. Cameo glass was made with the D'Argental mark from 1919 to 1925. Of special interest is the glass made by Paul Nicolas. Paul Nicolas became chief designer at Galle in around 1895 when he was barely 20. He was clearly Émile Galle's favored protégée, but when Galle died 9 years later he left the business to his son-in-law. He continued to design for Galle for a further 10 years. After the war he went to St Louis. St Louis had been and still is one of the great old glass houses of France; they had gone to the Paris exhibition in 1900 expecting to be crowned king of glass, only to be completely out-classed by the cameo glass of Émile Gallé. In the early 1920s Paul Nicolas cut a deal with St Louis –he would make cameo glass for them using their facilities and then also he could use their facilities to make cameo glass for himself too. The pieces Nicolas made for St Louis were signed a number of ways, but quite soon they settled on 'D'Argental' (the brand name they had established for their own previous, unsuccessful attempts at cameo glass). Nicolas added a cross of Lorraine to the mark to indicate when he personally made a piece. When he made Cameo for himself pieces were signed 'P. Nicolas' usually followed by 'Nancy'.

A red on yellow D'Argental landscape cameo vase, depicting 'Mont Saint Michel', signed D'Argental, with a cross of Lorraine, made by Paul Nicolas.
c1920 *9in (23cm) high*
$3,000-4,000 **MDM**

A large early 20thC D'Argental cameo glass vase, cut with a tree lined lakeside landscape, cameo signature to the body.
12.5in (32cm) high
$2,250-3,000 **FLD**

A brown on red large D'Argental landscape cameo vase, depicting a river inlet and trees, signed D'Argental, with a cross of Lorraine, made by Paul Nicolas.
c1920 *13in (33cm) high*
$3,000-4,000 **MDM**

A brown on orange large D'Argental landscape cameo vase, depicting trees and a village in the distance, signed D'Argental with a cross of Lorraine, made by Paul Nicolas.
c1920 *9in (23cm) high*
$1,800-2,250 **MDM**

A monumental blue and purple D'Argental landscape cameo vase, depicting a river, trees and castles, signed D'Argental, designed by Paul Nicolas.
c1925 *14in (35.5cm) high*
$5,250-6,000 **MDM**

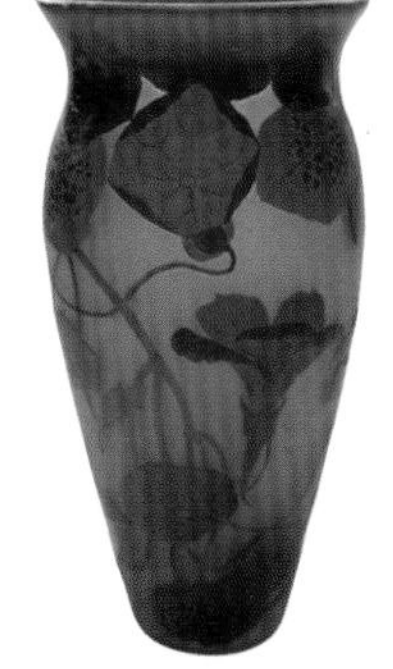

A monumental red on orange D'Argental cameo vase, depicting nasturtiums, signed D'Argental, with cross of Lorraine, made by Paul Nicolas.

This vase was a gift from Paul Nicolas to his brother Émile (founding secretary of the École De Nancy).
c1920 *14in (14cm) high*
$4,000-4,500 **MDM**

A red/brown on orange D'Argental cameo vase, depicting orchids, butterflies and dragonflies, signed D'Argental, with cross of Lorraine, made by Paul Nicolas.
c1920 *12in (30.5cm) high*
$4,000-4,500 **MDM**

A small Art Deco blue on pink D'Argental cameo vase, depicting a stylised deco pattern, signed D'Argental, with cross of Lorraine, made by Paul Nicolas.
c1925 *4in (10cm) high*
$1,800-2,250 **MDM**

A purple on blue D'Argental cameo vase, depicting irises, signed 'St Louis Nancy', made by Paul Nicolas.
c1920 *8in (20.5cm) high*
$1,800-2,250 **MDM**

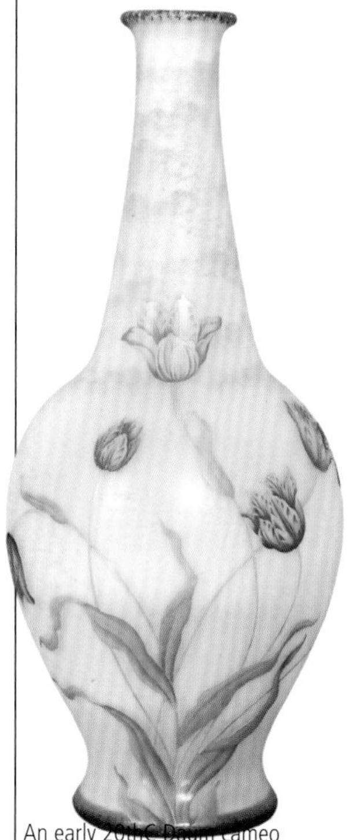

An early 20thC Daum cameo enamel vase, decorated with cameo-cut tulips picked out with hand enamel color over an opalescent ground, gilt Daum Nancy signature.

12in (30cm) high

$3,300-4,000 **FLD**

A large early 20thC Daum enamel cameo landscape vase, decorated with a tree landscape with farmhouse to cornfields, with cross of Lorraine and B.S.

13.5in (34cm) high

$9,000-10,500 **FLD**

An early 20thC Daum enamel cameo landscape vase, decorated with a summer forest view, with cross of Lorraine and artists monogram.

8.5in (21.5cm) high

$5,250-6,000 **FLD**

An early 20thC Daum enamel cameo landscape vase, decorated with an Autumn forest scene, with cross of Lorraine.

5.25in (13cm) high

$1,800-2,250 **FLD**

An early 20thC Daum enamel cameo landscape vase, decorated with an autumn tree lined river landscape, with cross of Lorraine.

5in (12.5cm) high

$4,400-4,800 **FLD**

An early 20thC Daum enamel cameo landscape vase, decorated with a winter forest scene, with cross of Lorraine.

4.75in (12cm) high

$2,700-3,300 **FLD**

An early 20thC Daum landscape cameo vase, with a winter woodland landscape, enamel signature.

8in (20cm) high

$1,500-2,100 **FLD**

A large early 20thC Daum spring landscape cameo vase, enamel signature.

15in (38.5cm) high

$8,500-9,000 **FLD**

An early 20thC Daum cameo vase, enameled with flowering fuchsia, cameo signature to the body.

4.75in (12cm) high

$1,450-1,800 **FLD**

A Daum Nancy glass beaker vase, enameled with sweet-peas, cameo Daum Nancy mark.

3.5in (9cm) high

$2,700-3,300 **WW**

A Daum Nancy cameo glass vase, enameled with Rowan berry fronds, cameo signature.

3.5in (8.5cm) high

$2,250-3,000 **WW**

A Daum Nancy miniature bowl, enameled with red flowers, enameled Daum Nancy France to side.

2.25in (5.5cm) diam

$2,000-2,400 **WW**

A Daum Nancy cameo glass bowl, with enameled decoration of Aquilegia, signed in cameo Daum Nancy, with Cross of Lorraine.

3.5in (9cm) high

$1,400-1,800 **ECGW**

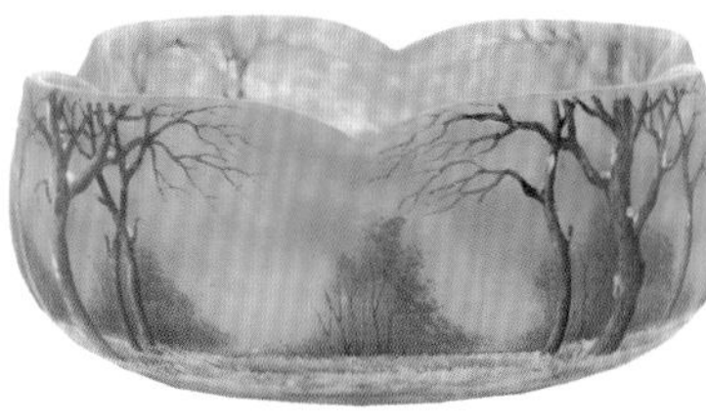

A Daum Nancy enameled glass winter landscape bowl, enameled Daum Nancy mark.

6in (15.5cm) wide

$2,400-3,000 **WW**

An early 20thC Daum cameo glass bowl, cut with wild orchids, cameo signature to the body.

4.75in (12cm) high

$750-900 **FLD**

A Daum Nancy cameo glass lamp shade, acid etched with a lakeside landscape, with metal mount, cameo Daum Nancy mark.

6in (15.5cm) high

$2,250-3,000 **WW**

A Daum acid etched amethyst glass vase, with geometric panels, engraved Daum Nancy France to foot.

8.75in (22cm) high

$1,150-1,300 **WW**

A Daum Nancy acid-etched glass vase, etched 'Daum Nancy France'.

9.5in (24cm) high

$400-450 **WW**

A large late 19thC Gallé loving cup, enamel decorated with stylised armorials, enamel signature to the base.

8in (20cm) high

$300-400 **FLD**

A Gallé blue mountain vase, unusually internally polished along mountain line and lake to reveal blue in purple, blue and orange, singed in cameo.

c1900 *5in (13cm) high*

$3,300-4,050 **M&D**

A Gallé blue mountain moon flask vase, in brown, blue and orange, signed in cameo.

c1900 *7in (18cm) high*

$3,000-4,000 **M&D**

A monumental Gallé 'impressionistic' aquatic vase, with irises, in yellow, blue and true black, signed in cameo.

c1900 *15in (38cm) high*

$9,000-10,500 **M&D**

An impressive Gallé squat vase, with dramatic internally polishing behind Anemones, in opal-orange, blue and purple, signed in cameo.

c1900 *8.5in (22cm) high*

$6,750-8,250 **M&D**

An unusual Gallé vase, with ornate tulips, in brown green and orange-red, signed in cameo.

c1900 *10.5in (27cm) high*

$4,800-5,700 **M&D**

A Gallé squat flowering 'Celandine' vase, purple and blue over opal, internally polished, signed in cameo.

c1900 *5in (13cm) high*

$3,000-4,000 **M&D**

A Gallé flat-top botanical vase, in purple, yellow and blue, signed in cameo.

c1900 *5in (13cm) high*

$2,400-2,700 **M&D**

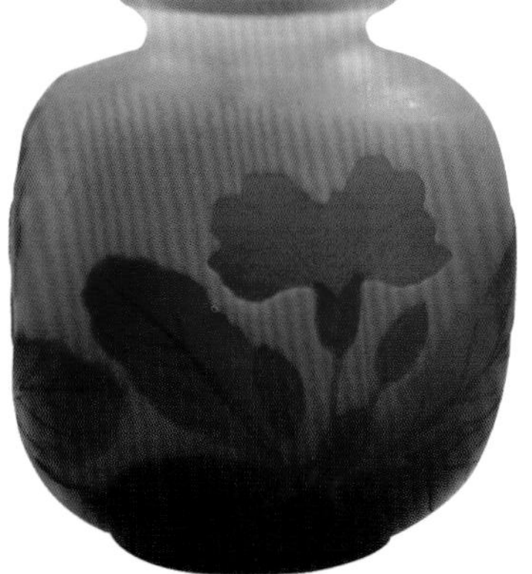

A Gallé internally polished small cube Primula vase, in red and pink over yellow, signed in cameo.

c1900 *4.5in (11.5cm)*

$2,700-3,300 **M&D**

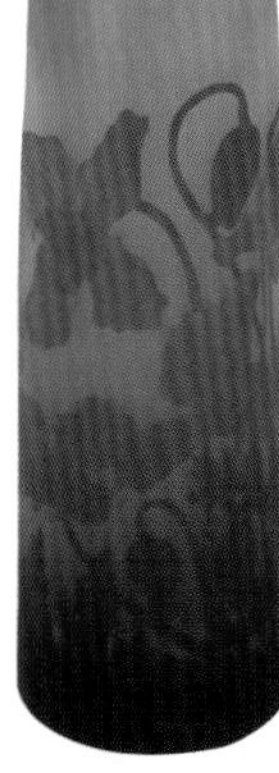

A Gallé unusual color 'Wild Poppy' vase, in green over pink over blue, signed in cameo.

c1900 *9in (23cm) high*

$1,800-2,250 **M&D**

Judith Picks: 'Formosa' Vase

I had to pick this vase as I fell in love with it at the NEC Antiques for Everyone and bought it. The decoration is superb with the opal red glass, with combed threads of green aventurine, gilded and enameled with horse chestnuts. It looks dramatic when the light strikes it. The Harrach glass factory is one of the oldest glass houses still in operation today. Harrach was initially run by Count Harrach, and opened in 1712. It's located in the small town of Harrachov in Northern Bohemia, which is now the Czech Republic. For a relatively small glass factory, Harrach produced a staggering amount of glass. Harrach glass blanks were used by most of the major Bohemian glass houses including Moser, J & L Lobmeyr, Egermann etc. This can make attribution complicated.

A Harrach four handled 'Formosa' vase, designed by Julius Jelinek.

c1905 *7in (17.75cm) high*

$1,800-2,250 **MDM**

A monumental Harrach cameo vase, gilded pink over green/gray, attributed to Julius Jelinek.

This is from a series of vases first shown at the Paris 1900 exhibition where Harrach earned a gold medal.

c1900 *16in (40.5cm) high*

$3,000-4,000 **MDM**

A Harrach cameo vase, 'in the English style' white opal on blue, depicting flowers, designed by Josef Petricek, with a Harrach shape code on the base.

1885 *5in (12.75cm) high*

$1,500-2,250 **MDM**

A small Harrach cameo vase, gilded with red over orange depicting flowers.

c1900 *4in (10cm) high*

$700-850 **MDM**

A classic Harrach cameo vase, gilded with opal white over green with the sun in clouds.

This vase is often wrongly attributed to Daum

c1900 *8in (20.5cm) high*

$1,800-2,250 **MDM**

A Harrach cameo vase, depicting Hydrangea, designed by Rudolf Schwedler, signed in cameo.

c1925 *8in (20.5cm) high*

$1,800-2,250 **MDM**

A Harrach cameo vase, depicting deer, designed by Rudolf Schwedler, signed in cameo.

c1925 *8in (20.5cm) high*

$3,000-4,000 **MDM**

A Harrach green lobster vase, enameled over gray glass.

This was probably made for the English wholesalers 'Silber and Fleming'.

c1880 *7in (17.75cm) high*

$450-600 **MDM**

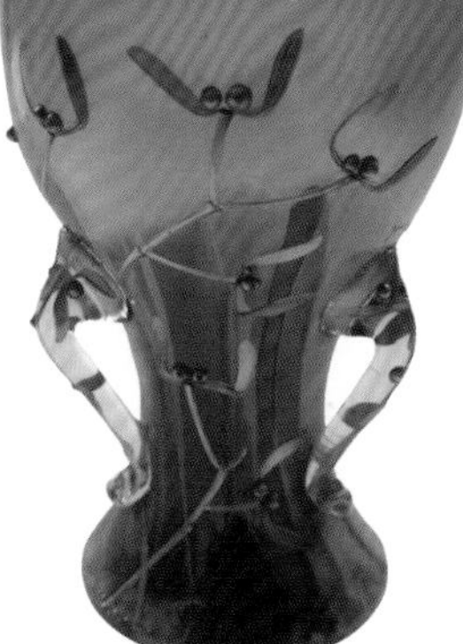

A Harrach 'Heckla' vase, designed by Julius Jelinek, polychrome colors and gilded with mistletoe.

c1905 *6in (15.5cm) high*

$1,800-2,250 **MDM**

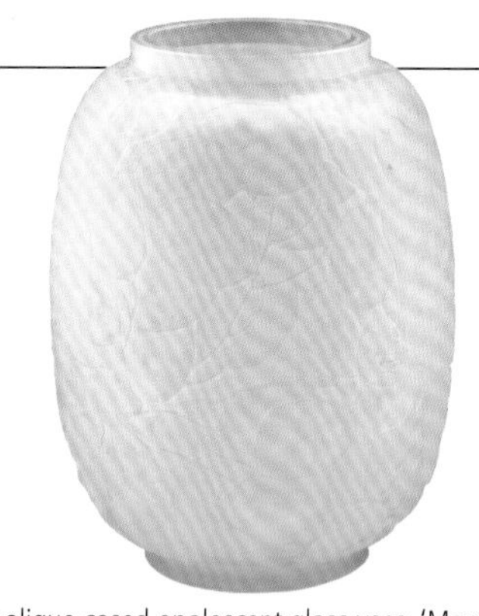

A Lalique cased opalescent glass vase, 'Monnaie De Pape', No.897, designed by Rene Lalique, with remains of blue staining, engraved 'R Lalique' to the foot.

1914 *9in (23cm) high*

$4,500-5,250 **WW**

A Lalique 'Spirales' frosted opalescent glass vase, no. 1060, stencil etched mark 'R. LALIQUE/ FRANCE'.

1930 *6.5in (16cm) high*

$3,000-4,000 **L&T**

A Lalique cased opalescent glass vase, 'Ormeaux', no.984, designed by Rene Lalique, etched 'R Lalique France'.

7in (17cm) high

$1,800-2,250 **WW**

A pair of Lalique glass vases, molded in the 'Ronces' pattern, no. 946, in electric blue.

designed 1922 *9in (23cm) high*

$5,250-6,000 **HT**

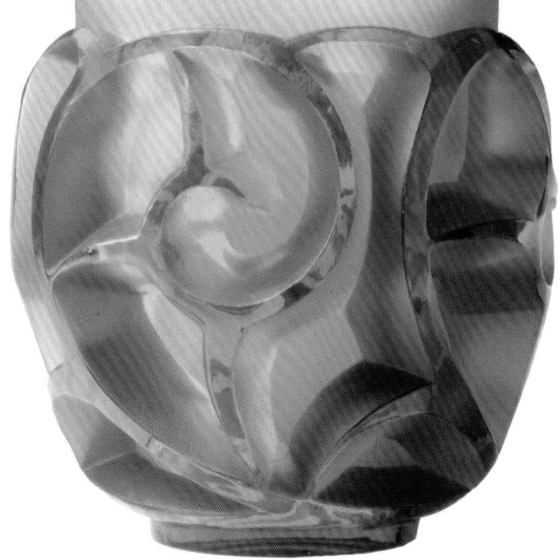

A Lalique 'Tourbillons' amber glass vase, wheel engraved 'R Lalique FRANCE' and etched 'No.973'.

8in (20.5cm) high

$21,000-27,000 **TEN**

A Lalique counter top display perfume bottle and stopper, 'Worth - 4 Dans La Nuit', by Rene Lalique, molded 'R Lalique' to base.

10in (25cm) high

$1,150-1,300 **WW**

A Lalique 'Le Jade' perfume bottle, for Roger et Gallet, molded 'ROGER ET GALLET PARIS, LE JADE, R. L. FRANCE', both stopper and bottled etched '6251'.

3.25in (8.3cm) high

$3,300-4,400 **DRA**

A Lalique frosted opalescent glass bowl, 'Madagascar', no.2481, designed by Rene Lalique, cast 'R Lalique' to rim, minor pin head nicks, wear to base rim.

13in (33cm) diam

$12,750-14,250 **WW**

A Lalique smokey with amethyst hue glass car mascot, 'Coq Nain', no.1135, molded 'R LALIQUE FRANCE'.

8in (20cm) high

$2,700-3,300 **TEN**

A Loetz 'Persica' vase, in purple/ pink spreading over yellow, gilded and enameled with a Greek/Roman figure.

1894 *7in (18cm) high*

$600-750 **MDM**

A pair of Loetz 'Arcadia' vases, spreading opalescence on pale green, with enamel pattern codes to base.

1896-7 *5in (12.7cm) high*

$1,200-1,500 **MDM**

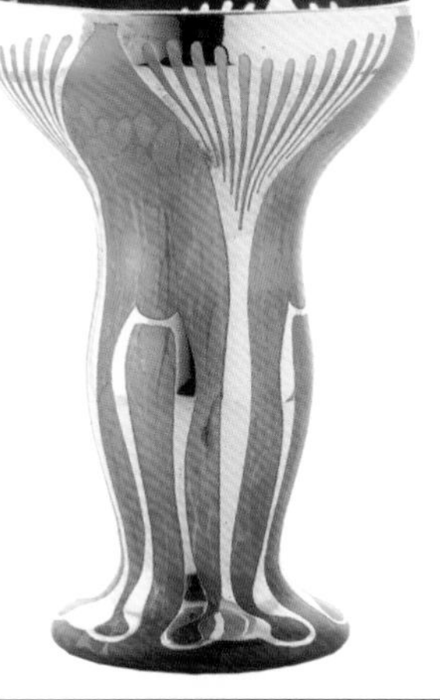

A Loetz 'Arcadia' vase, with stylised polychrome enamelling, spreading opalescence on pale green.

1896-7 *9in (23cm) high*

$1,700-1,800 **MDM**

A Loetz silver overlaid glass vase, in translucent rose colored glass with iridescent purple, blue and green stretched oil spot motifs against a gold ground, painted marks to base '3/781/H789'.

c1900 *8in (20cm) high*

$3,000-4,500 **L&T**

A Loetz 'Crete' green 'Papillon' (Butterfly wing) vase, with silver overlay.

c1900 *4in (10cm) high*

$1,200-1,500 **MDM**

A Loetz green 'Metalin' vase, with silver overlay, stylised acanthus leaves.

1905 *5in (13cm) high*

$1,500-1,800 **MDM**

A Loetz brown 'Metalin' vase, with silver overlay.

1905 *6in (15.5cm) high*

$1,20-1,400 **MDM**

A Loetz 'Cytisus' glass vase, surface decorated with golden iridescent spots.

4.75in (12cm) high

$2,400-3,000 **WW**

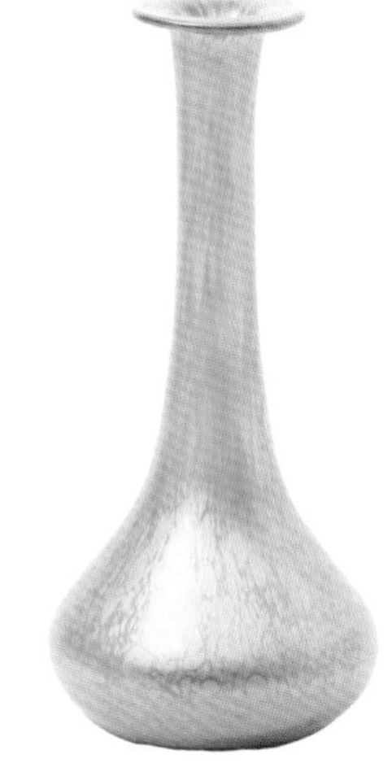

A Loetz iridescent glass vase, in a splashed blue iridescence.

9in (22.5cm) high

$550-600 **WW**

An A.V.E.M. 'Reazioni Policroma' glass vase, designed by Guilio Radi, unmarked.

c1948 *7in (18cm) high*

$1,450-1,800 **DRA**

A Barovier glass vase, with murrines, designed by Giuseppe Barovier, AB murrine.

c1920 *4.5in (11.5cm) high*

$1,150-1,300 **DRA**

A tall Laguna Gemmata glass vase, designed by Ercole Barovier, with flaring fan shaped mottled azure cased in clear, unsigned.

12.5in (32cm) high

$4,800-6,000 **WW**

A 'Nerro e Rosso' glass vase, attributed to Napoleone Martinuzzi for Zecchin Martinuzzi.

c1930 *6.25in (15.5cm) high*

$1,400-1,800 **L&T**

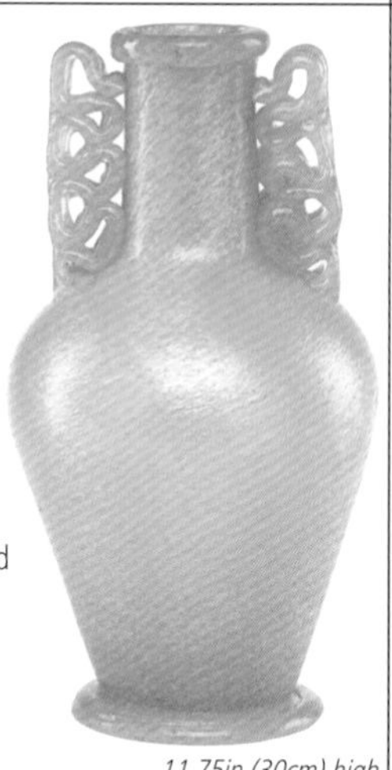

A 1930s attributed to Napoleone Martinuzzi 'Pulegoso' glass vase, unmarked.

11.75in (30cm) high

$1,500-2,100 **DRA**

An enameled S.A.L.I.R. glass vase, attributed to Anzolo Fuga, remnant of original decal label.

c1930 *9in (23cm) high*

$1,300-1,450 **DRA**

A Fratelli Toso 'Floreali' glass vase, with daisies, unmarked.

c1910 *9.75in (25cm) high*

$2,700-3,300 **DRA**

A 1930s blown glass vase, attributed to Fratelli Toso, unmarked.

8in (20.5cm) high

$975-1,150 **DRA**

An early 20thC glass vase, attributed to Venini, the pale green body with aventurine inclusions.

12.5in (32cm) high

$300-400 **L&T**

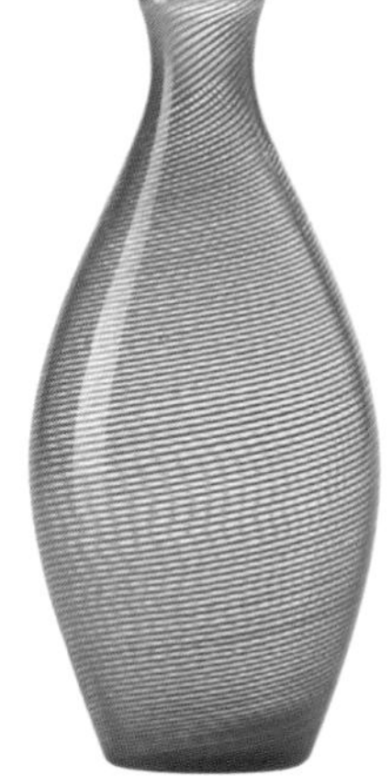

A small Venini 'Mezza Filigrana' vase, designed by Carlo Scarpa, acid-etched mark 'VENINI MURANO MADE IN ITALY'.

1935-43 *5.5in (14cm) high*

$1,200-1,500 **DRA**

A Stevens & Williams glass vase, by H Cook, cut and etched with an otter swimming amongst a shoal of fish, etched 'H Cook No.79'.

9in (23cm) high

$280-340 WW

A late 19thC Stevens & Williams 'Dolce Relievo' vase, cased in a butterscotch over opal, acid cut with 'The Three Graces', unmarked.

6.75in (17cm) high

$1,000-1,500 FLD

A late 19thC Stevens & Williams vase, possibly by John Northwood, cased in purple over opal and polished intaglio cut with a squirrel in a fruiting pine nut bough.

10.25in (26cm) high

$4,400-5,100 FLD

A late 19thC Stevens & Williams 'Osiris' vase, cased in yellow over opal and pink interior and decorated with wrythen spiralled ruby pulled loop threads.

10.5in (26.5cm) high

$3,300-4,400 FLD

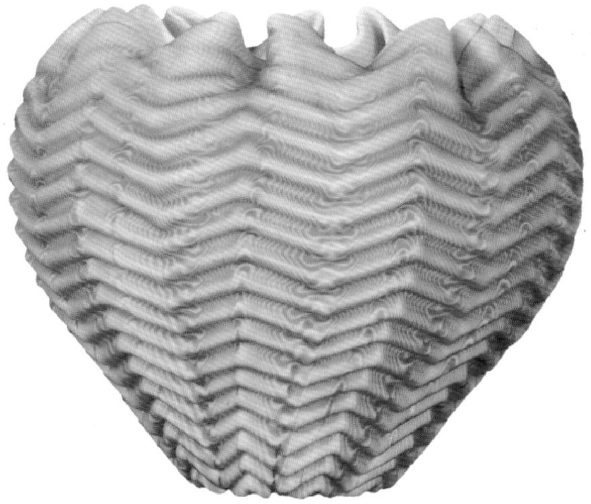

A late 19thC Stevens & Williams 'Osiris' style bowl, cased in peach over opal with a fine pulled threaded design over a tight herringbone-molded body.

5.25in (13cm) high

$3,000-4,000 FLD

A late 19thC Stevens & Williams 'Oisris' pattern posy bowl, cased in pale yellow with pulled cranberry spiral threads, acid patent mark.

5.5in (14cm) wide

$2,000-2,700 FLD

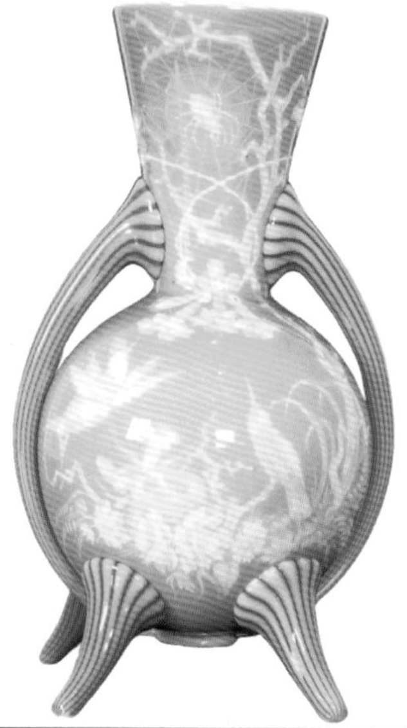

A late 19thC Stevens & Williams vase, cased in pink over opal and polished intaglio cut with hummingbirds and a flowering tree with spiders web above.

8.25in (21cm) high

$1,300-1,450 FLD

ESSENTIAL REFERENCE - CYPRIOTE TECHNIQUE

In the Cypriote technique, Tiffany sought to simulate the corrosive qualities of glass excavated from archaeological sites on Cyprus. To replicate the devitrified surfaces of buried artifacts, particles of metallic oxides were applied to a mass of molten glass. This created a chemical reaction that, in turn, pitted the surface of the glass when it was held to a flame. Alternatively, a gather of molten glass was rolled over a marver (i.e. steel plate) covered in pulverized silica rock, a process which also pitted its surface. Often additional decorative effects, such as silvery-blue leaves on trailing stems, were applied to the encrusted ground before it was iridised.

A Tiffany Studios 'Cypriote' vase.

1902 *10in (25.5cm) high*

$18,000-22,500 MIC

A Tiffany Studios 'Cypriote' vase, in the classical Ancient Roman form, signed on base '6215 N L.C. Tiffany'.

6.5in (16.5cm) high

$6,000-7,500 MIC

A Tiffany Studios 'Lava' vase, inscribed 'L.C. Tiffany Favrile 9166C'.

A visit to Mount Etna in Sicily during one of its eruptions is said to have inspired Tiffany to capture in glass the force and beauty of the molten volcanic flows.

4.25in (10.5cm) high

$4,000-5,250 MIC

A Tiffany Studios agate vase, bronze mount inset with eight jeweled glass scarabs, glass, inscribed 'L.C. Tiffany-Favrile'.

One of the first pieces of mounted agateware, perhaps the technique's prototype was included in Bing's Tiffany exhibition at the Grafton Galleries, London, 1899.

8.25in (21cm) high

$52,500-60,000 MIC

A Tiffany Studios 'Lava' vase, inscribed 'L.C.Tiffany-Favrile 26 A-Coll'.

This is one of the most monumental lava vases recorded, a factor no doubt in Tiffany's decision to reserve it as a study piece. Another reason is the satiny salmon iridescence on the gold volcanic flow. Whereas the technique became one of the most innovative developed at Corona, the precarious nature of its manufacture led to a high attrition rate and consequently, high production costs.

12.5in (32cm) high

$180,000-200,000 MIC

A Tiffany Studios gold favrile glass compote, with purple and pink highlights, signed '1705 L.C. Tiffany Inc. Favrile'.

4in (10cm) diam

$975-1,150 MIC

A Tiffany Studios 'Jack in the Pulpit' vase, the deep purple body decorated with gray green design allover strong iridescence, signed 'LCT Favrile'.

9.75in (25cm) high

$12,000-13,500 MIC

A Tiffany favrile glass goblet, in gold iridescence with purple, pink and blue highlights, signed 'L.C.T. 05999'.

8.5in (21.5cm) high

$1,300-1,450 MIC

A Tiffany Studios 'Sunset' landscape window, with birch trees on the right and evergreens on the opposite side, signed Tiffany Studios in enamel.

34.5in (87cm) high

$180,000-200,000 **MIC**

A Tiffany Studios 'Angel' window, in multihued blue and orange favrile glass, inscribed 'LIVI 'and now abideth faith hope and charity these three'.

39in (99cm) long

$37,500-45,000 **MIC**

A Tiffany leaded glass window, depicting 'Christ on the Road to Emmaus', commissioned for a New Jersey church.

105in (267cm) high

$82,500-90,000 **MIC**

ESSENTIAL REFERENCE - ACID ETCHING

The setting sun behind the mountains is sending rays of light up into the sky. This effect was achieved by selective acid etching on rear layers of glass. The inclusion of magnolia blossoms within the composition allowed Tiffany to include a selection of his drapery glass, which he had developed initially to portray the folds in the vestments in his figural windows. The glass, while still molten, was thrown on to a marver and rolled into a disk. The glassmaker, clad in thick asbestos gloves and with tongs, then manipulated the glass mass, as one would pastry dough, by taking hold of it from both ends and pulling and twisting till it fell into folds. Where necessary, pliers were used to form the corrugations. In this window, the deep crevices and undulations in the glass capture precisely those of the magnolia petal.

A Tiffany Studios 'Magnolia' landscape window, with a flowering magnolia tree and a river and a mountainous pass to a lake, unsigned.

c1910 *44.25in (112.5cm) high*

$180,000-200,000 **MIC**

ESSENTIAL REFERENCE - AQUAMARINE GLASS

Introduced around 1911-12, Aquamarine glass was the last major technique publicized by the firm.

- **Compositions of aquatic plants and other marine life were fashioned out of small colored glass canes that the glassblower pulled into their required forms with a metal hook not unlike a crochet needle. At various stages in the process, the composition was encased in layers of clear or tinted glass gathered on a blowpipe from a crystal pot. The result provided the viewer with the impression of looking into a fishbowl or pond, better examples providing a sense of motion within the water. The effect is illusionary as the decoration is far smaller than it appears, the thick outer mass of glass acting as a magnifying lens. In addition to flora, aquamarine glassware includes fish, algae, sea anemones, jelly fish and molluscs, in many instances presented within a complete ecological environment.**

A Tiffany Studios 'Aquamarine' vase, inscribed 'L.C. Tiffany-Favrile 5249G'.

10.5in (26.5cm) high

$90,000-105,000 **MIC**

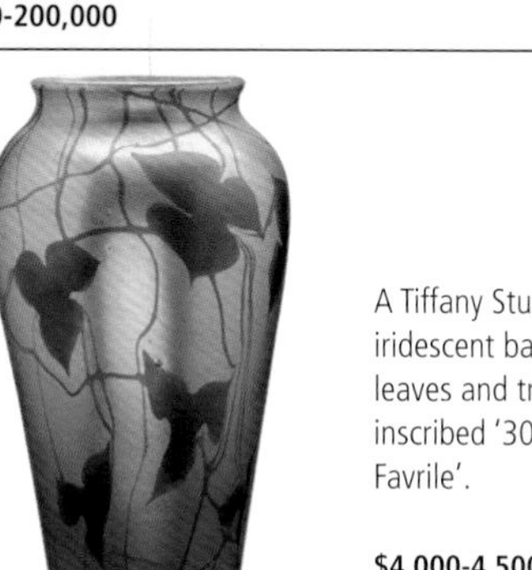

A Tiffany Studios vase, the gold iridescent background with green leaves and trailing vines, base inscribed '3041 C L.C. Tiffany Favrile'.

13.25in (34cm) high

$4,000-4,500 **MIC**

A Tiffany Studios scent bottle, designed by Paulding Farnham, glass with guilloché (engine-turned) and enameled gold mount set with twelve diamonds and an upper peridot, mount impressed 'TIFFANY & CO'.

c1900 *4.5in (11cm) high*

$85,000-97,500 **MIC**

A late 19thC Thomas Webb & Sons 'Queens Burmese' cameo glass vase, cased in opal over magenta over a pink to yellow ground, cut with flowers, foliage, unmarked.

6.25in (16cm) high

$25,500-30,000 FLD

A large late 19thC Thomas Webb & Sons cameo moon flask vase, cased in opal over blue and carved in the Chinese taste with flowers and foliate scrolls, unmarked.

10.25in (26cm) high

$28,500-34,500 FLD

A late 19thC Thomas Webb & Sons triple color cameo vase, cased in ruby over opal over blue and cut in a repeat over lapping scroll work, original paper labels.

4.25in (10.5cm) high

$10,500-12,000 FLD

A late 19thC Thomas Webb & Sons ivory cameo vase, decorated in the Chinese taste with ribbon tied fruiting boughs with scroll work pattern to the shoulders, full acid mark.

6in (15cm) high

$4,500-5,250 FLD

A Stourbridge cameo glass vase, probaby Thomas Webb & Sons.

5in (12cm) high

$450-600 L&T

A late 19thC Stourbridge cameo glass vase, possibly Thomas Webb & Sons, cased in opal over citron and cut with insects around a flowering wild rose, unmarked.

6.75in (17cm) high

$1,500-1,800 FLD

A late 19thC Stourbridge cameo glass vase, possibly Thomas Webb & Sons, cased in opal over cinnamon and cut with an abstract scroll.

4.75in (12cm) high

$1,400-1,800 FLD

A late 19thC miniature Stourbridge cameo glass posy vase, possibly Thomas Webb & Sons, cased in opal over ruby over yellow with opal interior.

2in (5cm) high

$900-1,200 FLD

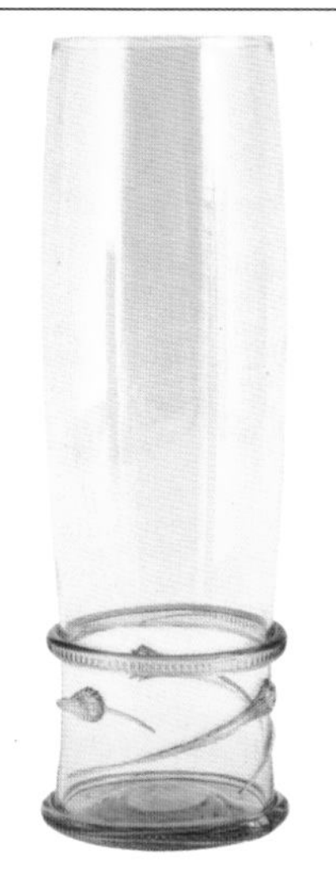

A James Powell & Sons, Whitefriars amber glass 'Serpent' vase, designed by Harry Powell.

c1910 *9.25in (23.5cm) high*

$330-420 **WW**

A James Powell & Sons (Whitefriars) Ltd. sea green 'Serpent' vase, by Harry Powell, etched with the arms of the Glaziers Company on their 250th Anniversary.

1913 *8in (20.5cm) high*

$550-600 **SWO**

A James Powell & Sons Whitefriars solifleur vase, pale blue-green glass streaked with red and white, with aventurine inclusions, unsigned.

4.25in (10.5cm) high

$975-1,150 **WW**

A James Powell & Sons Whitefriars glass lampbase, shouldered flint glass with ruby threads.

14.25in (36cm) high

$280-360 **WW**

A 1930s James Powell & Sons Whitefriars Ltd. sapphire chevron-cut vase, designed by William Wilson, pat. no.9035.

10in (25.5cm) high

$300-450 **SWO**

A 1930s Whitefriars bubble vase, by Barnaby Powell, in spinach green.

8in (20cm) high

$150-225 **SWO**

A James Powell & Sons Whitefriars cut glass 'Comets' vase, by William Wilson, emerald blue glass, cut with star and lens design, unsigned.

8.5in (21.5cm) high

$1,800-2,250 **WW**

A James Powell & Sons Whitefriars glass vase, by James Hogan, the sky blue body with amethyst bubbled ribbon trail, unsigned.

9.5in (24cm) high

$400-550 **WW**

A James Powell & Sons Whitefriars sapphire blue ribbon trailed vase, designed by Barnaby Powell.

9in (23cm) high

$240-300 **WW**

A 1880s James Powell & Sons Whitefriars Ltd. flint glass tazza, possibly by T G Jackson, with blue inclusions.

c1880s *5.3in (13.5cm) high*

$180-240 **SWO**

A late 19thC James Powell & Sons Whitefriars blue opal bonbon dish, on triform stand.

5.25in (13cm) high

$300-400 **SWO**

A James Powell & Sons Whitefriars straw opal glass dish, on a triform stand.

4in (10cm) high

$280-360 **SWO**

A pair of Guild of Handicrafts Ltd salts, with James Powell & Sons, Whitefriars green glass bowls, stamped marks, London.

1903 *2.5in (6.5cm) diam*

$1,20-1,400 **WW**

A James Powell & Sons Whitefriars 'Sea Green' bowl, with blue threaded decoration and tinting.

10.25in (26cm) diam

$280-360 **WW**

A rare James Powell & Sons, Whitefriars 'Minerbi' glass goblet, with green pulled down melted in threads, on twisted stem.

7.5in (18.5cm) high

$4,000-4,500 **WW**

A pair of James Powell & Sons Whitefriars Ltd. sea-green vinaigrette bottles and stoppers.

c1900 *7in (18cm) high*

$180-225 **SWO**

A Guild of Handicraft Limited decanter, designed by Charles Robert Ashbee, with James Powell & Sons Whitefriars green glass body, the silver neck chased with Art Nouveau entrelac design, set with five green chrysoprase stones, stamped marks, London.

1903 *8.25in (21cm) high*

$9,750-11,500 **WW**

A James Powell & Sons Whitefriars green glass decanter and stopper, designed by Harry Powell.

9.75in (24.5cm) high

$300-400 **WW**

A Gabriel Argy-Rousseau pâte de verre glass bowl, with a frieze of blackberry, cast 'G Argy-Rousseau' to side.

4.25in (10.5cm) wide

$3,000-4,000 **WW**

A James Couper & Sons, Glasgow, 'Clutha' glass vase, with milky inclusions.

'Clutha' (the Gaelic word for Clyde) glass was invented by James Couper in the 1890s. George Walton and Christopher Dresser designed for the range.

c1900 *3.5in (9cm) high*

$550-600 **L&T**

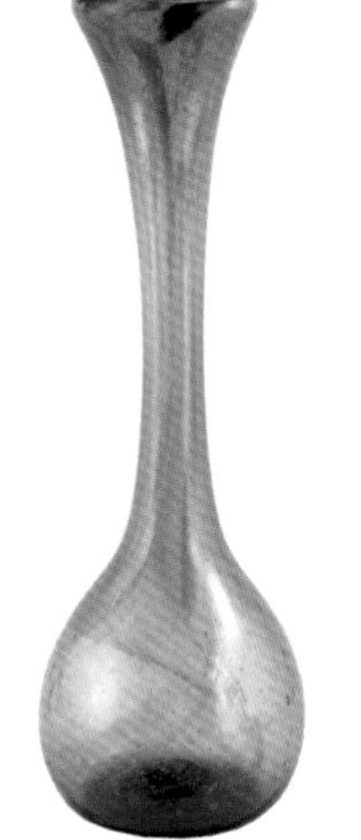

A James Couper & Sons 'Clutha' glass vase, designed by Dr Christopher Dresser, mottled glass with air bubble inclusions and white and aventurine swirls, unsigned.

22in (55.5cm) high

$1,800-2,250 **WW**

A James Couper & Sons 'Clutha' glass vase, designed by Dr Christopher Dresser, glass internally decorated with brown streaks and air bubbles, unsigned.

7in (17.5cm) high

$600-750 **WW**

A Degue cameo glass vase, orange body cased with red and blue flower stems, acid etched cameo mark to body.

9in (23cm) high

$600-750 **WW**

An early 20thC André Delatte cameo glass vase, cut with a fruiting orange bough with blossom, cameo signature to the body.

10.75in (27cm) high

$750-900 **FLD**

A 1930s Elferson's glass vase, after a design by Dunne Cooke, with 'chip' decoration.

9.75in (24.5cm) high

$180-240 **SWO**

A 1920s French Art Deco vase, by Marcel Goupy, enamel decorated with a landscape scene, black enamel signature to the base.

6in (15cm) high

$300-400 **FLD**

A 1930s Gray-Stan vase, the neck with bronze aventurine flecks and pulled loops, acid signature.

7in (18cm) high

$750-900 **FLD**

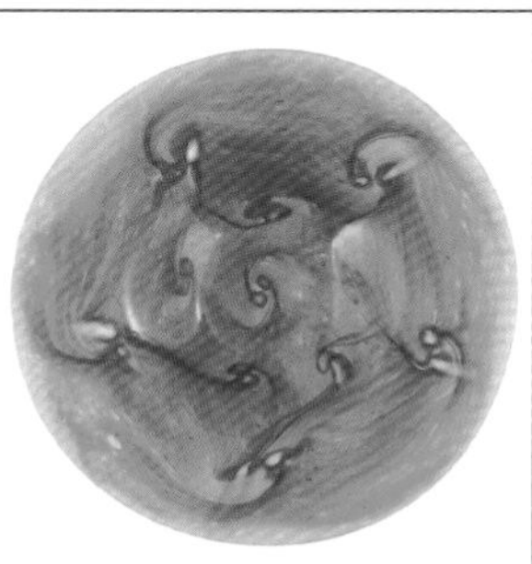

A Gray-Stan glass plate, designed by Mrs Graydon-Stannus, decorated with white swirls, on patinated metal stand, acid etched signature.
10.75in (27cm) diam
$255-300 WW

A Gray-Stan glass tazza, designed by Mrs Graydon-Stannus, foot etched Gray-Stan mark.
12in (30cm) diam
$255-300 WW

A Hadeland Norway glass vase, etched 'Hadeland 1074'.
10.25in (26cm) high
$95-115 SWO

A Kosta clear crystal 'Rodeo' vase, designed by Vicke Lindstrand, cut and engraved with a figure riding a rodeo horse, engraved marks.
c1950 8.5in (21cm)
$550-600 FLD

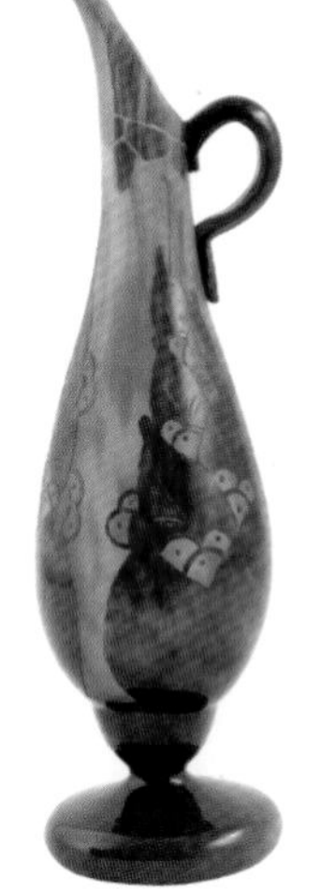

A La Verre Francais cameo glass ewer, etched 'La Verre Francais'.
14.75in (37.5cm) high
$900-1,000 WW

A John Moncrieff Ltd 'Monart' glass table lamp, the mottled orange and yellow glass with green, orange and aventurine inclusions, with maker's label, 'MONCRIEFF SCOTLAND/ MONART GLASS/ P/ 23.39*', original brass fittings.
c1930 13in (33cm) high
$1,200-1,800 L&T

A Monart glass bowl, decorated in a 'Feather and Bubble' pattern in green, highlighted in aventurine, remains of paper label.
9in (22.5cm) diam
$400-450 WW

A Monart glass vase, mottled blue glass with purple striped the shoulder with green, with air bubble inclusions.
9.5in (24cm) high
$600-750 WW

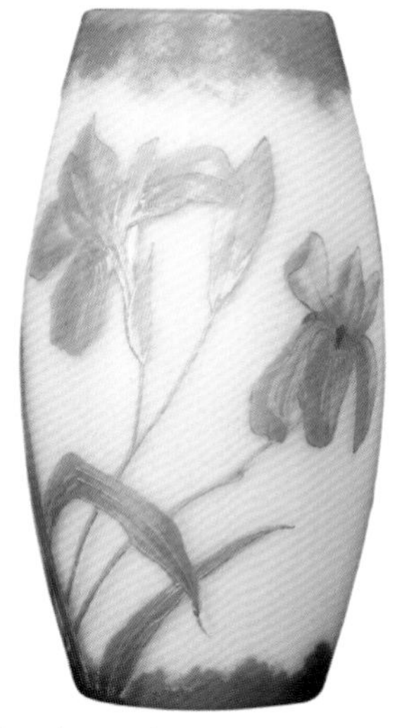

An early 20thC French Art Nouveau vase, in the manner of Mont Joye & Cie, unmarked.
8.5in (21cm) high
$420-510 FLD

An early 20thC Moser scent bottle and stopper, intaglio cut with Convolvulus.
6.5in (16cm) high
$330-420 FLD

A 1930s Orrefors Art Deco vase, designed by Edward Hald, decorated in a repeat honeycomb cut, engraved signature.

11in (28cm) high

$255-300 **FLD**

A late 19thC Richardsons cameo glass vase, cased in opal over ruby and cut with various fruiting and flowering boughs with insects, unmarked.

9in (23cm) high

$11,250-12,000 **FLD**

A Schneider glass tazza, the mottled green glass bowl with air bubble inclusions, on applied aubergine foot, etched 'Schneider' to the foot.

13in (32cm) diam

$450-600 **WW**

A 1920s Schneider Le Verre Français bowl, cased in mottled magenta over a burnt orange ground, engraved signature.

10in (25cm) wide

$450-750 **FLD**

A Schneider glass pedestal bowl, etched Schneider signature.

13.5in (34cm) diam

$400-450 **WW**

An Art Deco Schneider electric blue glass bowl, acid-etched Schneider signature.

13.5in (34cm) diam

$400-450 **WW**

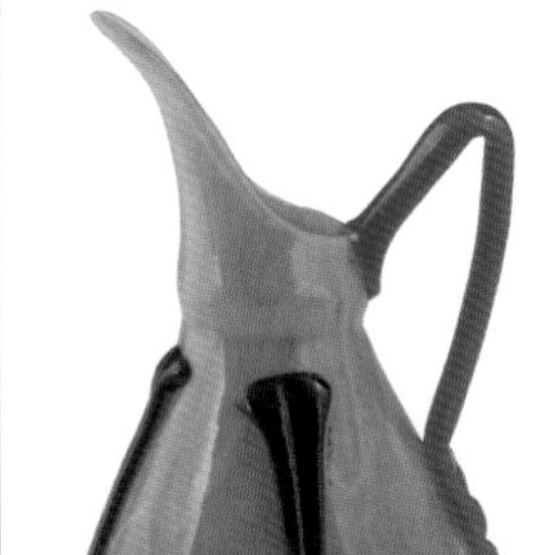

A Schneider cameo glass ewer, tapering aubergine and yellow streaked body, with purple tear-drop columns, acid etched Schneider mark.

13.25in (33.5cm) high

$750-900 **WW**

A Stuart & Sons engraved glass flower vase, acid etched mark, facsimile signature.

This was designed by Graham Sutherland, for the 1934 Art in Industry Exhibition, Harrods.

1934 *6in (15cm) high*

$4,500-5,250 **WW**

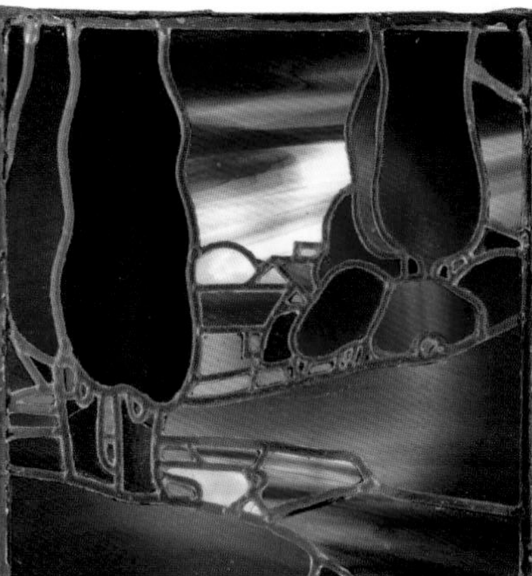

An Ernest Archibald Taylor (1874-1951) stained and leaded glass landscape panel.

c1910 *7.75in (20cm) high*

$3,000-4,000 **L&T**

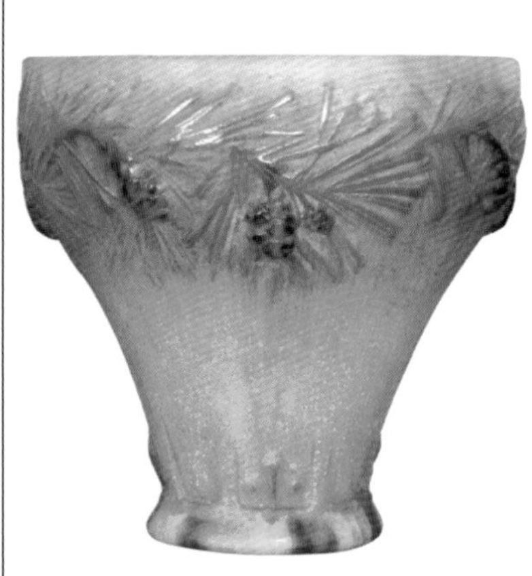

An early 20thC Amalric Walter pâte de verre vase, molded with pine boughs with cones, engraved signature.

4in (10cm) high

$1,500-2,100 **FLD**

A Hannah Moore Walton (1863-1940) glass 'Trumpet' vase, decorated with harebells and moths, painted monogram mark 'HW'.

Hannah Walton worked from the family home at 5 Belmont Terrace in Hillhead, Glasgow, where her sister Helen had established her studio in 1881. The sisters specialized in this type of painting on commercial glassware, and chose decorative subjects associated with water.

c1900 *7.75in (20cm) high*

$1,400-1,800 **L&T**

A WMF 'Ikora' glass table lamp, with spiral inclusions of green, indigo and red, the chrome mounting with an interior light, stamped 'WMF Ikora'.

11in (28cm) high

$400-450 **SWO**

A W.M.F 'Ikora' glass 'Dexel-Ei' vase, designed by Walter Dexel, unsigned.

6.75in (17cm) high

$255-300 **WW**

A W.M.F 'Ikora' 'Unica' glass, streaked green glass with red and yellow striations, with chrome fittings stamped mark to fittings.

12in (30cm) high

$150-225 **WW**

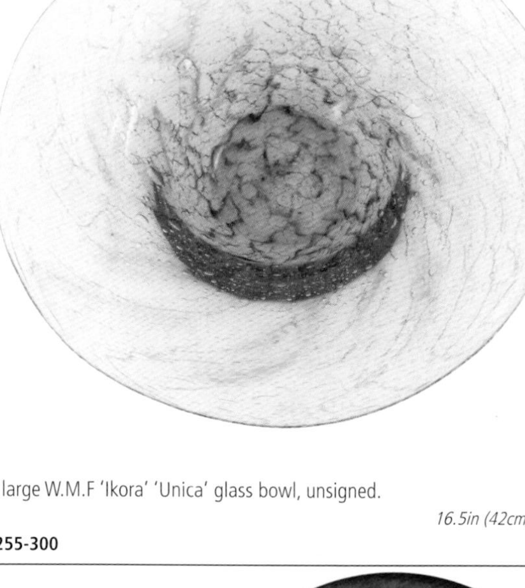

A large W.M.F 'Ikora' 'Unica' glass bowl, unsigned.

16.5in (42cm) diam

$255-300 **WW**

A WMF 'Ikora' glass vase, designed by Karl Weidmann, cased in clear crystal over a tonal gray, blue and ocher marbled ground, unmarked.

13in (33cm) high

$450-600 **FLD**

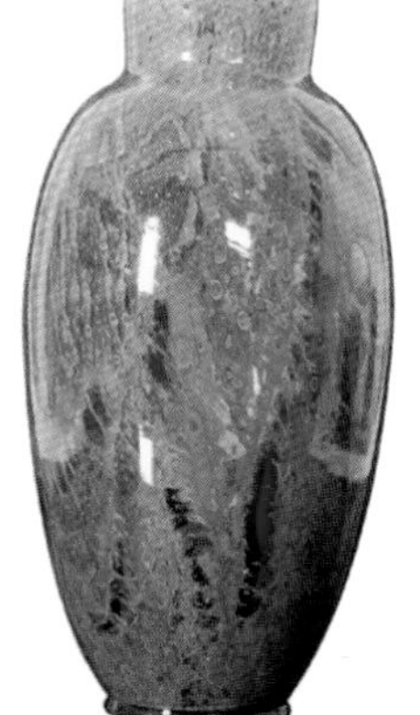

A Paul Ysart paperweight, decorated with a lamp work flower with bronze aventurine foliage over a mottled powder blue ground, with 'PY' signature cane.

2.75in (7cm) diam

$420-510 **FLD**

An Aesthetic Movement ebonized mantel clock, the blue and white enameled dial with Arabic numerals, with an eight-day movement striking on a gong.

13.5in (34.5cm) high

$300-450 **L&T**

An Arts and Crafts oak bracket clock, attributed to George Walton, with camera cuss movement.

c1902 *23in (59cm) high*

$3,000-4,500 **PUR**

A trapezoidal mantle clock, designed by Peter Hansen for L. & J.G. Stickley, Handcraft decal.

c1910 *22in (56cm) high*

$11,250-14,250 **DRA**

An Art Deco guilloché enamel, ivory and amber desk timepiece, the case with amber frog finial, the niche with an ivory female, possibly by Ferdinand Preiss, dial signed 'Kendall/17, Rue de la Paix/Paris', the eight-day key-less wind movement with lever escapement.

c1925 *6in (15cm) high*

$2,700-3,300 **CHEF**

An Arts & Crafts hammered copper mantle clock, inset with Ruskin cabochons above 'Dum Spectas Fugit' ('While One Watches, It Passes'), unmarked.

17.5in (44cm) high

$3,000-4,000 **DRA**

An Art Deco longcase clock, with a three-train movement.

75in (190cm) high

$450-600 **SWO**

A Stanislaw Czapek Goldscheider large clock case, Goldscheider mark, signed Capeque, professional restoration, new clock work, with mallet.

The Latin inscription on the front is from the famous poem 'The Song of the Bell' by Friedrich Schiller and loosely translates to 'I call the living, I mourn the dead, I repel lightning.'

25in (63.5cm) high

$3,000-4,000 **DRA**

An early 20thC miniature travel clock/photograph frame, by Cartier, contained in a tooled red leather fitted case, inscribed 'CARTIER'.

2in (4cm) wide

$6,750-8,250 **L&T**

An Art Deco marble and spelter mantle clock, the dial inscribed 'Marlière Frères, Valencienne'.

22in (56cm) wide

$300-400 **SWO**

An Art Deco onyx mantel clock, the dial inscribed 'Feunteun, Brest', chiming half-hourly.

21.25in (54cm) wide

$700-850 **SWO**

An Art Deco marble-faced clock, with two spelter models of alsatians.

27in (68cm) wide

$300-450 **DN**

An Art Deco spelter and marble mantle clock, unsigned.

13in (32.5cm) wide

$450-750 **WW**

An Art Deco mantel clock, the dial inscribed 'Türler Zürich', in a green veined and black marble case.

10in (25cm) high

$4,000-4,500 **SWO**

An Art Deco silver dressing table timepiece, maker Mappin Bros., Birmingham, with a Swiss movement.

1938 *2.75in (7cm) high*

$180-225 **HT**

An Art Deco enameled and chrome strut clock.

6.5in (165cm) high

$550-600 **SWO**

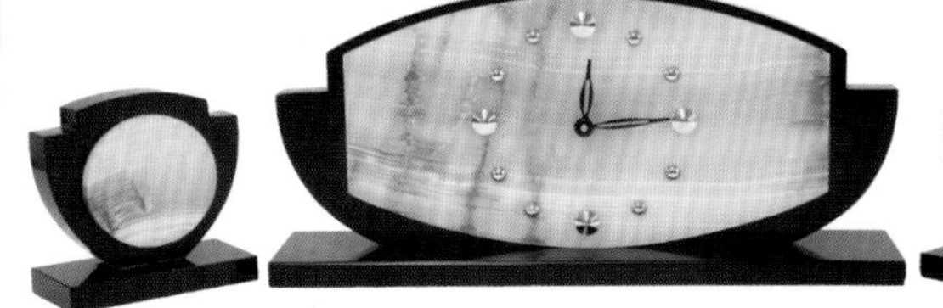

An Art Deco marble and onyx mantle clock garniture.

5.5in (14cm) high

$330-420 **SWO**

ESSENTIAL REFERENCE - WILLIAM QUARRIER

These are from Mount Zion Church, Quarriers Village, Renfrewshire which was founded as the 'Orphan Homes of Scotland' in 1876 by Glasgow shoe-maker and philanthropist William Quarrier. Quarrier had a vision of a community allowing the young people in his care to thrive, set in a countryside environment and housed in a number of grand residences under a house-mother and father. This vision was realized by a number of donations from Quarrier and his friends, who had a free hand in choosing the style that their cottage was built in. As a result the village is an unusual mix of Gothic, French, Old English, Scottish Baronial and Italian. Despite this virtually all of the buildings were the responsibility of one architect, Robert Bryden of Clarke & Bell in Glasgow, who worked free of charge on Quarrier's projects over a course of some twenty-eight years.

A pair of Gothic Revival overpainted and gilded wrought iron electroliers, associated frilled shades.

c1890 *55in (140cm) high*

$4,000-4,500 L&T

A pair of Artificer's Guild silvered metal twin-branch candlesticks, stamped Artificers Guild marks

10in (25.5cm high

$4,000-4,500 WW

A W.A.S Benson copper and brass chamberstick, designed by George Heywood Sumner, unmarked.

9in (22.5cm) high

$975-1,150 WW

A pair of W.A.S Benson copper and brass candlesticks, stamped 'WAS Benson'.

11in (27cm) high

$750-900 WW

A W.A.S Benson copper and brass wall/desk light, the adjustable brass body with copper flower head shade stamped marks.

15in (38cm) high

$3,000-4,500 WW

ESSENTIAL REFERENCE - SMITH BENSON

One of the most significant and forward looking of the Arts & Crafts designers is William Arthur Smith Benson (1854 – 1924). It is clear from Benson's sale catalogs of 'useful and artistic gifts' that he generated designs for an enormous number of saleable items. The 1899/1900 catalog, for instance, lists over 800 lines. His designs were ingenious, too, with double-jacket dishes pre-dating Pyrex oven-to-tableware and reflecting social changes, with people now cooking for their guests and serving them. With relaxed, informal living in mind, Benson designed for forward-looking people, in an age when much new product was based on Victorian ideals and formal living. The new, mercantile middle classes were not looking back to drawing room life, but instead cooking and entertaining guests themselves. Benson designed within the ethos of the Arts & Crafts, with simple, well thought through decoration, and joints, wires and mechanisms plainly visible on his pieces.

A pair of Birmingham Guild of Handicraft brass and copper table/wall lights, model no. 44, stamped maker's mark 'B.G.H.'.

c1898 *17.7in (45cm) high*

$4,500-6,000 L&T

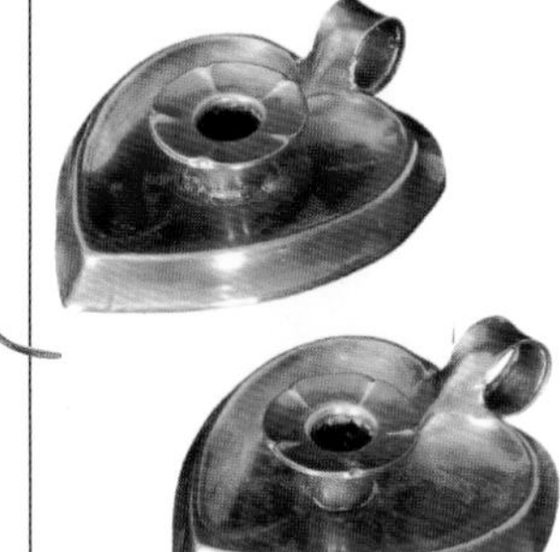

A pair of Arts and Crafts copper chambersticks, by Joseph Sankey & Sons, stamped, some later repair.

6.5in (16cm) wide

$90-105 FLD

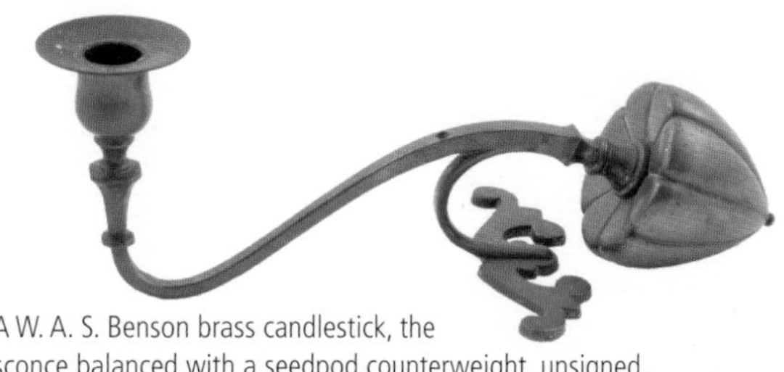

A W. A. S. Benson brass candlestick, the sconce balanced with a seedpod counterweight, unsigned.

12in (31cm) wide

$750-900 WW

A Tiffany Studios 'Acorn' table lamp, the shade is mounted on an urn base originally oil burning with original canister fitted with a one bulb socket, shade signed with metal tag 'Tiffany Studios New York', base impressed 'Tiffany Studios New York 14'.

20in (50cm) high

$10,500-15,000 **MIC**

A Tiffany Studios 'Apple Blossom' table lamp, bearing a dash number (351-1), shade impressed 'TIFFANY STUDIOS NEW YORK 351-1', base impressed 'TIFFANY STUDIOS NEW YORK 351'.

The reason dash numbers were appended to some models remains unresolved. One interpretation is that if a shade was considered to be of exceptional artistic and technical quality, it was assigned a dash number. Another interpretation is that a dash number identified a special commission. Whatever the reason, dash-number lamps are invariably of surpassing quality.

28in (71cm) high

$180,000-225,000 **MIC**

A Tiffany Studios 'Overall Swirling Daffodil' table lamp, shade signed 'Tiffany Studios New York', base signed 'Tiffany Studios New York 29940'.

shade 20in (51cm) diam

$37,500-45,000 **MIC**

A Tiffany Studios table lamp 'Laburnum on a Tree Trunk Base', the leaded glass shade is executed in yellow blossoms of favrile glass set against a deep purple background with vibrant green leaves, base signed 'Tiffany Studios New York 553'.

33.5in (85cm) high

$240,000-300,000 **MIC**

A Tiffany Studios 'Poppy' table lamp, mounted on a 'Pond Lily' base, shade impressed 'TIFFANY STUDIOS NEW YORK 1531'.

1906 *25.5in (65cm) high*

$225,000-300,000 **MIC**

A Tiffany Studios 'Snowball' table lamp, with original Edison Patent light fittings, stamped '250 V 50 C.P.' and Bakelite Bryant switches, stamped 'Tiffany Studios New York' and numbered '481' and '1571-1'.

c1905 *26in (66cm) high*

$60,000-75,000 **DEN**

A Tiffany Studios table lamp in the Venetian motif, shade is mounted on a gilded bronze base signed: 'Tiffany Studios New York 515'.

This model features some of the smallest pieces of Favrile glass and the finest lead work of all Tiffany models.

20.5in (52cm) diam

$135,000-180,000 **MIC**

A Tiffany Studios 'Wisteria' table lamp, shade impressed 'TIFFANY STUDIOS NEW YORK', base impressed 'TIFFANY STUDIOS NEW YORK 5795'.

Tiffany depicted the different colorations of the wisteria species faithfully in his lamps, creating examples in blue-purple-gray, pink-burgundy and white tinged with yellow. The design for the model was credited to a client, Mrs. Curtis Freschel, who in 1901 submitted to the firm a sketch of the lamp she wished made for her.

27in (68.5cm) high

$300,000-450,000 **MIC**

A Tiffany Studios twelve-light 'Lily' lamp, with favrile glass shades, signed 'L.C.T.' and a patinated bronze lily pad base, the base unmarked.

21in (53.5cm) high

$6,750-8,250 **POOK**

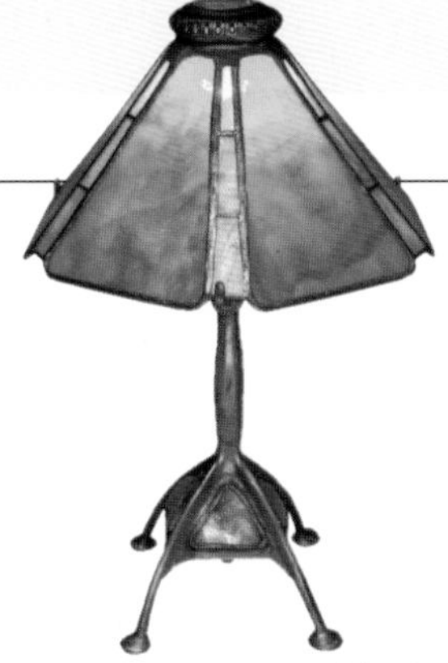

A Tiffany Studios hexagonal favrile glass table lamp, the shade is surmounted by a bronze crown which encloses an iridescent round blue turtleback, impressed 'TIFFANY STUDIOS NEW YORK'.

1906 *16.75in (42.5cm) diam*

$21,000-27,000 **MIC**

A Tiffany Studios carved leaf damascene desk lamp, shade signed, 'L.C. Tiffany Favrile 1115K', base signed, 'Tiffany Studios New York 470'.

10in (25.5cm) diam

$22,500-30,000 **MIC**

A Tiffany Studios jeweled damascene desk lamp, the shade signed 'S9069', base signed 'Tiffany Studios New York S934 and 324'.

shade 7in (18cm) diam

$10,500-15,000 **MIC**

A Tiffany Studios counterbalance desk lamp, base Impressed 'Tiffany Studios New York 416', shade impressed 'L.C.T.'

shade 7in (18cm) diam

$10,500-13,500 **MIC**

A Tiffany Studios double candlestick with jeweled bobèches, base, signed 'Tiffany Studios New York 4292', shades signed 'L.C.T'.

18in (46cm) high

$10,500-13,500 **MIC**

A pair of Tiffany Studios 'Prism Sconces', each featuring eleven green glass prisms, unsigned.

14in (35.5cm) high

$12,000-15,000 **MIC**

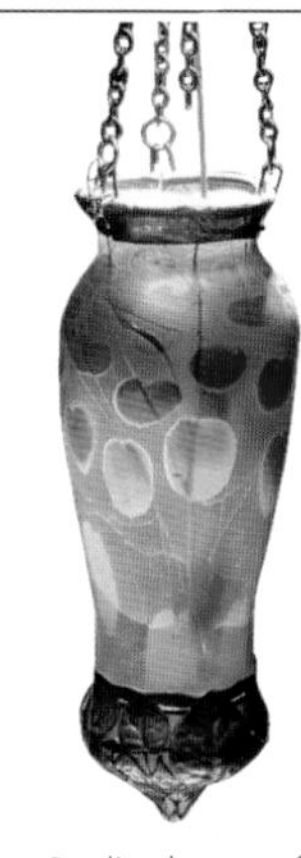

A Tiffany Studios lantern, from Laurelton Hall, inscribed 'o3449'.

23.75in (60.5cm) high

$90,000-105,000 **MIC**

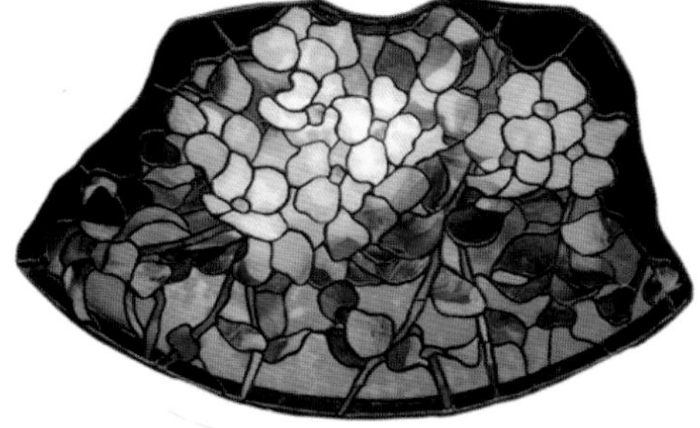

A Tiffany Studios 'Dogwood' lampshade, salesman's sample panel, unsigned.

To assist it's sales staff in the promotion of the firms wares the Tiffany Studios Design Department created a series of sample panels, such as this one, which incorporates a repeat segment of the lamp's overall design. Very few of these sample panels, have survived, this one was taken from the surviving inventory of the Tiffany Studios showroom when it closed in 1933.

16in (41cm) high

$21,000-27,000 **MIC**

A Tiffany Studios 'Poinsettia' chandelier, the shade has a beaded lower border, impressed 'Tiffany Studios New York 1331'.

29in (73.5cm) diam

$330,000-450,000 **MIC**

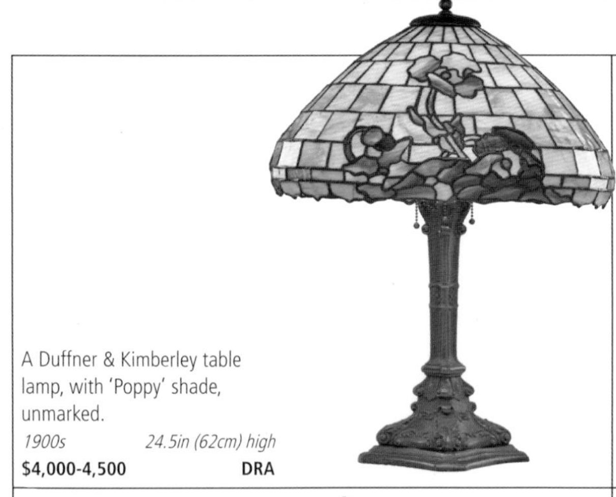

A Duffner & Kimberley table lamp, with 'Poppy' shade, unmarked.

1900s *24.5in (62cm) high*

$4,000-4,500 **DRA**

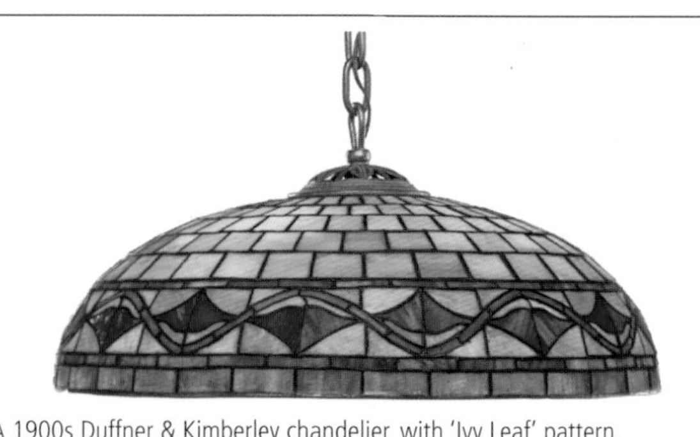

A 1900s Duffner & Kimberley chandelier, with 'Ivy Leaf' pattern, unmarked.

45.5in (116cm) diam

$4,000-4,500 **DRA**

A Duffner & Kimberly table lamp, in 'Louis XV' pattern, marked 'THE DUFFNER & KIMBERLY COMPANY NEW YORK'.

c1910 *29.5in (75cm) high*

$45,000-52,500 **DRA**

An early 20thC leaded glass 'Fleur de Lys' chandelier, attributed to Duffner & Kimberley, three panels with cracks.

23in (58.4cm) diam

$1,500-2,100 **DRA**

An early 20thC Handel leaded glass 'Iris' table lamp, shade signed and numbered '1816', base signed.

30in (76cm) high

$5,250-6,750 **DRA**

An early 20thC Handel leaded glass table lamp, electrified, shade signed and numbered '5351', patent number 979864.

20in (51cm) high

$6,000-7,500 **DRA**

An early 20thC Handel bronze lamp base, with period unassociated leaded glass shade, marked.

24in (61cm) high

$1,500-2,250 **DRA**

A Handel hanging hall lamp, with an obverse painted shade decorated with parrots.

shade 9.5in (24cm) high

$1,500-2,100 **POOK**

A 1910s Pairpoint 'Puffy' table lamp, 'Apple Blossom' shade with bumblebees and butterflies, tree trunk base stamped 'PAIRPOINT MFG CO 3091'.

23.5 (60cm) high

$24,000-30,000 **DRA**

A 1910s Pairpoint 'Puffy' table lamp, 'Open Apple Blossom' shade with bumblebees and butterflies, tree trunk base stamped 'PAIRPOINT MFG CO 3091'.

26in (66cm) high

$24,000-30,000 **DRA**

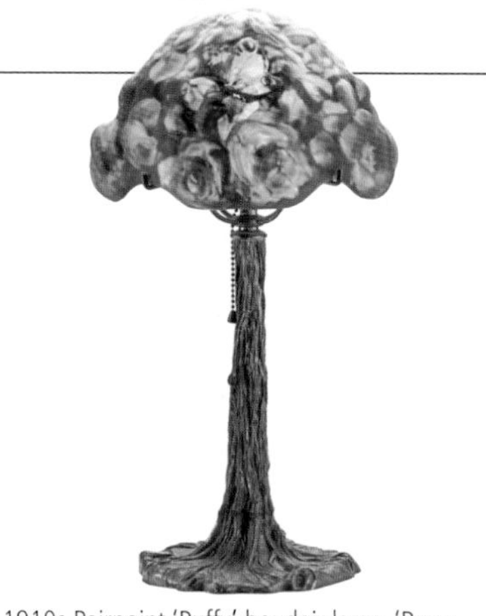

A 1910s Pairpoint 'Puffy' boudoir lamp, 'Rose Tree' shade on tree trunk base stamped 'PAIRPOINT MFG CO B3078'.

17.5in (44.5cm) high

$12,000-15,000 **DRA**

A 1910s Pairpoint 'Puffy' table lamp,' Rose Bouquet' shade on associated base, 'PAT. APPLIED' stamp to shade, base unmarked, some damage.

18in (46cm) high

$6,750-7,500 **DRA**

A 1910s Pairpoint adjustable 'Puffy' table lamp, 'Papillon' shade with butterflies and roses, base stamped 'PAIRPOINT 3047', rewired.

20in (51cm) high

$3,000-4,000 **DRA**

A 1920s Pairpoint boudoir lamp, with autumnal scene with deer, on amphora base, acid-etched and reverse-painted glass, base stamped 'PAIRPOINT D3013 MADE IN U.S.A.', with diamond.

16in (40.6cm) high

$1,000-1,400 **DRA**

A 1920s Pairpoint table lamp, with parrot tulips and classical base, acid-etched, obverse- and reverse-painted glass, shade signed, 'The Pairpoint Co', base stamped 'PAIRPOINT MFG CO B3030', with diamond.

18.5in (47cm) high

$1,400-1,800 **DRA**

A 1920s Pairpoint table lamp, with autumnal scene with deer and farmer, by William Macy, on classical base, acid-etched and reverse-painted glass, shade signed 'W. Macy', base stamped 'PAIRPOINT D3063' with diamond.

21.5in (54.6cm) high

$3,000-4,000 **DRA**

A 20thC Pairpoint table lamp, with a reverse painted floral shade and a bronze and marble base.

22.5in (57cm) high

$1,500-2,100 **POOK**

A French Art Nouveau wrought iron pendant light, signed 'DEGUJ?'.

41.75in (106cm) high

$450-600 **SWO**

An Art Deco wrought iron hanging light pendant, with rose and leaves.

31.5in (80cm) high

$300-400 **SWO**

An Art Deco hanging brass electrolier, with molded shades by Hettier & Vincent, France, and two matched wall lights, one damaged.

34.25in (87cm) high

$3,000-4,000 **SWO**

A rare Charles J. Weinstein Company chandelier, cast blue glass, gilt bronze, single socket, glass etched 'Made in Czechoslovakia'.

1931 *24in (61cm) high*

$19,500-24,000 **DRA**

A pair of Kayserzinn twin-branch pewter candelabra, stamped marks.

17.5in (44.5cm) high

$700-850 **WW**

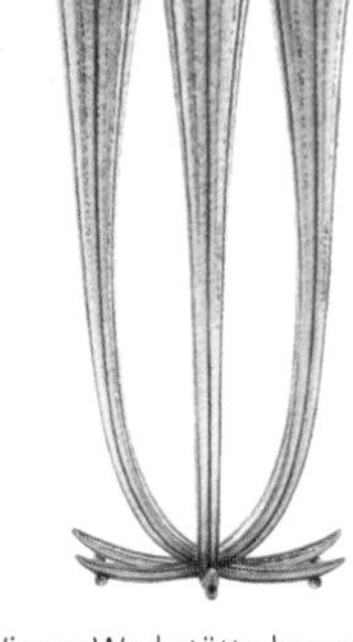

A 1920s Wiener Werkstätte hammered silver six-light candelabrum, designed by Josef Hoffmann (1870-1956), stamped 'MADE IN AUSTRIA/WW/JH/900/2W'

12.5in (31.8cm) high

$45,000-52,500 **DRA**

A 1920s gilt bronze 'La Tentation' table lamp, designed by Edgar Brandt (1880-1960), with carved alabaster, stamped 'E. BRANDT'.

21in (53.5cm) high

$21,000-27,000 **DRA**

A pair of early 20thC bronze cobra lamps, after Edgar Brandt, electrified, unsigned.

12in (30cm) high

$3,000-4,000 **SK**

A Poul Henningsen table lamp 'PH-4/3', for Louis Poulsen, Copenhagen, bronze base, marked 'PH lamp PATENTED'.

1926 *19in (48cm) high*

$4,000-4,500 **QU**

A Liberty & Co 'English Pewter' butter dish and knife, designed by Archibald Knox, model no. 0162, with green glass liner stamped marks.

5.7in (14.5cm) diam

$700-850 **WW**

A Liberty & Co 'Cymric' silver sugar basin and milk jug, with hammered finish, stamped marks, Birmingham.

1903 *sugar basin 6in (15cm) wide*

$1,300-1,450 **WW**

A Liberty & Co 'Cymric' silver and enamel bowl, designed by Archibald Knox, model no.9631, cast with Celtic knot designs, stamped marks, Birmingham, etched model mark to base.

1903 *7in (18cm) wide*

$7,500-9,000 **WW**

A Liberty & Co 'Tudric' pewter pedestal vase, designed by Archibald Knox, model no. 0276, with later glass liner, stamped marks.

6.3in (16cm) high

$600-750 **WW**

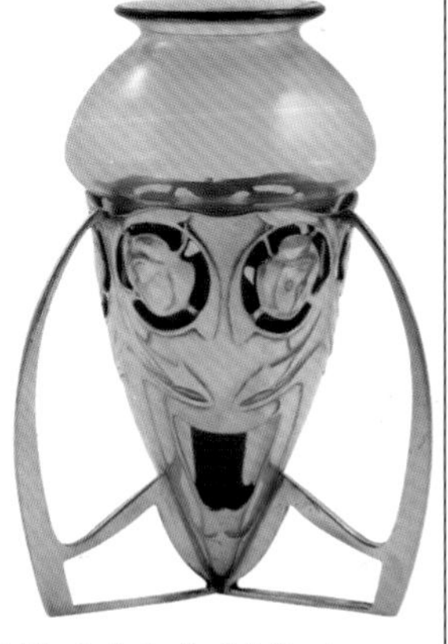

A Liberty & Co English Pewter vase, designed by Archibald Knox, model no.0226, with glass liner, stamped marks.

6.9in (17.5cm) high

$750-900 **WW**

A Liberty & Co 'Cymric' silver vase, enameled with Celtic entrelac panels in green and blue, stamped marks, Birmingham.

1901 *6.7in (17cm) high*

$3,000-4,000 **WW**

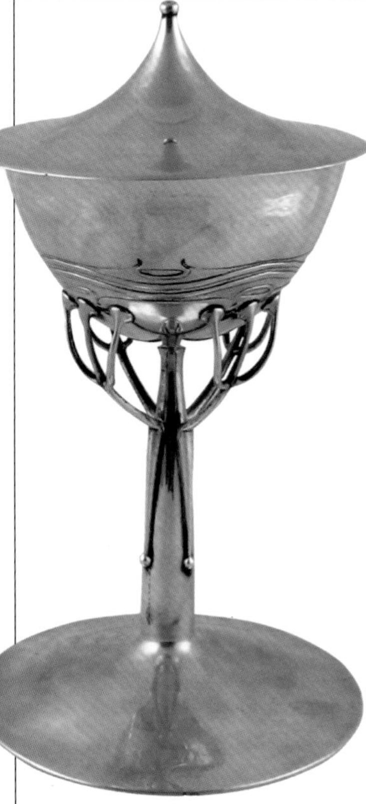

An Arts & Crafts silver standing cup and cover, designed by Archibald Knox for Liberty and Co, the bowl with embossed undulating wave forms and supported on the tapering stem by four three armed branches, hallmarked for Birmingham, Rd. 369132.

For a similar but enameled example see 'Archibald Knox' by Stephen Martin, p.179. For an enameled example from the collection of Mr. Brad Pitt, see 'The Liberty Style' catalog for an exhibition of Knox's work held in Japan, 1999/2000, p.102 fig. 134.

1901 *11in (27cm) high*

23oz weight

$75,000-90,000 **HPA**

A 'Cymric' silver and enamel vase, by Archibald Knox for Liberty & Co. London, the body cast and chased with Celtic knots and set with enamels, stamped maker's marks 'L&CO/ CYMRIC' and hallmarked Birmingham.

1902 *8.7in (22cm) high*

$27,750-30,000 **L&T**

A William H Haseler silver vase, designed by Archibald Knox, probably retailed by Liberty & Co, stamped marks, 'WHH, Birmingham'.

1910 *9.3in (23.5cm) high*

$3,000-4,000 **WW**

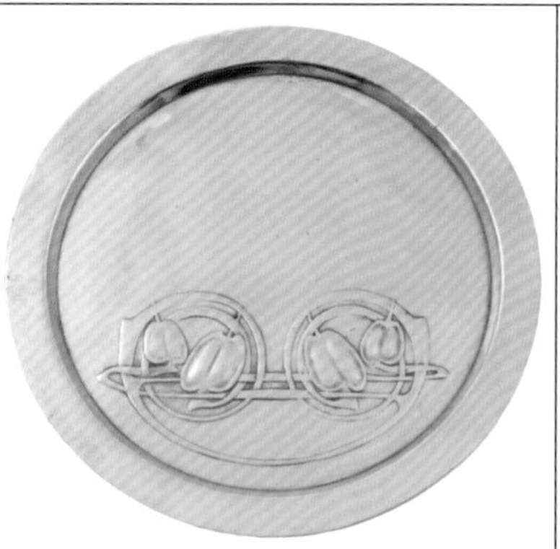

A Liberty & Co 'Tudric' pewter card tray, designed by Archibald Knox, model no.0163, stamped marks.

10in (25.5cm) diam

$750-850 **WW**

A Liberty & Co 'English Pewter' 'Bollellin' tray, designed by Archibald Knox, model no.044, stamped marks.

10.4in (26.5cm) diam

$600-700 **WW**

A Liberty & Co 'English Pewter' and enamel tray, designed by Archibald Knox, model no.0357, with over-slung handle, stamped marks

12in (30.5cm) wide

$1,000-1,200 **WW**

A Liberty & Co 'Cymric' silver tea set, designed by Archibald Knox, model no. 5237, each cast with stylised honesty and green agate stones, stamped marks, Birmingham.

1903 *teapot 7in (18cm) high*

$18,000-22,500 **WW**

A Liberty & Co 'Cymric' silver picture frame, designed by Archibald Knox, with pierced Celtic knot motif, stamped marks, 'Cymric Birmingham'.

1902 *7.5in (19cm) high*

$9,000-10,500 **WW**

A small Liberty & Co 'Cymric' silver and enamel box and cover, stamped marks, Birmingham.

1903 *3in (8cm) wide*

$1,000-1,200 **WW**

A Jessie Marion King for Liberty & Co., silver, enamel and Mother of pearl buckle, with two cloisonné panels with longboats, makers mark 'L&CO', stamped 'no.10197', Birmingham, dated.

1910 *3.75in (9.5cm) wide*

$4,500-5,250 **L&T**

A set of 'Cymric' silver and enamel buttons, by Liberty & Co. Birmingham, each depicting a peacock.

1900

$1,500-2,250 **SWO**

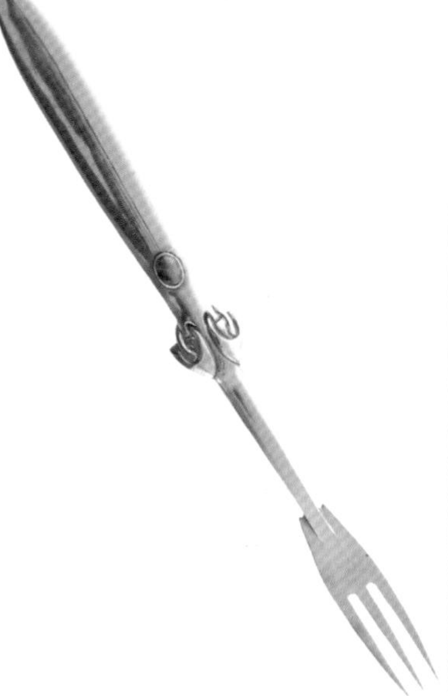

A rare Liberty & Co 'Cymric' silver fork, designed by Archibald Knox, cast with a Celtic knot, the handle set with a turquoise stone, stamped' L & Co mark, Cymric', Birmingham.

1903 *7.3in (18.5cm) long*

$5,400-6,000 **WW**

ESSENTIAL REFERENCE - ARCHIBALD KNOX

Archibald Knox (1864-1933) was a Manx designer of Scottish descent. Archibald, started his schooling at St. Barnabas Elementary School, and later attended Douglas Grammar School and Douglas School of Art, developing a lifelong interest in Celtic art. In 1897 Archibald Knox went to London, where he worked with the designer Hugh Mackay Baillie Scott, who also came from the Isle of Man. With Christopher Dresser, Archibald Knox designed metalware for the Silver Studio, which also supplied Liberty & Co. His design talent covered a wide range of objects, ornamental and utilitarian, and included silver and pewter tea sets, jewelry, inkwells, boxes, much for Liberty's Tudric (pewter) and Cymric (precious metals) ranges. The gravestone of Liberty's founder, Arthur Lasenby Liberty, was designed by Knox.

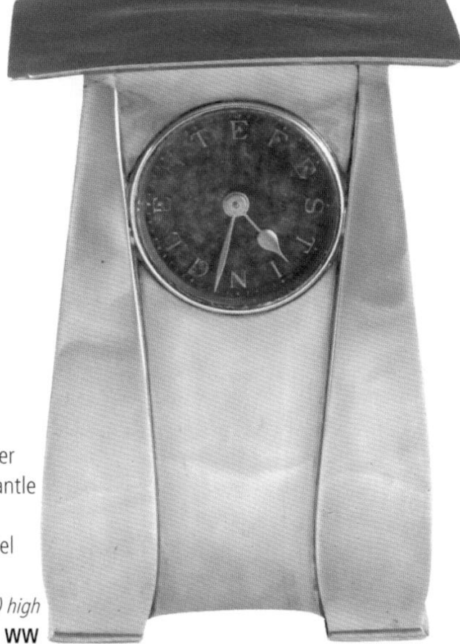

A Liberty & Co pewter silver and enamel mantle clock, designed by Archibald Knox, model no. 0761.

8in (20cm) high

$4,400-5,100 **WW**

A rare Liberty & Co 'Tudric' pewter mantle clock designed by Archibald Knox, model no.095, with Art Nouveau arabic numerals stamped marks.

13.4in (34cm) high

$45,000-52,500 **WW**

A Liberty & Co 'Tudric' Pewter mantle clock, designed by Archibald Knox, model no. 0255, cast in low relief with Art Nouveau foliage panel, cast Arabic numerals and patinated metal hands stamped marks.

9in (22.5cm) high

$9,000-10,500 **WW**

A 'Tudric' pewter, enamel, and copper carriage clock, designed by Archibald Knox, stamped 'TUDRIC 0756 ENGLISH PEWTER LIBERTY & CO'.

c1905 *4in (10cm) high*

$2,000-2,400 **DRA**

A Pewter, enamel, and copper 'Tudric' clock, designed by Archibald Knox, stamped 'TUDRIC 0629 ENGLISH PEWTER LIBERTY & CO'.

c1905 *7.75in (20cm) high*

$4,500-5,250 **DRA**

A 'Tudric' pewter and enamel mantel clock, by Archibald Knox for Liberty & Co., with single train Lenzkirch movement, stamped maker's marks 'TUDRIC/ 0252/ MADE IN ENGLAND'.

c1902 *6.8in (17.3cm) high*

$6,000-6,750 **L&T**

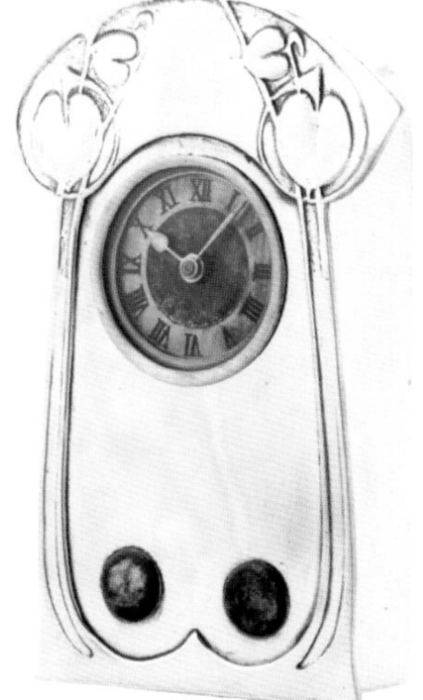

A 'Tudric' pewter and enamel clock, by Archibald Knox for Liberty & Co. with single train Lenzkirch movement, stamped marks 'TUDRIC/ 0370'.

c1902 *8in (20.5cm) high*

$6,600-7,500 **L&T**

A 'Tudric' polished pewter, copper and enamel clock, by Archibald Knox for Liberty & Co. with single train Lenzkirch movement, stamped marks 'ENGLISH PEWTER/ MADE BY/ LIBERTY & CO/ 0366'.

c1902 *8in (20.5cm) high*

$15,000-22,500 **L&T**

ESSENTIAL REFERENCE - GEORG JENSEN

Georg Jensen was born in 1866, the son of a Danish knife grinder. Jensen established his silvesmithy in Copenhagen in 1904, having apprenticed as a goldsmith aged 14, graduated in sculpture at 26, and been the recipient of a grant-aided two-year tour of Europe to witness the Arts and Crafts and Art Nouveau movements at first-hand. On return critical acclaim for his hollowware designs was instantaneous in Europe. In 1915 he also cracked the American market after the newspaper magnet and billionaire William Randolph Hearst purchased the entire Jensen display at the Pan Pacific Exhibition in San Francisco. From the outset, he employed exceptionally talented designers. Eminent examples, excluding Georg Jensen himself, include Johan Rohde (1865-1935); Harald Nielsen (1892-1977); Henning Koppel (1918-1981), and Vivianna Torun Bülow-Hübe (better-known as Torun, 1927-2004). When he died in 1935, the New York Herald saluted Georg Jensen as 'the greatest silversmith of the last 300 years'. The company he founded continues.

A Georg Jensen grape-style wine coaster, designed by Georg Jensen, design no. 229.

1920s *5.5in (14cm) diam*

$4,500-6,000 **PC**

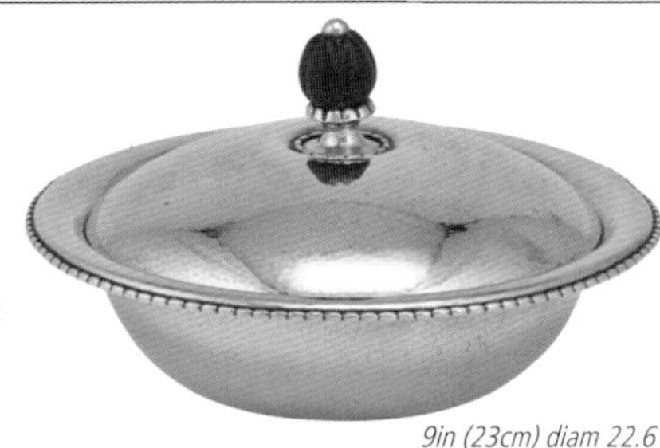

A Georg Jensen 'Bead Edge' silver covered bowl, with vertically fluted ebony final, 290A.

1925-1930 *9in (23cm) diam 22.6 oz*

$2,000-2,400 **DRA**

A Georg Jensen silver compote, designed by Johan Rohde.

1925-32. *6.25in (16cm) high 13.5oz*

$1,500-2,250 **DRA**

A Georg Jensen silver 'Grape' bowl, flared with four grape cluster drop handles, on lobed and vine column, designed by Georg Jensen in 1919, in production

1933-44. *14in (35.6cm) wide 64.62oz*

$10,500-15,000 **DRA**

A Georg Jensen silver 'Pyramid' baby food set, the footed bowl with stepped handles, inscribed 'Marguerite Grace, 1930', and a silver spoon, designed by Harald Nielsen, monogrammed.

bowl 16in (40.6cm) diam 7.86 oz

$1,000-1,500 **DRA**

A Georg Jensen silver pitcher, designed by Johan Rohde, Danish marks for post-war production.

This organic, minamalist pitcher, no432A was designed by Johan Rohde in 1920 but was considered too modern for the day and production was delayed until 19 25. Since then, this pitcher has been admired for some 90 years, demonstrating the enduring appeal of its design and its ability to transcend a century's worth of design. A pre-war example could cost anything from $15,000 up.

9in (22.9cm) high 17.74oz

$2,500-3,500 **DRA**

A Georg Jensen four-piece 'Blossom' tea set on tray, designed by Georg Jensen, design no. 2.

c1910

$22,500-30,000 **PC**

An Art Nouveau W.M.F electroplated tea set, cast in low relief with whiplash berried foliage, stamped marks.

tray 18.7in (47.5cm) wide

$450-600 **WW**

A silver-plate W.M.F centerpiece, cast with an Art Nouveau maiden, replacement liners, stamped makers mark and numbered 22.

23.6in (60cm) high

$850-975 **BELL**

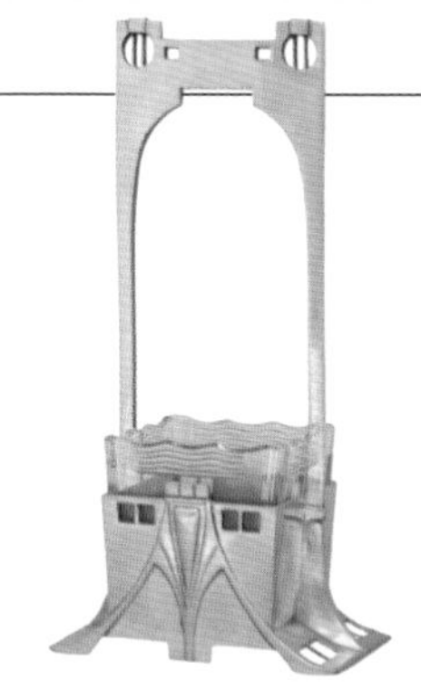

A W.M.F electroplated table basket, with a glass insert, with a wavy rim and engraved details, stamped marks.

11.8in (30cm) high

$600-750 **SWO**

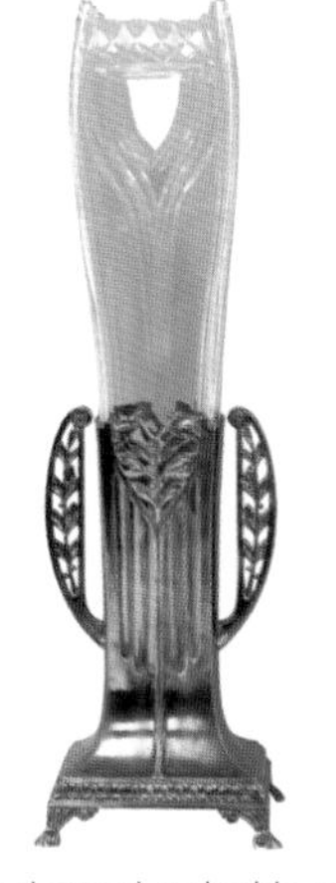

A W.M.F electroplated table vase, the clear cut glass sleeve inset into a twin-handled and pierced stand, stamped marks, with molded pattern number '665A'.

18.3in (46.5cm) high

$600-750 **SWO**

An early 20thC W.M.F silver-plate centerpiece figure of a panther, standing on a platform with clear glass insert.

24in (61cm) high

$1,500-2,250 **DRA**

A pair of Art Nouveau W.M.F pewter vases, with clear glass liners, stamped marks.

14in (36cm) high

$2,250-3,000 **WW**

An Art Nouveau W.M.F pewter dish, centered with a lady, her dress billowing down to the sides, stamped 'WMF'.

8.3in (21cm) high

$600-750 **SWO**

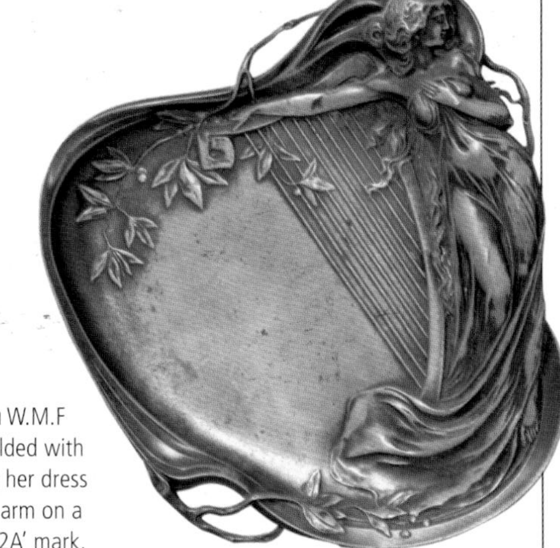

An Art Nouveau W.M.F pewter tray, molded with a lady clutching her dress and resting her arm on a harp, raised '252A' mark.

8.7in (22cm) wide

$180-225 **SWO**

ESSENTIAL REFERENCE - TIFFANY

As in this example, the repousse enamel decoration required several intricate steps. Firstly, the areas designated for relief treatment on the sheet of copper were raised into their desired shapes from the reverse by a metalworker who hammered and chased the surface with a variety of tools, including an anvil, snarling iron, and assortment of chisels and burins. Secondly, detailing was achieved with a series of chasing tools and punches which the metalworker interchanged as he manipulated the decoration on the copper into its final form. Thirdly, the completed sheet was rolled around a cylinder-formed block and neatly soldered along its vertical seam, before the circular foot was attached, likewise by soldering. Now in its final form, the vessel was, forthly,decorated by an enamelist, who painted the composition on to its surface. Using a painterly technique, the enamelist applied the superimposed layers of transparent pigments with a brush until the desired level of definition and richness of color was attained.

A Tiffany Studios 'Cala Lily and Poppy' enamel-on-copper vase, impressed 'Louis C. Tiffany SG 79'.
c1900 *14.5in (37cm) high*
$150,000-210,000 **MIC**

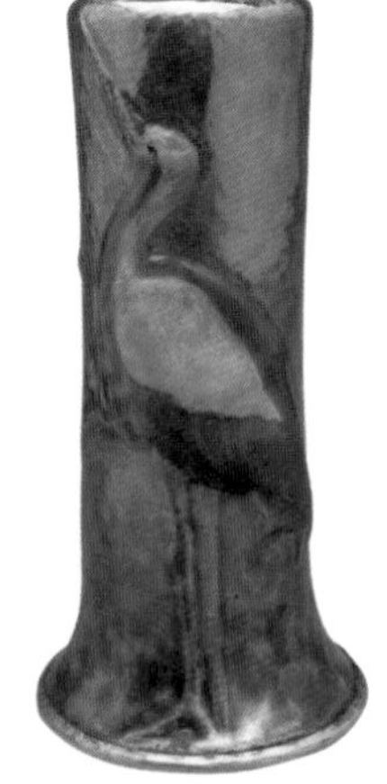

A Tiffany Studios 'Crane' enamel-on-copper vase, with crane and bamboo motifs, inscribed 'SG 96 L.C.T'.

This vase emphasises the stylistic influence exerted by Japanese artists on their western counterparts in the late 19thC.
c1900 *5.75in (14.5 cm) high*
$21,000-27,000 **MIC**

A Tiffany Studios enamel-on-copper 'Sagittaria' vase, the upper edges of the plant's leaves delineate the contour of the vessel's lip, inscribed 'Louis C. Tiffany, impressed SG 76'.
c1900 *9.75in (25cm) high*
$180,000-225,000 **MIC**

A Tiffany Studios bronze 'Saxifrage' candlestick, model #1331, impressed 'TIFFANY STUDIOS NEW YORK 11485'.

Like his contemporary, Emile Galle in France, Tiffany drew artistic inspiration from the humblest species of meadow plants, in this instance, a herb which grows in the clefts of rocks. Here,the plant's seed pods have been fashioned into a candle bobeche supported by a slender stalk rising from a symmetrical band of leaves that form the foot. Tiffany has turned a simple household appliance has into a work of art.
1906 *17.75in (45cm)*
$19,500-24,000 **MIC**

A Tiffany Studios favrile glass and bronze candlestick, impressed 'TIFFANY STUDIOS NEW YORK'.

The Price List for this model #1223, in 1906 was $30. Tiffany Studios continued to produce a wide range of candlesticks after the commercialization of Thomas Edison's incandescent filament bulb in the 1890's. For many householders the cost of immediate transition from combustion fuels to electricity was prohibitive, while for others, candles were kept on reserve for those moments when the electric bulb faltered, which it did with some frequency during its infancy.
1906 *15in (38cm) high*
$37,500-45,000 **MIC**

A Tiffany Studios bronze and favrile glass 'Fish' mosaic inkstand, with glasswell and plastic liner, impressed with 'Tiffany Studios New York D 1121' with the firm's logo.
7in (18cm) wide
$97,500-112,500 **MIC**

A Tiffany Studios bronze and glass 'Pine Needle' picture frame, impressed 'Tiffany Studios New York'.
8in (20.3cm) high
$2,250-3,000 **MIC**

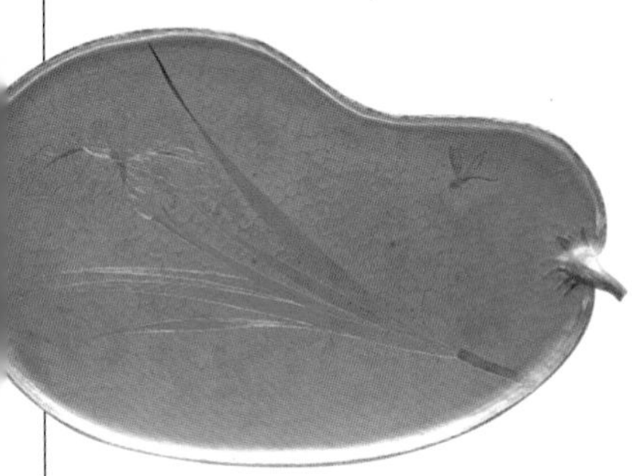

A Tiffany & Co. tray, the lily pad with an engraved 'Iris' stem with copper and gilt inlays, a gold and copper dragonfly, impressed 'TIFFANY & CO. 5391 M 607. STERLING SILVER. OTHER METALS.435. PATENT APPLIED FOR', with French control marks.

Exhibited: Exposition Universelle, Paris, 1878;

c1878 *Length: 16 inches (40.5 cm) long 34.7oz*

$75,000-90,000 **MIC**

A Tiffany & Co. sugar, applied mixed metal maple branches, with fauna,spider, bumblebee and fly, Impressed 'TIFFANY & CO. 5388 M 607. STERLING SILVER-ANDOTHER-METALS. 429', with French control marks.

Exhibited: Exposition Universelle, Paris, 1878

c1898 *Diameter: 4in (10cm) 7oz*

$15,000-18,000 **MIC**

A Tiffany & Co silver pitcher, with repoussé bands of Athenaeum leaves, impressed 'Tiffany and Company, 5066 Makers 6772. Sterling Silver. 925-1000'.

c1878 *8.25in (21 cm) high 27.25oz*

$4,000-4,500 **MIC**

A Tiffany & Co. repousse silver tea caddy, impressed 'Tiffany and Company. 7970 Makers 9064. Sterling Silver. 925-1000. T'.

c1884 *4.25in (11cm) high 7.8oz*

$1,150-1,300 **MIC**

A Tiffany& Co silver chafing dish, with a bone handle, the waisted, impressed 'TIFFANY AND COMPANY 11469 Makers 5571. STERLING SILVER. 925-1000. T'.

c1892 *11in (28cm) high*

$9,000-10,500 **MIC**

A Tiffany Studios bronze 'Turtleback' casket inkwell, the interior with three pens and inkwells, the front drawer for stamps. unsigned.

1906 *8.5in (22 cm) wide*

$52,500-60,000 **MIC**

A Tiffany Studios bronze and favrile glass 'Pine Needle' glove box, signed 'Tiffany Studios New York'.

13.5in (34.3cm) wide

$4,000-4,500 **MIC**

A set of four Tiffany Studios bronze door knobs, in the Moorish taste.

2.2in (5.6cm) diam

$8,500-9,000 **MIC**

A Guild of Handicrafts silver porringer, designed by Charles Robert Ashbee, set with green chrysoprase, inscribed 'E H C H Xmas 1904', London.

1904 *7.3in (18.5cm) wide*

$3,000-4,000 **WW**

A silver and enamel tea caddy, by Omar Ramsden And Alwyn Carr, incised 'OMAR RAMSDEN ET ALWYN CARR ME FECERVNT', London.

A fine and rare example, each panel showing a different plant.

1902 *3.75in (9.5cm) high*

$7,500-9,000 **DRA**

A pair of silver salts and spoons, by Charles Robert Ashbee for the Guild of Handicrafts, with glass liners, stamped maker's marks 'G/OF/H/LTD', hallmarked London.

1900 *salts 3in (8cm) diam*

$1,500-2,250 **L&T**

A silver napkin ring, by Omar Ramsden, with 'M.E', London.

c1927 *2.4in (6.2cm) high 1.6oz*

$400-450 **WW**

An Arts and Crafts hammered silver bowl, by Omar Ramsden, inscribed, 'MARY ROSE MCMXXXVI', the base engraved 'OMAR RAMSDEN ME FECIT'. London

c1935 *4.5in (11.5cm) wide 6.8oz*

$2,100-2,700 **WW**

An Arts and Crafts silver and enamel tea canister and cover, by Ramsden & Carr, the lid with an enameled panel of fish amongst weeds, the body with a female figure wrapped in seaweed with boats and mountain in the distance, opposing a cherub with a seaweed wreath and with dolphin heads to each corner, stamped to base 'Designed & Made by Ramsden & Carr, London', with an Arts & Crafts silver cabochon enameled caddy spoon, some damage, fully hallmarked London. the box 1902, the spoon 1906,

box 5.5in (14cm) long

$15,000-21,000 **APAR**

A silver toast rack, by Charles Boyton, with spot-hammered decoration, signed 'C. Boyton, London'.

c1932 *4.4in (11.2cm) long 3.8oz*

$450-550 **WW**

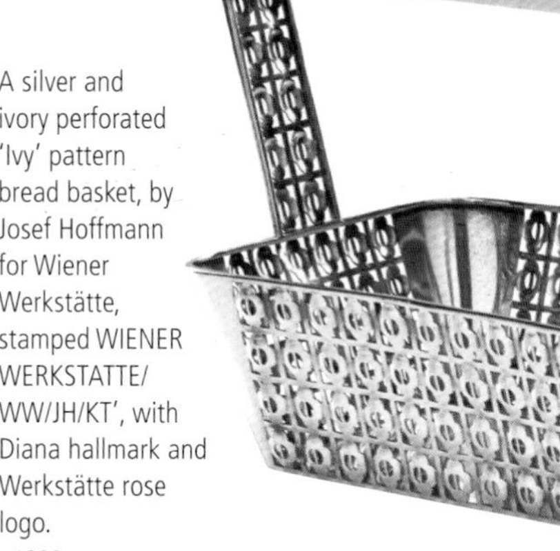

A silver and ivory perforated 'Ivy' pattern bread basket, by Josef Hoffmann for Wiener Werkstätte, stamped WIENER WERKSTATTE/ WW/JH/KT', with Diana hallmark and Werkstätte rose logo.

c1909 *9.75in (24.8cm) wide*

$37,500-45,000 **DRA**

An Arts Crafts silver tea service, by Jones and Compton, Birmingham.

1905 *36ozs*

$1,500-2,250 **ECGW**

An Art Deco silver tea service, by Mappin & Webb, Sheffield.

c.1938 *teapot 11.25in (28.5cm) long 47.1oz*

$1,400-1,800 **DN**

A French Art Deco silver colored tea and coffee service, by Henin & Cie., Paris.

c1930 *the coffee pot 7in (18cm) high 58.9 oz*

$5,250-6,000 **DN**

Judith Picks: Mocha Service

Mocha - an espresso-style coffee with a bit of milk and sometimes even a bit of chocolate - was very popular in Germany in the 1920s. Dell was the foreman at the metal workshop of the Bauhaus in Weimar from 1922-25 and while he was there he exeuted several pieces to his own designs, including a ewer, various candlesticks and a mocha service. The latter is only known from three historic photographs, its whereabouts is still unknown and it is not the mocha set shown which varies in several details. This set does conform to the characteristic specifications of the pieces from the Bauhaus workshop, using cylinders, spheres and hemispheres for the basic forms. As with many other objects designed by Bauhaus artists, the handles are formed as segments of circles.

A nickle-silver three-piece mocha service, designed and made by Christian Dell, with ebony handles, marked with Christian Dell's monogram.

coffee pot 8in (20cm) high

$90,000-105,000 **NAG**

An American hammered silver tea canister, by The Whiting Manufacturing Company, New York, with copper and silver maple leaves.

c1880 *4in (10cm) high 9.oz*

$1,800-2,250 **WW**

An Arts & Crafts silver tyg, with inscription, 'Captain's Prize for Golf, Woolton Golf Club', London marks.

1905 *23oz*

$750-900 **HW**

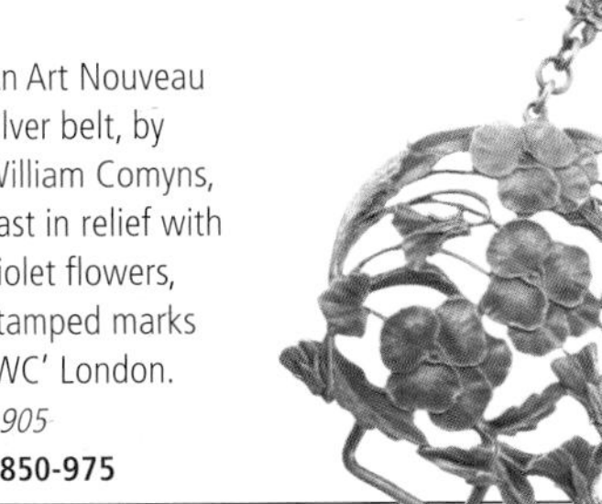

An Art Nouveau silver belt, by William Comyns, cast in relief with violet flowers, stamped marks 'WC' London.

1905 *25.6in (65cm) long*

$850-975 **WW**

ESSENTIAL REFERENCE - ELKINGTON & CO

This kettle represents the earliest provable Dresser design for electroplated silver. The kettle's pattern number 10272 places the design to 1866-1867. In 1865 'The Building News', page 916, stated that Elkington were producing Dresser's electroplated silver designs. As this example was not manufactured until 1884 (year letter Y) and its design not registered until 1885 (no.22876), the design initially appears to be later and of less importance than the iconic undecorated Hukin & Heath and Dixon & Sons designs by Dresser of 1878-1879. These have previously been regarded as evidence of a fundamental shift in Dresser's design philosophy after his visit to Japan in 1876-1877. The 1867 date of the design of this Elkington kettle contradicts this notion and advances Dresser's electroplated silver designs by a decade. Although metalwork designs annotated 'Dresser' are recorded in the Elkington pattern books from 1885, there are earlier examples (including this kettle) which retained their old pattern numbers when old pattern books were updated; these earlier original numbers were then carried forward to new pattern books and included amongst the later designs.

A rare and possibly unique Elkington & Co electroplated kettle, designed by Dr Christopher Dresser, model no.10272, registration number 22867, stamped marks.
c1867 *9.5in (24cm) high*
$30,000-38,000 **WW**

A Christofle silver-plated tea and coffee set, designed by Luc Lanel, with a tray.
19.25in (49cm) wide
$700-850 **SWO**

A Hukin & Heath articulated letter rack, by Dr Christopher Dresser, model no.2555, rod-and-ball construction on base, stamped marks.
1881 *5in (12.5cm) high*
$2,250-3,000 **WW**

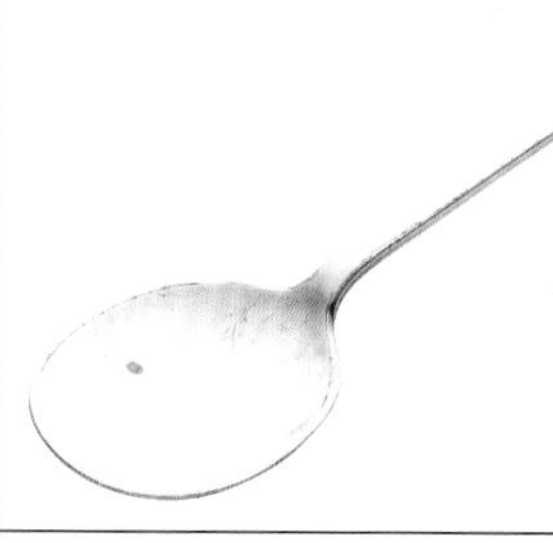

A silver-plate teaspoon, by Charles Rennie Mackintosh for Miss Cranston's Tearooms, indistinct stamped mark.
c1905 *5in (12.5cm) long*
$450-550 **L&T**

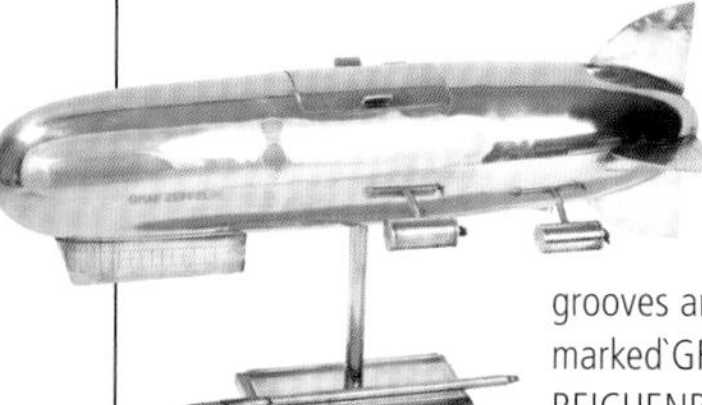

A silver-plated 'Zeppelin' inkwell, the lid opening to reveal, two original inkwells, the 'Zeppelin' having four engines with moving propellers, the base with two pen grooves and one silver plated pen, body marked'GRAF ZEPPELIN', and'FRANZ REICHENBERG, BERLIN D.R.P.'.
13.8in (35cm) wide
$9,000-12,000 **LOCK**

A Stickley Brothers hammered copper jardinière, stamped '300'.
c1910 *18in (45.7cm) diam*
$3,000-4,000 **DRA**

A Dirk Van Erp hammered copper vessel, stamped 'DIRK VAN ERP SAN FRANCISCO' with windmill.
1916 *12.5in (31.8cm) high*
$4,500-5,250 **DRA**

A Roycroft buttressed hammered copper bud vase, by Karl Kipp, with nickel silver, early orb and cross mark.
1906-10 *8in (20.3cm) high*
$4,500-5,250 **DRA**

A hammered copper, brass and horn chocolate pot, School Of Theodore Pond, Rochester Mechanics Institute, stamped 'Hand, WF' with dragonfly.
c1905 *9in (22.9cm) high*
$9,000-10,500 **DRA**

A W.A.S Benson copper and brass egg holder and spirit burner, with ebonized wood final, stamped Benson mark.

Although usually referred to as W.A.S. his names were William Arthur Smith.

7.9in (20cm) high

$200-350 **WW**

A W.A.S Benson brass inkwell and pen tray, stamped Benson.

10in (25.5cm) wide

$400-450 **WW**

A W.A.S Benson patinated copper jardinière, unsigned.

8.5in (21.5cm) high

$600-700 **WW**

A rare W. A. S. Benson flowerpot holder, with floriform stem and six petal jardinière, unsigned.

30.3in (77cm) high

$1,300-1,450 **WW**

A Birmingham Guild of Handicrafts copper jardinière, with applied pewter swagged garlands and abalone shell panels.

12.2in (31cm) high

$700-750 **FLD**

An Arts and Crafts copper cigarette box, in the manner of A.E. Jones, with central blue and green enameled roundel.

6in (15.5cm) wide

$400-450 **FLD**

A mid-19thC brass lectern, attributed to AWN Pugin (1812-1852) for John Hardman & Co. (1838-1900), the spread eagle clutching a globe in its talons, the base on six lions, impressed marks.

74in (188cm) high

$7,050-7,500 **SWO**

A Wiener Werkstätte brass inkwell, with a revolving lid, by Josef Hoffmann (1870-1956), stamped 'Made in Austria, Wiener Werkstätte', with 'JH' monogram.

The original design is in the WW archive, held by The Museum of Decorative Arts, Vienna.

9in (22.5cm) wide

$6,000-6,750 **SWO**

An Arts & Crafts copper box and cover, with ebony handle, stamped 'TH' and 'REGISTERED MARK', on a wrought iron frame.

23.5in (59.7cm) high

$150-225 **WW**

An Art Nouveau Continental, probably French, gilt-bronze mounted onxy desk tray.

12.6in (32cm) wide

$600-750 **DN**

An Art Nouveau gilded bronze vide poche, cast from a model by Leon Dusouchet, signed 'L Dusouchet'.

7in (18cm) wide

$600-750 **WW**

A Dunhill gold-plated 'Baby Sylph' lighter and key chain, marked 'Dunhill Made in England', with a bead style bale to the filler screw.

c1953

$450-550 **SWO**

A Must de Cartier lady's lighter, in gilt metal and green enamel, No.45275, in original fitted case.

$300-400 **SWO**

An Art Deco French silver and enamel cigarette case, gilded interior, with import marks for London.

1925 *3in (8cm) long 3.2oz*

$300-450 **WW**

An Art Deco silver and enamel cigarette case, by Walser Wald and Co., with geometric enamel pattern to the front, stamped, with original Walser Wald presentation box.

c1930 *6in (15cm) long*

$4,000-5,250 **L&T**

An Art Deco silver-gilt and enamel compact/aide memoire, with Mount Fuji in the background, the interior with a mirror and aide memoire, a cord tassel concealing a silver-gilt lipstick holder, with importer's mark of Cohen and Charles.

1925 *3in (7.5cm) long*

$450-600 **WW**

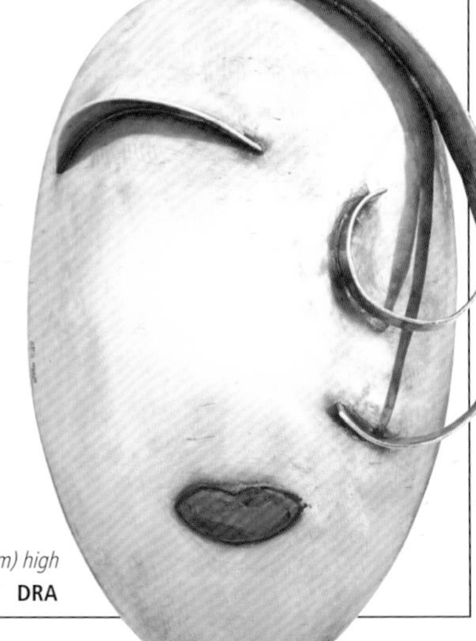

A 1930s Franz Hagenauer nickel-plated bronze and red enamel decorative mask, stamped 'WHW WERKSTATTEN HAGENAUER WIEN'

10.5in (26.7cm) high

$11,250-14,250 **DRA**

A late19thC/early 20thC Bergman cold-painted bronze figure of a seated exotic dancer, reverse with 'B' within vasiform mark and incised 'Nam-Greb'.

10.75in (27cm) high

$9,000-10,500 **SK**

An Austrian cold painted bronze figural table lamp, probably Franz Bergman, modeled as an Arab holding a string of beads, the shade formed as a hanging lampshade.

c1900 *20in (50.5cm) high*

$1,800-2,250 **DW**

A 19thC Bergman cold painted bronze of an Arab carpet seller, cast vase mark.

6.7in (17cm) high

$2,700-3,300 **SWO**

An early 20thC Austrian cold painted bronze figure of a partridge, by Franz Bergmann, realistically modeled and painted, stamped amphora foundry mark.

8.3in (21cm) high

$9,000-9,750 **L&T**

A 19thC painted metal Arab street vendor, with a monkey assistant.

25.6in (65cm) high

$1,200-1,800 **SWO**

A late 19thC/early 20thC Austrian cold painted bronze figure of a 'Whirling Dervish', by Franz Bergman, the back of his robes stamped with a 'B' in a vase.

7.8in (19.7cm) high

$975-1,150 **WW**

A late 19thC Austrian cold painted bronze group, of a hen and a cockerel standing on a plough, stamped '8'.

7in (17.5cm) long

$975-1,150 **SWO**

An Austrian cold painted bronze of a dachshund, stamped 'Geschutze'.

5.3in (13.5cm) long

$975-1,150 **SWO**

An early 20thC Austrian cold painted figure of a stag, realistically modeled and painted.

7.7in (19.5cm) high

$1,500-2,100 **L&T**

A pair of bronzes' 'The Marly Horses', after Guillaume Coustou the Elder,

23in (59cm) long

$1,800-2,250 **DN**

A bronze sculpture, 'Cat with Snake' by Wharton Esherick , wood signed 'Wharton Esherick 1926', bronze signed 'W.E. XXVI'.

1926 *18.25in (46.4cm) long*

$45,000-60,000 **DRA**

A mid-19thC patinated bronze and marble mounted group of a racehorse with monkey jockey, by Paul Gayrard (1807-1855), inscribed 'Gayrard' and 'Boyer' to the front.

5.5in (14cm) long

$900-1,000 **DN**

A 1920s silvered bronze figure of a stalking panther, by J. Hughes, signed to the rear leg.

16.5in (42cm) wide

$750-900 **FLD**

A late 19thC patinated French bronze animalier group 'L'Accolade', by Pierres Jules Mêne, signed in the maquette.

This famous group was first exhibited as a wax model in the Paris salon of 1852, apparently entitled 'Tachiani et Nedjebe, Chevaux Arabes'.

21.25in (54cm) wide

$11,250-14,250 **MAB**

A bronze cast from a model by Pablo Picasso, 'She-Goat', on black marble, unsigned.

12in (31cm) wide

$3,000-4,000 **WW**

A bronze 'Dachshund', by Edouard-Marcel Sandoz, signed, red/brown patina.

3.4in (8.5cm) high

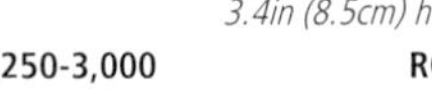

$2,250-3,000 **ROS**

A bronze model of an ibex, by Max Le Verrier, the base inscribed 'M. Le Verrier'.

c1930 *19in (48cm) high*

$975-1,150 **DN**

A pair of 19thC bronze models of mastiffs, later mounted on giltwood bases.

14¾in (37.4cm) wide

$1,800-2,250 **WW**

A German bronze lion aquamanile in the Gothic style, the proud animal stands gripping the water spout in his jaw.

5.5in (14cm) long

$5,250-6,000 **SWO**

A bronze figure, 'Hebe upon Jupiter's eagle', after Georges Marie Valentin Bareau, signed 'Georges Bareau', with Barbidienne foundry mark.

25½in (65cm) high

$3,000-4,500 SWO

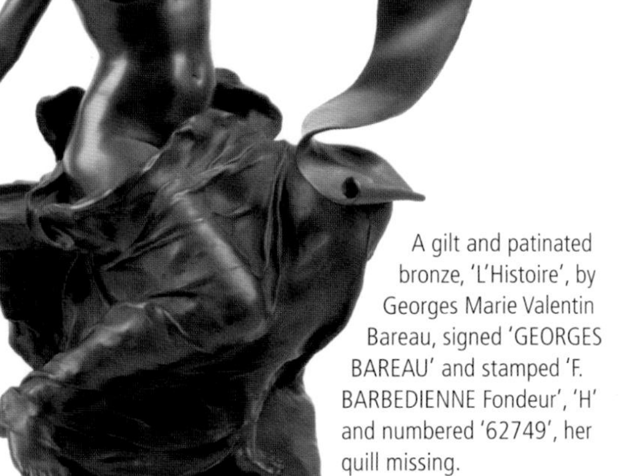

A gilt and patinated bronze, 'L'Histoire', by Georges Marie Valentin Bareau, signed 'GEORGES BAREAU' and stamped 'F. BARBEDIENNE Fondeur', 'H' and numbered '62749', her quill missing.

19.6in (49.7cm) high

$6,750-8,250 WW

A late 19thC cast bronze of a 'Cossack Mounted on a Pony', by Evgeni Alexandrovich Lancere, Wakelin factory.

8.7in (22cm) high

$4,500-6,000 TEN

ESSENTIAL REFERENCE - MASSIMILANO SOLDANI-BENZI

Soldani was Master of the Mint in Florence but, as perhaps the finest bronze caster in Europe in the late 1600s, extended his range well beyond the coinage of Tuscany. His workshop, conveniently situated opposite the entrance to the Uffizi Gallery, attracted the British 'Milordi', with Lord Burlington among the well-heeled English gentlemen who commissioned bronzes to be made from terracotta models. This statuette - with an Anglo-Irish provenance through the family of the late Countess of Lanesborough that might take it as far back as 1716 - may well be one of them.

- **Dr Charles Avery, former deputy keeper of sculpture at the V&A, who cataloged the piece, speculated it was purchased with its pair depicting Leda and the Swan (now missing) by the Countess's descendant Theophilus Butler (c1669-1723) probably from Soldani's representative GG Zamboni in London. The only other version of this model is in the Fitzwilliam Museum, Cambridge, who also own a version of Leda and the Swan.**

A bronze 'Cheyenne', after Frederic Remmington, depicting a Native American on horse back, on marble base.

20.5in (52cm) high

$1,500-2,100 PSA

An Italian baroque bronze, depicting 'Ganymede and the Eagle', by Massimilano Soldani-Benzi (1656-1740)

15in (38cm) high

$600,000-750,000 L&T

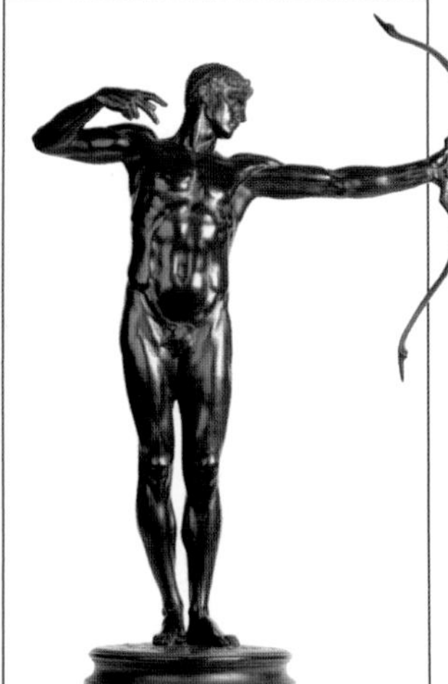

A bronze model of the archer, 'Teucer', by Sir William Hamo Thornycroft , signed 'HAMO THORNYCROFT 1881'.

28.7in (73cm) high

$9,750-11,500 TEN

A patinated bronze model of a dancer, cast from a model by Marcel-Andre Bouraine, balancing ivory balls on her hands, balancing on ball set on red marble tray, signed 'Bouraine'.

16.5in (42cm) high

$3,000-4,500 **WW**

A patinated bronze and ivory figure, 'Pierrot' by Demetre H Chiparus, signed, and 'ETLING' Paris, stamped in cast '9065 A B' and painted '9065'.

11.6in (29.5cm) high

$4,500-6,000 **TEN**

A bronze 'Egyptian Dancer' figure, by Claire Jeanne Roberte Colinet, signed, the plinth with button 'LN Paris JL' for Les Neveux de J. Lehmann Foundry.

16in (41cm) high

$4,500-6,000 **SWO**

A silvered bronze group, by J D Guirande, with a semi-nude dancer and a fawn, signed and stamped foundry mark 'MEDAILLE D'OR'.

24.8in (63cm) high

$4,500-6,000 **TEN**

A bronze on ivory figure of a Grecian lady holding a basket of fruit, by Karl Kretschmer, signed, dark splits to neck and arms.

10.6in (27cm) high.

$1,200-1,500 **SWO**

A pair of cold painted bronze figures, 'Autumn and Spring Dancers', by Pierre Laurel, on demi-lune onyx bases, signed, with foundry lozenge, 'L N PARIS J L' (Les Neveux de Jules Lehman).

taller 11in (28cm) high

$5,250-6,750 **TEN**

A silvered and cold-painted bronze figure, by Josef Lorenzl, modeled as a nude dancer, signed 'LORENZL', on onyx base.

c1925 26in (66cm) high

$8,250-9,750 **TEN**

A cold painted bronze figure of a nude, by Josef Lorenzl, signed 'Lorenzl' and with foundry mark 'BK', on onyx plinth.

10.8in (27.5)cm high

$3,000-4,000 **SWO**

A large silvered bronze model of a scarf dancer, cast from a model by Josef Lorenzl, on onyx base, signed 'Lorenzl'.

13in (33cm) high

$3,000-4,000 **WW**

A small gilt bronze sculpture of a dancer, cast from a model by Josef Lorenzl, on onyx base, signed 'Lorenzl'.

8in (20.5cm) high

$1,500-2,100 **WW**

A patinated bronze and ivory figure of a dancing girl, after Josef Lorenzl, on onyx base .

11.3in (28.5cm) high

$3,000-4,000 **CHOR**

A patinated bronze and ivory dancer, by Georges Omerth, on an onyx base, signed 'OMERTH' and stamped '1 5043', some cracks to ivory.

10.4in (26.5cm) high

$5,250-6,000 **TEN**

A gilt patinated bronze of an exotic dancer, 'Radha', cast from a model by Paul Philippe, with enameled decoration to dress, on onyx base, etched 'P Philippe'.

14.8in (37.5cm) high

$3,000-4,500 **WW**

A patinated and cold-painted bronze and ivory figure, 'Le Grand Ecart Respectueux' (The Respectful Splits), by Paul Philippe, signed, with foundry mark for Rosenthal & Maeder.

c1925 *11in (28cm) long*

$4,500-6,000 **TEN**

A patinated bronze and ivory figure, 'Dancing the Charleston', by Ferdinand Preiss, on a marble plinth.

15in (38cm) high

$24,000-30,000 **BIG**

A cold painted bronze and ivory figure, 'Autumn Dancer', by Ferdinand Preiss, on onyx and marble base, cast foundry mark.

14in (37cm) high

$21,000-27,000 **WW**

An Art Deco cold painted bronze and ivory figure of a woman, the 'Javelin Thrower', by Ferdinand Preiss, on a marble and onyx base, model no1176, signed.

c1925 *figure 7.5in (19cm) high*

$13,500-18,000 **HALL**

A bronze and ivory figure, 'Pierette', by Ferdinand Preiss, on a slate base, signed 'F. PREISS'.

c1925 *7.3in (18.5cm) high*

$2,100-2,700 **L&T**

A gilt patinated bronze and ivory figure 'The Tambourine Dancer', on a marble base, signed in cast 'F Preiss'.

13.4in (34cm) high

$6,000-7,500 **TEN**

A cold-painted bronze and ivory figure, by Ferdinand Preiss, of a violin player, on an onyx base, signed 'Phillippe' and the Preiss Kassler logo, missing bow, crack in top of head, repaied finger.

12.2in (31cm) high

$9,750-11,500 **TEN**

A cold-painted bronze figure, 'Girl on Wall', on alabaster base, stamped with the foundry mark for Preiss and Kassler.

9in (23cm) high

$3,000-4,500 **TEN**

An ivory figure 'Posing', on a signed green onyx pedestal.

c1925 *4in (10cm) high*

$8,250-9,750 **HALL**

An Art Deco ivory figure of a naked woman, titled 'Thoughts', by Ferdinand Preiss, on marble and onyx plinth, model no1131, signed.

c1925 *4in (10.5cm) wide*

$10,500-15,000 **HALL**

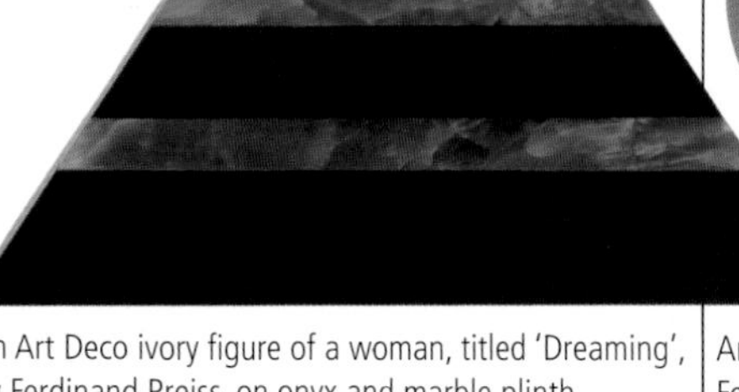

An Art Deco ivory figure of a woman, titled 'Dreaming', by Ferdinand Preiss, on onyx and marble plinth, variation of model no.1132, signed.

c1925 *figure 4in (10cm) high*

$15,000-22,500 **HALL**

An ivory and onyx pin dish, by Ferdinand Preiss, signed 'F Preiss'.

4in (10cm)

$750-900 **SWO**

A gilt bronze figure of a nude, by Julius Schmidt-Felling, signed, on a marble base.

13in (33.5cm) high

$900-1,000 **DN**

A gilt bronze figure of an Odeonesque dancer, by Victor Heinrich Seifert, signed, on a marble plinth,

17in (43.5cm) high

$1,500-2,250 **DN**

An Art Deco cold painted bronze and ivory matchstriker, by Peter Tereszczuk, with a Pierrot, signed AR for Arthur Rubenstein Foundry.

5.75in (14.5cm) long

$450-600 **SWO**

An Art Nouveau French gilt patinated bronze and ivory figure, modeled as a woman dancing, signed in cast 'Very 37', on an onyx base.

13in (33.5cm) high

$4,500-6,000 **TEN**

A magnificent cold painted and gilt bronze and hand carved ivory figure, of a striking Art Deco beauty in an uplifting stylised pose, raised on a shaped Potoro marble plinth, signed Bruno Zach and with foundry stamp.

c1925 *26in (66cm) high*

$150,000-172,500 **HICK**

An Art Deco spelter and ivorine figure, of a reclining lady and ibex, on a marble base, faced with onyx.

24.5in (62cm) long

$700-850 **SWO**

An Art Deco painted spelter group, of a maiden and two dolphins, on a black marble base.

31in (79cm) long

$850-900 **DN**

A bronze patinated figure of a nude African female dancer, possibly by Hagenauer, stamped '22'.

8.9in (22.5cm) high

$750-900 **SWO**

A bronze of a kneeling female and a goat, 'Jeune Femme au Cabri', by Victor Silvestre, inscribed signature and founder's mark 'Susse Fes Paris'.

32.5in (82.5cm) long

$2,250-3,000 **SWO**

An Art Deco patinated metal and marble figural tazza, unmarked.

15.8in (40cm) long

$700-750 **DN**

A 1920s bronze bust of a lady, by Frank Dobson, on a wood base with remnants of 'Internazionale D'arte Venezia 1928 label', inscribed in pencil 'Dobson' and in ink 'Belgrad'.

bust 11½in (29½cm) overall 15in (38cm)

$13,500-18,000 **SWO**

A bronze 'Bust of Nan (Condron)', by Sir Jacob Epstein, on wood base, inscribed in pencil 'A6751 Epstein'.

1909 *15.25in (39cm) wide*

$16,500-22,500 **SWO**

A bronze and marble sculpture, 'Pigeon a Queue Plate', by Jan and Joel Martel, signed in bronze 'J. MARTEL'.

c1925 *12in (30.5in) wide*

$9,000-10,500 **DRA**

A bronze, 'Nu et son Chien' (Nude and her Dog), by Henri Puvrez, signed and dated , and 'Fonderie Nat.le des bronzers Anc.ne, Firme J.Peterman, St Gilles - Bruxelles'.

1921 *11.75in (30cm) high*

$1,500-2,250 **SWO**

An Art Deco patinated bronze, 'Lapin Bijou', by Edouard Marcel Sandoz, cast marks 'E M Sandoz' and 'Susse Fres Es Paris'.

2in (5cm) high

$700-850 **FLD**

ESSENTIAL REFERENCE - ALVAR AALTO

Architect, designer, sculptor and painter, Alvar Aalto was born in 1898. During his prolific career – he died in 1976 – it is estimated he designed over 500 industrial, civic, and residential buildings, mostly in his native Finland, but also in Italy, France, Germany, and the United States. While his earlier works were conceived in the 'Nordic Classical' style, during the 1930s he embraced the 'International Modern' style – but developed an innovative and ultimately highly influential approach to it. Aalto's primary solution to this problem was to integrate an overtly organic material into his designs, and being a Finn that had to be wood. However, the manner in which Aalto used wood was often far from traditional. Indeed, his ground-breaking research, in conjunction with his wife Aino Marsio and carpenter-craftsman Otto Korhonen, into bending and molding laminated woods and plywood enabled him to deploy the material in revolutionary structural and aesthetic ways.

A pair of 'Tank' chairs, model 400, designed by Alvar Aalto.
Designed 1936
$4,500-5,250 **SWO**

A 1950s Jacques Adnet coffee table, unmarked.
19in (48.5cm) high
$12,000-15,000 **DRA**

A Ron Arad leather 'Rover' chair, with black lacquered aluminum, One Off label.
1981 *37in (94cm) high*
$2,700-3,300 **DN**

A 1930s Finmar beech drinks trolley, designed by Alvar Aalto, model no.98, applied label.
22in (56cm) high
$6,000-7,500 **WW**

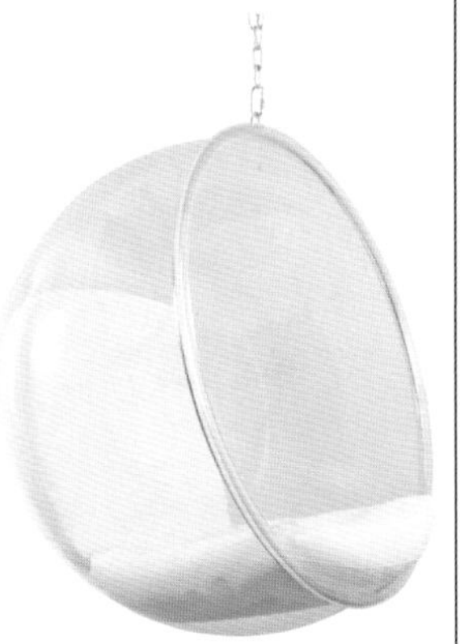

An Eero Aarnio 'Bubble' hanging chair, manufactured by Asko Oy, Helsinki.
Designed 1968 *27.5in (70cm) diam*
$3,000-4,000 **QU**

An Eero Aarnio 'Ball' (or 'Globe') chair, white molded polyester shell with red padded upholstery and cushions, restored.
51.25in (130cm) high
$1,150-1,300 **TEN**

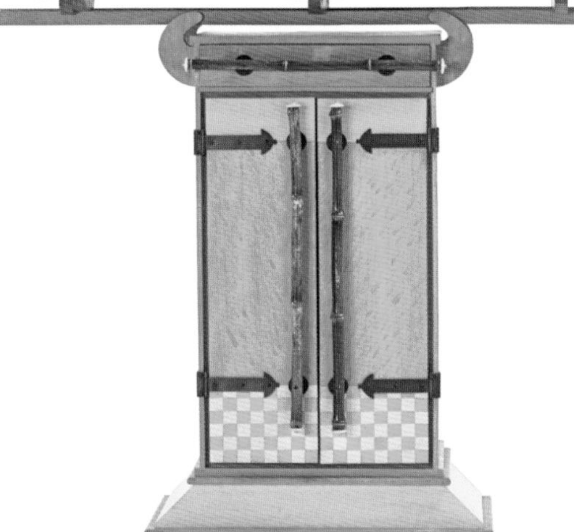

A Gary Knox Bennett cabinet, in satinwood, bamboo, maple, patinated brass and painted wood, unmarked.
38.5in (98cm) high
$5,250-6,750 **DRA**

A pair of 1970s Ward Bennett sled chairs, for Brickel Associates, in chromed steel, cane and upholstery, unmarked.
29.5in (75cm) high
$12,000-15,000 **DRA**

A 1950s Osvaldo Borsani coffee table, in stained and lacquered mahogany, brass and marble, unmarked.
43in (109.5cm) long
$21,000-27,000 **DRA**

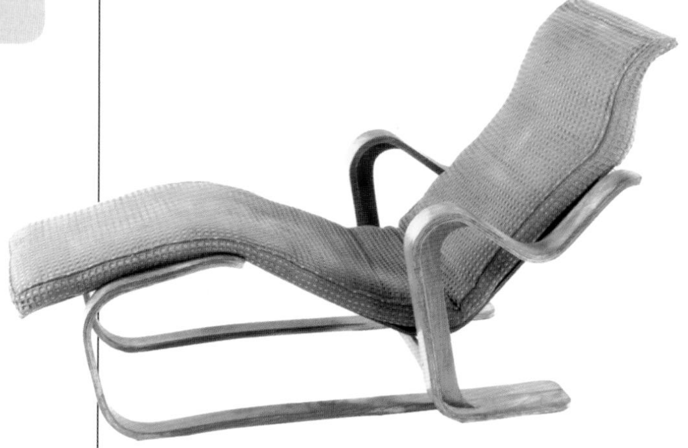

An Isokon bent-ply long chair, designed by Marcel Breuer, regd. no 812856.
51.25in (130cm) long
$11,500-12,750 **WW**

An Isokon bent-ply nest of tables, designed by Marcel Breuer.
largest table 17.75in (45cm) high
$7,500-9,000 **WW**

A 1950s Carlo Di Carli lounge chair, for Singer & Sons, unmarked.
32in (81.25cm) high
$4,000-5,250 **DRA**

A Wendell Castle crescent rocking chair, in ebonized wood and upholstery, signed and dated.
1980 *34in (86.5cm) high*
$12,000-15,000 **DRA**

A Wendell Castle grandfather clock, with carved, textured, and polychromed wood, signed and dated.
1993 *84in (213.5cm) high*
$11,250-15,000 **DRA**

Judith Picks: Wendell Castle

I think that Wendell Castle has got to rank as one of my favorite 20thC furniture designers or as he prefers 'artists'. He is often acknowledged as the father of the American craft furniture movement. He studied art and industrial design at the University of Kansas and made his first piece of furniture as a graduate student in sculpture. He once said 'To me the organic form offers the most exciting possibilities. It can never be completely understood in one glance.' He began working in oak and walnut but was soon to move into plastics in the 1960s. One of the most remarkable aspects of his work is the sheer variety, not just in the materials he has chosen but in the visual nature of his pieces in reponse to changes in developing technology.

A Wendell Castle crackle-lacquered wood coffee table, 'Theme and Variations I'.

16.5in (42cm) high

$27,000-33,000 **DRA**

A Wendell Castle 'Shelled Ladder' table, in ebonized mahogany, madrone burl veneer and gold leaf, signed Wendell Castle.

1991 *43in (109.5cm) high*

$12,000-15,000 **DRA**

A Wendell Castle cabinet, 'A Secret Kept', and mirror, 'A Secret View', in avodire veneer, pau amarello, painted wood and mirrored glass, cabinet signed and dated.

1997 *34in (86.5cm) high*

$21,000-27,000 **DRA**

A Wendell Castle 'Colt II' hall table, in chip-carved French walnut, polychromed, ebonized and crackle-glazed mahogany, signed 'Castle 94'.

1994 *39.75in (101cm) high*

$13,500-18,000 **DRA**

A 1990s Ceccotti Collezioni upholstered sculpted cherry bench, branded.

32.5in (81.25cm) high

$4,500-6,000 **DRA**

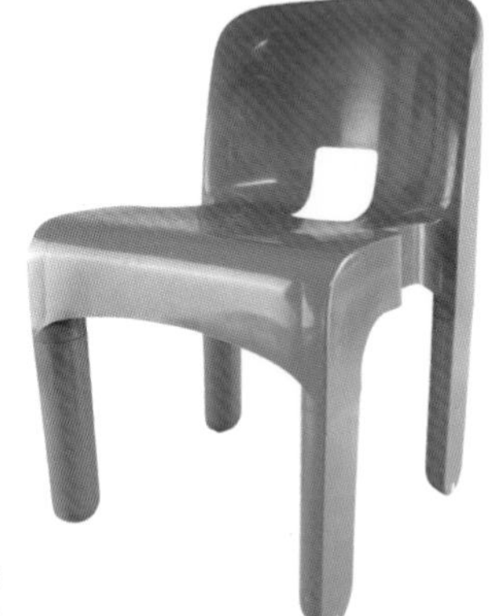

A Jo Colombo green 'Universale' chair, produced for Kartell.

This is an early model of the chair, numbered 4867.

1965 *28.5in (72.5cm) high*

$300-400 **ECGW**

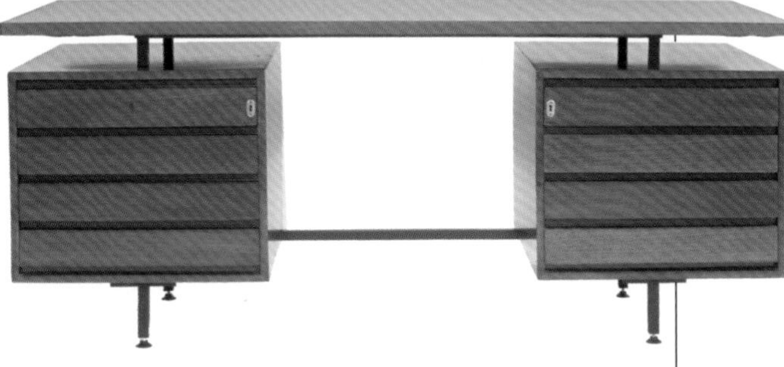

An executive desk, designed by Robin Day for Hille.

c1965 *29.5in (75cm) high 72.5cm (184cm) long*

$2,250-3,000 **SWO**

A pair of Herman Miller 'Time Life' aluminum chairs, designed by Charles & Ray Eames, with brown leather seats, applied label.

31.5in (80cm) high

$2,700-3,300 **WW**

A pair of Herman Miller 'Aluminium Group' armchairs, designed by Charles & Ray Eames, with tan leather seats, cast marks.

33in (84cm) high

$1,800-2,250 **WW**

A late 20thC Charles Eames black leather '670' and '671' chair and ottoman, with rosewood veneer ply frame and aluminum pedestal, both with a label for Hermann Miller.

Designed 1956 *33in (83cm) high*

$4,000-4,500 **DN**

A late 20th/early 21stC Charles and Ray Eames 'La Chaise' chair, for Vitra, raised on oak and chrome legs.

59.5in (151cm) long

$1,150-1,300 **ROS**

A Charles and Ray Eames cabinet, for Herman Miller, ESU 420-C, in birch, plywood, laminated walnut, zinc-plated steel, fiberglass and enameled masonite, manufacturer label.

1952 *58.5in (148.5cm) high*

$18,000-22,500 **DRA**

An exceptional Wharton Esherick figured walnut double pedestal desk, carved 'MCMXLV .W.E.'.

1945 *88in (223.5cm) long*

$52,500-67,500 **DRA**

A 1940s Wharton Esherick hammer handle chair, in hickory, cherry and painted canvas, unmarked.

29.75in (75.5cm) high

$11,500-12,750 **DRA**

Judith Picks: Cityscape

Born in Pennsylvania in 1931, Paul Evans studied sculpture, metalwork, and jewelry design at the School for American Crafters in Rochester, New York, and at Michigan's Cranbrook Academy of Art. After a visit to Philip Lloyd Powell's shop in New Hope, Pennsylvania, Evans began designing furniture. Initially selling his work through Powell (from 1954), and then collaborating with him, Evans went on (in 1964) to become the chief designer of the prestigious furniture manufacturer 'Directional' (until 1980), and then opened his own showroom in New York (in 1981), prior to his death in 1987. Evans success lies in the dynamic marriage of good old-fashioned craftsmanship by hand with the latest technological innovations. Above all, it's not just because his furniture is a brilliant fusion of furniture and art, of craftsmanship and technology, it's because it's uniquely attributable. Look at a piece of Paul Evans furniture and, whether table or cabinet, you will thereafter always recognise that look!

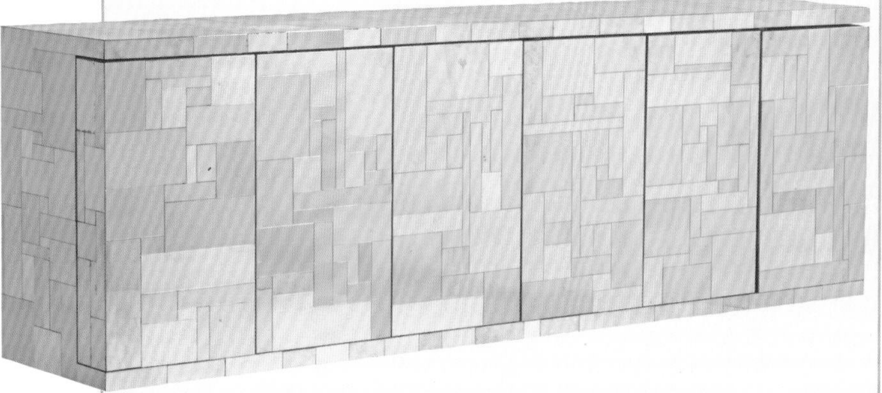

A Paul Evans wall-mounting 'Cityscape' cabinet, for Directional, in chromed steel and brass, unmarked.

84in (213.5cm) long

$14,250-16,500 **DRA**

A rare Paul Evans Studio four-door 'Patchwork' cabinet, in patinated copper and bronze, pewter, and enameled steel, unmarked.

c1970 *73.5in (187cm) high*

$39,000-45,000 **DRA**

A 1970s Paul Evans Studio custom two-door 'Argente' cabinet, in welded and dye-painted aluminum, laminate, polychromed wood and slate, unmarked.

48.25in (122.5cm) high

$37,500-45,000 **DRA**

A Paul Evans cabinet, for Directional, in welded and enameled steel, slate and bronze.

1969 *72in (183cm) long*

$30,000-38,000 **DRA**

A Paul Evans Studio occasional table, in polychromed and gilt steel, gilt wood and slate, unmarked.

1962 *30in (76.5cm) high*

$10,500-13,500 **DRA**

A Paul Evans sculptured metal dining table, for Directional, in bronzed composite and glass, signed 'PE 73'.

1973 *29.5in (75cm) high*

$9,000-11,500 **DRA**

A rare 1960s Paul Evans dining table (PE 23), for Directional, in welded and polychromed steel, bronze and glass, unmarked.

29.5in (75cm) high

$22,500-30,000 **DRA**

ESSENTIAL REFERENCE - PREBEN FABRICIUS

Fabricius was trained as a cabinetmaker by Niels Vodder before attending the School for Interior Design where he studied under Finn Juhl. It was there that he met the blacksmith Jørgen Kastholm. In 1961, they set up a design studio in a Gentofte cellar. In 1965, they exhibited at the furniture fair in Fredericia where the German furniture manufacturer Alfred Kill noticed their work. Kill had a reputation for high quality but initially Favricius and Kastholm were not keen to design furniture for factory production. Their international breakthrough came at the Cologne Fair in 1966 when they exhibited a whole series of office and home furniture leading to orders from ten large furniture concerns. The 'Tulip' chair, the 'Grasshopper' chair and the 'Scimitar' chair are among their most successful works. The pieces of furniture they produced during their seven-year period of cooperation from 1961 to 1968 were so distinctive that many are still produced today as classics.

A 1960s Preben Fabricius and Jørgen Kastholm 'Grasshopper' lounge chair, for Alfred Kill, in chromed steel, leather and canvas, unmarked.

28.25in (72.5cm) high

$7,500-9,750 DRA

A pair of 1990s Richard Ford nightstands, in sculpted and painted poplar, unmarked.

29in (61cm) high

$7,500-9,750 DRA

A 1940s Paul Frankl mahogany 'Station Wagon' dresser with mirror, no. 1041B-195, by Johnson Furniture Co., branded and stenciled numbers,

Dresser 66in (168cm) wide

$11,250-13,500 DRA

A Preben Fabricius and Jørgen Kastholm 'Scimitar' chair, manufactured by Ivan Schlechter, Copenhagen, in stainless steel and leather, needs restoring.

1962

$12,000-12,750 QU

A Piero Fornasetti brass umbrella stand, lacquered and lithographic transfer of hats, printed marks 'FORNASETTI/ MILANO/ MADE IN ITALY'.

c1950 *22.25in (56.5cm) high*

$1,500-2,100 L&T

A 1950s Piero Fornasetti 'Palazzo' coffee table, transfer-decorated lacquered wood, mahogany and brass, manufacturer label.

39in (100cm) wide

$10,500-13,500 DRA

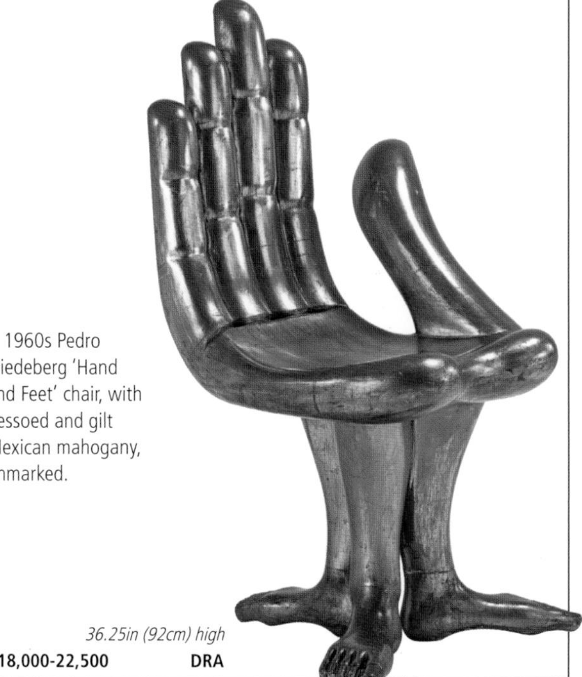

A 1960s Pedro Friedeberg 'Hand and Feet' chair, with gessoed and gilt Mexican mahogany, unmarked.

36.25in (92cm) high

$18,000-22,500 DRA

A pair of 1950s Pierre Jeanneret 'Senate' teak and leather armchairs, from the Chandigarh administrative buildings, unmarked.

36.5in (93cm) high

$14,250-18,000 **DRA**

A Bwana rosewood armchair, designed by Finn Juhl, for France & Søn.

$4,400-4,800 **SWO**

A 1960s Finn Juhl sculpted teak and leather NV-45 chair, for Niels Vodder, unmarked.

32.5in (82.5cm) high

$15,750-19,500 **DRA**

A 1980s Vladimir Kagan custom velveteen sofa, for Vladimir Kagan Designs Inc., unmarked.

129in (328cm) long

$18,000-21,000 **DRA**

A Vladimir Kagan walnut 150BC custom sofa, for Vladimir Kagan Designs Inc., unmarked.

31in (79cm) high

$9,000-11,500 **DRA**

A Vladimir Kagan contour sculpted walnut lounge chair and ottoman, no. 175E, for Vladimir Kagan Designs Inc. New York, with Mali mud cloth upholstery.

34.5in (88cm) high

$18,000-22,500 **DRA**

A 1990s Vladimir Kagan 'Cloud' sofa, for Directional, with sculpted wool and acrylic, manufacturer's label.

28in (71.5cm) high

$33,000-42,000 **DRA**

A rare 1950s Vladimir Kagan and Kagan-Dreyfuss mosaic tri-symmetric walnut dining table, with bronze and glass tesserae, unmarked.

30.5in (77.5cm) high

$30,000-38,000 **DRA**

A pair of 1950s Edvard and Tove Kindt-Larsen, cherry and vinyl chairs, for Gustav Bertelsen & Co., unmarked.

28.5in (72.5cm) high

$9,750-12,000 **DRA**

A Poul Kjaerholm 'PK22' chair, for E Kold, in black leather and polished steel, stamped mark.

27.5in (70cm) high

$1,800-2,250 **WW**

A Bodil Kjaer rosewood and chrome 'Model 901' desk, for E Pedersen & Son.

Bodil Kjaer was born in 1932 and has spent her career working in Denmark, Great Britain and in the USA. This desk is a very desirable piece of mid century furniture. The 'Model 901' received huge amounts of publicity after being used in two James Bond films, 'From Russia with Love' and 'You Only Live Twice'.

1959 *78.7in (200cm) wide*

$15,000-21,000 **SWO**

A Kai Kristensen rosewood and leather lounge or 'Paper Knife' chair, for Magnus Olesen Furniture.

$1,000-1,500 **SWO**

A 1960s Philip and Kelvin Laverne 'Chan' coffee table, patinated, and polychromed bronze, pewter, raised signature and paper label.

17.5in (44.5cm) high

$8,250-10,000 **DRA**

A Le Corbusier 'B301 LC1' chair, for Cassina Basculant, with hide seat and back, cast marks.

$700-850 **WW**

A 1970s Raymond Loewy 'DF 2000' cabinet, for Compagnie D'Esthetique Industrielle, in enameled steel, acrylic, laminate and rosewood, manufacturer's label.

49.5in (126cm) high

$7,500-9,000 **DRA**

A 1950s Carl Malmsten beech sofa, unmarked.

62in (157.5cm) long

$4,000-5,250 DRA

An Alchimia Ollo cabinet, designed by Alessandro Mendini, from an edition of three, lacquered and inlaid wood, applied Atelier Zav paper label.

1989 *83in (210cm) high*

$2,000-2,700 WW

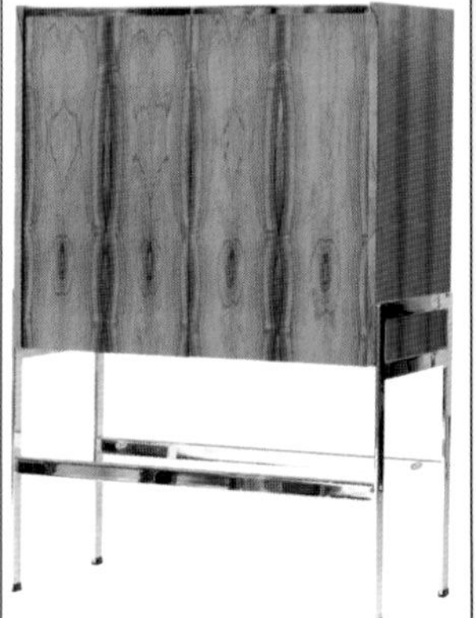

A 1970s rosewood and chrome cocktail cabinet, possibly Merrow Associates.

54in (137cm) high

$2,250-3,000 SWO

ESSENTIAL REFERENCE - SAM MALOOF

Sam Maloof was a furniture designer and woodworker. Maloof moved to Ontario, California in 1948, and set up a furniture workshop in the garage. Maloof designed and built a suite of furniture for his home using salvaged materials. Commissioned pieces followed and, from 1949 to 1952, Maloof continued working in the garage of his Ontario home. In 1953, Maloof relocated to Alta Loma, California. Over time, he added 16 rooms, including a furniture-making shop and studio, to the original 6-room house. Maloof's work is in the collections of several major American museums, including the Metropolitan Museum of Art, the Los Angeles County Museum of Art, the Philadelphia Museum of Art, and the Smithsonian American Art Museum. In 1985 he was awarded a MacArthur 'Genius' grant. Presidents Jimmy Carter and Ronald Reagan have both owned Maloof rockers. People magazine dubbed him 'The Hemingway of Hardwood.' But he regarded himself as a woodworker which he descibed as an 'honest word'.

A Sam Maloof sculpted walnut armchair, Alta Loma, CA, signed, dated and numbered with dedication.

1980 *31in (79cm) high*

$15,750-19,500 DRA

A Merrow Associates rosewood and chrome desk, on T-shaped chrome supports.

Merrow Associates was started by Richard Young, who is a former Royal College of Art student who later studied at the Royal Art Academy Copenhagen under Professor Ole Wanscher. Richard Young is obsessed by quality and the kind of meticulous detailing typical of Scandinavian furniture of the 1950s. He uses beautifully finished glossy surfaces - a juxtaposition of rosewood, steel and glass - as substitutes for patina and marquetry. He trained as a cabinet maker, another reason why materials feature high in his design priorities. Distribution was restricted to specialist retailers. Heal's and Harrods. Although the firm's idiom is essentially traditional, they prefer to call it modern classic. Merrow Associates has proved that British workmanship, properly directed, matches Scandinavian.

30in (76cm) high

$3,000-4,000 SWO

An oak 'Shaker' table, designed by Børge Mogensen for Fredericia Furniture, stamped 'Made in Denmark, 66 12 3' with hexagonal 'FDB' mark.

28.5in (72.5cm) high

$900-1,200 SWO

A George Nakashima walnut slab free-form coffee table, with rosewood butterfly joint.

59.5in (151cm) long

$16,500-22,500 **POOK**

A George Nakashima English oak burl 'Minguren I' side table, for Nakashima Studios, signed with client's name.

1973 *25in (63.5cm) high*

$27,000-33,000 **DRA**

A fine George Nakashima figured walnut and rosewood Minguren I coffee table, for Nakashima Studios, unmarked.

77.5in (197cm) long

$30,000-38,000 **DRA**

A George Nakashima walnut 'Conoid' bench, for Nakashima Studios, signed with client's name.

1974 *57in (145cm) long*

$24,000-30,000 **DRA**

A George Nakashima walnut 'Conoid' cushion chair and 'Green Rock' ottoman, for Nakashima Studios, signed with client"s name.

1976 *chair 34in (86.5cm) high*

$14,250-16,500 **DRA**

A George Nakashima walnut triple dresser, for Nakashima Studios, signed with client's name.

1963 *96in (244cm) long*

$21,000-27,000 **DRA**

A George Nakashima figured walnut single slab top Minguren III dining table, for Nakashima Studios, signed with client's name.

1977 *96in (244cm) long*

$25,500-30,000 **DRA**

A George Nakashima walnut and pandanus cloth wall-hanging cabinet, for Nakashima Studios, signed on back with client's name.

104in (264.5cm) long

$52,500-67,500 **DRA**

A fine George Nakashima double-pedestal desk, figured and book-matched walnut, rosewood, signed with client's name.

1975 *27.5in (70cm) high*

$37,500-52,500 **DRA**

A 1950s Isamu Noguchi Knoll walnut and chromed steel rocking stool, no. 86T, unmarked.

16.5in (42cm) high

$6,750-8,250 **DRA**

A 1960s Kurt Østervig rosewood elliptical gateleg table, for Jason Mobelfabrik, the top with exposed joints and drop down leaves, on a stained mahogany frame.

28.5in (72cm) high

$4,000-5,250 **L&T**

A Verner Panton 'Heart' chair, K3 with ottoman, for Vitra, marked Original Verner Panton Vitra.

1959 *chair 35in (88cm) high*

$2,250-3,000 **QU**

A Tommi Parzinger cabinet, for Parzinger Originals, lacquered wood, brass, unmarked.

100.25in (255cm) long

$10,500-13,500 **DRA**

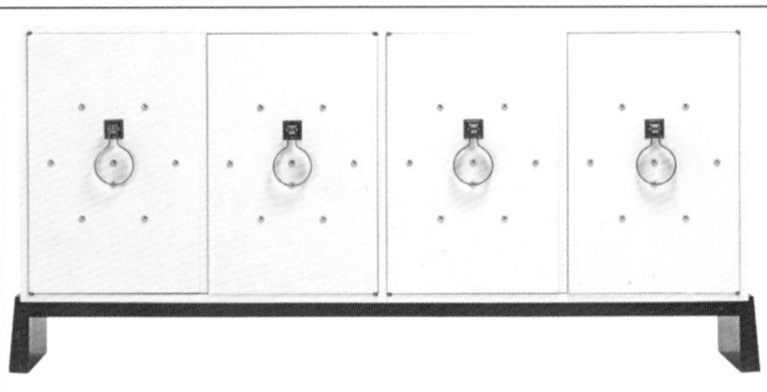

A 1950s Tommi Parzinger studded cabinet, for Parzinger Originals, lacquered wood, brass branded.

68.5in (174cm) long

$13,500-18,000 **DRA**

A 1950s Tommi Parzinger studded cabinet, for Parzinger Originals, with lacquered wood, brass branded.

68in (173cm) long

$21,000-27,000 **DRA**

A 1970s Warren Platner settee, for Knoll International, chromed steel and mohair, manufacturer's labels.

67in (170.5cm) long

$4,500-5,250 **DRA**

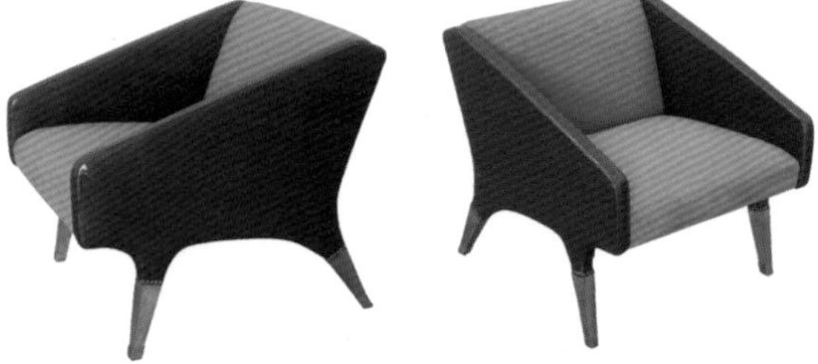

A pair of Gio Ponti lounge chairs, on oak splay legs, re-upholstered in blue leather and red fabric.

The Gio Ponti design lounge chairs were commissioned after the original for the Hotel Parco dei Principi, Rome.

27.5in (70cm) high

$7,500-9,000 **PW**

A 1950s Gio Ponti figured walnut four drawer dresser, for Singer & Sons, manufacturer's label.

47in (119.5cm) long

$14,250-16,500 DRA

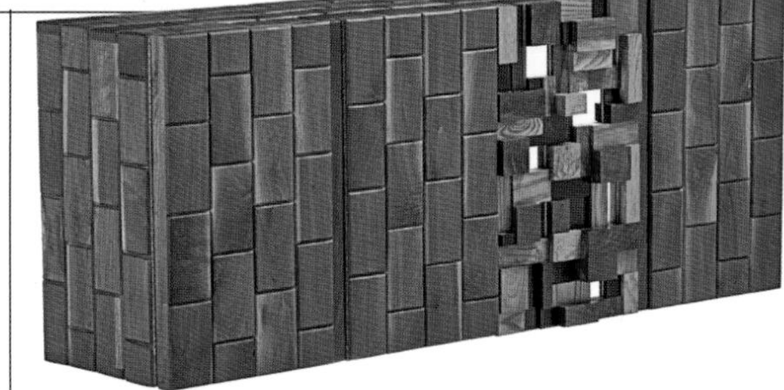

A fine Phil Powell wall-hanging cabinet, walnut, oak, rosewood, ebony, burlwood and mirrored glass, unmarked.

1977 *60in (152.5cm) wide*

$27,000-33,000 DRA

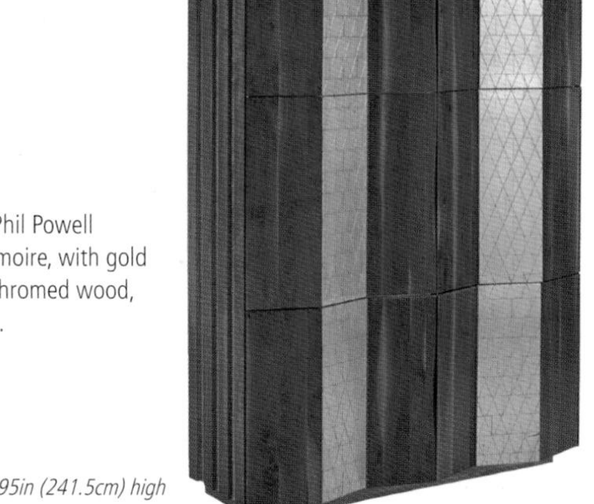

A 1960s Phil Powell walnut armoire, with gold leaf, polychromed wood, unmarked.

95in (241.5cm) high

$27,000-33,000 DRA

An Ernest Race 'Donkey' mark II bookcase, for Isokon.

15.75in (40cm) high

$550-700 SWO

An Ernest Race bent ply roebuck chair, enameled metal frame, stamped marks to seat.

29in (74cm) high

$550-700 WW

A 1950s T.H. Robsjohn-Gibbings Widdicomb chaise longue, bleached walnut, wool, unmarked.

59in (150cm) long

$5,250-6,750 DRA

A 1950s Jean Royère mahogany desk, with brass, lacquered cane, integrated lamp, unmarked.

30in (76.25cm) high

$21,000-27,000 DRA

An Afra and Tobia Scarpa 'Artona' walnut dining suite, for Maxalto, with ebonized details, comprising a dining table, and a set of six 'Africa' chairs, with black leather seats.

1975 *table 27.5in (70cm) high*

$12,000-15,000 SWO

A 1990s William Sofield marble and gilt wood coffee table, unmarked.
68.25in (173.5cm) long
$4,000-5,250 **DRA**

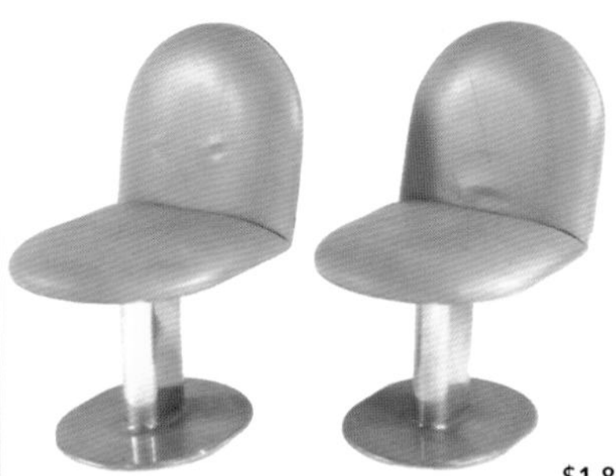

A pair of Ettore Sottsass polished steel 'Harlow' chairs, for Poltronova, with cream leather seats, cast marks.
31.5in (80cm) high
$1,800-2,250 **WW**

An Ettore Sottsass 'Harlow' aluminum and glass coffee table, cast marks.
38.5in (98cm) wide
$975-1,150 **WW**

An Ettore Sottsass Memphis cocktail cabinet, with veneered finish.
40in (100cm) high
$5,250-6,000 **WW**

A 1980s Karl Springer polychromed wood console table, for JMF, unmarked.
29in (74cm) high
$9,000-11,500 **DRA**

A Philippe Starck thermal treated aluminum rocking side chair, for Emeco Hudson, Emeco molded mark and label.
c2000 *35.5in (90cm) high*
$850-975 **DN**

A late 20th/early 21stC Philippe Starck silver 'Swan' armchair.
$550-700 **ROS**

A Studio 65 Stendig 'Marilyn' sofa, upholstered in red jersey.
1972 *81.25in (206cm) long*
$2,100-2,700 **DRA**

An Ilmari Tapiovaara 'Domus Lux' armchair, made by Keravan Puuteollisuus Oy, in birchwood, birch plywood.
c1948 *33in (84cm) high*
$6,000-6,750 **QU**

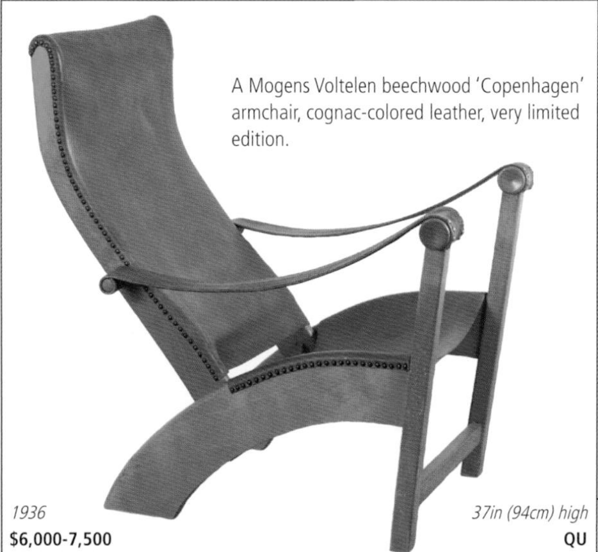

A Mogens Voltelen beechwood 'Copenhagen' armchair, cognac-colored leather, very limited edition.

1936 *37in (94cm) high*

$6,000-7,500 **QU**

An oak occasional table, designed by Peter Waals.

26.75in (68cm) diam

$9,750-10,500 **CHOR**

A Danish rosewood desk, designed by Ole Wanscher, and made by cabinet maker AJ Iverson.

Ole Wanscher was the second professor at the Copenhagen Academy of Fine Arts, (between Kaare Klint and Poul Kjarholm) and, like Klint, his work draws on 18th century English cabinet making. The tradition of handcrafted furniture was protected in Denmark until the 1960s by a punitive tax levied on imported mass-produced furniture. That said, 99% Danish Design (France and Sons, Jeppersons) was still mass-produced, leaving the cabinet maker items exclusive and sought after.

29in (74cm) high

$2,550-3,000 **SWO**

A Danish rosewood coffee table, designed by Ole Wanscher, and made by cabinet maker AJ Iverson.

41in (104.5cm) long

$900-1,000 **SWO**

A Hans Wegner oak single bed, for Getama, with a woven bamboo lattice headboard and integral bedside cabinets.

bed 39.25in (100cm) wide

$400-550 **SWO**

A Hans Wegner oak day bed.

81in (205.5cm) long

$750-900 **SWO**

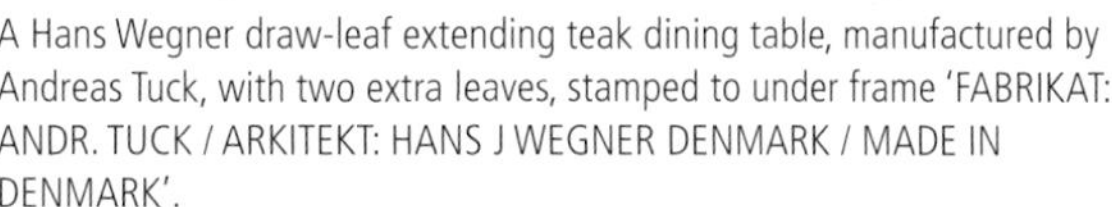

A Hans Wegner draw-leaf extending teak dining table, manufactured by Andreas Tuck, with two extra leaves, stamped to under frame 'FABRIKAT: ANDR. TUCK / ARKITEKT: HANS J WEGNER DENMARK / MADE IN DENMARK'.

28.25in (71.5cm) high

$1,800-2,250 **TEN**

A 1960s Hans Wegner and Johannes Hansen teak valet chair, brass, leather, branded.

37.25in (95cm) high

$10,500-15,000 **DRA**

Judith Picks: Hans Wegner

As I have recently bought a Hans Wegner dining table and 'Wishbone' chairs, he is a firm favorite. Hans Wegner was a world renowned Danish furniture designer. His high quality and thoughtful work, along with a concerted effort from several of his manufacturers, contributed to the international popularity of mid-century Danish design. His style is often described as Organic Functionality, a modernist school with emphasis on functionality. This school of thought arose primarily in Scandinavian countries with contributions by Poul Henningsen, Alvar Aalto, and Arne Jacobsen. In his lifetime Wegner designed over 500 different chairs, over 100 of which were put into mass-production and many of which have become recognizable design icons. One of his earliest objects, an armchair with sloping armrests like relaxed wrists (a 1937 design for an exhibit at the Museum of Decorative Arts), exhibited Wegner's approach of 'stripping the old chairs of their outer style and letting them appear in their pure construction.'

A 1950s Hans Wegner teak 'Papa Bear' chair, for A.P. Stolen, unmarked.

39in (99cm) high

$9,000-12,000 **DRA**

A pair of Frank Lloyd Wright folding benches, birch plywood, steel chain, branded mark 'FLW 51'.

These benches came from the Meeting House, First Unitarian Society, Madison, Wisconsin.

1951 *20in (51cm) high*

$7,500-9,000 **DRA**

A Memphis style laminated wood and glass dining table, and four white leather and chrome chairs (not shown).

table 31.5in (80cm) high

$975-1,150 set **WW**

A 1950s bar cabinet, stained and lacquered wood, parchment, nickeled brass, unmarked.

42in (107cm) long

$2,700-3,300 **DRA**

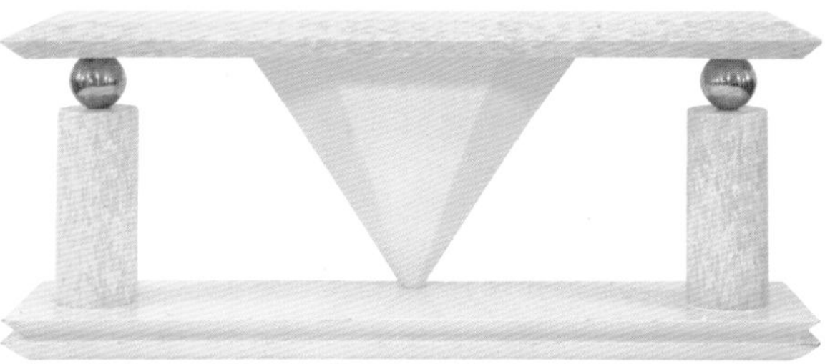

A composition and lacquered console table, the top with yellow fossil-type incusions, labeled 'Inexpor Ltda Hand Made in Colombia'.

72.5in (184cm) long

$2,000-2,400 **SWO**

A bulbous porcelain vase, designed by Laura Andreson, green and blue crystalline glaze, signed and dated.
1976 *7.5in (19cm) high*
$1,000-1,400 DRA

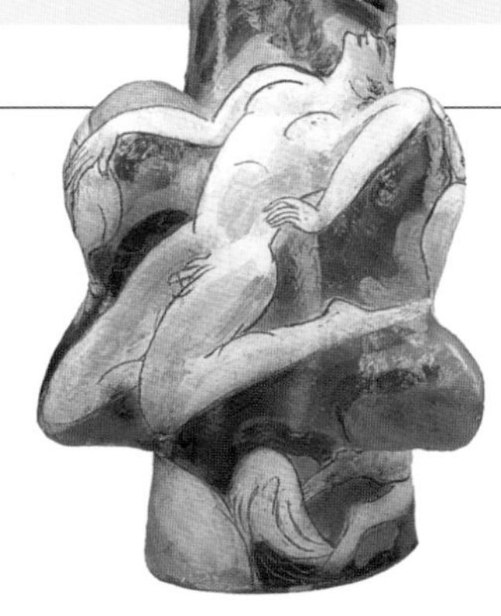

A three-sided glazed stoneware sculpture, designed by Rudy Autio, signed and dated.
1991 *36.25in (92cm) high*
$13,500-16,500 DRA

A porcelain vessel, designed by Brother Thomas Bezanson, with copper red glaze, signed Benedictine Monks, Weston, VT MX 30/15/20/1.
8in (20.5cm) high
$10,500-12,750 DRA

ESSENTIAL REFERENCE - THOMAS BEZANSON

Brother Thomas Bezanson was a Canadian born artist who is best known for his finely thrown porcelain vessels and complex glazes. After studying philosophy at the University of Ottawa, he spent twenty-five years as a Benedictine monk at Weston Priory, Vermont, before becoming the artist-in-residence at Mount Saint Benedict in Erie, PA. Bezanson believed in art as the language of the spirit, and he approached pottery as a monk would their daily duties and prayers: with equal measures of practice, concentration, and repetition. His ceramic experimentation yielded an astoundingly beautiful array of glazes and shapes. Heavily influenced by Japanese and Sung Dynasty ceramics, he valued perfection in his craft, leading him to destroy nearly 80% of each firing. His works can be found in over eighty museum collections worldwide.

A porcelain vessel, designed by Brother Thomas Bezanson, 'Chrysanthemum' glaze, signed Benedictine Monks, Weston, VT 2/1 3014/25, ichthys symbol.
7in (18cm) high
$13,500-16,500 DRA

A Bitossi 'Yantra' vase, designed by Ettore Sottsass.
15.5in (39cm) high
$850-975 WW

A Bitossi spool vase, designed by Ettore Sottsass, black painted 'Bitossi Sottsass' to base.
12.25in (31cm) diam
$850-975 WW

ESSENTIAL REFERENCE - ROSE CABAT

Rose Cabat (June 27, 1914–January 25, 2015) was an American studio ceramicist, classified as part of the Mid-Century Modern movement who was best known for her innovative glazes upon small porcelain pots called 'feelies' often in the shape of onions and figs and bowls. She was the oldest known actively practicing pottery artist in the United States. She and Erni began development of glaze formulas, which applied to the later developed 'feelie' forms would become Rose Cabat's signature pieces. In about 1960, Rose hit upon the basic form of the vessel which would become the foundation of the 'feelies'. She created a weed pot with a delicate closed neck, which cannot hold even one slender stem or stalk, quoted as saying, 'A vase can hold weeds or flowers, but can't it just be a spot of beauty?'

A large 'feelie' vase, designed by Rose and Erni Cabat, turquoise and green glaze, signed.
7in (18cm) high
$4,000-4,500 DRA

A Jean Cocteau ceramic plate, 'L'après Midi d'un Faune', signed and numbered 'Jean Cocteau/38/40'.
1958 *12.5in (31.5cm) diam*
$2,700-3,600 ROS

An early stoneware vase, designed by Hans Coper, impressed seal mark.
14.5in (36.5cm) high
$10,500-12,000 WW

A massive sculptural vessel, designed by Rick Dillingham, 'Gas Can', signed and dated.
1990 *28in (71.5cm) high*
$5,250-6,000 DRA

A 1940s/50s large glazed ceramic and glass mermaid sculpture, by Perth Amboy, signed.
25in (63.5cm) high
$4,000-4,500 DRA

A Shoji Hamada glazed stoneware jar, with ash glaze and wax-resist designs, signed, with original box.
c1960 *9in (23cm) high*
$6,000-7,500 DRA

A 1980s raku-fired covered vessel, designed by Wayne Higby, chop mark.
13in (33cm) high
$8,250-9,750 DRA

A glazed earthenware charger, designed by Jun Kaneko, signed and dated.
1987 *3in (8cm) high*
$4,500-5,250 DRA

A Marilyn Levine for Pillow Pottery box sculpture.

Marilyn Levine taught at the University of Regina 1966-73, the University of Utah, Salt Lake City 1973-76 and University of California, Berkeley 1976-80.

15.5in (39cm) wide
$1,300-1,450 CHOR

An anthropomorphic jug head 'Baby in Stroller' sculpture, designed by Michael Lucero, from the New World series, dated,
1996 *34in (86.5cm) high*
$8,250-10,000 DRA

A glazed hand-built faience pitcher, designed by Salvatore Meli, 'Gli Amori' ('The Lovers'), signed 'Meli 53 Roma', with original gallery label.
1953 *21.5in (55cm) high*
$10,500-12,000 DRA

A low bowl, designed by Otto and Gertrud Natzler, with flame red glaze, signed 'NATZLER' with paper label 'H387'.
1957 *2.75in (7cm) diam*
$30,000-38,000 DRA

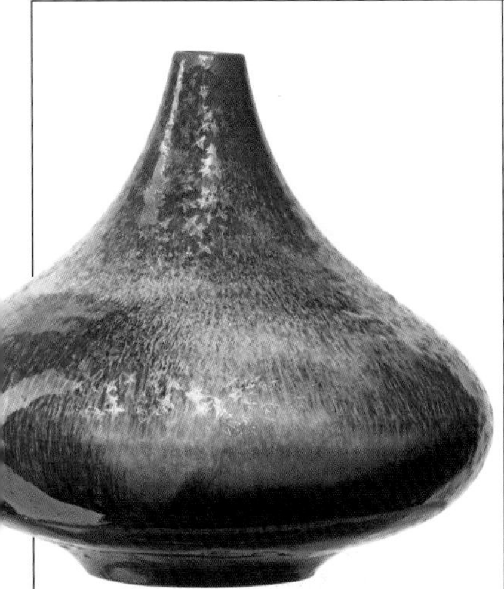

A teardrop bottle, designed by Otto and Gertrud Natzler, green crystalline glaze, signed 'NATZLER' with original paper label 'N653'.

1965 *4.75in (12cm) high*

$9,750-11,500 **DRA**

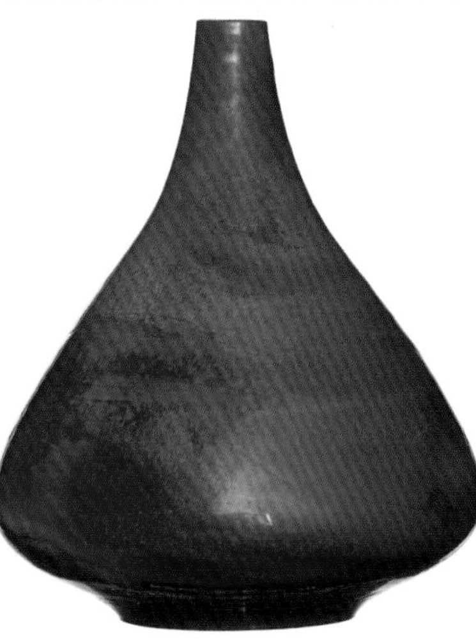

A reduction-fired vase, designed by Otto and Gertrud Natzler, iridescent sang nocturne glaze with melt fissures, signed 'NATZLER', paper label 'N786'.

1966 *9.75in (25cm) high*

$15,750-18,000 **DRA**

A Vallauris limited edition jug, 'Yan Soleil', no.516, designed by Pablo Picasso, incised marks, '131/300'.

Conceived 30th August 1963 in an edition of 300.

10.75in (27cm) high

$1,800-2,250 **WW**

A Pablo Picasso Madoura glazed earthenware plate, 'Face no. 130 (Visage no. 130),' signed 'No. 130 EDITION PICASSO 54/500 MADOURA'.

1963 *10in (25.5cm) diam*

$9,000-10,500 **DRA**

A Madoura jug, designed by Pablo Picasso, 'Pichet Tête Carrée' Ramie No.233, painted '293/300 Edition Picasso', limited edition.

5.5in (13.5cm) high

$6,750-7,500 **WW**

A glazed ceramic vase, designed by Gio Ponti and Rolando Hettner, Italy, signed.

1954 *28in (71.5cm) high*

$22,500-27,000 **DRA**

A Henry Varnum Poor glazed faïence bowl, decorated with fruit still life and leaping cats, signed and dated.

1952 *18in (46cm) wide*

$5,250-6,000 **DRA**

A Ken Price for Gemini G.E.L glazed earthenware coffee cup, 'North of El Prado', signed 'KP '93, 16/25, KP92, 2179, copyright/II', with box.

1993 *3.25in (8.5cm) high*

$8,250-9,750 **DRA**

ESSENTIAL REFERENCE - LUCIE RIE

Lucie Rie was born Lucie Gomperz in Vienna. She studied pottery under Michael Powolny at the Vienna Kunstgewerbeschule, a school of arts and crafts associated with the Wiener Werkstätte.

- **She set up her first studio in Vienna in 1925 and exhibited the same year at the Paris International Exhibition. In 1937, she won a silver medal at the Paris International Exhibition. In 1938, she emigrated to England, where she settled in London. Around this time she separated from Hans Rie, a businessman whom she had married in Vienna. During and after the war, to make ends meet, she made ceramic buttons and jewelry, some of which are displayed at London's Victoria and Albert Museum.**
- **In 1946, she hired Hans Coper, a young man with no experience in ceramics, to help her fire the buttons. As Coper was interested in learning sculpture, she sent him to a potter named Heber Mathews, who taught him how to make pots on the wheel. Rie and Coper exhibited together in 1948. Coper became a partner in Rie's studio, where he remained until 1958. Their friendship lasted until Coper's death in 1981. Rie's small studio was at 18 Albion Mews, a narrow street of converted stables near Hyde Park. The studio remained almost unchanged during the 50 years she occupied it and has been reconstructed in the Victoria and Albert Museum's ceramics gallery.**
- **Rie was a friend of Bernard Leach, one of the leading figures in British studio pottery in the mid-20th century. But despite his transient influence, her brightly colored, delicate, modernist pottery stands apart from Leach's subdued, rustic, oriental work. She taught at Camberwell College of Arts from 1960 until 1972. She stopped making pottery in 1990.**

A flaring vase, designed by Lucie Rie, with frothy white glaze, chopmark.
c1980 *10.5in (27cm) high*
$14,250-18,000 **DRA**

A porcelain bowl, designed by Lucie Rie, covered in a yellow glaze, impressed seal mark, original Albion Mews paper label.
9.25in (23.5cm) high
$4,500-6,000 **WW**

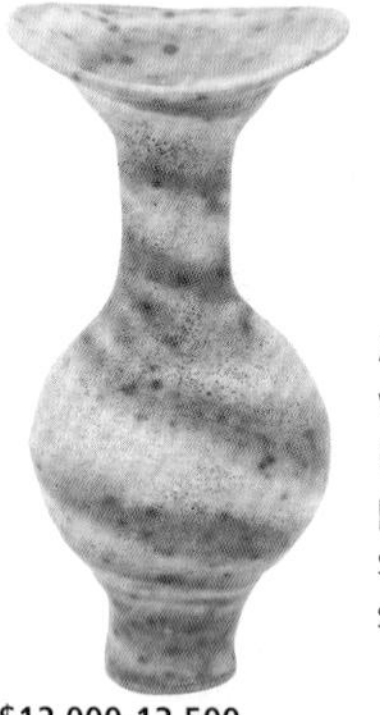

A stoneware bottle vase, designed by Lucie Rie, covered in a pitted pink glaze with brown stripes, with impressed seal mark.
11in (27.5cm) high
$12,000-13,500 **WW**

A porcelain footed bowl, designed by Lucie Rie, the exterior white with manganese bands and inlaid vertical lines, the interior sgraffito decorated, covered in a manganese and bronze glaze, impressed seal mark.
8.75in (22cm) diam
$13,500-15,000 **WW**

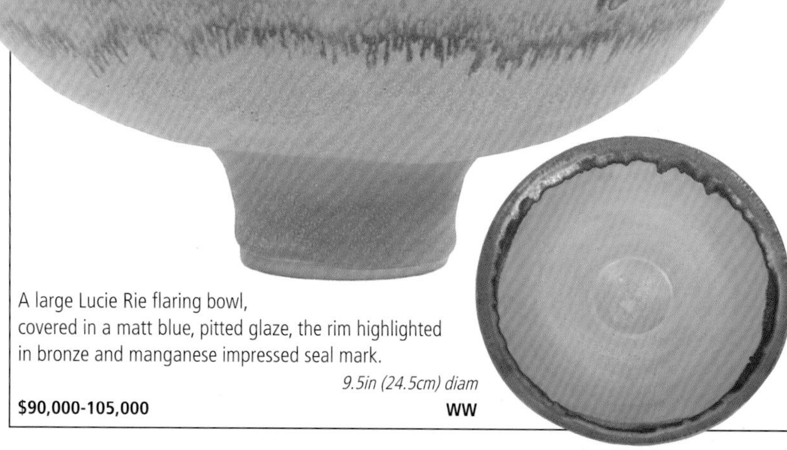

A large Lucie Rie flaring bowl, covered in a matt blue, pitted glaze, the rim highlighted in bronze and manganese impressed seal mark.
9.5in (24.5cm) diam
$90,000-105,000 **WW**

A porcelain bowl, designed by Lucie Rie, with pale green with gray and pink shading, the rim picked out with manganese, impressed seal mark.
9in (23cm) diam
$12,000-13,500 **WW**

A salt-glazed stoneware covered vessel, designed by Don Reitz, rare crystalline glaze, signed.

22.5in (51.5cm) high

$5,250-6,750 DRA

A large figural wood sculpture, designed by Edwin Scheier, signed and dated.

1972 *61in (155cm) high*

$12,000-13,500 DRA

ESSENTIAL REFERENCE - PAUL SOLDNER

Paul Soldner (1921) was an American ceramic artist, noted for his experimentation with the 16thC Japanese technique called raku introducing new methods of firing and post firing, which became known as American Raku. Soldner earned degrees in art education and art administration from Bluffton College and the University of Colorado, then turned his attention to ceramics. He focused first on functional pottery. In 1954, Soldner became Peter Voulkos' first student in the ceramics department at the Los Angeles County Art Institute (now the Otis College of Art and Design). As Soldner helped his teacher establish the program, he made several changes to the studio pottery equipment, which lead to him founding Soldner Pottery Equipment Corp. In 1955, to market his inventions, he held seven patents related to pottery equipment. After receiving his MFA in ceramics in 1956, Soldner began teaching at Scripps College. In the 1960s Soldner helped found Anderson Ranch Arts Center in Snowmass Colorado. Soldner developed a type of low-temperature salt firing. Along with Voulkos, Soldner has been credited with creating the 'California School' of ceramic arts by combining Western materials and technology with Japanese techniques and aesthetics.

- **Soldner retired from Scripps in 1991.**

A slab-built raku-fired sculpture on pedestal, designed by Paul Soldner, signed.

26in (66cm) high

$14,250-16,500 DRA

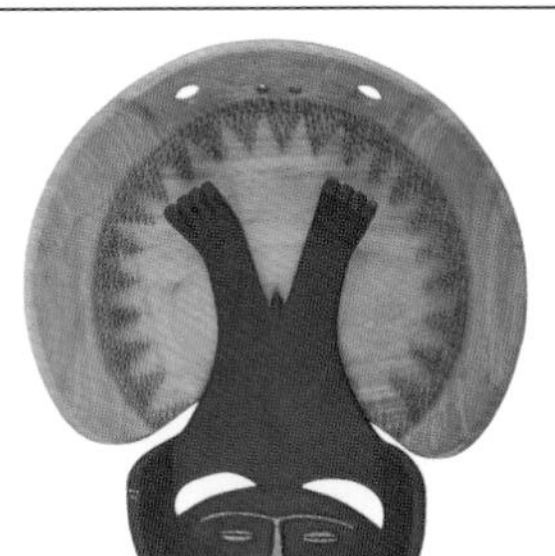

A 1960s wall-hanging sculpture, designed by Edwin Scheier, unmarked.

29.5in (75cm) high

$4,000-4,500 DRA

A lidded coupe, with figural finial, designed by Edwin and Mary Scheier, with manganese, gunmetal and blue glaze, signed and dated.

1990 *20in (51cm) high*

$8,500-9,000 DRA

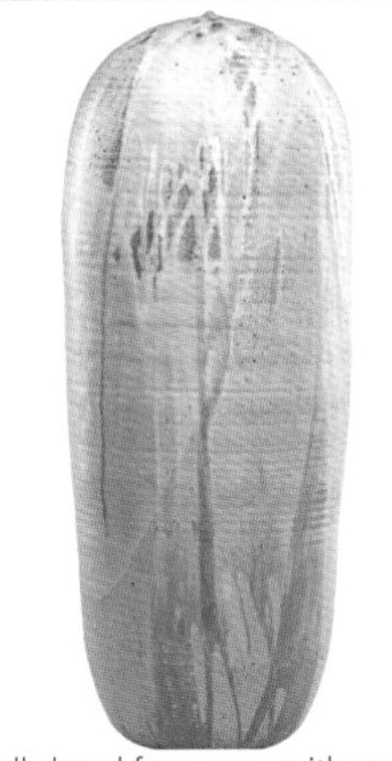

A tall closed form vase, with modest rattle, designed by Toshiko Takaezu, shino glaze, signed 'TT'.

35in (89cm) high

$10,500-13,500 DRA

An exceptional wood-fired stoneware stack pot, designed by Peter Voulkos, signed and dated.

Voulkos made a bronze edition of seven of this pot in 1986.

1975 *26in (66cm) high*

$30,000-38,000 DRA

A glazed faïence shadow box sculpture, designed by Carl Walters, 'The Death of Art', Woodstock, NY, signed.

This was Walter's response to the Museum of Modern Art, New York and art critics at the time who claimed that representational and figurative art was no longer art.

c1950 *10in (25.5cm) high*

$3,000-4,000 DRA

A folded bowl, by Beartrice Wood, verdigris volcanic glaze, Ojai, CA, signed 'BEATO'.

5.5in (14cm) high

$5,250-6,000 DRA

ESSENTIAL REFERENCE - DALE CHIHULY

Dale Chihuly enrolled at the College of the Puget Sound in 1959. A year later, he transferred to the University of Washington in Seattle to study interior design. In 1961 he learned how to melt and fuse glass. In 1962 he dropped out of school to study art in Florence. Chihuly began experimenting with glassblowing in 1965, and in 1966 he received a full scholarship to attend the University of Wisconsin–Madison. He studied under Harvey Littleton, who had established the first glass program in the United States at the university. In 1967, Chihuly received a Master of Science degree in sculpture. After graduating, he enrolled at the Rhode Island School of Design. Chihuly earned a Master of Fine Arts degree in sculpture from the RISD in 1968. That same year, he was awarded a Louis Comfort Tiffany Foundation grant for his work in glass, as well as a Fulbright Fellowship. He traveled to Venice to work at the Venini factory on the island of Murano, where he first saw the team approach to blowing glass. After returning to the United States, Chihuly spent the first of four consecutive summers teaching at the Haystack Mountain School of Crafts in Deer Isle, Maine. In 1971, Chihuly cofounded the Pilchuck Glass School near Stanwood, Washington. In 1976, while Chihuly was in England, he was involved in a head-on car accident and he was blinded in his left eye. After recovering, he continued to blow glass until he dislocated his right shoulder in a 1979 bodysurfing accident. No longer able to hold the glass blowing pipe, he hired others to do the work. Chihuly explained the change in a 2006 interview, saying 'Once I stepped back, I liked the view' and pointed out that it allowed him to see the work from more perspectives.

One of a set of five seaform glass pieces, designed by Dale Chihuly, blue lip wrap, signed and dated.

1994 *largest 11.5in (29.5cm) high*
$10,500-13,500 set **DRA**

A massive macchia bowl, designed by Dale Chihuly, with blue lip wrap, signed and dated.

2000 *25.75in (65.6cm) high*
$18,000-22,500 **DRA**

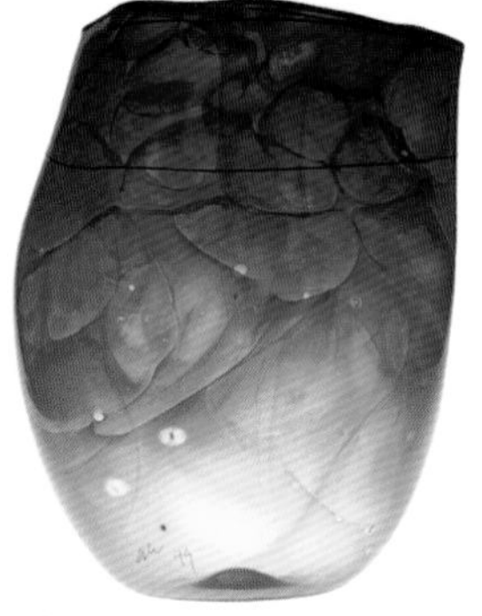

A large blown glass, designed by Dale Chihuly, with topaz basket with brown lip wrap, signed and dated.

With copy of original 'slick' from the studio (registration no. 99.3102.bl).

1999 *12.5in (32cm) high*
$7,500-9,000 **DRA**

A blown glass Venetian vase, designed by Dale Chihuly, with gold leaf, signed and dated.

1990 *27in (68.5cm) high*
$27,000-33,000 **DRA**

A two-piece blown glass sculpture with gold leaf, designed by Dale Chihuly and Pino Signoretto, Murano, Italy, signed and dated.

1998 *30in (76.5cm) high*
$18,000-21,000 **DRA**

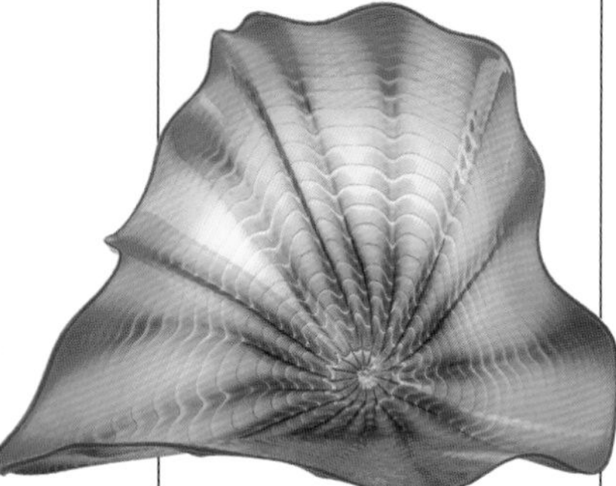

A large seaform piece, designed by Dale Chihuly, red-lip wrap,signed and dated.

1991 *13.5in (34.5cm) high*
$9,000-10,500 **DRA**

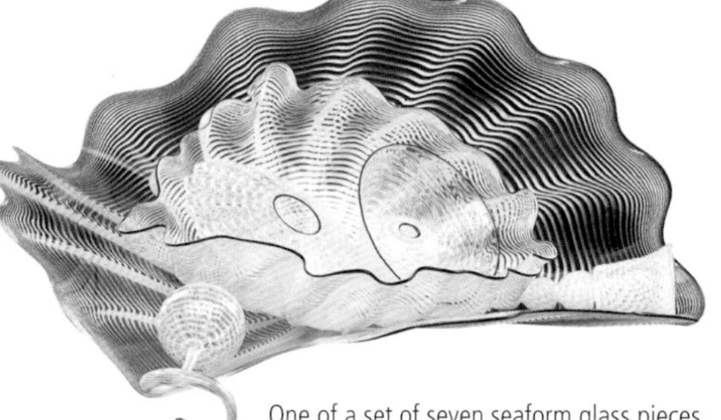

One of a set of seven seaform glass pieces, designed by Dale Chihuly, black lip-wrap, signed and dated.

2000 *largest 11in (28cm) high*
$15,000-18,000 set **DRA**

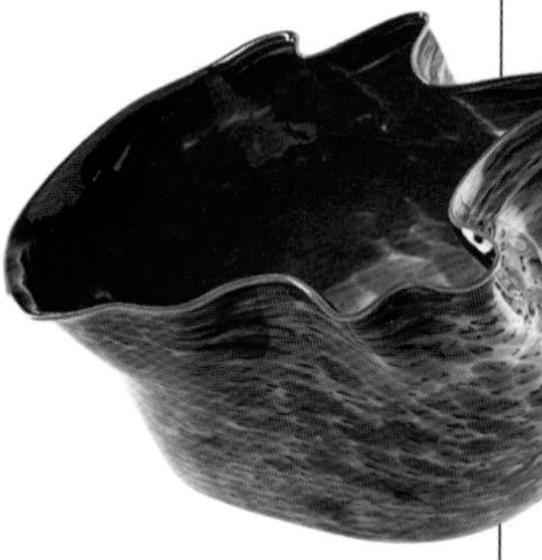

A large macchia bowl, designed by Dale Chihuly, with chartreuse lip wrap, signed and dated.

1986 *14in (35.5cm) high*
$25,500-30,000 **DRA**

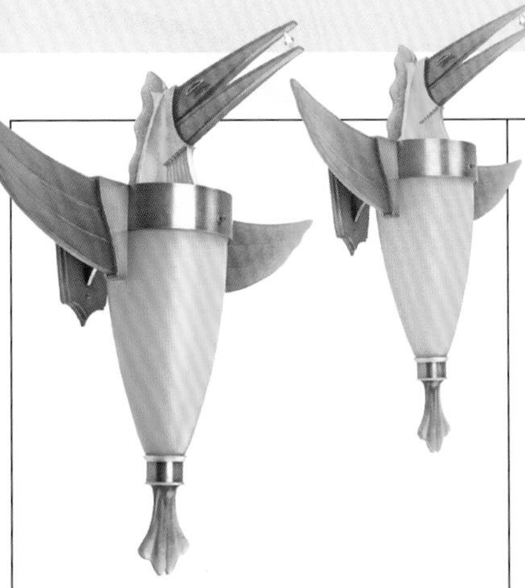

A pair of sculptural blown glass sconces, 'Birds with Diamonds', designed by Dan Dailey, pâte-de-verre, nickel and gold-plated bronze, unmarked.

2005 *24in (61cm) high*

$60,000-75,000 **DRA**

A fish 'Graal' Orrefors vase, designed by Edvard Hald, internally decorated with fish swimming amongst seaweed, engraved mark with full Hald signature, date and number 2638.

1945 *5.25in (13cm) high*

$750-900 **FLD**

A Mdina 'fish' vase, designed by Michael Harris, in clear, purple and mottled blue, with yellow inclusions, etched 'Michael Harris, Mdina Glass, Malta'.

c1970 *10.5in (26.5cm) high*

$1,20-1,400 **SWO**

A Harvey Littleton 'Implied Movement' glass sculpture, all signed, five dated, 'HKL 1-1987-6'.

1987 *tallest 37.75in (96cm) high*

$37,500-45,000 **DRA**

A 1950s Orrefors 'Ariel' vase, designed by Ingeborg Lundin, cased in clear glass over a sea green interior decorated with air trap disc forms, full engraved signature.

7in (18cm) high

$700-850 **FLD**

A Per Lütken vase, for Holmegaard Glasvaerk, Copenhagen, manufactory mark and artist's signature, '15972' engraved.

c1950

$750-900 **QU**

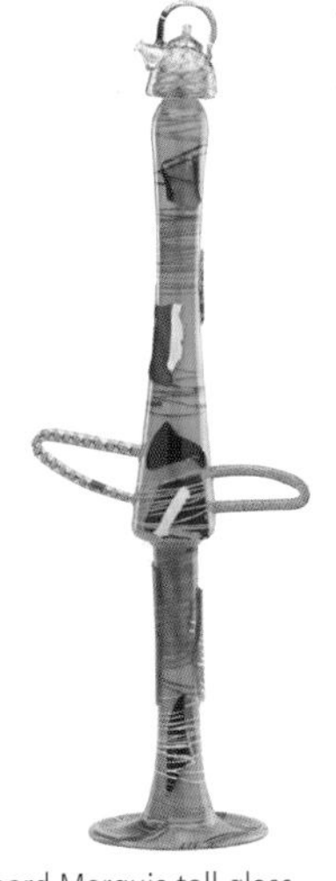

A Richard Marquis tall glass sculpture, 'Teapot Trophy,' signed, dated, and copyrighted.

1989-92. *34in (86.5cm) high*

$21,000-27,000 **DRA**

A Richard Marquis glass teapot sculpture, 'Crazy Quilt Coffee Pot', signed and dated in murrine and on base.

1990 *7.5in (19cm) high*

$11,500-12,750 **DRA**

A two-part glass sculpture, designed by William Morris, 'Artifact: Tooth', signed and dated.

This is one of a small edition made for a fundraiser at the Seattle Art Museum, 1994.

1994 *6.5in (16.5cm) high*

$15,000-18,000 **DRA**

A Mary Ann 'Toots' Zynsky filet-de-verre vessel, 'Birthday Chaos', signed.

16.5in (42cm) long

$12,000-15,000 **DRA**

A Barovier & Toso 'Oriente' blown glass vase, with silver leaf, designed by Ercole Barovier, unmarked.

c1960 *11in (28cm) high*

$21,000-27,000 **DRA**

A 1970s Venini threaded glass vase, designed by Fulvio Bianconi (1915-96), unmarked.

10.5in (26.7cm) high

$2,400-3,000 **DRA**

A Michele Burato blown and iridized glass vase, 'Dicro', etched 'Michele Burato 99 P.U. 'Dicro'.

1999 *16.75in (42.6cm) high*

$600-750 **DRA**

A Venini 'Incamiciato' cased glass vase, designed by Tomaso Buzzi, with label.

1965-70 *14in (35.6cm) high*

$700-850 **DRA**

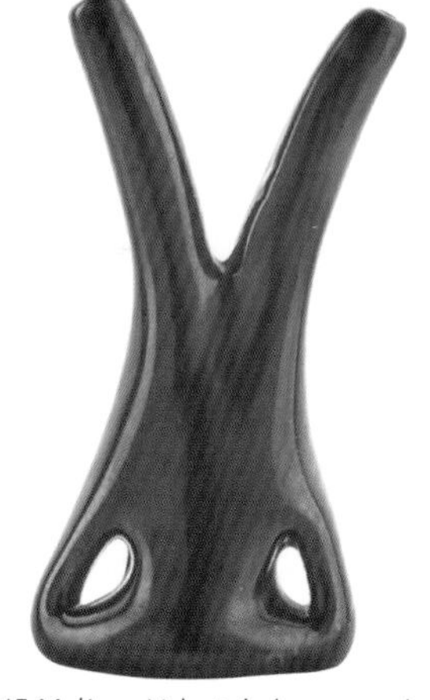

An A.V.E.M. 'Anse Volante' glass vase, designed by Giorgio Ferro, unmarked.

1952 *6.5in (16.5cm) high*

$600-750 **DRA**

A Salviati & Co two-piece sculpture, by Luciano Gaspari, blown and applied glass, signed 'L.G. 59'.

17in (43cm) high

$2,100-2,700 **DRA**

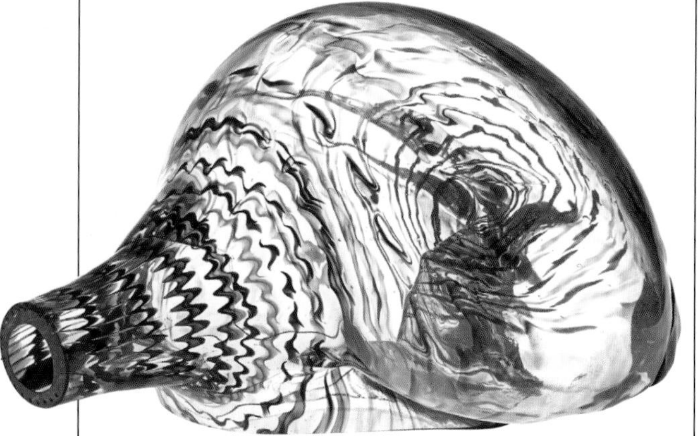

A Fratelli Toso mold-blown, cut and polished glass vessel, designed by Marvin Lipofsky and Gianni Toso, signed and dated.

1979 *10.5in (27cm) high*

$9,000-10,500 **DRA**

An Aureliano Toso glass ewer, designed by Dino Martens, in mauve aventurine with green and red stripes.

c1950 *13in (33cm) wide*

$4,000-5,250 **SWO**

An Aureliano Toso blown and iridized glass mace pitcher, with smoke line, designed by Dino Martens (1894-1970), original 'MADE IN ITALY' paper label to base.

c1950 *13.5in (34.3cm) high*

$1,500-2,250 DRA

A Yoichi Ohira 'Le Luci Sommerse' vase, blown glass, powder inserts, partial battuto surface, executed by Maestro Livio Serena and Maestro Giacomo Barbini, fully markedwith artist cipher.

Exhibited: Barry Friedman Ltd., New York, 2001Published: Yoichi Ohira: A Phenomenon in Glass, Barry Friedman Ltd., New York, 2002, p. 231

2000 *6.5in (16.5cm) high*

$25,500-33,000 DRA

A Yoichi Ohira 'Catena' vase, blown glass canes, murrine and powder inserts, executed by Maestro Livio Serena, fully marked and with artist cipher.

1998 *6in (15.2cm) high*

$11,500-12,750 DRA

ESSENTIAL REFERENCE - YOICHI OHIRA

Yoichi Ohira, who presently lives in Venice, Italy, was born and raised in Japan. He graduated from Tokyo's Kuwasawa Design School in 1969, and moved to Venice in 1973 to study sculpture at the Accademia di Belle Arti. Ohira began working with glass on Murano at the Fucina degli Angeli in 1973.

In 1987, he was offered the position of artistic director at Murano's de Majo glassworks, where he worked with some of the island's most accomplished and talented glass masters.

- **In 1992, he began working as an independent artist. In 1993, he began working with the Muranese master glassblower Livio Serena. In 1995, the master glass cutter Giacomo Barbini joined Ohira's artistic team. Ohira takes his inspiration from both cultures, taking the bright colors of Muranese glass and the restrained forms of Japanese applied arts.**

A Yoichi Ohira (b1946) 'Rosso e Nero' vase, blown glass canes, powder inserts, polished, executed by Maestro Livio Serena and Maestro Giacomo Barbini, fully marked.

2001 *7.5in (19cm) high*

$13,500-18,000 DRA

A Vistosi 'Pulcini' glass bird, by Alessandro Pianon, with a blue and green band of squares, with murrine eyes, on wire legs, now affixed to a marble base.

c1960 *8in (20.5cm) high*

$1,500-2,250 DN

A Seguso Vetri D'Arte sommerso glass vase, designed by Flavio Poli, unmarked.

c1960 *10.5in (26.7cm) high*

$1,200-1,800 DRA

A Venini set of four blown glass 'Canne' tumblers, designed by Gio Ponti, unmarked.

c1950 *4in (10.2cm) high*

$450-600 DRA

A 1950s Archimede Seguso alabastro glass figure of a peasant, foil label, tip of backpack broken off and reground.

10in (25.4cm) high

$255-300 **DRA**

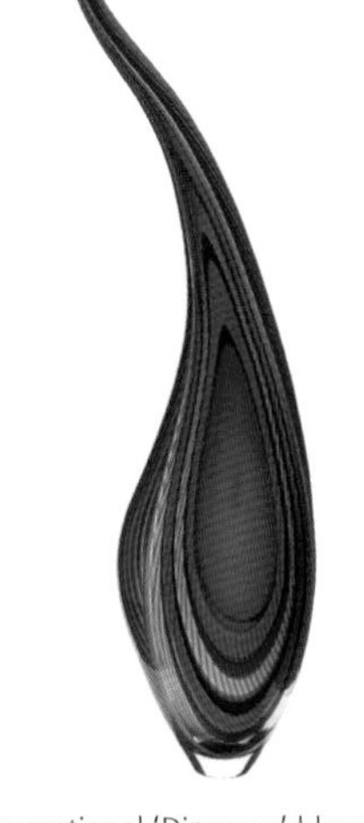

An exceptional 'Dinosaur' blown and carved glass vessel, designed by Lino Tagliapietra, signed.

2001 *48in (122cm) high*

$30,000-38,000 **DRA**

A Lino Tagliapietra 'canne' glass vessel, etched 'F31 Murano 44/100'.

1984 *10in (25.4cm) wide*

$1,200-1,800 **DRA**

A Venini blown glass bowl, with paper label, 'VENINI MURANO VENEZIA MADE IN ITALY'.

1961-1962 *6in 15.2cm) diam*

$1,000-1,200 **DRA**

A Vistosi 'Cocoon' sculpture, cased and blown glass and patinated iron, designed by Steve Tobin (b1957), glass signed, 'Tobin'.

1991 *81in (206cm) high*

$3,300-4,400 **DRA**

A Fratelli Toso blown glass vase with silver foil, unmarked.

13.25in (33.7cm) high

$2,700-3,300 **DRA**

A 1960s Venini 'Clessidra', unmarked.

9.75in (24.8cm) high

$900-1,000 **DRA**

A Venini 'Tessuto' glass vase, etched 'Venini Italia 85', original 'VENINI MURANO MADE IN ITALY' decal label.

1985 *9.75in 24.8cm) high*

$1,150-1,300 **DRA**

An Alvar Aalto white enameled aluminum ceiling lamp, 'A 337 - Flying saucer', manufacturer Valaistustyö Ky, Helsinki for Artek.

1954 *14in (35cm) high*

$1,000-1,400 **QU**

A large Barovier-Toso flush-mount chandelier, in clear and gold-foiled glass, brass and enameled steel, unmarked.

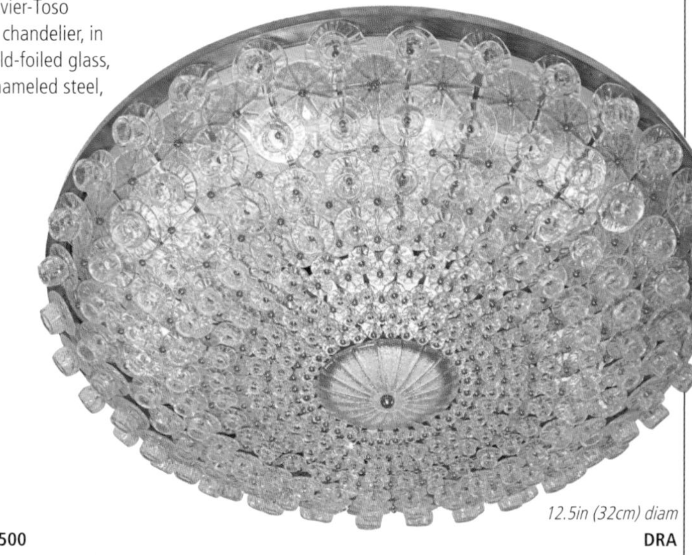

12.5in (32cm) diam

$12,000-13,500 **DRA**

A 1950s Maison Charles table lamp, patinated bronze, brass, two sockets, impressed Charles.

16.5in (42cm) high

$5,250-6,750 **DRA**

A Fornasetti 'Architettura' lamp base, lithographed with an 18thC building, brass mounted on ball feet, unmarked.

19.5in (49cm) high

$900-1,000 **SWO**

A 1950s adjustable floor lamp, designed by Greta Magnusson Grossman and Ralph O. Smith, enameled steel, enameled aluminum, brass, single socket, unmarked.

50.25in (128cm) high

$11,500-12,750 **DRA**

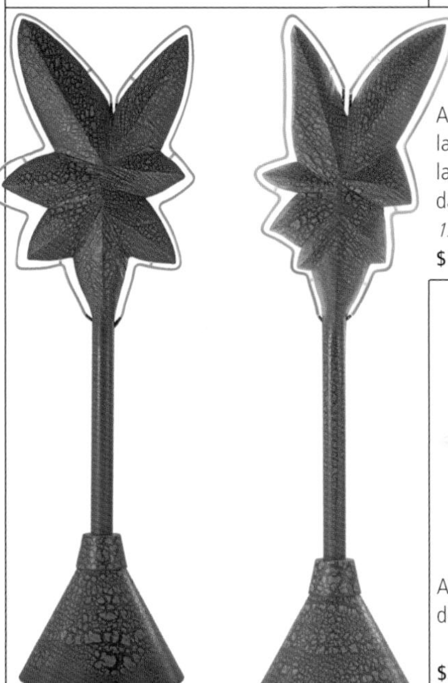

A pair of Wendell Castle large sculptural floor lamps, 'Burning Desire', carved and crackle-lacquered wood, neon tubing, both signed and dated.

1996 *85in (216cm) high*

$19,500-24,000 **DRA**

A Louis Poulsen 'PH5' hanging light pendant, designed by Poul Henningsen, labeled.

20in (50cm) diam

$300-450 **SWO**

A ceiling lamp, designed by Poul Henningsen and Kurt Nörregaard, 'Memory/Centrum', for Louis Poulsen Copenhagen, white enameled aluminum.

This was designed by Kurt Nörregaard based on Poul Henningsen's drawings from the 1960s.

1990 *42.5in (107cm) high*

$4,000-5,250 **QU**

A 200s 'Artichoke' chandelier, designed by Poul Henningsen, for Louis Poulsen Denmark, enameled aluminum, chromed steel, plastic, manufacturer's label.

This is the largest of the artichokes.

body 28in (71.5cm) square

$3,300-4,400 DRA

A Poul Henningsen 'Artichoke' ceiling light, for Louis Poulsen, Copenhagen, chrome-plated metal structure, copper-plated aluminum slats, manufacturer's mark.

1957 29.5in (75cm) high

$5,250-6,000 QU

A Sam Herman glass and chrome metal floor lamp, with twelve irregular glass panels forming the shade signed to one panel.

1971 64.5in (164cm) high

$2,250-3,000 WW

A pair of 1960s Georges Jouve table lamps, glazed ceramic, brass, linen shades, single sockets, signed Jouve with cipher.

bases 12in (30.5cm) high

$12,000-13,500 DRA

A 1950s pair of adjustable floor lamps, designed by Boris Lacroix, brass, enameled steel, vellum, two sockets.

68in (173cm) high

$12,000-13,500 DRA

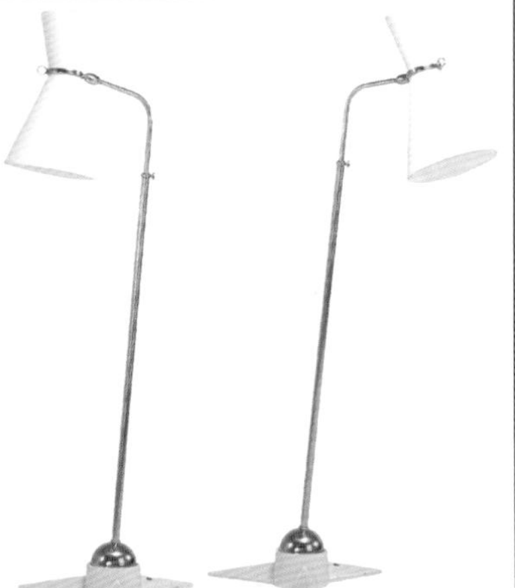

A pair of 1950s adjustable floor lamps, designed by Boris Lacroix, brass, enameled steel, paper shades, two sockets, unmarked.

fully extended 68in (173cm) high

$11,500-12,750 DRA

A pair of Albert Paley candlesticks, Rochester, NY, forged and fabricated blackened steel, signed 'ALBERT PALEY'.

1994 14.25in (36.5cm) high

$10,500-12,000 DRA

An Albert Paley floor lamp, forged and fabricated steel, frosted glass, single socket, signed and dated.

1999 90in (229cm) high

$21,000-24,000 DRA

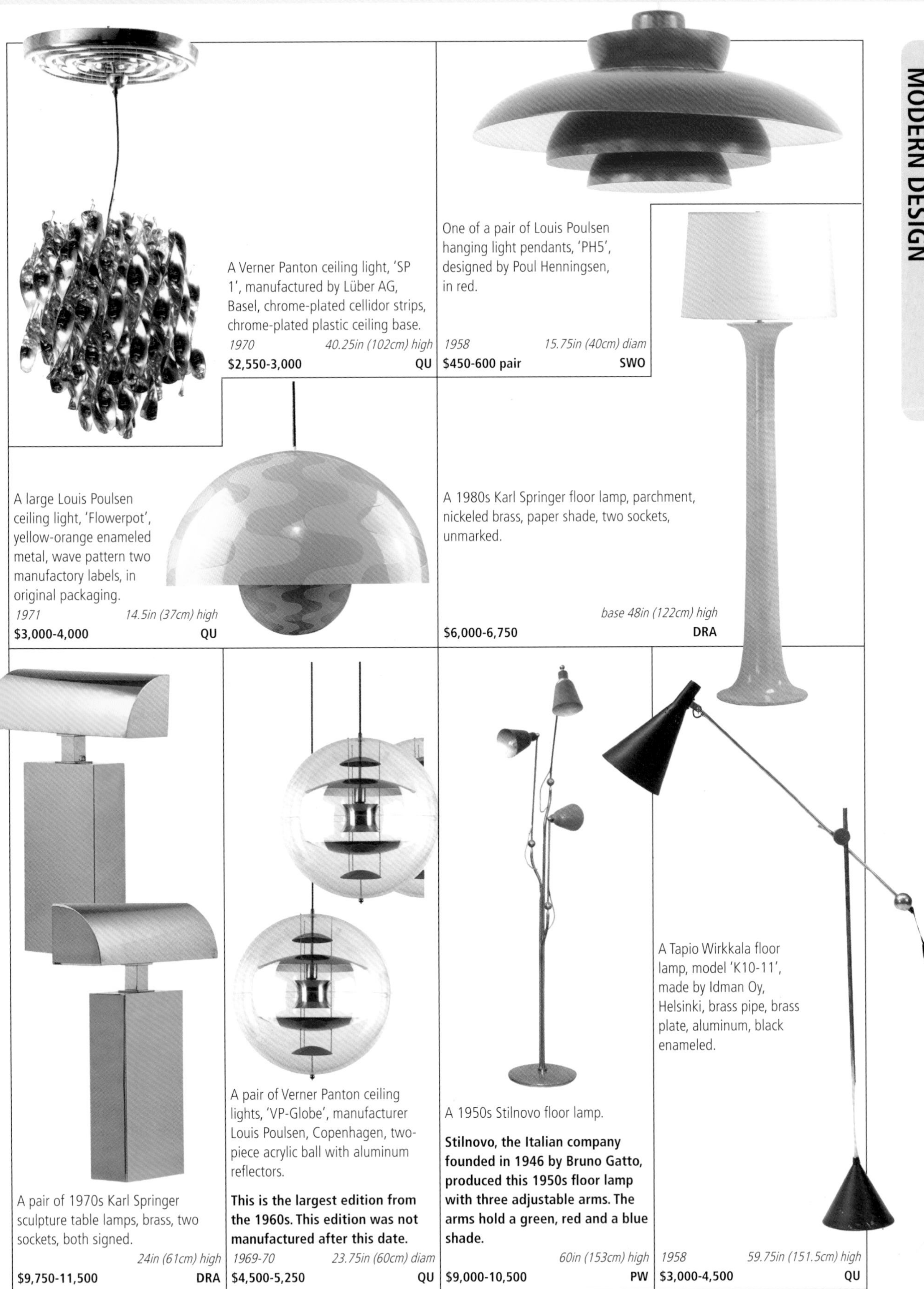

A Verner Panton ceiling light, 'SP 1', manufactured by Lüber AG, Basel, chrome-plated cellidor strips, chrome-plated plastic ceiling base.

1970 *40.25in (102cm) high*

$2,550-3,000 **QU**

One of a pair of Louis Poulsen hanging light pendants, 'PH5', designed by Poul Henningsen, in red.

1958 *15.75in (40cm) diam*

$450-600 pair **SWO**

A large Louis Poulsen ceiling light, 'Flowerpot', yellow-orange enameled metal, wave pattern two manufactory labels, in original packaging.

1971 *14.5in (37cm) high*

$3,000-4,000 **QU**

A 1980s Karl Springer floor lamp, parchment, nickeled brass, paper shade, two sockets, unmarked.

base 48in (122cm) high

$6,000-6,750 **DRA**

A pair of 1970s Karl Springer sculpture table lamps, brass, two sockets, both signed.

24in (61cm) high

$9,750-11,500 **DRA**

A pair of Verner Panton ceiling lights, 'VP-Globe', manufacturer Louis Poulsen, Copenhagen, two-piece acrylic ball with aluminum reflectors.

This is the largest edition from the 1960s. This edition was not manufactured after this date.

1969-70 *23.75in (60cm) diam*

$4,500-5,250 **QU**

A 1950s Stilnovo floor lamp.

Stilnovo, the Italian company founded in 1946 by Bruno Gatto, produced this 1950s floor lamp with three adjustable arms. The arms hold a green, red and a blue shade.

60in (153cm) high

$9,000-10,500 **PW**

A Tapio Wirkkala floor lamp, model 'K10-11', made by Idman Oy, Helsinki, brass pipe, brass plate, aluminum, black enameled.

1958 *59.75in (151.5cm) high*

$3,000-4,500 **QU**

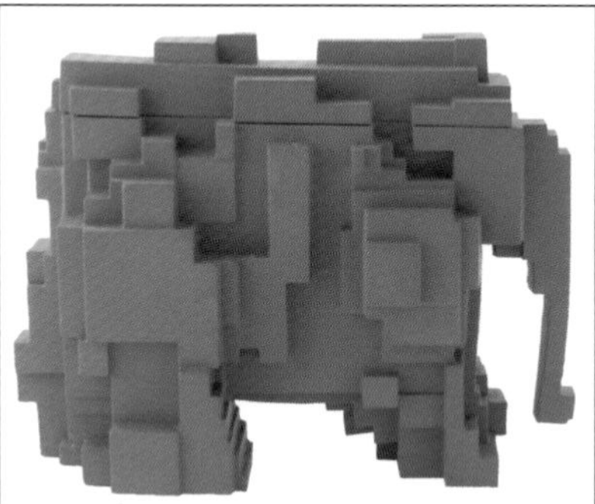

A limited edition molded plastic elephant, designed by Edouardo Paolozzi R.A, for Nairn Floors ltd the geometric case and cover holding advertising pamphlets, signed to the leg, numbered.

1973 *14in (35.5cm) long*

$1,500-2,100 **WW**

A turned vessel, designed by Ed Moulthrop, 'Rare Ash-Leaf Maple', chopmark, signed 'MOULTHROP RARE ASHLEAF MAPLE ACER NEGUNDO 306830'.

9.5in (24.5cm) high

$11,500-12,750 **DRA**

An important 1960s Paul Evans for Paul Evans Studios steel patchwork sculpture, welded and polychromed steel, painted wood, unmarked.

78in (198.5cm) high

$45,000-52,500 **DRA**

ESSENTIAL REFERENCE - PETER VOULKOS

A total of nine bronzes belonging to two editions were cast from the original ceramic Stack pot created in 1999. While celebrated as one of the most important pioneers of studio ceramics in the 21stC, Peter Voulkos also cast a number of his abstract impressionist pots in bronze. The present lot, 'Anasazi S13', belongs to the second, posthumous edition from a group of nine bronzes cast under the direction of Piero Mussi of the Artworks Foundry in Berkeley, CA. Mussi has also worked with artists such as Ruth Asawa, Jun Kaneko.

A monumental Peter Voulkos patinated bronze stack pot, 'Anasazi S13', Berkeley, CA, number 2 from an edition of 5, signed and dated 'VOULKOS 99', numbered '2/5' and stamped 'VOULKOS FAMILY TRUST'.

74in (188cm) high

$90,000-105,000 **DRA**

A 1960s Harry Bertoia suspended sound gong, Pennsylvania, hammered bronze, steel wire.

26in (66cm) long

$27,000-30,000 **DRA**

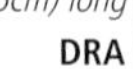

A James Bearden patinated steel sculpture, 'Passage', Voids Series, Des Moines, IA, signed B.

2013 *68in (173cm) high*

$4,500-6,000 **DRA**

A rare Guanacastle double sculpture, designed by Edwin Scheier, Mexico, signed and dated.

1972 *48in (122cm) high*

$13,500-16,500 **DRA**

A Fater Mel enameled steel outdoor sculpture, signed 'Mel'.

1989 *65in (165cm) high*

$5,250-6,750 **DRA**

A set of Stelton Cylinda Line stainless steel tablewares, designed by Arne Jacobsen & Magnus Stephensen, a fondue set on a teak lazy susan.

$300-450 **SWO**

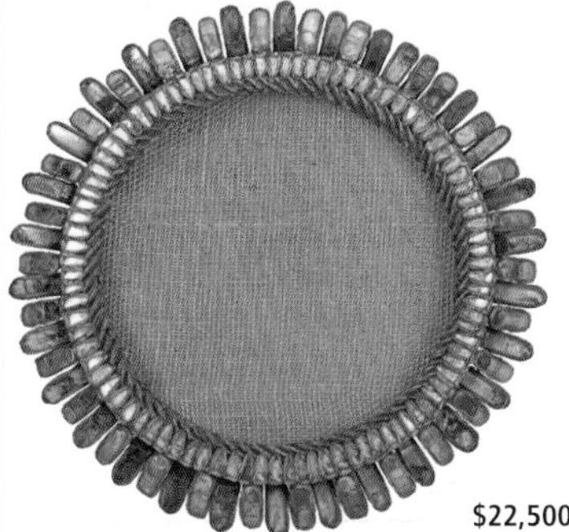

A 1960s Line Vautrin wall-hanging mirror frame, silver leaf, glass, talosel, etched Line Vautrin.

11in (28cm) diam

$22,500-30,000 **DRA**

A 1960s fourteen-piece enamel on steel composition, designed by Stefan Knapp, unmarked.

This was probably from the facade decoration at Alexander's Department Store, New York.

84in (213.5cm) long

$13,500-18,000 **DRA**

ESSENTIAL REFERENCE - LINO SABATTINI

Lino Sabattini, a brilliant and entirely self-taught Italian designer, was a leading designer of cutlery and tableware. His designs are beautiful, elegant, and distinguished by consummate craftsmanship. It was thanks to Gio Ponti, who raved about Lino Sabattini's designs, that Sabattini became known to a wide following. In 1956 Gio Ponti presented Lino Sabattini's metal objects in 'Domus'. This visual presentation was followed that same year by an exhibition Gio Poni organized for Lino Sabattini in Paris. Lino Sabattini became director of design at the prestigious Christofle Orfèvrerie, where he created metalware notable for abstract organic and elegant between 1956 and 1963. During that period, Lino Sabattini also designed metal, glass, and ceramic objects for Rosenthal, Nava, and Zani&Zani. In Bregnano, south of Como, Lino Sabattini established Argenteria Sabattini (1964) to execute his designs in limited editions.

A Christofle Gallia electroplated metal tea set, the design attributed to Lino Sabattini.

teapot 7.5in (19cm) wide

$975-1,150 **WW**

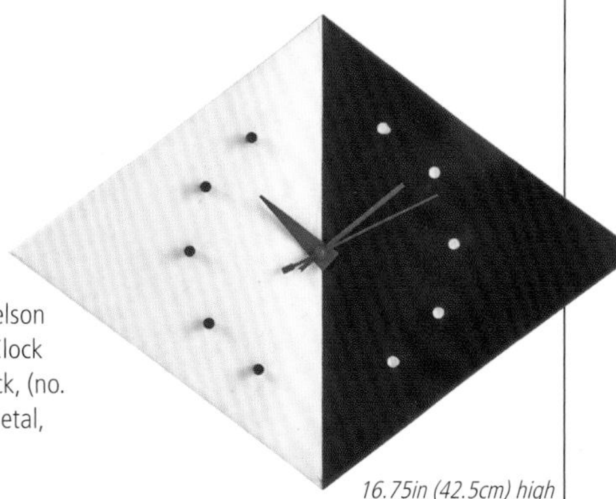

A 1950s George Nelson for Howard Miller Clock Company 'Kite' clock, (no. 2201), enameled metal, wood, decal label.

16.75in (42.5cm) high

$2,000-2,400 **DRA**

A Roy Lichtenstein for Multiples Inc. pin, 'Modern Head', with engraved signature, stamped 'copyright 1968 ROY LICHTENSTEIN FOR MULTIPLES INC'.

One of a limited edition designed by Lichtenstein for the Philadelphia Pop Art Show in 1968.

1968 *3in (8cm) high*

$6,000-6,750 **DRA**

A pair of rare gear-shaped bookends, designed by Albert Drexler Jacobson for Cowan Cincinnati, OH, both with circular 'COWAN RG stamp'.

1929 *4.75in (12cm) high*

$8,250-9,750 **DRA**

'FOLIES-BERGÈRE/Loie Fuller', designed by Jules Chéret (1836-1932), printed by Chaix, Paris.
1897 *49in (124cm) high*
$3,000-4,000 **SWA**

'LITHOGRAPHIES ORIGINALES', designed by Georges de Feure (1868-1943).
1896 *24in (63cm) high*
$3,000-4,000 **SWA**

'MELE/MODE NOVITÀ', designed by Leopoldo Metlicovitz (1868-1944), printed by G. Ricordi & C., Milan.
1910 *79in (202cm) high*
$20,000-30,000 **SWA**

'SARAH BERNHARDT/AMERICAN TOUR', designed by Aphonse Mucha, (1860-1939), printed by The Strobridge Lith, Co, Cincinnati.
1896 *78in (200cm) high*
$8,000-10,000 **SWA**

ESSENTIAL REFERENCE - ALFRED LEETE

This rare and iconic poster is one of only four known to exist. There are examples in the Imperial War Museum, State Library of Victoria Melbourne and the Robert Opie Collection. Last year it was wrongly reported in the press that the poster's existence was an urban myth and it was never used as a recruiting poster but this was not the case. Proof of the poster being displayed publicly in 1914 has now come to light in two photographs, one showing the poster on a hoarding with others published by the Parliamentary Recruiting Committee (PRC) at Liverpool Station on 15 December 1914 and the other posted on pillars of Chester's Town Hall. It would be reasonable to say that the rarity of this poster could be put down to the numbers printed being far less than other PRC issued posters, of which there was a surplus available for sale after the war. This poster is pure ephemera as it would appear to have been torn down from display either in disgust or as a future collectors item.

'BRITONS (Kitchener) WANTS YOU JOIN YOUR COUNTRY'S ARMY! GOD SAVE THE KING', designed by Alfred Leete (1882-1933), printed by the Victoria House Printing Company Co. Ltd., original recruiting poster.
1914 *29.75in (75.5cm) high*
$40,000-45,000 **ON**

'REMEMBER SCARBOROUGH! ENLIST NOW', designed by Edith Kemp-Welch (1870-1941), printed by David Allen, original Parliamentary Recruiting Committee poster, no.41., mounted on linen.

Edith Kemp-Welch was the less known older sister of Lucy and was a painter of portraiture and landscapes.
1915 *59in (150cm) high*
$1,600-2,000 **ON**

'Daddy, what did YOU do in the Great War?', designed by Savile Lumley (d1949), printed by Johnson Riddle & Co Ltd, original Parliamentary Recruiting Committee poster, no.79.

The title of this now-famous poster was one of the most memorable among the World War 1 posters. The idea for this design came to the owner of the printing company Johnson Riddle when he wondered what the outcome of not volunteering might be after the war; following the poster's publication he volunteered. The poster, although popular, was later criticised on the grounds of distortion and exploitation.
1915 *30in (76cm) high*
$2,000-2,500 **ON**

ESSENTIAL REFERENCE - KEEP CALM AND CARRY ON

This poster has now become one of the most famous propaganda icons of World War 2, and the irony is that the poster was never displayed in public. In September 1939 Keep Calm and two other letterpress posters had been put into production, Freedom is in Peril... and Your Courage..., were displayed in public places but the third, now recognized the world over with its unforgettable slogan, was not. It is now widely accepted that it was held back in anticipation of an invasion of Britain by the enemy or a severe air raid. The 'Phoney War' being the period September 1939 to May 1940 proved to be largely uneventful for the Home Front and the poster was never used. A change in the attitude to the wording probably contributed to the poster never being used. Although many thousands in several sizes were printed, only a few examples have appeared. This example is in the larger double crown format of which according to HMSO records 496,500 were printed.

'KEEP CALM AND CARRY ON', original WW2 poster, mounted on linen, restored tear.
1939 *29.5in (75cm) high*
$27,000-30,000 **ON**

'MARSEILLE PORTE DE L'AFRIQUE DU NORD', designed by Roger Broders (1883-1953), printed by Lucien Serre & Cie., Paris., minor creases and abrasions in margins and image, minor repaired tears at edges.

This geometrically appealing image manages to convey the hustle and bustle of the harbor, yet creates a stylized order out of the chaos.

1929 *39.5in (100cm) high*

$6,500-7,500 SWA

'VICHY/COMITÉ DES FÊTES', designed by Roger Broders (1883-1953), printed by Lucien Serre & Cie., Paris., creases, abrasions and restoration in margins and image, pin holes in corners.

One of Broders' most evocative posters, visually encapsulating the decadence and luxury of the Jazz Era.

c1928 *41.25in (104cm) high*

$6,000-8,000 SWA

'TRIPLEX', designed by Adolphe Mouron Cassandre (1901-68), printed by Alliance Graphique, Paris.

1931 *47in (119cm) high*

$25,000-30,000 SWA

'NEW STATENDAM/ HOLLAND-AMERICA LINE', designed by Adolphe Mouron Cassandre (1901-68), printed by Nijgh & Van Dittmar, Rotte.

1928 *40in (102cm) high*

$13,000-18,000 SWA

'CIRCUITO DEL LAGO DI GARDA', designed by Arduino Colato (1880-1954), printed by Barabino & Graeve, Genova, minor repaired tears and restoration.

In this Futurist-inspired landscape, a tour bus emerges from a tunnel like a bullet into a landscape of carefully graded colors and contrasting angles. Colato was a painter who designed only this one poster.

1937 *39.25in (100cm) high*

$5,000-6,000 SWA

'IN 1939/THE NEW YORK WORLD'S FAIR', designed by Nembhard N. Culin (1908-90).

1937 *30in (76cm) high*

$6,000-7,000 SWA

'EXACTITUDE', designed by Pierre Fix-Masseau (1905-94), printed by Edita, Paris.

1932 *39in (99cm) high*

$12,000-18,000 SWA

'DUNCAN YOYO', designed by Raymond Gid (1905-2000), printed by Bedos & Cie, Paris.

1930. *31in (79cm) high*

$6,500-7,500 SWA

'WIRELESS WAR', designed by Pat Keely (died 1970), printed by Haycock Press, original GPO poster PRD 323.

1943 *36.25in (92cm) wide*

$1,400-1,800 **ON**

'IMPERIAL AIRWAYS', designed by Harold McCready, printed by John Horn Limited, London & Glasgow, repaired tear through bottom edge into image.

Pictured at London's Croydon Airport is the Armstrong Whitworth Argosy Mk I, The City of Wellington, which operated for Imperial Airways between 1926 and 1935 on the London to Paris route. Only three of these particular three-engine aircraft were ever constructed.

1929 *30in (76cm) high*

$6,000-7,000 **SWA**

'CUNARD/WHITE STAR', with Queen Mary and Queen Elizabeth, designed by A. Roquin, printed by Publimp-Nadal, Paris, crease affecting image.

To announce the launch of the Cunard White Star line's service between New York and Cherbourg, Roquin visually equated two behemoths of the sea with the ultimate symbol of the Art Deco era, the Chrysler Building.

c1938 *40in (101.5cm) high*

$4,000-5,000 **SWA**

'KASSNER/ILLUSIONEN', unknown designer, printed by Adolph Friedlander, Hamburg.

c1930 *81in (205cm) high*

$2,000-3,000 **SWA**

'RAVEL', designed by Lucien Pillot (1882-1973), printed by Fournier, Besancon.

c1925 *62in (157cm) high*

$6,000-7,000 **SWA**

'IN 2 DAYS TO NORTH AMERICA!/ DEUTSCHE ZEPPELIN-REEDEREI', designed by Jupp Wiertz (1881-1939), printed by Eschebach & Schaefer, Leipzig, repaired tears and restorations.

The Hindenburg Zeppelin (LZ-129) pictured soaring over the skyscrapers of Manhattan. A gap in the cloudy sky illuminates the spire of the Empire State Building. The Hindenburg's illustrious career was terminated on May 6, 1937, when she burst into flames upon landing in Lakehurst, New Jersey.

1936 *33in (84cm) high*

$16,000-20,000 **SWA**

'Royal Scot leaves Euston', railway lithograph poster, designed by Norman Wilkinson R.A. (1878-1971), printed for L.M.S. by McCorquodale & Co., Ltd, London and Glasgow.

c1930 *45.5in (115cm) wide*

$4,000-5,000 **FLD**

'39 ¾ HOURS TO CHICAGO!/ SOUTHERN PACIFIC', unknown designer, minor repaired tears and restoration.

1936 *23in (58.5cm) high*

$5,000-6,000 **SWA**

'ZERMATT', designed by Emil Cardinaux, printed by J.E. Wolfensberger, Zurich, minor restoration.

The Matterhorn has appeared in countless posters. Cardinaux's image of the dawn-drenched mountain, revolutionary in its design, smashed the old mold.

1908 *40.5in (103cm) high*
$10,000-14,000 **SWA**

'Sports Invernali nel - L'ALTA AUSTRIA', designed by Franz Lenhart (1898-1992), printed by Steyrermuhl Wien.

c1937 *37.5in (95cm) high*
$3,500-4,500 **ON**

'Winter Sports in Italy', designed by Franz Lenhart (1898-1992), printed by B.V. Levi, Cortina.

c1930 *39.25in (99cm) high*
$4,000-5,000 **SWA**

'FLEXIBLE FLYER/ALEX TAYLOR & Co., Inc', designed by Sascha Maurer (1897-1961), minor restoration in margins and image.

c1935 *37in (94cm) high*
$3,500-4,500 **SWA**

'VILLARS-BRETAYE', designed by René Michaud, printed by Simplon, Lausanne, repaired tears in margins, repaired pin holes in corners.

1920 *39in (100cm) high*
$5,000-6,000 **SWA**

'NEWQUAY/CORNWALL'S FINEST ATLANTIC RESORT', designed by Bruce Angrave (1914-83), printed by Dangerfield, London, some restoration.

1932. *49in (126cm) wide*
$5,000-6,000 **SWA**

'CATTOLICA/adriatico', designed by Achille Dal Lago (1910-81), printed by Longo & Zoppelli, Treviso, repaired tears and staining at edges.

1937 *39.5in (100cm) high*
$4,000-6,000 **SWA**

'Bananas', designed by E. Mcknight Kauffer (1890-1954), printed by Haycock Cadle & Graham Ltd, original poster No 5 issued by the Empire Marketing Board.

1926 *60in (152cm) wide*
$2,000-2,500 **ON**

'THE YORKSHIRE COAST', designed by Laura Knight (1877-1970), printed by John Waddington, London, minor repaired tears at edges and in image.

A pioneering female artist, Laura Knight became the first woman elected into the Royal Academy in 1936. From humble origins, she focused much of her art on disenfranchised groups, such as gypsies and performers. She designed seven posters for London Transport and this for the LNER.

1929 *49in (124.5cm) wide*
$5,000-6,000 **SWA**

'SOUTHPORT/FOR A HOLIDAY IN WINTERTIME', designed by Fortunino Matania (1881-1963), printed by Waterlow & Sons Ltd., London, minor restoration.

An elegant assemblage of theatre-goers bedecked with minks, monocles and top hats, are exiting Southport's Garrick Theatre into a rainy evening. The theatre, considered an Art Deco masterpiece, was designed by a local architect, George Tonge. It opened a week before Christmas in 1932.

1925 *49.75in (126.5cm) wide*
$5,000-7,000 **SWA**

'MOSTRA DEL CICLO E DELL AUTOMOBILE/MILANO', designed by Leopoldo Metlicovitz (1868-1944), printed by G. Ricordi, Milan.

1907 *78in (199cm) high*
$30,000-40,000 **SWA**

'Canadian Pacific Happy Cruises', designed by Tom Purvis (1888-1959), repaired tears, minor restoration.

Purvis went on to design several posters for Canadian Pacific. His designs are all notable for their simple, powerful graphics.

1937 *40in (101cm) high*
$3,500-4,500 **SWA**

'SUNNY RHYL', designed by Septimus Edwin Scott (1879-1965), printed by Jordison & Co Ltd, London, minor repaired tears and restoration.

1927 *50in (127cm) wide*
$4,500-5,500 **SWA**

'ST. IVES THE CORNISH RIVIERA', designed by Borlase Smart (1881-1947), original poster printed for the Great Western Railway by Jarrold, mounted on linen.

c1930 *50in (127cm) wide*
$2,000-2,500 **ON**

'KLOSTERS', designed by Eduard Stiefel (1875-1967), Gebr. Fretz, Zurich, repaired tear and overpainting in upper right corner.

c1925 *40in (101cm) high*
$6,500-7,500 **SWA**

'SPORT ON THE L.M.S.', yachting lithograph poster, designed by Norman Wilkinson R.A. (1878-1971), printed for L.M.S. by McCorquodale & Co., Ltd, London and Glasgow.

c1924 *43.75in (111cm) wide*
$3,000-4,000 **FLD**

Judith Picks

One of my favorite places! This bright, abstract, kaleidoscopic view of Times Square, with its billboards, lights, traffic, energy and excitement depicted in Day-Glo, electric colors which further convey the visual splendor of the city. Originally issued in 1956, the poster featured a detailed image of a TWA Constellation. The image was so popular that the airline reused it when it fully entered the Jet Age, changing the image to feature the silhouette of a jet plane. A year after it was first issued, a copy of this poster was acquired by the Museum of Modern Art for their permanent collection.

'FLY TWA/NEW YORK', designed by David Klein (1918-2005).

c1960 *40in (102cm) high*
$7,500-8,500 **SWA**

ESSENTIAL REFERENCE - AUSTRALIA

The Sydney Harbour Bridge was constructed between 1923 and 1932. Influenced by the design of New York City's Hellgate Bridge, it is the world's tallest steel-arch bridge and among the world's top ten longest-spanning arch bridges. With eight lanes, it is also one of the widest. Although the Great Depression struck in the middle of construction, the building continued, employing over a thousand men in the process. Not only was it an economic lifeline for the city at the time, but perhaps more importantly, it served as a rising beacon of hope for the city and as a national showpiece for the world. The bridge was the greatest engineering challenge of its day anywhere on earth. Nothing like it had ever been attempted. It not only altered the life of a city forever, it became a symbol of a bold, young nation and a changing world.

'Still building - AUSTRALIA', designed by Percy Trompf (1902-1964), printed by Moore-Young, Melbourne, some restoration.

1930 *49.25in (125cm) high*

$5,500-6,500 **SWA**

'TRAVEL/AIR • LAND • SEA/ Book through BURNS, PHILP & CO LTD', designed by Walter Lacy Jardine (1884-1970), printed by H & G Pty Ltd, some repairs.

Burns, Philp & Co. was a trading company that used their own ships to keep their stores supplied, and later also delivered mail and carried passengers.

c1930 *39.25in (99cm) high*

$6,500-7,500 **SWA**

'AUSTRALIA', designed by Eileen Mayo (1906-94), printed by McLaren & Co. Pty. Ltd., Melbourne.

British-born Mayo moved to Australia in 1953 and designed a series of posters highlighting some of the continent's wildlife. With its typography influenced by Aboriginal art, this is a notable Australian travel poster.

1957 *39.5in (100cm) high*

$3,500-4,500 **SWA**

'AUSTRALIA/GREAT BARRIER CORAL REEF', designed by James Northfield (1888-1973), printed by J.E. Hackett, Melbourne, minor tears at edges.

c1935 *39.75in (101cm) high*

$4,500-5,500 **SWA**

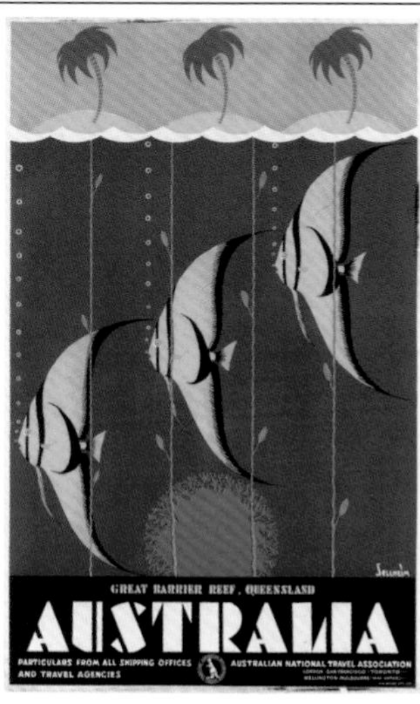

'GREAT BARRIER REEF, QUEENSLAND/ AUSTRALIA', designed by Gert Sellheim (1901-70), printed by F.W. Niven Pty. Ltd., Melbourne, repaired tears and some overpainting.

1937 *39.75in (101cm) high*

$6,000-7,000 **SWA**

'ENGLAND TO AUSTRALIA/WORLDS GREATEST AIR RACE', designed by Percy Trompf (1902-64), printed by Moore-Young, Melbourne.

1934 *40in (101cm) high*

$4,000-5,000 **SWA**

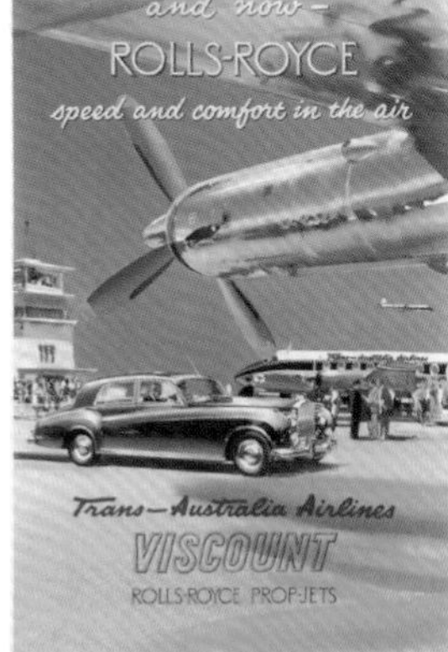

'and now - ROLLS-ROYCE/speed and comfort in the air/ Trans-Australia Airlines', designed by Frank Wootton (1914-1998), restored losses and overpainting in margins and image.

This poster originally appeared advertising British European Airways, bearing the slogan, 'Fly the Rolls-Royce way to London.' Trans-Australia Airlines was formed in 1946 and merged with Qantas in 1992. They began operating the Vickers Viscount in 1954.

c1954 *40in (101cm) high*

$5,500-6,500 **SWA**

Every antique illustrated in Miller's Antiques has a letter code which identifies the dealer or auction house that sold it. The list below is a key to these codes. In the list, auction houses are shown by the letter A and dealers by the letter D. Inclusion in this book in no way constitutes or implies a contract or a binding offer on the part of any of our contributors to supply or sell the goods illustrated, or similar items, at the prices stated.

A&G Ⓐ
ANDERSON & GARLAND
www.andersonandgarland.com

ADA Ⓐ
ADAMS
www.adams.ie

AH & HT Ⓐ
HARTLEY'S
www.andrewhartleyfinearts.co.uk

APAR Ⓐ
ADAM PARTRIDGE AUCTIONEERS & VALUERS
www.adampartridge.co.uk

AS&S Ⓐ
ANDREW SMITH & SON
www.andrewsmithandson.com

ATQ Ⓐ
ANTIQUORUM
www.antiquorum.com

BARB Ⓐ
BARBERS FINE ART
Tel: +44 (0)1483 728939

BC2AD Ⓓ
BCIIAD
www.bc2ad.co.uk

BE & H&L Ⓐ
BEARNES, HAMPTON & LITTLEWOOD
www.bearnes.co.uk

BEJ Ⓓ
BÉBÉS ET JOUETS
Tel: 0044 131 3325650
Email: bebesetjouets@tiscali.co.uk

BELL Ⓐ
BELLMANS
www.bellmans.co.uk

BER Ⓐ
BERTOIA AUCTIONS
www.bertoiaauctions.com

BIG Ⓐ
BIGWOOD FINE ART AUCTIONEERS
www.bigwoodauctioneers.com

BLO Ⓐ
DREWEATTS & BLOOMSBURY
www.bloomsburyauctions.com

BON Ⓐ
BONHAMS
www.bonhams.com

BRI Ⓐ
BRIGHTWELLS
www.brightwells.com

BW Ⓐ
BIDDLE & WEBB
www.biddleandwebb.co.uk

CAN Ⓐ
THE CANTERBURY AUCTION GALLERIES
www.thecanterburyauctiongalleries.com

CAPE Ⓐ
CAPES DUNN & CO.
www.capesdunn.com

CENC Ⓓ
CENTRAL COLLECTABLES
www.centralcollectables.com

CHEF Ⓐ
CHEFFINS
www.cheffins.co.uk

CHOR Ⓐ
CHORLEY'S
www.simonchorley.com

CHT Ⓐ
CHARTERHOUSE
www.charterhouse-auctions.co.uk

CLAR Ⓐ
CLARS AUCTION GALLERY
www.clars.com

CLV Ⓐ
CLEVEDON SALEROOMS
www.clevedon-salerooms.com

CM Ⓐ
CHARLES MILLER
www.charlesmillerltd.com

COT Ⓐ
COTTEES AUCTIONS
www.cottees.co.uk

CR Ⓐ
CHARLES ROSS
www.charles-ross.co.uk

CRIS Ⓓ
CRISTOBAL
www.cristobal.co.uk

CZER Ⓐ
CZERNY'S INTERNATIONAL AUCTION HOUSE
www.czernys.com

D&H Ⓐ
DOE AND HOPE
www.doeandhope.com

DA&H Ⓐ
DEE, ATKINSON & HARRISON
www.dahauctions.com

DEN Ⓐ
DENHAMS
www.denhams.com

DMC Ⓐ
DUMOUCHELLES ART GALLERY
www.dumouchelle.com

DN Ⓐ
DREWEATTS & BLOOMSBURY
www.dnfa.com/donnington

DOR Ⓐ
DOROTHEUM
www.dorotheum.com

DOY Ⓐ
DOYLE NEW YORK
www.doylenewyork.com

DR Ⓐ
DEREK ROBERTS ANTIQUES
www.qualityantiqueclocks.com

DRA Ⓐ
RAGO ARTS
www.ragoarts.com

DS Ⓐ
DUNBAR SLOANE
www.dunbarsloane.co.nz

DURR Ⓐ
DURRANTS
www.durrants.com

DUK Ⓐ
DUKE'S
www.dukes-auctions.com

DW Ⓐ
DOMINIC WINTER
www.dominic-winter.co.uk

ECGW Ⓐ
EWBANK CLARKE GAMMON WELLERS
www.ewbankauctions.co.uk

FELL Ⓐ
FELLOWS AUCTIONEERS
www.fellows.co.uk

FIS Ⓐ
AUKTIONHAUS DR FISCHER
www.auctions-fischer.de

FLD Ⓐ
FIELDINGS AUCTIONEERS
www.fieldingsauctioneers.co.uk

FOM Ⓐ
FONSIE MEALY'S
www.fonsiemealy.ie

FRE Ⓐ
FREEMAN'S
www.freemansauction.com

G&M Ⓐ
GORNY & MOSCH
www.gmcoinart.de

GBA Ⓐ
GRAHAM BUDD AUCTIONS
www.grahambuddauctions.co.uk

GHOU Ⓐ
GARDINER HOULGATE
www.gardinerhoulgate.co.uk

GORL Ⓐ
GORRINGES
www.gorringes.co.uk

GTH Ⓐ
GREENSLADE TAYLOR HUNT
www.gth.net

H&C Ⓐ
HISTORICAL & COLLECTABLE
www.historicalandcollectable.com

H&D Ⓐ
HENRY ADAMS AUCTIONEERS
www.henryadams.co.uk/auctions

HALL Ⓐ
HALLS
www.hallsestateagents.co.uk/fine-art

HAN Ⓐ
HANSONS AUCTIONEERS
www.hansonsauctioneers.co.uk

HARR Ⓐ
HARRISON AUCTIONS
www.jubileeauctions.com

HICK Ⓓ
HICKMET FINE ART
www.hickmet.com

HPA Ⓐ
HAMPSTEAD AUCTIONS
www.hampsteadauctions.co.uk

HT Ⓐ
HARTLEY'S
www.hartley-antiques.com

HW Ⓐ
HOLLOWAY'S
www.hollowaysauctioneers.co.uk

IMC Ⓐ
I M CHAIT
www.chait.com

J&H Ⓐ
JACOBS & HUNT
www.jacobsandhunt.com

J&J Ⓐ
JONES & JACOB
www.jonesandjacob.com

JACK Ⓐ
JACKSON'S
www.jacksonsauction.com

JDJ Ⓐ
JAMES D JULIA INC
www.juliaauctions.com

JN Ⓐ
JOHN NICHOLSONS
www.johnnicholsons.com

JON Ⓐ
ROGERS JONES
www.rogersjones.co.uk

JPOT Ⓓ
JONATHAN POTTER LTD.
www.jpmaps.co.uk

KAU Ⓐ
AUKTIONSHAUS KAUPP
www.kaupp.de

KEY Ⓐ
KEYS
www.keysauctions.co.uk

L&T Ⓐ
LYON & TURNBULL
www.lyonandturnbull.comk

LA Ⓐ
DAVID LAY FRICS
www.davidlay.co.uk

LAW Ⓐ
LAWRENCE'S FINE ART AUCTIONEERS
www.lawrences.co.uk

LHA Ⓐ
LESLIE HINDMAN AUCTIONEERS
www.lesliehindman.com

LOCK Ⓐ
LOCKDALES
www.lockdales.com

LOW Ⓐ
LOWESTOFT PORCELAIN AUCTIONS
www.lowestoftchina.co.uk

LSK Ⓐ
LACY SCOTT & KNIGHT
www.lsk.co.uk

M&D & MDM Ⓐ
M&D MOIR
www.manddmoir.co.uk

M&K Ⓐ
MELLORS & KIRK
www.mellorsandkirk.co.uk

MAB Ⓐ
MATTHEW BARTON LTD.
www.matthewbartonltd.com

MAI Ⓐ
MOORE ALLEN & INNOCENT
www.mooreallen.co.uk

MAR Ⓐ
FRANK MARSHALL & CO.
www.frankmarshall.co.uk

MART Ⓐ
MARTEL MAIDES LTD.
www.martelmaidesauctions.com

MAX Ⓐ
MAXWELLS
www.maxwells-auctioneers.co.uk

MBA Ⓐ
MULBERRY BANK AUCTIONS
www.mulberrybankauctions.com

MEA Ⓐ
MEALY'S
www.mealys.com

MELL Ⓐ
NICHOLAS MELLORS AUCTIONEERS
www.nicholasmellorsauctioneers.com

MIC Ⓐ
MICHAAN'S
www.michaans.com

MITC Ⓐ
MITCHELLS ANTIQUES & FINE ART
www.mitchellsantiques.co.uk

MM Ⓐ
MULLOCK'S
www.mullocksauctions.co.uk

MOR Ⓐ
MORPHETS
www.morphets.co.uk

MTZ Ⓐ
METZ AUKTION
www.metz-auktion.de

NAG Ⓐ
NAGEL
www.antiques.cl/nagel_antiques

ON Ⓐ
ONSLOWS
www.onslows.co.uk

PBE Ⓐ
PAUL BEIGHTON AUCTIONEERS
www.pbauctioneers.co.uk

PFR Ⓐ
PETER FRANCIS
www.peterfrancis.co.uk

POOK Ⓐ
POOK & POOK
www.pookandpook.com

PSA Ⓐ
POTTERIES AUCTIONS
www.potteriesauctions.com

PUR Ⓐ
PURITAN VALUES
www.puritanvalues.co.uk

PW Ⓐ
PETER WILSON FINE ART AUCTIONEERS
www.peterwilson.co.uk

QU Ⓐ
QUITTENBAUM
www.quittenbaum.dem

REEM Ⓐ
REEMAN DANSIE
www.reemandansie.com

RGA Ⓓ
RICHARD GARDNER ANTIQUES
www.richardgardnerantiques.co.uk

ROK Ⓐ
ROBERTSONS OF KINBUCK
www.robauctions-dunblane.co.uk

ROS Ⓐ
ROSEBERY'S
www.roseberys.co.uk

ROW Ⓐ
ROWLEY'S
www.rowleyfineart.com

RTC Ⓐ
RITCHIES
www.ritchies.com

RW Ⓐ
RICHARD WINTERTON AUCTIONEERS
www.richardwinterton.co.uk

SAS Ⓐ
SPECIAL AUCTION SERVICES
www.specialauctionservices.com

SCA Ⓓ
SCARAB ANTIQUES
www.scarabantiques.com

SHAP Ⓐ
SHAPES
www.shapesauctioneers.co.uk

SK Ⓐ
SKINNER INC.
www.skinnerinc.com

SOTH Ⓐ
SOTHEBY'S NEW YORK
www.sothebys.com

SPL Ⓐ
SUMMERS PLACE AUCTIONS
www.summersplaceauctions.com

STA Ⓐ
STAIR GALLERIES
www.stairgalleries.com

SWA Ⓐ
SWANN GALLERIES
www.swanngalleries.com

SWO Ⓐ
SWORDERS
www.sworder.co.uk

T&F Ⓐ
TAYLER & FLETCHER
www.taylerandfletcher.co.uk

TARQ Ⓐ
TARQUIN BILGEN WORKS OF ART
www.tarquinbilgen.com

TBW Ⓓ
TEDDY BEARS OF WITNEY
www.teddybears.co.uk

TCAL Ⓐ
THOMAS DEL MAR LTD.
www.thomasdelmar.com

TEN Ⓐ
TENNANTS
www.tennants.co.uk

THE Ⓐ
THERIAULT'S
www.theriaults.com

TOV Ⓐ
TOOVEY'S
www.tooveys.com

TRI Ⓐ
TRING MARKET AUCTIONS
www.tringmarketauctions.co.uk

VEC Ⓐ
VECTIS AUCTIONS
www.vectis.co.uk

W&W Ⓐ
WALLIS & WALLIS
www.wallisandwallis.co.uk

WAD Ⓐ
WADDINGTON'S
www.waddingtons.ca

WES Ⓐ
WESCHLER'S
www.weschlers.com

WHP Ⓐ
W & H PEACOCK
www.peacockauction.co.uk

WHT Ⓐ
WHITE'S AUCTIONS
www.whitesauctions.com

WOT Ⓐ
WOTTON AUCTION ROOMS
www.wottonauctionrooms.co.uk

WW Ⓐ
WOOLLEY & WALLIS
www.woolleyandwallis.co.uk

This is a list of auctioneers that conduct regular sales. Auction houses that would like to be included in the next edition should contact us at info@millers.uk.com.

ALABAMA
Flomaton Antique Auction
www.flomatonantiqueauction.com

Vintage Auctions
Tel: 205 429 2457

ARIZONA
Dan May & Associates
Tel: 480 941 4200

Old World Mail Auctions
www.oldworldauctions.com

ARKANSAS
Hanna-Whysel Auctioneers
Tel: 501 855 9600

Ponders Auctions
www.pondersauctions.com

CALIFORNIA
Bonhams & Butterfields
www.bonhams.com

I M Chait Gallery
www.chait.com

Cuschieri's Auctioneers & Appraisers
Tel: 650 556 1793

eBay, Inc.
www.ebay.com

H R. Harmer
Tel: 714.389.9178

Michaan's
www.michaans.com

San Rafael Auction Gallery
www.sanrafaelauction.com

L H Selman Ltd.
www.paperweight.com

Slawinski Auction Co.
www.slawinski.com

Sotheby's
www.sothebys.com

NORTH CAROLINA
Robert S Brunk Auction Services Inc.
www.brunkauctions.com

Raynors' Historical Collectible Auctions
www.hcaauctions.com

SOUTH CAROLINA
Charlton Hall Galleries Inc.
www.charltonhallauctions.com

COLORADO
Pacific Auction
www.pacificauction.com

Pettigrew Auction Company
Tel: 719 633 7963

Priddy's Auction Galleries
Tel: 800 380 4411

Stanley & Co.
Tel: 303 355 0506

CONNECTICUT
Braswell Galleries
www.braswellgalleries.com

Framefinders
www.framefinders.com

The Great Atlantic Auction Company
Tel: 860 963 2234

Norman C Heckler & Company
www.heckleraution.com

Lloyd Ralston Toys
www.lloydralstontoys.com

Winter Associates Inc.
www.auctionsappraisers.com

NORTH DAKOTA
Curt D Johnson Auction Co.
www.curtdjohnson.com

SOUTH DAKOTA
Fischer Auction Company
www.fischerauction.com

FLORIDA
Auctions Neapolitan
www.auctionsneapolitan.com

Burchard Galleries/ Auctioneers
www.burchardgalleries.com

Arthur James Galleries
Tel: 561 278 2373

Kincaid Auction Company
www.kincaid.com

Albert Post Galleries
Tel: 561 582 4477

TreasureQuest Auction Galleries Inc.
www.tqag.com

GEORGIA
Arwood Auctions
Tel: 770 423 0110

Great Gatsby's
www.greatgatsbys.com

My Hart Auctions Inc.
www.myhart.net

Red Baron's Auction Gallery
www.redbaronsantiques.com

Southland Auction Inc.
Tel: 770 818 2418

IDAHO
The Coeur d'Alene Art Auction
www.cdaartauction.com

INDIANA
AAA Historical Auction Service
Tel: 260 493 6585

Heritage Auction Galleries
www.historical.ha.com

Lawson Auction Service
www.lawsonauction.com

Schrader Auction
www.schraderauction.com

Stout Auctions
www.stoutauctions.com

Strawser Auctions
www.strawserauctions.com

ILLINOIS
Bloomington Auction Gallery
www.bloomingtonauctiongallery.com

The Chicago Wine Company
www.tcwc.com

Hack's Auction Center
www.hacksauction.com

Leslie Hindman Inc.
www.lesliehindman.com

Mastro Auctions
www.legendaryauctions.com

Sotheby's
Tel: 312 475 7900

Susanin's Auction
www.susanins.com

John Toomey Gallery
www.johntoomeygallery.com

IOWA
Jackson's Auctioneers & Appraisers
www.jacksonsauction.com

Tubaugh Auctions
www.tubaughauctions.com

KANSAS
CC Auction Gallery
Tel: 785 632 6062

Spielman Auction
Tel: 316 256 6558

KENTUCKY
Hays & Associates Inc.
Tel: 502 584 4297

Steffen's Historical Militaria
Tel: 859 431 4499

LOUISIANA
Estate Auction Gallery
Tel: 504 383 7706

New Orleans Auction Galleries
www.neworleansauction.com

MAINE
Cyr Auctions
www.cyrauction.com

James D Julia Auctioneers Inc.
www.jamesdjulia.com

Randy Inman Auctions Inc.
www.inmanauctions.com

Thomaston Place Auction Galleries
www.thomastonauction.com

MARYLAND
Hantman's Auctioneers & Appraisers
www.hantmans.com

Ilsennock Auctions & Appraisals Inc.
www.isennockauction.com

Richard Opfer Auctioneering Inc.
www.opferauction.com

Sloans & Kenyon
www.sloansandkenyon.com

Theriault's
www.theriaults.com

MASSACHUSETTS
Douglas Auctioneers
www.douglasauctioneers.com

Eldred's
www.eldreds.com

Grogan & Company Auctioneers
www.groganco.com

Shute Auction Gallery
Tel: 508 588 0022

Skinner Inc.
www.skinnerinc.com

White's Auctions
www.whitesauctions.com

Willis Henry Auctions Inc.
www.willishenry.com

MICHIGAN
Frank H. Boos Gallery
Tel: 248 643 1900

DuMouchelle Art Galleries Co.
www.dumouchelles.com

MINNESOTA
Tracy Luther Auctions
Tel: 651 770 6175

Rose Auction Galleries
www.rosegalleries.com

MISSOURI
Ivey Selkirk Auctioneers
www.iveyselkirk.com

Simmons & Company Auctioneers
www.simmonsauction.com

MONTANA
Allard Auctions
www.allardauctions.com

Stan Howe & Associates
Tel: 406 443 5658 / 800 443 5658

NEW HAMPSHIRE
Paul McInnis Inc. Auction Gallery
www.paulmcinnis.com

Northeast Auctions
www.northeastauctions.com

R O Schmitt Fine Art
www.roschmittfinearts.com

NEW JERSEY
Bertoia Auctions
www.bertoiaauctions.com

Dawson & Nye
www.dawsonandnye.com

Rago Arts & Auction Center
www.ragoarts.com

NEW MEXICO
Altermann Galleries
www.altermann.com

NEW YORK
Antiquorum
www.antiquorum.com

Christie's
www.christies.com

Copake Auction Inc.
www.copakeauction.com

Samuel Cottone Auctions
Tel: 716 658 3180

Doyle New York
www.doylegalleries.com

Guernsey's Auction
www.guernseys.com

William J Jenack Auctioneers
www.jenack.com

Keno Auctions
www.kenoauctions.com

Mapes Auction Gallery
www.mapesauction.com

Phillips de Pury & Company
www.phillipsdepury.com

Sotheby's
www.sothebys.com

Stair Galleries
www.stairgalleries.com

Sterling Auction House
www.sterlingauctionhouse.com

Swann Galleries Inc.
www.swanngalleries.com

OHIO
Belhorn Auction Services
www.belhorn.com

Cincinnati Art Galleries LLC
www.cincinnatiartgalleries.com

The Cobbs Auctioneers LLC
www.thecobbs.com

Cowan's Historic Americana Auctions
www.cowanauctions.com

Garth's Auction Inc.
www.garths.com

Treadway Gallery Inc.
www.treadwaygallery.com

Wolf's Auction Gallery
Tel: 216 575 9653

OKLAHOMA
Buffalo Bay Auction Co.
www.buffalobayauction.com

OREGON
O'Gallery
www.ogallerie.com

PENNSYLVANIA
Noel Barrett
www.noelbarrett.com

William Bunch Auctions
www.williambunchauctions.com

Concept Art Gallery
www.conceptgallery.com

Freeman's
www.freemansauction.com

Hunt Auctions
www.huntauctions.com

Pook & Pook Inc.
www.pookandpook.com

Sanford Alderfer Auction Co.
Tel: 215 393 3023
Email: info@alderauction.com

Charles A. Whitaker Auction Co.,
www.whitakerauction.com

RHODE ISLAND
Gustave White Auctioneers
Tel: 401 841 5780

TENNESSEE
Kimball M Sterling Inc.
www.sterlingsold.com

TEXAS
Austin Auctions
www.austinauction.com

Dallas Auction Gallery
www.dallasauctiongallery.com

Heritage Auction Galleries,
www.ha.com

UTAH
America West Archives
www.americawestarchives.com

VERMONT
Eaton Auction Service
www.eatonauctionservice.com

VIRGINIA
Green Valley Auctions Inc.
www.greenvalleyauctions.com

Ken Farmer Auctions & Estates
www.kenfarmer.com

Phoebus Auction Gallery
www.phoebusauction.com

WASHINGTON DC
Seattle Auction House,
www.seattleauctionhouse.com

Weschler's
www.weschlers.com

WISCONSIN
Milwaukee Auction Galleries
Tel: 414 271 1105

Schrager Auction Galleries Ltd.
www.schragerauctions.com

CANADA
ALBERTA
Arthur Clausen & Sons, Auctioneers
www.clausenauction.com

Hall's Auction Services Ltd.
www.hodginshalls.com

Hodgins Art Auctions Ltd.
www.hodginshalls.com

Lando Art Auctions
www.landoartauctions.com

BRITISH COLUMBIA
Maynards Fine Art Auction House
www.maynards.com

Robert Derot Associates
www.robertderot.com

Waddington's West
www.waddingtonsauctions.com

Heffel Fine Art Auction House
www.heffel.com

ONTARIO
Empire Auctions
www.empireauctions.com

Ritchies
www.ritchies.com

A Touch of Class
www.atouchofclassauctions.com

Waddington's
www.waddingtonsauctions.com

Walkers
www.walkersauctions.com

Deveau Galleries, Robert Fine Art Auctioneers,
www.deveaugalleries.com

Heffel Fine Art Auction House,
www.heffel.com

Sotheby's
www.sothebys.com

QUEBEC
Empire Auctions
www.montreal.empireauctions.com

Iegor - Hôtel des Encans
www.iegor.net

Montréal Auction House
pages.videotron.com/encans

Pinneys Auctions
www.pinneys.ca

Specialists who would like to be listed in the next edition, or have a new address or telephone number, should contact us at info@millers.uk.com. Readers should contact dealers before visiting to avoid a wasted journey.

AMERICAN PAINTINGS

James R Bakker Antiques Inc.
www.bakkerart.com

Jeffrey W Cooley
www.cooleygallery.com

AMERICANA & FOLK ART

American West Indies Trading Co. Antiques & Art
www.goantiques.com/members/awindiestrading

Augustus Decorative Arts Ltd.
www.portrait-miniatures.com

Axtell Antiques
www.axtellantiques.com

Thomas & Julia Barringer
Tel: 609 397 4474
Email: tandjb@voicenet.com

Bucks County Antique Center
Tel: 215 794 9180

Sidney Gecker
www.sidneygecker.com

Garthoeffner Gallery Antiques
www.garthoeffnergallery.com

Allan Katz Americana
www.allankatzamericana.moonfruit.com

Olde Hope Antiques Inc.
www.oldehope.com

Pantry & Hearth,
www.pantryandhearth.com

Raccoon Creek Antiques
www.raccooncreekantiques.com

J B Richardson
Tel: 203 226 0358

Cheryl & Paul Scott
Tel: 603 464 3617
Email: riverbendfarm@tds.net

The Splendid Peasant
www.splendidpeasant.com

The Stradlings
Tel: 212 534 8135

Patricia Stauble Antiques
Tel: 207 882 6341
www.staublechambersantiques.com

Throckmorton Fine Art
www.throckmorton-nyc.com

Jeffrey Tillou Antiques
www.tillouantiques.com

ANTIQUITIES

Frank & Barbara Pollack
Tel: 847 433 2213
Email: barbarapollack@comcast.net

ARCHITECTURAL ANTIQUES

Garden Antiques
www.bi-gardenantiques.com

Hurst Gallery
www.hurstgallery.com

Cecilia B Williams
Tel: 301 865 0777

ARMS & MILITARIA

Faganarms
www.faganarms.com

BAROMETERS

Barometer Fair
www.barometerfair.com

BOOKS

Bauman Rare Books
www.baumanrarebooks.com

CARPETS & RUGS

John J Collins Jr. Gallery,
www.bijar.com

Karen & Ralph Disaia
www.orientalrugsltd.com

D B Stock Antique Carpets
www.dbstock.com

CERAMICS

Charles & Barbara Adams
Tel: 508 760 3290
Email: adams_2430@msn.com

Mark & Marjorie Allen
www.antiquedelft.com

Jill Fenichell
By appointment Tel: 212 980 9346
Email: jfenichell@yahoo.com

Mellin's Antiques
www.mellinsantiques.com

Philip Suval, Inc
Tel: 540 373 9851
Email: jphilipsuval@aol.com

COSTUME JEWELRY

Aurora Bijoux
www.aurorabijoux.com

Deco Jewels Inc.
Tel: 212 253 1222

Terry Rodgers & Melody
www.melodyrodgers.com

Roxanne Stuart
Tel: 215 750 8868
gemfairy@aol.com

Bonny Yankauer
bonnyy@aol.com

CLOCKS

Kirtland H. Crump
www.crumpclocks.com

RO Schmitt Fine Art
www.roschmittfinearts.com

DECORATIVE ARTS

Susie Burmann
Tel: 603 526 5934
rsburmann@tds.net

H L Chalfant Antiques
www.hlchalfant.com

Brian Cullity
www.briancullity.com

Gordon & Marjorie Davenport
Tel: 608 271 2348
Email: GMDaven@aol.com

Ron & Penny Dionne
Tel: 860 487 0741

Peter H Eaton Antiques
www.petereaton.com

Gallery 532
www.gallery532tribeca.visualnet.com

Leah Gordon Antiques
www.leahgordon.com

Samuel Herrup Antiques
www.samuelherrup.com

High Style Deco
www.highstyledeco.com

R Jorgensen Antiques
www.rjorgensen.com

Bettina Krainin
www.bettinakraininantiques.com

William E Lohrman
Tel: 845 255 6762

Lorraine's
www.lorrainesantiques.com

Gary & Martha Ludlow Inc.
www.ludlowantiques.com

Macklowe Gallery
www.macklowegallery.com

Milly McGehee
Tel: 410 653 3977
Email: millymcgehee@comcast.com

Jackson Mitchell Inc.
Tel: 302 656 0110
Email: JacMitch@aol.com

Lillian Nassau
www.lilliannassau.com

Perrault-Rago Gallery
www.ragoarts.com

Sumpter Priddy Inc.
Tel: 703 299 0800
www.sumpterpriddy.com

James L Price Antiques
Tel: 717 243 0501
Email: jlpantiques@earthlink.net

R J G Antiques
www.rjgantiques.com

John Keith Russell Antiques Inc.
www.jkrantiques.com

Israel Sack
Tel: 212 399 6562

Lincoln & Jean Sander
Tel: 203 938 2981
EMail: sanderlr@aol.com

Kathy Schoemer American Antiques
www.kathyschoemerantiques.com

Thomas Schwenke Inc.
www.schwenke.com

Jack & Ray Van Gelder
Tel: 413 369 4660

Van Tassel/Baumann American Antiques
Tel: 610 647 3339

Anne Weston & Associates LLC
www.anne-weston.com

DOLLS

Sara Bernstein Antique Dolls & Bears
www.sarabernsteindolls.com

Theriault's
www.theriaults.com

FURNITURE

American Antiques
Tel: 207 354 6033
Email: acm@midcoast.com

Antique Associates
www.aaawt.com

Antiquebug
www.antiquebug.com

Barbara Ardizone Antiques
www.barbaraardizone.com

Artemis Gallery
www.artemisantiques.com

Joanne & Jack Boardman
Tel: 815 756 359
Email: boardmanantiques@comcast.net

Boym Partners Inc.
www.boym.com

Joan R Brownstein
www.joanrbrownstein.com

Carswell Rush Berlin Inc.
www.american-antiques.net

Evergreen Antiques
www.evergreenantiques.com

Douglas Hamel Antiques
www.shakerantiques.com

Eileen Lane Antiques
www.eileenlaneantiques.com

Lost City Arts
www.lostcityarts.com

Alan Moss
www.alanmossny.com

GENERAL

Alley Cat Lane Antiques
www.rubylane.com/shops/alleycat-lane

Bucks County Antiques Center
Tel: 215 794 9180

Camelot Antiques
www.about-antiques.com

Manhatten Arts & Antiques Center
www.the-maac.com

Showcase Antiques Center
www.showcaseantiques.com

South Street Antique Markets
Tel: 215 592 0256

GLASS

Brookside Art Glass
www.wpitt.com

Holsten Galleries
www.holstengalleries.com

Antiques by Joyce Knutsen
Tel: 315 637 8238 (Summer)
Tel: 352 567 1699 (Winter)

Paul Reichwein
Tel: 717 569 7637

JEWELRY

Ark Antiques
Tel: 203 498 8572

Arthur Guy Kaplan
Tel: 410 752 2090
Email: rkaplan8350@comcast.net

LIGHTING

Chameleon Fine Lighting
www.chameleon59.com

MARINE ANTIQUES

Hyland Granby Antiques
www.hylandgranby.com

METALWARE

Wayne & Phyllis Hilt
www.hiltpewter.com

ORIENTAL

Marc Matz Antiques
www.marcmatz.com

Mimi's Antiques
www.mimisonline.com

PAPERWEIGHTS

The Dunlop Collection
Tel: 704 871 2626 or (800) 227 1996

SCIENTIFIC INSTRUMENTS

Edison Gallery
www.edisongallery.com

SILVER

Alter Silver Gallery Corp.
Tel: 212 750 1928 or 917 848 1713
Email: aftersilvergallery@mac.com

Argentum
www.arguentum-theleopard.com

Chicago Silver
www.chicagosilver.com

Jonathan Trace
Tel: 914 658 7336

Imperial Half Bushel
www.imperialhalfbushel.com

TEXTILES

Pandora de Balthazar
www.pandoradebalthazar.com

Colette Donovan
Tel: 978 346 0614
Email: colettedonovan@adelphia.net

M Finkel & Daughter
www.samplings.com

Cora Ginsburg
www.coraginsburg.com

Nancy Goldsmith
Tel: 212 696 0831

Andrea Hall Levy
Tel: 646 441 1726
barangrill@aol.com

Stephen & Carol Huber
www.antiquesamplers.com

Fayne Landes Antiques
Tel: 610 658 056

Charlotte Marler
Tel: 212 367 8808
Email: char_marler@hotmail.com

Stephanie's Antiques
Tel: 212 633 6563

TRIBAL ART

Arte Primitivo
www.arteprimitivo.com

Marcy Burns American Indian Arts
www.marcyburns.com

Domas & Gray Gallery
www.domasandgraygallery.com

Hurst Gallery
www.hurstgallery.com

Morning Star Gallery
www.morningstargallery.com

Myers & Duncan
Tel: 212 472 0115
Email: jmyersprimitives@aol.com

Elliot & Grace Snyder
www.elliotandgracesnyder.com

Trotta-Bono American Indian Art
www.trottabono.com

20THC DESIGN

Mix Gallery
www.mixgallery.com

Moderne Gallery
www.modernegallery.com

Modernism Gallery
www.modernism.com

R Gallery
www.r20thcentury.com

CANADIAN SPECIALISTS

CANADIANA

Antiquites Gerard Funkenberg & Jean Drapeau
Tel: 819 842 2725

The Blue Pump
Tel: 416 944 1673
Email: john@thebluepump.com

Ingram Antiques & Collectibles
Tel: 416 484 4601

CERAMICS

Cynthia Findlay
www.cynthiafindlay.com

Pam Ferrazzutti Antiques
www.pamferrazzuttiantiques.com

FINE ART

Barbara M Mitchell
Tel: 416 699 5582
Email: fineartsbarbara@hotmail.com

FURNITURE

Croix-Crest Antiques
Tel: 506 529 4693

Faith Grant
www.faithgrantantiques.com

Lorenz Antiques Ltd.
Tel: 416 487 2066
Email: info@lorenzantiques.com

Maus Park Antiques
www.mausparkantiques.ca

Milord Antiques
Tel: 514 933 2433
Email: showroom@milordantiques.com

Richard Rumi & Co. Antiques
www.rumiantiques.com

Shand Galleries
Tel: 416 260 9056

GENERAL

Can/Am Antiques
www.canamauctionzone.com

Floyd & Rita's Antiques
www.floydrita.com

Toronto Antiques Centre
www.torontoantiquesonking.com

JEWELRY

Fraleigh Jewellers
www.fraleigh.ca

Fiona Kenny Antiques
www.fionakennyantiques.com

ORIENTAL

Pao & Molkte Ltd.
www.paoandmoltke.com

Topper Gallery
www.topperart.com

SILVER

Richard Flensted-Holder
By appointment only
Tel: 416 961 3414

Louis Wine Ltd.
www.louiswine.com

TRIBAL

Jamieson Tribal Art
www.jamiesontribalart.com

Page numbers in **bold** refer to pages with special features

INDEX TO ADVERTISERS